ROCK THE POTOMAC

BOOKS BY MARK OPSASNICK

CAPITOL ROCK

WASHINGTON ROCK AND ROLL

MISCELLANEOUS AND UNKNOWN

THE CULTURAL BADLANDS TOUR

THE MARYLAND BIGFOOT DIGEST

THE LIZARD KING WAS HERE

THE REAL STORY BEHIND THE EXORCIST

Gary

ROCK THE POTOMAC

POPULAR MUSIC
AND EARLY-ERA ROCK AND ROLL
IN THE WASHINGTON, D.C. AREA

Enjoy RTP!

Mark Opsasnick

Best Regards,
Mark Opsasnick

BookLocker

ISBN: 978-1-64438-283-7

Published by BookLocker.com, Inc., St. Petersburg, Florida.

Printed on acid-free paper.

BookLocker.com, Inc.
2019

First Edition

DEDICATION

To the fans of Washington, D.C. area popular music

CONTENTS

INTRODUCTION

Rock and roll emerged in America during the early 1950s as a new, intriguing and controversial form of popular music. By that point in time the general media, taking its lead from a magazine called the Billboard and other trade publications that covered the entertainment industry, had divided all of popular music into three basic classifications: pop; country & western; and rhythm & blues. Each of these different musical styles had its own unique lineage dating back centuries. Pop, it was argued, could be traced back to the sounds created by earliest man in the prehistoric age, though for practical purposes most scholars marked its beginnings with the violin bands and orchestras of 16th century Italy; country & western is believed to have evolved from traditional Gaelic singing of 9th century Kingdom of Scotland (later mixing with fiddle-fueled Scottish folk songs during the 17th century); and rhythm & blues had its origins in the shouts, chants and work songs of African slaves who labored on the plantations of Virginia and Maryland during Colonial times. Elements from all three of these musical forms were acquisitioned by the earliest rock and roll performers, resulting in the emergence of an unstructured type of music that could take on almost any manner and still retain its own unique character.

Shortly after its inception, rock and roll music gained momentum across America, initially being offered as a live entertainment option in night clubs, restaurants, auditoriums and similar establishments. During the early 1950s this music drew a youthful audience, gained widespread recognition as the unofficial sound of the city, and thrived as a specialized art form as regional music scenes grew in size and evolved in scope. The Washington, D.C. area, with a long history as a center of popular music, emerged as a hotbed of rock and roll talent, though many of the region's most talented musicians eventually felt compelled to leave the nation's capital to seek band jobs and recording opportunities in other locations such as Los Angeles and New York City. While numerous musicians found grander venues in which to play, many more stayed behind and in time achieved lofty status as legendary rock and rollers in their own backyard.

"Rock the Potomac" will transport readers through time and space as it studies eras that are vital to understanding how popular music evolved in the Washington, D.C. area and advanced the development of a rock and roll scene that has persevered through time. The book was created to serve as an educational tool, a reference source and an item of entertainment for anyone interested in the history of Washington, D.C. area popular music. It examines the area's musical past and commemorates the corresponding players, sounds, night clubs, landmarks and social movements that have defined the region's popular music scene and its colorful history.

MARK OPSASNICK
Greenbelt, Maryland
September 2018

PART ONE

CHAPTER ONE
BILLBOARD:
ESTABLISHING CLASSIFICATIONS OF MUSIC

(*Author's Note: For this book, one of the primary sources for musical classification is the publication currently entitled "Billboard." For decades this periodical has offered popular music charts that provide specific names for each style of music being surveyed. Through time the names of these musical styles have been appropriated from Billboard and used in practice by those working within the music industry and the popular media. For these reasons, and to ensure clarity when discussing different musical styles in this text, this work will begin with a chapter on Billboard magazine. In addition, for purposes of brevity and simplicity, when discussing classifications of music in this text, "country & western" will be commonly referred to as "C&W" and "rhythm & blues" will be commonly referred to as "R&B.")

In the late 19th century, as the number of circulating newspapers and publications grew, the media was increasingly called upon to publicize all manner of popular music. An American music trade publication entitled "Billboard Advertising" was created and contributed to the growth and prosperity of the industry by providing advertisements, articles and reviews that contained detailed information on musical bands and performers, their recorded work and the nationwide venues in which they performed.

As the commercial popularity of disc records increased with each passing year, it became necessary for the entertainment industry to establish some sort of system that would separate and categorize the various types of music that were being made available to the public. Basically, informal classifications emerged that gave definition to distinct types of music providing descriptive categories from which record consumers could choose from. Though informal in nature, these classifications gained wider public recognition and acceptance with the advent of the Billboard charts in the 1930s, a unique offering that rated the popularity of different types of popular music based on radio play and music store sales. (The Billboard charts remain an important component of music promotion, evaluation and consumption to this day.)

The inaugural edition of Billboard Advertising appeared on Thursday, November 1, 1894 and its opening page stated the publication was "devoted to the interests of advertisers, poster printers, bill posters, advertising agents and secretaries of fairs." The magazine was published by William H. Donaldson and James H. Hennegan out of Cincinnati, Ohio and in February 1897 its moniker was shortened from "Billboard Advertising" to "The Billboard." With the Monday, January 9, 1961 issue, the publication was retitled "Billboard Music Week." In the Saturday, January 5, 1963 issue the name was shortened to "Billboard" and that moniker has been retained to the present day.

In the early 20th century the Billboard gradually switched its format towards comprehensive coverage of the entertainment industry and was billing itself "The World's Foremost Amusement Weekly." The Billboard specialized in raw entertainment data and as time progressed began supplementing its extensive articles and features with various lists, rosters and charts of information pertaining to various forms of show business.

The very first popular music chart ever listed in the Billboard appeared in the Saturday, June 30, 1934 issue under the title "Network Song Census." Presented within the "Radio-Orchestra" section of the publication, the Billboard offered the following description of this chart: "Selections listed below represent the Billboard's accurate check on three networks via WJZ, WEAF and WABC. Only songs played at least once during each program day are listed. Idea is to recognize consistency rather than group score. Period covered is from June 15 to June 21, inclusive." In this inaugural list, a total of 19 songs were listed, with number one on the chart being "Sleepy Head" by the Mills Brothers.

Two weeks later in their Saturday, July 14, 1934 edition the Billboard added a second chart to their "Radio-Orchestra" section entitled "Sheet-Music Leaders." Accompanying this new chart was the explanation: "Based on reports from leading jobbers and retail music outlets from Coast to Coast, the songs listed below are a consensus of music actually moving off the shelves from week to week. The 'barometer' is accurate, with necessary allowance for day to day fluctuations." A total of 12 songs were listed in this first "Sheet-Music Leaders" chart with the number one selection being "I'll String Along with You" (words by Al Dubin and music by Harry Warren).

The Billboard took its music charts to a higher level when another new list, this one entitled "10 Best Records," was first introduced in the Saturday, October 12, 1935 edition. Appearing as part of the "Weekly Music Notes" column in the "Amusement Machines" section, the chart was described as "Ten 'best sellers' for automatic phonograph operators reported this week by record firms..."

The inaugural listing for the "10 Best Records" chart provided the 10 best sellers for seven different record labels in two different cities, Chicago and New York City. There were three number one hit songs listed for Chicago: "I'm Painting the Town Red" by Teddy Wilson and His Orchestra with vocals by Billie Holiday (Brunswick); "Joe Louis Strut" by Memphis Minnie and Orchestra (Vocalion {race records}); and "I'm on a See-saw" by Joe Haynes and His Orchestra (Melotone).

For New York City, the list had four number one hit songs: "What a Wonderful World" by Richard Himber and His Orchestra (RCA-Victor); "Cheek to Cheek" by Phil Ohman and His Orchestra (Columbia); "Cheek to Cheek" by Fred Astaire, Leo Reisman and Orchestra (Brunswick); and "Accent on Youth" by Henry Biagini and Orchestra (Melotone). The "10 Best Records" list was based on actual reported record sales and is considered to be the precursor for the modern-day "Billboard Hot 100."

The Billboard's charts changed through time. Its Saturday, March 23, 1940 issue offered a new heading in its "Music" section entitled "The Billboard Comprehensive Guide to Song Popularity" which included two charts: "National and Regional Sheet Music Best Sellers" and "Songs with Most Radio Plugs." Four months later several major changes were instituted. The heading in the Saturday, July 27, 1940 issue was changed to "The Billboard Music Popularity Chart" and four pop music charts were offered: "Records Most Popular on Music Machines;" "National and Regional List of Best Selling Retail Records" (10 listings each for National, East, Midwest, West Coast and South); "National and Regional List of Sheet Music Best Sellers;" and "List of All Songs with Most Radio Plays." Number one on all four of these charts was "I'll Never Smile Again" by Tommy Dorsey and His Orchestra, featuring vocals by Frank Sinatra (Victor).

Throughout the 1940s, a plethora of different best-selling record charts appeared in the pages of the Billboard, which was then being widely recognized as the most respected entertainment industry publication in circulation. During this time many of its advertisements, articles and reviews on musical groups and recordings often employed the use of three standard classification terms to categorize the various forms and styles of popular music that were discussed within its pages. These three terms were: "folk" (which included such forms and styles as camp music, country music, cowboy music, fiddle music, hillbilly music, mountain music, old-time music, rural music and Western swing music); "pop" (almost any type of music performed by White musicians); and "race" (which generally replaced the term "Negro music" in the 1930s and included any type of music performed by Black musicians including blues, jazz and spirituals).

In the 1940s, as circulation of the Billboard expanded, its popular music charts experienced alterations. The first momentous change occurred in its Saturday, October 24, 1942 edition when records by Black recording artists were listed under a new chart entitled "Harlem Hit Parade." The name of this chart was later switched to "Most Played Juke Box Race Records" in the Saturday, February 17, 1945 issue, marking the first time the publication assigned the term "race" to one of its music charts.

Another significant change occurred in the Saturday, January 8, 1944 issue of the Billboard (which, in this edition, offered no fewer than 10 different music charts) when a chart entitled "Most Played Juke Box Folk Records" made its debut.

In the Saturday, June 25, 1949 edition of the Billboard the musical classifications of "folk" and "race" were replaced with the terms "country & western" and "rhythm & blues" in the listings of "The Billboard Music Popularity Charts." First, the subheading of that issue's "Folk Record Section" was changed to "Folk (Country & Western) Record Section" with the three corresponding charts being renamed "Most-Played Juke Box (Country & Western) Records," "Best-Selling Retail Folk (Country & Western) Records," and "Advance Folk (Country & Western) Record Releases." In similar fashion, the subheading of "Race Records" was changed to "Rhythm & Blues Records" and the three corresponding charts were retitled "Best-Selling Retail Rhythm & Blues Records," "Most-Played Juke Box Rhythm & Blues Records," and "Advance Rhythm & Blues Record Releases."

By the time 1950 rolled around, largely due to the standards set by the Billboard, most commercially issued music was being described and categorized by newspapers, music publications and record company promotional material in the United States as either country & western, pop, or rhythm & blues. The stage was then set for rock and roll to develop from a commingling of all three styles. It emerged as a new and separate classification of popular music that quickly permeated global popular culture.

Despite these developments, it wouldn't be until the publication of a short, uncredited article in the Billboard on Saturday, December 4, 1954 entitled "Freed Enjoined from Use of 'Moondog' Label" that the term "rock and roll" (used as a noun to describe a separate classification of music) first appeared within its pages.

The article reads as follows: "NEW YORK, Nov. 27 – Alan Freed, key r.&b. deejay broadcasting over station WINS here, was enjoined this week from using the nick-name 'Moondog,' or any variation thereof, on his radio show... Freed stopped using the 'Moondog' name on his program as of the injunction date (24). He has not been using the 'Moondog Symphony' record for a few months. Freed is now calling his program the 'Rock and Roll Show.'"

From that point forward the Billboard treated rock and roll as a separate classification of popular music though it wouldn't be until its Saturday, March 21, 1981 edition that it published its first rock and roll music chart, a listing entitled "Rock Albums & Top Tracks."

CHAPTER TWO
WHEN COLONISTS RULED THE EARTH

In order to better appreciate the importance of a given regional music scene it is imperative to define the geographic area in question and obtain some measure of understanding regarding the general history of its people and the social movements they generated. Accordingly, a treatment of any aspect of the popular music scene of the Washington, D.C. area should first provide fundamental information pertaining to the establishment of the city itself and then offer an overview of how different forms of music evolved within the cultural context of the region and its residents.

Founded in 1791 on land ceded by the states of Maryland and Virginia as a permanent home for the nation's capital, the City of Washington harbored a growing population, endured political conflict and wars, and hosted a dynamic cultural arts scene, ultimately emerging as the heart and soul of the United States of America. Here, in the middle of the 20th century, rock and roll music began airing over local radio airwaves and emanating from night club stages, opening a special chapter in Washington, D.C.'s colorful entertainment history. In order to adequately illustrate exactly how rock and roll music emerged in the nation's capital, it is necessary to step back in time and begin an analysis of the region's social and cultural evolution from its earliest days.

Historians tell us that Italian explorer Christopher Columbus (1451-1506), while searching for a trade route to India, sailed across the Atlantic Ocean and discovered America on October 12, 1492 when his three ships, the Nina, the Pinta and the Santa Maria, landed on a piece of land that would later become one of the Bahama Islands. However, while Columbus named the island he landed upon San Salvador and declared its territory for the King and Queen of Spain, he initially thought he had landed on an outpost of Asia.

America, it turns out, was actually named after Amerigo Vespucci, a 15th century merchant from Florence, Italy who had been part of at least two significant voyages shortly after Columbus' excursions: a four-ship expedition that had explored the present-day coast of Brazil and visited Trinidad in 1499, and a more ambitious journey that again visited Brazil in 1501 and ventured as far south as the Rio de la Plata (the estuary that forms part of the border between Argentina and Uruguay) and the coast of Patagonia (the southernmost part of South America, located in Argentina and Chile). When he returned home from his second expedition Vespucci wrote numerous letters describing his experiences in what he called the New World and eventually had them published in two separate volumes, "Mundus Novas" in 1503 (written to Pier Francesco de'Medici) and "Lettera" in 1505 (written to Piero Soderini, the Gonfaloniere of Florence).

These published letters were studied by a group of German scholars which included two young cartographers named Martin Waldseemuller (1470-1520) and Matthias Ringmann (1482-1511). Inspired by Vespucci's writings, the group published a new manuscript that updated the scientific treatise "Geographia" (a discussion of the world's geography) which had been produced by the ancient Roman mathematician-geographer-astronomer Claudius Ptolemaeus (83 A.D.-168 A.D.). Entitled "Cosmographiae Introductio" and published on April 25, 1507, the new treatment included an introduction by Ringmann that included the following passage (as translated from Latin): "But now these parts (Europe, Asia and Africa) have been exclusively explored and a fourth part has been discovered by Americus Vespuccius. I do not see what right anyone would have to object to calling this part after Americus, who discovered it and who is a man of intelligence, and so to name it Amerige, that is, the Land of Americus, or America, since both Europa and Asia got their names from women."

This new geography also included in its appendix a substantial map of the world created by Waldseemuller with the New World prominently labeled "America." This geography and its map are believed to be the first to show the name "America" in print and serve as the earliest record of its use.

Serious attempts at colonizing America began when Queen Elizabeth I of England (1533-1603) took the throne in 1558. One of her favorite subjects, an explorer-writer-poet named Walter Raleigh (1552-1618), was instrumental in organizing several expeditions to the New World late in the 16th century. Raleigh is also credited for granting the name "Virginia" to the entire Atlantic Coast of North America from Florida to Newfoundland in 1584 in honor of Elizabeth the Virgin Queen (who, in turn, knighted him "Sir Walter Raleigh" a year later). However, a variety of dangerous circumstances prevented any of these expeditions from establishing permanent colonies in America and Queen Elizabeth began losing interest in such ventures as the century came to a close. The notion of colonizing America would regain momentum after her death on March 24, 1603.

A few hours after the passing of Queen Elizabeth, His Grace James VI, King of Scots (1566-1625) became His Majesty King James I of England through a proclamation issued by Elizabeth's chief minister, Sir Robert Cecil. Three years later on April 6, 1606 he authorized the Virginia Company of Plymouth and the Virginia Company of London to establish colonies in North America. The latter company, consisting of three separate ships – the Susan Constant (mastered by Captain Christopher Newport, carrying 71 people), the God Speed (commanded by Captain Bartholomew Gosnold, carrying 52 people) and the Discovery (led by Captain John Radcliffe, carrying 20 people) – set sail on the River Thames on December 19, 1606, on course for the Atlantic Ocean. The three vessels ultimately sailed into the Chesapeake Bay on April 26, 1607 and landed ashore that day at a place they called Cape Henry. A rude welcoming to the New World was delivered at dusk, as the English settlers were subjected to an unprovoked attack courtesy of several Powhatan Indians, various tribes of which inhabited the surrounding lands.

A seven-member governing council of Virginia was immediately established, which included a man named John Smith, who eventually was appointed Cape Merchant of the council and took on the self-imposed title of Captain. A member of the council named Edward Maria Wingfield was elected president of the colony.

Wingfield's first act in his new leadership role was to lead an exploring party up the Chesepiooc Sinus, a large body of water that was given its name by the Chesepiooc Indians, a Powhatan tribe whose territory ranged south of Cape Henry. (The Chesepiooc Sinus first appeared in print on a map by Theodor De Bry – based on drawings by John White – entitled "America" and published in Europe in 1590. Today this body of water is known as the Chesapeake Bay.) Wingfield first led his group out into the Chesepiooc, but opted to travel up a waterway on the eastern side of the bay which they subsequently named the James River (in honor of King James I of England).

On May 14, 1607 Wingfield's party established the first permanent English settlement in America at a location on the river they called Jamestown. (It seems appropriate to mention at this point that when Edward Maria Wingfield and his company settled in Jamestown, it is almost certain that they kept up their spirits by singing catches around their campfires and psalms in their simple houses of worship, thus introducing European folk music to the region.)

On June 16, 1608 Captain John Smith led his own exploring party up the Chesapeake Bay toward a river the Powhatan Indians called the Patawomeke (Smith later referred to the river in his writings as Patowomek and Patawomek – today we know it as the Potomac

River). He next explored the Eastern Shore of what would later become Maryland and then crossed over and searched along the Western Shore in the area of what is today known as the Calvert Cliffs. Smith's party eventually entered the Patawomeke and worked their way northwards, becoming the first English colonists to ever set sight on lands that would later become Prince George's County, Maryland and Washington, D.C. They ventured up to the area now known as Great Falls, Maryland, returned back to the Rappahannock River and ultimately returned to Jamestown.

During these early years, very few potential colonists could afford to leave their European homeland and cross the ocean to build another life in the New World. It became a common practice for ship captains, under the financial backing and guidance of European promoters, to offer service contracts to poor White migrants from Ireland, Scotland, England and Germany to become indentured servants in America where they would provide manual labor for a period of four to seven years in exchange for eventual freedom and small parcels of land.

In 1619 the first Black African indentured servants were imported to Virginia by a Dutch trader who exchanged his collection of bodies for a cargo of food. Initially the White and Black servants worked in conjunction with other in the settlements of Virginia and Maryland. As the century wore on an influx of Africans replaced the original White servants as the primary source of labor in the colonies. In 1656 these Africans were labeled "slaves" and lost their promises of freedom.

The English maintained efforts to colonize America and in 1629 George Calvert, First Lord Baltimore in the Irish House of Lords, applied to King Charles I of England for a land charter that would become the Province of Maryland. Unfortunately, George Calvert passed away in April 1632 and the charter for Maryland Colony, which covered a sizable portion of land north of the Potomac River and was named after Henrietta Maria, the Queen Consort of King Charles I, was granted to his son Caecilius (Cecil) Calvert, Second Baron Baltimore on June 20, 1632.

A group of 140 settlers under the leadership of 28-year-old Leonard Calvert (younger brother of Cecil Calvert) boarded two ships, the Ark and the Dove, and departed from Cowes on the Isle of Wight in England on November 22, 1633. With a human cargo of Catholics and Protestants, the two ships landed at St. Clement's Island in Southern Maryland on March 25, 1634. After their arrival, Leonard Calvert and a handful of intrepid colonists traveled up the river and met with the Emperor of the Piscataway Indians, who granted permission to the newcomers to settle where they pleased. Upon returning to the Island, the colonists celebrated the very first Catholic mass in the New World under the direction of Father Andrew White.

Calvert and his associates subsequently traded for "thirtie miles of ground" from the local Piscataway Indian tribe (exchanging axes, hoes, hatchets and cloth for the land) and renamed the territory Augusta Carolina, with the town of St. Maries serving as Maryland's first permanent settlement. It is believed that for a period of three years the colonists maintained these names, as it wasn't until 1637 that the names St. Mary's County and St. Mary's City surfaced in local records. There is no documentation verifying how these names were proposed or when the name changes were made official, but they have sustained to the present day. It is a fact, however, that at that point in time, the geographic region informally called St. Mary's County covered the entire state. In the ensuing decades Maryland's population grew as large numbers of dissenters from England, France, Germany, Ireland, Scotland and Wales arrived in the province in search of land and religious freedom and began forming small settlements along the Potomac River and its tributaries.

With the implementation of an agricultural economy based on tobacco growth and exportation, the settlers prospered and continued to move northwards, eventually working their way up to what is today the Pennsylvania border. As their settlements became increasingly self-reliant, the Province saw fit to erect additional counties. By 1674 10 counties were functioning in Maryland: Cecil, Dorchester, Kent, Talbot and Somerset east of the Chesapeake Bay, and St. Mary's, Anne Arundel, Calvert, Charles and Baltimore on the Western Mainland. By 1695, Maryland's overall population had exceeded 30,000.

As the 17th century came to a close, Maryland Governor Francis Nicholson and members of the General Assembly actively began making plans to reshape the boundaries of Calvert County and Cecil County to accommodate the formation of a new one named for Prince George of Denmark, consort of Princess Anne (younger sister of the deceased Queen Mary II) and next in line for the throne of England.

On May 8, 1695 "An Act for the Division and Regulating Severall Countys within this Province and Constituting a county by the name of Prince Georges County within the same Province" was passed, with the new region including all of the land west of the Patuxent River, east of Swanson Creek and north of Mattawoman Creek. A year later on St. George's Day, April 23, 1696, the Commissioners of the Peace held a meeting in a small town on the Patuxent River called Mount Calvert, took their oaths of office, and completed the formalities necessary to bring Prince George's County into existence.

Thereafter, Prince George's County, with a total population of approximately 1,700, served as Maryland's Western Frontier and its range included land that today constitutes Washington, D.C. and the counties of Montgomery, Frederick, Carroll, Washington, Allegany and Garrett. The boundaries of current-day Prince George's County were not established until the middle of the 18th century.

When Prince George's County was erected, its only town was Mount Calvert, which had been created through the General Assembly of the Province of Maryland's "Act of 1684 for the Advancement of Trade." It was situated on the western side of the Patuxent River, and had originally been a part of a 1,000-acre land grant bestowed upon Philip Calvert in 1652 in what was then Calvert County. A stately manor bearing the name of the town was erected on the property in 1657. Reportedly, the two-story brick home was constructed as a hunting lodge for its owner and most likely served in that capacity for several years. In 1667 the entire 1,000-acre property was sold to a gentleman named William Groome, who, 10 years later, passed the land to his son William Groome, Jr.

Sometime around 1680, William Groome, Jr. opened an inn within the town of Mount Calvert and many historians believe the actual location of this establishment was the Mount Calvert manor itself. (An inn was generally defined at the time as being a public lodging house that primarily served food and drink to travelers.)

When the commissioners met on that historical day in April 1696 and established Prince George's County, one of their more significant acts was to officially change the name of Mount Calvert to Charles Town. With these actions, William Groome Jr. then became designated as the very first known innkeeper in Prince George's County history, though to this day no one can ascertain exactly where in Charles Town his establishment was situated.

Prince George's County Court records show that in September 1697 three different individuals – William Groome, Jr., Jonathan Wilson and Charles Tracy – were all operating separate inns within the boundaries of Charles Town, as all three had been called before the court to verify that their inns were qualified "with accommodations for men and horse." It should be noted that some six years later the Prince George's County Court began officially referring to these establishments as ordinaries, which was basically an inn or an eating house that served regular meals at fixed prices. As the 18th century progressed, the preferred names for such establishments became tavern and saloon. As the county's only town, Charles Town flourished under a tobacco economy and developed as a center of trade and commerce. In due time more than a dozen different stores and warehouses existed within the town's limits.

CHAPTER THREE
THE REGION'S EARLIEST MUSICAL PERFORMANCES

When studying the general history of popular music in the Washington, D.C. area, it should be noted that all of the city's land, and most of the land that comprised the entire federal territory, was once a part of Prince George's County, Maryland. The first wave of English colonists to arrive here were responsible for bringing music and musical instruments to this region, though to this day it remains unproven as to where they actually staged their initial musical performances. While historians in Prince George's County speculate that churches, inns and ordinaries were settings for the very first popular musical performances in the region, there is no surviving documentation from the Colonial era that proves such was the case. However, it can be verified that some of the earliest public popular music performances in what would become the Washington, D.C. area were actually theatrical presentations replete with accompanying orchestras that were staged in the county seat of Marlborough in 1752. These events greatly impacted the social calendars of Alexandria and Georgetown, whose taverns and theatres eventually followed suit with considerably less public notice.

Attempts at establishing the types of musical instruments the first English colonists imported from their homeland and the very nature of the music they first performed here has proven to be problematic. Music was forged from random sounds and evolved to become a constituent of human civilization. Anything that produces sound can be considered a musical instrument and scholars are in general agreement that there are no universally accepted methods for determining when musical instruments came into existence. Musical performance initially functioned as a reflection of the dynamic relationship between human beings and the natural surroundings they lived in. The human body in and of itself was probably the very first object to serve as a musical instrument during the prehistoric age, only to be followed by such external devices as rattles and drums. When human impulse directed patterns of sound to be added to dancing and other rhythmic movements, the outcome ensured that a plethora of percussion, string and wind instruments would eventually be added to the mix.

When analyzing the earliest examples of popular music in America, two of the most basic instruments in use were the guitar and violin. Accordingly, when the colonists first took the stage in Prince George's County to perform their music, these instruments were their probable tools of trade. Both instruments were relatively lightweight, could be easily transported and played by single performers, and required no elaborate set-ups or accompaniments. While it may have required some measure of practice for the earliest musicians to perform these instruments in consort, it took little effort for a single player to mount a makeshift stage and entertain crowds for hours.

The guitar, which has existed in various forms and under a variety of names for over 4,000 years, was employed in the earliest musical sessions in America. It is believed to be a direct descendant of a stringed musical instrument called the chetarah, which originated sometime around 2000 B.C. in Assyria, a political state located on the Upper Tigris River in Mesopotamia which today is a part of Iraq. A related instrument was the kitharis, which first appeared in Greek literature of the 8th century B.C. By the 7th century B.C. the kithara, as it was then being called, had emerged as a popular instrument throughout Greece, and the direct ancestor of the modern-day guitar had been born.

The violin, which also figures prominently in the evolution of popular music, descended from the vitula, a bowed string instrument of 4th century Europe. Alternately known as the fidula or fiedel, the vitula is believed to have originated in Rome, Italy around 352 A.D. Evolving into the modern fiddle or violin, this instrument emerged as the primary component of orchestral playing which had its origins in the theatre and opera presentations of early 17th century Italy. As this mode of entertainment gained favor with the public during the Baroque period (1600-1750 A.D.), music was increasingly written for groups of players in combination, with orchestras and similar types of instrumental ensembles quickly spreading to France, Germany, England, Scotland and other European countries. It is believed that modern popular music directly evolved from these orchestras and violin bands that had become a treasured source of entertainment throughout Europe.

Music would have had a limited impact in the lives of the early colonists if it had not been for the existence of several public houses in the region in which they could perform. It is evident that the lives of the early colonists were guided by notions of Godliness, as illustrated by their churches and religious practices, and neighborliness, as evidenced by the significant number of inns and ordinaries that were established throughout the land as the population of the region increased.

These inns – also referred to as houses of entertainment, public houses, tipping houses and roadhouses – eventually began sharing some general characteristics. In terms of physical layout, the typical inn consisted of a small parlor for the general visitor, a separate sitting room for female travelers, a larger tap room which featured a finished floor, a fireplace, several seats and chairs, and at least one large table or writing desk to conduct personal business. In many instances hooks adorned the walls for the placement of firearms, and drawers were available to store tobacco, pipes and smoking tongs. Liquor flowed liberally within these structures, and cleared spaces within the tap rooms of these inns allowed for live musical exhibitions.

When the earliest colonists arrived in America from Europe, one of their primary objectives was to establish churches where they could practice freedom of religion. The Maryland General Assembly's May-June session of 1692 included the passing of legislation entitled "An Act for the Service of Almighty God and the Establishment of the Protestant Religion within the Province" which established the Church of England within the Province of Maryland, some four years before Prince George's County was established. This act specified that each county was to be divided into parishes by its justices and principal freeholders, who were then responsible for selecting a vestry consisting of six of the parish's most able men. The first duty of the vestry was to build a church or chapel, except in those parishes where a church or chapel had already been built.

When this act was passed, there were already several churches dotting the landscape. One of these was St. Paul's Church in Mount Calvert, which had been constructed in 1684 and was located on the west side of the town on a tract of land owned by a man known as Mr. John Davis. With the establishment of Prince George's County in 1696 the town of Mount Calvert had its name changed to Charles Town and St. Paul's Church was recognized as the first operating church within the new county's boundaries.

From the very beginning an integral part of the services of St. Paul's Church was the singing of hymns, psalms, spirituals and various types of religious songs, all of which were probably augmented by any number of guitarists or fiddlers. These occasions would certainly have been among the first instances where music was performed before a public audience within Prince George's County. However, documentation on this subject is lacking and the song titles and types of instruments utilized cannot be verified.

In addition to St. Paul's Church, the three Colonial-era inns of Charles Town could very well have been locations of the first public musical performances ever staged within the region. It is probable that these early inns of Charles Town, and certainly the ones that opened for business in other parts of the county during the ensuing years, hosted a range of assemblies and social events including dinners, parties, balls, concerts and dances of European origin (country dances, circle dances, highland dances, step dances, quadrilles, reels, jigs, etc.). These sessions most likely featured a single fiddler or guitarist-balladeer and quite possibly inspired the formation of small ensembles consisting of Scottish, Irish and Welsh musicians. The inns and ordinaries of Colonial times served not only as lodging facilities for travelers but also as centers of social gathering for townsfolk. It was only logical that at some point musical entertainment would be provided for visitors to the premises.

As the population of Prince George's County, Maryland expanded and recent European immigrants settled in clusters at various points along the local waterways, provisions were made to bring official recognition to the developing villages. In 1706 the General Assembly of the Province of Maryland passed the "Act for the Advancement of Trade" and established five additional towns in the growing county: Queen Anne, Nottingham and Mill Town (all on the Patuxent River), Marlborough (on Western Branch, just beyond the Patuxent) and Aire (on Broad Creek near the Potomac River). A year later a Supplementary Act was passed that brought the town of Piscataway, adjacent to Piscataway Creek and due east of the Potomac River, into existence.

The new towns prospered as tobacco ports and a number of ordinaries were opened in the busier commercial areas. It is known that the first ordinary to operate in the county outside of Charles Town was opened in 1703 by Robert Robertson in Marlborough, three years before the town was officially established. The lodging of travelers and comfort of townsfolk became a profitable business venture and the number of ordinaries in the country soon expanded.

Court records reveal the following individuals were issued licenses to operate ordinaries in Prince George's County throughout the first half of the 18th century: Nicholas Sporne (Marlborough; November 25, 1707); Mary Boyd (Queen Anne; August 28, 1711); Joseph Belt (Marlborough; August 28, 1711); Catherine Robinson (Marlborough; August 28, 1711); William Chillingsworth and Ruben Ross (Queen Anne; November 24, 1713); Matthew Browne (Marlborough; June 28, 1715); Mary Beard (Marlborough; June 28, 1715); Roberta Cherry (Queen Anne; March 24, 1718); Elizabeth Linton (Upper Marlborough; March 23, 1725); Martha Yoakley (Upper Marlborough; November 22, 1726; license issued to operate an ordinary and house of entertainment); John Boyd (Queen Anne; March 27, 1727; license issued to operate an ordinary and house of entertainment); James Chapman (Upper Marlborough; March 27, 1727; license issued to operate an ordinary and house of entertainment); Thomas Middleton (Piscataway, June 1741; exact day unknown); Catherine Playfay (Piscataway, June 1741; exact day unknown); Henry Watson (Bladensburg; 1942; exact date unknown); Elizabeth Brooks (Upper Marlborough; August 22, 1749); Benjamin Bing (Upper Marlborough; August 22, 1749); Thomas Morton (Nottingham; August 22, 1749); Zachariah Lanham (Piscataway; November 28, 1749); Henry Lowe (Broad Creek; March 27, 1750); Mary Noble (Piscataway; March 27, 1750); Jane Martin (Bladensburg; March 27, 1750); and William Malloy (Bladensburg; March 27, 1750).

In the largest session of the time, new licenses to operate ordinaries and public houses were granted to the following individuals on August 28, 1750: Thomas Chittam (Bladensburg); Richard Wright (Welch's Ferry); Benjamin Berry (Upper Marlborough); Elizabeth Taylor (Nottingham); Mary Townley (Upper Marlborough); Cavey Magruder (Upper Marlborough); John Brown, Jr. (Bladensburg); Henry Lowe (Broad Creek); Charles Dawson (Piscataway); Elizabeth Brooks (Upper Marlborough); and William McKay (Nottingham).

By 1750 the population of Prince George's County was approximately 10,000. With such a large number of ordinaries in operation throughout the growing region, it seems likely that scores of balladeers, fiddlers, guitarists, banjo players, horn blowers and percussionists – all schooled in traditional European folk music – conducted practice sessions and public performances within these establishments for the entertainment of their families and friends. In time, organized playing in consort became a feature of these ordinaries and a popular music scene was in the making.

CHAPTER FOUR
THE ASSEMBLY ROOM OF UPPER MARLBOROUGH

A major change occurred in Prince George's County, Maryland when the county seat was moved from Charles Town to Marlborough on Tuesday, March 28, 1721. In the wake of this change, Charles Town quietly faded from view and within 12 years had ceased operations as a town altogether with all of its businesses having shut down and its residents having moved on.

Marlborough, situated in the heart of tobacco country, was named after John Churchill, the first Duke of Marlborough and an ancestor of Winston Churchill. It had been officially established as a town in 1706 and had been attracting settlers as early as 1695. In 1744 the General Assembly of Maryland passed an act that would redesign the physical layout of the town and in the process called for a name change to Upper Marlborough. (In 1893, official county documents began referring to the town as Upper Marlboro.)

During the middle of the 18th century Upper Marlborough solidified its stature as the county's most prominent social center and landed itself a lasting place in local entertainment history when it introduced a facility known as the Assembly Room.

While it is commonly believed that the ordinaries of early Prince George's County were the settings of informal musical performances by some of the more artistically inclined colonists, there is no published documentation on those events to serve as confirmation. The situation is different when discussing 18th century Upper Marlborough.

The earliest known published reference to a musical celebration in this region appeared in the Maryland Gazette newspaper of Friday, August 2, 1745. The article included the following passage: "On Tuesday last, at Upper Marlborough in Prince George's County, were Great Rejoicings on Account of the Reduction of Cape Breton, a handsome subscription being raised by the Gentlemen of the said County, and all Demonstrations of Joy shewn on this Occasion." While details are lacking, it is not unreasonable to assume that some sort of musical performance was employed in these rejoicings to enhance the celebration at hand.

There is a considerable amount of documentation pertaining to 18th century theatre presentations in Prince George's County. The earliest colonists brought with them a taste for drama along with their various English customs. Their theatre productions, simple and basic events given the limited resources at their disposal, did include the fundamental properties that such presentations required: hand-painted scenery, crude machinery, various habits and popular live music.

Theatrical programs during those days usually offered a major play, a shorter afterpiece and the presentation of assorted musical numbers. Various songs and musical interludes were often added to the programs to showcase the skills and abilities of featured actors and performers. Companies that toured and performed throughout Virginia and Maryland during those times fell into one of three classifications: amateur companies consisting of inexperienced actors who took the stage for their own amusement; mixed companies which included both aspiring and established professional actors; and full professional companies whose actors subsisted on the income brought in by their appearances.

The earliest known theatrical presentation performed in the New Land was an amateur play which was staged in the Colony of Virginia in 1665, though details of this event are non-existent. References have been made to a 1690 performance of Benjamin Colman's tragedy "Gustavus Vasa" by Harvard students in Cambridge, Massachusetts and a 1702 offering of "A Pastoral Colloquy" by a troupe of students at William and Mary College in Virginia.

It is believed the first actual theatre in Colonial America was a venue called the Playhouse which was built in 1716 in Williamsburg, Virginia by a dance school instructor named William Levingston. Other theatres to open during this period included the New Booth Theatre in Philadelphia, Pennsylvania in May 1724, the New Theatre in New York City in December 1732 and the Queen Street Theatre in Charleston, South Carolina in February 1736. In the ensuing years similar venues were erected in port towns up and down the Atlantic Coast.

Of great significance is an entry that appeared in the Thursday, June 18, 1752 edition of the Maryland Gazette which reported on what turned out to be the first recorded theatrical production within the Province of Maryland. The article stated: "By permission of his Honour the PRESIDENT, at the new theatre, in Annapolis, by the Company of Comedians from Virginia, on Monday next, being the 22d of this Instant June, will be perfrom'd The BEGGAR'S OPERA: Likewise a FARCE call'd The LYING VALET."

This advertisement was then coupled with a smaller passage which announced: "N.B. The Company immediately intend to Upper Marlborough, as soon as they have done performing here, where they intend to play as long as they meet with encouragement, and so on to Piscataway and Port Tobacco. And hope to give satisfaction to the gentlemen and ladies in each place, that will favour them with their company." This performance, the article told, would begin "precisely at 7 o'clock" with "tickets to be had at the Printing Office."

In the aftermath of this initial announcement, articles in the Maryland Gazette reported that the following plays were scheduled at the theatre in Annapolis: "The Busy Body" coupled with the farce "The Lying Valet" on Monday, July 6, 1752; "The Beaux Sratagem" coupled with the farce "The Virgin Unmask'd" on Monday, July 13, 1752; "London Merchant: or, the History of George Barnwell" coupled with the ballad opera "Damon and Philida" on Monday, July 27, 1752; "A Bold Stroke for a Wife" coupled with the farce "The Beau in the Suds" on Friday, July 31, 1752; and "Drummer, or the Haunted House" coupled with the farce "The Devil to Pay, or, the Wives Metamorphos'd" on Monday, August 3, 1752.

The Thursday, August 13, 1752 edition of the Maryland Gazette reported that, for the first time, an evening of entertainment would be presented in Upper Marlborough: "By permission of his Honour the President, At the New Theatre at Upper Marlborough, by the Company of Comedians from Annapolis, on Thursday next, being the 20th of this instant August, will be perform'd The BEGGAR'S OPERA, likewise a FARCE call'd The LYING VALET. To begin precisely at 7 o'clock."

This advertised bill is nearly identical to the performance staged in Annapolis on Monday, June 22, 1752, with the lone exception on the program being the change in the credited performing troupe from "Company of Comedians from Virginia" to "Company of Comedians from Annapolis." It is likely the actors and musicians remained the same, with the company name being changed to create more interest amongst the residents of the Prince George's County seat. It is also probable that, at the very least, some manner of rudimentary musical accompaniment was employed in these presentations, though the newspaper advertisements neglected to indicate if such was the case.

A closer examination of the content of this particular theatrical presentation reveals that "The Beggar's Opera" was a three-act ballad opera written by poet-dramatist John Gay of Barnstaple, England. The opera satirized poverty, politics and social injustice, focusing on the premise that corruption exists at all levels of society. The main characters of Mr. Peachum and Macheath represented the infamous gangster Jonathan Wild and the cockney thief Jack Sheppard. The production utilized fiddle tunes, ballads and opera melodies, and debuted at Lincoln's Inn Fields, the largest public square in London, England, on Sunday, January 28, 1728.

The original production of "The Beggar's Opera" garnered controversial reviews in the local press and drew such sizable crowds that John Rich, manager of the facility, was able to use the proceeds to construct a new venue, the Theatre Royal-Covent Garden, which was considered to be the forerunner of the Royal Opera House. "The Beggar's Opera" has had a lingering effect on all British stage comedies that have since been produced and was especially influential on 19th century British comic operas and general musicals.

At the time it was standard practice that after the completion of what was usually a three- or five-act play there followed a short farce or comedy set to music which served to close the theatergoer's evening. In this instance David Garrick's "The Lying Valet," originally produced in England in 1741, served as the afterpiece to "The Beggar's Opera." It told the story of how the poverty-stricken protagonist, Charles Gayless, attempts to win the hand of the heiress Melissa and in the process seeks the assistance of his valet, Timothy Sharp, to bring about the marriage.

The company of comedians responsible for these entertainment spectacles in Maryland was headed by the somewhat mysterious team of Walter Murray and Thomas Kean, two actor-managers who had originally worked together on Shakespearean and Restoration plays and revivals in Philadelphia in 1749 and New York in 1750. In later years they worked together on similar theatrical presentations farther down the Atlantic Coast in Williamsburg and Norfolk, hence the name Company of Comedians from Virginia.

Unfortunately for historians, the announcements for these initial Maryland performances fail to identify cast members, rendering it impossible to ascertain if the troupe employed seasoned professional actors or rank amateurs drawn from the local towns. It is also impossible to determine exactly what type of orchestra was originally provided for the opera; speculation runs the gamut from a fiddler or two to a small ensemble comprised of locally recruited musicians to professional hands who employed different string and percussion instruments.

In its edition of Thursday, August 27, 1752, the Maryland Gazette issued an announcement for an additional performance of "The Beggar's Opera" and this time around indicated the presence of instrumental songs and music to accompany the players onstage: "By Permission of his Honour the President, At the New Theatre, in Upper Marlborough, by the Company of Comedians from Annapolis, on Thursday next, being the 14th of September, (at the request of the Ancient and Honourable Society of Free and Accepted Masons) will be perform'd THE BEGGAR'S OPERA: with instrumental music to each air, given by a set of private gentlemen and 'A Solo on the French Horn' also a Mason's Song by Mr. Woodham with a Grand Chorus, to which will be added a farce call'd The LYING VALET. Tickets to be had at Mr. Benjamin Berry's." (It should be noted that this performance took place on the day of the change from the Julian to the Gregorian calendar, when 11 days were dropped from the calendar and Thursday, September 14, followed Wednesday, September 2.)

This second performance in Upper Marlborough proved to have great historic implications, as no less an authority then Oscar G. Sonneck, in his book "Early Opera in America" (1915) wrote of this example: "We have to look to Upper Marlborough for the place where, for the first time in the history of opera in America, the employment of an orchestra is recorded."

Theatrical presentations continued in Annapolis and were publicized in the pages of the Maryland Gazette throughout the fall months of 1752. In Upper Marlborough, the New Theatre, or Ball Room as it was sometimes called, temporarily suspended such events, but did host other forms of entertainment. The Maryland Gazette of Thursday, October 12, 1752 included the following announcement: "We are told there will be a Concert of Music at the great Ball-Room in Upper Marlborough on Wednesday next, by several Gentlemen, for the benefit of Talbot County Charity School."

This entry serves as the earliest known advertisement for a concert event in the Province of Maryland. While one can only speculate as to what types of instruments were employed, it should be reminded that the modern-era popular music concerts in the Washington, D.C. area had their start with this lone advertised performance.

Another concert advertisement for Upper Marlborough that appeared in the Maryland Gazette of Thursday, June 14, 1753 indicated that these musical events probably occurred with some measure of regularity. On this occasion the notice read: "Upon Thursday the 28th of this instant June, will be performed at Upper Marlborough, a grand Concert of Music with many instruments, in the Ball Room: The evening will be concluded with a BALL. Tickets may be had at Mr. Benjamin Barry's, Mr. Benjamin Brookes's and at Mrs. Hillary's in Marlborough."

From 1754 to 1759 there was no mention in the Maryland Gazette of any type of entertainment being offered in Upper Marlborough. However, an article which told of a fascinating night of celebration in the county outside of Upper Marlborough appeared in the Maryland Gazette of Thursday, November 8, 1759: "Piscataway, October 30, 1759. On Friday last was a Day of Public Rejoicing here for the Success of his Majesty's Arms in the Reduction of Quebec. This was the greatest Concourse of People assembled upon the Occasion that was ever seen at one Time in this Place; Upwards of Fifty Gentlemen and Ladies dined in a most elegant Manner and many loyal and patriot Toasts were drank. At Night the Town was Illuminated, and a Ball given at Mrs. Playfay's, at which the Ladies made a brilliant Appearance."

The location of this event merits special recognition. Playfay's Ordinary was owned and operated by Catherine Playfay, who had opened the business in a private dwelling in Piscataway in June 1741 (according to land records, the house had been constructed in 1700). In 1780, the structure was torn down and was replaced in 1798 by a new brick building owned by a gentleman named Isadore Hardy. The new owner continued the lot's tradition by operating a public house out of the new structure, which came to be known as Hardy's Tavern. His son, William G. Hardy, eventually took over the business and continued to operate the tavern well into the middle of the 19th century. Just prior to the Civil War, the Brandt family acquired the property and converted the tavern into a private residence, which is still standing today with a listed address of 2305 Floral Park Road, Clinton, Maryland.

Although the Maryland Gazette failed to advertise any additional musical events in Piscataway, it did publicize many theatrical shows with musical accompaniment that were staged at the Assembly Room in Upper Marlborough throughout 1760. The lineup for these shows reads as follows: "Douglass" followed by "A Prologue spoken by Mr. Hallum" followed by the dramatic satire "Lethe, or, Aesop in the Shades" (Thursday, May 22, 1760); "The Provok'd Husband, or, A Journey to London" followed by the farce "The Virgin Unmask'd, or, An Old Man Taught Wisdom" (Monday, May 26, 1760); "The Stratagem" followed by the farce "Miss in Her Teens" (Monday, June 2, 1760); "King Richard III" followed by the dramatic tale "The King and the Miller" (Monday, June 9, 1760); "The Revenge" followed by the farce "The Devil to Pay, or, The Wives Metamorphosed" (Monday, June 16, 1760); "The Gamester" followed by the dramatic satire "Lethe, or, Aesop in the Shades" (Tuesday, June 24, 1760); and "Romeo and Juliet" followed by the farce "The King and the Miller" (Tuesday, July 1, 1760).

In late 1760 the New Theatre or Ball Room in Upper Marlborough was renamed the Assembly Room. The change came about when a group of gentlemen known as the Managers of the Upper Marlborough Assembly began using the facility for their party celebrations that featured live musical entertainment, dancing, food and spirits. These grand events were held twice a year, usually in the spring and fall. The first reported assembly was held on Thursday, November 13, 1760, with the last of these events taking place on Tuesday, November 8, 1785.

There are two additional announcements of great significance that appeared in the pages of the Maryland Gazette. The first of these provided publicity for yet another musical concert to be staged in Upper Marlborough. The Maryland Gazette of Thursday, February 23, 1769 ran the following announcement: "A PRIVATE CHARITY CONCERT will be perform'd in the Assembly Room at Upper Marlborough, on Wednesday the 29th of March next, by a Number of the best Hands, on different instruments; the first Violin by Mr. Leonard. TICKETS at 7s. 6d.. each, to be had of the Managers, Major Joseph Sim, Messieurs Charles Digges, John Hepburn, Jun. and Christopher Richmond, who will have the application of the Money arising for the intended Charity."

The second announcement, appearing in the Maryland Gazette of Thursday, April 24, 1783, stated: "By Authority, For Four Nights only, At the Theatre in Upper-Marlborough. On Wednesday, the 30th Day of April, 1783, Will be presented a Tragedy called The GRECIAN DAUGHTER. To which will be added a FARCE called The LYING VALET, To conclude with DANCING. Tickets to be had at the tavern, at one dollar each, as no money will be received at the theatre. The doors to be opened at six, and to begin at seven."

The Assembly Room in Upper Marlborough had been constructed in 1752 and for most of its first eight years had been referred to as the New Theatre or the Ball Room. One of the first reliable descriptions of the facility appeared in the book "Travels through the Middle Settlements in North-America in the Years 1759 and 1760 with Observations upon the State of the Colonies" by the Rev. Andrew Burnaby, A.M., Vicar of Greenwich, (1775). In this work, a journal entry taken from the year 1760 reads: "At Colonel Washington's... I took leave of Mount Vernon the 11th of June. I crossed over the Potowmac into Maryland...and proceeded on my journey to Marlborough 18 miles. I here met with a strolling company of players, under the direction of one Douglas. I went to see their theatre, which was a neat convenient tobacco-house, well fitted up for the purpose. From hence in the afternoon I proceeded to Queen Anne..."

Further descriptions of the Assembly Room, and the general entertainment scene in Upper Marlborough, are provided by author J. Thomas Scharf, who wrote extensively of the town is in his book, "History of Maryland from the Earliest Period to the Present Day: Vol. I" (1879). In a chapter entitled "The Assemblies and the Clubs," Scharf wrote: "Each town of any consequence in the province had its assembly-room where public meetings, and especially balls, were held, and where theatrical performances were held. We have seen from the Goldsborough papers, a rude sketch of the assembly-room and club-house at Marlborough, a one-storied structure of modest proportions, with hip-roof, but large windows."

Scharf then provided detailed information on the Assembly Room and provided substantial testimony from Colonel Richard Burgess, who provided ample details on his memories of the venue. Scharf wrote: "Amongst the papers of the late George L.L. Davis we have found some minutes of a conversation which he had some twenty-two or three years ago with Colonel Richard Burgess of Washington City, apropos of the old Marlborough Assembly balls, once so famous."

Scharf quoted Colonel Burgess as having said: "I retain a vivid recollection of the state of society during my youth in Prince George's County, and I attended many of the horse-races, balls, plays, and other diversions of that period. They were then under the management of the oldest and most distinguished gentlemen of the county; the strictest order and decorum were observed and a special regard was paid to the nicer points of etiquette..."

Colonel Burgess also stated: "The ruins of the old assembly rooms at Upper Marlborough are still conspicuous. It was used for a variety of purposes – for plays, balls, recitations by a musical class, of which I was a member, and which Bishop Claggett sometimes attended, and anniversary dinners on the Fourth of July...Those at Upper Marlborough were kept up to a very late house, sometimes till nearly daybreak...When we had a grand theatrical season or entertainment, the houses at Upper Marlborough were crowded and so also was every householder living within five miles of the town...A ball was given the first night after the play. There was generally a dance on the third night also, on which the races and theatrical season usually ended...The most fashionable dances were those simple 'contra dances,' called country dances; with which the ball was both opened and closed, cotillions, reels, etc. As yet, the waltz was not – on this continent, at least. The music comprised two or three violins, with maybe a flageolet, a flute, or a clarionet and, for the end sought, was nearly always good."

The only other first-hand account of the old Assembly Room to be found is one that appeared in the Prince George's Enquirer, a newspaper that began publishing in Upper Marlboro in 1887. In the edition of Friday, September 10, 1920, editor Frederick Sasscer, in his column entitled "Reminiscences II," provides a rare account of the old Assembly Room. His column reads: "Among the landmarks in the ancient town fifty years ago was the old Assembly Hall, or Ball Room, where, according to a very reasonable tradition, General Washington attended dances. I well remember the old building which was located at the foot of the hill where the High School now is, or immediately in front of the home of Dr. Beanes, the uncle of Francis Scott Key. It was a rectangular building of brick with a roof sloping back from the four sides, and, when new, must have been an attractive structure. At the time of its erection there was undoubtedly, as shown by old plats, a street running past it and the fine old brick residence on the adjoining lot, in the direction of the first Court House which was located where Mr. Buck's Garage stands, said street being parallel with the present Main Street or State road."

Sasscer continued: "No one seemed to exercise authority over the old Assembly Room. It had apparently been abandoned for years. In fact it was, at the time of which I am writing, scarcely habitable, and was occupied by anyone who dared to encroach upon the swallows and bats that made their resting places there. The writer remembers that it was successively used as a stable, an undertaker's shop, and as a blacksmith's shop. In this last capacity it served for many years, and the premises were strewn with broken wheels, old iron and the other usual debris surrounding such a shop...The memories of the old Ball Room have long since been obliterated by time. The crumbling building itself was torn down about the year 1870 when the first Act of Incorporation was passed for the town, and the broken brick were used for making foot paths by the side of the muddy streets."

Susan Pearl of the Prince George's County Historical Society, in private correspondence, provided information on the location of the Assembly Room: "Based on my own research: The Assembly Hall/Ball Room was located on the east side of Elm Street, about half way between Dr. Beanes' tomb and Main Street (approximately where the Circuit Court Annex Building is now). It must have been newly built in 1752, and it served as a facility for balls, concerts and theatrical productions for approximately a century...The Ball Room had ceased to function as such by the mid-nineteenth century. The lots around it were by then owned by prominent Marlborough attorneys Caleb Clarke Magruder and Thomas G. Pratt (the latter served as Governor of Maryland, 1845-48). After the Civil War, Magruder bought up from Pratt (by then removed to Baltimore) the lots adjoining the Ball Room, and in June 1870 he purchased from the Town of Marlborough

Commissioners the Ball Room lot itself (Prince George's County Deed HB#3:502). The old building was almost certainly no longer standing at that time. Magruder proceeded to develop the lots into a complex of professional/commercial establishments, and the northerly part of it later became the lumber yard."

Today, the town of Upper Marlboro doesn't even remotely resemble its 18th century layout. However, with Susan Pearl's information as a guide, it can be verified that the former site of the Assembly Room is now occupied in full by the Circuit Court Annex building, marked 14701 Governor Oden Bowie Drive (the building itself has gone through several name changes since its construction in 1976). Although its grounds have been completely paved over and not a trace of this legendary structure is to be found, the importance of the Assembly Room as the scene of the first orchestral performances in Maryland will survive for all eternity.

CHAPTER FIVE
GEORGE WASHINGTON AND THE FEDERAL DISTRICT

George Washington, the first president of the United States of America, was instrumental in the formation of the Federal District and the forward movement of the new nation's capital. Washington was born on Tuesday, February 22, 1732 in Westmoreland County, Virginia to a planter named Augustine Washington and his second wife, Mary Ball Washington. He was the eldest of six children from his father's second marriage and spent his childhood years living with his family on Pope's Creek near the Potomac River.

After his father passed away in 1743, Washington moved into Mount Vernon, a plantation on the Potomac owned at the time by his half-brother Lawrence. As a teenager he developed a special interest in land surveying and in 1748 was called upon to survey the lands of Lord Fairfax in the Shenandoah Valley. A year later he helped lay out the new town of Alexandria, Virginia. When his brother Lawrence passed away in 1752, Washington inherited Mount Vernon and spent much of his time tending to the estate's grounds and crops.

George Washington's duties as property caretaker ended abruptly in 1753 when the British and the French began sparring over control of the Ohio Valley region, a conflict that escalated into the French and Indian War (1754-1763). Washington was appointed an adjutant of one of Virginia's four military districts by Governor Robert Dinwiddie and was assigned to Fort Le Boeuf, Pennsylvania. There, his main task was to warn French authorities to cease encroachment on British-occupied land.

In preparation of this mission, Washington spent much of his time during March 1754 recruiting troops in Alexandria and training them in Market Square (which is still located on the north side of King Street, between Fairfax and Royal). His service to his country was so valiant he was eventually appointed commander in chief of the Virginia militia. He eventually left the Army in 1758 and returned to his Mount Vernon estate where he set about refurbishing the home and tending to the surrounding property. On Saturday, January 6, 1759 Washington married Martha Dandridge Custis, a wealthy young widow with two small children, and turned his attention towards politics.

As the century progressed, George Washington continued his political ascent and served in Virginia's House of Burgesses from 1759 to 1774. During these years he was a familiar figure in Alexandria and frequently conducted personal business and made social calls in the town. For these reasons, in 1769 he had a small townhouse built at 508 Cameron Street which came to serve as both a second private home and a personal office. In 1774 and 1775 Washington served as a delegate to the First and Second Continental Congresses and his sterling performance in this position of leadership made him the logical choice to guide the colonies through their greatest challenge.

One of the great moments in history occurred when the 13 colonies rejected the governance of British Parliament and the legitimacy of the monarchy and sought to become the sovereign United States of America, which led to the onset of the American Revolutionary War (1775-1783) between North America and the Kingdom of Great Britain. The first military engagements of the war were the Battles of Lexington and Concord, which commenced on Wednesday, April 19, 1775 in Middlesex County, Province of Massachusetts Bay and marked the outbreak of armed conflict between the two sides. With the escalation of war, George Washington quickly became the logical choice for military leadership. On Thursday, June 15, 1775 he was unanimously selected by Congress to serve as commander-in-chief of the Continental Army.

A little over one year into the war with the Kingdom of Great Britain, American patriots decided to make their separation from British rule a formality. On Friday, June 7, 1776 Richard Henry Lee, who had served in the Virginia House of Burgesses from 1758 to 1775, appeared before the Second Continental Congress in Philadelphia and proposed a declaration that the colonies were free and independent states. A five-person committee, headed by Thomas Jefferson, was appointed on June 10 to draw up the formal Declaration of Independence. The committee presented a draft of the statement to Congress on June 28, which then voted unanimously to declare independence on July 2. After revisions were completed, the Declaration of Independence was adopted by Congress on July 4, 1776 and copies were subsequently forwarded to the individual states for approval.

The United States of America, under the military leadership of General George Washington, along with the assistance of French forces, ultimately achieved victory over the Kingdom of Great Britain at the Battle of Yorktown, which was fought in Yorktown, Virginia on Wednesday, October 17, 1781. It was the last major land battle of the American Revolutionary War, which was officially brought to an end with the signing of the Treaty of Paris on Wednesday, September 3, 1783. This treaty was ratified by the American Congress of the Confederation on Wednesday, January 14, 1784 and by the King of Great Britain on Friday, April 9, 1784, with the final versions exchanged in Paris on Wednesday, May 12, 1784.

At the conclusion of the American Revolutionary War, General Washington resigned as commander-in-chief on Tuesday, December 23, 1783. In May 1787 Washington re-emerged to lead a Virginia delegation to the Constitutional Convention in Philadelphia where he advocated a stronger central government and was consequently voted in as chairman. The states ratified the new Constitution and on Thursday, April 30, 1789 he was inaugurated as first president of the United States of America as a member of the Federalist Party. Washington would ultimately serve two terms as president through Saturday, March 4, 1797.

One of the issues President George Washington was immediately confronted with in 1789 was the placing of a new and permanent nation's capital. Prior to his election the capital had endured a nomadic existence, having been moved a total of 17 different times between eight different cities: Philadelphia, Pennsylvania (Carpenter's Hall; September 5, 1774 to October 24, 1774); Philadelphia, Pennsylvania (State House; May 10, 1775 to December 12, 1776); Baltimore, Maryland (Henry Fite's House; December 20, 1776 to February 27, 1777); Philadelphia, Pennsylvania (State House; March 4, 1777 to September 18, 1777); Lancaster, Pennsylvania (Court House; one day only on September 27, 1777); York, Pennsylvania (Court House; September 30, 1777 to June 27, 1778); Philadelphia, Pennsylvania (College Hall, and then State House; July 2, 1778 to March 1, 1781); Philadelphia, Pennsylvania (State House; March 1, 1781 to June 21, 1783); Princeton, New Jersey (Prospect Hall, and then Nassau Hall; June 30, 1783 to November 4, 1783); Annapolis, Maryland (State House; November 26, 1783 to August 18, 1784); Trenton, New Jersey (French Arms Tavern; November 1, 1784 to December 24, 1784); New York, New York (City Hall, and then Fraunche's Tavern; January 11, 1785 to the Autumn of 1788); New York, New York (Federal Hall; March 4, 1789 to August 12, 1790); and Philadelphia, Pennsylvania (Philadelphia County Building-Congress Hall; December 6, 1790 to May 14, 1800).

To address the situation, Congress approved the bill entitled "An Act for establishing the temporary and permanent seat of the Government of the United States" on Friday, July 16, 1790. Informally called the Residence Act, this bill effectively approved the creation of a "District of Territory" on the Potomac River that would serve as the permanent national capital. With the passing of this act, for all practical purposes, the District of Territory, and what would eventually be called Washington, D.C., came into existence, though no legal designation was granted for the actual naming of the new Seat of Government of the United States. Its first three sections of the Residence Act read as follows:

Section 1. Be it enacted by the Senate and House of Representatives of the United States of America in Congress assembled, That a district of territory, not exceeding ten miles square, to be located hereafter directed on the river Potomac, at some place between the mouths of the Eastern Branch and Connogochegue, be, and the same is hereby accepted for the permanent seat of the government of the United States. Provided nevertheless, That the operation of the laws of the state within such district shall not be affected by this acceptance, until the time fixed for the removal of the government thereto, and until Congress shall otherwise by law provide.

Section 2. And be it further enacted, That the President of the United States be authorized to appoint, and by supplying vacancies happening from refusals to act or other causes, to keep in appointment as long as may be necessary, three commissioners, who, or any two of whom, shall under the direction of the President, survey, and by proper metes and bounds define and limit a district of territory, under the limitations above mentioned; and the district so defined, limited and located, shall be deemed the district accepted by this act, for the permanent seat of the government of the United States.

Section 3. And be it enacted, That the said commissioners, or any such two of them, shall have power to purchase or accept such quantity of land on the eastern side of the said river, within the said district, as the President shall deem proper for the use of the United Sates, and according to such plans as the President shall approve, the said commissioners, or any two of them, shall, prior to the first Monday in December, in the year one thousand eight hundred, provide suitable buildings for the accommodation of Congress, and of the President, and for the public offices of the government of the United States.

President Washington quickly made progress towards the establishment of the permanent Seat of Government of the United States. By the issuance of letters patent Saturday, January 22, 1791 he appointed three commissioners – Daniel Carroll, Thomas Johnson and David Stuart – "for surveying the district of territory accepted by the said act for the permanent seat of government of the United States, and for performing such other offices as by law are directed, with full authority for them, or any two of them, to proceed therein according to law."

On Monday, January 24, 1791 President Washington issued "A Proclamation," which provided a description of the boundaries for what would become the district of 10 miles square. He wrote the territory was to fall within four lines of experiment which included sections of land around Hunting Creek in Virginia and both sides of the Eastern Branch in Maryland.

In an action that attempted to clarify the boundary situation, Congress passed the act of March 3, 1791, entitled "An Act to amend 'An act for establishing the temporary and permanent seat of Government of the United States,'" which read: "That so much of the act entitled, 'An act for establishing the temporary and permanent seat of the government of the United States,' as requires that the whole of the district of territory, not exceeding ten miles square, to be located on the river Potomac, for the permanent seat of the government of the United Sates, shall be located above the mouth of the Eastern Branch, be and is hereby repealed, and that is it shall be lawful for the President to make any part of the territory below the said limit, and above the mouth of Hunting Creek, a part of the said district, so as to include a convenient part of the Eastern Branch, and of the lands lying on the lower side thereof, and also the town of Alexandria and the territory so to be included, shall form a part of the district not exceeding ten miles square, for the permanent seat of the government of the United States, in like manner and to all intents and purposes, as if the same had been within the purview of the above retired act."

With land ready and waiting for development, President Washington enlisted the services of French engineer and American Revolution veteran Maj. Pierre Charles L'Enfant to lay out the yet-unnamed city within the District of Territory. Maj. L'Enfant designed a unique framework that divided the Seat of Government into four quadrants (Northwest, Northeast, Southeast and Southwest) and provided for several government buildings, including the Capitol and President's House. His design also offered a grid street pattern interspersed with circles and squares for monuments. The plan was approved by President Washington on Monday, August 1, 1791.

In September of that year President Washington requested that Maj. L'Enfant confer with a number of persons interested in the creation of the District of Territory including Thomas Jefferson and James Madison. L'Enfant, who was staying in Philadelphia at the time, made several suggestions regarding the venture and dispatched Jefferson and Madison to meet with commissioners Daniel Carroll, Thomas Johnson and David Stuart in Georgetown on Thursday, September 8, 1791 to discuss the details of the project.

According to the Record of the Commissioners' Meeting, Maj. L'Enfant recommended the name of the city and territory should be "City of Washington and Territory of Columbia." On Friday, September 9, 1791 – the day following the meeting – the commissioners wrote a letter to L'Enfant in Philadelphia that read, in part: "We have agreed that the federal District shall be called 'The Territory of Columbia' and the federal City 'The City of Washington.'" However, despite this written proclamation, the commissioners had no statutory authority to provide official legal names for either the territory or the city.

Much to President Washington's chagrin, Maj. L'Enfant became somewhat difficult to deal with as the project wore on. He was dismissed from his assignment on Thursday, March 1, 1792 and the work was completed by surveyor Andrew Ellicott. The City of Washington began accepting new residents in the fall of 1792.

Although the City of Washington was functioning as part of the Territory of Columbia, its existence was not without controversy. Debate entailed over what the actual legal names were for the city and territory. In reality, there were no legal names for either. Incredibly, this problematic issue remained unresolved for more than 80 years, with historians still debating the dynamics of these titles to the present day.

Another name, District of Columbia, first appeared in the title of an act of Congress approved on Friday, May 6, 1796 entitled "An act authorizing a loan for the use of the city of Washington, in the District of Columbia, and for other purposes therein mentioned." However, this act does not provide legal designation for any such name for the Seat of Government. In what can only be described as a remarkable fact, the original District of Territory had no legal, official name from 1790 until 1871.

The process of transferring the capital accelerated with the dawning of the new century. The actual date of the first meeting of Congress in the City of Washington was scheduled for the seventeenth day in November 1800. Instead, its initial meeting in the city took place inside a partially completed Capitol building four days later on Friday, November 21, which was the first day of the session when a quorum of both Houses was present. Two weeks later on Monday, December 1 the federal capital was officially transferred from Philadelphia to the City of Washington, whose population was recorded as 3,210, of which 2,464

(76.7%) were White and 746 (23.2%) were designated as Colored. At this time, the census also recorded the population of the entire Territory of Columbia as 14,093.

Adding to the confusion surrounding the name and content of the Territory of Columbia was "An Act Concerning the District of Columbia" (commonly known as the Organic Act) that was passed on Friday, February 27, 1801. With this act the District of Columbia was divided into two counties – the portion of land obtained from Virginia was named the County of Alexandria, while the Maryland portion was given the name the County of Washington. Despite the creation of these two counties, the charter of the "Town of Alexandria," which was recognized as part of the original District of Territory, remained intact, as did the charter of the "Town of Georgetown," which maintained its independent status while occupying federal property.

This political act served little purpose in the long run. In response to strong public opinion and lobbying, the General Assembly of the State of Virginia passed an act on Tuesday, February 3, 1846 expressing interest in accepting retrocession of the land the state had previously given to the City of Washington. On Thursday, July 9, 1846, an act of Congress stated that the Virginia cession had not been, nor would ever be, a necessary part of the Seat of Government and provided for retrocession, depending on a final vote by Alexandria citizens. A vote was held at the Alexandria Courthouse beginning Tuesday, September 1, 1846, with the end result being 763 votes cast for retrocession and 222 votes against. The result was finalized by President James K. Polk on Monday, September 7, 1846, who declared the retrocession in full force and effect; Virginia formally accepted the territory on Saturday, March 13, 1847. These actions left the County of Washington as the sole county in the District of Columbia.

It wasn't until Congress approved "An act to provide a government for the District of Columbia" on Tuesday, February 21, 1871 that direct legislation provided for an official name for the Seat of Government of the United States of America. The act proclaimed: "That all that part of the territory of the United States included within the limits of the District of Columbia be, and the same is hereby, created into a government by the name of the District of Columbia, by which name it is hereby constituted a body corporate for municipal purposes." This act effectively eliminated the County of Washington, and merged the City of Washington and the Territory of Columbia into a single entity legally called the District of Columbia and commonly known as Washington, D.C.

To make this part of the history lesson complete, it must be noted that Georgetown, which had been in existence as both an independent town and a topographical destination since 1751, was officially assimilated into Washington, D.C. on Monday, February 11, 1895 by the act entitled "An act changing the name of Georgetown, in the District of Columbia, and for other purposes." This act, enacted by the Senate and House of Representatives of the United States of America in Congress assembled, read, in part, that Georgetown: "shall be known as and shall constitute a part of the city of Washington."

The town of Alexandria, Virginia had a significant role in the formation of the District of Territory thanks to President George Washington, who, although having a permanent residence in Mount Vernon, spent a significant amount of time in the town, often frequenting the various taverns that littered the neighborhood west of Union Street prior to and during the years of his presidency. When President Washington obtained the necessary clearance to acquire land for the new District of Territory, he made sure the state of Virginia ceded the property west of the Potomac River that included the town of Alexandria. Ultimately this land would remain a part of the District of Territory from the approval of the Residence Act in 1790 until retrocession brought it back to Virginia in 1847.

Much of what constitutes current-day Alexandria was originally part of a 6,000-acre land grant that Virginia Governor Sir William Berkeley bestowed upon an English ship captain named Robert Howson on October 21, 1669. This land grant, which extended along the Potomac River from Hunting Creek in the south to Little Falls in the north, was initiated by King Charles II in recognition of Howson's efforts in helping more than 100 individuals immigrate to Virginia. However, six months later Howson sold off his land for 6,000 pounds of tobacco to a Scottish Stafford County planter named John Alexander. The land grant actually overlapped a previous 700 acre land grant to Mistress Margaret Brent, a close friend of Leonard Calvert, governor of Maryland. Consequently, John Alexander, in an effort to resolve the sticky land ownership issue, paid the Brent heirs 10,500 pounds of tobacco on January 14, 1674 for the undisputed rights to the 700 acres.

By 1730 much of the land along the Potomac River had been cleared and in 1732 the General Assembly of the Province of Virginia installed a tobacco warehouse along what is now Oronoco Street for the purpose of storing, weighing and inspecting wheat and tobacco crops that were awaiting shipment to Great Britain. At that time the surrounding area was inhabited by Scottish and English merchants, traders and landowners who called their community Belhaven in honor of Scottish patriot John Hamilton, the second baron of Belhaven.

In October 1748 the inhabitants of this region petitioned the General Assembly of Virginia for official recognition and on Thursday, May 11, 1749 a new town named Alexandria was established, with the moniker being selected to honor original landholder John Alexander. The General Assembly of Virginia appointed John West, Jr., assistant surveyor of Fairfax County, to design the town, and he selected a 17-year-old youth named George Washington to assist with the project. In July 1749 the construction of homes, buildings and roads began, with the earliest streets of downtown Alexandria laid out in grid-like patterns and named to show the founders' loyalty to Great Britain: running north-south were Royal, Fairfax and Water (now Lee) Streets, while east-west routes included Duke, Prince, King, Cameron, Queen, Princess and Oronoco Streets.

During this period Alexandria prospered as a Potomac River port town, and, similar to its Maryland neighbor Prince George's County, proved to be fertile ground for a number of ordinaries that hosted the local citizenry and offered refreshments for the weary travelers passing through. An excellent unpublished work entitled "The Development of Taverns in Alexandria, Virginia, 1750-1810" written by James C. Mackay, III (a thesis submitted in partial fulfillment of the requirements for the degree of Master of Arts at George Mason University in Fairfax, Virginia in the spring of 1995) provides an abundance of information on the dynamics of the town's early ordinaries. This work illustrates that during the 1750s a total of 19 men and women held ordinary licenses in the town, with an additional 15 tavern keepers identified during the 1760s and another 12 in the 1770s.

While it is believed that live music was periodically offered in these establishments, documentation of such activities is scant. As Mackay noted: "Beyond their role as watering holes, the taverns in Alexandria also served as the center of the town's social life and the setting for many of the most popular amusements of the period. Many tavern keepers both before and after the Revolution advertised their establishments as a 'house of entertainment,' leaving the specific types of food and fun to the mind of the reader. Parties, dancing, music and special occasions such as formal dinners and holidays all presented opportunities for people to gather in local taverns to socialize."

A highly significant first-hand account that sheds some light on what Colonial-era dances were like in Alexandria was presented by one Nicholas Cresswell (1751-1804), a 23-year-old writer from Derbyshire, England who came to America in 1774. Upon his arrival, Cresswell traveled throughout the states of Maryland, Virginia, Kentucky, Pennsylvania and New York looking for a suitable home and motivated by his thought that "a person with a small fortune may live much better and make greater improvements in America than he can possibly do in England."

In his book, "The Journal of Nicholas Cresswell, 1774-1777" (1924), Cresswell penned: "January 7th, 1775. (Alexandria) Last night I went to the (Twelfth-night) Ball...Here was about 37 ladies dressed and powdered to the life, some of them very handsome and as much vanity as is necessary. All of them fond of dancing, but I do not think they perform it with the greatest elegance. Betwixt the country dances they have what I call everlasting gigs. A couple gets up and begins to dance a jig (to some Negro tune) others comes (sic) and cuts them out, and these dances last as long as the Fiddler can play. This is sociable, but I think it looks more like a Bacchanalian dance than one in polite assembly."

While Creswell failed to mention the name of the ordinary or ball room that hosted this event (it is now speculated by historians that the ball took place at Hawkins' Ordinary, which at the time was operated by one Mary Hawkins and located on the site of the future Gadsby's Tavern), one can safely assume that the entertainment presented was representative of the era and constituted a scene most likely repeated in many of the Alexandria taverns of the day.

Much attention has deservedly been bestowed upon Gadsby's Tavern, an establishment that was noted to have been a favorite of President George Washington during his two terms in office, as well as the location of several Birthnight Balls that honored his birthday. Gadsby's has served Alexandria as a tavern, ballroom, theatre, hotel, military quarters and public house since the latter portion of the 18th century and still stands today at 138 North Royal Street as a two-building museum where the public can discover its storied past as a celebrated Colonial gathering place. While a number of ordinaries opened and closed in Alexandria during its first 30 years, Gadsby's Tavern was by far the most socially prominent in that it offered a variety of dances, concerts and theatrical performances that attracted local citizens as well as an array of distinguished including presidents such as George Washington, Thomas Jefferson, John Adams and James Madison.

Gadsby's Tavern dates back to 1785, when original owner John Wise constructed a two-story public house he called the Fountain Tavern on a lot located on the southwest corner of Royal and Cameron Streets. This particular plot of land already boasted an interesting history, as from 1749 to 1784 its site had been occupied by a small building which had served as an ordinary under a variety of different owners. In 1792 Mr. Wise oversaw the construction of a new three-story hotel structure which adjoined the original Fountain Inn building. This fresh addition boasted two spacious dining rooms, an elaborate ballroom, a well-stocked bar and 14 sleeping rooms. In January 1793 Wise opened up this Colonial conglomerate under the awkward new name of the City Tavern, at the Sign of the Bunch of Grapes.

In late 1796 John Wise leased the City Tavern to an enigmatic individual by the name of John Gadsby (1766-1844), who hailed from London, England and had arrived in Alexandria shortly after the Revolution in hopes of finding employment as an architect. Gadsby is remembered as having been a somewhat anonymous figure about the town during his early years there and was said to have managed or tended bar for several years in a rough, unnamed waterfront tavern on Union Street before taking control of Mr. Wise's operation.

Gadsby assigned the twin towers property the dual name of Gadsby's Tavern and City Hotel and kept watch over the successful business until 1808, at which time he backed out of the local scene and relocated to Baltimore. John Wise then passed the establishment to a man named William Caton, who would run the City Hotel all the way through the Civil War years.

Gadsby later returned to the City of Washington in 1823 and managed O'Neal's Tavern (alternately known as the Franklin House) for three years before overseeing the construction of the National Hotel at Sixth Street and Pennsylvania Avenue NW, which opened to the public on Saturday, February 20, 1827. Gadsby managed the National Hotel until 1840, at which time he retired from the business world and subsequently spent his final years living with his wife in the Decatur House on Jackson Place NW. Curiously, John Gadsby seemingly avoided his old home site of Alexandria during his final years and never returned to the famed tavern on the opposite side of the Potomac River that proudly bore his name.

Gadsby's Tavern was known for being the site of several illustrious Birthnight Balls, events originally created in Great Britain as gala celebrations to commemorate the birthday of the monarch. In the aftermath of the Revolution, Americans decided to carry on this grand tradition in Virginia beginning in 1779. Without a monarch to recognize, they focused their attention on their very own iconic leader George Washington.

The inaugural Birthnight Ball was held at Gadsby's Tavern on Friday, February 10, 1797, though Washington was still conducting business in Philadelphia at the time and could not make the trip to Alexandria for the celebration. However, in spite of the fact that his presidency had come to a close, he did attend the next two Birthnight Balls at Gadsby's, which took place on the nights of Monday, February 12, 1798 and Monday, February 11, 1799. (Discrepancies in the birth date of Washington are due to differences in the Julian and Gregorian calendar. The British Empire switched from the Julian to the Gregorian calendar in 1752 and on the Julian calendar Washington as born on February 11, with the change adding 11 days to the calendar, therefore placing Washington's birth date on February 22. Despite the modification, celebrations continued to take place on or around February 11 for many years).

The Birthnight Ball of Monday, February 12, 1798 proved to be a somewhat anticlimactic event for the Gadsby Tavern regulars. Reportedly, after George Washington arrived with entourage in tow, a cannon discharged outside the tavern and much raucous celebrating ensued in the streets. Unfortunately, the grand festivities seemingly proved unimpressive to the former president and his posse, as he unexpectedly cut the partying short and absconded with his following to a nearby public house called the Union Tavern for his evening meal and subsequent consumption of spirits.

In an effort to remedy the situation and prevent history from repeating itself, the Birthnight Ball of 1799, which proved to be the last that George Washington ever attended, was advertised throughout the Alexandria area, with notices in local newspapers and word-of-mouth accounts promising a visit from the local hero. The event was apparently so well-organized and so highly anticipated that George Washington had no choice but to stay the entire evening and from every indication he thoroughly enjoyed the festive occasion.

According to several accounts that reviewed the night's activities, the former president was met some distance away from Gadsby's by the Light Dragoons, who escorted him through the city and were greeted by a booming cannon and a raucous populace as Gadsby's Tavern came into view. After mayor Francis Peyton delivered an address of welcome in the main dining room, Washington replied with great emotion, calling the gathered Alexandrians: "My neighbors and friends, some of whom have been the companions of my juvenile years." His subsequent post-dinner toast at Gadsby's was direct and to the point: "Prosperity to the town and citizens of Alexandria!"

As taverns flourished in Alexandria throughout the late 18th century with irregular schedules of informal musical entertainment, theatrical performances were introduced to the town and attracted substantial interest among a growing arts community. Plays and afterpieces were staged during the year 1798 in specially prepared vacant rooms at both Gadsby's Tavern and Fulmer's Tavern.

The town's first professional theater was the Alexandria Theatre, which was originally owned by a theatrical impresario named Thomas Wade West, who served as manager of the Virginia Company and owned theatres in Charleston, Norfolk, Richmond, Petersburg and Fredericksburg. This venue stood on the north side of what is today the 400 block of Cameron Street (today the former site of this theatre is occupied by the buildings from 407 to 427 Cameron Street). Designed by a man known locally as Captain Stephenson, Architect of Washington City, the two-story building was 50x90 feet, constructed of brick and originally housed various shops in its basement and on its first floor, with a large theatre occupying the top level.

An article in the Columbian Mirror and Alexandria Gazette newspaper of Saturday, May 11, 1799 entitled "New Theatre" announced the facility's grand opening: "The public are respectfully informed that the New Theatre will positively be opened on Thursday, May 16th with O'Keefe's celebrated Opera of The Highland Reel, with the original OVERTURE, SCOTCH MEDLEY & The Opera to conclude with A DOUBLE LAMANDE & SCOTCH REEL, By Mr. M. Sully, Mrs. Green, and Miss Gillespie."

After this auspicious debut, the Alexandria Theatre continued to host a variety of comedies, tragedies, dances and musical performances until February 1845, at which time the building was sold and its basement and first floor converted into a produce warehouse and grocery store, with the top-floor theatre renamed Liberty Hall. The facility continued to host musical concerts and assemblies until the entire building was destroyed by fire on Saturday, June 22, 1872. The original Alexandria Theatre had certainly been a venue of great importance for those local citizens enamored with the performing arts.

When surveying the history of the Federal District it becomes imperative to give full consideration to the town of Georgetown, which soon after its inception became a noted entertainment center within the region. Georgetown was founded on Saturday, June 8, 1751 when the General Assembly of Maryland authorized the formation of a town on the Potomac River on 60 acres of land which at the time belonged to George Beall and George Gordon.

At the time of its inception, Georgetown was a part of Frederick County, Maryland. The town was believed to have been named in honor of King George II of Great Britain and Ireland (1683-1760), though the point is argued to the present day by many who believe it was actually named in recognition of the two Georges from whom the land was obtained. The town was never incorporated as a city, though it was erroneously called the City of Georgetown in numerous acts of Congress. When Montgomery County, Maryland was formed in 1776, it inherited the town of Georgetown, which fell within its newly established geographic boundaries. The town was issued a charter and incorporated by the General Assembly of Maryland in 1789.

Georgetown left Montgomery County behind in 1790 and then confusingly maintained separate municipal status while operating on federal land as an independent town and topographical destination. Reduced to simplest terms, the town of Georgetown was occupying federal land, but it was not a part of the newly created Federal District. In fact, Georgetown wasn't officially assimilated into Washington, D.C. until Monday, February 11, 1895 when an act entitled "AN ACT changing the name of Georgetown, in the District of Columbia, and for other purposes" was enacted by the Senate and House of Representatives of the United States of America in Congress assembled.

Georgetown's foremost contribution to the local entertainment scene during the late 18th century consisted of several well-regarded public houses which hosted assemblies, balls, dances, parties and all sorts of informal gatherings, in addition to providing living and working quarters to some of the era's top federal officials and social dignitaries. While it has been documented that by 1796 there were more than 15 taverns in operation in Georgetown, it was John Suter's Fountain Inn that garnered the most attention during the final years of the 18th century.

The history of the Fountain Inn begins with the construction of a Colonial tavern on lot 51 of the original Georgetown survey in 1760. Originally named the King's Arms and owned and operated by one Joseph Belt, the tavern fronted 133 feet on the east side of High Street (present-day Wisconsin Avenue NW), just north of the canal. Little is known about the King's Arms, aside from the fact that Belt remained in control of the business until 1775, at which time he relinquished his management duties to a man named John Beall, who remained on in that capacity until the fall of 1782. In November of that year a gentleman named Ignatius Simpson apparently assumed control of the property and advertised his business as "The Tavern." His reign was relatively short, as he lasted as proprietor of the business for approximately one year, at which time a farmer from Montgomery County, Maryland named John Suter came into the picture.

Official notice of the change in ownership came at the November 1783 session of the Montgomery County Court, where John Suter was bonded to keep an ordinary or public house of entertainment in Georgetown. His newly acquired property – the original King's Arms – consisted of four separate, but closely grouped buildings: one two-story wood house; one one-story wood dwelling; one one-story wood kitchen; and one brick stable. He renamed his tavern the Fountain Inn (though it was commonly known as Suter's Tavern) and would remain in control of the business until 1794. Under Suter's watchful eye, the Fountain Inn reportedly played a vital role in the refreshment and entertainment of emerging political heroes, prominent public figures and common citizens alike.

John Suter's Fountain Inn was held in high esteem among local politicians and commissioners and was used on a regular basis as a meeting ground, polling place, lodge, restaurant and assembly hall. The first actual documented reference of this establishment as a political gathering place was found in the manuscript minutes of the Commissioners of Georgetown, which used the building as its meeting place on a regular basis from 1784 to 1789. The minutes read: "At a special meeting of the Commissioners of Georgetown at the house of Mr. John Suter on Tuesday, 22 June 1784. Present, Messrs. Andrew Hough, Robert Peter, Williams Deakins, Jr., John Murdock, Bernard O'Neill, and Thomas Beall, of George, to consider the application of John House."

The Fountain Inn was known for having been George Washington's unofficial Georgetown headquarters throughout his presidency and reportedly was also frequented on a regular basis by such political luminaries as John Adams, Thomas Jefferson and James Madison. Washington frequently traveled between his home in Mount Vernon, Virginia and various cities to the north and his diary recounts numerous stops at the inn during these business trips.

An entry in his dairy with the heading "Monday, March 28, 1791" reads: "Left Bladensburg at half past 6 and breakfasted at Georgetown about 8, where, having appointed the commissioners under the residence law to meet me, I found Mr. Thomas Johnson, one of them (and who is now chief justice of the State), in waiting, and soon after came in David Stuart and Daniel Carroll, esqs., and others, too. A few miles out of town I was met by the citizens of the place, and, escorted in by them and dined at Suter's Tavern (where I also lodged), had a public dinner given by the Mayor and Corporation, previous to which I examined the surveys of Mr. Ellicott, who had been sent on to lay out the district of ten miles square for the Federal City; also the works of Maj. L'Enfant, who had been engaged to make a draft of the grounds in the vicinity of Georgetown and Carrollsburg on the Eastern Branch." In a later diary entry, George Washington also noted that on March

30th, while still at Suter's, he wrote his final and official "Proclamation Fixing the Permanent Seat of Government."

In 1791, private quarters in the Fountain Inn became the offices of Maj. Pierre L'Enfant and Andrew Ellicott. It was there that they designed and produced comprehensive blueprints for the new Federal District. As the vision of a new nation's capital materialized, Washington himself, during a formal evening dinner party at Suter's, oversaw the agreement of purchase that was signed between the federal commissioners (Thomas Johnson, chairman and chief justice of Maryland; Daniel Carroll of Duddington, brother of Archbishop Carroll; and Dr. David Stuart, family physician of the president) and the land owners. The very first lots sold to the public were later auctioned from the tavern's main meeting room.

When it came to providing for his customers, John Suter reportedly spared no expense in stocking his tavern with the finest libations. He imported whiskey from his native Scotland, rum from Jamaica and brandy from London, England. No less an authority than Thomas Jefferson himself, who during his time as Minister to France had actually visited the countries of Europe and had brought home prime selections for his own private stock, was quoted as saying: "No man on the Atlantic Coast could bring out a better bottle of Madeira or sherry than old Suter."

Government matters aside, it has always been speculated by local historians that entertainment of various sorts had long been a feature at the Fountain Inn going back to its earliest days as the King's Arms. The very first pieces of documentation that show the Fountain Inn offering theatrical presentations appeared in advertisements in the Times and Potowmack Packet newspaper of Wednesday, August 4 and Wednesday, August 11, 1790. These ads told of performances that month by McGrath's Company of Comedians of such plays as "The Beggar's Opera," "The Tragedy of Douglas," "The West Indian" and other short pieces.

Other precise examples of public entertainment at the Fountain Inn showed up periodically through the years: The Times and Potowmack Packet newspaper of Wednesday, October 27, 1790 advertised performances that weekend by the New American Company of a farce entitled "Tragedy of Jane Shore;" the Columbian Chronicle newspaper of Tuesday, December 3, 1793 contained a notice that read, in part, "The dancing assemblies commence this evening at Mr. Suter's;" and, according to the Columbian Chronicle newspaper of Tuesday, February 25, 1794, the McGrath Company staged an evening of entertainment featuring the play "Richard III," an interlude of dancing featuring a hornpipe performance by Mr. Kelly and a favorite song by Mrs. Fitzgerald, and an afterpiece entitled "The Prisoner at Large, or, the Irish Wedding."

At some point in early 1794, John Suter fell ill with cancer and retired to his farm in Montgomery County, where he passed away in November of that year. Upon leaving his business behind he handed management duties of the Fountain Inn over to his wife Sarah, who remained in charge until at least December 1795. While it is known that a gentleman named Henry Medley assumed control of the Fountain Inn in December 1796, it remains unknown as to how long he managed the business, as there are no published references to this establishment for all of 1797, 1798 and 1799.

From that point the history of the Fountain Inn becomes a bit more accessible. In June 1800 a man named Francis Kearns reopened the tavern as the Sign of the Ship and kept the inn going into 1802. Local newspapers infrequently referred to the business during this time as Kearns' Tavern. Historian Oliver W. Holmes documented that the next verifiable owner was one George Pitt, who operated the establishment as the Anchor Tavern and Oyster House from July 1803 until May 1816. Holmes also found newspaper references to the business as both the Anchor Tavern and the Golden Anchor Tavern during these years.

While nothing regarding the tavern could be uncovered for the year 1817, Holmes noted that from 1818 to 1821 it was in operation as Mr. Eno's Tavern and in July 1821 it was advertised as Mr. Howard's Tavern.

The famed tavern was next mentioned in a notice in May 1835 that announced: "An old building, formerly Pitt's Tavern, on High Street adjoining the Bridge over the Canal, for sale." Presumably, the cluster of buildings that comprised the famed Fountain Inn was torn down shortly after this notice appeared.

While the Fountain Inn and its many incarnations garnered attention for its esteemed political clientele, its role as birthplace of the Federal District and its colorful history of interesting and diverse entertainment, there were other prominent local taverns in operation during this time. Among these Georgetown establishments were: The Union Tavern, which was opened in December 1795 on the northeast corner of Washington and Bridge Streets (today 30th and M Streets NW), was originally operated by John Suter, Jr. and Samuel Huff and stood its ground until the wrecking ball came calling in 1936; the City Tavern, which was opened by Clement Sewall in December 1796 on Bridge Street, just west of High Street and is still standing today at 3206 M Street NW; and the Columbian Inn, which originally opened in 1799 on the northwest corner of Cherry and High Streets and remained in operation through the Civil War era (Today this location would be north of the canal, on the west side of Wisconsin Avenue NW, just above Grace Street NW).

As the 18th century came to a close, President George Washington, who had served two precedent-setting terms in which he provided the developing nation with stability and authority and created an executive structure that would service future presidents, developed severe health problems. Known as the Father of Our Country, he stood as a symbol of American virtue and spent his last two years in retirement at Mount Vernon, Virginia. He died of a throat infection at his estate on Saturday, December 14, 1799 at the age of 67.

CHAPTER SIX
THE UNITED STATES THEATRE

By 1800 the City of Washington was enjoying its status as the social, cultural and political center of the vast Middle Atlantic region. Prince George's County, Maryland, whose populace remained primarily concerned with the importation of goods from Europe and the exportation of tobacco, still boasted prosperous towns such as Upper Marlborough and Bladensburgh, both of which were important for the vast array of services and opportunities they offered the people of the region. However, those seeking the energy and excitement of a night on the town now set their sights on the City of Washington, which had begun offering plays and other unique stage presentations in a few specially constructed theatres, the success of which helped pave the way for an influx of entertainment-oriented playhouses, halls, hotels and taverns.

Many of the earliest residents of the City of Washington had migrated to America from Eastern European countries, bringing with them a taste for various types of visual and performing arts. To meet the desires of the people, ambitious entrepreneurs within the city gradually established a number of public stages in which they offered grand events such as plays, musical concerts, vocal recitals and dance assemblies. The manner of these presentations were of far greater sophistication and organization than those held in the shed-like Assembly Room of Upper Marlborough and the simple ordinaries that occupied the surrounding lands of Prince George's County, Maryland. Aiding the cause of these early theatres were articles and notices which appeared in the Daily National Intelligencer – the first regular newspaper of the City of Washington which had begun publishing in October 1800 – that publicized these highly anticipated stage presentations.

The three primary early-era venues in the City of Washington, all of which came to define public entertainment in the nation's capital during the first half of the 19th century, were the United States Theatre, the first version of the Washington Theatre (located at 11th and C Streets; it later housed Carusi's Saloon) and the second version of the Washington Theatre (located on Louisiana Avenue; it later housed such venues as the Assembly Rooms, the Olympic Saloon and Canterbury Hall).

All three of these establishments initially served as public theatres which offered farces, dramas, tragedies and miscellaneous stage productions. Their bills sometimes included various types of musical entertainment such as solo musical acts, vocal performances by leading actors and small ensemble and combo playing that was performed during intermissions or utilized to augment certain portions of the stage show.

As time progressed, musical performances took on an increasingly important role in stage productions throughout the city, as concert presentations served to both entertain the public and inspire local musicians who strived for professional status. Ultimately, these early-era venues, with their offerings of organized entertainment, served as predecessors to the restaurants and night clubs of the future that would carry on the legacy of live musical presentations.

The United States Theatre was the very first of its kind to ever operate within the City of Washington. It opened in August 1800 in the Union Pacific Hotel, a structure which offered a curious history itself, and, ironically enough, never actually served the general public as a hotel.

The story of the United States Theatre began when a New Hampshire native and astute businessman named Samuel Blodgett, Jr. (1757-1814), who was known for having established the Insurance Company of North America in Philadelphia, Pennsylvania in 1792, arrived in the City of Washington in January 1793 and began purchasing sizeable parcels of undeveloped land. One of the lots he purchased was along the north side of E Street, between 7th and 8th Streets, a location that would eventually become the heart of the Downtown area. Blodgett, Jr. transferred the land over to the city's commissioners and then devised a scheme to build a hotel on the site by lottery.

Plans for the hotel were drawn up by James Hoban, the architect of the President's house, with the actual construction of the building beginning in the fall of 1793. A total of $36,000 was ultimately spent on construction expenses, with the federal government providing a generous supply of freestone for the basement walls. Once completed, the building's large, central brick frontage measured 120 feet and included two extensive wings. The structure itself stood two stories in height, with a basement and an attic completing the package. Formally named the Union Pacific Hotel, the facility was declared by its backers as the biggest and finest hotel building in America, a somewhat misleading statement, as the building itself never served as an actual hotel or boarding house. Nonetheless, the citizens of the City of Washington began informally referring to the looming structure as the Great Hotel or Blodgett's Hotel. It would take almost 10 years for the building's construction to be completed.

As the Union Pacific Hotel slowly took shape, other developments of local significance were in the works. In August 1799 there arrived in the town of Georgetown a troupe of actors from Pennsylvania calling themselves the Philadelphia Company. This group had left the Chestnut Street Theatre, where they had worked under the moniker the New Company and settled in at Suter's Tavern where they staged six separate plays over the course of an eight-week period.

The Philadelphia Company was led by two Englishmen, actor Thomas Wignell (1753-1803) and composer-organist Alexander Reinagle (1756-1809), who, during their relatively short stay, traveled about the City of Washington in their free time and were so impressed with the vitality of the local residents and the considerable success they enjoyed in Georgetown they vowed to soon return and bring their theatre presentations to the heart of the developing city. When their commitment at Suter's Tavern ended, Wignell, Reinagle and their company made their way back to Philadelphia to resume theatrical presentations at the Chestnut Street Theatre. However, they kept good on their promise to return to the City of Washington and late in the summer of 1800 they set their sights on the Union Pacific Hotel, where the proprietors of the new building enlisted the group to stage the very first professional theatrical presentations within the city.

The United States Theatre opened within the Union Pacific Hotel on the night of Friday, August 22, 1800. The building, still unfinished at the time, consisted of a bare, 300-seat, candle-lit room void of stage or scenery. According to a generous advertisement in that day's edition of the Centinel of Liberty, and George-Town Advertiser, this very first theatrical presentation by the Philadelphia Company consisted of a prologue spoken by Mr. Wignell himself, followed by a featured tragedy entitled "Venice Preserved; Or, a Plot Discovered," after which was a two-act farce entitled "The Spoil'd Child." On this first evening the doors of the theatre opened at 6pm and the curtain rose at precisely 7pm, with a reported 130 theatre-goers in attendance. Despite the somewhat barren conditions of the building, box and pit seats were priced at one dollar. The performance was repeated one more time on the night of Monday, August 25.

The Philadelphia Company consisted of at least 18 known actors and actresses and the troupe remained consistent throughout its Washington stay. For their opening night performance of "Venice Preserved; Or, a Plot Discovered," no fewer than 11 separate actors were employed, including Mr. Wignell himself who took on the role of "Jaffier." For the farce-afterpiece, "The Spoil'd Child," the remaining seven members of the troupe were utilized, along with a gentleman named Mr. Warren who had also participated in the main attraction. Of significance here is that within the newspaper known as the Centinel of Liberty, and George-Town Advertiser there is a detailed section where the entire cast and their respective roles for each presentation are listed in full.

Interestingly enough, the roster for "The Spoil'd Child" shows the following line: "Little Pickle (with songs) – Miss Arnold." While no other details are available in this reference, the scant information provided serves as the first documented instance of a vocal performance, with, presumably, some measure of accompanying popular music, being performed in conjunction with a theatrical presentation within the City of Washington. With this performance popular music made its public debut in the City of Washington.

The Philadelphia Company remained in town for less than 30 days. During their stay they offered five additional stage presentations at the United States Theatre (within the Union Pacific Hotel): The tragedy "Hamlet, Prince of Denmark" followed by the farce "Lovers Quarrels, or Like Master-Like Man" (Wednesday, August 27, 1800); the comedy "The Wheel of Fortune" followed by the farce "The Horse and the Widow," with the Epilogue song by Mr. Bernard, Mrs. Touchwood and Mrs. Francis (Friday, August 29, 1800); the comedy "Comedy of the Secret; or Partnership Dissolved" with entertainments (Monday, September 1 and Wednesday, September 3, 1800); the tragedy "Romeo & Juliet" (including Act I, "A Masquerade," in which the Minuet de la Cour and a New Gavot were introduced by Mister Harris and Miss Arnold; and Act V, "A Funeral Procession and Solemn Dirge," which featured vocal parts by Messrs. Danley, Francis, Bliffet, Robins, Miss Arnold, Miss Solomon, Mrs. Warren, and Mrs. Stuart), followed by the farce "The Village Lawyer" (Friday, September 5; Saturday, September 6; Monday, September 8; Wednesday, September 10; and Friday, September 12, 1800); and the comedy "The Road to Ruin, or the Rural Rumpus" (Saturday, September 13; Monday, September 15; Wednesday, September 17; and Friday, September 19, 1800).

With the conclusion of the first theatrical season of the United States Theatre, the Philadelphia Company returned to its home state, where it continued to stage well-received presentations at various theatres. After Thomas Wignell passed away in 1803, Alexander Reinagle relocated to Baltimore, Maryland, where he enjoyed a prosperous association with the Holiday Street Theatre which endured until his death in 1809.

The Union Pacific Hotel, meanwhile, never did host another theatrical presentation by the United States Theatre or any other entity. The building sat vacant and largely unused until it was sold to Congress in 1810 for the sum of $10,000. It subsequently housed the General Post Office until the entire structure was destroyed by fire on Tuesday, December 13, 1836. A new, all-marble structure designed by architect Robert Mills was erected on its site and reopened in 1842, maintaining its previous title of General Post Office. The building would house many different government offices up to 1988. After a decade of neglect, the vacant General Post Office property was sold in 1998 to the Kimpton Hotel and Restaurant Group of San Francisco, which extensively renovated the property and reopened the historic building on Sunday, June 23, 2002 as the Kimpton Hotel Monaco, with its front address marked 700 F Street NW.

CHAPTER SEVEN
CARUSI'S SALOON

As the Union Pacific Hotel stood silent and memories of its former tenant, the United States Theatre, hovered about the quiet downtown streets, plans were being formulated by two distinguished gentlemen of the city, William Levell and John P. Van Ness, to bring a new theatre to the City of Washington. Levell and Van Ness had observed how the United States Theatre had been managed and were greatly impressed by the way its presentations had accentuated the importance of musical and vocal performances. In April 1803 they began soliciting subscribers to invest in the construction of a new building within the City of Washington that would house a professional theatre for the presentation of plays, musical concerts and miscellaneous recitations. Levell and Van Ness then selected a site at the northeast corner of 11th and C Streets NW, just south of Pennsylvania Avenue NW, as the future home of their new enterprise. Groundbreaking of the new theatre building occurred in early June 1803 and upon completion the building would ultimately front 135 feet on 11th Street NW and 64 feet on C Street NW.

Progress on the new theatre was relatively slow. On Thursday, June 7, 1804, as construction of the theatre building was finally nearing completion, a meeting of the theatre's stockholders chaired by Washington Mayor Robert Brent was held at Rhodes Tavern in which a five-man Board of Directors for the Theatre Company was established. The five individuals elected to this Board – John P. Van Ness, Samuel Harrison Smith, Robert Brent, William Brent, and Thomas Law – were granted to "have the power generally to manage the affairs of the institution during the period for which they are elected." The written resolution further provided the Board of Directors with full control of the theatre's funds and instructed them to see to the completion of the building and secure a dramatic company that would provide theatrical presentations. The proceedings of the meeting were published in the Daily National Intelligencer newspaper of Wednesday, June 13, 1804.

The Daily National Intelligencer of Friday, November 16, 1804 announced that, after a two-day postponement due to inclement weather: "The public are respectfully informed that the WASHINGTON THEATRE will open on Friday evening Nov. 16, 1804, with a GRAND MEDLEY of entertainments by the celebrated Mr. Maginnis, from London, who has performed in the most capital cities of Europe, and America."

The evening opened with nine separate performances in succession: A rendition of the celebrated song "Ode to Freedom;" a new comic song entitled "Satire upon all Trades;" an act billed as the Wonderful Magic Goblets; a comic song by an individual named Nathan; an "astonishing experiment" called "Confederate Counters" by a presumed psychic named Don Diego; a patriotic song; a variety of deception with cards; and two concluding songs, including a rendition of "America, Commerce and Freedom."

The featured attractions of the evening were then presented by the Wonderful Group of Artificial Comedians (described as standing "three feet and a half high") and consisted of the plays "Patrick's Return; or, the Merry Humors of Darby" and "Neptune, God of the Ocean, and His Queen," the latter of which was introduced by "an ingenious piece of machinery displaying a splendid representation of a sea engagement." The doors of the theatre opened at 6pm, with the performance commencing one hour later. Admission was one dollar for box seats and 75 cents for the pit. The Daily National Intelligencer concluded its advertisement with the statement: "The above performance will be accompanied by the Italian Band of Music."

The Washington Theatre continued on with fall-winter seasons for more than 14 years until it went down in flames under somewhat suspicious circumstances. An article in the

Daily National Intelligencer of Thursday, April 20, 1820 entitled "Our Theatre is Destroyed by Fire!" announced: "About 7 o'clock yesterday morning, the THEATRE in this city was discovered to be on fire. There was scarcely an interval of a moment from the discovery of the fire before the whole roof and interior were in flames and in less than fifteen minutes the roof fell in. The opinions of those who have enquired into the matter vary as to the cause of the fire: Some suspect it to have been the work of an incendiary, whilst others suppose it to have been the result of accident."

In June 1821 the burned-out shell of the original Washington Theatre building at 11th and C Streets NW was purchased by a 20-year-old musician and dance instructor named Lewis Carusi. (A new version of the Washington Theatre was later reopened in August 1821 at Louisiana Avenue NW and Sixth Street NW.) The name Carusi was well-known in the City of Washington, as his father Gaetano had been personally recruited by Thomas Jefferson in 1805, along with 17 other musicians, to move from Catania, Sicily, to the nation's capital in an effort to upgrade the United States Marine Band. Upon the arrival of the new musicians, Jefferson had a change of heart and Gaetano Carusi pursued a career in teaching music performing with orchestras at the Washington Theatre. Gaetano had brought two sons with him to Washington in 1805, Lewis and Samuel, and had schooled both youths in the skills of dance and music.

After purchasing the original Washington Theatre property, Lewis Carusi enlisted the services of architect George Hadfield to reconstruct the building from the ground up, which upon completion featured a spacious ground-floor dining room measuring 48x80 feet with a 22 foot high ceiling. Upon the building's completion in the summer of 1822 Lewis brought his brother Samuel on board to co-manage the facility. The Carusi brothers then renamed the venue the Washington Assembly Hall and began planning to open a school of dance and music on the premises.

The establishment had its grand opening on Tuesday, October 22, 1822, with two articles in the Daily National Intelligencer announcing its arrival. The first, entitled "The Washington Assembly Hall," read: "Being now prepared for the reception of scholars, Samuel Carusi solicits his friends, and the citizens at large, to call and inspect the Hall for themselves and they will be convinced of the complete adaptation of this room for all species of amusements. The expenses have been severe and grinding, and have involved his father deeply, relying solely upon the generosity of his fellow citizens. He offers gratuitously to the amateurs of music a fine and spacious Hall, where they will find all kinds of instruments, and where they may daily resort for practice and pleasure. He offers on moderate terms, to teach thoroughly the whole theory and grounds of music, and, in short time, insure a sufficient knowledge, so as to enable his pupils to compose. He will teach signing, and instruct on the piano forte, harp, guitar, and all other stringed and wind instruments..."

The second of the two articles was simply entitled "Dancing" and stated: "Mr. Lewis Carusi has opened his Dancing School at the Washington Assembly Hall, where he invites his pupils to attend generally. The floor is in fine order, and large enough to enable thirty cotillions to dance at the same time. He solicits the attention of parents, to enter their children at once. His price for the season will be very reasonable."

The Carusi Brothers immediately began booking live entertainment in the Washington Assembly Hall. Weekly dances and balls with live musical groups were introduced in 1823 under such banners as "Cotillion Party," "Practising Ball" and "Rational and Philosophical Amusements." Large concert presentations became a popular attraction at the Hall after the Friday, November 12, 1824 edition of the Daily National Intelligencer ran an advertisement for a Vocal and Instrumental Concert to be held at the hall on the following Monday featuring a vocalist named Mrs. Green, assisted by a large orchestra. Solidifying the facility's status as the City of Washington's most esteemed entertainment venue were three glorious Inaugural Balls celebrating newly elected presidents: President John Quincy Adams (Friday, March 4, 1825); President Andrew Jackson in his first term (Wednesday, March 4, 1829); and President Andrew Jackson in his second term (Monday, March 4, 1833).

While officially operating as the Washington Assembly Hall, the venue was also informally referred to in the pages of the Daily National Intelligencer as the Washington Assembly Rooms, Carusi's Assembly Rooms, the Assembly Rooms and the Washington Saloon.

When Lewis Carusi opened his dancing school for the 1833 season, the name of the hall was changed to Carusi's Saloon, a moniker which endured until the late 1850s. The change was made official with an entry in the Daily National Intelligencer on Tuesday, November 19, 1833 entitled "Dancing and Waltzing School at Carusi's Saloon," which, in part, read: "Lewis Carusi having commenced his school for the season, respectfully informs the citizens of Washington and its vicinity, that he is prepared to receive pupils at his Hall, on 11th Street West. His mode of instruction will be of the latest and most improved style of dancing and waltzing, and every attention paid to deportment and address; he anticipates, by exertion to improve those committed to his charge, the continuance of their patronage."

During the venue's subsequent 24-four-year existence as Carusi's Saloon, the steady offerings of entertainment fell into five basic categories: balls and dances; celebrations, dinners and parties; musical and vocal concerts; plays and theatrical presentations; and recitations, exhibitions and miscellaneous events. Of special note were four additional Inaugural Balls held in the venue: President Martin Van Buren (Saturday, March 4, 1837); President William Henry Harrison (Thursday, March 4, 1841); President James K. Polk (Tuesday, March 4, 1845); and President Franklin Pierce (Friday, March 4, 1853).

At this time the brick building fronted 100 feet on 11th Street NW (all the way to Pennsylvania Avenue NW) and 55 feet on C Street NW. It had been redesigned to offer a large saloon and four separate rooms on the ground floor, with a second floor offering a spacious two-room saloon complete with a specially constructed orchestra gallery. When nationally recognized entertainers descended upon the nation's capital, it was Carusi's Saloon that hosted their local premiers.

Some of the more distinguished performers to grace the stage of Carusi's Saloon in its final years included the Ethiopian Singers (Messrs. Germon, Stanwood, Harrington, Pell, White and Howard) who appeared for several evenings in January 1848; the young French violinist Paul Julien, who gave his Grand Farewell Concert on Monday, April 4, 1853 assisted by Signorina Anna Vezentini (Prima Donna from the Grand Opera, Milan), Signor Atilio Arnoldi (Tenore from Maretzek's Italian Opera, New York) and Herr Charles Becht (pianist, from the Grand Conservatorine, Berlin); Miss M.E.M. Makeah, an accomplished American actress who gave a program of dramatic readings on Thursday evening, January 19, 1855; and the famed Italian opera contralto Madame D'Angri, who gave her only concert in Washington on Saturday, April 25, 1857 assisted by her daughter M'dlle Mathilde D'Angri, Mr. Thomas on violin, Mr. Screiber on trumpet and pianist Sig. Abella.

The very last public performance to ever be held at Carusi's Saloon was a lecture given by Mrs. Frank R. Wright on the subject of "Beautiful Men" on the night of Thursday, December 16, 1857, with her delineation of Miss Flora McFlimsey, in character, and recitation of Butler's "Nothing to Wear." The venue fell dark the following day and Lewis Carusi settled into a comfortable retirement.

After the Carusi contingency vacated the premises, it took a little less than three weeks for lessee Mr. W. Stuart (also of Wallack Theatre, New York) and director Mr. Dion

Bourcicault to clean and rearrange the premises and reopen the venue as the Washington Theatre, which advertised a seating capacity of 1,300.

The opening night of Wednesday, January 6, 1858 offered the play "Our Wife" featuring Miss Dolly Marshall and Miss Louisa Marshall and a ballet pantomime entitled "Flora and Zephyr" featuring Signorina Teresa Rolla of Niblo's Corps de Ballet, of the Academie Imperiale of Paris and Her Majesty's Theatre of London. With this gala event leading the way, the Washington Theatre then prospered for more than a decade as the city's most celebrated public entertainment venue, maintaining the tradition of excellence initiated by Carusi's Saloon.

The opening of the Washington Theatre ushered in a new era for the celebrated building at 11th and C Streets NW, one in which a series of playhouses would enjoy tremendous success within its quarters for more than 70 years. After the Washington Theatre closed on Thursday, August 17, 1871 the lineup of theatres to grace the building was quite impressive: The Theatre Comique (August 1871 to Tuesday, September 19, 1882); the New Theatre Comique (Wednesday, September 20, 1882 to Friday, January 18, 1884); the Theatre Comique (it again operated under this moniker from Saturday, January 19, 1884 to Tuesday, February 23, 1886); the National Museum (Saturday, February 27, 1886 to Sunday, September 19, 1886); Kernan's Washington Theatre (Monday, September 20, 1886 to Saturday, April 28, 1888); Kernan's New Washington Theatre (after a five-month dark period, Monday, October 1, 1888 to Saturday, May 16, 1891); Kernan's Lyceum Theatre (after a three-month dark period the theatre reopened on Monday, August 17, 1891 with a new listed street address as 1014 Pennsylvania Avenue NW; the theatre then changed its name to the New Lyceum Theatre on Saturday, September 1, 1906 and closed on Sunday, March 16, 1919; it subsequently sat dark and unused for the next 23 months); the Capitol Theatre (Sunday, February 20, 1921 to Saturday, October 14, 1922); and the President Theatre (Sunday, October 15, 1922 to Sunday, March 3, 1929).

Within a week after the President Theatre closed, the building was torn down and construction began almost instantly on the new Internal Revenue Building, which ultimately was completed on the former theatre site on Sunday, June 1, 1930 and opened for business six weeks later on Monday, July 14. The United States Internal Revenue Service Building is still standing today on the plot of land that used to be the southeast corner of 11th Street NW and Pennsylvania Avenue NW, though its rerouted front entrance is now on the building's south side and marked 1111 Constitution Avenue NW.

CHAPTER EIGHT
THE GREATEST HALL OF ALL

When the original Washington Theatre at 11th and C Streets NW burned down in April 1820, it left a void in the City of Washington's developing performing arts scene. Fortunately for the patrons of the arts, it was not long before a new professional theatre building was erected on the southeast corner of 6th Street NW and Louisiana Avenue NW (today known as Indiana Avenue NW), two blocks north of Pennsylvania Avenue, in the heart of what was developing into Downtown Washington. Officially named the Washington Theatre in deference to its storied predecessor, the 700-seat brick structure was initially managed by Messrs. William Warren and Burke Wood of the Philadelphia and Baltimore Company, whose sophisticated theatrical presentations were eagerly welcomed by the public.

This newer version of the Washington Theatre had its grand opening on the night of Wednesday, August 8, 1821 with an address by Mr. Wood himself, followed by a comedy play entitled "She Stoops to Conquer, Or, the Mistakes of a Night." The bill also included an afterpiece in the form of a musical dance performance called "A Pas Seul" by Mrs. H. Wallack. The evening concluded with a comic opera entitled "The Spoiled Child."

The venue itself was operated in a first-class manner, with box seats priced at one dollar, pit seating available at 75 cents and a special place appropriated to People of Color for a 50-cent admission. In addition, smoking was prohibited in every part of the theatre and proper officers were appointed by the police to "rigidly notice any breach of decorum."

The Washington Theatre carried on for more than 14 years at this location and offered eagerly anticipated stage performances featuring many of the nation's most renowned actors, comedians, singers and musicians. Some of the venue's more storied evenings of entertainment during the 1820s included: A five-night performance of Shakespeare's celebrated tragedy "Richard 3d" beginning on Thursday, August 1, 1822 featuring the Washington debut of 26-year-old lead actor Junius Brutus Booth (father of John Wilkes Booth, future assassin of President Abraham Lincoln), late of the Theatres Royal Drury Lane and Covent Garden in England; a series of performances by British-born actor Thomas Abthorpe Cooper beginning with an appearance in Shakespeare's "MacBeth" on Tuesday, September 3, 1822; a full-scale offering of John Howard Payne's opera, "Clari; or, The Maid of Milan" on Monday, March 29, 1824 that included the performance of such songs as "Sweet Home," "The Rose of Love" by Mrs. Waring, "Little Love is a Mischievous By" and "Love the Young Deceiver" by Mrs. Allen, "The Ladies," "Chit Chat," and "The Sun that Lights the Roses" by Mr. Moreland, and the duet of "I Love Thee" by Mrs. Allen and Mr. Moreland; an appearance by Philadelphia-born actor Edwin Forrest as the character of Rolla in the play "Pizarro" on Monday, October 2, 1826; and a four-performance stand by the celebrated French dancer Mademoiselle Celeste, who began her stay on Saturday, March 29, 1828 with the lead in the melodrama "The Dumb Girl of Genoa; Or, The Mountain Robber" and followed up with roles in the farce "Honest Thieves" on March 31, the melodrama "The Broken Sword" on Tuesday, April 1, and the French play "Deaf and Dumb; or, The Orphans Protected" on Wednesday, April 2 – each night she augmented each performance with a special Grand Turkish Pas Seul dance.

Perhaps the most interesting character of all to work the Washington Theatre was the famed T.D. Rice (1808-1860), who performed in black-face makeup as a hapless slave named Jim Crow in a song-and-dance act which was responsible for inspiring the extremely popular minstrel shows of the 19th century.

Born a White American named Thomas Dartmouth Rice in New York City, the innovative playwright and comic actor first introduced the Jim Crow character onstage in Louisville, Kentucky in 1828, replete with a heavy Black accent and ragged slave attire. He extensively toured America and Europe, garnering rave reviews and enjoying tremendous success for what was then considered to be progressive humor. His popularity was such that Jim Crow became a generic term for all White comedians' black-face portrayal of slaves, and, long after Rice's passing, the illogical namesake of racial segregation laws.

T.D. Rice made his local debut on the night of Wednesday, October 3, 1832, appearing at the Washington Theatre as Mammon in the melodrama "The Devil's Ducat" and as Tristrain Fickle in the farce "The Weathercock." In between the two offerings, he provided a full schedule of comic songs as the famed Jim Crow. His performances were enthusiastically received and T.D. Rice returned to the Washington Theatre repeatedly in 1832 and 1833.

The Washington Theatre continued on in fine fashion with theatrical presentations featuring nationally recognized talent until the night of Monday, November 23, 1835. On that particular date the Theatre offered a play entitled "Rob Roy McGregor" and ended the evening with a farce entitled "The Wrong Box." Included on the program, according to the Daily National Intelligencer, was "a variety of other entertainments, as will be expressed in the bills of the day." For reasons never made clear, the Washington Theatre shut its doors for good at the conclusion of this presentation, though the venue did not stay dark for long.

In its edition of Friday, December 25, 1835, the Daily National Intelligencer offered a notice with the heading "American Theatre – Louisiana Avenue" which stated: "F.C. Wemyss respectfully informs the public that, having leased the old theatre in the City of Washington, he will open it for the season on Christmas Day. The following distinguished actors are already engaged: Mr. Booth, Mr. Hill, Miss Waring, Mr. A. Addams, Mr. Ingersoll, Miss Mary Duff, who will appear in rapid succession. The stock company will be such as he trusts will meet the approbation of the public. Price of admission to any part of the theatre, fifty cents."

The ad then advertised the Christmas day performance of the melodrama "Therese; or, The Orphan of Geneva" featuring Miss Mary Duff in the lead role. Opening the evening was a farce entitled "Raising the Wind" and the evening concluded with another farce entitled "Kill or Cure."

Of special interest is the man who leased the old Washington Theatre and worked hard on its reincarnation, the American Theatre. Francis Courtney "F.C." Wemyss (1797-1859) was a native Londoner who came to America in 1822 to join the Chestnut Theatre Company in Philadelphia, Pennsylvania. He developed into a skilled comedian, quickly graduated to dramatic roles and eventually became the manager of his home venue. He later managed theatres in Baltimore, Pittsburgh and New York. When the opportunity came to refurbish an empty venue in the nation's capital and reopen it in his vision as the American Theatre, he jumped at the chance. Wemyss is best remembered as the author of the book "Twenty-Six Years of the Life of an Actor and Manager" (1847), an autobiography focusing on his vast range of theatrical experiences. Wemyss also served as editor of a series of book volumes of early American plays entitled "The Acting American Theatre" (1826).

Unfortunately the dream of F.C. Wemyss was short-lived, as the American Theatre barely made it through a scant six-week run. Their final weekend performance took place on the night of Saturday, February 6, 1836 with what was advertised as "Mr. Watson's Benefit" which consisted of the play "School of Reform" with the role of Tyke performed by Mr. Watson. Also on the bill was a "Hornpipe Song" by Durang Russell and a concluding farce entitled "Turnpike Gate" which included comic songs by Mr. Painter.

Two nights later the American Theatre offered its final program, "Mr. Russell's Benefit," which was highlighted by a comedy entitled "Wild Oats" and also included a musical mélange of melody, glee and songs and climaxed with the laughable farce "My Uncle Sam." With Mr. Wemyss packing his bags and heading for seemingly greener pastures, the storied venue then sat vacant and forgotten for the following five years, ignored by the city's entrepreneurs and seemingly on the verge of permanent extinction.

Suddenly and surprisingly, the weathered building on Louisiana Avenue NW was brought back to life. On Tuesday, March 2, 1841 the Daily National Intelligencer ran the following notice: "The New Assembly Rooms: The Old Theatre on Louisiana Avenue, so admirably situated for public amusements, has just been converted into two spacious and elegant assembly rooms. These rooms will be opened next Thursday night for the Inauguration ball, and will, no doubt, from the extensive preparations now in the course of completion, form a most splendid and brilliant appearance. The Washington Assembly Rooms, it is calculated, will accommodate two thousand, five-hundred persons. The two dancing rooms measure 85 feet by 45. To each of these dancing rooms are annexed two supper rooms, measuring 60 feet by 20. These rooms are intended, the one for gentlemen, and the other for gentlemen and ladies accompanying them. The ladies' dressing room measures 37 feet by 7. The gentlemen's dressing room measures 18 feet by 6 and ½. We understand the dancing rooms will be most brilliantly lighted. Two choice bands of music are engaged, and the supper will be provided by Kinchy in his best style. It is believed that this ball will be of the most splendid kind ever got up in this metropolis."

With that grand announcement, the Assembly Rooms, as they were christened, reopened to the public with the Inauguration Ball of President William Henry Harrison on the night of Thursday, March 4, 1841. No fewer than 76 managers were appointed to the event, with tickets being hawked at Dr. Watkins' Store and the Gadsby's and Brown's Hotels. There was formidable competition in the city that evening as two other Inauguration Balls were also being staged by competing venues: the Central Masonic Hall just down the street at 4½ Street NW and Louisiana Avenue NW offered the "First Native American Inauguration Ball" while the popular Carusi's Saloon was the scene of the "People's Tippecanoe Inauguration Ball."

On Friday, March 5 the Daily National Intelligencer announced that: "The several ball-rooms and places of amusement were filled with crowds of gentlemen and ladies attracted to this city by the novelty and interest of the great occasion. In the course of the evening, the President of the United States paid a short visit to each of the Assemblies held in honor of the Inauguration, and was received with the warmest demonstrations of attachment and respect."

The Inauguration Ball of President Harrison kicked off a period of steady activity in the Assembly Rooms that lasted for nearly four years. An assortment of concerts and dances were the featured programs of entertainment from the spring of 1841 until November 1844, at which time a new entrepreneur, identified in the local newspapers of the day as Mr. T. Ward, came into the picture and leased the venue. Operating the Assembly Rooms as a well-conducted place of amusement, Mr. Ward's first offering was an act known as the Campanologian Band of Swiss Bell Ringers, who staged a four-night grand concert beginning Wednesday, December 4, 1844.

In the wake of this initial performance, Mr. Ward evidently saw fit to invest time and money into the refurbishment of the venue on Louisiana Avenue NW, as it wasn't until the second week of January 1845 that he would again enlist seasoned performers to entertain the citizens of the City of Washington. This time, however, Mr. Ward would introduce a new name for his assembly hall and unknowingly make history with his choice of entertainment.

The Friday, January 10, 1845 edition of the Daily National Intelligencer included the following paragraph in its "Local News" column: "The Olympic Saloon, advertised in this day's paper by Mr. Ward, will be opened on Monday night, for popular dramatic entertainments, vaudevilles, petit operas, etc. The location of the Olympic Saloon (in the Washington Assembly Room, Louisiana Avenue) is certainly eligible and, should the performances be good, as we have been led to anticipate, it will gratify us to find that Mr. Ward's new enterprise is liberally patronized."

Elsewhere in the same edition, a sizable notice was published under the enticing headline, "Ward's New Olympic Saloon, near Coleman's Hotel. New Era in Histrionics." Part of the notice read: "The lessee begs to announce that the arrangements for the efficient opening of the above establishment being completed, the season will positively commence on Monday, January 13, with a new and effective force, expressly selected with a view of affording talented performances of comedy, vaudeville, and petite opera."

This article provided extensive information on the performers who were scheduled to grace the stage of the new venue: "Mrs. Timm, the popular singer and actress, from Mitchell's Olympic, New York; Miss McBride, from the Chestnut Street Theatre, Philadelphia; Mrs. Hautonville, from the Chestnut Street Theatre, Philadelphia; Miss Pauline, from the Walnut Street Theatre, Philadelphia; Miss Nicholls, from the National Theatre, Philadelphia; Mr. John Sefton, the popular comedian from the New York theatres; Mr. Brunton, from the Chestnut Street Theatre, Philadelphia; Mr. Thompson, from the Arch Street Theatre, Philadelphia; Mr. Anderton, from the Charleston Theatre; Mr. McDonald, from the Park Theatre, New York; Mr. Ward. Introductory to the performance, a Pictorial Allegory, written for the occasion and named, Our Country in 1770, and its glorious destiny revealed. The local scenery by Lee – the music arranged by Mr. Weber. On Monday and Tuesday, January 13th and 14th, the performance will commence with the new and highly interesting piece, Theresa's Vow, or the Maid of Croissy. To conclude with, for the first time in Washington, a new and original vaudeville, with the author's music, new dresses, new and peculiarly constructed machinery, and as performed with great success at New York, Philadelphia, called the Blue Domino, or Anthony and Cleopatra...For terms, apply at Coleman's Hotel."

The significance of this notice is of great importance, as it rates as the very first time in history that vaudeville entertainment was offered to the public in America. While there have been vague references to vaudeville-type shows having been staged in saloons of the West during this general time period, this particular notice marked the first documented example of vaudeville entertainment being advertised in the United States of America.

The term "vaudeville" has its origin in the town of Vire (located within the Normandy region of France), which during the 15th century was well-regarded as a place of country ballads laced with sharp satire, local humor and true-life adventure. These pastoral folk songs came to be referred to as "Un Chanson du Vau de Vire" ("A song of the Valley of Vire") and were frequently associated with the French poet Olivier Basselin (1400-1450), who owned and operated a fulling mill in Vire and created numerous songs and pieces of prose that touched upon such endearing topics as love, war, and, of course, hilarious drinking escapades of the French countrymen.

By the year 1500 the shortened term "vaudevire" was in common use to describe these catchy songs that permeated the valleys surrounding Normandy. As an accepted part of the French vocabulary, "vaudevire" eventually coalesced with a separate style of love song, Voix de Ville (Voice of the City) and during the 17th century the term "vaudeville" was in widespread use throughout the whole of France to describe a light, entertaining song or ditty. The opening of the Theatre du Vaudeville in Paris, France on Thursday, January 12, 1792 served to advance the term throughout all of Europe and the word "vaudeville" gradually came to refer to the actual variety shows, as opposed to the individual songs being performed within the shows themselves.

In the United States, vaudeville shows became a featured theatrical attraction in the 19th century, with a generally accepted heyday spanning from 1875 to 1932. While there was never a standard vaudeville formula, programs evolved through time to eventually offer audiences a diverse menu of entertainment in anywhere from 8 to 14 brief acts or turns.

The content of these presentations was aligned without regard to narrative plot or theme and included musical and vocal performances (with an emphasis on solo or duet numbers), dance numbers, magic acts, acrobatics, gymnastics, juggling, clowning, comedy routines, animal acts and guest appearances and cameos by a variety of celebrity actors and noteworthy personalities. The performers themselves shaped the stage acts, combining music and dialogue with costumes, props and the power of their own personal charisma to magically captivate their enthralled audiences.

Locally, vaudeville became the driving force of theatres in Washington, D.C. in the early 20th century and dissipated after the repeal of Prohibition in 1933, giving way to the increased popularity of motion pictures, and, eventually, the newer wave of live music night clubs.

The Olympic Saloon remained under the direction and management of Mr. T. Ward throughout January 1845, offering live entertainment several nights per week with a company of local players led by actors named Mrs. Timm, Mr. John Sefton, Miss McBride and Mr. Brunton. Dramas, farces, unique vaudevilles and various types of musical performances filled each multi-act bill, and, according to press reports of the day, drew enthusiastic crowds.

On Monday, January 27, 1845 actress Mrs. Timm assumed the role of director of the Olympic Saloon (the reasons for Mr. T. Ward's rather sudden departure have since remained a mystery, though he apparently maintained ownership of the building for an unspecified period of time) and her first booking for that particular evening was topped by the first appearance of Mr. John Dunn, the celebrated comedian and buffo singer. She maintained operational control of the facility for a period of approximately five weeks, her most significant booking being the Ebon Minstrels, who made their Washington debut at the Olympic Saloon in a headlining role on the night of Saturday, March 1, 1845. This was another entertainment first, as it marked the first time "minstrel" entertainment was featured in the City of Washington.

The Saturday, March 8, 1845 edition of the Daily National Intelligencer contained a notice informing the public that one William E. Burton, who had previously managed the National Theatre (which had just closed in the aftermath of a calamitous fire), had reached an agreement with Mr. T. and had taken control of the Olympic Saloon with the intent of maintaining the employment of his dramatic corps. Burton, the notice stated: "Invites his friends to witness a nightly series of entertainments of sterling merit."

Evidently, Mr. Burton's reign over the Olympic Saloon lasted a mere two nights. Saturday night's program consisted of a play entitled "Border Beagles; or, The Yankee in Mississippi," a "Fancy Dance" by someone only identified as Miss Gertrude, a comedetta entitled "A Kiss in the Dark," and a concluding farce "The Artful Dodger" (which included songs by lead actor Mr. Chapman). The show for Tuesday night, March 11, 1845, which turned out to be the final night of the Olympic Saloon, featured the dramatic, two-act play "Lone Star; or, Trouble in Texas" followed by the concluding farce, "His Own Ghost."

For a six-month period following the demise of the Olympic Saloon, the building on Louisiana Avenue NW was once again called the Assembly Rooms and was subsequently utilized by a succession of individual entrepreneurs who mainly staged musical concerts and dinner parties within the facility.

In the fall of 1845 one Moses Copp came onto the scene, redesigned the Assembly Rooms to house six separate bowling lanes and reopened the facility on Monday, November 29 as Copp's Bowling Saloon. Advertised in the pages of the Daily National Intelligencer as "the most spacious and magnificent establishment of the kind in the world," the saloon offered a ground-floor restaurant replete with several separate party rooms and bathing rooms and a second-floor bowling saloon and pistol gallery. Copp's Bowling Saloon was open to the public through January 1849.

When Moses Copp dropped out of the picture, the venue reverted back to a concert hall and from February 1849 until October 1861 was available to the public as the Assembly Rooms (also advertised in the local newspapers of the day as the Washington Assembly Rooms).

In grandly celebrated event, the Assembly Rooms hosted a concert on the night of Tuesday, December 22, 1857 headlined by the renowned opera singer Miss Juliana May, assisted by tenor Signor Tiberini, baritone Signor Rudolphsen and the young, highly acclaimed pianist Harry Sanderson.

Bookings in the Assembly Rooms had slowed considerably by the summer of 1861. At that time a new team of managers arrived on the scene with intentions of revitalizing the building and installing a new theatre on the premises. After several weeks of renovating the property, gentlemen named Leonard Grover and William Sinn assumed control of the Louisiana Avenue NW building and installed a third party named George Percival as their manager. Together, this team introduced Canterbury Hall on the premises with opening night occurring on Wednesday, November 13, 1861.

Plays, musical performances and variety shows were the order of the day. Some of the earliest entertainers at Canterbury Hall included black-face/minstrel performers Frank Bower (billed as the Philadelphia Darkey, he had been an original member of the Virginia Minstrels troupe), Dick Parker (the popular Ethiopian comedian), singer-dancer Harry Fox (a featured attraction at minstrel shows up and down the East Coast) and the legendary Billy Emerson (born William Emerson Redmond in Belfast, North Ireland, he became one of the most noted minstrel song and dance men of the day).

Over the next several years among the more famous entertainers to take the stage at Canterbury Hall were Agnes Robertson (a Scotland-born actress of great acclaim), Julia Mortimer (the noted British actress), Kate Pennoyer (the famed dancer and pantominist who was billed as the Queen of Terpsichore), the Rabineau Sisters (highly regarded ballet dancers), the Rollande Brothers (acrobats), Marietta Ravel (an actress and tight-rope artist), comedian W.B. Cavanaugh, the St. George Sisters (singers and dancers), John Denier (tight-rope walker), Cherry Belle (vaudeville dancer and actress), Tony Pastor (billed as the Dean of Vaudeville, he was one of the nation's most popular minstrel show-vaudeville actor-singers), the Fowler Sisters (dancers), Louisa Wells (circus star and equestrienne) and just about all of the top theatrical and vaudeville entertainers that were touring the Eastern United States at the time.

Canterbury Hall suffered a premature closing when a fire destroyed the facility on the night of Friday, July 23, 1869. It marked the end of the famed venue that had enjoyed so many wondrous moments in Washington, D.C. performing arts history. It is interesting to note that the former site of Canterbury Hall remained a vacant lot for over 100 years. Bulldozers arrived in 1974 to begin construction on the District of Columbia Courthouse, which ultimately was opened to the public in May 1978. The building was officially renamed H. Carl Moultrie, I Courthouse of the District of Columbia in July 1992 and is still standing today at 500 Indiana Avenue NW.

In retrospect, it is clear that the three primary early-era venues of the City of Washington – the United States Theatre, the Washington Theatre (Carusi's Saloon) and the

Washington Theatre (Assembly Rooms) – served as cultural cornerstones for the city's evolving performing arts scene.

Each of these three stages was recognized for offering innovations that contributed to the advancement of theatre and music within the framework of popular culture in the nation's capital: The United States Theatre introduced the fundamentals of English theatre to the City of Washington and served as the pioneer venue of the local theatre arts community; the Washington Theatre (Carusi's Saloon) widened the scope of the local performing arts scene by booking a steady procession of plays, concerts, dances and special events that always featured an impressive array of amateur and professional talent; and the Washington Theatre (Assembly Rooms) made its mark in entertainment history, when, as the Olympic Saloon, it became the very first venue in America to advertise and book vaudeville entertainment, thus giving birth to a unique type of multi-act variety show that would later dominate local theaters and eventually play an instrumental role in the advent of night clubs in Washington, D.C.

As the population of the City of Washington expanded throughout the course of the 19th century, interest in the performing arts steadily increased and a variety of assembly rooms, hotels, taverns and theatres were opened to the public to accommodate the needs of the socially active public.

Two of the more storied taverns of this era were Rhodes Tavern and the Ebbitt House. The former was built in 1799 as an unnamed boarding house at the northeast corner of 15th and F Streets NW and became Rhodes' Hotel in 1801. It was soon renamed Rhodes' Tavern and was known for hosting lavish dancing assemblies. The Ebbitt House was built in 1835 on the southeast corner of 14th and F Streets NW and initially operated as an unnamed boarding house and grocery store. In 1865 it was named the Ebbitt House and during its early years was known to employ local banjo players and guitarists for individual performances.

Two of the most popular hotels of the time were the Willard Hotel and the National Hotel. The Willard Hotel building was constructed in 1816 at the northwest corner of 14th and Pennsylvania Avenue NW as a row of six, two-story residential houses. It was converted into Strother's Hotel in 1818 and then changed hands and titles numerous times before being refurbished and reopened as Willard's City Hotel in October 1847. It ultimately became the Willard Hotel in May 1853.

The building that housed the National Hotel was also constructed in 1816 and sat at the northeast corner of 6th Street NW and Pennsylvania Avenue NW. It originally consisted of a series of residential row houses. In 1826 it was opened to the public as Gadsby's Hotel and in 1844 it was transformed into the National Hotel, operating until January 1931. Both the Willard and the National hosted formal balls, dances and assemblies.

Among the several multi-purpose assembly halls where all manner of popular music concerts and miscellaneous entertainment offerings were staged were: Apollo Hall, which opened in 1841 on the south side of Pennsylvania Avenue NW, between 13th and 14th Streets NW; Odd Fellows' Hall, which opened in 1845 on the east side of 7th Street NW, between D and E Streets NW; and Metzerott Hall, which opened in 1851 on the north side of Pennsylvania Avenue NW, between 9th and 10th Streets NW.

High-class theatres stocked with professional talent thrived in the nation's capital during these years and among the favorites were: the National Theatre, which was first opened along the north side of E Street NW, between 13th and 14th Streets NW, on Monday, December 7, 1835 (through the years there would be five different versions of this theatre at various locations in the city); the Odeon, which opened in February 1845 on the northeast corner of 4½ Street NW and Pennsylvania Avenue NW; the Adelphi Theatre, which opened in December 1847 on the south side of Pennsylvania Avenue NW, between

4½ and 6th Streets NW; and Ford's Theatre, which was originally built in 1833 as Parson Brown's Baptist Church on the east side of 10th Street NW between E and F Streets NW and became George Christy's Opera House in 1861; it became Ford's Athenaeum on Wednesday, March 19, 1862 and then changed its name to Ford's Theatre in 1863.

CHAPTER NINE
ALONG THE EASTERN BRANCH

Throughout the 18th century the towns that achieved greatest cultural significance within Prince George's County, Maryland were situated along rivers and grew in economic stature as the businesses of exporting farm crops and importing goods prospered. Second to Upper Marlborough, the most important town to emerge in the region was Bladensburgh, which was situated in the outer stretches of the county on the Eastern Branch, some 15 miles northwest of the county seat, where it later served as the heart of a main transportation route for travelers voyaging to the City of Washington or Baltimore. Through the years Bladensburgh would develop a colorful reputation as a party town, a place where socializing, eating, drinking, dancing, music-making and fighting were interchangeably mixed.

The population of Prince George's County increased from approximately 10,000 in 1750 to 21,185 in 1800, necessitating the gradual establishment of additional towns throughout the territory to accommodate the expanding number of inhabitants. Despite the growth, Upper Marlborough, mainly because of its role as the county seat and its early distinction as a port town and commerce center, would maintain a sterling reputation as a town of high-quality entertainment well into the late 19th century. However, as the population of Prince George's County steadily grew, other developing towns became designated as suitable locations for ordinaries, taverns and restaurants. As a result, local residents found themselves inundated with a plethora of dining and entertainment options throughout the county. Upper Marlborough was no longer the single unchallenged option for a night on the town.

Bladensburgh was established in 1742 by an Act of the General Assembly of Maryland "for laying out and erecting a Town on the South Side of the Eastern Branch of the Potomack River in Prince Georges County near a place called Garrison's Landing." The town is believed to have been named after one of two individuals: William Bladen, a graduate of Oxford University who had served as the Attorney General of Maryland in 1707; or his son Thomas Bladen, who was elected governor of Maryland in 1742 and held the post through 1747.

Commissioners were appointed and instructed to purchase 60 acres of land on the site with the intent of laying out the town in 60 separate one-care lots. Once established, Bladensburgh immediately became a busy port town for the shipping of tobacco and the reception of imported goods from overseas, with a number of wharves, stores, ordinaries and other private businesses fueling its growth and economic development.

The town's name was officially recognized as "Bladensburg" with the passing of the Chapter 137 of the Laws of Maryland, which stated: "An act to incorporate the village of Bladensburg, in Prince Georges County, Mar. 9, 1854." However, this seemed a somewhat inconsequential act, as the town had used both spellings both before and after the passing of the law.

Bladenburgh's reputation as a nocturnal retreat for spirits and celebrations had its origins in two prime establishments that were constructed in the port area long before the town itself was established. These two ordinaries, the George Washington House and the Palo Alto Hotel, stood opposite each other on the road to Baltimore and offered the most festive dances, the finest liquor and the most raucous musical entertainment to be found in the county.

The George Washington House, which is still standing today at 4302 Baltimore Avenue in Bladensburg, was reportedly built in 1732, though its earliest land record that can be referenced is dated Saturday, March 14, 1747. This document refers to the structure as the Brick Store and lists Israel Folsom as owner. The next transaction occurred when Jacob Wirt purchased the property on Thursday, June 2, 1763, with the land area consisting of the original 24x36-foot brick store structure, referred to as the Indian Maid, and an adjoining two-story frame tavern referred to as the Indian Queen Tavern. From 1774 until 1784 the Brick Store complex was rented out by Peter Carnes, an attorney who is noted for making the first authenticated balloon ascents in America during the spring and summer months of 1784. The business was later owned by Jasper Wirt, while a fellow named Baley Earles Clarke ran the operation from 1792 until 1832.

Sometime between 1809 and 1831 the Indian Queen Tavern portion was torn down, with the original Brick Store subsequently being altered to form the main brick section of what is today the George Washington House. When stage lines were flourishing, the Brick Store was a coaching house and relay station. During this same time when the Bladensburg Dueling Grounds were in favor, many participants spent what might have been their final night on this planet at the inn. It is said that cannon balls from the 1814 Battle of Bladensburg were embedded in the tavern's walls at the time.

Land records illustrate that in 1835 the building was still being called the Brick Store. In 1854 the property was registered as both a store and tavern. It became a hotel in 1857 and in 1876 was being referred to as the George Washington Hotel (on the premise that George Washington had spent the night there during his presidential term, though in reality he had stayed over in the adjoining Indian Queen Tavern). In 1894 it was renamed the George Washington House.

During its time the George Washington House frequently hosted a variety of dances, balls and concert performances. Word-of-mouth accounts transmitted from one generation to another are the primary source of information pertaining to the venue's music offerings, with no known first-hand accounts, either written or recorded, having survived through the years. While details on these long-lost nights of entertainment are scant, the George Washington House was reportedly considered to be one of Bladenburgh's classiest establishments of the day, with small ensembles, violin bands and proper orchestras frequently employed for their events. Meanwhile, the town's other smaller taverns and saloons favored fiddlers, banjo players and country singers for their nights of entertainment.

In recent times the George Washington House operated as a hotel, restaurant or tavern before closing its doors in 1970. The building's last private owner, Florence Morgan, sold the property to the Prince George's Jaycees on Friday, June 30, 1972 for the sum of $42,000. Today the George Washington House still stands and currently houses the Anacostia Watershed Society. Famous names from the past who are said to have spent the night here at various points in time are Patrick Henry, Thomas Jefferson, Henry Clay, Daniel Webster, John C. Calhoun, Stephen Decatur (the night before his fateful Wednesday, March 22, 1820 duel with James Barron), and, of course, George Washington himself, once in 1774 on his way to the first Continental Congress and again in 1790 during the journey that led to the agreement on a national capital.

Just north of the George Washington House on the opposite side of the Road to Baltimore was the equally famous Palo Alto Hotel, which had been constructed in 1734. Though initially functioning solely as a house of lodging, the Palo Alto was notorious throughout much of the 19th century for its cocking main, where the killer birds would tear each other to shreds much to the delight of the drunken throngs. Reportedly, a regular visitor for these special events was President Andrew Jackson, who reportedly delighted in the bloody bird battles and could frequently be seen on a favorite bar stool sloshing down cold ones. Throughout its existence the Palo Alto was saddled with a rough reputation, as gentle folk music in the early evenings often gave way to drunken fiddle jamborees in the wee hours, with arguments, fisticuffs and outright brawls frequently transpiring.

The Palo Alto Tavern, as it came to be called, is allegedly the birthplace of the term "cocktail." During the period of time in which Hyattsville to the north was a dry town, the Palo Alto offered travelers a two-way sign. The side that faced the road into Hyattsville read "Last Chance," while the reverse side read "First Chance" and welcomed incoming thirsty travelers to the sporting port of Bladensburg.

The Palo Alto Tavern remained in operation until 1963, at which point its name was changed to Bresnahan's Tavern. In 1966 the establishment, whose listed street address at the time was 4409 Baltimore Avenue, closed for good and the building was subsequently torn down in 1969. Its former site is now occupied by an unmarked work building belonging to Security Fence Manufacturing and Supply Company (whose main office is at 4301 46th Street, Bladensburg).

Prince George's County, Maryland endured social and economic changes during the course of the 19th century. The population remained remarkably stable during the century in terms of sheer numbers – in 1800 the county recorded 21,185 residents, with the number increasing modestly to 29,898 in 1900. Agriculture, with tobacco firmly established as the staple crop, remained the backbone of the economy during this time, though as the century came to a close there was a noticeable reduction in large plantations and a notable increase in the number of small farms across the land. Commercial life gradually expanded in the county as small industries took hold, stores and taverns thrived, transportation routes improved and towns took shape beyond the waterways. The population of the county increased dramatically as the 20th century progressed, with new arrivals attracted by the plethora of job opportunities, available goods and services, and superior cultural offerings afforded by nearby Washington, D.C.

The 19th century did not start well for the people of Prince George's County. While the county had not engaged in any type of extensive military action during the Revolutionary War, things were drastically different during the now-infamous War of 1812. The United States of America, in an effort to end the impressment of American sailors by the British, stop foreign aid to the Indians and add land in British-controlled Canada and Spanish-inhabited Florida to the Union, declared war on the Kingdom of Great Britain on Thursday, June 18, 1812.

By the summer of 1814, the British had repelled several American advances on Canada and decided to make diversionary attacks on the nation's capital and nearby Baltimore. British forces landed on Benedict Pier on the Patuxent River in Southern Maryland on Saturday, August 20, 1814 and over the next several days marched 50 miles northwards. Shortly before 1pm on Wednesday, August 24, 1814 they were met on the banks of the Anacostia River in Bladensburg, Maryland by a poorly trained and ill-prepared defensive force of American militia largely from Prince George's County. The Battle of Bladensburg ensued.

The reported number of participants in this battle has never been verified. It is estimated by many historians that approximately 4,000 to 4,500 British soldiers under joint command of Major General Robert Ross and Admiral George Cockburn advanced that day upon an American force of 5,041 led by General William Henry Winder and commanded by Brigadier General Tobias Stansbury. They met on the banks of the Anacostia River at the foot of Lowndes Hill in Bladensburg. By 4pm the British had routed the disorganized American militia mainly with the utilization of their advanced Congreve rockets.

The victors then marched towards the seemingly deserted City of Washington and at approximately 7pm began burning down the Capitol, the President's House, the Treasury and the War Department building with little opposition. Within 24 hours most of the city's prominent buildings had been reduced to smoldering embers and President James Madison had fled for his life to rural Virginia.

When the British invaded Prince George's County in August 1814 Ross and Cockburn had made their headquarters at the home of Dr. William Beanes in Upper Marlboro, whom they subsequently took as a prisoner and held on shipboard in the Chesapeake Bay as they prepared to attack Baltimore. A young lawyer from Georgetown named Francis Scott Key (born in a farmhouse called Terra Rubra in what was then Frederick County, Maryland on Sunday, August 1, 1779) knew Dr. Beanes personally and was called upon by mutual friends to negotiate his release.

Key, along with a United States Prisoner Exchange agent named John Stuart Skinner, sailed up the Chesapeake Bay in a Flag of Truce vessel and met with General Robert Ross, who released Dr. Beanes to their custody, but on the condition that the three remain detained on their ship, some eight miles off shore from Fort McHenry, until the Battle of Baltimore had been concluded.

The fighting commenced early on the morning of Tuesday, September 13, 1814 and the three men watched the fiery exchange from their ship throughout the entire day and into the evening hours. They noted that American forces had raised a large American flag over the fort which was in view until the night arrived and then only during the glare of battle. Just before dawn on Wednesday, September 14, the fighting stopped. The morning light revealed that the American flag was still there. Key was so inspired at the sight before his eyes, he began writing a poem on the back of a letter which ultimately became "The Star Spangled Banner."

Later set to music that was written by John Stafford Smith for the poem "To Anacreon in Heaven," "The Star Spangled Banner" became our national anthem through an Act of Congress on Tuesday, March 3, 1931. Ultimately, the British were defeated by the United States in the Battle of New Orleans on Sunday, January 8, 1815. A month later on Friday, February 17, 1815 the two countries exchanged a peace treaty and President Madison declared the war at an end.

In the early 19th century the Palo Alto Hotel served as primary quarters for those brave individuals who had agreed to settle personal disputes on a nearby field of honor known informally as Blood Run or the Dueling Grounds. The grounds themselves were tucked away in a little stream valley just off of the Road to Bladensburg and were allegedly the site of no fewer than 52 duels between the years 1814 and 1868. (Today the location of the Dueling Grounds is just southwest of the intersection of 38th Avenue and Bladensburg Road, adjacent to Anacostia River Park and Fort Lincoln Cemetery, in what is now known as Colmar Manor, Maryland.)

The most famous duel to ever take place on the Dueling Grounds occurred in 1820 between naval officers James Barron and Stephen Decatur. The 52-year-old Barron was a disgraced officer, having been court-martialed in 1807 for negligence in keeping his vessel prepared for war by allowing several of his men to be imprisoned by the British. Barron blamed the 41-year-old Decatur for the decision, pointing out that Decatur sat on the Board of Inquiry and had a prominent role in the court martial procedure itself.

On Wednesday, March 22, 1820 the two adversaries met at the Dueling Grounds, with the terms being pistols at eight paces. Decatur, then in his prime and an expert marksman, was the odds-on favorite to snuff out the portly, near-blind Barron. Such was not the case, as when the shots rang out, Barron was hit in the hip and Decatur was struck in the abdomen. The former would recover in time while the latter died later that evening in his mansion at Lafayette Square in the City of Washington.

The Palo Alto Hotel, as the nearest public house to the field of honor, became the home base for the participants of these duels. It was here that the contestants secured lodgings for the night prior to the deadly contests, were served square meals, and were entertained by evening sessions of fiddle playing. It has also been reported that many of the injured participants received post-duel treatments here within the Palo Alto, with many staying on as lodgers until their period of convalescence was complete.

It should be noted that the Palo Alto Hotel was also credited as having been the site of the invention of the cocktail, a story which is told in detail in an uncredited article in the Washington Post of Sunday, December 20, 1908 entitled "History of the Cocktail: Intellectual Bartender Recalls Duel That was Responsible for its Invention." As the story goes, on the surprisingly snowy evening of Tuesday, April 16, 1846 a dueling party consisting of 12 gentlemen left the old John Adams house in Washington and galloped towards northward toward Bladensburg. The party rode in two groups: the first contained Baron Henri de Vrie et Challono (an attaché of the French Legation), his fellow diplomat Chevalier Luigi Lugno (representative of the King of the Two Sicilles), Messrs. Jones, Lorrimore and Burton (members of the lower house of Congress) and Drs. John Malone and Guilford Calloway of the Army Medical Corps; and the second contained individuals identified as Mr. John A. Hopkins, Colonel Denmead Magione and Messrs. George William Mattingly, J. Upton Benson and Frederick G. Allison (reportedly Baron Challono and Mr. Hopkins were the principals, with Chevalier Lugno and Colonel Magione serving as their seconds). Shortly after 9pm the gentlemen reached the Palo Alto and there enjoyed an excellent supper. An hour later they retired for the night and awoke at daylight the next morning to journey to the Dueling Grounds.

On the field of honor on the morning of April 17, Baron Challono was badly wounded. The ground where he fell was drenched with blood and he required the services of both surgeons for more than two hours. His adversary, Mr. Hopkins, rushed to his side as soon as he fell and immediately became ill at the sight before him. He was escorted by his party back to the Palo Alto and arrived on the premises shortly after 8am.

Inside the hotel they sat Challono down in the old tap room and called upon bartender John Welby "Jack" Henderson to set up something stimulating at once. Henderson, noting that something unusually powerful was needed, grabbed a champagne glass and filled it half full of Maryland rye. He next added portions from a bottle of bitters and added a swig of syrup. He then offered up the mixture to Mr. Hopkins and the first Manhattan cocktail was born. Mr. Hopkins reached for the glass, gulped down the potion and made an immediate full recovery. "Another!" he cried. Jack Henderson then made a second one with more care, topping the drink by dropping a brandied cherry into it. Mr. Hopkins gulped it down and then ordered a round for his party. When the men sat down to breakfast a half-hour later, they were all in high spirits.

Colonel Magione saw before him a historic moment and notified the Daily National Intelligencer of the event. He proposed the drink be labeled Royal Jack, in honor or bartender Jack Henderson, but for reasons still unknown the name "cocktail" became attached to it and has survived to the present day. For the record, the gentlemen who were actually present when the first cocktail was mixed and consumed were Mr. Hopkins, Colonel Magione, Mr. Benson, Mr. Allison and bartender Jack Henderson.

Documenting the popular music scene in Prince George's County from this century is problematic, as very little material pertaining to this subject has survived through time. Available information on the county during these years is sketchy and comes from limited newspaper accounts and second-hand sources. It is known that as the 19th century came to a close a series of taverns in Bladensburg employed individual musicians to perform on weekends for their customers. Among these establishments were: the Green Tree Tavern, owned by Herman Bohnke and located on the eastern end of what would become Bladensburg Road; Coldenstroth's Saloon, which was built in the 1850s as a grocery store on Water Street, was taken over by George W. Coldenstroth in 1861 who soon converted it into a hotel and saloon, and survived well into the 20th century as the original Dixie Pig Restaurant and Barbecue on Annapolis Road; and the famed Palo Alto Tavern.

Among those now-forgotten folk musicians that toiled on the makeshift stages of these public houses during the late 1800s and very early 1900s were: banjoists Howard Burr, Harry Weber and George Dreager; and fiddlers Lloyd Williams, Richard Heygster and Philip Hill (the legendary "One-Man Orchestra" from Forestville). Meanwhile, the town's top establishment, the George Washington House, was known to stage more formal balls and dances during the final years of the century, with Frank Pistorio's Orchestra often providing the entertainment.

Perhaps the lively spirit of Prince George's County during this time is best captured by a fascinating account which appeared in the Washington Post on Monday, September 26, 1898. Entitled "Fired into a Crowd," the article reads: "September 25 – A shooting affray occurred at Bladensburg last night, Alex Cooper firing five times into a crowd congregated in the rear of Penn's Saloon. One of the bullets passed through the muscular part of the arm of Herbert Galloway. It appears that someone in the crowd spoke in an uncomplimentary way of Cooper's banjo playing. Without any warning he drew a pistol and began firing. Cooper fled, but was arrested this morning by Constable Vincent. He was hidden in a barn."

CHAPTER TEN
THE INTRODUCTION OF NEGRO MUSIC

During the 19th century, particularly after the Civil War years, newspapers in the City of Washington and around the country commonly used the term "Negro music" in their various articles to describe most any type of music performed by Blacks. As a result, a new genre of music – one based solely on the race of its performers, as opposed to the content of the music – joined pop and folk as main classifications of popular music in America. The first performers of what was to be called Negro music were the slaves, who, when they first were imported in the 17th century, could not speak English. In time they began mimicking the songs they heard and saw performed by the White American plantation owners, family members and workers who had originally brought the music with them from Europe. What the slaves began adding to the mix was percussion, which was not an African invention in the first place. Eventually, their plantation work songs, field hollers, spiritual chants and blues shouts became the foundation of what would become Negro music, race music, and, eventually, R&B.

Minstrelsy, the impersonation of Negroes in action and song by White men, played an important role in the development of Negro music. The portrayal of Negroes by White actors in black-face makeup began occurring in theatres across America in the early 1800s. Such characters were frequently featured in lead roles in the various dramas, farces, dances and songs offered by these venues, with many entertainers, perhaps the most esteemed being T.D. Rice (who was noted for his Jim Crow characterizations), achieving great fame for their performances that both lampooned and celebrated plantation Negroes.

The term "minstrelsy" came into public consciousness with the formation of a band called the Virginia Minstrels, consisting of fiddler Daniel Decatur Emmett, banjoist Billy Whitlock, tambourine player Dick Pelham and percussionist Frank Bower, who performed their first full-length music-and-comedy show at the Masonic Temple in Boston, Massachusetts on Tuesday, March 7, 1843. Minstrel performers soon began appearing on stages throughout the country in theatre presentations, circuses, medicine shows, and, eventually, vaudeville routines. When Negroes themselves began performing in black-face makeup as parts of their own minstrel troupes later in the century, it furthered the popularity of their own race-defined classification of music.

Negro music in Washington, D.C was greatly advanced by the abolition of slavery, which gave Blacks the freedom to live their lives as they saw fit. A monumental moment in history occurred with the approval of an act of Congress entitled "An Act for the Release of Certain Persons held to Service or Labor in the District of Columbia" on Wednesday, April 16, 1862, which officially abolished slavery in the nation's capital. This act, in part, read: "Be it enacted by the Senate and House Of Representatives of the United States of America in Congress assembled, that all persons held to service or labor within the District of Columbia by reason of African descent are hereby discharged and freed of and from all claim to such service or labor; and from and after the passage of this act neither slavery nor involuntary servitude, except for crime, where of the party shall be duly convicted, shall hereafter exist in said District." The end result was the freeing of approximately 3,100 slaves within the City of Washington.

On a national level, the subject of slavery was addressed by the Emancipation Proclamation, a statement issued by President Abraham Lincoln on Thursday, January 1, 1863, which, in part, declared: "All persons held as slaves within any State or designated part of a State, the people whereof shall then be in rebellion against the United States, shall be then, thenceforward, and forever free."

Strangely, though, President Lincoln's curious action only applied to the 11 states that comprised the Confederacy and left slavery untouched within the Union states, thus allowing Blacks to serve in the Union Army and Navy. It is an often overlooked fact that with this proclamation President Lincoln basically granted freedom over slaves for which he had no control, but kept in bondage the slaves over which he could have set free, had he so desired.

Ultimately, it was the Thirteenth Amendment to the United States Constitution, ratified by Congress on Wednesday, December 6, 1865, that officially brought an end to slavery in the United States of America. It stated, in part: "Neither slavery nor involuntary servitude, except as a punishment for crime whereof the party shall have been duly convicted, shall exist within the United States, or any place subject to their jurisdiction." With that decision, approximately 3.9 million slaves were granted their freedom.

The years surrounding the abolition of slavery were also highlighted by the conflict known as the Civil War. It should be noted, however, that the term "Civil War" itself is technically erroneous, as it implies a battle between two factions attempting to establish control of a single government. In fact, the Civil War, or more appropriately, the War for Southern Independence, was a battle between two separate nations, the Union and the Confederate States of America, the primary purpose of which was to deny the Confederacy its constitutional right to self-government. The war was fought over exorbitant taxation, expansion of federal power and loss of states' sovereignty.

The North was constantly trying to raise taxes on the states in the South through exorbitant tariffs on imported goods in order to bolster their own increasingly inefficient businesses. The South increased its trade with England and France, exchanging cotton for various manufactured goods which the North could not offer.

With the election of President Abraham Lincoln, the South was paying more than 80% of America's collected tariffs, though as a region they only comprised approximately 30% of the country's total population. These oppressive taxes combined with the denial of the constitutional right for the states to govern themselves pushed for the states in the South to legally withdraw from the Union and form the Confederate States of America. The only way the North could collect these high taxes and maintain their existence was to invade the Confederate states and physically force them back into the Union, denying their right to self-government and independence.

After Abraham Lincoln of the Republican Party won the presidential election on Tuesday, November 6, 1860, the political debate over Southern independence intensified and on December 20 of that year South Carolina became the first state to secede from the Union. The Confederate States of America officially came into existence on Saturday, February 9, 1861 with a membership consisting of Alabama, Florida, Georgia, Louisiana, Mississippi, South Carolina and Texas.

As this situation unfolded, Union forces maintained armed occupancy of Fort Sumter in Charleston, South Carolina and refused to vacate the premises. Their actions belied the South's new independence and with no other choice General Pierre Beauregard of the Confederate Army opened fire on Fort Sumter on Friday, April 12, 1861, thus igniting the Civil War. Three days later President Lincoln issued a proclamation declaring the existence of a state of insurrection in the seceded states and called for 75,000 militia volunteers. The Confederacy responded by adding Virginia, Arkansas, North Carolina and Tennessee to their nation, with their ranks then numbering 11 states in all and more than nine million people.

In March 1862 Robert E. Lee (1807-1870), who had spent most of his youth and young adult years living in Alexandria, Virginia, became a military advisor to Confederate President Jefferson Davis. On Sunday, June 1, 1862 he assumed command of the Army of

Northern Virginia, the main Confederate force and was ultimately appointed general-in-chief of the Confederacy in February 1865.

However, the Civil War came to an end on Sunday, April 9, 1865 when General Lee surrendered to General Ulysses S. Grant and the Union troops at the Village of Appomattox Courthouse in Virginia. General Lee was later elected president of Washington College in Lexington, Virginia (today known as Washington and Lee University) and urged Southerners to strive for peace in a united country. Because of the way he kept the Confederacy alive despite the great odds he faced, he is looked upon by many as a military genius, an ideal of the South and an American hero.

One of the most horrific chapters of the Civil War era included a macabre tie-in to the City of Washington's performing arts community. On the evening of Friday, April 14, 1865 during the presentation of the comedic play "The American Cousin" at Ford's New Theatre, President Abraham Lincoln was assassinated by a promising 26-year-old actor named John Wilkes Booth (1838-1865). A native of Harford County, Maryland and the son of British Shakespearean actor Junius Brutus Booth, the young Booth had ties to the Confederacy and was angered over President Lincoln's taxation policies of the South.

Booth had been performing regularly in plays at Ford's New Theatre (his last appearance there had taken place on Saturday, March 18, 1865 when he portrayed Duke Pescara in the tragedy "The Apostate") and at 10pm on the night in question he somehow slipped unnoticed into Lincoln's box and shot him in the back of the head with a .44 caliber Derringer. Jumping from the box to the stage he then raised his knife and shouted "Sic semper tyrannis" (Latin for "Thus always to tyrants") before fleeing through a stage door to the alley. President Lincoln was taken to William Petersen's house across the street from the theatre immediately after the shooting and died there the following morning, April 15, 1865, at 7:22am.

After shooting President Lincoln, Booth and associate David Herold escaped on horseback and at midnight arrived at Surratt's Tavern in Southern Prince George's County, Maryland where they had stored guns and supplies. The pair eventually made it to Garrett's Farm in Virginia, with Booth being shot in a tobacco barn just before dawn on the morning of Wednesday, April 26, 1865. He died three hours later on the porch of the Garrett's farmhouse.

In the wake of the Civil War, the number of newly freed Blacks living in the City of Washington grew. They gravitated towards a certain section of the city which became known as Hell's Bottom, a run-down and dangerous slum area renowned for harboring a large contraband camp and a sympathetic Baptist church which provided shelter and relief for the growing Black population. Saloons within this compact geographic zone provided settings for informal rounds of singing, shouting and simple musical performances. These establishments were predecessors of the halls, night clubs and restaurants that would eventually proliferate along in the U Street NW area, whose development would accelerate during the early decades of the 20th century.

Shortly after the onset of the Civil War, the Union Army had to deal with an unusual situation. A number of Black slaves walked off the plantations in Maryland and Virginia and sought protection in the Union Army within the City of Washington. Initially, the Union had no established policy for dealing with such individuals and final decisions on the status of the slaves were rendered by individual commanders. Not surprisingly, most were put to work for the Union troops. However, so many escaping slaves began showing up at Union camps that a decision was eventually made to classify these new arrivals as contraband of war. This meant that once fleeing slaves from Maryland and Virginia crossed over into the ranks of the Union Army, it was immediately determined that their labor had previously been used to aid the Confederacy and thus became classified as property. Any and all enemy property that fell into Union possession constituted contraband and would not be returned. Once found to be contraband, these escaping slaves were then declared to be free by the Union Army.

In May 1862, a month after slavery was abolished in the City of Washington, Union General James Samuel Wadsworth, commander of the Military District of Washington, instructed a White Methodist minister named Danforth B. Nichols, who served as the Washington Representative of the American Missionary Society, to establish a small contraband camp consisting of tents and wooden shanties in an abandoned square of vacant land bounded by 12th and 13th Streets NW (which ran north and south) and Q and R Streets NW (which ran east and west). Nichols named the settlement Camp Barker and originally intended the barracks to serve as a makeshift hospital for sick and injured Black Union contraband soldiers.

Within months of its establishment Camp Barker was being overrun with several hundred of the city's 3,185 freed slaves who had nowhere else to turn for food, shelter and medical supplies. Appearing on the scene at this time was one Reverend Henry Bailey, a Black preacher who ministered the men at Camp Barker and attempted to make organized spiritual services a part of their lives. Human traffic through the camp remained constant and by December 1863 more than 5,000 contrabands had been processed by Camp Barker.

In 1864 Reverend Henry Bailey, with the help of 10 associates, purchased a piece of land directly across the street from Camp Barker for $2,500 (today this land comprises the 1200 block of R Street NW and is largely occupied by the building that houses Unity of Washington, D.C.). He filled the lot with large tents and founded the Fourth Baptist Church with hopes of recruiting members from the hundreds of newly freed Blacks that were idly combing area streets. Within a year a brick-and-wood house had been constructed on the lot, and the church, which had previously operated out of a tent on the lot, began holding services in its basement. It was there in the basement church that the singing and music performed by the free Blacks – spirituals, blues shouts and other songs offered by the former slaves and soldiers – became a regular feature of the religious services.

As a side note, Reverend Henry Bailey remained on as pastor of the Fourth Baptist Church until 1870 and was then succeeded by Reverend Robert Johnson, who served in that role until 1903. The original Fourth Baptist Church building was torn down in 1882 and subsequently replaced with a new structure. On Saturday, June 18, 1892 it became Metropolitan Baptist Church and carries that name to this day.

The overcrowded conditions of Camp Barker and the Fourth Baptist Church were probably a major reason why other similar camps were established in this general area of the city. Before the Civil War had ended other settlements in operation included the Campbell Hospital (6th Street NW and Florida Avenue NW), the Wisewell Barracks (7th and O Streets NW), the Colfax Industrial Mission (11th and R Streets NW) and the Cliffburne Barracks (15th Street NW along Meridian Hill).

In addition, an offshoot of Camp Barker named Freedman's Hospital was established in a mansion at Iowa Circle (known today as Logan Circle). In 1867 Freedman's Hospital relocated to a site east of 7th Street NW, where it still stands today. Residents of this area were also serviced by several churches and saloons, both of which kept their doors open for anyone passing through the neighborhood.

By the summer of 1865 thousands of Blacks, mainly former slaves and Union soldiers without jobs or homes, had landed in the vicinity of Camp Barker and the Fourth Baptist Church. The main problem with this situation was that the throngs of homeless people who shuffled about the neighborhood were desperate for food, money and whatever shelter they could obtain. Survival of the fittest became the rule of the streets and the area developed a sinister reputation as loitering, violence, crime and public drunkenness became rampant.

The White Americans who once occupied most of the homes in this region moved away. That summer the neighborhood became known as Hell's Bottom, with its loose boundaries encompassing several blocks extending from 8th Street NW to 13th Street NW (east-to-west) and U Street NW to P Street NW (north-to-south). Within Hell's Bottom a number of saloons opened their doors, providing late-night shelter and cheap booze that mainly fueled an increasingly criminal element. Hell's Bottom became the City of Washington's first Black ghetto.

Hell's Bottom wasn't the City of Washington's only dangerous neighborhood during the latter years of the 19th century, as a number of sections within the nation's capital developed reputations as hotbeds of vice and crime. Among the most feared of these zones included Swampoodle, which extended from 2nd Street NW to 2nd Street NE (east-to-west) and K Streets NW and NE to F Streets NW and NE (north-to-south); Bloodfield, whose boundaries were marked 1st Street SW to 4th Street SW (east-to-west) and G Street SW to M Street SW (north-to-south); and the notorious stretch known as Goat Alley, which was located in the square created by 6th Street NW to 7th Street NW (east-to-west) and M Street NW to L Street NW (north-to-south).

The legend of these locales was captured in an article in the Washington Post on Wednesday, September 17, 1902 entitled "Rival to Boom Towns: Washington Has Had its Wild and Wooly Days" which told: "The vast horde of enfranchised slaves, discharged soldiers and a cloud of riffraff, bummers, and camp followers, who, while they swelled the city's population, were absolutely worthless as citizens, and their arrival soon made this city one of the most disorderly places in America. Fights, murders, stabbings and shooting scrapes were of daily occurrence."

The article continued: "The arrival of this vast horde of riffraff resulted in an enormous increase in the number of gambling houses and dives. This horde congregated, or, rather, settled in three places – Bloodfield, Swampoodle, and Hell's Bottom, which in those days were perfect hotbeds of vice. Murders occurred there frequently, and crime of all sorts was rampant."

On the northernmost edge of Hell's Bottom, the pathway known as U Street NW had been paved in stone in 1872 and served as the neighborhood's most heavily traveled avenue, making it the ideal location for a bustling business district. Late in the 19th century as Hell's Bottom began to lose its fearsome reputation, U Street NW did become the target of local developers and entrepreneurs, who began constructing homes and buildings in its open spaces and soliciting local businessmen to take advantage of its offerings. In 1895 there were reportedly some 15 black-owned businesses in operation in the U Street corridor and the surrounding streets that flowed into it. By 1920 that number had reportedly increased substantially, firmly establishing U Street NW as the primary economic and social center for Washington, D.C.'s Black population.

Hell's Bottom was widely written about in the pages of the Washington Post. At the center of the neighborhood was a ramshackle structure officially known by the city as Sutherland's Barroom which was operated by Keith Sutherland, a well-known character in the area.

Sutherland had been born into slavery in 1855 in Charles County, Maryland and moved to the City of Washington in the spring of 1862. His parents settled in the "Negro" section of the city and purchased a small piece of property at 1643 Vermont Avenue NW, which included a house and a small, one-story stable on the north side of the yard that faced out onto nearby R Street NW. In 1878 Keith Sutherland converted the stable into a simple saloon which offered a counter, a small billiard table and a small bar and serving area. He was granted a liquor license for his crude establishment and he filed under the name Sutherland's Barroom, though a makeshift sign on the premises announced the surroundings as the Northern Lights Poolroom.

The actual structure for Sutherland's Barroom was given the address of 1112-1114 R Street NW. It sat on the southeast corner of Vermont Avenue NW and R Street NW, several feet north of where 12th Street NW merged with Vermont. This triangle became known far and wide as the geographic center and heart and soul of Hell's Bottom itself. Sutherland's Barroom was one of several saloons that operated within the confines of Hell's Bottom and catered solely to Black customers.

Keith Sutherland began his ascent to local celebrity when the Washington Post of Sunday, February 4, 1900 ran an article entitled "Ex-King of the Bottom: Once Dominated a Notorious Section of the City; Where Crime and Evil Reigned." The lengthy piece introduced Sutherland as the "King of Hell's Bottom" and described the barroom owner as the "overlord and supreme ruler of the Negroes in the vicinity" and "monarch of all he chooses to survey."

The uncredited article then provides an entertaining description of what Hell's Bottom had once been: "It is still within the memory of the present generation when 'Hell's Bottom' was a fact and not a memory. The swampy, low-lying ground bred mosquitoes, malaria and thugs. It was the quarter set apart for and dominated by the tough element of the colored population. A white man with money in his pocket studiously avoided the locality after dark, or else set a fast pace to which he adjusted the accompaniment of a rag-time whistle. Half a dozen saloons congested within the radius of a block served the barroom habitués with whisky as hot as chili con carne and as exhilarating as Chinese pundu. Fights arose approaching the dimensions of a riot, and the guardians of the law had all they could do to quell the disturbances. A policeman or two was killed, and that, together with the growth of the city, led to the rehabilitation of 'Hell's Bottom.' Now it is interesting mainly in its wealth of reminisces."

The article provides extensive details on Sutherland, who was known as "Keitt" by the locals: He was born a slave in Charles County, Maryland and arrived in the city of Washington in 1862; he had worked as a bootblack around the Treasury building and remembered seeing Abraham Lincoln's funeral pass by, with a white horse tied behind a hearse; he had inherited the pool room-saloon building (a former stable) from his parents; and he stood six foot one, weighed 250 pounds and was known as a fearless fighter whose exploits in local brawls was legendary. In one telling passage, the article tells: "If one hints robbery or burglary, 'Keitt' simply rolls his eyes expressively, and enough has been said. No one cares to tamper with his till."

The article also provides the following description of the barroom: "The saloon on the outside looks like a combination coal and wood shed...On Saturday night the place takes on something of its old glory. In the smoke-begrimed room – hardly 12 by 12 – are found thirty or forty men eating and talking. Through the thick clouds of smoke, the lamps throw out a dim gleam, and the odor of frying fish and the fumes of the pipe struggle for mastery. The crowd gets noisy at times, but any attempt at boisterousness is quieted by a word from the dominant spirit of the gathering. If anyone gets obstreperous he is thrown out on the pavement, and it makes little difference to the bouncer whether the mutinous one lands on his head or not. This is the Negro Bohemia. They who live from hand to mouth love to come here. The boot-black with a dime receives as much consideration as the belated teamster with a roll of one-dollar bills."

Keith Sutherland himself is then quoted on the history of Hell's Bottom: "Hell's Bottom began to get its name shortly after the close of the war in 1866. There were two very lively places in those days. One was a triangular square at Rhode Island Avenue and 11th Street.

It was here that an eloquent colored preacher, who went by the name of John the Baptist, used to hold revival services which were attended by the newly freed slaves. The revival was alright, but the four or five barrooms in the neighborhood used to hold the overflow meetings and when the crowds went home at night you couldn't tell whether they were shouting from religion or whisky. Then there was what was known as the contraband camp on S Street, between Twelfth and Thirteenth. The Negroes who had just been freed stayed there waiting for white people to come and hire them. They got into all sorts of trouble and many of them settled in the neighborhood. Money was scarce and whisky was cheap – a certain sort of whisky and the combination resulted in giving the place the name which it held for so many years. The police force was small. There was no police court and the magistrates before whom offenders were brought rarely fixed the penalty at more than $2. Crime and lawlessness grew terribly and a man had to fight whenever he went into the 'Bottom.'"

The most significant aspect of Keith Sutherland's Hell's Bottom narrative, as reported by the Washington Post, was his description of how the saloons of Hell's Bottom handled the human overflow from the neighborhood's churches, with shouting becoming an accepted part of the revival-like gatherings. This passage is significant because it is the earliest documented example we have of the transformation of Negro music from slave songs to church spirituals to saloon singing which was occurring in settings located close to the U Street NW area. In effect, this was the origin of Negro music performance within the City of Washington and marked the beginning of the legacy of race and R&B music within Washington, D.C.

As for Keith Sutherland, the King of the Bottom maintained his barroom on R Street NW until 1908, at which time he sold off the property, moved around the corner to a home at 1640 11th Street NW and opened up a small, one-story shack-like structure he called the Fairview Hotel on the southwest corner of 1st Street NE and Florida Avenue NE. Far from being a hotel, the wooden building was little more than a lunch and dinner counter surrounded by three walls where Sutherland served up simple meals and bootlegged whiskey for his regular Black customers, many of whom worked nearby in the local B&O freight yard.

In August and September of 1916 the Washington Post ran many articles telling of efforts by the city's health department officials to close Sutherland's establishment, which they found to be unsanitary. The articles mainly served to spread the legend of Sutherland as a "colored philosopher and prophet" by telling of the various words of wisdom he had scrawled all over the walls of his cook-shop. Sutherland was eventually granted a pardon and maintained his business until his death on Sunday, February 19, 1933 at the age of 79.

The demise of Hell's Bottom occurred over a roughly two-year period and was triggered by the shooting of a rookie police officer that raised the ire of city officials. The trouble began when two Black young men reportedly well-known for criminal behavior in Hell's Bottom, 26-year-old George Bush and 19-year-old Osborne Basey, engaged in fisticuffs over a young Black woman named Rosie Briscoe on Sunday, November 3, 1889. Two nights later, Bush, who had lost the fight, appeared outside of Steve Wall's Saloon on the southeast corner of 11th and Q Streets NW – deep in the heart of Hell's Bottom – and called for Basey to meet him on the street. When Basey emerged from the saloon, Bush fired four shots from a revolver, two of which struck Basey – one in the shoulder and one in the right lung. He died at Freedman's Hospital five hours later.

The shots were heard by a 40-year-old, White Metropolitan Police private named A.N. Crippen, who was stationed at a patrol box one block away at 12th and Q Streets NW. George Bush proceeded to dart past Private Crippen and stormed into Bob Brown's Saloon on the northwest corner of 12th and Q Streets NW, where he climbed a flight of stairs and entered a small room on the second floor. Private Crippen trailed close behind the subject, but when he entered the room he was immediately shot in the chest by Bush. As he staggered backwards, Private Crippen managed to fire two shots, both of which reached their target, striking Bush in his right lung and liver. Wounded and desperate, Bush advanced on Private Crippen and pointed the revolver at his head from point-blank range. Crippen grabbed the gun's barrel, but Bush pulled the trigger one final time, shooting the policeman through his right eye and killing him instantly. Bush, however, was losing blood quickly and when backup police arrived on the scene they found him slumped in the saloon's upstairs hallway. He died at 8am the next morning in Freedman's Hospital.

Fallout from the shooting of a White police officer by a Black criminal was severe and proved to be the primary reason for the dismantling of Hell's Bottom. Despite his age, Private Crippen had only been on the force for three months and local newspapers made it a point to publish detailed coverage of the horrific shootings.

A feature article in the Washington Post of Wednesday, November 6, 1889 entitled "Two Murders" included the passage: "His (Private Crippen) beat was one of the worst in the city and is in the heart of 'Hell's Bottom.' Fighting is a nightly occurrence and the neighborhood is infested with a lot of Negroes, who, when they are not in jail are drinking and fighting. Wall's Saloon is a notorious resort and is kept by Steve Wall, a son of Squire O.S.B. Wall."

Pressure to clean up Hell's Bottom intensified in the wake of Private Crippen's shooting and both Steve Wall's Saloon and Bob Brown's Saloon were closed within six months of the shootings. The area was growing steadily and a series of new homes were constructed in 1890 in the area of what was once Camp Barker. Many of the newer Black residents to the area began voicing their concerns to local church officials about the degenerate nature of the old neighborhood and centered their complaints on the litany of notorious saloons that still littered the area and housed the neighborhood's roughest characters.

On the afternoon of Tuesday, November 17, 1891 Rev. George W. Moore of Lincoln Memorial Church, located within Hell's Bottom at the southeast corner of 11th and R Streets NW, appeared before the commissioners of the city on behalf of the concerned residents of the neighborhood and appealed the issuance of liquor licenses to all of the saloon owners within Hell's Bottom. His presentation included the offering of petitions signed by many property holders and church members denouncing the saloons of the area, along with a passionate personal appeal to put an end to the notorious establishments that he felt were responsible for so much vice, violence and crime in the immediate district.

At the conclusion of the session, the commissioners had rejected the renewal of liquor licenses for the following saloon owners: Hugh McCann (1626 11th Street NW); Thomas Bannagan (1609 12th Street NW); Robert R. Brown (1600 12th Street NW); Patrick F. Nelligan (1016 Rhode Island Avenue NW); John M. Stutz (1100 Q Street NW); Samuel G Stewart (1003 Rhode Island Avenue NW); Daniel Donavan (1622 Vermont Avenue NW) and Felix Shannon (1433 11th Street NW). With the closing of these saloons, the human flotsam of Hell's Bottom absconded to Parts Unknown and the neighborhood's sordid reputation quickly dissipated. What was once Washington, D.C.'s worst ghetto soon became a lower-middle class neighborhood whose residents began gravitating towards the developing U Street NW area for their goods, services and entertainment.

CHAPTER ELEVEN
NEW COLORS FOR THE ENTERTAINMENT SPECTRUM

During the final decades of the 19th century, Washington, D.C. experienced constant cultural and technological change that directly impacted public entertainment within the city. The number of theatres and halls steadily increased, with their plays and musical presentations receiving substantial advertising and coverage in two new daily newspapers, the Evening Star and the Washington Post. Inventor-businessman Thomas Edison introduced two devices that would assume monumental roles in entertainment history – the phonograph, which would revolutionize the way music was recorded and listened to; and the kinetoscope, the first device to record and reproduce objects in motion, thus giving birth to motion pictures which would eventually replace vaudeville as the primary form of entertainment in Washington, D.C. theatres in the 20th century. All of these advances changed the local performing arts landscape as Washington, D.C. celebrated its first century of existence and prepared to usher in the coming 20th century.

In the wake of the Civil War, changes to the City of Washington's physical and cultural landscapes ensued. New streets were carved out and homes and commercial buildings were constructed throughout the city. According to census figures, in 1800 the population of the entire Federal District was 14,093 (of which 10,066 or 75.6% where White), while in 1900 the total population of Washington, D.C. was 278,718 (of which 191,532 or 68.7% where White).

As the city grew, its entertainment scene became more advanced. Two newspapers, the Evening Star (which debuted on Wednesday, December 22, 1852) and the Washington Post (which debuted on Thursday, December 6, 1877) provided comprehensive coverage of the city's musical and theatrical presentations. The nation's capital also began receiving national attention for its performing arts programs when a new and unique entertainment trade publication entitled "Billboard Advertising" began publishing in late 1894. In the years ahead this magazine would help revolutionize the entertainment industry in the United States. Washington, D.C. was one of many American cities whose entertainment scene benefited from its publication.

The increased media coverage given to the local entertainment scene brought the informed citizens out of their homes and into the venues of the city. With amusements flourishing in late 19th century Washington, D.C., the theatres and halls of the city seemed to open, close and change names with regularity. These stages, for the most part, hosted vaudeville programs, plays and musical concerts, with many theatres mixing their bills to include all three sets of entertainment during the course of a single evening.

Entertainment in Washington, D.C. during the post-Civil War years was defined by storied venues like the National Theatre, the Theatre Comique (formerly Carusi's Saloon) and Ford's Theatre. Other top-flight theatres and assembly halls of notable status in operation at this time included: Lincoln Hall (in operation from 1869 to 1884 on the northeast corner of 9th and D Streets NW); the Avenue Theatre (situated on the southwest corner of 11th and D Streets NW, it opened as the Avenue in 1878 and underwent six different name changes before closing in 1891); Albaugh's Grand Opera House (which was located on the northeast corner of 15th and C Streets NW – later marked 1424 Pennsylvania Avenue NW – and was open to the public from 1884 to 1900); and Harris' Bijou Theatre (which sat on the southwest corner of 9th and C Streets NW – later marked 900 C Street NW – and was in operation from 1886 to 1892). On these stages the finest offerings of popular music, vaudeville and theatre were made available to the citizenry of the nation's capital. In time competition arrived in the form of night clubs and sound recordings that altered the way music was made available to the public.

When considering the major technological innovations of the entertainment world, two that dramatically impacted the performing arts in Washington, D.C. were the phonograph, which introduced and eventually revolutionized sound recordings; and the kinetoscope, which was the first device to produce moving pictures and marked the beginning of the motion picture industry. Both inventions were created by Thomas Alva Edison (1847-1931), an American inventor, scientist and businessman who had been born in Milan, Ohio and raised in Port Huron, Michigan. Edison spent his adult years in Menlo Park, New Jersey and produced many incredible inventions during his time there. In all, he held a staggering 1,093 patents in his name in the United States alone and also included the electric light bulb as one of his many significant creations.

The phonograph is the very first machine that could record and reproduce sound and is one of the most important inventions in music history. Edison developed this device during the summer of 1877 while experimenting with a telegraph transmitter. While transcribing telegraphic messages through indentations on paper tape, he noted that the machine's tape gave off noises resembling spoken words when played at a high speed. He speculated that a telephone conversation could possibly be recorded in a similar manner and began experimenting by attaching a needle to a telephone receiver diaphragm and holding it against moving paraffin paper. Edison's thinking was that the needle, propelled by speaking vibrations, would scrape the paper tape, with the indentations leaving a message. He recorded a short message, "Mary Had a Little Lamb," and played it back using a stylus on a tinfoil cylinder. It was the first sound recording in history.

Edison named his invention the phonograph and later refined his machine by changing the paper to a metal cylinder with tin foil wrapped around it. He added two diaphragm-and-needle units, one for recording sound and one for playback, with the initial phonographs playing cylinders rather than discs. Edison's phonograph was completed on Sunday, August 12, 1877 and he filed for its patent on Monday, December 24 of that year, with the patent being issued on Tuesday, February 19, 1878. He established the Edison Speaking Phonograph Company on Thursday, January 24, 1878 with the intent of making a new device and making it available for public consumption. His promotional tour took him to Washington, D.C., where he provided a public display on Thursday, April 18, 1878 in an exhibition sponsored by the Academy of Sciences at the Smithsonian Institution.

For almost 10 years, Thomas Edison's phonograph served as the primary device to capture and play back sound recordings. However, technology moved forward and in November 1887 a patent was issued to a German-born inventor named Emile Berliner (1851-1929) for a similar machine called a gramophone, which employed a simpler way of recording sound onto a flat disc.

Emile Berliner was born in Hanover, Germany on Tuesday, May 20, 1851 and emigrated to the United States of America at age 19, where he lived in Washington, D.C. and worked in the Gotteilf, Behrend, and Co. Dry Goods Store for several years. In 1875 he moved to New York City, became interested in laboratory experimentation and 12 months later began a six-year stint with the American Bell Telephone Company. He returned to Washington, D.C. in 1883 and purchased a house at 1458 Columbia Road NW. He then began experimenting in his home laboratory with sound recording, questioning the efficiency of cylinders in Thomas Edison's phonograph and searching for alternative ways of capturing and playing back pieces of sound.

After several years of research and experimentation, Berliner constructed a machine whose primary component was an arm with an attached needle that read spiral grooves via vibration, etched the acquired sound information into a flat record, transmitted the information to a speaker and played back the sound using a stylus that followed the lateral grooves (the earliest of these records were made of various materials including metal and hard rubber). Berliner called this device the gramophone and the discs he created were the first 78rpm sound recordings that could be mass-produced from master sound molds. He filed a patent for this invention on Wednesday, May 4, 1887 and was granted his patent on Tuesday, November 8, 1887.

Berliner gave his first public exhibition of the gramophone in Washington, D.C. during an event sponsored by the Technical Society of Washington on the night of Friday, October 5, 1888 at the Grand Army Hall on Pennsylvania Avenue. More than 300 people attended the two-hour performance of recitations and music by gramophone. The set-up was something Washingtonians had never seen before – a platform holding an immense black-painted cone resembling a large cannon, to the left of which sat a small table holding a recording apparatus. On an adjoining table sat a device used to exhibit the undulations of sound waves.

Addressing the crowd, Mr. Berliner first explained the process of speaking and told how sound waves, generated by the voice, made impressions on the brain by means of the auditory wave. He then spoke of the principal differences between other existing devices and his gramophone and emphasized that with his machine the sound waves were etched on a flat metal disc, while by the former they are recorded on a wax cylinder. Berliner explained the production by process by telling how the etching upon the metal disc is produced by putting a thin coat of fatty substance over its surface, allowing the stylus of the recording apparatus to make adulatory representations there on, and finally immersing the plate in acid, thereby etching it. He stated that the greatest accomplishment of the gramophone is that it reproduced sound for an entire audience.

In the wake of his first public displays of the gramophone, Berliner began pressing hundreds of discs, or records, from each mold he created and began offering them to the public. In April 1893 he transferred all patents to his own newly formed company, the United States Gramophone Company, and established a new professional sound laboratory within company headquarters at 1205 G Street NW. It was there that he began recording the top professional singers in the nation's capital.

In 1897 the first records to be pressed on shellac appeared, with mass production of such items beginning a year later. At that time the shellac in use was actually a molding material consisting of shellac resin and filler materials such as cotton compound, powdered slate and wax lubricants. Today such a concoction would be defined as a thermoplastic. The rotations speeds of these early records varied widely, with most being recorded between 74rpm and 82rpm.

The United States Gramophone Company soon had competition in the form of the Columbia Phonograph Company, which was founded by Edward D. Easton on Tuesday, January 15, 1889 and was situated in Washington, D.C. at 919 Pennsylvania Avenue NW. By 1891 Easton's company had a catalog of more than 200 cylinders and in 1898 they began pressing discs. Wary of the local rivalry and desirous of greater opportunities, Emile Berliner and an engineer associate named Eldridge R. Johnson teamed up in 1901 to form a new business called the Victor Talking Machine Company in Camden, New Jersey. In 1929 this company was purchased by the Radio Corporation of America (RCA), thus becoming RCA-Victor. The recording industry had taken off on a national level.

By 1925, 78rpm was the standard speed of commercial recordings because of the newly introduced electric synchronous turntable motor. In the 1940s these records became known as 78s as a way to distinguish them from the other record formats that began appearing. Commercial music was revolutionized when the 12-inch 33rpm long-play record was developed by Columbia Records and introduced to the public in June 1948. RCA

Victor responded by creating the seven-inch 45rpm single record and marketing it in February 1949. (The 33rpm and 45rpm records were made from vinyl plastic; although both examples are still being pressed today, vinyl records were largely supplanted in popularity by digital media in the late 1980s.)

Another technological innovation that greatly impacted local popular culture, the kinetoscope, was a device that recorded and reproduced moving objects and was the first projector of its kind. The kinetoscope came into existence when inventor Thomas Edison, working from his New Jersey laboratory, filed a caveat with the Patents Office on Wednesday, October 17, 1888 describing his idea for a machine which would "do for the eye what the phonograph does for the ear" – record and reproduce objects in motion.

Edison's new contraption consisted of an upright wooden cabinet 18 inches by 27 inches by four feet high with a peephole and magnifying lenses on top. Inside the box, a 50-foot band of film was passed through a series of spools, with a sprocket continuously drawing the film under a lens, thus producing a series of moving pictures. Edison called his new piece of equipment a kinetoscope using the Greek words kineto (meaning "movement") and scopos (meaning "to watch").

The first public demonstration of the kinetoscope was held in New York at the Brooklyn Institute of Arts and Sciences on Tuesday, May 9, 1893, with the production and distribution of the device and accompanying films officially assumed by the Edison Manufacturing Company on Sunday, April 1, 1894. In Washington, D.C., the very first public showing of the kinetoscope and its scenes of everyday life took place on the night of Saturday, October 6, 1894 at the Columbia Phonograph Company (919 Pennsylvania Avenue NW).

An advertisement in the Evening Star newspaper of that date read: "It is here! Edison's Kinetoscope!!! Marvelous! Realistic! True to Life! The most wonderful and interesting invention of this century of science. The only actual and literal 'Living Pictures' ever produced. Words fail to describe it – you must see it to get an idea of its remarkable qualities! Exhibition begins this evening and continues day and night."

A month later, the kinetoscope was given another exhibition in Washington, D.C. at the Corcoran Building (527 15th Street NW). An advertisement in the Washington Post of Tuesday, November 6, 1894 announced that "Edison's Latest Marvel" would be on display with several subjects being offered for public viewing including "the Skirt Dance," "Caicedo, the Rope Walker," "the Blacksmiths at Work," "Sandow, the Strong Man" and "The Chicken Fight." Each short moving picture cost five cents per viewing.

Other projectors soon followed in the kinetoscope's footsteps and the competition for public attention was keen in the nation's capital. Theatrically projected one-hour screenings of these moving pictures became a new addition to entertainment scene. On Friday, January 1, 1897 Willard Hall (on F Street NW, between 14th and 15th Streets NW) began a month-long exhibit of Lumiere's Cinematographe with "moving pictures true to life" of maneuvers by soldiers of Europe, royal wedding processions, street scenes including Pennsylvania Avenue and the El Puerto del Sol in Madrid. Admission prices were 25 cents for adults and 15 cents for children.

Next up at Willard Hall was a series of regular showings of another type of moving picture projector called the American Biograph which lasted through all of February and the first two weeks of March. Another Thomas Edison offering, a new-and-improved projection device called the Vitascope, was showcased for all of March and April of that year at a specially prepared facility in Washington, D.C. called Vitascope Hall which adjoined the Columbia Theatre (1116 F Street NW).

Washington's theatre owners and vaudeville managers observed the new entertainment trend and began presenting moving pictures and scenes-in-motion from around the world, along with short films with military and political themes, including footage associated with the Spanish-American War. Early in the 20th century, movie exhibition earned a regular spot on most local vaudeville bills, with short films eventually replacing several of the variety show's live acts.

As the 1800s closed out it became increasingly evident that the very essence of popular music in Washington, D.C. and the ways it was being presented to the public were changing, particularly with regards to the categorization and presentation of the music itself. Up to that point in time, the public had learned of entertainment programs through newspaper notices, posters, handbills and word-of-mouth transmission. As popular music became more complex the dependence on local media outlets for ads and notices became greater.

In terms of categorization, the expanding number of musical forms and styles called for the newspapers and publications of the era to provide more detailed descriptions and definitions of the various genres being discussed, advertised and reviewed. A derivative of such treatment was the repetitive placement of these forms and styles into a series of broad, general headings, the most common of which were "folk music," "Negro music" and "pop music."

The ways in which music was being presented and listened to was affected by various technological and cultural changes, with the phonograph, the gramophone and sound recordings fueling the notion of home entertainment. There was competition in the city between the existing theatre companies, vaudeville troupes, musical ensembles and moving picture groups that sought bookings for their appearances. It was this competition for stage time that eventually introduced night clubs to the nation's capital.

During the first half of the 20th century a series of technological innovations and social episodes swept across the United States of America and transformed the daily lives of its citizens. With regards to increasingly sophisticated technology, the first automobile to be mass-produced in the country – the three-horsepower, curved dash Oldsmobile – debuted in 1901 and kicked off a revolution in the field of transportation. A total of 425 of the vehicles were sold that year, with the number climbing to over 5,000 in 1904. By 1908 there were 241 automobile manufacturing firms in business and thousands of Americans were getting behind the wheel and taking to the road.

Other technological breakthroughs introduced new options in terms of home entertainment. The introduction of such inventions as the radio (1922) and the television (first exhibited for the American people at the New York World's Fair in April 1939) encouraged people to explore indoor amusement options. The field of music was also experiencing upgrades, with the fragile and fading 78rpm discs eventually being replaced by two new types of vinyl records: the twelve-inch 33rpm long-play record introduced by Columbia Records in 1948; and the seven-inch 45rpm single record produced for the masses a year later.

While technological advancements were occurring with regularity, the country's social climate was replete with uncertainties as the realities of World War I (1914-1918), the Great Depression (1929-1939), and World War II (1939-1945) forced citizens to contemplate methods of survival and redesign their futures. It was a rapidly transforming world on many different levels.

The residents of the nation's capital took the changes in stride and watched as a substantial number of new arrivals made their homes in the city. The population of the entire region grew rapidly during this time due to the President Franklin D. Roosevelt's New Deal venture which greatly expanded the size of the federal government and created a plethora of job openings during the 1930s. In Washington, D.C. the population rose from 278,718 (68.7% White) in 1900 to 802,178 (64.5% White) by 1950, while neighboring

Prince George's County, Maryland saw their numbers jump from 29,896 (59.9% White) in 1900 to 194,182 (88.1% White) in 1950.

The new arrivals spilled over into the developing suburbs, causing growth in the neighboring counties of Maryland and Virginia and fueling a burgeoning metropolitan area. During this period, music continued to enrich lives of the region's people, with its popularity increasing through time as musicians and musical venues of every persuasion appeared in the region and were met with enthusiastic audiences eager to embrace the various styles of popular music presented for their enjoyment.

CHAPTER TWELVE
THE MARCH KING

In the late 19th century United States Marine Band leader John Philip Sousa emerged as a musical hero in Washington, D.C. Sousa was a talented composer, conductor and musician who was known for his American military and patriotic marches. The United States Marine Band (which had been established by an act of Congress on Wednesday, July 11, 1798 and today ranks as the oldest of the military bands and the oldest professional musical organization in the United States) regularly performed throughout the area at assembly halls, theatres, military events and political functions. Sousa came to be known as the March King for his mastery of march composition and earned a worldwide reputation for the way his patriotic compositions reflected the country's spirit.

John Philip Sousa was born on Monday, November 6, 1854 in the City of Washington in a house at 636 G Street SE. This childhood home was located near the United States Marine Barracks (later known as "Marine Barracks, Washington, D.C.") where his father, John Antonio Sousa, was a trombonist in the United States Marine Band. Sousa then spent most of his youth living in a house at 502 7th Street SE, during which time he attended a series of private and public school only blocks from his home, the last of which was Wallace Grammar School. In addition to his formal schooling, in 1861 he began attending the Conservatory of Music operated by John Esputa, who ran the school from his home at 511 8th Street SE. During his four years there, Sousa studied voice, violin, piano, flute, cornet, trombone and baritone and alto horn under Esputa's guidance.

At age 13 Sousa was approached by a circus band musician, who attempted to recruit the youngster into his fold. His father learned of the ploy and instead enlisted his son in the United States Marine Corps on Tuesday, June 9, 1868 as an apprentice musician. Simultaneously, Sousa studied harmony, composition and violin under local musician George Felix Benkert. Sousa remained in the United States Marine Band as a violinist and wind instrumentalist until being discharged on Tuesday, May 18, 1875. He then began playing professionally in orchestras at Ford's Theatre and the Theatre Comique.

In June 1876 Sousa moved to Philadelphia, Pennsylvania where he worked as an orchestra violinist for several theatre companies and also held a side job correcting proofs for the W.F. Shaw Publishing Company. He returned to the United States Marine Band as its 14th different leader (and its first American-born) on Friday, October 1, 1880. He remained in that position until submitting his resignation on Saturday, July 30, 1892.

Sousa ultimately created a total of 136 marches and approximately 200 different songs and compositions during his professional career. During his 12-year run as leader of the United States Marine Band he guided the 40-musician outfit into the studio on numerous occasions where together they made their first recordings, with 50 cylinders of their music being released by the Columbia Phonograph Company in the fall of 1890 alone.

By the end of the century more than 400 different titles were for sale, making Sousa's marches among the very first pieces of popular music ever recorded. Some of the more popular of Sousa's marches that were written and recorded with the United States Marine Band during his time with them were: "The Gladiator March" (1886); "Semper Fidelis" (the Official March of the United States Marine Corps, 1888); "The Washington Post" (1889); "The Thunderer" (1889); and "The High School Cadets" (1890). Later in his career after leaving Washington, D.C., Sousa composed such acclaimed marches as "Stars and Stripes Forever" (the National March of the United States, 1896); "Hail to the Spirit of Liberty" (1900); and "Glory of the Yankee Navy" (1909).

The popularity of John Philip Sousa grew to such heights in the nation's capital that David Blakely, who acted on occasion as tour manager for the United States Marine Band, began encouraging the band leader to strike off on his own and form his own touring civilian concert band. With a guaranteed salary of $6,000 per year plus a percentage of all performance profits, Sousa decided, after a 12-year run during which time he achieved the rank of Warrant Officer, to make his break from the United States Marine Band.

After making his intentions public, a grand farewell celebration entitled "Testimonial Concert to John Philip Sousa" was staged on Friday, July 29, 1892 at the New National Theatre Grand Opera House in Washington, D.C. The evening featured such performers as Mrs. Kitty Thompson Berry (soprano), Mr. Herndon Morsell (tenor), Mr. Herman Rakemann (violinist), the Franz Art Club and the United States Marine Band led by John Philip Sousa himself. The very next day, Sousa directed a concert on the White House lawn that was attended by President Benjamin J. Harrison. He was discharged immediately at the conclusion of the performance.

The following Monday Sousa went to New York City and rehearsed with his new band on Thursday, August 4. From 1892 to 1931, Sousa and His Band, as the new musical outfit was most often called, was based out of Chicago, Illinois and became the most popular musical act in the world. They toured the globe, traveled more than one million miles, performed in front of more than one million people and ultimately performed an astounding 15,623 concerts. John Philip Sousa died on Sunday, March 6, 1932 at the age of 77.

CHAPTER THIRTEEN
THE RADIO DIAL

The radio was introduced in Washington, D.C. in the 1920s and from the onset included musical programming among its on-air broadcasts. While few at that time could have realized the worldwide cultural impact radio would come to have in the years ahead, its significance as a source of regional information, news and musical enjoyment was immediately evident to all who tuned in. During this time, many night clubs and other venues in the nation's capital that offered live musical entertainment, along with the musicians and bands that worked their stages, greatly benefited from the programs that aired on local radio stations which featured their evening performances. These segments raised the listener's awareness of local music, enhanced their appreciation of the work of area musicians and generated tremendous overall interest in the continuously evolving popular music scene of the nation's capital.

The story of the radio begins early in the 20th century, when experimental broadcasts were aired on an intermittent basis by a number of federally operated government stations in the United States. The experiments seemed to work and official regulation through the Bureau of Navigation of the Department of Commerce was granted in 1912. However, it wasn't until December 1921 that a broadcast service was formally established by the Department of Commerce which provided a 360-meter wavelength for entertainment program broadcasts. That month, radio stations around the country applied for and received broadcast licenses and an entirely new world of entertainment opened up to the public.

In the Washington, D.C. area, the first publicly broadcasted AM radio program aired at 10am on the morning of Friday, March 24, 1922 when a 30-minute segment entitled "Radiophone Weather Report" was broadcast on station WXX-Washington Post Office Department Station. Two other separate radio stations were in operation that day including WPM-Washington, Thomas Williams (1324 New York Avenue NW, Washington, D.C.) which offered "News Items" at 12:30pm, and NAA-Washington Naval Radio Station, which aired 30-minute segments entitled "Musical Program" at 8:30pm and 9:15pm. While it is uncertain exactly what type of music was actually aired by NAA on this date, it seems likely that a performance by some type of Navy band or orchestra was featured, as the station had been constructed as a naval radiograph station back in 1913 and was located adjacent to Fort Myer in Arlington County, Virginia. For all practical purposes, NAA's "Musical Program" rates as the very first popular music program ever aired on broadcast band radio in the Washington, D.C. area.

The number of operating radio stations in the nation's capital began to grow. On Thursday, March 30, 1922 a fourth AM radio station joined the ranks, WMU-Doubleday-Hill Electric Co. (715 12th Street NW, Washington, D.C.). Not much is known about their first day of limited programming, which was only listed in local newspapers as "Music" from 4:30pm to 5:30pm and again from 7:30pm to 8:30pm. While the contents of those programs remain unknown, it nevertheless established WMU as the second area radio station to ever broadcast some type of music over the local airwaves.

The following Tuesday, April 4, WMU went on the air at 4:30pm with another one-hour program again simply listed as "Music" that advertised the following lineup of classical music and waltzes: "Mother O'Mire" (Tours), "Praeludium" (Jarnefeldt), "Ballet Egyptien" (Luigini), "Musettes Waltz" (Puccini), "Tommy Lad" (Tschmacher-Margetson), "Wild Flower Waltz" (Martens and Earle), "Hawaiian Smiles" (Mary Earle), "On the Road to Mandaley" (Kipling-Speaks), "Alda" (Verdi), "Minuet" (Boccherini), "Star of Eve" (Wagner), "Souvenir"

(Drdia), "Florodora Sextette" (Stuart), "Florodora Selections" (Stuart), "Forge into the Forest" (Michaelis) and "On the Bosphorous" (Lincke). With this roster of talent, WMU must be recognized as having aired the first identifiable program of popular music in Washington, D.C. area radio history.

Later that day, WMU was joined by another station by the name of WJH-White & Boyer Company (812 13th Street NW, Washington, D.C.) which called on members of the Raleigh Hotel Orchestra to partake in a popular music broadcast entitled "Music and the Masses" which began at 7:45pm. This particular offering differed from WMU's program in that they aired the Orchestra's performances as a live concert, quite probably the first such radio venture of its kind. It was a feature they would frequently repeat with a variety of local hotel orchestras.

The first episode "Music and the Masses" offered the following: an opening address by Mrs. Hamlin Cogswell, national officer, League of American Penwomen; Violin Solos performed by violinist Helen Dodge and pianist Byron Blodgett; Baritone Solos sung by Claughton West with Miss Willie Pope on piano; Violin Solos performed by violinist Daniel Chwalow, assistant director of the Raleigh Hotel Orchestra; Piano Solos performed by Milton Davis; Baritone Solos sung by Mr. Fred Kemlo with pianist Byron Blodgett; Cello Solos performed by Mr. J.S. Zebley; Soprano Solos sung by Miss Eddie Misletts with pianist Ralph Garren on piano; Orchestra Selections by the Raleigh Hotel; Piano Solos performed by Mr. Ralph Garren; and Trios for Violin, Cello and Piano performed by Daniel Chwalow, J.S. Zebley and Ralph Garren, under the direction of Theodore Hoffman.

On the evening of Wednesday, June 7, 1922 a new station, WEAS-The Hecht Co., aired for the first time with a one-hour block of programming that began at 7pm. Among their featured segments were two songs under the heading "Mandolin-Banjo Selection," one of which was the set-closing number "Goodnight Ladies" by The Stone Brothers. While today little is known about this musical group and the actual style of their songs, the selection titles listed for this particular evening, along with other listed performances the Stone Brothers gave on WEAS in future broadcasts, seem to indicate that "Mandolin-Banjo Selections" could be considered the first example of the airing of country music over the radio in the Washington, D.C. area.

In order to keep up with the budding competition, WMU deliberately made musical programming the primary focus of their broadcasting in the ensuing weeks and aired a great variety of performances during their evening broadcasts. On Thursday, June 22, 1922 they broadcasted a number of musical selections from 4:30pm until 5:30pm, including an interesting entry entitled "Negro Spirituals." This stands as the first known example of such music being played over a radio station in the Washington, D.C. area.

A month later WEAS caught the attention of radio listeners when they aired a one-hour program of popular music and entertainment on Friday, July 7, 1922 entitled "Radio Vaudeville." The inaugural broadcast of this program was arranged by Ted Lesser and offered the following lineup: 7:30pm – Bill Barker's White Owl Orchestra performing "Do It Again" and "Highbrow Blues;" 7:40pm – Miss Anne Suter singing "Some Sunny Day" and "Angel Child;" 7:45pm – Bill Barker's White Owl Orchestra performing dance selections; 7:50pm – Miss Anne Suter singing "Finale Hoppers;" 7:55pm – Mrs. David H. Kincheloe (wife of Representative Kincheloe of Kentucky) providing songs, novelty whistling, and recitations; 8:05pm – Miss Ruth Ayler, accompanied by Miss Edith M. Gallant, singing "Tell Her I Love Her So" and "Believe Me If All Those Endearing Young Charms;" and from 8:15pm to 8:30pm – Julius Zancig, famous mental telepathist, giving a demonstration of mind reading by answering any questions submitted over the radio, in writing, or via telephone. "Radio Vaudeville" proved to be a very popular program for WEAS throughout the year and was instrumental in other local stations adopting the practice of offering variety shows that featured live, on-air performances by an array of talented entertainers.

During the 1920s the number of radio stations in the Washington, D.C. area multiplied, with musical programming becoming a primary reason for the steady growth in radio's popularity during this decade. While most stations in the area eventually offered a variety of music and talk programs for their listening audiences, one station in particular, WTFF, quickly became affiliated with country music shortly upon its inception and today should be considered the first radio station of its kind in the nation's capital.

WTFF appeared on the local airwaves in August 1927 and was owned and operated by the Independent Publishing Company, publishers of a fraternal newspaper called the Fellowship Forum. While its transmitter was located in the woods surrounding Mount Vernon, Virginia, the station's modest broadcast studio was located within the Forum's headquarters at 339 Pennsylvania Avenue NW, Washington, D.C. From the very beginning, the 50-watt station made various styles of folk music and country music its primary offering. For the first few months the station could be heard nightly for two hours, with a number of local acts such as the Mandolin and Guitar Club directed by Walter T. Holt, pianist Burrus Williams, violinist John Slaughter, and the station's own Fellowship Forum Quartet regularly performing live in the studio.

As winter approached, the station began broadcasting four hours per night, with a typical evening's entertainment exemplified by the following schedule which aired on Sunday, December 11, 1927: Fairfax Women's Choir (7pm); Fairfax Male Choir (7:25pm); Guitar and Banjo Solos (7:45pm); Dr. A.H. Moore, Violinist (8pm); George Dixon Thompson, Pianist (8:15pm); Orchestra (8:35pm); Mrs. Albert R. Klaas, Soprano (9pm); Old Fashioned Sermon (9:15pm); Vocal and Instrumental Selections (9:30pm); Trombonist (10pm); and Hawaiian Orchestra (10:40pm).

Among the many popular acts to appear in 20-minute slots on WTFF throughout the remainder of 1927 and into 1928 were country singer-yodeler-guitarist Jimmie Rodgers, pianist Jack Wells, the Duckett Trio, Joe Hopkins and the Old Time Fiddlers, Billy Pendleton's Dixie Syncopators, singer-banjoist Bill Herron, the Old Time Trio and "Woodville Brown – The Southern Troubadour." On Sunday, November 11, 1928, WTFF changed its call letters to WJSV and later became WTOP on Sunday, April 4, 1943. The station remains in operation today under those call letters.

CHAPTER FOURTEEN
THE FACE OF YOU STREET

By 1900 the notorious ghetto neighborhood of Hell's Bottom had become a fading memory as its boundaries dissolved and its streets hosted an influx of better-class Black residents. A number of Black-owned businesses began to open their doors along U Street NW and its arteries. At this point in time, the area was simply being referred to as You Street and it wouldn't be until after Shaw Junior High School displaced McKinley Manual Training School at 1625 7th Street NW in September 1928 that the neighborhood, which included most of the boundaries of what was once Hell's Bottom, became informally known as Shaw, a moniker which is still in use today. (As a side note, Shaw Junior High School had been named after a White Civil War hero named Col. Robert Gould Shaw, who had been an officer in the Union Army and commanded the all-Black 54th Regimen of the Massachusetts Volunteer Infantry. The building that once housed this school still stands on the southeast corner of 7th Street NW and Rhode Island Avenue NW and currently houses Asbury Dwellings, a senior citizen housing complex whose address is now listed as 1616 Marion Street NW.)

The population of the You Street area grew steadily in the early years of the 20th century, as it became the first destination of Blacks who had relocated to the city. The presence of such institutions as Howard University, Freedman's Hospital and the Washington Bee newspaper, along with available housing and assorted Black churches, made it an obvious choice for these newcomers to the city who were seeking opportunities for better lives. It was logical for entertainment venues to open within the You Street area and in time several community buildings and theatres were constructed that served that purpose.

By the 1920s several well-regarded restaurants and night clubs were operating in the area, many of which featured what the local newspapers called "Negro music." The entertainment scene was fueled by the introduction of True Reformer's Hall in 1903, and scores of theatres, including the Howard Theatre which opened in 1910. From this era a product of the neighborhood was jazz pianist Duke Ellington, who early in his career played many dances and night club jobs within the You Street area. Although Ellington departed Washington, D.C. in 1923 at age 24, he became a community hero for his musical accomplishments and made many triumphant returns to the Howard Theatre in the ensuing years.

The very first building to impact the future of entertainment in the You Street area was True Reformers' Hall, which was opened at 1200 U Street NW on Wednesday, July 15, 1903. Constructed by the United Order of True Reformers (a benevolent society based in Richmond, Virginia that offered insurance, banking and other financial services to Blacks) and designed by supervising architect J.A. Lankfort, the building was a four-story, 85 foot high structure with dance halls on the second and third floors, business offices on the ground floor and a basement banquet hall that accommodated 1,000 guests. Its opening was a major event for the community and the hall became a looming landmark for the You Street area.

Dedicatory services for True Reformers' Hall began on opening day at 10:30am and consisted of an assembly which featured many readings and speeches by local dignitaries in addition to several musical selections by local groups. According to published press accounts, an uncredited choir performed "Solomon's Prayer," Mozart's "Gloria" and several other selections that morning while an unnamed band provided renditions of "The Star Spangled Banner" and "America." An afternoon session featured songs by the Monumental

Orchestra, including a performance of "Star of the Sea." The festivities concluded with an evening concert and banquet in the basement with music provided by an ensemble under the auspices of Dr. D.A. Lane and Prof. R.J. Daniels.

In the years ahead, music remained an important component of True Reformers' Hall. In 1903 and 1904 the Washington Conservatory of Music, established by Oberlin-trained pianist Harriet Marshall Gibbs, had its headquarters within the building and staged many evenings of entertainment for the public. Local churches and religious organizations such as the Beacon Light Gospel Tent, the People's Seventh-Day Adventist Church and the Second Evangelical Christian Science Church frequently used the building for their weekend services and often offered recitals and musical performances by various members. Schools and community organizations also held dances and socials on the building's second and third floors.

One highly anticipated event took place at True Reformers' Hall on Monday, January 21, 1907 when a double quartet under the direction of Thomas Johnson and consisting of musicians from Mrs. A.C. Barney's Studio, along with singer Lottie Wallace and singer-violinist Clarence C. White, performed at a reception for the benefit of the Clarkes Domestic Training School and the Colored Social Settlement. Another significant performance took place in the hall on Saturday, June 15, 1907 when the two-act comic opera "The Isle of Never" was given for the benefit of the building committee of the Colored Young Women's Christian Association. The libretto and lyrics of the opera were by G. Luther Sadgwar, with music provided by a 15-piece orchestra conducted by local bandleader Clarence C. White, who had previously studied violin, piano and harmony at the Oberlin Conservatory in Ohio.

Various musical groups made stops at True Reformers' Hall as the You Street area grew as a business and entertainment district. One such attraction that made several appearances throughout 1910 was the Famous Juvenile Troubadours, a group of Black singers from Baltimore under the direction of J. Ellsworth Toomey, who appeared in conjunction with the Lyric Orchestra for themed presentations and general dances. Beginning in 1911 and continuing on for several years were performances by the Wilberforcian Orchestra, an all-Black local outfit of great esteem. The band's lineup was comprised entirely of Washingtonians and was directed by J. Sherman Hunnicutt, who also performed with the outfit as lead violinist. Other band members were: W. Calvin Chase, Jr. on cornet; Nathan Nesbit on clarinet; K.F. Phillips on piano and violin; E.L Burns on drums; C.W. Jones on cornet and piano; W.P. Bayless on second violin; J.B. Clark on trombone; J.H. Anderson on cello; W.C. Hunnicutt on flute; F.G. Haley on trombone; and Mr. Preston on viola.

Other local jazz musicians who entertained at the hall's various social events during this time were singer Gertrude Wells and pianists Claude Hopkins and Louis Brown. In addition, rare stage presentations by some of the top Black vaudeville entertainers of the day were also made at True Reformers' Hall during these early years, with such personalities as S.H. Dudley and Aida Overton Walker making special appearances in between engagements at the nearby Howard Theatre.

In early 1917 True Reformers' Hall was sold to the Knights of Pythius of the District and renamed Pythian Hall. At that time a jazz band called Duke's Serenaders provided music for a dance in the hall, marking the very first professional gig of the teenaged bandleader-pianist known as Duke Ellington. During these years the hall played a prominent role in making live music and entertainment a feature in the You Street area and brought together most of the top Black musicians of the city. Throughout the 20th century the building originally known as True Reformers' Hall housed many different businesses and community agencies, and also endured periods of vacancy and neglect. It is still standing today as a significant landmark of the Shaw neighborhood.

Adding prestige to the You Street area were several theatres that offered such events as plays, live music and motion pictures. The most popular of these venues was the Howard Theatre (620 T Street NW), which opened with a program of vaudeville entertainment on the night of Monday, August 22, 1910 and in later years was known for hosting multi-act musical shows featuring some of the best jazz and R&B artists in the country.

Other theatres in the neighborhood included: the Dunbar Theatre (1901-1903 7th Street NW), which was located one block south of U Street NW in a four-story office and apartment building built by the Southern Aid Society of Virginia and was opened to the public on Monday, October 18, 1920. The Dunbar had seating for 395 and offered all of the latest feature-length motion pictures, with local organists Professor George E. Battle and Carroll Boyd providing on-the-scene sound effects and intermission music; the Republic Theatre (1343 U Street NW), which opened on Monday, May 30, 1921 and featured motion pictures until its demolition in 1976; and the larger and more prestigious Lincoln Theatre (1215 U Street NW), which opened on Monday, February 27, 1922, had a seating capacity of 1,600 and offered the public both first-run motion pictures from the Metro Pictures Corporation and live entertainment, though its musical presentations were infrequent and on a much smaller scale than those offered by the nearby Howard Theatre.

One of the Lincoln Theatre's most significant early offerings was a program entitled "Three Period of Negro Music" which was presented under the auspices of the National Negro Music Center Campaign Committee on the evening of Saturday, May 13, 1922. This exhibition included primitive African songs interpreted by Kathleen Easmon and C. Kamba Simango, Negro music of the antebellum period performed by the Wooding Jubilee Quintette and modern Negro music composed by Coleridge Taylor, H.T. Burleigh and Nathaniel Dett as interpreted by singers Florence C. Talbert and Maeme F. Moon, accompanied by cellist David J. Martin, Jr. In the early 1930s the Lincoln mixed motion picture offerings with sporadic live performances by such major stars of the day as comedian Stepin' Fetchit, pop-opera singer Jules Bledsoe, and a dancing trio known as the Three Gobs.

In February 1923, an underground ballroom with a capacity of 3,000 occupants called the Lincoln Colonnade opened underneath the Lincoln Theatre's back parking lot and initially featured dances and assemblies which mainly employed Louis Brown's Orchestra or Bill Baldwin's Orchestra as its house bands. From the 1930s until its closing in 1956 this basement space offered special events featuring a variety of local and national jazz bands. During its time some of the best ensembles to perform there included Don Redman and His Orchestra (featuring singer Myra Johnson), Lionel Hampton and His Orchestra, Eddie "Mr. Cleanhead" Vinson and His Orchestra, Earl Bostic and His Band and the James Moody Orchestra. In addition, jazz saxophonists were a regular attraction and among those to work the underground stage included Gene Ammons, Buck Hill, Snooks Riley and Stan Getz.

The You Street area's entertainment scene was enhanced with the opening of a number of live music night spots in the 1920s. Three establishments in particular, the Oriental Grill and Dining Room, the Murray Casino and Night Club Bohemia, brought people and music together and strengthened the neighborhood's cultural identity.

The first of these establishments to make its mark was the Oriental Grill and Dining Room, which opened on Friday, November 26, 1920 in two levels (the basement and the first floor) of a three-story Victorian building at 901 R Street NW. The restaurant was owned by Louis T. Thomas, a local jazz pianist, who had operated the Louis Tomas' Clef Club booking agency in the same building since 1916. Thomas simultaneously led his own ensemble which was called the Capital City Clef Club Orchestra. The Washington Bee newspaper ran several months of ads proclaiming the Oriental Grill and Dining Room to be "Headquarters of Washington's Superior Colored Musicians," and sometimes referred to the club in articles as Louis Thomas' Cabaret.

In April 1921 the name of the Oriental Grill and Dining Room was officially changed to Oriental Gardens. While Louis Thomas and the Capital City Clef Club Orchestra, which at times included a young Duke Ellington on piano, held down house band duties, other blues and jazz entertainers regularly made appearances throughout the 1920s. Their ranks included bands such as Billy Griffin Prince Trio; singers Ethelene Jordan, Gladys Rose, Virginia Johnson and Amelia "Babyface" Simms; singer-dancer Ada "Bricktop" Smith; banjoist Sterling Conaway; singer-pianist Agnes McGill; pianist Claude Hopkins; and singer-drummer Sonny Greer. The building that once housed the Oriental Gardens is still standing today as a private residence.

The next You Street area hot spot to appear was the Murray Casino, which was owned and operated by the three-man team of Raymond Murray, Morris Murray and Norman Murray, proprietors of Murray Printing Company Inc. The casino opened on the night of Saturday, January 1, 1921 in a two-story building at 920 U Street NW. During the 1920s some of the jazz artists who worked engagements there were Gertie Wells' Aces, Carroll Boyd's International Invincibles, Gertie Monk and Her Six Jazz Jiggs, Lucille Hegamin and the Syncopated Jazz Band, Elmer Snowden's Jazz Band, Doc Perry's Society Band, Mayo's Jazz Band, G. Frank Jones' Jazz Band, Trixie Smith and Her Jazz Band, Percy Glascoe's Jazzeolas, Carroll Boyd's Jazzers, Sylvester Thomas' Columbian Orchestra, Bill Reeve's International Jazzers, Louis Brown's Jazz Babies, and, throughout 1927, several appearances by Duke Ellington and the Washingtonians. In the 1930s the club utilized two main house bands, the Tommy Myles and His Playboys and Hartwell Cook and His Orchestra. During the club's final years, the Sepia Syncopators were the main entertainers. The Murray Casino closed in 1942, though its building still stands.

The third primary night spot of the You Street area during its early years was Night Club Bohemia, which was owned and operated by James Fletcher in the basement of the Lewis Building at 2001 11th Street NW. The opening night bill on Friday, October 22, 1926 consisted of Claude Hopkins and His Harmony Band, blues singer Miss Bea Foote and singer-dancer Miss Billie Griffin. For the remainder of the 1920s the featured house band was the Henry Sheppard Orchestra, an outfit that often invited guest jazz musicians to perform with them including pianist Duke Ellington, who worked with the band through one of their engagements in April 1927.

Night Club Bohemia went through different owners and name changes, operating as the Crystal Caverns Club, Club Caverns, the Caverns, and then, beginning in September 1960, Bohemian Caverns. Some of the top jazz performers to appear at the club in the 1930s included Harold Francis' Caverneers and such singers as George Craft, Doris Rhubottom, Bea Morton and Max Bailey.

Several other live-music establishments were operating in the You Street area in the 1920s and made cultural contributions to the neighborhood. Among these entries were: the Poodle Dog Cabaret (2009 Georgia Avenue NW), which was in operation from October 1920 to July 1922, was owned and managed by Abraham L. Mitchell and boasted such attractions as the Claude Hopkins Orchestra and Duke Ellington's Serenaders; the Dreamland Cabaret (1827 7th Street NW), which was open from November 1921 to December 1923, was owned by Benjamin S. Moore and managed by Charles Johnson and served up local blues singers such as Mabel White, Louise Walker and Blanche Clarke, along with orchestras led by the likes of Sonny Greer, Bill Miller and Claude Hopkins; and the Paradise Café (2011 Georgia Avenue NW), which lasted from October 1922 to

February 1924, was managed by Robert H. Thomas and boasted Claude Hopkins' Agate-Cracking Jazzers as its regular house band.

The You Street area, which became established as a separate section within the Shaw neighborhood, was enhanced by the opening of the Masonic Temple Building in October 1929. The looming six-story structure had taken more than seven years to construct and was located on the southwest corner of 10th and U Streets NW. City directories at the time listed it as having two separate addresses: a front entrance marked 1008 U Street NW, and a side door marked 1930 10th Street NW. (This building is still standing today as Prince Hall Freemason and Eastern Star Charitable Foundation, Inc. at 1000 U Street NW, though it is still informally referred to as the Masonic Temple Building.)

The sixth floor of the Masonic Temple building was outfitted for use as a night club and on Friday, November 1, 1929 the Bamboo Inn opened in its quarters with Elmer Calloway and His Orchestra supplying the music. In early 1930 the establishment changed its name to Club Prudhom, with the same house band flipping its moniker to Elmer Calloway and His Club Prudhom Orchestra.

In December 1933, a White Jewish owner named Louis Hurwitz came on board, redesigned the business as the Cotton Club and actively recruited both Black and White patrons to his new enterprise. During its two-year run the Cotton Club offered such Negro music entertainers as Duke Eglin and His Orchestra and Tommy Myles and His Cotton Club Orchestra; and singers Bobby Chapman, Benny Fonville, Sid Sisko, Gladys West, Helen Wiggins, Georgetta Bryant and Sally Gooding. Also making appearances were such comedians as Rastus Murray, Drucilla Drew and the team of Peanuts and Rinky, along with specialty dancers Betty Bee and Amy Spencer. Hurwitz also booked some top-flight White entertainers into the Cotton Club including Ozzie Nelson and His Orchestra, pop singer Estelle Taylor, pianist Eddie Duchin, vaudeville comedian Roscoe Ates and the comedy team of Bert Wheeler and Robert Woolsey.

Another significant night club to emerge in the You Street area was Republic Gardens. This night club had its origins in an eatery called the Republic Café that opened in 1928 at 1350 U Street NW. The business was moved across the street into a converted row house at 1355 U Street NW by owner William Govan Tindel in September 1932 and remained a popular food service restaurant for several months. In January 1933 Tindel changed the name of the establishment to Republic Gardens and began booking Black dancers, singers and jazz bands.

Throughout the 1930s and 1940s house band duties at Republic Gardens were served by such jazz ensembles as Willie Fair's Orchestra, Henry Johnson's Orchestra and Al Dunn's Combo. Some of the better-known jazz musicians to appear in the night club during these years were pianist Duke Eglin and singers such as Bea Foote, Julia Bryant, Jackie Johnson, Scotty Harrison, Jesse Johnson, Virginia Maples, Harry Dias, Mary Hall, Catherine Davidson, Elizabeth Fair, Sarah Deans, Sis Brooks, Clara Jay, DeWitt Davis, Helen Randall, Gordon McKay, George Craft, Ann Edwards, Ada Boulden, Doris Knighton, Lou Porter, Ethel Lacy, Gladys Bradsher, Bernice Arnold, Uria Bailey, Donnie Morrison, Thelma Cobb, Billie Stewart, Doris Brown, June Norton, Jeri Ann, Ann White, Harriet Jefferson, Grace Smith, Betty Logan, George Screene and Maude Thomas. Republic Gardens remained a You Street area hot spot until its closing in October 2007.

Another popular night club in the You Street area during the 1930s was the Jungle Inn (1211 U Street NW), which replaced the Little Tavern Restaurant in 1935 and remained in operation for six years. The Jungle Inn sat two doors away from the Lincoln Theatre in the heart of the neighborhood's business district. This storied night club is famed for having hosted two very famous entertainers: a teenaged singer from Newport News, Virginia named Pearl Bailey who was the featured vocalist through all of 1935 and 1936; and New

Orleans native-jazz legend Jelly Roll Morton (real name Ferdinand Joseph LeMott), who landed in this night club in early 1937 and served as its manager, bartender, cook, doorman and house pianist until he departed the city in December 1938. During his tenure, Morton had briefly renamed the club twice, calling it the Blue Moon Inn and the Music Box at different times, though it always officially traded as the Jungle Inn. Other regulars to work the long, narrow, second-story establishment included jazz pianists Toby Walker, Julius "Skinny" Warren and Tippecanoe.

In 1942 the Jungle Inn was replaced by a night club called the Casbah Restaurant, which then remained one of the You Street area's most popular destinations for more than 40 years. There were a few interruptions in the Casbah Restaurant's history – from November 1947 to January 1950 it traded as the Louis and Alex Restaurant and from April 1952 until December 1957 it operated as the Marina. In early 1958 it was back in action under its original name, the Casbah Restaurant. During the 1940s the Casbah Restaurant emphasized Black jazz entertainers and among those to perform in the long, narrow second-floor room were bands such as the Casbahians, the Four Deuces of Rhythm, Billy Taylor and His Trio, Ray Nance and His Trio, the Harlemaires, Johnny Malachi and His Trio, the Four Blazes, Rector Bradley and His Trio, Skeets Tolbert and His Trio, Eddie Warren's Quartet, the Teddy Brannon Trio, the Vocaliers, and the trio of Plink, Plank and Plunk. Other headliners included pianists such as Vivian Smith, Bill Halsey, Tommy Chase and Johnnie Weatherspoon. Jazz and blues singers to perform included Rita Grenae, Kitty Warren and Wynonie Harris.

During its stretch as the Marina from 1952 to 1957, this night club offered shows that featured jazz and R&B performers, comedians and occasional exotic dancers. Among those to perform there during those years included Gene Ammons and His Orchestra featuring Earl Coleman, the Milestone Trio, Warren Jackson and His Four Kings, Sarah McLawler and Her Trio (featuring violinist Richard Otto), Bobby Fielder's Band, Lester Young and His Orchestra, Arthur Prysock and His Band, Calvin "Hound Dog" Ruffin and His Band, Buck Hill and His Jazz Quartet, the Snooks Riley Quintet, Art Blakey and the Jazz Messengers, Kenny Dorham and His Jazz Prophets, the Max Roach Quintet, the J.J. Johnson Quintet, the Terry Gibbs Quartet, the Horace Silver Quintet (featuring trumpeter Art Farmer), the Kai Winding Septet, the Lee Konitz Quartet, the Miles Davis Quintet, the Julius Watkins Jazz Modes Quintet, Otis Winfield and the Jazz Stylists, Flap McQueen and His Ray-O-Vacs, the Eddie Hill Combo, the Van Perry Quintet, Tiny Grimes and His Highlanders and Frank Motley and His Crew (featuring singer Angel Face).

In addition, other jazz performers to make stops at the Marina during its existence were such singers as Rea Parker, Jimmy McPhail, Shirley Field, DeWitt Davis, Don Wheeler, Hazel Davis, Rea Palmer and Big Maybelle Smith. Other major attractions included singer-guitarist Chuck Berry; singer-pianists Bubber Johnson and Shirley Horn; organist Jimmy Smith; and saxophonists Julian "Cannonball" Adderley and Sonny Stitt.

In 1958 the moniker of the night club was switched from the Marina back to the Casbah Restaurant and for the remainder of the decade the club's headliners included such bands as VI Burnside and Her All-Stars, the Three Sounds, the Bobby Robinson Trio and Roland Kave and His Diablos; jazz singer Lee Richardson; R&B singer Ernie Brown; and organist James Drayton. The Casbah Restaurant remained a live music hot spot until its closing in 1985. Since that time a number of businesses and night clubs inhabited the building and since December 2008 the premised have been occupied by the Next Door Restaurant and Bar.

Other night clubs of this era within the You Street area were: the Green Parrot (1218 U Street NW), a lesser-known establishment which operated from 1935 to 1940 and offered blues singer Sid Sisko and pianist Duke Eglin as its main attractions; the Barksdale

Cafeteria (1934 9th Street NW), which opened in 1935, featured local blues singer Mabel White for several years, and kept its doors open under this name for more than 20 years; the relatively short-lived Norfolk Grill (1810 14th Street NW), which opened in 1936 with ads shouting out "Hep! Hep! The Jumpin' Jive" and for several years featured the Harold Francis Orchestra (this group's lineup also included pianist Harold Francis, saxophonist Alfred Page, drummer Bill Mason and a trumpeter named Georgetown), the jazz group Johnny Highsmith and His Rhythm Makers, blues singers Berenice Burns and Slim Jones, singer-comedian Jack Meredith, and jazz singers Rocksey Turner and Bob Davis; and the action-packed Little Harlem (1851 7th Street NW), which operated from 1939 to 1947 and boasted such performers as jazz pianists John Malachi and Sir Charles Thompson, and jazz saxophonist Benny Golson.

Another significant night club of this time that sat on the outskirts of the You Street area was the notorious Club Madre (2204 14th Street NW), which was in operation from 1945 to 1949 and often featured jazz singer Una Mae Carlisle and a band called the Metrotones. After Club Madre closed in June 1949, its building sat vacant for nearly four years before La Comeur Lounge opened in its space in November 1953.

Jazz was the style of music served up by La Comeur Lounge and during its three-year existence a number of impressive Black and White performers graced its stage. Among those to work the establishment were the George Shearing Quintet, Charlie Barnet and His Orchestra, the Beryl Booker Trio, the Bill Doggett Trio, Buddy DeFranco and His Combo, Billy Taylor and His Trio, Oscar Peterson and His Trio, the Flip Phillips Quartet, the Mert Oliver Quintet, Al Dunn and His Jazz Combo, the Gerry Mulligan Quartet, the Max Roach Quintet, Chet Baker and His All-Star Quintet, Clifford Brown and the All-Stars, the Australian Jazz Quartet, the Jackie London Quartet, Joe Loco and His Mambo Quintet, the Three Rockers, saxophonist Lee Konitz and His Band, singer-pianist Freddie Cole and His Band, and the jazz trombone duo of Kai Wending and J.J. Johnson. Among the top jazz singers to work the club were Chris Connor, Dolores Parker, Lee Talbert, Laura Pettaway, Rea Parker and Sallie Blair. In 1956 the Cue Tavern replaced La Comeur Lounge and the house band slot was filled by the Buck Hill Trio. Later, from 1957 to 1995 this building housed the Flamingo Lounge.

Entrepreneurs Richard Cannady and Freddy Woods opened the Off Beat Club (1849 7th Street NW) in 1942 and enjoyed a 15-year run as one of the You Street area's liveliest night spots. The Off Beat Club mainly booked local Black entertainers who offered up jazz and blues under the under the race music banners, though the club's clientele included Blacks and a smattering of Whites.

Among the Off Beat Club's main attractions during the 1940s were pianists Clifton Springs and Tommy Chase, and bands such as Peter Rabbit and His Off Beat Band, the Off Beat Serenaders, Teddy Polk's Orchestra, Slim Jim Jones and His Trio, the Three Specks, the Raymond Jackson Trio, the Royal Hoagland Band and the Brother Moncur Quintette. Featured singers during these years included Ruby Smith, Esther Gardner, Marie Ricardo, Sonny Lee, Edna "Yak" Taylor, Hattie Green, Kitty Warren, Claudia McNeil, Helen Stewart, Clara Seawright, Ida Harris, Saundire Lee, Lee Richardson, Teddy Coles, Leroy Stevenson, Rubberlegs Williams, Nudie Williams, Sammy Lee, Charles McCormick, Bobby Chapman, Sonnie Pokes and Jimmie Young.

During the 1950s the Off Beat Club offered such performers as Floyd Taylor's Combo; singers Mable Small, George Eades, Edy James; and singer-comedian emcees like Jimmy Green, Jimmy Reds and Ray Murray. The Off Beat Club closed in 1957 and two years later Key's Restaurant opened in its former space.

The husband-and-wife team of Bill and Jean Clore opened Clore's Restaurant and Cocktail Lounge (1855 7th Street NW) in 1943 in the space formerly occupied by the

Cornelius Scott Restaurant. With the You Street area established as an entertainment mecca, they offered a variety of Black jazz artists in their night club including bands such Ted Sinclair and His Rhythm Kings, Clyde Wright and His Stomping Aces of Rhythm, Tommy Myles and His Trio (featuring Ruth Bostic and Pop Griffin), the Four Monotones; and singers such as Irene Baptiste, Doris Knighton, Kay Hedgeman, Ruby Bryant, Pauline Martin, Barther Lee, Purcell Green, George Craft and Red Roscoe Simmons. Clore's closed in early 1950 and was replaced on April 15 of that year by the Seven-Tee Restaurant.

Another favorite night spot that arrived in the You Street area during the 1940s was Club Bengasi (1423-1425 U Street NW). Opening on Wednesday, July 28, 1943 inside a turn-of-the-century row house that had formerly been occupied by a night club called the Rock Inn, Club Bengasi was located on the western end of the You Street area a block away from Club Bali. The establishment was initially owned by a man named Von Blaine, who was quickly bought out by a local entrepreneur named Paul Mann.

An impressive roster of jazz and blues acts mounted the Club Bengasi stage during the 1940s including bands such as the Billy Moore Trio, the Palmer Brothers, the Jones Brothers, Peter Rabbit and His Rhythmic Trio, the Eddie South Trio (featuring pianist Billy Taylor), the Poinciana Trio, Stuff Smith and His Trio, Leon Abbey and His Quartet, the Al Casey Trio, Ben Webster and His All-Time Esquire Quartette, John Kirby and His Orchestra, the Henry Wells Quintet, Earl Bostic and His Groovy Band, Ben Webster and His Quartet, the Ravens, Charlie Shavers and His Orchestra, the Slam Stewart Quartet, Arnett Cobb and His Combo, Savannah Churchill and the Trio Tones, Pearl Bailey and the Five Metrotones, the Loumell Morgan Trio, Chubby Jackson and His Band, Eddie "Cleanhead" Vinson and His Band, Charles Brown and His Smarties and Frank West and His Combo.

Featured pop and jazz singers at Club Bengasi during the 1940s included Helen Humes, Ethel Waters, Ella Fitzgerald, June Christy (one of the rare White performers to entertain in the night club), Johnny Hartman and Billy Eckstine. Other headliners on the premises included saxophonist Don Byas and pianists Hazel Scott, Connie Berry, Milton Gregory, Eddie Haywood, Maurice Rocco, Mary Lou Williams, Maurita Gordon and Erroll Garner.

During the 1950s Club Bengasi booked such entertainers as the Erroll Garner Trio, the Jackie Davis Trio, Eddie South and His Trio, Herbie Fields and His Orchestra, Stan Getz and His Orchestra, the Cecil Young Quartet, the Blue Note Quintet, Stuff Smith and His Sensational Combo, Lester Young and His Combo, George Stribling's "Sepia Review" (featuring dancers Ray Sneed and Audrey Armstrong and singer Marie Wright), Lou Powers' Band, Dave Brubeck and His Band, the Three Strings, Paul "Hucklebuck" Williams and His Great Band (featuring singer Danny Cobb), Thelonius Monk and His Trio and the Gene Bonnike Trio.

Club Bengasi carried on until the summer of 1963, at which time it was renamed the Living Room and proceeded to offer local folk and jazz groups for the following six years. In 1970 it reassumed its original moniker and operated as Marion's Bengasi until its 1974 closing. The building was subsequently torn down and since September 1986 the former Club Bengasi space (the first half of the north side of the 1400 block of U Street NW) has been occupied by part of the Frank D. Reeves Center for Municipal Affairs, an eight-story office building whose front entrance is currently listed as 2000 14th Street NW.

Other favorites in the You Street area during the 1940s included the Beachcomber (1803 14th Street NW), the Boulevard Grill (1218 U Street NW), the Capital Grill (1228 U Street NW; it later became the Turf Restaurant and Bar), Club Cimmaron (1914 13th Street

NW), the Hollywood Tavern (1940 9th Street NW), the Old Rose Social Club (1848 7th Street NW) and the Success Café (1357 U Street NW).

As the You Street area soldiered on, yet another active venue of the late 1940s and early 1950s was Club 20-11, which operated out of the Dunbar Hotel (2011 15th Street NW). Noted jazz entertainers to work there included the Jones Brothers, the King Cole Trio, the Lennie Tristano Sextet, the Slam Stewart Trio, the Don Shirley Trio, Al Sears and His All-Star Combo, Arnett Cobb and His Orchestra, Tiny Grimes and His Combo, Erroll Garner and His Trio, pianist Johnny Malachi, and a number of singers including Maxine Sullivan, Al Hibbler and Pearl Bailey.

Just a block off of You Street was a later arrival to the scene, Abart's Internationale and Cocktail Lounge (1928 9th Street NW), which, at various times during its 1956-1964 existence, was alternately advertised in the local media as Abart's Lounge, Abart's Jazz Mecca, the International Club, the International Jazz House and the International Jazz Mecca. The night club was a hot spot for local and visiting jazz talent and boasted the finest players one could imagine.

From its opening in December 1956 through 1959 performers in Abart's Internationale and Cocktail Lounge included bands such as the Grassella Oliphant Trio, the Sarah McLawler Trio (featuring violinist Richard Otto), Freddie Cole and His Trio, the Gus Simms Trio, the Ramsey Lewis Trio, the Shirley Horn Trio, the Jimmy Smith Trio, and the Three Sounds Trio; singer Frances Burnett; singer-pianist Nina Simone; guitarist Ray Crawford; clarinetist Tony Scott; saxophonists Lou Donaldson, Lucky Thompson, Charlie Rouse, Buck Hill and Ben Webster; trumpeters Art Farmer and Donald Bird; and French horn player Julius Watkins.

In the 1960s the jazz entertainment surged on at Abart's and from 1960 until its closing in 1964 headliners in the night club included ensembles such as the Buck Clarke Quintet, the Buck Hill Quartet, Julian "Cannonball" Adderley's Quintet, the Ruben Brown Trio, Lambert-Hendricks-Ross (a vocalese trio consisting of Dave Lambert, Jon Hendricks and Annie Ross), the Shirley Horn Trio, Art Blakey and the Jazz Messengers, the Wild Bill Davis Trio, the Les McCann Trio, the Johnny Griffin Quintet, the Yusef Lateef Quartet, the Montgomery Brothers (guitarist Wes, bassist Monk, and pianist-vibraphonist Buddy), the Horace Silver Quintet, the Bobby Timmons Trio, the Jimmy Heath Quintet, the Shirley Scott Trio (featuring saxophonist Stanley Turrentine), and the John Coltrane Quartet; singers Aretha Franklin, Etta Jones and Sallie Blair; saxophonists Eddie "Lockjaw" Davis, Stan Getz, Sonny Stitt and Leo Parker; trumpeters Mouse Johnson and Lee Morgan; and trombonist Slide Hampton.

CHAPTER FIFTEEN
THE DUKE

Of all the talented musicians and entertainers who performed in the You Street area before the rock and roll era, by far the most celebrated was Duke Ellington, the now-legendary ragtime piano player, jazz composer and bandleader. Ellington spent the first 24 years of his life in Washington, D.C. before moving to New York where his engagements at the famed Cotton Club in Harlem earned him considerable fame. His journey is an interesting study in that he honed his considerable musical skills for years in local venues, but left town with his band and established a reputation in what he deemed to be a more lucrative market. This act of relocation became a regular practice of local musicians in later decades who also felt the need to move beyond the confines of the Washington, D.C. area in order to achieve national recognition for their talents. Ellington's move ultimately paid off, as he led his professional band for more than five decades, composed thousands of jazz scores and is credited with creating one of the most distinctive big band sounds in all of popular music.

Edward Kennedy "Duke" Ellington was born on Saturday, April 29, 1899 to James Edward and Daisy Kennedy Ellington in their home at 2129 Ward Place NW, Washington, D.C. His father worked as a driver and a butler and frequently moved his family about the city, occupying no fewer than 10 different homes from the time of Duke's birth through 1918. Both parents were piano players and they introduced their son to the instrument when he was seven years old. Duke Ellington attended Garnet School and Garrison Junior High School, and in 1914 enrolled at Armstrong Manual Training School, a vocational high school for Black students, to study commercial art. Exhibiting a stronger interest in music, he dropped out of Armstrong in February 1917, some three months before he was scheduled to graduate.

Ellington periodically took private piano lessons from various teachers in Washington during his pre-teen years, but it wasn't until he entered high school that he entertained thoughts of performing in public. During this time he studied other piano players at neighborhood parties and frequently hung out at Frank Holliday's Poolroom (626 T Street NW), right next to the Howard Theatre. There, he observed the behavior of scores of local musicians during their idle hours, the ranks of which included such esteemed jazz pianists as Ralph Green, Claude Hopkins, Shrimp Bonner, Phil Word, Roscoe Lee, Oliver "Doc" Perry, Louis Brown, Louis Thomas, Clarence Bowser, Lester Dishman, Sticky Mack and Blind Johnny. His experiences inspired him to work the stage at several Armstrong school assemblies where he played piano for his classmates as they danced the night away.

In the spring of 1917, shortly after leaving Armstrong Manual Training School, Ellington formed his own jazz band, the Duke's Serenaders. Their very first professional date was at a dance held in room 10 of True Reformers' Hall on U Street NW. They played that evening from 8pm until 1am and were paid a sum total of 75 cents for their efforts.

The composition of Ellington's band varied from gig to gig, but usually consisted of the Duke on piano, along with a drummer, a saxophonist, and either a banjo or guitar player. Among the local musicians who passed through the Duke's Serenaders over the next few years were guitarists Bill Miller and William Escoffery, banjoist Elmer Snowden, bass fiddler Otto "Toby" Hardwick, saxophonist Felix Miller, trumpeter Arthur Whetsol and several different drummers including Brother Miller, Lloyd Stewart and Sonny Greer.

The Duke's Serenaders performed a mixture of originals and jazz covers, mixing Ellington's own compositions such as "Soda Fountain Rag," "What You Gonna Do When the Bed Breaks Down?" and "Bitches Ball" with popular selections like Scott Joplin's "Maple

Leaf Rag," Irving Berlin's "Alexander's Ragtime Band," W.C. Handy's "St. Louis Blues" and Tony Jackson's "Pretty Baby."

In March 1918 Ellington moved out of his parents' house at 1703 8th Street NW and into his own home at 1955 3rd Street NW. On Tuesday, July 2, 1918 he married a girl he knew from high school named Edna Thompson and their only child, a son they named Mercer Kennedy Ellington, was born on Tuesday, March 11, 1919. Another move subsequently followed, with Ellington relocating his family to 2728 Sherman Avenue NW, a residence that would be his last Washington, D.C. address.

During this time Ellington supported his family with the money he made working with the Duke's Serenaders and other local jazz bands including the Capital City Clef Club Orchestra, led by Louis Thomas, and Wooding's Smart Set Orchestra, directed by Russell Wooding. From 1920 to early 1923 he worked in a number of bands that performed at the Murray Casino and also served as the house pianist at Oriental Gardens. During this time the Industrial Café (2006 11th Street NW), which had opened on Wednesday, September 29, 1920 and was situated next-door to the Hiawatha Theatre, became a regular late-night hangout for Ellington and his musician friends.

In 1922 Ellington put his art skills to use and took a daytime job as a designer-painter for Ewell Conaway Sign Painter (610 T Street NW), a few doors down from the Howard Theatre. Even with the added income, his financial situation remained precarious and Ellington concluded that in order to achieve fame and fortune as a ragtime jazz pianist, he would have to pursue greater musical opportunities outside of Washington, D.C.

In February 1923 Ellington left the nation's capital and moved to New York City to pursue night club work, taking drummer Sonny Greer and bass fiddler Otto "Toby" Hardwick with him. He then spent the next four years leading his own orchestra, the Washingtonians, in various New York night clubs including the Club Kentucky, the Exclusive Club, Connie's Inn, Ciro's and the Plantation Club. From 1927 to 1931 his band worked the Cotton Club in Harlem, a prestigious job which included a weekly live radio broadcast that enabled Ellington to finally achieve the stardom he sought.

Duke Ellington reached his creative peak during the 1930s when he became a major star of the swing era and produced such classics as "Moon Indigo," "Creole Rhapsody," "Sophisticated Lady" and "Solitude." He recorded hundreds of jazz songs for such record labels as Victor, Brunswick and Okeh, appeared in motion pictures and played on radio broadcasts with some of the greatest figures in popular music, performed with his orchestra at venues throughout the United States and Canada and embarked on extensive concert tours throughout Asia, Africa, Europe, Australia and South America. Faithful to his roots, he always booked his bands into the Howard Theatre when he returned home to visit family and friends in Washington, D.C. Ellington continued to write and perform music until his death from lung cancer on Friday, May 24, 1974 at the age of 75.

CHAPTER SIXTEEN
THE HISTORY OF THE HOWARD THEATRE

A document on file with the DC Historic Preservation Office Building Permits Database shows that the original order to approve the construction of the Howard Theatre on the plot of land at 620 T Street NW, Washington, D.C. was issued in permit number 4639 on Friday, February 25, 1910. The two-story, concrete, brick-and-stone building with a frontage of 80 feet and a depth of 126 feet was designed by architect C. Edward Storck and built by Baltimore construction specialist Henry L. Maas at a cost of $49,000. The original owner of the building was National Amusement Co. with no corresponding individual names provided. Information gleaned from local newspaper articles revealed that National Amusement Co. was a Baltimore, Maryland-based business and the theatre was named after Oliver Otis Howard, a White General in the Union Army who had also served as Howard University's third president. The theatre was equipped with 1,200 seats.

In researching this book, research requests for information on the National Amusement Co. were filed with three present-day organizations: the Maryland Department of Labor, License and Regulation (Division of Occupational Professional Licensing); the Maryland Business License Information System; and the Maryland Department of Assessments and Taxation (Taxpayers Services Division). All three of these agencies claimed they could not locate any information whatsoever on the business in question. A check was made with the Enoch Pratt Free Library in Baltimore, Maryland, where a 1910 Polk Baltimore City Directory from their collections revealed an entry for the National Amusement Co. that listed Marion S. Pearce as president and Philip J. Scheck as secretary and treasurer.

The fact that Pearce and Scheck, both White Americans, were officers of the National Amusement Co. and owners of the Howard Theatre made perfect sense, given their well-established history in the motion picture business. Marion S. Pearce (1874-1953) and Philip J. Scheck (1877-1932), both Baltimore natives, met while working together at United Railways and shared a mutual interest in electricity, which led to an interest in motion pictures. The two formed a partnership in 1901 and began exhibiting movies in various churches and halls throughout Maryland in the cities of Baltimore, Towson, Frederick, and Ellicott City. By 1905 they had expanded their operations and opened both a moving picture equipment business and a small short-lived movie house in Baltimore. They continued to expand their holdings and by 1909, according to various published sources, were operating as many as six different movie houses in Baltimore alone, including the Grand, the Amusea, the Ideal and the Victoria. They later opened the 3,000-seat Hippodrome Theatre in Baltimore in November 1914.

In 1910 Pearce and Scheck formed the National Amusement Co. and their first course of action was to build the Howard Theatre in a long-established Black neighborhood in Washington, D.C. At this time, the You Street area already hosted three small Black vaudeville-movie houses: the Minnehaha Theatre at 1213 U Street NW (1909-1912); the Hiawatha Theatre at 2008 11th Street NW (1909-1924); and the Ford Dabney Theatre at 2001 9th Street NW (1910-1911). Pearce and Scheck never publicly commented on their new theatre, so one can only speculate that they saw the move as profitable in that both Whites and Blacks together were prospective customers, a daring practice of integration that was uncommon during that particular era.

The first action taken by the Howard Theatre owners was the assignment of two associates, Messrs. Jacob S. Rosenthal and someone known only as Mr. Benedict, to oversee the theatre's management and present themselves to the general public and local media as owners, though in fact they served as front men for the two real proprietors. In one of their first administrative actions, they hired a Black theatre manager named W. H. Smith, who had formerly held a similar position at the Pekin Theater in Chicago, Illinois.

Amid a flurry of articles in the Washington Bee newspaper, the Howard Theatre opened for business on the night of Monday, August 22, 1910 with an evening of entertainment entitled "Vaudeville Perfected" that consisted of nine separate performing acts. Of these nine featured acts, five happened to feature White entertainers.

The opening night show, which ran until the following Sunday, offered the following bill: the Five Largards (a troupe of White European acrobats and gymnasts); Abbie Mitchell (though promoted throughout her career as a Black songstress, in reality this American soprano opera singer, billed as the Queen of Song, was the offspring of a White Jewish father and a Black mother); E. Warren Hatch & Co. (a White comedy troupe that presented the playlet "Miss Cupid"); the Rice Brothers (a White German comedian team); Mr. & Mrs. Tom Lancaster (a White American musical comedy duo); the Pekin Trio (a Black threesome from Chicago that later gained some measure of acclaim for their jazz music); an act billed as Johnson Brothers & Johnson (which, in reality, was the Black minstrel trio of Bob Cole, J. Rosamond Johnson and James Weldon Johnson); Frank Clermonto & Etta Minor (this Black cornet-playing duo, when off the stage, went by their legal names of Frank Clermont and Etta Minor Clermont); and Dem Black Dragoons (an all-Black minstrel group). Prices for the show included balcony admission at 15 cents, balcony reserved at 25 cents, orchestra reserved at 25 and 50 cents, lower box seats at $1, upper box seats at 75 cents, and entire six-seat boxes at $4 and $5.

The Howard Theatre followed up that first week's offering with another week-long round of mixed-race entertainment. For the week beginning Monday, August 29, 1910 their bill offered the following performers: Mr. J. Aldrich Libbey and Miss Katherine Trayer (two White singers, late of the Bostonian Grand Opera Company, who performed a comedy satire); Cameron and Toledo (two White acrobats who performed an extravaganza entitled, "The Enchanted Grotto"); the Great English (a hoop rolling marvel who presented "the greatest novelty act ever presented by a single colored performer"); Rose Fox (a Black actress, late of the Empire of London, England, who gave a performance entitled "Little African Knights"); the Dark Town Trio (a Black threesome described as "noiseologists and terpsichoreans"); Queen Dora (a White European novelty dancer who performed a series of fire, serpentine, rainbow, and electrical ribbon dances); Brown and Delx (a "colored singing and dancing sister act"); and the added attraction of a troupe of White actors led by Joseph Maddern and Katherine and Company (who presented a race track society sketch entitled "Too Many Darlings").

The Howard Theatre kicked off the fall months by bringing in a 50-member Black performance troupe called the Smart Set headed by vaudeville comedian Sherman Houston "S.H." Dudley and supported by comedian Aida Overton Walker who presented the classical comedy "His Honor the Barber" from Monday, September 5 through Sunday, September 11. In addition, the night of Sunday, September 11 saw the theatre host a "Grand Sunday Night Concert" featuring the Famous Smart Set Quartette and soprano vocalist Miss Lillian Brown, marking the first concert to ever be presented on the Howard's stage. The week of Monday, September 12 saw Hawley Alcott and Company present the novelty playlet "Monday Afternoon" which featured the Rays (a group of "colored singers and dancers") and six other novel acts.

After a three-week break the Howard Theatre reorganized with a week-long visit by Stetson's Uncle Tom Cabin Company beginning Monday, October 10 and followed that up with two offerings from the newly created 40-player Howard Stock Company, which staged a two-week run of the musical comedy "My Friend from Dixie" beginning Monday, October

24th and then another two-week staging entitled "Big Minstrel Carnival" featuring J. Leubrie Hill and W.H. Vodrey beginning Monday, November 7.

On Sunday, November 20 the Howard Theatre underwent a rather significant change in its operations when manager William H. Smith was replaced by a White administrator named Sidney Bieber. While the theatre had enjoyed a rousing opening week, attendance had steadily dwindled in ensuing weeks. Bieber's first responsibility as manager was to oversee the week-long engagement of an all-White company that performed Neil Twomey's play "St. Elmo" beginning Monday, November 21. The second week-long show to be staged under Bieber's watch was the melodrama "Anita, the Singing Girl," which ran from Monday, November 28 until Saturday, December 3. This particular stage event was presented by an all-Black company known as the Philadelphia Players and featured Clara Turner in the lead role and a supporting cast that included Jim Hammond, Maxwell Driscoll, Billy Barry, Ira Moore, Lee Wesely and Deville Wesely.

Bieber then continued the practice of emphasizing Black entertainment, as the remainder of December 1910 saw him book such stage presentations as "A Girl's Best Friend," a play featuring Clara Turner; a performance by an outfit called the American Minstrels; and a musical entitled "A Blackville Corporation" that featured J. Leubrie Hill, Brown and Shelton, Louie Mitchell, Leona Marshall and the music of Will Vodrey. More than two-and-a-half years later, the last live stage show at the Howard Theatre under Sidney Bieber's management was the Corwell and Nye vaudeville presentation of "The Mississippi Minstrels and Musical Maids" featuring the Fagan Trio, Happy Sam Gardner and Funny Al Strauder which was in residence from Monday, April 28 through Saturday, May 3, 1913.

On Monday, September 1, 1913 the National Amusement Company installed a new Black manager by the name of Andrew J. Thomas to handle the Howard Theatre's bookings. Thomas, who had previously owned and operated the Minnehaha Theatre a few blocks away on U Street NW, immediately scheduled several weeks of live stage presentations and motion picture offerings. The very first event under his management took place on Friday, November 7, 1913 and was billed "A Unique Concert of Negro Music" featuring the Clef Club Orchestra of New York conducted by James Reese Europe and a chorus of 60 that provided an evening of plantation melodies, syncopated rhythms and tango tunes.

From 1913 to 1919 the Howard Theatre continued to offer programs of theatre, vaudeville and motion pictures that featured Black, and, to a lesser extent, White entertainers. According to local press accounts, theatre attendance during these years was fully integrated. Many of the theatrical presentations of this period showcased Black troupes like the Smart Set and the Quality Amusement Company of New York and among the more popular Black headliners were J. Leubrie Hill, the tandem of Salem Tutt Whitney and Homer Tutt, and S.H. Dudley.

Among the more intriguing shows from this period at the Howard Theatre that featured White actors and musicians were: a Saturday, May 22, 1915 appearance by Mr. Lewis H. Murray and Company, which presented "The Evolution of Dance," an exhibition of modern society and classique dances accompanied by an orchestra under the direction of Mr. James Reese Europe; and a week-long run beginning Monday, March 25, 1918 of a show billed as "Big Time Vaudeville" which featured Fiddler and Cole, Harry and Kid, and Oliver's Beauty Chorus.

The Howard Theatre underwent a significant change when manager Andrew J. Thomas resigned from his position in early 1922 and the theatre's lease was subsequently assumed by the Dudley-Murray United Theater Corporation on Monday, March 6 of that year. Under new Black manager Sherman Dudley, the Howard Theatre mainly hosted three different types of live entertainment shows: plays and musical revues by Black theater companies; musical concerts featuring individual performers; and vaudeville bills headlined by White entertainers.

Among the more esteemed Black theater companies to regularly perform at the Howard Theatre during the 1920s were: the Quality Amusement Corporation of New York City, the plays of which featured such actors and entertainers as Cleo Desmond, Lawrence Chenault, Shelton Brooks, Babe Townsend, Inez Clough, Susie Sutton, Elizabeth Williams and the music of pianist C. Luckeyth Roberts; the Lafayette Players, whose major performers were Abbie Mitchell, Evelyn Ellis, Arthur Simmons; the Smarter Set, which featured the team of Salem Tutt Whitney and J. Homer Tutt; and a number of presentations by actor-entrepreneur Irvin C. Miller including the "Brown Skin Models" revue and the popular stage show "Broadway Rastus."

Concert performances were also given during this time by such nationally renowned blues singers as Mamie Smith, who appeared at the Howard nine separate times during the 1920s, the first of which was an engagement where Mamie Smith and Her Jazz Hounds Revue headlined an eight-act, two-hour show that ran from Monday, December 20 to Saturday, December 25, 1920. In similar fashion, jazz singer Ethel Waters debuted at the Howard as Ethel Waters and Her Jazz Masters, top-billed over the Black Swan Troubadours and an all-star vaudeville revue for a one-week run that began on Monday, June 19, 1922. She would perform at the Howard a total of five times during the decade.

Black comedians also garnered the spotlight at the Howard, including such favorites as and Jackie "Moms" Mabley, who debuted at the Howard on Monday, April 27, 1925 with a supporting spot in the musical revue "Fun in a Cabaret," and the duo of Butterbeans and Susie, a couple of singer-dancer-comedians who made the first of four stops at the Howard during the decade with a week-long run beginning Monday, April 4, 1927.

During the 1920s many renowned White entertainers appeared onstage at the Howard Theatre. In one vaudeville offering that began on Monday, November 14, 1921, singer-dancer-actress Lillian Devere headlined the show and was supported by other acts such as the Tennessee Four, Male Lucile, Tenderlo, and the team of Marlin and Bell. Beginning Sunday, January 29, 1922 the Howard offered the stage comedy "Some Show" which featured Dutch comedian-actor Danny Murphy and the Great Zita ("The Only Posing Woman of Her Kind in America") and a cast that included Harry Evans ("The Hebrew Funster"), Elmer Brown, Emma Kekler, Florence Whitford and Mildred Simmons. In what was advertised as "The Season's Best Offering," the legendary Italian comedian Ralph "The Jazz Wop" Rogers, along with singer Harry "Hickey" Levan, co-headlined a show entitled "The Big Review" presented by Henry P. Dixon beginning Sunday, February 26, 1922. Some of the other White performers to grace the Howard stage during the decade were mentalist Dr. C. Harmon ("The Reader of Destiny"), the Russian acrobat duo of Al and Daisy Pissore, a New York vaudeville comedy team known as the Phun Fiends, and the stars of the Knight Brothers Circus.

The Howard Theatre started the 1930s on somewhat shaky ground. After three-and-a-half months of seemingly well-received shows, the Howard closed at the conclusion of a week-long run of a musical revue billed as "The Stars of Blackbirds" featuring the Famous Howardettes on Saturday, April 12, 1930. The theatre then sat dark from Sunday, April 13, 1930 until Friday, September 25, 1931.

During the summer of 1931 Abe Lichtman, the latest in a long line of White entrepreneurs to have leased the theatre business, broke his contract with the building's owners, thus allowing another White entertainment outfit, the Stiefel Brothers of Philadelphia, Pennsylvania (Oscar, Harold, Barney and Morris), to come in and assume operational control. The first move of the new lessees was to install a 41-year-old Black manager from Chicago named Sheppard "Shep" Allen to run the house. Despite numerous changes in ownership, he would remain in that capacity until June 1970. The first show the new team staged featured local favorite Duke Ellington and His Cotton Club Orchestra that ran from Saturday, September 26 to Friday, October 2, 1931.

As the 1930s progressed, the Howard's musical programs, which increasingly took on the style of modern-era, multi-act concerts and featured all manner of both Black and White performing artists, gained tremendous creative momentum that would characterize the venue for the next three decades. Among the noted Black jazz entertainers to headline the Howard Theatre from 1930 to 1939 were singers Noble Sissle, Blanche Calloway, Cab Calloway, Baron Lee, Ethel Waters, Bessie Smith, Lena Horne and Billie Holliday. Also featured were a number of pianists including Duke Ellington, Bennie Moten, Earl Hines, Fletcher Henderson, Eubie Blake, Claude Hopkins, Luis Russell, Coleridge Davis, Count Basie and Edgar Hayes. Other Black jazz acts to perform during this time were Lucky Millinder and His Orchestra, Chick Webb and His Jazz Orchestra (featuring singer Ella Fitzgerald), the Mills Brothers, the Four Ink Spots, singer-pianists Tiny Bradshaw and Fats Waller, saxophonists Jimmie Lunceford and Andy Kirk, saxophonist-clarinetist Don Redman, singer-trumpeter Louis Armstrong, trumpeter Erskine Hawkins and violinist Stuff Smith,. Rounding out these bills were comedians such as Stepin Fetchit, the team of Butterbeans and Susie and Jackie "Moms" Mabley.

White performing artists were also booked into the Howard Theatre during the 1930s, though their appearances during this time were irregular at best. On several occasions manager Shep Allen booked lavish Black and White revues which featured the best of both factions in what were often times billed as head-to-head competitions.

These unique, week-long bills included such match-ups as: A "Black and White Revue" consisting of 30 "Colored" stars led by Bert Howell and 30 "White" stars led by the singing Stoner Brothers (beginning Saturday, April 2, 1932); a "Black and White Battle of Music" sending Al "The Sepia Guy Lombardo" Jenkins and His Orchestra against "The Hottest White Band from the West" Victor Lopez and His Orchestra (beginning Friday, November 9, 1934); Harold Woods and His Royal Crest Orchestra was matched against an "All Star Sepia Review" consisting of Amanda Randolph, Slim and Eddie, the Three Brown Jacks, Smith and Sink, Troy Brown and Baby Cox (beginning Friday, April 12, 1935); a "Black and White Revue" that sent a squad of Black entertainers that included Dusty Fletcher, Cora Green, Monty Hawley, Billie McLaurin, Lillian Fitzgerald, Clarence Robinson, the team of Ford, Bowie and Dailey, and 16 dancing girls against the White lineup of "George Burns and Company" which featured the legendary comedian George Burns himself, comedian-actor Ben Linn, dancer Lee Murray, singer York Tracy, and 16 Earl Carroll Beauties (beginning Friday, January 24, 1936); "The Battle of Music" with a White band, Little Jack Little and His Orchestra, going head-to-head with a Black outfit, Baron Lee and His Orchestra (beginning Friday, February 12, 1937); "The Battle of Swing Jamboree" with White headliners Charles Barnet and His Broadway Favorites featuring singer Judy Ellington playing opposite Lucky Millinder and His Harlem Rhythm Orchestra (beginning Friday, October 28, 1938); and another exciting "Black and White Revue" with the Savoy Sepia Follies taking on an all-White company known as Earl Taylor's Revue Glorified which included a squadron of acrobats known as the Bellfords, the female swing-singing Udell Triplets, Hollywood songstress Connie Cella, the Rover Boys comedy team and sweet-throated tenor Gordon Bennett (beginning Friday, March 24, 1939).

The 1940s decade saw the Howard Theatre enter into one of its greatest chapters, with a staggering number of now-legendary musical performers – both Black and White – gracing its stage. Multi-act bills were very much the norm during this time, and jazzy, big-band orchestras held down the fort as all manner of entertainers gave it their all on a nightly basis. Throughout this period the Howard Theatre continued to actively pursue mixed audiences, as evidenced by the diverse nature of the largely out-of-town and nationally acclaimed singers, comedians and musicians they booked for the viewing and listening pleasure of the hometown crowds.

Some of the most popular Black jazz entertainers to perform at the Howard during this decade included bands such as Andy Kirk and His Clouds of Joy (featuring singer June Richmond), Count Basie and His Orchestra, Earl "Fatha" Hines and His Orchestra, Lucky Millinder and His Orchestra, Erskine Hawkins and His Orchestra, Cab Calloway and His Steaming Swingcopators, Fats Waller and His Orchestra, Duke Ellington and His Orchestra, Claude Hopkins and His Orchestra, Jimmie Lunceford and His Band, Fletcher Henderson and His Orchestra, Lionel Hampton and His Victor Recording Orchestra, the King Cole Trio (led by Nat King Cole), Cootie Williams and His Band, Noble Sissle and His Orchestra, Louis Jordan and His Tympany Five, Louis Armstrong and His Orchestra, Dizzy Gillespie and His Orchestra, Art Tatum and His Trio and Arnett Cobb and His Flying Home Sextet. Vocal groups to headline the theatre during these years included the Mills Brothers, the Golden Gate Quartet, the Ink Spots and the Red Caps. Featured singers included Billy Eckstein, Wynonie Harris, Ella Fitzgerald, Pearl Bailey, Billie Holiday, Ethel Waters and Lena Horne and among the favorite comedians to work the stage were Stepin Fetchit and Jackie "Moms" Mabley.

Although it is almost completely overlooked today, there were also a tremendous number of White jazz headliners at the Howard Theatre during these years. Among these performers were Louis Prima and His Orchestra (featuring singer Lily Ann Carol), Charlie Barnet and His Orchestra (featuring singers Jean Dick and Louise Baldwin), Tony Pastor and His Orchestra (featuring singer Patti Powers), Georgie Auld and His Band (featuring singer Ann Solloway), Randy Brooks and His Orchestra (featuring singers Loretta Vale and Phil Michel), Johnny "Scat" Davis and His Orchestra (featured singers during his band's multiple appearances included Louise Douglas, Sonny Morgan, Nadine Vaughn and Jeff Lane), Tommy Reynolds and His Orchestra (featured singers during their many appearances included Judy Tremaine, Laura Watson and Sid Gary), Herbie Fields and His Victor Recording Orchestra (featuring singer Pat Flaherty), Stan Kenton and His Orchestra (featuring singer June Christy), Freddie Slack and His Orchestra (featuring singer Lynne Stevens), Ray Anthony and His Music in Action Orchestra (featuring singers Frances Foster and Dick Noel), Boyd Raeburn and His Orchestra (featuring trumpeter Maynard Ferguson and singer Gwen Bell), Charlie Ventura and His Band (featuring singer Jackie Cain and singer-pianist Roy Kral), and a special visit by dancer-pianist-trumpeter Jerry Brandow. In addition, another famed White entertainer to perform on the Howard Theatre stage that decade was country singer-guitarist Roy Rogers.

Perhaps the most incredible White act the Howard booked during this time was a week-long engagement by the famed comedy team the Three Stooges, who embarked on a rare live Washington, D.C. engagement on the Howard stage that ran from Friday, September 27 to Thursday, October 3, 1946.

The Howard's great days of mixed-race entertainment continued throughout the 1950s, with hundreds of talented entertainers performing onstage to capacity audiences. Throughout much of the decade the Howard, under longtime Black manager Shep Allen, billed its live music as jazz, though numerous pop, R&B and rock and roll performers were included on their multi-act bills.

A sizeable number of nationally known Black entertainers worked the Howard Theatre during the 1950s and some of the best bands to make appearances were Lionel Hampton and His Orchestra, Lucky Millinder and His Mighty Orchestra, Dizzy Gillespie and His Recording Orchestra, the Will Mastin Trio (featuring singer Sammy Davis Jr.), Bull Moose

Jackson and His Buffalo Bearcats, Arnett Cobb and His Sizzling Six, Paul Williams and His Hucklebuck Sextette, Louis Jordan and His Big Orchestra, Erskine Hawkins and His Tuxedo Junction Orchestra, the Clovers, King Cole and the Trio, Count Basie and His Orchestra and Revue, Cab Calloway and His Orchestra, Duke Ellington and His Orchestra, Frank Motley and His Orchestra (featuring drummer T.N.T. Tribble), the Heartbreakers, Charlie Parker and His Combo, Earl "Fatha" Hines and His Big Orchestra, the Drifters, Lloyd Price and His Orchestra, Little Richard and His Orchestra, the Coasters and Art Blakey and the Jazz Messengers. Other esteemed headliners included: singers Ella Fitzgerald and Pearl Bailey; singer-guitarists Bo Diddley and Chuck Berry; singer-pianist Ray Charles; and comedians Jackie "Moms" Mabley and Redd Foxx.

Some of the great White jazz bands to perform at the Howard during the 1950s included drummer Gene Krupa and His Mighty Columbia Recording Orchestra (featuring saxophonist Buddy Wise, trombonist Urbie Green, bassist Don Simpson, trumpeter Don Fagerquist and singers Frances Lynn and Bill Black), saxophonist Charlie Ventura and His Big Orchestra, clarinetist Artie Shaw and His Orchestra, clarinetist-saxophonist Woody Herman and His Orchestra, drummer Johnny Otis and His Barrelhouse All-Stars (Otis was the offspring of Greek immigrants and in reality was a White American), clarinetist-saxophonist Herbie Fields and His Orchestra, saxophonist Charlie Barnet and His Orchestra, clarinetist Buddy DeFranco and His Orchestra, pianist Dave Brubeck and His Quartet, saxophonist Boyd Raeburn and His Orchestra, saxophonist Stan Getz and His Quintette, saxophonist Lee Konitz and His Combo, jazz guitarist Johnny Smith and His Trio, the Big Band (featuring drummer Joe Theimer), the Lennie Tristano Quartet (featuring Tristano on piano, along with saxophonist Warne Marsh and bassist Peter Ind), the Crickets (featuring singer-guitarist Buddy Holly), the Del Vikings (a racially mixed, five-piece doo-wop group featuring two White vocalists, David Lerchey and Gus Backus), Dion and the Belmonts, the Elegants, the Skyliners, drummer Louis Bellson and His Orchestra and the Crests (a racially mixed doo-wop group whose lead singer was a White American named Johnny Maestro). Other headliners during the decade included: singer Bobby Darin; singer-guitarist Dale Hawkins; and saxophonist Allen Eager.

In the 1960s the Howard Theatre continued with their multi-act bills, but placed greater emphasis on offering Black jazz and R&B acts while limiting the number of White performers that took the stage. Among the big names in Black entertainment that appeared at the Howard during this decade were groups such as Little Anthony and the Imperials, the Drifters, the Flamingos, Rick Henderson's All Stars, Buddy Johnson and His Mighty Orchestra, the Coasters, Bo Diddley and His Trio, the Isley Brothers, Louis Jordan and His Tympany Five (featuring singer Dottie Smith), the Four Tops, Ray Charles and the Raelets, Julian "Cannonball" Adderley and His Quintette, Harvey and the Moonglows, James Brown and the Famous Flames Orchestra, the Miracles, Hank Ballard and the Midnighters, the Drifters, Ike and Tina Turner, the Four Tops, the Shirelles, Lloyd Price and His Big Band, the Miles Davis Quintette, the Clovers, the Spinners, Gladys Knight and the Pips, Duke Ellington and His Orchestra, the Ramsey Lewis Trio, the Supremes, Martha and the Vandellas, Quincy Jones and His Famous Orchestra, the Temptations, Patti LaBelle and the Bluebelles, the O'Jays, Sam and Dave and Peaches and Herb. Other major headliners included: singers Ruth Brown, Sam Cooke, Brook Benton, Screaming Jay Hawkins, Ben E. King, Pearl Bailey, Etta James, Aretha Franklin, Gene Chandler, Marvin Gaye, Otis Redding, Dionne Warwick and Wilson Pickett; singer-guitarists John Lee Hooker, Chuck Berry, Freddie King and Muddy Waters; singer-pianists Fats Domino and Billy Stewart; and comedians Jackie "Moms" Mabley and Redd Foxx.

While much smaller in numbers than previous decades, White musicians did make rare appearances and among those bands the Howard Theatre highlighted during this decade were: jazz saxophonist Charlie Barnet and His Big Orchestra, the Crests (a pop vocal group), jazz drummer Louis Bellson and His Orchestra, the Capris (a doo wop group), the Del Vikings (a racially mixed doo wop group) and the Dovells (a pop vocal group). Appearances were also made by: jazz guitarist Charlie Byrd; C&W-R&B singer-pianist Ronnie Milsap; and the blue-eyed soul singer Wayne Logiudice.

After the riots in Washington, D.C. that followed the assassination of Dr. Martin Luther. King, Jr. in April 1968, the Howard Theatre lost just about all of its White audience. Overall attendance dipped so low the theatre began spacing out its concerts presentations and live music shows took place on a sporadic basis from 1969 to 1970. The last major live music event of this era on the Howard Theatre stage was an R&B show that ran from Friday, March 27 to Sunday, April 5, 1970 featuring singer Joe Simon, the Soul Children, the Fawns, the Vibrations, singer Bill Morgan and comedian Sad Sam. After a series of Friday-Sunday night "Capital City Talent Shows" in the month of June 1970, the theatre went dark and remained shuttered from Monday, June 22, 1970 to Wednesday, April 16, 1975.

Only two shows were offered at the Howard Theatre in 1975. The first was an R&B event that ran from Thursday, April 17 through Thursday, April 24 featuring: jazz singers Arthur Prysock and Melba Moore; jazz trumpeter Harry "Sweets" Edison; and comedians Redd Foxx, Jackie "Moms" Mabley, Pigmeat Markham, LaWanda Page and Butterfly McQueen. The second show ran from Friday, April 25, through Thursday, May 1 and featured: R&B singer Joe Simon; the Fatback Band; and jazz singer-pianist Garland Green. The venue then again went dark until a one-night R&B vocal group concert event on Friday, April 29, 1977 offered the Jewels, the Spaniels, the Clovers and the Rainbows.

Throughout the remainder of 1977 and continuing through July 1980 live music at the Howard Theatre was presented on an intermittent basis. The venue was dark from August 1980 through July 1982 and then from August 1982 to August 1985 bookings included occasional live go-go music shows. The Howard Theatre, which had changed ownership on numerous occasions through the years, was purchased by Ellis Development in 2006 which then enlisted Howard Theatre Restoration, Inc. to oversee management of the facility. After a $30 million renovation, the Howard Theatre reopened to the public on Monday, April 9, 2012 with a performance by rapper Wale. It currently hosts concerts by a variety of popular music acts.

CHAPTER SEVENTEEN
THE BLUE YODELER

As different styles of popular music evolved in the Washington, D.C. area in the 1920s, a man who would become a legend in the realm of country music named Jimmie Rodgers quietly relocated to the nation's capital where he furthered his ascent to national recognition. Known far and wide as "The Blue Yodeler" and "The Singing Brakeman," and, more recently, "The Father of Country Music," Rodgers was the archetypical hillbilly singer-guitarist whose music emphasized folk traditions from the American South and West.

Born James Charles Rodgers on Wednesday, September 8, 1897 in the Pine Springs community of Lauderdale County, Mississippi (10 miles northwest of the city of Meridian), he began performing as a teenager, singing and playing guitar at talent shows and dances around his home state. As the son of a railroad man, he spent many years as a section hand and brakeman on various railroads, including a 1917-1918 stint with the New Orleans & Northeastern Railroad.

After years of odd jobs and gigs as a pick-up guitarist, mandolinist and banjoist around Meridian, Rodgers joined a traveling musical outfit called Billy Terrell's Comedians in the fall of 1923 for an eight-week tour of several states in the South. In early 1924 he quit the tour and went back to working railroad jobs in several Western states including Texas, New Mexico and Colorado, but was diagnosed with tuberculosis later in the year, thus slowing his railroad career considerably. He next worked with a medicine show that toured the states of Tennessee, Kentucky, Ohio and Indiana. In 1925 and 1926 he held jobs with the Florida East Coast Railroad in Miami and the Southern Pacific Railroad in Tucson, Arizona, among other companies. In the fall of 1926 Rodgers was back in Meridian with his second wife Carrie and five-year-old daughter Anita when he decided to devote all his time to a career in music.

In January 1927 Rodgers ventured to Asheville, North Carolina where he worked odd jobs for three months before gaining a weekly program in April on local radio station WWNC playing novelty selections and specialty numbers with guitarist Otis Kuykendall. Later that month he came across a string music group from Bristol, Tennessee called the Tenneva Ramblers which consisted of singer-guitarist Claude Grant, his brother Jack Grant on mandolin and fiddler Jack Pierce. In May when the band had exhausted its bookings, Rodgers hired the group to be his backing band and called his new outfit the Jimmie Rodgers Entertainers. The band began working square dances and high school auditorium shows throughout the Asheville area, playing a peculiar mix of dance numbers, pop tunes, traditional ballads and folk tunes.

In August of that year the Jimmie Rodgers Entertainers went to Bristol, Tennessee for a recording session with agent-producer Ralph Peer of the Victor Talking Machine Company, but an argument ensued as soon as they hit town and Rodgers decided to leave the group and record the sessions as a solo act. Consequently, On Thursday, August 4, 1927 he cut two songs for the Victor label, "The Soldier's Sweetheart" and "Sleep, Baby, Sleep." The next day he and his wife, who had sent their daughter Anita to live for a while with his parents in Alabama, headed for Washington, D.C. where relatives had invited them for an extended stay.

Rodgers arrived in the nation's capital on Friday, August 5, 1927 in the middle of a sweltering summer. He and his wife Carrie moved into the brick row house of Alex and Annie R. Nelson at 1151 3rd Street NE. (Annie Nelson, who worked at the time as a cataloguer for the Government Printing Office, was Carrie's sister.) At that point in time the house was facing a large vacant lot, which some 14 years later would be the site of Uline

Arena, which later became the Washington Coliseum in 1961. (To this day the front door of the old Rodgers home directly faces the large entrance area of the long-dormant coliseum structure.)

The activities of Jimmie Rodgers during his time in the nation's capital are somewhat mysterious. It is known that he sought work as a professional musician during his years in Washington, D.C., but there is little documentation pertaining to where he actually performed at. His wife Carrie wrote a book entitled "My Husband Jimmie Rodgers" (1935) which unfortunately provides little information regarding their time in Washington. In one passage in the book she writes that Rodgers worked playing as a "fill-in between pictures in neighborhood theatres" out in the suburbs, though she did not state if the theatres were in Maryland or Virginia. In another section she mentions that "Jimmie's various engagements were fairly steady and well-paying," but offers no other details.

What is known is that during his stay in Washington, D.C., Rodgers secured a weekly radio program of his own on station WTFF, with his first on-air segment occurring on Sunday, December 18, 1927 from 9:20pm to 9:40pm. Rodgers' rural music was characterized by lines of blues singing with yodeling between verses. He became an immediate hit with the people of the nation's capital, where an influx of Southerners looking for government work was developing. An announcer at WTFF named Ray McCreath took note of the listeners' love for Rodgers' unique vocalizations and is credited for naming Jimmie "The Blue Yodeler." He reportedly became his local manager and secured paid jobs for him around the nation's capital until the final airing of Rodgers' popular WTFF radio program on Sunday, May 21, 1928.

Local appearances by Jimmie Rodgers, as documented in the Washington Post and other dailies, included: a benefit performance for the Veterans of Foreign Wars organization on Thursday, February 23, 1928 at the Mount Alto Nursing Home (3021 Tunlaw Road NW, Washington, D.C.); a banjo performance hosted by emcee Ray McCreath on Tuesday, April 24, 1928 at a luncheon for the Washington Advertising Club at Harvey's Restaurant (1016 Pennsylvania Avenue NW, Washington, D.C.); and a headlining role at a minstrel show benefit for the Gadsby's Tavern Fund on Thursday, May 31, 1928 at Lyceum Hall in Alexandria, Virginia, an event presented by Alexandria Hive No. 48 of the Maccabees, an American Legion auxiliary.

Rogers' most prestigious local performance was his greatly heralded week-long engagement at the Earle Theatre in Washington, D.C. where he headlined a revue entitled "Moonlight and Roses" from Saturday, August 4 to Friday, August 10, 1928. The show featured several seasoned vaudeville performers including rube fiddler Charlie Althoff, a teenaged sister dance act called the Lovey Girls, the singing team known as the Kardo Brothers ("The Boys of 1,000 Songs"), popular dancer Frank Siefert and emcee Joe Bonbrest. The fast-paced, 30-minute revue ran four times per day in between showings of the feature film "Home, James" (Universal Pictures, 1928).

During this engagement Rodgers appeared each night in his brakeman's outfit which included a blue jumper and striped cap and took his place onstage as the house orchestra struck up the song "Frankie and Johnny." Placing one foot on a cheap drugstore chair and picking away on his new Weymann guitar, Rodgers performed such songs as "Blue Yodel," "Brakeman's Blues" and "Ben Dewberry's Final Run" and was reportedly met with encore demands after each showing. The Washington Post gave Rodgers a rave review in their Monday, August 6, 1928 edition, stating: "Jimmie Rodgers, 'The Singin' Brakeman,' would have come back some five times if a certain Saturday audience had had their way about it."

Rodgers' star had risen rapidly during his time in the nation's capital. He had established a local reputation through his WTFF radio show and live appearances. He had also managed to complete recording sessions in November 1927, February 1928 and June

1928 for the Victor Talking Machine Company in Camden, New Jersey, resulting in a total of 21 songs including "Blue Yodel," which was released on Friday, February 3, 1928, sold over one million copies, and rocketed Rodgers to national stardom.

Throughout 1928 health problems continued to put a damper on Rodgers' activities. His tuberculosis continued to simmer and the prospect of fighting through a second harsh Washington, D.C. winter did not seem appealing to the Blue Yodeler. Accordingly, Jimmie and Carrie Rodgers left the nation's capital in the middle of September 1928. Though his time in Washington, D.C had been brief, he had been a very influential performing artist on the local country music scene and paved the way for future C&W musicians in the nation's capital.

Rodgers and his family spent their final years in Kerrville, Texas. He made solo appearances throughout the South, toured with the Paul English Players, appeared in the short movie "The Singing Brakeman" (Columbia Pictures, 1929), co-headlined a Red Cross tour of the Midwest in 1931 with humorist Will Rogers, and performed short tours with the J. Doug Morgan Show in 1932 and 1933. Jimmie Rodgers died on Friday, May 26, 1933 due to complications from tuberculosis at the age of 35.

Jimmie Rodgers was the very first inductee of the Country Music Hall of Fame in 1961 and was inducted into the Rock and Roll Hall of Fame in the "Early Influences" category on Thursday, January 23, 1986. His song "Blue Yodel No. 9" was subsequently selected by the Hall as one of their "500 Songs that Shaped Rock and Roll." During his six-year recording career, Rodgers recorded a total of 110 songs for the Victor label. Today Jimmie Rodgers is widely referred to as "The Father of Country Music."

CHAPTER EIGHTEEN
GOIN' DRY

Prohibition was a period from Thursday, November 1, 1917 to Wednesday, April 5, 1933, when, under the Sheppard Act, the sale, manufacture and importation of liquor was outlawed in Washington, D.C. With liquor being prohibited, a number of speakeasies quietly went into operation throughout the city and the suburbs, though the featured attraction was the bootlegged whiskey and not so much musical entertainment. When Prohibition was eventually repealed, there was a surge in the issuance of liquor licenses and the openings of new bars, night clubs and restaurants, resulting in an immediate and substantial demand for musicians and other entertainers.

It must be accentuated that temperance movements against the consumption of alcohol had a lengthy history in the United States that dated back to the early 19th century. In 1815 Maine became the first state to go totally dry, banning the sale of alcohol except for "medicinal, mechanical or manufacturing purpose." By 1855, 12 states had adopted policies of total prohibition, though most had rejoined the wet ranks by 1880. Early in the 20th century a number of pro-dry political factions were gaining influence, including the Women's Christian Temperance Union and the Anti-Saloon League. The influence of these groups was substantial and their agendas dominated local elections around the country and ultimately resulted in increasing numbers of dry states.

In the 1916 presidential election both Democratic incumbent Woodrow Wilson and Republican candidate Charles Evans ignored the Prohibition platform. Both parties had strong wet and dry factions and with the expectations of a close election, neither candidate wanted to lose any part of their respective voting bases. Consequently, the presidential candidates stood idly by as the 65th United States Congress met at the end of 1916, with the Democratic drys outnumbering the wets by 140 to 64 while dry Republicans outnumbered their wets by 138 to 62.

President Wilson was in a precarious position, as 17 of the 30 states he had carried in 1916 were dry. When the issue of prohibition in the District was raised, he determined any such laws would be within Congress's responsibility, and, with World War I looming, obviously considered the matter to be a disposable issue. The first measure to pass was the Sheppard Act, named after dry Senator John Morris Sheppard of Texas, which prohibited the sale, manufacture and importation of liquor in the District of Columbia, thus rendering the city totally dry. President Wilson signed the bill on Saturday, March 3, 1917 and the measure officially went into effect at 12am on the morning of Thursday, November 1, 1917. A total of 356 licensed liquor establishments in Washington, D.C. had to close their doors.

It took more than 15 years for Prohibition to come to an end. In the summer of 1932, Franklin Delano Roosevelt, governor of New York, accepted the nomination of the democrat party to be their presidential candidate. Cornerstones of his campaign were promises of a New Deal series of programs that would span a five-year period and were intended to provide relief, recovery and reform to the people and economy of the United States of America. Along with the New Deal there also came a pledge to repeal Prohibition.

After winning the election on Tuesday, November 8, 1932 and being inaugurated on Saturday, March 4, 1933, Roosevelt immediately focused his work on two main issues – building the size of the government and bringing alcohol back to the people. While his New Deal agencies ultimately improved the lives of those adversely affected by the Great Depression by increasing the number of federal jobs from 63,000 in 1930 to 166,000 in 1940, it also gave the federal government greater control over the economic and social affairs of the nation. President Roosevelt's other priority, his attack on Prohibition, moved quickly and almost without opposition.

The wait for a legal happy hour in Washington, D.C. had reached its conclusion. At 4:05pm on the afternoon of Wednesday, April 5, 1933, President Franklin Delano Roosevelt, using five different pens, signed the District Beer and Wine Bill, effectively striking down the Sheppard Act and ending Prohibition in Washington, D.C. At 12am on the morning of Friday, April 7, 1933, 3.2% alcohol began flowing once again in the nation's capital. Despite heavy intermittent rain showers, large crowds had gathered in the Downtown area and restaurants filled to capacity as automobiles blew their horns in the streets of the city. The Beverage Permits Board, which had been flooded with somewhere between 1,200 and 1,500 applications for liquor licenses in the preceding days, immediately issued 150 temporary licenses.

The very first beer delivery in the city was made from the Abner-Drury Brewer to the White House at 12:05am that Friday morning. The beverages arrived in a van that featured a string orchestra that performed "Happy Days Are Here Again" as it made its way down Pennsylvania Avenue. A banner pasted on the side of the vehicle read: "Here's to you – President Roosevelt. The Nation's first real beer in years." Citizens cheered wildly as two motorcycle policeman cleared a pathway through the crowd that led to the west side of the White House. With great ceremony, the drivers of the van approached the building's entrance with two gaily decorated bottles of beer – one light and one dark – along with two cases of additional brew, only to be informed that President Roosevelt and most of the White House staff were sound asleep! Undaunted, the potions were dropped off with best regards and the van next sped over to the National Press Club Building at 14th and F Streets NW, where a dozen cases and six halves were hustled up to the top floor quarters of the club. As the wee hours of the morning wore on, supplies were quickly exhausted and beer was shipped in from Baltimore and Pittsburgh, with calls for additional supplies put in to breweries in Milwaukee and St. Louis.

While alcohol drinkers in Washington, D.C. had languished under the Sheppard Act, the neighboring states of Maryland and Virginia had experienced federal-implemented Prohibition under Article XVIII of the Constitution of the United States of America, which went into effect on Friday, January 16, 1920. Officially entitled "The National Prohibition Act," it read, in part: "...the manufacture, sale, or transportation of intoxicating liquors within, the importation thereof into, or the exportation thereof from the United States and all territories subject to the jurisdiction thereof for beverage purposes is hereby prohibited."

Eventually, the 72nd United States Congress proposed Article XXI of the Constitution of the United States of America, which repealed Article XVIII and brought an end to national Prohibition. The ratification of this Twenty-first Amendment on Tuesday, December 5, 1933 meant that alcohol was once again flowing freely throughout the land and the entire Washington metropolitan area was ready to experience the dawning of a new cultural era fueled by changes in the population, the social atmosphere and the business landscape.

CHAPTER NINETEEN
PROHIBITION-ERA NIGHT CLUBS

Night clubs became an important component of Washington, D.C. area popular culture during the 1920s, a decade that saw several of these extraordinary places of entertainment open their doors largely in response to the numerous theatres of the nation's capital that were mixing their nightly programs with vaudeville productions, plays and motion pictures. The night clubs combined the functions of the restaurant, tavern and assembly hall, but placed special emphasis on their menus of live musical entertainment. Each of Washington's earliest night clubs cultivated its own unique clientele, and, with a little scouting, citizens from all levels of society were able choose appropriate social environments and enjoy comfortable evenings on the town. In the 1930s, with vaudeville waning, motion pictures beginning to dominate the city's theatres, and the repeal of Prohibition (1917-1933) on the books, the number of night clubs in the Washington, D.C. area greatly expanded.

East of the city, live music in Prince George's County, Maryland was available in the form of informal performances in a variety of down-home settings and would remain in this mode throughout the Prohibition era. A plethora of saloons, taverns and halls continuously offered live country music, a style that strongly remained the county's music of choice for years to come.

Much of the musical offerings in Prince George's County, Maryland during this period emanated from Bladensburg, which granted licenses to a total of 12 taverns in the year 1900 alone, thus cementing the town's status as an on-going land of revelry. During these early years and into the days of Prohibition many of these Bladensburg establishments, and other similar taverns throughout the county, played host to a variety of country musicians who would take to their makeshift stages alone or with a friend or two to churn out sets of what was variously called camp music, country music, cowboy music, fiddle music, hillbilly music, mountain music, old-time music, rural music and Western swing music – the earliest versions of what would later become formally classified as country & western (C&W) music. Among these establishments were the Pan Electric House, the Palo Alto Restaurant and Hotel, the Spa Hotel, and the Gentleman's Driving Club (all located in Bladensburg), the Ram's Horn Inn in Chillum, the White House Tavern in Beltsville, the Piscataway Tavern in Piscataway, the Mistletoe Inn in Brandywine and the Horsehead Inn in Baden. Regular performers at these establishments during the Prohibition era included such accomplished musicians as banjoists Joe Cullen, Morris Hale and Tom Wilkinson and guitarist-mandolinists Clarence Whitmore, Dennis O'Brien and Bob Green.

While the rough-edged taverns of the county were alive with swing and strings, the more professional country music entertainers of the area such as Gene Beck's Band or banjoist Walter Holt accepted jobs at balls, dances and concert presentations that were frequently scheduled in a number of higher-class assembly halls. These venues included the Masonic Hall in Hyattsville, the Town Hall in Upper Marlboro, Grange Hall in Beltsville and the Academy of Music in Laurel. It was certainly an interesting alternative to country music performances in Washington, D.C., which at the time were mainly confined to fairs and festivals at different parks and churches, or at special events at facilities like the Benning Race Track. This system of taverns and halls as primary musical venues remained intact in Prince George's County all the way through to the end of Prohibition, during which time the night club began fostering significant interest and support throughout the Washington, D.C. area.

A contributing factor to the growing prestige of night clubs in the Washington, D.C. area throughout the Prohibition era was the fact that local theatres were increasingly offering motion pictures as featured forms of entertainment, a practice that eventually spelled the downfall of vaudeville. During this era the theatres of the nation's capital mainly offered four main types of entertainment: plays, vaudeville, burlesque shows and photoplays (motion pictures).

At that time Washington, D.C. was home to dozens of now-legendary theatres and competition between these storied venues for public attention was intense. Among the entries were: the Cosmos Theatre (919-921 Pennsylvania Avenue NW) and B.F. Keith's Theatre (619 15th Street NW), both of which booked extravagant vaudeville shows with nationally renowned performers; the Belasco Theatre (17 Madison Place NW) and the National Theatre (1317-1325 E Street NW), which both offered highly acclaimed plays; the Gayety Theatre (513 9th Street NW), which flaunted its tantalizing burlesque attractions; and the Columbia Theatre (1112 F Street NW) and the Empress Theatre (416 9th Street NW), theatres that introduced the latest photoplays.

As the popularity of motion pictures grew and demand for the latest movie releases increased, local theatre owners found it impractical to spend large sums of money booking touring vaudeville troupes and theatre company productions. As a result, movie theatres in the Washington, D.C. area flourished while out-of-work orchestra musicians searched for jobs. With the advent of Prohibition, many restaurant owners in the city looked for different types of amusements in which to tide over their supposedly alcohol-free audiences. The most obvious source of entertainers for these entrepreneurs to consider was the growing pool of unemployed musicians in the area and it was from this collection of performing artists that the restaurant owners began recruiting orchestras and ensembles to entertain their patrons late into the evenings. As a result of this new trend a vibrant night club scene took hold during the Prohibition era.

Something similar to the modern-era night club first emerged in Washington, D.C. prior to Prohibition in two main parts of the city, Downtown and the You Street area. While the fundamental concept of the night club itself had existed for centuries, its emergence in America in the 20th century as a distinct type of entertainment establishment had a significant impact on contemporary popular culture.

Basically, a night club in its modern form is defined as being a place of evening entertainment that serves food and drink and offers its patrons music, dancing and different types of floorshows. The term itself is of American origin and probably came into public use during the late 1800s. However, the night club was little more than a variation of the historical tavern or saloon, with special emphasis placed on music that was being offered during extended hours. In practice, the night club actually came into existence when the term was used by the media to advertise it as a specialized type of entertainment establishment.

In Washington, D.C. the very concept of the modern-era night club was set in motion with the opening of the Café Republique on the night of Tuesday, September 27, 1910. Located in the heart of Downtown on the first floor of the Corcoran Building on the southwest corner of 15th and F Streets NW (now the site of W – formerly the Washington Hotel at 515 15th Street NW), the elegantly furnished café was managed by J.W. Gibson and boasted the finest French cuisine in the city. The main dining room of the café, awash in green decorations and flashing electric lights with a large flowing fountain in the center, accommodated some 300 patrons and offered evening entertainment consisting of lavish floorshows featuring the music of Imperatori's Orchestra, which performed from a special balcony overlooking the room. A unique underground grotto operated in the basement of the building, providing a bohemian retreat for those so inclined. Despite the fact that the café enjoyed brisk business each night after the theatres of the city closed, the overhead of running such a venture ultimately proved too costly to continue and the Café Republique closed its doors in October 1913.

The next night club of note in Washington, D.C. was the infamous Krazy Kat, a bohemian lair that rated as the city's first alternative hangout for artists, painters, sculptors, poets, writers and actors. The Krazy Kat indeed enjoyed a crazy existence for several years and was constantly under the surveillance of local law enforcement authorities who seemed offended by the various art exhibits, painting classes and late-night parties the night spot hosted.

The Krazy Kat opened during the summer of 1918 in a large brick stable situated at 3 Green Court NW. The general area of this hangout was in an alley bordered by Massachusetts Avenue NW to the north, 13th Street NW to the east, L Street NW to the south, and 14th Street NW to the west. (Today this building is long-gone and its former site is occupied by Balance Gym at 1339 Green Court NW, directly next-door to a gay bar called the Green Lantern at 1335 Green Court NW). It was owned and operated by a trio of artists consisting of Cleon Throckmorton, John Don "Jawne" Allen and John Stiffen.

The proprietors put their creative talents to work and fixed up the old stable as a dining room and lounge area. They then cleared a small courtyard area behind the stable and furnished it with several tables and chairs. They also installed a wooden shed-like structure that backed up against the main building and served as a kitchen and restroom. A small painting on the front door announced "Syne of ye Krazy Kat," with a warning at the top of the door announcing, "All soap abandon ye who enter here." Rounding out the Krazy Kat complex was the famous tree-house, a flat wooden platform built some 15 feet off the ground into a large tree adjacent to the stable which held a table and several chairs and could only be accessed by scaling a 12-step ladder.

Painter-designer Cleo Throckmorton made a noble attempt at conveying the correct bohemian atmosphere throughout the stable and surrounding grounds, adding candles in wax-covered bottles as table placements, hanging swinging lanterns from the stable's ceiling and adorning the walls with various impressionist and abstract paintings. The looming tree-house apparently served as private quarters for friends of the owners, and the shed-kitchen offered only hot chocolate and gingerbread on its menu. Donations for musical instruments were tossed into an old cigar box on a mantelpiece in the stable and a used piano was eventually acquired for impromptu performances by visiting musicians. Unfortunately for the bohemian contingency, it was these very visiting musicians that eventually led to a much-publicized raid of the Krazy Kat.

The city's Health Department, increasingly wary of any alley structures that encouraged human inhabitation or congregation, heard allegations of late-night parties and weirdo revelry in the ominous Green Court alley and enlisted the aid of the police force to keep the Krazy Kat under tight surveillance. Things came to a head at 1am on the morning of Friday, February 21, 1919, when shots were heard somewhere around the stable's courtyard, prompting Policeman Roberts to bolt for the alley and bust in on a massive, drunken free-for-all in progress with the amped-up bohemians slugging out with a group of staggering, inebriated musicians. When the smoke cleared, police rounded up a total of 22 men and three women, eventually charging Allen, Throckmorton and Stiffen with keeping a disorderly house, and 11 others with various counts of assault, drinking in public, and disorderly conduct. In the wake of this momentous bust, the Krazy Kat persevered and remained a bohemian hangout until 1925, at which time its managers dispersed and the club ceased operation.

With widespread publicity heaped upon the Krazy Kat, it didn't take very long for two other bohemian-flavored establishments to rise up in the city, further advancing the notion of what would soon come to be known as the night club within the nation's capital. Like the Krazy Kat, these were also places where the artistically inclined gathered and celebrated into the evening hours, though their operations were far more formal in nature.

The first, Café St. Mark's, opened at 913 15th Street NW on Wednesday, March 12, 1919 and was known for its high-society patrons and advertised supper dances and tea dances featuring the Meyer Davis Orchestra. It remained open to the public until May 1921. Café St. Mark's should not be confused with Club St. Mark's, a similar establishment which operated out of the ballroom of the Draper Mansion at 1011 Connecticut Avenue NW from October 1926 until September 1928 and featured the Spencer Tupman Orchestra.

The second, simply known as the Better 'Ole, staged an opening night gala on Saturday, October 1, 1921 from the second floor space at 1515 U Street NW and was directly modeled after the coffee houses of New York's Greenwich Village. The artists of the city and their followers, described at the time by the Washington Post as "long-haired men and short-haired women," flocked to the Better 'Ole during its seven-year existence on the outer western fringe of the You Street area.

The Better 'Ole was owned and operated by a local artist named Clarence Smith and was unusual for its time in that it catered to a White clientele, but featured both Black and White singers and dancers as entertainment. The house band was the Better 'Ole Orchestra which was directed by Roscoe Lee from 1921-1924, and then Joe Bombrest from 1925 to 1928. An article in the Washington Post of Sunday, February 10, 1935 entitled "Washington Night Life Puts on Grown-up Airs" by Osgood Nichols called it "the first real night club of the so-called 'night club era.'"

In the middle 1920s the term "night club" began experiencing common public use in the nation's capital as a description for a particular type of establishment offering evening entertainment for the public. The prime examples of its early promotion were advertisements surrounding the popular club known as Le Paradis ("A supper club – favored with unusual popularity because of its unusual advantages") which began offering what they called "The Saturday Night Club" featuring dancing to the Meyer Davis Orchestra until 2am. This new feature was first publicized in a small box ad in the Washington Post of Saturday, February 14, 1925, which stated: "We are pleased to announce the first celebration tonight, Saturday, February 14th of the Saturday-Night Club Valentines – a novelty Valentine party will greet the opening of this new club." Subsequent advertisements for Le Paradis in the dailies of the nation's capital simply referred to the weekend theme as "The Saturday Night Club" and the term "night club" was quickly appropriated by numerous other café and restaurant owners around the city, thus introducing an entirely new social entry to local popular culture.

Le Paradis first opened its doors on the third and top floor of a building at 1 Thomas Circle in the heart of Downtown Washington on the evening of Monday, October 23, 1922. It boasted a large combination dancing-and-dining room with seating for 300 and was fitted in Italian and Spanish design, including a $10,000 black-and-ivory ceiling, and offered a summertime roof garden that overlooked the city. The establishment was officially owned by a corporation known as National Cafes Inc., which listed Meyer Davis as president and Howe Totten as owner of the building and property.

Meyer Davis, an Ellicott City, Maryland native, was a locally prominent 29-year-old pianist and violinist who had gotten his start in Washington in 1912 as a free-lance violinist in several different theatre and hotel orchestras. In January 1915 he put together his first Meyer Davis Orchestra and for the next seven years worked many of the top establishments in and around the city including the Willard Hotel, the Raleigh Hotel Roof Garden, Chevy Chase Lake, the Café St. Mark's, the Hadleigh Hotel and the Wardman Park Hotel. During the first two weeks in October 1922, his band headlined at B.F. Keith's

Theatre, a prestigious gig which cemented his stature as the leading orchestra director in the nation's capital.

Davis' considerable local success was instrumental in his decision to enter into the world of night club management, where he aspired to hold down a dual role as club manager and orchestra leader. Upon establishing Le Paradis he used his vast network of musician contacts to put together a new house band that specialized in the latest jazz tunes. His initial group, billed as the Meyer Davis Le Paradis Band, was comprised exclusively of Washington, D.C. area musicians and consisted of himself on piano and violin, pianist Spencer Tupman, banjoist-saxophonist Bob Foster, violinist Nathan Brusiloff, saxophonists Joe Smith, Charles Williams and Franklin Edson, drummer Ben Franklin and musical arranger A. Borguno.

The Meyer Davis Le Paradis Band scored a major coup when they were called upon to give a live musical broadcast over budding local radio station WEAS. This initial appearance, presented as an on-air program entitled "Meyer Davis Le Paradis Band in Special Concert," aired live from the Hecht Company (618 F Street NW, Washington, D.C.) on Thursday, December 28, 1922 at 9pm. The band subsequently gave live concert broadcasts over local station WCAP in 1923 and was then a regular feature attraction on local radio station WRC for several years to come, particularly during the summer months when their performances were aired live from the Le Paradis roof garden. Davis did an admirable job balancing club management duties and musical bookings, as his talented group was recognized as the top orchestra in the city throughout the 1920s. He expanded his musical enterprises and established a number of separate touring Meyer Davis Orchestra units that worked up and down the East Coast of the United States for years to come.

During its first two years Le Paradis attracted capacity crowds on a nightly basis, resulting in a business so rewarding that Meyer Davis saw it necessary to open up a second night club called Club Chanticler on the building's second floor in November 1924. The new club's walls, ceiling and fixtures were completely decked in gold colors, adorned with emerald green velour draperies and bathed in subdued rosette lighting. It was somewhat small in physical space, accommodating only 125 patrons at any one time, and operated as a private club with entrance granted only to card-carrying members. Charles Garbett was installed as manager, and, for entertainment duties, Davis brought in pianist Paul Fidelman who then put together a basic four-piece ensemble called the Club Chanticler Orchestra.

For several years Le Paradis regularly booked local performers and visiting acts to headline their evening programs. In January 1928 decisions were made by Meyer Davis to add midnight revues featuring groups from New York City, enlarge the Le Paradis Orchestra, and place its direction under long-standing member Nathan Brusiloff. The initial midnight offering on Monday, January 23, 1928 included a singing and dancing team from the Casa Lopez called the Phelps Twins, an acrobatic dancer direct from the Frivolity Club named Al White, and a former prima donna of the Ziegfeld Follies named Alice McKenzie. The revamped Le Paradis Orchestra now consisted of singer Walter Scott Kolk, violinist Nathan Brusiloff, banjoist "Fish" Walker, saxophonists Jack Powers and Bob Buch, bassist Jose Torres and drummer Al Spieldock.

The eventual demise of Le Paradis can be attributed to two catastrophic events that clouded its image and turned away many of its regular customers. First, despite the laws of Prohibition, the managers of Le Paradis regularly served set-ups consisting of alcoholic beverages to its patrons. The illegal practice finally caught up with them when Justice Charles S. Hatfield acted upon a series of formal complaints and declared the night club a nuisance in an opinion handed down in District Supreme Court on Tuesday, July 31, 1928.

His written statement instructed government attorneys to prepare an injunction that would close the establishment for one year.

On the night of Saturday, August 4, 1928 Le Paradis was padlocked, with the roof garden and the Club Chanticler on the second floor also being closed to the public. One year later the padlocks were removed and Le Paradis was reopened on the night of Thursday, September 19, 1929, still under the management of Meyer Davis. However, the scene was changing. Many new night clubs had appeared on the landscape and competition was more intense than ever.

The second event which damaged Le Paradis was the bizarre case of 27-year-old Robert Shaw Montgomery, who early on the morning of Sunday, May 17, 1931 shot two people in the night club building with a .45 pistol before taking his own life. Apparently the trouble began when Montgomery argued with Club Chanticler night manager Charles Garbett over the availability of a table near the dance area in the second-floor night club. Denied a his seat of choice, Montgomery pulled the automatic pistol from an arm holster and shot Garbett in the chest as they stood in the middle of the club, badly wounding the manager (Garbett eventually made a full recovery). As the gunman exited the club, he encountered Patrolman Jesse Taylor of the Second Precinct, who was entering the premises, and shot him twice in the chest, killing him instantly. When Montgomery reached the pavement of Thomas Circle, he stopped and shot himself twice under his own heart, ending the horrific fiasco. Meyer Davis, haunted by the nightmarish episode, increasingly focused his attention on his stable of touring orchestras and shut down the night club operation in September 1931. Willing entrepreneurs quickly came along and on Saturday, October 24, 1931 Club Michel opened in the former Le Paradis space.

As Le Paradis reigned as one of the city's premier night clubs throughout much of the Prohibition era, several other establishments around the Downtown area opened their doors with similar regimens. Among these converts were several well-established hotels that opted to implement the night club format in their spacious ballrooms and newly renovated lounges. Some of the more familiar names included in this gathering were: the Franklin Square Hotel (1010 14th Street NW), which housed a lounge called La Java headlined by Irving Boernstein's La Java Orchestra; the Hamilton Hotel (1001 14th Street NW), which featured a night club called Club Lido that offered Emory Daugherty's Lido Orchestra; the Mayflower Hotel (1127 Connecticut Avenue NW), which featured the Vincent Lopez Orchestra in its Presidential Room; the Wardman Park Hotel (2660 Woodley Road NW), whose main ballroom brought in several different bands during the decade including Irving Boernstein's Orchestra and Paul Specht's Orchestra; and the Willard Hotel (1401 Pennsylvania Avenue NW), which at the time called its night club the Palm Room and offered the Meyer Davis Trio as its house band.

Also included in the new wave of Prohibition-era entertainment were several other night clubs in the city that booked orchestras, small-scale vaudeville revues and individual musicians and entertainers for the growing number of people who were anxious to experience a night on the town. One of the more interesting of these entries was the Swanee (501 13th Street NW), which operated out of the basement of the famed Earle Theatre from February 1925 to September 1929. This night club offered the Swanee Syncopators as its house band, a group that had operated at different times under such musical directors as Sam Brown and Al Kamon and was called upon to back a cavalcade of vaudeville entertainers who took the stage after the theatre upstairs had closed for the night. The Swanee was surprisingly owned and operated by Le Paradis proprietor Meyer Davis. On Tuesday, April 11, 1939 the Swanee was converted into a new night club called the Neptune Room, with the Earle Theatre up above being renamed the Warner Theatre in 1947.

Three other noteworthy Washington, D.C. night clubs of the Prohibition era were the Spanish Village, the Lotus Restaurant and the Aster. The Spanish Village (1304 G Street NW) was a pretty little place above the popular Restaurant Madrillon in the Washington Building that was owned and managed by Peter Borras and served up Johnny O'Donnell and the Madrillon Orchestra as its tropical-costumed house band. This second-floor night club, which existed from October 1925 to November 1928, was designed to resemble a village in Spain and was noted for having installed little individual huts over the tables in which the patrons could lock themselves in and enjoy complete privacy.

The Lotus Restaurant (727 14th Street NW), "A Chinese and American Restaurant of Distinction," opened on Saturday, January 21, 1928, was owned by Mr. D.G. Lam, and offered Archie Slater's Orchestra as its house band. (The Lotus Restaurant would remain one of the city's most prestigious night clubs and offered the best in local and national performing artists until its closing in August 1961.)

The last of the Prohibition-era night spots, the Aster (804 14th Street NW) was billed as "Washington's newest, most artistic and largest Chinese-American restaurant" when it opened on Wednesday, October 31, 1928. It offered Emory Daugherty and His Aster Orchestra as its nightly featured attraction. (The Aster, which was owned by Mr. Dow On, closed in July 1932, with its building going on to host numerous popular restaurants in the ensuing years, including the legendary Casino Royal Theatre Restaurant.)

CHAPTER TWENTY
SWING TOWN

The 1930s and 1940s were pivotal decades for the popular music scene of the Washington, D.C. area. The music was constantly evolving as social and demographic changes swept the region. The 1930s started off with the advent of the decade-long Great Depression, which kicked in with the stock market crash of Black Tuesday on October 29, 1929 and devastated the nation. In 1933 President Franklin Delano Roosevelt began to institute his New Deal economic recovery programs while the repeal of Prohibition, both in Washington, D.C. and on a national level, allowed for the flow of alcohol, which, in turn, directly influenced the opening of dozens of new restaurants and night clubs throughout the entire area that emphasized live music. The nation's capital was growing rapidly, with Washington, D.C.'s population jumping from 486,869 (72.6% White) in 1930 to 663,091 (71.5% White) in 1940 to 802,178 (64.5% White) in 1950 and Prince George's County, Maryland's count going from 60,095 (76.6% White) to 89,490 (81.8% White) to 194,182 (88.1% White) during the same period. Most of these new arrivals were working-class folk from the South and their arrival would signal a change in culture that would resonate through these parts for the better part of the next three decades.

During the 1940s, the people of the Washington, D.C. area, like most of America, found themselves exiting the Great Depression and entering an era dominated by the advent of World War II (1939-1945). The city itself had undergone an influx of White Southerners looking for government jobs. Economic growth combined with population growth was transforming the nation's capital into a bustling metropolitan area.

The local music scene was also experiencing significant changes. Long-play albums and 45rpm single records were both introduced to the public, thus revolutionizing the way recorded music was accessed. A magazine called the Billboard was the country's top music trade publication, and, in addition to publishing different charts that ranked the record sales and popularity of songs, had established an unofficial classification system for popular music that would facilitate the eventual emergence of rock and roll. Perhaps the most significant change of all was the substantial increase in the number of night clubs and restaurants offering live music throughout the area, creating demand for more musicians, new bands and a greater variety of music.

One of the earliest venues to offer live orchestral music, both before and during the swing era, was Chevy Chase Lake, a multi-faceted recreation area located 40 yards due east of Connecticut Avenue in Chevy Chase, Maryland (1.8 miles north of Washington, D.C.). The property included a lake 160 yards wide by 240 yards long, an amusement park, shops, a bowling alley, a shooting gallery, a swimming pool, a boating area and a large dance pavilion with a seashell-shaped bandstand overlooking the lake.

Chevy Chase Lake had opened in 1894 and during its early years was known for evening entertainment sessions consisting of local and visiting military brass bands. By the 1930s top-flight orchestras had become the norm and some of the more popular bands to play the Lake's pavilion during this time were the Meyer Davis Orchestra (directed by Ben Levine), Barnes Thompson and His Ambassadors, William Alexander and His Orchestra, George Hall and His Hotel Taft Orchestra (featuring singer Loretta Lee), Mac Hallet and His Orchestra, Ted Black and His Orchestra and Lee Field and His Orchestra (featuring singer Leigh Windham). Chevy Chase Lake discontinued live music after its 1936 summer season and was closed to the public shortly thereafter. Today its former site is partly occupied by 8101, a condominium building at 8101 Connecticut Avenue (on the southeast corner of Connecticut Avenue and Chevy Chase Lake Drive).

The 1930s and the 1940s were considered to be the swing era of the Washington, D.C. area and many of the area's night clubs featured this type of music. Among those night spots of the city held in highest esteem were the series of night clubs that operated out of the legendary building marked 804 14th Street NW. In 1927 a building on this site that had housed a business called Blackistone Florists was demolished. In its place a new structure was constructed and from 1928 to 1932 it housed a restaurant called the Aster. Following the Aster at this address were such favorite live music clubs as the Regal (October 1932-October 1933) and La Paree (November 1933-June 1937). Both of these night spots were similar to the Aster in that they retained Emory Daugherty and His Orchestra as the house band, with a variety of local guest vocalists such as Ray Beck, Marie Fowler and Jane Whitney brought in for short engagements. In addition, La Paree featured Al Sokol and His Orchestra, with Washington's own Buddy Shaner handling the lead vocals, for much of 1935 and 1936, along with more ambitious floorshows featuring guest singers, comedians, dancers and acrobats.

La Paree closed its doors on Saturday, June 12, 1937, and a new restaurant, Bamboo Gardens, opened for business in its place on Tuesday, September 28, 1937. New proprietors Henry K. Wong and Hugh K. Liang worked hard to make their venue the best in the city in terms of local and national entertainment. During their two-year run they assigned house band duties to such top local outfits as Russ Cullen and His Orchestra, Emory Daugherty and His Orchestra and Al Norton and His Orchestra. Gala floorshows were the attraction at Bamboo Gardens and some of the better-known entertainers to work the club during its time included: pop singers such as Leo Lisee, Sam Richardson, Mary Martin, Judith Gales, Marion Dawn and Judy Acton; dancers such as Mildred King and Mary Jane Brown; and comedians Peter Wells and Jimmy Walker. The legacy of 804 14th Street NW would continue on for years to come, as the Bamboo Gardens was converted into the Casino Royal Theatre Restaurant in early 1940.

One block down the street from Bamboo Gardens in Washington, D.C. was the Lotus Restaurant (727 14th Street NW). Prominent in the city since the late 1920s, the Lotus Restaurant also offered the best in local and national talent, with their flashy floorshows anchored for most of the swing era by Bill Strickland's Capitolians, a swinging orchestra that featured singing emcee Al Norton and backed the club's nightly revues of singers, comedians, dancers, magicians, acrobats, jugglers and almost every type of entertainer one could imagine. Some of the more prominent performers that enjoyed great success at the Lotus Restaurant during this time included pop music singers Charlie Mayer, Ray Donahue, Judy Ellington, Odette Borde, Lillian King, Virginia Sims, Evelyn Knight and Sally Winston. Joining the parties were such dancers as Dorothy Ray, Audrey Gibson, George Kiddon, the Van Sisters and Virginia Brown, and the comedy team of Morosco and Hayden.

Another prestigious Washington, D.C. night club was Restaurant Madrillon, a very popular hangout owned and operated by Peter Borras which originally opened on Monday, April 5, 1920 at 1304 G Street NW. The business was later relocated to new quarters on the second floor of the Washington Building (1434 New York Avenue NW) on Saturday, December 31, 1927 with a highly publicized grand reopening that featured Johnny O'Donnell's Madrillon Band, Stafford Pemberton's Cyclonic Dancers, jazz singer Orville Rennie and Spanish dancer Rosita Fantanay.

During the swing era, the Restaurant Madrillon's music schedule featured such pop and jazz performers as Johnny Robb and the Madrillonians, Herb Gordon and His New Yorkers, Leon Brusiloff's Dance Orchestra (featuring singer-trumpeter Jack Schafer, drummer Ralph Hawkins and singers Anita Cazenova and Carmen Cortez), Johnny Shaw and His Orchestra (featuring singer Helen Forrest), Johnny Slaughter's Orchestra, Carr and Don's Orchestra, the Hurtado Trio, the Echevarria Trio, the Lazala Trio, violinist Harry Cherkassky and pianist Sasha Bartnowsky. Pop singers to work extended engagements included Eddie Poindexter, Sue Milroy and Bob Ellis. Restaurant Madrillon would enjoy a long and life at this location and eventually closed its doors on Saturday, January 4, 1958.

There was a series of exciting night clubs in Washington, D.C. during this time that enjoyed great success. Of these entries, one of the more interesting rose from the remains of the old Le Paradis night club at Thomas Circle. A number of different establishments enjoyed varying levels of success in that storied building during the decade, with Club Michel leading the way. Their opening night bill of Saturday, October 24, 1931 featured German singer Thora Hojgaard, the Hollywood dance team of Fawn and Jardon and house orchestra John Slaughter and His Aristocrats, a 10-piece outfit that backed singer-comedian-emcee Larry Guterson.

Club Michel lasted until December 1934 and during its time boasted such top-flight pop music entertainers as singers Marty Rubin, Skin Young, Walter Scott Kolk, Ken Murray and Victoria Regal. Dancers to entertain the crowds included Jack Meyers, Marion Wilkins, Elaine Pring and Norma Gallo. All of these performers were backed by such bands as Pete Macias and His All Star Orchestra, Harry Albert and His Orchestra and Charlie Wright's Orchestra.

Other night clubs to occupy the building during this decade were: the Pilgrim Club (December 1934-June 1935), which offered the Bert Bernath Orchestra and the Al Weiner Orchestra; Club Volga Boatman (October 1935-January 1938), whose house band was led by accordion player Matt Windsor and specialized in Russian and Gypsy entertainers such as singer Michel Michaeloff; and the Melody Club (June 1938-November 1938), whose regular attractions were Wingy Mannone's Orchestra (featuring singer Bert Sherry), Dick Kuhn and His Fountain of Music and Bill Mundy and His Swingsters.

West of Thomas Circle sat the night club known as Troika (1011 Connecticut Avenue NW), which opened its doors under the ownership of Helen Hamilton in February 1933. Troika operated within quarters that had once been the ballroom of the stately Draper Mansion and had most recently housed a night club called the Silver Slipper (November 1932-January 1933). Many establishments had come and gone through the years in this room, including Club St. Mark's (October 1926-September 1928), which was one of the city's earliest night clubs.

In the 1940s Troika moved away from the Gypsy entertainment that had been its staple during the 1930s. Among the top pop music entertainers to work the night club were the Roger Kay Orchestra, the Sasha Lukas Orchestra, and a procession of singers including Nadya Norskaya, Patricia Prochnik, Irene Bordoni, Sophie Tucker, Sheila Barrett, Terry Lawlor, Terri LaFranconi, Josephine Houston, Keith Clark, Nan Wynn, Benny Fields, Don Lamont, the duo of Owen and Parker, Joe E. Lewis, Walter O'Keefe and Harry Richman. Other featured entertainers included: dancer Eunice Healy; and such comedians as Frank Fay, Jack Marshall, Paul Rossini, the sister team of Topsy and Eva Duncan (with Topsy working the crowd with satirical songs and Eva accompanying on piano) and the adagio comedy trio of Hibbert, Byrd and LaRue. Troika closed in 1946.

A few blocks south of Thomas Circle sat the Mayfair Restaurant (The Remington Building, 527 13th Street NW). This establishment opened its doors on Monday, March 11, 1935 and was considered to be one of the city's better establishments. Its night club segment operated as the Café of All Nations from its inception until August 1957, at which time the room's special moniker was dropped.

The walls of the Mayfair Restaurant's main dining room were covered in murals of nationalistic life and maps of countries from all over the world. The main room was lined with benches covered with turquoise fabricoid and filled with similarly treated chairs. The tables had black tops and chromium pedestals. Separating these arrangements were alcoves walled with sheets of black glass reaching from the tops of the benches to the ceilings; these held groups of up to eight people. From the main room one could enter the bar area, whose walls were covered with panoramas of Washington, the Potomac River, the Capitol and the White House.

During the 1940s the Mayfair Restaurant's Café of All Nations booked local pop and jazz bands such as Lyle Smith and His Trio (featuring bassist Fabyan Wright, guitarist Cub Higgins and Smith himself playing a range of instruments including the piano, vibraphone, saxophone, accordion and clarinet), the Rhythm Boys, the Gentlemen of Rhythm, the Chordsmen, the Senators, Dick Abbot's Four, Paul Kain and His Orchestra, Al Yurdin and His Music, Joe Masters and His Music Masters, Sammy Ferro and His Orchestra and the Dick Young Trio. Others to appear onstage there included: singer Mary Byrne, pianists Dorothy Hutchenson and Helen Myer; and organist Lee Potter.

From 1948 to 1951 the Mayfair Restaurant's house band duties were handled by the esteemed Sammy Seymour Trio (singer-keyboardist Nini Baker, saxophonist-clarinetist Sammy Seymour and bassist Hugh Barteman). For the remainder of the 1950s, some of the night club's headlining bands included Nini Baker and Her All-Star Trio, the Capital City Dixielanders, Peggy Holt and Her Continentals, Ben Miller's Red Sox, Country Thomas and His Dixieland Band, Veo and His Duo, and the Mayfair Jazz Ensemble (featuring guitarist Bill Leonhart, bassist Norman Williams, pianist John Eaton, clarinetist Wally Garner and drummer Buddy Dean). Individual jazz performers to appear included: organist Tommy Johnson; keyboardist Ronnie Stancil; and violinist Stuff Smith.

The Mayfair Restaurant closed its doors in February 1964 with its building later housing the Two Caesars Restaurant (October 1964-September 1978) and the Thai Room 2 (October 1978-1985) before being torn down in 1986. Since April 1987 the former site of the Mayfair Restaurant has been occupied by Columbia Square, a 13-story office building at 555 13th Street NW.

To the west at Dupont Circle an establishment called the Heigh Ho Club (1536 Connecticut Avenue NW) opened its doors on Tuesday, October 2, 1933. Modeled after the trendy night spots of London and billed in the local newspapers as "Washington's Smart Social Embassy," the Heigh Ho Club was owned and operated by Pete Macias, who also served as its house orchestra director until the club's closing in January 1939. The night club was unusual in that it featured an impressive marble staircase at its entrance and included several open fireplaces throughout its interior. Featured vocalists with the Pete Macias Orchestra included Marty Rubin, Charley Wright and Jimmy Nichols, with pianist Grace Shannon a regular added attraction. Dance teams such as Joseph and Ellen Corbett and Adam and Jane DiGitano also proved to be popular draws at this unique night club.

Across town in the Southeast quadrant of the city was Brinkley's (533 8th Street SE), which initially opened in 1931. After several years as a quiet local watering hole in an unassuming commercial strip near the Marine Barracks, Washington, D.C., Brinkley's owner Eugene Brinkley and manager Dick Richards made the decision to usher in live pop music. In March 1936 they hired Johnny Rice and His Aces as their house orchestra, with Jimmy Crandell frequently appearing as a featured vocalist. For the next three years several bands worked engagements at the night club including Jimmy Bright and His Orchestra, Jack Torry's Orchestra, Biff Johnson's Orchestra, Mac McCaffrey and His Orchestra, along with special attractions like saxophonist Carl Gunther and pianist Eddie Brown. Brinkley's remained in operation through September 1949. A year later after a change in ownership it was reopened as the Round Up Club, a rough-and-tumble C&W music dive that would eventually include rock and roll bands in their offerings throughout the 1950s and 1960s.

During the swing era a very important entry in the local night club scene was introduced in the Northeast quadrant of the city. There, in the brick building that had housed the old Beuchert Tavern from 1880 to 1895, a new establishment was opened to the public that would figure prominently in the local popular music scene. In November 1927 a candy store called Louis Kavakos and Sons Confectioners replaced a market called the Sanitary Grocery Company at 727 H Street NE. In the fall of 1933 the business was expanded into an eatery and renamed Louis Kavakos and Sons Restaurant; later in November 1935 the name was simplified to Louis Kavakos Restaurant. In September 1937 the establishment was converted into a live music night club and renamed Kavakos Grill, with Brownie's Nighthawks Orchestra installed as the main attraction. Renamed Club Kavakos in January 1945, this hot spot on the outer edge of the city would offer every conceivable type of music until its closing in December 1955.

The Uptown area of the city was represented by the Brown Derby (3333A Connecticut Avenue NW), whose building had been constructed in 1928 and for more than a decade housed only the Albert Footer Delicatessen. The Brown Derby moved into a vacant portion of the large structure in December 1938 and started off as a musical comedy club that was billed in local newspaper ads as the "Nuttiest Nitery in the Country" with a motto that proclaimed "Where Stars are Made and Stars are Shattered." The Brown Derby was owned by Al Simmonds, a talented singer-comedian, and his longtime vaudeville partner George Berg, an accomplished pianist. Early on they worked the club together by providing nightly entertainment via humorous skits and musical numbers. The pair had met in New Orleans a decade prior and had previously owned and operated the Club Subway in Newark, New Jersey, and the Club Swanee in Hartford, Connecticut. During its first year pop singer Marian Martin was also a regular attraction at the Brown Derby, along with a vocal act called the Three Little School Girls.

From 1940 to 1942 a series of local pop music performers worked the Brown Derby including: bands such as the Three Loose Nuts and the Variety Boys; singers Dot Garcia, Beth Calvert and Jack Curtis; pianist Margie Capp; and harmonicist Eddie Manson. Another regular was famed boogie-woogie singer-pianist and Decca recording star Erskine Butterfield, who lived in Newark, New Jersey and had previously worked for several years with the Noble Sissle Orchestra. Butterfield evidently took a liking to the night club and made stops here for several years beginning in 1942.

Things changed at the Brown Derby in 1943, with a number of nationally known pop and jazz acts topping the bills. Among those to perform in the club that year were the Hickory Nuts, the Novelites, the Art Tatum Trio, the Jones Brothers, Ella Fitzgerald and the Four Keys, T-Bone Walker and the Three Pork Chops, the Four Palmer Brothers and the Golden Gate Quartet. Other regular attractions that year included the Washington, D.C.-born-and-bred pop singer Buddy Shaner and jazz singer-pianists Harry "The Hipster" Gibson and Fats Waller.

There were many notable jazz performers at the Brown Derby during the middle 1940s. In 1944 favorites included bands such as the Three Tucker Sisters, the Pete Brown Quartet and Clinton "The Deacon" Hobbs and His Orchestra. For much of the year the house pianist was Sam Krupit and among the headlining singers were Danny Sullivan, Jack Wyatt, Mildred "Mrs. Swing" Bailey, Rita Ray, Greta Van Kirk and Margie McCloin.

The year 1945 saw a number of jazz pianists take the stage at the Brown Derby including Hal Thornton, Joe Sullivan, Corky Williams, Sammy Price, Meade Lux Lewis, Albert Ammons, Pete Johnson and Harry "The Hipster" Gibson. Also making visits that year were a series of nationally known jazz outfits such as the Loumell Morgan Trio, the Art Tatum Trio, Sidney Beschet and His New Orleans Feet Warmers, Coleman Hawkins and His Orchestra and Dizzy Gillespie and His Band.

From 1946 to 1949 the Brown Derby continued in this vein, with appearances made by such jazz bands as Slam Stewart and His Deuces, Cats and the Fiddle, the Phil Moore Four, Joe Marsala and His Seven Instrumentalists, Sidney Bechet and His Dixieland Feet Warmers, the Bill Johnson Quartet, Eddie South and His Trio, the King Cole Trio, the Toppers, Eddie Heywood and His Orchestra, John Kirby and His Orchestra, George Berg and His Trio, the Kings of Swing and the Three Chords. Featured pianists included Harrison Cass, Horace Gerlach, Kirby Walker, Larry Boyd, Earle Palmer, Erskine Butterfield and organist Carl Parker. Headlining singers included Susan Shepard and Ethel Waters.

From 1950 to 1953 the Brown Derby continued on as one of the city's finest jazz night clubs. This period saw the night club host such acts as the Three Stars, Carl Mark and His Holiday in Rhythm Quartet, the Hollywood Rangerettes, Buster Bailey and His Dixieland Combo, the Slam Stewart Trio, Wally Coombs and His Dixielanders, Sidney Bechet and His New Orleans Feet Warmers, Wild Bill Davison and His Dixie Six, Bud Freeman and His Dixieland All-Stars, the Windy Dixiecrats (featuring saxophonist Mason "Country" Thomas), the Capital City Dixielanders, Roddy Conway and His Jazzmen, Little Bobby Conway and His Dixie Sextet, the Basin Street Five (featuring saxophonist Ben Lary and drummer Al Pometto) and the Wild Bill Davis Trio. Others to take the Brown Derby stage during this time were: jazz singers Billie Holliday, Jimmy McPhail and Eddie Miller; pianists Joe Sullivan, Jan Dumond, Harvey Chown, Hal Thornton and Jack Rowland; saxophonist Coleman Hawkins; and drummer George Wettling.

Thereafter the Brown Derby began winding down and for most of 1954 the house band was the Basin Street Boys, a jazz group that was sometimes billed as the Basin Street Five. The Brown Derby closed its doors later that year and its space went on to host some popular live music night clubs in the years ahead including P.L.'s Café (1962-1964) and Sam's Place (1968-1971).

In 1939 the Fat Boy Restaurant (2201 New York Avenue NE) moved into the space formerly occupied by the Transit Mixed Concrete Company and for the next 12 years offered a variety of orchestras and pop and jazz music ensembles for their patrons. Among the popular local bands to work the restaurant during the 1940s were Johnny Graham and His Orchestra, Lyle Howard's Swingmasters, Bill Mundy and His Orchestra, De Vaughn Clement and His Orchestra (featuring singer Gene Power), Bernie Carroll and His Orchestra, the Joe Cochran Orchestra, Jack Morton's Orchestra, Henry Mack and His Orchestra, the Art Calevas Trio and Jack Maggio's Quartet. In 1952 the Fat Boy was replaced by Newland's Cafeteria.

Across town, restaurateurs Paul and David Young purchased the Wun Kow Restaurant (815-817 13th Street NW) in 1936 and replaced it with the Roumanian Inn. Four years later they decided to outfit their main lounge as Paul Young's Romany Room and usher in live entertainment for their patrons. Opening night for their new format was on Tuesday, October 15, 1940 with a star-studded bill of entertainment featuring Al Spieldock and His Orchestra (Spieldock having just completed a succession of tours drumming for Artie Shaw and Benny Goodman), singer Biddie Dunn, pianist Dee Lloyd McKay, emcee-comedian Ralph Lewis and the rhythm dance team of Alman and Roland. Because of menus like this, Paul Young's Romany Room was immediately established as one of the city's top live entertainment night spots.

During the first half of the 1940s the Romany Room offered an impressive assortment of jazz entertainers including bands such the ever-present Al Spieldock and His Orchestra, Paul Neff and His Orchestra, the King Cole Trio (led by the now-legendary crooner Nat King Cole, the band's two-week engagement at the Romany Room – their Washington, D.C. debut – began on Tuesday, April 22, 1941 and ended on Monday, May 5, 1941), Ray

Hyman's Orchestra, Charlie Frankhauser and His Orchestra, Felix Zimmer and His Orchestra and Lenny Rogers and His Orchestra.

Other featured performers at Paul Young's Roman Room during the 1940s included an array of pop and jazz singers such as Jerry Brandow, Biddie Dunn, Louise Lee, Sonny Shaw, Rae Marsh, Ben Perry, Marie Austin, Pearl Williams, Marion Powers, Paula Drake, Harriet Brent, Bob Preble, Helene Standish, the Dennis Sisters, Marjorie Capp, Elaine Jordan, Marjorie Garretson, Betty Reilly, and the duo of Owen and Parker. Featured pianists included Dee Lloyd McKay, Hilda Simmons, and Marvelle Myles. Dancers to fill the bills included Emilee Adreon, Rosalind Gordon, Diane Nelson, Barbara Blaine, Doris Ruby and tap star Steve Condos. Comedians were also a hot commodity in the night club and among those to headline were Ralph Lewis, Alan Gale, Eddie White, Al Merin, Al Schenk, Jerry and Turk, Alan Ross, Mousie Garner, Jackie Phillips, Al Stone, Bud Sweeny, Gene Baylos, Eddie Shaeffer, Allan Stone, Tiny Kaye, Cliff Conrad, Jackie Miles and Buddy Lester.

Paul Young's Romany Room gained special acclaim for hosting the Washington, D.C. debut of a red hot young crooner-and-comedian team known as Dean Martin and Jerry Lewis. Fresh off an engagement at the Latin Casino in Philadelphia, Pennsylvania, Martin and Lewis began a two-week engagement in the Romany Room that ran from Tuesday, December 3 to Monday, December 16, 1946. During their stay, they headed a bill that included Lenny Rogers and His Orchestra and dancing star Doris Ruby. Of special note is that there was no cover charge for these shows, which were scheduled for 8:15pm and 11:30pm each evening, and dinners were priced at a mere $1.50.

The duo of Martin and Lewis went over so well that Paul Young subsequently made a concerted effort to emphasize comedians in his night club throughout 1947. Some of the top comedians to work the club that year were Mischa "The Mad Russian" Auer, Emil Boreo, Joey Bishop, Sid Caesar, Alan Gale and regulars Buddy Lester and Alan Gale. After a brief closing due to an inexplicable downturn in business, the Romany Room reopened in March 1948 with a new policy that featured the rhumba music of Tito Rodriguez and His Rhumba Orchestra for the remainder of the decade.

Two streets over, a new night spot entered into competition with Paul Young's Romany Room in 1942. Herb Sach's Del Rio Restaurant in flood-plagued Bladensburg, Maryland burned to the ground in January 1941, causing the owner to search for safer ground in which to open a new night club venture. He found a spacious area in Downtown Washington at 727 15th Street NW, a building that had previously been the site of Laidlaw and Company Stocks and Bonds, but had been sitting vacant since said business closed its doors in December 1940. Sachs moved into the building and reopened a new version of the Del Rio Restaurant on the premises on Wednesday, January 28, 1942. The club's opening night bill featured the modern pop music of Dick Stabile and His Orchestra (featuring singer Gracie Barrie).

The Del Rio Restaurant only lasted until July 1945, but during its time booked an impressive array of local and big-name pop and swing orchestras. Bands to perform engagements at the night club included Henry King and His Orchestra, Enric Madriguera and His Orchestra, Nat Brandywine and His Orchestra (featuring singer June Robbins), Carl Hoff and His Orchestra (featuring singer Al Noble and the vocal duo known as the Murphy Sisters), Richard Himber and His Orchestra, Carl Ravazza and His Orchestra, Arturo Arturos and His Orchestra (featuring singer Wendy Bishop), Caney and His Rhumba Orchestra, Bernie Cummins and His Orchestra, Enric Madriguera and His Orchestra (featuring singer Connie Baxter), Frankie Masters and His Orchestra, Edith Lorand and Her All-Male Recording Orchestra, Leo Reisman and His Orchestra, Eddy Rogers and His Orchestra, Carlos Molina and His Orchestra, Del Courtney and His Orchestra (featuring singers Mary Jane Dodd and Jack Milton), Bud Waples and His Orchestra, Gray Gordon and His Tick Tock Rhythm Band (featuring singers Lana Lane and Danny Baxter), Blue Baron's Orchestra, Peter Rotunda and His Orchestra, Art Kassel and His Kassels in the Air, Dinorah and Her Latin America Orchestra, Ray Kinney and His Musical Ambassadors and Vincent Pirro and His Orchestra.

The building at 727 15th Street NW continued to play an important role in local popular culture for many years to come. In 1946 a short-lived night club called Delmonico's followed the Del Rio and featured pop music singer Gene Archer and comedian Artie Dann during its run. Later, in April 1948, the Playhouse Theatre took over the space and enjoyed tremendous local success until its closing in September 1983.

A couple blocks away, the Western Auto Supply Company went out of business in 1940 and its building sat vacant until a restaurant called Ruby Foo's Den (728 13th Street NW) opened in its place in September 1942. Owner Joel Pike introduced a live music room called Trade Winds on the restaurant's second floor, replete with striking royal blue and yellow walls and strange white palm trees bearing phony white coconuts.

The opening night show at Trade Winds took place on Wednesday, December 29, 1943 and featured Jerry Rodis and His Orchestra, pop singer Sonny King, singing satirist Reni Revel, a singer-guitarist known only as Spivy, organist Sid Willoughby and a magician known as the Great Maurice. Rodis remained the house band leader until the night club closed in December 1947, but many other excellent musicians graced the Trade Winds stage during its time. Among those to perform there in the 1940s were Jack White's Orchestra, Jack Lane and His Love Birds, the Terry Sisters, singer-guitarist Christine Johnson, blues singer Lillias MacLellan and pop singers Margaret Phelan, Francine White and Lee Rogers. Other favorites to work the room included novelty musician Jackie Jay, comedians Norman Duke and Bob Shepard and dancers Beverly Bogart and Virginia McGraw.

Another major venue of the city was the Arcadia Ballroom (3134-3138 14th Street NW), which was created within the popular Arcadia Market complex that had been opened in 1910 and closed to the public in 1948. The ballroom was always a well-known venue for live swing music and for most of the 1940s the house band was Jack Corry and His Orchestra. On the rare occasion when Corry and his ensemble took a night off, the band box was filled by such groups as Buddy Garrison and His Orchestra and DeVaughn Clements and His Rhythm Five.

Throughout the Prohibition era, a building in the city marked 1016 14th Street NW seemed to host different restaurants every few years. Later on, from 1944 to 1949, this space was occupied by an establishment called the China Clipper, with owner Sam Wong bringing in an impressive array of local orchestras, pop music bands, singers and dancers. During its first three years regular entertainers in the restaurant included Joe Ford and His Orchestra, Sid Willoughby and His Band, Curly Fox and His Orchestra and Joe Masters and His Orchestra. Among the singers to headline during this time were Joan Campbell, Eleanor Kade, Sally Rowe, Ruth Chin and Lee Paige. During the club's final three years the top attractions were Clinton Hobbs and His Orchestra, Jimmy Santmyer and His Orchestra, Al Shea's Trio (which consisted of Shea on guitar, organist Carl Parker and accordionist-cellist-pianist Stan Jones), and the Three Jays, an outfit that mixed together blues, jazz and pop in a lively style which at the time defied categorization.

Alexandria, Virginia was largely treated as an outpost of the Washington, D.C. area music scene, but offered several popular night clubs through the years that attracted bands from around the region. In the swing era the most celebrated establishment from this region was Club Nightingale (originally listed at 2808 Richmond Highway, Alexandria, Virginia; in 1965 this building would have its street address changed to 7407 Richmond Highway), which opened its doors on Wednesday, June 16, 1937 with the Ralph Garren Orchestra leading the way. Club Nightingale, a family operation in every sense, was owned by Ellsworth "Elliot" Nightingale, and consisted of a large log cabin-type structure with a dance floor area measuring 1,100 square feet. From 1937 to 1939 swing ensembles to work the club were Ralph Garren's Orchestra, Jack Hawley's Orchestra, Watson Powell and His Moods in Blue Orchestra and Bill Downer's Orchestra.

Club Nightingale maintained its momentum throughout the 1940s with a series of local and nationally known musical artists including Bill Downer's Orchestra, Rodd Raffell and His Orchestra (featuring singer Tommy Lawrence), Jack Maggio and His Orchestra (featuring singer Reathis Stevens), Tommy May's Orchestra, Jack "Jive" Schafer and His Orchestra (featuring singers Kitty McCormack and Louise Lee), Brownie and His Night Hawks, Kenneth Gorham and His Orchestra, Bob Siedell and His Orchestra (featuring singer Kay Linton), Boyd Raeburn and His Orchestra, Eddy Howard and His Orchestra, Clinton Hobbs and His Orchestra, Frankie Condon's Orchestra (featuring singer Leah Matthews), the Decker Brothers Orchestra (featuring singer Don Andrews), Gene Krupa and His Orchestra, Berk Motley and His Orchestra, Ira Sabin and His Orchestra, Buzzy Ellis and His Orchestra, Larry Panza and His Orchestra, the Merry Makers, Rip Rice and His Music Makers, and singers Oliver Nelson and Sonny Boy Vallie.

Throughout the 1950s Club Nightingale carried on with the Music Makers serving as house band for the first half of the decade and Dale Turner and His Orchestra playing on a nightly basis for the last half of the decade. Special appearances were also made during these years by the Dynamics, the Woody Free Combo and the Art Lochner Swinget. From 1960 until its closing in 1965 the house band duties were held by Buddy Gale and His Orchestra, with special appearances made by the likes of the Tommy Dorsey Orchestra and Berk Motley and His Orchestra.

Richmond Highway's other main attraction, the Club Log Tavern, opened up just a couple of doors down from the Club Nightingale (originally listed at 2814 Richmond Highway, Alexandria, Virginia; in 1965 this building would have its street address changed to 7415 Richmond Highway) in October 1939 for owner Jack Breedan. As its name implied, it was a large log cabin structure, rectangular in design, and boasted an interior replete with a stage and accompanying dance floor and big open fireplaces around its dining area, with a backside veranda equipped for outdoor dancing. Seeking to compete with the Club Nightingale, the Club Log Tavern initially mirrored the musical style offered by its neighbor and from October to December 1939 brought in several high-profile big bands as entertainment including Jimmy Gandley and the Jitterbugs' Delight, Dick Davis and His Orchestra, Jimmy Gray's Orchestra (featuring pianist-singer Dardanelle Breckenridge) and Bill Summer's Orchestra.

During the 1940s Club Log Tavern was a hot spot for big band music and featured a number of the region's top musical performers including singer-pianist Dardanelle Breckenridge, Gerry Black's New York Orchestra, Charley Parrish and His Orchestra, Paul Perkins and His Bayou Band, Don Collins and His Orchestra, Lester Diggs and His Orchestra, and Frankie Mann's Orchestra. This night club would change owners several times during its lifetime and during the 1950s would offer a variety of different musical styles including C&W, R&B and rock and roll. A fire brought Club Log Tavern to a close in 1965, but it was reconstructed and reopened later that year as the 1320 Club and went on to become one of Northern Virginia's top rock and roll night clubs.

Many other Washington, D.C. night clubs showcased local pop and jazz ensembles and orchestras during the swing era. Their ranks included the Old New Orleans Restaurant (1214 18th Street NW), which featured such entertainers as Jack Allyn's Continental Music, Bob Simpson and His Orchestra, Les Williams and His Southern Rhythm Band, violinist

Sasha Lucas, and such singers as Marian Carl, Jody Miller, Gay Lou, Dwight Fiske, Johnny Bradford and Tony Romano; Club Habana (1118 Connecticut Avenue NW), whose long-standing house band was Moe Baer and His Club Habana Orchestra; Ramon's (1341 Connecticut Avenue NW), which offered Rudy Schramm and His Orchestra; the Venus (509 14th Street NW), which weighed in with Hugh Alexander and the Venus Orchestra; the Crescent Café Rathskeller (723 14th Street NW), whose featured entertainer was songstress Libby Frazier who was backed for long stretches by either George Gaul's Band or Ralph Garren's Orchestra; the Cocoanut Grove (505 K Street NW), which liked to bring in pop music singers such as Bennett Green, Carl Addison and the Bradley Sisters; the Gingham Club Restaurant (1423 Pennsylvania Avenue NW), whose top attractions were Jimmy Santmyer's Orchestra and Phil Lynch and His Dance Orchestra; and the Rendezvous (809 H Street NE), which featured Jerry Rodis and His Orchestra (featuring singer Joe Bell).

Joining the area's roster of rousing live music venues was a beautiful ballroom just beyond the city's limits in a spacious park in Montgomery County, Maryland. Glen Echo Park (7300 MacArthur Boulevard, Glen Echo, Maryland) opened up as an institution of learning overlooking the Potomac River on Tuesday, June 16, 1891 under the name the National Chautauqua at Glen Echo. It offered six separate instructional schools, which initially went under the headings of the Art School, School of Business, Delsarte, Physical Training, Kindergarten and Institute of Sacred Literature. In May 1898 the name of the entire compound was changed to Glen Echo Park and live music, mainly in the form of orchestras and brass bands, was presented on a special stage in what they called the Amphitheatre. The following summer a merry-go-round and other rides were installed and its metamorphosis into a full-blown amusement park had begun. Music was an integral part of the park's success for several decades and on Saturday, May 6, 1933 they opened a lavish, $50,000 facility called the Spanish Gardens Ballroom which had a capacity of 1,800 occupants and was specifically designed to host live summer concerts.

The pop and swing music orchestras that performed on summer evenings in Glen Echo Park's Spanish Gardens Ballroom during the 1930s were quite impressive. From 1933 to 1937 the Dave MacWilliams Orchestra (directed by Phil O'Brien) held court. From May to September 1938 several big bands worked weeks at a time including Henry Halstead and His Orchestra, Larry Funk and His Band (featuring singers Helen O'Connell and Buddy Hayes), the Howard Becker Orchestra, Ralph Webster and His NBC Orchestra, Ray Herbeck and His Orchestra, Little Joe Hart and His Orchestra Dave MacWilliams and His Orchestra (featuring singer-trumpeter Jack Schafer, who, in the ensuing years, would front his own band and become one of Washington's biggest attractions).

The 1939 summer season saw appearances at the Spanish Gardens Ballroom by the likes of Herbie Holmes and His Orchestra (featuring singer Nancy Hutson), Cecil Golly and His Orchestra (featuring singer Nancy Gay), a special week-long engagement beginning Monday, May 29, 1939 by Lawrence Welk and His Orchestra (featuring singer Mildred Stanley), Wally Stoefler and His Orchestra (featuring singer Thelma Mitchell), Lang Thompson and His Swing Specialists, Little Joe Hart and His Orchestra, Carl Lorch and His Orchestra (featuring singer Shirley Dean), Tiny Hill and His Dance Orchestra (featuring singer Allan DeWitt and someone named Ozzie Osborne on vibraharp), and Jimmy Livingston and His Orchestra (featuring singers Nolan Canova and Jack Crawley).

From 1940 to 1943 Glen Echo Park's Spanish Ballroom featured Paul Kain and His Orchestra as the house band. When the park opened for the 1944 summer season the name of this facility was officially changed from Spanish Gardens Ballroom to Spanish Ballroom. Kain's band then remained the venue's top attraction through the summer of 1948. for the 1949 season a number of different bands were brought in for shorter engagements including George Towne and His Orchestra of Twelve, Gene Williams and His Orchestra, Lee Castle and His Orchestra, Skitch Henderson and His Orchestra, Victor Lombardo and His Orchestra, Glen Gray and the Casa Loma Orchestra (featuring singer Julie O'Brien), and Sammy Ferro and His Orchestra.

The Spanish Ballroom expanded its offerings during the 1950s with the standard swing orchestras being joined by a litany of C&W, pop, and rock and roll acts. In terms of popular orchestras, among those groups to perform during the decade were Sammy Ferro and His Orchestra, the Vaughn Monroe Orchestra, Tommy Dorsey and His Orchestra, the Dorsey Brothers (Tommy and Jimmy; featuring singer Lynn Roberts), Johnny Long and His Orchestra (featuring singer Barbara Hammond), Freddie Shaffer and His All-Girl Orchestra, Ralph Flanagan's Orchestra, Charlie Spivak and His Orchestra, Tom Darlington and His Orchestra, Ray Anthony and His Orchestra, Roy Stevens and His Orchestra, Woody Herman and the Third Herd and Art Mooney and His Honey Babe Orchestra.

During these years C&W music also made a splash at Glen Echo as Connie B. Bay booked his Thursday night "Town and Country Square Dancing" parties in the Spanish Ballroom from June to September 1951. Live music was supplied by a band called the Radio Ranchmen, who at the time were featuring singer-guitarist Billy Grammer and square dance caller Ralph Case.

In the ensuing years Gay frequently booked the Spanish Ballroom for his live music events. During one fruitful stretch from May to August 1955 he lined up a series of Friday night concerts with Jimmy Dean and the Texas Wildcats (featuring lead guitarist Roy Clark) as his opening act house band. Among the top C&W performers to appear at these events were Carl Smith and the Tunesmiths, Little Jimmy Dickens and His Country Boys, Hank Thompson and His Brazos Valley Boys, Hank Snow and His Rainbow Ranch Boys, Ernest Tubb and His Texas Troubadours, Clyde Moody and His Carolina Woodchoppers, Webb Pierce and His Wondering Boys, the Maddox Brothers and Rose (an act comprised of five members of the Maddox family – Rose, Fred, Carl, Henry and Don), female pianist Del Wood, singer-banjoist Grandpa Jones, singer-guitarist-pianist Marty Robbins and comedian Peach Seed Jones.

A number of special musical attractions were also offered in the Spanish Ballroom during the 1950s, including a rock and roll concert by Bill Haley and His Comets on Monday, September 5, 1955. Performing there on several occasions in 1958 and 1959 was Vernon Taylor and the Southerners, and late in the decade a number of Don Dillard Record Hop extravaganzas were booked with local rock and roll favorites Terry and the Pirates leading the way. One of these special Dillard-booked shows took place on Monday, July 24, 1959 and was headlined by pop singer Connie Francis.

In the 1960s different types of live music events were offered in the Spanish Ballroom on a sporadic basis. Early in the decade different concerts were staged featuring C&W singer-guitarist Hank Locklin, the bluegrass band led by Flatt and Scruggs (guitarist-mandolinist Lester Flatt and banjoist Earl Scruggs) and a local rock and roll group called the Newports, who were booked there throughout the 1962 summer season. In 1963 and 1964 several appearances were made by the legendary rock and roll band Link Wray and His Ray Men. On Saturday, May 15, 1965 a C&W show offered singer-guitarist Hank Williams, Jr. and the Compton Brothers, and a week later on May 22 the famed rock and roll singer-piano player Jerry Lee Lewis was featured in-concert. In one of the Spanish Ballroom's last concert events, R&B singer Little Richard headlined a show on Wednesday, July 20, 1966 that was presented by radio station WUST and emceed by disc jockey-promoter Barry Richards.

Glen Echo Park closed after the 1968 season concluded and with it went the live music concerts of the Spanish Ballroom. The park was purchased by the federal government in

1971 and was maintained in the ensuing years by the National Park Service. In 2003 renovation began on the facilities of Glen Echo Park and it was reopened to the public. Today, an organization called the Glen Echo Park Partnership for Arts & Culture, Inc. oversees Glen Echo Park's arts and cultural programs and maintains the property's historic facilities. Glen Echo Park currently operates as a visual and performing arts site that hosts resident arts and cultural organizations, artist studios, a social dance program, a restored carousel and classes in visual and performing arts. The Spanish Ballroom, which today has an adjusted capacity of 870 occupants, largely operates as a swing ballroom, but still frequently stages concerts, special events and social dances.

CHAPTER TWENTY-ONE
HOTEL LOUNGES AND ROOMS OF THE SWING ERA

Contributing to the local popular music scene during the swing era were a number of upscale hotels within Washington, D.C. which opened night clubs on their premises, creating a competitive atmosphere where managers waged recruiting battles against each other for the best available local orchestras and out-of-town entertainers. The majority of these hotels were centrally located in the Downtown area of the city within blocks of each other and just a short distance from an array of neighboring night clubs and restaurants.

During this era the attitude towards live music was different in the hotels than it was in the standard night clubs of Washington, D.C. for a number of reasons. The hotels were primarily concerned with providing lodging for guests and secondarily concerned with presenting music for their overnight customers, while the sole focus of the standard night clubs was to provide live entertainment for their regular patrons. Many of the hotels of this era, in an effort to project a higher-class image and keep their tourists and travelers on the premises, designated their bar areas as lounges or rooms, enforced dress codes for their customers and made concerted efforts to book swing ensembles, big band orchestras and the occasional national act. The standard night clubs had a tendency to book a much wider range of bands and individual performers and were more willing to experiment with different musical forms and styles.

Leading the way through the swing era was the Ambassador Hotel (1412 K Street NW), which opened on Monday, September 30, 1929, closed in August 1978, and was torn down in 1980. The Hi-Hat Cocktail Lounge opened within this hotel in March 1934 and closed in August 1978. Throughout much of the swing era the house band was Jack Neal and the Banner Boys. Other pop and jazz entertainers to appear at the night club during these years were the Four Ms, Jerry Salisbury and His Three Ambassadors, Ray Harts and His Diplomats, Opalita and Her Trio, the Paul Kain Quartet, pianist Paul Homer, and a number of different singers including Camilla Lazari, Angie Rodante and Peggy Leonard.

The Hotel Annapolis (1111 H Street NW) opened in March 1925, changed its name to the Manger-Annapolis Hotel in December 1954 and closed in April 1980 when it was sold to Maharishi International University College of Natural Law, which opened up a campus in the building in January 1982 and closed in 1987. The building was torn down in 1988. The Anchor Room opened within this hotel on Wednesday, September 15, 1937 with a performance by Johnny Slaughter's Orchestra (featuring singer Evelyn Knight). The Anchor Room closed in July 1955, at which time it was renovated and renamed the Surf Room. Pianist Matt Windsor and singer Eileen George were the nightly regulars from 1940 to 1943. Other pop music entertainers to work the club during this decade were singer-pianist Don Makin, the duo of singer Georgia Butler and pianist Jerry King, the team of singer-harpist Peggy Norton and singer-guitarist Cassi Cassano, the Latin Linos (a duo consisting of singer-musicians Betty and Dubby Lino), and singers such as Virginia Pollard and the duo Ivory and Blue.

The Cairo (1615 Q Street NW) was a hotel that opened as the Cairo Flats in November 1894, changed its name to the Cairo in April 1895, and remained a hostelry until 1978. At that time the hotel was converted to a condominium building and remains in business as the Cairo to the present day. Club Cairo operated as a night club in the hotel's ballroom from 1946 to 1949. Although short-lived, this night club emerged as one of the grandest in the city and hosted some great entertainment during its day.

Among those to perform in Club Cairo were bands such as Evelyn Tyner and Her Trio, Bob Simpson and His Orchestra, Ted Lewis and His World-Famous Orchestra (featuring singer Geraldine Dubois), the Bell-Aires, the Modernaires, Paul Kain's Orchestra, the Jerry Rodis Orchestra, the Art Calevas Trio, Nilda Ramos and Her Cuban Boys, Sparty Donato and His Orchestra, the Ted Alexander Trio, the Barton Brothers Band and Mousie Garner and His Trio. Featured pop and jazz singers at the club were Carl Ravazza, Phil Brito, Dale Belmont, June Edwards, Judy Lynn, Sarah Ann McCabe, Marilyn Ross, Sonny Skylar, Eileen Ayres, Terry Allen, Frances White, Sylvia Froos, Belle Baker, Jerri Blanchard, Betty Reilly, Kay Vernon, and singer-comedians Bill McGraw and Al Schenk. Special attractions in the night club included singer-accordionist Joyce Aimee and singer-pianist Valerie Lee.

In addition, Club Cairo brought in many comedians to round out their bills. Among those to perform here were Sheila Barrett, Ollie Franks, Ben Blue, Dick Buckley, Martha Raye, Phil Foster, Henny Youngman, Artie Dann, Arthur Blake, Larry Kent, Professor Irwin Corey, the Crosby Sisters, Jay Jason, Elroy Peace, the Duncan Sisters, Allan Drake and Bob Shepard. Dancers to grace their bills included Eileen Franks, Pat Rooney, Eleanor Powell, the Andrew Twins, Paul White, the Mayo Brothers, Phyllis Claire, Beatrice Kay, Bobby Brandt and the Wally Wanger Girls. Late in the decade Club Cairo was replaced by the Royal Palm Room, whose opening night of Thursday, September 29, 1949 was headlined by the Ralph Hawkins Orchestra (featuring singer Patricia Lane).

What was once Club Cairo remained in periodic operation during the 1950s as either the Cairo Room or the Cairo Ballroom. During this time a variety of musical entertainers were brought in to entertain the crowds. Among those to appear included: jazz bands such as Don Bestor and His Orchestra, the Three Jones Brothers, Sammy Ferro and His WTTG Television Orchestra, Johnny Wolford's Orchestra, Matt Windsor and His Orchestra, Fran Grady's Cairo Caravans, Buddy Rowell and His Cubanairs, Frank Grady and His Orchestra, Earl Swope and His Quintet, the Sauter-Finnegan Orchestra, the Billy Johnson Orchestra (featuring singer Ann Read), the Orchestra (featuring pianist Bill Potts), Washie Bratcher's Orchestra and Wee Hour Jazz (featuring saxophonist Ted Efantis). Other jazz performers to headline included singer Thelma Carpenter, singer-pianist Shirley Horn, saxophonist Buck Hill and drummer Stump Saunders. Also making appearances were pop singer Marion Klatta, comedian Louise Potter, and the C&W outfit known as Smitty Smith and the Town and Country Timers, whose lineup consisted of featuring square dance caller Ralph Case, singer-guitarist Smitty Smith, guitarist Kenny Smith, singer-accordionist Stoney Rigsby, fiddler Curley Smith and drummer Jimmy Burkett.

Several blocks south of the Cairo sat the Hotel Claridge (820 Connecticut Avenue NW). This building was constructed in 1921 and housed several businesses during its first few years before hosting the Women' National Democratic Club from 1924 to 1927. It was then converted into a hostelry and housed the Army-Navy Hotel from September 1928 until May 1934, with its lounge area called the Army-Navy Coffee Shop. On Sunday, May 13, 1934 the name of the establishment was changed to the Hotel Claridge and it remained in operation under that banner until its closing on Saturday, May 31, 1975.

The King Cole Room opened within the Hotel Claridge in March 1937 in the old coffee shop space and closed on Thursday, May 1, 1958. Pop and jazz oriented piano players and torch singers were the specialties of this night club and during the late 1930s and 1940s regular entertainers included pianists Bob Brewer and Nap Lipton, and singers Evelyn Knight, Linda Carroll, Peggy Wood, Bob Pace, Arthur Todd, Elaine Moore, Dona Mason, Mildred Kirke and Jody Miller. During the 1950s featured entertainers included such pop singers as Betty Madigan, Pat Lockwood, Kyra Marie and Eileen Todd.

The Hamilton Hotel (1001 14th Street NW) opened in December 1922 and closed in 1972 with its replacement being the Salvation Army. In 1994 the building was sold, renovated and reopened as the Hamilton Crowne Plaza, and is still in operation under that name today. The Rainbow Room opened within this hotel on Wednesday, July 31, 1935 and closed in November 1952. During the swing era this night club featured big bands and among those groups to work engagements in the room were the Meyer Davis Orchestra, Milton Davis and His Orchestra, Roy Kyser and His Orchestra and Jimmy Nichols and His Orchestra. The room was then quickly given a make-over and reopened on Wednesday, November 19, 1952 as the Purple Tree Lounge with pianist Mariana Sarrica headlining.

A hotel named the Lee House (1100 15th Street NW) was opened to the public on Friday, April 21, 1922. In April 1940 the name of the hotel was changed to the Lee Sheraton Hotel; in June 1950 the name was changed to the Lee House Hotel; and in September 1958 the name was changed to the Pick-Lee House Hotel. The hotel closed in November 1979 and the building was torn down in February 1980.

The Dubonnet Room operated within the Lee Sheraton Hotel at this address from Friday, July 17, 1942 to February 1948, with its name being changed to the Sheraton Lounge in February 1948. Among the swingin' bands to be featured in this night club were the Adrian Rollini Trio, Davy Crocker and His Trio (featuring singer Earline King), Eddie Fogel and His Orchestra, Alden Ray and His Orchestra, Russ Cullen and His Orchestra and George Berg and His Orchestra (featuring singer Lew Davie). Keyboardist Rodney Davis was the headliner in the Sheraton Lounge throughout 1948 and 1949.

The Hotel Mayflower (1127 Connecticut Avenue NW) opened in 1925 and is still in operation today as the Renaissance Mayflower Hotel. The Mayflower Lounge opened within this hotel on Monday, April 2, 1934 and closed in March 1957. From 1940 to 1947 Dick Koon's Orchestra held down house band duties in the lounge, with a number of pop singers making appearances including Ha Cha Gardner, Joan Whitney, Linda Carroll, Bonnie Boyd, Hildegarde, Cynthia Cavanaugh, Bernice Byres, Elayne Hume and Gini Bogart. In 1948 and 1949 two different bands, Dick Barlow and His Orchestra and Pierson Thal and His Orchestra, were often booked in conjunction with singers such as Dick Smart, Nancy Donovan and Eric Thorson.

The Raleigh Hotel (401 12th Street NW) opened on Thursday, November 1, 1894, went through extensive alterations in 1911, closed in September 1963, and was torn down in July 1964. The Pall Mall Room opened within this hotel on Tuesday, November 24, 1936 and closed in September 1963. Featured bands during the swing era in this night club included Bert Bernath and His Orchestra, Russ Cullen and His Orchestra, Oscar Davis and His Dance Orchestra and Bob Callahan and His Orchestra. Other headliners included singers Patricia Prochnik, Nan Garcia and Mitzi Greene, and pianists Eddie Chase and Les Colvin.

The Hotel Powhatan (1763 Pennsylvania Avenue NW) was opened to the public on Saturday, October 12, 1912. In March 1937 new owners changed its name to the Roger Smith Hotel and it remained in operation until Thursday, May 1, 1975. The Café Caprice opened within this hotel on Thursday, October 27, 1938 and closed in September 1958. Featured musical performers in the café during the 1940s included Tiny Meeker's Orchestra, Eddie Whitesel's Rhythmaires, Eddy Mayehoff and His Orchestra, the Don Carper Four, Miles Hallett and His Music, Eddie Brown and His Music, and pianists Frank Irving and Paul Berlin.

The Hadleigh Apartment Hotel (2101 16th Street NW) opened on Wednesday, September 15, 1920 and became the Roosevelt Hotel in January 1923. The Roosevelt Hotel was converted into apartments for elderly residents in April 1963; in 1987 it was purchased by the Washington, D.C. government and renamed the Roosevelt Hotel for Senior Citizens. In 2002 it was sold and its new owners renamed it the Camden Roosevelt.

The Victory Room opened within the Roosevelt Hotel in January 1942 and closed in February 1953.

The Victory Room was noted for its lighting scheme of Capri blue and deep rose and its opening night program on Monday, January 26, 1942 featured an all-star lineup of Glenn Miller and His Orchestra, singers Marion Hutton and Ray Eberle, singer-saxophonist Tex Beneke and a vocal group known as the Modernaires. Miller and his cohorts drew a packed house of over 800 followers, but were only booked for the one performance. The very next night the room's headliner was Tony Pastor and His Orchestra.

Roosevelt Hotel owner Maria Kramer did all the booking for the Victory Room, and in the year 1942 alone some of the top flight swing entertainers to make appearances in the night club were Mitchell Ayres and His Fashions in Music, Lou Breese and His Orchestra, Benny Goodman and His Orchestra, Will Bradley and His Orchestra, Les Brown and His Orchestra, Ray Kinney's Hawaiians (featuring singer Meymo Holt and the Aloha Maids), Sonny Dunham and His Orchestra, Louis Prima and His Orchestra, Chuck Foster and His Orchestra (featuring singers Dottie Dotson and Ray Robbins), Blue Baron and His Orchestra, Harry James and His Orchestra, Georgie Auld and His Orchestra, Tommy Dorsey and His Orchestra, Duke Ellington and His Orchestra, Count Basie and His Orchestra, Shep Fields and His Orchestra, George Salb and His Orchestra, Will Bradley and His Orchestra, Ina Ray Hutton and Her Orchestra, Alvino Ray and His Orchestra, Jimmy Dorsey and His Orchestra, Charlie Spivak and His Orchestra, Abe Lyman and His Orchestra, Bob Chester and His Orchestra, Charlie Barnet and His Orchestra, Larry Clinton and His Orchestra, Vaughn Moore and His Orchestra, Jack Teagarden and His Orchestra, Russ Morgan and His Orchestra, Claude Thornhill and His Orchestra, Bobby Byrne and His Orchestra, Sam Donahue and His Orchestra and Mel Hallett and His Orchestra.

The remainder of the 1940s saw a procession of big band talent pass through the Victory Room. Among these performers were Denny Becker and His Merry Madcaps, Justin Stone and His Band, Tommy Reynolds and His Orchestra, Denny Beckner and His Madcap Merrymakers, Bobby Sherwood and His Orchestra, Dean Hudson and His Orchestra, Milt Davis and His Orchestra, Rodd Raffell and His Orchestra, Lawrence Welk and His Champagne Orchestra, George Barr's Orchestra, Tony Pastor and His Orchestra (featuring singers Ruth McCullough and Dick Dyer), Johnny Richards and His Orchestra (featuring singer Dotty Reed), Eddy Stone and His Orchestra, Ann Dupont and Her Orchestra (featuring pianist George Marshall), Bud Waples and His Twelve Men of Melody (featuring singer Miss Charee Moyse), the Don Roth Trio, Eddy Rogers and His Orchestra, Bob Lee and His Orchestra Lee Castle and His Orchestra, George O'Dell and His Organaires, Bill McCune and His Orchestra (featuring singer Bette Buckner), Sammy Marks and His Orchestra and Toby Tyler and His Orchestra.

In one of the final shows of the decade, the Victory Room scored a major coup when they booked a special, one-night-only "Grand Ole Opry" presentation on the evening of Friday, December 16, 1949 that featured C&W music singer-guitarists Hank Williams and Cowboy Copas, Shorty Long and His Santa Fe Rangers, singer Dolly Dimples (wife of Shorty Long, this vocalist's real name was Gladys Vagnoni) and Ralph Case and His Eight Tennessee Square Dancers.

The Shoreham Hotel (2500 Calvert Street NW) opened on Thursday, October 30, 1930 and is still in operation today as the Omni Shoreham Hotel. The Blue Room opened within this hotel on Friday, October 1, 1937 and closed in 1975. The Barnee-Lowe Orchestra held down house band duties in the Shoreham from its 1930 opening until 1956 and was stationed in the Blue Room throughout the 1940s. They backed an impressive array of pop and jazz singers during the swing era including Gene Archer, Alberta Mansfield, Earl

Lawrence, Cyril Rodney, Barrington Sharma, Barbara Lee, Jack Murray, Betty Bryant, Gene McCarthy and Tommy Farrell.

The Statler Hotel (1001 16th Street NW) opened in September 1942 and had its name changed to the Statler Hilton in 1958. It became the Capital Hilton in 1977 and is still in operation today under that name. The Embassy Room opened within this hotel on Tuesday, December 1, 1942 and closed in December 1945.

Among the musical entertainers to display their wares in the Embassy Room during the 1940s were Xavier Cugat and His Orchestra, Carmen Cavallaro and His Orchestra, Ramon Ramos and His Orchestra, Bob Knight and His Orchestra, Nat Brandywine and His Orchestra, Ted Straeter and His Orchestra, Cal Gifford and His Orchestra, Ray Benson and His Orchestra, Guy Lombardo and His Royal Canadians, Emil Coleman and His Orchestra and George Duffy and His Orchestra. Other attractions in the club were such pop singers as Morton Downey, Monica Lewis, Carl Brisson, Hildegarde and Dorothy Shay; and pianists Evelyn Tyner and Jan August.

The Meridian Mansions Apartments Hotel (2400 16th Street NW) opened in 1917, had its name changed to Hotel 2400 in November 1938 and closed in December 1963. New owners reopened the building as an apartment complex under the name of Envoy Towers Apartments in September 1964. After another change in ownership in 1976 the name was shortened to the Envoy and it is still in operation under that moniker today.

The Lounge Riviera opened within Hotel 2400 on Friday, November 18, 1938 and closed in January 1959. From 1940 to 1947 the main house band of the lounge was Pete Macias and His Orchestra. During those years they backed a number of talented pop singers including June Bartlett, Harriet Berck, Adele Van, Jack Norton and Mary LaMarr. Other special attractions during those years included Roy Comfort and His Guardsmen and organist Ida Clarke. From 1948 to 1950 guitarist Bob Knight and His Orchestra were the featured attraction. In the 1950s regular entertainers included Jack "Jive" Schafer and His Orchestra (featuring singer June Elliot), Bob Simpson and His Orchestra and Beach Johnson and His Orchestra with either Betty Madigan or Nona Wallace as the featured vocalist.

The Wardman Park Hotel (2660 Woodley Road NW) opened on Saturday, November 23, 1918, became the Sheraton Park Hotel in 1953 and was torn down in 1977. A new Sheraton Park Hotel was constructed on its site and in 1998 it became the Marriott Wardman Park Hotel. It remains open under that name to the present day. The Metronome Room opened within this hotel on Friday, December 25, 1936, closed in June 1950, and was soon replaced by a new night club called Caribar.

During the swing era one top orchestral outfit after another appeared in the Metronome Room including Eddy Brandt and His Orchestra (featuring the Rhythm Boys and singer Phyllis Usher), Little Jack Little and His Orchestra (featuring singer Kathleen Quinn), Grant Thompson and His Orchestra (featuring singer Madge Marley), the Reggie Childs Orchestra, Sonny James and His Orchestra, Tommy Marvin and His Orchestra (featuring singer Marion Stanfield), Jack Coffey's Rockin' Rhythm Orchestra (featuring singers Beverly Blayne, Dick Kaps and Tipsy Walters), Layton Bailey's Orchestra (featuring singers Jean Janis, Don Wilson and Kay Griffith), Alan Holmes and His Orchestra (featuring singer Kay Hunt), Ray Heatherton's Band (featuring singer Judy Clark), Leonardo and His Orchestra (featuring singer Nina Orla), Sandy Sandifer and His Orchestra (featuring singer L'il Betsy Jones), Bill Grassick and His Orchestra (featuring singer Betty McHugh), Eddie Camden and His Orchestra (featuring singer Sally Powell), Lee Barrett and Her Orchestra, Benny Ribble and His Orchestra (featuring singer Joan Carroll), George Sterney and His Orchestra, Al Navarro and His Orchestra, Paul Kain and His Orchestra, Ken Harris and His Orchestra and Bob Ellis and His Orchestra.

The Willard Hotel (1401 Pennsylvania Avenue NW) opened on Tuesday, October 15, 1901, had its name changed to the Willard Intercontinental Hotel in 1986 and since 1996 has been in operation as the Willard Intercontinental Washington. The Willard has always featured some sort of musical entertainment, with the Palm Room hosting events from its opening until the early 1930s and the Bamboo Room serving as its main night club from March 1934 until January 1940. The action subsequently switched to the Willard Room, which opened on Tuesday, April 14, 1942, and, for the next several years, featured such pop music entertainers as the Meyer Davis Orchestra, Blue Baron and His Orchestra, Xavier Cugat and His Orchestra, the Melodaire Four and pianist Tommy Johnson. The Willard Room closed as a public restaurant in April 2009, though its space can currently be rented out for special events.

To illustrate the intensity of the popular music that was being performed in these hotel night clubs, there appeared a curious entry in the "News of Capital Night Clubs" column by Mary Harris in the Friday, March 3, 1939 edition of the Washington Post that struggled to identify the style of music that a particular band was aptly performing. Her commentary left the reader wondering if the musical performance she described was bordering on what would later become rock and roll. The column read in part: "Sweet Jam: Around midnight, Paul Kain's Metronome Room Orchestra is likely to play a whirligig of sparkly tunes that you won't be able to recognize, for the life of you. If you ask what they're playing, you'll be told, 'Sorry, but there's no name for it.' The answer is that the boys are doing a flock of melodies that they have evolved cooperatively and casually. Paul leads the themes with his saxophone. It's really a 'jam session,' sweetened aplenty."

CHAPTER TWENTY-TWO
THE FIRST FEMALE POP STARS OF THE NATION'S CAPITAL

When the big band swing era kicked into gear in the 1930s, a number of bands featured female vocalists to handle the songs and please the crowds. Female singers came and went, but two in particular, Helen Forrest and Evelyn Knight, not only became top attractions in the night clubs of the Washington, D.C. area, but went on to achieve tremendous national fame. Both of these pop stars worked with some of the biggest orchestras in the entertainment industry and sang on records that went to the top of the Billboard charts. Forrest and Knight remain two of the brightest stars to ever have graced the music scene of the nation's capital.

Helen Forrest was one of the most popular female pop singers of the big band era and during her time served as vocalist for swing orchestras led by Artie Shaw, Benny Goodman and Harry James. She was born Helen Fogel in Atlantic City, New Jersey on Thursday, April 12, 1917 and dropped out of high school in the 1930s to pursue a singing career. She moved to New York City where she performed with various bands and became a featured radio singer for stations such as WNEW, where, in 1934 she adopted the stage name of Helen Forrest. During this time she also sang on broadcasts for station WCBS, where she performed as Bonnie Blue.

In 1936 Forrest relocated to Washington, D.C. and in December of that year became the featured vocalist for Johnny Shaw and His Orchestra at Restaurant Madrillon, an engagement that lasted until November 1938. At that time she was recruited out of the Madrillon by bandleader Artie Shaw, who was looking for a vocalist to replace Billie Holliday. Forest toured with Shaw's orchestra for two years and recorded more than 40 songs with his band, one of which, "Thanks for Everything" (Artie Shaw and His Orchestra, Vocal Refrain by Helen Forrest; Bluebird Records, 1939), went to number one on the "Songs With Most Radio Plugs" chart in the Saturday, January 7, 1939 edition of the Billboard. She remained with Shaw until November 1939.

A month after leaving Artie Shaw, Forrest joined Benny Goodman's Orchestra and ultimately made more than 50 recordings with his band over a two-year period. Forrest left Goodman's band in August 1941 and briefly worked with Nat King Cole and Lionel Hampton. She would continue to record with Goodman well after her main tenure with the band was over and one of these recordings, "Taking a Chance on Love" (Benny Goodman and His Orchestra, Vocal Chorus by Helen Forrest; Columbia Records, 1943) reached number one on the Billboard magazine's "National and Regional Best Selling Retail Records" pop chart on Saturday, June 12, 1943.

In late 1941 Forrest passed an audition with bandleader Harry James and remained his vocalist for more than two years. Two of her single recordings with James went all the way to top of the Billboard magazine's "National and Regional Best Selling Retail Records" pop charts: "I Had the Craziest Dream" (Harry James and His Orchestra, Vocal Chorus by Helen Forrest; Columbia Records, 1942), which went to number one on Saturday, February 13, 1943; and "I've Heard That Song Before" (Harry James and His Orchestra, Vocal Chorus by Helen Forrest; Columbia Records, 1942), which went to number one on Saturday, March 6, 1943.

In 1944 Forrest embarked on a solo career and subsequently released numerous singles for Decca Records, including the hit song "Time Waits For No One." She also performed and recorded with Dick Haymes and appeared in several movies as a vocalist with the Harry James Orchestra including "Private Buckaroo" (Universal Pictures, 1942),

“Springtime in the Rockies “ (Twentieth Century Fox Film Corporation, 1942), “Bathing Beauty” (Metro-Goldwyn-Mayer, 1944) and “Two Girls and a Sailor” (Metro-Goldwyn-Mayer, 1944). She returned to Washington, D.C. on numerous occasions, performing engagements at Club Kavakos in 1948, 1949 and 1952, the Capitol Theatre in 1951, the Blue Mirror in 1952, the Casino Royal Theatre Restaurant in 1953 and the Lotus Restaurant in 1959.

In the early 1960s Forrest was the featured vocalist with the Tommy Dorsey Orchestra under the direction of Sam Donahue. In August 1964 she was back in the nation’s capital and made a highly publicized engagement with the band at the Shoreham Hotel. She continued singing in night clubs, cabarets and with big band reunion tours into the early 1990s. Ultimately she recorded more than 500 songs and at her peak was regarded as the most popular female singer in the United States. Helen Forrest died of heart failure on Sunday, July 11, 1999 at the age of 82.

Joining Helen Forrest as a local female singing star who went on to national prominence was Evelyn Knight. Born Evelyn Davis on Monday, December 31, 1917 in Reedville, Virginia, she relocated with her mother to Washington, D.C. in 1930 where they resided in an apartment at 1424 K Street NW. She then spent several years dropping in and out of local schools and attending stage and screen shows at such Downtown venues as the Fox Theatre, the Palace Theatre and the Earle Theatre. Inspired by the singers she observed in the theatres of Washington, she took the stage name of Honey Davis and began her local musical career singing with John Slaughter and His Orchestra at the Willard Hotel’s Bamboo Room in May 1935. In October of that year she moved with Slaughter’s band over to the Wardman Park Hotel where they remained the featured attraction for three months.

Through her work with Slaughter, Davis became a popular attraction in the city and caught the eye of numerous orchestra leaders. In May 1936 she accepted an offer as lead vocalist for Jimmy Harris and His Orchestra at the Maryland Club Gardens on Marlboro Pike in Hillside, Maryland. After several months with Harris, she next became the lead singer with Al Sokol and His Orchestra and performed with them throughout October and November 1936 at LaParee in Washington, D.C. On Friday, December 4, 1936, three weeks before she turned 19, she wed a photographer from the Washington Daily Times newspaper named Andrew Knight and moved with him to an apartment in Arlington, Virginia. (While “Arlington” is offically a county with no incorprated cities or towns, it is commonly considered to be an unincorporated city.)

The marriage brought on a name-change to Evelyn Knight and a new engagement at the Lotus Restaurant with Bill Strickland and His Capitolians that lasted from December 1936 through the end of June 1937. She then worked her way as lead vocalist through a series of groups including the John Slaughter Trio at the Anchor Room of the Annapolis Hotel in Washington, D.C. from September to December 1937, Howard Gale and His Steel Pier Orchestra at the Hotel Emersion in Baltimore from January to March 1938, and Howard Pyle’s CBS Orchestra at Boulevard Farms on Mount Vernon Highway in Alexandria, Virginia throughout the month of April 1938. In May 1938 she began performing as a featured pop music singer at the Claridge Hotel’s King Cole Room on Connecticut Avenue NW in Washington, D.C. She remained there until September 1943, during which time she established herself as one of the greatest female singers to ever come out of the nation’s capital.

Towards the end of her run at the King Cole Room, Knight was offered an opportunity to relocate to New York City and work several prestigious night clubs. In early 1944 she made the change and went on to headline the Blue Angel and Plaza Hotel’s Persian Room. She signed with Decca Records and became one of their top artists and performed and recorded with some of the biggest names in the music industry including Bing Crosby. In the late 1940s she moved to Los Angeles, California and headlined at two of the city's top establishments, Ciro's and the Cocoanut Grove.

Knight made innumerable recordings through the years, including more than a dozen that reached various music popularity charts in the Billboard magazine. One of her single releases, "A Little Bird Told Me" (Evelyn Knight and the Stardusters; Decca Records, 1948) reached number one on the Billboard magazine's "Best-Selling Popular Retail Records" chart on Saturday, January 22, 1949. Her next hit release, "Powder Your Face with Sunshine" (Evelyn Knight and the Stardusters; Decca Records, 1948), reached number three on the same chart in the magazine's Saturday, February 19, 1949 edition. She also recorded two songs with Bing Crosby that were coupled together on one single: "Everywhere You Go" and "How it Lies, How it Lies, How it Lies!" (Bing Crosby and Evelyn Knight with Jud Conlon's Rhythmaires; Decca Records, 1949). In one of her final and most popular hit songs, she sang a duet with Red Foley on the song "My Heart Cries for You" (Red Foley and Evelyn Knight; Decca Records, 1950).

Knight became a popular television attraction and made appearances on "The Colgate Comedy Hour" (hosted by comedians Bud Abbott and Lou Costello; Sunday, January 7, 1951), "The Milton Berle Show" (three different episodes from 1948-1951), "Paul Whiteman's Goodyear Revue" (1951), and "The Ed Sullivan Show" (three different episodes in 1951 and 1952). In the early 1950s she toured the country working the supper club circuit before abruptly retiring from the entertainment business in 1954 at the age of 37.

Knight spent the rest of her years living quietly in Arizona and California. Her celebrity was cemented when she was included among the original 1,500 stars on the Hollywood Walk of Fame in 1960. She is considered today to be one of the greatest popular music singers the Washington, D.C. area has ever produced. Evelyn Knight died of lung cancer on Friday, September 28, 2007 at the age of 89.

CHAPTER TWENTY-THREE
HAPPY HOUR IN PRINCE GEORGE'S COUNTY

In Prince George's County, Maryland a significant change in the cultural landscape took shape in the years following Prohibition when a number of bars, night clubs and restaurants began opening up along several different artery-like roadways that branched out from Washington, D.C. into the eastern suburbs. The most prominent of these developing roadway-business districts were: Rhode Island Avenue, running from Mt. Rainier towards Hyattsville and College Park, where it was then called Washington-Baltimore Boulevard and would later be known under the more popular name of Route One; Bladensburg Road, which bisected Colmar Manor and Cottage City and was then referred to as Baltimore Boulevard as it rounded its way through parts of Bladensburg and Hyattsville; Central Avenue, the main thoroughfare through the northern parts of Capitol Heights and Seat Pleasant; Marlboro Pike, a long stretch that ran from Coral Hills and Hillside all the way out through District Heights and Forestville; Branch Avenue, an alternate name for the Southern Maryland Pike, which led away from Silver Hill towards Clinton; and Livingston Road, the roadway that cut through Oxon Hill and led travelers towards Accokeek; it would be widened and renamed Indian Head Highway in 1949. While the majority of the new bars and night clubs that appeared on these landscapes did not offer live music at first, that situation would gradually change as Great Depression subsided.

During the 1930s and 1940s each of these Prince George's County roadways seemed to have had at least one or two bars or night clubs that distinguished themselves from the other surrounding establishments by offering entertainment that brought in the post-Prohibition revelers. These establishments increasingly depended on advertising and coverage in local newspapers to attract new customers and stimulate business. Such announcements proved to be especially beneficial to club owners in the county who could not compete for radio exposure with the high-powered night clubs of Washington, D.C., many of which regularly had their house orchestras featured on different programs that went out over local airwaves. In time this situation would change, with hundreds of bars and night clubs opening up throughout the entire Washington, D.C. area in the coming years. This situation fostered a growing field of music lovers that were becoming less concerned with geographic boundaries, transportation routes and territorial loyalty and more interested in finding a suitable venue that featured their music of choice.

The first roadway of note in Prince George's County, Maryland during this time was Rhode Island Avenue, which enjoyed a concentration of burgeoning businesses close to the District as it sliced through Mt. Rainer and then merged with Washington-Baltimore Boulevard in Hyattsville. North of this point the highway was simply called Baltimore Boulevard and would eventually come to be known as Route One. The more prominent post-Prohibition era night clubs that were situated along this roadway were Klein's Tavern (which later became Bass' Restaurant and Bar), Waldrop's Restaurant (which later became Jimmy Comber's Supper Club), the 4400 Club (which began booking live rock and roll music in the 1950s), and, farther up the road, the Dude Ranch, which gained popularity when it became Club LaConga in the early 1940s.

The first establishment of interest on the Maryland side as Route One exited Washington, D.C. was Klein's Tavern (3208 Rhode Island Avenue, Mt. Rainier), which was opened in 1934 by Carl Klein and featured Hildreth Harrison at the piano for the remainder of the 1930s. In 1941 Klein's Tavern was sold to Jack, Sol and Benny Bass and was renamed Bass' Restaurant and Bar.

For much of the 1940s entertainment on the main ground floor of Bass' Restaurant and Bar was supplied by local jazz pianist Tommy Chase. During the 1950s the night club featured accordionist Nat Bader and a pop music trio called the Merry-Tones (Paul Adams, Arty Freda and Dick O'Lare). In the middle 1960s the basement space was converted into the Turntable Lounge under the management of Sonny Melcher. It quickly became a noted location for late-night rock and roll jam sessions which featured such bands and musicians as the Saxtons, blues rock guitarist Roy Buchanan and R&B singer-pianist Big Al Downing. Live music was eventually phased out of Bass' Restaurant and Bar in the middle 1980s, though it remained open as a seedy neighborhood hangout until June 2006. The historic building was sadly torn down without fanfare in June 2009 and today its plot is the home of a nondescript parking lot.

A few blocks to the north and just off of the avenue was the Melody Ballroom (3806 34th Street, Mt. Rainier), which had been constructed in 1920 as a dance hall and meeting space. During the 1930s some of the pop and country music bands that performed there were the Hobey Lobist Orchestra, Bernie Jarboe and His Nite Hawks, Bob Garber and His Melody Makers, Jimmie Gandley and His Relaxed Rhythm Band and the Riverside Ramblers.

Continuing north on Route One was Waldrop's Restaurant (4318 Rhode Island Avenue, Brentwood), which opened for business on Thursday, May 14, 1942. Named after original owner Hugh Morgan Waldrop, who also owned the Dixie Pig Restaurant and Barbecue in nearby Bladensburg, this supper club establishment specialized in pop music orchestras which management had perform in the restaurant's ground floor dining area. Among the ensembles to play here during the 1940s were Van Camp's Orchestra, Phil Genther and His Band, Bob Lawrenson and His Orchestra, Charlie Mosher and His Orchestra and Paul Kline and His Quartet.

From 1950 to 1955 Waldrop's Restaurant offered multi-act bills of orchestras, singers, comedians and burlesque dancers. Some of the bigger name musical acts to work the night club during these years were Jack McCollim's Orchestra, Charley Walp and His Orchestra, the Lou Rossi Trio, Frank Condon and His Orchestra, the Charlie Chase Quartet and Jimmy Dean and the Texas Wildcats (featuring lead guitarist Roy Clark). Headlining pop singers during these years included Mickey Carmichael, Pat O'Dare, Gloria Gall, Jean Farnay, Kathy Mann, Peggy Stevens, Marita Morell, Jimmy McCall, Lea Mathews, Johnny Vann and Gene Rand.

Comedians were especially popular at Waldrop's Restaurant and among those to make appearances were Johnny "Rubberface" Frisco, Jack Morgan, Smoky Joe Harmon, Frankie Donato, Louise Potter, Tony Rizzo, Dick Wilson, Lee Allen, Burt Gehan, Jack Count, Joe Laurel and the duo of Bill Layne and Don Hines. Rounding out the festivities were scores of burlesque dancers, with some of the more popular being Carmen Hope, Teena Christine, Pat "Amber" Halladay and the now-legendary Blaze Starr.

On Thursday, September 15, 1955 the liquor license for Waldrop's Restaurant was transferred from Joseph Loskorn to Jimmy Comber, who immediately renamed the restaurant Jimmy Comber's Supper Club. Much like his predecessor, the new establishment began offering large floorshows that featured a house orchestra and a parade of comedians, exotic dancers and special guest singers and bands. Jimmy Comber's Supper Club would last until January 1959, though it should be noted that the live music action switched from the ground floor to the basement, with the opening of the Submarine Room on Tuesday, January 29, 1958, a venture that lasted 12 months.

From its opening in 1955 to the end of 1957 some of the pop and jazz ensembles to work Jimmy Comber's Supper Club were the Tu-Tones, Bill Cooper and His Orchestra, Billy Ford and His Thunderbirds, Paul Dumire's Orchestra, the Four Tunes, the Four Joes, the Four Mascots, the Hilites, the Rhythmettes, the Par Four; the Murraymen, Eddie Pierce's Orchestra, Frankie Garner's Orchestra, the Gaylords, the Charmonaires, Louis Jordan and His Tympany Five, the Bon Bons, Dave Appell and the Applejacks, the Jodimars, Bobby Boyd and the Jazz Bombers, Mike Sarge and His Sergeants, the Ink Spots, Frankie Mayo and His New Yorkers, Woody Herman and His Orchestra, Steve Gibson and His Red Caps, the Harvey Boys, the Ames Brothers, Buddy Morrow and His Orchestra, Charlie Ventura and His All Stars, the DeMarco Sisters, Si Zuckor and His Band, the Golden Gate Quartet, Si Seymore's Orchestra, the Bon Bons, Johnny Long and His Orchestra and the Glenn Miller Orchestra (directed by Ray McKinley).

A number of pianists were also featured at the club during that time including Bob Petty, Herb George, Larry Girard and Jackie Lee. Pop singers were also on display during this time and among those to make appearances were Vicki Young, Meg Myles, Dottie Smith, Pat Kirby, the Baker Sisters, Jerry Vale, Dorris Lynn, Cozy Morley, Jerri Adams and Alan Dean. Most of the club's nightly bills also included comedians, the ranks of which included the Goofers, Alan Drake, Nat Ray, Bobby Charles and Dusty Brooks. In addition, notable burlesque dancers to display their talents on the stage were Betty Sawyer, Patti Call, Tania Velia, Betty Howard, Libby Jones, Desiree Cyn, Pat "Amber" Holliday and Lynn Storm.

When the Submarine Room was in operation at Jimmy Comber's Supper Club from January 1958 to January 1959 it offered a mix of entertainment from swing orchestras and pop singers to rock and roll bands and burlesque dancers. Featured entertainers during that year-long period included Frankie Mayo and His New Yorkers, Murray Schaff and His Aristocrats, the Chords, Lee Allen and His Orchestra, the Four Tunes, Woody Herman and His Orchestra, the Tyrones and Steve Gibson and His Red Caps. Featured burlesque dancers during this time included Lynn Storm, Evelyn West, Barbara Lee, Betty Howard, Marla Grant, Tawny Tremaine and Judy Gibbs.

The building that once housed Waldrop's Restaurant and Jimmy Comber's Supper Club is still standing and since 1993 has been occupied by a church called the Faith Outreach Center.

Farther north, beyond the University of Maryland campus where Route One's name was switched from Rhode Island Avenue to Baltimore Avenue, sat the Dude Ranch (9410 Baltimore Avenue, College Park). Opened by Milton F. Barrett in April 1934 in what was then a neighborhood called Berwyn, the Dude Ranch was a Spanish-themed restaurant, which, for a very short time in the early 1940s, was called the Casa Grande Club.

From 1940 through the summer of 1942 a number of highly regarded pop music ensembles were brought in to anchor the colorful floorshows that were offered at the Dude Ranch. Among these bands were Rafael Lopez's Orchestra, Charlie Parrish's Casa Grande Orchestra, Clyde Martin's Orchestra (featuring singer Tommy Martin), Don Collins' Music, Bruce Van and His New Yorkers, Al Massey and His Orchestra (featuring singer Connie Smith), Ralph Garren and the Dude Ranch Orchestra, the Phil Barrett Orchestra, Berk Motley and His Orchestra, Dick Hummer and the Carolina Club Orchestra, Paul Kurzen's Orchestra, Al Shea and His Dance Orchestra, Charley King and the Crazy Cowboys and Ann Mix and Her Western Entertainers. Among the headlining pop singers at the Dude Ranch during its relatively short existence were Agnes Harris, Peggy Paige, Beverly Lee, Dixie Dyer, Dolly Dare, Dick Bae, Jimmy Staley, Texas Eddy and Johnny Pinkard.

On Friday, September 18, 1942 Barrett renamed his establishment Club LaConga and kept the Spanish theme intact. At different times during the 1940s he briefly called his establishment Club Rayburn and Café LaConga. Some of the entertainers to perform at Club LaConga during this decade included Herbert Curbelos and His South American Orchestra, Olivera DeDuca and His Latin American Orchestra, Chevez and His Famous Rumba Band, Louis Betancourt and His Rhumba Band, Bill Abernethy and His Orchestra,

Oscar Calvert and His Rhumba Band, Donnelly James and His American Orchestra, Errol Vernon and His Orchestra (featuring singer Janice Lynn), the Jack Gandy Quartet, Manny Cavalier and His Orchestra, the Jesse Mack Trio, the Magic Notes Trio, Charlie Parrish and His Cuban American Orchestra, Dick Truette and His Orchestra (featuring singer Lyda Allen), the Four Tunes, the Jolly Five, the Hi-Lo Quartet, the Jones Brothers, singer-pianists Mary Keefe and Barbara Johnstone and jazz pianist Ace Harris.

In the 1950s Barrett ushered in star-studded, multi-act floorshows to the Club LaConga that covered almost every aspect of the entertainment field. Orchestras, singers, dancers, comedians and all types of musical groups worked the stage – including an occasional rock and roll outfit.

During this decade some of the big-name groups to appear on its stage included Chico Cortez's Rumba Orchestra, Bob Lawrenson and His Orchestra (featuring singer Doris Hart), Al Dunn and His All-Star Combo (featuring singer VeRonnee), Frankie Condon's Trio, the Dee Clements Orchestra, Gordon Mitchell and His Orchestra, Ken Kaiser's Combo, Gordon Marshall and His Orchestra, Bill Spooner and His Orchestra, Lou Simonton and His Orchestra, the Frank Moore Four, the Rhythm Masters, Joe Stanley and His Sophistikats (featuring singer Kitty Cutler) and the Topnotes.

Other entertainers at Club LaConga during the 1950s included: pop singers Ronnye Nelson, Anita Marios, Vicki Lynn, Tom August, Lee Davis, Joe Martini, Peggy Stevens, Norty Michaels, Nancy Ford, Jack Laurence, Lynn Martin, Arlene Defaye, Marion Dawn, Jerry Toronto, Guy Tano, Danny Winchell, Rena Lyndon, Bobby Todd and Polly Rochelle; comedians Stan Stanley, Eddie Black, Russ Byron, Jimmy Judge, Hal Berry, Dick Hayman, Janice Walker, Bobby Doyle, Stan Howard, Tubby Boots, Jack Lester, Bob Shelton, Hank Greenburg, Billy Roberts and the duo of Joe Blow and Sally Rose; and burlesque dancers Hillary Dawn, Sandra Seers, Joann Merritt, Joan Swanson, Margie Grey, Cynthia Ames, Rita Rose, Toni Adams, Lois Baker, Echo Day and Dolores Delraye.

Club LaConga was destroyed in a fire on Tuesday, June 16, 1959 and was never rebuilt. Its former site is currently occupied by a car dealership called College Park Honda (9400 Baltimore Avenue, College Park).

Just to the south of Rhode Island Avenue was Bladensburg Road, which during the Prohibition years was known as Baltimore Boulevard as it entered Prince George's County traveling east away from Washington, D.C. This roadway served as a buffer between the towns of Cottage City and Colmar Manor as it moved towards the Anacostia River and the Peace Cross monument. It was a historic route that figured prominently in the Battle of Bladensburg, with much of the actual fighting that fateful day having taken place on what is now the town of Colmar Manor. Upon their crushing defeat of the Prince George's County militia in 1814, the British traveled this roadway all the way into the City of Washington where they subsequently set about burning down various federal buildings.

Bladensburg Road had hosted ramshackle roadhouses since the late 1800s, but began taking shape as a recognizable business strip with the construction of new shops and taverns in the early 20th century. After the repeal of Prohibition, a number of neighborhood-oriented establishments on Bladensburg Road obtained liquor licenses and opened their doors to a new generation of drunks. Their ranks included such watering holes as Joe Moran's Bar, the Horseshoe Inn, Stuart's Restaurant, Pincus' Restaurant, Walter Shelton's Place, Tony Bresnahan's Tavern and the Rustic Cabin Restaurant (all of which were located on the south side of the roadway in Colmar Manor, Maryland).

Across the street in Cottage City, Maryland was Bill's Place, which had opened in 1934 and then in 1936 became the P&C Drive In Café and later during the rock and roll era operated as the Dixie Pig. It should be noted that the street addresses of these establishments changed several times during the 1930s and it wasn't until the middle

1940s when the roadway had its name officially changed from Baltimore Boulevard to Bladensburg Road that permanent street addresses were assigned.

Perhaps the most unique establishment to operate on Bladensburg Road during and after Prohibition was the Maryland Athletic Club (3200 Bladensburg Road, Mt. Rainier), which in reality was an expansive illegal gambling casino inside a large converted mansion near the Washington, D.C. line that was informally known as Jimmy's Place. The Maryland Athletic Club occupied the northeast corner of what is now Eastern Avenue NE and Bladensburg Road and was owned and operated by the now-legendary gambling baron Jimmy LaFontaine.

The mansion that housed the Maryland Athletic Club had long been known as Rives Station and had been owned for decades by Col. Wright Rives, a longtime trusted aide to President Andrew Johnson. In 1919 James A. "Jimmy" LaFontaine, a 51-year-old native of Southwest Washington, D.C. who had previously owned the Ivy Club in Northern Virginia, purchased the property and set up his operations which included craps, poker, roulette and thoroughbred wagering.

LaFontaine managed to stay clear of the law for much of the 30 years he was in business through an intricate system of banking, campaign contributions, special gifts and protection money to local law enforcement officials. However, in 1931 he was sentenced to nine months by a federal judge on income tax evasion. It was said that the Maryland Athletic Club averaged a net profit of over $200,000 a year every year it was in existence. While this establishment went out of business after the death of LaFontaine on Monday, November 21, 1949, it served as a legendary casino that set the stage for the tawdry strip of bars that was slowly developing further east along Bladensburg Road.

In the wake of Prohibition tavern and club owners along Bladensburg Road slowly began incorporating live music entertainment into their night spots. This stretch of roadway from the Washington, D.C. line to the Peace Cross monument became informally known as the Strip and developed into a mini Las Vegas with new sights, lights and sounds. In time, a stretch of rough-and-tumble bars and gaudy night clubs dotted the Strip, a roster that included such now-legendary live music hangouts as the Romano Inn, the Wheel Bar, the Dixie Pig, the Surf Club, the Rustic Cabin Restaurant, and, just over the Anacostia River, the Cross Roads.

The Strip became so notorious in the post-Prohibition era, it was immortalized in Jack Lait and Lee Mortimer's best-selling book "Washington Confidential: The Low-Down on the Big Town" (1951). Chapter Nine of this book was entitled "The Overflow" and dealt with the wild world of Prince George's County, Maryland in fine fashion. Some descriptive quotes included: "Prince George's is a long strip predominantly devoted to gaiety, night life, gambling, and whoring" and "There are usually more floating crap-games, illegal bookies, and after-hours spots in Prince George's than there are in Reno, where all such things are legal."

Best of all was the authors' overall take on the legendary Bladensburg Road Strip, of which we are told: "The latter is Rum Row, with several blocks of dirty drinking-joints where wind-broken broads solicit drinks, roll drunks, and whore, often as a pastime when no dough is available."

The Romano Inn (3705 Bladensburg Road, Colmar Manor), was one of the more popular clubs on the Strip and was the very first night club one encountered on the right-hand side of the road while traveling away from Washington, D.C. towards the Peace Cross monument. It occupied a seemingly ancient structure originally marked 111 Baltimore Boulevard. Earlier in the 20th century this building housed a long-forgotten roadhouse owned by Alex Merrill called the Horseshoe Inn. Today, there are no existing land records to tell exactly when this building had been constructed, though it is highly likely it had been erected sometime around the turn of the century along with several others in the immediate vicinity. Furthermore, there are no published transactions of the Board of License Commissioners of Prince George's County, Maryland that verify exactly when the Horseshoe Inn went out of business or what happened to its liquor license.

Information has been provided by many past and present Colmar Manor residents who tell that the Horseshoe Inn, which was known for its square dance jamborees, was sold and converted into a night club called the Romano Inn sometime during the middle 1940s. A liquor license transaction made by the Board of License Commissioners of Prince George's County, Maryland that was published in the Thursday, September 12, 1946 edition of the Hyattsville Independent newspaper tends to confirm some of this information by showing that the Romano Inn came into existence on Thursday, September 19, 1946 at 3703 ½ Bladensburg Road under the ownership of Pauline Fratantuano, though no mention is made of the Horseshoe Inn.

The Romano Inn, whose official street address was changed to 3705 Bladensburg Road upon its formal opening, was operated by the husband-and-wife team of Joe and Pauline "Frat," who immediately began booking live entertainment for their growing customer base. From 1946 to 1948 house entertainment was alternately supplied by pop singer-pianists Margie McCloin and Ola Mae Bishop, and local piano favorite Tommy Chase. In 1949 and 1950 featured acts were the versatile boogie-woogie singing team of Fred and Faye Wakefield, pianist Andy Mindale and a pop music outfit known as Tommy Nourgis and His Trio.

When the rock and roll era gained momentum in the middle 1950s the Romano Inn responded by bringing in the Three Jacks (though they quickly lost them in 1954 to the neighboring Wheel Bar), and later offered a variety of pop and jazz music entertainers including pianist Harvey Chown, the Three Romeos (Jay Calomeris, R. Smith, Ted Efantis), the Grayden Parker Trio, Mert Oliver and His Band and Gene Bonnike and His Band. The Romano Inn enjoyed a long 26-year stay on the Bladensburg Road Strip before closing in July 1973 and being felled by the wrecking ball shortly thereafter.

The Wheel Bar sat right next to the Romano Inn on Colmar Manor side of the Bladensburg Road Strip in one of the many ancient, now-untraceable buildings that have long since been torn down and wiped off the map. While no land records or business licenses exist regarding this establishment or its predecessors, neighborhood old-timers have stated that the Wheel Bar building, along with others that were clustered around it, probably went up in the early 1900s and housed a variety of roadhouses through the years. These sources tell that shortly after the repeal of Prohibition a saloon called Joe Moran's Bar was opened on the premises, which at the time was marked 119 Baltimore Boulevard. In 1944 the building address was changed to 3817 Bladensburg Road and a year later Spruce Baird bought out Joe Moran and opened up the Wheel Bar on the premises. In the late 1940s the Wheel Bar featured the pianist known only as "Lennie," with occasional performances by pop singer Jerry Toronto.

In the 1950s the Wheel Bar was under the ownership of Solomon Alex Stern, who experimented with many different musical styles for his patrons during his management reign. From 1950 to 1952 the Wheel operated as a type of neighborhood piano bar for older gamblers – a somewhat strange situation given the circus-like atmosphere that dominated the Bladensburg Road Strip at the time. During that time different pianists, including longtime house keyboardist "Lennie the Wizard" (as he was then being called) tickled the keys on a nightly basis.

In 1953 and 1954 things picked up and joining Lennie the Wizard were some versatile popular music aggregations such as: Jerry Rodis and His Orchestra, who provided standards and classic dance tunes; the Ray Marshall Trio (a threesome of multi-instrumentalists from West Virginia consisting of real-life brothers Ray, Jesse and Clyde – advertised as "The Craziest Trio in Town"), who played everything from chart-topping pop songs to obscure R&B numbers to some early Bill Haley rock and roll selections; and Al Dunn and His Music (featuring vocalist VeRonnee), an outfit that had worked most of the city's top R&B night clubs. Others making appearances during this period were the pop music outfit Danny Powell Trio, the jazz-oriented Shirley Horn Trio, and the C&W trio of singer-fiddler-guitarist Blackie Skiles, singer-steel guitarist Billy Strickland and guitarist-bassist Ulysses White.

During the fall of 1954 rock and roll music began making its presence felt in the Wheel Bar, a move that contributed greatly to Bladensburg Road's developing reputation as one of the region's hottest live music corridors. Earlier that summer a hot rocking local trio known as the Three Jacks left the Quonset Supper Club in Silver Hill, Maryland and took a job at the Romano Inn on the western edge of Bladensburg Road in Colmar Manor, a gig that lasted several weeks until after the Labor Day weekend. In September of 1954 the band took a week-long engagement next door at the Wheel Bar and proved to be such a popular commodity they were called back for periodic appearances over the next six months.

In a send-off to C&W music on Tuesday, June 21, 1955, the Wheel Bar offered a "Hillbilly Jamboree" that lasted for two consecutive weeks and featured mixtures of local musicians including: singer Dick Thomas; singer-fiddler-guitarist Blackie Skiles; singer-guitarist Dub Howington; singer-steel guitarist Billy Strickland; steel guitarist Ray Chillum; guitarists Ulysses White, Benny Simpson, Pete Pepper and Aubrey Warder; and drummer Jim Burkett.

In March 1955 the Three Jacks were called upon to take over house band duties at the Wheel Bar for good and replace the Marshall Brothers, who had long been popular headliners in the club. While working the Wheel that year, the Three Jacks were responsible for kicking off the legendary Sunday jam sessions that later became a featured attraction in numerous other Prince George's County night clubs. In November of that year, Billy Williams and His Band (Williams being the former Lionel Hampton tenor saxophonist; his group at the time featured singer Eva Foster) joined the Three Jacks on the Saturday and Sunday rock and roll sessions, a venture that lasted for the next 12 months.

In 1956 the Wheel Bar introduced a bevy of locally based striptease dancers to its audience and they remained a popular commodity for the remainder of the decade. The Three Jacks remained the main musical attraction and performed six and seven nights a week at the club all the way through March 1960. When they took a rare short vacation, other rock and roll bands like the Rhythm Rockets and the Three of Us Trio were called upon to fill the bills. On Thursday, March 16, 1961 Solomon Alex Stern sold the Wheel Bar to Russell and Juanita Crews, who changed the name of the establishment to the Basin Street Lounge and ushered in Dixieland and ragtime jazz for their customers.

Across the street from the Wheel Bar on the northeast corner of 38th Street and Bladensburg Road sat a building, which, after Prohibition, first housed Bill's Place and then the P&C Drive In Café. In the late 1940s and early 1950s this space hosted such popular music night clubs as the Chesapeake Musical Bar and the Oriental House. In December 1952 the Dixie Pig opened for business in this building and became one of the area's top C&W bars before switching its format and maintaining its popularity as a high-powered rock and roll night club.

Moving farther west down the Strip was the Surf Club (4201 Bladensburg Road, Colmar Manor), which became established as one of the most revered country music night clubs in the area, though its origins have been obscured through time and an aura of mystery envelopes its history. There are no existing business or land records for the old Surf Club building and there are only two known pieces of documentation that mention the bar. First, a small ad for the Surf Club appears in the Friday, January 31, 1941 edition of the Prince Georgean newspaper. Second, a transaction notice for the Board of License Commissioners of Prince George's County, Maryland in the Friday, October 2, 1942 edition of the same newspaper states that ownership of the liquor license was transferred from Surf Club, Inc. to Helen Resnick, with the listed address of the restaurant being given as 501 Washington-Baltimore Boulevard (all of the buildings along this stretch of roadway – that would soon be renamed Bladensburg Road – underwent changes in their listed addresses during the 1930s and 1940s). At this point in time there is no way of verifying when the building at this address was constructed or when the name Surf Club was appropriated for business trading.

On Friday, April 30, 1943 Helen Resnick sold the business to Tony Bresnahan, who renamed his new establishment Tony Bresnahan's Tavern. He kept the business going until May 1951, at which time the liquor license was transferred to Charles F. Pincus and the restaurant was renamed the Surf Club. On Thursday, August 2, 1951 the liquor license was transferred again, this time to the team of John Biro, Robert "Bob" Beckelman and William Faussett, three musicians who collectively ushered live jazz music into the Surf Club for the first time. For the remainder of 1951 Beckelman held down chores as the club's singer-comedian-emcee, while Biro's jazz band, the Capital City Dixielanders, assumed house band duties. When Biro took a break from the action, top-billing at the Surf Club was given to Scotty Laurence and the River Boat Jazz Trio.

From 1952 to 1954 Bob Beckelman remained the featured emcee and the Capital City Dixieland Band, which at times featured drummer Al Pometto, continued as the designated Surf Club house band. Other jazz groups to work extended engagements at the night club during these years included the Scott Trio (singer-saxophonist Jimmy Scott, solovox player Irene Scott and drummer Ernie K.), Booker Coleman and His Bopsters and Two Kings and an Ace (singer Harriet King, guitarist Dick Griffin and saxophonist Hector Barroso).

During this period, Bob Beckelman added and dropped names of various associates from the restaurant's liquor license in rapid-fire succession. Eventually he sold the restaurant and had the liquor license transferred outright to a former business partner named Murray Kanner. Throughout 1955, with Kanner overseeing the club's operation, the Capital City Dixielanders were joined by a C&W-jazz outfit called the Chick Hall Trio, which consisted of singer-guitarist-banjoist Milford Willard "Chick" Hall, singer-guitarist Dick Williams and bassist-rhythm guitarist Ulysses White.

Chick Hall made an offer to purchase the Surf Club and in December 1955 the business became his. On Thursday, March 15, 1956 the Board of License Commissioners of Prince George's County, Maryland for Alcoholic Beverages Licenses approved the transfer of the Class B liquor license from Murray Kanner, Mary Kanner and Jack Sapienza to Milford Willard Hall (president-treasurer), Martha Ann Hall (vice president) and Clarence P.T. Lockhart (secretary).

Under Chick Hall's watch, the Surf Club proceeded to become one of the area's top C&W night clubs, mainly because the new owner and his cohorts took over nightly entertainment chores. For the remainder of the 1950s and throughout the 1960s the Chick Hall Trio was mainly comprised of Hall, Sr., rhythm guitarist Ulysses White and bassist-rhythm guitarist Roy Green. Other top bands to work the Surf Club stage during these years included Dub Howington and the Tennessee Haymakers, Smokey Mac and the Twilighters and Wade Holmes and His Town and Country Boys.

With Bladensburg Road targeted for extensive redevelopment in the early 1970s, the Surf Club closed its doors on Sunday, March 2, 1975, but reopened under the same trading name three nights later on Wednesday, March 5 in a new building at 4711 Kenilworth Avenue in nearby Hyattsville, Maryland. The Chick Hall Band, which originally consisted of

Hall singing and playing lead guitar, rhythm guitarist Roy Green, singer-bassist Wade Holmes (who on weekends was replaced by Chick's son Chris Hall on bass and vocals) and drummer Bob Redding, was the featured nightly attraction in the new Surf Club for more than 16 years.

When Chick Hall retired from the night club business in 1991, his son Chris Hall maintained control of the Surf Club. At that point a new house band named Heroes and Friends took over, with its initial lineup consisting of singer-lead guitarist Milford Chick Hall (the son of Milford Willard "Chick" Hall and commonly referred to as "Chick Hall, Jr."), singer-bassist Chris Hall, keyboardist Brin Reed and drummer Tim Jarvis. With musicians coming and going, Heroes and Friends remained the club's main attraction for 17 years, though in its final days the band operated as a trio, with the Hall brothers being joined by drummer Mike Toole. Towards the end of its run under Hall's ownership, the Surf Club also featured a variety of local blues, jazz and rock and roll acts.

Chris Hall sold the Surf Club to James Byrum on Monday, January 14, 2008, who reopened the business as Surf Club Live on February 1 of that year. After more than three years of hosting a variety of popular music acts, the club shut its doors for good after a final night of live music on Saturday, October 29, 2011. Since May 2012 this legendary building has been occupied by the Kenilworth Laundromat.

Rounding out the Strip was the Rustic Cabin Restaurant (4321 Bladensburg Road, Colmar Manor), which was initially owned by Louis Rosenfield and opened for business on Tuesday, July 19, 1938 on the far eastern end of Bladensburg Road, a few yards away from the western bank of the Anacostia River (its original street address was listed as 619 Baltimore Boulevard). Made from cured cedar logs, the rectangular, one-story Rustic Cabin was a bit higher class than many of the rough-and-tumble bars which by that time had already lined up on both sides of the Strip. Rosenfield booked high-quality orchestras for his evening supper crowd and tended to maintain these house bands for long engagements. Featured entertainers at the Rustic Cabin during the 1940s included Al Shea and His Orchestra, the R.C. Orchestra, Jack Myerly and His Melody Men, the Rustic Melodeers, Berk Motley and His Orchestra and pop singer Jerry Toronto.

Alonza Berkley "Berk" Motley was certainly the most significant personality to frequent the Rustic Cabin during those days and would eventually become its proprietor. Berk Motley was born in Danville, Virginia on Saturday, September 27, 1913 and was raised in both Virginia and North Carolina. He learned the saxophone, clarinet, trumpet and trombone and became a professional musician at the age of 14. In the 1930s he played saxophone on tours with such acts as Glenn Miller and His Orchestra, Sammy Kaye and His Orchestra, the Dorsey Brothers, the Hal Kemp Orchestra and the Glen Gray Casa Loma Orchestra. He often worked large vaudeville revues where he backed up such stars as comedians Red Skelton and Bob Hope.

Berk Motley first worked the Washington, D.C. area with his own 16-piece orchestra at the Dude Ranch in Berwyn, Maryland in 1936. In the late 1940s he settled in this area and made appearances at Club Nightingale on Richmond Highway in Alexandria, Virginia before obtaining the house band job at the Rustic Cabin Restaurant in 1948. Motley enjoyed the night club so much he purchased the building and business outright on Thursday, June 23, 1949.

Pop music was still the choice at the Rustic Cabin throughout the first half of the 1950s, with Motley himself often leading the 12-piece house orchestra, a job that had him playing saxophone and clarinet and providing corny comedy routines. Other bands to work lasting engagements during those years included Jack Myerly and His Melody Men, Dianne Dawn and Her Men of Music, the Tri-Tones and the jazz group Nancy Leach and Her Fandango Four. Among the headlining pop singers of this time were Betty Travis and Rena Lyndon.

Throughout 1955 and 1956 Motley repeatedly booked a band known as the House Rockers, a versatile, high-energy pop music outfit that allowed rock and roll to make inroads in the Rustic Cabin. The rock invasion began in full force in September 1956 when nightly bills at the club featured the extremely popular C&W band Jimmy Dean and the Texas Wildcats paired with two rock and roll outfits, the Three of Us Trio and Frankie Mayo and His New Yorkers. Some of the other bands to work the Rustic Cabin during the final months of that year included pop groups such as the Wilde Winds; jazz acts such as Joe Hockaday and His Orchestra and Wild Bill Whelan and His Dixie Six; rock and roll bands such as Joey Nave and His Five Points and Johnny Logan and His Royal Crowns; R&B-rock singer Rosa LaKing ("The Queen of Rock and Roll"); and R&B singer-pianist Billy Stewart.

From 1957 to 1959 the primary forms of musical entertainment at the Rustic Cabin Restaurant were rock and roll and R&B, with a number of out-of-town and nationally known performers, both White and Black, headlining the night club. Among those acts to perform during these years at this Bladensburg Road hot spot included Joe Bruce and the Steppers, Mike Sarge and His Sergeants, the Nite Caps, the Five Stars, Chris Powell and His Blue Flames, Ricky Ricardo and His Blues Four, the Valentinos, the Tyrones, the Five Stars, the Jodimars, Red Prysock and His Band, La Playa Sextet, the Nu-Tones, Murray Schaff and His Aristocrats, Doc Stark and His Nite Riders, Braden Parker and His Band, the Top Notes, Freddie Bell and the Bell Boys, Birdie Castle and His Stardusters, Pat the Cat and His Kittens and Howard Litt's Four Sharps.

Other special headliners at the club during those years included: jazz greats such as singer-pianist Ray Charles and saxophonist Earl Bostic; pop singers such as Jo Ann Campbell, Joe Lagana, Toni Price, Valerie Grimaldi, Jan Kelly and Betty Bucik; R&B artists such as singers Rocking Joe Thomas and Lloyd Price, singer-pianists Ruth Brown and Bubber Johnson; and the ever-present Berk Motley and His Orchestra.

In the 1960s Motley eased off the practice of booking national acts and mainly featured his own orchestra on weekends. On Thursday, April 7, 1966 he changed the name of the Rustic Cabin Restaurant to Berk Motley's Sirloin Room and from that point forward Motley himself would perform by playing saxophone and clarinet and telling jokes, backed only by a guitarist and accordionist. By the 1990s, Motley was still valiantly making weekend appearances, though health issues slowed his stage time and the changing demographics of the surrounding neighborhoods caused the restaurant's business to slowly dry up.

Berk Motley's Sirloin Room closed in September 1997 with little fanfare. Sadly, Motley passed away on Friday, July 23, 1999 at the age of 85. After a period of vacancy, the Family Buffet opened on the premises in May 2000 and closed that December. In September 2003 a new establishment called JTK Restaurant and Bar tried its hand with rap and go-go music, but closed in December 2005. This legendary landmark was torn down in January 2006 and its former site now serves as a parking lot for the nearby National News Agency.

Further out past the eastern end of Bladensburg Road, across the Anacostia River and a few steps past the Peace Cross monument, sat two other highly significant night clubs that stood in close proximity to each other, the Dixie Pig Restaurant and Barbecue (4500 Annapolis Road, Bladensburg) and the Cross Roads (4103 Baltimore Avenue, Bladensburg). The first of these, the Dixie Pig Restaurant and Barbecue, occupied the building that once housed Coldenstroth's Saloon and served as the area's primary country music establishment from 1925 until its demise by fire on Saturday, November 22, 1952. A new Dixie Pig was opened the following month on Bladensburg Road in Cottage City in a building previously occupied by the Oriental House. The Cross Roads, meanwhile, was rebuilt from the ashes of the fire-stricken Del Rio Restaurant and opened on Wednesday,

November 19, 1941 to a new world of pop music and burlesque entertainment before turning towards C&W music in the 1960s. The club later gained recognition in the music world for being the home of blues rock guitarist Roy Buchanan in the early 1970s.

Due south of Bladensburg Road was Central Avenue, which exited Washington, D.C. and made its way eastwards through the town of Capitol Heights and the city of Seat Pleasant, Maryland. In the smallish downtown area of Capitol Heights there were scores of bars open to the public along Central Avenue during the immediate post-Prohibition years including such long-forgotten, down-home beer taverns and saloons as the Wagon Wheel, the Stumble Inn, Margie's Place, the Midway Tavern, Luckett's Bar, Kelly's Tavern, Great's Tavern, Charlie's Tavern and Roses' Tavern. (The road that was originally known as Central Avenue in that era is still in existence today as Old Central Avenue.)

Situated on Central Avenue just outside of Capitol Heights in Seat Pleasant, Maryland were such live music night clubs as the Dixie Tavern, Chubby's Restaurant and Bar, and Armstrong's. The Dixie Tavern figured prominently on the local country music scene from 1934 until its sale in September 1948, at which time it became Club Hillbilly. Chubby's Restaurant and Bar and Armstrong's were also significant parts of this scene for their roles in mixing C&W with bluegrass music.

Chubby's Restaurant and Bar was a prototype Prince George's County roadhouse that was known for its cheap beer, nightly brawls and country music. It opened in November 1944 and was located 1.3 miles east of Washington, D.C. at 7101 Central Avenue in Seat Pleasant, Maryland (this address was changed to 6715 Central Avenue in 1967). Chubby's Restaurant and Bar was one of a number of such establishments that dotted this highway as one traveled eastwards away from Washington, D.C.

In the 1940s the Stoneman Family was Chubby's Restaurant and Bar's main nightly attraction. In the early 1950s C&W acts such as singer-guitarists Roy Clark and Carl Lukat, Jimmy Dean and the Texas Wildcats, Dub Howington and the Tennessee Haymakers, the Blue Grass Champs, Leon Baxter and His Band and the Tennessee Troopers (singer-guitarist-mandolinist Buzz Busby, fiddler Scotty Stoneman and guitarist Jack Clement) made frequent appearances at the night spot. In the summer of 1953 Chubby's Restaurant and Bar became one of the first of the local night clubs to introduce rock and roll music when they brought in the Frank Shegogue Combo, a group whose namesake was one of the area's most dynamic electric guitarists.

In the late 1950s Chubby's Restaurant and Bar was advertising itself in the local dailies as "The Hottest Rock n' Roll Club in America." Performers at the night club during that time included Frankie Mayo and the New Yorkers, the Pete Rubino Quintet, Joe Stanley and His Building Rockers, the Rocking Kings and singer-pianist Mark Ruslander (today he is known as the political comedian Mark Russell).

In the 1960s some of the regular performers at Chubby's Restaurant and Bar included bluegrass singer Mac Wiseman, Chubby Wise and the Florida Playboys, Danny Denver and the Sound Tracks and the Ozark Playboys. Remarkably, this night club carried on as a live C&W music spot for several decades as the neighborhood around it experienced significant demographic change. Chubby's Restaurant and Bar closed on Wednesday, December 20, 1989 and was eventually torn down without fanfare in May 1996.

Further out on Central Avenue, just over the Seat Pleasant border, was Armstrong's (101 Brightseat Road, Landover, Maryland), which was opened in 1941 by Ethel M. Armstrong and specialized in live bluegrass and C&W music. In the 1940s the Stoneman Family performed there on a regular basis. In the 1950s some of the better known headliners were the Blue Grass Champs, Smokey Mac and his Twilighters and the Tennessee Troopers (singer-guitarist-mandolinist Buzz Busby, fiddler Scotty Stoneman and guitarist Jack Clement). Armstrong's was replaced by the Ranch House in 1959, which remained in operation until April 1966.

To the south of Central Avenue, as Alabama Avenue SE exited Washington, D.C. into Maryland it became Marlboro Pike, which by the end of Prohibition in the middle 1930s was filling up with a series of bars and night clubs that serviced an all-White clientele from surrounding areas that included the community of Coral Hills, town of Capitol Heights, city of District Heights and community of Forestville. New arrivals to these parts tended to be Southern in nature and through time their cultural flavor would strongly influence the live music establishments of the Pike. During the post-Prohibition era, Marlboro Pike was steadily developing as a destination for musical entertainment and hosted a number of bars and night clubs of all persuasions. Among the more visible of these establishments were the Campus Club, Mike Young's Café, the Hilltop Restaurant, the Senate Inn, Maryland Club Gardens, Detta's Musical Bar, the Homestretch Tavern and Griffith Farms.

The first stop on Marlboro Pike as one advanced away from Washington, D.C. and moved through Prince George's County was the Campus Club, whose original address was marked 1429 52nd Avenue, Capitol Heights, Maryland. (Today this reconfigured building is occupied by the Freedom Way Missionary Baptist Church and its street address is marked 1266 Benning Road.) This smallish beer joint opened in 1936 in what was then called the Hillside neighborhood of Capitol Heights, was known for its mind-boggling brawls, and enjoyed the distinction of being the first Washington, D.C. area night club to cater to motorcycle riders, serving for many years as the unofficial home base for the D.C. Ramblers, one of the area's first organized motorcycle clubs.

The Campus Club long employed local country music guitarists and banjo players, who placed a kitty at the foot of the stage and worked for beer money. The club stepped up its schedule when owner Vernon "Jack" Biedler purchased the business from Sadie Strohl in July 1946. He continued to allow single musicians to take his stage every night, but upgraded the operation when he booked a high-quality local band, Dub Howington and the Tennessee Haymakers, throughout 1948 and 1949.

In the early 1950s some of the better-known musicians to appear at the Campus Club were the C&W duo of singer-guitarists Roy Clark and Carl Lukat, and a bluegrass trio called the Tennessee Troopers which consisted of singer-guitarist-mandolinist Buzz Busby, fiddler Scotty Stoneman and guitarist Jack Clement. The Campus Club continued to feature bluegrass music until its closing on Thursday, December 21, 1961.

A step away from the Campus Club in the Hillside neighborhood was Mike Young's Café, whose original address was 5200 Marlboro Pike, Capitol Heights, Maryland. (In 1967 this building's address was changed to 4856 Marlboro Pike.) Mike Young opened his night club here in December 1937 and originally booked pop music orchestras for his patrons. For a brief spell in the 1940s the establishment was advertised as Club 5200. Entertainers to perform here during these early years included Tony Costello and His Paradise Islanders (featuring singer George Stribling), Harry Lacy and His Orchestra, Fuzz Mooney and His Music, Jack Russell's Quintet, the Southern Serenaders (featuring singer Joshua Hayseed and fiddler Hink Dean) and Johnnie Galo and His Orchestra.

In the 1950s Mike Young's Café did a turnaround and booked C&W music, with a very young Roy Clark serving as house guitarist at different times. A fire set back Mike Young's Café in August 1954 and the following year new owner Raymond Williams changed the name of the business to Ray's Bar and Grill, which remained in operation until November 1999. It then became a restaurant called Flavors of the South, which turned over to J.C. Liquors on Thursday, May 1, 2014.

In August 1939 Richard Dolph opened the Hilltop Restaurant in the unincorporated Coral Hills community of Maryland at what was then 5211 Marlboro Pike right at the intersection with Benning Road and directly across the street from Mike Young's Café. (In 1961 this building – then occupied by the Las Vegas Club – burned to the ground. A new building was constructed on its site in 1966 and a McDonald's Restaurant opened on the premises in 1967. At that time this building's street address was changed to 4857 Marlboro Pike, Capitol Heights.)

Marlboro Pike was developing into a Southland paradise in the years following Prohibition and the Hilltop Restaurant was created with the idea that it would establish itself as one of the highway's alternatives to the tougher working-class bars that were beginning to surface throughout the area. While the Hilltop Restaurant brought in some classy musical outfits to please the crowds, it too had a rough veneer and attracted some of the local community's harder partiers.

During the 1940s pop music entertainers to work the Hilltop Restaurant included We Three (guitarist Al Shea, organist Larry Hendrick and accordionist Stanley Jones), Larry Hendrick and the Hilltoppers, James Scott and His Orchestra, Bob Deardorff and His Orchestra, Jimmy Calomeris and His Musical Moods, Bob Lee's Orchestra, the Lee Barton Trio, Sonny Kast and His Jump Trio, and singers Jerry Toronto and Millie Harvey.

In 1950 and 1951 the Hilltop Restaurant continued the practice of offering top-flight entertainment by presenting bills consisting of orchestras, pop singers, burlesque dancers and comedians. House band duties were alternately filled by such acts as Sonny Kast and His Band, Billy Burke and His Band and Lee Mason's Orchestra. Pop singers to headline the night club included Jeannie Lee, Judy Sentino, Carman Velez, Kathy Mann, Nancy Ford, Marian Dawn, Dolores Rebel, Bobby Doyle, Norty Michels, Al "Luigi" Baker and Peggy Stevens.

The Hilltop Restaurant then made its mark in local rock and roll history when owners Lucy Gentile and Bayless Smith booked a band from Philadelphia called Murray Schaff's Aristocrats into their night club beginning the night of Tuesday, March 25, 1952. In what turned out to be a critical move in local music history, they used the full term "rock and roll" in local newspapers to advertise the band's extended appearances.

The night club then featured a number of highly regarded popular music acts of all styles in 1952 and 1953 including Lee Mason's Orchestra, the Riff Robbins Quartet, a trio called Plink, Plank, and Plunk (featuring former Red Caps singer Arthur Davey), the Louise Stuart Quartet, the duo of Kast and Abernathy, Billy Burke's Extraordinaires, the Jive Bombers, the Marveleers, the Goofers, the Dee Clements Band, Frank Motley and His Crew, the Heartbreakers, the Kirby Stone Quintet, Len Carrie and His Kracker Jacks, the Ink Spots and Duke Ellington and His Famous 15-piece Orchestra. In addition, other featured performers at the night club during those years were jazz saxophonist Arnett Cobb and such pop music singers as Betty Allyn, George Eades, Dee Darling, Nancy Ford, Paul Mann and Mel Torme.

The closing of the Hilltop Restaurant in September 1953 was quickly followed by the opening of a bottle club called the Lyre Club at the same address later that month. The Lyre Club fell under heavy surveillance from the local law enforcement authorities because of the gamblers it attracted, but managed to stay in operation until April 1956. The structure sat vacant for several months as new owners refurbished the building's interior and gave the exterior a much-needed facelift.

The Las Vegas Club opened for business under owner Bernadette Fletcher in the former Hilltop Restaurant and Lyre Club space on Thursday, September 13, 1956. The opening night bill was headlined by Al Dunn's Orchestra (featuring singer VeRonnee), an outfit that would serve as the house band for most of the next year. During its five-year run the night club offered floorshow entertainment featuring dancers, comedians and a variety of pop, rock and R&B bands. Ownership of the night club also changed surprisingly frequently during its existence and passed through the hands of such individuals as Roy Law and the three-man team of Robert Plympton, Isidor Schonberger and Bernard Fell.

Musical performers that worked the Las Vegas Club in the late 1950s included singer-pianist Mark Ruslander (he would later become political satirist Mark Russell), and a mix of pop and jazz acts that included the likes of Two Kings and Two Aces, Kitty Cutler and the Las Vegas Quartet, Sammy Ferro and His Trio, the Ted Efantis Quartet, the Tops, the Crawford Brothers, the Merry-Tones, the Vince Michael Trio and the Vince Fabrizio Trio. A number of pop singers were also featured late in the decade including Patsy Grady, Joe Lagana, Eddie Beavers, Spud Duto, Fran Grady, Ray Damore, Pete Horn and Patti Phillips.

Beginning in late 1958 and continuing throughout 1959 a number of C&W performers were booked into the Las Vegas Club including Dub Howington and His Tennessee Haymakers, Smokey Mac and His Rhythm Rockers, Smokey Mac and His Yellowstone Valley Boys and Roy Clark and His Stardusters. In 1960 and 1961 the format was wide open, with a number of different musical styles being offered to the public. Bands and musician to work the night club during that period included rock and roll acts such as the Naturals, the Downbeats, the Saxtons, Barry Darvell and the Blazers and the Three of Us Trio; R&B outfits such as the Ink Spots, Chet Ivey and His Band and the Pyramids; and C&W performers such as Bobby Stephenson and the Famous Four, singer-guitarist Buck Owens, Flatt and Scruggs, Hank Thompson and His Brazos Valley Boys and singer-fiddler-guitarist Benny Martin.

The Las Vegas Club closed on Thursday, September 21, 1961 and in December of that year the building burned to the ground. A McDonald's Restaurant occupied the site from 1967 to September 2013 and was subsequently razed. Since Sunday, December 14, 2014 the lot has hosted a 7 Eleven food store.

A little farther east down the roadway sat the Senate Inn, a legendary roadhouse whose address was originally listed as 5704 Marlboro Pike, Capitol Heights, Maryland. (In 1967 this building's address was changed to 5000 Marlboro Pike.) The building was constructed in the Hillside neighborhood of town in 1930 and served as a private residence until 1939, at which time it was purchased by Juell R. "Dick" Richardson, who was impressed by its night club potential.

In 1940 Richardson leased out the building to Eugene and Bernard Owens, who opened a gay night club on the premises called Club Esquire. This establishment was certainly unique for its time and during its two-year existence hosted floorshows featuring a plethora of male dancers and female impersonators. In May 1942 Otis Robinson, a previous owner of the Homestretch Tavern a bit further down Marlboro Pike, assumed the night club lease, had the liquor license transferred to his name, and renamed the business Club Bali, all the while maintaining its status as a gay club. In December 1942 Club Bali shut down and the female impersonators and their followers had scattered.

In January 1943 Dick Richardson took control of his property and named his new night club the Senate Inn. So began the odyssey of one of the region's most colorful establishments, a tough roadhouse that through its lifetime would offer almost every conceivable type of music and hosted a slew of incredible entertainers, both local in nature and nationally known. In the 1940s, however, things were slow to accelerate. House band for those years was Charlie Parrish and His Orchestra, with pop singer Lily Saunders and comedian Marty Aument making regular appearances.

In the 1950s Richardson stepped up the quality of entertainment and placed an emphasis on "Exotic Revues" – nightly shows that featured a small house orchestra, an emcee-comedian, a featured pop singer or band, and a bevy of burlesque dancers that changed on a weekly basis.

From 1950 to 1954 the dancers were mainly backed up by Dee Clements and His Trio. When that house band took a short break from the action, groups that took their place included Peter Donak and His Orchestra, Al Dugan and His Orchestra, Charlie Parrish and His Orchestra, Rick Kenny and the Kentones, the Mello Rhythm Boys, the Senators, Jimmy Vallin and His Merrymakers and Lou Rossi and His Orchestra.

During those years some of the featured pop singers to appear at the Senate Inn were June Elliott, Bobby Doyle, Prairie Sue, Vicki Lynn, Bascom Doyle Smith, Sandy Moss, June Martin, Lee Barry, Johnny Fortune, Armen Camp, Allen Kane, Grady Wilson, Lucille Marra, Betty Lynn, Rena Lyndon, Toni Rae, Johnny Fortune, Don Stephan, Bunny Rose, Sandy Moss, Grady Wilson, Betty Lynn, Lucille Marra and Don Stephan. C&W artists were also booked on occasion, with some of the biggest favorites being singer-guitarist Smitty Smith, and the singing duo of Lily and Curly (Lily Pickens and Sloan "Curly" Kimbler).

Noteworthy emcee-comedians of this period to handle the Senate's stage were Ezra Candler, Louise Potter, Danny Bishop, Russ Byron, Hal Nevers, Johnny Gilford, Tommy Rizzo and Tommy Monaghan. In addition, the club's exotic revues featured such burlesque dancers as Marlene O'Hara, Margie Gray, Wanda Lee, Princess Leilani, Rita Grable, Terri Lane, Cynthia Ames, Kitty King, Margerita Sparks, Judy Carroll, Mitzi Dallas, Sherry Kelly, Carol Dawn, Gloria Jean, Lorraine Sterling, Jean Carson, Dawn Jabot and Maxine Sullivan.

In 1955 Dee Clements and his band left the Senate Inn and their place was filled by a succession of pop music ensembles including Lou Rossi and His Men of Music, Freddie Merkle and His Orchestra, Buddy Garrison and His Quartet and Bob Massey and His Orchestra. Featured singers during the year included Ken Arthur, Lucille Marra, Joyce Dunn, Toni Garrett, Mark Leonard and Terry Gayle.

In 1956 Bob Massey and His Orchestra took over as the house band of choice and singer Rena Lyndon was featured nightly. When Massey took a weekend off, other groups to be called upon for duty included Peter Donak's Band, Charlie Parrish's Band and Al Graps and His Band. These groups continued to provide the musical backing for the floorshows that featured comedians such as Bill Roberts, Paul East, Jack High, Johnny Henderson, Danny Bishop, Jerry Sheldon, Bobby O'Day and Johnny Frisco, and exotic dancers such as Lois Lee, Polly Rochelle, Gloria Jean, Dixie Darling, Judy Gibbs, Beverly Styles, Justine Judge, Lana London, Luna Rose, Pat Storm and Dawn Jabot.

In October 1956 the Senate Inn introduced rock and roll to its patrons when they booked the Super Jets, a popular quartet in the night clubs of Marlboro Pike. The kept the band on their bills for weeks at a time throughout the late 1950s, adding variety to what was already an eclectic mix of entertainment offerings.

From 1957 to 1959 the Senate Inn continued to offer the exotic revues, with a number of house bands coming and going, including Charlie Parrish's Band, the Ken White Orchestra and the Sophistikats. Rena Lyndon remained the club's featured singer, with guest appearances made by other pop singers such as Mardi Emerson and Bob Marco. Emcee-comedians to pass through during this period included Bobby O'Day, Johnny Henderson, Jerry Sheldon, Paul East, Jeff Davis, Billy Rosser, Paul East, Johnny Savoy, Johnny "Rubberface" Frisco, Allen Reno, Jack High, Buddy Dean and Louise Potter. Top exotic dancers to perform were Marla Grant, Diane Duvall, Sunny Pierce, Lisa Andre, Bonnie Peel, Flame O'Hara and Fern Monahan.

As the decade rounded out, comedian Mickey Rooney appeared as emcee for a week-long engagement that lasted from Monday, December 29, 1958 to Saturday, January 3, 1959. He actually headed what was billed as a "Sensational Exotic Revue" that consisted of Debby Day (dazzling exotic star), Sunny Pierce (wow!), Diane Duval (daring!), Terri Russell (sex-otic), dancing to the Sophisti-Kats, and Rooney himself handling the ceremonies. At this point in time, the 39-year-old Rooney had already appeared in more than 100 feature-length motion pictures and dozens of stage productions and television shows. Unfortunately, despite his celebrity, he reportedly ran into money problems and in the late 1950s returned to theatrical productions and night club work to stay connected with the entertainment industry. At the time it was still a great surprise to see him booked into a rollicking Prince George's County roadhouse like the Senate Inn.

Changes hit the Senate Inn when, in early 1960, live music became the primary entertainment with the dancing girls being slowly phased out. Bands that worked the club from January to August of 1960 included the Sophistikats and two rock and roll groups, the Three Jacks and the Perry Mates.

The club then adopted a C&W format in September 1960 when the Texas Wildcats (fiddler Buck Ryan, rhythm guitarist Herbie Jones, banjoist Smitty Irvin and lead guitarist Jack Leadbetter), an outfit that had previously backed singer Jimmy Dean, took over as the house band. From late 1960 through 1965 other bands and musicians to perform at the Senate Inn included: bluegrass acts such as Don Reno and Red Smiley and the Tennessee Cutups, the Stanley Brothers (Carter and Ralph), the Clinch Mountain Boys, and singer Mac Wiseman; C&W acts such as Dub Howington and the Tennessee Haymakers, the Western Swingsters (featuring steel guitarist Johnny "Pancake" Norris), and the Justis Brothers; singer Patsy Cline; singer-guitarists Billy Grammer, Roy Clark, Smitty Smith, Little Jimmy Dickens and Marvin Rainwater; singer-guitarist-comedian Lonnie "Pap" Wilson; the husband-and-wife duo of singer-banjoist Grandpa Jones and fiddler Ramona Jones; banjoist Donnie Bryant; and rockabilly singer Wanda Jackson.

In 1966, another change was implemented and the Senate Inn began booking R&B bands. This format only lasted for two years and some of the groups to perform were Little Charles and the Reflections, Little Teddy and the Soul Set, King Henry and the Four Knights, Steve Charles and the Prodigals and Big Al Downing and His Band. In 1968 C&W music was reinstated and Dub Howington and the Tennessee Haymakers served as house band until the end of 1969. In the early 1970s regular attractions at the Senate Inn included the Deltas, Rambunctious, Tobacco Road and the Rosslyn Mountain Boys. Because of the increasingly rough nature of its clientele, the Senate Inn ended live music in 1973, but remained a local watering hole until closing for good in April 2007. The building was torn down without fanfare in September 2014 and its former space is now nothing more than a vacant lot.

Maryland Club Gardens was an amazing night club complex that sat 0.8 miles east of the Washington, D.C. line on a 42-acre parcel of land at the edge of the Hillside neighborhood which at the time was marked 6100 Marlboro Pike, Capitol Heights, Maryland. Opened to the public in 1934 by the husband-and-wife couple of Emil "Eddie" Stamm and Mary Inez "Dolly" Stamm, Maryland Club Gardens was a cabaret entertainment center which consisted of a two-story main building that housed a large dining area and aluminum-walled ballroom, the entrance of which was bordered by silver-green walls leading to a large, horseshoe-shaped crystal bar with a staggered front and mirrored back. The interior of the building was decorated with a variety of marbled wing figures throughout and featured a lighted, bubbling fountain. Immediately in front of this main building sat an Olympic-sized, color-lighted swimming pool, with a long terrace balcony overlooking it and a stage across the water on the opposite side. Scores of tables were scattered around the pool area and throughout the great outdoors, each adorned with beach umbrellas, comfortable seating, and an array of party favors. Picnic tables were strategically placed on the grounds surrounding the Maryland Club Gardens.

Lavish floorshows were the main attraction of Maryland Club Gardens, with great programs of professional entertainment presented on a nightly basis. Even more celebrated – though only discussed in hushed tones – was the legendary, unmarked apartment above the bathhouse next to the pool that was kept by Dolly Stamm and served as her own private party room for a seemingly endless parade of lifeguards, waiters, bartenders, musicians, club patrons and special guests of all persuasions. Mrs. Stamm was described as a big woman with auburn hair and icy blues eyes who loved to dance the night away with almost any man aside from her husband and reportedly primed herself for each evening by downing two bottles of Johnny Walker black label after dinner.

Entertainment at Maryland Club Gardens was quite impressive, with local musicians employed in house band positions for months at a time and nationally known entertainers brought in for special occasions. For most of 1934 Maryland Club Gardens offered a floorshow anchored by Fran Trappe's Garden Orchestra which featured emcee Bryan McDonald, baritone singer Charles Mayer, blues singer Helen Wright, the dance team of Janis and Jeanet and fan dancer Joan Miller. In 1935 some of their regular headliners were: Al Barkley and His New Yorkers, the Three Harmonics, Sid Allan and His Orchestra, Jimmy Harris and His Orchestra and Luzak and His Violin; accordionist Bob Dunnington; blues singer Sally Winston; pop singers Marjorie King, Sherry Louise and Gracie Barrie; and the ballroom dance team of Lewis and Peggy Harper.

The remainder of the 1930s saw a tremendous array of pop music entertainers grace the Maryland Club Gardens terrace stage including: Charlie Jeter and His Orchestra, Harold Veo and His Orchestra, the Lou Williams Orchestra and the Three Betas; singers Ben Alley, Dave Barnum, Lou Williams, Sydney Void, Virginia Simms, Lucille Wray, Honey Davis, Wanda Dean, Phyllis Page and Priscilla Bennet; accordionist Joe Cravers; pianist Ann Curwood; and organists Ann Leaf. In addition, a number of different professional dancers worked the club including Erma Lane, Mary Eller, Frances Black, Hillary Gabriel, Gail Lee, Joan Miller, Leila Salipsky, the team of Alma and Roland and tap dancer Walter Doe.

In 1940 Maryland Club Gardens brought in an all-female orchestra known as Nadine's Coeds as its house band and also booked such pop music performers as Peggy Dennis' Continentals, singers Louise Chandler and the Sidney Boys and guitarist Bob Miller. At this time the night club came under intense law enforcement scrutiny when reports began circulating that the establishment was ignoring the provisions set forth in its liquor license by continuing to service its patrons around-the-clock on weekends. Reportedly, a group of local, high-ranking law enforcement officers were determined to force Eddie and Dolly Stamm out of business and eager to usher in Washington, D.C. gambling baron and Maryland Athletic Club proprietor Jimmy LaFontaine, who was waiting in the wings to pick up the pieces and convert the property into a gambling casino. (Ironically, Eddie Stamm had previously worked at LaFontaine's Bladensburg Road casino before acquiring Maryland Club Gardens.)

The Stamms shrugged off rumors of an impending visit by law enforcement officials and reportedly were genuinely surprised when, early on the morning of Sunday, October 20, 1940, an eight-man squad of Maryland State Police, under the orders of state's attorney H. Winship Wheatley, Jr. and directed by Sgt. W.H. Conroy, conducted a raid on the Maryland Club Gardens on charges of selling liquor after-hours.

Arrested that morning were waiter Mike Ruiz and waitress Joan Karee who were both charged with selling liquor without a license. The Stamms were gently persuaded by unknown parties to abstain from fighting the charges, relinquish the club's liquor license, and sell the property to the first bidder who came along. Within a year Jimmy LaFontaine had bought the property and reopened Maryland Club Gardens as a high-powered gambling casino, without any offerings of live entertainment. With LaFontaine's passing in November 1949 the establishment shut its doors for good.

The abandoned Maryland Club Gardens property was sold to a group of doctors in November 1954. They refurbished the buildings and the swimming pool and opened the Oakcrest Country Club on its grounds on Saturday, May 28, 1955. The club was closed in 1967 and its buildings sat vacant until the Maryland National Capital Park and Planning Commission, which had purchased the property in July 1970, opened the Oakcrest Community Center there in May 1971 (its new street address was 5200 Marlboro Pike, Capitol Heights). The original restaurant building of Maryland Club Gardens remained standing and was used as a boxing training center until the spring of 1982, at which time it was torn down and replaced with a ball field. Today the former site of Maryland Club Gardens hosts two large buildings: the Oakcrest Community Center (1300 Capitol Heights Boulevard, Capitol Heights); and the William Hall Academy (5200 Marlboro Pike, Capitol Heights).

Not far down the road from where Maryland Club Gardens once stood was a lesser-known live music establishment of great interest. In June 1946 Ethel Thomas purchased the Roadside Café, which had been built in 1936, and renamed it Detta's Musical Bar (The original address of this night club was 6254 Marlboro Pike, Capitol Heights, Maryland; it was changed to 5256 Marlboro Pike in 1967).

The entertainment menu at Detta's Musical Bar was diverse for its time and location. Among the pop music bands to work this establishment in the late 1940s and into the early 1950s were Tony Gaudio and His Orchestra, the Star Dust Quintet, the Tune Twisters, the Rhythm Four and the Duffy Trio. Other headliners included pop singer Jerry Toronto and blues singer-pianist Ola Mae Bishop.

Detta's Musical Bar closed in the middle 1950s, reopened for a short while as Jack Maggio's Whitehouse Restaurant, and in 1956 was converted into a night club called Billy's Tavern. Among the local musical entertainers to appear at Billy's Tavern in the late 1950s were: C&W bands Roy Brown and the Texas Swingsters and Roy James and His Outlaws; and rock and roll groups such as Charlie Burgee and His Sophisticators, the Louis Ray Trio, Bobby Stephenson and His Rock and Roll Band and the Four Jacks. In August 1979 Billy's Tavern was replaced by Oakcrest Liquors, which is still in business at this location today.

A couple blocks away from Detta's Musical Bar was a country music roadhouse called the Homestretch Tavern, which was in operation from 1928 to 1972. (The original address of this night club was 6301 Marlboro Pike, Capitol Heights; it was changed to 5401 Marlboro Pike in 1967; the building was torn down shortly after its closing.) The Homestretch Tavern's golden years were the 1950s, during which time it welcomed in such C&W performers as Jimmy Dean and the Texas Wildcats, Bill Peer and His Melody Boys (featuring singer Patsy Cline), the Maryland Playboys, Dub Howington and the Tennessee Haymakers, the Orbits (featuring Don and John Presley) and Smokey Mac and His Twilighters; singer-guitarist Roy Clark; comedian Tiny Jenkins; and the jazz band known as the Capital City Dixielanders.

Further out on Marlboro Pike in Forestville, Maryland, approximately 3.2 miles east of the Washington, D.C. line sat another one of the region's top night club attractions, Griffith Farms. Situated one-third of a mile down a single-lane dirt road off the main highway in the middle of an 80-acre parcel of farmland (today that dirt road has been paved and renamed Donnell Drive), Griffith Farms was actually an old, Colonial-style plantation house that had been refurbished and prepped for use as a public restaurant and night club. It was owned for many years by George Griffith and featured a large dining area and a screened-in brick terrace where orchestras provided dance music for dinner guests and visitors. The surrounding grounds were filled with broad lawns, stately trees, umbrella-topped tables and gaggles of clucking chickens that were given free reign over the land and thoroughly aggravated more than a few guests.

From June 1935 to June 1939 Griffith Farms featured such bands as Brick Dornin and His Varsity Six Orchestra, Raymond and His Hawaiian Serenaders, Bill Cassi and His Orchestra, Manuel Bofill and His Filipino Orchestra, Happy Walker's Band, the Three Hawaiians and accordionist Charlie Bates.

In June 1939 Tom O'Donnell took over the establishment, changed the name to O'Donnell's Farm and kept the business in operation until October 1952. Soon after closing the restaurant, O'Donnell sold the property to developers, who began clearing the land in March 1957 for a future center of commerce. On Thursday, November 19, 1959 the Pen Mar Shopping Center opened on the farm's former site. For those in search of the approximate location of the old plantation house, its general area is occupied by BB&T Bank (3448 Donnell Drive, Forestville).

Joining the popular strips of Rhode Island Avenue, Bladensburg Road, Central Avenue and Marlboro Pike were two additional Prince George's County roadways that hosted several notable night clubs during the post-Prohibition era. These two avenues, Southern Maryland Pike, which in the 1930s became known as Branch Avenue, and Livingston Road, which was widened and renamed Indian Head Highway in 1948, both exited the Southeast quadrant of Washington, D.C., traveled through parts of Prince George's County which had the time had a distinctly Southern feel, and led away from the city to more rural sections of Southern Maryland. Branch Avenue was home to two now-legendary Silver Hill night spots, the Quonset Inn and Strick's Restaurant, while Indian Head Highway boasted the Sunnybrook Tavern.

From 1934 to 1943 a gentleman named Alexander Matthews owned a watering hole called the Alex Tavern that was located just over the Washington, D.C. boundary line at 3225 Naylor Road in Silver Hill, Maryland, a roadway that closely paralleled Branch Avenue. In 1947 he tore down the tavern building, cleared the land, and had a unique Quonset hut constructed in its place. He named his new establishment the Quonset Inn and began booking all types of musical entertainment.

Among the pop music acts to appear at the Quonset Inn from 1947 to 1949 were the Al Shea Trio, Art Calevas and His Orchestra, the Sammy Ferro Trio, the Jones Brothers, the Magic Notes (featuring singer Toddy Stewart), the Novel-Aires, Curley Fox and His Quintet, Dick Bailey and His Quartet, Pete Donak's Dance Band, the Tunesmen, the Four Tunes, the Four Robbins, the Five Kings, the Joe Venuta Quartet and the Mann Sisters Quartet. Other entertainers to perform at the Quonset Inn during those years included: singers Norma Sheppard, Valerie Lee, Nora Wells, Bob Eberly and Jack Leonard; accordionist Joyce Aimee; pianist Les Colvin; and singer-pianists Dee Lloyd McKay, Lee Carroll and Dot Furlette.

On Thursday, July 17, 1952 the Quonset Inn changed its name to the Quonset Supper Club and through the years experienced a number of different owners including legendary gambler Sam Wong, Alice Meyers, Catherine McCully, George Bopp, Edward Hines, Daniel Volm and Madeline David. All of the night club's proprietors showed a commitment to maintaining the establishment's status as one of the area's leading popular music venues. The Quonset Supper Club contributed to a unique entertainment zone by offering evening floorshows that usually featured a house orchestra, a headlining group or vocalist and a variety of comedians and dancers.

From 1950 to 1952 some of the pop music orchestras that held house band duties at the Quonset included Al Shea and His Trio, Jack "Jive" Schafer and His Orchestra, Frankie Condon's Band, the Lee Maxfield Orchestra, Les Elgart and His Orchestra, Bill Beach and His Orchestra (featuring singer Diane Jayson), Lee Mason's Band, Carr Von Sickler's

Quartet and Peter Donak's Orchestra. Other featured groups and musicians to perform during this time were the Four Blues, the Four Tunes, the Tune Twisters, the duo of singer Dell Adams with pianist Tommy Howe, the Fred and Faye Wakefield Trio, the Solidaires, the Three Galli Sisters, the Charioteers and the Tic-Tac-Toe Trio. Also to headline were the Singing Cowboy Johnny Wise, pianists Maurita Gordon and Tommy Chase and R&B singer Earl Plummer.

This early 1950s period also saw the Quonset Supper Club offer a number of highly regarded pop singers such as June Elliott, Berry Frank, Betty Cardinal, Vicki Villani, June Morgan, Mary Elaine, Nikki Williams, Vicki Lynn, Kathy Mann, Nancy Ford, Sunny Amber, Eddie Kinley, Carol Knight, Karen Andrews and Ted Ruddick. Visiting comedians included Charlie Taylor, Isabelle Dawn and Harry Shafran, and favorite burlesque dancers of the day were Beverly Styles and Pat "Amber" Halladay.

The year 1953 was a pivotal period for the Quonset Supper Club, as they moved towards rock and roll for the first time by pairing the dynamic pop singer Mary Martell with the Three Jacks, a band that would soon be billed as a rock and roll outfit at various night clubs in the area. The Three Jacks went on to work such area establishments as Maynard's Restaurant, the Romano Inn and the Wheel Bar. During their residence at the Quonset Supper Club, it appears the Three Jacks mainly covered general pop music and the latest hit singles on the Billboard charts. Other pop acts to be featured at the night club that year included Eddie Beavers and His Band, Buddy Garrison and His Quartet, the Four Jays and pianist Dick Wade.

In 1954 the Three Jacks continued to make appearances at the Quonset Supper Club. Arriving on the scene that year was the pop music outfit known as Al Dunn and His Orchestra (featuring singer VeRonnee). Dunn's band remained the house band throughout the remainder of the 1950s and often worked shows in conjunction with pianist Tommy Chase.

As the decade rounded out some of the other pop and jazz bands to work the Quonset Supper Club included the Sammy Ferro Trio, the Lou Rossi Band (featuring singer Ted DeFrancis), the Nephews, the Gene Bonnike Trio, the Bill Jackson Combo, the Eric Stevens Quartet, the Krazy Kats and the Jazz Bombers. Also headlining were pop singer Monica Layne, pianists Tony Ryan and Hal Thornton and saxophonist Hector Barroso.

Throughout the 1960s the Quonset Supper Club brought in a variety of pop and rock and roll entertainers and among the more popular attractions were Jimmy Vee and the Scamps, Joe Bruce and His Steppers, the Nini Baker Trio, the Tommy Charles Trio, Mildred Kohler and the Galaxies, Crystal Dawn and the Day Breaks, Mildred Kohler and the Celebrities, Rickie and the Gents, the Saxtons, the Naturals, Tommy Cole and the Belvederes (featuring singer Richie Kay), Take Five, singer Johnny Staggs, pianist Tommy Fessler and comedian Dave Astor.

During the 1970s the Quonset Supper Club began experimenting with different forms of music and entertainment, bringing in everything from national R&B acts like the Drifters and the Coasters to local rock bands like Sugar Bear, Libra and Tahoka. In the 1980s and 1990s the club turned towards an R&B-flavored schedule. The Quonset Supper Club changed owners and on Wednesday, December 22, 1993 was converted into the Legend Restaurant and Night Club, which maintained live music and catered to a Black clientele. In May 2013 the Legend went out of business and the building has been vacant ever since.

Strick's Restaurant was built just steps away from the Washington, D.C.-Maryland line in 1934 by Julius H. Strickland, a Colonial Beach, Virginia native who relocated to Kentland, Maryland as Prohibition was winding down. He and his wife Agnes chose to enter the restaurant business and decided to give his new establishment a portion of the family name. (In somewhat confusing fashion, the street address of Strick's Restaurant from 1934 to 1966 was listed in local phone directories as 3350 Naylor Road SE, Washington, D.C. despite the fact the building actually sat on the Prince George's County side of the dividing line – an official change was made to the building's current address of 3211 Branch Avenue, Silver Hill, Maryland on Sunday, July 31, 1966.)

After years as a neighborhood bar and eatery Strickland brought in a local trio known as the Mello Rhythms in the early 1950s to perform light jazz music for his restaurant's customers. On Thursday, February 11, 1954 Giles E. Fletcher Sr. of Hillcrest Heights, Maryland purchased the restaurant, added a new stage and dance floor area and redesigned its interior space to accommodate 110 patrons. He quickly transformed the establishment into one of the Washington, D.C. area's most popular C&W night clubs.

Bars and night clubs dotted the Branch Avenue corridor during the post-Prohibition years, with a rough-and-tumble roadhouse called Yesterday's situated close behind Strick's Restaurant, the Quonset Inn going strong with their pop music orchestras and singers a block away, and the Half Shell Restaurant, another smallish bar that booked local rock and roll bands, situated directly across the highway from these establishments. In addition, not far from Strick's Restaurant were two popular C&W night clubs, the Village Barn on Suitland Road in Morningside, and the Sunnybrook Tavern on Indian Head Highway (then called Livingston Road) in Oxon Hill. Strick's Restaurant combined with all of these night spots to create a unique and exciting zone of revelry that attracted patrons from all over the Washington, D.C.'s developing metropolitan area.

Throughout 1954 some of the area's best C&W performers worked at Strick's Restaurant including: bands such as Frankie Robinson and the Virginia Playboys, the Cactus Mat Trio (singer-accordionist Stoney Rigsby, guitarist Jimmy Groves and steel guitarist Dickie Thompson), Smokey Mac and His Sons of the South, the Roane Brothers, Jimmy Dean and the Texas Wildcats (featuring guitarist Roy Clark), the Four Pirateers, Buddy Gayer and His Ranch Hands and the Sunset Ramblers; singer Miss Dale Turner; singer-guitarist Jack Rodgers; and singer-steel guitarist Johnny "Pancake" Norris.

In 1955 the regular house band at Strick's Restaurant was the Cactus Matt Hillbilly and Western Band, which had changed its name but still consisted of Rigsby, Groves and Thompson along with singer Miss Dale Turner and singer-guitarist Jack Rodgers. In addition, bands such as the Pirateers, the Sunset Ramblers and Frankie Robinson and the Virginia Playboys continued to make nightly appearances throughout the year.

One of the more important footnotes in the musical history of Strick's Restaurant is that the legendary singer Patsy Cline performed there every Sunday afternoon as the featured singer of Bill Peer and His Melody Boys from Sunday, March 6 through Sunday, September 11, 1955. Other headliners at the night club during the year included the Matt Matson Quartet, Bill Pollard and His Pleasant Valley Boys, Al Gardner and His Quartet, Reds Goatee and His Mountain Boys and Country Thomas and His Dixieland Swing Band (featuring drummer Eddie Phyfe). Special attractions in 1955 included singer-guitarists Dick Williams and Billy Grammar, guitarist Scotty Johnson, fiddler-pianist-vibraphonist Johnny Foster and comedian Tiny Jenkins.

Rock and roll music was first introduced to Strick's Restaurant when Charlie Burgee and the Sophisticators were added to their bills beginning Friday, February 17, 1956 (ads in the Washington Daily News newspaper proclaimed the saxophone-playing band leader as "Rock and Roll Charlie"). C&W was still the music of choice, though pop and rock and roll bands were often booked for special engagements.

Bands to work Strick's Restaurant in 1956 also included the Cactus Matt Hillbilly and Western Band (which was now a quartet with Rigsby, Thompson and Groves being joined by singer Frankie Robinson), Ed Beavers and His Five Beavers, Jimmy Dean and the Texas Wildcats, the Buckskins, the Four Rhythm Rockers, Stoney Rigsby and the Dixie

Dudes, Dub Howington and the Tennessee Haymakers, Ernie Armand and His Vikings, Bob Kessler and His Rhythm Rocket Boys, the Buddy Garrison Quartet, the Lazy River Boys (a quartet consisting of singer Clyde Bowie, guitarist Aubrey Warder, steel guitarist Ray Chillum and bassist Roy Brown), and the Country Lads. Other featured C&W performers included: singer-guitarists Smitty Smith and Billy Grammar; steel guitarist Zack Allen; the house rhythm section of bassist Bob Elliot and drummer Jimmy Burkett; comedian Tiny Jenkins; and pop singer Jerry Toronto.

In 1957 and 1958 a mix of old favorites and rising newcomers were commingled at Strick's Restaurant. Among those bands that topped the bills were: the Texas Swingsters, Dub Howington and the Tennessee Haymakers, the Moonshiners (featuring singer Dick Williams), Doc Bartley and His Country All Stars, the Blue Grass Champs, Smokey Mac and His Twilighters, Smokey Mac and His Yellowstone Valley Boys and Roy Clark and His Stardusters (a quartet that also included singer-guitarist Jack Rodgers, steel guitarist Ray Sherman and drummer Duke Maddox). Other headliners included: singer Joe Lagana; singer-bassist Mary Klick; singer-guitarist Billy Grammer (whose band consisted of fiddler Buck Ryan, banjoist Smitty Irvin and drummer Duke Maddox); comedian Tiny Jenkins, and Jerry Toronto's Amateur Talent Show (featuring bands such as the Bobolinks and the Rhythm Makers).

By 1959 Strick's Restaurant's primary headliners were two different C&W music acts – the Texas Wildcats (minus lead singer-accordionist Jimmy Dean, who had moved on to host his own television show in New York) and Roy Clark and His Stardusters. In addition, a number of local rock and roll bands like the Naturals and the Three of Us Trio were regularly featured. Some of the better-known C&W acts to make special guest appearances that year were singer-guitarist Billy Grammer, singer-bassist Mary Klick and the ventriloquist act of Alex Houston and Elmer (the dummy). Also, the popular Sunday afternoon jam sessions that had long been a staple at Strick's Restaurant often featured Roy Clark and His Stardusters facing off opposite Charlie Daniels and His Jaguars throughout the year.

In the 1960s Strick's Restaurant continued on with a unique mix of C&W and rock and roll entertainment. Bands and musicians to appear at the night club during this decade included Roy Clark and the Stardusters, the Three of Us Trio, the Sportsmen, the Fabulous Furies, the Rivieras (featuring singer Carole Church), the Naturals, Danny Denver and the Sound Tracks (featuring guitarist Roy Buchanan), the Saxtons, Lamont and the All Stars (featuring drummer TNT Tribble), Tommy Cole and the Belvederes, Little Hugh and the Embers, the Starliters, the Nine Kingsmen, Wanda Jackson and Her Party-Timers, the Wanderers, the Impacts, Eddie Shugart and His Pop-Tops, the String Masters (featuring singer Dick Williams), the Outlaws (featuring singer-guitarist Johnny Hopkins), Scotty Stoneman and His Little Fugitives, the Blue Grass Champs, the Rangers, Link Wray and His Ray Men, the Sundowners, the Country Kats, the Case Brothers, Take Five (featuring guitarist Danny Gatton), Fabulous King Henry and the Knights, the Gang, the Impossibles and Joe Miller and the Country Plowboys.

In the aftermath of the Riots of 1968 Strick's Restaurant suffered a decline in business. Beginning in 1970 its live music schedule was reduced to weekend-only C&W and rock and roll bands. In the early part of the decade musical acts to make appearances included Vallie Ray and the Rhythm Ramblers and Tobacco Road, the latter of which served as house band for most of 1971 and 1972.

The family and friends of Strick's Restaurant suffered a terrible tragedy when owner Giles Fletcher Sr. was shot and killed on the premises during an attempted robbery on Wednesday, July 25, 1973. The night club last offered live music in the spring months of 1975, with the last group to play the night club being A Special Blend, a largely instrumental jazz rock band from Hyattsville, Maryland consisting of singer-guitarist Dan Hovey, bassist Jim Earl, keyboardist Gary Harmon, saxophonist Dave Waldo and drummer Rex Wilson. Strick's Restaurant is still open today, but only as a liquor and package goods store.

The southernmost roadway of the group, Livingston Road (known more recently as Indian Head Highway), hosted a number of smaller bars in the post-Prohibition era. One of these, the Roadhouse, was opened in 1934 and became the Sunnybrook Tavern in 1945 (The original address of this establishment was marked 6980 Livingston Road, Oxon Hill, Maryland; the building's address was changed in the late 1960s to 9001 Livingston Road, Fort Washington, Maryland.) The Sunnybrook Tavern became known for its C&W entertainers and among those to perform there in the late 1950s included Dub Howington and His Tennessee Haymakers, Jimmy Dean and the Texas Wildcats, singer-guitarist Roy Clark and singers Patsy Cline and Miss Dale Turner. The original Sunnybrook Tavern building was torn down in early 1992, with a new structure being rebuilt on its lot and opened to the public on Thursday, March 12, 1992. It is still in operation today, though its glory days as a music venue are now just distant memories.

CHAPTER TWENTY-FOUR
SURROUND SOUNDS

Leading a charge of dynamic night clubs in Washington, D.C. that surrounded the rock and roll era was the Lotus Restaurant (727 14th Street NW), a Chinese and American restaurant that was owned by Mr. D.G. Lam and was opened to the public on Saturday, January 21, 1928. It immediately became one of Washington, D.C.'s most popular night spots when it featured Archie Slater's Lotus Restaurant Orchestra as its initial house band. Other top swing bands to appear on the Lotus Restaurant stage in 1928 and 1929 were Emory Daugherty and His Lotus Orchestra, Irving Boernstein and His Lotus Orchestra and Fred Slasor and His Lotus Orchestra.

In the 1930s the Lotus Restaurant expanded its entertainment schedule to include, in addition to a nightly house orchestra, floorshow revues that featured singers, comedians, dancers, magicians, acrobats, jugglers and almost every type of entertainer one could imagine. During this decade the programs were anchored by Bill Strickland's Capitolians, a swinging orchestra that featured singing emcee Al Norton. Some of the nationally known pop music singers that graced the Lotus Restaurant stage during this era were Charlie Mayer, Ray Donahue, Judy Ellington, Odette Borde, Lillian King, Virginia Sims, Evelyn Knight, Sally Winston and Marion Dawn.

From 1940 to 1945 manager Dick Lam maintained Bill Strickland and His Orchestra as the Lotus Restaurant house band, with Washington's own Buddy Shaner, a former basketball and football star at Central High School, as the featured singer. Some of the touring revues to appear during these years were Al Davis' Top Hat Revue, the Broadway Capers Revue (featuring comedian Harry Reso), the Fantasies Broadway Revue (featuring dancers Latasha and Laverne), Jim Wong's Vaudeville Troupe, the Marvelettes Revue (featuring dancer Joyce Graham), the Champagne Revue (featuring acrobatic dancer Patsy Marr), the Pretty Colleens Revue (featuring Bob and Betty DeWitt), the Blossom Revue (featuring the Eight Dancing Buds), the Swingette Revue (featuring a team of novelty singers called the Laska Sisters), the Rhythm Revue (featuring South American tap dancers Jason and Belle), the Parade of the United Nations (featuring singer-dancer Bunny Hare), the Strutting Along Revue (featuring dancer Peggy Kraft), and the Jean Davis Girl Revue (featuring singer Gloria Evans).

In addition, during these years bands like the Continental Trio and the Four Jitterbugs were welcomed attractions at the Lotus Restaurant and a number of individual singers made appearances including Dixie Roberts, Mary LaMarr, Leslie Hare, Yvonne Moray, Sheila Rogers, Judy Ellington and Patricia Lane.

In 1946 Bill Strickland and His Orchestra relinquished their post to Al Sokol's Orchestra, though Buddy Shaner remained as the primary emcee-singer for the remainder of the decade. During the latter portion of the 1940s the pop music entertainment remained strong, with appearances made by such bands as the Belmonts, the Three Arnauts (a musical novelty act), the Four Hearts and the Three Fontaines. Other featured acts included: singers Bob Preble, John Kirby, the Castle Sisters and the Dewey Sisters; fiddler Johnny Ladher; aerial acrobat Linda Ravel; magician Joan Brandon; and dance troupes called the Dancing Springers and Winnie Hoveler and Her Pretty Dancers.

More changes took place at the Lotus Restaurant late in the decade. In 1948 Jack Corry's Orchestra replaced Al Sokol's Orchestra and went on to work the night club on a regular basis all the way through 1957. During those years they anchored a floorshow format that usually featured an array of dancers, comedians and headlining singers. When Corry and his unit were unavailable, the club's first option was Sam Jack Kaufman and His

Capitol Orchestra. Among the more prominent performers at the Lotus Restaurant during the early 1950s were organist Nina Baker and such pop music singers as Buddy Shaner, Clara Mitchell, Lois King, Joyce Swanson, Marc Leonard, Jack Maggio and Cathy Johnson.

From 1955 to 1957 the cavalcade of stars continued at the Lotus Restaurant, with pop music vocalists the main attraction. Making appearances during these years were Norman Brooks, Rusty Draper, Alan Dean, Jackie Paris, Georgie Shaw, Burt Taylor, Bill Farrell, Lee Kane, Bob Eberly, Art Lund, Teddi King, Jackie Lee, Billy Fields, Felicia Sanders, Jo Ann Tolley, Pete Hanley, Alan Dean, Sonny Graham, Lillian Briggs, Ray Eberle, Bob Manning, Jim Lowe, Ralph Young, Helen Aimee, Lynn Roberts, Vicki Young, Terri Stevens, Alan Dale, the Baker Sisters, Steve Lawrence, Richard Hayman, Eileen Rodgers, Lou Monte, Anita Ellis, Bob Manning, Judy Lynn, Rita Raines, Mona Carol, Mae Sagan, Arlene Fontana, Connie Francis, Elaine Gordon, Eugenie Baird, Lee Kane, Helene Dixon, Jana Mason, Bob Carroll, Joe Valino, Bobby Darin, Janice Harper, Sam Cooke, Tony Reynolds, Danny Costello, Pete Hanley, Maureen Cannon, Arlene DeMarco, the Jaye Sisters, Gene Nash, Tina Robin, Billy Albert, Eugenie Baird, Trudy Richards, Maureen Arthur, Betty Summer, Don Rondo, Barbara McNair, Karen Chandler, Rudy Hansen, Johnny Mathis, Betty Johnson, Terri Stevens, Denise Darcel, Don Cherry, Dick Haymes, Don Cornell and Janice Harper. Among the headlining groups were Joe Maize and His Chordsmen, the Diamonds, the Four Coins and the Coronados.

In 1958 and 1959 headliners at the Lotus Restaurant included bands such as the Playmates, Woody Herman and His Orchestra, Johnny Puleo and His Harmonica Gang, the Four Preps, the Kirby Stone Four and the Will Mastin Trio (featuring singer Sammy Davis Jr.). Other attractions included: singer-pianist Liberace; and such comedians as Dave Astor, Sue Carson, Alan Drake and Phyllis Diller.

Featured singers during those years included Rusty Draper, Betty Madigan, Meg O'Shaughnessy, the Lane Brothers, Judy Scott, Marion Marlowe, Monique Van Vooren, Meg Lyles, Billy Albert, the Ardrey Sisters, Enzo Stuarti, Kay Brown, Laureanne Lemay, Kathy Barr, Jennie Smith, the Holly Twins, Betty George, the Bon Bons, Chanson D'Amour, Alan Copeland, Wyoma Winters, Bernadine Read, Beverly Kenney, Steve Karmen, Betty Anne Steele, Pat O'Day, Lyda Fairbanks, Don Rondo, Peggy King, the Poni Tails, Terri Stevens, Patricia Wilson, Norman Brooks, Denise Darcel, Ginny Simms, Gretchen Wyler, Kathy Crosby, Eileen Barton, Gwen Harmon, Gale Robbins, the Giovannis, Dolly McVey, Jo Ann Campbell, Coby Dijon, Joan Weber, Roger Coleman, Toni Carroll, Teddy Randazzo, Bob Eberly, Helen Darcel, Christine Jorgenson, Keefe Brasselle, Kathy Linden, Al Alberts, Alan Copeland, Helen Aimee, the Jamal Sisters, the Rover Boys, Sheila Reynolds, the Ink Spots, Teal Joy, Tom Allen, Ann Hathaway, Ralph Young, Jaye P. Morgan with the Morgan Brothers, the DeJohn Sisters, Meg Myles, Connee Boswell, the Andrews Sisters, Dick Roman, Billy Daniels, the Four Aces, Billy Eckstine, Lillian Briggs, Dor Ann Gray, Tony Martin, Patrice Wymore, Bob McFadden, the Barry Sisters, Betty Reilly, Helen Forrest, Bob Eberly, Al Alberts, Peter Palmer, Cathy Carr and Mary Lou Brewer.

In 1960 and 1961 the Lotus Restaurant offered bills topped by many nationally known entertainers. During those years, as the club's final days approached, some of the stars to perform were pop singers such as Ray Peterson, Diahann Carroll, Tommy Leonetti, Enzo Stuarti, Billy Eckstine, Nat King Cole, Paul Anka, Sammy Davis, Jr., Anita Bryant, Ruth Wallis, Al Alberts, the team of Eydie Gorme and Steve Lawrence, Frankie Laine, Beatrice Kay, Bobby Breen, Peter Palmer, Sunny Gale, Toni Fisher, Tina Scott, Roy Hamilton, Johnny Nash, Noreen Parker, Duke Hazlett, Linda Roman, the Kalin Twins, Bobby Rydell, Gene Barry, Brook Benton, Jack Basco, Frank Gari, the Andrews Sisters, Bobby Breen, Don Rondo, Bob Eberly and Paula Sydney.

Also making appearances those years were: groups such as Vaughn Monroe and the Four Voices, the Louis Prima Orchestra (featuring singer Keely Smith), the Nini Baker Trio, the Quaker City Boys, the Ed Dimond Orchestra, Gene Austin and His Whippoorwills and the Platters; rockabilly singer Crash Craddock; and comedians such as Al Mack, Lee Allen, Mort Sahl, Jackie Vernon, Stanley Dean, Buddy Lester, Dick Capri, Harry Shafran, Alan Gale, Rip Taylor and Mickey Rooney.

Due to the increased asking price of top-flight entertainers and a sharp drop in business, the Lotus Restaurant shut down operations in November 1961. One year later a People's Drug moved into its space, with the building address being changed to 717 14th Street NW. People's Drug became CVS Pharmacy on Thursday, May 5, 1994. Today that CVS still inhabits the old Lotus Restaurant building.

The Neptune Room (501 13th Street NW) appeared on the scene in the spring of 1939 in the basement of the Earle Theatre, a space that had previously been occupied from 1925 to 1929 by a night club called the Swanee. (The Warner Theatre took over from the Earle Theatre on Thursday, September 11, 1947 and is still in operation today with an updated address of 513 13th Street NW.) The Neptune Room, which was owned by Ramon Lurba, could accommodate some 400 patrons and projected an underwater theme replete with a long aquarium bar framed with marine blue mirrors and decked with colored inlays of octopi, sea horses and other oceanic creatures. The club opened on the night of Tuesday, April 11, 1939 to a packed house with Johnny De Leon and His Hawaiians leading the way.

From its opening through 1941 some of the top performers to work the Neptune Room included pop music singers Bert Granoff, Gene Archer, Alice O'Connell, Mary Martin, Earline King, and Leslie Hare. Organist Glen Hardman and pianists such as Evelyn Tyner, Grace Shannon and Johnny Hartsfield also topped many bills. Among the jazz and pop bands to headline the club during that period were Milt Herth and His Trio (advertised locally as "His Herth-Quake Trio"), the Danford Trio, the Blackfriars Players, the Dalton Boys, Joe Collins and His Mad Hatters, the Arnold Trio and Don Baker and His Musicomics.

Probably the Neptune Room's greatest historical booking occurred during this time when it served as the scene of singer-pianist legend-to-be Wladziv "Walter" Liberace's Washington, D.C. debut, who worked an extended engagement at the club from Saturday, September 20, 1941 until Friday, November 7, 1941.

Throughout the remainder of the 1940s the Neptune Room enjoyed visits by a number of outstanding pop music entertainers. Their ranks included Grant Thompson and His Swingcopators (featuring singer Penny Paige), Andy Padova's Streamliners, the Four Keyboard Orchestra (pianists Bob and Bertie Hellman along with organists Arlo and Collins), the Mat Jaffee Trio, Henry Daye and His Knights, Dave Roberts and His Rhythm Band, Billy Arnold and His Biggest Little Band in the World, Art Hinett and His Radio Rhythms, the Milt Raymond Trio, Bill Thompson's Gleesome 3-Some and Sammy Ferro and the Tidesmen. Other headliners included: singers Dennise Dawson and Kay Arden; organist Leonard Friendly; and pianists Dick Maguiness, Linda Johnson, Lynn Reynolds and Rodolfo Cornejo.

In the 1950s the Neptune Room hosted such pop music acts as the Carl Horvath Trio, the Billy Arnold Trio, the Manhattanites, Ralph and Buddy Bonds and their Twin Organs, the Triads, the Bill Thompson Trio, Art Swanson's Temptunaires, the Nye Mayhew Trio, the Connie Thomas Trio, the Charmers, the Dante Trio, the Teri Trio, the Ray Jenkins Trio, the Carmen Rios Trio, the Hal Hoffer Trio, the Milt Raymond Trio, the Larry Nolan Trio, the Musical Keyboards Trio and the Californians. Also featured were: pop singers Roger Miller and Linda Griner; singer-pianist Jesse Gunther; pianists Charmaine Berkley, John Gilder and Dorothy Lee; jazz pianist Ahmad Jamal; organists Maurice Fitchard, Lorette Charon, Renan Decamp and Sal Trippe.

In the 1960s the Ralph Hawkins Trio took over house band duties and remained the primary entertainers for several years. Numerous pianists were booked as headliners during this time including Paul Humphrey, Marianne Arden, Beatrice Grandet, Ilene Kelley, Connie Thomas and Irene Broni.

The Neptune Room closed in February 1966, with a short-lived discotheque called Arthur opening in its space in November 1968. Up above, the Warner Theatre persevered throughout the changes and still exists today as a popular concert venue in the nation's capital.

A couple blocks north of the Neptune Room was El Patio, which operated under its original moniker from 1940 to 1954 and then underwent a name change and remained in business as the Patio Lounge until 1957. When the Novelty Cafeteria closed its doors on the second floor of 711 13th Street NW in 1940, it didn't take long for Jimmy Flakas to come along and lease the vacant space for his new restaurant which he christened El Patio. With an interior that boasted the likeness of a Spanish castle (but, despite its name, did not offer any type of patio), El Patio was opened to the public on the night of Tuesday, October 15, 1940 with pianist Jack Campbell and singer Honey Dalzell headlining.

In its first 18 months El Patio featured an array of such pop music entertainers including: the Stylists; singers Lina D'Acosta and Virginia Joy; pianist Hildreth Harrison; organist Larry Hendricks; and accordionist Nick Hope. In 1942 the night club was sold to Johnny Longo, who, for the remainder of the decade and into the early 1950s, brought in several top popular music acts including: Don Rinaldo's Four Men of Note, the Four Men of Rhythm (featuring guitarist Dave Appel), the Four Toppers, the Adrian Rollini Trio, Little Jack Little and His Orchestra, Myles Hallett and His Orchestra, Rocco Terrone and His Continentals and Wally Taylor and His Trio; singers Kathleen Quinn, Anita Boyer, Justine Wayne and Vicki Lee; and guitarists Frank Victor and Roy Smeck.

In November 1954 the business was sold to Olivia Davis, who changed the name of the night club to the Patio Lounge and converted it into one of the city's most popular jazz night spots by bringing in top national talent. During its 26-month run, the Patio Lounge featured such performers as Joe Nardy's Combo, Dizzie Gillespie and His Orchestra, Stan Getz and His All-Stars, Miles Davis and His Quartet, the Ralph Sharon Trio, Lester Young and His All-Stars, the Modern Jazz Quartet, the Erroll Garner Trio, the Oscar Peterson Trio, the Roy Eldridge All-Stars, the Wild Bill Davis Trio, the Art Tatum Trio, the Billy Taylor Trio, Joe Loco and His Mambo All-Stars, George Shearing and His Quintet, George Wallington and His Trio, the Teddy Charles Trio (featuring double bassist Charles Mingus), Benny Green and His Quintet, Johnny Smith and His All-Star Combo, the Rick Henderson Quartet, Art Blakey and the Jazz Messengers, the Serge Chaloff Sextet, the Gerry Mulligan Sextet, Carmen McRae and the Australian Jazz Quartet, Bud Powell and His Trio, Johnny Smith and His Trio, the Ralph Sharon Trio (featuring singer Chris Connor), Gene Bonnike's Trio, Bobby Conway and His Dixie Six, Milt Buckner and His Trio, Gene Krupa and His Quartet, the Four Tunes, Al Cohn and His Quintet (featuring trumpeter Conte Candoli), the Bud Powell Trio, the Pia Beck Trio, the Eddie Phyfe Quartet, the Shirley Horn Trio, the Gerry Mulligan Sextet, the Paul Bley Trio, the Chet Baker Quintet, Paul Bley's Trio, the Herbie Mann Quartet, the Joe Saye Trio, Al Belletto's Sextet, the Phineas Newborn, Jr. Quartet, the Bobby Scott Trio, the Barbara Carroll Trio, the Bud Shank Quartet, the Matt Dennis Trio, the Zoot Sims Quintet, the Mitchell-Ruff Duo, the Don Shirley Duo, the Marion McPartland Trio, the Greco Quartet, the Villegas Trio, the Chico Hamilton Quintet, the New Jazz Quintet, the Buddy DeFranco Quintet, the duo of drummer Max Roach and trumpeter Clifford Brown, the duo of trombonist Kai Winding and trombonist J.J. Johnson, and the Bill

Potts Trio (which consisted of pianist Bill Potts, bassist Willie Williams and drummer Jim Lucht).

In addition, the Patio Lounge featured an array of individual jazz headliners during that period including: pianists Larry Boyd, Hampton Hawes, Meade Lux Lewis, Bruce Raeburn, Bernard Peiffer, Karl Coleman and Eugene Sermely; saxophonists Sonny Stitt and Johnny Hodges; and flutist Sam Most. Top-billed singers at the club included Patti Phillips, Terri Morel, Ann Read, Billie Holliday, Mel Torme, Jerri Southern, Herb Jeffries, Betty St. Clair, Ruth Brown, Joe Derise, Chris Connor, Teddi King, Al Hibbler, Beverly Kenney and Sarah Vaughan.

The Patio Lounge closed on Monday, January 14, 1957, and in what must be considered one of the fastest flips in Washington, D.C. area night club history, was replaced the very next day by the Peking Restaurant.

A couple blocks away from the Patio Lounge was the Merry-Land Club (1405 L Street NW), which Olivia Davis opened in March 1941 in a space previously occupied by the Tyrolean Brau Haus Restaurant. For much of its 37-year existence, the Merry-Land Club offered pop and jazz music and mixed local bands with occasional national acts.

During its first year the Merry-Land Club booked such entertainers as Jack Norman's Trio, the Paul Adams Trio, De Vaughn Clements and His Trio, singer Lorraine Provon and pianist Hildreth Harrison. In 1942 Al Norton and His Instrumental Trio was installed as the house band and held that position for the better part of three years, working with headliners such as: singers Mary LaMarr, Jean Lee and Alice Winstead; guitarists Paul Adams, Frank Flanigan and Keith Young; pianist Cliff Jones; vibraphonist Johnny Graham; and singer-accordionist Ward Duval.

Replacing Norton's group in 1944 were two main bands, Swanee's Trio (featuring singer Lorrie Lamm), and the Frank Oxley Trio (featuring singer Kitty McCormick). In 1945 one of the main headliners was a local jazz band called the Guardsmen, whose lineup consisted of singer Lorrie Lamm, guitarist Chick Howe, bassist Frank Corcoran and vibraphonist Johnny Graham. Other groups to work the club that year included the Tony Rand Trio, Dave Crocker's Trio and the Rollickers.

From 1946 to 1948 the Merry-Land Club mainly featured local talent and among the bands to regularly appear there were the Pat Monte Trio, the Debonairs, the Tony Rand Trio, the Four Jays (featuring singer Florence Lorraine), the Lee Foster Trio, the Allen McPaige Trio, Hope Arnold and the Gold Coasters, the Three Pages of Rhythm, the Merry-Tones, Roy Kyser's Trio (featuring singer Margie Dare) and the Ko-Ko Nuts (a trio consisting of Jack Norman, Ray Marshall and Dick Celdran). In addition, a number of individual performers headlined the club during these years including: singer Judy Ellington; singer-guitarist Bill Huggins; singer-pianists Shirley Allen, Hal Thornton and Erskine Butterfield; and organist Nate Shanks.

In 1949 a mix of talent enjoyed success at the Merry-Land Club including such groups as the Al Dunn Trio, the Ko-Ko Nuts, Jimmy Summerville and His Ohio Boys, the Merry Makers, the Merry-Tones, the Versatones (featuring singer Marian Caruso), the Dolores Vogue Trio, Three Aces and a Queen and the Golden Gate Quartet. Individual headliners that year included: guitarist Slim Gaillard; pianists Larry Campo, Hal Thornton, Count Smith, Art Tatum, Maurice Rocco, Eddie Heywood, Rose Murphy and Skeets Light; singer-guitarist-keyboardist Cass Cassano; and accordionist Ruth Hamilton. Jazz singers were also favored and giving performances that year were Pearl Bailey, Ella Fitzgerald, Savannah Churchill, Marion Bruce and Derry Falligant.

In the early 1950s the Merry-Land Club continued to offer a variety of well-known pop, jazz and R&B entertainers. Among the top groups they presented during that time were the Hey Jackson Quintet, the Rhythm Rascals, the Ko-Ko Nuts, the King Cole Trio, Lou Style and His Stylists, the Ray Marshall Trio, the Mary Ellen Quartet, the Fabulous McCormicks, the Novelaires, the Dell Trio, Lou Styles and the Stylists, the Merrylanders, the Stan Jasen Trio, the Norval Reid Trio, the Four Beavers, the Hot Peppers, the Dick Handel Trio, Haven Johnson and His Orchestra, Jack White and His Trio, the Tunesmiths, the Condijacs, the Jodijacs and the Todds. Also headlining were two highly regarded C&W bands, Jimmy Dean and the Texas Wildcats and Hawkshaw Hawkins and His Hillbilly Band.

During that period the club also featured a number of multi-styled pianists such as Art Tatum, Larry Campo, Kirby Walker, Denny Miles, Maurita Gordon, Tony Parker, Marion Page, Harry Taylor, Martin Rocklin, Jimmy Woods, Meade Lux Lewis, Maxine Adams, Frankie Dash, Mike Hunnicutt, Lee Black, Tommy Chase, Ralph Cooper, Johnny Knapp, Wayne Carmichael, Bill Seldon, Kenneth Shaefer, Hal Thornton and singer-pianist Rose Murphy. Other musicians to headline at that time included singer-guitarist Lazy Bill Huggins and organist Nate Shanks.

Among the Merry-Land Club's top singers of that time were Hadda Brooks, Bill Jacoby, Jimmy McPhail, Pearl Bailey, Bob Scott, Mildred Bailey, Ray Eberle, Stuart Foster, Bobby Breen, Bob Carroll, Lily Ann Carroll, Dick Todd, Sandy Evans, Bob Eberly, Patsy Abbott, Patti Phillips, Grady Wilson, Jackie Burns, Jack Wakefield and Jack Maggio.

In the late 1950s the Merry-Land Club entered its final era as a live music venue. At that time the club offered such outfits as the Bernard Peiffer Trio, Ray Marshall and the Ko-Ko Nuts (featuring singer Jack Maggio), the Bill Potts Quartet (featuring trumpeter Joe Bovello), the Mitchell-Ruff Duo, the Alex Kallao Trio, Bill Beach and the Band, Buddy Garrison and His Orchestra, the Eddie Phyfe Orchestra, the George Rice Band and the John Fichetti Band. Special attractions included R&B guitarist Bill Harris and several pianists including Tommy Maulding, Beryl Booker and Mark Russell. In addition their bills often featured talented pop singers such as Patsy Grady, Jeannie Smith, Joe Lagana, Rena Lyndon, Scotty Goings and Sunny Stewart.

In the 1960s the Merry-Land Club changed its format and primarily offered revues featuring dancers of all types, including programs of exotic and burlesque dance entertainment. They continued this practice throughout the 1970s up until its closing in January 1979. The structure was then demolished that summer to make way for 1101 Vermont Avenue, a 12-story office building which, since April 1981, has occupied the entire north side of L Street NW from 14th Street to Vermont Avenue NW.

Far across town in the Northeast quadrant of the city sat a smaller night club called the Melody Inn (1122 Bladensburg Road NE). The construction of this building began in September 1940 and a year later Angelo Scandolos opened the Melody Inn to the public. Black jazz entertainers were featured and among the more popular entertainers to grace its stage in the 1940s were singer Rita Grenae, pianist Tommy Chase and the Ray Jackson Trio.

Performers at the Melody Inn during the 1950s included: bands such as the Woody Woods Combo, Billy Fair's Band, Big Steve and His Combo, the Clovers, the Val-Tones and the John Malachi Combo; singers such as Paul Breckenridge, George Craft, Jimmy Moultrie, Dolores Brown, Harry Robinson, Betty Harris, Jimmy McPhail, Irma McGinnis, Betty Carter and Ethel Ennis; singer-pianist Freddy Cole; and comedians Redd Foxx (who appeared here regularly throughout 1958 and 1959), Shuffle McDonald, Nubby Neill and Willie Lewis.

In 1959 R&B singer Jimmy McPhail, who had appeared at the Melody Inn on a regular basis for years, purchased the business and renamed the night club Jimmy McPhail's Gold Room. He maintained the club's status as one of the city's hottest jazz spots until its closing in 1997.

Far off the beaten path in an area below the Marine Barracks, Washington, D.C. in the Southeast quadrant of the city was the Penguin Restaurant (1218 11th Street SE), which opened in December 1945 in the space formerly occupied by the Ralph Perry Restaurant. The Penguin offered an eclectic group of musical entertainers during its time.

From 1945 to 1947 the emphasis at the Penguin Restaurant was on blues and pop, with regular appearances made by: pop bands such as the Penguin Trio, Al Massey and His Band and Phil Genthner and His Orchestra (featuring singer George Gelser); blues singers such as Ola Mae Bishop, Grace Thomas and Nora Wells; and emcee-comedians Mel Walton and Bill Abbey.

From 1948 to 1950 the Penguin Restaurant was catering to a heavily Southern clientele and to appease the masses a number of country music bands were brought in including Franky French and His Band, Billy Strickland and His Hillbilly Gang, Bill Morfield and His Mountain Boys, Andy Burton and His Rhythm Rangers, Johnny Lee and His Band and Chubby Wise and His Florida Playboys. Other acts to headline included: pop bands such as the Tune Twisters (a quartet consisting of guitarist Ollie Haas, accordionist Pat Patterson, guitarist Andy Burton and bassist Hank Rowe) and Sonny Kast and His Icelanders; and the ever-present blues singer Ola Mae Bishop.

After the Penguin Restaurant closed in 1950, the building sat vacant for a year before reopening in October 1952 as the Booker T Restaurant, a Black night club with live music presented in a separate lounge they called the Flamingo Room. The building later housed a store called Thompson and Cook Hardware from 1956 to 1963 and was torn down in 1964.

Club Players (486 K Street NW) opened up in 1947 in a three-story building that been constructed in 1889 and for much of the early 20th century had housed the William Boyle Saloon. Replacing a short-lived bottle club called the Spotlight, Club Players staged floorshows which, though somewhat less lavish than what could be seen in competing night clubs such as the Casino Royal Theatre Restaurant, the Lotus Restaurant and the Merry-Land Club, offered interesting lineups of exotic dancers, comedian, dancers and live pop music entertainment.

In the early 1950s some of the more notable bands to work engagement at Club Players were Jimmy Lee and His Rhythm Maniacs, Phil Loria's Orchestra, Jimmy Sedlar Orchestra, Pete Pogue's Trio (featuring singer Warren Jackson), the Rhythm Kings, Al Dunn and His Orchestra (featuring singer VeRonnee) and the Bobby Wilkes Combo. Featured pop singers at the club during these years included Nora Wells, Betty Combs, Bob Preble, Johnny Fortune, Jerry Toronto, George Eades, Gene Cunneff, Gene Ford and Bobby Todd. In addition, an array of comedians and exotic dancers rounded out every nightly show.

Club Players became known as the launching point for the Kalin Twins, the popular local singing duo that had a major hit single on Decca Records called "When," which entered the Billboard magazine's "The Billboard Hot 100" music popularity pop records chart on Monday, June 30, 1958 and peaked at number five on Monday, August 4, 1958 (it remained on the Top 40 charts for 12 weeks). A follow-up single, "Forget Me Not," peaked at number 12 on "The Billboard Hot 100" chart on Monday, October 27, 1958.

The Kalin Twins, Hal and Herb, hailed from Port Jervis New York and entered the world of pop music early in their lives. After graduating from Port Jervis High School in 1952, Hal Kalin joined the United States Air Force and was sent to Japan and Herb Kalin developed a night club act based on the style of pop singer Johnnie Ray. In June 1953 Herb moved to Washington, D.C. and began working the stage at Club Players, first under his own name and then later on under the moniker of Buddy Ladd. Herb remained at Club Players well into 1957, at which time brother Hal decided to join him onstage as Nicky Ladd and they performed as the Ladd Twins. The brothers soon struck a deal with Decca Records, began using their given name, and scored big with the smash hit single "When." Backing the pair up during these years at Club Players was the Bobby Wilkes Combo, which maintained house band status at the night club throughout much of the decade.

During the 1950s other top attractions at Club Players included: pop singers such as Shirley Neal, June Hayes, Joe Lagana, Rena Lyndon and Valerie Ellas; R&B singer Don Covay; exotic dancers such as Judy Gibbs, Sue Travis, Margie Grey, Bonita Secret, Stunning Smith, Bobbi Rogers, Louise Angel, Bobbi Collins, Ruth York, Venus DeCarlo and Sandra Sears; and comedians such as Art Baker, Dan E. Bishop, Buzz Barrie, Ralph Sherman, Johnny Frisco, Charlie Delmar and Barry Thomas.

In the 1960s Club Players became a room that mainly featured a succession of exotic and burlesque dance revues. The house band throughout the decade was Bobby "Dual Sax" Wilkes and His Orchestra, who anchored these shows that combined comedians, dancers and interludes of orchestral and pop music. Club Players closed in 1972 and since that time a number of bars and restaurants have occupied its former premises. The entire building is currently occupied by a multi-level adult entertainment lounge called Cloakroom.

The Showboat Lounge replaced the Superior Inn in the basement of 2477 18th Street NW in the Adams Morgan neighborhood of Washington, D.C. in May 1935 and remained in operation through 1979. The establishment came into its own when owner Harry Lambros converted it into a live jazz night club in 1957 and installed the Charlie Byrd Trio (jazz guitarist Charlie Byrd, bassist Keter Betts and drummer Eddie Phyfe) as the house band, a position they more or less maintained for over ten years. From 1957 to 1959 other headlining jazz entertainers at the Showboat Lounge included: bands such as the Mose Allison Trio, the Charlie Schneer Quartet, the Shirley Horn Trio; singers Joe Lagana and Joyce Carr; clarinetist-flutist-saxophonist Sam Most; saxophonist Bob Wilber; trumpeter Gene Brusiloff; and violinist Stuff Smith.

During the early 1960s a number of folk music entertainers were brought in to alternate with the various jazz acts that appeared at the Showboat Lounge. In that period some of the folk acts to perform included: singers Charlotte Daniels, Dick Flood, Lynn Gold, and Geula Gill; singer-guitarists Mike Seeger, Carolyn Hester, Donald Leace, Joe Glazer, Bob Grossman, Bob Coltman, Paul Clayton, John Bassette and Allen Damron; guitarists Pat Webb and Robbie Basho; and dulcimer player Howard Mitchell. In addition, among the unique special attractions brought in were blues singer Jimmy Witherspoon; blues singer-guitarist Mississippi John Hurt; and comedian Bill Cosby.

The Showboat Lounge was always primarily a jazz night club and in the 1960s some of the groups and ensembles to appear at the venue, both on evenings when the Charlie Byrd Trio held court, as well as their off-nights, included: the Dick Morgan Trio (featuring singer Ginny Byrd), the Tee Carson Trio, the Shirley Horn Trio, the Art Farmer Quartet (featuring guitarist Jim Hall), the Kenny Burrell Jazz Quartet, Sal Salvador and His Quartet (featuring singer Sheryl Easly), the Wes Montgomery Quartet, the Barnes-Kress Duo (jazz guitarists George Barnes and Carl Kress), the Karl Boxer Trio, the Roland Kirk Quartet, the Oscar Peterson Trio, the Dizzy Gillespie Quintet, Lambert-Hendricks-Bavan (a vocalese trio consisting of Dave Lambert, Jon Hendricks and Yolande Bavan), the Neil Wolf Trio, the Village Stompers, the Art Farmer Quartet, Gene Krupa and His Quartet, Teddy Wilson and His Trio, Maynard Ferguson and His Sextet, Louis Jordan and His Tympany Five, Gene Krupa and His Quartet, the Vince Guaraldi Trio (featuring Brazilian jazz guitarist Bola Sete), Jon Hendricks and His Trio, the Tommy Gwaltney Trio, Carmen McRae and Her Trio, Al Cohn-Zoot Simms Quintet, the John Handy Quintet, the Ahmad Jamal Trio, the Earl "Fatha" Hines Quartet, Jackie and Roy (singer Jackie Cain and singer-pianist Roy Kral), the Dukes of Dixieland, Orlando Smith and His Jazz Trio and the Coasters.

In addition, that decade saw a number of individual jazz musicians brought in as featured attractions and their ranks included singers Marilyn Maye, Astrud Gilberto, June

Christy and Chris Connor; singer-guitarist Frank D'Rone; guitarist Herb Ellis; guitarist-harmonicist Toots Thielemans; Brazilian singer-guitarist Joao Gilberto; Brazilian guitarist Bola Sete; Flamenco guitarists William Dockins and Anita Sheer; bassist Joe Byrd; singer-pianists Mose Allison and Matt Dennis; pianist Eddie Heywood; singer-accordionist-organist Joe Mooney; pianists Teddy Wilson and Bill Evans; saxophonists Zoot Simms, Coleman Hawkins and Roland Kirk; trumpeter Jonah Jones; and rock and roll guitarist Johnny Knight.

The summer of 1969 saw the Showboat Lounge undergo a metamorphosis when new management was introduced and the jazz acts were replaced with local, psychedelic-tinged rock and roll bands. Among the featured acts that year were Urch Perch, Claude Jones and Natty Bumpo. The night club passed through the hands of different owners in the 1970s with jazz trumpeter Bobby Sanchez and His Quintet holding down house band duties for a spell early in the decade. Live R&B music became the feature for the remainder of the decade. The Showboat Lounge closed in 1979 and a number of different restaurants (including another version of the Showboat Lounge from 2000 to 2002) have inhabited its basement space through the years.

Back in Northeast Washington, D.C., the Village Inn (1606 Rhode Island Avenue NE), which was owned by the legendary professional wrestling referee Bennie Bortnick, began an 11-year run when it replaced Nesline's Restaurant in 1947. Main attractions in this establishment during the late 1940s included the musical novelty act known as the Wacky Keys, the pop-oriented Tunesmiths and the blues-country-jazz outfit known as the Tune Twisters.

In the 1950s the Village Inn booked a mix of pop and C&W bands including Art Fred and His Merrytones, Smitty Smith and the Georgia Boys, Chubby Wise and the Florida Playboys, the Cavaliers, the Merry-Tones, the Teddy Carter Quartet, the Rhythm Pioneers and Jimmy Marlon and His Rockabilly Kats. Also headlining was guitarist Danny "String King" Rae. The Village Inn closed its doors in 1958 and a year later its place was taken by Barclay's Steak House, a restaurant void of live music.

A few blocks south of the Village Inn at 1300 Rhode Island Avenue NE was Rhode Island Plaza, an eight-story, 422-unit red brick apartment building that was constructed in 1952 on a plot of land that had previously been the site of the historic structure known as Hilltop House (which had been constructed in 1773 and had once served as the interim President's House for President James Monroe after the British had burned down the official residence in the War of 1812).

The ground floor of Rhode Island Plaza hosted a number of businesses, one of which was an ambitious 150-seat jazz night club called the Celebrity Room, which opened in early 1953. Some of the headlining bands during its brief existence included: the Oscar Peterson Trio, the Cecil Young Quartet, George Shearing and His Combo, Nat King Cole, Count Basie and His Orchestra, the Joe Holliday Combo (featuring singer Savannah Churchill) and Al Dunn and His Orchestra (featuring singer VeRonnee). Among the top jazz singers to perform were Sarah Vaughan, Pearl Bailey, Patti Page, Ella Fitzgerald and Billie Holiday. In November 1953 a short-lived night club called Café Celebrity replaced the Celebrity Room only remained in operation for a few months, during which time its featured entertainer was the Shirley Horn Trio.

After a two-year vacancy, the Spotlite Room replaced Café Celebrity on the night of Thursday, May 24, 1956. For the remainder of the 1950s this new establishment booked an impressive array of jazz talent. A number of star performers, both White and Black, played here including such bands as Charlie Buck and His Famous Combo, Frankie Condon's Orchestra, Bobby Felder's Quintet, the Montclairs, Al Dunn and His Combo (featuring singer VeRonnee), the Kuturas, the Orchestra (under the direction of Bill Potts), the Randy

Weston Jazz Trio, Art Blakey and the Jazz Messengers, the Dizzie Gillespie Jazz Quintet, the J.J. Johnson Jazz Quintet, Shirley Horn and the Three Sounds, the Bill Harris Trio, the Dick Williams Quintet, Bobby Felder's Jazz Prophets, the Jimmy Smith Trio, the Sonny Stitt Jazz Quintet, the Lou Donaldson Jazz Quintet, the Miles Davis All-Stars, the Ahmad Jamal Jazz Trio, the Joe Rinaldi Quintet, the Horace Silver Jazz Quintet, the Milt Buckner Jazz Trio, the Buddy Rich Jazz Quintet, the Fabulous Dorsey Orchestra (under the direction of Lee Castle), Maynard Ferguson's Big Band, the Harry James Orchestra and the Neal Martin Jazz Trio.

Also appearing at the Spotlite Room in the late 1950s were such featured attractions as: singers Danny Knight, Betty Carter, Evelyn West, Dakota Staton and Ethel Ennis; jazz guitarist Domenico Modugno; bassist Oscar Pettiford; pianists Dini Clark and Andre Previn; clarinetist-saxophonist Flip Philips; saxophonists Julian "Cannonball" Adderley, Cecil Payne, Jack Nimitz and Buck Hill; trumpeter Roy Eldridge; trombonist Curtis Fuller; and percussionist Buck Clark.

In the early 1960s the Spotlite Room hosted such entertainers as: singers Jimmy Ricks and Sam Hawkins; and such bands as the Spaniels, El Trinados, Big Ernie and His Band, the Three of Us Trio, TNT Tribble and His Band, Chuck Booker and the Blues Messengers, the Gordon Twins, the Swingers, the Stump Washington Jazz Combo, the Clovers and the Van Perry Combo.

The Spotlite Room closed in June 1963 and was replaced that same month by a very short-lived folk music night club called the Evil Eye. In later years, different social service agencies occupied the ground floor area of the Rhode Island Plaza building that once housed these night clubs. Rhode Island Plaza was eventually torn down in 1996.

For several years one of the city's most popular jazz night clubs was Charlie Café's Lounge (1359 Connecticut Avenue NW), which existed on the outside shell of Dupont Circle from 1958 to 1966. During its first two years house band duties went to the Eddie Phyfe Three, a trio that featured the legendary local drummer Eddie Phyfe and backed up such featured headliners as singer-pianist Shirley Horn, saxophonist Angelo Tompros, trombonist VI Dickerson, trumpeter Jerry Blumberg, and vibraphonist Fred Tatman. In the early 1960s regular entertainers in the café were the Vince Fabrizio Trio and the Tee Carson Trio, and from 1963 to 1966 the Billy Taylor Trio held court with such rotating jazz singers as Bobbie Kelley, Ann Read, Suzanne Greene, Ricky Lynch and Linda Cordry. Charlie's Café Lounge closed for good after a devastating fire destroyed its premises early on the morning of Saturday, December 3, 1966.

CHAPTER TWENTY-FIVE
KNOWN THE WORLD OVER!
CLUB KAVAKOS

In November 1927 the Louis Kavakos and Sons Confectioners replaced the Sanitary Grocery Company in the ancient Beuchert Tavern building (1880-1895) at 727 H Street NE in Washington, D.C. In 1933 the Kavakos family converted their candy store into the Louis Kavakos and Sons Restaurant and from November 1935 until August 1937 the business operated under the shortened name of the Louis Kavakos Restaurant. In September 1937 the name was changed to Kavakos Grill and the eatery's interior was redesigned and assigned a capacity of 400 occupants. Brownie's Nighthawks Orchestra was installed as the jazz-pop house band where they reigned supreme for the remainder of the decade.

In 1941 and 1942 Brownie's Nighthawks Orchestra remained the house band at Kavakos Grill, though management gradually began bringing in different local entertainers to round out the bills. During these two years featured singers at Kavakos Grill included Barbara Brown and Barbara Gray. The club also brought in different types of musical acts in an experiment to see what types of crowds would follow, as evidenced by a December 1940 booking of the Cowboy Ramblers, who specialized in what was billed as hillbilly music. In 1942 Brownie's Orchestra was replaced by Louie's Orchestra, which featured singers Nell Deacon and Sandra Phillips throughout much of the year.

The two-year period covering 1943 and 1944 was a pivotal time for Kavakos Grill, as the entertainment offerings were changed on a weekly basis. Pop and jazz singers, dancers and small revues were the nightly feature. During this time a number of out-of-town performers were booked in an effort to expand the club's entertainment base. One of the mainstays of the club during this time was emcee-comedian Frankie Donato who charged up the floorshows and proved to be a very popular and capable personality to carry the evenings.

Bands to work the Kavakos Grill during these years included George Grand and His Orchestra, Al Shea and His Band, Ralph Garren and His Orchestra and Hal Black and His Orchestra. Among the more popular singers to be featured were Joan Harvey, Kay Wayne, Patsy Gallagher, Elaine Webber, Betty Carr, Ann Carroll, Adeline Niece and George Aiker. Some the top dancers to be highlighted at this time were tap specialist Jean Mason, the team of Dennis and Lee, the ballroom team of Jack and Sally Taylor and the tap dancing Van Sisters. Special acts on display included accordionist Les Sechrist, magician John Simms, novelty acrobat Dale Adams and a team of jugglers known as the New Yorkers. Guest singer-emcee-comedians to grace the stage when Donato needed a break included Johnny Patchen, Marty Wayne, Artie Brooks and Happy Wilcox.

In 1945 and 1946 Club Kavakos continued to mix local talent with traveling stars to keep up with the Washington D.C. area's other top night spots. During this period the main house band was Clinton "The Deacon" Hobbs and His Orchestra, with other groups making periodic stops including Charlie Drake and His Orchestra, Don Lamond and His Orchestra and Hook's Novelteers. Frankie Donato continued his lengthy run as nightly the emcee-comedian and featured pop singers included Vickie Lawn, Sherry Lynn, Naomi Stevens, Louise Lee, Johnny Keeler, Bob Edwards, George Arnold, Gracie Smith, Patsy Gallagher, Bob Paquin, Ray Hawk and Joan Campbell. The top comedy team of the day was the Barbary Coast Boys (Eddie Gold and Harry Reed).

The year 1947 saw Club Kavakos spare no expense in bringing in top pop music talent. Frankie Donato was still on board for much of the year as emcee and main performers included such bands as Ina Ray Hutton and Her Sensational Orchestra (featuring singer

Danny Ricardo), Bill Burke's Music Makers, Glen Gray and His Famous Casaloma Orchestra, Boyd Raeburn and His Orchestra (featuring singers Ginny Powell and Ray Johnson), Jimmy Crawley and His Musical Chips (featuring singer Cortland Carter), Ray McKinley and His Band, Ray Eberle and His Orchestra, Bob Astor and His Laughing Musical Makers, Johnny Bothwell and His Orchestra, Freddie Masters and His Musical Merrymakers, Ray Anthony and His Click, Dean Hudson and His Orchestra and Will Goff's Music Makers.

Showcased singers in 1947 included the very popular Gracie Smith, George Arnold, Ruth Rogers, Lillian Bowman, Ray Hawk, John Barry, Claire Hogan, the team of Patterson and Jackson, and the duo of Jesse and James. Other attractions included comedians Dave Hecht, Harry Delmont, Phil Fletcher and Cousin Ida, and the comedy dance team of Moke and Doke. Other featured entertainers that year were: pianist Harvey Chown; vibraphonist Val Eddy: and dancers such as Sue Ronson, the Dancing Byrons, Honey Holder, Helen Carroll and the Clark Brothers.

The year 1948 saw some incredible national acts visit Club Kavakos which caused the establishment's reputation for high-quality entertainment to soar. Among the top groups to take the Kavakos stage that year were Jerry Wald and His Orchestra, Ted Weems and His Heartaches Orchestra, Buddy Rich and His Orchestra, Johnny Bond and His Band (featuring singer Rosemary Calvin), Sam Donahue and His Band of Stars, Larry Clinton and His Orchestra, Dean Hudson and His Show Band, Louise Sheldon and Her All-Girl Orchestra, Buddy Moreno and His Orchestra, Gene Krupa and His Orchestra, Chris Cross and His Orchestra, Freddie Masters and His Musical Merry-Makers, Freddie Cook and His Cookies (featuring singer Betty Dorsett), the Orioles, the Doles Dickens Quintette, the Tunesmen, Clinton Hobbs and His Orchestra, Tony Pastor and His Orchestra, Louis Prima and His Orchestra, Jack Emerson and His Orchestra, Woody Herman and His Orchestra (featuring double bassist Chubby Jackson and drummer Don Lamont), Herbie Fields and His Jazz All Stars, George Hipp and His Ballroom Orchestra, Jerry Trotta and His Orchestra, David Townsend and His Orchestra, Lee Maxfield and His Orchestra, Tommy Reynolds and His Orchestra and the pop trio known as the Three Suns (singer-organist Artie Dunn, guitarist Al Nevins and accordionist Morty Nevins).

Other popular acts to appear that year included: singers Helen Forrest, Ken Griffin, Marshall Young, Fred and Fay Wakefield, Ray Eberle, Connie Haines, Jack Leonard, Bob Eberly, Nellie Lutcher, the Sherry Sisters, Helen Lee and Russell Sessions; pianist Harvey Chown; and comedians Ken Barry, Cy White, Allan Drake, the duo of Stump and Stumpy, Chic Kennedy, Ted Buccola, Tony Lane, Tommy Phillips and the team of Bobby Sheldon and June Burnett.

Rounding out the decade, Club Kavakos maintained its well-deserved reputation as a top-flight entertainment venue by booking top talent throughout 1949 including bands such as Gene Williams and His Orchestra, Tony Pastor and His Orchestra, Pee Wee Hunt and His Orchestra, Ray Anthony and His Orchestra, the Skyliners Quartet, Chris Cross and His Orchestra, Johnny Bothwell's Orchestra, Freddie Gray and His Orchestra, Daryl Harpa and His Orchestra, Dean Hudson and His Orchestra, Louis Jordan and His Tympany Five, Al Dunn and His All Star Combo, Count Basie and His Orchestra, Tommy Ryan and His Orchestra, Buzz Ellis and His Orchestra, the Treniers, the Gene Gilbeaux Quartet, Chris Powell's Five Blue Flames, Johnny Wolford and His Orchestra, the Prestels, the Velvetones and Natalie and the Beachcombers.

Also topping the bills that year were such pop music singers as Alan Dale, Fran Warren, the duo of Fred and Fay Wakefield, Bobby Lucas, Margo Page, Janet Brace, Patti Page, Helen Forrest, Buddy Baer, Gracie Smith, Nellie Lutcher, Laura King, Bobby Lucas, Tony Lazarus, the Sherry Sisters and Lenny Love. In addition, pianist Junie Mays paid the club a visit, and favorite comedians to appear included Sid Blake, Bob Melvin, Tommy Thompson and the duo of Al Fisher and Armen Camp. Featured dancers during the year included Marie Styles, Arlene Joyce, Astra Andra and Jessie Vicks.

Club Kavakos remained one of the city's best night clubs in the 1950s in terms of quality of entertainment, which makes its demise during the middle part of that decade all the more puzzling. They offered an assortment of music, comedy and dance presentations on their stage, but reports of tax troubles began surfacing as the decade wore on. Despite the money problems that were developing behind the scenes, Club Kavakos offered some amazing bands and performers in their final years.

In 1950 headlining popular music orchestras at Club Kavakos included Ray Anthony and His Orchestra, Ralph Hawkins and His All-Washington Band, Bartolo and His Authentic Rhumba Orchestra and Stan Kenton and His Orchestra. Featured singers at the club included Marian Callahan, Irene Knight, Fay Wakefield, Lily Ann Carol, Rita Montoya, Dick Merrick, Al Morgan, Walter Long, Carmen D'Antonio, Dolores Hawkins and Mel Torme. Some of the club's top-billed comedians included Buddy Lester, Mickey Shaughnessy, Dolly Dawn, Paul Gray, Joe Rio, Ken Barry and the duo of Pepper Davie and Tony Reese. In addition, among the favored dancers to grace the stage were Elisa Jayne, Hillary Dawn, Stormy Lynn, Polly Shaw, Maxine Holman, Pat "Amber" Halladay, Hawaiian dancer Wanda Hillard, fan dancer Sally Rand and acrobatic dancer Nadine Ames.

Club Kavakos kept its momentum going in 1951 with such headlining musical outfits as Stan Kenton and His Artistry in Rhythm Orchestra, Larry Fotine and His Orchestra (featuring singers Cathy Cordovan and Guy Ross) and Ralph Hawkins and His Orchestra. Among the top pop singers to appear at the club that year were Johnnie Ray, Verna Leeds, Bill Darnell, Vince Carson, June Christy, Art Lund, Roy Roberts, Nellie Lutcher, Jim Perrin, Phyllis Miller, Dolores Hawkins, Gene Williams, Bobby Wayne, Irene Knight and Jerry Woodson. A frequent added attraction was accordionist Tony Lavelli, while headlining comedians included Mickey Shaughnessy, Buddy Lester, Alan Carney, Joe E. Ross, Tiny Sinclair, Jay Weston, Barry Thomas, Jackie Winston and Bobby Baxter. In addition, the club's bills were filled out by such dancers as Julie Martin, Hillary Dawn, Pat "Amber" Halladay, Pat Hobson, Sheila "The Peeler" Ryan, tap dancers Walter Long and Doris Hart, and the Doris Kemp Dancers.

One of the biggest stars to emerge from Club Kavakos was pop singer Johnnie Ray (1927-1990), whose first engagement at the club ran from Monday, August 20 to Sunday, August 26, 1951. That week, Ray, described in local ads as "Broadway's Latest Singing Discovery," headlined a bill that included the Raven Sisters, dancers Madeline and Linda and comedian Ben Perry. Ray had been born in Dallas, Oregon, was raised on a farm in Hopewell, and spent his teen years living in Portland. He first started singing at teen dances while at Franklin High School in Portland and after graduation moved to Hollywood, California in the late 1940s to pursue a singing career. Connections he made on the West Coast persuaded him to move to Detroit, Michigan, where better opportunities awaited.

In 1950 Ray was headlining in a Black blues night club in Detroit called the Show Bar and was signed to Okeh Records. His first single, "Whiskey and Gin" backed with "Tell the Lady I Said Goodbye" (Johnnie Ray with Maurice King and His Wolverines; Okeh Records, 1951) was recorded in May 1951 and released in August of that year. Ray appeared at Club Kavakos while promoting that single in the Mid-Atlantic region.

Ray's second single, "Cry" backed with "Little White Cloud That Cried" (Johnnie Ray and the Four Lads; Okeh Records, 1951), was recorded and released in October 1951, shortly after his initial Club Kavakos engagement. "Cry" peaked at number one on the Billboard magazine's "Best Selling Pop Singles" chart on Saturday, December 29, 1951 and remained in that position for 11 straight weeks, selling over two million copies and establishing Ray as a major singing star.

In 1952 Club Kavakos welcomed such pop and jazz bands as Pee Wee Hunt and His Dixieland Band, the Ralph Hawkins Orchestra, Woody Herman and His Orchestra, the Orchestra (directed by Willis Conover), the Four Lads, Ben Lary's Combo and Al Cohn and His Band. Special attractions included jazz pianist Erroll Garner and jazz saxophonist Stan Getz. Among the top singers to appear on the stage that year were Shirley Powell, Dolly McVey, Betty Clooney, Bobby Shields, Ruth Rogers, Gene Cunneff, Terry Ward, Vince Carson, Dolores Hawkins, Danny Winchell, Gene Williams, Margie Robinson, Bert Taylor, Terry Ward, Sally Blair, Pearl Bailey and Nellie Lutcher. Rounding out the bills were comedians Mickey Shaughnessy, Buddy Lester, Alan Carrier, Jackie Kahane, Bobby Bell, Jackie Winston, Phil Kaye, Johnny Savoy, the Three Nuts Brothers and the Jerry and Turk Revue. Top dancers included Buster Burnell, Monica Lake, June Powers, Lee Sharon, Carmen Hope, tap dancers Frances Martin and Amelia Gilmore and Hawaiian dancer Wanda Hilliard.

The night club moved along through 1953 with appearances made by top bands such as Tommy Dorsey and His Orchestra, Louis Prima and His Orchestra, the Goofers, Ralph Hawkins and His Orchestra, Zoot Sims and the Big Band, Stan Getz and His Band, Lionel Hampton and His Orchestra, the Bud Powell Trio (featuring double bassist Charles Mingus), Ed Leddy's Cool Figs, the Afro-Cubans, Charlie Parker and His Big Band, Joe Theimer and the Big Band, Billy May and His Orchestra, Charlie Barnett and His Orchestra, the Modern Sounds Trio, Dizzy Gillespie and His Orchestra, Woody Herman and His Orchestra (featuring singer Eddie Henley) and the Fred Merkle Quintet.

Among the popular singers to perform in Club Kavakos that year were Dick Brown, Kenny Milton, Georgie Shaw, Pearl Bailey, Billy Gilbert, Rickie Vallo, Leonard Conner, Toni Ross, Rickey Vallo, Varetta Dillard, Harriett King, Grady Wilson and Buddy Jayson. Other entertainers to appear included: pianists Thelonious Monk, Harvey Chown and Nat Bader; comedians Don Young, Monroe Seaton, Jackie Kahane, Herkie Styles, George Hopkins, Buddy Lester, Wally Dean, Irene Boyd, Bill Brown, Groggy, Lee Allen and Rummy Bishop; and a variety of dancers including Joan Shields, Margie Robinson, Estrilita, Linda Scott and Pat Rooney.

The year 1954 saw Club Kavakos continue to usher in the big bands and among the groups to appear were Toby Tyler and His Orchestra, Count Basie and His Orchestra, the Joe Theimer Quintet, Ralph Hawkins and His Orchestra, Frankie Condon and His Orchestra, Bill Reichenbach's Orchestra, TNT Tribble and His Band, Woody Herman and His Orchestra and the Capital City Dixielanders. Top singers to work the club that year included Linda Francis, Guy Dennis, Danny Winchell, Bob Stefan, Joe Lagana, Frankie Richardson, Nellie Lutcher and Vince Carson. Others to perform on the 1954 bills were singer-pianist Jackie Lee; pianist Harvey Chown; saxophonist Angelo Tompros; comedians Stan Stanley, Dick Carson and Jackie Kahane; dancer Hotcha Drew; and a wave of burlesque dancers that included Shirley Kelly, Falene Marvea, Jackie DePaul and Carmen Hope.

In 1955 the problems Club Kavakos was facing came to light when agents of the Internal Revenue Service padlocked the establishment on Tuesday, February 8, 1955 and revealed that a tax lien representing $16,000 in withholding, cabaret and social security taxes had been filed against the contents of the building. If the owners of Club Kavakos, identified at the time as William, John and George Kavakos, failed to meet the tax bill by Saturday, February 19, the night club could have gone on the auction block within 10 to 40 days of seizure.

On Saturday, February 12, the Kavakos Brothers made a $4,000 down payment on the tax debt and then met with IRS officials on Monday, February 14 to set up a repayment schedule. While the night club was allowed to reopen, it was now evident the business was in dire financial straits.

For the remainder of 1955 some of the entertainers to work Club Kavakos under this cloud were Jack "Jive" Schafer and His Orchestra, the Orchestra (featuring drummer Joe Theimer), Dizzy Gillespie and His Orchestra, Dale Turner and His Orchestra, Buzz Busby and the Bayou Boys, Brownie and His Circle Ranch Boys, Sonny James and His Melody Boys, Sam Wool and His Orchestra and Dave Willis' Orchestra (featuring singer Jean Muncy). Among the headlining singers that year were Teddi King, Joe Lagana, Norval Reid, Billy Stanton, Tony Zang and Bill Storme.

By January 1956 the financial woes of Club Kavakos became too significant to overcome and the establishment was basically operating on a night-to-night basis. For that entire month the night club offered a scaled-down floorshow consisting of Bob Charlton's Quartet, pop singer Ken Tash, blues singer-tap dancer Maria Hudson, tap dancer Jimmy Peterson and exotic dancer Sherri LaRosa. Club Kavakos closed up shop for good at the conclusion of the Sunday, January 29, 1956 performance.

Later in 1956 the Miles Sandwich Shop moved into the Club Kavakos building and remained there until 1977. A number of businesses came and went until the building was demolished in 1999. Today the former site of Club Kavakos is occupied by a new two-story commercial building listed as 775-777-779 H Street NE.

CHAPTER TWENTY-SIX
WASHINGTON'S ONLY THEATRE RESTAURANT: THE CASINO ROYAL THEATRE RESTAURANT

For more than two decades in the early 20th century a building then marked 800-804 14th Street NW in Washington, D.C. housed a popular business called Blackistone Florists. The business was sold in 1927 and the new owners had the original structure torn down, with a new, two-story restaurant building erected on its site that same year. From 1928 to 1940 a number of entertainment-oriented restaurants operated out of the second floor of the new building marked 804 14th Street NW including the Aster Restaurant, the Regal Restaurant, Café LaParee and the Bamboo Gardens Restaurant. In early 1940 a new venue appeared on the scene – the Casino Royal Theatre Restaurant. It would ultimately prove to be one of the greatest entertainment night clubs in Washington, D.C. music history.

In a very fast overnight transaction, the owners of the Bamboo Gardens Restaurant, Henry K. Wong and Hugh K. Liang, sold their business to a mysterious gentleman named King Lai Yee, who then opened the second-floor, 600-seat restaurant on the night of Tuesday, March 12, 1940 under the new name of the Casino Royal Theatre Restaurant. Continuing in the vein of its predecessor – it was virtually impossible to tell any difference at all in the two establishments except for the name on the front awning – the Casino Royal Theatre Restaurant maintained an emphasis on quality live entertainment featuring swing orchestras and multi-act floorshows for its ready-made audience.

Opening night at the new enterprise consisted of Wally Wanger's Broadway Revue led by the dance team of Labrun and Campbell and shadowgraph artist Ed Rickard, with music supplied by Eddy Wald and His Dance Orchestra. Doors opened at 6pm with no cover charge, shows were presented at 7:30pm, 10pm and 1am, and dinner cost 60 cents.

The Casino Royal Theatre Restaurant carried on the popular entertainment floorshow tradition of the Bamboo Gardens Restaurant and was immediately rated as one of the city's top night clubs. One of the main reasons for its success in the 1940s was the presence of Jack "Jive" Schafer's Dance Orchestra, which held house band duties and backed the dazzling array of floorshow revues that worked the club from 1940 until 1945. Schafer's band then returned intermittently for shorter engagements from 1946 to 1949. Schafer himself was an animated lead singer and engaging trumpeter who specialized in risqué novelty songs that proved wildly popular with the Washington, D.C. set. His nightly routine included an original humorous composition called "Ants in My Pants" and a rendition of something called "Yas, Yas, Yas," an adults-only song for which Schafer had more than 300 verses to choose from.

Writing in his "Swing Sessions" column in the Sunday, July 26, 1942 edition of the Washington Post, jazz expert Bill Gottleib called Schafer "One of the town's top trumpet players, orchestra leaders and arrangers" and that he was "recognized as a thoroughly hep musician."

Before reaching the Casino Royal Theatre Restaurant, the Baltimore born-and-raised Jack Schafer had honed his craft during the 1920s playing accompaniments for several years in a silent movie house in his hometown of Baltimore. He then spent several years working at the Ritz in New York City where he sang and played trumpet in the Morgan Baer Orchestra. In 1935 Schafer relocated to Washington, D.C. and spent the next few years playing trumpet in the house bands at the Restaurant Madrillon and the Gayety Theatre.

In 1939 an offer came for Schafer to tour and record with the legendary Harry James Orchestra and thus began an eight-month association that led to engagements in top night clubs across the United States and numerous recordings for Columbia Records. Schafer's trumpet can be heard on such Harry James hit songs as "Cross Country Jump," "Saturday Night Special" and "Avalon," among others. He returned to Washington, D.C. in early 1940 and worked briefly in the house orchestra at the Gayety Theatre (again) before moving over to the Flagship in Georgetown in May where he was a featured singer, comedian and trumpeter with the Jack O'Brien Flagship Orchestra (directed by Buff Amorosi).

When the Flagship closed in June 1940, Schafer immediately put together his own band of local swing musicians and passed an audition for the Casino Royal Theatre Restaurant job. During his first year there, Schafer's band also worked nightly sets at the Capitol Theatre, running back-and-forth between venues every night to maintain his contractual agreements. It was a grueling schedule that the band somehow managed to pull off without a hitch, but by early 1941 the Casino Royal Theatre Restaurant was firmly established as their home turf.

During their first five years at the Casino Royal Theatre Restaurant Jack "Jive" Schafer's Dance Orchestra usually worked in conjunction with singer-emcee Bob Preble. Together they hosted hundreds of touring multi-act revues consisting of talented dancers, acrobats, jugglers, magicians, psychics, skaters and other assorted performers. Some of the more esteemed outfits they backed at the night club during the first half of the 1940s were Earl Lindsay's Cavalcade Revue, Ann Grace and Her LaConga Girls, Jack Lane and His Love Birds, the Sharon Lynn Girls, the Muriel Kretlow Dancers, the MacArthur Dance Troupe, the Claire Ray Dancers, the Vee Ames Dancers, and the Rainbow Revue (which featured acrobatic dancer Margie Greene, tap dancer Mary Jane Brown and the magic of Dagmar and Company).

From 1945 to 1949 Jack "Jive" Schafer made only periodic appearances at the Casino Royal Theatre Restaurant. The night club began rotating swing orchestra house bands, but all the while continued to book large entertainment revues. During these years headliners included Ralph Hawkins and His Band (featuring singer Mary LaMarr), Frank Garner and His Orchestra (featuring singer Linda Allen), Jack Wyatt and His Band (featuring singer Kay Linton), and trombonist Toby Tyler and His Band. They also brought in such pop singers as Carol James, Marianne Dunne, Louise Lee, Patricia Lane and Ann Nichols, along with comedians such as Wally Dean, Walter Murray and Tony DeMarco. Featured dancers during these years included tap dancer Walter Long, contortionist dancer Betty Wagner and the madcap dance team known as the Halloway Sisters.

During the early 1950s the Casino Royal Theatre Restaurant continued the practice it had established in the previous decade and employed a house orchestra to back up the assorted local pop singers, dancers and comedians that passed through. In 1950 Jack "Jive" Schafer and His Band and Clinton Hobbs and His Society Band were the main attractions, and in 1951 and 1952 the house band was Bob Simpson and His Band, which often backed up the popular singer Bob Preble and special guests like singers Ann Gibson, Herb George and Jilla Webb.

In 1953 the Casino Royal Theatre Restaurant changed its format and began bringing in big-name national acts from the fields of pop and R&B, and, to a lesser extent, rock and roll and C&W music. Some of the better-known bands to work the club that year included: Bob Simpson and His Band (featuring singer Bob Preble), the Billy Williams Quartet, the Mills Brothers, the Four Aces, the Gaylords, the Chordettes, the Royal Sapphires, the Slate Brothers and Ralph Melendez and His Orchestra. Other featured attractions included: pop singers Guy Mitchell, Mindy Carson, Buddy Greco, Helen Forrest, Johnnie Ray, Christine Jorgensen, Vaughn Morrow, Rudy Vallee, Al Martino, Don Cornell, Linda Bishop and Janis Paige; jazz-pop organist Milt Slosser; jazz singers Billy Eckstine, Georgia Gibbs, Ella

Fitzgerald and Pearl Bailey; jazz singer-trumpeter Louis Armstrong; jazz bassist Al Morgan; R&B singer Dolores Hawkins; and singer-comedian Galeena Netchi.

Top musical outfits to appear at the Casino Royal Theatre Restaurant in 1954 included Louis Jordan and His Band, Cab Calloway and His Orchestra, Ann Sothern and Her Escorts, Ted Lewis and His Orchestra, Murray Schaff's Aristocrats, Harry Ranch and His Orchestra, the Sauter-Finegan Orchestra (featuring singer Sally Sweetland), the Hilltoppers, Steve Gibson and His Red Caps, the Mills Brothers, the Crew Cuts, the Four Knights, the Four Lads, the Three Suns, Spike Jones and His Band, Archie Bleyer and His Band, the Gaylords, the DeCastro Sisters, the Four Tunes and Ernie Rudy and His Orchestra.

Special headliners at the Casino Royal Theatre Restaurant that year included: pop singers Micki Marlo, Billy Daniels, Julius La Rosa, Jo Ann Tolley, Maureen Cannon, Joni James, Lillian Roth, Snooky Lanson, Tony Bennett, Jerry Vale, Betty Madigan, Penny Singleton, Kitty Kallen, Johnnie Ray, Linda Weisbrod, Fifi D'Orsay, Val Valente, Frances Langford, Maureen Cannon, Georgie Shaw, Joni James, Mindy Carson, Snooky Lanson and Connee Boswell; jazz singers Ella Fitzgerald, Alan Dean, Monica Lewis and Sarah Vaughan; jazz singer-pianist Nat King Cole; pianist Jan August; dancer Gypsy Rose Lee; and comedians Buddy Lester and Myron Cohen.

The entertainment calendar at the Casino Royal Theatre Restaurant was quite impressive for 1955 as well, with some of the era's top popular music performers making stops. Their ranks included the Hilltoppers, the Mills Brothers, Bill Haley and His Comets, the Four Lads, the Four Aces, Tony Pastor and His Orchestra, Bob Simpson's Orchestra and Nini Baker's Combo. Others featured artists included: jazz singers Sarah Vaughan and Olga James; jazz singer-pianist Nat King Cole; pop singer-pianist Little Jack Little; pop-R&B singer Al Hibbler; R&B singers Dolores Hawkins and Roy Hamilton; singer-comedian Mae West; burlesque dancer Lili St. Cyr; and comedians Dick Shawn, Jerry Martin and Mickey Shaughnessy.

Headlining pop singers in 1955 included Eydie Gorme, Joan Weber, Eileen Todd, Cathy Carr, the Laurie Sisters, Bill Hayes, Tony Bennett, Frankie Laine, Richard Hayman, Frank Parker, the DeJohn Sisters, Danny Machin, Cathy Carr, Betty Clooney, Vicki Young, the Paulette Sisters, Richard Hayman, Frank Parker, Sophie Tucker, Walter O'Keefe, Pat Boone, Bill Lawrence, Denise Lor, Betty Madigan, June Valli and Peggy Lee.

The year 1956 saw another impressive array of musicians and entertainers visit the Casino Royal Theatre Restaurant. Among the best bands and ensembles to appear were Vince Martin and the Tarriers, Steve Gibson and His Red Caps, the Esquires, the Topnotchers, the Platters, Cab Calloway and His Orchestra, the Mills Brothers, the Ames Brothers, the Mariners, the Esquires and Kenny Davis and the Red Heads. Other headliners that year included: C&W singer Eddy Arnold; jazz singers Bobby Scott, Ella Fitzgerald, Helen O'Connell, Mel Torme; jazz singer-pianist Bob Howard; jazz pianists Erroll Garner and George Shearing; jazz trumpeter Don Cherry; jazz-pop pianist Carmen Cavallaro; R&B singer-pianist Fats Domino; rock and roll singer Lillian Briggs ("The Queen of Rock and Roll"); rock and roll singer-guitarist Gene Vincent; singer-comedian Mae West; and semi-classical singer Enzo Stuarti.

Other entertainers at the Casino Royal Theatre Restaurant in 1956 included: pop singers such as Joan Weber, the Bonnie Sisters, Kitty Kallen, Jaye P. Morgan, Gloria Mann, Cathy Carr, Pat Boone, Julius LaRosa, Jan Welles, Teddi King, Guy Mitchell, Sunny Gale, Eydie Gorme and Johnny Mathis; comedy teams such as Fisher and Marks, Rowan and Martin, Olsen and Johnson, and Bill Layne and Don Hines; burlesque dancer Lili St. Cyr; and fan dancer Sally Rand. The year also saw the Casino Royal Theatre Restaurant offer a special rock and roll show hosted by WEAM disc jockey Jay Perri that included:

singers Clyde McPhatter, LaVern Baker, Don Covay and Billy Clarke; and bands such as the Jay Hawks and the Rainbows. There was also a special C&W presentation featuring Jimmy Dean and the Texas Wildcats, singer Patsy Cline and singer-guitarist George Hamilton IV.

In 1957 some of the top groups to play Casino Royal Theatre Restaurant were the Four Aces, the Four Voices, the Ivory Joe Hunter Trio, the Drifters, the Hilltoppers, the Kirby Stone Four, the Vagabonds and the duo of Mickey and Sylvia. The best of the pop singers to appear there that year were Steve Lawrence, Roberta Sherwood, Lori Taylor, Johnnie Ray, Connie Francis, Carmel Quinn, Johnny Mathis, Dorothy Lamour, the Shepherd Sisters and Hildegarde. Other top performers included: blues singer Big Joe Turner; jazz singers Mel Torme, Sarah Vaughan and Della Reese; jazz singer-pianist Dinah Washington; jazz pianist Eddie Heywood; jazz-pop pianist Carmen Cavallaro; rock and roll singer-pianist Jerry Lee Lewis; rock and roll singer-guitarist Charlie Gracie; R&B singer Ruth Brown; dancer Nelja Ates; burlesque dancer Georgia Sothern; fan dancer Sally Rand; and comedians Alan Drake and Henny Youngman.

The trend of national entertainment continued throughout 1958 at the Casino Royal Theatre Restaurant, with a steady parade of major acts on display including Ralph Marterie and His 16-Piece Orchestra, the Four Lads, the Four Esquires, the Ink Spots, Danny and the Juniors, the Diamonds, the Hi-Los, the Mills Brothers and Count Basie and His Orchestra. Some of the pop singers to perform that year were Roberta Sherwood, Eileen Rodgers, Betty Madigan, Gene Courtney, Corinne Calvet, Jerry Vale, Vicki Benet, Jimmy Casanova, Jimmie Rodgers, Robert Clary, Julie Newmar, Marilyn Davies, Mary Lou Brewer, Domenico Modugno, Geoffrey Holder, Carmen D'Oro, Abbe Lane, Xavier Cugat and Arlene Blaine.

In addition, other top performers of 1958 included: jazz singers Sarah Vaughan, Ernestine Anderson, Abbey Lincoln and Carmen McRae; opera singer Marguerite Piazza; and comedians Mickey Shaughnessy, Charlie Applewhite, Jonathan Winters, Sid Gould, Dave Gardner, Will Jordan, Phil Terry, Shelley Berman, Mort Sahl, Rip Taylor, Phil Foster, Don Adams, and the duos of Mike Nichols and Elaine May, and Phil Ford and Mimi Hines.

The year 1959 saw the Casino Royal Theatre Restaurant close out the decade with another strong procession of popular music entertainers. Some of the headliners that year included such groups as the Kingston Trio, the Modernaires, the Dukes of Dixieland, Frank Virtue and the Virtues, the Treniers, the Playmates, the Hi Los, the Mills Brothers, Turk Murphy and His San Francisco Jazz Band, Woody Herman and His Orchestra, the Jonah Jones Quartet and the team of multi-styled guitarist Les Paul and singer-guitarist Mary Ford. Other featured performers included: singer-pianist Liberace; folk singer Josh White; jazz singers Sylvia Syms, Nina Simone and Sarah Vaughan; jazz-pop singer-pianist Earl Grant; pop pianist Martin Denny; and R&B singers Roy Hamilton and Sam Cooke.

In 1959 a number of top pop singers headlined the Casino Royal Theatre Restaurant including Johnnie Ray, the Hi Los, Genevieve, Monique Van Vooren, Tommy Leonetti, Dick Haymes, the Castle Sisters, Jennie Smith, Denise Darcel, Tommy Sands, Mary Meade French, Bobby Darin, Carmen D'Oro, Billy Storm, the Crosby Brothers, Connie Francis, Yvonne DeCarlo, Ivo Robic and Dorothy Dandridge. Comedians that made appearances were Roger Price, Jack Martin, Joe E. Ross, Morey Amsterdam, Bob Charles, Jack E. Leonard and the comedy team of Phil Ford and Mimi Hines. For burlesque fans, dancer Tempest Storm remained a club favorite.

The Casino Royal Theatre Restaurant continued on into the 1960s with the best available national talent. The year 1960 saw the night club bring in headlining bands such as the Brothers Four; Guy Lombardo and His Royal Canadians, the Mills Brothers, the Four Coins, the Four Freshmen, the Memory Laners, Woody Herman and His Orchestra, the

Dukes of Dixieland, Marty Emerson Orchestra (featuring singer Ginny Palles), Les Brown and His Band of Renown, Buddy Morrow and His Orchestra, Billy May and His Band and Larry Elgart and His Orchestra. Favorite pop singers to work engagements included Andy Williams, Jane Froman, Suzanne Lake, Peggy King, Lillian Roth, Dorothy Shay, Betty Madigan, Kitty Kallen, Margaret Whiting, Frankie Avalon, Cathy Carr, Bobby Darin, Andy Mastro, Pat O'Day, Teal Joy and Al Martino. Special attractions that year included opera singer Anna Marie Alberghetti and singer-pianist Helene Aimee.

The year 1961 saw more big names from the national popular music scene invade the Casino Royal Theatre Restaurant. This roster included: bands such as the Earl May Trio, Danny and the Juniors, Charlie Parrish and His Collegians, the Paris Sisters and the Count Basie Orchestra; pop singers such as Guy Mitchell, Ray Peterson, Cathy Carr, Barbara Russell, Tony Pastor, Betty Johnson, Gloria Lynne, Neil Sedaka, Dion, Kitty Kallen and Johnny Maestro. Special attractions included: jazz singer-saxophonist Tony Pastor; the duo of multi-styled guitarist Les Paul and singer-guitarist Mary Ford; R&B singers Aretha Franklin, Chubby Checker and Lloyd Price; rock and roll guitarist Duane Eddy; and rock and roll-C&W singer-guitarist Conway Twitty. Rounding out the bills were comedians such as Bobbi Baker, Ned Walsh, George Kirby, Rummy Bishop, the team of Mason and Ross, and dancers such as Marcia Edgington, Lee Sharon and burlesque star Julie Gibson.

The years 1962 and 1963 saw the Casino Royal Theatre Restaurant continue to attract top national acts of various musical styles to the nation's capital. Among the groups to perform at the club during that period were the Dovells, Jay and the Americans, the Highwaymen, Count Basie and His Orchestra, the Lettermen, the Angels, the Four Seasons, the Halifax Three and a folk outfit called Knob Licker Upper 10,000. Pop singers to work the club during those years were Vivian Blaine, Tommy Roe, Jayne Mansfield with Mickey Hargitay, Johnny Tillotson, Bobby Vinton, Gene Pitney, Johnnie Ray, Neil Sedaka and Dion. Other headliners included: blues rock singer-guitarist Bobby Mack; C&W singer Molly Bee; folk singer Lynn Gold; jazz singers Della Reese, Sarah Vaughan and Gloria Lynne; R&B singers Chubby Checker, Gene McDaniels and Dee Dee Sharp. In addition, comedians to make appearances were Rusty Warren, Phyllis Diller, Belle Barth, Pearl Williams, Dick Gregory, the Smothers Brothers, Jackie Mason and Bob Holiday.

By late 1963 the Casino Royal Theatre Restaurant was experiencing a sharp drop in business, a strange occurrence given the quality entertainment the night club had continued to provide. Competition with other night clubs in the city had taken its toll and it had become difficult to book the steady stream of top acts that had been its practice for years.

During the first half of 1964 the Casino Royal Theatre Restaurant valiantly attempted to move forward and leading the way were bands such as Count Basie and His Orchestra, the Serendipity Singers and Si Zentner and His Big Band. Other headliners included pop singers Johnnie Ray, Linda Scott, Lenny Welch, John Gary, Vic Dana and Jane Russel; jazz singers Connie Haines and Beryl Davis; and R&B singer Chubby Checker. Comedians to work the club during this period included Poncie Ponce, Forest Tucker, Mickey Rooney and pop singer-comedian Bobby Van.

The Casino Royal Theatre Restaurant then offered its final week of live entertainment with a "Country Jamboree" that ran from Monday, July 13, 1964 to Saturday, July 18, 1964 and featured singer Sheb Wooley (performing sets as both himself and separately in disguise as drunken C&W singer "Ben Colder"), singer-guitarist Bobby Sykes and the singing duo of Bill Wilburn and Cathy Morrison.

After a five-month dark period, the Casino Royal Theatre Restaurant reopened as a discotheque on Thursday, December 31, 1964 and remained in operation as such for more than seven years. The basement, meanwhile, was still hosting the Speakeasy Lounge which had been in operation since 1960. During a brief period in May 1971, another attempt at bringing in live music was made. Two rock and roll bands, the Five Staircases and the Intruders, were given bookings, but by the end of the month the restaurant had returned to its discotheque ways.

In June 1972 the legendary Casino Royal Theatre Restaurant space again went dark, with the Speakeasy Lounge being closed for business as well. After several years, the second-floor night club space was opened up as an adult movie house called the Casino Royal Theatre, and was in operation from Wednesday, August 24, 1977 to Monday, June 5, 1989. The building was torn down in 1990 and since 1991 the former site of the Casino Royal Theatre Restaurant has been occupied by a 10-story office building called City Center (1401 H Street NW).

CHAPTER TWENTY-SEVEN
AT THE PEACE CROSS – THE PLACE TO BE: THE CROSS ROADS

In 1937 a budding entrepreneur named Herbert Sachs went looking for a site on the outskirts of Washington, D.C. in which to build a restaurant that featured live entertainment. He found his place on a vacant lot (which had formerly been the site of an old wood frame house) on the western edge of Bladensburg, Maryland just north of the Dixie Pig Restaurant and Barbecue and the Peace Cross monument at the three-way intersection of Bladensburg Road, Annapolis Road and Baltimore Avenue. His new establishment, which he named the Del Rio Restaurant, featured a Spanish theme in décor and food, and opened for business at 4103 Baltimore Avenue in January 1938.

Sachs decked out a special Fiesta Room on the premises and featured Spanish swing music by house band Max Zinder and His Orchestra from its opening into early 1940. A number of additional pop music bands were introduced to the night club throughout 1940 including Rollin Webber's Orchestra, Maxine Patrice and Her Orchestra (featuring singer Carolyn Wells), Ray Bradford and His Orchestra (featuring singer Penny Pepper) and Don Martinic and His Conga Rumba Orchestra. In addition, featured pop singers at the Del Rio Restaurant included Leon Lafell, Bonny Fleming, Trudy Chandler, Mary Martin, Olive White, Cleo Mayfield and Nora Williams. Other Del Rio favorites included: Jimmy Lackore and His Phantom Harmonica, singer-pianists Tony Ryan and Jack Wells; dancer Shirley Gae; the dancing Statler Twins; and comedians Don Rice, Steve Evans and George Beattie.

Unfortunately, the Del Rio Restaurant suffered a dramatic demise. Shortly before 8am on the morning of Thursday, January 16, 1941 an explosion erupted in a boiler room of the establishment and the resulting fire quickly consumed the building. Despite the fact that within minutes some 75 firemen were on the scene, including members from the Bladensburg, Brentwood, Cottage City, Mt. Rainier, Hyattsville, Tuxedo, Riverdale and Cheverly departments, the damage was severe. Included in the loss was a library of Spanish music valued at $700, about $2,000 worth of musical instruments, and an elaborate bar valued at $10,000. The structure was a complete wreck, with only the lower cinder block foundation and a couple of charred walls remaining as the smoke cleared.

In the aftermath of the Del Rio Restaurant's burning, Sachs sold the building to the local tandem of Edgar Smith and Edgar Baum, who immediately set about having a new structure with dimensions of 60x60 feet built on the Del Rio's char-broiled hearth. The new owners called their new enterprise the Cross Roads and on Wednesday, November 19, 1941 they opened the night club, which had a capacity of 350 occupants, to a world of gangsters, gamblers, working girls and local habituates of the Bladensburg Road Strip who came to hear contemporary pop music.

From its opening until the waning months of 1945 the house band of the night club was Ralph Hawkins and His Cross Roads Band, with a revolving cast of featured female singers passing through including Carol James, Lydia Allen, Mary LaMarr, Sharon Terry and Lee Barrett. Hawkins, one of the area's top jazz-pop drummers, had previously toured and recorded with Artie Shaw and Harry James, and had assembled a tight Cross Roads ensemble which consisted of guitarist Randy Ryan, saxophonist Clinton "The Deacon" Hobbs, bassist Jack Wyatt and pianist Ralph Hawley Garren. When this group took a rare night off, bands to fill his spot included Joe Ricardels and His Orchestra (featuring singer Peggy Paul), Al Massey and His Band (featuring singer Lynn Lee) and Jack Wyatt's Orchestra (featuring singer Lyda Allen).

From 1946 to 1949 Ralph Hawkins and His Orchestra, as they were then being billed, continued to work extended engagements at the Cross Roads, though a number of different bands and entertainers (both White and Black) were rotated in and out. When Hawkins worked the night club during these years, Betty Madigan was his usual featured singer.

Other ensembles to make appearances during this time at the Cross Roads were bands such as Toby Tyler and the Cross Roads Band (who usually featured the singers Paula Rae and Gene Conrad), the Art Calevas Trio, the Doles Dickens Quintet, the Bob King Trio, the James Quintet, the Loumell Trio, Bill Norvas and the Upstarts, the Andy Andrusia Orchestra and the Paul Mann Orchestra.

In addition, these years saw a cavalcade of different entertainers take the Cross Roads stage including: pop singers Sherry Sherwood, Donna Mason, Joyce Aimee, Terry Stevens, Georgie Gerety, Lily Ann Carol, Patti Page, Bill Warfield, Marion Bruce, Betty Holiday, Carolyn Marsh, Barbara Leeds, Sonny Howard and Bill Darnell; pop singer-guitarist Bill Huggins; pianists Kirby Walker and Maurice Rocco; pianist-dancer Jerry Brandow; and comedians Allan Drake, Janis Walker, Lionel Standler, Ken Barry, Marc Ballero, Gerri Gale, the Terp Toonsters and a musical comedy act called the Three Arnauts. Rounding out the festivities were a number of talented dancers including Wynn Seeley, Martha Ann Bentley, Ann Connors, Betty Percy, Kathy Skylar, Vera Love and the dancing Clark Brothers.

One of the most intriguing engagements in Cross Roads history occurred when a star-studded two-week show featuring Lenny Bruce ("America's Latest Comedy Find"), singer Doreen Day, Shirley Paige's Dancing Adorables and Ralph Hawkins and His Orchestra was offered at the night club from Monday, February 28 to Saturday, March 12, 1949.

This incredible engagement marked the Washington, D.C. debut of Lenny Bruce (1925-1966), who had been born in Mineola, New York, had grown up in nearby Bellmore, and after a three-year hitch in the United States Navy began working as a stand-up comedian in Brooklyn in 1947. His uncensored and innovative performances, which covered everything from satire to social criticism to jazz and personal experiences, made Bruce one of the top comedians in the country, though several arrests on drug and obscenity charges would ultimately frame his extraordinary career.

On Wednesday, August 3, 1966 Lenny Bruce was found dead in the bathroom of his home in the Hollywood Hills, with the official cause of death recorded as acute morphine poisoning caused by an accidental overdose. He was the subject of the 1974 biographical film "Lenny" (United Artists, 1974) starring Dustin Hoffman, and in 2004 was listed at number three on Comedy Central's list of the "100 Greatest Stand-Ups of All-Time."

During the 1950s the Cross Roads underwent a steady succession of ownership changes – a sizeable litany of now-legendary proprietors that included such names as Henry Burgess, Victoria Morgan, Russell Herzog, Stanley Zeleneski and Esther Turisi – though the night club's commitment to top-flight live entertainment never wavered. Their offerings were diverse and featured orchestras, local and nationally renowned pop music singers and an array of burlesque dancers.

From 1950 to 1952 the main house bands at the Cross Roads were Andy Andrusia's Orchestra and Jerry Rodis and His Orchestra, with special appearances made by such groups as the Merrymakers, the Spotlighters and the Jimmy Middleton Sextet (featuring singer Joyce Kerr). Pop singers to appear these years were Janet Lord, Ann Beebe, Eileen Peters, the Palmer Sisters, the Croydons, Joan King, Doris Paige, Carmen Carr, Phyllis Manning, Bettie MacDonald; Betty Jo Morgan, Beverly Alber, Evelyn Shelby, Tom Barry, Jane Cooper, Ronnie Sterling, Johnny Val, Marilyn Rogers, Jack DeLeon, Bill McArthur, Carole Winters, Vince Carson, Alan Carrier, Ronnie Sterling, Georgia Reed, Kaye Gayle,

Jack Leonard, Joe Rio, Jimmy Nelson, Kay Cahill, Tommy Sosebee, Don Kidwell, Carol Knight, Libby Dean, Pat Cameron, Mike Hunnicutt and Guy Mitchell. Other entertainers of this time included: comedians Dick Shawn, Alan Carrier, Sosimo Hernandez, Bobby Sheldon, June Burnett and Dusty Brooks: and burlesque dancers such as Irma the Body, Pat "Amber" Halladay and Carmen Del Carmen.

From 1953 to 1955 the Cross Roads remained a pop music palace, with Jerry Rodis and His Orchestra remaining the primary house band. Other ensembles to play the club when Rodis took a few nights off were Al Dunn and His Orchestra (featuring singer VeRonnee), Buddy Garrison and His Orchestra, Gene Ammons and His Orchestra, Jack "Jive" Schafer and His Orchestra, Ralph Hawkins and His Orchestra and Buddy Mack and His Orchestra. Headlining pop singers to perform during this time were Frances Faye, Mark Andrews, Guy Mitchell, Fran Carroll, Georgia Carr, Dolores Parker, Betty Holliday, Frances Colwell, Tony Bennett, Betty Allen, Ethel Ryder, Johnny Fortune, Lorraine Marsh, Patti Page, Linda Bishop, Ruth Rogers, Patti Phillips, Kaye Gayle, Jimmy Hutchins, Joy Rogers, Ray Eberle, Liza Eldon, Shirley Neal, Jack Maggio, Eve Carroll, Barbara Walters, Buddy Ladd, Gus Savalas, June Nelson, Gail Mathews, Joe Lagana, Rena Lyndon and Diane Edwards.

This middle 1950s period also saw the Cross Roads bring in a number of top-flight comedians including Ronnie Sterling, Jimmy Evans, Mickey Shaughnessy, Joe Louis, Ned Walsh, Lee Allen, Mousie Garner, Jackie Farrell, the Nuts Brothers, Ish Kabibble, Jay Jayson, Buddy Lewis, Don Phillips, Bobby Barton, the team of Jerry and Turk, Dick Havilland, the duo of Danny Rogers and Jerry Cooper, Armen Camp, Jeff Davis, Buzz Barrie, Johnny Hall and Joe E. Ross. Entertainment bills also included the obligatory burlesque dancers, the ranks of which included Hillary Dawn, Joyce Lennett, Bunny Holliday, Sally Sweet, Pat Meschelle, Lonnie Lovejoy, Pat "Amber" Halladay, Ann LaRoche, Ruby Rose, Betty Howard, Judy Gibbs, Irma the Body, Dolores Delraye, Dusty Dare, Tempest Storm, Blaze Starr, Beverly Styles, Bubbles Darlene and Lynn Storm.

The years 1956 to 1959 marked the final phase of the pop music glory years of the Cross Roads, with a plethora of great entertainers making their final stand in the club. During this period main house band duties were held by Buddy Garrison and His Orchestra, with a number of other bands making occasional appearances including Johnny Johnstone's Orchestra, TNT Tribble and His Five Sticks of Dynamite, Al Dunn and His Orchestra, DiAngelo and His Thunderbird Five, the Five Satellites, the Blue Chips Quartet and the Twin Tunes. Top-billed pop singers that passed through included Helen Phillips, Ginger Cole, Lillyn Whitmore, Kim Elliot, Randy Robbins, Eddie Kinley, Jody Sans, Patti Stewart, Allan Kaye, Pat Grady, Toni Price, Nancy Ford, Joyce Damone, Audrey Gaylor, Marian Dawn, Grady Wilson, Doris Lee, Bill Lewis, John Cooley, Betty Allyn, Rena Lyndon and Joe Lagana.

Special attractions at the Cross Roads as the 1950s came to a close included singer-accordionist Judy Santino and blues singer Smokey McGuire, along with a stream of comedians whose ranks included Jack High, Lee Wyler, Buzz Barrie, Joey Altee, Jackie Whelan, Jack Soo, Tony Santoro, the team of Sally Rowe and Joe Blow, Alan Reno, Danny Foster, Dick Havilland, Johnny Frisco, Jimmy Murphy, Charlie Delmar, Joe Little, Jimmie Judge, Barney Long, Barry Thomas, Louise Potter, B.S. Pulley and Carnation Jimmy Lake. The final round of burlesque dancers included Vicki Palmer, Stunning Smith, Dolores Del Raye, Donna Christie, Nina Reye, Lois Lee, Falene Marvae, Nikkie Masters, Lana London, Blaze Starr, Sherri Winters, Tawney Tremaine, Mitzie Dore, Ruth York and Judy Gibbs.

In January 1960 the Cross Roads business was purchased by George Saslaw, a former C&W-pop singer who had spent years performing in night clubs all over the Washington, D.C. area and had been a longtime favorite at the Crosstown Restaurant in the Mount

Pleasant neighborhood of the city. Saslaw introduced country music to the Cross Roads and during the course of the decade made several structural additions to its original building, thus significantly expanding the night club's capacity. These changes were instrumental in converting the Cross Roads into the Washington, D.C. area's premiere C&W music venue.

For much of the 1960s the house band at the Cross Roads was Dub Howington and the Tennessee Haymakers. Other C&W entertainers to perform at the night club during this decade included: bands such as Roy Clark and the Stardusters and Jimmy Dean and the Texas Wildcats; singer-guitarists Luke Gordon, Little Jimmy Dickens and Ernest Tubb; and singers Jimmy Byron, Patsy Cline, Faron Young, Lefty Frizzell and Mac Wiseman.

Late in the 1960s Saslaw brought in a new house band by the name of Danny Denver and the Soundmasters. This group, which featured the revered lead guitarist Roy Buchanan, was adept at playing a range of musical styles including C&W, blues, pop and rock and roll. In the early 1970s Buchanan broke away from Denver and headlined the Cross Roads with his own bands, first simply performing as Roy Buchanan, and later being billed as Roy Buchanan and the Snake Stretchers. It was here that Buchanan established his legend as one of the world's greatest blues rock guitarists.

During the 1970s some of the popular C&W bands and musicians to appear at the Cross Roads were the Baxter Brothers, the Carter Brothers, the Osborn Brothers, Teenie Chenault and the Country Rockers, Roy Self and the Country Younguns, Mark Baxter and Cross Country Freight, Jimmy Martin and the Starlighters, Bobby Jay and 301 Country, J. W. Martin and Heavy Country, the Freedom Ryders, Vallie Rae and the Raemen, Al Johnson and the North Star Band, the Virginia Renegades, Whitewater, Country One, Ranger Joe and the Buffalo Band, Tapestry and Country USA. Special appearances were also made during these years by rock and roll performers such as guitarist Link Wray and Danny and the Fat Boys (a trio consisting of guitarist Danny Gatton, singer-bassist Billy Hancock and drummer Dave Elliott).

In the 1980s a mix of pop, country and rock and roll musical entertainers played the Cross Roads including the Hubcaps, Sunburst, the Rainbow Riders, Crystal Clear Country, the Chick Hall Band, Michael Hoover and Clearwater, Casual Country, Second Coming, Smoky River Breakdown, the Silver Band, the Memories, Landslide, the Sidewinders and singer Ronnie Dove. The Cross Roads remained one of the Washington, D.C. area's top live music venues until Saslaw sold the operation in April 1987 to Andrew Rucci, Robert Rucci and Barbara Brooke.

The Cross Roads carried on with country music until March 1993. In February 1995, after a change in ownership, it reopened under the same name as a Caribbean-themed night club and later went on to host rap, hip-hop and R&B performers. In September 2012 the Cross Roads closed its doors for good and its quarters have been vacant ever since. The building was sold on Friday, April 19, 2013 to J&J Medical Health Care and Equipment.

CHAPTER TWENTY-EIGHT
SHOWPLACE OF STARS:
THE BLUE MIRROR CLUB

The building that housed the Blue Mirror Club (824 14TH Street NW) in Washington, D.C. was constructed in the 20th century and for many years had been the site of the Firestone Tire and Rubber Company (1915-1919) and the E.J. Quinn Motor Sales Company (1920-1923). After two years as the Coal Merchant's Board of Trade, the building was converted into a restaurant and alternately served as Stouffer's Buffet Sandwiches (1926-July 1936), Blanken's Restaurant (August 1936-September 1938), the Old Vienna Restaurant (October 1938-1939), and the New Bavarian Restaurant (1939-April 1940).

On Tuesday, April 23, 1940 a gentleman named Herman Daiker opened Daiker's Restaurant on the premises. On the restaurant's very first night live music was offered in the form of violinist Evva S. Noel and pianist Frank J. Meyer, a pair that performed in the dining room throughout the year. From January 1941 until July 1945 the building was occupied by the Plymouth Restaurant, which was owned by Charlie Braden and began as a Gypsy music venue with the headlining acts of Bob Straszny's Gypsy String Ensemble and Michel and His Violin. In time a move was made towards a more standard pop music format with two duos regularly holding court – pianist Sammy Marks and organist Leonard Friendly, and the team of guitarist Jack Norman and accordionist Eddie Whitesel.

With the closing of the Plymouth Restaurant, the Blue Mirror Club opened its doors in August 1945 under the ownership of Ameen David and immediately sought to separate itself from the competition by offering unique designs and interior innovations. The night club had a capacity of 200 occupants and featured an elevated, circular stage that revolved throughout the night and walls consisting of blue plate glass with etched figures and cut-out designs throughout, all decked along the edges with red and gold trimmings. A huge mirrored bar took up one end of the main room and completed the decor.

During its first few months and into early 1946 evening pop music entertainment was supplied by the Keithly Quartet (featuring singer Dee Saunders). For the next two years they specialized in pianists and featured such performers as Johnny Andrews, Ted Bauers and Maurita Gordon. During this time they also booked such pop music ensembles as the Four New Yorkers, the Five Esquires, Lisa and Her Zephyrs, the Stan Nelson Trio, the Freddie Gray Quintet (featuring singer Nancy Lee), Niguel San Miguel and His Quartet (featuring singer Lisa Alonso) and Larry Lane and His Melo-Men.

In 1948 the Blue Mirror Club began adding out-of-town acts to its roster like the Jones Brothers, a jazz group that performed at the night club frequently over the next two years. Other jazz acts to work the club in 1948 were the Kirby Stone Quintet, the Nocturnes, the Stan Nelson Trio and singer-pianist Kirby Walker.

By 1949 the transformation of the Blue Mirror Club to a major music venue was complete, with a number of up-and-coming and nationally known pop, jazz and R&B acts being featured. Among the big names to visit were the Tunesmen, the Don Renaldo Quintet, Freddie Gray and His Graytones, Steve Gibson and His Red Caps, Art "Guitar Boogie" Smith and the Crackerjacks, the Lenny Ensign Quartette, the Charioteers, Louis Armstrong and His Esquire Combo (which, besides singer-trumpeter Armstrong, consisted of singer Velma Middleton, pianist Earl "Fatha" Hines, bassist Arvell Shaw, clarinetist Barney Bigard, trombonist Jack Teagarden and drummer Cozy Cole), Dick Thomas and His Guitar, the Four Tunes, the Three Flames, Fletcher Henderson and His Orchestra, Chubby Jackson and His Quintet, the Caldwells and the team of Fred and Faye Wakefield.

Headlining singers during that time included Marion Page, Nancy Lee, Dee Lloyd McKay, Billie Holiday and Ethel Waters.

The Blue Mirror Club would go on to feature a mix of national jazz, R&B and rock and roll acts throughout the 1950s. In the year 1950 groups to appear at the night club included the Tunesmen, Lisa Alonso and Her Tropicaires, Al Dunn and His Trio, the Deep River Boys, the Mills Brothers, the Four Keys, Louis Armstrong and His All-Star Concert Court (featuring trombonist Jack Teagarden and pianist Earl "Fatha" Hines), the Nocturnes, Louis Jordan and His Famous Tympany Five, Red Ingle and His Natural Seven, Three Chaps and a Chic, Gay Crosse and His Good Humor Six, Steve Gibson and the Red Caps, Hugo Malan and His Orchestra, Two Sparks and a Flame, the Marveleers, the Three Peppers, the Two Nifties, Doles Dickens and the Whispers, the Four Keys, the Al Shea Trio, the Page Cavanaugh Trio and the Piccadilly Pipers. Other headliners included pop singers Bob Eberly and Jack Leonard; singer-pianists Dee Lloyd McKay and Maurice Rocco; and pianist Jackie Davis.

In 1951, as rock and roll music loomed on the horizon, the Blue Mirror Club brought in a variety of top acts including the Three Tunesters, the Ravens, the Tunesmen, Erroll Garner and His Trio, Steve Gibson and the Red Caps, Buddy Hawkins and His Keynotes, the Four Vibra-Tones, the Treniers, the Gene Gilbeaux Quartet, Louis Armstrong and His All-Stars, the Marveleers, the Charioteers, the Bell-Tones, Herbie Fields and His Orchestra, the Billy Williams Quartet, Murray Schaff and the Aristocrats, Savannah Churchill and the Striders, Ralph and Buddy Bonds, Pee Wee Hunt and His Band, the Novelites and the Austin Powell Quintet. Among the headlining singers to appear in the Blue Mirror Club that year were Phil Brito, Sarah Vaughan, Bob Eberly, Nat King Cole, Dinah Washington, Bill Darnell and Ella Fitzgerald. Favorite pianists to work engagements included Eddie Heywood and Don Shirley.

The year 1952 started off with Murray Schaff's Aristocrats working an extended engagement at the Blue Mirror Club, with jazz singer Ella Fitzgerald coming in during the month of January as a special headliner. Other headliners that year included groups such as Pete Rubino and His Crackpots, the Four Tunes, the Ink Spots, Cab Calloway and His Combo, Earl "Fatha" Hines and His Combo, Steve Gibson and the Red Caps, the Nat King Cole Trio, the Three Sharps, Chris Powell and His Blue Flames, the Heartbreakers, the Stan Freed Trio, the Four Keys, the Johnny Hamlin Quintet, the Bobby Wilkes Combo, the Dick Bailey Trio, Max Kaminsky and His Fabulous Dixieland All Stars, the Four Blues, Wild Bill Davison and His All-Star Jazz Sextet, Bill Bowen and His Butterball Four, the Pied Pipers, the Jackie Davis Trio, Doles Dickens and His Band, the Bob Evett Quartet, the Van Perry Quartet and Powell Austin and His Quintet.

Other featured musicians on the Blue Mirror Club stage in 1952 included jazz pianist Eddie Heywood and jazz saxophonist Anthony Johnson. Among the top-billed pop and jazz vocalists to appear were Sarah Vaughan, Helen Forrest, Ella Mae Morse, Steve Lawrence, Joe Allegro, Ethel Waters and Billie Holliday. Added attractions were a variety of dancers, with Pat "Amber" Halladay and June Powers leading the way.

Top groups in 1953 at the Blue Mirror Club included the ever-present Murray Schaff's Aristocrats, the Tunesmen, Herbie Fields and His Orchestra, Muggsy Spanier and His All-Star Dixieland Jazz Group, the legendary initial booking of the rock and roll outfit known as Bill Haley and His Comets (which took place in June of that year), the Treniers, Jack "Jive" Schafer and His Orchestra, Sammy Robbins and His Quartet, the Van Perry Quartet (featuring singer Eva Foster), the Four Lads, the Four Dukes, the Mary Ellen Quartet, the Four Tunes, the Cecil Young Quartet, the Marveleers, Stan Getz and His Band, the Dave Brubeck Quartet, the University Four, the Topnotes and Al Dunn and His Orchestra (featuring singer VeRonnee). Other performers of note from that year included: C&W singer

Rusty Draper; pop singer Bob Manning; singer-pianist Buddy Greco, pianist Stomp Gordon; and R&B singer Jimmy McPhail. Dancers included the likes of Lee Sharon, Sally Rand, Toni Adams, Ann Perri, and Princess Alexandra, while popular comedians at the night club included Jack Lester, Dick Haviland and the singing comedy team known as the Happy Jesters.

The year 1954 saw a variety of jazz, R&B, rock and roll and pop music performers pass through the Blue Mirror Club. Their ranks included Dave Brubeck and His Orchestra, Muggsy Spanier and His All-Star Orchestra, the Madcaps, Romaine Brown and the Romaines, the Five Bluenotes, Murray Schaff's Aristocrats, Buddy Garrison's Orchestra, Willie Restum and His Kats, Ray McKinley and His Orchestra, Dick Davis and His Nu-Tones and Bobby Boyd and His Jazz Bombers. Pop singers to headline included Scotty Goings, Patti Phillips, Julia Lee and Marian Dawn.

Entertainment in this night spot continued along the same lines in 1955 and appearing onstage were: groups such as the Kerry-Pipers, Murray Schaff's Aristocrats, the Al Belletto Quintet, Willie Restum and His Krazy Kats, Svata Ciza and His All-Stars, the Three Sharps and Jack "Jive" Schafer and His Orchestra; pop singers such as Joe Lagana, Grady Wilson, Claire Nicken and Matt Windsor; comedians Don Rickles and Bob Freed; and exotic dancers such as Jacqueline Turner, Candy Coley, Beverly Styles and Judy Gibbs.

The Blue Mirror Club altered its entertainment schedule in 1956 when it began exclusively offering exotic shows with female dancers as the main attraction, a practice that continued all the way into the early 1970s. For the remainder of the 1950s and throughout the 1960s Matt Windsor served as the singing emcee as the house bands switched on-and-off. Primary orchestras during this time included Jack "Jive" Schafer and His Orchestra, Louie Bellucci and His Music Makers, Bebe Cohen and His Music Makers and Earl Abrams and the Music Makers.

Scores of exotic dancers paraded across the Blue Mirror Club stage during this era with some of the more popular names being Crystal Dawn, Lana London, Rita Dare, Nina Rosee, Georgia Peaches, Renee DeMilo, Bobbie Pierson, Jill Parker, Louise Angel, Stunning Smith, Judy Gibbs, Adele Latour, Beverly Styles, Dee-Ann Dawn, La Faithia, the now-legendary Blaze Starr, Fawzia Amir, Marla Grant, Mitzi Dore, Lucy Martelli, Pat "Amber" Halladay, Carol Lee, Flame O'Hara, Jessie Young, Peggy West, Tinker Bell, Debbie Starr, Queen Estrella, Sandra Sears, Angel Robbin, Laline Francis, Kim Heather, Bobbi Collins, Susan Smart, Dixie Diamond, Lynn Arden, Mira Slova and Wanda Deel.

The Blue Mirror Club remained in business until July 1972. A month after its closing the building was razed to make way for one of the city's Metrorail stations and a proposed office building complex. Since September 1982 the former site of the Blue Mirror Club has been occupied by 1400 Eye Street, a 12-story office building; underneath the ground floor of this building is the McPherson Square Metro station.

CHAPTER TWENTY-NINE
THE HOME OF STARS:
CLUB BALI

One of the most storied night clubs in Washington, D.C. area popular music history was Club Bali, which operated out of a turn-of-the-century, two-story building at 1901 14th Street NW in Washington from 1943 to 1951. This establishment was located right at the intersection of 14th and T Streets NW, one block south of U Street NW in a bustling section of the You Street area which at the time hosted a number of jazz night spots. Club Bali mainly booked Black jazz acts, but did bring in White entertainers on occasion, and hosted racially mixed crowds during its existence. Many of the top local and nationally known jazz musicians performed on the Club Bali stage, making it one of the most highly acclaimed night clubs the city ever hosted.

The building that housed Club Bali has a long and colorful history. Constructed in 1907, it originally hosted a business called Casino Bowling Alleys, which enjoyed an 11-year occupation of the premises. From 1919 to 1920 the building was home to the Columbia School of Drafting, after which the growing automobile industry came calling for its space. In the ensuing years, the following businesses worked their way through the large, square building: Liberty Auto Sales (1920); the Washington Templar Motor Company (1921); the R.L. Taylor Motor Company (1922); the Luttrell Chevrolet Sales Company (1923-1926); the Fisk Tire Company (1927-1928); the R.L. Taylor Motor Company (a second run from 1929-1936); and Arcade Pontiac Company (December 1936-1938).

When the automobiles shipped out, a pool hall called Danridge Burrell Billiards moved into the space and remained in business at 1901 14th Street NW from 1939 to 1941. However, the building's prime location on the busy section of 14th Street NW drew the attention of an enterprising restaurateur who sought to transform the long, two-story structure into a unique hangout.

In the summer of 1941 an enterprising entertainer-entrepreneur named David Rosenberg purchased the building at 1901 14th Street NW with the idea of converting it into a live music night club that would attract both Black and White customers from the You Street area and surrounding neighborhoods. When the sale was complete, Rosenberg, along with his wife Tillie, refurbished the property and in October of that year opened a restaurant called the Spot in the former pool hall. Not much information is available about this initial venture, as the restaurant was very low key and the owners did not take out advertising in the local newspapers, though it is believed that David Rosenberg himself often sang pop standards for his seemingly small clientele.

The Spot was short-lived, as Rosenberg changed the name of the venture to Club Bali in the spring of 1943 and hired Black entertainer-promoter Sherman H. Dudley, Jr. (his father was a well-known vaudeville performer and producer who had brought innumerable stage shows to the nearby Howard Theatre) to book live jazz music and floorshows into the new night club, which had a capacity of 300 occupants.

Club Bali's much-celebrated opening night extravaganza took place on Tuesday, March 23, 1943 and featured a star-studded lineup that consisted of Sherman H. Dudley, Jr. himself as emcee, blues singers Edna "Yack" Taylor and Betty Sinclair, comedians Dick Montgomery and the team of Allen Drew and Mickey, exotic dancer Joy LaJoia, tap dancer Satchel Robinson, music by the Tan Balinese Septet, and an orchestra known as Club Bali's Deuces of Rhythm. The night club was packed to the rafters and Dudley, Jr.'s next move was to hire Coleridge Davis and the Hardy Brothers Orchestra as his house band, an arrangement that would last throughout all of 1943 and 1944.

Dudley Jr. then shaped his Club Bali evenings as small-scale knock-offs of what was being presented at the Howard Theatre, with multi-act bills featuring local and out-of-town bands, single musicians, singers and an array of dancers (from tap to exotic) under the headings of themed vaudeville-like revues. During the club's early years, almost all of the performers were Black, though the night club's clientele remained racially mixed. With weekly coverage in the Washington Afro American and periodic ads in the Washington Post and Washington Daily News, Club Bali immediately became one of the You Street area's top establishments.

For the remainder of 1943 some of the featured jazz artists to work Club Bali were: bands such as Ella Fitzgerald and the Four Keys, Johnny Malachi's Orchestra, Jimmie Hinsley and His Maniacs of Rhythm, the Beachcombers, the Cats and the Fiddle, the Three Riffs and the Swing Maniacs; singers Victoria Vigal, Rhapsody Underhill, Una Mae Carlisle, Rita Grenae, Edna Mae Harris, Bea Roxy, Valaida Snow, Nina Mae McKinley, Bea Morton, Monette Moore, Billy Eckstine, Bobby Caston, the Palmer Brothers, George Clark and Avis Andrews; singer-comedian Red Roscoe Simmons; comedians Joe Frazier, Snooky Morris, Buddy Bowser, Eddie LeMonte, Johnny Hudgins, Willie Green, Dick Montgomery and Warren Banks; and dancers Peckin' Joe Steele, Slim Thomas, Roaul and Ronnie, Billie and Vivien, Earl and Francis, Doris Smart, Honey and Honey, Vashti, Helen Penn, Slim and Sweets, Tony and Marita, Moore and Larry, David and Wittye, Lakita and Zora, the Smith Sisters, Princess Valda, Iron Jaw Wilson, the Two Zoot Suiters, the Baliettes, the Club Bali Girls; and dancing vibraphonist Jimmie Smith.

In December 1943 a major change took place as David Rosenberg, with his sights set on building a much larger music hall on the eastern end of the corridor, sold Club Bali outright to a Black businessman from the neighborhood named Benny Caldwell. With Sherman H. Dudley, Jr. still in the manager's chair and Coleman Davis and His Hardy Brothers Orchestra still providing the nightly musical backdrop, Club Bali continued to offer the best available jazz, blues and novelty talent.

Performers in Club Bali in 1944 included: bands such as Louis Jordan and His Tympany Five, Coleman Hawkins and His Orchestra, Roy Eldridge and His Orchestra, the Beachcombers, the Charioteers, Billy Eckstine and His Orchestra, Dizzy Gillespie and His Orchestra, the Mills Brothers and the Three Jacks; singers Pearl Bailey, Louise Beavers, the Smith Sisters, Billie Holiday, Sarah Vaughan, Lillian Fitzgerald, Ann Cornell, Tina Dixon, Maxine Johnson, Marva Louis, Doris Bradley, Minta, the Cabin Girls and Ray Sneed Jr.; singer-pianists Margaret Watkins and Audrey Thomas; singer-comedians Willie Bryant and Mercer Marquez; singer-drummer King Johnson; pianists Maurice Rocco and Ann Jenkins; and fiddler Tosh Hammond.

Other entertainers to appear that year included: comedians Billy Mitchell, the Musical Madcaps, Kenneth Harris and Doc Wheeler; dancers such as the Four Congaroo Dancers, the Four Crackerjacks, the Baliettes, the Brown and Brown Trio, Princess Sonya, Helen Penn and the Pennettes, Zamba, Bill Bailey, Eddie Rector, Big Time Crip, Apus and Estrelita, Billy Williams, Satchel Robinson, Chinky Grimes, Ray and Ray, Ernie and Uzie, Taliaferro and Vance, Zamba, Tarzanya, Princess Orelia, Connie Harris, the Sun Tan Girls, Leon Collins, the Nicholas Brothers, the 52nd Street Girls, Lakita and Zora, Ray and Ravida, and the team of Troy Brown and Barron Lee; acrobat Martha Please; contortionist Jigsaw Jackson; and the amazing skater Count Leroy.

In 1945 Al Dunn and His Orchestra became the new Club Bali house band, eventually being billed under the name of Al Dunn and His Bali Hoofers. They maintained their nightly slot all the way through the end of 1946 and backed an incredible assortment of talented performers during their stay. The lineup for this band consisted of Dunn on drums, the

Pogue brothers, Peter and Wilbourne, on saxophones, pianist John Thomas, trumpeter Reginald Corley, trombonist William Simms and bass violinist William Eldridge.

Making appearances at Club Bali in 1945 were such groups as Coleridge Davis and His Band (although they were no longer the house band, they continued to make frequent visits to the night club), Louis Jordan and His Tympany Five, the Cats and the Fiddle, the Five Red Caps, the Four Notes, the Mello-Tones, the Charioteers, the Beachcombers, the Three Peppers, Deek Watson and His Brown Dots, and a White jazz band called the Jack Wyatt Trio.

Other Club Bali headliners that year included: singers Ella Fitzgerald, Bea Roxy, Lillian Fitzgerald, Phyliss Smiley, Mary Stewart, the Rogers Sisters, Melrose Colbert, Mary Jefferson, Inez Washington, Boogie Woogie Joe, Baby Hines, Cousin Ida, Sunny Lee, Gladys Bentley, Doris Woods, the Little Four, Gwen Tynes, Annastean Haines, Marcellus Wilson, Baby Hines, Larry Steel, Zorrita Abbey, Nevo Peoples, Flora Washington and Bobby Keyes; pianist Maurice Rocco; trumpeter King Brigham; singer-trumpeter Crawford Price and vibraharpist Pete Diggs. Favorite comedians to appear were Billy Mitchell, Jackie "Moms" Mabley, Moke and Doke, Dick Montgomery, Joyner and Foster, Warren Banks and Peckin' Joe Steel. Rounding out the bills were dancers Sadie and Stella, the Manhattan Debs, Little Flash, Ralph Brown, Von and Gertrude, Johnny and Henny, the Hottentots, Smooth and Mellow, Lovi Lane, Blair and Tirp, Lopez and LaSalle, Peg Leg Parker, Brown and Brown, Boyd and Chapman, Gypsie, Miller and Boogie, Doris Smart, Valda, Tomago and Queda, Iron Jaw Wilson, Jackie Petite, Heckle and Jive, Jimmy Smith, Linn Camp, Lolita and Carmensita, Tony and Tanya, the Three Barons, Al Gusto, Peck and Peck, Candy Reed, Rocky and Vivian, Kay DuCongie, Lucky and Lucky, Ray Pearl and Yo-Yo, and Teddy Quarles.

Although Sherman H. Dudley, Jr. had bowed out of the picture by the end of 1945, there was no break in the high caliber of entertainment Club Bali offered during the late 1940s. In 1946 the night club booked bands such as the Phil Moore Four, Al Cowan and His Seven Musical Madcaps, Slam Stewart and His Little Band, the Cats and the Fiddle, Deek Watson and His Brown Dots, Riff Robbins and His Instrumental Quartette and the Three Loose Nuts.

Other featured entertainers that year included: singers Margaret Watkins, Chester Crumpler, Savannah Churchill, Alberta Hunter, Claudia McNeal, Connie Lewis, Baby Hines, Lillian Fitzgerald, Ella Fitzgerald, Phyliss Smiley, Nina Mae McKinney, Una Mae Carlisle, Valaida Snow, Ray Sneed Jr., Caleb Peterson, Miss Rhapsody and Sam Fouche; singer-dancer Baron Lee; singer-drummer King Johnson; pianist Dorothy Donegan; comedians Della Wiggins, Warren Banks, Doc Wheeler, Billy Thomas, Bob Brown, Lillian Fitzgerald, Della Wiggins and Dusty Fletcher; ventriloquist John Hopkins; and dancers Princess Valda, Princess Auriela, Satchel Robinson, Ray and Ray, Marnoni, Frankie Que, Saxy Williams, Dorothy Adams, Spic and Span, Sandy Brown, Fajor and Tyenna, Baby Lazar, Tato and Marth, Princess Sallo and Waggo, Marimoni, Rhythm Red, Tobie Winters, LaRoche and Reina, Congo and Chela, the Brown and Brown Dance Trio, Billy and Eleanor Byrd, Luck and Lucky and Carmensita Romero; and baton specialist Willie Lewis.

In the late 1940s Club Bali begin to shy away from the large multi-act bills that had been its staple since its opening and concentrated more on bringing in single national acts that performed longer sets and didn't have to share the stage with a cavalcade of entertainers. Coinciding with this change in policy the night club experimented with the name New Bali from late 1946 to early 1948, after which it reverted back to its traditional moniker.

In 1947 New Bali headliners included: bands such as Illinois Jacquet and His Orchestra, the Skeets Tolbert Quartet, Lester Young and His Orchestra, the Gaylindon Trio, Charlie Rouse and His Quartet, Eddie Heywood and His Sextet, the Cats and a Fiddle, J.C. Heard and His Orchestra (featuring singer Etta James), Ace Harris and His Combo, Lester Young and His Combo, Earl Bostic and His Recording Combo, Al Dunn and His Trio, Henry "Red" Allen and His Orchestra and the Four Radars of Rhythm; and jazz singers Sarah Vaughan, Ella Fitzgerald and Viola Jefferson.

Continuing in this vein, the year 1948 saw Club Bali switch back to its original name and bring in such bands as Claude Hopkins and His Combo, the Jimmy Shirley Trio, Herbie Fields and His Orchestra (one of the few White bands to work the night club), the Five Kings, Ben Webster and His Quartet, Louis Armstrong and His All Star Band (featuring pianist Earl Hines, bassist Arvell Shaw, trombonist Jack Teagarden, clarinetist Barney Bigard, drummer Sid Catlett and singer Velma Middleton), the Four Tunes, Phil Phillips and His Streamlined Combo, Johnny Moore and His Three Blazers, the Charioteers, Al Dunn and His Orchestra, the Ravens, Bull Moose Jackson and His Buffalo Bearcats, the Ink Spots, Rick Henderson's Combo, Lester Young and His Combo and the Mid Towners. Other attractions included: singers Ella Fitzgerald, Savannah Churchill, Pearl Bailey, Billie Holliday, Isabelle Cooper, Una Mae Carlisle, Hadda Brooks, Helen Humes, Marian Bruce, Ann Cornell, Lee Richardson, Ida James and Marcellus Wilson; and singer-pianists Rose Murphy and Ivory Joe Hunter.

Club Bali then rounded out the decade with a series of popular jazz performers in 1949, including three top White musical combos, Herbie Fields and His Orchestra, Charlie Ventura and His Orchestra and Jackie Cain and Her Orchestra featuring her husband, singer-pianist Roy Kral. Other well-known performers to work the club that year included: bands such as Cab Calloway and His Orchestra and Illinois Jacquet and His Orchestra; singers Billie Holiday, Sarah Vaughan, Marian Bruce, Cathy Graves, Pearl Bailey, Dinah Washington, Ruth Brown, Johnny Hartman, Teal Joy, Norval Reid and Marcellus Wilson; up-and-coming R&B guitarist Clarence Dillard; guitarist Tiny Grimes; singer-saxophonist Jimmy Preston; and pianist Erroll Garner.

Despite the big names and large crowds, Club Bali did not survive very far beyond the 1940s. In 1950 the club brought in such entertainers as Louis Jordan and His Tympany Five, Louis Armstrong and His Orchestra and Jimmy Campbell and the Jolly Four. On Wednesday, March 28, 1951 the night club was closed when owner Benny Caldwell was arrested on charges of jury tampering in the highly publicized November 1950 jury tampering trial of notorious local gambler William "Snags" Lewis.

The night club at this address later went through a series of owners and name changes in the early 1950s, operating as the Piccadilly Social Club (January 1952 to February 1953) and the Stage Door Club (June 1953 to December 1953). Next up was the Café Trinidad (December 1953 to December 1954), which hosted such headlining jazz and R&B entertainers as: the Harlem Scandals of 1954, Jack "Jive" Schafer and His Orchestra, the Four Tunes, Frank Motley and His Orchestra, the Zephyrs, Count Basie and His Orchestra and the Four Tunes; singers Connie Carroll, Dorothy Parker, Billie Holliday and Jimmy McPhail; and jazz pianist George Shearing.

In January 1955 the business changed hands again and was reopened as the Spa Restaurant, embarking on a notorious 15-year run as a rough-edged R&B-rock night club that somehow endured much of the tumultuous late 1960s period where the surrounding neighborhood burned in the riots and descended into a haven for heroin and prostitution. The Spa closed in October 1971 and sat vacant for nearly two years until it was reopened as Jack's Lounge (July 1973 to March 1975). After sitting empty for eight years the building was purchased by the Arena Stage theater group, which operated the Living Stage Theatre Company on the premises from 1984 to 2003. From 2004 to 2012 it operated under the name of Arena Stage at 14th and T. In October 2012 a restaurant called Matchbox opened on the premises.

CHAPTER THIRTY
MUSIC IN THE GROOVE: THE MUSIC HALL

Today the spacious building at 815 V Street NW, the 9:30 Club, rates as one of Washington, D.C.'s most prestigious concert halls, with nationally known performing musical artists of every persuasion including it on their schedule as they pass through the nation's capital. However, like many other long-standing night clubs in the city, its history has been somewhat obscured through time, with few having knowledge of the extraordinary musical events that have transpired within its walls through time.

The history of this venue begins with David Rosenberg, the original owner of nearby Club Bali, who had this structure designed by architect Alber I. Cassell and constructed on V Street NW in 1946 for a cost of $50,000. Rosenberg wanted to create a multi-event amusement center for the You Street area's community which went beyond the typical night club operation. Because of his extensive background in the local entertainment industry, Rosenberg christened his new venue with the rather unimaginative title of the Music Hall. He then installed Louis Mitchell as the venue's manager, who immediately began booking appearances by some of the top jazz artists in the country.

The Music Hall opened to the public with a week-long engagement by Louis Armstrong and His Orchestra that began on Sunday, January 12, 1947 and concluded the following Saturday. The Sunday show started with a 2pm-6pm matinee performance and the week included nightly performances by Al Dunn and the 12-Piece Music Hall Orchestra, an act that provided house band duties in the night spot throughout its first year. Local ads in the Washington Daily News referred to the venue as "Washington's New Beautiful $200,000 Ballroom and Concert Hall" and made note of its "special spectator section," a second-floor balcony that circled the dance floor.

The Music Hall enjoyed an auspicious debut, as an article in the Washington Afro American of Saturday, January 18, 1947 entitled "Music Hall's First Night Attracts More Than 5,000" proclaimed: "A crowd that at times, reached almost mob proportions, and estimated at no less than 5,000 persons, attended the opening of Washington's new dance palace, the Music Hall, at 9th and V Sts., N.W., here Sunday night as Louis (Satchmo) Armstrong and his band began a one week stand."

This attendance figure, however, seems to be greatly exaggerated, as directly below this article on the Washington Afro American's same page, another piece entitled "Capital Night Spots" stated: "Approximately 3,200 swing-crazed fans jammed the hall to the music of jazzdom's all-time trumpet king, Louis Armstrong and His Orchestra." In reality the hall had a capacity of 1,200 occupants, but the main issue is that the venue enjoyed a surge of interest from its very start.

For the next 18 months the Music Hall offered a variety of impressive Black and White musical acts in the hopes that a diverse entertainment bill would attract patrons from all over the area. Some of the Black jazz performers to make appearances in the concert hall during this time included bands such as Billy Eckstine and His Orchestra, Cootie Williams and His Orchestra, Lionel Hampton and His Orchestra, J.C. Heard and His Orchestra, Luis Russell and His Band, Cab Calloway and His Cotton Club Orchestra, Jimmie Lunceford and His Orchestra, Erskine Hawkins and His Tuxedo Junction Orchestra, Illinois Jacquet and His Orchestra, Andy Kirk and His Orchestra, Dizzy Gillespie and His Orchestra, Art Tatum and His Orchestra, Eddie "Cleanhead" Vinson and His Orchestra and Eddie Durham and His New Combo (featuring singer Jean Parks); singers Ella Fitzgerald and singer Lee Richardson; pianists Mary Lou Williams and Hank Jones; saxophonist Charlie Shavers;

bassist Curley Russell; cornetist Rex Stewart; drummer Sid Catlett; and a special engagement by the Calypso Carnival featuring the Great MacBeth and His Band along with singers King Wilmoth Houdini, the Lord Invader and the Stick Fighters.

Among the White jazz musicians to be featured in the Music Hall were: bands such as Tony Pastor and His Orchestra, Sam Donahue and His Orchestra and Charlie Ventura and His Orchestra; guitarists Bill DeArango and Mary Osborne; bassist Bob Leininger; pianist Ralph Burns; trombonist Bill Harris; and drummer Dave Tough.

During the spring of 1948, a local 27-year-old radio personality named Willis Conover, who, since March 1946, had hosted a jazz music program on station WWDC entitled "Tune Shop," staged a series of afternoon "Jam Session" events which pitted Dixieland vs. be-bop music at various area venues. What made these events so intriguing was the fact that Conover made it a point to include both Black and White players in these sessions, a brave and ambitious venture given the era in which they occurred.

"Jam Session No. 1" took place on Saturday, April 24, 1948 at Pierce Hall inside All Souls Unitarian Church (located at 1500 Harvard Street NW, Washington, D.C., today it goes by the name All Souls Church Unitarian) and featured such Black jazz musicians as trumpeter Cootie Williams, saxophonist Otto Hardwick and pianist Sir Charles Thompson. Also on the bill were White jazz musicians such as saxophonist Angelo Tompros, trombonist Marty Emerson, bassist Mert Oliver and singers Helen Martin and Joe Dosh.

"Jam Session No. 2" was held on Sunday, May 9, 1948 at the F Street Auditorium on the 13th floor of the National Press Building and featured a be-bop lineup of White saxophonist Charlie Ventura, Black saxophonist Ben Webster and Black pianist Sir Charles Thompson going against the Dixieland crew of White cornetist Wild Bill Davison, White trombonist Miff Mole and Black clarinetist Albert Nicholas.

For the third offering in this series, Conover brought his racially mixed group of jazz stalwarts to the Music Hall and on Sunday, May 23, 1948 his "Jam Session No. 3" offered a free-for-all session that included Black musicians such as saxophonist Charlie "Bird" Parker and pianist Sir Charles Thompson, and White musicians such as cornetist Wild Bill Davison, pianist Joe Sullivan and drummer George Wettling.

In the summer of 1948 the Music Hall stopped taking bookings for live performances and went dark. This situation soon fostered inquiries from a number of entrepreneurs including a three-man set that felt the venue had great potential as a night club if effectively managed. That fall a deal was struck between building owner David Rosenberg and the local, Black-and-White team of legendary local pianist Duke Ellington, Prince George's County night club owner Benjamin Bass, and Del Rio Restaurant owner Herbert Sachs. The three managers then turned the Music Hall's former space into a night club operation called Duke Ellington's that would feature the best in national jazz entertainment. The grand opening of Duke Ellington's occurred on Friday, October 22, 1948 with the headlining act being, not surprisingly, Duke Ellington and His Orchestra (featuring singer Kay Davis). Their engagement lasted 10 consecutive nights.

In the wake of what was a promising debut, Duke Ellington's, under the management of Charles Nelson, featured a number of great entertainers in what would unfortunately prove to be a short-lived venture. Among the jazz performers that appeared in the night club from November 1948 to January 1949 were: groups such as Hal Swinger and His Swing Sensations, the Golden Gate Quartet, Joe Morris and His Orchestra (featuring saxophonist Johnny Griffin), the Lionel Hampton All Stars, Mercer Ellington and His Orchestra, Illinois Jacquet and His Band and Buddy Rich and His Orchestra; singer Billy Eckstine; and a week-long, multi-act revue entitled "Harlemania" that began on Tuesday, December 28, 1948 and featured John Kirby and His Orchestra, the jazz quartet Three Bs and a Bop, singer Martha Short, singer-comedian Dusty Fletcher, the comedy duo Harris and Scott, dancer Tarzanys and tap dancer Shorty Howell.

Unfortunately, due to poor attendance, Duke Ellington's shuttered its doors after the conclusion of "Harlemania." The building would house a number of businesses in the ensuing years including the National Institute of Painting and Paperhanging (1950), another run as the Music Hall with very sporadic social events (1951-1953), the Caravan Ballroom (1954-1956), and the WUST Radio Music Hall (1958-1995). The building then became the new location of the 9:30 Club, which moved over from its previous F Street NW location and opened its doors to the public at 815 V Street NW on Tuesday, January 9, 1996 with a performance by the Meters.

CHAPTER THIRTY-ONE
JOE TURNER ARENA

The story of Joe Turner Arena (its façade displayed "Joe Turner's Arena" and it was commonly referred to as "Turner's Arena," though its business license had it officially listed as "Joe Turner Arena") begins with William Joseph "Joe" Turner, who was born in 1885 in Bowie, Maryland and moved with his parents to Washington, D.C. in 1890. He was a legendary local sportsman, having taken up professional wrestling in his teens and winning the world's middleweight championship from Pinky Garner at Jimmy Lake's Gayety Theatre on 9th Street NW in Washington, D.C. in 1907. He went on to tour carnivals across the United States, taking on all comers in wrestling sideshows for several years, and retired as an undefeated champion in 1926. In 1930 he returned to Washington, D.C. and began promoting professional wrestling shows at the Gayety Theatre and other local venues.

In 1934 Joe Turner began promoting professional boxing in the city and began actively looking for his own venue in which to stage his sporting events. In 1935 he purchased a vacant garage-like building formerly occupied by the Safety Auto Glass Corporation at 1341 W Street NW, Washington, D.C., installed 2,800 seats, and renamed his new acquisition Joe Turner Arena. The arena opened on Monday, December 2, 1935 with a professional boxing match that saw Phil Furr successfully retain his District Welterweight Championship against Sid Silas. Joe Turner Arena subsequently became Washington, D.C.'s primary venue for professional boxing and wrestling and was also the location of live concerts featuring all manner of jazz and popular music orchestras throughout the 1940s. During that decade Turner also owned and operated the nearby Kit-Mar Restaurant on 14th Street NW, which at that time specialized in live country music.

Joe Turner died from liver failure on Tuesday, February 18, 1947. His wife Florence inherited his holdings and soon married Gabe Menendez, who had been her late husband's professional boxing matchmaker, and together the pair owned and operated Joe Turner Arena for many years.

On Thursday, December 18, 1952 the Menendez duo announced that they had sub-leased the facility to a four-man syndicate headed by Vincent James McMahon (better known as Vince McMahon, Sr.), who would go on to found the World Wide Wrestling Federation (the precursor to today's WWE) and whose son Vincent Kennedy McMahon would become a household name in the world of professional wrestling.

Later in the 1950s Gabe and Florence Menendez sold Joe Turner Arena to the C.E. Finch Company, who allowed McMahon's group to continue to exclusively lease and operate the facility, which they renamed Capitol Arena in January 1956. In June 1964 the C.E. Finch Company sold the property to the Washington City Orphan Asylum and in July 1965 the facility was closed to the public and subsequently torn down. Today the arena's former site is occupied by 14W Apartments.

Joe Turner Arena was somewhat unique as a musical entertainment venue in that it offered both Black and White orchestras and jazz ensembles and welcomed integrated audiences throughout the 1940s. Their various musical concerts were regularly advertised in such local newspapers as the Washington Afro American, the Washington Daily News and the Washington Post, and there was never any adverse publicity pertaining to the race mixing of their musicians or audiences.

A rare and widely advertised event at Joe Turner Arena entitled "Dancecapades of 1941" featured a "Battle of Swing" pitting the all-White Gene Krupa Orchestra against the all-Black Jimmie Lunceford Orchestra. The concert took place on Tuesday, April 15, 1941 and apparently went on without any problems, as the venue continued to host bands from both worlds throughout the decade.

Some of the popular musical outfits that performed at Joe Turner Arena in the 1940s were Count Basie and His Orchestra, Tommy Dorsey and His Orchestra (featuring singer Frank Sinatra, trumpeter Ziggy Elman, and a vocal group called the Pied Pipers), Buddy Rich and His Orchestra, Charlie Barnet and His Orchestra (featuring singer Bob Carroll, trombonist Ford Leary, and a vocal group called the Quintones), Andy Kirk and His Clouds of Joy, Fats Waller and His Orchestra, Coleman Hawkins and His Orchestra, Lionel Hampton and His Orchestra (featuring singer Dinah Washington), Cab Calloway and His Cotton Club Orchestra, Eddy Durham and His Band, Ella Fitzgerald and the Four Keys, Duke Ellington and His Orchestra, Erskine Hawkins and His Orchestra, Sonny Durham and His Orchestra, Will Osborne and His Hollywood Orchestra, Al Cooper and His Savoy Sultans, Lucky Millinder and His Orchestra (featuring singer Sister Rosetta Tharpe and singer-guitarist Trevor Bacon), Hot Lips Page and His Orchestra, Jimmie Lunceford and His Orchestra, Coleridge Davis and His Hardy Brothers Orchestra, Benny Goodman and His Orchestra (featuring drummer Gene Krupa), Buddy Johnson and His Grand Orchestra, Earl "Fatha" Hines and His Orchestra, Don Redman and His Orchestra (featuring singers Dolores Brown and Dick Vance), Eddie Durham's All-Star Girl Band, Luis Russell and His Orchestra, Louis Prima and His Orchestra (featuring singer Lily Ann Carol), Billy Eckstein and His Orchestra, Tiny Bradshaw and His Orchestra, Cootie Williams and His Orchestra, the King Cole Trio, Benny Carter and His Orchestra, Jimmy Adams and His Orchestra, the Dixie Hummingbirds, Johnny Moore's Three Blazers, Illinois Jacquet and His Orchestra, Woody Herman and His Orchestra and singer Sarah Vaughan.

Joe Turner Arena was also the site of what was billed as a folk music "Hootenanny" on Thursday, March 18, 1948 that was headlined by singer-guitarist Pete Seeger, Black singer-guitarist Lead Belly and singer Betty Sanders. This proved to be an unusual concert attraction for this particular venue, as the type of music they offered would find much more receptive audiences a decade later in the city's coffee house scene of the late 1950s and early 1960s. Its occurrence illustrates that Gabe Melendez was willing to book most any type of musical event in his facility and bring in any and all patrons who wished to attend such celebrations.

In one of the venue's more interesting booking trends, country music entrepreneur Connie B. Gay, who had relocated to the nation's capital from Lizard Lick, North Carolina in 1945 and since January 1947 had hosted a daily C&W music radio program on WARL entitled "Town and Country Time," hosted live country music programs at Joe Turner Arena throughout the late 1940s. These events proved to be extremely popular with Washington, D.C.'s growing Southern population and filled the arena to capacity.

The first country music show Gay ever held at Joe Turner Arena was called "Radio Ranch" and took place on Saturday, November 22, 1947. Headlining the program, which aired on local radio station WINX, were singer-banjoist Grandpa Jones, singer-yodeler-harmonicist Tex Cherry and the house band known as the Radio Ranchmen.

After a year of irregular bookings at the arena, Gay announced the inception of a new concert program he called "Gay Time," with the inaugural show of Friday, November 12, 1948 headlined by singer-mandolinist Bill Monroe and His Blue Grass Boys and filled out by bluegrass singer-guitarist Clyde Moody, the blind singer-guitarist Pete Cassell, fiddler Chubby Wise, singer Linnie Ayleshire, the husband-and-wife duo of singer-banjoist Grandpa Jones and fiddler Ramona Jones, and the Radio Ranchmen. Gay continued booking his "Gay Time" C&W shows throughout 1949 and into the early 1950s featuring regulars like singer-banjoist Grandpa Jones and the Stoneman Family along with visiting talent like singer-guitarists Tex Ritter and Lefty Frizzell and Bill Peer and His Melody Boys.

From 1950 to 1953 when Connie B. Gay was busy elsewhere the arena was frequently rented out by WEAM disc jockey Cactus Matt (Matthew Warren) for "Barn Dances" that featured top local and national C&W talent. Some of the musicians to perform at these events included: bands such as the Dude Ranchers (featuring singer-steel guitarist Billy Strickland), Frankie Robinson and the Virginia Playboys, Bill Peer and His Melody Boys, Sons of the Pioneers, the Hoosier Hotshots, Jack Clement and the Tennessee Troupers, Woody Carlyle and His Pine Valley Boys and the Stoneman Family; singers Paul Jones and Dotty Lee Carlyle; the duo of Ralph Case and Pop Sugar; singer-guitarists Roy Clark, Arthur "Guitar Boogie" Smith, Pete Cassell, Tex Ritter and Lefty Frizzell; bassist Lum York; singer-mandolinist Buzz Busby; guitarist-mandolinist Lew Wade; singer-harmonicist Wayne Raney; fiddlers Fiddlin' Shorty Lindsey, Fiddlin' Shorty Smith, Chubby Wise and Jack Youngblood; and the musical comedy duo of Homer and Jethro ("Homer" being guitarist Henry D. Haynes and "Jethro" being mandolinist Kenneth C. Burns).

Perhaps the greatest on-going musical event ever staged at Joe Turner Arena was Connie B. Gay's "Town and Country Jamboree" presentation which aired on WMAL-TV, Channel 7 on Saturday nights from October 1, 1955 to August 31, 1957. The program was a live broadcast that aired from 10pm to 1am and was hosted by Gay, Jimmy Dean, Jackson Weaver and Phil Long. Local stars were mixed with some of the best entertainers from "The Grand Ole Opry" in a marathon concert setting that would extend well into the morning hours.

Among the headliners on "Town and Country Jamboree" were: bands such as Bob Wills and the Texas Playboys, Little Jimmy Dickens and His Country Boys, Ernest Tubb and His Texas Troubadours, Jimmy Dean and the Texas Wildcats, Bill Peer and His Melody Boys (featuring singer Patsy Cline) and Dub Howington and the Tennessee Haymakers; singer Miss Dale Turner; singer-bassist Mary Klick; singer-banjoist Grandpa Jones; singer-guitarists Lefty Frizzell, George Hamilton IV, Marvin Rainwater, Billy Grammer and Chick Hall; and singer-steel guitarist Billy Strickland.

Although Connie B. Gay left the Washington, D.C. area as the 1950s came to an end, the jam sessions continued on Friday and Saturday nights at Capitol Arena from 1959 to 1962 under the management of several local promoters including Don Owens. These events mainly highlighted local C&W talent such as Roy Clark and the Stardusters, the Texas Wildcats and singer-guitarist Vernon Taylor, along with the occasional visiting headliner like R&B singer-guitarist Jimmy Reed. By 1963 the music had stopped and the arena spent its final years mainly hosting professional wrestling events.

CHAPTER THIRTY-TWO
D.C.'S LARGEST HILLBILLY NIGHT CLUB: THE DIXIE PIG

One of the most interesting country music night clubs to ever grace the Washington, D.C. area music scene was the Dixie Pig Restaurant and Barbecue, which was originally located slightly east of the Peace Cross monument in a seemingly ancient, weather-worn, two-story roadhouse marked 4500 Annapolis Road in Bladensburg, Maryland. The structure that housed this bar-restaurant had been constructed circa 1850 as a grocery store on what was then called Water Street. From 1861 to 1925 it had operated as Coldenstroth's Saloon – a hotel, package goods store and bar owned by George W. Coldenstroth, and, subsequently, by various surviving family members. The ground floor dimensions of this building initially measured 40x40 feet and its main entertainment room could accommodate 125 occupants (later additions to the building expanded its size).

Documenting the early years of this establishment has proven difficult, though it is known that in the late 1800s and very early 1900s some of the musicians that performed on the Coldenstroth's Saloon stage were banjoists Howard Burr, Harry Weber and George Dreager; and fiddlers Lloyd Williams, Richard Heygster and Philip Hill (the legendary "One-Man Orchestra" from Forestville).

Coldenstroth's Saloon was purchased by Hugh and Lonnie Waldrop in 1925. The brothers immediately changed the name of the operation to the Dixie Pig Restaurant and Barbecue. For a short time in 1934 they attempted to run the business under the name of the Pig 'n' Whistle, but the moniker proved unpopular with the locals and they quickly changed it back to its previous tag.

The Waldrop brothers continued to book country music into the Dixie Pig Restaurant and Barbecue throughout the Prohibition era and the ensuing years. Some of the bands they brought in were: Al Shea's Orchestra, Norman Bell and His Orchestra, Don Collins and His Orchestra, Bill Strickland and His Hillbilly Kings, Blackie Skiles and His Lazy K Ranch Boys, Tex and His Mountain Rangers, Speedy Baker and His K-Y Boys, Jack Myerly and His Melody Men, Dub Howington and His Tennessee Haymakers (featuring singer-accordionist Jimmy Dean and guitarist Herb "Toothless" Jones), Johnny Lee and His Band, the Stoneman Family, Charlie King and His Virginia Ramblers, the Lazy River Trio, the Southern Troubadours, the Barnyard Revelers, the Mountain Music Makers, the Silver String Revelers, the Potomac Highlanders, the Hayshakers, the Happy Hicks Band, Harry King and His Hillbilly Band, and the Swinging Strings.

Other entertainers that headlined the night club included singer-guitarist Billy Grammer; yodeler Earl O'Neill; banjoists Newt Beall and Eddie Leger; and singer-square dance caller Paul Jones. In the early 1950s C&W regulars at the Dixie Pig Restaurant and Barbecue included Gene Bridget and the Melody Boys, singer-guitarist Roy Clark, singer-accordionists Jimmy Dean and Stoney Rigsby, guitarist Chick Hall and fiddler Chubby Wise.

The Dixie Pig Restaurant and Barbecue unfortunately succumbed to a devastating fire on Saturday, November 22, 1952. A month later two local entrepreneurs named Harry Isikoff and Reuben Bonnett opened a new night club, simply called the Dixie Pig, at 3804 Bladensburg Road in Cottage City, Maryland, a building that had most recently housed a popular music establishment called the Oriental House. This particular location had a long and colorful entertainment history and the Dixie Pig would be the last in a fascinating line of night spots to occupy the premises.

The structure at 3804 Bladensburg Road had been constructed in 1934 and during its first decade of existence housed a straightforward restaurant called Bill's Place (1934-1935) and a similar establishment called the P&C Drive In Café (1936-1949). On Wednesday, June 15, 1949 new owner Albert Smith converted the business into the Chesapeake Musical Bar and placed a premium on live music entertainment.

In 1949 and 1950 a mix of pop, jazz and R&B bands and musicians appeared at the Chesapeake Musical Bar including such groups as Al Dunn and His Combo, the Four Tunes, the Tune Timers, the Ko-Ko Nuts, the Tune Twisters, Freddy Merkle and the New Sounds (featuring saxophonist Ted Efantis), Col Nemeth and His Instrumental Trio, the Five Keynotes and a trio called Plink, Plank and Pluck. Also giving performances were: pop singers Jo Metee and Bobbie Todd; singer-pianist Dick Wade; keyboardist Bill Abernathy; pianists Jan Dumond, Erskine Butterfield and Alyce Brooks; and such comedian teams as Cook and Tyler, Murray and Palmer and the Jolly Jesters.

In 1951 the Chesapeake Musical Bar changed its trading name to Club Chesapeake and maintained its pop music format with appearances by Jack "Jive" Schafer and His Orchestra, Jack Wyatt and His Trio, singer Vince Carson, and the R&B group known as the Jones Brothers. Club Chesapeake continued in this vein throughout early 1952 with bills offering the Doug Jones Orchestra, the ever-present pop singer Vince Carson, singer Betty Allyn, burlesque star Georgia Sothern and various comedians and dancers.

Club Chesapeake was sold and after a quick facelift a new night club called the Oriental House opened in its space on Saturday, March 22, 1952. The pop music format was retained and for the remainder of the year the house band was Jerry Rodis and His Orchestra, who backed a range of floorshow entertainers. Among the main event pop singers to perform at the night club were Vince Carson, Rose Marie, Bob Stevens, Buddy Laciana, Terry Ward, Kathy Mann and Gene Arcade. Special appearances were also made by such R&B bands as the Four Tunes and the Jones Brothers. Featured burlesque dancers included Pat "Amber" Halladay, Sheila "The Peeler" Ryan, Carmen Del Carmen, Jai-Leta, Carmen Hope and Hillary Dawn. Among the regular comedians to perform were Ben Perry, Johnny Hall, Norty Michels, Ray Hastings, Chick Mullery, Johnny Frisco, Danny Bishop, Bobby Byron and Ronnie Sterling.

In late 1952 Harry Isikoff and Reuben Bonnett purchased the Oriental House and on Sunday, December 28 of that year they opened a C&W night spot on the premises called the Dixie Pig. With a capacity of 250 occupants, the new establishment quickly became one of the area's best C&W night clubs and throughout most of 1953 and 1954 featured the duo known as Chick and Johnny (singer-guitarist Chick Hall and fiddler-pianist-vibraphonist Johnny Foster), with frequent stops made by Jimmy Dean and the Texas Wildcats (featuring guitarist Roy Clark), Clyde Aaron and His Boys, and singer Texas Jim Robertson. In 1955 the popular C&W outfit Dub Howington and the Tennessee Haymakers handled the house entertainment chores, with regular appearances made by Country Thomas and His Dixieland Swing Band, Sonny James and His Swingin' Country Cousins, the ever-present singer-guitarist Roy Clark (who had branched out and was headlining as a solo artist) and singer-comedian Tiny Jenkins.

In October 1954 Benjamin Minovitz and William Rubin, the last owners of the original Dixie Pig Restaurant and Barbecue near Peace Cross, reappeared on the scene and purchased the newer Dixie Pig. For more than a year they continued booking C&W music. However, competition on the Strip was heating up, as the Wheel Bar across the street was packing them in with a rock and roll band called the Three Jacks. On Friday, February 24, 1956 Minovitz and Rubin offered a rock and roll show featuring the new music of the Five Rockets and Lou Rossi's Trio, two rock bands from the Philadelphia-Wildwood circuit.

The Dixie Pig's proprietors continued to tap that well and throughout 1956 they offered engagements by such rock and roll acts as Al Rappa and His New Riffs, Joey Nave and the Points, Bobby Boyd and His Jazz Bombers, Lee Raymond and the Kerry Pipers, the Bombadier Quartet, the Day Brothers, Johnny Belmont and His Las Vegas Jazz Kats, Birdie Castle and His Famous Stardusters, Joey Preston and His Five Rockets, Tex Daniels and His Rockin' Six, the Fabulous Dynatones, Red Prysock and His Band, Jack Murdock and His Five Stems, the Rockin' Horses, the Five Sins, the Royal Crowns, the Henry Mac Quartet, Romaine Brown and the Romaines, the Tilters, Doc Stark and His Nite Riders, Freddie Bell and the Bell Boys, the Fabulous Playboys, the Nu Tones, the Nite Caps, the Tyrones, and a young singing sensation from Philadelphia named Frankie Avalon (who appeared at the Dixie Pig on Tuesday, September 4, 1956).

As the decade came to a close, competition arose between the Dixie Pig and a new entry to the local rock and roll music scene, the 4400 Club on nearby Rhode Island Avenue in Brentwood, Maryland. To keep up with the action, from January to April 1957 the Dixie Pig offered rock bands like the Rockin' Horses, Red Prysock and His Band, the Dynatones, Stanley Gaines and His Hurricanes, Pat the Cat and His Kittens, the Tyrones, Lloyd the Fat Man, Roland Cook and His Band, Mike Sarge and His Sergeants, Doc Stark and His Nite Riders and R&B singer Joan Proctor.

In May of 1957 the format of the Dixie Pig abruptly switched back to C&W music with Dub Howington and the Tennessee Haymakers resuming their house band duties. Other performers at the Dixie Pig through the remainder of 1957 and 1958 included: bands such as the Blue Grass Champs and Smokey Mac and His Twilighters; bluegrass singer Mac Wiseman; singers Dale Turner and Patsy Cline; and singer-guitarist Roy Clark. The Dixie Pig flipped back to rock and roll music in early 1959 and for the duration of the year headliners included Al Pometto and the Jazz Bombers, the Off Keys, Charlie Daniels and the Rockets (who became Charlie Daniels and the Jaguars that spring), the Savoys, the Belvederes and Smokey Mac and His Twilighters.

Beginning in the late 1950s and continuing into the 1960s the Dixie Pig experienced several changes in ownership. Despite the unstable business atmosphere, the night club continued to operate as one of the area's top live music establishments.

From 1960 to 1965 some of the rock and roll acts to headline the Dixie Pig were Charlie Daniels and the Rivieras, the Tornadoes, Jimmy Vee and the Scamps, the Saxtons, Jackie "Shotgun" Powers and the Intruders, the Van Dykes, the Nutrones, the Tyrones, the High Hopes, the Holidays, Bill Haley and His Comets, the Joy Riders, the Quaker City Boys, Big Al Downing and His Band, the Bill Black Combo, Audrey and Her Riot Men, the Day Brothers, Don Hawkins and His Band (featuring singer Babs Tino), Jimmy J and the Js, the Jaye Birds, the Ink Spots, Little Joe and His Thrillers, the Quaker City Boys, the Don Daumit Quintet, the Upsetters (featuring singer Don Cooper), the Royals, the Buck Clarke Quintet, the Three of Us Trio, the Peppermint Stix, Chuck Booker and the Blues Messengers, the Flamingos, the Jay Price Revue, the Jokers, the McGraw Brothers, the Skylarks, the Magnatones and the Perry Mates.

Although its live music business was reportedly strong, the Dixie Pig mysteriously closed its doors for good on Thursday, June 17, 1965. The building was then without takers for more than two years. Next up, a business called R.A. Donley and Son Retail Stationary operated in the old night club space from 1967 to 1988. Several businesses came and went and today the structure that once housed the Dixie Pig is occupied by the Universal Dialysis Center.

CHAPTER THIRTY-THREE
DOWN ON THE BAYOU

The storied brick structure that once sat at 3135 K Street NW in Washington, D.C. is firmly established as one of the most heralded buildings in local popular music history. It was known for being the home of the Bayou, the legendary night club that operated there from 1953 to 1998. A Dixieland music night spot for its first dozen years, the Bayou turned to rock and roll music in September 1965 and quickly became the city's most important live music venue, hosting local and national acts alike. However, the Bayou was only one segment in what was a truly amazing litany of night spots that passed through this building before it was ultimately closed on Thursday, December 31, 1998.

The history of 3135 K Street NW – "The Bayou Building" as it has been retroactively named – had been largely cloaked in obscurity until David Lilling, executive producer of the 87-minute documentary "The Bayou: D.C.'s Killer Joint" (Metro Teleproductions, 2013), enlisted the services of architectural historian Emily Hotaling Eig to research the building's origins. Eig skillfully unearthed fascinating documentation showing that the building dated back to a warehouse called Cooper's Shop, which had been constructed in 1888 by owner James O.R. Kuhn as a place where one could build and store barrels.

On Monday, April 17, 1916 Kuhn sold the building to Richard H. Gaskins, who, in turn, sold it to Joseph H. Cranford on Thursday, September 16, 1920. At that point the building became the home of Cranford Paving Company, which remained in business through 1936. In 1937 and 1938 Cranford was apparently leasing the building to Simeon E. Dockstader, who operated what city directories listed as the Simeon Dockstader Warehouse on the premises.

On Tuesday, November 22, 1938 Cranford sold the structure to Merwin A. Mace, who evidently had extensive construction work done on the building, but in the process retained the large back retaining wall and a side wall that had been a part of the original Cooper's Shop.

Mace had the building redesigned as a restaurant with a total capacity of 500 occupants and leased the premises to a local entrepreneur named Don Dickerman, who promptly redecorated the building's three-level interior and opened it to the public as a unique, sea vessel-styled night club he called the Pirate's Den.

After a series of what were called public dress rehearsals where certain local dignitaries and socialites were invited in for lavish costume-optional dinner parties, the Pirate's Den officially opened its doors on the night of Tuesday, February 7, 1939. Ads in the local newspapers proclaimed the new night spot as the "jolliest, most unique and colorful rendezvous in the whole cock-eyed world." Owner "Captain" Don Dickerman would appear each night in full pirate garb and captivate patrons with his greetings and gab. As the Captain carried on, his 40 buccaneer waiters and waitresses danced about the premises, serving customers their food and beverages and providing songs and short entertainment skits for all who looked on.

Music at the Pirate's Den was provided by Piper Manning and His Orchestra, which served as the night club's house band throughout its 12-month tenure. In February 1940 Dickerman abruptly announced he was pulling up his stakes and moving to Miami, Florida with the intention of opening up another Pirate's Den, a move that necessitated the closure of his Washington, D.C. operation.

A series of different owners and short-lived night clubs followed in the wake of the Pirate's Den's passing. First up was the Flagship – a half-hearted stab at maintaining the Pirate's Den seafaring theme, though without the theatrical staff – which opened on the night of Wednesday, April 10, 1940 and was operated by the team of Brooke Johns and Jack O'Brien. Entertainers at the Flagship during its short eight-week run included: bands such as Sam Korman and His Orchestra and Jack O'Brien's Flagship Orchestra (directed by Buff Amorosi); singers Lynn Allison and Jerry Junkin; singer-trumpeter Jack Schafer (who would soon depart for the Casino Royal Theatre Restaurant where he fronted his own orchestra and became a local icon as Jack "Jive" Schafer); harpist Marian Wilkinson; and accordionist Martha Madison. The Flagship closed on the night of Sunday, June 9, 1940.

After a four-month period where the building sat unused, it was converted into the Veterans' Club in October 1940, an operation of which almost nothing is known, aside from the fact that live music was not offered to the public. The Veterans' Club closed in August 1941.

Next in line was the Viking, which opened on the night of Friday, November 7, 1941. For entertainment purposes, owner Percy Klein hired Stan Hall and His Philadelphia Serenaders and the Paul Perkins Orchestra as his alternating house bands and regularly showcased pop singer Ginger James. The Viking failed to generate the desired business and was sold during the first week of March 1942.

On the night of Monday, March 9, 1942 a new night club called Club Louisiana opened in the vacated Viking space. Nothing had changed in the establishment's physical layout or decor, but a new owner by the name of Julius "J.T." Richards was on the premises. Club Louisiana's very first night featured entertainment in the form of Jack O'Brien's Dance Orchestra (featuring singer Marilynn Pinnix), the same basic musical outfit that had held house band duties during the building's Flagship days.

That month J.T. Richards hired Ray King and His Orchestra as his regular house band, a position they maintained until June 1944. During that two-year period other guest performers to appear at the club were Juanito Velasquez and His Orchestra, Johnny Velasquez and His Rumba Band, Stan Hall and His Orchestra, Rae Scott's All-Girl Band (featuring singer Dot Jefferson), Phil Hartwell's Orchestra, Bob Neal's Orchestra, and pop singer Virginia Pearson.

In June 1944 J.T. Richards sold Club Louisiana to a Black entrepreneur named Frank Moore, who wanted to present mainly Black jazz entertainers to racially mixed crowds. Opening night for the new Club Louisiana was Friday, August 18, 1944 with a bill that featured Earl "Fatha" Hines and His Orchestra, singers Betty Roche and Jesse Barry, pianist Clifton Smith, whistler Jesse James and the dance teams of Claudia Oliver and the Louisiana Girls.

For the next four months a series of jazz performers worked the club, including bands such as George Auld and His Orchestra (the saxophone-playing Auld being one of the very few White musicians to work the club under Moore's Ownership), Andy Kirk and His Clouds Of Joy, John Kirby and the Biggest Little Band in the World and Dennis Briscoe and His Swing Orchestra.

Featured singers at Club Louisiana during this time included George Craft, Fats Pinere, Pattie Powers, Gwen Tynes, Evelyn Purvis, Bea Booze and Helen Stewart. Comedians to work the stage included Ben Jenkins, the Two Zephyrs, and the teams of Waters and Saunders, Carl and Harriette, Roule and Ronnie, and Bob and Benny. Also highlighted were such dancers as Sue Williams, LaZanda, Peckin' Joe Steele, Stumpy and Slim, Pops and Louie and Helen Penn and Her Pennettes. Unfortunately, Moore's vision never reached fruition and Club Louisiana closed its doors in December 1944 due to poor turnouts.

For the remainder of the 1940s the building at 3135 K Street NW housed two different bottle clubs, the Culinary Arts Club (Monday, January 1, 1945 to Friday, August 20, 1948) and the Town and Country (Saturday, August 21, 1948 to Saturday, December 31, 1949).

Both clubs operated on the premise that patrons bring their own bottles, which would then be marked by the bartender and filed away in the back of the bar until called into use. Setups for ice and soda and other drinks were then sold for 25 cents.

At the end of 1949 the Town and Country closed up shop and in January 1950 another bottle club, the Hide-Away, opened on the premises. Listing William K. Benjamin as owner and Joseph B. Horowitz as president and manager, the club abstained from live entertainment and became known as a late-night hangout for the city's most notorious gamblers and gangsters, who would gather in the wee hours, discuss the day's business and plot new transactions over breakfast. Somewhat ironically, District policemen also favored the bottle club and seemingly ignored the swirl of vice around them, as evidenced by the relative tranquility the club enjoyed during its first year of operation. All of that would change after the Hide-Away celebrated its first anniversary.

At 4:50am on the morning of Wednesday, January 10, 1951, the now-legendary Washington, D.C. bootlegger and gambler Joseph F. Nesline, then 36, shot and killed 39-year-old underworld finger man George P. Harding with a .45 semi-automatic pistol on the Hide-Away's second-floor balcony. The two had reportedly known each other since childhood and until recent months had still been fast friends. At the time of this incident, both men gave home addresses in Prince George's County, Maryland with Nesline residing at 1903 Chillum Road in Hyattsville and Harding living with his girlfriend Lorraine Nichols at her house at 3824 Queens Chapel Terrace in Avondale (several years later the jurisdiction of this address would be changed from Avondale, Maryland to Washington, D.C.). The reason for the falling out between Nesline and Harding has never been disclosed.

According to accounts in the Washington Post and other newspapers that covered the murder and subsequent trial, George Harding had told Hide-Away waitress Juanita Gilbert that earlier in the evening he had shot a bartender between his legs and pistol-whipped him inside the Club Chesapeake on Bladensburg Road in Prince George's County and had also "slapped down" a waitress at the Cross Roads. He allegedly told her about five or ten minutes before the shooting that, "I'm going to take care of Nesline now."

Harding had reportedly arrived at the Hide-Away that morning with two other men, one of whom was convicted White-slaver George Clainos. The two took a table with a bartender named Edward T. Digman, after which Clainos left the club, only to return a few minutes later and hand Harding a gun which he slipped into his pocket. Joseph Nesline reportedly saw Harding in the club when he arrived at 2am, but managed to steer clear of his nemesis.

Sometime after 4:30am Nesline climbed the stairs leading to the second floor where he went to the men's room. As he exited the room, he saw Harding standing at the head of the steps facing him, both hands in his pockets. Nesline testified that as Harding began to approach him he pleaded with him to stop, but Harding began to curse him and reached into his open coat. Nesline, fearing for his life, pulled out the pistol he had tucked between his pants and shirt and shot Harding on the left side of his chest at point-blank range.

Two police officers of the Seventh Precinct, Lieutenant Karl G. McCormick and Sergeant Arthur Gernhoffer, had been drinking coffee at a downstairs table (one published account said the officers were eating breakfast at the time) when they heard the gunshot and ascended the staircase. They were met at the top by Joseph Nesline, who told the officers, "I just had to do it. He forced me into it." Lieutenant McCormick then turned a flashlight on the shadowy walkway and saw George Harding's body sprawled on the floor between the top of the stairs and the men's room. The policemen found a loaded .38 caliber Remington revolver in Harding's hip pocket. Hospital personnel quickly arrived on the scene, but Harding died on the premises shortly after 5am.

Three months later Joseph Nesline went to trial on charges of first degree murder and carrying a deadly weapon and was represented by attorneys Charles E. Ford and H. Clifford Allder. On Wednesday, April 18, 1951, a jury of eight men and four women, after deliberating for one hour and 20 minutes, acquitted Nesline on the murder charge, but found him guilty on the weapons charge. District Court Judge Alexander Holtzoff gave him the maximum sentence possible under the law – one year in jail and a $1,000 fine. The Hide-Away never reopened its doors after the Harding shooting.

On Wednesday, May 23, 1951 a liquor license was granted to Marion Reid Flagg who had leased the vacant property at 3135 K Street NW and hoped to open a restaurant and live music venue on the premises. The new night club, which was dubbed Jazzland, eventually opened its doors on Friday, November 9, 1951 with Wild Bill Whelan's Dixie Six holding down regular house band duties.

During this time ads for the night club in the Washington Daily News proclaimed "You Can Now Hear Authentic Dixieland Jazz." The newspaper's "Tips on Tables" column by Hal Rosen in the Saturday, November 10, 1951 edition described the establishment as offering "The flavor of New Orleans offered in the seaport motif as well as the music, with remnants of old sailing vessels decorating the club."

Wild Bill Whelan's Dixie Six had been formed in January 1950 by local radio personality Willis Conover and had been recruited into the Jazzland after a two-year residency at the Charles Hotel (1338 R Street NW, Washington, D.C.). Offering a unique brand of Dixieland jazz, the band consisted of local Western High School graduate William F. Whalen on cornet, pianist Bob Conway, bass fiddler Bob Deardorff, trombonist Leo Hackley, clarinetist Wally Garner and drummer Francis X. Dean. Other jazz bands to work Jazzland in 1952 and early 1953 included Scotty Lawrence and His River Boat Boys, the Five Men of Jazz and Norval Reid and His Trio.

A part-owner of the Jazzland was writer-publicist Joe Hall, who specialized in creating newspaper ads for many of the Washington, D.C. area's restaurants and night clubs. When Marion Flagg decided to leave the restaurant business and close the Jazzland in April 1953, Hall opted to stay behind and keep the night club going. After a quick remodeling job, which mainly consisted of changing the night club's front facade, Hall assumed the lease on the building and reopened the restaurant on Friday, April 24, 1953 as Captain Joe's Port of Georgetown Supper Club, with the Hall-composed ads in local newspapers proclaiming: "Excitement Awaits You...behind these doors! Exciting food, exciting décor, exciting entertainment and music at Washington's new nite spot."

During Captain Joe's Port of Georgetown Supper Club's four-month run, the house band was a Dixieland jazz quintet known as the Foggy Bottom Five. Unfortunately for Hall, business dropped as the summer months wore on and as Labor Day approached he put the word out that his restaurant enterprise was up for sale.

Entering into the picture at this point was the three-man team of Vince Tramonte, Tony Tramonte and Mike Munley. The group had become acquainted while hanging out at the Knights of Columbus Edward Douglass White Council 2473 in Arlington, Virginia. Munley reportedly heard of Captain's Joe's sinking vessel and approached the two brothers about entering the restaurant business. It took little urging to get the two Tramontes to join the plan.

Vince Tramonte was a real estate attorney who had in part financed his undergraduate education at the University of Virginia by singing in various bands. He brought a love of music and a wealth of legal knowledge to the team. Tony Tramonte was a dentist in Northern Virginia with a thriving practice. In August 1953 the sale of the business was completed and Joe Hall closed the Jazzland. The new operators moved in, cleaned the premises, changed the name on the façade once again, and a new night club had arrived on the scene.

The Bayou, as the new establishment was called, opened to the public on the night of Friday, September 11, 1953 and for entertainment offered live Dixieland music by Bobby Conway and His Dixie Six (featuring cornetist Wild Bill Whelan). They remained the primary headliner for the remainder of 1953 and throughout 1954, with Country Thomas and His Basin Street Six getting the call when Conway had other engagements. This particular style of jazz music defined the night club throughout the 1950s and into the 1960s.

House band duties at the Bayou from 1955 to 1959 went to Wild Bill Whelan and His Dixie Six, with a number of esteemed jazz musicians making guest appearances. Among these added attractions were: bands such as Will Alger and His Salt City Six, Joe Rinaldi's Swanee Six, the Orchestra (directed by Bill Potts and featuring saxophonist Stan Getz), the Jack Nimitz Quartet and Ron Erwin's Seldom Fed Five; singer-banjoist Danny Barker; pianist Willy "The Lion" Smith; clarinetists Pee Wee Russell, Tony Parenti, Peanuts Hucko, Sol Yaged and Hank D'Amico; saxophonists Bud Freeman, Coleman Hawkins and Illinois Jacquet; cornetists Rex Stewart and Wild Bill Davison; trumpeters Jimmy MacPartland, Billy Butterfield, Phil Napoleon, Pee Wee Erwin, Bobby Hacket, Max Kaminsky, Bobby Hackett, Ruby Braff, Charlie Shavers and Roy Eldridge; trombonists Cutty Cutshall, Big Chief Russell Moore and Miff Mole; and violinist Joe Venuti.

From 1960 to 1963 the Bayou maintained its Dixieland jazz format and their top attractions included: bands such as Wild Bill Whelan and His Dixie Six, Big Bill Decker and His Dixie Six, Clyde McCoy and His Famous Dixieland Band, Joe Renaldi and the Foggy Bottom Six, Wally Garner and His New Orleans Jazz Band, Eddie Dimond and the Foggy Bottom Six and the Gaslight Trio; singers Gloria Hudson and Fats Pinere; singer-pianist Calvin "Hound Dog" Ruffin; pianist Don Ewell; and several all-star jazz sessions that featured such musicians as: trumpeters Hal Posey and Kenny Fulcher; trombonists Charlie Butler and Slide Harris; and bassist Tom Moultry. In addition, a new attraction was added to the Bayou's roster in 1963 in the form of burlesque dancer Julie Gibson, who became an immediate fan favorite.

Jazz continued to be the Bayou's featured musical style through the summer of 1965. Some of the talented performers to appear during this time were Eddie Dimond and the Foggy Bottom Six (featuring trumpeter Hal Posey), Woody Herman and His 16-Piece Band, Count Basie and His Orchestra, and a number of guest pop singers including Jodie Sands, Grace Markay, Rita Carol, Lynn Cornell, Gloria Hudson and Julie Taylor. During this time burlesque dancers to fill the bill when Julie Gibson took a night off included Penny Damone, Judy Kelly, Lisa Duran and Nina Rosee.

In the summer of 1965 Vince Tramonte scouted a red-hot rock and roll band called the Telstars that was packing them in at a night club called the Beachcomber in Ocean City, Maryland. In September of that year after the beach season had concluded he brought the band into the Bayou and their performances filled the club to capacity. Overnight, jazz was out, rock and roll was in, and the Telstars remained the Bayou house band for the next three years.

The Bayou went on to become the Washington, D.C. area's premiere rock and roll night club. In the early 1970s they primarily booked several local bands on a regular basis. These included Innocent Color, Billy Budd, Wizzard, Tahoka, the Cherry People, Face Dancer, the Nighthawks, Cherry Smash and Sinbad. In 1974 they began bringing in national rock and roll acts on an occasional basis, with the first concerts of note being Kiss on Monday, March 25, 1974 and Badfinger on Tuesday, March 26, 1974. Later in the year Mike Tramonte, son of Vince Tramonte, stepped up as manager and continued to book a mix of local groups and big-name talent. Through the years some of the biggest acts in popular music appeared at the Bayou including U2, Foreigner, Dire Straits, the Police, the Talking Heads, Billy Joel and Robin Trower.

The Bayou closed its doors on Thursday, December 31, 1998 and in 2000 the historic building marked 3135 K Street NW was torn down. Since April 2003 the former site of the Bayou has been occupied by a movie theatre complex called AMC Loews Georgetown 14 with a new listed address of 3111 K Street NW.

CHAPTER THIRTY-FOUR
THE HOME OF SOUL JAZZ: BOHEMIAN CAVERNS

In 1922 the Lewis Building was constructed at 2011 11th Street NW in Washington, D.C. for owner John W. Lewis, founder of the Industrial Savings Bank. During its early years the structure's ground floor housed the George Davis Drugstore, which utilized the basement below as storage space. In 1926 a local entrepreneur named James Fletcher leased out the basement area and opened a private club in its space called Night Club Bohemia which had a capacity of 100 occupants. Ads in local newspapers proclaimed the new night spot to be "A nice place for nice people." Opening night at the establishment occurred on Friday, October 22, 1926 with a bill consisting of Claude Hopkins and His Harmony Band, blues singer Miss Bea Foote and singer-dancer Miss Billie Griffin.

The Friday, October 15, 1926 edition of the Washington Tribune newspaper ran an advertisement that described Night Club Bohemia as "Rich in Appointment, Grand in Environment: A beautiful cozy love nest filled with a continuous chant of sweet and pretty melodies, embroidered with an increasing flow of rich and tuneful harmonies," and proclaimed it to be a "beautiful harbor of enchantment."

For most of the night club's first three years, the Henry Sheppard Orchestra retained house band duties, with special guest appearances frequently made by visiting musicians of note, including Duke Ellington, who joined the Sheppard's band on piano for a week-long engagement at the club from Saturday, April 16 to Sunday, April 24, 1927.

Night Club Bohemia underwent changes in ownership and trading names. From 1928 to 1934 it was in operation as the Crystal Caverns Club and from 1935 to 1958 it went by the name Club Caverns. For most of the 1930s new owner Elston Nightengale operated Club Caverns as a private blues and jazz club and retained Harold Francis' Caverneers as his house orchestra, with such singers as George Craft, Jack Meredith, Doris Rhubottom, "Queen o' Jump-Jive" Bea Morton and Estrelita Brooks making regular appearances. Other acts that enjoyed extended engagements at the Club Caverns during those years were Bea Lemmons and Her Comedy Club Chorus and a number of blues singers including Mary Dixon, Maxine Johnson and Max Bailey. In addition, the club featured comedians such as Apus Brooks, Rastus Murray and Joe "Mother" Smothers, along with dancers such as Bay Scruggs and the team of Spic and Span.

For much of the 1940s Club Caverns was owned and operated as a private club by the trio of Bennie Caldwell (who also owned Club Bali), Alonza Collins and Blanche Calloway, with memberships selectively offered to both Black and White applicants who met management's approval. As a result, Club Caverns maintained an air of high-society stuffiness, while enjoying some of its finest years in terms of talent offerings and overall popularity.

During the 1940s it was customary for a typical Club Caverns evening to offer a jazz orchestra, featured singers, and several comedians and dancers on the undercard. From 1940 to 1949 some of the club's featured bands and star musicians were: Brother Hill and His Caverneers, Harold Francis' Orchestra, Streamline and His Orchestra, Rookie Davis and Her Orchestra, Tommy Chase and His Band, the Club Harlem Ensemble, the Palmer Brothers, Johnny Malachi and His Orchestra, the Three Loose Nuts (featuring singer-bassist-pianist Eddie Cole), the Three Riffs, the Edwards Sisters, Sonny Lee and His Orchestra, the Choraliers Quartette, Phil Phillips and His Orchestra, Coleridge Davis and His Orchestra, Sir Charles and His Six Madcaps of Swing, Ray Abrams and His Orchestra, Al Dunn and His Trio, the Gaylindon Trio, the Harlemaires, the Four Tunes, the Cat

Anderson Quartet, the Doles Dickens Quartet; pianist Marlow Morris; trumpeter-dancer Taps Miller; and pianist-trumpeter-dancer John Zella.

Jazz vocalists were always prominently featured at Club Caverns, a number of whom have since achieved legendary status in the music world. During the 1940s some of the headlining singers to appear in the night club were George Craft, Willie Dukes, Jimmy Young, Doris Rhubottom, Bea Morton, Maxine Johnson, Kay Hedgeman, Alma Turner, Doris Woods, Marian Harrison, Mae Diggs, Dorothy Lee, Louis Diggs, May Arthur, Blanche Coles, Drusilla Drew, Marie Young, Alice Dixon, Marion Miller, Dolores Brown, Naomi Price, Rita Costello, Bob Brown, Babe Wallace, Connie Alcaines, Edna Sourez, Willie Bryant, Bobby Caston, Lora Pierre, Esty Cooper, Viola Vanderhill, Mae Joy, George Clark, Ginger Neale, Marshall Haley, Betty Logan, Starling Hatchett, Buster Cromwell, Betty Bartlett, Bernice Arnold, Viola Jefferson, Lucille Towns, Rita Grenae, Dinks Patterson, Bunny Briggs, Manhattan Paul, Maxine Gomez, Nan Snow, Billie Holiday, Gordon McKay, Pearl Bailey, Evelyn Keys, Honey Brown, Alberta Prymes, June Evans, Billie Stewart, Lillian Fitzgerald, Lee Richardson, Edna Mae Harris, Louis Brown, Johnny Gardner, Alberta Adams, Myra Johnson, Gladys Bentley, Margaret Watkins, Becky Corbett, Delores White, Johnny Davis, Nellie Forman, Mae Daniels, Gwen Tynes, Rena Collins, Marie Sayles, Eva Foster, Savannah Churchill, Ida James, Alberta Hunter, Albina Jones, Bobby Keys, Rita Greenway, Ann Maxwell, Ollie Potter, Ulla Bryant, Gatemouth Moore, Billy Williams, Melrose Colbert, June Norton and Gracie Allen.

Supplemental entertainment also contributed to the success of Club Caverns during the 1940s and joining the bands and singers during this time were such comedians as Sporty-O-Dee, Rastus Murray, David Whitty, Short and Shorty, Snooky Marsh, Snooky Morris, Leon "Chops" Oden, George Williams, Slap and Happy, Joe "Mother" Smothers, Badie and Tuffy, Gussie Washington, Dick Montgomery, Billy Mitchell, Shorty Daniels, Eddie Lemons, Bunkley Redding, Eddie Jenkins, Al Wilson and comedian-dancer Johnny Gardner.

Rounding out the action were dancers of various styles; their names included Baby Scruggs, Catherine Randall, May Joy, Pauline Bryant, Lois Campbell, Myrtle Wilson, Atta Blake, Olivia Gordon, Connie Harris, Edna Mae Waters, Princess Minnola, Dollie Pembrooke, Neeta Johnson, Estella Young, Pauline Moore, Delores Wade, Rosebud Thomas, Dolores Dennis, Gladys Ellis, Jeanette Reeves, Chinky Grimes, Watina Allen, Lovey Lane, Viola Kemp, Hotcha Drew, Billie McLaurence, Dodo Proctor, Ralph Brown, Walter Green, Jimmie Mordecai, Tom Collins, Ray Sneed, Jr., S.H. Dudley, Jr., Leroy Carrington, Peckin' Joe Steele, Teddy Quarles, Eddie Rector, Snake Hips Hill, Duke Jenkins, Artie Brook, Tommy Thompson, Bobby Simpson, Harvey Collins, Satchel Paige, Apus and Estrelita Brooks, Helen Penn and Her Pennettes, Spic and Span, Two Giants of Rhythm, Rae Pearle and Yo-Yo, Luck and Lucky, Candy and Pepper, Randolph and Purvis, Saunders and Vinson, Von and Gertrude, Leonado and Zola, Phillips and Wald, Zorro and Margo, Hon and Bunny and the Three Johnnies.

During the 1950s Club Caverns went through many changes including transfers of ownership, phases as a private membership bottle club, and several different periods of inactivity. Early in the decade the house band was jazz drummer T.N.T. Tribble and His Band (often advertised as T.N.T. Tribble and His Recking Crew). In 1952 and 1953 some of the top headliners were Chris Powell and His Blue Flames, Frank Motley and His Orchestra, the Heartbreakers, and singers Dolores Parker and Pearl Bailey.

In the middle part of the 1950s Club Caverns operated as a private bottle club, first under owner Thomas Dent, and then under his successor Robert Rucker. After what seemed like a constant battle with the Government of the District of Columbia Alcoholic Beverage Control Board over various infractions, the establishment rebounded in 1958 by installing the Billy Spooner Trio as its house band and featuring such performers as blues singers George Craft, Jimmy Moultrie and Little Sammy Ward.

In December 1958 the name of the night club was shortened to the Caverns and an effort was made to bring in more nationally known jazz talent. In 1959 the action picked up and from January to July of that year headliners at the Caverns included Johnny Lytle and His Hammond Organ Trio, the Wild Bill Davis Trio, the Richard Otto Organ Trio, Willis "Gator Tail" Jackson and His Swinging Organ Group (featuring guitarist Bill Jennings), the Johnny Griffin Quartet, the Max Roach Quintet, and singer-keyboardist Sarah McLawler. In addition, featured musicians at the club included: saxophonists Sonny Stitt, Jackie McLean and Benny Golson; trumpeters Webster Young and Kenny Dorham; trombonists Bob Brookmeyer and Calvin Jones; cornetist Nat Adderley; and drummer Philly Jo Jones.

In July 1959 the Caverns was sold to Angelo Alvino, who immediately enlisted his friend Tony Taylor as club manager and booking agent. Taylor, given name Anthony Elias, had been born and raised in Washington, D.C. and had founded the Washington Jazz Society in 1953 at the age of 26. By profession he was an illustrator with the Navy Hydrographic Office. In his spare time he played guitar and piano, though he specialized in evaluating musical talent. Legend has it he crossed paths with Alvino in the middle 1950s while both were observing homeless musicians playing for handouts on the corner of 11th and U Streets NW. Alvino vowed to bring Taylor aboard should he ever purchase a night club and after acquiring the Caverns he kept his word.

Angelo Alvino honored the scheduled bookings for his new night club for approximately eight weeks. During the late summer of 1959 headliners at the Caverns included such jazz performers as: the Wilber Little Trio, the Max Roach Quintet and the Pepper Adams Quintet; pianist Phineas Newborn; cornetist Nat Adderley; saxophonists Benny Golson and Jackie McLean; singer-trumpeter Kenny Dorham and trumpeter Bill Hardman.

Tony Taylor made the Thelonius Monk Quartet his first official booking and the foursome worked an engagement at the Caverns from Wednesday, August 26 through Monday, August 31, 1959. Taylor then brought in the Paul Chambers Trio, which performed on Tuesday, September 1 and Wednesday, September 2, 1959. After Wednesday evening's performance the Caverns went dark for reasons still not entirely clear. It took Angelo Alvino a full year to resolve a myriad of issues between his private investors and the Government of the District of Columbia Alcoholic Beverage Control Board, in addition to completing extensive interior renovations. He reopened the night club under the new name of Bohemian Caverns on Monday, September 12, 1960 with jazz singer-pianist Shirley Horn and Her Trio as his new house band, a position they would hold through January 1961.

Shirley Horn was a beloved Washington-born singer-pianist and her bandmates at the time were bassist Lewis Powers and drummer Stump Saunders. The trio's sets regularly included such favorite numbers as "Mountain Greenery," "Wild is the Wind" and "City of Blues." Horn later embarked on a solo career and released albums for a number of major record labels including Mercury and ABC-Paramount. Bohemian Caverns then progressed through the 1960s as the city's most prestigious jazz night club.

From 1961 to 1964 some of the jazz ensembles to appear at Bohemian Caverns included the JFK Quintet, the Reuben Brown Trio, the Butch Warren Trio, the Maurice Roberts Quintet, the Shirley Horn Trio, Bill Dockens and His Band, the John Coltrane Quartet, the Betty Gray Trio, the Ramsey Lewis Trio, the Wynton Kelly Trio, the Jackie McLean Quartet, the Roland Kirk Quartet, the Kenny Duca Trio, Art Blakey's Jazz Messengers, the Horace Silver Quintet, the Sam Dailey Trio, the Manny Logan Quartet, the Horace Parlan Trio, the Albert Daly Trio, the Junior Munce Trio, the Bobby Timmons Trio, the Dorothy Ashby Trio, the Yusef Lateef Quintet, the MGM Trio, the Thelonious Monk

Quartet, the Les McCann Trio, the Max Roach Quartet, the Bill Evans Trio and the Brother Jack McDuff Quartet.

Other headliners during that period included: jazz singers Joe "Everyday" Williams and Abbey Lincoln; R&B singers Lou Rawls and Valentine Pringle; classical guitarist Miguel Justin; jazz saxophonist Eric Dolphy; and the folk duo of Gary and Bart.

The late 1960s saw Bohemian Caverns survive the Riots of 1968, but close in October of that year due to a downturn in business. From 1965 until its closing appearances were made by bands such as the Don Patterson Trio, the Three Sounds, the Eddie Harris Quartet, the Bobby Timmons Trio, the Dorothy Ashby Trio, the Chico Hamilton Quartet, the Les McCann Trio, the Ramsey Lewis Trio, the Julian "Cannonball" Adderley Sextet, the Herman Foster Trio, the John Coltrane Quartet, Arthur Prysock and His Band, the Barry Miles Jazztet, the Donald Criss Trio, the Miles Davis Quintet, the Charles Able Trio, the Horace Silver Quintet, the Sole Brothers, Jud Watkins and the Soulfuls, the ESP Trio, the Modern Jazz Quartet, the Stan Getz Quartet, the Shirley Horn Trio, the McCoy Tyner Trio, the Willie Bobo Sextet, the Echoes, the Latin Jazz Cookers, the Eddie Henderson Quintet, the Stanley Turrentine Quartet, the Young Holt Trio, the Roy Merriweather Trio, the Kenny Burrell Quartet, the Lou Donaldson Quartet, the Jack McDuff Quartet, the Richard "Groove" Holmes Trio, Art Blakey and the Jazz Messengers, the Roland Kirk Quartet, the Rufus Harley Quartet, John Bartell and the Soul Masters, the Dave Aiken Trio, the Hugh Masekela Quintet, the Ray Bryant Trio, the Wes Montgomery Quartet, the Freddie McCoy Quartet, the Sonny Stitt Quartet, the Bill Evans Trio, Andy and the Bey Sisters and the Larry Young Trio.

Others to perform at the club during its final years included: blues singer-guitarist Muddy Waters; jazz singers Jean DuShon and Joe Carroll; R&B singers Aretha Franklin, Lou Rawls, Carla Thomas, Erma Franklin and Walter Jackson; jazz pianist Shirley Scott; jazz flutist Herbie Mann; jazz singer-guitarist George Benson and jazz vibraphonist Gary Burton.

During the 1960s three major jazz albums were recorded at Bohemian Caverns: "The Ramsey Lewis Trio at the Bohemian Caverns" (The Ramsey Lewis Trio; Argo Records, 1964); "The In Crowd" (The Ramsey Lewis Trio; Argo Records, 1965); and "Live at Bohemian Caverns – Washington, D.C." (Les McCann; Limelight Records, 1967).Of these recordings, the album "The In Crowd" peaked at number two on Billboard magazine's popular music "Billboard Top LP's" chart on Saturday, November 6, 1965, while the single "The In Crowd" reached number two on their "Top Selling Rhythm & Blues Singles" chart on Saturday, September 25, 1965 and number five on their "Billboard Hot 100" pop singles chart on Saturday, October 9, 1965.

After Bohemian Caverns closed in October 1968, several attempts were made to keep the basement space in operation as a night club. From December 1969 to March 1969 it housed a night club called Frank's Cave. It then sat vacant until February 1970, at which time it opened for three weeks as the Caverns and offered two R&B house bands, the Young Senators and the Ronnie Clark Quintet. The building sat vacant for the remainder of 1970 and all of 1971. It then operated as the Underground Supper Club from 1972 to 1983 and as the New Underground Supper Club from 1984 to 1989.

After a period of vacancy that lasted several years, the Lewis Building was purchased by Al Afshar in 1998. He reopened Bohemian Caverns to the public on Friday, July 7, 2000 with jazz organist Jimmy Smith as the headlining act. In 2006 Afshar sold the night club business to an outfit headed by Omrao Brown called Mahogany LLC, and Bohemian Caverns continued to offer local and national jazz and R&B acts. As the You Street area underwent a revitalization that saw dozens of new restaurants and night clubs open up along it streets, Bohemian Caverns suffered a drop in business and closed its doors after a performance by Kris Funn and Cornerstone on Saturday, March 26, 2016.

CHAPTER THIRTY-FIVE
THE WASHINGTON COLISEUM

The Washington Coliseum (1140 3rd Street NW, Washington, D.C.) was constructed in 1940 and originally opened as Uline Arena on the night of Tuesday, January 28, 1941 with an ice revue entitled "Ice-Capades of 1941." The arena was owned by Migiel J. "Mike" Uline, who had been born in the Netherlands in 1874 and arrived in the United States at age 16, where he settled in Cleveland, Ohio and worked as a cigar box maker and later in a quarry and ice plant. He went on to own ice plants in Cleveland, Toledo and Warren, Ohio and relocated to Washington, D.C. in 1931, where he eventually racked up a total of 69 patents on devices used in his ice industry.

Uline Arena was built with a $450,000 loan from the Reconstruction Finance Corporation and hosted all sorts of sporting and entertainment events including professional boxing and wrestling, skating, rodeo, circus, roller derby, indoor track and field events for Catholic University and hockey games for Georgetown University. The arena was also home to two of the city's first professional sports teams, the Washington Lions of the Eastern Hockey League, and the Washington Capitols of the Basketball Association of America, who were coached by Red Auerbach from 1946 to 1949 (the BAA was a precursor to the NBA).

Soon after its opening Uline Arena began offering musical concerts which added additional seating to its large ground floor that resulted in a capacity of 8,000 occupants. The first musical act to appear in the arena was baritone singer Paul Robeson, who, in an event sponsored by the Washington Committee for Aid to China on Friday, April 25, 1941, sang ballads and spirituals while backed by the Washington People's Chorus under the direction of Alfred Manning.

Other major musical events to take place in Uline Arena in 1941 included a mixed-race swing concert that featured Erskine Hawkins and His Orchestra and Benny Goodman and His Orchestra on Tuesday, July 8, 1941, and a patriotic musical revue entitled "It's Fun to be Free" that took place on Tuesday, November 4, 1941, was hosted by Burgess Meredith, and featured Betty Field, Jesse Matthews, Ray Bolger, Martha Scott, Gladys Swarthout, Kitty Carlisle, Larry Adler, Fred Keating and Sergeant York.

In June 1942 the facility began booking dance orchestras as part of their "Uline Arena Summer Garden" program. The house band for most of the summer was Jack Coffey and His "Rockin' Rhythm" Orchestra featuring singers Pat Murphy, Dick Kaps, Ginny Braynard and the Rockette Choir. When Coffey took a night off, Chick Lloyd and His Orchestra usually stepped in to fill the void.

The next major popular music event at the arena was an event billed as "Concert in Jazz" which took place on Monday, May 17, 1943 and featured a team consisting of cornetist-guitarist-trumpeter Bobby Hackett, clarinetist Pee Wee Russell, banjoist-guitarist Eddie Condon and double bassist Bob Haggert playing opposite a band comprised of trombonist Marty Emerson, trumpeter Charlie Frankhauser, pianist Eddie Finckel, bassist Mert Oliver, saxophonist Lee Hardesty and drummer Ralph Hawkins.

That summer the Uline Arena Summer Garden returned, with appearances made by such bands as Ted Fio Rito and His Orchestra (featuring singers Lynn Stephens and Jimmy Baxter), Shep Fields and His New Music (featuring singer Buddy Clark), Freddy Mack and His Orchestra and Freddie Shaffer and His Orchestra (featuring the Victory Sweethearts). Victor Lopez and His Orchestra made an October visit, and on Monday, November 15, 1943 the arena hosted "A Cavalcade of Negro Music" that featured the Four Ink Spots, the Art Tatum Trio, the Silver Echo Quartette, Cootie Williams and His

Orchestra, singer Ethyl Wise and singer-pianist Erskine Butterfield. The year was rounded out with a concert by Duke Ellington and His Famous Orchestra on Monday, December 6, 1943.

Musical events were lightly scheduled at Uline Arena throughout the remainder of the 1940s and among those bands making concert appearances during the decade were drummer Buddy Rich and His Orchestra, Ray Anthony and His Orchestra (featuring singer Dick Noel), Woody Herman and His Orchestra, the King Cole Trio and Horace Heidt and His Orchestra.

Various types of musical concerts were staged at Uline Arena in the 1950s including two significant shows by C&W promoter Connie B. Gay: a concert labeled "Gay Time" on Saturday, February 16, 1952 headlined by Jimmy Dean and the Texas Wildcats and singer-guitarists Rosalie Allen, Elton Britt and Ann Jones; and a New Year's Eve country music spectacular on Friday, December 31, 1954 featuring Jimmy Dean and the Texas Wildcats and singer-guitarists Red Foley, Ernest Tubb and Andy Griffith. A rock and roll concert in the arena on Friday, November 11, 1955 was headlined by Bill Haley and His Comets, and jazz concerts in 1957 and 1958 featured Illinois Jacquet and His Orchestra and the Lionel Hampton Orchestra, respectively. On Friday, February 20, 1959 a rock and roll spectacular offered singer Frankie Avalon, pop singer Linda Laurie, rockabilly singer Jessie Lee Turner, the Crests, the Chantels, Dickie Do and the Don'ts and the Show Club Orchestra.

Mike Uline died on Saturday, February 22, 1958 and Uline Arena was then sold to Harry Lynn, who changed the name of the facility to the Washington Coliseum on Sunday, September 17, 1961 – the first day of an eight-night stand by Rev. Morris Cerullo's Great Miracle Crusade. The coliseum then landed a permanent place in rock and roll history when it hosted the first American concert by the Beatles on Tuesday, February 11, 1964.

Other significant Washington Coliseum concert headliners of the decade included: The Dave Clark Five (Wednesday, May 27, 1964); the Four Seasons (Sunday, June 7, 1964); Chuck Berry (Friday, February 12, 1965); the Beach Boys (Saturday, April 24, 1965); Gerry and the Pacemakers (Thursday, May 13, 1965); the Rolling Stones (Saturday, November 13, 1965); Bob Dylan (Sunday, November 28, 1965); the Rolling Stones (again; this time on Sunday, June 26, 1966); the Mamas and the Papas, Mitch Ryder and the Detroit Wheels, Question Mark and the Mysterians, the Left Banke and Webster's New Word (Saturday, October 15, 1966); Herbie Mann and His Quintet (Saturday, December 3, 1966); the Beach Boys (Saturday, April 15, 1967); "Soul-O-Rama '67" featuring the Young Holt Trio, King Curtis, the Manhattans, Jimmy Castor, Lorraine Ellison and the Paul Hawkins Jazz Quintet (Sunday, October 15, 1967); the Temptations (Sunday, October 29, 1967); and Wilson Pickett, the Magnificent Men and Phil Flowers (Saturday, May 25, 1968).

Things slowed considerably in the 1970s, with only two major rock and roll events taking place in the coliseum: a concert headlined by Blood, Sweat and Tears on Sunday, March 7, 1971 and a show offering Rare Earth, the Funkadelics and the Ohio Players on Monday, October 15, 1973.

The last live music concert to be held at the Washington Coliseum was headlined by Run DMC on Saturday, December 1, 1984. The building then sat unused for two years before being leased for a mere 30 days in December 1986 by the Takoma Park Christian Faith Center. The building was then vacant for the next seven years before being used as a refuse transfer station by a company called Waste Management from 1994 to 2003. For several years thereafter the facility was used by Tag-B Group Valet Services as an indoor parking lot. In 2004 the building was purchased by developer Doug Jemal, who established ownership under the legal name of Jemal's Uline LLC. Jemal renamed the structure Uline Arena and today the refurbished building exists as an office-retail redevelopment.

CHAPTER THIRTY-SIX
THE MUSIC MOGULS

Through the years, many individuals had interesting behind-the-scene roles in the Washington, D.C. area music scene. Musicians and night club owners aside, there were various entrepreneurs that contributed to the local music industry, particularly during the 1940s and 1950s, whose vision, independence and accomplishments still resonate among area music fans today. Among those who made their mark on the local music scene are Ahmet Ertegun, who co-founded Atlantic Records, the Feld Brothers, who were noted for their lavish concert presentations, and Lillian Claiborne, who worked tirelessly to record many of the region's musical artists when the local recording industry was in its infant stages.

When evaluating the Washington, D.C. area's contributions to the worldwide music industry, a name that repeatedly surfaces is Ahmet Ertegun, a man who spent his teenage and young adult years in the nation's capital and is noted for being co-founder, president and chairman of the board for Atlantic Records. His contributions to popular music led him to become one of the world's most highly esteemed rock and roll moguls.

Ahmet Ertegun was born Tuesday, July 31, 1923 in Istanbul, Turkey and lived in Switzerland, France and England before moving to Washington, D.C. in 1935 with his father Mehmet Munir Ertegun, mother Hayrunnisa, sister Selma and older brother Nesuhi. At that time his father was appointed Ambassador E&P Turkey to the United States of America and the family moved into the Turkish Embassy at 1606 23rd Street NW.

Ertegun attended St. Albans School in Washington, D.C. before finishing his high school education two years early in 1940 at Landon School in Bethesda, Maryland. As a teenager he acquired a love for race music, and, along with his brother, began collecting 78rpm discs, eventually amassing more than 25,000 records and establishing one of the largest private collections in the world. He also attended the Howard Theatre on a weekly basis where he saw such performers as Duke Ellington and His Orchestra, Louis Armstrong and His All Star Band, Cab Calloway and His Cotton Club Orchestra and Jimmie Lunceford and His Orchestra.

A major event occurred in Ertegun's life when the Quality Music Company replaced the J&B Market at 1836 7th Street NW in the You Street area of Washington, D.C. in 1938. The store specialized in radio sales and repairs and also offered a small area devoted to the sale of 78rpm records, a practice that would expand with the introduction of 33rpm long-play records and 45rpm single records in the late 1940s. Eventually their record sales department replaced the radio services division altogether.

In the late 1930s and early 1940s Ertegun and his brother spent many hours in the store several days a week, picking out old jazz and blues records which they purchased at the price of three for a quarter. The store was owned by Max Silverman, who, because of his love of record sales, came to be known in the shop as "Waxie Maxie." In October 1953 the name of the store was changed to Waxie Maxie Quality Music and in 1965 the chain began developing, with several stores opening their doors throughout the Washington, D.C. area as Waxie Maxie's Quality Music Stores. Unfortunately, the original Quality Music Company store on 7th Street NW was burned down in the riots of April 1968 and never reopened at that location.

Ertegun graduated from St. John's College in Annapolis, Maryland in 1944 with a Bachelor of Arts in philosophy. His father passed away that same year, after which Ertegun moved out of the Turkish Embassy, and, along with his mother, took an apartment nearby in Washington, D.C. at 2500 Q Street NW #109. He spent most of the next three years taking graduate courses in philosophy at Georgetown University, though he never completed his master's degree.

It was during this time that Ertegun and Max Silverman reportedly visited a number of night clubs in the You Street area including the Off Beat Club, Club Caverns, the Casbah Restaurant, Republic Gardens and Club Bengasi to witness the town's top jazz and blues talent in action.

Ertegun also reportedly invited many of the musicians he scouted to informal jam session at the Turkish Embassy. These activities culminated in a number of live concert presentations organized and directed by Ertegun, the first of which was an event entitled "Jazz Concert" for the Washington Jazz Society that was staged on Monday, April16, 1945 at Joe Turner Arena in Washington, D.C. and featured a band consisting of clarinetist-saxophonist Pee Wee Russell, cornetist Muggsy Spanier, trombonist Marty Emerson, bassist Mert Oliver and drummers Ralph Hawkins and Sid Catlett.

These musical experiences inspired Ertegun to form his own independent record label. In October 1947, with a $10,000 investment from family dentist Dr. Vahdi Sabit, Ertegun co-founded Atlantic Records with Herb Abramson, who worked as a producer for National Records while studying dentistry at New York University. Their first offices were in the Ritz Hotel in Manhattan, New York, with Abramson serving as president and Ertegun serving as vice president in charge of A&R, production and promotion.

Atlantic Records originally specialized in R&B music and included Ruth Brown, Big Joe Turner, the Drifters, the Coasters, the Clovers and Ray Charles among their early acts. In 1967 the company became a subsidiary of Warner Bros.-Seven Arts (now the Warner Music Group) and expanded into rock and roll music, signing up such groups as Cream, CSNY, Led Zeppelin, Yes, Foreigner, the Rolling Stones and Phil Collins. Atlantic Records became one of the world's preeminent music companies and Ertegun would remain with the company in various capacities until his death on Thursday, December 14, 2006 at age 83. Ertegun was inducted into the Rock and Roll Hall of Fame, an organization he co-founded, in the "Non-Performer" category on Wednesday, January 21, 1987.

While Ahmet Ertegun was working his way towards Atlantic Records, the Feld Brothers emerged as one of the most prominent entrepreneurial duos in Washington, D.C. entertainment history. Their odyssey began in a discount drug store in a run-down Black neighborhood, saw them operate a short-lived independent record label that surprisingly yielded a million-selling single, continued on as they became one of the country's major rock and roll promotion and management outfits, and culminated in the acquisition of Ringling Bros. and Barnum & Bailey Circus. Employing a combination of business instinct, music appreciation and innovative practices, the pair enjoyed worldwide fame for their show business exploits which were achieved without ever vacating the nation's capital.

Israel "Izzy" Feld, born Sunday, September 25, 1910 in Whitmer, West Virginia, and Irvin Feld, born Friday, April 19, 1918 in Hagerstown, Maryland, were groomed for the entertainment business early in their lives. They spent much of their youth living in Hagerstown, where they and their four sisters lived with their parents and helped out with the family's clothing store. The two brothers spent the summer of 1931 traveling with a local carnival outfit where they sold half-ounce bottles of snake oil from a makeshift podium. The Feld family moved to Baltimore in 1934 and it was there that Irvin finished his formal schooling.

In 1940 both Israel and Irvin Feld moved to Washington, D.C. where they immediately became involved in the establishment of Super Drugs, Inc., a discount drug store at 1108-1110 7th Street NW, whose building had previously been occupied by the New York Whole Merchandise Company. For the first two years the company's officers were listed as Albert Skylar (president), Milton Skylar (vice president), Sidney Sweren (secretary) and Irvin Feld (treasurer). By 1942 Irvin Feld had taken over as president of the company and his brother Israel was being listed as vice president.

Super Drugs functioned as a pharmacy and variety store and included a large lunch counter and soda fountain. Due to the Feld brothers' love of music, the store also offered a sizeable record section where blues and jazz 78s were sold. The business operated under the name Super Drugs from 1940 to 1942, Super Cut Rate Drugs from 1943 to February 1954, and, lastly, Super Music City from March 1954 to April 1968, after which it closed due to damage from the rioting that took place in the wake of the shooting of Dr. Martin Luther King, Jr.

The Feld Brothers did so well with Super Cut Rate Drugs they decided to expand their holdings, with an emphasis on home entertainment. With record sales greatly stimulating their cash flow, they opened a second store in the city called Super Music and Appliances at 1327 H Street NE on Monday, July 1, 1946, replacing the Sun Radio Company. They operated the business under the shortened name of Super Music from January 1951 to July 1952, and then as Super Music City from August 1952 to February 1963. A third installment of this small chain appeared in 1946 when the Felds opened yet another Super Music City in the National Press Building at 1350 F Street NW. It remained in operation there until 1964.

The Feld brothers were impressed by the tremendous interest in music among the patrons of their stores. To capitalize on this situation they formed their own independent record label, Super Disc, in the summer of 1945, and began recording local and national performing artists from the fields of blues, folk, gospel, jazz and pop.

Over the course of the following three years more than 100 different 78rpm singles were issued on the Super Disc label by such artists as the Loumell Morgan Trio, the Bantam Blues Quartet, the Tennessee Ramblers, the Don Byas Quartet, the Erskine Butterfield Quartet, the Slim Idaho Trio, the Jordan River Boys, the Sid Catlett All Stars, Jimmy Crawley and His Musical Chips, the Sunny Williams Trio, the Doles Dickens Quintet, the Capital Hillbillies, the Singing Crusaders, Viola Watkins and the Super Jazzmen, Ronnie Deauville with the Ram Ramirez Quartet, Elder Lightfoot Solomon, the Blues Boys (featuring Guitar Slim), the Velvetones, Rev. Kelsey's Congregation, Snub Mosley and His Orchestra, the Singing Crusaders, Lena Phillips, Winnie Scott and Bull Moose Jackson.

In addition, there were two known short-lived subsidiaries of Super Disc Records operated by the Feld Brothers in the late 1940s: Scoop Records, which issued singles by Rev. Kelsey's Congregation, Bill Grammer's Shenandoah Valley Boys ("Bill" being singer-guitarist Billy Grammer, who later had a major hit in 1958 with "Gotta Travel On" on Monument Records) and the Christian Leaders Quartet; and Quartet Records, which issued singles by two bands, the Sunset Harmonizers and the Harmonizing Four.

By far the most successful act offered by the Feld Brothers was the now-legendary Arthur "Guitar Boogie" Smith, who released several singles on the Super Disc label, including his signature tune entitled "Guitar Boogie." Issued in 1945, the single reportedly sold more than one million copies, making it the first independent record label to register such a sale.

How Irvin Feld, who had taken on the personal responsibility of recruiting musical talent for the Super Disc record label, came across Arthur Smith is an interesting tale in itself. Smith was born Friday, April 1, 1921 in Clinton, South Carolina and entered the United States Navy in 1943 during World War II. He was stationed at the U.S. Naval Training Center, Bainbridge in Port Deposit, Maryland where he spent what little spare time he had honing his guitar playing and writing songs, showing considerable skill in the styles of folk and jazz.

After competing training in 1944, Smith was assigned to a clerical position at the Naval Transportation Service in Washington, D.C. and began sitting in with the United States Navy Band, then under the direction of band leader Commander Charles Brendler, as a guest guitarist on occasional weekend engagements. He also spent several nights per week throughout 1944 and 1945 performing as a lead guitarist for folk groups in various Washington, D.C. night clubs, including the Shamrock Restaurant in Georgetown and the Covered Wagon Restaurant on 14th Street NW, just north of Thomas Circle. When the Blue Mirror Club opened in June 1945, Smith became their house guitarist and it was there that he caught the attention of Irvin Feld, who was searching for a versatile guitarist to fill out his Super Disc recording sessions.

Arthur Smith proved to be far too talented to remain a session man for long and in late 1945 Irvin Feld had him record a 78rpm single record for Super Disc entitled "Guitar Boogie" (The Rambler Trio Featuring Arthur Smith – Guitar; Super Disc Records, 1945). The B-side of the single was "Beaty Steel Blues" ("The Tennessee Ramblers Featuring Cecil Campbell – Guitar; Super Disc Records, 1945). The up-tempo, 12-bar boogie style instrumental was promoted heavily on local radio stations and reportedly sold more than one million copies, making it the highest selling independent single of the time.

Arthur Smith, meanwhile, moved to Charlotte, North Carolina late in 1945 where he hosted and performed on various radio shows including "Carolina Calling" on station WBT. He later became a C&W music superstar and began hosting "The Arthur Smith Show" on WBTV in Charlotte in 1951, a program that would air for 32 years in 90 markets across the nation. He also recorded and toured for many years with his own group, Arthur Smith and the Cracker-Jacks.

In the late 1940s and early 1950s Arthur Smith and his band returned to Washington, D.C. to perform at such night clubs as the Blue Mirror Club, Club Bali, Café Celebrity and Club Kavakos (where he played with drummer Gene Krupa). In 1955 Smith composed a banjo instrumental entitled "Feudin' Banjos" and recorded the tune with Don Reno. The song later appeared in the film "Deliverance" (Warner Bros., 1972) as "Dueling Banjos." Smith proceeded with legal action that eventually gave him songwriting credit and back royalties in a landmark copyright infringement suit. Arthur Smith retired from the music business in 2006 and passed away on Thursday, April 3, 2014 at the age of 93.

After its initial release, the success of "Guitar Boogie" attracted the interest of several major record companies who were looking to buy out the smaller Super Disc label. In July 1948 Irvin Feld sold the entire Super Disc catalog of released and unreleased master tapes, along with the contracts of several of his performers including Arthur "Guitar Boogie" Smith, to M-G-M Records of New York City, effectively marking the end of his independent record company.

In October 1948 M-G-M had Smith re-record his signature tune and in November the new version of the song was released on the major label as "Guitar Boogie" by "Arthur (Guitar Boogie) Smith and His Cracker-Jacks" (the B-side was a song entitled "Boomerang"). The single subsequently entered the Billboard magazine's "Most-Played Juke Box Folk Records" music popularity chart on Saturday, December 25, 1948 and peaked at number eight on Saturday, January 22, 1949, remaining on this chart for a total of seven weeks and reportedly selling more than three million copies in the process.

With the sale of Super Disc, the Feld brothers next entered the world of concert promotion when they accepted an offer by RCA-Victor to stage a live music event to commemorate the new 45rpm single record format that had just been introduced to the music industry. The concert was staged on Saturday, November 20, 1948 at the District of Columbia National Guard Armory in Washington, D.C. and was headlined by jazz singer Vaughn Monroe and His Orchestra. Tickets, which were priced at $1.00 in advance and

$2.00 at the door, were only available at the Willard Hotel Theatre Ticket Bureau and the Super Music City store on F Street NW. The event drew a near-capacity crowd and the Feld brothers, who had named their new promotional enterprise "Super Attractions," had found a new line of business that would keep them occupied for the next two decades.

Under the banner of Super Attractions, the Feld brothers went on to manage the government-owned Carter Barron Amphitheatre in Washington, D.C. from 1954 to 1976. They eventually built a multi-million dollar empire by booking large rock and roll package tours and managing the careers of numerous big-name entertainers including Paul Anka. On Saturday, November 11, 1967 the Feld brothers achieved their lifelong dream when they purchased, along with Roy Hofheinz (builder of the Houston Astrodome and owner of the Houston Astros baseball team), the Ringling Bros. and Barnum & Bailey Circus – "The Greatest Show on Earth" – for $8 million.

Since their arrival in Washington, D.C. the Feld brothers had lived at various addresses in the city with their respective spouses and families. For most of the 1950s the brothers shared an apartment at 4545 Connecticut Avenue NW #911. After Irvin's wife died in 1958, he moved into a unit at 4501 Connecticut Avenue NW #716, while Israel moved in at apartment #717. After a 10-year stay in that building, the brothers moved their families into penthouse suites at the Colonnade (2801 New Mexico Avenue NW), where they remained until their respective passings. Israel Feld died of a heart attack on Friday, December 15, 1972 at the age of 62 and Irvin Feld died of a cerebral hemorrhage while vacationing in Venice, Florida on Thursday, September 6, 1984 at the age of 66. Irvin's son, Kenneth Feld, inherited all of his father's holdings and took charge of Feld Entertainment, which owns and produces Ringling Bros. and Barnum & Bailey Circus. He is still chairman and CEO of the operation today.

On the local scene, one of the earliest and most active record producers was Lillian Claiborne, who actively recruited local musicians into local studios for recording sessions long before it was common practice. Lillian N. Claiborne was born in Newport News, Virginia in 1898, and, although much of her young adult life is cloaked in mystery, it has been reported she spent many years living in New York City before relocating to the nation's capital where she pursued her unique musical interests.

Lillian Claiborne and her husband Samuel Homer Claiborne arrived in Washington, D.C. in 1941 and took an apartment in the Taylor Towers at 4021 9th Street NW #201, a unit they would call home for the next six years. "Homer," as Mr. Claiborne was commonly called, worked as a CPA for Snyder, Farr and Company during his years in the nation's capital and his financial stability allowed Lillian Claiborne to indulge herself in her music-related projects. She scoured the night clubs and recording studios of the city throughout the early 1940s, searching for unrecognized and under-appreciated musical talent, hoping to build a stable of musicians that would record for her independent record label and achieve national recognition and financial prosperity for everyone involved. She has little trouble recruiting a number of acts that were eager to lay their music on the line for her fledging record company.

In 1946 Claiborne joined forces with local music publisher Haskell Birchfield Davis to form an independent record label called DC Records which exclusively featured local homegrown talent, including a number of C&W acts. For 13 years this company, which utilized a mailing address of 1425 Van Buren Street NW, Washington, D.C. for much of its existence (this address was actually the private home of Haskell Davis' parents), rented studio time at various studios throughout the area for their projects, most often utilizing the U.S. Recording Company at 1121 Vermont Avenue NW. More than 50 single releases were commercially released on the label in a variety of musical categories during the company's existence.

A unique record label for its time, the first DC Records releases were a pair of orchestral 78rpm single records issued in January 1947: "No Wonder" by "Ted Alexander, Tiny Meeker's Orchestra," backed with "Yes" by "Ann Hayden – Ted Alexander, Tiny Meeker's Orchestra;" and "A Moment of Madness" backed with "Born to Love You," both credited to "Tiny Meeker's Orchestra."

These were followed up with releases by a procession of pop music acts such as Bill McCune and His Orchestra, Bill Dillard with the Jack Pleis Trio, Larry Laurence with the Quintones and Bob Berry with the Ziggy Travers Trio. There were also records by such C&W groups as the Howington Brothers, Sleepy McDaniel and His Radio Playboys, Ray Davis' Band, Dudley Callicutt and the "Go" Boys and Bob Dean and His Southern Serenaders. In addition, Claiborne produced recordings by several race music acts including the Progressive Four, the Gospel Stars, Three B's and a Honey, Frank Motley and His Crew, the Heartbreakers, the Cap-Tans and the Corinthian Singers.

During her tenure as music entrepreneur, Claiborne also released recordings on two more of her own independent record labels, Loop and Gamma, and leased out innumerable selections from her vast library of locally crafted tapes and recordings to a number of outside record labels including Atlantic, Chess, Decca, Specialty, Gem, Josie, Hawkeye, Savoy, Sabu, Golden Crest, Design, Guest Star and others.

In terms of personal endeavors, after the Claibornes left their apartment in Washington, D.C. in 1948, they purchased a home on Montpelier Road in the Manor Club Estates in Rockville, Maryland and remained there until 1970.

From 1957 to 1959 Claiborne, in addition to her work with DC Records, also operated her own music publishing agency, Claiborne Music, out of an office in Washington, D.C. at 1129 Vermont Avenue NW #221. From 1960 to 1963 this agency operated at this address under the name of the Claiborne Agency. From 1964 to 1969 the headquarters for the Claiborne Agency was listed at 930 F Street NW #615, an address in the Atlantis Building, which, in later years, would stake its own place in local music history as the home of the original Nightclub 9:30. From 1970 to 1975 Washington city directories listed Lillian Claiborne's residence as 2939 Van Ness Street NW #1006. When Lillian Claiborne passed away on Wednesday, April 9, 1975 at the age of 77, most of her personal papers, tapes and music-related materials were reportedly destroyed.

CHAPTER THIRTY-SEVEN
SWINGING TOWARDS ROCK AND ROLL

The seeds of rock and roll music were being planted in the Washington, D.C. area during the swing era in many ways. Although the term was not yet being used to describe a particular category of music, several different forms and styles were being experimented with in different settings, with the results wielding indescribable, though seemingly enjoyable, sounds. It was from this increased experimentation with music that the very spirit of what would later become rock and roll emerged within a steadily evolving popular music scene.

After rock and roll music appeared on the scene in the 1950s it didn't take long for the electric guitar to become one of its major musical components, with the instrument achieving increased popularity among both musicians and music followers alike. The electric guitar eventually became the primary point of identification for rock and roll by providing a signature sound, which, when coupled with a back beat rhythm, provided for a new musical experience that would take the music world by storm. While the guitar in its earliest form dates back over 4,000 years to the stringed chetarah of Mesopotamia, the electric guitar did not appear until approximately 20 years before rock and roll was established as a separate classification of popular music.

The electric guitar was created in 1931 by the Ro-Pat-In Corporation of Los Angeles, California, a company founded by Adolph Rickenbacker, Paul Barth and George Beauchamp. With an interest in discovering new ways in which string instruments could be amplified, Beauchamp produced an electromagnetic pickup in which strings passed through two horseshoe magnets and over a coil, creating a magnetic field which amplified the vibration of the strings. He then enlisted the services of his friend Rickenbacker to help manufacture a new product, which was a specially designed aluminum guitar complete with the new electric pickup that required being played on a person's lap using a steel slide, much like today's steel guitars. They initially referred to these new guitars on an informal basis as frying pans, but marketed them as Electro String Instruments.

With Rickenbacker as president, Barth as vice president and Beauchamp serving as secretary-treasurer, the company was established as the Ro-Pat-In Corporation on Thursday, October 15, 1931, and began production of the electric guitar in August 1932. Later, in May 1934, the name of the company was changed to Electro String Instrument Corporation and in advertisements and literature the new guitars were referred to as Rickenbacker Electros. Today those Rickenbacker Electros are recognized as having been the first commercially viable electric guitars.

In the Washington, D.C. area, the electric guitar first appeared on the scene as part of a radio program simply entitled "Electric Guitar" which first aired on station WOL at 7:15pm on the night of Monday, September 30, 1935. Today nothing at all is known about this program as information on its producers, hosts, performers and content has never been uncovered, though it must have generated some measure of interest among local radio listeners at the time.

Several months later, these instruments became available to area musicians, as local newspapers began carrying print advertisements in February 1936 for the electric guitar being sold for $150 (complete with amplifier) at a music store called Droop's (1300 G Street NW). These ads proclaimed: "Not an experiment, but the results of extensive and thorough research. See how it's built with electro magnetic pick-up...and amplification that's the last word in sound."

Local musicians were apparently somewhat slow to add the electric guitar to their night club shows, but local newspapers did mention such instances as they occurred: a band called Raymond and His Hawaiians, while performing at Griffith Farms on Marlboro Pike in Forestville, Maryland, featured "the only electric guitar used in these parts" (Washington Post, Wednesday, August 5, 1936); David Naeole, fiddler and leader of a different band called the Royal Hawaiians at the Ambassador Hotel's Hi-Hat Cocktail Lounge, was noted for taking a turn on the "hard-to-play electric guitar" (Washington Post, Wednesday, December 9, 1936); the same band and the same venue made news again a month later for their rendition of a Mexican cowboy number entitled "Rancho Grande" in which "Clarence Blake, billed as the only electric guitar player in town, is reported to produce some amazing sounds with his tricky instrument" (Washington Post, Wednesday, January 6, 1937); an article entitled "Band Features Electric Guitar at Madrillon" stated: "Seems like the Madrillon Orchestra, under Johnny Shaw's supervision, is always seeking something new. Last week we mentioned the tin fife as a new piece of equipment. This week the orchestra is going Hawaiian and one of the first electric guitars in the District is in the hands of Hugh Barteman. Shaw predicts it will be one of the most popular band instruments" (Washington Post, Wednesday, January 26, 1938); and, in what was probably the first time the instrument was ever played on the Potomac River, Sidney's Swing Orchestra, directed by vocalist Ray Cullen, appeared on board the Wilson Liner for a river cruise, a journey that featured one Ray Nelson, who "plays string bass in the band and presents specialty numbers on the electric guitar" (Washington Post, Sunday, May 22, 1938).

A prime example of the curious path popular music was taking within the Washington, D.C. area is illustrated by an article that appeared in the Washington Post on Friday, April 3, 1936 entitled "'Swing Music' Session is Set for Oak Room: Whoop-la Orchestra, with Toby Walker, Hot Pianist, at Raleigh." The article stated: "You can get the problem of 'what is swing music' off your chest Sunday afternoon by going to the Oak Room, Raleigh Hotel, where a 'swing music jam session' will be held. All the local exponents of whoop-la orchestrations will be there with a special guest in Toby Walker, 'hot' pianist. Ask 20 band men what is 'swing music' and you get 20 different answers ranging from 'It's musician's music' to 'The soul of rhythm' and such. Make up your own definition."

It is obvious from this piece that the content of the music being performed by these Oak Room musicians was unlike anything local music followers had heard before and sessions like these opened new avenues of musical thought and performance.

The complexities of swing music and the direction it was taking would soon surface again in the area. In an article published in the Washington Post on Friday, February 18, 1938 entitled "Evolution of 'Swing' Shown to Kiwanians," it is told how a local orchestra leader named Sidney Seidenman presented a talk on the evolution of swing music to the Washington Kiwanis Club during their weekly meeting at the Mayflower Hotel. Seidenman was quoted as saying: "It is not fair to say that modern dance music is bad just because we don't like it. Anyone who doesn't tap his feet with the rhythm in modern day swing music might as well say he is ready to consign himself to a rocking chair." Seidenman, along with some of the top local orchestra leaders and musicians including Bobby Simpson, Dick Koons, Ralph Hawkins, and Maxine Tappan, then proceeded to demonstrate the latest swing music styles through a rousing live performance.

Seidenman's statements, which came decades before the advent of rock and roll, must be considered somewhat visionary in the way they encouraged acceptance for what was then regarded as a progressive development in the field of popular music. His sentiments would be echoed time and again in the years ahead by ground-breaking musicians who pontificated on new types of musical styles looming on the horizon. In his commentary he emphasized the rhythm of the new music and also displayed with his "rocking chair" reference his conviction that new types of music hold merit, despite their varying levels of acceptance among listeners.

During these early years there were other indications that music was evolving, both in name and content. An article in the Washington Post of Tuesday, December 27, 1938 entitled "Oberlin Students to Give Concert Here Tomorrow" told of a musical event to take place the following night featuring the Oberlin College Varsity Men's Glee Club, which was presenting a program of concert-dance music in the auditorium of the Interior Building. The 35-man dance band from Ohio, whose grand tradition dated back to 1897, thus making them one of the oldest groups of its kind, was in the middle of a tour that would ultimately lead them through the states of Ohio, Pennsylvania, Delaware, Maryland and the District of Columbia where they gave public performances before thousands of enthusiastic fans. Local newspapers noted that the Glee Club was led at the time by a Baltimore, Maryland native named Ad Mueller and called their music "rocking rhythm."

The first time the term "rock and roll" ever appeared in local newspapers occurred in a column in the Washington Post of Monday, December 4, 1939 entitled "News of Capital Night Clubs" by Marry Harris. In the column's final paragraphs, Harris wrote that a local figure named Leroy Thayer, who at the time was the 37-year-old national president of the Dancing Masters of America, related to her that in his opinion the two coming dances in the country were the polka and the "Rock-and-Roll."

The latter dance had been invented by Irene Castle (nee Foote), the legendary New York-born dancer-actress, who, in May 1911 at the age of 18, wed English actor Vernon Castle and subsequently joined him to form a talented and popular dance duo. While the Castles made such dances as the Bunny Hug, the Texas Tommy and the Grizzly Bear world famous, her arrangement of the Rock-and-Roll in 1939 apparently sank without a trace. While the term failed to catch on in the field of popular dance, it would later come to life in the field of popular music.

During the 1940s articles and advertisements in such local newspapers as the Washington Afro American, Washington Daily News, and Washington Post began utilizing what we now call "rock and roll terminology" to help illustrate certain types of live music that were being presented in local night clubs. (The five main components of rock and roll terminology are the words "rock," "rocks," "rockin'," "rocking" and the complete term "rock and roll") While the term "rock and roll" – which was considered to be a euphemism for sex and had actually been sporadically appearing in song titles since the 1920s – was not yet being used to describe a distinct classification of popular music, these and other related words were being used with increasing frequency to energize and intensify the promotional material that served to fuel the local popular music scene.

The use of rock and roll terminology by the local media began when Milt Herth and His Herthquake Trio, a Chicago-based, high-energy jazz outfit that recorded for Decca Records and had proven to be a favorite in the nation's capital, reappeared in Washington, D.C. for an engagement at the Neptune Room that began on Saturday, June 29, 1940 and lasted until Friday, August 9, 1940. Herth proved to be a master Hammond organist (the trio was rounded out by pianist Morty Jacobs and marimba player-drummer Jack Conner) and the Washington Post, which gave substantial coverage to the band during their stay, ran an impressive picture ad on Wednesday, July 3 with the prominent caption "Rocking the Town with Rhythm."

Local journalists had a hard time placing a handle on Herth's musical output. In the "Ringside Table" column of the Washington Post of Friday, July 5, 1940, Mary Harris wrote: "'Precision Boogie-Woogie' is the only phrase to describe the amazing rhythms being rolled out by the new Milt Herth Trio in the Neptune Room. They're a combination prairie fire and train wreck in such numbers as 'Runnin' Wild.' But it's all absolutely precision as well as explosive rhythm. There's not an ounce of 'jam' in it. And they can play anything."

The next noticeable "rock" reference was again attributed to Mary Harris, who in her "Ringside Table" column in the Wednesday, March 19, 1941 edition of the Washington Post wrote: "Party-of-the-week will be the opening of Wardman's new Burgundy Room tomorrow eve and the simultaneous debut of Jack Coffey's 'Rockin' Rhythm' orchestra with full floorshow. This is a double-header with a vengeance. The big new Burgundy Room, a symphony in silver-and-wine, is being opened a day ahead of schedule for the Coffey symposium of dance music and vaudeville, a diversion pattern new to Washington."

Augmenting this account was the "Tips on Tables" column by Paul Ream in the Thursday, March 20, 1941 edition of the Washington Daily News. While reporting on Coffey's Burgundy Room engagement, Ream noted: "Coffey has another innovation with his band in a new system developed by his guitarist, Byron Henry, for amplifying the tones of the piano, guitar and two violins, adding a new range of tone and rich musical color to the Coffey dance music."

For the record, Jack Coffey was the first bandleader in town to incorporate the word "rockin'" into his outfit's moniker and experiment with volume and sound, making his band one of the region's most prominent popular music ensembles of the 1940s.

During this time the King Cole Trio, fronted by famed crooner Nat King Cole, had a big hit on Decca Records with the song "Honeysuckle Rose." To promote the single, the group took an engagement in Washington, D.C. at Paul Young's Romany Room along with emcee Al Merin and Al Spieldock and His Orchestra that lasted from Tuesday, April 22, 1941 until Monday, May 5, 1941. While in town they searched for an after-hours hot spot in which to continue their music-making and found it nearby at Restaurant Madrillon.

There were riotous musical jam sessions informally held at the Restaurant Madrillon and the best musicians to pass through town usually stopped by for the parties. The ever-present Mary Harris, writing in her Washington Post "Ringside Table" column of Monday, April 28, 1941, announced: "The King Cole Trio rolls on like ten tons of anthracite. When they're joined by Al Spieldock's band and Jerry Brandow's trumpet for an after-sweetly at Madrillon, will open at midnight 'jive concert,' the building rocks. Many of our town's rhythm boys drop in for this late 'jam' symphony. We met Madrillon's Hugh Barteman and pianist Sammy Marks hurrying in just as we left. There's a sizzly rumor that Mary La Marr, who used to sing so Paul Young's tomorrow." (Note – that is the verbatim account that appeared in the Washington Post, grammatical errors and all.)

Later that summer, the Washington Afro American ran an intriguing picture advertisement in their Saturday, August 30, 1941 edition for an upcoming Howard Theatre stage show that pronounced: "Rock! To the Rhythm of Andy Kirk and His Clouds of Joy." Also listed on the bill's undercard, which ran from Friday, August 29 to Thursday, September 4, 1941, were June Richmond ("Tunes Torrid and Tantalizing"), Mary Lou Williams ("Sweetheart of the Ivories"), Floyd Smith ("Wizard of the Guitar"), Henry Wells ("Romance in Song"), Stump and Stumpy ("2 Classy Clowns"), and Billy Nightingale ("Tapping T.N.T.").

This would be the first of several examples of the Howard Theatre incorporating rock and roll terminology into their ads and notices. Several months later, the Washington Afro American ended the year with an advertisement in their Saturday, December 6, 1941 edition for Club Caverns that proclaimed: "Bob Brown and Jimmie Hill present their Rockin' n Rhythm Revue starring Six Glamorous Ladies of the Ensemble headlined by Naomi Price – A Ball of T.N.T. – and Marion Hairston, Hill & Hill, Rita Costello, and Bunny Briggs."

Several important examples of rock and roll terminology surfaced in local newspapers in 1942. First was a box ad in the Saturday, January 17, 1942 edition of the Washington Afro

American that featured the announcement: "Another Thrilling Show Beginning Friday, Jan. 16 at Club Caverns. Brilliant Parade O' Stars – Manhattan Paul (Singer-Dancer, Fun Provoker) and His Rockin' & Rhythm Revue – Slim & Slim ('Sensational Dance Team'), Edna Soarez ('Dynamic Soubrette and Thrilling Dancer'), Bobby Caston ('Decca Record Star'), Naomi Price ('Singing Dynamo of Red Hot Tunes'), and Helen Penn and Her Fast-Stepping, Saucy, Exotic Club Harlem Ladies O' Ensemble."

The Washington Afro American next published a Howard Theatre advertisement in their Saturday, February 14, 1942 edition that stated: "Rock to the Rhythm of Earl 'Father' Hines and His Great Orchestra with Washington's Own Composer-Singer Billy Eckstein." Filling out the bill were Madeleine Green ('Lovely Mistress of Melody'), Sahji ('Exotic Queen of the Shakes'), Son & Sonny ('Dancomaniacs on the Loose'), and Joyner and Foster ('Frolicsome Funsters'). This engagement lasted from Friday, February 13 to Thursday, February 19, 1942.

In ensuing years the word "rock" would appear in Washington Afro American ads for many of Earl Hines' Howard Theatre performances. His very next engagement at this venue ran from Friday, September 18, to Thursday, September 24, 1942 and was publicized through similar Washington Afro American ads that proclaimed "Rock to the Rousing Rhythm of Earl 'Father' Hines and His Mighty Orchestra."

A couple of months later the focus switched back to Paul Young's Romany Room when Washington Post journalist Mary Harris, writing in her "Ringside Table" column of Wednesday, April 29, 1942, announced: "Mirthquakes are rocking Paul Young's twice a night. This is the new kind of Paul Young floorshow, unscheduled as 'Information, Please,' riotous as 'Helzapoppin',' Jerry and Turk, emcee Alan Ross, dancer Joan Wood, singer Lila Barbour, also half the waitresses and bus boys in the place are in and out of this panicking revue."

A few weeks later, the Washington Afro American published a Howard Theatre picture advertisement in their Saturday, May 30, 1942 edition that announced: "On Stage – One Week – Opens Friday, May 29. The Newest Sensation of Modern Swing, Lionel Hampton and His Victor Recording Orchestra. Thrill...To the Rhythm That's Rocking the Nation! Hear...The Sophisticated Syncopation of the Future." This particular Howard Theatre lineup was rounded out with appearances by Cholly & Dotty ("Those Rhythm Rounders"), the Bye Sisters ("Harmony Honeys"), and Pops & Louie ("Frolicsome Funsters").

The summer of 1942 was highlighted by the opening of a specially prepared dance floor at Uline Arena that featured one of the region's most popular dance bands. The Saturday, July 18, 1942 edition of the Washington Post included a large advertisement for this new attraction at this venue that read: "Opens Tonight – Uline's Summer Garden. Largest Dance Floor in the South. Jack Coffey and His Rocking Rhythm 13-Piece Orchestra with Pat Murphy (Drummer-comedian), Dick Kaps (vocalist), Ginny Braynard (Charming Songstress) and the Rockette Choir." The bill also included a floorshow featuring singer Chago Rodrigo (formerly with Xavier Cugat), ballroom dancers Montez and Adele, singer-accordionist Helen Dexter, tap dancer Betty Jane Brown, and emcee Will Kreamer.

While Coffey's output probably cannot be categorized as a style that would become rock and roll, its energy pointed in that direction, as descriptions in subsequent articles in the Washington Post referred to his band as a "high tension crew," proclaimed their music as "unpredictable swing" and referred to the Summer Garden's dance floor as "jitterbug heaven."

Another reference to Coffey's rocking nature was made by Mary Harris, who wrote the following in her Washington Post "Ringside Table" column of Monday, August 3, 1942: "Ginny Braynard, songstress with Jack Coffey's Orchestra at Uline's Summer Garden, does all the new ones-up brown, but when she gets out that old 'Rockin' Chair,' she rocks the whole place."

For the next few years there were additional examples of rock and roll terminology in local media music coverage. Mary Harris' "Ringside Table" column in the Friday, October 8, 1943 edition of the Washington Post mentions: "The Louisiana over in Georgetown is rocking with the rhythms of Ray King's 13 swing men" (ironically, this same building would later house the Bayou, which became one of the most storied rock and roll night clubs in Washington, D.C. history). Next, the Saturday, November 10, 1945 edition of the Washington Afro American included an advertisement for Club Caverns that proclaimed: "Washington's Most Intimate Night Spot Presents 'Rockin' in Rhythm' starring Viola Jefferson ('The Girl with the Wistful Eyes') and featuring: Bobby & Sue ('Dance Act'), Dick Montgomery ('Star of Carmen Jones'), Manhattan Paul ('One-Man Variety act'), Jeanette Reeves ('Dancer'), and Brother Hill and His Caverneers." A month later, the Saturday, December 8, 1945 edition of the Washington Afro American ran a large box advertisement for the King Cole Trio's week-long engagement at the Howard Theatre with the prominent caption "Royal Rockin' Rhythm."

In addition, Mary Harris weighed in with two separate entries in her Washington Post "Ringside Table" columns. In the edition of Monday, February 11, 1946 she wrote: "The Brown Derby will rock with the roasting rhythm of Phil Moore, composer of 'Shoo, Shoo, Baby.' It's Phil's first Washington appearance, though the hurricane jive of his recently organized quartet is already familiar on the records and radio." The following week in the edition of Monday, February 18, 1946 she wrote: "The rocking arrangement of Ellington's 'A Settin' and a Rockin' being played by Eddy Rogers in the Victory Room."

"Rock" references in the local media resurfaced some two years later when the "On the Town" column in the Sunday, April 21, 1948 edition of the Washington Post ran the following passage: "Club Kavakos is rocking to the music of Buddy Mareno and His Orchestra. Buddy, who sings as well as leads his orchestra, was the featured vocalist with Harry James, Dick Jurgens, and a number of the bigger bands in the country for some time before organizing his own outfit. Buddy won favor with the bobby soxers over the country and they even went so far as to form a fan club for him, which always helps when the booking agent goes into a club."

Later in the year, the Washington Afro American of Saturday, August 21, 1948 ran a "Now Playing" ad for a Howard Theatre show that proclaimed: "The Band That Rocks! Jimmie Dale & Orch. Featuring Leon 'Skylark' Ketchum." Later, the Washington Daily News of Friday, October 15, 1948 ran a box ad for the Cross Roads in Bladensburg that rang out: "Stop, Look, Listen to the Rockin' Rhythm of Maurice Rocco, Beginning Tuesday, October 19."

When the famed gospel music group the Golden Gate Quartet came to Washington, D.C. for and engagement at the newly opened Duke Ellington's that lasted from Tuesday, November 9 through Sunday, November 14, 1948, their box ads in the Washington Daily News of November 9 and the Washington Post of November 10 both featured the caption: "Duke Ellington's Club Presents Rhythm Rocking Kings of Harmony The Golden Gate Quartet."

The Washington Post, in its "On the Town" column of November 10 included the following write-up: "The New Duke Ellington Club will rock and roll to the rhythms of the Golden Gate Quartet for the next few days. The boys make a specialty of swinging the old spirituals. Hardly anyone had ever heard of this musical aggregation until a few years ago when they stopped the show night after night in one of the New York night spots. They haven't stayed in the night clubs exclusively. Since they got their first break they've been in Carnegie and Constitution Hall, the Library of Congress and even the White House. The rest of the music at the club is being furnished by Joe Morris and His Boys. They include a number of men from the old Lionel Hampton Orchestra."

This entry marked the very first time the full term "rock and roll" was described in the local media in conjunction with a local live music performance, although it wasn't being used to describe a particular classification of music. Its presence, however, is highly significant in that it opened up a new entry into popular music jargon and most likely contributed to the evolution of two verbs without an innate musical association seamlessly being joined together to create the noun, "rock and roll."

Two other items of interest rounded out the decade as the advent of rock and roll loomed on the horizon. First, Arnold Fine's "Tips on Tables" column in the Friday, January 21, 1949 edition of the Washington Daily News included a feature on singer Mary Martell, who was top-billed at a night club called the 400 (1425 F Street NW). The headline read "Mary Martell's 'Bidi' Rhythm Really Started in Her Cradle" and reported: "Bidi-bidi-bi, bidi-bidi-ba. That's Mary Martell (The 400) singing. Course the listener doesn't have any idea of what the song is about, but the rhythm rocks. Far as modern music is concerned, that's about all that counts anyway."

As the year closed out R&B piano star Maurice Rocco was featured at the Merry-Land Club from Monday, November 28, 1949 to Monday, December 4, 1949. The Washington Daily News of Tuesday, November 29, 1949 included an ad for this engagement that cried out: "Olivia Davis Presents...Hear His Rockin' Rhythm – Maurice Rocco, Dynamic Piano Star of Stage, Screen & Radio."

The presence of rock and roll terminology in the Washington, D.C. print media during the 1940s served to energize the existing styles of music that were being discussed and formed a descriptive basis for what would become rock and roll in the following decade. Though the initial appearances of these references were almost subliminal in nature, they impacted local musicians, promoters, disc jockeys, night club owners, record executives and fans of the local music scene in the way they energized the presentation of popular music at the time. When the journalists of the 1940s wrote of a musical performer's "rockin' rhythm" or noted how a certain type of music "rocks" they unknowingly turned onto a twisting pathway that, when mixed with other artistic elements, would eventually deposit them into an amorphous musical territory that would take America, and the world, by storm.

CHAPTER THIRTY-EIGHT
SONGS THAT ROCKED

The origin of rock and roll has been debated ever since its emergence in the early 1950s as a distinct classification of music and legitimate instrument of worldwide popular culture. The main question that fans, historians and journalists have attempted to answer is whether or not rock and roll came into existence when a musical combo first performed what can today be identified in terms of musical structure as a "rock and roll" tune, or, if it was first defined when the term "rock and roll" was used to label a separate type of popular music. Unfortunately, this intriguing issue can never be clearly settled. Strong cases can be made for either scenario, as there is no plausible method to determine when this particular type of music, which draws from most every other available idiom, separated itself from other established musical styles and became an entity unto itself. Most published articles and books that have attempted to clarify the origin of rock and roll music have presented extensive research on the subject, but have ultimately offered conclusions culled from selected resource material that reflects the personal agendas and emotional responses of their respective authors.

It has been widely written that the term "rock and roll" has been most commonly used throughout the 20th century as a euphemism for sex, though it has never been pinpointed exactly when such a definition was established. In similar fashion, it has also been declared that the words "rock" and "rocking" have been generally used through this same period of time to describe such acts as the motions of a nautical craft, the gyrations of dance, moments of spiritual fervor, and rhythmic movements in general, among other examples. Despite the shady inception of the term and its various uses, it is an established fact that prior to 1952 numerous songs from the spectrum of popular music used elements of rock and roll terminology in either their titles or lyrics.

The first known recorded instance of the term "rock and roll" was on a phonograph record entitled "Campmeeting Jubilee" by the Haydn Quartet (Monarch Record, Victor Talking Machine Co, number 4003). This particular song had been recorded on Thursday, February 7, 1901 in a Camden, New Jersey studio and released as a single by Victor in 1904. The Haydn Quartet was a White, New York-based, vaudeville-minstrel outfit consisting of John Bieling (tenor), Harry MacDonough (tenor), Samuel Holland Rous (baritone, stage name S.H. Dudley – not to be confused with the Black vaudeville performer Sherman H. Dudley) and William F. Hooley (bass). Spiritual in nature, the song included the lyrics, "We've been rocking and rolling in your arms, rocking and rolling in your arms, rocking and rolling in your arms – in the arms of Moses."

A different version of this same song was issued in 1916 under the title "The Camp Meeting Jubilee" on the Little Wonder Record label (No. 339) and credited to "Male Quartette." No other information is available pertaining to the recording session that produced it or the musicians involved with the project, though it is evident the Haydn Quartet was not involved. While the influence of these intriguing recordings on the world of popular music may have been limited at best, their very existence provides for a viable starting point from which one can begin tracing the lineage of rock and roll terminology in recorded music.

In September 1922 a young, Black vaudeville singer known as Trixie Smith, with a backup band known as the Jazz Masters, recorded a J. Berni Barbour-penned song entitled "My Man Rocks Me" (With One Steady Roll) for Harry Pace's Harlem, New York-based Black Swan Records, America's first Black-owned record company. This race music tune, which was actually released in January 1923 and surprisingly loaded with sexual innuendos, included the chorus line of "My man rocks me with a steady roll, there's no slippin' when he once takes hold," thus marking the introduction of the words "rock" and "roll" in the same line to mainstream recorded music.

Although this recording sold in limited quantities, it did spur the interest of other musicians of the day, with the following seven remakes being issued in the ensuing years: "My Man Rocks Me (With One Steady Roll)" (The Southern Quartet, 1924); "My Man Rocks Me (With One Steady Roll)" (The Golden Gate Orchestra, 1924); "My Daddy Rocks Me (With One Steady Roll)" (Charles Creath's Jazz-O-Maniacs, Vocal Chorus by Floyd Campbell, 1925); "My Daddy Rocks Me (With One Steady Roll)" (Harold Ortli & His Ohio State Collegians, 1925); "My Daddy Rocks Me (With One Steady Roll)" (Husk O'Hare's Wolverines, 1928); "My Daddy Rocks Me" (Tampa Red's Hokum Jug Band, 1929); and "My Daddy Rocks Me" (Jimmy Noone and His Orch., 1929).

In 1934 two Hollywood film studio songwriters, Sidney Clare and Richard Whiting, authors of the song "On the Good Hip Lollipop" for Shirley Temple, wrote another for the child star entitled "Rock and Roll," but reportedly had their offering turned down by Fox Pictures for reasons never made known. The pop song was then offered to the Boswell Sisters, three White siblings from New Orleans, who recorded "Rock and Roll" with Jimmie Grier and His Orchestra for Brunswick Records. They were subsequently recruited to perform the song in the movie "Transatlantic Merry-Go-Round" (Reliance Pictures, Inc., 1934) which starred Jack Benny. Clearly a pop song in every sense, the tune's nautical theme was clearly evident in its lyrics: "It's the rollin' rockin' rhythm of the sea...rock and roll like a rockin' chair."

There was a steady procession of songs throughout the 1930s and 1940s that utilized elements of rock and roll terminology and several achieved great heights of popularity with music lovers. One song in particular which has proven to be quite influential in the world of popular music is "Good Rocking Tonight," a race music single that was written and performed by New Orleans-raised Roy Brown (the record was credited to "Roy Brown with Bob Ogden & Orch.") and released on the DeLuxe label in 1947. A saxophone-heavy cover of the tune was recorded a year later by a Black singer-guitarist from Omaha, Nebraska named Wynonie Harris and released on King Records as "Good Rockin' Tonight." The song went all the way to number one on the Billboard magazine's "Best Selling Retail Race Records" chart in June 1948. An impressive array of musical artists have since covered this timeless song including Elvis Presley, the Treniers, Ricky Nelson, Pat Boone, James Brown, the rock group Montrose, and even Robert Plant and the Honeydrippers, who had a hit in 1984 with a revamped and somewhat lightweight version entitled "Good Rockin' at Midnight."

The presence of rock and roll terminology in 20th century popular music has been well documented, with innumerable examples of such vernacular appearing in the titles of all manner of recorded songs by Black and White singers, musicians and groups. However, prior to the early 1950s, in almost every instance where such terminology occurred the words were used as verbs describing some type of motion, as opposed to nouns describing a separate style or classification of music. To better illustrate this point, the following is a selected list of 125 songs that were recorded prior to 1953 and included elements of rock and roll terminology in their titles:

"My Man Rocks Me (With One Steady Roll)" (Trixie Smith and the Jazz Masters, 1922)
"Rock, Aunt Dinah, Rock" (Coot Grant and Kid Wilson, 1925)
"Old Country Rock" (William Moore, 1928)
"Detroit Rocks" (Montana Taylor, 1929)
"Rock That Thing" (Lil Johnson, 1929)

"Rock Me Mama" (Banjo Ikey Robinson & His Bull Fiddle Band, 1929)
"Rocking and Rolling" (Robinson's Knights of Rest, 1930)
"Rockin' in Rhythm" (Duke Ellington and His Orchestra, 1931)
"Rollin' Mama Blues" (Ruby Glaze – Blind Willie, 1932)
"Rock and Roll" (The Boswell Sisters with Jimmie Grier & His Orchestra, 1934)
"Rock and Roll" (Joe Haymes Orchestra, 1934)
"Rock and Roll" (Harry Reser Orchestra, 1934)
"Rock and Rye" (Earl Hines and His Orchestra, 1934)
"Rockin' and Swingin'" (Don Albert and His Orchestra, 1936)
"Let's Reel and Rock" (Big Bill, 1937)
"Rock Me Daddy" (Georgia White, 1937)
"Rock It for Me" (Teddy Grace, 1937)
"Rock It for Me" (Chick Webb and His Orchestra with Ella Fitzgerald, 1938)
"Rock It for Me" (Mildred Bailey, 1938)
"Rockin' Rollers' Jubilee" (Erskine Hawkins and His Orchestra, 1938)
"Rock It in Rhythm" (Tampa Red and the Chicago Five, 1938)
"Rockin' the Town" (Johnny Green and His Orchestra, vocals by Gertrude Niesen, 1938)
"Rockin' Rollin' Mama" (Buddy Jones, 1939)
"The Heebie Jeebies are Rockin' the Town" (Lionel Hampton and Orchestra, 1939)
"Rocking the Blues" (Port of Harlem Jazz Men, 1939)
"Rock and Rollin' Daddy" (Merline Johnson, 1939)
"Keep Rockin'" (Harlan Leonard and His Rockets, 1940)
"Rock and Ride" (Harlan Leonard and His Rockets, 1940)
"Rock Me Mama" (Art Tatum and His Band, Vocal Chorus by Joe Turner, 1941)
"Baby, That's Rock 'n' Roll" (Art Tatum and His Band, Vocal chorus by Joe Turner, 1941)
"Rock Me in the Groove" (Sweet Georgia Brown, 1941)
"I Want to Rock" (Cab Calloway and His Orchestra, 1942)
"Rock Me" (Lucky Millinder & His Orchestra, Vocal Chorus by Sister Rosetta Tharpe, 1943)
"Rock Me Mamma" (Arthur "Big Boy" Crudup, 1944)
"The Boogie Rocks" (Albert Ammons, 1944)
"Rockin' the Boogie" (Hadda Brooks, 1945)
"Rock-A My Soul" (The Four Blue Jackets, 1946)
"Rockin' Mama Blues" (John Sellers, 1946)
"Rock the Joint Boogie Woogie" (Big Joe Turner, 1947)
"Rockin' the Blues" (Pee Wee Crayton, 1947)
"Prelude in C # Minor (Rockin' Ol' Rocky Rachmaninov)" (Harry "The Hipster" Gibson, 1947)
"Rock That Voot" (The Nelson Alexander Trio, 1947)
"Rockin' the House" (Memphis Slim, 1947)
"Good Rocking Tonight" (Roy Brown with Bog Ogden & Orch., 1947)
"Shout 'N' Rock" (Billy Williams and His Jump Band, 1948)
"Rock and Roll" (Manhattan Paul with Paul Bascomb's Orchestra, 1948)
"We're Gonna Rock" (Bill Moore featuring Paul Williams – Bar. Sax. 1948)
"Good Rockin' Tonight" (Wynonie Harris, 1948)
"Rockin' Boogie" (Joe Lutcher and His Society Cats, 1948)
"Rock and Roll" (The Flairs, 1949)
"Rock and Roll" (Bill Mathews and the Ballardiers, 1949)
"Rock and Roll" (Doles Dickens and His Quintet, 1949)
"Rock and Roll" (Wild Bill Moore, 1949)
"Rockin' at Midnight" (Roy Brown with His Mighty-Mighty Men, 1949)

"Rock that Boogie" (Little Jimmy and Orchestra, 1949)
"Rockin' Jenny Jones" (Hattie Noel, 1949)
"Rock Awhile" (Goree Carter & His Hepcats, 1949)
"Let's Rock" (Goree Carter & His Hepcats, 1949)
"Rock the Joint" (Jimmy Preston and His Prestonians, 1949)
"Rock the Joint" (Chris Powell and the Five Blue Flames, 1949)
"Rock and Roll Blues" (Erline "Rock and Roll" Harris, 1949)
"Rock the House" (Lowell Fulson, 1949)
"All She Wants to Do Is Rock" (Wynonie Harris, 1949)
"Rockin' the Blues" (Max {Blues} Bailey, 1949)
"Rockola" (Joe Lutcher and His Society Cats, 1949)
"I'm Gonna Rock" (Ralph Willis and Spider Sam, 1949)
"Rock the House" (Tiny Grimes Quintet, 1950)
"Rock It" (Jimmy McCracklin, 1950)
"Rock With Me Mama" (Buddy Tate's Orchestra, 1950)
"Rockin' All Day" (Jimmy McCracklin, 1950)
"We're Gonna Rock" (Gunter Lee Carr, 1950)
"Rock H-Bomb Rock" (H-Bomb Ferguson and Charlie Singleton Orch., 1950)
"How About Rockin' With Me" (Piney Brown with Orchestra, 1950)
"I'm Gonna Rock (Till My Rocker Breaks Down)" (Connie Jordan Combo, 1950)
"Rockin' Blues" (Johnny Otis Orchestra with Mel Walker, 1950)
"Rockin' with Red" (Piano Red, 1950)
"Rock and Roll" (John Lee Hooker and His Guitar, 1950)
"Rock Mister Blues" (Wynonie Harris, 1950)
"Rock Around the Clock" (Hal Singer and His Orchestra, vocal by Spo-Dee-Odee, 1950)
"Sausage Rock" (Doc Sausage and His Mad Lads, 1950)
"Rockin' the Blues" (Pee Wee Crayton, 1950)
"Rock With It" (Johnny Moore's Three Blazers, 1950)
"Rockin' Rhythm" (Peewee Barnum with Orchestra Accompaniment, 1950)
"Rocking After Midnight" (Lowell Fulson, 1950)
"She's Gone Rock Away Blues" (Stick McGhee and His Spo-Dee-O-Dee Buddies, 1950)
"Rockin'" (The Robbins, 1951)
"Rockin' and Rollin'" (Tommy Scott, 1951)
"Rockin' and Rollin'" (Lil' Son Jackson, 1951)
"Rockin' at Home" (Floyd Dixon and His Band, 1951)
"All I Do is Rock" (The Robins, 1951)
"Let's Rock Awhile" (Amos Milburn, 1951)
"Good Rockin' Man" (Roy Brown and His Mighty-Mighty Men, 1951)
"I'm A Good Rockin' Baby" (Ray Snead, 1951)
"We're Gonna Rock" (Gunter Lee Carr, 1951)
"Rock Little Baby" (Cecil Grant, 1951)
"Rock the Joint" (Jimmy Cavallo and His House Rockers, 1951)
"Rock-a-Bye Baby" (Roy Brown and His Mighty-Mighty Men, 1951)
"Shout and Rock" (Elmore Nixon with Henry Hayes and His Rhythm Kings, 1951)
"Rockin' and Jumpin'" (Freddie Mitchell Orch. with Honey Brown, 1951)
"Rock Savoy, Rock" (Andrew Tibbs, 1951)
"Rock Little Daddy" (Eunice Davis with Freddie Mitchell Orch., 1951)
"'Gonna Rock this Mornin'" (Doles Dickens Quintet, 1951)
"I Want to Rock" (Little Miss Sharecropper, 1951)
"I'm Your Rockin' Man" (Herman Manzy and Orchestra, 1951)

"My Kind of Rockin'" (Rene Hall Trio, 1951)
"The Band's A-Rockin'" (Johnnie Lee Wills and His Boys, 1951)
"Rock-Roll" (Gene Ammons and His Band Prestige, 1952)
"Rock 'N Roll Blues" (Anita O'Day and Her Orchestra, 1952)
"Rock, Daddy, Rock" (Big Bertha Henderson with Al Smith Orch., 1952)
"The Last of the Good Rocking Men" (The Four Jacks, 1952)
"Rockaway Rock" (Billy Mitchell, 1952)
"Rock, Rock, Rock" (Willis Jackson and His Band, 1952)
"Rockin' on Sunday Night" (The Treniers, 1952)
"It Rocks! It Rolls! It Swings!" (The Treniers, 1952)
"We're Gonna Rock This Joint" (Jackson Brothers Orchestra, 1952)
"Rock Me All Night Long" (The Ravens, 1952)
"Rock Around the Clock" (Wally Mercer, 1952)
"Rock the Joint" (Bill Haley with the Saddlemen, 1952)
"Real Rock Drive" (Bill Haley with Haley's Comets, 1952)
"Rock the Bottle" (Earl Forest with the Beale Streeters, 1952)
"Rock This Morning" (Jesse Allen, 1952)
"Rockin' the Blues Away" (Tiny Grimes His Guitar and Rocking Highlanders, 1952)
"Rockin' With Fes" (Roy "Bald Head" Byrd, 1952)
"House Rockers Jamboree" (Tucker Coles Orchestra, 1952)
"I'm Going to Rock Some More" (Piano Red, 1952)

CHAPTER THIRTY-NINE
KING OF THE MOONDOGGERS

Any comprehensive study of popular music must give full consideration to the contributions of famed disc jockey Alan Freed, who laid claim to creating the term "rock and roll" and applying it to a separate classification of music in 1951. While there is ample evidence that such a term (and related terminology) existed and was utilized as a verb in various popular music songs during previous decades, there is no disputing that it was Freed who promoted and popularized the term "rock and roll" and presented it as a noun that described a new style of music in the early 1950s.

Aldon James "Alan" Freed, son of Charles and Maude Freed, was born on Wednesday, December 21, 1921 in Johnstown, Pennsylvania. His family lived for several years in Windber, Pennsylvania before making brief stays in Oklahoma City, Oklahoma and Alliance, Ohio. In 1933 the family settled in Salem, Ohio where Freed spent the remainder of his teen years. After graduating from Salem High School in June 1940, he enrolled at Ohio State University in Columbus as a journalism major, but dropped out after a semester. He next enlisted in the United States Army in early 1941 and was stationed at Camp McCoy in Wisconsin. Years later Freed would publicly state that he had earned a Master of Science in mechanical engineering from Ohio State University, but there is no evidence that he ever attended the school beyond that one semester.

After receiving a medical discharge from the Army in the fall of 1941, Freed returned to Salem, Ohio where he worked for a year for the federal government as an assistant ordinance inspector. While employed with the feds he aspired to switch careers and become a radio newscaster, and began taking lessons at a local broadcasting school conducted by WKBN Radio in Youngstown. In October 1942 he was hired by WKST Radio in New Castle, Pennsylvania where he hosted a nightly classical music program in addition to conducting administrative work. During his time at this station, Freed married his girlfriend Betty Lou Bean who hailed from Lisbon, Ohio.

In February 1943 Freed returned to the station in Youngstown where he had first taken broadcasting lessons and took a job as a newscaster and sports announcer at WKBN Radio. In early 1945 he moved over to WAKR Radio in Akron, Ohio where he initially provided a nightly sports wrap-up after the 11pm news and also did play-by-play coverage for the various Akron University athletic teams. One evening, after filling in for a missing disc jockey, Freed took over a nightly listener call-in program entitled "Request Revue" that featured pop and race music recordings. Songs by the likes of Ella Fitzgerald, Count Basie, Woody Herman and Lionel Hampton were regularly aired and the popular show became the station's top money-making program.

In early 1950 contractual problems with WAKR led to a court-ordered injunction against Freed that prohibited him from working on any other radio stations in the Akron area. Freed was forced to look elsewhere for work and he landed in Cleveland at television station WXEL where he hosted the afternoon movie and also occasionally played popular records on an obscure, late-night television program that featured pianist Grant Wilson.

In the spring of 1951, approximately one year after arriving in Cleveland, Freed reportedly had a chance encounter in a local bar with a man named Leo Mintz, who figured prominently in the local popular music scene. Mintz was well-known throughout Cleveland, Ohio as the owner of a phonograph record store called Record Rendezvous and had enhanced his status among area music fans by sponsoring several programs on radio station WJW (850 on the AM dial). Reportedly, when Alan Freed told Mintz of his desire to jumpstart his radio career, the record store owner arranged to have Freed hired by WJW as a classical music disc jockey.

According to the "Plain Dealer Radio Schedule" that was published on a daily basis in the Cleveland Plain Dealer newspaper, Alan Freed first appeared on the air on station WJW on the night of Wednesday, July 4, 1951. His program, simply listed as "Allan Freed" (sic), aired that evening at 11:30pm and ran for one hour. The type of music that Freed aired on his new radio program was never mentioned in the "Plain Dealer Radio Schedule," or anywhere else in the newspaper, and has never been conclusively verified, though it is likely that classical music was the main material offered. For the remainder of 1951, Freed's radio show, which ran from 60 to 90 minutes in length, was aired up to six nights per week on WJW at either 11:15pm or 11:30pm.

Freed's situation took an interesting turn when Leo Mintz, after noticing that sales of R&B records in his store were on the upswing, devised a plan to sponsor an on-air program on WJW that would feature this type of music. He told Freed of his plans to buy a weekly block of time for his new radio program, contingent upon Freed's agreement to leave his classical music show behind and host the R&B show. Freed initially balked at Mintz's offer, but soon did an about-face and began airing a new program that featured R&B music. A check with the "Plain Dealer Radio Schedule" shows that Freed's radio show switched its title to "Moon Dog House" on Wednesday, November 14, 1951. The show aired that night from 11:15pm-1am and marked the beginning of Freed's practice of airing high-energy R&B music for his listeners.

Alan Freed quickly became infamous for his on-air antics. Things reportedly were very interesting from the onset when the innovative disc jockey, while airing an obscure 1949 tune called "Moondog's Symphony" that featured a howling canine, began manically pleading over the airwaves with the "Moondog" to stop its howling or it would "wake up the neighbors!" ("Moondog's Symphony" was credited to a recording artist known only as "Moondog," who in real life was a blind, Viking-garbed poet named Louis Thomas Hardin, Jr. who haunted the streets of New York City and in later years became somewhat of a cult avant-garde figure). In response, the phones immediately lit up on the station's switchboard with puzzled callers wanting to know what the host's problem was.

The following nights saw Freed playing an instrumental throughout his show that had been recorded in 1947 by the Todd Rhodes Orchestra entitled "Blues for the Red Boy." He jokingly announced the title of the tune as "Blues for the Moondog" and subsequently began using it as his own personal theme. Freed began introducing his show by doing some howling himself. He then proclaimed himself "King of the Moondoggers," referred to his listeners as the "Moondog Kingdom," and greeted his audience every night with a rousing, "Hello everybody and welcome to the 'Moon Dog House!'"

Freed became a wildman on the airwaves. He screamed out song introductions, clanged a cowbell and pounded on a telephone book in time with the tunes, spewed forth maniacal jive patter before and after the numbers he played, and frequently punctuated the driving music with animated shouts of "Go! Go! Go! Go! Go!" The show caused a sensation among Cleveland's teenaged music fans and in time became the city's most popular radio program.

Somewhere in the midst of this on-air turmoil Alan Freed created a new classification of music when he began referring to the music he aired on WJW as "rock and roll." Determining the exact date of this landmark event has been problematic. It is a matter of historical fact that in the back cover notes of the record album "Alan Freed's Top 15" (Alan Freed; End Records, 1962), Freed penned the now-infamous line: "It is impossible for me to present this album without thinking back to 1951 in Cleveland, where I named our music 'rock n roll.'"

However, It must be noted that there is no independent corroboration in the form of audio tapes of his on-air broadcasts or published documents such as newspaper or magazine advertisements, articles or listings that conclusively prove Freed ever used that particular term on his radio show that year. In addition, Freed never publicly revealed exactly where he got the inspiration for the term "rock and roll," though one must assume he appropriated the term from a song title or lyric that had caught his attention. Still, the very fact that Freed made a public proclamation in which he credited himself for the invention of rock and roll must be noted by music historians as a valid point of origin because of the claimant's status as a recognized music industry innovator and visionary.

Alan Freed's bold assertions sparked a great debate that has raged to the present day: Should the birth of "rock and roll" be credited to the various musicians of the 1920s, 1930s and 1940s who had actually played songs whose musical content was strikingly similar to what we now accept as rock and roll music, or should its invention solely be attributed to Freed himself, who was undoubtedly responsible for using the term as a noun to describe a new category of music in the early 1950s? Many rock and roll purists are of the opinion that musical content trumps categorical definition, though in reality it seems erroneous to give songs from the early 20th century a musical label that was not actually introduced to popular culture until 1951.

During his time in Cleveland, Alan Freed's most highly publicized endeavor was his co-organization of a now-historic event known as the "Moondog Coronation Ball." Considered by many music historians to have been the first rock and roll concert (this despite the fact that the term "rock and roll" was never used in any of the events promotional materials and there is no evidence showing that Freed ever used such terminology in promoting the show on his "Moon Dog House" radio show), the live music event took place at the Cleveland Arena on Friday, March 21, 1952 and was booked by local music promoter Lew Pratt. Bands were recruited by Freed, who also acted as the concert's emcee, and financial backing was provided by Leo Mintz. Posters for the event proclaimed it to be "The Most Terrible Ball of Them All!" and promised that Freed would be conducting an in-person live broadcast of the event over his WJW "Moondog Radio Show."

The live concert was supposed to feature the R&B acts Paul Williams and the Hucklebuckers, Tiny Grimes and the Rockin' Highlanders, the Dominoes and singers Danny Cobb and Varetta Dillard. Problems began, however, when the doors opened at 9:30pm and the arena quickly filled to its 10,000 capacity, with thousands more lining the streets outside the building fighting to get in. Estimates vary as to how many eventually crashed the gate: The "Cleveland Plain Dealer" claimed that 6,000 additional concert-goers forced their way inside; the "Cleveland News" put the total number of attending "hepcats" at an improbable 25,000; and Freed himself went on his radio program the next day and told that 7,000 people without tickets smashed open the doors and bulged the insides of the arena.

The reckless behavior of the crowd inside the arena intensified and after only one song by Paul Williams and the Hucklebuckers, Cleveland Police Captain William Zimmerman called for the lights and shut down the show. The concert attendees, the vast majority of whom were Black, reluctantly vacated the premises. While the show's premature ending was anticlimactic, Freed saw the potential in having R&B bands perform in large venues and he began booking such events on a regular basis, a course of action that brought him national attention as a concert promoter and music business entrepreneur.

Alan Freed remained at the helm of the "Moon Dog House" radio show on WJW until September 1954, at which time he moved to New York City where a disc jockey position awaited him at station WINS. In the Big Apple, Freed's exploits were legendary as he hosted his own radio program entitled "Rock 'n' Roll Party," promoted concerts, and appeared in several rock and roll-themed movies and television programs.

However, in the late 1950s Freed's incredible career took a turn for the worse when he became embroiled in the infamous payola scandal that rocked the entertainment industry. Record companies and distributors had long instituted the practice of paying cash to disc jockeys to play their products and even though he steadfastly maintained he never played a rock and roll record he didn't genuinely like, Freed was dragged through the courts for years to face charges of commercial bribery and federal tax evasion.

Alan Freed ultimately left WINS in May 1958 and over the next several years went through short stints at WABC in New York, KDAY in Los Angeles and WQAM in Miami. In the early 1960s he left the entertainment industry behind and retired for good with his third wife Inga to Palm Springs, California. He was inducted into the Rock and Roll Hall of Fame in the "Non-Performer" category on Thursday, January 23, 1986. The iconic Alan Freed, the man known worldwide for creating and promoting rock and roll music, died of uremic poisoning due to kidney failure on Wednesday, January 20, 1965 at the age of 43.

CHAPTER FORTY
ROCKING THE NATION'S CAPITAL

The emergence of rock and roll music was a highly significant addition to America's changing cultural landscape in the 1950s. The nation was going through a great transition between the end of World War II and the political and social uprisings of the 1950s: The population was exploding as thousands of servicemen returned to America and ignited the baby boom; republican President Dwight D. Eisenhower spent two terms in the White House as Senator Joseph McCarthy (R-Wisconsin) stepped up the fight against the growing communist threat; the economy, fueled by corporate growth, was thriving; suburbia was developing; and television broadcasting, which had been suspended during the war years, became the primary component of mass media. Music as a worldwide commodity was becoming increasingly popular with younger audiences. The stage was set for a revolution in music.

Around the time of the accepted Alan Freed-pronounced rock and roll starting point of November 1951, a number of Washington, D.C. area night clubs and venues attained significant recognition for the tremendous musical quality and diversity of their performers and it seemed logical that some of these establishments would be suitable landing spots for different types of new musical styles as they emerged in the region. During this time there were several venues that laid the foundation for live rock and roll in the Washington, D.C. area through their booking of high-energy musical acts, the most notable of which were the District of Columbia National Guard Armory, the Blue Mirror Club, the Howard Theatre, and, over the line in Prince George's County, Maryland, the Hilltop Restaurant.

The first of several examples of rock and roll terminology to surface in the local media during this time was in the "Tips on Tables" column by Hal Rosen in the Friday, May 4, 1951 edition of the Washington Daily News. In that piece Rosen wrote about a show entitled "Lionel Hampton – His Orchestra and His Variety Show of 1951" featuring Hampton along with pianist Milt Buckner and drummer Curly Hamner that took place at the District of Columbia National Guard Armory (2001 East Capitol Street, Washington, D.C.) on the following Sunday evening. His article states: "There's a gent known as the 'Hamp' who threatens to set the National Guard Armory a-rockin' this Sunday night... Hampton brings his orchestra and variety show to the Armory this Sabbath for a three-hour concert and show."

In terms of local night clubs, the Blue Mirror Club had noticeably stepped up its entertainment schedule in the late 1940s to include more nationally known pop, jazz and R&B acts. They continued that practice into the following decade and in 1950 and 1951 the night club featured appearances by such performers as Louis Armstrong and His Esquire Combo, the Tunesmen, the Four Tunes, the Red Caps, the King Cole Trio, the Mills Brothers, the Four Keys, Louis Jordan and His Tympany Five, the Ink Spots, the Marveleers, Doles Dickens and the Whispers, Chris Powell and the Blue Flames, Erroll Garner and His Trio, the Treniers, the Billy Williams Quartet and jazz singers Sara Vaughan and Ella Fitzgerald.

Of note is the fact that Herbie Fields and His Orchestra, co-billed with pop singer Bob Eberly, worked the Blue Mirror Club from Monday, November 12 through Sunday, November 18, 1951. Hal Rosen, in his "Tips on Table" column in the Washington Daily News of Wednesday, November 14, 1951, wrote: "Mister Fields is no stranger to Washington. His seven-piece orchestra rocks the Blue Mirror with a brand of rock 'em, sock 'em jazz that has customers hopping in their seats."

The Howard Theatre, which was now emphasizing a mix of jazz and R&B acts in their live music extravaganzas, made some rock and roll overtures in advertisements for their shows that they placed in the Washington Afro American newspaper. From Friday, September 7 through Thursday, September 13, 1951 a show was co-headlined by "The All Time All American Alto King" Johnny Hodges and His All Stars and Tiny Grimes and His "Rocking" Highlanders. Next, a show that ran from Friday, September 28 to Thursday, October 4, 1951 was headlined by Herbie Fields and His Great Orchestra and included a performance by R&B singer Madame Marie Knight, whose promo implored fans to "Rock to the rhythm of 'On Revival Day' and 'Shady Green Pastures.'" Lastly, a special "Battle of the Blues" at the Howard that ran from Friday, December 7 through Thursday, December 13, 1951 pitted Larry "Rocking Rhythm" Darnell ("Star of 'I'll Get Along Somehow'") against Wynonie "Mister Blues" Harris ("Star of 'Bloodshot Eyes'").

Another major night spot in the area that experimented with a variety of musical entertainment was the Hilltop Restaurant, which was located in Coral Hills, Maryland, right at the intersection of Marlboro Pike and Benning Road, directly opposite from what was then Mike Young's Café. Throughout 1950 the Hilltop Restaurant featured the fast-paced "jive" music of Sonny Kast and His Band, a high-energy jazz-pop group which in the ensuing years would morph into the Three Jacks and gain prestige as one of the area's first and most dynamic rock and roll bands. While Kast and his mates held down house band chores, the Hilltop Restaurant brought in pop singers such as Tod Mason, Jeanne Lee and Cathy Mann, and an array of exotic dancers like Fifi Darlene, Autumn Rhaiens, Jo-Jo Denning and Sandra Seers to please the crowd. They also included in their bills comedians such as Freddie Vincent and Frankie Farr, and often hosted specialty acts like the London Dancers.

In 1951 Sonny Kast moved his outfit from the Hilltop Restaurant over to the Penguin Restaurant in Southeast Washington, D.C. The Hilltop Restaurant then employed two house bands, Billy Burke's Orchestra and Lee Mason and His Orchestra, and brought in entertainers such as pop singers Harold Terry, Nancy Ford, Norty Michels and George Ackers, comedienne Louise Potter, and exotic dancers Bobby Todd, Therese Carroll, Laura Paterson, Gloria Marlowe and Jane Cooper.

Things took an intriguing turn on the local music scene when a Philadelphia-based jazz-R&B outfit called Murray Schaff's Aristocrats descended upon the nation's capital in the fall of 1951. The band's non-stop upbeat music mixed traditional jazz covers and raucous R&B originals and their dynamic stage show literally had audiences rocking and rolling in the seats. The band's Washington, D.C, debut took place with an electric run at the Blue Mirror Club where they were second-billed to the Billy Williams Quarter from Monday, November 19 through Sunday, November 25, 1951.

The appearances of Murray Schaff's Aristocrats as a support act to the Billy Williams Quartet went over so well, the Blue Mirror Club decided to bring the band back for an extended four-week stay that began on Monday, December 24, 1951 and lasted until Sunday, January 20, 1952. Included in this engagement was a second-billing to jazz singer Ella Fitzgerald from Monday, January 14 to Saturday, January 19, 1952 that reportedly drew capacity crowds every night. By this time Schaff and his band, for all practical purposes, were performing music that was in the process of being classified as rock and roll, complete with sides of up-tempo jazz featuring three-part vocal harmonies.

When the Blue Mirror Club bookings concluded, Murray Schaff's Aristocrats moved over to the Hilltop Restaurant. They opened there on the night of Tuesday, March 25, 1952, headlining a bill that included trapeze artist Alma Bray and the duo of Kast and Abernathy (Frank "Sonny" Kast and Bill Abernathy, "Washington's Favorite Jivesters").

A box advertisement in the Washington Daily News on their opening day cried out, "HERE THEY COME. 1952'S Skyrocketing Quintet. Rock and Roll to Their Exciting Jazz." It marked the first time the full term "rock and roll" was used to promote the appearance of a live music group in Prince George's County, Maryland and subsequent notices of a similar nature that appeared in local dailies cemented their status as the Washington, D.C. area's first legitimate rock and roll attraction.

Hal Rosen, in his "Tips on Tables" column in the Saturday, March 29, 1952 edition of the Washington Daily News helped spread the legend when he wrote: "Here's a group who wants to make you rock and roll in your seats. It's Murray Schaff and his Aristocrats, currently featured at the Hilltop...the music these boys provide is more than slightly frantic."

The band was repeatedly brought back for lengthy engagements at the Hilltop Restaurant throughout 1952 and most of 1953. During this time, ads for the group in the night club section of the Washington Daily News screamed out "Go! Go! Go!," and "Still Rocking the Town." Reviews from this popular daily announced that the band played "spine-tingling music and songs that will make you rock, roll, and bounce."

In the wake of these media announcements and the enduring success of Murray Schaff's Aristocrats, other local and out-of-town rock and roll performers began to materialize all over the Washington, D.C. area music scene. It was clear, however, that throughout the entire year of 1952 the local press didn't always know how to label these performers. When the Marveleers, a Philadelphia-based doo-wop outfit, came down to the Hilltop Restaurant for a week-long engagement that began on Tuesday, June 3, 1952, ads in the June 4 Washington Daily News announced them as "The Marveleers and their 'Rockin' Rhythm.'"

Other examples of how local newspapers struggled when it came to properly advertising performing artists in Washington, D.C. night clubs who were in the process of becoming rock and roll artists in 1952 include: Jack Rowe's Restaurant, which was headlined by local Black vocalist George Eades, who was touted as a "Sensational New Singing Discovery;" Maynard's Restaurant, which was headlined by the dynamic local singer Mary Martell, whose music was described as "bounce version of pop tunes" while she herself was crowned "the go-go-go girl;" the Covered Wagon Restaurant, a notorious C&W joint a block south of Maynard's at 14th and Rhode Island Avenue NW, which was booking an up-tempo, Black, guitar-and-sax outfit called the Three of Us Trio with the simple heading "Don't Miss;" and the Howard Theatre, which promoted a week-long visit by Roy Brown and His Mighty Mighty Men that began on Friday, September 5, 1952 with ads in the Washington Afro American that pronounced Brown as "America's Foremost Exponent of Rockin.'" All of these aforementioned acts were soon being billed throughout the land as rock and roll performers, though at this point in time the term was still being digested by local media outlets and was being used sparingly.

CHAPTER FORTY-ONE
BILL HALEY AND HIS COMETS INVADE WASHINGTON, D.C.

If one accepts the notion that Alan Freed appropriated the term "rock and roll" in 1951 and applied it to a new classification of music, it would be a logical presumption that the very first rock and roll song – a tune that was recorded and subsequently promoted under such a classification – would have to have appeared in the wake of Freed's initial use of the term on his "Moon Dog House" radio program on station WJW. However, just about all of the songs recorded in 1951 and 1952 that had elements of rock and roll terminology in the title or lyrics were promoted as "rhythm & blues" songs despite the fact that the term "rock and roll" was already indoctrinated into popular culture. The reason for this is that most of these songs were recorded by Black artists who automatically had their work classified as R&B for marketing purposes, regardless of the actual musical content of the songs themselves. This situation began to change when a Philadelphia-based C&W singer-guitarist named Bill Haley crossed over and achieved widespread national popularity with two early-era rock and roll tunes, "Rock the Joint" in 1952 and "Crazy Man, Crazy" in 1953, the latter of which was the first legitimate rock and roll song to ever reach the Billboard popular records music charts.

The man known to this day as "The Father of Rock and Roll," William John Clifton Haley Jr., was born in Highland Park, Michigan on Monday, July 6, 1925 and raised by musical parents. The Haley family relocated to Boothwyn, Pennsylvania in 1932 and by his early teens Bill Jr. was playing guitar and singing Western swing tunes for a dollar per night at the nearby Booth Corners Auction Mart. In 1943 Bill Haley signed on as a guitarist and yodeler with a Wilmington, Delaware-based Western swing music group known as the Cousin Lee Band. Two years later he joined a group called the Downhomers in Fort Wayne, Indiana as a singer, and in 1946 he took to the road and began traveling the country as a pickup guitarist. Haley eventually ended his tours in the fall of 1947 and settled down in Chester, Pennsylvania.

In Chester, Haley took a job as a disc jockey at radio station WPWA and formed his first country music band, the Four Aces of Western Swing. This group released four singles in 1948 for Cowboy Records and one in 1949 for Center Records. In April 1949 Haley formed a similar band called the Aces and two months later changed the group's name to the Saddlemen. In 1950 they released singles on two popular Philadelphia labels, Keystone Records and Atlantic Records. By early 1951 Yodeling Bill Haley and the Saddlemen were still playing C&W music, though around this time they began experimenting with a different musical style that can best be described as a mix of blues and C&W. Advertisements for the group in Philadelphia newspapers labeled their music as "jive," "popular," "cowboy" and "hillbilly" and described them as "the most versatile band in the land."

During this time, Haley began opening his shows with a rousing song entitled "Rock the Joint," which had been a significant R&B hit in 1949 for Jimmy Preston and His Prestonians. The charging, up-tempo tune drove the working class crowds wild. The commotion caught the attention of a local Philadelphia entrepreneur named Dave Miller, who felt that Haley's band was the perfect crossover group to record a cover of another scorching R&B number entitled "Rocket 88," which had been released as a single on Chess Records in April 1951 by Jackie Brenston and His Delta Cats. Released in May 1951 on Miller's Holiday Records label by "Bill Haley and the Saddlemen," this newer version of "Rocket 88" (the B-side was "Tearstains on My Heart") was an exciting, mind-bending fusion of C&W music and hard-edged R&B, with lightning lead guitar chords by session player Danny Cedrone, an innovative funky bass line and grunt-like vocals by Bill Haley himself. The recording left its listeners somewhat bewildered and reminds many present-day music aficionados of the early Rolling Stones. It was simply a classic recording that blurred the boundary lines of popular music. Haley's band released four additional C&W singles on Holiday Records in 1951 and early 1952.

In April 1952 Dave Miller formed a new company called Essex Records and the label's inaugural 45rpm single record release was a rousing version of "Rock the Joint" backed with "Icy Heart" credited to Bill Haley with the Saddlemen. Haley made some minor lyrical changes of his own to this classic, which had been written by three musicians who worked for the New York-based Gotham Records company named Harry Crafton, Wendell "Don" Keane and Harry "Doc" Bagby. His version of the song also featured an inspired solo by session guitarist Danny Cedrone, which somewhat ironically would reappear two years later in their famed hit single "(We're Gonna) Rock Around the Clock."

The single "Rock the Joint" reportedly sold over 75,000 copies and despite the fact that when performing before live audiences Haley would take the stage wearing a cowboy hat and western shirt, radio stations from Philadelphia to Chicago promoted the song as "rock and roll," thus causing a major change in musical direction for the band. A strong case can be made that this version of "Rock the Joint" was indeed the first rock and roll song ever recorded and promoted as such.

At this point It should be noted that many music historians have claimed the 1951 single "60 Minute Man" by the Black, New York-based R&B group the Dominoes should be considered the first rock and roll song because of its repeated phrase, "I rock 'em, roll 'em, all night long." The sex-laden song reached number one on the Billboard magazine's "Best Selling Retail Rhythm & Blues Records" chart on Saturday, June 30, 1951 and spent a total of 14 weeks in that position. It also made the magazine's "Best Selling Pop Singles" chart, making it the first R&B song to ever achieve such a distinction. "60 Minute Man" stayed on the pop chart for a total of four weeks, peaking at number 23 on Saturday, September 22, 1951. This particular single had been promoted as an R&B record upon its release, as the term "rock and roll" had yet to be popularized by disc jockey Alan Freed. For that reason it seems unreasonable to literally define it as a "rock and roll" song.

In November 1952, Haley officially adopted rock and roll for good by changing the name of his group to "Bill Haley and His Comets," with the original lineup of this landmark band consisting of Haley playing guitar and handling vocals, guitarist Billy Williamson, pianist John Grande and bassist Marshall Lytle. It is interesting to note that Haley's band originally had no regular percussionist. Their first road drummer was Charlie Higler, who debuted with the group in June 1953 at Washington, D.C.'s Blue Mirror Club. Higler was soon replaced by Dick Richards, who then became the first full-time Comets drummer.

In the spring of 1953 Bill Haley and His Comets became one of the most popular rock and roll bands in the world with the release of their single "Crazy Man, Crazy" backed with "Whatcha Gonna Do" (Bill Haley with Haley's Comets; Essex Records, 1953). The song debuted on Saturday, May 23, 1953 as number 15 on the Billboard magazine's "Best Selling Singles" chart, which was listed under the general heading of "Top Popular Records." While the song never advanced beyond this numerical ranking, it did remain on this chart for a total of six weeks. Its emergence was a musical milestone, as it marked the first time in history that a legitimate rock and roll song had ever cracked the Billboard magazine's popular music chart.

While touring in support of their smash rock and roll hit single, Bill Haley and His Comets included in their travels a stop in Washington, D.C., where they performed in front of sold out crowds at the Blue Mirror Club in an engagement that ran from Monday, June 29 to Saturday, July 4, 1953. Opening for the headliners was a local group called the Top

Notes. At this point in time Bill Haley and His Comets were considered the number one rock and roll band in the world and it is interesting to note that for their Washington debut they opted to work the Blue Mirror Club, as opposed to being booked into a larger concert hall such as Joe Turner Arena or Uline Arena.

Bill Haley and His Comets went over very well in the nation's capital and influenced innumerable other local bands to adopt rock and roll as their music of choice. They reportedly enjoyed their time here and returned several times throughout the decade, making stops at such venues as the Casino Royal Theatre Restaurant (week-long engagements in January and April 1955), Glen Echo Park's Spanish Ballroom (Monday, September 5, 1955), Uline Arena (Friday, November 11, 1955), the District of Columbia National Guard Armory (Sunday, February 5, 1956) and Ritchie Coliseum on the University of Maryland's College Park campus (Saturday, December 27, 1958).

Bill Haley and an ever-changing lineup of Comets continued to rack up the hits and reached "The Billboard Music Popularity Charts" under the "Popular Records" classification on 14 different occasions between 1953 and 1958. They scored significant hits during this period with the following songs: "(We're Gonna) Rock Around the Clock," which reached number one on the "Best Sellers in Stores" popular records chart on Saturday, July 9, 1955 and eventually sold more than 30 million copies worldwide; "Burn That Candle," which reached number 16 on the "Best Sellers in Stores" popular records chart on Saturday, January 14, 1956; and "See You Later Alligator," which reached number six on the "Best Sellers in Stores" popular records chart on Saturday, February 11, 1956.

Bill Haley and His Comets enjoyed worldwide popularity, especially before the British Invasion of the middle 1960s. In the late 1960s and throughout the 1970s Haley worked with different band lineups and gave electrifying performances. He spent his final years in Harlingen, Texas, and died on Monday, February 9, 1981 at the age of 55.

CHAPTER FORTY-TWO
ON EVERY HIT PARADE

From a historical perspective the advancement of the term "rock and roll" in the Washington, D.C. area during the 1950s was largely facilitated by advertisements and articles in local newspapers such as the Evening Star, the Washington Daily News and the Washington Post. The music itself was also celebrated through other forms of popular media, most notably radio and television broadcasts. Information regarding the transmission of early-era rock and roll in the nation's capital can be gleaned from miscellaneous sources and pieced into a cultural framework of the period, thus creating a more complete understanding of the evolution of popular music in this region.

Radio played an important role in the spread of rock and roll during the 1950s. When attempting to identify the first disc jockey to ever broadcast rock and roll music over the radio in the Washington, D.C. area, it is imperative to establish a reasonable time frame in which such music initially became accessible to those working in the local radio industry. If one accepts the proclamations of disc jockey Alan Freed, it seems probable that the musical term he popularized in Cleveland did not transfer over to disc jockeys in other cities for several weeks after his "Moon Dog House" radio program went on the air in November 1951.

Freed's "Moondog Coronation Ball" in March 1952, combined with the release of the popular single "Rock the Joint" by Bill Haley with the Saddlemen in April 1952, would indicate that a practical time frame in which to begin looking for examples of the term "rock and roll" in the local media outlets would be the spring months of 1952. A second logical area of concentration would be the months surrounding the May 1953 release of the single "Crazy Man, Crazy" by Bill Haley with Haley's Comets, which holds special designation as the first legitimate rock and roll single to ever reach the Billboard magazine's "Best Selling Singles" pop music chart. Both of these single releases were instrumental in advancing the popularity of rock and roll music on a national level.

Although it is generally accepted that rock and roll music is an invention of the early 1950s, the task of identifying the Washington, D.C. area's pioneering rock and roll disc jockey, and the program he or she hosted in which the first rock and roll song was broadcast, has proven to be problematic for several reasons. A review of the area's daily newspapers reveals that from 1951 to 1953 there were no listed radio programs for this area with the term "rock and roll" in their title, nor were there any published radio program print advertisements offering or promoting rock and roll music. Furthermore, there are no known published articles or books that name a particular disc jockey as having been the first to play rock and roll music on the airwaves in the Washington, D.C. area from 1951 to 1953; no disc jockey who was on the local airwaves from the years 1951 to 1953 has ever stepped forward claiming to be the first to have played rock and roll music for his or her audience; and no actual sound recording of a disc jockey playing rock and roll music over the local airwaves from 1951 to 1953 has ever surfaced. Consequently, at this point in time it is simply impossible to identify the first disc jockey that played rock and roll music on the air in the Washington, D.C. area. While such a person did exist at some point in time, he or she has, thus far, escaped detection.

At this point little can be done to solve this lingering mystery besides examining the various radio programs that were broadcasting over the local radio airwaves during select time periods and speculating as to whether or not any of them offered rock and roll songs as part of their programming. For example, a review of the "Radio Programs" listings for the top several AM radio stations in the Washington Post and the Washington Daily News for the month of April 1952 reveals numerous popular music programs that were airing at that time and may be considered potential candidates. Among the programs that were on the air that month were "Dancing Party" (WMAL), "Hit Parade" (WRC), "Hollywood Music Box" (WRC), "Bandstand 1260" (WWDC), "1260 Club" with Willis Conover (WWDC), "Parade of Hits" (WWDC), "Dance Party" (WWDC), "Dance Time" (WWDC), "Musical Caravan" (WEAM), "Dancing Party" (WEAM), "Request Granted" with Milt Grant (WOL), "High School Hit Parade" (WOL), "House Party" (WTOP), "Tip Top Record Shop" (WTOP), "Record Shop" (WGMS), "Record Releases" (WGMS), "Night Music" (WOL), and more than a dozen others including programs hosted by such personalities as Milton Q. Ford (WWDC), Art Brown (WWDC), Mike Hunnicutt (WOL) and Eddie Gallaher (WTOP).

While the search to reveal which radio program first aired rock and roll in the Washington, D.C. area has thus far proved futile, there is an item from an area newspaper rates as the first example of a local disc jockey writing about a rock and roll band's music. Eddie Gallaher, who had hosted popular music programs entitled "Sundial" and "Moondial" for radio station WTOP since September 1946, also penned a column for the Washington Post entitled "On Records" where he discussed the latest single releases from various popular bands that he played on the air.

In the newspaper's Sunday, July 26, 1953 edition Gallaher writes in his column: "Another small label, Essex Records, named after the car I drive, has had a bonanza lately with an outfit called Bill Haley's Comets. Their record of 'Crazy, Man, Crazy' (Essex 321), a song as jivey as its title, became quite a popular item around the country; so naturally the record company, not having much else to do, put out a sequel. One side is 'Pat-A-Cake,' and the other is 'Fractured' (Essex 327). You may not be absolutely fractured, but at least you might find this latest record somewhat amusing."

Because of this documentation, and despite the likelihood that rock and roll music had been played on other radio stations in the nation's capital prior to this article's publication, Eddie Gallaher gets the nod as the first Washington, D.C. area disc jockey to grant recognition to a rock and roll band and introduce their music to his audience.

While the radio remained a prestigious and treasured component of home entertainment throughout the 1950s, its colleague in modern electronic gadgetry, the television, was rapidly growing in popularity during these years and also served as a source of musical programming. Two locally aired television shows, "Chuck Richards Talent Hunt" and "Capital Caravan," offered live, onstage R&B performances in an innovative broadcast format that predated both "The Milt Grant Record Hop," which debuted on WTTG Channel 5 in the Washington, D.C. area on Saturday, September 22, 1956, and "American Bandstand," which was hosted by Dick Clark and made its national debut for ABC on Monday, August 5, 1957. Unfortunately, published articles regarding program content on these two local shows is minimal and no videotaped episodes or tape recordings of either "Chuck Richards Talent Hunt" or "Capital Caravan" are known to exist.

The only available documentation regarding the first of these shows, "Chuck Richards Talent Hunt," is a short piece that appeared in the Saturday, June 9, 1951 edition of the Billboard. In his column entitled "Rhythm & Blues Notes," reporter Hal Webman writes: "Chuck Richards, r. and b. deejay in Baltimore, kicked off a new video show designed to bring to light new r. and b. talent. Tagged 'Chuck Richards Talent Hunt,' the show will run for nine weeks, with local celebs as judges. The final show will provide a winner to be selected by a special panel of judges. Winner gets a free trip to New York, three suits of clothes and other prizes including a disking paper with either King or DeLuxe Records. The Richards show, believed to the first of its kind, is aired every Thursday at 4:30p.m. and is seen in Baltimore on WMAR-TV and in Washington via WMAL-TV."

A bit more information is available on "Capital Caravan," thanks to regular listings in the local newspapers. The show premiered at 6pm on the night of Saturday, July 25, 1953 on WTTG Channel 5 and broadcasted from the Caravan Ballroom (815 V Street NW, Washington, D.C.), which had formerly operated as the Music Hall and Duke Ellington's. A listing for the program in the "Saturday TV Highlights" section of the Washington Post that day simply stated: "A new program, 'Capital Caravan,' features all-Negro music and talent."

"Capital Caravan" was hosted by a White American named Bob McEwen and offered the Three of Us Trio as its rock and roll house band for several years. Local and national jazz and R&B entertainers were featured on every show and among the regular attractions included bands such as: Duke Ellington and His Orchestra, Les Williams and His Orchestra, the Musical Bops, the Van Perry Combo, the Harry Watkins Combo, Rick Henderson and His All Stars, Los Diablos and the Mambo Cyclones, the Orioles, the Ravens and the Heartbreakers; singers such as Fats Pinere, Jimmy McPhail, June Gaskins, Loretta Holmes, Dee Smith, Doris Holb, Jo Ann Winston, Johnny Ace, LaVern Baker and Jean Vegas (wife of comedian Redd Foxx); singer-pianists such as Ray Charles, Billy Stewart, Ivory Joe Hunter and Amos Milburn; pianists such as Betty Gray, Ellsworth Gibson and Clarence Williams; saxophonist Illinois Jacquet; and conga player Buck Clark. In addition, the show included an array of dancers in their programming including Ray Sneed, Roland "Mambo King" Kane and pantomimist Ernie Ingram. "Capital Caravan" switched over to WMAL-TV on Saturday, November 15, 1958, with its final episode airing at 10:30am on Sunday, December 18, 1960.

The earliest documented live rock and roll music performances in the Washington, D.C. area night clubs and venues took place in 1952 and 1953 at the Blue Mirror Club, the Hilltop Restaurant and the Howard Theatre. In the ensuing years this new classification of music spread to similar establishments throughout the area and rock and roll terminology was showing up on a weekly basis in night club ads and entertainment columns that appeared in such local dailies as the Washington Daily News, the Evening Star and the Washington Post.

In the middle 1950s rock and roll bands were giving live performances at night spots throughout the entire Washington, D.C. area: Club LaConga featured the Frank Moore Four; Chubby's Restaurant and Bar brought in the Frank Shegogue Combo and Joe Stanley and His Building Rockers; the Dixie Pig brought in bands from Wildwood and Philadelphia such as Al Rappa and His New Riffs, Joey Nave and the Points and Bobby Boyd and His Jazz Bombers; the Wheel Bar featured the Three Jacks; the Rustic Cabin Restaurant offered the Three of Us Trio and Johnny Logan and His Royal Crowns; the 4400 Club featured the Jodimars Quintet, Don Haven and the Hi Fis and the Blockbusters (featuring drummer Al Pometto); Benny's Rebel Room was headlined by the likes of Big Steve and His House Rockers and the Saxtons; the Ozarks Restaurant had singer Lucky Wray (Ray Vernon); the Jo Del Bar and Grill had the Jimmy Case Trio switch from C&W to rock and roll; the Kit-Mar Restaurant acquired local rock and roll singer George Eades; Bob White's Hideaway offered Bernie Kessler's Rhythm Rockers and Lucky Wray and His Rock and Roll Trio; the Rendezvous was headlined by Roy Clark and the Power Pacs, followed by a long run by Link Wray and His Ray Men; the Marina brought in singer-guitarist Chuck Berry and Tiny Grimes and His Rockin' Highlanders; the Senate Inn booked the Super Jets; and Strick's Restaurant began offering the rocking sounds of Charlie Burgee and the Sophisticators.

CHAPTER FORTY-THREE
A LITTLE BIT OF TOWN AND AN AWFUL LOT OF COUNTRY

Early in the 20th century folk music was still the primary name of the musical genre that encompassed such commonly referred-to styles as camp music, country music, cowboy music, fiddle music, hillbilly music, mountain music, old-time music, rural music and Western swing music. It wasn't until 1949 that the "folk" classification was replaced in the mainstream media with the "country & western" heading. While the content of the music itself remained the same through the years, the name of its classification was transformed into a more representative moniker as its following grew across the United States.

In the Washington, D.C. area during the Prohibition years, much of the folk music being performed in night clubs and at local events was referred to as hillbilly music, which at the time was not a derogative term. One of the main reasons for this was the local presence of a pianist from Watauga County, North Carolina named Al Hopkins (1889-1932) and his band which he called "The Hill Billies." The group formed in 1924 in Galax, Virginia and consisted of Al Hopkins and his brother Joe on guitar, fiddler Tony Alderman and banjoist John Rector. In late 1925 the quartet relocated to Washington, D.C. and on Saturday, January 9, 1926 they performed live on radio station WRC in a special 30-minute program beginning at 10pm simply entitled "The Hill Billies."

An article in the Washington Post that day entitled "Fiddling Program Scheduled" reported: "'Plain and fancy' fiddling, together with selections from the traditional music of the hill countries of the South, will be presented by the 'Hill Billies,' one of the country's most unusual musical organizations, from WRC tonight. Included in the ranks of the 'Hill Billies' is Charles Bowman, champion fiddler of Tennessee, and winner in 28 out of 32 fiddling contests in all parts of the United States. Also with the Hill Billies are the Hopkins Brothers, Al, John, and Joe; A.E. Alderman, a second of the leading American fiddlers, and John Rector, recording banjoist..."

Two nights later the Hill Billies performed a concert of what the Washington Post described as "old songs in vocal, violin, banjo and guitar music" in Washington, D.C. at the Columbia Heights Christian Church (1435 Park Road NW). Throughout the remainder of 1926 and all of 1927, the band's Saturday night radio show was aired irregularly on WRC and the group made several additional appearances in Power Hall at the Columbia Heights Christian Church.

During their time the Hill Billies appeared on radio and vaudeville shows across the country, issued several 78rpm records on the Okeh and Vocalion labels, and also released recordings as Al Hopkins and His Buckle Busters on the Brunswick label in 1927. Their popularity served to increase the identification of their style of hillbilly music with the established classification of folk music both locally and nationwide. The Hill Billies recorded and performed until the death of leader Al Hopkins in an automobile accident on Friday, October 21, 1932.

Throughout the 1930s and 1940s country music was on display and attracting strong interest at venues and night clubs throughout the Washington, D.C. area. In November 1933 Club Michel featured hillbilly singer Charlie Wright; in July 1934 a hillbilly band known as the Southern Mountaineers gave concerts at several local Maryland theatres including the Cameo Theatre in Mt. Rainier and the Arcade Theatres in Hyattsville and Rockville; in March 1936 the Mountain Music Makers made a stop at the Loyal Order of Moose Columbia Lodge (1414 I Street NW, Washington, D.C.); and in May 1937 the Wardman Park Hotel auditorium was the site of the American Federation of Arts Convention, which featured a number of mountain music performers including blind balladeer Horton Barker, fiddler Jess Johnson and banjoist C.B. Wohlford. Perhaps the area's most popular country music showcase was the Dixie Pig Restaurant and Barbecue in Bladensburg, which had replaced Coldenstroth's Saloon in 1925 and eventually burned to the ground in November 1952.

A less-celebrated, but equally significant country music night club of the time was Farran's Restaurant (1216 Bladensburg Road NE, Washington, D.C.). Samuel W. Farran was a coal dealer who had been operating out of a tiny cinder block building at 1214 Bladensburg Road NE for several years when he decided to expand his horizons and have a new restaurant building constructed on the adjoining lot. In 1936 the building was completed and Farran's Restaurant was opened to the public.

In 1940 Farran began calling the dining room area of his restaurant the Boots and Saddle Club and began booking country music bands as entertainment. The house band for much of the late 1930s and 1940s was a local outfit called Hutch and His Senators (featuring Red DeMarcus and Bill O'Day). Others to work the club during the 1940s included: a trio called We Three, and Billy Strickland and His Gang; singer George Grande; and singer-fiddler-guitarist Blackie Skiles. In the early 1950s the business was leased out to Billy King who ushered in jazz by introducing King Herbert and His Jump Trio as the new house band. After more than 16 years of continuous operation, Farran's was sold and new owner Paul Mann opened Club Afrique in its place on Tuesday, February 24, 1953 with a bill that featured the Milt Buckner Trio, jazz saxophonist Ben Webster and the Three of Us Trio.

Over in Central Prince George's County, Maryland was the Dixie Tavern (6900 Central Avenue, Seat Pleasant; today this site is occupied by Central Exxon which is marked 6400 Central Avenue), which had been opened in 1934 for owner Hugh Waldrop, who also owned the Dixie Pig Restaurant and Barbecue in Bladensburg. Among the regular country music entertainers there during the post-Prohibition years were Roland Cumberland and His Swing-O-Pators, Alice and Her Wonderland Boys, Al Shea's Orchestra, Blackie Skiles and His Orchestra, Norman Bell and His Orchestra, the Jay-Gee Orchestra and Billy Strickland and His Hillbilly Kings.

In September 1948 the Dixie Tavern was sold to the trio of Connie B. Gay, Jane E. Trimner and Percy W. Carrick, who converted the premises into Club Hillbilly. In addition to retaining much of the country music talent that had worked the Dixie Tavern, the new owners booked such entertainers as: the Stoneman Family, Dub Howington and the Tennessee Haymakers (featuring singer-accordionist Jimmy Dean), the Town and Country Ranchmen and the Sons of the Pioneers; singers Ken Curtis and Jimmy Wakely; singer-guitarist George Jones; and the musical comedy duo of Homer and Jethro. Club Hillbilly closed its doors for good in 1951.

Across the street from Joe Turner Arena in the Uptown area of Washington, D.C. was the Kit-Mar Restaurant (2300 14th Street NW). In 1932 the Kit-Mar Coffee Pot moved into quarters formerly occupied by the Hall Tire and Rubber Company. In 1939 new owners changed the name of the business to the Kit-Mar Restaurant and ushered in what would be a decade of hillbilly music. Favorite performers at this night club throughout the 1940s included Billy Strickland and His Hillbilly Kings, Boogie Woogie Johnny, and the Three Corns (Andy Burton, Jesse Marshall and Jimmie Ivie). The Kit-Mar Restaurant was advertised for a while in the late 1940s as the Kit-Mar Drum Bar and for a stretch was owned by entrepreneur Joe Turner.

Among the C&W acts to work the Kit-Mar Restaurant during the 1950s were Dub Howington and the Tennessee Haymakers (featuring singer-guitarist Smitty Smith, guitarist Ulysses White and fiddler Buck Ryan), Mac Wiseman and the Country Boys, the Sons of the Southland (featuring singer-guitarist Smokey Mac and fiddler Buck Ryan) and singer-steel guitarist Billy Strickland. Pop and rock and roll performers to appear in the night club included Russ Bello's Band, the Jets, Dan Daumit's Trio, and singers Jerry Toronto, Lou Frazier, Bob McQuain and George Eades. In addition, a number of exotic dancers worked the Kit-Mar stage including the Salome Sisters, Jean Russell and Rosalie Lynn. After its closing in 1959 two different R&B night clubs occupied the premises: the Cuban Lounge (December 1960-September 1962); and the Diamond Jim Club (October 1962-April 1968).

Further down 14th Street towards Thomas Circle was the Covered Wagon Restaurant (1402 14th Street NW), which, in March 1938, replaced the Coffey Brothers Screen Company at this address and quickly established itself as one of the top country music night clubs in the area. Original owners James Saunders and Anthony Seidl booked the top local entertainers of this genre during the 1940s and among those to work the night club included: bands such as Dub Howington and His Tennessee Haymakers (featuring singer-accordionist Jimmy Dean and guitarist Herb White), Billy Strickland and His Gang, the Melody Boys String Band (featuring singer Paul Jones) and Harry Rodcay and His Hillbilly Band; singer-fiddler-guitarist Blackie Skiles; singer-guitarist Billy Grammer; guitarists Zeb Turner and Ulysses White; fiddler Chubby Wise; and drummer Jim Burkett.

The Covered Wagon Restaurant explored new territories in November 1952 when they brought in the Three of Us Trio, a Black trio consisting of singer-saxophonist Charley Kelly, guitarist Clarence Dillard and drummer Laurence Farrell that had the distinction of being one of the first area groups to be billed in local night clubs as a rock and roll band. In the middle 1950s another regular headliner at this night club was an outfit called Three Kings and a Queen (featuring saxophonist VI Burnsides). The Covered Wagon Restaurant closed its doors in October 1958.

In the Southeast quadrant of Washington, D.C., not far from Capitol Hill on what was then called Sailor's Row, was the Band Box (747 8th Street SE). This night club, which replaced the Thomas Hines Restaurant in January 1943, was owned by Jimmy Pagliochini and specialized in C&W music for just about all of its 17-year run.

Among the main attractions to work the Band Box during the 1940s were the Diplomats, the Tune Twisters, Blackie Skiles and His Band, Billy Strickland and His Gang and Mason Thomas and His Dixieland Jazz Band. During the 1950s Billy Strickland and the Band Boxers held down the house band position and some of the more popular musicians to play in the night club during those years included: guitarist Andy Burton; bassist Hank Rowe; and multi-instrumentalist Clyde Marshall. The Band Box was later replaced by Jack's Cocktail Lounge in November 1960. Since 1980 this building has housed the Southeast Uniform Company.

One of the more storied C&W night clubs in Washington, D.C. was the Jo Del Bar and Grill (719 9th Street NW), which was in operation from 1950 to 1958 and ultimately closed after a gruesome murder took place on its premises. A long line of restaurants had inhabited this ancient building including the short-lived Acropolis Club, which had replaced the Cactus House Restaurant in January 1950 and was a favorite of the city's Greek gambling community. The Acropolis closed in April of that year and in October 1950 George P. Kaldes opened the Jo Del Bar and Grill in its quarters.

From the very beginning the Jo Del Bar and Grill offered C&W music and during the first half of the decade some of the bands and musicians to work the night club were Dub Howington and the Tennessee Haymakers, Billy Strickland and His Gang, Harry Rodcay and His Hillbilly Band, Smokey Roberts and His Bear Cats, Whitey Murphy and His Rhythm Riders, Smokey and His Rhythm Makers, Jimmy Dean and the Texas Wildcats and a number of singer-guitarists including Pete Pike, Roy Clark and Carl Lukat, all of whom often worked in conjunction with house bassist Buck Austin.

In 1955 Sonny James and His Country Melody Boys (featuring steel guitarist Vernon Edwards and drummer Bobby Vargas) took over house band duties at the Jo Del Bar and Grill. In 1956 they gave way to the Jimmy Case Trio, who also went by the name Jimmy Case and the Cherokees and were the first group to be advertised by the night club as a rock and roll band. For the next two years Case's band worked at the Jo Del, alternating sets with country music guitarist Kenny Fisher and blind pianist Bernard Mainer.

Tragedy struck the Jo Del Bar and Grill, when, at 1:45am on the morning of Friday, December 27, 1957 46-year-old Henry Clay Overton (aka Jack Owens) and 21-year-old Russell Wayne Carpenter, both of Southeast Washington, D.C. were ejected from the night club by Kaldes after refusing to pay a $20 whiskey tab. At 2am Overton and Carpenter returned to the night club with a loaded .45 automatic and opened fire. Killed instantly were Kaldes, who was struck by bullets four times, and 32-year-old house guitarist Kenneth Fisher, who was shot five times. Also shot in the melee was blind pianist Bernard Mainer, who groped helplessly for cover when the gunfire broke out and was struck in the hip and kidney. Mainer later passed away from his injuries on Friday, March 7, 1958.

After a wild getaway run through several states in the South, Overton was killed in a fiery, head-on automobile crash in Augusta, Georgia on Sunday, December 29, 1957 (ending a 110 mile per hour chase with Georgia State Police). Carpenter was arrested 24 hours later in West Palm Beach, Florida. He was convicted on Friday, April 25, 1958 in Federal Court in Alexandria, Virginia on kidnapping and car theft charges (stemming from his getaway run on the night of the Jo Del murders). On Thursday, May 8, 1958 he was sentenced to life imprisonment on each of two kidnapping charges, five years each on two car theft counts, and 12 months for contempt of court after refusing to answer questions about the shootings. He later pleaded guilty to a plea-bargained charge of manslaughter in Federal District Court in Washington, D.C. on Monday, May 9, 1960, which carried a 15-year maximum. He was paroled in May 1973.

The Jo Del Bar and Grill reopened on Tuesday, January 7, 1958 but closed for good the following week, as Pandora Kaldes, widow of the slain owner, opted to place the establishment for sale. The building was subsequently torn down and for many years thereafter its space served as a parking facility. The Jo Del Bar and Grill's former site is now inhabited by an 11-story office building called Edison Place (701 9th Street NW).

During the 1950s there were more night clubs in the area offering C&W music than ever before. Among the favorites in Washington, D.C. were: the Anchor Grill (1913 Nichols Avenue SE) in Anacostia, whose main attraction was the Blue Grass Champs; Bob White's Hideaway (319 Pennsylvania Avenue SE) on Capitol Hill, whose main headliners were Frankie Robinson and the Virginia Playboys, Smitty Irvin and the Tri-State Ramblers and Roger Allen and His Western Swing Boys; the Camden Tavern (1252 H Street NE), whose frequent headliners were Billy Strickland and His Gang, Harry Rodcay and His Hillbilly Band, Bob King and the Camdeneers, Smokey Roberts and His Bear Cats and singer-guitarists Pete Pike, Roy Clark and Carl Lukat; the Casablanca Tavern (421 11th Street NW), which hosted the Shenandoah Ramblers (featuring guitarist Eddie Nesbitt) and singer-guitarist-mandolinist Buzz Busby; the Crosstown Restaurant (3201 Mount Pleasant Street NW) in Mount Pleasant, which was home to hillbilly singer-guitarist Zeb Turner; Elmer's (a night club located within the Franklin Park Café at 829 13th Street NW), whose regulars were Red Seal's Rhythm and Strings (featuring singer Kitty Cutler), the Stoneman Family, Roy Perkey and his Country Favorites and pianist Roy Perkins; the Famous Restaurant (1215 New York Avenue NW), which regularly booked Jimmy Dean and the Texas Wildcats, Bill Peer and His Melody Boys (featuring singer Patsy Cline), the Stoneman Family, the Blue Grass Champs, singer Dick Williams, singer-guitarist Roy Clark and guitarist Tommy Johnson; the Harmony Restaurant (511-512 2nd Street NE), whose favorites were Jimmy Dean and the Texas Wildcats, Smokey Mac and His Sons of the South, Country Thomas and the Tune Twisters, the Short Brothers, Joe Carroll's Rhythm Masters, Little Bobby Stevenson and His Hillbilly Trio, the trio of singer-fiddler-guitarist Blackie Skiles, singer-steel guitarist Billy Strickland and bassist-rhythm guitarist Ulysses "Useless" White, steel guitarist Johnny "Pancake" Norris, singer-accordionist Stoney Rigsby, and an occasional visit by the rock and roll band the Three of Us Trio; Harry's Tavern (1200 New York Avenue NW), whose house band for years was Dub Howington and the Tennessee Haymakers; the Ozarks Restaurant (929 10th Street NW), whose earliest house bands were Pete Pike and the Ozark Four and the Blue Grass Champs; the Penguin Restaurant (1218 11th Street SE), which featured Chubby Wise and His Florida Playboys; the Shamrock Restaurant (3295 M Street NW) in Georgetown, whose regulars included Jimmy Dean and the Texas Wildcats, the duo of steel guitarist Mickey Woodward and guitarist Roger Woodward, Texas Jim Robertson and His Gang and singer Goldie Hill; the Starlite Restaurant (1419 Irving Street NW), whose main attractions were Butterball Paige and the Starliters, Jimmy Dean and the Texas Wildcats, Bill Peer and His Melody Boys (featuring singer Patsy Cline), singer Dick Williams and singer-guitarist Carl "Curly" Sluder; Ted's Grill (601 Pennsylvania Avenue SE) on Capitol Hill, whose best performers were the Tune Twisters and the Billy Strickland Trio; and the Victory Grill (1117 Good Hope Road SE), Anacostia's other main C&W bar of the time, whose top attractions were Stoney Rigsby and the Rock and Roll Westerners and the Buckskins.

In the 1950s the population in Prince George's County, Maryland was arguably even more Southern than that of Washington, D.C. and the popularity of C&W music was at an all-time high. Scores of night clubs competed to book the best available talent and several establishments in the growing suburbs gained reputations as country music hot spots.

Among the very best of these establishments were: the Dixie Pig (3804 Bladensburg Road, Cottage City), which, despite frequently switching its format back-and-forth between rock and roll and C&W during its existence, regularly booked such names as Chick Hall and His Gang, Dub Howington and the Tennessee Haymakers, Jimmy Dean and the Texas Wildcats, singer Patsy Cline, bluegrass singer Mac Wiseman, singer-guitarist Roy Clark and comedian Tiny Jenkins; the Homestretch Tavern (6301 Marlboro Pike, Capitol Heights; its address was later changed to 5401 Marlboro Pike), which was home to Jimmy Dean and the Texas Wildcats, Dub Howington and the Tennessee Haymakers, Smokey Mac and His Twilighters, the Capital City Dixielanders, the Maryland Playboys, the Orbits (featuring Don Presley and John Presley) and comedian Tiny Jenkins; the Sea Shell (4918 Livingston Road, Oxon Hill; its address was later changed to 4916 Indian Head Highway), a smallish bar whose longtime house band was led by singer-accordionist Stoney Rigsby; Strick's Restaurant (3211 Branch Avenue, Silver Hill), which hosted the top C&W acts available including the Cactus Matt Trio (singer-accordionist Stoney Rigsby, lead guitarist Jimmy Groves and steel guitarist Dickie Thompson), Frankie Robinson and the Virginia Playboys, Smokey Mac and His Twilighters, Bill Peer and His Melody Boys (featuring singer Patsy Cline), Jimmy Dean and the Texas Wildcats, Dub Howington and the Tennessee Haymakers, the Blue Grass Champs, Roy Clark and His Stardusters, the Buckskins, and such singer-guitarists as Billy Grammer, Dick Williams, Smitty Smith and rockabilly star Wanda Jackson; the Surf Club (4201 Bladensburg Road, Colmar Manor), which was purchased by Chick Hall in 1955 and featured, in addition to Hall himself, singer-guitarists Wade Holmes and Pete Pike; the original Sunnybrook Tavern (6980 Indian Head Highway, Oxon Hill; the bar was rebuilt on the original site in 1992 and is now marked 9001 Livingston Road, Fort Washington), which brought in such talent as Dub Howington and His Tennessee Haymakers, singer-guitarist Roy Clark and singers Patsy Cline and Miss Dale Turner; and the Wheel Bar (3817 Bladensburg Road, Colmar Manor), which often staged

"Hillbilly Jamborees" featuring the likes of singer-fiddler-guitarist Blackie Skiles, singer-steel guitarist Billy Strickland and guitarist-bassist Ulysses White.

Contributing to the growing popularity of country music in the Washington, D.C. area was its availability in mediums other than night clubs and concert events. Country music had been offered on different radio stations in the Washington, D.C. area since the 1920s, but it wasn't until 1948 that the relatively new device of television began offering such music in their programming. Two of the earliest of these on-air country music programs were "Gay Time" (WNBW, Channel 4; Saturday nights, July-October 1948) and "Hayloft Conservatory of Musical Interpretation" (WTTG, Channel 5; Thursday nights, August 1948-March 1949).

When it came to musical programming, television had a decisive advantage over radio in that those who could afford to purchase the sets could actually see and hear their favorite stars perform in a live music setting. While both mediums were invaluable in terms of promoting the work of these musicians, the imagery and visuals provided by television generated greater excitement within a particular musician or band's fan base.

In the 1950s as technological advances were made and the number of television stations and programs in the Washington, D.C. area expanded, additional C&W music television shows were introduced to the local viewing public. Most of these specialized television programs, all of which were hosted by local celebrity musicians and featured both local and national musical entertainers who performed live in studio settings, are now largely forgotten. Despite the lack of information on these shows, all should be recognized as historically significant for the contributions they made to the advancement of C&W music on a regional level. The following is a list of some of the more popular of these television programs of the 1950s:

"Town and Country Time"
(WMAL-TV, Channel 7)
Tuesday nights at 10pm; April 10, 1951 to September 18, 1951
Produced by Connie B. Gay, this 30-minute program was an offshoot of the radio show of the same name and usually featured singer-banjoist Grandpa Jones and a revolving series of musicians who performed on a small set fashioned after a country store.

"Showcase: The Cactus Matt Show"
(WTTG, Channel 5)
Monday nights at 8:30pm; March 22, 1954 to April 12, 1954
"Showcase" was a 30-minute experimental television program that aired pilots and short-run episodes of varying content. "The Cactus Matt Show" was presented on "Showcase" for four consecutive Monday nights as a C&W variety music show. Hosted by Matthew "Cactus Matt" Warren, the show featured such musicians as guitarist Roy Clark, Frankie Robinson and the Virginia Playboys and the Cactus Matt Trio (singer-accordionist Stoney Rigsby, lead guitarist Jimmy Groves and steel guitarist Dickie Thompson). Cactus Matt served as an alter-ego for several years for Matthew Warren, who for much of the late 1940s and early 1950s was program director at radio station WEAM, where he also hosted a C&W music show entitled "Cactus Matt." During this time Cactus Matt also promoted live music shows on a regular basis at venues throughout the area including Joe Turner Arena and Strick's Restaurant. Simultaneously, under his real name of Matthew Warren, he served as a sportscaster, news reporter and highly regarded host of "Georgetown University Forum" on television station WTTG Channel 5. In the early 1960s he left the C&W music bookings behind and was news editor at WTTG. By the middle 1960s Warren was hosting a show entitled "Perspective" on radio station WMAL, after which he faded from the local scene.

"Town and Country Time"
(WMAL-TV, Channel 7)
Various weeknights and times; Monday, January 17, 1955 to Friday, January 24, 1958
This second installment of "Town and Country Time," an extension of the 1951 series, was produced by Connie B. Gay and hosted by Jimmy Dean. This program aired anywhere from 30 to 60 minutes and showcased Dean and his band, the Texas Wildcats. During its three-year run nearly every C&W musician in town appeared on the show including regulars such as Dub Howington and the Tennessee Haymakers, Roy Clark, Grandpa Jones, Billy Grammer, Marvin Rainwater, Mary Klick, Dale Turner and Patsy Cline. Also making appearances were innumerable stars of "The Grand Ole Opry" that were in town to perform on the featured Saturday night television show "Town and Country Jamboree" and the summertime "Moonlight Cruises" that Gay booked on the S.S. Mount Vernon along the Potomac River.

"Town and Country Jamboree"
(WMAL-TV, Channel 7)
Saturday nights at 10pm; October 1, 1955 to August 31, 1957
This program was a live Saturday night broadcast from Joe Turner Arena that aired from 10pm to 1am. Hosted by Connie B. Gay, Jimmy Dean, Jackson Weaver and Phil Long, these marathon concerts offered all the established local stars from the "Town and Country Time" radio and television programs, as well as some of the biggest names of "The Grand Ole Opry" including Bob Wills and the Texas Playboys, Little Jimmy Dickens and His Country Boys, Ernest Tubb and His Texas Troubadours and singer-guitarist Lefty Frizzell.

"Hayloft Hoedown"
(WNBW, Channel 4)
Weekdays at 2pm; Monday, September 13, 1954 to Friday, March 4, 1955
This 30-minute program was hosted by Mike Hunnicutt ("Champion Jug Blower of East Tennessee") and featured a five-piece band fronted by singer-guitarist Pete Pike and mandolinist Buzz Busby, and rounded out by fiddler John Hall, banjoist Don Stover and bass fiddler Lee Cole. The group performed the program's theme song, "Bile Them Cabbages Down," on every show and Pike and Busby often appeared in comedy skits as Ham and Scram, a couple of cut-ups who told jokes and played music while dressed in overalls, broad hats, and phony glasses, noses and mustaches.

"The Jimmy Dean Show"
(WTOP, Channel 9)
Various days and times; Monday, April 8, 1957 to Saturday, August 30, 1958
"The Jimmy Dean Show" was a 45-minute program that debuted at 7am on Monday, April 8, 1957 with a lineup that included the Texas Wildcats, pop singer Jan Crockett, the Country Lads (Dick Flood and Billy Graves), ventriloquist Alex Houston, rockabilly singer-guitarist Wanda Jackson and C&W singer-guitarist George Hamilton IV. It went on to become the Washington, D.C. area's premier C&W music variety show. Dean went on to bigger and better things in the 1960s including his own nationally syndicated television show on ABC.

"Country Style"
(WTOP, Channel 9)
Weekdays at 7:45am; Monday, April 8, 1957 to Saturday, August 31, 1957
The featured house band on this 15-minute program was Johnny Lyndon and the Country Stylists, who were advertised as offering "toe-tapping music and songs." The singing duo known as the Country Lads and singer-guitarist Roy Clark made frequent appearances.

"Don Owens TV Jamboree"
(WTTG, Channel 5)
Saturday nights at 9pm; August 3, 1957 to December 3, 1960
WARL C&W music disc jockey-promoter Don Owens hosted this one-hour program, which was listed in the local newspaper program listings as "Live Country Music Show" during the month of August 1957 (though its official title was "Don Owens TV Jamboree"). The show's house band was Vernon Taylor and the Circle-O-Boys.

"Buckskins' TV Jamboree"
(WTTG, Channel 5)
Friday and/or Saturday nights at various times; Saturday, September 28, 1957 to Friday, May 9, 1958
The Buckskins were a popular local cowboy music band and were regularly appearing at Strick's Restaurant in Silver Hill, Maryland and the Victory Grill in the Anacostia neighborhood of Washington, D.C. when they landed this 30-minute, primetime program. Their lineup consisted of lead vocalist Frankie Robinson, tenor vocalist Joe Reagan, lead guitarist-baritone vocalist Jimmy Groves, accordionist Dick Johnson and bassist Slim Vick.

"The Blue Grass Champs"
(WTTG, Channel 5)
Saturday nights at 8:30pm; February 22, 1958 to September 20, 1958
The Blue Grass Champs first formed in 1953 with three members of the Stoneman family of Carmody Hills, Maryland – Scotty, Jimmy, and Donna – and family friend Jimmy Case, a guitarist who resided nearby in Capitol Heights, Maryland. Throughout the decade the band worked regularly in Washington, D.C. at the "Town and Country Jamborees" at Joe Turner Arena, as well as such night clubs as the Famous Restaurant, the Ozarks Restaurant and the Anchor Grill in the Anacostia neighborhood of the city. They also performed at several night spots in neighboring Prince George's County, Maryland including Strick's Restaurant, the Dixie Pig, Chubby's Restaurant and Bar and Armstrong's. While at the height of their local popularity, they were granted this 30-minute, live music television program.

"The George Hamilton IV Show"
(WTOP, Channel 9)
Various days at 12noon; Saturday, September 6, 1958 to Friday, May 29, 1959
George Hamilton IV, born Monday, July 19, 1937, was an 18-year-old C&W singer-guitarist from Winston Salem, North Carolina when he ventured to the nation's capital in the summer of 1955 to make a special appearance on a "Town and Country Jamboree" show at Joe Turner Arena. That fall Hamilton returned to his home state and enrolled as a freshman at the University of North Carolina at Chapel Hill. He quickly became a popular performer around the college town and scored a local hit with the single "A Rose and A Baby Ruth," which was initially released on the independent Colonial Records label in June 1956. The song's enormous popularity led Hamilton to sell the rights to ABC-Paramount, which rereleased "A Rose and A Baby Ruth" as a single backed with "If You Don't Know" in

October 1956. The single placed in several of "The Billboard's Music Popularity Charts" including peaking at number six on "The Top 100" chart on Saturday, December 22, 1956, number seven on the "Best Sellers in Stores" chart on Saturday, December 15, 1956, number seven on the "Most Played By Jockeys" chart on Saturday, January 5, 1957, and number eight on the "Most Played in Juke Boxes" chart on Saturday, January 12, 1957. Connie B. Gay, meanwhile, had persuaded Hamilton to transfer from the University of North Carolina to American University in Washington, D.C. in the fall of 1956 and made him a regular on his "Town and Country Time" television show. Hamilton's popularity as both a pop and C&W entertainer soared and he was later a featured performer on "The Jimmy Dean Show." When Dean left the area for his own nationally broadcast show in New York City, Hamilton IV became his logical replacement on local television. The first episode of his new one-hour program, "The George Hamilton IV Show," aired one week after Dean left town and featured pop singer Jan Crockett, C&W singer Jo Davis, the Country Lads, the Texas Wildcats, singer-bassist Mary Klick and ventriloquist Alex Houston. George Hamilton IV went on to become one of the music's industry's biggest crossover stars.

"Music Fair"
(WTTG, Channel 5)
Wednesday nights at 10pm; March 25, 1959 to May 27, 1959
"Music Fair" was a short-lived, 30-minute C&W program that featured the Buckskins and singer Alice Sharon.

CHAPTER FORTY-FOUR
THE BEN ADELMAN EMPIRE

With radio and television spreading the popularity of C&W music to fans throughout the Washington, D.C. area, a number of record producers inspired by the introduction of 33rpm long-play records and 45rpm single records sought to capture these musicians in the studio and make the sounds available to the public for their listening pleasure. Lillian Claiborne and the Feld Brothers were among the first to capture local country musicians on record when they started their respective record labels back in the 1940s. Joining them in the 1950s was Benjamin "Ben" Adelman, who established himself on the local music scene first as a music publisher, then, as C&W music flourished throughout the region, as operator of a series of recording studios which enabled him to produce records that he either released on his own private labels or farmed out to larger companies across the country. Most of the top C&W musicians in town, and many pop and rock and roll acts as well, worked with Adelman at some point during his lengthy reign in Washington, D.C.

Ben Adelman was reportedly born and raised in upstate New York and ultimately spent 16 years in the United States Navy, during which time he performed as a multi-instrumentalist in the United States Navy Band. In 1934, towards the end of his service, he was stationed in Washington, D.C. and late that year started a music publishing company in the city with his brother Samuel called Adelman Brothers Music Company (527 9th Street NW, Room 601). The business closed in 1941.

In 1942 Adelman and his wife Katherine ("Kay"), who was employed as a manager with the American Research Bureau, lived together in an apartment in Washington at 1315 Peabody Street NW #105 and jointly operated a music publishing company called Mayflower Music Company. They also wrote songs that they hoped local musicians would record, as Ben's main source of income during those years was as a taxi driver for the Arrow Cab Company. The Mayflower Music Company stayed in business until 1951.

In the fall of 1951 the Adelmans moved to a house at 239 Missouri Avenue NW in Washington, D.C. and Ben opened a now-legendary recording studio called Truetone Recording Company on the second and top floor of an oddly shaped, two-story building at 5506 Illinois Avenue NW, right at the intersection with Georgia Avenue NW, some seven blocks west of their home (in more recent years, a third floor was added to this building). The sparsely furnished studio was little more than an empty room which contained a desk, a chair, a couch, several plug-in outlets for amplifiers, and, in terms of actual studio equipment, one microphone and one Magnatone tape recorder. The Truetone Recording Company remained at the Illinois Avenue address for a little over three years, during which time Adelman made hundreds of recordings of some of the area's best C&W musicians.

Adelman dreamed of writing and producing a series of hit songs that would make him rich and establish himself as a major player in the national music scene. He felt the best way to accomplish this goal was to farm out his recordings to major record labels across the United States. Adelman soon discovered that making such contacts was a difficult task and that when such business arrangements were established, it would be he, the local producer, who would come up on the short end of the stick. Adelman found an interested party in Bill McCall, owner of 4 Star Records in Pasadena, California, who was more than happy to make low-risk deals for large helpings of Adelman's recordings.

One of Adelman's earliest projects involved arranging and producing singer-accordionist Jimmy Dean, who fronted his own band the Texas Wildcats, and was a regular on the Connie B. Gay-produced "Town and Country Time" radio show on WARL. Dean was recruited by a local music aficionado named Fred Foster (later the president of Monument

Records) to make several demo recordings in the cramped confines of Truetone Recording Company.

In the spring of 1952 Fred Foster sent a Jimmy Dean demo of a song entitled "Bumming Around" (written by someone named "P. Graves") to several independent record companies he had learned of through the Billboard directory. Bill McCall of 4 Star Records in California quickly responded and asked Foster to rerecord the song in a better facility in Washington, D.C. Foster complied and in July 1952 took Dean and his band into a recording studio called Sound Studios Inc. (1124 Vermont Avenue NW). McCall then released the single "Bumming Around" backed with "Picking Sweethearts" (Jimmy Dean; 4 Star Records, 1952) in August of that year and it eventually charted on three different C&W records charts in the Billboard magazine, peaking at number five on the "Most Played by Jockeys" country & western records chart on Saturday, March 21, 1953.

Ben Adelman's name was never mentioned in conjunction with "Bumming Around," though his wife Kay was credited as the songwriter of the B-side, "Pickin' Sweethearts," despite the fact that song was actually written by Fred Foster. Adelman was reportedly stunned by the success of "Bumming Around" and stung not only by Fred Foster's role as Dean's producer on the sessions, but also by the fact that he never capitalized monetarily on what became a nationwide hit song. He immediately began recording additional songs by Jimmy Dean and the Texas Wildcats and other local C&W musicians in his Truetone Recording Company studio. He also continued to send recorded material to McCall, an indication that, to some extent, money was changing hands between the two.

From 1951 to 1954 Adelman made recordings at his Truetone Recording Company that featured such local C&W musicians as: singer-guitarists Roy Clark, Wade Holmes, Pete Pike and Luke Gordon; singers Marvin Rainwater and Patsy Cline; and singer-guitarist-mandolinist Buzz Busby. Dozens of musicians including Clark, Holmes and Pike, along with others like steel guitarist Mickey Woodward, guitarist-bassist Roger Woodward and fiddler Buck Ryan, also served as studio musicians on numerous songs recorded by Adelman. The fate of these recordings varied greatly. Some were sold to other record labels such as McCall's 4 Star label and released as 33rpm long-play records or 45rpm single records, some were released in later years by Adelman on his own budget record labels like Spin-O-Rama and Mount Vernon Music, and others were simply never heard from again.

Many of these recordings, despite the rather primitive conditions under which they were crafted, sound surprisingly good in today's high fidelity world. The songs of the Adelman early 1950s sessions, some of which would be packaged and released more than 10 years after being recorded, range from mundane to fascinating.

Some of the more intriguing examples of these recordings are two 45rpm single records by Roy Cark: "Mysteries of Life" backed with "Sugar Coated Sweetheart" (Roy Clark and His Wranglers; 4 Star Records, 1954); and "Stepping Stones" backed with "The Day That I Found You" (Roy Clark; Coral Records, 1956). With Clark's subsequent rise to country music stardom, these selections became rare collector's items and are still highly sought-after items today.

Albums from these Adelman sessions include: "Featuring the Country Singing of Jimmy Dean with Luke Gordon" (Jimmy Dean with Luke Gordon; Spin-O-Rama Records, 1963); "Jimmy Dean and the Town and Country Men" (Jimmy Dean and the Town and Country Men; Guest Star Records, 1964); "Country Comedy – Songs & Frolic by Ham & Scram Featuring Buzz Busby" (Ham & Scram featuring Buzz Busby; Mount Vernon Music, 1963); "The Country's Favorite Country Singer" (Marvin Rainwater; Mount Vernon Music, 1952); "Marvin Rainwater" (Marvin Rainwater; Guest Star Records, 1962); "Golden Country Hits Sung by Marvin Rainwater with Wade Holmes" (Marvin Rainwater with Wade Holmes; Spin-O-Rama Records, 1963); and the two-part album series from Wade Holmes, "Mr.

Lean Sings Country Favorites, Volume 1" (Mr. Lean; Mount Vernon Music, 1963) and "Mr. Lean Sings Country Favorites, Volume 2" (Mr. Lean; Mount Vernon Music, 1963).

In the fall of 1954 Adelman opted to move his Truetone Recording Company to more spacious quarters within the city and found a suitable location downtown in the elegant Portland Building (1129 Vermont Avenue NW), a structure that was erected in 1880 and would later face the wrecking ball in August 1962. In September 1954 the move was officially made and the new True-Tone Recording Company (note the new spelling of the company's name) opened up in Room 101 of the aging building.

One of the top local artists Adelman recorded in his studio during this time was singer-guitarist Lucky Wray (real name Vernon Wray), who performed a mix of C&W, pop, rockabilly and early rock and roll material. His studio sessions for Adelman had musical backing provided by his two brothers, guitarist Link Wray and drummer Doug Wray, along with bassist Shorty Horton – a quartet that later became Link Wray and His Ray Men. Adelman arranged to have three rockabilly 45rpm single records from these tapes released for Lucky Wray on Starday Records. He continued recording local musicians in the new quarters for approximately three years during which time he and his wife Kay moved about the city with great frequency.

In 1957 Adelman rendered the True-Tone Recording Company defunct and then spent several weeks contemplating his next move. That summer he opened a new studio called Empire Records and Recording Studios (323 Cedar Street NW) in the Takoma neighborhood of Washington, D.C. In 1960 Adelman and his wife moved from 7002 5th Street NW to a home at 1615 Juniper Street NW, where they remained for the duration of their time in the city.

Adelman went on to record a variety of musicians and bands in his studio and in the late 1950s and early 1960s he released 45rpm single records on Empire Records by such performers as Jack Donovan and the Knight Caps, Joey Kay, Roy Franklin, Phil Flowers, Wayne Busby, Buzz Busby, Skip Manning (a pseudonym for Phil Flowers), the Country Kings, Carl & Norman, Johnny Brown, Keith Daniels and His Blue Ridge Ramblers and Luke Gordon.

In 1965 Ben Adelman closed Empire Records and Recording Studios, though he continued to maintain offices at the Cedar Street NW location under the name of B&F Record Distributing Company. In 1968 he shut down operations altogether and he and Kay left the nation's capital and moved to Florida. Ben Adelman reportedly passed away in 1970, with his wife Kay joining him in 2001.

In recent times there has been a substantial amount of erroneous material in published articles and on Internet web sites pertaining to the dates and locations of recordings produced by Ben Adelman in his various Washington, D.C. studios. It should be noted that in most instances, Adelman did not create records for public consumption from his master tapes until several years after the recordings were actually made. He usually attempted to sell such material to more prominent record labels. If these record companies declined his offer, he would then release the material on one of his own budget record labels. In many cases such records were issued that contained music he had recorded more than 10 years prior.

As a result of this practice, many articles and published discographies list sessions for performers such as Luke Gordon, Marvin Rainwater, Buzz Busby and others as having been recorded by Adelman in 1953 and 1954 in his studio at 323 Cedar Street NW. However, that would have been impossible as Adelman did not actually move his studio to that location until 1957.

The reason for these errors is that Adelman shipped off recordings to various record companies in the 1950s and 1960s that included documentation that listed his business address of 323 Cedar Street NW and not the name and address of the studio where the material had actually been recorded. For the record, any Ben Adelman-produced recordings from 1951 to August 1954 were made at the Truetone Recording Company's Illinois Avenue NW studio, most recordings made from September 1954 to the summer months of 1957 were made at the True-Tone Recording Company's Portland Building studio on Vermont Avenue NW, and any recordings after the summer of 1957 were made at Adelman's Empire Records and Recording Studios on Cedar Street NW.

In his time Ben Adelman recorded local musicians and made their music available to regional and national audiences. Through this process he fostered the dreams of local musicians who hoped to one day have hit records, provided inspiration for musicians to continue making music and to pursue recording and performing opportunities, and produced permanent records of their work. Though he never attained the levels of personal fame and fortune he desired, Ben Adelman did earn a place of distinction in the history of Washington, D.C. area popular music for his efforts in recording, publishing and distributing the musical works of scores of local performing artists.

CHAPTER FORTY-FIVE
FROM LIZARD LICK TO ARLINGTON

The one individual who has been credited with doing more to shape, promote and sustain the local C&W music scene during the 1950s is Connie B. Gay, whose exploits as a disc jockey, manager, concert promoter and music entrepreneur have rendered him a legendary figure in the annals of Washington, D.C. area music history.

Connie Barriot Gay was born on Saturday, August 22, 1914 in Lizard Lick, North Carolina, some 18 miles east of Raleigh. He grew up on a 17-acre tobacco farm and graduated from North Carolina State University with a Bachelor of Science in agriculture in 1935. He then embarked on a succession of jobs: throughout 1935 he worked as a soil analyst for the Soil Erosion Service; in 1936 he was publisher of a magazine entitled "Rural Electrification Guide;" he worked all over the country for most of 1937 as a carnival pitchman; and in 1938 he worked as a field administrator with the Farm Security Administration where he implemented programs designed to alleviate rural poverty. In the early 1940s Gay switched over to the United States Department of Agriculture and eventually hosted the agency's "National Farm and Home Hour" radio show. Gay was a natural on the microphone and he began scheming to create his own musical radio show.

In 1946 Gay left his government job behind and called Frank Blair, who at the time was the program director at radio station WARL in Arlington, Virginia. He presented to Blair his idea of an on-air show devoted entirely to country music. Blair, who would go on to hold the position of news desk anchorman for NBC's "Today" show from 1953 to 1975, agreed with Gay's proposal, granted him a 30-minute, 12noon slot, and on Thursday, November 7, 1946 the new radio show, entitled "Town and Country Time," went on the air. Gay, who had spent the previous 10 years moving about the country, bought a house at 845 N. Lincoln Street in Arlington, Virginia. Along with his wife Hazel and their two children, he called this residence home for the next eight years.

While WARL was located on the second floor of a building at 3102 Tenth Road N. in Arlington, Gay originally broadcasted his show from the basement of his new home, temporarily using a primitive telephone hook-up that linked him to the station's transmitter in nearby Clarendon. Offering "country news and country views," Gay passed on a salary and instead took a percentage of the advertising revenue obtained from sponsors. The show proved so popular it was soon expanded from 30 minutes to three hours of total programming and WARL quickly changed the majority of its programming to feature country music.

When Gay eventually began broadcasting directly from the WARL studio in 1947, he anchored his radio broadcasts by assembling a group of musicians he called the Radio Ranchmen who would often perform live on the air for his expanding audience. The initial lineup of this band consisted of four musicians: singer Joe Wheeler, steel guitarist Buddy Wheeler, fiddler Curly Parker (formerly of the Blue Sky Boys) and singer-guitarist Billy Grammer.

The Ranchmen subsequently went through a number of personnel changes with some original members departing and some popular names in country music taking their places. New additions in the late 1940s included singer-guitarist Clyde Moody (formerly with Bill Monroe and His Blue Grass Boys) and fiddler Robert "Chubby" Wise (who had previously been a member of Bill Monroe and His Blue Grass Boys, and would go on to work with Lester Flatt and Earl Scruggs and the Foggy Mountain Boys, and Hank Snow and His Rainbow Ranch Boys). Other musicians to pass through the Radio Ranchmen included bassist-guitarist Red Seal, accordionist Pat Patterson and blind singer-guitarist Pete Cassell.

In addition to his disc jockey duties, Gay booked local country music performers into area fairs, fire departments, high schools, shopping centers, theatres and VFWs. It was a move that would eventually establish him as the Washington, D.C. area's premier entrepreneur of hillbilly music entertainment. Gay mainly employed local bands in his initial efforts to infiltrate the night club scene of the nation's capital, but found that bringing in nationally recognized talent greatly boosted the size of the turnouts.

The first country music star Gay brought in for his shows was Louis Marshall "Grandpa" Jones, the now-legendary singer-banjoist who had born in Henderson County Kentucky in 1913 and raised in Akron Ohio. Jones spent much of the early 1940s in Cincinnati performing in conjunction with radio station WLW and recording for King Records. After a stint in the United States Army he moved to Nashville, Tennessee where he became a regular performer on "The Grand Ole Opry" and married fellow musician Ramona Riggins on Monday, October 14, 1946. In 1947 Jones moved to Northern Virginia to join forces with Connie B. Gay where he became a featured attraction on his radio program and live music presentations.

Another regular performer Gay called upon shortly after arriving in the Washington, D.C. area was Pete Cassell, a blind singer-guitarist who was known as both "The King of the Hillbillies" and "The Blind Minstrel." Born Monday, August 27, 1917 in Cobb County, Georgia, Cassell was a self-taught musician who worked his way through special education schools in his home state, but gave up his dream of becoming a lawyer to perform country music on a variety of radio stations including WSB in Atlanta and WWVA in Wheeling, West Virginia.

While checking out the Washington, D.C. night club scene, Cassell was told about Connie B. Gay's brand new radio show and volunteered his musical services. Gay began using him on his broadcasts and live shows and the blind minstrel's performances were so well-received he was granted his own country music radio show on WARL. Cassell, who had also released singles on the Decca, Mercury and Majestic record labels, continued working with Gay into the early 1950s before slowing his schedule due to heart problems. He passed away of coronary thrombosis in 1954 at the age of 37.

In the summer of 1947 Gay ventured to Nashville, Tennessee where he met with Jim Denny, who at the time was the director of the WSM Artist Service Bureau and the unofficial manager of "The Grand Ole Opry" (the weekly "Opry" concerts were booked through Nashville radio station WSM at the time). Gay came away with a business arrangement that allowed for him to have exclusive access to "Grand Ole Opry" acts. It was a business move no other music promoter in the nation's capital could match and Gay quickly went to work lining up a venue for the nationally known talent that was now at his disposal.

Gay's first event was a highly publicized "Grand Ole Opry" concert at DAR Constitution Hall in Washington, D.C. on the night of Friday, October 31, 1947 featuring singer-guitarist Eddy Arnold and comedians Rod Brasfield and Minnie Pearl. Tickets were offered at the then-exorbitant price of $6 and both the 7pm and 9:15pm shows were completely sold out, with a large number of local politicians, dignitaries and socialites among the attendees.

Six months later Gay began booking "Gay Time" revues that featured live country music entertainment at DAR Constitution Hall on a weekly basis. The first of these events took place on the night of Saturday, April 17, 1948 and featured bluegrass singer-guitarist Clyde Moody, country singer-guitarist T. Tex Tyler, and country singer-banjoist Grandpa Jones.

All told, 27 consecutive Saturday night "Gay Time" programs were staged at DAR Constitution Hall. The run eventually came to an end on the night of Saturday, October 16,

1948 with a concert that featured singer Dave Denny, the husband-and-wife duo of singer-banjoist Grandpa Jones and fiddler Ramona Jones, bluegrass singer-guitarist Clyde Moody, fiddler Chubby Wise, and the singing duo of Lily and Curly, all of whom were backed by the latest version of the Radio Ranchmen.

The success of these unique live concert programs attracted the interest of local television stations and Gay was quick to take advantage of this intriguing opportunity. He signed up with station WNBW (Channel 4) for a program that broadcasted portions of these concerts live from DAR Constitution Hall over a period of 12 weeks. Entitled "Gay Time," the first installment aired on Saturday, July 31, 1948 from 9pm to 10pm. Inexplicably, WMAL-TV (Channel 7) somehow became involved in the mix and "Gay Time" aired on its network for one Saturday only – August 21, 1948 – and then just as suddenly returned to WNBW for its remaining eight installments.

Not surprisingly, another local country music television program entitled "Hayloft Conservatory of Musical Interpretation" attempted to take advantage of the sudden interest in country music and aired on Thursday nights from August 5, 1948 until March 31, 1949 on WTTG (Channel 5). Although it gave local musical entertainers a chance to display their wares in a studio setting, it failed to capture the electricity of the concert experience and its popularity eventually waned.

Despite his impressive accomplishments as a disc jockey, manager and promoter, Connie B. Gay did run into some tense situations. In one very bizarre incident, Gay was badly beaten in an altercation with singer-steel guitarist Billy Strickland, whom Gay was managing at the time. An article entitled "Guitar Player Charged with Beating Rival" in the Washington Post of Friday, June 11, 1948 detailed how Gay, while seated at the Dixie Pig Restaurant and Barbecue in Bladensburg, Maryland on the previous Wednesday night, was approached by the 35-year-old Strickland who battered him with his fists and feet, leaving the entrepreneur with cuts, bruises and possible broken ribs.

According to the article, Gay claimed the beating stemmed from "professional jealousy." Strickland, admitting he had a "bitter tooth" for Gay, admitted to his role in the assault and claimed he waited until the latter tried a "backhand blow and then I let him have it." The exact reason for the bad blood between Gay and Strickland (his real name was Billie E. Strickland, but he used "Billy" as his stage name), who had come to the nation's capital from his hometown of Smithfield, North Carolina and was one of the area's top country music guitarists, has never been ascertained. However, it did prove to be a bad career move for the guitarist, who remained a well-known attraction in the night clubs of the Washington, D.C. area throughout the 1950s, but went several years before working again on Gay-promoted live music shows.

Connie B. Gay was undaunted by the fact that DAR Constitution Hall's management had inexplicably pulled the plug on his successful concert schedule and corresponding television program. He found new life when he learned that the owners of Joe Turner Arena in the Uptown area of the city were open to bringing in different types of live music entertainment. Gay had utilized this facility in the past, having held a "Radio Ranch" concert there in November 1947, and he quickly negotiated a deal to relocate his "Gay Time" live presentations to the arena. His first show, a live concert with no television coverage, was held on Friday, November 12, 1948 and featured Bill Monroe and His Blue Grass Boys, singer Linnie Ayleshire, singer-guitarists Clyde Moody and Pete Cassell, fiddler Chubby Wise, the husband-and-wife duo of singer-banjoist Grandpa Jones and fiddler Ramona Jones, and the Radio Ranchmen.

With his "Gay Time" concerts being staged on a semi-regular schedule at Joe Turner Arena, Gay continued to expand his local country music enterprise and booked live musical events into every available local venue. On Thursday, September 16, 1948 Gay, along with

Jane E. Trimner and Percy W. Carrick, purchased the Dixie Tavern (6900 Central Avenue, Seat Pleasant) and changed its name to Club Hillbilly, installing Dub Howington and the Tennessee Haymakers (featuring singer-accordionist Jimmy Dean) as the house band. Major stars like singer-guitarist George Jones were brought in as featured attractions. Club Hillbilly would stay in operation until a fire severely damaged the premises in 1951.

In the summer of 1949 the general media, taking a cue from the entertainment industry publication known as the Billboard, began referring to country and hillbilly music as country and western music, or C&W for short. Despite this trend, Gay had no problem referring to the musical style that was offered on his live shows as hillbilly music and often used that heading in the advertisements for his events for years to come.

Gay also booked "Grand Ole Opry" acts into larger local venues like the District of Columbia National Guard Armory in Washington, D.C. His initial concert event there was entitled "A Hillbilly Weekend" and took place over two days, Saturday, April 22, 1950 (9pm-1am) and Sunday, April 23, 1950 (3pm-6pm). Featured C&W entertainers on these two shows were singer-guitarist Hank Snow and Gay's regular team of singer-banjoist Grandpa Jones, singer-guitarist Pete Cassell and the singing duo of Lily and Curly. He later staged a C&W New Year's Eve 9pm-2am extravaganza at the District of Columbia National Guard Armory on Sunday, December 31, 1950 that featured singer-guitarist Red Foley, comedians Rod Brasfield and Minnie Pearl and square dancing led by caller Paul Jones.

In 1950 Gay began booking C&W musical riverboat tours on two different ships that sailed the Potomac River from the piers at Maine Avenue SW to Marshall Hall and back. His very first tour, advertised as a "Moonlight Cruise" for "Hillbillies," was aboard the S.S. Bear Mountain of the Potomac River Line Company and was staged on Saturday, May 27, and Sunday, May 28, 1950 (start times were 8:30pm and 12:30am on Saturday, and 2:30pm and 8:30pm on Sunday). Featured performers four this weekend package tour included singer-guitarists Rosalie Allen, Elton Britt and Pete Cassell, the husband-and-wife duo of singer-banjoist Grandpa Jones and fiddler Ramona Jones, the singing duo of Lily and Curly and Don Patton and His Swing Boys.

His next S.S. Bear Mountain "Moonlight Cruise" took place the following week on Thursday, June 1, 1950 and featured Bill Monroe and His Blue Grass Boys and Don Patton and His Swing Boys. Gay's third and final S.S. Bear Mountain "Moonlight Cruise" of that summer took place on Friday, August 18, 1950 and featured Little Jimmy Dickens and His Country Boys, Don Patton and His Swing Boys and local singer Prairie Sue.

For his last event of the 1950 season, Gay switched over to the S.S. Mount Vernon, a four-tiered ship that was operated by a company called the Wilson Line, one of several to operate ships on the Potomac River. The ship could hold 2,452 passengers and featured a spacious, glass-enclosed ballroom on its third level. On Thursday, September 7, 1950 Gay ended the summer season in fine fashion, bringing in C&W superstar Hank Williams to headline the program.

Gay continued to book his "Grand Ole Opry Moonlight Cruises" on the S.S. Mount Vernon every summer season through 1957, with Jimmy Dean and the Texas Wildcats serving house band duties. Among the C&W performers that performed on these cards were groups such as: Fiddlin' Curley Smith and the Blue Mountain Boys, Ernest Tubb and His Texas Troubadours, Don Patton and His Swing Boys, Curley Smith and His Blue Valley Boys, the Skyline Boys, the Foggy Mountain Boys, the Candy Kids, the Lone Pine Mountaineers, the Tennessee Mountain Boys, Bill Monroe and His Blue Grass Boys, Little Jimmy Dickens and His Country Boys, the Carter Sisters, the Carlisles, the Maddox Brothers and Rose, Mac Wiseman and His Country Boys, Elvis Presley and His Blue Moon Boys, Dub Howington and the Tennessee Haymakers, Hank Snow and His Rainbow Ranch Boys, the duo of Lester Flatt and Earl Scruggs and the vocal duo of Johnnie and Jack

(Johnnie Wright and Jack Anglin); singers Bill Franklin and Betty Cody; singer-guitarists such as Cowboy Copas, Hank Thompson, George Morgan, Lone Pine, Autry Inman, Kitty Wells, Carl Smith, Webb Pierce, Ken Marvin and Lefty Frizzell; guitarist Mother Maybelle; singer-steel guitarist Jerry Byrd; female pianist Del Wood; the husband-and-wife duo of singer-banjoist Grandpa Jones and fiddler Ramona Jones; the singing duo of Lily and Curly; and comedians Minnie Pearl, the musical comedy duo of Homer and Jethro and singer-comedian Lazy Jim Day.

The year of 1951 was a busy time for Gay, who, in addition to maintaining his radio programs on WARL, was building a stable of C&W performers and booking them into venues of all sizes all over the Washington, D.C. area, as well as sending them out on Department of Defense-sponsored "Special Services Road Shows" to Europe, Asia and the Caribbean.

During this time Gay made a triumphant return to local television when, on Tuesday, April 10, 1951 a new 30-minute C&W program he produced and hosted entitled "Town and Country Time" debuted on WMAL-TV (Channel 7) at 10pm. The show broadcasted from the station's Washington, D.C. studio inside the Evening Star Broadcasting Company (4461 Connecticut Avenue NW). The initial program featured a lineup of singer-banjoist Grandpa Jones, singer-guitarist Smitty Smith and square dance caller Ralph Case, all of whom performed in a country store setting. The show reportedly had a substantial following and remained on the air for several months, with the final episode airing on Tuesday, September 18, 1951.

In addition, Gay had his monthly "Grand Ole Opry Moonlight Cruise" on the S.S. Mount Vernon operating on schedule during the summer months of 1951, and also hosted "Town and Country Square Dancing" parties at Glen Echo Park's Spanish Ballroom in Montgomery County, Maryland on Thursday nights from June to September of that year. Music for these events was supplied by the Radio Ranchmen, which at this time were featuring singer-guitarist Billy Grammer, with Ralph Case providing the square dance calling.

Gay next staged what proved to be his biggest show to date when he booked an ambitious two-day live concert presentation simply entitled "Grand Ole Opry" into Griffith Stadium in Washington, D.C. on Saturday, September 22 (8:30pm) and Sunday, September 23, 1951 (2pm). The double event featured singer-guitarists Hank Snow, Lefty Frizzell, Ernest Tubb, Carl Smith; the duo of Lester Flatt and Earl Scruggs; singer-pianist Moon Mullican; and the comedian known as the Duke of Paducah. The event reportedly drew a two-day crowd of more than 28,000 fans, a stunning turnout for the time that firmly established Washington, D.C. as one of the nation's leading C&W music centers.

Gay followed up this event with another sold-out New Year's Eve presentation at the District of Columbia National Guard Armory on Monday, December 31, 1951 that featured singer-guitarists Hank Williams and Lefty Frizzell, singer Redd Stewart, singer-pianist Moon Mullican and singer-accordionist-fiddler Pee Wee King. After this show, Gay struck up a close friendship with the troubled and now-legendary country star Hank Williams, who subsequently spent several weeks at a time living in Gay's Arlington, Virginia home prior to his untimely death at on Thursday, January 1, 1953 at age 29.

Gay took his next big-venue C&W show to Uline Arena, where his first "Gay Time" concert in the facility took place on Saturday, February 16, 1952 and drew several thousand attendees at $1.25 a head. The event was promoted in the local dailies as "One of the Nation's Great Hillbilly Shows" and promised floorshows and dancing from 9pm to 2am. The evening was headlined by singer-guitarists Rosalie Allen, Elton Britt and Ann Jones, with second-billing going to the duo of singer-harmonicist Tex Cherry and singer Little Mary, singer-guitarist Don Kidwell and steel guitarist George Trummell. Rounding out the show were groups such as Jimmy Dean and the Texas Wildcats, Fiddlin' Curley Smith and the Blue Mountain Boys, Dub Howington and the Tennessee Haymakers, Roy Jackson's Silver Greek Jamboree and the singing duo of Lily and Curly. Joining these performers were singer-guitarists Smitty Smith, Don Owens and Smokey Mac; singer-fiddler-guitarist Blackie Skiles; singer-steel guitarist Billy Strickland, steel guitarist Mickey Woodward, singer-accordionist Stoney Rigsby, fiddler Chubby Wise and square dance caller Ralph Case.

This "Gay Time" Uline Arena show was especially significant in that it marked the first documented appearance of Jimmy Dean and the Texas Wildcats on a Connie B. Gay-promoted event. Gay and Dean would share a tumultuous relationship from 1952 to 1958, a period in which Gay was granted managerial control over Dean's career. The two eventually parted company when Dean was granted a national television show on CBS in New York City, a development that necessitated the buying out of his contract by the network. The split was finalized only after a sizeable amount of money changed hands in Gay's favor and Dean's great displeasure.

Jimmy Dean was a tall, lanky West Texan who had come to the nation's capital while serving in the United States Air Force in the late 1940s. While in the service he spent his evenings singing and playing accordion with Dub Howington and the Tennessee Haymakers in local officers' clubs, as well as at a Washington, D.C. night club called Harry's Tavern. In his autobiography Dean claims he met Connie B. Gay in 1952 when he took it upon himself to approach the promoter with an offer where his new band the Texas Wildcats would play on Gay's WARL "Town and Country Time" radio program for free in exchange for nightly plugs for their upcoming gigs.

In reality Gay and Dean had actually become acquainted years earlier during Dean's time with Dub Howington, as Gay had made it a point to check out every C&W musician in town. Gay had undoubtedly seen Dean performing with Howington at Harry's Tavern, the Covered Wagon Restaurant and the Dixie Pig Restaurant and Barbecue in the late 1940s, and while it is not known exactly when and where the two were actually introduced, it has been verified that when Gay booked Dub Howington and the Tennessee Haymakers into his own Club Hillbilly in Seat Pleasant, Maryland in 1948 and 1949, Dean was the group's featured lead singer.

In 1951 Dean put together his own band from the remnants of Dub Howington's group and began playing out as Jimmy Dean and the Texas Wildcats at the Harmony Club on 2nd Street NE near Union Station in Washington, D.C. Beginning in 1952 and continuing on for several years Dean and his band were booked almost exclusively by Gay and worked a variety of local night clubs and special events. They were part of the "Gay Time" extravaganza at Uline Arena on Saturday, February 16, 1952 headlined by singer-guitarists Rosalie Allen, Elton Britt and Ann Jones. When Gay brought in singer-guitarists Red Foley and Hank Snow to headline his Wednesday, December 31, 1952 New Year's Eve show at the District of Columbia National Guard Armory, it was Jimmy Dean and the Texas Wildcats who served as the house band.

In January 1953 Gay began booking live Saturday night shows into the Oxon Hill Volunteer Fire Department in Oxon Hill, Maryland and for much of the year his headlining act at these dances was Jimmy Dean and the Texas Wildcats. The band also appeared regularly for Gay during the summer and early fall months of 1953 at the Super Chief Drive-In Theater on Indian Head Highway in Oxon Hill, Maryland, as well as Sidney Lust's Marlboro Theatre in Upper Marlboro, Maryland. They were also on the bill for Gay's Thursday, December 31, 1953 New Year's Eve extravaganza at the District of Columbia National Guard Armory that featured Hank Thompson and His Brazos Valley Boys, Hank

Snow and His Rainbow Ranch Boys, Ray Price and the Drifting Cowboys, singer-banjoist Grandpa Jones and the Echo Inn Cloggers.

The popularity of Jimmy Dean and the Texas Wildcats soared in 1954, thus cementing their role as Connie B. Gay's top in-house attraction – a role held in previous years by the Radio Ranchmen. Gay's faith in the band's drawing power resulted in them headlining the multi-celebrity "Home Show," a week-long, home appliance exhibition and entertainment affair that was staged at the District of Columbia National Guard Armory from Saturday, April 24 to Sunday, May 2, 1954.

Shortly after this event Dean replaced lead guitarist Jimmy Groves with Roy Clark and the band took on a more up-tempo dimension. They spent the remainder of the year anchoring Gay's "Town and Country Time" radio show, worked local night clubs and special events several nights per week, and served as the house band and co-headliners of Gay's Friday, December 31, 1954 New Year's Eve C&W spectacular at Uline Arena that featured singer-guitarists Red Foley, Ernest Tubb and Deacon Andy Griffith, singer-bassist Mary Klick, and the Midwestern Hayride Dancers. The partnership between Connie B. Gay and Jimmy Dean endured for more than six years, during which time both sides enjoyed considerable success on the local music scene.

From 1951 to 1957 Gay served as promoter and master of ceremonies for an event entitled "The National Championship Country Music Contest" at the Warrenton Horse Show Grounds in Warrenton, Virginia, a competition sponsored by the Warrenton Junior Chamber of Commerce and the Association for Greater Warrenton. During these early years the annual contest (which would continue on for years after Gay withdrew his involvement with the festival) would allow hundreds of musicians to compete for "National Champion" awards in the following five separate categories: "Best Band," "Best Banjo Player," "Best Fiddler," "Best Miscellaneous" and "Best Vocal."

In August 1953 Jimmy Dean and the Texas Wildcats were called upon to back up an unknown female singer from Winchester, Virginia named Patsy Cline in one of the competitions. Although it has never been conclusively verified which category Cline competed in that year, it has been reported that she did perform onstage, but did not win her respective competition. It has also been reported that Cline made a lasting impression on many who witnessed her performance in that year's contest and caught the attention of Connie B. Gay, However, there are no stories of Gay actively courting the unknown female singer into his stable of stars at that time.

It has been widely written in a number of published biographies and articles on Patsy Cline that the singer from Winchester, in full cowgirl regalia, entered "The National Championship Country Music Contest" for a second time in 1954. She reportedly performed the Bob Wills hit song "Faded Love" while backed by Bill Peer and His Melody Boys, and walked away with a first place prize. While some of these published accounts claim Cline won her award in the "Best Female Vocalist" category, it has since been verified that no such award was ever given out in the 1954 competition. (It is a fact that the first female singer to ever win an individual competition in this contest was Brenda Lee Anthony, who walked away with the "Best Vocals" award in 1963.)

It is likely Cline competed in either the "Best Vocalist" or "Best Miscellaneous" contest that summer, though at this point in time there is no way to verify this information. A check with an article in the Fauquier Democrat newspaper of Thursday, August 12, 1954 entitled "Town Throbs to Hillbilly Music" reveals that the five actual winners in the competition that year were Slim Morrison of Silver Spring, Maryland ("Best Vocalist"), Roy Clark of Alexandria, Virginia ("Best Banjo Player"), Scotty Stoneman of Carmody Hills, Maryland ("Best Fiddler"), the Bayou Boys of Washington, D.C. ("Best Band") and guitarist Chick Hall of Washington, D.C. ("Best Miscellaneous"). Patsy Cline, in fact, was not a winner in any division of the 1954 contest. Still, it is assumed that she did participate in the contest and Connie B. Gay himself has been quoted as saying it was there in August 1954 that he first watched her perform and subsequently made the decision to manage her career.

Gay immediately went to work finding music-related endeavors for Cline. She became a regular in-studio performer on his "Town and Country Time" radio show, took part in recording sessions in Washington, D.C. at Ben Adelman's Truetone Recording Company on Illinois Avenue NW (which led to her first record deal with Bill McCall of 4 Star Records), and, along with Bill Peer and His Melody Boys (a band in which she still assumed the position of lead singer), was booked throughout the late summer and fall months of 1954 into such local night clubs and venues as the Starlite Restaurant, the Covered Wagon Restaurant, the Famous Restaurant and the Oxon Hill Volunteer Fire Department. She remained a vital part of Gay's empire for the next three years during which time she regularly headlined his live music events and performed on his various television programs.

In the fall of 1954 Gay was approached by WMAL-TV (Channel 7) and asked to revive his "Town and Country Time" music television show, which had previously aired under the same name on the same local network back in 1951. At the time WMAL-TV was licensed by the Evening Star Broadcasting Co. and owned by the Evening Star Newspaper Co. WMAL-TV's network affiliate was ABC-TV, which, after the WMAL deal was inked, reportedly offered Gay a three-year, $2 million contract that would syndicate the television show to more than 40 stations across the country. It was a blockbuster deal that gave Gay complete control over all of the show's logistics including who his daily guests would be and what events and products would be promoted.

This new and improved version of "Town and Country Time," which shared the same name of Gay's long-running radio show, debuted on Monday, January 17, 1955 on WMAL TV Channel 7 and aired every weekday in a 5pm-5:30pm time slot. The show, which would air for a little over three years, emanated from the WMAL studios on Connecticut Avenue NW, was hosted by Gay, employed Mark Hamilton as its announcer and utilized Jimmy Dean and the Texas Wildcats featuring singer-standup bassist Mary Klick of Hagerstown, Maryland as its regular house band. The final showing of "Town and Country Time" was on Friday, January 24, 1958.

As his television show flourished, Gay began booking Friday night concerts into Glen Echo Park's Spanish Ballroom, a practice that lasted from June to August 1955. With Jimmy Dean and the Texas Wildcats (who at this time were featuring Roy Clark on lead guitar) serving as the opening act on every show, some of the stars to perform that summer in the ballroom were Carl Smith and the Tunesmiths, Little Jimmy Dickens and His Country Boys, Hank Thompson and His Brazos Valley Boys, Hank Snow and His Rainbow Ranch Boys, Ernest Tubb and His Texas Troubadours, the Maddox Brothers and Rose, Clyde Moody and His Carolina Woodchoppers, Webb Pierce and His Wondering Boys, female pianist Del Wood, singer-banjoist Grandpa Jones, singer-guitarist-pianist Marty Robbins and comedian Peach Seed Jones. All of these entertainers, along with others that appeared on his S.S. Mount Vernon Moonlight Cruise excursions down the Potomac River, were special guests on the "Town and Country Time" television program that summer.

In addition, that summer also saw Gay work out an agreement with Joe Turner Arena, a facility he had often booked in the past, where he would take over the premises on Saturday evenings from 9pm to 2am and sponsor a weekly event he called "The Barn Dance." House band for these weekly hoedowns was the ever-present Jimmy Dean and the Texas Wildcats, with singer Miss Dale Turner, who hailed from Arlington, Virginia. The first "Barn Dance" to take place at Joe Turner Arena that summer season occurred on Saturday, June 18, 1955 and reportedly attracted a standing-room-only crowd. Both the

Glen Echo and Joe Turner Arena concerts were heavily publicized on Gay's television program and proved to the hottest live events in the Washington, D.C. area that summer.

The success of the Saturday night "Barn Dances" combined with the consistently high ratings of the "Town and Country Time" television program led managers at WMAL-TV to implement an extended C&W music concert program that would air from Joe Turner Arena for several hours on Saturday nights. This new show, "Town and Country Jamboree," first aired on Saturday, October 1, 1955 on WMAL-TV (Channel 7) from 10pm to 1am and was the first music-themed television show of any kind to air in three-hour blocks on a weekly basis.

This inaugural episode of "Town and Country Jamboree" featured Bob Wills and His Texas Playboys, Jimmy Dean and the Texas Wildcats (featuring guitarist Roy Clark and singer Miss Dale Turner), Dub Howington and the Tennessee Haymakers, singer-steel guitarist Jerry Byrd, singer-guitarists Marvin Rainwater and Luke Gordon, singer Autry Inman, fiddler-pianist-vibraphonist Johnny Foster and comedian Tiny Jenkins. Four emcees were on hand to handle the announcing and commercial duties: Connie B. Gay himself; house band leader Jimmy Dean; WMAL radio announcer Jackson Weaver, who was known for being one-half of the station's popular "The Frank and Jackson Show," which in 1960 would become "The Harden and Weaver Show;" and WARL disc jockey Phil Long, who was the long-running host of the station's "Lawn Party" C&W music show.

The production set-up for "Town and Country Jamboree" was also somewhat unique for its time and basically served as a model for future local concert broadcasting. Joe Turner Arena, located on the northeast corner of 14th and W Streets NW, had been established in 1935 as a small, 2,800-seat boxing arena by Joe Turner. After Turner's death in 1947 the ownership of the building passed to his widow, who sub-leased the premises to a syndicate headed Vincent McMahon in 1952. Connie B. Gay was allowed to construct a stage on the east side of the building, with elevated bleachers installed against the back wall and a sizeable dance floor separating the two. The show was directed by Thomas Winker, who worked from a remote television truck parked just outside of the arena in the alley east of the building and gave instructions to the three cameramen who worked the stage and dance floor areas and a fourth cameraman who worked from a separate room within the arena where he shadowed announcer Jackson Weaver.

Jimmy Dean served as one of the stage emcees for "Town and Country Jamboree," and his group, the Texas Wildcats (featuring lead guitarist Roy Clark), maintained the role of house band throughout the show's entire run. Three female singers, Mary Klick, Dale Turner and Patsy Cline, regularly performed on the show, as did dozens of other talented performers including singer-banjoist Grandpa Jones, singer-guitarist Billy Grammer, singer-guitarist Luke Gordon, and the Echo Inn Cloggers.

Two noteworthy mainstays on the program were Marvin Rainwater and George Hamilton IV. Rainwater was a part-Cherokee singer-guitarist from Wichita, Kansas who had relocated to Northern Virginia in the early 1950s and sang C&W songs at the Annandale Grill before being scooped up by Connie B. Gay for his various live music presentations. Rainwater went on to record singles and albums for M-G-M Records from 1955 to 1960 and had a major crossover hit song with "Gonna Find Me A Bluebird," which went to number three on the Billboard magazine's "C&W Best Sellers in Stores" chart on Monday, July 29, 1957.

George Hamilton IV was a 19-year-old college student at the University of North Carolina when he scored with a local hit in Chapel Hill entitled "A Rose and a Baby Ruth." Connie B. Gay made a trip to the South and brought the young singer-guitarist up to the Washington, D.C. area in the summer of 1956 for a series of live performance dates. Hamilton opted to stay in the area for a spell and Gay assumed management of his career.

Just as "Town and Country Jamboree" was being prepared for television broadcast, Gay was setting his sights on a new, dynamic performer who was still relatively unknown, but whom he thought had the potential to explode on the national scene. An article in the Washington Post of Saturday, September 4, 1955 entitled "Just Grit Your Teeth and Sit Still for 'Medic'" included the following passage: "Connie B. Gay says that a 19-year-old boy named Elvis Pressley (sic) will be the next sensation of the country & western (hillbilly) music field. Pressley has crossed bebop with country music and, according to Gay, 'is the hottest thing in the hillbilly field.'"

Gay obviously knew talent when he heard it and in six months he would corral the young country music sensation – and future King of Rock and Roll – for a headlining spot on one of his S.S. Mount Vernon Moonlight Cruises. It was a historic night that stands as the one and only time Elvis actually performed in Washington, D.C., as the ship remained docked in Pier 4 for the entire evening due to a malfunctioning high pressure valve.

The now-legendary gig took place on the cold, windy and rainy night of Friday, March 23, 1956 and consisted of Elvis Presley and His Blue Moon Boys headlining a "Moonlight Cruise" on the S.S. Mount Vernon that also included an opening act called Melvin Price and the Santa Fe Rangers, a band from Easton, Maryland. Earlier in the evening at 6:30pm Jimmy Dean had conducted an unspectacular interview with a near-mute Presley on his WMAL-Channel 7 television program "Town and Country Time," which broadcasted live from the Evening Star Broadcasting Company on Connecticut Avenue NW in Washington, D.C. The uneventful and mercifully short exchange between Dean and Presley unfortunately revealed nothing about either the forthcoming night's activities or the star performer himself. Neither an audio tape nor a written transcript of the show is known to have survived.

Gay had shelled out $4,500 to charter the ship for the evening and priced tickets at a paltry $2, feeling certain that the 2,452-person capacity would be met. However, he became alarmed when, upon his arrival to the concert scene that evening, he learned that the ship would be unable to sail the river. To make amends he offered immediate refunds to anyone who didn't want to stay for the show, which he had expanded to a full three hours. Few took him up on his offer.

Elvis Presley, who was actually 21 years old at the time of his Washington, D.C. visit, had just hit the big time with his first chart-topping hit, "I Forgot to Remember to Forget," which was released on RCA Records in December 1955 and had reached number one on the Billboard magazine's "Best Sellers in Stores" country & western records chart on Saturday, February 25, 1956 (this song would spend a total of 40 weeks on that particular chart). He had performed at the Mosque Theatre in Richmond, Virginia the night before his visit to Washington, D.C., and was scheduled to be at CBS TV Studio 50 in New York City on Saturday morning to make his sixth and final appearance on "Stage Show," a variety program hosted by the Dorsey Brothers.

The entertainment on the S.S. Mount Vernon that evening began shortly after 8pm and consisted of two 80-minute sets separated by a 20-minute intermission, with Melvin Price and the Santa Fe Rangers opening and Elvis Presley and His Blue Moon Boys closing each show. The concert took place in the glass-enclosed ballroom of the ship's main deck, directly below the top-level observation deck, and attracted a near-capacity crowd which stayed behind for the show even after being informed the ship would not be leaving Pier 4.

Presley, guitar in hand, took the small stage under a two-police officer escort and reportedly cranked out a variety of gospel, C&W and rock and roll songs including such classics-to-be like "Heartbreak Hotel" and "Blue Suede Shoes." He kept the between-song banter to an absolute minimum and many attendees now recall that shortly after the show as the crowd filed out, the soon-to-be King of Rock and Roll casually walked over to a spot on the open dance floor close to the stage and quietly chatted away with any fans who happened by.

What Elvis Presley and his bandmates did after the S.S Mount Vernon performance, or where they spent the night, remains unknown. Despite unsubstantiated rumors of Presley and his entourage having partied at various Washington, D.C. area night clubs into the wee hours of that morning, many have speculated that the band simply packed up and left town via automobile that same night, a likely scenario given their Saturday morning television appearance in New York City.

There has been some measure of controversy regarding the exact lineup of bands that performed on the Elvis Presley-S.S. Mount Vernon "Moonlight Cruise." While all of the published newspaper advertisements for the event have only listed Elvis and His Blue Moon Boys and Melvin Price and the Santa Fe Rangers as the evening's entertainment, other pieces of documentation have raised some interesting questions about this concert presentation. At this point there is no question that Presley's backup band at the very least consisted of his usual group of guitarist Scotty Moore, bassist Bill Black and drummer D.J. Fontana. Nor is there any disputing the fact that Mel Price and the Santa Fe Rangers worked the show as well. A detailed account of the three-hour evening of entertainment, along with interesting quotes from Price himself, appears in an article in the Washington City Paper of Friday, February 16, 2007 entitled "Elvis on the Potomac" by Peter Golkin.

The first piece of supplemental information regarding this situation to be taken under consideration appeared in an article entitled "Billy Poore Sez: Fill the Gaps in Your Family's Education with this Amazing Made Simple Teaching Program" by Billy Poore in issue number six of Kicks magazine (published in 1988). In this article, Poore, who later authored the book "RockABilly: A Forty-Year Journey" (1998), reminisces on his own Washington, D.C. area rock and roll experiences and includes a segment on the S.S. Mount Vernon cruises where he tells: "I saw Bunker Hill play and met him on a REAL crazy river boat gig! He was performing on the Wilson Line Moonlight Cruise on the Potomac River on a hot summer night in 1962. This was the same Moonlight Cruise that a few years earlier had featured a show by Elvis, Scotty & Bill with Jimmy Dean and the Texas Wildcats!" Poore, however, fails to elaborate on the role that may have been played by Jimmy Dean's band and without further details one can only speculate on the source of this information and the degree of its reliability.

Adding to the mystery are select lines that appear in C&W singer-guitarist Roy Clark's autobiography, "Roy Clark: My Life in Spite of Myself" (1994). On page 62 of the first edition hardback, Clark writes: "On his way through Washington one time, Colonel Tom Parker came by with Elvis Presley to pay a call on Connie B. Gay and arrange for the band to back up Elvis on a gig..." and later on the same page, "I remember at the time we backed up Elvis, the colonel was trying to sell Presley's contract to Connie. Parker wanted something like $8 million dollars, and he was willing to take it in payments over time. Connie told the colonel, 'I think he's great but I don't think he's got a future.'"

Unfortunately, Clark, who did, in fact, play guitar with Jimmy Dean and the Texas Wildcats from the summer of 1954 to the summer of 1956, does not identify anywhere in the book the name of the venue in which he backed up Presley, an event which he surely must remember the details of, but for reasons unknown opted not to divulge. The mystery endures to this day.

In the middle 1950s Gay began shifting his interests towards what he felt was a more lucrative career path – radio station ownership. In 1954 his success as a local C&W music entrepreneur enabled him to sell his house on N. Lincoln Street in Arlington and relocated to a much larger house in Vienna, Virginia. Despite the move, he continued to manage his operations as the Town and Country Network, Inc. (1122 N. Irving Street, Arlington, Virginia) from 1956 to 1959.

The time required to produce his television programs led Gay to withdraw his show on radio station WARL, with his last on-air broadcast taking place on Saturday, November 5, 1955 (WARL was later sold and had its call letters changed to WAVA in January 1961). Gay then began purchasing radio stations around the country, an endeavor that required more of his time than he had anticipated. Despite the tremendous success of his two local television programs, he decided to bring an end to both programs. "Town and Country Jamboree," his Saturday night show from Joe Turner Arena, aired for the last time on Saturday, August 31, 1957, while his daily early evening show, "Town and Country Time," had its final episode air on WMAL-TV on Friday, January 24, 1958.

Gay's withdrawal from the local music scene as a manager, promoter and producer was completed when he purchased local radio station WGAY in Silver Spring, Maryland on Sunday, November 9, 1958 for a reported price of $460,000. (The similarity between the station's call letters and the Gay's last name was pure coincidence.) It became one of nine such stations Gay would eventually come to own, joining stations WTCS (Fairmont, WV), WTCR (Ashland, KY), WFTC (Kingston, NC), KLRA (Little Rock, AR), KITE (San Antonio, TX), WYFE (New Orleans, LA), WVOM (Huntington, WV) and WQMR (Silver Spring, MD).

During this time Gay maintained a corporate office in the Wisconsin Building, which was located in Washington, D.C. on the southeast corner of the intersection of Wisconsin Avenue NW and Albemarle Street NW. The front of the Wisconsin Building was marked 4000 Albemarle Street NW, with a side entrance marked 4435 Wisconsin Avenue NW. From 1958 to 1960 Gay's business in this building went by the name Connie B. Gay Enterprise, Inc. and from 1961 to 1962 it operated under the name of the Connie B. Gay Broadcasting Corporation. Gay's operation folded in late 1962.

Gay had founded the Country Music Association in Nashville, Tennessee in 1958, which was noted for being the very first trade association for a single genre of music. He then created the Country Music Hall of Fame in 1961. Gay served as the CMA's Founding Board President from 1958 to 1960. After going through a divorce from his wife Hazel he remarried to a woman named Katherine in 1961. They moved from Vienna to McLean, Virginia, which would become his primary residence for the remainder of his life, and had two more children. He spent the 1960s managing his various radio stations and making frequent vacation trips to the Virgin Islands.

In November 1970 Gay sold off his four remaining radio stations, including local stations WGAY and WQMR, in a package deal to Greater New York Media, Inc. for $3.3 million, bringing his reported net worth to more than $50 million. He then spent his retirement years traveling the country with his family. He was inducted into the Country Music Hall of Fame in 1980. Connie B. Gay died of cancer on Sunday, December 3, 1989 at Fairfax Hospital in Fairfax, Virginia at the age of 75.

CHAPTER FORTY-SIX
THE STONEMAN FAMILY

The Stoneman Family is a legendary bluegrass musical outfit from the western side of Virginia whose members began making their mark in the Washington, D.C. area during the Depression era and went on to become one of the region's most beloved musical families. Their story begins with Ernest Van "Pop" Stoneman, who was born on Thursday, May 25, 1893 in Iron Ridge, a small, rural community in Carroll County, Virginia. Pop sang and played several instruments including guitar, harmonica, autoharp, and, to a lesser extent, banjo and fiddle. In November 1918 he married 13-year-old Hattie Frost and the couple settled in Galax, Virginia. Mr. Stoneman began working in the region as a carpenter and in 1924 and 1925 he made several trips to New York City where he embarked on recording sessions for producer Ralph Peer. These recordings resulted in six separate 78rpm single record releases as "Ernest V. Stoneman" on Okeh Records, including the hit song "The Titanic."

In December 1932 Ernest and Hattie and their nine children moved to the Washington, D.C. area, taking a home in a large house at 1205 King Street in Alexandria, Virginia (the couple would eventually have a total of 23 children, of which 13 survived to adulthood). Ernest struggled for carpentry work, necessitating a move back to Galax, Virginia in the summer of 1934. In March 1935 the Stonemans moved back to Washington, D.C., taking a home at 4768 Reservoir Road NW. Upon his return to the nation's capital, Pop maintained a hand in show business, performing as a solo artist on a weekly Saturday night program entitled "Old Barn Loft" on radio station WJSV.

The Stonemans then proceeded to move about the Washington, D.C. area frequently. From the fall of 1936 to the fall of 1939 they resided in homes at 1816 Wisconsin Avenue NW, 203 Anacostia Road NE, a house in Bladensburg, Maryland, and houses on Higden Road NE and Minnesota Avenue SE. During the 1920s and 1930s Ernest Stoneman recorded for a variety of record labels including Okeh, Edison, Gennett, Victor, Plaza and Vocalion.

In the fall of 1941 "Pop" Stoneman, as Ernest was now being called, moved his musical family, which now consisted of 11 children, to the community of Carmody Hills in Prince George's County, Maryland. There, he had a home constructed at 307 74th Place. (This house was torn down in the late 1960s. A new structure was built in its space in 1974 and given the address of 417 Goldleaf Avenue.)

Once settled in, Pop and various family members began singing and playing bluegrass music, usually billed as "The Stoneman Family," in a number of local night clubs including Armstrong's, Chubby's Restaurant and Bar and the Wagon Wheel, all of which were situated nearby along Central Avenue in either the town of Capitol Heights or the city of Seat Pleasant.

For the most part the Stoneman Family performances featured Pop and six of his children – Patsy, Scotty, Donna, Jimmy, Roni and Van. They also made regular appearances on Connie B. Gay's "Town and Country Time" radio show in the early 1950s, as well as all of his television shows of the era including "Gay Time," "Town and Country Time" and "Town and Country Jamboree."

In August 1953 Scotty Stoneman tied with Chubby Wise for first place in the "Best Fiddler" competition in "The National Championship Country Music Contest" in Warrenton, Virginia. He would go on to win the award a total of four times when the event was promoted by Connie B. Gay during the 1950s. (Scotty Stoneman also won the title in 1954 and 1956 and tied with John Hall for the honor in 1957.) Throughout the 1950s and 1960s, the Stoneman Family performed at such local night clubs as the Dixie Pig, Elmer's, the Famous Restaurant (they worked there on-and-off from 1954 to 1966), and the Ozarks Restaurant. They were also regular participants in the extravagant weekend country music shows held at Joe Turner Arena.

In the spring of 1955, Scotty (fiddle), Jimmy (bass fiddle), and Donna Stoneman (mandolin), along with family friend Jimmy Case (guitar), formed a band called the Blue Grass Champs. They began playing regularly at the Famous Restaurant in Washington, D.C., a gig that would last for most of the following 10 years. Early in their career they added a banjo player from Bristol, Tennessee named Porter Church, and throughout the late 1950s, when taking a break from the Famous Restaurant, they worked other local night clubs such as Chubby's Restaurant and Bar, the Dixie Pig, and the Anchor Grill in Southeast Washington, D.C. They also made several appearances every year at Strick's Restaurant in Silver Hill, Maryland from 1957 to 1967.

The Blue Grass Champs competed in "The National Championship Country Music Contest" in Warrenton, Virginia for several years, winning the "Best Band" competition in 1956 and 1957. The band gained national attention when they won first prize in a televised contest on "Arthur Godfrey's Talent Scouts" in New York City in 1956. The band's popularity in the nation's capital was such that they were granted their own local television show "The Blue Grass Champs," which aired on WTTG Channel 5 on Saturday nights from February 22, 1958 to September 20, 1958. In 1962 an album entitled "Bluegrass Champs," credited to Ernest V. Stoneman and the Stoneman Family, was released to enthusiastic fans on Starday Records.

With the folk music revival of the 1960s the Stoneman Family began branching out in search of more prestigious engagements away from home. A major milestone for the band was reached when they performed for the first time at "The Grand Ole Opry" in February 1962. They left Carmody Hills in 1966, eventually settling in Tennessee, and went on to record singles and albums for more than two-dozen different record labels including Ace, Capitol, Folkways, M-G-M, RCA Victor, Starday and World Pacific. In addition, a number of Stoneman Family members embarked on individual solo projects, the most notable of which was fiddler Scotty Stoneman, who released albums on the Briar, Design and Old Homestead record labels.

In 1966 the Stoneman Family was granted its own national television show entitled "Those Stonemans," which broadcasted from Nashville, Tennessee. A year later were named "The Country Music Association 1967 Vocal Group of the Year." In 1973 Roni Stoneman joined the cast of the television show "Hee Haw," assuming the comedic role of bedraggled Ida Lee Dagger, in addition to singing and playing banjo in regular segments.

Ernest "Pop" Stoneman passed away due to complications from stomach surgery on Friday, June 14, 1968 at age 75. He was ultimately inducted into the Country Music Hall of Fame in 2008. Scotty Stoneman, regarded by many as one of the greatest fiddlers in the history of bluegrass music, passed away on Sunday, March 4, 1973 at the age of 40. For a complete overview of the family's spectacular musical career, look up Ivan M. Tribe's book "The Stoneman's: An Appalachian Family and the Music That Shaped Their Lives" (1993).

CHAPTER FORTY-SEVEN
BILLY GRAMMER

Billie Wayne "Billy" Grammer was born on Friday, August 28, 1925 in Benton, Illinois, strummed his first song on the guitar at age four, and began learning chords from a cousin and playing country music a year later. As the eldest of 13 children, he obtained his musical inclinations from his father, who played fiddle and trumpet. He graduated from Sesser-Valier High School in In Sesser, Illinois in June 1943 and served in the United States Army for a short while, receiving an honorable discharge due to vision problems. He married his high school sweetheart, Ruth Burzynski, in their home church in Rend City, Illinois in October 1944 and a year later the couple moved to Washington, D.C. where Grammer briefly worked as an apprentice toolmaker in the Washington Naval Gun Factory. After being laid off, the couple moved back to Benton, Illinois.

In 1947 Grammer received a letter from a friend in Vienna, Virginia named Bob Beck who told him of Connie B. Gay's WARL radio program, "Town and Country Time." Grammer then hitchhiked to Arlington, Virginia and secured an audition with Gay, who immediately hired him to be a singer-guitarist with a band he was finalizing called the Radio Ranchmen. This outfit then served as Gay's house band both on radio programs and live dates around the nation's capital for several years. From 1947 to 1949 Grammer worked programs, shows and concerts almost exclusively for Connie B. Gay.

In 1948 Grammer recorded a 78rpm single record consisting of "Part of My Soul" backed with "Jealous Heart" that was credited to Bill Grammer's Shenandoah Valley Boys and released on the Feld Brothers' local Scoop Records label. Other single releases credited to Billy Grammer included the 45s "When You Know" backed with "I Almost Lost My Mind" on the Plaza label and "Take Me Back South" backed with "Wabash Cannonball" on the Guest Star label, two tracks that are believed to have been recorded in the middle 1950s at Ben Adelman's Truetone Recording Company and released many years later.

In 1948 Grammer took side jobs working with singer-fiddler-guitarist Blackie Skiles at the Dixie Pig Restaurant and Barbecue in Bladensburg, Maryland and was a regular performer at Joe Turner Arena on its various C&W music extravaganzas throughout this period. During these years Grammer worked live dates regularly with the Radio Ranchmen and singer-banjoist Grandpa Jones, among others.

In the early 1950s Grammer began traveling the country with his family pursuing musical jobs. In 1950 he was in Wheeling, West Virginia where he regularly played guitar for the husband-and-wife team of Doc and Chickie Williams on the radio program "The World's Original WWVA Jamboree" (which broadcasted live from the Virginia Theatre). During that time he also backed stars like singer-banjoist Grandpa Jones and singer-guitarist Hawkshaw Hawkins on their live performances in the region.

Grammer was back in Washington, D.C. in 1951 working on Connie B. Gay's "Town and Country Time" radio show. In August of that year Grammer won the "Best Guitarist" competition in "The National Championship Country Music Contest" in Warrenton, Virginia. He would later return and win the same contest again in 1955.

From 1952 to early 1955 Grammer and his growing family lived in various locations including Benton (Illinois), Phoenix (Arizona), Boulder (Colorado) and Billings (Montana). In March 1955 he returned to the nation's capital, moving into a duplex on what was then Presley Lane in the town of Riverdale, Maryland. They stayed in that home for a year before moving into a larger house also situated on Presley Lane, which would then remain their home base throughout the decade. (The Grammer house was one of several homes on the property of Floyd Presley, which was located just off of Riverdale Road less than a mile due east of and across the street from Wildecroft Elementary School – these houses were torn down in the 1960s and the entire Presley tract was cleared away long ago.)

Grammer was a featured attraction on Gay's "Town and Country Time" and "Town and Country Jamboree" television programs from 1955 to 1958, as well as "The Jimmy Dean Show" and "Don Owens TV Jamboree" later in the decade. In the summer of 1956 he replaced guitarist Roy Clark in Jimmy Dean and the Texas Wildcats, appearing with his new band most frequently at Glen Echo Park's Spanish Ballroom, the S.S. Mount Vernon Moonlight Cruises, the Rustic Cabin Restaurant on Bladensburg Road, and the Hayloft in Washington, D.C. He also spent much of 1958 and 1959 headlining as a solo artist at Strick's Restaurant in Silver Hill, Maryland.

Grammer's ascent to national stardom was accelerated through the release of the single "Gotta Travel On" on Monument Records in 1958. The single came about after Grammer had struck up a friendship with a local music fan and budding entrepreneur named Fred Foster, who was in the process of forming his own record company which he named after the Washington Monument.

Fred Foster, who had been born in 1931 in Rutherford County, North Carolina, came to the Washington, D.C. area in 1947, and, before entering the music industry, worked a series of jobs with the local Hot Shoppes restaurant chain. (Foster initially worked as a car hop at the restaurant's Arlington and Silver Spring locations before being assigned manager at the Hot Shoppes at 1400 Rhode Island Avenue NE in Washington, D.C.) He spent the 1950s living in various residences in Langley Park, Maryland and Adelphi, Maryland. In 1952 he served as a studio arranger on the recording of Jimmy Dean's hit song "Bumming Around." During this period he also spent two years as a field representative for Mercury Records and then worked for two additional years in a similar position with ABC-Paramount Records.

Late in the 1950s Foster was working as a music distributor for J&F Wholesale Record Distributors in Baltimore, Maryland when he encountered Walt Maguire, marketing director for London Records, who encouraged him to form his own record label. Foster spent these years living in an apartment at 7910 18th Avenue in Adelphi, Maryland. He formed Monument Records on Tuesday, March 11, 1958 and began scouting local talent for his new company. In August 1958 Foster purchased a house at 1701 Avalon Place in Chillum, Maryland and operated Monument Records out of his residence until he left the area in July 1960.

Foster liked Billy Grammer's playing with Jimmy Dean and the Texas Wildcats and the singer-guitarist was the first solo act he signed to Monument Records. He took Grammer to Nashville, Tennessee and on Friday, August 22, 1958 they went to work at the RCA Victor Studio on Hawkins Street with producer-bassist Bob Moore, guitarist Chet Atkins, the Anita Kerr Singers and several never-unidentified studio musicians. The end result of this session was the single "Gotta Travel On" backed with "Chasing a Dream," which became the inaugural release on Monument Records on Wednesday, October 1, 1958.

"Gotta Travel On" was adapted from an 18th century British folk song entitled "Done Laid Around" by a music collector from Brown's Cave, Virginia named Paul Clayton who was an acquaintance of Fred Foster. After making some minor lyrical changes, Foster gave the song a new title (though the writing credit remained with Paul Clayton). After the Nashville session was completed he placed his other projects on hold and made Grammer's recording the first release on his new Monuments Records label.

The song "Gotta Travel On" by Billy Grammer first entered the Billboard magazine charts in November 1958 and eventually placed on four different music popularity charts: under the category of "Pop Records," the song peaked at number four on "The Billboard Hot 100" chart on Monday, January 12, 1959; within the same musical category it reached number seven on the "Honor Roll of Hits" chart on Monday, January 19, 1959; under the category of "Country & Western Records" it peaked at number five on "The Billboard Hot C&W Sides" chart on Monday, February 16, 1959; and under the category of "Rhythm & Blues Records" it reached number 14 on "The Billboard Hot R&B Sides" chart on Monday, February 9, 1959.

In less than five months, "Gotta Travel On" had sold more than 900,000 copies and Billy Grammer was on his way to stardom. Fred Foster's Monument Records enterprise flourished after this initial hit release, with the company signing up such artists as Roy Orbison, Boots Randolph, Grandpa Jones, Dolly Parton, Kris Kristofferson, Willie Nelson and numerous others. "Gotta Travel On" proved to be an enduring song indeed, as it was later covered by such artists as Jerry Lee Lewis, June Carter and Bob Dylan, who recorded a version of it for his 1970 double album "Self Portrait." Grammer, meanwhile, continued to record for Monument Records and later in his career would go on to release singles and albums on the Decca and Epic record labels.

In June 1959 Billy Grammer and his wife and three children moved to Nashville, Tennessee, where he became a featured performer at "The Grand Ole Opry," a role that endured for more than five decades. He frequently performed in the Washington, D.C. area in 1961 and 1962, including several engagements at the Senate Inn on Marlboro Pike in Capitol Heights, Maryland. He became involved in the design and manufacturing of custom-made guitars and in 1964 was a founding member of a guitar-making company in Nashville with Clyde Reid and J.W. Gower called RG&G Musical Instruments, Inc. He was the namesake for the Grammer guitar, a flat-top model built to his specifications.

Grammer continued to perform live concerts and on Monday, May 15, 1972 Billy Grammer and the Travel On Boys performed at the campaign rally in Laurel, Maryland for then-Alabama governor and Democratic presidential candidate George Wallace. The band was playing Wallace's exit song, "Under the Double Eagle," when Wallace was shot and paralyzed from the waist down. Grammer was also a highly sought-after session man for many years and recorded with the likes of Patti Page, Louis Armstrong, Eddy Arnold and many others. Several years after retiring to Sesser, Illinois, Billy Grammer died of a brain hemorrhage in his hometown of Benton, Illinois on Wednesday, August 10, 2011 at the age of 85.

CHAPTER FORTY-EIGHT
DUB HOWINGTON

Charles William "Dub "Howington Jr. was born in Bristol, Virginia on Saturday, June 23, 1928 and learned to sing and play guitar by listening to a variety of musicians including jazz guitarist Django Reinhardt and country music artists such as Sons of the Pioneers, Bob Wills, Jimmie Rodgers, the Carter Family and Ernest Stoneman. In 1947 he relocated to Washington, D.C. where he and his older brother Roy, an upright bass player, first performed as the Howington Brothers in several night clubs including the Covered Wagon Restaurant on 14th Street NW and the Dixie Pig Restaurant and Barbecue in Bladensburg, Maryland. Dub Howington, as a guitarist and singing bandleader, went on to spend the next 24 years as one of the most highly acclaimed C&W musicians the Washington, D.C, area has ever known.

Several months after arriving in town in 1947, Dub Howington put together a backup band he called the Tennessee Haymakers which included his brother Roy and a revolving cast of musicians and performed at area night clubs, military base officers' clubs and picnics. They quickly caught the eye of local music entrepreneur Lillian Claiborne, who ushered them into the United States Recording Company (1121 Vermont Avenue NW). There, Howington's band recorded more than a half-dozen different songs that were released in the 78rpm single record format on Claiborne's DC Records label in 1947 and 1948, including the local hit favorite "Boil 'Em Cabbage Down" backed with "Don't Play With Love" (credited to "Howington Brothers with the Tennessee Haymakers, fiddle Speedy Baker").

In 1948 Dub Howington came across a tall, lanky singer-accordionist from Texas named Jimmy Dean performing with guitarist Lee "Brownie" Callaway, Jr. in a C&W dive in Washington, D.C. called Harry's Tavern (1200 New York Avenue NW), which had just replaced a bar called the Bowery. Howington was greatly impressed by Dean's gift of gab and in 1949 decided to reorganize the Tennessee Haymakers. The new band now consisted of Dub and Roy Howington, guitarist Herbie Jones and singer-accordionist Jimmy Dean. This outfit became the house band at Harry's Tavern and also worked a number of other night clubs throughout the area including the Covered Wagon Restaurant, the Camden Tavern, the Jo Del Bar and Grill, the Dixie Pig Restaurant and Barbecue, the Campus Club, the Homestretch Tavern, Chubby's Restaurant and Bar, Club Hillbilly and barn dances at the Pythian Temple on 9th Street NW in Washington, D.C.

Later In 1949 Howington's band was back in the United States Recording Company studio under the direction of Lillian Claiborne, where they recorded a two-sided 78 that was released later that year on her Loop Records label – the A-side of this recording consisted of the song "A Wonderful Dream" (credited to "Roy Howington") and the B-side contained a song entitled "Haymakers' Shuffle" (credited to "Howington Brothers and the Tennessee Haymakers").

Claiborne next leased out the master tapes of two other previously unreleased Howington recordings to the major label Atlantic Records, which released the single "I'm On Pins and Needles" backed with "Alabama Jubilee" (credited to "Howington Brothers") on 78rpm in April 1950. This situation repeated itself in 1953 when she again leased out two previously recorded Howington classics to a major label. This time the recipient company was Decca Records with the resulting 78rpm single record consisting of "Tennessee Rooster Fight" backed with "Two Faced" (credited to "Howington Brothers"). In the ensuing years Dub Howington would go on to release other singles on the Gotham and Quincy record labels.

In the early 1950s Dub Howington and the Tennessee Haymakers were regularly featured on Connie B. Gay's "Town and Country Time" WARL radio show. During the summer of 1952 Dub became a regular performer at the Kit-Mar Restaurant on 14th Street NW, across from Joe Tuner Arena, where he appeared with singer-guitarist Smitty Smith, guitarist Ulysses White and fiddler Buck Ryan. In 1953 Dub Howington was drafted into the United States Army and served in the Korean War. During his time in the service he was a singer-guitarist in the United States Army Band. In his absence, many of his bandmates defected to other groups in the area, including Jimmy Dean and Herbie Jones, who, just prior to Dub's departure for service duty, became founding members of Jimmy Dean and the Texas Wildcats.

After his tour of duty ended in 1955, Dub Howington returned to the Washington, D.C. area, and, later in the decade, purchased a house at 7759 Frederick Court in Hyattsville, Maryland. He and his first wife Wilma started a family which eventually consisted of daughters Clara, Vickie Mae and Stephany, and a son, Charles III. During these years he was also frequently called upon to do studio work for local producer Ben Adelman. As a result of these recording sessions he and several of his bandmates appeared on numerous 45rpm single records for C&W singer-guitarist Luke Gordon that came out on such record labels as World Artists, Starday and Mount Vernon Music.

Dub Howington and the Tennessee Haymakers remained major players in the local C&W music scene throughout the 1950s and 1960s. One of the most popular versions of the band consisted of Dub Howington on lead guitar and vocals, steel guitarist Don West, bassist Fuzzy Groves, drummer Jessie Parrish, and any one of several fiddlers from the ranks of Homer "Curley" Smith, Marvin West and Buck Ryan. Many other musicians passed through the band during these years including guitarists Wade Holmes and Benny Simpson, pianist Johnny Foster and drummer Flip Bacher.

In terms of live performances, Dub Howington and the Tennessee Haymakers spent the late 1950s making regular appearances on Connie B. Gay's television programs, "Town and Country Time" and "Town and Country Jamboree." They were also featured on various C&W music presentations at Joe Turner Arena and aboard the S.S Mount Vernon Moonlight Cruises.

During these years and throughout the 1960s the band regularly performed at such area night clubs as the Dixie Pig, the Surf Club, the Wheel Bar, the Homestretch Tavern, the Cross Roads, the Village Barn, the Famous Restaurant, the Ozarks Restaurant, the Round Up Club, Guy's Place, Strick's Restaurant, the Sunnybrook Tavern and the Las Vegas Club. In 1969 and 1970 some of the group's last club engagements were in the Maryland suburbs at the Senate Inn in Capitol Heights, the Cross Roads in Bladensburg and the Turf Club in Laurel.

In 1971 Howington left the nation's capital and moved to Homosassa, Florida where he married his second wife Margaret and spent his free time fishing and playing music. In the 1980s he was a singer-guitarist in 90 Proof, one of Florida's top C&W bands. Dub Howington passed away in Florida on Sunday, December 29, 1991 at the age of 62.

CHAPTER FORTY-NINE
CHICK HALL

Milford Willard "Chick" Hall rates as one of the most creative and talented singer-guitarists to ever emerge from the Washington, D.C. area. Noted for his innovative abilities in the fields of pop, jazz and C&W music, his road to becoming a master musician began early in life and continued on after relocating to the nation's capital in his middle 20s, where he went on to spend more than four decades establishing himself as one of the finest gentleman players the region has ever known.

Exhibiting an independent approach in the ways he created and shared his music with the public, Hall balanced his time owning, managing and performing in the now-legendary Surf Club, which originally sat on the Bladensburg Road Strip in Colmar Manor, Maryland and enjoyed a heyday that lasted from the middle 1950s to the middle 1970s. It was there that he opted to focus on pleasing his family, friends and followers instead of pursuing record deals and high-profile performances that would have landed him the national recognition he so richly deserved. In the larger scheme of life Hall became a richer man for his decisions, as his indomitable spirit lives on to this day as an inspirational presence in the lives of innumerable musicians and performing artists throughout the Washington, D.C. area.

Milford Willard Hall was born on Monday, August 20, 1923 in Snowden, North Carolina and grew up in the city of South Norfolk, Virginia (which today exists only as a neighborhood within the city of Chesapeake). Known from an early age as "Chick," he picked up a Stella acoustic guitar at the age of 13 and began playing along to songs he heard on local radio stations, with selections featuring the work of such guitarists as Charlie Christian, Les Paul, Django Reinhardt and George Barnes becoming personal favorites. Hall was completely self-taught and learned tunes note-for-note by ear. At age 15 he joined his first band, a local Western swing band called the Virginia Cavaliers, and his reputation as a guitar virtuoso began to spread throughout the Tidewater region.

After working with different jazz and country music groups in and around Norfolk, Hall was hired in 1941 to play lead guitar with Norman Phelps and the Virginia Rounders, a country music band that featured the three Phelps brothers, Norman (bass vocals, bass guitar and lead and rhythm guitar), Willie (baritone vocals, drums, washboard and rhythm guitar), and Earl (tenor vocals, fiddle and mandolin).

Norman Phelps and the Virginia Rounders had a fascinating history. In 1936 the brothers ventured to New York City and recorded several singles for Decca Records under the names "Norman Phelps Virginia Rounders" and "Norman Phelps and His Virginia Rounders." They next relocated to Hollywood, California, where from 1937 to 1941 they were featured as singing cowboy musicians in no fewer than 12 motion pictures, including the movies "Hittin' the Trail" (Grand National, 1937) and "Painted Desert" (RKO Radio Pictures, 1938). Upon returning to the Norfolk area the three Phelps brothers acquired the best available guitarist on the local music scene, a young Chick Hall, and began playing at dances, night clubs and social events as Norman Phelps and the Virginia Rounders. They quickly established themselves as the top musical outfit in the region.

Towards the conclusion of his two years of work with the Phelps Brothers, Chick Hall married Martha White on Thursday, April 1, 1943. He was then drafted into the United States Army and served in the division that was then called the United States Army Air Forces (the United States Air Force was not designated as a separate branch of military service until Thursday, September 18, 1947). He spent most of his three-year hitch in Peoria, Illinois and at Yuma Test Branch in Yuma, Arizona. During his military service he often performed with the United States Army Air Force Band, which at the time was under the direction of the now-legendary composer-arranger-trombonist Glenn Miller, who is regarded as one of the swing era's greatest orchestral bandleaders and recording artists.

Hall was utilized as a guitarist on many of Miller's live radio broadcasts that were aired over various programs across the country on the Armed Forces Radio Service. He also had the opportunity with Miller's band to work live concerts where they backed up many top popular music performers including such singers as Eddy Arnold and Helen Forrest.

It's a given that Hall's guitar work has appeared on a number of Glenn Miller's recorded songs, though his studio work was never properly documented and pinpointing his playing on these Miller selections has proven to be problematic. There were more than three-dozen military 12-inch V-Disc records recorded between July 1943 and June 1944 featuring Miller's band, with most having been issued with labels that read "War Department Music Branch Special Services Division" and credited to "Capt. Glenn Miller and the Band of the AAF Training Command." Many of these recordings feature either Johnny Desmond or Bob Carroll on lead vocals. At this point in time it is almost impossible to determine which of these recordings Hall played on, with the only possible way to identify such work is to have one of his sons (Chick Jr. or Chris) sit down and give each selection a close listening.

After the conclusion of World War II, Hall was discharged from the United States Army in 1946 and subsequently moved back to the Norfolk area. There, he rejoined Norman Phelps and the Virginia Rounders and worked with them at Fernwood Farms Picnic Ranch (formerly the Norfolk Country Club), a night club-recording studio that the Phelps brothers owned and operated.

Hall spent the better part of the next three years playing with Norman Phelps and the Virginia Rounders at Fernwood Farms Picnic Ranch and other night clubs in the area, with a young guitarist named Link Wray becoming one of his biggest followers. Wray actually sat in with the Rounders on occasion at Fernwood Farms Picnic Ranch and would play rhythm to Hall's leads. In later years Wray would often credit Chick Hall as one of his biggest influences, describing him as a "fantastic" player and comparing him to one of his other major influences, guitarist Chet Atkins. A decade later, Link, Vernon and Doug Wray took Hall's advice and made the move to Washington, D.C. to capitalize on the fertile popular music scene that had blossomed in the nation's capital.

In 1948, at the urging of C&W singer-pianist Moon Mullican and singer Marvin Rainwater, Chick and Martha Hall moved to Washington, D.C. and lived at various residences over the next 12 years. In 1960 they moved into a house at 4506 24th Avenue in Mt. Rainier, Maryland, which would remain their home for the rest of the guitarist's life. He embarked on a career as a professional musician and his talents as a singer-guitarist-banjoist were in great demand throughout the region.

In the late 1940s Chick Hall was a regular headliner at the Kit-Mar Restaurant on upper 14th Street NW where he worked with fiddler-pianist-vibraphonist Johnny Foster and steel guitarist Marvin Carroll. He was also featured at the Wagon Wheel in Capitol Heights, Maryland, where he and Foster worked as a duo. During this time Hall and Foster also settled in as part of a C&W trio with singer-steel guitarist Billy Strickland at two other night spots, the Camden Tavern on H Street NE and the Covered Wagon Restaurant on 14th Street NW just north of Thomas Circle. Hall could also be seen during this period sitting in with singer-fiddler-guitarist Blackie Skiles and his band at Bob White's Hideaway on Capitol Hill and Chubby Wise and the Florida Playboys at the Penguin in Southeast Washington.

Hall frequently sat in with a number of C&W and jazz musicians in the area and always made himself available when a versatile guitarist was needed to round out a roster. He got to know the great jazz guitarist Charlie Byrd early in his career and would often take the stage with him at the Crosstown Restaurant in the Mount Pleasant neighborhood of

Washington, D.C. In the early and middle 1950s he also worked the big weekend barn dances at Joe Turner Arena where he backed the likes of singer-banjoist Grandpa Jones, Frankie Robinson and the Virginia Playboys, Jimmy Dean and the Texas Wildcats and Bill Peer and His Melody Boys, who at the time were featuring Patsy Cline as their lead singer.

Perhaps Chick Hall's favorite hangout during his early years in the Washington, D.C. area was the original Dixie Pig Restaurant and Barbecue in Bladensburg, which was situated at the foot of the Peace Cross monument only a couple of miles from his Mt. Rainier home. It was there that he first saw singer-accordionist Jimmy Dean fronting Dub Howington and the Tennessee Haymakers, and struck up what would become a close friendship with the lanky Texan. At the Dixie Pig Restaurant and Barbecue Hall worked with every C&W musician to pass through town and still found time on his breaks to talk with and tutor young musicians, including an up-and-coming fast guitarist from Southeast Washington, D.C. named Roy Clark, who was enamored with Hall's innovative techniques.

On Saturday, November 22, 1952 the original Dixie Pig Restaurant and Barbecue burned to the ground in the midst of flooding conditions and was never reopened at that location. Two entrepreneurs, Harry Isikoff and Reuben Bonnett opened a new version of the Dixie Pig a mile away on Bladensburg Road in Cottage City, Maryland on Sunday, December 28, 1952, and installed the duo of "Chick and Johnny" as their house band ("Johnny" being the ever-present fiddler-pianist-vibraphonist Johnny Foster, a regular comrade of Hall's for many years).

For all of 1953 and 1954 Hall was the Dixie Pig's main attraction, with his bands variously billed as Chick Hall and His Hillbillies, Chick Hall and His Gang and the Chick Hall Trio. (As a side note, the last owners of the old Dixie Pig Restaurant and Barbecue in Bladensburg, Benjamin Minovitz and William Rubin, reappeared on the scene and purchased the new Dixie Pig in Cottage City from Isikoff and Bonnett in October 1954.)

While working the Dixie Pig in 1953 and 1954, Hall was regularly being called upon by promoter Connie B. Gay to play guitar on the weekend C&W "Barn Dance" extravaganzas he was staging at Joe Turner Arena, though he reportedly never accepted the entrepreneur's offers to manage his career. Supposedly, it was Gay who talked Hall into competing in "The National Championship Country Music Contest" in Warrenton, Virginia the weekend of Saturday, August 7 and Sunday, August 8, 1954, and, to no one's surprise, Hall walked away with first prize in the "Best Miscellaneous" competition. As legend has it, Hall was such a runaway winner that year, Gay, who apparently exercised great influence in picking the various contest winners, actually paid him not to enter the 1955 competition.

During this time Hall became a regular at a lively jazz bar called the Surf Club which was situated at 4201 Bladensburg Road in Colmar Manor, Maryland, across the street and three blocks east of the newer Dixie Pig. At the time the Surf Club featured the Capital City Dixielanders as its house band and Hall would sit in with them several times a week playing jazz and pop music.

In early 1955 Hall put together a band at the Surf Club billed as the Chick Hall Trio that would alternate sets on a nightly basis with the Capital City Dixielanders throughout the year. His new group consisted of himself on guitar, five-string banjo and vocals, singer-guitarist Dick Williams, and his brother-in-law Ulysses White, who played bass and rhythm guitar. The Surf Club had gone through a number of different owners through the years and when the latest group of proprietors expressed concern over their abilities to continue operating the establishment, Hall stepped in with an offer to buy the business.

In December 1955 the sale went through and on Thursday, March 15, 1956 the Board of License Commissioners of Prince George's County, Maryland for Alcoholic Beverages Licenses approved the transfer of the Class B liquor license from Murray Kanner, Mary

Kanner and Jack Sapienza to Milford Willard Hall (president-treasurer), Martha Ann Hall (vice president), and Clarence P.T. Lockhart (secretary).

Under the new ownership team, the Surf Club became one of the Washington, D.C. area's most popular C&W music venues, with Hall and his various bandmates providing incredible music in a unique social environment for the next 19 years. The headlining house band during this run was the Chick Hall Trio, whose early lineup consisted of Hall, Ulysses White, and rhythm guitarist-bassist Roy Green. Forsaking drummers, Hall had several notable musicians pass through his three-man outfit, including bassists Durwood Potter and Red Seal and singer-bassist-rhythm guitarist Wade Holmes.

Many other top local C&W bands worked the Surf Club through the years including Dub Howington and the Tennessee Haymakers, Smokey Mac and the Twilighters, Wade Holmes and His Town and Country Boys and Danny Denver and the Sound Tracks. On top of that, innumerable high-profile visitors made their way to the club for one-night stands or unannounced performances including singer Jim Reeves and a slew of singer-guitarists such as Lefty Frizzell, Faron Young, Elton Britt, Mac Wiseman, Little Jimmy Dickens, Luke Gordon, Ernest Tubb and local guitar hero Danny Gatton.

Hall himself like to recount the story of how one slow weeknight in the spring of 1959, as the other night clubs on the Strip were in the middle of their evening's entertainment presentations, he took the stage in the Surf Club with his band for a middle set, looked out into the rather sparse audience and saw several of his regulars sitting with their respective entourages at separate tables waiting for their mentor to captivate them with his tone, taste, timing and technique.

On this particular historic occasion, the "regulars" consisted of: Jimmy Dean and several members of his former band the Texas Wildcats at one table (Dean had been a Surf Club regular ever since Hall had purchased the club and on this occasion he was back in town from New York and sitting in with the Saxtons at the nearby 4400 Club); Roy Clark, who was hunkered down alone near the foot of the stage (Clark would often sit down in the Surf Club for guitar lessons from Hall in between his sets at the Cross Roads nearby); Patsy Cline and her group at another table along the side of the room (Cline was passing through town as her career had begun to accelerate); and a new band on the Strip named Charlie Daniels and the Jaguars who were quietly parked in the rear of the room (Daniels had relocated from Wilmington, North Carolina and was so enamored with Hall's guitar work he would gather his bandmates and venture to the Surf Club almost every night after completing their performances at the nearby Dixie Pig).

When Hall finished his 40-minute set, his energized followers nodded and applauded with great enthusiasm, then shuffled out of the club in single file and returned to their respective night clubs to finish their own appearances for the night.

The Surf Club also gained a bit of notoriety for its appearance in the book "Hard Living On Clay Street: Portraits of Blue Collar Families" by Joseph T. Howell (1973). The non-fictional work chronicled the real-life experiences the author had while spending a year (August 1970 to August 1971) with the White, blue-collar residents of a particular section of Mt. Rainier, Maryland. In the text, Howell actually provides a classification system for the neighborhood bars and taverns that the locals frequented, with the two most prominently featured being "The Dixie Club," which was a pseudonym for the Cross Roads in Bladensburg, and "The Bronco," which was based on the Surf Club on Bladensburg Road. In the book Howell details his conversations with "Larry," a neighborhood tough who during his three weeks in the neighborhood spent his free time shooting pool and fighting in the Bronco.

Chick and Martha Hall had two sons together and both have made their marks on the local music scene. Milford Chick Hall, was born in 1945 and to this day is commonly referred to as "Little Chick" or "Chick Hall, Jr." During his teenage years Chick Hall, Jr. played lead guitar for the Rhythm Rockers and the Majestic Neons, two of the top teen rock and roll bands in the area. He then went on to work with a plethora of C&W musicians in addition to frequently making music with his father at the Surf Club on Bladensburg Road. Today he is considered to be the best all-around guitarist in the entire Washington, D.C. region.

Chris Hall was born in 1952 and began playing bass guitar for his father on the weekends in 1966, filling out the trio that usually consisted of Chick Hall and rhythm guitarist Roy Green. Chris remained an "on-call" bassist for his father for decades to come, always ready to perform when other players left the fold. As one of the Washington, D.C. area's most talented singer-bassists he has carried on the family's musical legacy in fine fashion.

In 1973 developers descended on Bladensburg Road and began buying up commercial properties, with the owners of most of the Strip's storied night clubs succumbing to the purchase offers that came their way. Chick Hall, in anticipation of the inevitable sale of his old Surf Club, made arrangements to have a new Surf Club constructed at 4711 Kenilworth Avenue in nearby Hyattsville, right on the Bladensburg line. On Sunday, March 2, 1975 he closed the doors on his Bladensburg Road establishment for good and on Wednesday, March 5, 1975 he opened up his new venture on Kenilworth Avenue.

The newer Surf Club carried on without missing a beat and from the night of its opening until 1991 the Chick Hall Band held court with a lineup of Chick handling lead vocals and lead guitar, rhythm guitarist Roy Green, singer-bassist Wade Holmes and drummer Bob Redding, with Chris Hall carrying on his regular practice of subbing for Holmes on the weekends. Other drummers to work on-and-off for Hall during these years included Dave Chandler, Tim Jarvis and Lefty Corr.

In 1991 Chick Hall retired from the music business and turned the Surf Club over to his family, with his son Chris assuming management duties. A new house band named Heroes and Friends was installed, with the inaugural lineup of this C&W group consisting of singer-guitarist Chick Hall, Jr., singer-bassist Chris Hall, keyboardist Brin Reed and drummer Tim Jarvis. This group remained the club's primary attraction for years, though a variety of top bands from around the Washington, D.C. area were occasionally booked, including the Ruthie and the Wranglers, the Paulverizers, the hard rocking Slickee Boys and special blues night events featuring Blue Lou and Friends.

In the Surf Club's final years Heroes and Friends performed as a trio, with the Hall brothers being joined by drummer Mike Toole. However, changing social conditions in the neighborhood caused a steep drop in business and the Halls sold the Surf Club to James Byrum in January 2008. The new owner made a gallant attempt at bringing in the best in local blues, country rock and Zydeco music, but business failed to escalate and the final evening of entertainment in the club took place on Saturday, October 29, 2011 with a performance by the White R&B combo King Soul. Byrum then sold the building to VMS Enterprises. Inc. in November 2011. Today the former Surf Club structure is occupied by the Kenilworth Laundromat.

While the Surf Club was soldiering on, Chick Hall was enjoying a quiet retirement in Mt. Rainier with his wife Martha at his side and his family close by. He was known by all as a devoted family man and regarded as one of the finest guitarists the Washington, D.C. music scene has ever known. Rejecting the notion of leaving town and taking his skills on the road, he embraced the Surf Club folk and reveled in the joy and satisfaction of performing his music in his own way, free of constraints and artistic compromises. He proved one could become a legendary musical figure right in one's own backyard. Chick

Hall passed away quietly from complications of Alzheimer's disease on Tuesday, November 18, 2008 at the age of 85.

CHAPTER FIFTY
ROY CLARK

Roy Clark is firmly established as one of the greatest musical entertainers of all time. A master of the guitar, banjo and fiddle, Clark is recognized worldwide for his incredible accomplishments in C&W music and is known for holding audiences spellbound with his humor, vocal abilities and musical wizardry. Many followers of Clark are surprised when they discover the talented guitarist grew up in Washington, D.C. and lived in Prince George's County, Maryland for over four years during the 1950s, during which time he was a fixture at local night clubs and dances where he offered sets of C&W mixed with rock and roll. When he left the area, he found fame as a performing artist in Las Vegas, Nevada, headlined venues all over the world, and was a regular attraction for many years at his own Roy Clark Celebrity Theatre in Branson, Missouri. Clark still tours the country regularly today and rates as one of the brightest stars this locale has ever produced.

Born Roy Linwood Clark in Meherrin, Virginia on Saturday, April 15, 1933, the master guitarist spent portions of his early years living in Staten Island, New York and St. Clairsville, Ohio. In January 1942 his father Hester Clark relocated the family (consisting of wife Lillian, sons Dick, Dwight, and Roy, and daughters Jean and Susan) to Washington, D.C. The Clark family moved into a home at 739 Yuma Street SE in the heart of a government housing project informally known as Highland Dwellings. Hester Clark obtained clerical employment at the Washington Navy Yard making telescope and periscope lenses in the optical department.

The Clark family was very musical, as Hester played guitar, banjo and mandolin at square dances throughout Virginia, Maryland and Washington, D.C. Several of Roy Clark's uncles also played and it was only natural that he was exposed to the world of country music early in his life. At age 13 Clark discovered that his next-door neighbor, Johnny Schwartz, owned a Harmony Weymann archtop-style guitar and would visit his home and play it whenever he could. On Christmas morning 1946, waiting under the tree was a brand new Silvertone model guitar – right from the Sears catalog – and an obscure instruction book on how to play guitar. After receiving these gifts Clark began practicing at home for hours on end.

While attending Kramer Junior High School in Southeast, Washington, D.C. Clark began showing proficiency in the visual arts. He enrolled at nearby Chamberlain Vocational High School a couple of years early to take courses in drafting and art. He also developed his athletic skills and played on the varsity football and baseball teams, the latter of which prompted scouts from the St. Louis Browns to offer him a tryout. During his teenage years Clark began playing guitar at square dances along with his father, and also with other young musicians at functions booked by Ralph Case. His first television show performance was at the age of 15 in 1948 for WTTG-TV's "Hayloft Conservatory of Musical Interpretations." On that program he appeared with his father as "Roy Clark and Dad." Together they performed the song "One Has My Name (The Other Has My Heart)," a tune written by Eddie Dean, Dearest Dean and Hal Blair.

While at Chamberlain Vocational High School, Clark worked extensively for Ralph Case and played square dances every Monday night in the city at the Strong John Thompson School (1200 L Street NW). He also played on weekends at the Fort Belvoir Officers' Club in Fairfax County, Virginia and worked a regular Saturday morning country music show at radio station WBUZ, which was located on the Washington, D.C.-Prince George's County line at 4421 Southern Avenue in Bradbury Heights, Maryland. A regular companion of

Clark's at these various jobs was Ralph's son Jimmy Case, who was also a highly regarded early-era country and rock and roll musician in Washington, D.C.

In early 1948 Clark began working with an unnamed trio at small local bars in and around Southeast Washington, D.C. including the Shanty, the Stage Coach Tavern, the Victory Grill and the Oxon Run Inn (informally known as the Bucket of Blood). That summer the band also obtained a job in North Beach, Maryland on the Chesapeake Bay at Rose's Musical Bar. The two other teenagers in the group quickly returned home, but Clark stuck it out and was hired to play guitar for a country music band led by Smokey Rice. This group also included an advanced guitarist named Carl Lukat, who had grown up not far from Clark at 1810 Fairlawn Avenue SE in Washington, D.C. and had graduated from Anacostia High School.

Roy Clark returned to Washington, D.C. in September 1948 and continued to play radio broadcasts for station WBUZ and square dances with Ralph Case. Through Case, Clark was hired by a square dance band to work a two-week show that was headlined by country music star Hank Williams at Baltimore's Hippodrome Theatre. He also backed singer-banjoist Grandpa Jones on a four-day tour that traveled from Baltimore, Maryland to Rochester, New York. With music becoming the dominant force in his life, the 15-year-old Clark quit Chamberlain Vocational High School in early 1949, only a half-semester away from graduation.

Roy Clark's real education began when he entered the Washington, D.C. night club world as a full-time performer at the age of 16. He first worked with Carl Lukat at the Camden Tavern (1252 H Street NE), where the duo took requests, played assorted Hank Snow and Hank Williams tunes and scooped their pay from the kitty on the front of the stage. He also played in combos at Pete's Restaurant in Georgetown and the Jo Del Bar and Grill on 9th Street NW with singer-guitarist Pete Pike and bassist Buck Austin.

For the better part of the next two years through late 1951, Clark and Lukat also worked in Prince George's County, Maryland at such night clubs as the Wagon Wheel, Club Hillbilly, Chubby's Restaurant and Bar, the Campus Club, Mike Young's Café, the Homestretch Tavern and the Senate Inn. In addition to the steady night club work, Clark also found time to pursue other activities, including an abbreviated professional boxing career where he went 15-1 under promoter Goldie Ahearn. In August 1951 he won the "Best Banjo Player" competition in "The National Championship Country Music Contest" in Warrenton, Virginia, with his first place finish resulting in $500 cash, a chance to perform at "The Grand Ole Opry" in Nashville, and the attention of local C&W music promoter Connie B. Gay. (Clark later won the same "Best Banjo Player" competition for a second time in 1954.)

In his autobiography "Roy Clark: My Life in Spite of Myself (1994) Clark mentions that at the time of Carl Lukat's induction into the United States Army in 1951 the two of them were playing the Campus Club, a rough motorcycle club hangout near the Washington, D.C. line. Owned at the time by Vernon "Jack" Biedler, the Campus Club was a legendary Prince George's County night spot located just off of Marlboro Pike in Hillside, Maryland and was known for its mind-boggling brawls. The establishment enjoyed the distinction of being the first Washington, D.C. area night club to cater to bikers, as it was then an unofficial home base for the D.C. Ramblers, one of the area's first organized motorcycle clubs. When Clark and Lukat left the Campus Club, their spot was filled by other local legends, the Tennessee Troopers, a trio consisting of singer-guitarist-mandolinist Buzz Busby, fiddler Scotty Stoneman and guitarist Jack Clement.

With his friend Carl Lukat in the United States Army, Clark spent several months in late 1951 and early 1952 in Nashville, Tennessee where he backed up the C&W musical comedy duo Lonzo and Oscar ("Lonzo" being singer-guitarist Lloyd George and "Oscar" being singer-mandolinist Rollin Sullivan) at "The Grand Ole Opry." Upon his return to Washington, D.C. he married a woman named Ruby and the couple resided in a house at 1226 Simms Place NE. While the marriage lasted only a short while, the union did produce a son named Roy L. Clark Jr. who was born in 1953.

Beginning in early 1952 Clark spent two years working as a solo performer in a variety of Washington, D.C. night clubs including the Bob White Club, the Covered Wagon Restaurant, Matt Windsor's Restaurant, the Potomac Restaurant, the B&J Restaurant (formerly Pete's Restaurant), the Famous Restaurant, the Jo Del Bar and Grill, Harry's Tavern and the Harmony Club. In addition to his night club work, he also began playing the large C&W "Barn Dances" for Cactus Matt at Joe Turner Arena on Saturday nights, and became a regular on Connie B. Gay's "Town and Country Time" radio show on station WARL.

Clark spent a lot of time on the Prince George's County side of the line and worked the original Dixie Pig Restaurant and Barbecue on Annapolis Road in Bladensburg, Maryland on a regular basis. That night club mysteriously burned down in November 1952 and a new Dixie Pig quickly reopened over on the Bladensburg Road Strip a month later. Clark moved his act over to the new Dixie Pig and shared his mix of singing, playing and comedy with other popular country musicians such as singer-fiddler-guitarist Blackie Skiles, singer-guitarist Smitty Smith, singer-accordionist Stoney Rigsby, fiddler Chubby Wise and drummer Jimmy Burkett. He also performed in other Bladensburg Road establishments such as the Wheel Bar, the Romano Inn, the Surf Club and the Rustic Cabin Restaurant.

While working these night clubs Clark did a significant amount of recording for Ben Adelman at his two Washington, D.C. studios, the Truetone Recording Company on Illinois Avenue NW (1951 to 1954), and then his relocated and renamed True-Tone Recording Company in the Portland building on Vermont Avenue NW (1954 to 1957). While it is unknown how the two came to meet, it is known that Clark recorded many songs both as a featured singer-guitarist and as a session guitarist for Adelman over a period of several years. Many of these songs have surfaced, while many more have vanished without ever having seen the light of day.

Among those songs that were released without Clark's knowledge or consent was a pair of singles recorded in 1953 and released posthumously: "Mysteries of Life" backed with "Sugar Coated Sweetheart" (Roy Clark; 4 Star Records, 1954); and "Stepping Stones" backed with "The Day That I Found You" (Roy Clark and His Wranglers; Coral Records, 1956). There was also an album release of material recorded from 1953 to 1956 entitled "Roy Clark" (Roy Clark; Guest Star Records, 1960) which included the songs "Sugar Coated Sweetheart," "Mysteries of Life," "Folsom Prison Blues," "Release Me," "Kansas City," "Home Sweet Home" and "Alabama Jubilee."

In February 1954 Roy Clark had just finished playing the Famous Restaurant on New York Avenue NW with singer-guitarist Dick Williams when he decided to accept an offer to join Jimmy Dean and the Texas Wildcats at a salary of $150 a week. Besides Clark and Dean, the group consisted of steel guitarist Marvin Carrol, rhythm guitarist Herbie Jones, fiddler Buck Ryan, with a number of guest musicians coming and going over the following two years. In addition to playing Connie B. Gay's WARL "Town and Country Time" radio show on a daily basis, the band worked a grueling schedule and played nightly at every conceivable local function including picnics, political rallies, television shows and night clubs all over the entire Washington, D.C. area.

Jimmy Dean and the Texas Wildcats were the undisputed kings of the local C&W music scene during Roy Clark's tenure with the band in the middle 1950s. They headlined the grand opening of a Washington, D.C. night club called the Starlite Restaurant on Irving Street NW in July 1954. They also performed at such Prince George's County, Maryland night clubs as the Surf Club, the Dixie Pig, the Rustic Cabin Restaurant, the Sunnybrook Tavern, the 4400 Club and Waldrop's Restaurant (where during the fall of 1954 Clark met his future wife Barbara Rupard during one of their performances).

During the summer of 1955 Jimmy Dean and the Texas Wildcats, with Roy Clark prominently featured as lead guitarist, worked Friday nights at Glen Echo Park's Spanish Ballroom where they opened for such acts as Little Jimmy Dickens and His Country Boys, Hank Snow and His Rainbow Ranch Boys and Ernest Tubb and His Texas Troubadours. They were also the featured house band on the WMAL-TV "Town and Country Time" and Town and Country Jamboree" live music television shows during this time. Clark's tenure with Jimmy Dean and the Texas Wildcats came to an end during the summer of 1956 due to his excessive tardiness to band performances.

Apparently, bad blood between Clark and Dean lasted for several months, as evidenced by a now-legendary tale of how Clark exacted some mischievous revenge on his former bandleader. As the story goes, shortly after Labor Day in September 1956, Clark, still smarting from his dismissal from the Texas Wildcats, discovered that Jimmy Dean's group was headlining at the Rustic Cabin Restaurant on Bladensburg Road in Colmar Manor, Maryland. Clark cut loose on his motorcycle early one night from where he was performing at the Rendezvous in Washington, D.C. and made his way back to the Bladensburg Road Strip where he made stops at his usual hangouts including the Dixie Pig and the Surf Club. While at the Surf Club, Martha Hall, wife of the great guitarist Chick Hall, told Clark about Jimmy Dean and the Texas Wildcats' engagement a few doors down at the Rustic Cabin, and suggested Clark should pay the band a visit – and ride his motorcycle right through the restaurant. Evidently, Clark thought this was a great idea – the doors to the Rustic Cabin burst open, the former Texas Wildcats guitarist revved up the engine on his bike, and circled the club's main floor in a thunderous roar and cloud of smoke as Dean and his bandmates looked on in bewildered disbelief. Clark then waved to his buddies and sped off into the night, presumably back to the Rendezvous to finish his evening's set. This story of his final farewell to Dean has resonated in Prince George's County music circles for decades.

Earlier in 1956 Hester Clark, then a project planner with HEW, had moved the family from Yuma Street SE to 3812 First Street SE, Washington, D.C. Later that year when Roy Clark became more serious with Barbara Rupard, he moved from the First Street SE home to the Rupard residence at 2307 57th Avenue in Tuxedo, Maryland where Barbara lived with her parents and siblings. Taking over an enclosed porch area of the house, Clark's new quarters marked the beginning of his four-year stay in Prince George's County.

During the summer of 1956 Clark began putting together his own combos that mainly performed C&W music. In July of that year he formed Roy Clark and the Power Pacs with steel guitarist Bill Bagent and played the summer and early fall months at the Rendezvous in Washington, D.C. From October 1956 until April 1957 he played the Famous Restaurant, most often with steel guitarist Tommy Johnson. In December 1956 Clark and Johnson were advertised as the Country Kut-ups (other musicians in the band at that time were singer-rhythm guitarist Freddie Stafford and drummer Duke Maddox) and throughout April 1957 the Famous Restaurant advertised their house band as Roy Clark and the Country Stylists. During the summer months of 1957 the band was still working the Famous Restaurant, but had changed its name to Roy Clark and the Country Cousins. During this time he also backed up C&W singer Marvin Rainwater on guitar and banjo throughout the Washington, D.C. area, most often at the Saturday night "Town and Country Jamboree" performances at Capitol Arena.

Clark's divorce from his first wife Ruby was finalized in April 1957. On Saturday, August 31, 1957 he married Barbara Joyce Rupard. The wedding was held in Prince George's

County at the First Methodist Church of Hyattsville, then-located at 5300 Baltimore Avenue. In September 1957 Roy and Barbara Clark moved into a one-bedroom apartment at 5364 Quincy Place #101 in the Merilee Arms Apartments in Hyattsville (today this complex is called Hillcrest Woods Apartments). He stayed there until September 1960. It was his last Prince George's County home.

After the marriage and the move to Hyattsville, Clark appeared as a solo headliner at local night clubs such as the Dixie Pig and the Famous Restaurant, and also worked the Shamrock Restaurant in Georgetown as part of the Shamrock Trio with steel guitarist Mickey Woodward and guitarist-bassist Roger Woodward. Although the "Town and Country Jamboree" went off the air at the end of August 1957, Clark continued to appear on the various live Friday and Saturday night C&W music shows staged at the Capitol Arena by promoter Don Owens. In June 1958 Clark put together a new band called Roy Clark and the Stardusters, and, after a three-week engagement at the Las Vegas Club on Marlboro Pike in Coral Hills, Maryland in August of that year, settled in for a long stay at the legendary Prince George's County night club known as Strick's Restaurant.

Built in 1937 by a Colonial Beach, Virginia native named Julius Strickland, Strick's Restaurant was located at 3211 Branch Avenue in Silver Hill, Maryland. The night club was purchased by a Hillcrest Heights resident named Giles Fletcher Sr. in February 1954. It was the classic rough-and-tumble Prince George's County roadhouse of the 1950s – a square, one-floor, brick-and-concrete building in the margin between the Branch Avenue and Naylor Road intersection that could hold approximately 110 patrons.

Strick's Restaurant offered live C&W music (with some rock and roll thrown in for good measure), fine food, cheap booze and a rugged Southern clientele determined to have a wild time. Festive full-scale brawls were a nightly feature. Strick's Restaurant went mainly country after the Fletcher purchase and regularly featured the top stars of the area such as Jimmy Dean and the Texas Wildcats, Dub Howington and the Tennessee Haymakers, singer-guitarists such as Smokey Mac and Billy Grammer, singer-accordionist Stoney Rigsby, rockabilly singer-guitarist Wanda Jackson and Bill Peer and His Melody Boys (featuring singer Patsy Cline). Later in the 1960s, Strick's Restaurant went rock and roll and among those that performed in the night club were Link Wray and His Ray Men and guitarists Roy Buchanan and Danny Gatton. Strick's Restaurant still stands today, though it functions only as a liquor store and the stars of yesteryear are now just distant memories.

In the late 1950s Strick's Restaurant became known for holding Sunday afternoon jam sessions that were informal gatherings of the best C&W music stars in the Washington, D.C. area. Other popular Sunday attractions at the night club during this time were the extravagant talent shows hosted by either Jerry Toronto or Ed Beavers. When he first performed at these events, Clark's backup band consisted of singer-guitarist Jack Rodgers, steel guitarist Ray Sherman and drummer Duke Maddox, a lineup that would stay intact throughout the summer and fall of 1958 and into 1959. In early and middle 1959 Roy Clark and the Stardusters had some Sunday sessions at Strick's Restaurant with Charlie Daniels and the Jaguars, an interesting tale that Clark recounts in his autobiography.

During the course of Roy Clark's stay at Strick's Restaurant, Barbara Clark heard about the Off Keys, a popular teenage rock and roll band from her alma mater Bladensburg High School that was drawing large Friday night crowds to the Bladensburg Volunteer Fire Department, a facility not far from the apartment she and Roy occupied. She scouted the band in the summer of 1958, liked what she heard, and got her husband to invite the boys down to a Friday night jam session at the Capitol Arena, an event that soon turned into a regular weekend sojourn for the band.

In September 1958 Clark signed a one-shot contract with the New York-based Debbie Records label, a company that was owned by Ray Rainwater, brother of C&W singer-guitarist Marvin Rainwater, whom Clark had backed up on many live dates in and around the nation's capital. For musical backing on the resulting session, Clark called upon the Off Keys and ushered the group into a studio called Capitol Transcriptions Inc. (located on the sixth floor of 620 11th Street NW, Washington, D.C.).

The single Clark recorded that month was "Please Mr. Mayor" backed with "Puddin'" (Roy Clark; Debbie Records, 1958). The A-side featured Clark on lead guitar and vocals, backed by seven members of the Off Keys: rhythm guitarist Clarence Perry, bassist Luman Perry, pianist Sam Paladino, saxophonists Dick Moody, Art Gould and Roger Hughes, and drummer Jack Henderson. For the B-side, Clark utilized only the Perry Brothers, Paladino and Henderson to provide the musical backing. Although an excellent pair of rock and roll songs, the single, which was released to the public in November 1958, failed to make the Billboard magazine charts.

After a year as the main nightly attraction at Strick's Restaurant, Clark revamped the Stardusters in August 1959 and invited former Off Keys piano player Sam Paladino to join the fold as a full-time member. The new lineup for his band now consisted of Clark, Paladino, bassist Johnny Powell, fiddler-saxophonist Marvin West and drummer Flip Bacher. They spent afternoons rehearsing at Flip Bacher's home in Palmer Park, Maryland and embarked on a grueling schedule of nightly playing in the immediate area that lasted until September 1960. Among the establishments they regularly graced were Vinnie's Grill, the Cross Roads, the Dixie Pig, the 4400 Club, the Village Barn, Strick's Restaurant, Hunter's Lodge and the Oxon Hill Volunteer Fire Department (where they would perform on Saturday evenings and upon the completion of their set would race to the Capitol Arena in Washington, D.C. to partake in the lively C&W jamborees that were being staged there by Don Owens).

During this run Clark took up an offer from C&W music promoter Don Owens to record a single for his newly formed record label, Owens International Corp. In May 1960 Clark gathered together bassist Johnny Powell, pianist Sam Paladino, saxophonists Marvin West and Dick Moody and drummer Flip Bacher. He took the group into the confines of Capitol Transcriptions Inc. where they quickly cut two dynamic rock and roll instrumentals in one afternoon session. The result of this effort, "Rock, Maggie, Rock," backed with "Man, Like Long Ago" (Roy Clark and the Versitals; Owens International Corp., 1960), was released that June 1960 and quickly faded from view, a victim of non-existent promotion. It remains the only record ever commercially released by Owens International Corp.

Roy Clark's departure from Prince George's County and introduction to fame and fortune in Las Vegas, Nevada happened suddenly. In September 1960 Wanda Jackson was searching for a lead guitarist to join her band in Vegas at the Golden Nugget and some female friends of Jimmy Dean told her about the former Texas Wildcats guitarist who was still working the local circuit. Jackson journeyed to Strick's Restaurant and after witnessing one of his Sunday performances she offered Clark the job. He left on a moment's notice, telling only his wife and immediate family, with his Stardusters becoming aware of his departure only after he failed to show for a gig.

Clark subsequently spent several years as Wanda Jackson's frontman and lead guitarist and from there went on to establish himself as one of the most popular C&W music and television entertainment personalities in history. (Though Clark left for Vegas in 1960, he returned to Maryland and owned a house at 3521 Williamsburg Road in Davidsonville, Maryland from 1963 to 1976. In 1976 he moved to Tulsa, where he still resides.)

Roy Clark's status as a nationally known performing artist was greatly enhanced when he signed with Capitol Records in 1961. During his years with Capitol he released a total of nine albums and saw his first hit single on that label, "Tips of My Fingers," reach number ten on Billboard magazine's "Hot Country Singles" chart on Saturday, September 7, 1963.

During his career Clark released more than 70 albums and 70 singles on a variety of national and independent record labels including Capitol, MCA, Dot and ABC. Nine of his singles have reached the top ten on Billboard magazine's country music charts, including the 45rpm "Come Live With Me" backed with "Darby's Castle" (Roy Clark; Dot Records, 1973), which went all the way to number one on the "Hot Country Singles" chart on Saturday, May 12, 1973. Much of his back catalog has been reissued in recent years on compact disc and numerous compilations of his most popular songs are available in this medium.

Roy Clark's incredible accomplishments include having appeared on dozens of television shows, everything from "The Beverly Hillbillies" in the early 1960s to hosting "The Tonight Show" in 1963 to his position as host and featured performer on "Hee Haw," a role he accepted back in 1969 and held for more than 23 years. He's held starring roles in such feature-length motion pictures as "Matilda" (American International Pictures, 1978) and "Uphill All the Way" (New World Pictures, 1986). He's headlined in Las Vegas at the Sands, the Frontier, the Desert Inn, and Caesar's Palace. He's taken the stage at "The Grand Ole Opry" in Nashville, performed at every major arena in the country, and has extensively toured Europe and Asia. From 1983 to 1997 he headlined at his own Roy Clark Celebrity Theatre in Branson, Missouri, and also toured the United States for years with his own nine-piece backup band, Rodney Lay and the Wild West, which included another Washington, D.C. area rock and roll veteran, guitarist Vernon Sandusky (formerly of the Chartbusters). In 2009 Roy Clark was inducted into the Country Music Hall of Fame. He continues to record, tour and perform for his fans around the world.

CHAPTER FIFTY-ONE
JIMMY DEAN

Jimmy Ray Dean was born on Friday, August 10, 1928 in Olton, Texas and grew up in nearby Seth Ward, a neighborhood situated in the northeast section of the city of Plainview. He learned the fundamentals of music at an early age, as his mother played piano and Dean himself enjoyed singing on Sundays at the Seth Ward Baptist Church. He also frequently sang with his friends in impromptu vocal groups around town.

At age 17 Dean's mother enrolled him in the United States Merchant Marine and during his year-long tour he traveled from California to South America. In 1946 Dean joined what was then called the United States Army Air Forces (the United States Air Force was not designated as a separate branch of military service until Thursday, September 18, 1947) and was stationed at Bolling Air Force Base in Washington, D.C. where he served most of his two-and-a-half-year tour of duty.

While stationed at Bolling Air Force Base, Dean began frequenting a rough country music bar called Harry's Tavern, which was located in the Downtown area of Washington, D.C. on New York Avenue NW right next to a Greyhound Bus terminal. During its earliest years the building at this address had housed a succession of markets and fruit stores, and most recently had hosted the White Coffee Pot Restaurant from 1928 to 1942, Traveler's Grill from 1943 to May 1946, and a live music bar called the Bowery from June 1946 through early 1948.

When Harry's Tavern opened on the premises in the summer of 1948 a guitarist named Lee "Brownie" Callaway, Jr. and his makeshift country music group, which included fiddler Scotty Stoneman, was hired to handle house band duties. Dean and other servicemen would frequent the club and eventually Dean himself began singing songs and playing accordion with Callaway's group. He was soon accepted as a full-time band member.

While Dean was performing with Callaway's band at Harry's Tavern, he caught the attention of Dub Howington, one of the Washington, D.C. area's hottest young guitarists, who offered him a position in his band the Tennessee Haymakers. Howington was enjoying success in the nation's capital as a performing and recording artist with his brother Roy, a standup bass player, and was looking to expand his popular country music outfit to capitalize on the growing number of night clubs that were switching over to that style of music as the Southern population of the area grew.

Upon Dean's discharge from the United States Air Force in 1949, he joined Dub Howington and the Tennessee Haymakers, whose lineup at that time consisted of Dub on vocals and guitar, singer-bassist Roy Howington, rhythm guitarist Herbie "Toothless" Jones (who was eventually replaced by guitarist Jimmy Groves), and Dean, who, in addition to playing accordion and piano, handled master of ceremony duties on the microphone. For the next two years the band worked regularly at Harry's Tavern and a number of other area night clubs including the Covered Wagon Restaurant, the Camden Tavern, the Jo Del Bar and Grill, the Dixie Pig Restaurant and Barbecue, the Campus Club, the Homestretch Tavern, Chubby's Restaurant and Bar, the Wagon Wheel, Club Hillbilly, the Oxon Run Inn and barn dances at the Pythian Temple on 9th Street NW in Washington, D.C.

In 1951 Dean married a woman from Takoma Park, Maryland named Mary Sue Wittauer who resided at the time with her parents at 8115 Roanoke Avenue (the marriage would end in divorce in 1991 and shortly thereafter Dean married his second wife Donna Meade). Later in that same year Dean parted company with Dub Howington and subsequently put together his own band with remnants of Dub's fast-disintegrating Tennessee Haymakers. The inaugural lineup for this new band consisted of Dean on lead vocals and accordion, lead guitarist Jimmy Groves, rhythm guitarist Herbie Jones and bassist Bob Elliot.

Advertised as Jimmy Dean and the Texas Wildcats, this group worked throughout 1952 at local military base officers' clubs, as well as a number of night clubs in the area including the Harmony Restaurant, the Covered Wagon Restaurant, the Kit-Mar Restaurant, the Homestretch Tavern, Ted's Grill, and several bars in the Anacostia neighborhood of Washington, D.C. including the Shanty, the Victory Grill, the Anchor Lounge and the Stagecoach Tavern. Within a couple of months after forming, several personnel changes transpired within the group, with Jimmy Groves departing, Quincy Snodgrass replacing Bob Elliot on bass, and fiddler Buck Ryan and steel guitarist Marvin Carrol joining up.

Dean and his band pledged their services to Connie B. Gay, who immediately booked the group to perform on the "Gay Time" extravaganza he staged at Uline Arena on Saturday, February 16, 1952, an event that was headlined by singer Rosalie Allen and singer-guitarists Elton Britt and Ann Jones. At this time the band also performed daily on Gay's "Town and Country Time" radio show on station WARL in Arlington, Virginia.

In the spring of 1952 Jimmy Dean and the Texas Wildcats were working at the Covered Wagon Restaurant on 14th Street NW in Washington, D.C. when an aspiring songwriter-producer named Fred Foster approached Dean offstage about making some demo records at Ben Adelman's Truetone Recording Company on Illinois Avenue NW. Foster sent one of these demos, a song entitled "Bumming Around," to 4 Star Records in Pasadena, California. Company president Bill McCall responded and asked them to record a higher fidelity version of the song at a better-equipped facility. Foster took Dean and the band into a Washington, D.C. facility called Sound Studios Inc. in July of that year and a month later the song was released nationally as a 45rpm single record on 4 Star Records. The single "Bumming Around" backed with "Picking Sweethearts" (Jimmy Dean; 4 Star Records, 1952) eventually peaked at number five on the Billboard magazine's "Most Played by Jockeys" country & western records chart on Saturday, March 21, 1953.

Throughout the early 1950s Dean and his band recorded dozens of songs at the Truetone Recording Company that producer Ben Adelman would, years later, release on a variety of albums on independent labels. This was done entirely without Dean's knowledge or consent. Among these albums, were "Jimmy Dean with Luke Gordon Featuring the Country Singing of Jimmy Dean and Featuring the Country singing of Luke Gordon" (Jimmy Dean with Luke Gordon; Spin-O-Rama, 1963), and "Jimmy Dean and the Town and Country Men" (Jimmy Dean and the Town and Country Men; Guest Star, 1964). These albums included material that was recorded more than 10 prior to their release. Dean maintained that he never received royalties or any type of compensation for any of these independent album releases.

With the impressive showing of the single "Bumming Around," Jimmy Dean and the Texas Wildcats worked a steady round of live dates around the nation's capital throughout 1953 and 1954. They kicked things off as the house band at Connie B. Gay's Wednesday, December 31, 1952 New Year's Eve show at Washington's District of Columbia National Guard Armory, backing up singer-guitarists Red Foley and Hank Snow and many others. They were regulars on most Saturday nights at the Oxon Hill Volunteer Fire Department in Prince George's County, Maryland throughout 1953 and also played numerous dates at the nearby Super Chief Drive-In Theatre on Indian Head Highway that summer season. On Saturday, June 6, 1953 they co-headlined a one-day concert with guitarist Chet Atkins at Captain Joe's Port Georgetown Supper Club, a night club that would soon become the Bayou, and also appeared at the high-class Merry Land Club on L Street NW, a block off the 14th Street Strip.

Connie B. Gay also employed Dean and his group as the house band for all of his S.S. Mount Vernon Potomac River "Moonlight Cruises" that 1953 summer season where they backed up such C&W music stars as singer Mac Wiseman, singer-banjoist Grandpa Jones, singer-guitarists Little Jimmy Dickens, Carl Smith, Webb Pierce and Marty Robbins, the quintet known as the Maddox Brothers and Rose, and the musical comedy duo of Homer and Jethro. They also alternated sets on one engagement with Ernest Tubb and the Texas Troubadours. They again worked with Gay on his Thursday, December 31, 1953 New Year's Eve show at the District of Columbia National Guard Armory, where they worked an all-star bill headlined by Hank Thompson and His Brazos Valley Boys and Hank Snow and His Rainbow Ranch Boys.

After his discharge from the United States Air Force in 1949 Dean moved through various addresses in and around Washington, D.C. In early 1954 he and his wife, along with certain members of the Texas Wildcats, moved into a large rooming house at 3303 18th Street NW in the Mount Pleasant neighborhood of Washington, D.C. This residence was only four blocks away from the Starlite Restaurant on Irving Street NW, which opened as a C&W night club in July of that year. Jimmy Dean and the Texas Wildcats worked the Starlite Restaurant several nights a week for the remainder of 1954 and into 1955, and more often than not walked their way to and from work.

In April 1954 Jimmy Dean and the Texas Wildcats worked both the Dixie Pig on Bladensburg Road in Cottage City, Maryland and the Famous Restaurant in Washington, D.C., venues that were fast becoming two of the area's premier C&W night clubs. Connie B. Gay also had them headline "The Home Show" at the District of Columbia National Guard Armory in Washington, D.C., a week-long home appliance exhibition and entertainment affair that ran from Saturday, April 24 to Sunday, May 2, 1954.

In the summer of 1954 Dean added lead guitarist Roy Clark to the Texas Wildcats lineup, with Herbie Jones moving from lead guitar back to rhythm guitar. In addition to working the Starlite Restaurant on a semi-regular basis, the band appeared regularly at Glen Echo Park's Spanish Ballroom, the Shamrock Restaurant on M Street in Georgetown, and frequent "Moonlight Cruises" down the Potomac River aboard the S.S. Mount Vernon. In the fall months they added weekly performances at Waldrop's Restaurant on Rhode Island Avenue in Brentwood, Maryland to their schedule. On Friday, December 31, 1954 they worked another one of Connie B. Gay's New Year's Eve shows, this one at Uline Arena that featured singer-guitarists Red Foley, Ernest Tubb and Deacon Andy Griffith, among others.

In 1955 Dean and his wife moved into a house at 1708 N. Roosevelt Street in Arlington, Virginia, a residence that would remain their home until Dean accepted a television show offer from CBS and departed for New York City in September 1958.

On Monday, January 17, 1955 Connie B. Gay returned to live local television with the show "Town and Country Time," which aired on WMAL-TV (Channel 7) on various weeknights at various times until Friday, January 24, 1958. This live C&W music program, which would run anywhere from 30 to 60 minutes, featured Jimmy Dean himself as the host and his band the Texas Wildcats as the house band. At this point in time Dean's group consisted of lead guitarist Roy Clark, rhythm guitarist Herbie Jones, steel guitarist Marvin Carroll, fiddler Buck Ryan, singer-standup bassist Mary Klick, and Dean himself playing accordion and handling emcee and lead vocal duties. Other musicians came and went during this time, including banjoist Jesse Smith "Smitty" Irvin and longtime fill-in bassist Bob Elliot.

On Friday, May 6, 1955 Jimmy Dean and the Texas Wildcats kicked off another May-to-September season as the house band at Glen Echo Park's Spanish Ballroom with a headlining performance. On Friday, May 13 they opened up on a triple bill headlined by

Little Jimmy Dickens and His Country Boys and female pianist Del Wood. Among the other top C&W acts they opened for that summer at the Spanish Ballroom were Hank Thompson and His Brazos Valley Boys, Hank Snow and His Rainbow Ranch Boys, Carl Smith and the Tunesmiths, Ernest Tubb and His Texas Troubadours, Webb Pierce and His Wondering Boys, the Maddox Brothers and Rose, and singer-guitarist-pianist Marty Robbins.

Later in 1955 Connie B. Gay expanded his empire and added "Town and Country Jamboree," a three-hour Saturday night live music broadcast beginning at 10pm from Joe Turner Arena. This expanded program, which aired on WMAL-TV, ran from Saturday, October 1, 1955 until Saturday, August 31, 1957, also employed Jimmy Dean as its main host and the Texas Wildcats as the all-purpose musical team. Both television shows featured the best in locally based talent such as singer-guitarists Billy Grammer and Marvin Rainwater, singer Patsy Cline, and nationally established stars like fiddler Bob Wills, singer-guitarists Lefty Frizzell and Ernest Tubb and all of the stars of "The Grand Ole Opry" that passed through town.

In 1956 Dean and his band supplemented their television jobs with appearances at a number of area night clubs including Strick's Restaurant, the Sunnybrook Tavern, the Surf Club, and the 4400 Club. During the summer months they appeared on numerous S.S, Mount Vernon "Moonlight Cruises" where they supported such acts as Bill Monroe and His Bluegrass Boys, Hank Snow and His Rainbow Ranch Boys, the husband-and-wife duo of singer-banjoist Grandpa Jones and fiddler Ramona Jones and singer-guitarist Lefty Frizzell.

That summer Dean replaced lead guitarist Roy Clark with Billy Grammer, and on Tuesday, September 11, 1956 Jimmy Dean and the Texas Wildcats were featured at the Rustic Cabin Restaurant on Bladensburg Road on a rock and roll bill that included Frankie Mayor and His New Yorkers and the Three of Us Trio. The band closed out the year headlining a show of C&W music entitled "Town and Country TV Stars" at the prestigious Casino Royal Theatre Restaurant in Washington, D.C. The program ran from Monday, December 17 to Sunday, December 23, 1956 and also included singer Patsy Cline and singer-guitarist George Hamilton IV, both of whom were backed by Dean and the Texas Wildcats.

In December 1956 one of the premier Downtown night clubs in Washington, D.C., the Wayne Room, closed its doors on H Street NW. After a change in ownership it reappeared a month later as a C&W night club called the Hayloft. On Monday, January 14, 1957 the Hayloft opened to a packed house with a bill featuring Jimmy Dean and the Texas Wildcats, Bobby Stephenson and His Hayloft Boys and steel guitarist Bud Isaacs. Dean's band worked the Hayloft for seven consecutive nights before opting to concentrate on their radio and television performances for the remainder of the year. The Hayloft, despite their successful opening week, was converted into a rock and roll night club a mere month after its opening, and eventually became one of the city's most popular night spots.

Jimmy Dean went over so well on the televised programs "Town and Country Time" and "Town and Country Jamboree" he was selected by WTOP-TV (Channel 9) to host his own 45-minute musical variety show, appropriately entitled "The Jimmy Dean Show," which aired on various days at various times from Monday April 8, 1957 to Saturday, August 30, 1958. The debut episode of this program featured the Texas Wildcats as the house band, along with pop singer Jan Crockett, the Country Lads, ventriloquist Alex Houston, rockabilly singer-guitarist Wanda Jackson, and C&W singer-guitarist George Hamilton IV.

The local success of the program led to CBS offering Dean a New York-based, nationally syndicated television 30-minute show, also entitled "The Jimmy Dean Show," which aired from Monday to Saturday afternoons at 2pm from Monday, September 15,

1958 to Wednesday, June 24, 1959 (in the Washington, D.C. area, this program aired on WTOP-TV, Channel 9).

Of note is that despite Dean's life in the Big Apple, he reportedly kept an apartment at the Gregory Estates Apartments in Seat Pleasant, Maryland from 1959 to 1961, utilizing it when he had business in the nation's capital. During his visits back to the Washington, D.C. area, many musicians recall seeing Dean trudging along the roadside back to this apartment in the wee hours after a night of drinking and informal singing and playing at the nearby Palmer Restaurant (which is still standing today at 7222 Martin Luther King Junior Highway, Landover, MD).

During his career Jimmy Dean recorded more than 30 studio albums and 30 singles for over a dozen different record labels, large and small. He scored with a number of C&W hits for Mercury, Columbia, and RCA including the single "Big Bad John" which was released on Columbia Records in September 1961 and reached number one on Billboard Music Week's "Hot 100" pop music chart on Monday, November 6, 1961. This popular tune, the B-side of which was "I Won't Go Hunting With You Jake," remained in that chart's top slot for five weeks and ultimately sold over six million copies. The song also went to number one in Billboard Music Week's "Easy Listening" and "Hot C&W Sides" charts.

With the success of "Big Bad John" and other well-received singles and albums, Dean was recruited by a major television network to host yet another nationwide version of "The Jimmy Dean Show." This time his one-hour program aired weekly on Thursday nights on ABC, and lasted for three full seasons from Thursday, September 19, 1963 to Friday, April 1, 1966 (locally, the program aired on WMAL-TV, Channel 7). He went on to perform his music in concert halls all over the country and regularly headlined "The Grand Ole Opry."

Dean became a C&W music icon and starred in a number of television programs such as "Daniel Boone" (1967-1970) and movies such as "Diamonds Are Forever" (United Artists, 1971), where he played the role of reclusive billionaire Willard Whyte. In 1969 he and his brother Don formed the Jimmy Dean Meat Company, which became world-renowned for its pure pork sausages. In 1991 Dean divorced his first wife and married singer-songwriter Donna Meade. He was inducted into the Country Music Hall of Fame on Tuesday, February 23, 2010. Jimmy Dean passed away in Varina, Virginia on Sunday, June 13, 2010 at the age of 81.

CHAPTER FIFTY-TWO
BUZZ BUSBY

The extraordinary singer-guitarist-mandolinist Buzz Busby was born and raised in the rolling farmlands of Northern Louisiana, but as a young adult in the 1950s moved to the Washington, D.C. area where he ultimately became a legendary figure in the field of traditional bluegrass music. Offering a unique repertoire of original songs that combined spirited instrumental performance with heartfelt vocals, Busby created bluegrass-flavored musical portraits of his personal experiences, many of which illustrated the trials and tribulations he endured in his walk through life. To the present day, Busby is recognized as the Father of Bluegrass in the nation's capital. He was an iconic and somewhat tragic figure who possessed musical genius, but struggled with a legion of personal demons that prevented him from capitalizing on the adulation he received from fans and fellow musicians alike.

Buzz Busby was born Bernarr Busbice on Wednesday, September 6, 1933 on a farm in Eros, Louisiana, not far from the city of Monroe. The youngest boy of nine children, he grew up listening to country music stars of the era like Webb Pierce, Bob Wills, Roy Acuff and Bill Monroe on radio shows broadcasted over local stations, including "The Grand Ole Opry." He took up guitar at age eight and learned chords from his brothers Wayne and LeMoyne. By the age of 14 he was proficient on the mandolin and fiddle and was working bars, night clubs, dances and church functions in and around Monroe with his older brother Wayne and pickup bands mainly comprised of various family members. After graduating from high school at age 17, he took a job with the FBI as a fingerprint technician and moved to Washington, D.C.

When Busby arrived in the nation's capital in the summer of 1951 he first frequented a C&W night club called the Rendezvous on 10th Street NW and struck up a friendship with Frank Dunsmore, a mandolinist who was working in the bar. The pair, along with two other fellows, began renting a house on 10th Street SE, not far from the Marine Barracks, Washington, D.C. The four had a penchant for partying and were soon evicted from the premises, with Busby living for a very short time in a house on 17th Street NW, near the White House.

In the fall of 1951 Frank Dunsmore found a house just over the District line on 58th Avenue in Hillside, Maryland, a couple blocks away from bustling Marlboro Pike (this particular house is still standing and today is marked 1111 Mentor Avenue, Capitol Heights, Maryland). Busby moved into Dunsmore's new abode and began frequenting the various C&W bars that lined the Pike and also made it a point to check out other similar establishments throughout the Washington, D.C. area. During this time it was at one of these night clubs, the Shamrock Restaurant in Georgetown, where he met a young fiddler named Scotty Stoneman who lived in Carmody Hills, Maryland, not far from Hillside.

Busby discovered a bar situated just off of Marlboro Pike in Hillside called the Campus Club and during the summer months of 1951 would go there to watch a couple of spellbinding C&W guitarists named Roy Clark and Carl Lukat perform a wide range of pop and country tunes. The Campus Club was a very rough dive that catered to motorcycle riders – the original D.C. Ramblers had made it their unofficial home base – and brutal fights were a regular occurrence. Musicians, however, were basically viewed as untouchable by the bar's patrons. Busby would frequently take his mandolin to the club and sit in with Clark and Lukat whenever he could. That summer when Lukat was inducted into the United States Army and Clark moved on to other engagements, owner Vernon "Jack" Biedler asked Busby to form a group and take over house band duties.

During this time Busby had been venturing out to the Shamrock Restaurant with Frank Dunsmore to see Pop and Scotty Stoneman perform. On one occasion Scotty asked Busby to join a new bluegrass trio he was forming with guitarist Jack Clement (who would later move to Nashville and become a highly regarded producer) that he wanted to call the Tennessee Troopers. Busby agreed and made arrangements for this new band to begin working the Campus Club several times a week, an engagement that would last on-and-off for approximately two years.

Busby resigned from his FBI post in the summer of 1952 to pursue music on a full-time basis. The Tennessee Troopers, in addition to their steady job at the Campus Club, worked throughout the early 1950s at such local night clubs as Mike Young's Café, Chubby's Restaurant and Bar, Armstrong's, the Victory Grill, the Stage Coach Tavern, the Jo Del Bar and Grill, the Casablanca, the Famous Restaurant, the Rendezvous, the Shamrock Restaurant and the Charles Hotel down in Hughesville, Maryland. It was during these years that Busby perfected his bluegrass style of playing and word spread of his unique vocal delivery and prowess on the mandolin.

In January 1953 Busby married a woman from Carmody Hills, Maryland named Patricia Padgett and for most of the following two years they lived in various residences in Riverdale, Maryland (the marriage lasted until 1961 and produced two children). In the summer of 1953 Vernon Biedler told Jack Clement he would be retained as the house band leader, but vanquished Busby and Scotty Stoneman from the premises, allegedly because he discovered that both musicians were under the age of 21. Undaunted, the pair immediately trekked over to the Kit-Mar Restaurant on upper 14th Street NW, across from the Joe Turner Arena, where they secured positions with Mac Wiseman, who labeled his backup band the Country Boys (banjoist Wayne Brown rounded out the new quartet). The Kit-Mar Restaurant engagement soon came to an end and the band began performing daily at Johnny's Used Cars in Baltimore, Maryland and made regular live appearances on the "WRVA Old Dominion Barn Dance," a Saturday night radio show broadcast from the WRVA Theatre in Richmond, Virginia.

Late in 1953 Busby left Wiseman's outfit and reunited with Jack Clement. They relocated to Wheeling, West Virginia where they performed on the "The World's Original WWVA Jamboree" live radio program for several months and also worked as backing musicians for singer-guitarist Hawkshaw Hawkins on appearances throughout the region.

During the winter of 1953-1954, Busby, along with Jack Clement and Scotty Stoneman, packed up and followed Hawkins' manager Aubrey Mayhugh to Boston, Massachusetts, where they regularly performed on "The WCOP Hayloft Jamboree," a live music radio program. They also worked shows in the Boston area at such venues as Symphony Hall, John Hancock Hall and the King Philip Ballroom. Despite the steady work, the frigid seasonal weather caused them to make their stay a short one.

In the spring of 1954 Busby got together with guitarist Pete Pike, who had been working the Pine Tavern on Massachusetts Avenue NW with bassist Herschel G. "Curly" Irvin and his son, banjoist Jesse Smith "Smitty" Irvin, both of whom were transplants from Shelby, North Carolina. Simply billed as either Pete Pike and His Band or Pete Pike and His Pine Tavern Boys, the group saw several musicians come and go, but when Buzz Busby arrived on the scene he decided to stay for a while. Over the summer months the lineup continued to change, with the Irvins departing, and Busby and Pike eventually being joined by banjoist Don Bryant, fiddler John Hall and bassist Lee Cole. Busby eventually took over the reins of the outfit and renamed the band Buzz Busby and the Bayou Boys.

On Saturday, August 7 and Sunday, August 8, 1954 the Bayou Boys appeared as a quartet in the Connie B. Gay-promoted "National Championship Country Music Contest" in Warrenton, Virginia (Pete Pike did not participate in these events) and walked away with a

"National Champion" award in the "Best Band" competition. Three other band members also finished as second place winners in their respective contests: John Hall in the "Best Fiddler" category (first place was a tie between Scotty Stoneman and Chubby Wise); Don Bryant in the "Best Banjo" category (first place went to Roy Clark); and Buzz Busby himself in the "Best Vocal" category (first place went to Slim Morrison).

In the wake of this success, Buzz Busby and the Bayou Boys were recruited out of the Pine Tavern to star in a new, 30-minute bluegrass music television show entitled "Hayloft Hoedown" which aired on weekdays at 2pm on WNBW-TV (Channel 4). The show was produced by Carl Dagan and hosted by local radio-television personality Mike Hunnicutt. The band now consisted of Busby, Pike, Cole (who was eventually replaced by bassist Buck Austin), Hall, and newcomer Don Stover, who replaced Don Bryant on banjo.

One of the show's features was a musical comedy sketch featuring Ham and Scram, two barnyard characters portrayed by Busby and Pike who simultaneously delighted and dazzled their audiences with their corny jokes and masterful string music. "Hayloft Hoedown" aired from Monday, September 13, 1954 to Friday, March 4, 1955, and, despite its reported success, eventually met its downfall due to the disinterest of several of its prominent sponsors and salary disputes amongst almost everyone involved in its operation.

Buzz Busby and the Bayou Boys continued to make music throughout the late 1950s. Musicians came and went, with singer-guitarist Charlie Waller replacing Pete Pike and bassist Vance Truell replacing Lee Cole. Other musicians to pass through the group included banjoists Smiley Hobbs and Bill Emerson, banjoist-bassist Pete Kuykendall and fiddler Carl Nelson. The band left the Washington, D.C. area and performed on the Louisiana Hayride – the live C&W music show broadcast over radio station KWKH from the Municipal Auditorium in Shreveport – for most of 1955 and supported singer-guitarist George Jones on package show tours throughout the Deep South. Later, from 1956 to 1958, the band was back in the Washington, D.C. area and performed daily segments on radio station WARL in Alexandria.

During these years Busby and his wife had moved from Riverdale, Maryland to Greenbelt, Maryland, where they passed through two residences, 30-A Crescent Road and 10-F Southway. In late 1958 they moved into a house at 6302 41st Place in Riverdale, Maryland. Busby began working with different musicians on the side and his music was regularly featured on area radio stations such as WINX, WGAY and WARL. He rounded out the decade playing rock and roll and C&W music with Pete Pike at Rose's Musical Bar in North Beach and the Dock in Leonardtown, Maryland, and appearing with fiddler Paul Justis at the Harvard Grill on upper 14th Street NW in Washington, D.C.

During the late 1950s Busby began participating in recording sessions at Ben Adelman's Empire Records and Recording Studios in the Takoma neighborhood of Washington, D.C. Busby had previously issued 45 rpm single records on different independent labels, including one he and his band did in Louisiana that consisted of "Lost," backed with "Just Me and the Juke Box" (Buzz Busby and His Bayou Boys; Jiffy Records, 1955). The material he recorded for Adelman spanned many years from the late 1950s to the early 1960s, with much of it being leased out to Starday Records, which then went about issuing various songs as 45rpm single records.

Some of the more highly regarded of these singles include: "Talking Banjo," backed with "Lonesome Road" (Buzz Busby and the Bayou Boys; Starday Records, 1958); "Lonesome Wind," backed with "Lost" (Buzz Busby and the Bayou Boys; Starday Records, 1958); and "Don't Come Runnin' Back To Me," backed with "Cold and Windy Night" (Buzz Busby; Starday Records, 1960).

Other recordings Busby made for Adelman resulted in singles for artists such as Bill Harrell and the Virginians, Bill Emerson and John Hall, singer-guitarist Luke Gordon, and his brother Wayne Busbice, who also released singles under the name Wayne Busby. One curiosity to appear from the Adelman master tapes was an album that featured the duo of Pete Pike and Buzz Busby entitled "Country Comedy – Songs & Frolic by Ham & Scram Featuring Buzz Busby" which was recorded in 1954, but issued in 1963 on the Mount Vernon Music label.

Busby spent much of the 1960s traveling back and forth between Louisiana, Arkansas and Washington, D.C. and supported himself by working a variety of odd jobs. During this decade he lived in three different apartments in Takoma Park, Maryland, and worked on-and-off as a truck driver for Ben Adelman's B&F Record Distributing Company. In 1969 Busby moved into a house at 7209 Dartmouth Avenue in College Park, Maryland. He remained there for more than 14 years during which time he supported himself as a service station attendant at a nearby Homoco Gas Station on Route One.

Despite the tough breaks he endured, Busby continued to play music during his years in College Park, most notably with Leon Morris in the early 1970s and the Johnson Mountain Boys later in that decade. In 1978 and 1979 he was a regular performer with his own band at Bambino's, a pizza restaurant on Kenilworth Avenue in Riverdale, Maryland (which in the 1980s would go through many incarnations including a stint as a rock and roll night club called the Riverside Inn).

Though Busby never scored a major hit song or reached the Billboard magazine charts during his career, he released singles and albums on a number of different record labels including Rebel, World Music, Jessup, Webco, Rounder and Patuxent Partners. In the middle 1980s Busby entered into a self-imposed retirement, dealing with Parkinson's disease and a deteriorating heart condition that caused him to move into a nursing home facility. In his later years he could only perform sporadically with his brothers at area bluegrass festivals and special events. He died of heart failure on Sunday, January 5, 2003 at the age of 69.

CHAPTER FIFTY-THREE
BILL HARRELL

With a career that spanned several decades, singer-guitarist Bill Harrell is one of the most popular figures in bluegrass music. Known for his easy-going, traditional approach to music, Harrell was responsible for spreading bluegrass to a wide audience in the nation's capital and across the United States. He got his start in music while living in the Washington, D.C. area in the 1950s, and was known for fronting his own band, Bill Harrell and the Virginians, and for playing in the nationally acclaimed outfit Don Reno and Bill Harrell and the Tennessee Cutups. In his time, Harrell was a featured performer at night clubs, concerts and festivals all over the country and remains a revered figure in bluegrass music.

George William "Bill" Harrell was born in Marion, Virginia on Friday, September 14, 1934 and received his first guitar at the age of nine. As a youth he took piano lessons and learned to read music. While still a youngster, Harrell's family relocated to the Washington, D.C. area and bought a house at 5408 Riverdale Road in Riverdale, Maryland.

Harrell graduated from Bladensburg High School in 1952 and then enrolled at the University of Maryland. During his college years he played guitar and mandolin in local bluegrass night clubs like the Pine Tavern and the Shamrock Restaurant with such local musicians as mandolinist Smiley Hobbs, fiddler Carl Nelson, bassist Roy Self, and banjoists Eddie Adcock, Smitty Irvin and Donny Bryant.

In the 1950s Harrell began putting together his own bands. In the middle part of the decade he led an outfit he called Bill Harrell and the Rocky Mountain Boys. In 1957 he joined the United States Army, but was sidelined for a year after being involved in an automobile accident. Upon his discharge in 1959, he returned to the Washington, D.C. area and formed another band, Bill Harrell and His Virginia Mountaineers, which included Harrell on lead guitar, singer-rhythm guitarist Buzz Busby, banjoist Bill Emerson, fiddler Carl Nelson and bassist Roy Self. Often joining this group were fiddler Scotty Stoneman and mandolinist Smiley Hobbs. This group conducted several recording sessions for Ben Adelman at his Empire Records and Recording Studios in Washington, D.C., with several of the resulting songs being released as 45rpm single records on Starday Records.

In 1960 Harrell put together the first edition of Bill Harrell and the Virginians, whose lineup was rounded out by banjoist Smitty Irvin, fiddler Buck Ryan and bassist Stoney Edwards. They soon recorded and released their first album, "The Wonderful World of Bluegrass Music" (Bill Harrell and the Virginians; United Artist Records, 1963). During the early 1960s they performed regularly in Washington, D.C. at the Famous Restaurant and the Shamrock Restaurant. In 1965 Smitty Irvin was replaced by banjoist Don Stover. The band went on to headline concerts, fairs and festivals up and down the Atlantic Coast, in addition to performing regularly on "The Jimmy Dean Show" television program.

Through the years Bill Harrell and the Virginians have gone through several personnel changes and have recorded and released more than a dozen albums on such record labels as United Artists, Adelphi, Rebel, and Leather. Despite a few breaks in the action, Bill Harrell and the Virginians continued to perform and record into the 21st century.

In 1963, while keeping up with his own band the Virginians, Harrell began performing with banjoist Don Reno in a group billed as Don Reno, Bill Harrell and the Tennessee Cutups. Don Reno was born in Buffalo, South Carolina on Monday, February 21, 1927 and was raised in Haywood County, North Carolina. In 1939 he joined a bluegrass band known as the Morris Brothers and in the ensuing years performed with guitarist Arthur Smith and a group called the Bluegrass Boys. Throughout the 1950s and into the early 1960s he led a band with Red Smiley called Reno and Smiley and the Tennessee Cutups.

Bill Harrell got the call to replace Smiley in Reno's outfit and in 1963 they recorded and released their first album, "The King of Bluegrass" (Don Reno/Bill Harrell and the Tennessee Cut-Ups; Derbytown Records, 1963). The group headlined fairs, carnivals and bluegrass music festivals all over the United States. In 1967 Don Reno moved to Riverdale, Maryland and for several years during the late 1960s and early 1970s Don Reno, Bill Harrell and the Tennessee Cutups performed on a regular Friday-night basis at the Oxon Hill Volunteer Fire Department in Southern Prince George's County, Maryland.

Reno and Harrell remained musical partners into the late 1970s. Through the years they released more than two-dozen albums on such record labels as Derbytown, King, Starday, Viechi, Monument, Gusto, Rebel, Wango, London, Jalyn, King Bluegrass, Atteiram, Rural Rhythm Classic and CMH.

In early 1977 Bill Harrell and the Virginians reformed with a lineup of singer-guitarist Bill Harrell, bassist Ed Ferris, fiddler Carl Nelson and banjoist Darrell Sanders. They concentrated on playing two particular venues in the Washington, D.C. area – DiGennaro's Restaurant in Laurel, Maryland, where they performed on a weekly basis from 1977 to 1980, and Bambino's Restaurant in Riverdale, Maryland, where they were a regular attraction from 1978 to 1981. Under the name of Bill Harrell and the Virginians, this group recorded and released the album "Bluegrass and Ballads" (Bill Harrell and the Virginians; Adelphi Records, 1978).

In 1979 mandolinist Larry Stephenson joined the group, but soon left to join the Bluegrass Cardinals. Mandolinist Paul Atkins performed with the band in the middle 1980s, but eventually departed to form the Borderline Band. Ferris and Sanders left the group in the late 1980s with bassist Billy Budd and banjoist Bob Lundy taking their places. Despite these and other changes in personnel, Bill Harrell and the Virginians remained one of the world's most highly acclaimed bluegrass bands and continued to perform and record into the 21st century. Bill Harrell passed away on Tuesday, June 4, 2009 at the age of 74.

CHAPTER FIFTY-FOUR
PATSY CLINE

Patsy Cline rates as one of the greatest female C&W singers of all time. Although reared in a number of locations throughout the state of Virginia, she spent the 1950s perfecting her stage demeanor and vocal delivery in venues throughout the Washington, D.C. area. It was here in what was then a burgeoning C&W music scene that she made the successful transformation from promising cowgirl singer to nationally recognized performing artist.

Patsy Cline was born Virginia Patterson Hensley on Thursday, September 8, 1932 in Winchester Memorial Hospital in Winchester, Virginia. At the time of her birth her family was residing in Gore, an unincorporated town in the western section of Frederick County, Virginia some 10 miles northwest of Winchester. Shortly after her birth the Hensley family moved to the town of Elkton in Rockingham County, some 100 miles to the south. The Hensley family remained in Elkton for approximately four years and then embarked on a series of moves around the state. Over the next 10 years the future superstar singer lived in a variety of cities and towns including Grottoes, Lexington, Winchester, Portsmouth, Edinburg, Middletown and Round Hill.

In 1947 the Hensley family was back in Gore, and when Hensley dropped out of Gore High School in November 1948 her formal schooling came to an end. That same month her family moved to 608 South Kent Street in Winchester and she took a job in town as a cook and waitress at a restaurant called the Snack Bar, working there from 1949 to June 1950. After leaving the Snack Bar she immediately began working as a soda fountain service attendant at Gaunt's Drugstore, a tenure that lasted until June 1952. She was not destined to work in the food service industry for long.

Upon her move to Winchester, Hensley began singing along to the broadcasts of local radio station WINC, which specialized in general pop music, but also included a Saturday hillbilly music program on its schedule. She approached WINC disc jockey-bandleader "Joltin'" Jim Coy and was allowed to sing on-air with his band, the Melody Playboys, on numerous occasions.

From September 1949 to November 1950 Hensley entered amateur shows emceed by local bandleader Jack Fretwell at the Palace Theatre, singing songs by the likes of Al Jolson, Jo Stafford and Margaret Whiting. She also periodically performed in assemblies and shows at John Handley High School and the Kiwanis Club of Winchester.

In 1951 Hensley joined Jack Fretwell's Orchestra as a lead singer and for the next year performed with the band at such Virginia venues as the John Marshall Inn (Front Royal), York's Inn (Winchester) and the Eagles' Club of Winchester. Throughout 1951 and 1952, while still a Winchester resident, she also worked a variety of pickup gigs in the area from Winchester north to Jefferson County, West Virginia. These jobs included dates at country clubs, carnivals and church functions with pianist William "Jumbo" Rinker. She also took bookings with Sonny Frye and the Playboys at a night club south of Winchester called the Rainbow Inn and one in Ridgeway, West Virginia called Chuck and Ray's Western Club.

In September 1952 Hensley became the lead singer of a C&W band called Bill Peer and His Melody Boys. The group's leader, guitarist Clarence William "Bill" Peer, lived in Charles Town, West Virginia where he was employed during the weekdays as a Buick salesman for the Goode Motor Company. During the weeknights and weekends he worked as a country music disc jockey on radio station WEPM in nearby Martinsburg. In 1941 he formed a band which was initially called the Melody Boys and Girls. The group regularly performed live on his Saturday morning radio show which was entitled "Bill's Melody Time."

With Hensley on board as the main vocalist, Bill Peer and His Melody Boys, who specialized in the songs of Hank Williams, spent most of the next two years performing in Maryland at the Loyal Order of Moose Brunswick Lodge No. 1582 in Frederick County, the Loyal Order of Moose Hagerstown Lodge No. 212, the CIO Union Club in Hagerstown, and carnivals in the towns of Middletown, Woodsboro and Clear Spring. When Hensley married a man named Gerald Cline on Saturday, March 7, 1953 in Frederick, Maryland, she assumed his last name and from that point on became known as Patsy Cline in both her personal and professional lives.

The career of Patsy Cline took an upward swing when she met C&W promoter Connie B. Gay in 1954. Most accounts state that Gay saw Cline competing in "The National Championship Country Music Contest" in Warrenton, Virginia in August 1954, an event promoted by Gay himself and sponsored by the Warrenton Junior Chamber of Commerce and the Association for Greater Warrenton.

Despite information provided in her later published biographies, Cline never actually won any awards in the 1954 contest, though one must assume her performances left indelible impressions on Gay, the Washington, D.C. area's premier C&W music entrepreneur. Throughout the fall of 1954 Connie B. Gay booked Bill Peer and His Melody Boys (featuring Patsy Cline) into Washington, D.C. night clubs for the first time at such establishments as the Covered Wagon Restaurant, the Starlite Restaurant and the Famous Restaurant. During this time Cline also became a regularly featured singer on Gay's "Town and Country Time" radio show on station WARL in Arlington, Virginia.

On Thursday, September 30, 1954 Patsy Cline signed a multi-year contract with Bill McCall's 4 Star Records of Pasadena, California. The details of how she became involved with McCall in the first place are still shrouded in mystery, as it has been reported that in August and September of that year Cline had been unsuccessfully courted by local music producer and DC Records proprietor Lillian Claiborne, and had also reportedly been recruited by Ben Adelman to record a dozen different songs at this Truetone Recording Company in Washington, D.C. However, neither Claiborne nor Adelman appeared to actually have Cline under any type of management contract, though it has been reported that Adelman supplied McCall with several Cline demos, along with information on her availability as a recording artist. Curiously, the recordings Cline allegedly made for Adelman in the late summer of 1954 have never surfaced.

Bill McCall had Cline record four songs under producer Owen Bradley at his Bradley Film and Recording Studios in Nashville, Tennessee on Wednesday, June 1, 1955. He then leased the songs out to Decca Records, which released them as two separate 45rpm single records on their subsidiary label, Coral Records. The first of these, "A Church, A Courtroom, Then Goodbye," backed with "Honky Tonk Merry Go Round" (Patsy Cline; Coral Records, 1955) was released on Wednesday, July 20 of that year. The second, "Hidin' Out," backed with "Turn the Cards Slowly" (Patsy Cline; Coral Records, 1955) was released a few months later on Saturday, November 5. These singles, along with others by Cline that appeared on Coral Records in the late 1950s, failed to reach the Billboard charts. When her contract with 4 Star Records expired in 1960 she signed with Decca Records, which remained her primary record company for the duration of her career. When Decca was purchased by MCA in 1962, the Cline masters were part of the deal.

Patsy Cline's popularity greatly increased in the Washington, D.C. area during the late 1950s. She was a regular performer on the two WMAL-TV (Channel 7) live music broadcasts, "Town and Country Time" and "Town and Country Jamboree." She appeared with Bill Peer and His Melody Boys every Sunday in 1955 from March 6 to September 11 at Strick's Restaurant in Silver Hill, Maryland and spent many weekend nights that year singing with the band at the Oxon Hill Volunteer Fire Department. Cline split with Peer in September 1955 and struck out on her own as a solo headliner.

From Monday, December 17 to Sunday, December 23, 1956 Patsy Cline co-headlined a triple bill at the Casino Royal Theatre Restaurant in Washington, D.C. with singer-guitarist George Hamilton IV and Jimmy Dean and the Texas Wildcats. Throughout the latter half of the decade some of the other local night clubs and venues she performed in were the Famous Restaurant, the Dixie Pig, the Surf Club, the Senate Inn, the Sunnybrook Tavern and Glen Echo Park's Spanish Ballroom.

On Monday, January 21, 1957 Cline made an appearance on the nationally syndicated television show "Arthur Godfrey's Talent Scouts" and walked away as the show's winner after a stirring performance of the song "Walking After Midnight." In the aftermath of that appearance her national reputation soared and she was headed for stardom in the pop and C&W music fields.

Cline divorced her first husband and in September 1957 remarried a man named Charles Dick and moved to Fayetteville, North Carolina. In 1960 the couple relocated to Nashville, Tennessee and their union produced two children, Julia Dick and Randy Dick. Cline maintained her professional career and headlined venues across the United States (including "The Grand Ole Opry") and overseas. She racked up several hit songs for Decca Records, including: "Walking After Midnight," which peaked at number three on Saturday, April 20, 1957 in the Billboard magazine's "C&W Best Sellers in Stores" chart; "I Fall to Pieces," which went to number one on Monday, August 7, 1961 in Billboard Music Week's "Hot C&W Sides" chart; "Crazy," which peaked at number two on Saturday, January 20, 1962 in Billboard Music Week's "Hot C&W Sides" chart; and "She's Got You," which reached number one on Saturday, March 31, 1962 in Billboard Music Week's "Hot C&W Sides" chart.

On Sunday, March 3, 1963 Patsy Cline performed at a benefit at the Soldiers and Sailors Memorial Hall in Kansas City, Kansas. Two days later on the evening of Tuesday, March 5 she died in a plane crash near Camden, Tennessee along with her manager Randy Hughes (who piloted the plane) and fellow C&W music stars Cowboy Copas and Hawkshaw Hawkins. She was 30 years old at the time of her passing. In 1973 Patsy Cline became the first female solo artist inducted into the Country Music Hall of Fame.

CHAPTER FIFTY-FIVE
COFFEE, CONFUSION AND THE BEATNIKS OF WASHINGTON

The Beat Generation emerged in the 1950s as a bohemian-fueled movement of visionary literary heroes, passionate poets and colorful, off-beat characters whose very lives were driven by an emotional quest for experience and an insatiable thirst for spontaneous poetry, unrestrained sex, bebop jazz, marijuana (which they called "tea"), impulsive travel and esoteric philosophy. Two main camps of the Beat Generation emerged in the United States as their presence permeated mainstream American culture: a New York contingency comprised of such luminaries as Jack Kerouac, John Clellon Holmes, William Burroughs, Gregory Corso, Allen Ginsberg and Herbert Huncke; and a West Coast faction whose ranks included Lawrence Ferlinghetti, Michael McClure, Gary Snyder, Philip Whalen and Lew Welch.

The creative power of these literary pioneers inspired devoted followings of like-minded writers and artists in hip coffee houses across the nation, with a particularly intense scene materializing in Washington, D.C., where a basement venue known as Coffee 'n' Confusion became an early focal point for the city's "beatnik" contingency. This particular establishment is remembered today for also having been the site of the very first public performance of rock and roll legend Jim Morrison, who as a teenager gave an original poetry recital on the coffee house's cramped, makeshift stage. Morrison later became an icon for his role as lead singer for the rock and roll band the Doors.

The term "Beat Generation" was first coined by Jack Kerouac during a conversation he had with fellow writer John Clellon Holmes in 1948 where he used those words to describe the writers and poets that comprised a developing literary circle in New York City. While it was Kerouac himself who initially used the term "beat" in his debut novel "The Town and the City" (1950) – he alludes to a woman named Liz wandering "beat" around New York City – it was Holmes who completed the exercise and wrote extensively of the Beat Generation – a collection of writers, artists, drug-users, hustlers, thieves and down-and-out philosophers – in his New York-based novel "Go" (1952). (In this thinly disguised autobiographical account, Homes wrote of himself as "Paul Hobbes," Jack Kerouac appeared as main character "Gene Pasternak" and Allen Ginsberg was brought to life as "David Stofsky.")

Holmes later authored an essay entitled "This is the Beat Generation" which appeared in the New York Times Magazine on Sunday, November 16, 1952 that attempted to define the very essence of the young people of the movement. He wrote that those of the Beat Generation harbored more than just weariness, but carried raw feelings of being used and endured a nakedness of mind and soul. Jack Kerouac countered in interviews by explaining that "beat" really meant "beatific" or "sacred," and many interpreted his works as exercises in capturing the holiness of the downtrodden.

While Jack Kerouac's first novel "The Town and the City" was not widely read, his second effort in 1957, "On the Road," was credited for announcing, in effect, a new consciousness. It was a major event in the annals of Beat Generation literature and fostered a special magic with its undirected raw energy, prose-poetry and larger-than-life protagonists "Sal Paradise" (Jack Kerouac himself) and "Dean Moriarty" (Neal Cassady – a major prototype hipster figure in both the Beat Generation culture of the 1950s and the hippie movement of the 1960s), who zoomed back-and-forth across the country in search of thrills and experiences.

As Beat Generation consciousness expanded during the late 1950s, San Francisco Chronicle reporter Herb Caen noted in his "Pocketful of Notes" column of Wednesday, April 2, 1958 that Look magazine had hosted a party in a North Beach house for 50 "beatniks" in preparation for a forthcoming article on the subject. It marked the first time the term "beatnik" had ever appeared in print and it quickly became the moniker bestowed upon those who ingratiated themselves into the Beat Generation world. The beatnik image was shaped by a wave of books and articles that projected images of shaggy, bearded, beret-topped, bongo-playing, marijuana-smoking men and sullen, straight-haired, black-dressed women.

The beatniks were already firmly established as staples of popular culture when the family of George S. Morrison relocated from Alameda, California to Alexandria, Virginia in January 1959. Morrison, a freshly promoted Captain in the United States Navy, had just landed a new assignment at the Pentagon in Arlington County and rented a home for his wife and three children in a quiet, upper class neighborhood named Jefferson Park.

The Captain's son, Jim Morrison, was 15 years old at the time of their arrival in Alexandria and enrolled as a sophomore at George Washington High School in the middle of the year. Even at that young age the future lead singer of the Doors reportedly found the literature and poetry of the Beats mesmerizing and strongly identified with their uninhibited attitudes, unbridled creativity, and underground lifestyles, as well perhaps with their poetry and spirituality. Though just a teenager, he was known to actively explore the coffee houses and bohemian-flavored night clubs of Washington, D.C. where he soaked up the local Beat culture whenever time allowed.

It is known that during his three-year stay in Alexandria, Jim Morrison's private library included the novel "Go" (1952) by John Clellon Holmes, and the Jack Kerouac novels "The Town and the City" (1950), "On the Road" (1957), "The Dharma Bums" (1958), "The Subterraneans" (1958) and "Doctor Sax" (1959). He also owned editions of "Howl and Other Poems" (1956) by Allen Ginsberg, "A Coney Island of the Mind" (1958) by Lawrence Ferlinghetti, "Gasoline" (1958) by Gregory Corso and "Naked Lunch" (1959) by William Burroughs.

It should be noted that bohemians, loosely defined as individuals with literary or artistic interests who live untroubled by middle-class social standards, had an established history in the nation's capital well before Jim Morrison landed in the area. Many veterans of Washington, D.C.'s counterculture maintain to this day that the spiritual ancestors of the beatniks of the nation's capital were a somewhat ephemeral and now largely forgotten congregation of remarkable Georgetown artists, writers and poets that had once inhabited a small, refuge-like compound known as Hamilton Arms.

Predating the Beat Generation movement by almost two decades, Hamilton Arms came into existence in 1939 when 58-year-old Lieutenant Colonel Milo Hamilton Brinkley purchased a small collection of old ivy-covered houses on 31st Street NW, quietly nestled between M and N Streets, in the heart of historic Georgetown. He set about refurbishing the neglected collection of structures and molded them into his own little European-flavored village. Feeling the need for a central meeting place to bring his tenants and the neighborhood folk together, he opened the Hamilton Arms Coffee House that year in the village's main structure at 1232 31st Street NW, a building had had been constructed in 1900 and had had previously housed the C&P Telephone Company's West Exchange for many years.

While Mr. Brinkley rented out the pink, yellow and turquoise Swiss village houses, his wife Emma Conger ran the Hamilton Arms Curiosity Shop, his son-in-law Howard Reid managed the coffee house, and daughter Mary "Molly" Brinkley Reid operated the Pottery while acting as artist-in-residence – she reportedly spent her days painting, designing and decorating the property's various rooms, gardens and buildings.

Hamilton Arms was basically a series of rental units, but offered living and working space for unique, creative individuals and soon developed into a little bohemian enclave tucked away within the brick-lined streets of residential Georgetown. A walk through the blue iron gate alongside the coffee house revealed a long, covered grape arbor, a myriad of beautifully landscaped gardens, a tile house and kiln, 30 apartment units fashioned from a former slave compound, balconies covered in ivy and a small rectangular swimming pool guarded by the Discus Thrower, a remarkable stone statue of a naked Greek athlete preparing to chuck his sphere. The pool itself, long a village trademark, was the scene of now-famous night-long parties before officials from the city's Health Department, citing the lack of a badly needed filter system, ordered the pool off-limits.

An article in the Washington Post of Monday, May 18, 1953 entitled "Hamilton Arms Folk Lose Swimming Hole in their Garden by City Condemnation Rule" by Warren Unna called the Hamilton Arms village "the Georgetown miniature of La Rive Gauche, Greenwich Village and San Francisco's Telegraph Hill." A resident named Chefik Haddad, former military attaché for Iraq, was quoted in the article as describing the village as "Something between a campus and a village. People are not less conventional here, but what you might call conventional in a different way."

What really made Hamilton Arms unique were the groups of incredible people that set up camp on the grounds of the village. A cast of indefinable characters predating the beatniks made the Hamilton Arms Coffee House their carefree playground. They began infiltrating the grounds, appearing from nowhere for friendly visits in the quaint apartment rooms and throwing wine parties that lasted for days and nights and wound throughout the gardens of the courtyard.

Several years after the Health Department raid, Lieutenant Colonel Brinkley reminisced to local journalists about the once-commonplace midnight raids made by unknown revelers on the notorious swimming pool. More telling, however, was a piece on the heyday of the Hamilton Arms that appeared in the Washington Post on Saturday, March 11, 1978 entitled "Georgetown's Eccentric Landmark" by Jane Ann Spotts that stated: "Residents swear that Georgetown's first 'pot party' took place there in the late 50s, along with several other recreational firsts."

Ultimately, the Hamilton Arms Coffee House closed its doors on Saturday, May 25, 1957, as the Brinkleys felt they could not keep the business alive without selling liquor, a practice forbidden at the time due to the presence of the Fifth Church of Christian Science two doors away. In time, the most of the bohemians that frequented the grounds of the Hamilton Arms scattered to other parts of the city in search of new scenes and the younger ones that remained became absorbed into the burgeoning hippie movement of the 1960s.

Through it all the apartments on the property remained occupied and the Hamilton Arms continued on as a small offbeat residential community until the spring of 1978, at which time the property was sold and the buildings renovated for an influx of various private businesses. Today the compound goes by the official name of Hamilton Court and the building that once housed the Hamilton Arms Coffee House is currently the home of Compass, a technology-driven real estate platform.

Despite the absence of the hip Hamilton Arms Coffee House, the evolving bohemians continued to congregate at different hangouts around the city. A unique event of the region's growing beat subculture in the late 1950s was a happening labeled "The Complimentary Essence in Poetry and Jazz" that took place at one of Washington, D.C.'s more respected establishments. In his "Tips on Tables" column in the Monday, July 28, 1958 edition of the Washington Daily News, Don Hearn wrote: "Tonight the new management of the Hotel 2400 premieres a rather novel – and somewhat fascinating – brand of nitery fare in its Lounge Riviera. T.S. Eliot and modern music. In other words, kiddies, the 'complimentary essence in poetry and jazz.' Tho the idea is nothing new – since it has become and exceedingly popular pastime with certain natives in San Francisco and Manhattan – it is a 'first' for our town. Performing the works of such gentlemen as T.S. Eliot, Robert Frost, Dylan Thomas and Conrad Aiken is youthful actor-poet Dan Cookman. Serving up the progressive background is the Webster Young Quintet, featuring Ben Dixon. (This accomplished crew has gained notable attention with their 'Prestige' platters.) For the records, this unique offering is on tap in the lounge three times nightly: 8:30, 10:30 and again at 12:30. It should be noted, I suppose, in between these avant garde sessions, there is music for dancing should anyone feel the least bit restless."

Details of what exactly transpired at this happening are non-existent, as no follow-up reviews of the performances were ever published in any of the Washington, D.C. area's dailies. While almost nothing is known about Dan Cookman, Webster Young was a popular Washington, D.C.-based jazz trumpeter who at the time of the event was 25 years old and had recorded several albums for Prestige Records – the most notable of which were "Tuba Sounds" (Ray Draper Quintet with Jackie McLean and Mal Waldron introducing Webster Young; Prestige Records, 1957) and "Strange Blues" (Jackie McLean; Prestige Records, 1957). During the late 1950s Young also performed with his own band at the Caverns in the You Street area.

The quintet's drummer, Ben Dixon, was 23 years old at the time of the Hotel 2400's Lounge Riviera event and had worked with Young on the "Tuba Sounds" album and later in the 1960s would appear on numerous albums by such jazz artists as Lou Donaldson, Grant Green, Big John Patton, Jack McDuff, Harold Vick and Baby Face Willette.

Apparently this avant-garde offering was a one-off affair, as in the days following this engagement, the Lounge Riviera brought in pianist Mark Rollins and His Orchestra to provide dance music for its patrons. The pairing of jazz and poetry – both staples in Beat Generation culture – was a new and curious concept for area music fans, but was eventually accepted as a popular practice by the progressive bohemian element that had taken hold in the nation's capital.

Not long after the Hotel 2400's Lounge Riviera poetry-jazz experiment, the more adventurous bohemian spirits of Washington, D.C. found a new sanctuary in a small, eclectic establishment known as Coffee 'n' Confusion. During the spring of 1959 the Beats emerged in Washington, D.C., embracing the writings of Jack Kerouac, John Clellon Holmes and Allen Ginsberg, and searching for places where they could congregate and share their love of art, jazz and poetry. They frequented a select number of gathering spots that accepted their ranks: Harrigan's Restaurant on the waterfront in Southwest Washington, where local artists displayed their paintings on the walls and held court every night in the unusual beer garden that overlooked the Potomac River; Julie's Café on M Street in Georgetown, where a low-key neighborhood watering hole slowly converted into a hip beatnik meeting place; and the Caverns, a legendary jazz basement in the You Street area where a diverse array of music fans could lounge all night. However, it was the introduction of Coffee 'n' Confusion that galvanized the burgeoning contingency of beatniks that had suddenly materialized amidst clouds of marijuana smoke and inspired voices of poetry and free expression.

Coffee 'n' Confusion was the creation of William Addison Walker, a charismatic bearded poet from Pinehurst, North Carolina who went by the name "Bill" and had arrived in Washington during the late 1950s just as Beat consciousness was on the rise. He married a local Vassar graduate named Ruth Murray and enrolled at George Washington University to study creative writing. Walker rented a house in the city at 809 22nd Street NW, which eventually became home for a horde of beatnik allies. Walker was 24 years old when he and his wife opened the first version of Coffee 'n' Confusion on Wednesday, April 1, 1959 at 912 New Hampshire Avenue NW, a smallish ground-floor storefront which had previously housed a grocery store called the Neighborhood Market.

Walker based Coffee 'n' Confusion on the coffee houses of New York City's Greenwich Village and during its first week of operation his establishment served approximately 100 patrons per night, an impressive feat considering they advertised solely through word-of-mouth contacts in the local bohemian community. The beatnik hangout offered coffee, tea, poetry readings, debates, bongos, folk songs, checkers and chess for its colorful clientele of students, poets and musicians. Although Coffee 'n' Confusion hadn't been open long enough to draw serious heat from the local police, Assistant Corporation Counsel Louis P. Robbins happened along one evening and found the coffee house in violation of numerous insignificant zoning laws. He ordered the business closed on Tuesday, April 7, 1959 and a wave of publicity followed the club's shutdown.

Bill Walker searched the city for a new location for his business and eventually found a suitable spot in the basement of the Zantzinger Building (945 K Street NW), a murky, underground space which had previously housed a series of short-lived restaurants. The Zantzinger Building, constructed in 1884 on the northeast corner of 10th and K Streets NW, was a two-story, brick Victorian mansion with wood detail, arched windows, framed balconies and a half-attic on top. It had actually served as a private residence in the Mount Vernon Square neighborhood until real estate mogul Otway Berryman Zantzinger, Sr. came along and purchased the structure in 1925. The property was immediately rezoned and later that year the new owner relocated his private real estate business, the O.B. Zantzinger Company, from 912 10th Street NW to his new K Street headquarters. It was a fascinating section of Downtown, as just around the corner was the seedy 9th Street Bowery and its used book shops, arcades, peep shows, liquor stores and run-down restaurants.

The new basement version of Coffee 'n' Confusion, which could accommodate 75 patrons, operated seven days a week from 8pm to 4am, requested a token donation at the door, and did not serve alcohol. An auspicious grand opening was staged on the night of Saturday, June 6, 1959 that advertised a poetry contest between some local heroes known as the Washington Poets and a squadron of Beats from New York City. Bill Walker addressed the crowd throughout the evening as manager Dick Dabney and other hip poets like Bill Jackson read original works, the titles of which ranged from "The Charlie Starkweather Blues" to "The Stream of Not-So Consciousness."

By the early morning hours Walker was being hailed by his customers as a folk hero in the making – the leader of a new generation committed to self-expression and artistic freedom. The shaggy-haired, goateed and bleary-eyed Walker relished his role as King Hipster and in the days following the impressive debut of his coffee house he told local reporters he didn't really like the term "beatnik" and objected to the way that people in America were slaves to routine. He said he hoped his protest would give other people guts and help them organize their own protests. Exactly what he was protesting, though, was never really made clear.

As Coffee 'n' Confusion simmered as a beatnik hot spot, it fell under intense scrutiny from local law enforcement authorities who seemed anxious to pounce on the club's patrons the moment they emerged from the smoky den and attempted to navigate their way down K Street. After a six-month undercover police investigation, the Narcotics Squad of the District Police, armed with search warrants based on material gathered by rookie policeman Private Jose L. Estrada (who had posed as a drug-buying beatnik), staged sweeping raids on the morning of Friday, April 1, 1960 on both Coffee 'n' Confusion and

Java Jungle, a similar coffee house that had opened in August 1959 at 2119 Pennsylvania Avenue NW.

A total of 12 local beatniks were arrested on drug charges during the two raids, including 24-year-old Java Jungle owner John F. Stevens and 26-year-old Dick Dabney, who had formerly been a manager of Coffee 'n' Confusion. Both were accused of unlawful transfer of marijuana. Stevens pled guilty and was eventually placed on probation, while Dabney was acquitted on grounds of entrapment. The bust sent waves of paranoia through the beatnik scene and was particularly devastating to Java Jungle, as the coffee house never reopened its doors after the unexpected raid.

Bill Walker, reeling after the police intervention, worried that his business would wane as the beatniks were targeted by law enforcement officials as major players in local marijuana distribution rings. Before the month of April was out, 27-year-old Angelo Alvino, a no-nonsense entrepreneur who owned the renowned jazz night club known as the Caverns (later renamed Bohemian Caverns) and had been a fixture on Washington's music scene for many years, made him an offer and came away with 50 per cent ownership of Coffee 'n' Confusion. Alvino wasted little time in augmenting the nights of poetry at the coffee house with late-night jam sessions that brought together some of the city's top folk and jazz musicians. Coffee 'n' Confusion soldiered on under the new part-owner and continued to pull in an eclectic crowd of artists, poets, beatniks and others who defied categorization.

It was said that Angelo Alvino had kept a watchful eye over the patrons of his night clubs and had somehow made the acquaintance of one of his teenaged regulars at Coffee 'n' Confusion – a reserved young man named Jim who in later years would turn out to be a famous rock and roll singer. Long after his reign as a night club owner had ended a number of local musicians pointed out to Alvino that a local fellow named Morrison had gone on to achieve fame and fortune with a rock and roll band called the Doors. When he saw the jacket of the band's first record album, he immediately recognized one of the members as a long-haired version of the teenager he had known only as "Jim." Several of Jim Morrison's friends from George Washington High School have since confirmed that Coffee 'n' Confusion had been one of his favorite haunts.

Reportedly, Jim Morrison, who was a member of George Washington High School's Class of 1961, was slow to get involved in the festivities at Coffee 'n' Confusion and initially seemed to prefer observing what transpired around him. However, in the spring of 1960 towards the end of his junior year of high school, Morrison actually got up onstage and performed at least one poetry recital at Coffee 'n' Confusion, a monumental event that marked the very first time he ever performed in public and shared his written work with a captive audience.

While the actual poem he read that evening has never been conclusively identified, it has been speculated by some in attendance that evening that a version of "Horse Latitudes" may have been the selection. This public recital was testament to how important Morrison felt the coffee house was and how strongly its patrons and their behavior influenced him. Coffee 'n' Confusion was not only the very first place where he ever saw poets in action; it provided the cramped stage where he cut his teeth as a performing artist.

As for Bill Walker, the years following his reign as Washington's top beatnik were difficult ones indeed. He and his wife Ruth gave up on Coffee 'n' Confusion in October 1960 because the Beats were happy to hang out, but reluctant to spend cash. The couple divorced and Bill moved to Paris, France where he became involved with arms traders. He was eventually arrested on gun-smuggling charges in Spain and subsequently spent several years in a Madrid jail. Upon his release he returned to the United States and lived in New York City, but years of alcohol abuse had severely damaged his liver. According to his daughter Brandel France de Bravo, William Addison "Bill" Walker died in June 1974.

The beatnik scene in Washington, D.C. was at its most intense from the inception of Coffee 'n' Confusion in the spring of 1959 until the massive marijuana busts of Friday, April 1, 1960. In the wake of those arrests several spirited entrepreneurs around the city, their eyes focused on the precarious situation surrounding Coffee 'n' Confusion and beatnik leader Bill Walker, quietly formulated plans to open similar coffee house establishments in hopes of attracting some of the beatnik clientele that was now growing wary of their old hangouts.

The Georgetown neighborhood of the city became home of the Cauldron, a beatnik den that was opened by Irwin Baron in May 1960 in the basement of 3263 M Street NW. This adventurous coffee house took over the underground space formerly occupied by Ward's Used Furniture Store and featured spontaneous entertainment, live jazz and folk music, primitive dance exhibitions and classic movies.

Unfortunately, because of the C&W music culture that prevailed on M Street at the time, the beatniks were slow to respond and the Cauldron didn't bubble for long. On Tuesday, November 1, 1960 the owner changed the name of the establishment to the Lamplighter and was out of business less than three weeks later. Before the month was out Melo's Italian Restaurant had taken over the top floor of the building and the Cauldron's basement dwelling had been remodeled and reopened as Melo's Subcommittee Room, a small-scale cabaret-theatre. In October 1962 Melo's closed and the basement was subsequently transformed into the French Quarter, a jazz night club that switched over to rock and roll with the arrival of the British Invasion a couple years later. The French Quarter thrived as a Georgetown hot spot until 1968. Today the ground floor of 3263 M Street NW houses a jewelry store called Aurate New York with the former Cauldron basement area serving as storage space.

Northeast of Georgetown in the Adams Morgan neighborhood was Potter's House (1658 Columbia Road NW), which opened in June 1960 at the former site of the Embassy Lunch Restaurant by the nondenominational Church of the Saviour under the guidance of Rev. Newton Gordon Cosby. Acting upon his belief that Christianity must always be open to new structures, Rev. Cosby designed Potter's House as "a quiet place where thoughtful people of any belief can relax, hear music, look at art, and talk."

Coffee, simple fare, poetry readings, live folk music and displays and shows by local artists gave the Potter's House a unique distinction in a section of the city which at the time was mainly known for its two other night spots, the Showboat Lounge on 18th Street NW, which for years featured now-legendary jazz guitarist Charlie Byrd, and the Underground at 14th Street and Columbia Road NW, which during most of 1961 offered jazz guitarist Bill Harris. The Potter's House differed from other beatnik hangouts in that its atmosphere was a bit more subdued and it closed at midnight on Fridays and Saturdays, a departure from the dusk-to-dawn hours that other local coffee houses adhered to. Remarkably, Potter's House remains open at its original location to this very day.

Several years after the inception of Potter's House, Adams Morgan welcomed another coffee house called Ontario Place (1811 Ontario Place NW), which replaced the Ontario Market in May 1963 and stayed in business until June 1965. Ontario Place was widely known for offering blues singer-guitarist Mississippi John Hurt and gained a reputation among Washington musicians as one of the hippest places in town after Bob Dylan stopped by for a visit, an event later chronicled in the book "Positively Main Street" (1972) by Toby Thompson. Ontario Place made a lasting mark in local music history, but faded far too quickly from the scene. The building that once housed this coffee house was torn down in recent years and today its former site is occupied by a newly constructed private residence.

Another major beatnik establishment to appear on the scene was the Unicorn (1710 17th Street NW), which emerged on the fringes of Dupont Circle long before that area had established its reputation as a refuge for counterculture devotees. The composition of the neighborhood surrounding the Circle changed drastically after the infamous June 1963 incident involving 23-year-old Eddie Hicks, a troubadour who had been arrested for vagrancy while sitting on the grassy lawn adjacent to the Circle and playing his guitar for the small crowd that had gathered around him. His arrest triggered a series of demonstrations around the Circle's fountain that would define the area as a gathering spot for bohemians, leftists, nonconformists and revolutionaries that exists to the present day.

While the pulse of the neighborhood had long circulated through such eclectic Dupont Circle bars as the Flame Restaurant, Charlie's Café Lounge, the Ben Bow Restaurant and the Brickskeller, the Unicorn quietly joined their ranks in January 1961 and offered folk music and a bohemian atmosphere for those who shied away from the hustle and bustle of nearby Connecticut Avenue NW. Six months after its opening the Unicorn was purchased by a neighborhood resident named Elliot Ryan, who would later become a significant figure in Washington, D.C.'s rock and roll scene as creator and publisher of Unicorn Times, a publication that initially had its offices adjacent to Dupont Circle at 1721 21st Street NW and covered the music scene in the nation's capital from 1973 to 1986.

Ryan was originally from New York, had graduated from Michigan State University, and after a two-year stint in the United States Army settled down in Washington, D.C. in May 1960. He took over the Unicorn with the idea of making it a live music coffee house and installed a Wednesday night "Hootenanny" where a bevy of folk musicians gathered and performed for the masses. Jazz musicians were featured on Monday nights and on weekends he booked such folk music performers as Tim Cameron, Allen Damron, Mario Illo, John Everhart, Robbie Basho, Pete LaFarge and Erik Darling. Local guitarists like John Fahey and Max Ochs regularly showed up for impromptu performances and the popular Joan Baez even stopped in one night to sing onstage with the resident folkies.

The Unicorn also staged art shows and Sunday afternoon movies, everything from Charlie Chaplin flicks to art films and foreign works to more unique selections such as "The Ruse" (Universal Pictures, 1928) and "The Room Upstairs" (Alcina, 1946). A total of 50 different kinds of tea and coffee were on the menu and patrons could play chess or sift through racks of newspapers and magazines. Citing financial reasons, Elliot Ryan closed the Unicorn in the spring of 1964 and today the former site of this unique coffee house hosts a six-story apartment building called the Admiral Dupont (1700 17th Street NW).

As Washington's original beatnik gathering spot and poetry performance space, Coffee 'n' Confusion lived off its reputation and remained in operation until April 1963, at which point Angelo Alvino closed up shop to devote his full attention to Bohemian Caverns. The local beatniks continued to use the structure at 945 K Street NW as home base, as the building's basement went on to host such coffee houses as the Open Way (July 1963 to March 1964), the Crow's Toe (April 1964 to December 1964), and a succession of similar establishments throughout the latter part of the decade including the Lute and Lyre, the Womb's Tomb, Porterchinko's Palace and the Blue Sparrow.

As the 1960s wore on the beatniks dwindled in number in Washington, D.C. and were eventually all but replaced by scores of long-haired hippies that mobilized a new cultural revolution driven by hard rock and roll, rampant drug use and fanatical opposition to the Vietnam War, capitalism and conservative values. As cultural staples, folk music gave way to the Beatles and the British Invasion, which, in turn, inspired a wave of psychedelia that infected both musical and social trends. As the authentic beatniks disappeared and the Summer of Love loomed on the horizon, the hippies descended upon Dupont Circle, dispensing LSD and offering visions of peace and tranquility to the young sycophants that hovered about.

Purple Haze aside, the empty and crumbling Zantzinger Building at 10th and K Streets NW eventually outlived its usefulness and was torn down in October 1969. The former site of Coffee 'n' Confusion then served for nearly 40 years as an asphalt parking lot for the Mount Vernon Place United Methodist Church. The lot was cleared in 2007 and in late 2009 a 12-story glass-and-concrete office building called 901 K Street was completed and began accepting tenants a year later. Sadly, no markers, monuments or plaques commemorate the former location of the basement lair that launched Washington, DC's Beat Generation and served as the very first stage for a rock and roll legend.

CHAPTER FIFTY-SIX
THE DROP INN – A MODEL FOR TEEN CLUBS

The very notion of organizing recreational activities for youths goes back to Colonial times when settlers in the first villages created games and contests within their developing communities to keep their children and young adults occupied. Through time, as the region that became the Washington, D.C. area developed in terms of size and population, a number of assemblies, clubs and meetings were established through churches, schools, community centers and other organizations that provided social events in which teenagers could participate and spend their free time in constructive ways. Elements such as musical entertainment and dancing became integral parts of these gatherings and in many instances became the primary reason for the establishment of such social outlets.

Beginning early in the 20th century the term "teen club" became one of several accepted monikers for a system of organized social events for teenagers in and around the Washington, D.C. area. One of the more influential teen organizations to emerge in the region was a "canteen" operated by the Greenbelt Recreation Department in a facility called the Drop Inn, an actual basement gathering place in Greenbelt, Maryland where various activities were offered including dances with both jukebox and live music. The Drop Inn was part of a series of teen social experiments that the Greenbelt community had been supporting since the city's founding in 1937. Greenbelt's various teen assemblies, including functions and meetings held in the Drop Inn, served as models for similar organizations that formed throughout the region in the ensuing years.

The first mention of a teen gathering in Greenbelt, Maryland was in a small article that appeared in the Greenbelt Cooperator newspaper of Wednesday, December 15, 1937 entitled "Young Peoples' Meeting Held December 10." The short piece told that the Young Peoples' Meeting actually took place in a private home at 1-G Gardenway and listed out the attendees: Stanley Provost, Varina Craig, Mary Clara Bonham, Nella Berkalew, Larry Childress, Dorma Ashley, Shirley Friedman, Mary Provost, Lossie Thurston, Lynn Ashley, Nathelia Sandman, Dolores Carr, Tommy Poston (this is the same Tom Poston who went on to become a leading Hollywood actor) and Mae O'Brien. Elected officers were Stanley Provost, president; Dorma Ashley, vice president; and Lossie Thurston, secretary and treasurer.

In January 1938 the organization changed its name to the Young Peoples' Club and continued the established practice of meeting in various private homes throughout Greenbelt. The pages of that same newspaper offered periodic updates on this group, culminating in the formation of a Greenbelt Junior Citizen's Association on Tuesday, June 21, 1938. Little was written about the organization in the pages of the Greenbelt Cooperator over the next few years, leaving its history incomplete.

Not to be outdone, other nearby communities began forming teen clubs and advertising their offerings in the local media. One of the earliest examples from the suburbs is an article that ran in the Prince George's Post of Thursday, November 30, 1939 which announced that an "Entertainment and Dance" sponsored by the Young People's Fellowship of Pinkney Memorial Church of Hyattsville was to take place at their church on the night of Friday, December 8.The article stated: "The theme for the entertainment will be that of a series of popular and well-known radio programs. There will be dancing all evening in between these various presentations." In 1940, the Fellowship organizers at Pinkney Memorial Church began calling these events Young People's Nightclubs and continued the monthly gatherings with radio entertainment throughout the decade.

Meanwhile, the situation in Greenbelt had slowly changed through time. The responsibility for the supervision of youth activities in the city was haphazard at best and reached a stage where the very administration of such events was left to anyone who desired to step in and take charge. To fill the void left by the disbandment of the Young People's Meetings, a woman identified in the Greenbelt Cooperator as Mrs. Anita Sauls was positioned as chairman of the dance committee. Her work resulted in the staging of nine "Young People's Dances," aimed at youths in elementary, junior high school and high school, in the auditorium of Center School between May 1943 and April 1944.

Popular dance music at these Young People's Dances was provided by a local band called the Serenaders, whose all-Greenbelt lineup consisted of pianist Jack Huntington, clarinetist-saxophonist Mahlon Eshbaugh, saxophonists Jimmy Griggs and Sam Downs, trumpeters Dick Palmer and Harry Benefiel, trombonist Jimmy McCarl and drummer Dick Coulter. The Serenaders, in addition to their appearances at these events, also performed at different school dances, variety shows and social functions throughout the area.

An article in the Greenbelt Cooperator of Friday, September 8, 1944 entitled "High School Hep-Cats' Hunt for New Headquarters is Happily Unhexed" told: "After six years of struggle the teen age group of Greenbelt has finally acquired a suitable place for a weekly 'hang-out' and headquarters for a youth club." This facility, it turns out, was actually the Greenbelt Athletic Club's clubhouse, located between Crescent Road and Braden Field, with Thursday night becoming the designated night for the teens to take over the premises.

The first event of the new Greenbelt Youth Club in the clubhouse, presumably to have taken place on Thursday, August 30, featured hot dogs, cokes, ping pong, dart-throwing and live music furnished by Bob Walker with His Guitar. The Greenbelt Cooperator reported that the event drew approximately 75 "hep-cats and cuddle-bunnies" and Mary Jane Townsend and Ellen Gussion were chosen president and secretary, respectively, of the new club. In middle October, after several weeks of dances in the clubhouse, the Greenbelt Youth Club moved its weekly events back to Center School's auditorium, and talk began of securing new quarters for the club in the basement portion of the fire and police station building.

According to a series of articles in the Greenbelt Cooperator in November 1944, the Greenbelt town council appropriated $2000 for the establishment of a canteen for teenagers and appointed Mary Jane Townsend to head a committee to plan and operate said facility. The Greenbelt Recreation Department, under the guidance of employees Miss Helena Knauer and Miss Eileen Mudd, sponsored the project and an executive committee was established to serve as the club's governing body.

On Saturday, December 23, 1944 the Drop Inn, as the teen facility came to be called, opened in the basement of the building marked 151 Centerway that housed the Greenbelt Police Department and the Greenbelt Fire Department (today this basement space has a separate address of 155 Centerway). The room could accommodate a total of 75 occupants. Entertainment that evening was offered in the form of group singing, Marilyn Maryn's reading of her original poem "Meet Me Here," and a jukebox stocked with the latest popular music tunes. For refreshments, a soda bar sold cokes and hot dogs Memberships were charged and the club's initial hours – which would change frequently during the club's existence – were 4pm-10pm on weekdays, 7pm-11:30pm on Saturday and 1pm-4pm Sunday.

On Friday, March 9, 1945, the Drop Inn first offered a program of live music featuring a barbershop quartet composed of George Jones, Jack Waldo, Wayne Hernberg and Billy Sauls backed by Fred Aydlett on accordion. Another accordionist, Herbert Hall, later played his famous "Laughing Song" and several duets were sung by Christie Richardson and June Brittingham.

The Drop Inn next offered live music for its members on Saturday, July 21, 1945 with a dance featuring the music of the Serenaders, whose lineup now consisted of LeGrand and Harry Benefiel, Mahlon Eshbaugh, Dick Palmer and Dick Burke. According to articles in the "Greenbelt Cooperator," dances were held in the Drop Inn on a semi-regular basis for the next 12 months, with music provided by a group called Jack Waldo's Orchestra.

At this time, other developing communities in Prince George's County, Maryland began to form teen clubs, leading Ralph Brown, who held dual roles as chairman of the county's Recreation Guidance Council and superintendent of the Prince George's County Police, to take it upon himself to raise money for these organizations. Brown organized a teen dance on Friday, January 18, 1946 at the Hyattsville Armory that served as a fundraiser with the proceeds going to implement and outfit what he called "teen-age canteens" and establish funds for future recreation buildings in the metropolitan area.

This event was the largest of its era and was widely publicized with an uncredited, front-page article in the Prince George's Post of Thursday, January 3, 1946 entitled "Dance Scheduled to Raise Funds for Teen-Agers." With live music provided by the Claude Nichols Orchestra, the event was a rousing success. Within a few months, more than a half-dozen new teen clubs had been established, with many holding dances that featured music from small, established orchestras or newly formed bands comprised of local teenaged musicians from neighboring communities.

On Monday, June 10, 1946 a private group in Greenbelt called the Youth Center and Memorial Park Committee completed negotiations to buy a vacant, L-shaped surplus building for $1,200. The structure had previously served as the administrative headquarters for the Federal Public Housing Authority, which sat on a lot at University Lane and New Hampshire Avenue in Silver Spring, Maryland. The one-story building, whose dimensions were 40x72 feet, was cut into five sections and in September 1946 was transported by truck to a cleared site at 9 Parkway Road, adjacent to the Greenbelt Center parking lot, where it would serve as the new Drop Inn facility. While this transplanted surplus building was being prepared, the old Drop Inn continued to operate in the basement of the police and fire station.

On Monday, March 31, 1947 the Greenbelt Town Council held a special meeting where it was determined that they would emerge as the controlling body of the new Drop Inn. The following month an Adult Advisory Board was established to approve rules and regulations for the new canteen as suggested by a Teen-Age Planning Committee. Members of the Adult Advisory Board were: Mrs. Leon Benefiel, chairman; Mrs. Alfred Sansone, ways and means and hostesses, Miss Eileen Mudd, secretary and program; Joseph Rogers, treasurer and equipment; Rev. Eric Braund, program and hosts; Allen Morrison, publicity and grounds; and James Wolfe, ways and means and canteen. Jimmy Williams was named Youth Canteen President. Membership was $2.00 per year and it was decided the Drop Inn would operate on weekdays from 2:30pm to 5:30pm, on Wednesday, Friday and Saturday nights from 7:30pm to 11:30pm, and Sunday evenings from 7:30pm to 10:30pm. Members must be aged 14 to 25, single, and residents of Greenbelt.

On the night of Saturday, May 3, 1947, the new Drop Inn off of Parkway Road opened its doors with an open house from 7pm to 9pm that attracted more than 400 visitors. Following the reception, a teen dance was staged in the packed facility featuring the music of Bill Baxter's Orchestra. The Drop Inn, which also came to be known informally as the Greenbelt Youth Center, flourished for the following six years despite being subjected to constant changes in its administration and policies.

A key organizational change in the Drop Inn's policy occurred at a Town Council meeting on Monday, April 5, 1948 where the facility and its corresponding teen club were placed under the permanent supervision of the Greenbelt Recreation Department, which oversaw the entire organization through a new, council-appointed, five-member Greenbelt Youth Center Advisory Board. This board was responsible for establishing the general rules and regulations of the Drop Inn, maintaining membership records for the Greenbelt Youth Center organization, and booking live musical entertainment for the Drop Inn's on-going weekend teen dances.

There were several quality teen bands that performed at the Drop Inn's dances during its seven-year existence, the most significant of which were Bill Baxter's Orchestra, the Off Beats and the Lewis Maddox Orchestra. From 1947 to 1949 Bill Baxter's Orchestra served as the main house band at these events. This four-piece band, which played pop and jazz songs of the era, consisted of Greenbelt teens Bill Baxter and Jimmy Griggs on horns, pianist Tommy Millet and drummer Ervin Dietzel. Unfortunately, the pages of the Greenbelt Cooperator, which included frequent small notices of the band's appearances at the Drop Inn, failed to provide any measure of biographical information on the youths who played in this band and their stories remain lost in time. However, the very fact that the band was repeatedly called upon to headline the numerous teen dances staged at the Drop Inn during these years is indicative of its popularity within the community.

Another favored band of the Drop Inn era was the Off Beats, a Dixieland jazz-pop band that originally consisted of several youngsters from University Park Elementary School and Hyattsville Junior High School in Prince George's County, Maryland. Formed in September 1947 to perform at the University Park Teen Club dances, the initial lineup of this congregation consisted of clarinetist Harvey Beavers, trumpeter Dickie Burgess, saxophonist John MacBride, pianist Bobby Charlton and drummer Tommy Donaldson. (At this time it should be noted that there was a different rock and roll band on the local scene in the late 1950s that used this same name and included guitarist Danny Gatton.)

Shortly after forming, demand for the Off Beats grew and the band members found themselves working other teen clubs in the area including the Bladensburg Teen Club, the Hyattsville Teen Club and the Cheverly Teen Club. In the early 1950s the band experienced personnel changes, but all the while made appearances at socials held at St. Hugh's Catholic Church in Greenbelt and St. Ambrose Catholic Church in Cheverly.

During the 1951-1952 school year, at which time all the band members were students at Northwestern High School in Hyattsville, the Off Beats made regular appearances at the Drop Inn, where they began experimenting with the latest tunes on the Billboard magazine music popularity charts. They would remain a top attraction at the Drop Inn for approximately three years. In the group's final days they began incorporating some early-era rock and roll tunes into their repertoire, most notably songs by Fats Domino. During the summer of 1954, with most of the band members having graduated from Northwestern High School, the Off Beats left the Drop Inn behind, changed their name to the Merry Makers, and began playing the local hotel circuit.

It can be argued that rock and roll music made its first splash on the Drop Inn scene during the 1953-1954 school year, when a jazz-oriented band called the Lewis Maddox Orchestra began performing at the facility's teen dances on nights when the Off Beats were busy tending to other engagements. Maddox, a resident of Cheverly, Maryland and a member of Bladensburg High School's Class of 1956, had first put his band together during his freshman year, with his group's initial lineup consisted of himself, singer-bassist Jack Otley, saxophonist Charlie Kelley, trumpeter Kermit Frye and drummer Stan Spiwak. They played everything from jazzy Dizzy Gillespie, Benny Goodman and Louis Prima compositions to early rock and roll-styled Bill Haley songs.

A number of different musicians were called upon to work with the Lewis Maddox Orchestra during its three-year existence, a span that saw them perform at St. Ambrose Catholic Church in Cheverly, the University Park Teen Club, the Bladensburg Teen Club, the Lewisdale Teen Club, the Hyattsville Teen Club, the Takoma Park Teen Club, the District Heights Teen Club, the Landover Services Teen Club and Greenbelt's Drop Inn. One of the more noteworthy musicians to play in the band was bassist Jack Otley, who lived in nearby Rogers Heights and later became a founding member of the Saxtons, a now-legendary Prince George's County-based rock and roll group.

After years of changes in the Drop Inn's Teen-Age Planning Committee and Greenbelt Youth Center Advisory Board, the Greenbelt Town Council ultimately came to the conclusion that after seven years of relatively smooth operations, the teenagers had outgrown the Drop Inn facility. The Greenbelt Cooperator of Thursday, May 6, 1954 ran an article entitled "Youth Center Outgrown, Will Use Center School" which stated that the Drop Inn was being vacated that month and future Friday and Saturday night dances would be held in the community center auditorium (in reality this facility was the Center School gymnasium).

With the issue dated Thursday, September 23, 1954, the Greenbelt Cooperator changed its name to the Greenbelt New Review. In that edition an article entitled "Recreation News: Grand Opening of Youth Center at Center School" by Donald Wolfe told that the Youth Center would be holding all of its future events in the Center School (presumably in the space that was commonly referred to as either the auditorium or gymnasium), beginning with a teen dance on the night of Saturday, September 25, 1954 (the Greenbelt News Review failed to name the band that was providing the entertainment that evening).

Ultimately, the government agency surplus Drop Inn building below Parkway was torn down in January 1955 and hauled away. At the end of 1956 the "Drop Inn" moniker for the dances in the Center School gymnasium was abandoned for good and future articles in the Greenbelt News Review referred to all teen activities in the school under the organizational heading of "Youth Center."

From 1957 to 1959 the Youth Center's Saturday night dances in the Center School gymnasium utilized either recorded music or live bands as entertainment. Regular bands to perform at these functions ranged from formal groups like Murray Tanner and His Orchestra to pop music outfits like the Hi Lites and the Nomads. Special events in the gymnasium included: A "Youth Center Dance" on Saturday, May 18, 1957 hosted by WEAM disc jockey Bob Rickman and headlined by the Diamonds; a Don Dillard Record Hop for the "Greenbelt Teen Club" on Saturday, September 14, 1957 that featured Terry and the Pirates; a return appearance for the Greenbelt Teen Club by Terry and the Pirates on Saturday, November 9, 1957; a "Youth Center Dance" on Saturday, January 25, 1958 featuring the Off Keys; and a "St. Patrick's Day Dance" for the Youth Center on Saturday, March 15, 1958, again featuring the Off Keys.

After years of lobbying by the citizens of Greenbelt who felt the teen population needed a new facility in which to congregate, a building called the Greenbelt Youth Center was constructed and formally opened on Saturday, December 31, 1960 with a New Year's Eve party that featured live music by the Capris. The event drew more than 250 teens and ushered in a new rock and roll-flavored decade for the youth of Greenbelt.

CHAPTER FIFTY-SEVEN
CULTIVATING TEEN INTEREST IN ROCK AND ROLL

During the 1950s rock and roll music in the Washington, D.C. area was usually directed towards teenagers through dances and special events presented by teen organizations, churches and schools, or towards adults through stage appearances and concerts held in night clubs and miscellaneous venues. Younger musicians comprised the bands that worked the teen dance circuit, while older musicians worked the night clubs. Despite occasional overlapping, the players involved with these two systems mainly operated separate of each other; though innumerable teen musicians stuck with the trade and went on to enter the area's professional ranks.

For some teenagers rock and roll music was identified as an expression of rebellion, while for other youths it was a cultural element that provided unique entertainment and provided opportunities for them to connect with peers who shared a common musical interest. Conversely, most adults who followed popular music seemed less concerned with songs that lyrically deviated from the norm and gravitated towards pop classics, dance tunes, instrumentals, and songs that offered simpler tales of love and everyday life. Rock and roll's signature back beat rhythm ensured that movement and dance would always be coupled with its performance, and the notion of sex – the very act for which the music had been granted its moniker – would forever remain a recurring theme in its delivery.

With the rock and roll era at hand in the 1950s, a number of factors contributed to a heightened interest amongst teens in the Washington, D.C. area's music scene. These included various television programs, radio broadcasts, motion pictures and other media components that served to raise public consciousness in terms of coupling teenagers with the new phenomena of rock and roll music. As a result of this public exposure, the number of teen dances in and around the nation's capital grew steadily throughout the decade, with rock and roll becoming firmly established as the primary form of entertainment being offered to the patrons of these functions.

One significant influence on the growth of teen interest in the local music scene was the television program entitled "Paul Whiteman's TV Teen Club" which broadcasted from Philadelphia, Pennsylvania and was aired over the ABC-TV network throughout the country during the early 1950s. In the Washington, D.C. area, this program, which usually lasted 30 minutes in length, aired on Saturday (and sometimes Sunday) evenings at either 9pm or 9:30pm over WMAL-TV (Channel 7) from Saturday April 2, 1949 until Sunday, December 13, 1953. The show was hosted by the legendary band leader Paul Whiteman, who was known as the King of Jazz and had achieved great popularity during the 1920s during which time his orchestras were regarded as the best in America.

Whiteman's show featured teenaged singers and dancers from Philadelphia performing live in front of a studio audience and rated as the first show of its kind to feature such entertainment. One bootleg tape of the show dated Monday, July 14, 1952 features a 16-year-old Charlie Gracie singing "Rock the Joint" (a song that had most recently been covered by Bill Haley with the Saddlemen) backed by Paul Whiteman's Orchestra, a fascinating artifact that illustrates the show's importance in exposing rock and roll music to a youthful viewing audience. That same year a young announcer named Dick Clark was hired to read commercials on the show for sponsor Tootsie Roll. He later went on to fame and fortune as the host of "American Bandstand," which made its network debut on Monday, August 5, 1957.

The second television show directed at the local teen population was "Bandstand Matinee," which aired on WMAL-TV (Channel 7) on weekday afternoons at 4:30pm from Monday, April 6, 1953 to Friday, October 9, 1953 (the show initially ran for 30 minutes, but expanded to one full hour beginning Monday, June 1). Emanating from the WMAL-TV studios within the Evening Star Television Center (4461 Connecticut Avenue NW, Washington, D.C.), the show offered a party format where teens danced to recordings of current pop music tunes and was hosted by Sherman Butler, who had led a news show on radio station WMAL since June 1952. In short time the show was enjoying great popularity, with as many as 1,000 teens attempting to crowd the studio's dance floor, whose show capacity was 195. Problems ensued as teens from all over the area descended upon the studio every weekday afternoon.

The situation was assessed in an article in the Washington Post of Wednesday, August 26, 1953 entitled "Special Police Patrol Established to Curb Teen-age Hoodlums Swarming TV Show, Terrorizing Merchants on Upper Connecticut Ave." by Ralph Reikowsky. The piece described how hordes of teenagers descended on the area each afternoon to attend the show, spurring numerous complaints from merchants regarding teens who were engaging in gang fights, vandalizing their stores and terrorizing anyone who got in their way. Capt. Daniel O. Fletcher, commander of the Eighth Precinct, was quoted as saying that most of the teenagers came by bus from the Southeast and Northeast quadrants of the city.

The article detailed numerous incidents of bad behavior attributed to the teenagers – who were described as having long wavy hair combed into duck-tails and wearing blue jeans and T-shirts or sweat shirts. John H. Ryan, head of the precinct's juvenile squad, was quoted in the article as saying that most of the culprits were members of the 14th Street Gang, a group of car thieves whose unofficial headquarters were in the vicinity of 14th and Irving Streets NW. According to Ryan, the gang was led by 19-year-old Charles R. James of 1743 Irving Street NW, who was known on the streets as "The Flame" and "Jimmy James." WMAL officials claimed this gang practically took over the show for several months. The article also mentioned that two other groups attended the show, the Ash Can Gang from upper 9th Street NW, and an unnamed gang from Anacostia.

Things apparently did not improve for the show, as an article in the Washington Post of Tuesday, September 22, 1953 entitled "Bandstand Matinee Issues New Rules to Curb Rowdiness" documented a series of rules and regulations the station had set up in order to screen out what they called "undesirables." Under the new guidelines, the number of persons admitted to the dance floor was now limited to 75, teenagers had to have reservations to attend each show as well as membership cards with their photographs in place in order to gain admittance, and no new applications were being accepted. Dancers were to be more formal in dress, with the boys being prohibited from wearing T-shirts and the girls prohibited from wearing slacks. In addition, while the teens were on the WMAL premises, rules prohibited the use of profanity, gum-chewing, smoking, pushing, shoving, rough-housing or defacing station property, and routes were established for going to and from the dance studio.

While there was never any word as to how the 14th Street Gang reacted to this menu of changes, an article in the Washington Post of Friday, October 9, 1953 entitled "TV Station Drops Teen Dance Show" by Larry Laurent stated that the show was being televised for the last time that day because WMAL-TV was reorganizing its schedule due to a change in ABC's daytime network programming. In all likelihood the trouble from the teens who were attending the show simply became too much for the officials at WMAL to handle and it was easier to cancel the program rather than work on any further crowd control strategies.

Despite its unfortunate demise, "Bandstand Matinee" served as a seminal television program in the way it ventured into the teen world and offered music and dance opportunities for a growing and increasingly restless segment of the population. Future television shows that offered rock and roll music for teen viewers borrowed heavily from this program.

Another development that encouraged interest in rock and roll music among the local teen population was the opening of WPGC, a brand new 250-watt radio station at 1580 on the AM dial (the station's power was increased to 1,000 watts after its first year of operation). Located inside a small concrete building off a dirt road in a field on the farm of Duval B. Evans between Pennsylvania Avenue and Suitland Road in Morningside, Maryland, the station had its on-air debut on Thursday, April 15, 1954. (Today the exact former site of this studio and its transmitter is occupied by a private home marked 3501 Dottie Kelly Court, District Heights, Maryland.)

Billed at the time in local newspaper ads as "The Voice of Prince George's County," WPGC offered "programs, sports, news, and music" and upon its opening was the only standard broadcast station situated in the county. General manager Harry Hayman employed a staff of nine and for most of the musical segments used a C&W band called the Happy Melody Boys who would play live in the studio for the station's growing audience.

One of the station's most popular disc jockeys during its first year of operation was local C&W musician Wade Holmes, who hosted a program entitled "Corn Shuckin' Time" which often included live studio performances by Holmes and his various musician friends. For the teen listeners Mr. Hayman placed Peg Huyck in charge of what was advertised as "teenage disc shows." Her pop music program included songs of the national hit parade by the likes of Bill Haley and His Comets, Pat Boone, Perry Como, the Chordettes, the Crew Cuts and Rosemary Clooney, as well as on-air announcements regarding local teen club dances and events. Her program marked the first time the local youths had popular music, and, specifically, rock and roll, aimed directly at them via radio.

During the 1950s more than two-dozen rock and roll-themed motion pictures were released theatrically in the United States, most of which were aimed at teenagers and young adults, and all of which served to promote the new classification of music as a staple of American pop culture. Some of these films contained actual concert footage, others offered plots based on teenage rebellion or confrontations with some sort of authority, and some were driven by simple story lines that illustrated the changing social concerns of the time. The one constant in these films is that at some point in each movie audiences were introduced to the top rock and roll stars of the era, which were often presented on the big screens in larger-than-life fashion.

Serving as an orientation to the rock and roll films on the horizon was the very popular box office attraction "Blackboard Jungle" (M-G-M Pictures, 1955), which starred Glenn Ford as Richard Dadier, a teacher at a vocational high school in Manhattan, New York who attempts to deal with the antisocial hoodlum students that surround him. While the movie did not offer a direct rock and roll plot, it did feature the music of Bill Haley and His Comets, whose hit song "(We're Gonna) Rock Around the Clock" served as the film's central theme song and was played in part or in whole a total of four times throughout the movie – during the opening credits, in the first scene, an instrumental treatment around the middle, and at the close of the film. "(We're Gonna) Rock Around the Clock" eventually reached number one in the Billboard magazine's "Best Sellers in Stores" popular records chart on Saturday, July 9, 1955 and would ultimately tally world-wide sales of over 30 million units.

"Blackboard Jungle" (with ads proclaiming it to be "A Drama of Teen-Age Terror!") made its Washington, D.C. premiere on Friday, April 22, 1955 at Loew's Columbia Theatre (1112 F Street NW) and was shown day and night through Tuesday, June 7. The movie reportedly set a box office record for attendance and ticket sales during its 47-day run. Coinciding with the film's local debut and serving as a brilliant marketing ploy, Bill Haley and His Comets worked three nightly sets at the Casino Royal Theatre Restaurant from Monday April 25, to Sunday, May 1, 1955, further bolstering interest in the film and simultaneously confirming their status as the nation's top rock and roll band. "Blackboard Jungle" paved the way for the production of a slew of major motion pictures during the 1950s that either featured rock and roll bands or mixed rock and roll music with the teen generation.

Most all of the rock and roll-themed motion pictures were shown in the Washington, D.C. area at some point and reportedly enjoyed considerable success. The first of such films to play area theatres was "Rock 'n' Roll Revue" (Studio Films Inc., 1955), a 37-minute movie that was filmed live at the Apollo Theatre in Harlem, New York. In this movie Willie Bryant hosts an evening of music and comedy that features performances by Louie Bellson, Ruth Brown, the Clovers, Nat King Cole, Duke Ellington, Lionel Hampton, Dinah Washington, Big Joe Turner and Mantan Moreland, among others. The movie was targeted at Black audiences in Washington, D.C. and had its local premier on Friday, October 14, 1955 at the Howard Theatre, where it enjoyed a two-night showing.

The next, and perhaps most significant rock and roll motion picture to show on local screens, was "Rock Around the Clock" (Columbia Pictures, 1956), a 77-minute musical adventure that starred Bill Haley and His Comets, Alan Freed, the Platters, Tony Martinez and His Band and Freddie Bell and His Playboys. The movie gives a fictionalized account of the birth of rock and roll with manager Steve Hollis (Johnny Johnston) discovering Haley's band at a local teenage dance. He then attempts to book his new discovery, but falls into a tangled web with agent Corinne Talbot (Alix Talton) and dancer and main love interest Lisa Johns (Lisa Gaye). Alan Freed portrays himself, and, in a major plot turn, is called upon by a blackballed Hollis to book Haley and his band, thus increasing their national exposure and setting up the movie's twist ending.

"Rock Around the Clock" is unique in local rock and roll history in that it marked the first time the actual featured performing artists made in-person promotional appearances at the movie's local premiere. The movie had its world premiere on Wednesday, March 14, 1956 at three different Washington, D.C. facilities, the Ambassador Theatre (2454 18th Street NW), the Metropolitan Theatre (934 F Street NW) and the Republic Theatre (1343 U Street NW), with Bill Haley and His Comets stopping off at each theatre for autograph signing sessions.

"Rock Around the Clock" is noted for being the first of its kind to show White and Black musicians performing in the same venue, and was targeted throughout the country at audiences of both races. In Washington, D.C., the Ambassador and the Metropolitan drew White movie patrons, and Haley and his band made early afternoon stops at both venues on Wednesday, March14. The Republic Theatre, however, was located in the heart of Black Washington in the You Street area, and, surprisingly, both Bill Haley and His Comets and the Platters made a special joint appearance there on opening night from 6:45pm to 8pm, signing autographed pictures and giving away 400 free records to the Black teenagers. The movie reportedly drew large and enthusiastic crowds during its first local theatrical run.

In terms of marketing strategy, a somewhat similar approach was taken by distributors of the movie "Rock Rock Rock!" (Vanguard Productions, Inc., 1956). The movie had its Washington, D.C. debut on Saturday, December 15, 1956 at Loew's Columbia Theatre (1112 F Street NW), and subsequently had a two-day showing the following Friday and Saturday afternoons and evenings at the Howard Theatre. "Rock Rock Rock!" is an 85-minute film that features a 13-year-old Tuesday Weld as Dori Graham, a young lady who desperately tries to earn money to buy a special gown to wear to the local high school rock and roll dance. The movie also features disc jockey Alan Freed as himself and songs from such artists as Chuck Berry, LaVern Baker, the Flamingos, the Moonglows, Frankie Lymon and the Teenagers and the Johnny Burnette Trio.

Two other extremely popular rock and roll movies of the 1950s that enjoyed success in the Washington, D.C. area were: "Rock, Pretty Baby!" (Universal-International Pictures, 1957), which included songs by Rod McKuen, Sonny Burke, Henry Mancini and Bobby Troup and debuted on Thursday, February 14, 1957 at both the Ambassador Theatre and Metropolitan Theatre; and "Don't Knock the Rock" (Columbia Pictures, 1957), which served as a follow-up to "Rock Around the Clock" and starred Alan Freed and Bill Haley and His Comets, with appearances by Little Richard, the Treniers and Dave Appell and the Applejacks, and debuted on Thursday, February 28, 1957, also at both the Ambassador Theatre and the Metropolitan Theatre.

CHAPTER FIFTY-EIGHT
THE EVENING STAR'S "TEEN" SECTION

The establishment of rock and roll as a new classification of popular music, combined with increased interest in the region's teen club situation, caused one of Washington, D.C.'s daily newspapers, the Evening Star, to begin publishing a special weekend section called "Teen," with the first 12-page segment appearing in the Sunday Star edition on November 18, 1956. Specifically aimed at area youths, Teen offered articles that focused on local high school events and included extensive coverage of the area's teen music scene, as well as articles on the top popular music entertainers in the country. This special section became a popular component of the Evening Star and greatly enhanced rock and roll's popularity with the area's younger population. The final installment of Teen appeared in the Washington Star-News (as the newspaper came to be called) of Saturday, May 11, 1974.

The very first appearance of Teen was framed with the subtitle "For and About Young People" and included a lead-off article entitled "Where Can We Go?" by George Flynn that illustrated the recent increase in teen club activity. The article stated: "A social phenomenon which has arisen entirely within recent years, the growth of the clubs reflects the fact that the teeming teens have overwhelmed the traditional facilities of churches, YMCAs and recreation departments. Mrs. Ellen Vinson, director of recreation in Prince George's County says pressure is stepping up for creation of new teen clubs, while attendance at existing clubs rose sharply this fall. The same trend was found in Montgomery County, Maryland, where Miss Sally Wilkinson is director of program services for the county's recreation department. The growth of teen clubs is clearly spelled out in the attendance records at teen events in Montgomery County. In the 1955-56 school year, 39,377 teens signed in at dances and parties and meetings, against 33,361 in 1954-5."

Teen proved to be immensely popular among youthful readers and for the duration of the 1950s included articles on teen activities and music-related subjects. One recurring feature was "Top Teen Tunes" which profiled different performing artists of national significance. A few of the major stars profiled of this era were Fats Domino, Andy Williams, Perry Como, Pat Boone, Chuck Berry, the Everly Brothers, Dale Hawkins, Johnny Mathis, Little Richard, Elvis Presley, Sam Cooke, Ray Charles, Jerry Lee Lewis, Danny and the Juniors, the Platters, the Coasters, Bobby Darin, Frankie Avalon, Conway Twitty, Lloyd Price and dozens of others.

Another regular was "Top Disc Jockeys Pick Top Ten Tunes," a popularity chart where local disc jockeys listed out their favorite songs. Those who participated were Don Owens (WARL), Jerry Strong (WMAL), Milton Q. Ford (WOL), Al Ross (WRC), Eddie Gallaher (WTOP), Lord Fauntleroy (WUST) and Jack Rowzie (WWDC), with other jocks such as Don Dillard (WDON), Bob Rickman (WEAM) and Milt Grant (WTTG) eventually being added to the mix. Another highlight of Teen was "Teen-to-Teen," a classified marketplace page which had two separate categories marked "Miscellaneous" and "Notices" that included advertisements and plugs for teen bands and their appearances at local dances, record hops and teen club events.

During the late 1950s the number of local teen bands to advertise in the "Teen-to-Teen" section gradually increased as new rock and roll bands formed and opted to take advantage of the service offered by the unique marketplace. Among these youthful bands from around the Washington, D.C. area that targeted the readers of Teen and increased their followings through its readership included the Bel Airs, the Belvederes, the Cadets, the Cavaliers, the Chain Gang, the Chessmen, the Chirps, the Continentals, the Corpse Combo, the Dukes, the Epics, the Fabulous Esquires, the Four Js, the Galaxies, the

Javelins, Jerry Dallman and the Knightcaps, the Knights, the Moderns, the Nomads, the Off Keys, the Partymakers, the Rhythm Makers, the Royals, the Savoys, the Serenaders, the Silvers, the Sonotones, the Sportsmen, Terry and the Pirates, the Thunderbirds, the Tri-Tones and the Zing Ding Daddies.

As pioneers of the local teen rock and roll scene, these bands took differing routes to their dates with destiny. Some bands faded from view after a limited lifespan, while others enjoyed considerable local success and spawned numerous musicians of note who remained integral parts of the local popular music scene for decades to come.

CHAPTER FIFTY-NINE
MILT GRANT

In the spring of 1956 a new rock and roll-oriented television show directed at teenagers entitled "Record Hop" hit the Washington, D.C. area, bringing pop and rock music into the homes of thousands and showcasing both musicians of national prominence and local bands on the rise. Hosted by Milt Grant, a veteran of the local radio airwaves who had successfully made the transition to television programming, the greatest contributions "Record Hop" made to local popular culture were the ways it inspired area teen musicians to hone their musical skills, broaden their horizons as performing artists and develop an appreciation for the works of other performing artists.

The story of "Record Hop" centers on the now-legendary radio and television personality Milt Grant. Born in New York City on Sunday, May 13, 1923 and raised in Plainfield, New Jersey, Grant reportedly studied economics and English at New York University and Columbia University before entering the radio world in the late 1940s. He served as news director at WNYC in New York City and then as program manager at WARM in Scranton, Pennsylvania before working his way down to the nation's capital in 1949.

Once in Washington, D.C., Grant worked as a staff announcer at local radio stations WTOP and WWDC before moving over to WINX, where he served as an on-air personality from February 1950 until November 1951. During his time at that station he hosted such popular music shows as "Grant's Good Deal" and "Cavalcade."

On Tuesday, November 27, 1951 Grant began a new job at radio station WOL, where he hosted a daily radio program entitled "The Milt Grant Show," which would remain on the air for more than four years. His show featured a different musical theme every night: "Blues" on Mondays, "Best Band in the Land" on Tuesdays, "Top Tunes of Tomorrow" on Wednesdays, "Oldies – Tunes Out of the Past" on Thursdays, "The Top Thirty Tunes" on Fridays, and "The Saturday Night Rhythm & Blues Jamboree" on Saturdays. (Grant's show aired on an intermittent basis on Sundays during this time.)

It was during this program's run on WOL that Grant built a devoted following and earned a reputation as one of the area's top disc jockeys and popular music personalities. During these years Grant was also called upon to host other popular music programs on WOL, including short-lived shows entitled "Request Granted" and "Disc-overer." His tenure with radio station WOL lasted until April 1956.

While he was with radio station WOL, Milt Grant entered the world of television programming when he accepted the role of host on a variety show entitled "Marion Showcase," which aired on WTTG-TV (Channel 5) on Sundays from March 7 to March 21, 1954. The program offered two hours of filmed drama, amateur talent and dance instruction. When the show began its fall season on Sunday, October 10, 1954, it had changed its name to "Marion Dance Program" and offered a medley of afternoon television entertainment from 12:30pm to 2pm consisting of a full-length movie, a 30-minute talent contest entitled "Star Showcase" and a program of dance instructions where the winners were awarded a week's engagement at the Casino Royal Theatre Restaurant.

Grant also hosted other local short-run television programs in the area, including a talent show entitled "Reward for Talent" that aired on Saturdays at 7:30pm on WMAL-TV (Channel 7) from Saturday, April 10 to Saturday, May 2, 1954.

Grant had impressed the powers at WTTG-TV to the extent that when a new variety program entitled "Featurama" was pegged for broadcast, he was immediately offered the job of master of ceremonies. "Featurama" was a 50-minute program that aired Monday through Friday nights beginning at 11:10pm and was advertised as a parade of short subjects of cartoons, comedy, sports, music, news and adventure. The program was a late-night success for WTTG and aired from Monday, June 20, 1955 to Friday, December 7, 1956. By the time "Featurama" had run its course, Grant was well entrenched as host of yet another ground-breaking television program – one that would make him a legend in the Washington, D.C. area rock and roll scene.

As the popularity of "Featurama" grew, Grant made note of the interest generated by the program's short musical segments. He formulated the idea of an afternoon teenage record hop television show and when he approached the WTTG administration with his proposal it was granted immediate approval. Grant installed himself as host and acquired use of the ballroom of the Raleigh Hotel (401 12th Street NW, Washington, D.C.), outfitting it as a dance studio where teenagers would appear live on camera and dance to the latest Top 40 songs.

Entitled "Record Hop," the program debuted on Saturday, July 21, 1956 with special guest performances by rock and roll singer-guitarist Gene Vincent and pop singer Teddi King. "Record Hop" was a hit from the start and initially aired on Saturdays from 4pm to 5pm. On Monday, August 19, 1957, the program switched its title to "The Milt Grant Show" and began airing on a Monday-to-Friday schedule from 5pm to 6pm, all the while maintaining its regular Saturday time slot as well. All told, the show remained on the air for more than four years.

A big part of the show's appeal was that, in addition to offering recordings of the top hits of the day and live performances by some of the top performing artists in popular music, local bands and musicians were showcased on every show. The kids that appeared on the show were largely plucked from various Washington, D.C. area high schools and teen clubs and the musicians and bands that made appearances reads like a virtual Who's Who of 1950s popular music.

Among the local acts to appear on Grant's show were the Off Keys, Jerry Dallman and the Knightcaps, the Triumphs (featuring future Jefferson Airplane and Hot Tuna members Jack Casady and Jorma Kaukonen), the Naturals, Terry and the Pirates, Vernon Taylor, Ray Vernon and others. The great rock guitarist Link Wray earned a spot as a house band musician and would reportedly dash off into the local night club scene the moment the cameras stopped rolling.

Among the featured national stars to appear on the show were the Platters, the Drifters, the Coasters, the Laurie Sisters, the Ames Brothers, the Four Aces, Mickey and Sylvia, Dion and the Belmonts, Les Paul and Mary Ford, the Everly Brothers, the Andrews Sisters, the Del Vikings, Danny and the Juniors, Ike and Tina Turner, Mitch Miller, Gogi Grant, Paul Anka, Frankie Avalon, Andy Williams, Tab Hunter, Bobby Darin, Connie Francis, Jimmy Clanton, Fabian, Ray Peterson, Sal Mineo, Johnny Mathis, Brenda Lee, Teddy Randazzo, Neil Sedaka, Anita Bryant, Clyde McPhatter, LaVern Baker, Jackie Wilson, Lloyd Price, Sam Cooke, Little Richard, Roy Hamilton, Brook Benton, Chubby Checker, Sarah Vaughan, Della Reese, Ella Fitzgerald, Fats Domino, Billy Grammer, Conway Twitty, Johnny Horton, Crash Craddock, Bobby Rydell, Freddy Cannon, Gary U.S. Bonds, Chuck Berry, Bo Diddley, Roger Miller, Duane Eddy and actor Charlton Heston.

"The Milt Grant Show" was advertised as a show for teenagers, about teenagers, and starring teenagers, and predated the inaugural broadcast of "American Bandstand" featuring host Dick Clark by some 13 months. The program shot straight to number one on Washington, D.C. area television and eventually reached an estimated audience of more than 250,000 teenagers. Milt Grant's popular program became an institution in the nation's capital and when WTTG aired the final episode on Saturday, April 15, 1961, an extremely important chapter in Washington, D.C. rock and roll history came to a close. To this day the real reason for the show's cancellation has never been revealed. It was widely speculated that one or two suits at WTTG simply didn't like seeing either the teenagers or the rock and roll bands taking precious camera time, despite the show's incredible success.

"The Milt Grant Show" was of great social and cultural significance in that it exposed rock and roll, R&B, and pop music to a wide and diverse audience, gave local teenagers a chance to see the major musical stars of the day, and provided incentive for local teenaged musicians to form bands by offering opportunities to perform before live audiences on a highly acclaimed, top-rated television program.

Contributing to the show's success were Grant's record hops and live concert shows that he staged at local high school gymnasiums and special venues of note such as the Hyattsville Armory, the Greenbelt Armory, the Silver Spring Armory and the Bladensburg Volunteer Fire Department. These events usually featured a headlining national act with several local teen bands rounding out the bill and were heavily promoted on his television show. It was a lucrative practice that was emulated by numerous area disc jockeys and music promoters throughout the late 1950s and into the 1960s.

After WTTG-TV canceled his program, Milt Grant formed the Capital Broadcasting Company, a corporation that created a new UHF television station called WDCA-TV (Channel 20). The channel began broadcasting on the night of Wednesday, April 20, 1966 in a studio located just outside of Washington, D.C. at 5202 River Road in Bethesda, Maryland. Grant served as chief operating officer until he sold the station on Thursday, August 16, 1979 to Taft Broadcasting for $15 million.

Grant then moved to Texas in 1980 where he purchased television stations in Houston and Dallas and reportedly sold them to Gulf Broadcasting in 1984 for $174 million. A year later he purchased three independent television stations in the cities of Philadelphia, Chicago and Miami, respectively. It proved to be a financial disaster, as his holdings reportedly ran up debts in excess of $419 million, forcing him to file for Chapter 11, Title 11, United States Code bankruptcy in December 1986. Unfazed, Grant spent the next 20 years purchasing and selling television stations in smaller markets all over the Unites States.

Milt Grant died of cancer in Fort Lauderdale, Florida on Saturday, April 28, 2007 at the age of 83. Various obituaries reported that he had been married twice and his survivors included three children, a sister and four grandchildren.

CHAPTER SIXTY
SOCK HOP

As "The Milt Grant Show" was capturing the interest of teenage viewers in the Washington, D.C. area, another less-heralded, dance-oriented show appeared on local television and attempted to capitalize on the youthful rock and roll following. "Sock Hop" aired on WTOP-TV (Channel 9) from Saturday, December 14, 1957 to Saturday, November 1, 1958, and, as its premiere was described in the "Saturday TV Preview" article in the Washington Post, was "a teenage dance session where kids leave their shoes at the door." "Sock Hop" failed to offer the big-name musical performers that its competitor "The Milt Grant Show" offered, but instead concentrated on recorded songs and lengthy shots of the various dancing teens as they moved to the music in the studio. Live musical performances by local bands and visiting entertainers were occasionally featured, but program inconsistencies and low ratings led to the show's eventual demise.

The initial host of "Sock Hop" was Jay Perri, who was born in 1931 in Farrell, Pennsylvania and served in the United States Army during the Korean War before locating to the Washington, D.C. area where he gained some measure of recognition as an R&B and rock and roll disc jockey at radio station WEAM in the middle 1950s. Perri switched over to radio station WTOP on Sunday, April 6, 1957 where he hosted a pop music program entitled "The Jay Perri Show."

Perri's popularity on WTOP radio was such that he was the obvious choice as host for the new television dance program WTOP's brass hoped would bump "The Milt Grant Show" from the top of the local ratings. Perri hosted "Sock Hop" from its opening show on Saturday, December 14, 1957 until Saturday, June 28, 1958, during which time it was situated in an 11am-12pm time slot. (Perri left radio work in the late 1960s and from 1972 to 1985 was an advertising salesman for the Journal newspapers in the Washington, D.C. area before joining the Washington Times as an account executive. He retired in 1995 and died on Sunday, June 5, 2011 of complications from a stroke.)

On Saturday, July 5, 1958, Bob Dalton replaced Jay Perri as the host of "Sock Hop," a move that also coincided with a change in the one-hour program's beginning broadcast time from 11am to 1:30pm. While he didn't have the rock and roll credentials that Perri displayed, Dalton did bring years of experience in local radio and television broadcasting to the table.

Dalton had first joined the announcing staff of WMAL radio and WMAL Television in May 1951 and worked with the company in various capacities for more than a year. In July 1952 he moved over to radio station WTOP and over the next six years hosted a variety of pop music shows included "Hour of Stars," "Sunrise Salute," "Holiday," "The Bob Dalton Show" and "Footsteps in Music." His transition to television as host of "Sock Hop" was reportedly a smooth one, but the immense popularity of "The Milt Grant Show" proved to be too great the program to overcome.

A prime example of the difference in quality between "Sock Hop" and the "The Milt Grant Show" was their advertised live television shows for Saturday, September 13, 1958. While "Sock Hop" and host Bob Dalton welcomed the relatively obscure pop singer Danny Mason (who had previously served a term as a master of ceremonies under the name "Danny Machin" at the Casino Royal Theatre Restaurant in Washington, D.C.), "The Milt Grant Show" featured the Mills Brothers, one of the biggest Black pop music singing acts of the day. The match-up was a no-contest in terms of viewer popularity and musical quality, with the Mills Brothers reportedly pulling in an impressive viewing audience. Similar one-sided head-to-head offerings eventually led to the demise of "Sock Hop" some six weeks later, while "The Milt Grant Show" continued on as a ratings leader until its unceremonious cancellation in April 1961. Host Bob Dalton was still aboard the sinking ship when the final episode of "Sock Hop" aired on Saturday, November 1, 1958.

CHAPTER SIXTY-ONE
SHOW OF STARS

By the time rock and roll music materialized in the 1950s, the notion of placing nationally recognized popular music acts in larger theatres, armories and arenas was already an established practice in the nation's capital. The first legitimate arena-filling rock and roll attraction to sweep into town was Bill Haley and His Comets, who had transformed from a night club act to a major concert attraction in a flash, titillating local promoters and rock and roll fans alike who witnessed their mercurial ascent to the top of the pop music world. After stops in the area during the middle 1950s at such establishments as the Blue Mirror Club and Casino Royal Theatre Restaurant, Haley and his group were soon called back to headline concerts at the city's two largest indoor venues, Uline Arena (1140 3rd Street NE; capacity 8,000) and the District of Columbia National Guard Armory (2001 East Capitol Street SE; capacity 10,000). These were landmark rock and roll events that stand as the first instances where this new style of music was presented in the nation's capital on stages of this magnitude.

The first of these large-scale rock and roll concerts took place at Uline Arena on Friday, November 11, 1955 with Bill Haley and His Comets headlining and the Eldorados and Gene Ammons and His Band filling out the undercard. By that point in time Haley and his band had placed a total of five different singles in various popular records charts in the Billboard magazine, including "(We're Gonna) Rock Around the Clock," which had reached number one on the "Best Sellers in Stores" chart earlier that summer on Saturday, July 9, 1955 and had already sold millions of copies worldwide.

The concert at Uline Arena was reportedly a terrific success, leading promoters Israel and Irvin Feld of Super Attractions to book a traveling show entitled "Rock 'n' Roll Show of '56" which hit Washington, D.C. on Sunday, February 1956 at the District of Columbia National Guard Armory. The show was headlined by Bill Haley and His Comets, with a large supporting cast that consisted of singer-guitarist Bo Diddley, the Platters, the Drifters, the Five Keys, the Turbans, Red Prysock and His Orchestra, the vocal duo Shirley and Lee, and R&B singers LaVern Baker and Roy Hamilton.

Super Attractions did extremely well with this concert, leading the Feld Brothers to book a similar extravaganza entitled "The Biggest Rock 'n' Roll Show of '56" into the District of Columbia National Guard Armory on Sunday, June 3, 1956. This concert event again featured Bill Haley and His Comets as headliners. Two shows, one at 3pm and another at 8:30pm, were scheduled to take place, with other listed attractions in the show being singer-guitarist Bo Diddley, the Drifters, the Platters, the Teenagers, the Teen Queens, the Flamingos, the Colts, Red Prysock and His Big Rock 'n' Roll Orchestra, blues singer Big Joe Turner, and R&B singers LaVern Baker and Clyde McPhatter. Unfortunately, things did not go so smoothly at this particular show.

An article in the Washington Post of Tuesday, June 5, 1956 entitled "Rock 'n' Roll Ban Urged After Melee" detailed the unfortunate series of events that transpired during the evening portion of the Sunday show: "A ban on shows at the National Guard Armory featuring 'Rock and Roll,' the torrid music with the 'big beat,' was urged yesterday by Police Capt. Thomas E. Edwards. Edwards called for the ban after a series of fights and knifings that sent four youths to hospitals during and after a Sunday night Armory show attended by 5,000 'Rock and Roll' fans, mostly teenagers."

The Washington Post then provided a time-table of Sunday night incidents at or near the Armory as the concert took place. At 8:30pm in front of the Armory, 24-year-old Charles Nichols of 5721 5th Street NE was cut on the right arm by an unidentified individual; at

10:30pm 17-year-old William Warfield of 4767 Edgefield Road, Bethesda, was hit on the head with a flying chair during a melee on the balcony; at 11:10pm, 19-year-old Jack L. Jones of1631 Euclid Street NE was struck on the head by an unknown object thrown by one of a group of boys at the corner of East Capitol Street and 15th Streets; at 11:18pm, 16-year-old Howard B. Mahoney of Culpeper, Virginia was cut on the left ear by an unidentified knife-wielding individual as he was standing in front of the Armory; at 11:25pm, A District jail guard named James E. Whalen reported a group of boys threw stones at his car at 19th and C Streets NE, breaking two of the vehicle's windows; and at 11:35pm, 19-year-old Aubrey M. Tolson, Jr. of 527 Oglethorpe Street NW said the windshield and right window of his car were broken by a stone-throwing group of boys at 19th Street NE and Benning Road NE. Capt. Edwards told the Post that 19 District policemen were assigned to Armory traffic details that evening and another 25 special police officers from the National Detective Agency were hired by the promoters of the show and assigned duty inside the Armory. He also stated that no arrests were made on the evening.

As a result of the disturbances that took place at the June 3 concert, the District of Columbia National Guard Armory Board, under the direction of Board Chairman George F. Shea, unanimously voted on Wednesday, October 24, 1956 to ban further rock and roll performances in the facility. The Board, in rendering its final decision, fell back on one of the Armory's statutes, which permits such things as athletic events and contests and "other activities as may be in the interest of the District of Columbia," and decided that rock and roll music did not fall under the latter category.

Although the District of Columbia National Guard Armory was now out of the picture as a viable rock and roll venue, other arena-like facilities were pegged to host the big-name acts that were being lured to the nation's capital and presented before the growing popular music fan base.

Aside from Bill Haley and His Comets, the biggest rock and roll performer to hit Washington, D.C. in the 1950s was 19-year-old teen idol Frankie Avalon, a Philadelphia native who had hit the Top 20 in the Billboard magazine's "Best Sellers in Stores" popular records chart with three different singles in 1958 – "Dede Dinah," "Ginger Bread," and "I'll Wait For You." Avalon also had a red-hot single entitled "Venus" that would eventually reach number one on the Billboard magazine's "The Billboard Hot 100" pop records chart on Monday, March 9, 1959.

On Friday, February 20, 1959, Super Attractions booked a multi-act rock and roll concert at Uline Arena that was headlined by pop singer Frankie Avalon, emceed by Milt Grant and filled out by pop singers Jesse Lee Turner and Linda Laurie, the Crests, the Chantels, Dickie Do and the Donts, and the Show Club Orchestra. Reportedly, this concert had none of the problems that had surfaced at the Bill Haley appearance at the District of Columbia National Guard Armory some three years prior.

The Feld brothers, meanwhile, had enjoyed tremendous success with Carter Barron Amphitheater (4850 Colorado Avenue NW, Washington, D.C.), a 4,200 seat government-owned venue that they had managed since 1954. The Felds had been booking concerts of different types of music all over the Atlantic Coast and decided to hold a week-long, multi-act event at Carter Barron that would accommodate the largest possible number of area rock and roll fans. They called the extravaganza "The Biggest Show of Stars for '59," brought the popular Milt Grant in to emcee, and broke the presentation into two parts with two main headliners.

The first of these shows, which ran for three consecutive nights beginning Tuesday, September 1, 1959, featured pop singer Frankie Avalon as the headliner with a supporting card that included the Clovers, the Kalin Twins, pop singers Annette Funicello, Ray Peterson and Gary Stites, R&B singer Clyde McPhatter, C&W singer-guitarist George

Hamilton IV, rock and roll guitarist Duane Eddy, and Paul Williams and His Show of Stars Orchestra The second part of the show, which ran for four consecutive nights beginning Friday, September 4, 1959, saw pop singer Paul Anka replace Avalon as the headliner, with the undercard losing Duane Eddy, but retaining all the other performers from the first show.

The concert at Carter Barron seemingly went over very well. In an article in the Washington Post of Wednesday, September 2, 1959 entitled "Avalon and Audience Set Rock Creek to Rockin,'" Tony Gieske wrote: "Sometimes it was hard to tell whether there would be entertainment or battle. When Avalon appeared before his young audience, they half-rose from their seats and his life seemed in danger. Ear-splitting screams rent the air like a jet plane squadron...At one point, a young girls stuck her fists in her eyes and wept deep, wracking sobs as her hair uncurled down her neck in the intermittent rain."

An article in the Evening Star of the same date entitled "Teen-Agers Brave Rain for Rock 'n' Rollers" by Roberta Hornig stated: "A series of cloudbursts failed utterly to dampen the ardor of a mob of teen-agers who packed Carter Barron Amphitheater last night to scream for their latest singing idol, Frankie Avalon...For nearly two hours they moaned, sighed, shrieked, and squealed through the rock and roll program. When brown-eyed Frankie appeared, the audience, mostly young women – and very few men – went into a sort of enraptured frenzy."

It was these large-scale shows of the 1950s that introduced arena rock and roll to the nation's capital and inspired promoters of the 1960s to continue the practice of booking such nationally known entertainment into the largest possible venues in the Washington, D.C. area. The appearances of Bill Haley and His Comets, Frankie Avalon and other acts reinforced the notion that rock and roll music was a cultural entity whose popularity would continue to grow and spread on both the local and national levels and remain in demand for years to come. These performers made lasting impacts on their younger teenaged fans, influenced musicians of all ages and provided dynamic entertainment for adult music-lovers as well. In the coming decades rock and roll would achieve even greater heights of popularity in the Washington, D.C. area as waves of new musical entertainers was loomed on the horizon.

CHAPTER SIXTY-TWO
RAY VERNON

Ray Vernon (real name Vernon Wray) was one of the Washington, D.C. area's great rock and roll singers of the 1950s. Later, as the owner and operator of several recording studios in and around the city, he was recognized for his talent as a producer, arranger and sound engineer. Along with two of his brothers he was also an original member of Link Wray and His Ray Men, an outfit now regarded as one of the greatest and most influential rock and roll bands of all-time. Ray Vernon helped kick-start rock and roll in the nation's capital and remained a presence on the local music scene throughout the 1960s, a decade that saw him spend much of his time ensconced on the Wray family estate in Accokeek, Maryland. There, he played and recorded with a procession of talented visiting musicians, all the while managing the musical affairs of his two brothers. With his local legend established, Ray Vernon left the area in 1971 and settled in Arizona where he embarked on new creative ventures.

Vernon Aubrey Wray was born on Monday, January 7, 1924 in the base hospital at Fort Bragg in Cumberland County, North Carolina, just outside the city of Fayetteville. He grew up with his family in the city of Dunn, North Carolina, some 30 miles northeast of the base. He was raised in a musical family and took up the guitar at age 11.

When Vernon Wray was 18 years old his father moved the household to Portsmouth, Virginia. During the late 1940s and early 1950s Wray participated in a succession of C&W bands as a singer-rhythm guitarist with his younger brothers Link and Doug, who had become proficient on lead guitar and drums, respectively. Another participant in these groups was a close family friend and skilled bassist named Brantley "Shorty" Horton, Jr. At this time, Vernon Wray took on the stage name of Lucky Wray and the quartet worked night clubs in Norfolk and Virginia Beach under such monikers as the Melody Four, Lucky Wray and the Lazy Pine Wranglers and Lucky Wray and the Palomino Ranch Gang.

In the summer of 1954 the Wray brothers and their wives relocated from Portsmouth, Virginia to Washington, D.C., where a burgeoning C&W music scene had taken hold. Vernon Wray and his wife Evelyn took a unit 1339 Saratoga Avenue NE #493A in the Brentwood Village apartment complex. Meanwhile, Link and his wife Elizabeth had moved into the same complex and lived a couple doors away at 1345 Saratoga Avenue NE #463D. Doug Wray and Shorty Horton had also made the trip north and would spend several months staying on-and-off with both brothers.

For most of the following year Vernon Wray performed under the stage name of Lucky Wray and worked nightly as the exclusive attraction at the Rendezvous on 10th Street NW. During this time he was singing and playing rhythm guitar and his backup band remained the same as ever – Link Wray on lead guitar, Doug Wray on drums and Shorty Horton on bass. Performing a mix of C&W and rock and roll music, they were still a few years away from shifting the focus of their music to Link's heavy, pre-heavy metal guitar sound and changing the name of their outfit to Link Wray and His Raymen.

In August 1955 a C&W night club called the Ozarks Restaurant opened up five blocks north of the Rendezvous on 10th Street NW in Washington, D.C. and within a month Vernon Wray had switched the band's operations to this new establishment. In early 1956, while performing at the Ozarks Restaurant, the group's performances caught the eye of local music producer Ben Adelman, who liked what he heard and quickly shuttled the quartet into the studio of his True-Tone Recording Company in the Portland Building in Downtown Washington, D.C.

Ben Adelman had a strong business relationship with Don Pierce, president and co-owner of Starday Records, an independent record label which at the time was based in Los Angeles, California that specialized in rockabilly and C&W music and boasted singer-guitarist George Jones as its biggest star. Adelman's recording session with Vernon Wray resulted in three separate 45rp singles that were leased to Starday and released to the public over the course of the next year: "It's Music She Says," backed with "Sick and Tried" (Lucky Wray; Starday Records, 1956); "What-Cha Say Honey," backed with "Got Another Baby" (Lucky Wray; Starday Records, 1956); and "Teenage Cutie," backed with "You're My Song" (Lucky Wray with Link and Doug Wray; Starday Records, 1957). Though these rockabilly singles failed to chart, they did serve to introduce the music of Vernon Wray as "Lucky Wray" to the national music scene.

In March 1957 the Wray brothers and their families moved to the Bolling View Apartments in Southeast Washington, D.C. Vernon Wray and Evelyn took a unit at 210 Orange Street SE #1 and Link and Elizabeth, along with brother Doug, moved into the same building and occupied apartment #4 (today this apartment complex is named River Hill).

The three Wray brothers and Shorty Horton resumed their house band job at the Rendezvous, where they were still being billed as "Lucky Wray." On occasion Vernon Wray took separate bookings at Bob White's Hideaway on Pennsylvania Avenue in the Capitol Hill neighborhood of Washington, D.C. where he worked with Shorty Horton on bass and Ray Scearce on drums as Lucky Wray and His Rock and Roll Trio. In late 1956 and early 1957 Lucky Wray, whose backup band now consisted of Doug Wray, Shorty Horton and guitarist Dick Williams (who temporarily replaced Link Wray, who was recovering from tuberculosis and a recent operation that required the removal of one of his lungs), performed regularly at the Charles Café, a night club on upper 14th Street NW in the Columbia Heights neighborhood of the city that offered both C&W and rock and roll music.

While playing the Charles Café in April 1957, Vernon Wray caught the attention of a visiting booking agent for a New York theater agency who was friends with Bernie Lowe, a producer-pianist-songwriter who was also founder and president of Cameo Records in Philadelphia, Pennsylvania. Lowe was looking for a Southern-flavored Pat Boone for his record label, and was told that Vernon Wray filled the requirements.

The following week Vernon Wray was taken to Lowe's house in the Wincote area of North Philadelphia, the basement of which contained Cameo's recording studio and business. There, he privately auditioned for the Cameo president and was promptly signed to a limited record deal. Lowe also informed Vernon Wray that his recordings would be released under the new stage name "Ray Vernon."

During the final week of April and the first week of May, Ray Vernon made return trips to a Philadelphia studio for two separate sessions (this time with his brother Link, who was still recuperating from his bout with tuberculosis and the loss of a lung). Together, the two Wray brothers, along with six other Cameo studio musicians and a chorus, recorded more than a dozen tracks. Ultimately, four pop music singles were released from this material: "Evil Angel" backed with "Remember You're Mine" (Ray Vernon; Cameo Records, 1957); "Evil Angel" backed with "I'll Take Tomorrow (Today)" (Ray Vernon; Cameo Records, 1957); "Terry" (You're Askin' Too Much) backed with "I'm Countin' On You" (Ray Vernon; Cameo Records, 1957); and "Window Shopping" backed with "I'll Be So Good To You" (Ray Vernon; Cameo Records, 1958).

With the Cameo singles on the market, Ray Vernon spent the remainder of 1957 (with brother Link Wray back in action on lead guitar) performing night club dates at both the Charles Café and the Rendezvous. Meanwhile, all of the Wray Brothers had developed close friendships with Milt Grant and regularly worked on "The Milt Grant Show" – Ray

Vernon as a part-time host and regular featured performer, Link as the lead guitarist for many of the show's featured attractions, and Doug as the house drummer.

Ray Vernon, with his two brothers and Shorty Horton backing him up, headlined record hops for both Don Dillard and Milt Grant at such locations as the Silver Spring Boys Club, the Silver Spring Armory, the Hyattsville Armory and the Bladensburg Volunteer Fire Department. At this time the music they performed was a mix of C&W, pop and rock and roll. Through Milt Grant, Ray Vernon also hosted his own short-lived television show, "Top Tunes with Ray Vernon," which aired on WTTG-Channel 5 on Fridays from 7pm-7:30pm from Friday, September 13, 1957 to Friday, October 18, 1957. On the show Ray would introduce, discuss and play five of the latest top singles moving up the Billboard magazine music popularity charts.

One of the group's more intriguing performances took place at the Silver Spring Armory on Friday, March 14, 1958. In what was advertised as "Milt Grant's Dance and Show," Chuck Berry, one of the nation's top R&B singer-guitarists, headlined a bill that included the Kalin Twins and Ray Vernon and Band. The event drew an audience of more than 1,000 young rock and roll fans and was typical of the star-studded bills that Grant and his friendly competitor Don Dillard offered in the area's larger armories and halls in the late 1950s.

Several weeks later on Sunday, April 20, 1958 Don Dillard staged a record hop at St. Camillus Church in Silver Spring, Maryland which featured Ray Vernon, Link Wray, the Belvederes, and rock and roll singer-guitarist Gene Summers. That summer Milt Grant presented a multi-act concert at the Hyattsville Armory on Friday, August 8, 1958 that was headlined by pop singer Bobby Darin and included appearances by Link Wray, Ray Vernon and rock and roll singer-guitarist Donnie Boyd.

In the spring of 1958 Link Wray, who had increasingly been playing live dates in a trio format with Shorty and Doug (billed simply as "Link Wray"), scored a major hit on the Billboard magazine pop charts with the roaring rock and roll instrumental "Rumble," which was issued on the Cadence record label. Subsequently, the band took on the name "Link Wray and His Ray Men." Ray Vernon, though he still performed rhythm guitar with the group on a semi-regular basis, was no longer the focus of the unit and increasingly took on more of a management role, securing bookings for the band and scouting potential musicians for the fold.

Link Wray and His Ray Men embarked on several abbreviated regional tours throughout the eastern and midwestern sections of the United States that year to support their popular single and Ray Vernon took it upon himself to oversee the band's finances and artistic direction. In early 1959 Link Wray and His Ray Men were signed to Epic Records and went on to release numerous singles for that label in the ensuing years.

In addition to his managerial duties, Ray Vernon kept his own solo career intact and as the decade rounded out released three singles on two different record labels: "Two Teen Age Hearts," backed with "It's So Easy" (Ray Vernon; Mark Records, 1958); "That's You" backed with "I Love You Darling" (Ray Vernon; Mark Records, 1958); and "My Sugar Plum" backed with "Pretty Blue Eyes" (Ray Vernon; Liberty Records, 1959). Unfortunately, these songs failed to enjoy the success of "Rumble" and none made the Billboard magazine charts.

Throughout 1959, Link Wray and His Ray Men, now with a growing cast of musicians in the fold that included singer-keyboardist Bobbie Howard, guitarist Johnny Sneed, keyboardist Bill Hodges, and Ray Vernon serving as a part-time vocalist, continued to perform on "The Milt Grant Show" and work at the Rendezvous in Washington, D.C., their unofficial home base throughout the late 1950s. Over the next several years the band released singles and albums for a number of record labels including Epic and Swan.

In the 1960s Ray Vernon spent much of his time producing records for other artists and managing Link Wray and His Ray Men. He hosted a short-lived rock and roll radio show entitled "Monster Party" on station WEEL out of Fairfax, Virginia in the spring and summer of 1960. In one of his increasingly rare solo appearances, he performed at a dance on Saturday, June 11, 1960 at the Connecticut Belair Country Club in Silver Spring, Maryland where he co-headlined with the Belvederes.

In October 1960 the Ray Vernon Recording Studio was opened in room 327 of the Portland Building at 1129 Vermont Avenue NW in Washington, D.C. Ray Vernon kept the studio going at that location for two years, during which time he produced recordings for a number of area artists including Ronnie Dove, the Fender Benders, Marvin Rainwater, and, of course, Link Wray and His Ray Men. When his lease in the Portland Building expired in October 1962, Ray moved his Ray Vernon Recording Studio to new quarters at 527 9th Street NW, but the studio closed before the year ended.

Throughout 1960 and 1961 Link Wray and His Ray Men featuring Ray Vernon appeared regularly at two different night clubs in the Downtown area of the Washington, D.C., the Ozarks Restaurant, and Vinnie's Grill. With "The Milt Grant Show" being canceled by WTTG in April 1961, the band began focusing on live appearances while Ray Vernon continued his practice of mass-producing singles by the band and either leasing them to independent labels around the country or issuing them in limited quantities on any one of a variety of labels of his own making.

During this time, Ray Vernon was still regarded as a fine rock and roll singer in his own right and continued to make occasional live appearances for a number of local promoters. One interesting event staged by Don Dillard was a "Fun-A-Rama" featuring "The Bootie Hop" – "The Newest, Most Exciting Dance in the Country" at the College Park Ice Skating Club (10203 Baltimore Boulevard, College Park, Maryland) on Friday, October 6, 1961, which was headlined by Link Wray and Vernon Wray, who were billed separately as solo acts. Also performing that evening were the Renaults, the Hot Tamales, R&B singer Prince Preston and rockabilly singer Little Jimmy Dee. Musical backing for all the acts that evening was supplied by Link Wray and His Ray Men.

On Friday, December 1, 1961, Ray Vernon and the Hot Tamales co-headlined a "Twist-a-thon" promoted by local disc jockey Jack Alix at Mackin High School in Washington, D.C. In one of his final area performances as a solo act, Ray Vernon headlined a dance with the Fender Benders at the Cherrydale Fire Department on Lee Highway in Arlington, Virginia on Friday, February 16, 1962. During this early 1960s period, Ray continued recording and issuing 45rpm single records in his own name which appeared on such labels as Ray Vernon, Scottie, Rumble and Mala.

In December 1962 Ray Vernon purchased a sizeable piece of property at 16706 Livingston Road in Accokeek, Maryland. The land contained one large house that served as the main residence, two smaller guest houses in the backyard away from the main road, and a large wooden structure which had served its previous owners as a chicken coop. He also purchased a lot across the street at 16403 Livingston Road which included a one-story, barn-like structure that he converted into Wray's Market and Pool Hall. A personal business office was set up in the basement of the main house and the chicken coop was converted into a private studio officially christened "Wray's Shack 3 Tracks." The worn-down wooden structure was then suitably stocked with an Ampex three-track recorder and innumerable reels of tape.

Ray Vernon then spent the rest of the decade managing Link Wray and His Ray Men, with a large pool of musicians passing through the group on an irregular basis. During these years the band worked lengthy engagements at such area night clubs as Vinnie's Grill, the 1023 Restaurant, the Famous Restaurant and Stick's Restaurant. Various family members, relatives and friends would live for varying periods of time on the Livingston Road compound throughout the nine years he owned the property.

Ray Vernon was also involved in the recording of two critically acclaimed albums in the Accokeek studio – a Link Wray solo effort he co-produced simply entitled "Link Wray" (Link Wray; Polydor Records, 1971), and an album that he co-engineered entitled "Mordicai Jones" (Mordicai Jones; Polydor Records, 1971), which was supposedly a solo effort by former British Walkers leader Bobbie Howard under an assumed name, but in reality featured lead vocals by Gene Johnson, Howard on piano and mandolin, and the musical backing of Link Wray and members of his Ray Men.

In December 1971 the Wray empire in Accokeek, Maryland came to an end. Ray Vernon sold all the property he held along Livingston Road, allegedly disposed of hundreds of cans of tape and the master recordings they contained, and packed up his three-track recorder and personal belongings. With his personal business taken care of, he then moved to Tucson, Arizona and reclaimed his birth name "Vernon Wray."

While various Wray family members scattered, brother Link eventually made his way to Tucson as well, where he and Vernon shared a trailer and established a new recording studio in the area which was dubbed Vernon Wray's Record Factory. While Link Wray put together different versions of the Ray Men in the 1970s and toured the country, Vernon Wray took to performing softer, countrified acoustic blues at venues from Tucson to Los Angeles, and issued a solo album of his work entitled "Wasted" (Vernon Wray; Vermillion Records, 1972).

Ray Vernon was a tremendous musical entertainer who should have been one of the biggest crossover singing stars of his time. Possessing a golden voice that fit perfectly with the country-tinged rockabilly and early-era rock and roll songs he offered, Ray Vernon entertained his fans as a 1950s solo performer and later as a featured singer with the hard-rocking pioneer band Link Ray and His Ray Men. His desire to highlight other musicians and bring out their best on recordings led him away from the spotlight and towards a place where he assumed management responsibilities for his brothers and friends and placed their needs to the forefront, while downplaying his own career aspirations and keeping personal projects in the background. In the late 1970s Ray Vernon's health took a turn for the worse and he died suddenly in Arizona on Sunday, March 25, 1979 at the age of 55.

CHAPTER SIXTY-THREE
VERNON TAYLOR

Vernon Taylor is one of the Washington, D.C. area's first rock and roll stars. The singer-guitarist was a local teen idol who released singles on the Dot and Sun record labels, made regular appearances on local radio and music-oriented television shows, embarked on regional tours throughout the East and Midwest, and during the height of his popularity even made an appearance on "American Bandstand" – a very rare occurrence for any musical performer from the nation's capital.

Vernon Taylor was born on Tuesday, November 9, 1937 in the Layhill community of Montgomery County, Maryland. He grew up in a family of Baptist farmers and spent much of his childhood on a cattle farm in Warrenton, Virginia. At age eight he took up guitar, began learning chords from his two brothers, and was an avid listener of radio programs that featured country music. At age eleven his family returned to Montgomery County and took up residence in Spencerville, Maryland. Taylor, who attended Sherwood High School and would be a part of the 1957 graduating class, was progressing as a singer-guitarist and included Roy Acuff, Gene Autry, Roy Rogers, Eddy Arnold, Grandpa Jones, Hank Williams and Ernest Tubb among his many influences.

During his years at Sherwood High School, Taylor joined a band called the Nighthawks, which played a mixture of pop and C&W songs. From 1954 to 1956 the band performed regularly on Saturday nights at the Beltsville Fire Department in Prince George's County, Maryland. At the time the group consisted of Taylor handling vocals and rhythm guitar, lead guitarist Jack Quaintance, bassist Denny Pilgrim and drummer Roger Pries. Quaintance, Pilgrim and Pries all lived in Silver Spring, Maryland at the time and all three finished high school at Emerson Institute in Washington, D.C.

When Elvis Presley hit the scene and began releasing singles on Sun Records, Taylor added several of his songs to his band's set list. At one point during their Beltsville Fire Department run, the Nighthawks served as the backup band for C&W fiddler Curley Smith, further increasing their reputation as one of the area's best and most versatile musical outfits. The Nighthawks also performed at Glen Echo Park's Spanish Ballroom, local USO concerts, and on live radio broadcasts over station WGAY.

In early 1957 Taylor put together a new rockabilly band he called Vernon Taylor and the Southerners. The initial lineup for this group consisted of Taylor on lead vocals and rhythm guitar, lead guitarist Joe Carroll, steel guitarist Danny Pendleton, bassist Denny Pilgrim and drummer Duke Maddox. That summer the band worked weekends at Glen Echo Park's Spanish Ballroom and during one of their performances were observed by the popular bluegrass singer Mac Wiseman. At the time Wiseman was recording for Dot Records, a record company based in Hollywood, California whose stable of artist included such acts as Pat Boone, Tab Hunter and the Del-Vikings.

Wiseman was impressed by what he saw at the Spanish Ballroom and promptly notified Dot president Randy Wood of the talented young rockabilly singer. Studio time was secured and in July 1957 Taylor traveled to Nashville, Tennessee and recorded four songs with studio musicians. The results of these sessions were the singles "Losing Game" backed with "I've Got the Blues" (Vernon Taylor; Dot Records, 1957) and "Why Must You Leave Me" backed with "Satisfaction Guaranteed" (Vernon Taylor; Dot Records, 1958). Only one of these songs, "Why Must You Leave Me," was actually written by Taylor.

As part of the promotional campaign behind his first Dot single release, Taylor made a live appearance on the new Philadelphia-based musical entertainment television show

"American Bandstand." The show was hosted by Dick Clark and aired for one hour on weekday afternoons at 3:30pm before a nationwide audience on the ABC network.

On the morning of Thursday, October 24, 1957 Taylor left Washington, D.C. with Don Owens' secretary and upon arriving at the WFIL-TV building on Market Street ran through a quick dress rehearsal in Studio B, the room from which the show was broadcast. During the live afternoon show that day, which also included a performance by 21-year-old pop singer Cathy Carr, Taylor sang his budding hit song "Losing Game." Unbeknownst to Taylor, the episode was watched by Sam Phillips, founder and owner of the Sun Record Company in Memphis, Tennessee. Phillips was impressed by Taylor's singing and made a note to establish contact with the young rockabilly singer from the nation's capital.

Just as his first Dot single was being released to the public, Taylor accepted an offer from Don Owens to lead the house band on the "Don Owens TV Jamboree" television program, which aired on Saturday nights from 9pm to 10pm on WTTG-Channel 5 in the Washington, D.C. area. Taylor's band was initially called the Circle-O-Boys before quickly switching their name back to the Southerners. They often performed their own selections on-camera, in addition to being called upon to back up some of the national acts who appeared on the show. Some of the pop and C&W performers they played behind included singers Patsy Cline and Eddy Arnold; singer-guitarists George Jones, Webb Pierce and George Hamilton IV; rock and roll singer-pianist Jerry Lee Lewis; and the team of multi-styled guitarist Les Paul and singer-guitarist Mary Ford. Vernon Taylor and the Southerners remained featured performers on the show for the duration of the program from Saturday, August 3, 1957 to Saturday, December 3, 1960.

In the summer of 1958 Sam Phillips approached Jack Clement, the main producer-songwriter for his Sun Record Company, and inquired about the possibility of adding Vernon Taylor to the Sun Records stable. Clement, a talented C&W singer-guitarist in his own right, had spent the early 1950s living and performing in the Washington, D.C. area where he had been friends with Don Owens for several years and was a longtime admirer of Taylor's musical talents.

In the summer of 1958 Clement, with Owens' blessing, arranged to have Taylor partake in several sessions at the Sun Studio at 706 Union Avenue in Memphis, Tennessee. Over the course of the next year Taylor would repeatedly return to Memphis, and, with the help of studio musicians, ultimately recorded several songs for the Sun Record Company. These sessions resulted in two single releases for Taylor on the Sun label: "Breeze" backed with "Today is a Blue Day" (Vernon Taylor; Sun Records, November 1958); and "Sweet and Easy to Love" backed with "Mystery Train" (Vernon Taylor; Sun Records, August 1959). Other Sun recordings by Taylor would remain in the vaults for years, with some eventually being reissued on rockabilly compilation CDs.

With the Sun singles on the market, Taylor opted to avoid the Washington, D.C. area night club circuit and instead focused on concert and festival performances. He balanced his weekly appearances on the "Don Owens TV Jamboree" television program with abbreviated regional tours throughout the East and Midwest in support of his single releases.

Taylor's local bookings tended to be special events, like a Sunday, December 21, 1958 concert at the Villa Theatre in Rockville, Maryland where he was second-billed to singer Patsy Cline on a program that also included singer-guitarist Luke Gordon. Taylor's band throughout this period remained the Southerners, who moved forward despite the occasional replacement of players. In the early 1960s Taylor and Maddox reorganized their quintet and picked up new members in guitarist Billie Copeland and bassist Steve Foster from the freshly disbanded Terry and the Pirates, along with steel guitarist Danny

Pendleton. With the reconstituted lineup, Vernon Taylor and the Southerners continued to perform as a unit throughout the first half of the new decade.

In the middle 1960s Vernon Taylor became disillusioned with the business side of the music industry and began to cut back on his musical activities, instead concentrating on family commitments and his career in the printing industry. He disbanded the Southerners, retreated to the northern reaches of Maryland, and only made public musical appearances on special occasions.

In recent years, when the music industry experienced an exciting rockabilly revival, Taylor's work was at the forefront. In 1995 he released a CD collection of his Dot and Sun material entitled "There's Only One…Your Lovin' Man" (Vernon Taylor; Eagle Records, 1995) and in 1999 a CD of new studio material was issued entitled "Daddy's Rockin'" (Vernon Taylor; Run Wild Records, 1999). In addition, a number of his recordings have been included on various rockabilly compilations, making his music available to a new generation of early-era rock and roll fans.

CHAPTER SIXTY-FOUR
THE THUNDERBIRDS

During the 1950s teen dances grew in popularity throughout the Washington, D.C. area. Accordingly, the number of teen rock and roll bands in the Washington, D.C. area expanded at a rapid pace throughout these years and into the 1960s. With rock and roll increasingly directed at teenagers and young adults through television programs, radio shows, record album and singles, and feature-length movies, its demand necessitated the formation of bands by the teens themselves, and the various teen organizations that offered dances and live music provided the inspiration necessary to keep such an artistic cycle in motion.

As teen rock and roll bands began to emerge throughout the nation's capital in the middle 1950s, one of the forerunners of the new musical movement was the Thunderbirds, a guitar-oriented quartet that hailed from Southeast Washington, D.C. and specialized in popular rockabilly and early-era rock and roll songs. The Thunderbirds came together during the summer of 1955 and when interest in rock and roll began to accelerate among the youths of the city the group acquired house band status at the St. Francis Xavier Parish Teen Club, which staged popular weekend CYO dances for the Southeast teens. The band eventually branched out and performed at similar-type dances and social events throughout the area.

The Thunderbirds established themselves as rock and roll pioneers in the talent-rich territory of Southeast Washington, D.C. and inspired scores of other area musicians practice their craft and follow in their footsteps. They are known to have been the favorite band of a young and upcoming rock and roll guitarist named Danny Gatton, who would watch them rehearse during his pre-teen years and later use those experiences as motivation to become a professional musician and create his own legend.

The Thunderbirds formed when Dick Grimes and Harry Early, two youths from the Congress Heights neighborhood of Southeast Washington, joined forces with two other youths, Jack Reid and Gene Newport, who hailed from a smallish, unnamed neighborhood that was sandwiched between Bolling Air Force Base and South Capitol Street SE. Grimes, born in 1940, was raised at 121 Trenton Place SE and at one point his parents rented out the basement of their home to a couple, the husband of which was a steel guitar player. This man's cousin, who played a regular guitar, would often stop by to rehearse, and at age 11 Grimes began watching the two practice, eventually learning their chords and playing guitar on his own.

A childhood friend of Dick Grimes was Harry Early, also born in 1940, who lived a couple blocks away in an apartment on Brothers Place SE. Early took up the drums and began joining Grimes in musical jam sessions. A friend introduced the pair to a guitarist named Gene Newport, who lived a couple miles to the south at 127 Darrington Street SE, which was situated in a residential area just west of South Capitol Street SE. One block over from Newport at 89 Elmira Street SW was a friend of Newport's named Jack Reid, also a guitar player, who had previously lived on Atlantic Street SE in the Highland Dwellings neighborhood of the city. (Elmira Street SW actually straddled the border of Southwest and Southeast Washington, D.C.)

The quartet came together in the summer of 1955, at which time Grimes, Early and Newport had finished their schooling at Kramer Junior High School in Anacostia and were preparing to enter the 10th grade that fall at Anacostia High School. Reid was a year younger and was set to begin his ninth grade year at Kramer Junior High School. When these four teenagers decided to form a band, they took their name from the Ford model car that had just hit the showrooms in 1955 – the Thunderbird – and they initially worked out C&W tunes in the basement of Dick Grimes' house on Trenton Place SE, a room that became their primary rehearsal space.

As the music of Elvis Presley began to figure prominently in the evolution of popular music, the Thunderbirds began concentrating on learning songs by Bill Haley and His Comets, Jerry Lee Lewis, Carl Perkins, Gene Vincent, the Everly Brothers, and, of course, Presley himself. They were unusual in their approach to making rockabilly and rock and roll music, as they featured a three-guitar attack, with Newport handling most of the lead vocals and often times tuning the strings on his six-string guitar down to play bass lines, and Early pounding along on a lone snare drum.

When not rehearsing in the Grimes basement, the band would get together and practice in the basement of Jack Reid's home on Elmira Street SW, while a young 10-year-old named Danny Gatton, who lived directly across the street at 88 Elmira Street SW, perched himself on the stairs and watched studiously as the band of older teens prepared their material. Gatton was tutored at times by both Reid and Newport and would go on to become recognized as one of the world's greatest popular music guitarists.

From the onset, the Thunderbirds based out of the St. Francis Xavier Parish Teen Club in Southeast Washington, D.C. Early on they picked up a gentleman named Mike Mead as their manager, who became instrumental in helping them obtain local bookings. The band performed at teen dances, schools and churches all over the Washington, D.C. area. They regularly appeared in Washington, D.C. at Immaculate Conception School, St. Cecilia's Academy, St. Ann's Catholic School, St. Ann Roman Catholic Church, the Church of the Assumption Teen Club, the St. Teresa of Avila Catholic Church Teen Club, St. Thomas Moore Catholic School and St. Timothy's Episcopal Church.

The Thunderbirds performed at a number of special events including a concert at Howard Hall on the campus of St. Elizabeth's Hospital and prom dances at Anacostia High School. They embarked on a special week-long tour in June 1957 of Fort Carson, an expansive United States Army installation located near Colorado Springs, Colorado, where they performed in officers' clubs and special on-base functions.

The Thunderbirds also frequently worked in Maryland at the Maryland Park Junior High Teen Club (Capitol Heights), Mount Calvary Catholic School (Forestville), the St. Bernard Catholic Church Teen Club (Riverdale) and the St. Ambrose Catholic School Teen Club (Cheverly). During its existence, the Thunderbirds were regularly booked to perform at local dances by radio station WPGC and worked several Milt Grant record hops in places like the Fredericksburg Armory in Virginia and Glen Echo Park's Spanish Ballroom in Montgomery County, Maryland.

To minimize distractions the Thunderbirds took to practicing at the Livingston Barber Shop, which had opened in 1957 at 4648 Livingston Road SE in Washington, D.C., just steps away from the Maryland line. The business was owned by Wade H. Sheppard (known to his customers and fellow musicians as "Shep"), a skilled barber and stand-up bass player in numerous C&W bands around the city.

Sheppard set up a back room in his shop as a sound studio and allowed scores of local musicians to come in and work on their material. Throughout the 1950s and into the early 1960s other top bands from the area including Terry and the Pirates and the Kalin Twins frequently used Shep's digs as a rehearsal space. (It should be noted that from 1957 to 1958 the Livingston Barber Shop was located at 4648 Livingston Road SE, then in 1959 it apparently was moved two doors down to 4652 Livingston Road SE, where it would remain for many years to come.)

The Thunderbirds continued their flight throughout the late 1950s, eventually landing and disbanding in the spring of 1959. Grimes, Early and Newport had all graduated from

Anacostia High School in 1958 and Reid was set to graduate in June 1959. One of the band's very last gigs took place on the S.S. Mount Vernon ship that sailed the Potomac River.

An article in the Prince George's Post of Thursday, April 30, 1959 entitled "Teen Club Cruise is Set for May 1" read: "Seventeen Teen Clubs representing Area C of the Prince George's County Recreation Department will hold their fourth annual Moonlight Cruise on May 1. The cruise, which will begin at 8p.m., will sail down the Potomac aboard the U.S.S. Mount Vernon, and will return to the Wilson Line pier by 11p.m. On the trip dancing will be held; the music and vocals being provided by the 'Thunderbirds.' A record attendance of over 1200 participants is expected for this event." The ship reportedly hosted an overflow audience that night and the festive evening served as a fitting conclusion to exciting reign of the Thunderbirds.

With the Thunderbirds grounded for good, the band members launched off in other directions. Gene Newport and Jack Reid landed in another rock and roll band called the Jesters, which played everything from country clubs and bar mitzvahs to Washington, D.C. night clubs like the Parkside Café. Later, in the middle 1960s, Gene Newport played bass in a version of the Saxtons at Benny's Rebel Room and then spent several years with the Classics. Dick Grimes went on to play guitar for the rock and roll band the Dominoes for several years in the early and middle 1960s at Washington, D.C. night clubs such as the Starlite Restaurant and the Shelter Room. He later spent eight years with a pop music band called the Four Sharps, which mainly worked American Legions, Moose Lodges and private club events throughout Northern Virginia. Harry Early, meanwhile, spent several years in the United States Marine Corps after leaving the Thunderbirds and never played in a formal band again.

CHAPTER SIXTY-FIVE
THE OFF KEYS

One of the earliest teen rock and roll bands on the local circuit was the Off Keys, who formed in Bladensburg, Maryland in the spring of 1956 and made their debut at a teen dance at St. Ambrose Catholic School in Cheverly, Maryland. The band was formed by piano player Sam Paladino and enjoyed tremendous local fame for their electrifying performances at the Bladensburg Volunteer Fire Department, the Hyattsville Armory, and a number of local high schools, in addition to regular appearances on "The Milt Grant Show" and at various area night clubs. The emergence of this band changed the face of the local teen club dances.

Sam Paladino, the force behind the Off Keys, grew up in a house on Annapolis Road in Bladensburg, Maryland just down the street from Bladensburg High School. In the spring of 1956, the young piano player was finishing his eighth grade year at St. Ambrose Catholic School and began attending the Bladensburg Teen Club, which was then held at Bladensburg Junior High School at 4915 Annapolis Road – today this brick building houses the Bladensburg Elementary School. Paladino brought with him to the teen club a love for R&B and the relatively new rock and roll sounds. Chaperones at the teen club asked Paladino to put together a band that could perform live for the teens and the talented pianist recruited two other Bladensburg youths into the fold, saxophonist Roger Hughes and drummer Jack Henderson.

As a rocking trio, the Off Keys specialized in songs by Fats Domino, Little Richard, Huey "Piano" Smith and Elvis Presley. The performed at teen dances at the Bladensburg Teen Club and St. Ambrose Catholic School, as well as private parties in the surrounding neighborhoods. In the fall of 1957 the three original Off Keys were joined by saxophonist Dick Moody, guitarist Marvin French and bassist Larry King. At that time the band began playing a regular 8pm-11:30pm Friday-night gig at the Bladensburg Volunteer Fire Department, a run that would last for more than 18 months and establish the band members as local rock stars.

In early 1958 the Off Keys expanded to nine pieces by replacing Marvin French with a dynamic lead guitarist named Clarence Perry, and adding a pair of saxophonists in Art Gould and Steve Merenshaw, and rhythm guitarist-bassist Luman Perry (brother of the aforementioned Clarence). With all nine band members then attending Bladensburg High School (all would graduate in either 1958 or 1959), the Off Keys became one of the most popular teen bands in the area.

One of the features of the Off Keys was Clarence Perry, who rates as one of the most dynamic guitarists to ever emerge from the Washington, D.C. area. Perry displayed reckless abandon onstage – dancing and jumping about, throwing his axe around and playing the guitar with his teeth. No one in Prince George's County had ever seen or heard anything like it before and it was during his stay with the Off Keys that the band's performances at the Bladensburg Volunteer Fire Department drew capacity crowds every Friday night.

Clarence Perry was born in Camden, Arkansas and his family eventually landed in Bladensburg, Maryland in the early 1950s. At the age of 17 in 1957 he picked up a guitar, learned basic chords from his mother (an excellent banjo player in her own right), and played along with Chet Atkins and Hank Williams tunes on the radio.

Sam Paladino recruited Perry into the Off Keys and the guitarist's first gig with the band was at a record hop at Bladensburg Junior High School that reportedly drew a standing-room-only crowd. Shortly after that, the Off Keys performed at a talent show at Bladensburg

High School and during a rendition of the song "Bo Diddley" Perry's crazy duck-walking and teeth-on-guitar antics caused the chaperones to pull the curtains on the band, only to have Perry jump through an opening before they closed for good and continue playing while the cafeteria full of teenagers went wild with cheers and screams. The following Friday night the Bladensburg Volunteer Fire Department was filled to capacity to see the Off Keys and their new manic guitarist. It was the beginning of a lengthy run of sold-out shows for the band in the spacious facility.

Throughout 1958 the Off Keys also performed at area teen dances at Center School (Greenbelt), St. Mary's School (Landover Hills), the Beltsville Fire Department, the Greenbelt Armory and the Denton Armory (in Caroline County on Maryland's Eastern Shore). That summer, after one of their exciting Friday night Bladensburg Volunteer Fire Department performances, the band ventured down to Capitol Arena in Washington, D.C. where they played onstage at the popular country music "Barn Dance" events that were staged by promoter Don Owens.

The journey to the Capitol Arena became a regular Friday late-night excursion for the Off Keys and it was during one of those jam sessions that the band came to the attention of C&W music guitarist Roy Clark, who was living with his wife Barbara at the time in Hyattsville, Maryland, not far from many of the Off Key members. Clark caught a glimpse of the Off Keys one evening and subsequently sent his wife Barbara – herself a graduate of Bladensburg High School – to scout the group at the Bladensburg Volunteer Fire Department.

Based on his wife's recommendation, Roy Clark then began inviting the Off Keys to join him onstage at Capitol Arena for some extended jamming at the dances, a practice which the band engaged in on a regular basis for several months during the second half of 1958 and into 1959 (the "Barn Dance" events were switched to Saturday nights at the Capitol Arena in January 1959). It was also the beginning of collaborations between pianist Sam Paladino and Roy Clark that would endure until the talented guitarist would depart the nation's capital for Las Vegas in September 1960.

In September 1958 the Off Keys entered into a Washington, D.C. recording studio called Capitol Transcriptions Inc. to record a single for Debbie Records, a New York City-based company owned and operated by Ray Rainwater, brother of C&W singer-guitarist Marvin Rainwater, who had seen the band performing at the Capitol Arena and wanted to lay down their sound on vinyl. The resulting single, "Walkin' the Dog" backed with "Baby Baby" (The Off Keys; Debbie Records, 1958), featured an eight-man version of the band (the lineup consisted of both Perry brothers – with Clarence handling lead guitar and vocals and Luman playing bass, Paladino, Moody, Hughes, Gould, Merenshaw and Henderson), but was poorly promoted and failed to make the Billboard magazine charts.

That same month several members of the Off Keys were called upon by their mentor, the soon-to-be-famous C&W-rock singer-guitarist Roy Clark, who enlisted their services to back him on the single "Please Mr. Mayor" backed with "Puddin'" (Roy Clark; Debbie Records, 1958), recordings that were made at Capitol Transcriptions Inc. and released that November.

Shortly after those recordings sessions were completed, Luman Perry recruited Fred Jaeschke to join the band as a bass player and fill the void left by the departing Larry King. Jaeschke hailed from Colmar Manor, Maryland and had graduated from Bladensburg High School back in 1956, during which time he had played with a C&W music band. His acceptance into the fold allowed Luman Perry to move over to rhythm guitar on a permanent basis and gave Clarence Perry more room to experiment with his innovative riffs and intricate leads. The dual guitar work provided by the dynamic Perry brothers created a fuller and more powerful sound for the band.

Throughout 1958 and into 1959 the Off Keys made several appearances on "The Milt Grant Show," the popular teen dance television program that aired six days a week on WTTG-TV Channel 5 from the Raleigh Hotel in Washington, D.C. It was on this show that the Off Keys once placed second in a televised "Battle of the Bands" competition and it was through their stellar on-camera performances that they became the house band at weekly record hops staged by Grant on Sunday afternoons at the Hyattsville Armory. During these concert-like events which took place throughout the fall months of 1958, the Off Keys appeared as headliners on numerous occasions, and were also called upon to serve back-up band duties for some of the era's top musical performers including the Silhouettes and a number of R&B singers including Ruth Brown, Jackie Wilson and Brook Benton.

With the advent of a new year, the Off Keys kicked things off by playing a Milt Grant record hop on Saturday, January 10, 1959 at their home base of Bladensburg High School, triple-billed with rockabilly singer-guitarist Vernon Taylor and Jerry Dallman and the Knightcaps. Not long thereafter, guitarist Clarence Perry left the band to join the Saxtons and was replaced by another Bladensburg High School student, Duke Duquette.

In the spring of 1959 the Off Keys played their first area night club gigs at the Dixie Pig on Bladensburg Road in Cottage City, Maryland. The headliner at the club at that time was a newly arrived act from Wilmington, North Carolina called Charlie Daniels and the Rockets. The various Off Keys members got to know the transplants quite well.

At one point Charlie Daniels and the Rockets were booked for a week at the Ocean Plaza Ballroom in Carolina Beach, North Carolina with Huey Smith and the Clowns. Daniels and his group played the first few days of that job while the Off Keys covered for them in Maryland at the Dixie Pig. For the final three nights – Friday, April 3 through Sunday, April 5 – the bands switched places and the Off Keys headed to North Carolina to finish the week off.

Later, while working the Dixie Pig, Daniels changed the name of his band to the Jaguars and continued to perform in Washington, D.C. area night clubs for the next two years. He later went on to great fame and fortune with a string of Southern rock hits including "The Devil Went Down to Georgia" (The Charlie Daniels Band; Epic Records, 1979) which reached number one on Billboard magazine's "Hot Country Singles" chart on Saturday, August 25, 1979 and peaked at number three on their "Billboard Hot 100" pop music chart on Saturday, September 15, 1979.

A major highlight in the Off Keys odyssey was their Sunday, April 12, 1959 appearance on the nationally broadcasted CBS television show, "Ted Mack and the Original Amateur Hour," which at that time originated from Studio 54 at Broadway and West 54th Street in New York City. A unique and innovative program for its time, this show was in existence from 1948 until 1970 and was one of the very few programs that aired over all four major television networks at different times during the Golden Age of Television. The band, described in promotional material for the show as "An Instrumental Combo from Bladensburg, Maryland," passed two separate auditions in Baltimore, Maryland before being accepted as contestants on the program. When their opportunity arrived they performed a rendition of Huey "Piano" Smith's "I Like Birdland." While the Off Keys didn't win first prize, their appearance on the program did provide them with the designation of being the very first Washington, D.C.-based rock and roll band to ever perform on the show.

The Off Keys remained active through May 1959. During their final weeks, in addition to working opposite Charlie Daniels and the Jaguars at the Dixie Pig, they played jobs at several Washington, D.C. rock and roll night clubs including Guy's Place in Southeast and the Parkside Café on 14th Street NW.

In the spring of 1959 after their Parkside Café engagement ended, the Off Keys disbanded, though many of their players remained on the local music scene including: Dick Moody and Duke Duquette, who joined the Savoys, a popular rock and roll band that mainly played dances at the West Lanham Hills Volunteer Fire Department; Clarence and Luman Perry, who formed the Perry Mates and regularly appeared at the Rocket Room (Clarence Perry later worked with the legendary singer-guitarist Roy Orbison in Nashville); and Sam Paladino, who joined Roy Clark and the Stardusters during the fall of 1959 and remained with the band until September 1960. Through the years he has worked with dozens of top bands and musicians including guitarists Danny Gatton and Roy Buchanan, the Orioles and blues singer Cathy Ponton King.

Fame and national recognition somehow eluded the Off Keys and although their dissolution marked the end of the 1950s teen rock era, their influence lingered for years throughout the county. The talents of these great musicians would still be heard for years to come in various professional bands on the Washington, D.C. area night club circuit.

CHAPTER SIXTY-SIX
JERRY DALLMAN AND THE KNIGHTCAPS

Jerry Dallman and the Knightcaps emerged from Laurel, Maryland in the fall of 1956 and became known for their popular single release "The Bug," a song written about a frenetic style of dance displayed by teens at the Fort George G. Meade Teen Club in Anne Arundel County, Maryland. Years after its initial release, the song unexpectedly turned up in the John Waters comedy movie "Hairspray" (New Line Cinema, 1988) sparking renewed interest in Dallman and his band among the followers of 1950s rock and roll music. When "The Bug" was initially released in December 1958 it was never properly marketed or distributed, thus dashing any chances the band had for national stardom. Still, they soldiered on and established themselves as one of the most popular teen rock and roll bands of the time in the Washington, D.C. area.

Jerry Dallman, the leader of the band, was born in Washington, D.C. and raised in Laurel, Maryland, where as a youth in the early 1950s he taught himself to sing and play guitar. He formed the Knightcaps in the fall of 1956 at the start of his senior year at Laurel High School. Originally a trio, the group was rounded out by pianist Bert Gosnell and guitarist Robert McKenzie, two classmates of his at Laurel High whom he'd met while they were in a classroom practicing the Elvis Presley song "Don't Be Cruel" for a school musical. The band took on the name Jerry Dallman and the Knightcaps and debuted on Saturday, November 17, 1956 in a talent contest at the grand opening of the Laurel Shopping Center. Also performing that day were country music acts such as Jimmy Dean and the Texas Wildcats (featuring guitarist Billy Grammer) and singer-guitarist George Hamilton IV. Dean later joined the boys for a late lunch that day at the White Coffee Pot restaurant and complimented them on their first place prize.

Jerry Dallman and the Knightcaps then began playing dances at teen clubs and schools throughout suburban Maryland. From 1956 to 1958 they were regulars at the Odenton Teen Club, the Laurel Teen Club, the Fort George G. Meade Teen Club, the Laurel Fire Department and the Knights of Pythius Hall in Annapolis, Maryland. Schools that booked them for dances included Waterloo Junior High School (Elkridge), Arundel High School (Gambrills), DeMatha Catholic High School (Hyattsville), St. Mary's High School (Annapolis) and Laurel High School (Laurel). They also were a popular attraction at officers' clubs at a number of local military bases including Fort George G. Meade and Bolling Air Force Base. The band specialized in songs by Elvis Presley, Roy Orbison and the Crickets (featuring singer-guitarist Buddy Holly).

In June 1957 the Knightcaps added Gary Edenfield on drums, a Laurel, Maryland native who was attending Arundel High School at the time. Edenfield told Dallman about an unusual dance being performed at the Fort George G. Meade Teen Club by teens that, when the right type of rhythm was being played, would stand in a circle and frantically pass around an imaginary insect. Later that year, using this particular dance exhibition as inspiration, Dallman penned "The Bug" in a single 30-minute session.

Edenfield's stepfather sold concessions at Uline Arena and in January 1958 a customer of his named Joe Drew introduced the band to music producer Ben Adelman. That month Adelman had Jerry Dallman and the Knightcaps record a demo of "The Bug" at his studio, Empire Records and Recording Studios, in the Takoma neighborhood of Washington, D.C. Drew then took the primitive recording to local television personality Milt Grant in an effort to get the band booked on his popular music-oriented television show.

Milt Grant loved "The Bug" and had the band rerecord the tune that summer at the newly opened Edgewood Recording Studio (1129 Vermont Avenue NW, Room 101,

Washington, D.C.). The end result of the Edgewood session was the 45rpm single record "The Bug" backed with "Honey Bee" (Jerry Dallman and the Knightcaps; Punch Records, 1958), with writing credits for both songs going to "Dallman-Davis-Cooper." ("Davis" was Cindy Davis, a pseudonym Kay Adelman, and "Cooper" was Fred Cooper, a pseudonym for Milt Grant, neither of whom had anything to do with writing the song.)

"The Bug" gained Jerry Dallman and the Knightcaps instant local fame and the band came very close to landing a major record label contract. The single was released in December 1958 and sold extremely well in the Washington, D.C. and Baltimore regions and was praised in such national publications as Billboard and Cash Box.

Under the direction of Baltimore-based road manager Stan Hoffman, Jerry Dallman and the Knightcaps embarked on an abbreviated tour of several Northeast states in support of the song, and made appearances on both "The Milt Grant Show" and "The Buddy Deane Show" in Baltimore. Unfortunately, Milt Grant allegedly rebuffed leasing offers from several national labels including Epic Records, thus dashing the group's hopes of national stardom. The single remained the only 45rpm record ever issued by Punch Records, which in reality was an independent label created by Grant. It seems that Grant basically had the band record the song, pressed a limited number of copies on his own fly-by-night record label, and inexplicably did nothing further with the product after the stock had been depleted.

Jerry Dallman and the Knightcaps pressed on throughout the late 1950s and into the early 1960s and played numerous dances at the Laurel and Fort George G. Meade Teen Clubs. They also performed at rock and roll record hops for both Milt Grant and Don Dillard at the Hyattsville Armory where they played on some amazing bills headlined by the likes of Link Wray and His Ray Men, singer-guitarist Bo Diddley and pop singer Annette Funicello. Another incredible gig for the band was the "Rock 'N Roll Spectacular" at the University of Maryland's Ritchie Coliseum on Saturday, December 27, 1958 where they were part of a bill that was headlined by Bill Haley and His Comets and included Terry and the Pirates, rockabilly singer-guitarist Vernon Taylor and others.

In the spring of 1959 Ben Adelman again brought the Knightcaps, minus founder Jerry Dallman, (who, during his final 18 months with the band, was frequently absent from the group's rehearsals and performances) into his Empire Records and Recording Studios. There, he matched the band with pop singer Jack Donovan to record a single that featured a song he felt had potential to appear as the theme song in a major science fiction movie that was in the works. The movie was entitled "Time Machine" (Galax Films, Inc., 1960) and its musical arranger was Russell Garcia, whom Adelman was well acquainted with. When Adelman was told by Knightcaps guitarist Robert McKenzie of a song of the same title written by Gary Edenfield, he felt he could profit by arranging a deal through Garcia with Galax Films, Inc. to lease the single to the studio, as well as issuing it on one of his own independent record labels.

The recording session for this project included Robert McKenzie on guitar, Bert Gosnell on piano, Gary Edenfield on drums, an individual from the Phil Flowers camp known only as "Whiskey" on bass and Jack Donovan handling lead vocals. The resulting single was "Time Machine" backed with "I Wanna Cry" (Jack Donovan and the Knight Caps; Empire Records, 1959). The song "Time Machine" was credited to "Drew-Davis-Edenfield," with "Drew" being the aforementioned Joe Drew and "Davis" being Cindy Davis, a pseudonym for Kay Adelman. These credits ensured profits for her husband Ben Adelman, with Knightcaps drummer Gary Edenfield receiving one-third of the credit for the song he wrote entirely by himself. The flipside of "I Wanna Cry" listed writing credits for "Blocker-Davis," with the true identity of "Blocker" remaining a mystery to the present day.

The "Time Machine" single was given a rush release in June 1959, but failed to make an impact on the national scene and was ultimately turned down by Garcia for inclusion in the film. The movie "Time Machine" was released in August of 1960 and garnered large viewing audiences and favorable reviews.

The Knightcaps soldiered on, though changes were on the horizon. They played their first night club engagement at the California Inn in Laurel, Maryland on Saturday, November 26, 1960 and after an appearance at the Fort George G. Meade Teen Club on Saturday, February 18, 1961, Dallman departed from the group. Bert Gosnell and Robert McKenzie also left the band at that time and Gary Edenfield went about reorganizing the outfit. He moved himself from drums to vocals and rhythm guitar and welcomed to the band lead guitarist Joe Ecker (from Howard County, Maryland), and bassist Bob Mitchell and drummer Bobby Kuykendahl (both from Montgomery County, Maryland). This quartet continued to perform as the Knightcaps at local night clubs in the Laurel area such as the Turf Club, the South Seas, the California Inn and Nuzback's Bar. The group ultimately disbanded in 1963.

An interesting side note to the Knightcaps saga is that in the early 1960s Gary Edenfield often performed on long-necked banjo with guitarist Bart Johnson as Gary and Bart at the now-legendary Washington, D.C. coffee house Coffee 'n' Confusion. The duo also made appearances at several other folk music night clubs in the city including the Cellar Door, the Brickskeller and Bohemian Caverns. Edenfield also performed during the middle and late 1960s in Laurel-based rock and roll bands called the Windjammers and the Streetwalkers – groups that included several of his former Knightcaps bandmates. Jerry Dallman, meanwhile, remained a legendary figure on the local music scene because of his involvement with "The Bug," though he rarely played in public after leaving the Knightcaps. In his later years he lived a quiet life in his hometown of Laurel, Maryland and passed away from heart disease on Tuesday, March 28, 2006 at the age of 66.

CHAPTER SIXTY-SEVEN
THE SAXTONS

An extremely popular and influential rock and roll band in the Washington, D.C. area during the late 1950s was the Saxtons, a Prince George's County, Maryland combo that rose to the top of the local night club scene, toured the country and had aspirations of becoming a national act. The band formed in December 1956 when two separate groups of musicians met and merged at the Wheel Bar on Bladensburg Road in Colmar Manor, Maryland. This union created the Saxtons, an outfit that jumped right into the local music scene and made a lasting impression on all who witnessed their collective talents in action.

One of the two groups to meet, the Rhythm Rockets, had formed in early 1956 and consisted of singer-accordionist Ken Selby, singer-bassist Jack Otley, saxophonist Jim Fowler and drummer Joe Jenkins, who hailed from the Eastern Shore and attended the University of Maryland at the time. The other group of rock and roll musicians was the Joe Stanley Combo, a constantly changing bunch that revolved around its singer-saxophonist namesake and singer-trombonist Robie Robinson. Stanley had already been working local night clubs for several years both as a sideman and a bandleader and had taken notice of the Wheel Bar's decision to move in a rock and roll direction. As the year came to an end Stanley brought in a pickup group of local musicians and talked the Wheel Bar managers into hiring his combo to work opposite the Rhythm Rockets, a group he was immediately impressed with.

The roots of the Rhythm Rockets go back to Bladensburg Junior High School in Prince George's County, when, during the 1952-1953 school year, a trio of young musicians first came together as the Harmony Hounds. The band's original lineup consisted of harmonica player Dave Reynolds, accordionist Ken Selby and guitarist Jan Bish – who was soon replaced by an acoustic bassist from Rogers Heights named Jack Otley.

The Harmony Hounds played only instrumentals and specialized in what can best be described as skiffle or jug band music. They became very popular in the county and during the middle 1950s performed pop music hits of the era at USO shows, talent contests and dances at the Bladensburg Teen Club (then located at the old Bladensburg Volunteer Fire Department at 4810 Annapolis Road - today it houses the Bladensburg Barber School), the Drop Inn in Greenbelt, the University Park Teen Club and the Landover Services Teen Club.

One interesting item of documentation for this outfit was a photo-announcement in the Thursday, February 25, 1954 edition of the Prince George's Post for a performance by Reynolds, Otley and Alan Young under the caption "Young Musicians" which read: "The Hillbillies shown here in rehearsal for the big Variety Show to be given at Bladensburg High School Feb. 26 are (l. to r.) Alan Young, Dave Reynolds and Jack Otley." In the photo Young is show at the piano, Reynolds is playing the harmonica and Otley is manning is stand-up bass. Absent from this group was Ken Selby, who evidently was otherwise engaged and did not perform in the show. While no name was provided for the three musicians in the picture, it was around this time that the band changed its name to the Harmony Boys, with Reynolds giving up the harmonica and switching to drums. This band continued to perform until the end of the 1955-1956 school year.

The three main members of the Harmony Boys all attended Bladensburg High School, with Jack Otley graduating in 1956 and Dave Reynolds and Ken Selby graduating a year later. During their high school years both Reynolds and Otley also performed on occasion with the Lewis Maddox Orchestra on the local teen club circuit.

In the summer of 1956 Selby (now handling lead vocals in addition to playing accordion) and Otley both joined a new local rock and roll quartet called the Rhythm Rockets, which also included another Bladensburg High School student named Jim Fowler on saxophone and a drummer from Cambridge, Maryland named Joe Jenkins. The band worked steadily at Club LaConga in College Park, as well as a number of different night clubs on the Eastern Shore of Maryland. In December 1956 the Rhythm Rockets moved to the Wheel Bar on Bladensburg Road in Colmar Manor, where they opened for a band called the Three Jacks, and alternated with another loose-knit outfit known as the Joe Stanley Combo.

Joe Stanley was born in Washington, D.C. and began taking saxophone lessons at age 12. After a year at Eastern High School in the District, his family moved out to Bladensburg, Maryland, where he went on to graduate from Bladensburg High School in 1954. During his teen years he mainly played along with records, but expanded his musical vocabulary by venturing to inner-city Washington where he would observe Black R&B bands that performed at the Howard Theatre and neighboring venues in the You Street area.

After completing high school Stanley began singing and playing saxophone with pickup bands in local American Legions, Moose Lodges and VFWs. It was while playing one of these assignments in 1955 that he met a singer-trombonist from Harrisburg, Pennsylvania named Robie Robinson. The two worked together in bands in Philadelphia, Pennsylvania for a short while, but returned to the nation's capital in 1956.

In the Washington, D.C. area Stanley and Robinson put together rock and roll bands that worked under such names as Joe Stanley and His Building Rockers and Joe Stanley and the Sophistikats. These groups performed throughout 1956 at such Maryland night clubs as Chubby's Restaurant and Bar on Central Avenue in Seat Pleasant and Club LaConga in College Park. As the year wore on the band name was switched to the Joe Stanley Combo and in December 1956 they obtained a job at the Wheel Bar. It was there that they meshed with the Rhythm Rockets.

The very first version of the Saxtons had Joe Stanley and Robie Robinson joining together with the four members of the Rhythm Rockets to form a hard rocking sextet that could cover almost any style of music. They rehearsed in the basement of Jack Otley's house at 5004 54th Place in Rogers Heights, Maryland and their first jobs together in early 1957 were in Washington, D.C. at the Moulin Rouge and the Parkside Café. Fowler and Selby soon left, reducing the Saxtons to a quartet. They looked to strengthen their roster and worked out a number of part-time members while they were at the Parkside Café, including singer-pianist Mark Ruslander (today he is the well-known political satirist Mark Russell) and singer Gail Ferguson. The band's goal was to travel around the United States and that year they took to the road and played night club dates throughout the Midwest and up and down the Atlantic Coast.

In the fall of 1957 the Saxtons returned home and from October to December of that year performed at Guy's Place in Southeast Washington, D.C. In January 1958 they were hired by local entrepreneur Herbert Hertz to be the house band at his 4400 Club in Brentwood, Maryland, where they played opposite such bands as Georgie Young and His Rockin' Bocs, the Nitecaps, the Applejacks featuring Dave Appell and the Frank Moore Four. Hertz thought the band had great potential and eventually became their manager on a limited basis.

In March 1958 the group added another full-time member in 22-year-old singer-guitarist Frank Shegogue, who had grown up in a musical family in the Huntington neighborhood of Bowie, Maryland on the eastern edge of Prince George's County. Shegogue learned to play the guitar from his parents and embarked on his first paid musical job at age 12 when he performed country tunes with his brother George at the Snug Harbor Inn on Annapolis Road in Lanham, Maryland. During his years at Laurel High School he met up with an accomplished country guitarist from Hyattsville named Reds Newkirk and together they assembled various musical combos and played local parties, weddings and dances at places like the American Legion Disney-Bell Post 66 in Bowie.

After graduating high school in 1953, Shegogue put together the Frank Shegogue Combo, a C&W band which consisted of himself on lead guitar, singer-rhythm guitarist Reds Newkirk, saxophonist Bobby Sauer and drummer Jimmy Hines. They played at a very popular country music roadhouse known as Chubby's Restaurant and Bar, which at the time was located 1.3 miles outside of Washington, D.C. on Central Avenue in Seat Pleasant, Maryland.

During the Frank Shegogue Combo's time at Chubby's Restaurant and Bar, the hit single "Crazy Man, Crazy" by Bill Haley with Haley's Comets was climbing the charts. Shegogue began covering this and other Haley tunes, thus adding a healthy dose of rock and roll to their nightly C&W music presentations. In the summer of 1954 the band added pianist Bobby Charlton and saxophonist Lewis Maddox to its roster and began playing the Pigeon House Inn on Route 3 in Crofton, Maryland (Anne Arundel County). Shegogue joined the United States Navy in the spring of 1955 and left the area. Upon his return later in the decade he was recruited into the Saxtons by Joe Stanley, who remembered watching him play guitar on numerous occasions at Chubby's Restaurant and Bar.

In 1958 the Saxtons, with its now-classic lineup of singer-trombonist Robie Robinson, singer-saxophonist Joe Stanley, guitarist Frank Shegogue, bassist Jack Otley and drummer Joe Jenkins, became one of the hottest bands on the Washington, D.C. area night club scene. They continued to be a featured attraction at the 4400 Club, and during the year also worked engagements at other top clubs in the area such as Benny's Rebel Room, the Parkside Café, the Dixie Pig, the Cross Roads, Jimmy Comber's Supper Club and the Village Barn.

Several major record labels showed interest in the Saxtons, but the band opted to maintain a heavy performance schedule which saw them playing every night of the week. Consequently, the Saxtons never recorded or released any singles or albums. Right when the band reached its highest point, splintering occurred. First, Joe Jenkins departed in October 1958 and his temporary replacement was Tommy Donaldson, who had previously drummed for the Off Beats. Shortly after that, Frank Shegogue joined Al Pometto and the Jazz Bombers and Robie Robinson accepted a lucrative offer to join Charlie Daniels and the Jaguars as a full-time member. As the year closed out, the Saxtons disbanded, though the group's inactive status lasted only for a matter of weeks.

Undaunted by the chaotic situation around him, Joe Stanley set about reforming the Saxtons in early 1959. He basically put together an entirely new band, a move that became a recurring activity in the years ahead. This new lineup saw Stanley joined by former Off Keys guitarist Clarence Perry, bassist Hugh Cassidy, a trombone player from Philadelphia named Al Leonard and former Harmony Boys drummer Dave Reynolds. That year they continued to work the 4400 Club, the Parkside Café and Benny's Rebel Room, in addition to embarking on short regional night club tours. As the 1950s came to a close the band experienced a whirlwind of personnel changes, with a number of musicians coming and going including former Thunderbirds bassist Gene Newport, guitarist Hugh O'Donnell and drummer Stan Weinberg.

From 1960 to 1969 a steady stream of local musicians passed through the Saxtons, as Joe Stanley's reputation was such that he could simply pick up the phone and bring in almost anyone he desired to fill existing vacancies. Stanley himself worked steadily throughout the decade with a variety of bands and was often called upon to work engagements with some of the best local and national musicians. Among those performers he worked with included the Bill Black Combo, Link Wray and His Ray Men, Charlie Daniels and the Jaguars, rockabilly singer-guitarist Dale Hawkins and C&W singer-guitarist Roy Clark.

One of the more interesting Saxtons lineups Stanley had was active in the spring of 1961 and consisted of himself, trombonist Al Leonard, saxophonist Ed Montini, bassist Vince Brando, drummer Stan Weinberg and the now-legendary guitarist Roy Buchanan. Both Montini and Buchanan had been recruited by Stanley from Dale Hawkins' band during their October 1960 Rocket Room engagement. This outfit performed a series of short engagements at such local night clubs as the Alpine Room, Guy's Place, the 4400 Club and the Dixie Pig. However, in due time, Stanley was working with singer-bassist Billy Hancock in yet another completely different version of the Saxtons.

During its 1960s reign the Saxtons tore through just about every rock and roll night club in town and altered their repertoire to suit the changing times. Every style of popular music was on their menu, along with their jazz and R&B favorites, and they skillfully tailored their offerings to appease their followings and please the various club owners.

The decade saw the ever-changing Saxtons play one-nighters and short engagements in Prince George's County at the Dixie Pig, the Rustic Cabin, the 4400 Club, Bass' Restaurant and Bar, the Cross Roads, the Village Barn, Strick's Restaurant, the Senate Inn, the Las Vegas Club and the Bladensburg Volunteer Fire Department. Over the line in Washington, D.C. they were headliners at the Hayloft, Rand's Night Club, Vinnie's Grill, the Rendezvous, the Parkside Café, Benny's Rebel Room, the Starlite Restaurant, Guy's Place, the Shelter Room, the Scene and the Rocket Room. The Saxtons played a critical role in Washington, D.C. area rock and roll history. They were leaders of their time for a younger generation of musicians who sought to establish reputations on the local night club scene and pursue dreams of becoming professional performing artists.

CHAPTER SIXTY-EIGHT
TERRY AND THE PIRATES

Terry and the Pirates emerged from Southeast Washington, D.C. in the late 1950s and during a relatively short-lived existence established themselves as one of the area's most popular rock and roll bands. Their origins were unusual, as they morphed from a group of musical FBI employees that performed show tunes at occasional Bureau functions into a regular headliner for local radio personality and music promoter Don Dillard at his various record hops and concert shows. The band was unique in that their only single release on a local independent label was acquired and reissued by Chess Records, a national label based in Chicago, Illinois, giving them a reputation that traveled far outside the nation's capital. In addition, many of the band's alumni went on to perform in later years with some of the best rock and roll and C&W acts the area had to offer.

The roots of Terry and the Pirates go back to January 1956, when 17-year-old Billie Copeland of Latham, Tennessee accepted an entry-level job with the Federal Bureau of Investigation in Washington, D.C. Copeland, who had learned to play guitar by listening to musical heroes such as Carl Smith, Webb Pierce and Hank Williams on the radio, had graduated early from Dresden High School in Dresden, Tennessee and came to the nation's capital by himself to start a new life. The Bureau found him a room in an apartment with five other young FBI employees at 1322 Congress Street SE in the Congress Park Apartments and word quickly spread of Copeland's guitar-playing prowess.

Another young FBI employee named Terry West, who hailed from Cordell, Georgia and lived in another building in the same apartment complex on Congress Street SE, was an aspiring singer and was told of Copeland's talent by mutual friends. Within weeks the two new employees, along with a youthful drummer from Clarksville, Tennessee named Andrew Earl, had been recruited by superiors to form the FBI Recreational Activities Band, a new musical congregation that performed classics, show tunes and a range of pop music songs at various Bureau dances, banquets and picnics. One of the local venues this band performed at regularly for the FBI was the American Legion Kenna Main Post 37, which at the time was located at 3201 Nichols Avenue SE in Washington, D.C.

During an autumn afternoon in 1956 a 21-year-old self-taught guitarist from Oxon Hill, Maryland named Steve Foster was visiting friends on Congress Street SE, when, as he walked by the apartment building marked 1322, he spied Billy Copeland playing guitar in the courtyard outside. He promptly introduced himself and the two immediately hit it off. Foster was also a fan of C&W music, with Ernest Tubb being a particular favorite, and although he had never played in a band before, he talked his new friend into letting him sit in with the FBI Recreational Activities Band at one of their rehearsals in Copeland's apartment. Right at that time the FBI informed the young musicians that their trio was being discontinued and future social events would no longer require their services.

In previous weeks an observer of several of the FBI Recreational Activities Band's performances informed local WDON disc jockey Don Dillard of the young group's talent. When Dillard eventually went looking to scout the band himself, he was dismayed to discover they were no longer performing for the Bureau. He put word out to West and Copeland that he would like to set up a gig at the American Legion Kenna Main Post 37 so he and his associates could watch the band play firsthand. West and Copeland retained drummer Andrew Earl and added their friend Steve Foster and as a quartet they performed in the hall in January 1957 as Terry and the Pirates for the first time, with the band's new name suggested by Dillard himself.

The band impressed Don Dillard immensely, who immediately offered his services as manager and stated that he planned on booking them on a regular basis into the various record hops he would be staging at venues throughout the Washington, D.C. area. However, the band suffered a temporary setback when Andrew Earl decided to resign from the Bureau and return to his home state of Tennessee, leaving the band without a drummer. They soon found his replacement in a promising 18-year-old percussionist named Jack Kerge, who resided in the Anacostia neighborhood of Southeast Washington, D.C. and had graduated from Anacostia High School the previous June. In addition, they picked up a 15-year-old Baltimore native named Marshal Folstein on saxophone, who, although he would perform with the band as often as he could, did not stay in the group very long. With their roster complete, the quintet of West, Copeland, Foster, Kerge and Folstein began working steadily for Dillard all over the region.

Throughout 1957 and into 1958 Terry and the Pirates rehearsed at the Livingston Barber Shop, which during those years was located at 4648 Livingston Road SE. The barber shop was owned by a man named Wade H. Sheppard, who was also a part-time musician and rented out the back room in his shop as rehearsal space to a number of local bands. Among the notables that held band practice there were the Thunderbirds – another popular Southeast Washington, D.C. rock and roll band – and the Kalin Twins, who were on the verge of national stardom with single releases on Decca Records. In late 1957 Terry and the Pirates had one last roster change when Marshal Folstein was replaced by Vince Gedeon, a guitarist-saxophonist from Adelphi, Maryland who had previously been a founding member of a top rock and roll band from Prince George's County called the Belvederes.

Under Don Dillard's management, Terry and the Pirates worked a variety of local armories and fire departments, as well as providing musical backing for groups like the Kalin Twins. Throughout 1957 and 1958 the band performed at such facilities as the Knights of Columbus Father Rosensteel Council 2169 (Silver Spring), the Reckord Armory (University of Maryland), the Oxon Hill Volunteer Fire Department, the Bladensburg Volunteer Fire Department, the Boulevard Heights Fire Department, the District Heights Fire Department, the Forestville Fire Department and regular weekend concerts at the Hyattsville Armory and the Silver Spring Armory. They also performed at smaller teen dances at places like Center School in Greenbelt, the College Park Skating Club, the Kentland Teen Club and the St. Francis Xavier Parish Teen Club in Southeast Washington, D.C.

One of the band's most important dates came when they were part of what was billed as a "Rock 'N Roll Spectacular" that was staged at Ritchie Coliseum on the University of Maryland's College Park campus on Saturday, December 27, 1958. The multi-act, three-hour concert was sponsored by the Laurel Junior Chamber of Commerce and was headlined by Bill Haley and His Comets, with Terry and the Pirates appearing in a supporting role along with the Kingsmen, the Mellow Kings, Vernon Taylor, the Crystals, Jerry Dallman and the Knightcaps, the Cool Breezes and the Starlighters. The event sold out the 1,500-seat venue and rated as one of the area's most important rock and roll extravaganzas of the year. In the wake of this concert, Terry and the Pirates were tabbed as the house band at Glen Echo Park's Spanish Ballroom, a position they held for most of 1959. It was at this facility where they eventually gave their final performance.

A high point for Terry and the Pirates occurred when one of their performances at the Silver Spring Armory in the spring of 1958 was observed by a friend of Don Dillard's named Paul Robertson, who at the time was a manager in the Washington, D.C. office for the Decca Distributing Corporation. Robertson, who resided in Silver Spring, Maryland and had previously worked for years as a record buyer for Hecht and Company in Washington,

D.C., was in the process of starting an independent record label which he named Valli Records, in honor of his daughter Valerie.

After observing Terry and the Pirates in action Robertson felt the band would be the prefect rockabilly act for his developing project and approached Dillard about having the band record what would be the inaugural single release for his new record label. Robertson brought the band into the Edgewood Recording Studio in Washington, D.C. and recorded several songs with the engineering and production assistance of Edgewood proprietor Ed Green. The result of this undertaking was the 45rpm single record, "What Did He Say" backed with "Talk About the Girl" (Terry and the Pirates; Valli Records, 1958).

This first and only single for Terry and the Pirates was initially released in May 1958 and was an immediate regional success. The single proved to be so well-received that Robertson approached the brother team of Leonard and Phil Chess at Chess Records in Chicago, Illinois and worked out a deal where the major label purchased the rights to the record, thus rendering the Valli version obsolete after a six-week lifespan. The song was then rereleased on Chess Records in June 1958.

Unfortunately for Terry and the Pirates, Chess failed to properly market and distribute the single, which consequently failed to make the Billboard magazine charts and subsequently dropped from sight. For these and other reasons now obscured through time, this 45rpm single record turned out to be the only two recorded songs ever released by the band and both the Valli and Chess companies disappeared from the band's radar as quickly as they had materialized. The group simply never heard from either Robertson or the officials at Chess Records ever again and never received royalties for their songs.

In late 1959 Terry and the Pirates called it quits and the band members went in separate directions: Terry West returned to Georgia and left the music business; Vince Gedeon worked with numerous bands including Danny Denver and the Sound Tracks, Little Hugh and the Embers, Sonny Gordon and the Panics and singer-pianist Big Al Downing, and later was a founding member of the Chartbusters in 1964; Jack Kerge went on to drum for the Rhythm Makers; Billie Copeland played guitar for rockabilly singer Vernon Taylor from 1960 to 1966; and Steve Foster spent the 1960s working with numerous acts including Vernon Taylor, Charlie Daniels and the Jaguars, the Saxtons, the Naturals and the Eddie Stitt Combo.

CHAPTER SIXTY-NINE
THE BOBOLINKS

The first area teen band devoted to performing doo-wop songs was the Bobolinks, who emerged from Southeast Washington, D.C. in the late 1950s as a unique a capella group that went on to become recording stars and a featured live attraction in area talent contests, USO shows and night clubs. The talented quintet, which got their start singing on street corners in their Anacostia neighborhood, included both original compositions and covers of popular hit songs in their repertoire. As a vehicle for a distinct brand of 1950s rock and roll, the Bobolinks served as a vibrant entry in the area's social and musical history which in all likelihood will never be duplicated.

The Bobolinks enjoyed tremendous popularity for their pleasing vocalizations and harmonies and were a marked departure from other 1950s rock and roll bands of the region that emphasized back beat rhythms tangled with jangles of guitars, saxophones and keyboards. With the advent of the 1960s, the Bobolinks changed their name to the Memories and would go on to achieve national recognition as one of the world's most talented doo-wop groups, ultimately being enshrined in the Vocal Group Hall of Fame in 1988. The band is still active today, performing concerts and benefits all over the United States.

The original lineup of the Bobolinks consisted of Jim Durst (baritone and some lead vocals), Ron Lutz (first tenor and some lead vocals), Robert "Boots" Dove (second tenor vocals), Gene Fitzgerald (first tenor and background vocals) and Lou Martin (first tenor and primary lead vocals).

While the exact starting point of the band has been a point of contention among the various original members, the general consensus is that the Bobolinks initially formed in May 1957 in Anacostia when Jim Durst, then 16 years old and finishing his sophomore year at Chamberlain Vocational High School, was introduced to 14-year-old Ron Lutz, who at the time was finishing his eighth grade year at nearby Kramer Junior High School. The word was out that Durst was an accomplished vocalist and was looking for fellow singers to join him in forming a band, and Lutz, who had been singing informally since elementary school, was the first recruit into the fold. The two teens lived two blocks from each other on the same street in Anacostia and began rehearsing and auditioning different singers in the basement of the Durst home at 1635 S Street SE. When the Durst and Lutz sought a live audience, the pair would move outdoors during the afternoon hours and sing in public on street corners along nearby Good Hope Road SE.

Soon to join Durst and Lutz in the late spring of 1957 were Robert "Boots" Dove and Gene Fitzgerald. Dove was born in 1938 and had previously attended Eastern High School in Washington, D.C., though he was living in District Heights, Maryland at the time he first encountered his future bandmates. One day during a journey into Anacostia, Dove happened across Durst and Lutz singing as they stood on the curb in front of the Rainbow Delicatessen, which at the time was situated at 1533 Good Hope Road SE and was in the process of becoming a favored hangout of the singing group. That very same day Dove was invited to the Durst basement for what turned out to be a successful band audition.

In similar fashion, Gene Fitzgerald, a long time Anacostia resident and a member of Anacostia High School's Class of 1958, first saw Durst and Lutz standing on Good Hope Road SE, singing right in front of the Rainbow Delicatessen. He also approached the pair about joining musical forces, passed his audition in the Durst basement, and became the fourth addition to the fast-growing Bobolinks nest.

The final member of what is generally recognized as the original Bobolinks group is Lou Martin, who has actually written a book about his experiences with the band entitled "The Memories: A Doo-Wop Journey" (2012). Martin had grown up in the Capitol Hill neighborhood of Southeast Washington, D.C. (west of the Anacostia River) and had graduated from Eastern High School in June 1957. During his teen years he had informally sung R&B songs with three other youths at dances held at a Capitol Hill community center called the Friendship House Association (619 D Street SE).

Shortly after graduating high school, Martin scouted the Bobolinks at one of their live performances at a night club in Waldorf, Maryland called the Lamplighter. He then approached the band several days later at their main hangout, the Hi Ho Snack Bar Restaurant, then-located in the heart of Anacostia at 1433 Good Hope Road SE, just one block down from the Rainbow Delicatessen.

The Hi Ho Snack Bar Restaurant was a typical 1950s teen hangout, the type that could have served as a model for Arnold's Drive-In in the popular television show "Happy Days" (which aired on ABC from 1974 to 1984 and starred Ron Howard as Richie Cunningham and Henry Winkler as Arthur "The Fonz" Fonzarelli). The place was stuffed to capacity every weekday afternoon with students from nearby Kramer Junior High School and Anacostia High School and it was there that Martin was introduced to Jimmy Durst and secured an appointment with the band to determine his Bobolink potential. The very next day Martin, accompanied by Durst's sister Susanne on piano, sang "In the Still of the Night" by the Five Satins for Durst's mother in the living room of their S Street SE home. After the song was completed, Mrs. Durst sent the accepted newcomer to the basement to meet with his awaiting bandmates.

With its roster settled, the Bobolinks began giving live performances in the area and during the late 1950s went through a series of managers including: Jerry Toronto, a former pop singer who especially liked to stage talent shows featuring younger bands and musicians at various night clubs; Gene Winters, a disc jockey at radio station WPGC, who booked the Bobolinks into a number of station-sponsored dances and events; and Philip "Buddy" Catzva, owner of the Hi Ho Snack Bar Restaurant, who had an interest in the band from the very beginning.

From 1957 to 1959 the Bobolinks were alternately booked by these three individuals into United Service Organization (USO) shows around the nation's capital and at officers' clubs on area military bases such as Bolling Air Force Base (Washington, D.C.), Walter Reed Army Medical Center (Washington, D.C.), Andrews Air Force Base (Prince George's County, Maryland), Fort George G. Meade (Anne Arundel County, Maryland), Fort Myer (Arlington County, Virginia), Fort Belvoir (Fairfax County, Virginia) and other military installations up and down the Atlantic Coast.

The Bobolinks competed in talent shows at places like the Victory Grill in Anacostia, the Alpine Room on Kennedy Street NW, Strick's Restaurant in Silver Hill, Maryland, and the Hyattsville Armory. They worked a number of teen dances in Southeast Washington, D.C. at the St. Francis Xavier Parish Teen Club, the St. Teresa of Avila Catholic Church Teen Club and the Hillcrest Playground, where, according to a letter in the "Play Back From Teen Readers" section in the Evening Star's "Teen" section of Sunday, November 23, 1958, a performance they gave at that location on Friday, October 31, 1958 drew an audience of more than 2,000 teens.

The Bobolinks also performed at such locations as the Hi Ho Snack Bar Restaurant (their home base on Good Hope Road SE), the Rainbow Delicatessen, O.U.A.M. Hall (officially titled the Junior Order of United American Mechanics Hall, this facility shared a building at the time with the Anacostia Temple at 2407 Minnesota Avenue SE, Washington, D.C.), Sarto Hall on Stewart Road in Forestville, Maryland, the District Heights Fire

Department, and Mama Bellosi's Italian Restaurant (then-located at 5158 Benning Road in Capitol Heights, Maryland, the building is marked 1252-1254 Benning Road today and currently stands vacant). In addition, the band made several appearances on "The Milt Grant Show" in Washington and "The Buddy Deane Show" in Baltimore.

Although basically an a capella singing group, the Bobolinks decided to add a couple of musicians to the mix to complement their sound. They first picked up guitarist and fellow Southeast Washington, D.C. resident Dick Grimes from the Thunderbirds to accompany them on various musical ventures. Grimes was followed by at least two other guitarists in the late 1950s including Tommy Saul and Dennis Smith, both products of Southeast Washington, D.C. Personnel changes in the band continued throughout the 1960s and 1970s as the band continued on as the Memories.

The Bobolinks were herded into various recording studios during their time to have their sound captured and released on vinyl, though the results of those sessions have largely been obscured through time. It is known that the band signed a limited contract with Colt 45 Records, a Washington, D.C-based independent record label owned and operated by the brother team of Jim and Ted Pedas, who today are well-regarded movie producers.

Several songs the Bobolinks recorded at the Pedas-owned-and-operated Circle Recording Studio (2138 Pennsylvania Avenue NW, Washington, D.C.) for Colt 45 Records were never released in single format. They did release one 45rpm single record, "I Promise," backed with "Mr. Frog" (The Bob-o-Links; Hi-Ho Records, 1959), which had been recorded at Edgewood Recording Studio in Washington, D.C. and issued on an independent record label owned by restaurateur Philip "Buddy" Catzva. The session reportedly featured backing music supplied by three players who happened to be visiting the studio that day, namely legendary jazz saxophonist Sonny Stitt, along with his regular pianist and drummer. The single was never marketed outside of the nation's capital and remains the only Bobolinks 45rpm single record ever released. To this day it ranks as a hard-to-find collector's item of great value.

In 1960 changes in personnel and musical direction transformed the band. Discussions ensued about a name-change that would better reflect their commitment to the doo-wop songs of yesteryear. In 1961 a formal name-change to "The Memories" was made and throughout much of the 1960s and early 1970s the band's lineup consisted of singers Lou Martin, Ronnie Lutz and Robert "Boots" Dove, along with guitarist Dennis Smith, bassist Jim Morrow and drummer Jerry Walmark. The Memories are still recording and performing today and have long been recognized as one of the world's finest doo-wop groups.

CHAPTER SEVENTY
THE BELVEDERES

The Belvederes were one of the premiere Washington, D.C. bands of the early rock and roll era and during their 1957-1967 existence displayed an impressive range of musical versatility and expertise in some of the region's best night clubs and venues. Formed in Adelphi, Maryland by brothers Tommy Dercola (accordion, keyboards and vocals) and Gino Dercola (guitar, bass and vocals), the band's original lineup also included singer-bassist Denny Rafkin, guitarist-saxophonist Vince Gedeon and drummer Sammy Grasso. As their journey progressed, the group combined unwavering artistic devotion with spirited performances that seamlessly weaved together different elements of popular music, a practice that influenced other area musicians to expand their musical boundaries and left audiences clamoring for more of the band's unique blending of pop, R&B, rock and roll and satire-laced songs.

The story of the Belvederes begins with Tommy and Gino Dercola, two brothers who were born in Washington, D.C. in the late 1930s and raised in the neighborhood surrounding 11th and C Streets NE. As pre-teen youths they were encouraged to take up music by their parents, with Tommy becoming proficient on the accordion and Gino mastering the guitar. For several years while attending Stuart Junior High School their father would take them to participate in various area talent shows and special events where they performed as a duet and offered up the top pop songs of the day.

In 1956 the Dercola family moved from Washington, D.C. out to Prince George's County, Maryland where they had a house built at 8616 Riggs Road in Adelphi. Once the move was complete, both the Dercola boys were enrolled at High Point High School in nearby Beltsville, where Tommy was a member of the Class of 1957 and Gino a member of the Class of 1959.

Upon their arrival in Adelphi, the Dercola brothers set about putting together a rock and roll band and began auditioning local musicians. During the 1956-1957 school year they acquired guitarist-saxophonist Vince Gedeon of Beltsville, who, like Tommy Dercola, was a member of High Point High School's Class of 1957, and bassist Denny Rafkin of Adelphi, who, like Gino Dercola, was a member of High Point High School's Class of 1959. The band was completed in June 1957 when Gedeon introduced them to a drummer named Sam Grasso, whom he had previously worked with in different jazz bands. Grasso hailed from College Park, Maryland and had graduated from Northwestern High School in 1955. The Belvederes became the first and only rock and roll band he would ever play in.

The group chose their name based on Tommy Dercola's fondness for the Plymouth Belvedere automobile, and continued group rehearsals in the lower-level recreation room of the Dercola house on Riggs Road. Their initial repertoire consisted of most of the songs that had placed on the Billboard magazine's popular music charts, with numbers by Fats Domino, Chuck Berry, Bill Haley and His Comets and the Crickets (featuring singer-guitarist Buddy Holly) rating as personal favorites.

The Belvederes debuted on Thursday, August 8, 1957 at the Adelphi Teen Club, located inside of Adelphi Elementary School (8820 Riggs Road), with a set list that included: "Ubangi Stomp" by Warren Smith; "Whole Lotta Shakin' Going On" by Jerry Lee Lewis; "Valley of Tears" by Fats Domino; "Hound Dog" and "(Let Me Be Your) Teddy Bear" by Elvis Presley; "That'll Be The Day" by the Crickets; "Over The Mountain; Across the Sea" by Johnnie & Joe; "Bony Moronie" by Larry Williams; and "Let The Good Times Roll" by Shirley and Lee.

The band quickly caught the attention of local entrepreneur Milt Grant and on Thursday, August 22 they gave a special in-studio performance on "The Milt Grant Show" television program at the Raleigh Hotel in Washington, D.C. The band was on its way and late in the year when WDON's Don Dillard staged one of his record hop dances at nearby High Point High School with Terry and the Pirates placed as headliners, the Dercola brothers contacted the WDON disc jockey-promoter and challenged the headlining band to a contest. Dillard was intrigued by the brash challenge and made an in-person visit to the Dercola home in Adelphi where he watched the band rehearse first-hand. He was duly impressed and immediately added the group to his stable, with the Belvederes working their first job for him at his record hop at the Silver Spring Armory on Saturday, February 8, 1958, where they co-headlined with Terry and the Pirates.

In 1957 and 1958 the Belvederes displayed their exciting brand of pop, R&B and rock and roll music at a variety of local teen clubs and dances including, in addition to the Adelphi Teen Club (Adelphi), the Rolling Crest Teen Club (Hyattsville), the Hollywood Teen Club (College Park), the Beltsville Teen Club (Beltsville) and dances at High Point High School (Beltsville) and various University of Maryland fraternities. Don Dillard also had the band perform on a regular basis at the various multi-act record hops he staged at such facilities as the Silver Spring Armory, the Hyattsville Armory, the Greenbelt Armory, and the Bladensburg Volunteer Fire Department. These Dillard-arranged events regularly drew several hundred teens and were in direct competition with similar shows booked by Milt Grant.

The popularity of the Belvederes was such that Dillard felt they were a necessity in order for him to compete with Grant on a weekly basis, leading him to offer a management contract with the band. However, the group had their sights set on entering the Washington, D.C. area's more lucrative night club world and they respectfully declined Dillard's generous offer.

The first Washington, D.C. area night club gigs the Belvederes played included engagements at the Village Inn in October 1957, the Dixie Pig in February 1958, the Alpine Room in March 1958 and an unusual teen-oriented night club called the Keen Klub in Rockville, Maryland in February and March 1958, where a singer named Mickey Gilley once opened for them. They also performed at such establishments as the Shamrock Restaurant from August through November 1958, the Village Barn from October through November 1958, the Famous Restaurant in December 1958 and another round of dates at the Dixie Pig in February 1959. The band also continued to play local school dances, teen clubs, military base officers' clubs, and fraternity and sorority parties at colleges such as the University of Maryland, American University and the University of Virginia.

In the early 1960s the Belvederes eventually settled on a lineup that saw singer-accordionist Tommy Dercola and singer-bassist Gino Dercola being joined by former Off Keys saxophonist Roger Hughes, and two former members of the Savoys, singer-guitarist Dickie Kibler and drummer Bill Jubane. The band refined its unique rock and roll style and Tommy Dercola experimented with different keyboard models including the Wurlitzer electric piano, the Gulbransen transistorized organ and the Hammond B-3 organ.

From May to November 1962 the Belvederes were the house band at an unusual venue called the Turn of the Century, which was located at 4233 Wisconsin Avenue NW in Washington, D.C. The night club was small and cramped and had no dance floor, but the band made the most of the circumstances and added a humorous twist to their shows when they began offering "Songs that Momma Never Sang." Numerous song parodies comprised this part of their show which included humorous and risqué lyrics, props, wigs and special sound effects.

During this time, as business picked up at the Turn of the Century, the band switched its name to Tommy Cole and the Belvederes (Tommy Cole being the new stage name for Tommy Dercola). They began exploring incoming offers from other establishments and worked an engagement at the Champagne Room in December 1962 and then accepted a house band offer from the Rocket Room which kept them busy from December 1962 through February 1963.

In 1960 and 1961 (as "The Belvederes") and from 1962 to 1964 (as "Tommy Cole and the Belvederes") the band worked the area's top night clubs including the Village Barn, the Rocket Room, Vinnie's Grill, the Alpine Room, Guy's Place, the Round Up Club, the Lyon's Den, the Skylark, the Champagne Room (in December 1962 the now-legendary bassist Jack Casady filled in with Tommy Cole and the Belvederes at this newly opened venue), the Turn of the Century, Strick's Restaurant (where they held house band duties for much of 1963 and 1964), the Palmer Restaurant, Ben's Hideaway, the Shelter Room, the Dixie Pig and the Starlite Restaurant.

Throughout the 1960s the mainstays of Tommy Cole and the Belvederes were Tommy Cole, Gino Dercola and drummer Bill Jubane. The group always worked as a quartet or quintet and several other musicians worked their way in and out of the band during these years including: guitarists Al Bautista and Marvin "Kim" Tsoy;" bassists Bernie Schmidt, Brad Fisher and Dick Brauer; saxophonists Dick Moody and Adrian "Switchy" Swicegood; guitarist-saxophonist Wally Simms; and return appearances from singer-guitarist Dickie Kibler, who would appear with the band under his new stage name Richie Kay. From 1965 to 1966 Tommy Cole and the Belvederes maintained their status as one of the region's top rock and roll outfits while headlining at night clubs such as Benny's Rebel Room, the Hayloft, the Keg, the Villa and the Silver Dollar Restaurant.

Tommy Cole and the Belvederes were especially popular during this time at the Quonset Supper Club in Silver Hill, Maryland. They worked engagements in the night club from August to November 1965, January 1966, June 1966 to February 1967 and June to November 1967. During their Quonset run, Gino Dercola left the band in August 1966 and filling his shoes proved to be a tall order. During the group's final year, the lineup was down to a four-piece consisting of Tommy Cole on organ and vocals, guitarist Wally Simms, saxophonist Adrian "Switchy" Swicegood and drummer Bill Jubane. Tommy Cole and the Belvederes eventually disbanded in November 1967.

In terms of studio work, Tommy Cole and the Belvederes had recorded songs in local studios at different times during their reign with hopes of having the material issued on major record labels. Unfortunately, the record deals never materialized and these recordings were never released to the public.

Of special interest is that Tommy Cole and the Belvederes did one recording session in 1962 with rock and roll singer Prince Preston (real name Preston Peters). From this session came the 45rpm single record "Dancing Girl" backed with "Wait for Me" (Congressional Records, 1962), with the A-side credited to "Prince Preston with the Belvederes") and the B-side credited to "Prince Preston" with "Vocal Background – The Barvells." The single achieved some measure of regional success, but failed to make the Billboard magazine charts. That same year Tommy Cole and the Belvederes backed up local country rock singer Sonny King (real name Clay Smith) on his 45rpm single record "Do You Love Me" backed with "Dig Yourself" (Sonny King; Marida Records, 1962).

After Tommy Cole and the Belvederes disbanded, their popularity lived on. To this day they rate as one of the very few Washington, D.C. area rock and roll bands to make an appearance in a major novel, as their performances at the Turn of the Century landed them a place in the Joe Haldeman novel "1968: A Novel" (1995).

Although Tommy Cole and the Belvederes were no longer part of the musical landscape as the 1960s concluded, founding members Tommy and Gino Dercola remained on the local music scene for several years to come. Gino Dercola was a singer-bassist with the Joe Carter Combo, a country rock band that performed at area military base officers' clubs from 1967 to 1976. Tommy Dercola formed the Tommy Cole Trio, a rock and roll group of the 1970s that performed at such Maryland night clubs as the Loft Room (Waldorf), Gus and John's Italian Villa (Camp Springs), the Oysterman's Inn (Deale) and the East West Garden (Hyattsville).

CHAPTER SEVENTY-ONE
THE SAVOYS

As the number of teen bands in the Washington, D.C. area increased during the late 1950s, one of the most dynamic additions to the scene proved to be the Savoys, a talented Prince George's County rock and roll outfit that became known for drawing capacity Saturday night crowds to the West Lanham Hills Volunteer Fire Department. The Savoy's tenure came to a close after an early 1960s stay at the Club Log Tavern in Alexandria, Virginia, an engagement that saw the band successfully bridge the gap between the sock hop teen dances and the adult-oriented night club world.

The Savoys were formed in the summer of 1958 when three members of a group called Bob Holliday and the Royals – Mickey Anderson, Warren Smith and Larry Brennan – recruited two brothers who had previously played in a teen band called the Rockets – Dickie and Dan Kibler – and organized themselves into what quickly became one of the most popular rock and roll quintets Prince George's County, Maryland would ever experience.

Mickey Anderson hailed from Ardmore, Maryland and first played guitar in a rock and roll band called the Rhythm Rockers at the Lanham Teen Club during his 1956-57 sophomore year at Bladensburg High School. During the course of that school year the band was hired by the Bowie Teen Club to play their dances at a nearby facility on High Bridge Road known as McNamara's Barn. Through his Bladensburg High School friends, Anderson heard of another dance band called Bob Holliday and the Royals and invited them to jointly work a dance with the Rhythm Rockers at McNamara's Barn in early 1957. Shortly thereafter, Anderson left the Rhythm Rockers and became lead guitarist for Bob Holliday's band.

At that point Bob Holliday and the Royals were a five-piece band whose lineup after the initial McNamara' Barn gig consisted of Holliday handling lead vocals, Anderson on guitar, keyboardist Larry Brennan, saxophonist Warren Smith and drummer Butch Lewis. Warren Smith, who had grown up in Riverdale, Maryland, had previously played saxophone in the school band at Greenbelt Junior High School and his first organized band experience had been with Holliday's outfit. Brennan, a skilled piano player from Bladensburg, had also gained valuable performance experience working with the Royals.

In early 1958, Anderson, Smith and Brennan – all members of Bladensburg High School's Class of 1959 – discussed plans to break away from the Royals and form their own band. While playing a job at the Hyattsville Theatre where they and other musical acts performed in-between feature film attractions, the three observed two brothers named Dickie and Dan Kibler performing as a duo and felt they would make fine additions to their new musical project.

The Kiblers had grown up on a farm in Hyattsville, Maryland that stood on land that is now occupied by Prince George's Plaza. Dan would graduate from Northwestern High School in 1961 while his brother Dickie Kibler would graduate from DuVal High School in 1962. From 1955 to 1957 during their years at University Park Elementary School, the Kibler brothers played together in a band called the Rockets that performed both C&W and rock and roll tunes at their school's dances. The group consisted of singer-guitarist Dickie Kibler, steel guitarist Dan Kibler, guitarist Doug Cashell and drummer Ron Nagers, who was later replaced by Ed Brown.

When the Rockets disbanded in 1957, Dickie Kibler, then 13 years old and a student at Hyattsville Junior High School, began playing guitar and singing Elvis Presley songs as a solo performer at places like the Hyattsville Theatre, the Beltsville Drive-In and Magruder

Park in Hyattsville. His brother Dan happened to accompany him on one of his Hyattsville Theatre performances, an event which marked the first time that future Savoy Mickey Anderson actually saw the tandem in action.

Dickie Kibler, while working a concession stand at a Bladensburg Volunteer Fire Department dance in early 1958 that featured the Off Keys, was approached by Warren Smith and queried about his musical skills. The Kibler brothers then agreed to join forces with the three Royals members to form a new band. Calling themselves the Savoys, the new quintet consisted of lead singer-lead guitarist Dickie Kibler, singer-bassist Mickey Anderson, singer-saxophonist Warren Smith, keyboardist Larry Brennan and drummer Dan Kibler. In the summer of 1958 the Savoys played a weekly Saturday night teen dance at the West Lanham Hills Volunteer Fire Department (7609 Annapolis Road, Hyattsville, Maryland), an engagement that lasted for most of the following two years.

During their stay at the West Lanham Hills Volunteer Fire Department, the Savoys, whose repertoire included songs by the likes of Fats Domino, Little Richard, the Treniers, Larry Williams, Lloyd Price, Ace Cannon, Chuck Berry and Frankie Ford, built a tremendous following with several hundred dancing teens cramming their way into the facility every Saturday night. Consequently, the band developed a friendly rivalry with the Off Keys, who were packing them in across the way at the Bladensburg Volunteer Fire Department on Friday nights.

The Savoys' success opened up new opportunities and in 1958 and 1959 the band worked country club parties, dances at area schools and facilities like the Landover Hills Fire Department, Center School in Greenbelt and the St. Hugh's Catholic Church Teen Club, also in Greenbelt. They also worked events for promoter Don Dillard at the Hyattsville Armory where they headlined on their own and also backed up the likes of pop singers Bobby Rydell and Barry Darvell. The Savoys also made appearances on "The Milt Grant Show" where on one occasion they backed up pop singer Annette Funicello and on another occasion placed first in a "Battle of the Bands" contest.

In 1959 the Savoys expanded in size and became a nine-piece band. Drummer Jack Henderson came over from the Off Keys and replaced Dan Kibler for a short while. He was then replaced by Bill Jubane, who had grown up in Hyattsville, Maryland, had graduated from Northwestern High School in 1957, and had previously drummed for the Washington Redskins Band. Next, after the Off Keys officially broke up in May of 1959, three of their saxophone players, Dick Moody, Art Gould and Steve Merenshaw, joined the Savoys and beefed up the band's sound. Luman Perry also came over from the Off Keys at that time to handle lead vocal duties. At one point during the year he took over the bass guitar role when Mickey Anderson briefly left the band.

In May 1959 the Savoys became the regular attraction at the Friday night dances at the Bladensburg Volunteer Fire Department, replacing the disbanded Off Keys. The Savoys also took their place at the Dixie Pig on Bladensburg Road in Cottage City, Maryland, where they worked several nights a week and were co-billed on occasion with Charlie Daniels and the Jaguars. It marked the band's first excursion into the Washington, D.C. area's rock and roll night club scene and they continued to work both the Dixie Pig and the Bladensburg Volunteer Fire Department for the remainder of the year. During this time, personnel changes within the band continued, with lead singer Robert "Mo" McCallum passing through the group and the horn section eventually departing.

By early 1960 the Savoys roster had stabilized at five pieces, with its final lineup consisting of singer-guitarist Dickie Kibler, singer-bassist Mickey Anderson, keyboardist Larry Brennan, saxophonist Dick Moody and drummer Bill Jubane. The group obtained a house band position at the Club Log Tavern on Richmond Highway in the southern stretches of Alexandria, Virginia, a rockin' roadhouse that was generally considered to be the bottom boundary line for the Washington, D.C. area music scene. The band continued to work the Club Log Tavern throughout 1961, and during the year also performed at several teen dances at the Greenbelt Youth Center in Greenbelt, Maryland. Shortly after they played a New Year's Eve dance in the Youth Center on Sunday, December 31, 1961, the Savoys disbanded.

The Savoys were truly one of the great young bands of the early rock and roll era in the nation's capital. They proved to be kings of all they surveyed, but their kingdom failed to expand beyond the outer eastern stretches of the Washington, D.C. suburbs, possibly because the band focused on live performances and passed on recording opportunities, a decision that limited major record label interest in the band. However, the individual musical talent within the band was extremely impressive, with several Savoy alumni remaining active in the ensuing years.

From the original lineup, Mickey Anderson would play throughout the 1960s with such bands as Barry Darvell and the Blazers, Mickey's Monkees and the Wheels of Progress. Warren Smith spent his post-Savoys years working area night clubs with the Saxtons, Joe Banana and the Bunch, the Partymakers, and also did a stint with the Wheels of Progress. Dickie Kibler worked with Tommy Cole and the Belvederes for several years, performed as pop singer Richie Kay at the Quonset Supper Club during the late 1960s, and from 1969 to 1974 served as lead singer for the band Octagon. Kibler then spent the early 1980s as the singer-bassist for a group called the Sliders.

CHAPTER SEVENTY-TWO
STARS OF R&B

In 1949 the Billboard and other mainstream media publications classified most of the music being performed by Blacks as rhythm & blues, a category that replaced the previously used headings of race music and Negro music. This new classification of music, commonly called R&B, encompassed almost any style they performed, from blues to jazz to pop to soul, and was based on the skin color of the performers rather than the content of their music.

During the 1950s and 1960s locally based R&B musicians mainly performed at night clubs in the You Street area, and, to a lesser extent, local teen dances throughout the surrounding area. During these years the Washington, D.C. area was home to a number of R&B performing artists that became favorites on the local music scene, and, in many instances, achieved some measure of national recognition for their talents.

The Clovers were a race music vocal group that formed in Washington, D.C. in 1946 and initially consisted of singers Harold Lucas, Billy Shelton and Thomas Woods, all students at Armstrong High School. A fourth vocalist, John "Buddy" Bailey, was soon added to the band roster. They performed at teen dances, amateur talent shows and on radio programs throughout Washington, D.C. In the late 1940s they also played their very first night club dates in the city at the Old Rose Social Club (1848 7th Street NW), which was located just around the corner from the Howard Theatre in the heart of the You Street area. At this point the band was signed to an independent record label which released their first single, "When You Come Back to Me" backed with "Yes Sir That's My Baby" (The Clovers; Rainbow Records, 1950). Guitarist Bill Harris joined the Clovers in 1950 and would spend more than two decades with the band.

In 1951 the Clovers were signed to Atlantic Records by Max Silverman and in the ensuing years released a string of albums and singles that raced up and down the Billboard magazine's R&B charts. Throughout the decade the band performed concerts and shows at venues around the country and endured a number of personnel changes.

In 1959 the band was signed by United Artists Records and the recordings continued. During its time the group issued two crossover singles that hit the pop music charts: "Love, Love, Love" (The Clovers; Atlantic Records, 1956), which reached number 30 on the Billboard's "The Top 100" pop music chart on Saturday, July 28, 1956; and "Love Potion No. 9" (The Clovers; United Artists Records, 1959), which peaked at number 23 on the Billboard's "The Billboard Hot 100" pop music chart on Monday, November 16, 1959.

The Rainbows were an R&B vocal group that formed in the Lincoln Heights neighborhood of Northeast Washington, D.C. in March 1953 and originally consisted of six singing teenagers: Henry Womble, Frank Hardy, James Nolan, Ronald Miles and John Berry; and singer-pianist Donald Watts. The group performed sporadically on the local teen dance circuit and at school functions, with word of their ability eventually reaching local music producer Lillian Claiborne.

In August 1953 Claiborne recorded sessions with the group at an unidentified studio in Washington, D.C. and that month they released their first 45rpm single record, "Can't You See I Love You So" backed with "My Heart Is Yours" (The Rainbows; Gem Records, 1953). In the fall of 1954 the group hit the recording studio again, resulting in the single "Evening" backed with "Mary Lee" (The Rainbows; Red Robin Records, 1954). This single was reissued in Feb 1956 on Pilgrim Records, a company out of Boston, Massachusetts.

The Rainbows reorganized in 1956 and moved on with a new lineup of four singers: Ronald Miles, John Berry, Don Covay and Chester Simmons. During this time other singers occasionally subbed for missing members at live gigs, including Billy Stewart and Marvin Gaye. The group worked a number of record hops that year for local radio disc jockey Jay Perri and also continued to record songs in local studios. In June 1956 they released a single, "Stay" backed with "Shirley" (The Rainbows; Pilgrim Records, 1956). Later in the year another single appeared, "They Say" backed with "Minnie" (The Rainbows; Rama Records, 1956). The Rainbows broke up at the end of 1956, but would reorganize and resurface with different lineups for the next 50 years.

Singer Jimmy McPhail was born in 1928 in Rocky Mount, North Carolina and moved to Washington, D.C. during his childhood. He began singing at age eight with the Galbraith AME Zion Choir and was a frequent participant in talent and variety shows during his years at Armstrong High School. In 1950 He began performing as an R&B singer at night spots throughout the Washington, D.C. area and became a headliner at some of the top venues in the nation's capital. Among the night clubs he appeared during the 1950s were the Brown Derby, the Merry-Land Club, the Blue Mirror, Café Trinidad (formerly Club Bali), the Marina, and, over in Prince George's County, Maryland, the Vista Ballroom. During those years McPhail also frequently performed on the star-studded bills at the Howard Theatre.

In the late 1950s McPhail was regularly headlining the Melody Inn, a small R&B night club tucked away on Bladensburg Road NE at the far edge of the city. He became so popular in the club he bought the business outright in 1959 and promptly changed the name of the establishment to the Gold Room. McPhail maintained ownership of the Gold Room until 1997 and actively performed in the club until its closing.

During his career, McPhail recorded and released several singles for RCA Victor Records and other smaller independent labels. When he wasn't tending to the Gold Room, McPhail often appeared as a vocalist with Duke Ellington's Orchestra, singing with the group at concerts and shows across the America. Jimmy McPhail died on Monday, March 16, 1998 at the age of 70.

Singer-pianist Shirley Horn specialized in jazz music and was known for her subtle ballads, though when called upon she could swing with the best of them. During her time she collaborated with some of the best jazz musicians in the world including Dizzy Gillespie, Miles Davis, Stuff Smith, Ray Charles, Antonio Carlos Jobim, Joe Williams, Carmen McRae, Toots Thielemans, Oscar Peterson, Clark Terry, Wynton Marsalis and numerous others. Horn was a fixture on the Washington, D.C. area night club scene during the 1950s and 1960s and later in her career as her reputation soared she continued to make most of her live appearances at venues in and around the nation's capital.

Shirley Horn was born in 1934 in Washington, D.C., and, with the encouragement of her organist grandmother, began taking piano lessons at age four. She graduated from Dunbar High School in the city and went on to graduate from Howard University with a degree in classical music. During her teen years she spent her free time listening to the records of such pianists as Erroll Garner, Oscar Peterson and Ahmad Jamal, and observing the performances of jazz and R&B musicians in the night clubs of the You Street area, which, despite being underage, she reportedly visited with regularity.

In 1954 Horn put together her first jazz trio and in March of that year they began playing out at the Wheel Bar on the Bladensburg Road Strip in Colmar Manor, Maryland. From 1955 to 1959 her outfit worked engagements at a series of night clubs in Washington, D.C. including the Marina, the Celebrity Room, the Patio Lounge, the Cairo Ballroom, Charlie's Café Lounge, the Spotlite Room (formerly the Celebrity Room), Abart's Internationale and Cocktail Lounge, the Brass Rail Bar and Restaurant, and the Amber Room (inside the Stevens Café). Horn worked with many different local musicians through the years, but during the late 1950s and throughout much of the 1960s her trio was usually rounded out by bassist Lewis Powers and drummer Stump Saunders.

In 1960 Horn recorded and released her first album, "Embers and Ashes: Songs of Lost Love Sung by Shirley Horn" (Shirley Horn; Stere-O-Craft Records, 1960). That year she continued to headline at the Amber Room and also worked engagements at the Flame Restaurant near Dupont Circle. In October 1960 the Shirley Horn Trio became the featured attraction at Bohemian Caverns in the You Street area for several months and made return appearances there all the way through 1967.

Other local night clubs the Shirley Horn Trio performed in during the 1960s included Lenardo, the Mayfair Restaurant, Abart's Internationale and Cocktail Lounge (which underwent a rapid-fire succession of name changes, and, for a short while, operated as the International Jazz Mecca), the Showboat Lounge, Los Josan and the Bridge. In the 1970s she also performed locally at Mr. Henry's Capitol Hill, Top-O-Foolery, the Corsican and the Howard Theatre. For much of the late 1960s and early 1970s she utilized bassist Steve Novosel and drummer George Brown on her local live dates.

In her time Shirley Horn recorded more than 30 albums for more than a dozen different record companies including such major labels as Mercury, ABC-Paramount and Verve. Several of her albums placed on Billboard magazine's various jazz album charts. In the late 1990s Horn's health declined and she began limiting her live performances. In 2005 she was awarded the National Endowment for the Arts Jazz Masters Award. Shirley Horn died on Sunday, October 20, 2005 at the age of 71.

Singer Don Covay was born Donald James Randolph in 1936 in Orangeburg, South Carolina. He moved to Washington, D.C. in the middle 1940s and attended Shaw Junior High School, where he began singing in school assemblies and talent shows. As a teenager in the early 1950s he sang in the Cherry Keys – his family's gospel quartet – and also with a local vocal group called the Bachelors. He later sang on an intermittent basis with the Rainbows.

In 1957 Covay began his professional career when he joined Little Richard's Revue, appearing as a singer under the name of Pretty Boy. In the late 1950s he appeared as a solo performer at such Washington, D.C. night clubs as Jack Rowe's Restaurant, Club Players and the Casino Royal Theatre Restaurant. He was a regular performer on the Chitlin Circuit in several Eastern states during the 1960s and made his first solo appearance at the Howard Theatre on a bill that ran from Friday, February 23 to Thursday, February 29, 1963 and offered the Miracles, B.B. King, Gene Chandler, Baby Jane and the Rockabyes and Henry LaMont.

Covay released 11 albums and numerous singles for more than a dozen different record companies including such major labels as Atlantic, Columbia and Mercury. His one major crossover hit song was "Mercy Mercy" (Don Covay & The Goodtimers; Rosemart Records, 1964), which reached number 35 on Billboard magazine's "Billboard Hot 100" music popularity chart on Saturday, October 24, 1964. He was also a prolific songwriter, with his compositions having been recorded by dozens of musical artists including Chubby Checker, Aretha Franklin, Gladys Knight and the Pips, Wilson Pickett, the Rolling Stones, the J. Geils Band, Etta James, Otis Redding, Little Richard, Gene Vincent, Wanda Jackson, Connie Francis, Steppenwolf and Small Faces, among others. Don Covay died on Saturday, January 31, 2015 at the age of 78.

Singer-guitarist Chuck Brown, regarded by some to be the Godfather of Go-Go, was born in Gaston, North Carolina in 1936 and moved to Washington, D.C. with his mother at age six. Information regarding his adolescence and teen years is fleeting, though it has been reported he was living on the streets at age 15, embarked on a short stint in the United States Marine Corps at age 17, and then spent much of the 1950s in and out of jail. As a young adult he spent several years at Lorton Correctional complex on a murder charge and it was during his years of incarceration that he taught himself to play guitar.

Back in Washington, D.C. in the early 1960s, Brown reportedly played guitar with an R&B group called Jerry Butler and the Earls of Rhythm. He then spent the middle 1960s in a local Top 40 band called Los Latinos. In 1966 he joined a local R&B band called the Soul Searchers, an outfit that initially performed on the local teen dance circuit. Among the group's earliest gigs were performances at the Cedar Lane Unitarian Universalist Church Teen Club in Bethesda, Maryland and the Greenbelt Teen Club at the Greenbelt Youth Center in Greenbelt, Maryland.

In the early 1970s, the Soul Searchers, with Brown on lead guitar and vocals, released two albums: "We the People" (The Soul Searchers; Sussex Records, 1972); and "Salt of the Earth" (The Soul Searchers; Sussex Records, 1974). At this time Brown began developing the go-go style of music that became his trademark. The band changed its name to Chuck Brown and the Soul Searchers and had a major hit with their third album, "Bustin' Loose" (Chuck Brown and the Soul Searchers; Source Records, 1979). From this record came their one major crossover hit song, "Bustin Loose Part 1," which peaked at number 34 on Billboard magazine's "Billboard Hot 100" popular music chart on Saturday, April 7, 1979.

To date, more than two-dozen albums featuring the music of Chuck Brown have been issued, a number that includes his recordings with the Soul Searchers, solo efforts, live sets and compilations. He is credited with creating the Washington, D.C. go-go scene and was responsible for spreading the popularity of that style of music across the globe. In recent years he was a popular concert attraction at some of the area's top venues including Nightclub 9:30 and the Howard Theatre. Chuck Brown died on Wednesday, May 16, 2012 at the age of 75.

Singer-pianist Billy Stewart was born in Smithfield, North Carolina in 1937 and raised in Washington, D.C. where he graduated from Armstrong High School. He had started singing at age 12 with his younger brothers Johnny, James and Frank as the Four Stewart Brothers, often performing live on radio station WUST. As a teenager he sang and played piano for the Rainbows and reportedly it was during one of the band's performances in 1956 that singer-guitarist Bo Diddley discovered Stewart and recruited him into his backup band.

In the late 1950s and early 1960s Stewart appeared as a solo R&B performer at a variety of local night clubs including the Rustic Cabin Restaurant in Colmar Manor, Maryland and the Colt Lounge on 14th Street NW in Washington, D.C. From 1962 to 1967 he frequently performed on the large R&B shows at the Howard Theatre.

With Bo Diddley's assistance, Stewart began recording for Chess Records and released a total of 19 singles and five albums on the label from 1956 to 1969. Stewart's biggest crossover single was "Summertime" (Billy Stewart; Chess Records, 1966) which peaked at number 10 on Billboard magazine's "Billboard Hot 100" pop music chart on Saturday, August 27, 1966. Billy Stewart died on Saturday, January 17, 1970 at the age of 32.

Marvin Gaye is considered to be one of the greatest singers in popular music history for the way he helped shape Motown and compiled a string of hit songs that made Billboard magazine's R&B and pop music charts. To this day his singing continues to influence musicians of all genres.

Marvin Gaye was born in Washington, D.C. in 1939 and grew up in the Southwest, Columbia Heights and Deanwood neighborhoods of the city. During his years at Cardoza High School in the middle 1950s he sang in such doo-wop vocal groups as the Dippers and the D.C. Tones. He dropped out of high school at age 17 and after a brief stint in the United States Air Force he returned to the nation's capital and began a professional singing career.

In the late 1950s Gaye joined a Washington, D.C. R&B vocal group called the Marquees, who were discovered by Bo Diddley and signed to Okeh Records. The band's first release for the company was the single "Hey Little School Girl" backed with "Wyatt Earp" (The Marquees; Okeh Records, 1957). In 1959 Harvey Fuqua hired the entire group, changed the outfit's name to Harvey and the New Moonglows, and had them record several singles for Chess Records. After the band broke up in 1960, Gaye signed on with Tri-Phi Records of Detroit, Michigan as a studio drummer and later in the year signed on with Tamla Records as a solo artist.

On the local level, Gaye often returned home to Washington, D.C. in the 1960s, but seemingly avoided the local night club scene. Instead, he preferred performing on the large R&B shows staged at the Howard Theatre where he was advertised as a solo singer. He made several appearances in 1962 and 1963 at the theatre, but as his star rose he began concentrating on working in larger concert halls across America.

During his career Marvin Gaye recorded and released more than 30 albums, with more than 20 compilations of his work having been released to date. From 1963 to 1982 Gaye released more than 80 singles, 33 of which hit the Billboard magazine pop charts. His various recordings were issued on more than two-dozen different record labels, including such majors as Tamla, Motown, Epic, Reprise, CBS, Columbia and Polydor. A total of 14 of his single releases reached the Top 10, with three of those going all the way to the top: "I Heard it Through the Grapevine" (Marvin Gaye; Tamla Records, 1968), which reached number one on the "Billboard Hot 100" chart on Saturday, December 14, 1968; "Let's Get It On" (Marvin Gaye; Tamla Records, 1973), which peaked at number one on the "Billboard Hot 100" chart on Saturday, September 8, 1973; and "Got To Give It Up Pt. 1" (Marvin Gaye; Tamla Records, 1977), which hit number one on the "Billboard Hot 100" chart on Saturday, June 25, 1977. Gaye was inducted into the Rock and Roll Hall of Fame in the "Performers" category on Wednesday, January 21, 1987. Marvin Gaye died on Sunday, April 1, 1984 at the age of 44.

Singer Van McCoy was born in Washington, D.C. in 1940 and at age 12 began writing songs and singing hymns at Metropolitan Baptist Church. During his years at Theodore Roosevelt High School in the late 1950s he sang in a neighborhood doo-wop group called the Starlighters. During those years he also handled lead vocals for the Marylanders, a rock and roll teen dance band from Montgomery County, Maryland. As the decade ended, he moved to Philadelphia, Pennsylvania and formed his own record company, Rockin' Records. At that time he recorded and released his first single as a solo R&B performer, "Never Trust a Friend" backed with "Mr. D.J." (Van McCoy; Rockin' Records, 1959).

During the 1960s McCoy worked as a staff writer and A&R man for Scepter Records and owned or co-owned a number of record companies including Vando Records, Share Records and Maxx Records. During this time he began writing songs for a number of independent and national recording artists and also produced and arranged singles and albums for a wide array of R&B artists including Peaches and Herb, Gladys Knight and the Pips, Aretha Franklin, Brenda and the Tabulations, the Stylistics, David Ruffin and Stacy Lattisaw.

From 1963 to 1979 McCoy, as either a solo R&B artist or bandleader, released more than a dozen albums and more than two-dozen singles on over a dozen different record labels including Columbia, Epic, Mercury, Buddah and MCA. His crowning achievement was the disco hit song "The Hustle" (Van McCoy & the Soul City Symphony; Avco Records, 1975), which reached number one on Billboard magazine's "Billboard Hot 100" pop music chart on Saturday, July 26, 1975. Van McCoy died on Friday, July 6, 1979 at the age of 39.

Peaches and Herb was a Washington, D.C. R&B vocal duo originally consisting of Francine "Peaches" Day (born Francine Edna Hurd in 1947), and Herb Fame (born Herbert

Feemster in 1942). The duo was put together in 1966 by Van McCoy and through the years employed many local musicians in their backup band. Their first album release was "For Your Love" (Peaches & Herb; Date Records, 1967). Fame retired the duo in 1970 and took a position with the Metropolitan Police Department in Washington, D.C. He quit the force in 1976 and put Peaches and Herb back together, with Linda Greene serving as the new "Peaches." To date seven different women have played the role of "Peaches" in the duo.

Peaches and Herb have a total of 10 studio albums and 12 compilation albums to their credit. They have placed a total of 22 singles on various Billboard charts, with their biggest hit being the song "Reunited" (Peaches & Herb; Polydor Records, 1978), which peaked at number one on Billboard magazine's "Billboard Hot 100" pop music chart on Saturday May 5, 1979. Among the record labels they have recorded for are Date, MCA, Polydor, Columbia and Imagen. Peaches and Herb are still active today, with Wanda Makle currently holding down the "Peaches" role.

In a city loaded with R&B talent, it was only natural for a television show for Black teenagers to emerge in the local market. The program in question, "Teenarama Dance Party," aired on UHF station WOOK-TV Channel 14 in Washington, D.C., Monday-through-Saturday, 5pm to 6pm, from Thursday, March 7, 1963 to Friday, November 20, 1970. The show broadcast from WOOK Radio (5321 First Place NE) and was created by the duo of local radio personality Al Jefferson and local teenager Cal Hackett. It featured local teenagers who selected and played the latest hit records, danced to the popular songs of the era and provided announcements of local high school events.

Most guests that appeared on "Teenarama Dance Party" were R&B artists who were in town working engagements at the Howard Theatre. Musical stars that were featured on the program included James Brown, Smokey Robinson and the Miracles, Chubby Checker, Major Lance, Mary Wells, Aretha Franklin, Lou Rawls, Billy Stewart, Martha and the Vandellas, the Supremes and the Four Seasons. Bob King hosted the program from 1963 to 1965, with a procession of WOOK radio personalities taking turns with that role through its final days.

CHAPTER SEVENTY-THREE
CHARLIE BYRD

Famed jazz guitarist Charlie Byrd moved to Washington, D.C. as a young adult in the early 1950s and made a name for himself during his long engagement at the Showboat Lounge in the Adams Morgan neighborhood of the city, a run that lasted more than 10 years and allowed him to perform with some of the biggest names in jazz music. Byrd recorded for a number of record labels during his time, but is best known for the album "Jazz Samba" he released with Stan Getz, a highly acclaimed effort that was recorded in Washington, D.C. at All Souls Unitarian Church and topped the Billboard charts in 1963. Byrd's specialty was Brazilian music, especially bossa nova, and ultimately he achieved legendary status among fans and fellow musicians in a town noted for its history of great guitarists.

Charlie Byrd was born in Suffolk, Virginia on Wednesday, September 16, 1925 and grew up in the city's Chuckatuck neighborhood. At age 10 he learned acoustic steel guitar from his father, a country store keeper, and a major influence on the young musician during his formative years was Gypsy guitarist Django Reinhardt. In 1942 he briefly attended Virginia Polytechnic University and played in various jazz bands during his time there. In 1943 he was drafted into the United States Army where he played guitar in the Army Special Services Band and toured Europe in the all-soldier production "G.I. Carmen." Upon his discharge he moved to New York and studied composition and jazz theory at the Harnett National Music School in Manhattan in the middle 1940s. During that time he began playing classical guitar.

Byrd moved to Washington, D.C. in 1950 and early in the decade played his first local night club dates at the Crosstown Restaurant in the Mount Pleasant neighborhood of the city. He moved to Rockville, Maryland, studied on-and-off with classical guitarist Sophocles Papas, and studied composition under Thomas Simmons at the Columbia School of Music. In the summer of 1954 he passed an audition in New York City and was chosen to attend a class in Siena, Italy taught by Spanish classical guitarist Andres Segovia.

In 1957 Byrd was regularly performing in several different jazz night clubs in the nation's capital including the Vineyard (1732 14th Street NW), the Crescent Restaurant (New York Avenue NW) and the Flame Restaurant (1629 Connecticut Avenue NW, just north of Dupont Circle). In October of that year he began headlining with his own band, the Charlie Byrd Trio (which included bassist Keter Betts and drummer Eddie Phyfe) at the Showboat Lounge in Adams Morgan, an engagement that would endure for most of the next 10 years. During that run, Betts remained his steady bassist, though Byrd went through a series of talented drummers after Phyfe's departure including Bertell Knox, Buddy Deppenschmidt and Bill Reichenbach.

Throughout his career Byrd toured foreign lands with impressive jazz combos. In May 1959 he played 27 concerts during a three-week State Department-sponsored Goodwill tour of England with Woody Herman and His Orchestra. For that outing the band was a 14-piece outfit that consisted of singer-clarinetist-saxophonist Woody Herman, guitarist Charlie Byrd, bassist Keter Betts, pianist Vince Guaraldi, cornetist Nat Adderley, trumpeter Reunald Jones, trombonist Bill Harris, drummer Jimmy Campbell and six English studio musicians.

In 1961 Byrd was part of another diplomatic tour of South America and came away enamored with musicians he had seen perform bossa nova tunes in Brazil. Upon his return to Washington, D.C. he met with saxophonist Stan Getz at the Showboat Lounge and discussed recording songs by Brazilian jazz singer-guitarist Joao Gilberto and Brazilian jazz pianist Antonio Carlos Jobim, both of whom are credited for creating the bossa nova style of music. Getz approached producer Creed Taylor about recording an album of bossa nova music for Verve Records and then set about recruiting musicians he had previously worked with to complete the project.

The recording session for this album of bossa nova music took place on Tuesday, February 13, 1962 in Pierce Hall, which was located inside All Souls Unitarian Church (1500 Harvard Street NW, Washington, D.C.). Musicians who played on the session were guitarist Charlie Byrd, tenor saxophonist Stan Getz, bassist Keter Betts, bassist-rhythm guitarist Gene Byrd and drummers Buddy Deppenschmidt and Bill Reichenbach. All but one song were recorded in one take. The resulting album, "Jazz Samba" (Stan Getz Charlie Byrd; Verve Records, 1962), was released in April 1962 and peaked at number one in Billboard's "50 Best Sellers – Stereo" chart in the "Billboard Top LP's" category on Saturday, March 9, 1963. It remains the only jazz album to ever top a Billboard pop music chart.

The success of "Jazz Samba" made Charlie Byrd one of the world's most famous guitarists. In the ensuing years he gave concerts and performed at jazz festivals across the United States and embarked on several tours of South America, Europe and Asia that saw him perform with some of the biggest names in jazz music.

In the Washington, D.C. area, Byrd played with his trio at the Showboat Lounge through late 1967. In November of that year opened his own night club with Showboat owner Peter Lambros and called it the Byrd's Nest (813 Ellsworth Drive, Silver Spring, Maryland). Despite Charlie Byrd's presence, the Byrd's Nest only lasted two years.

After the closing of the Byrd's Nest, the talented guitarist frequently headlined the Cellar Door in Georgetown for several years beginning in 1969. Later, from 1976 to 1978, Lambros and Byrd owned a night club called the Showboat Lounge at the Villa Rosa which was located in the former Byrd's Nest space. They tried one more joint venture, a night club a few doors down from the Bayou in the Georgetown neighborhood of Washington, D.C. called Charlie's Georgetown (3223 K Street NW). Upon its opening in June 1980 Byrd was the first entertainer to perform there. He was also the club's final headliner in June 1985.

In 1973 Byrd relocated to Annapolis, Maryland and for the next 26 years he based out of the King of France Tavern which was located within the Maryland Inn. Regular musicians to work in his various combos through the years included his brother, bassist Gene ("Joe") Byrd and drummers Bill Reichenbach, Wayne Phillips and Chuck Redd. To date, more than 90 albums of Byrd's music have been issued on a variety of record labels including Savoy, Washington, Offbeat, Riverside, Pickwick, Columbia, Milestone, CBS, Fantasy, Delta and Concord Jazz. Charlie Byrd died on Thursday, December 2, 1999 at the age of 74.

CHAPTER SEVENTY-FOUR
THE BEATLES INVADE THE NATION'S CAPITAL

From January 1960 to December 1963 nationally known rock and roll acts performing in the Washington, D.C. area were mainly showcased at armories, fire departments, select night clubs or the Howard Theatre. With the advent of the British Invasion – the moniker placed on a collection of musical groups from England that ventured to America in the middle 1960s and ultimately changed the course of rock and roll music – venues of greater capacity were secured by local promoters to accommodate the enormous fan base these bands were quickly cultivating. The British Invasion was initiated by the Beatles in 1964 when they performed their very first concert in the United States at the Washington Coliseum, a now-legendary event that launched the Fab Four to world fame, inspired innumerable young musicians to try to follow in their footsteps, and permanently moved star-studded rock and rollers into the arenas of the land.

On Tuesday, December 10, 1963 the British Invasion was set in motion when a 15-year-old ninth grader at Sligo Junior High School, Marsha Albert of Silver Spring, Maryland, saw a story about an upcoming rock and roll band from England called the Beatles on "The CBS Evening News with Walter Kronkite." She subsequently wrote to local radio station WWDC and asked to hear the group's music. Disc jockey Carroll James had an English pressing of their 45rpm single record "I Want to Hold Your Hand" flown in by a BOAC (British Overseas Airways Corporation) flight attendant friend and played it on the air on Tuesday, December 17, a month before its scheduled release in the United States. In the process, James unknowingly became the very first disc jockey to ever air the Beatles on American radio.

The Beatles quickly became a sensation, both locally and nationwide. Capitol Records, who held the American rights to the Beatles' recordings, began rushing their single "I Want to Hold Your Hand" backed with "I Saw Her Standing There" (The Beatles; Capitol Records, 1963) to radio stations across the country on Thursday, December 26, well in advance of the record's official Wednesday, January 8, 1964 release date. The single entered Billboard magazine's "Hot 100" popular music chart at number 45 on Saturday, January 18, soared to number three the following week and topped the chart at number one on Saturday, February 1, 1964.

With the Beatles suddenly dominating the Washington, D.C. area radio airwaves and their single racing up the charts, the possibility of having the band perform in the nation's capital was on every local promoter and music personality's mind. One of the more fascinating and overlooked aspects of this concert situation is that Don Dillard, the popular rock and roll disc jockey of Wheaton, Maryland-based radio station WDON, attempted to bring the Beatles into the Bladensburg Volunteer Fire Department, whose second-floor space he had rented out on numerous occasions for his own teen dances and record hops. Within days of Carrol James' initial airing of "I Want to Hold Your Hand" Dillard had personally contacted William Turner, the East Coast representative for Capitol Records who was lining up potential Beatles concert dates in America for the General Artists Corporation (the booking agency that manager Brian Epstein was working with to organize the band's American tour), in hope of booking the band into the Bladensburg facility sometime in January or February of 1964.

Dillard worked hard to sell the Bladensburg Volunteer Fire Department to Turner, even setting up a tentative date to meet with him in his office at WDON in Wheaton, Maryland to iron out the concert details. In 1962 and 1963 Dillard had booked such nationally known performers as Danny and the Juniors, Joey Dee and the Starliters, Tab Hunter, the Miracles, Chubby Checker, the Shirelles, the Supremes, Bo Diddley and Link Wray and His

Ray Men into the venue, and he insisted to Turner he could squeeze over one thousand teens into a facility whose legal capacity was a mere 354 occupants. However, as "I Want to Hold Your Hand" ascended the pop music charts, Turner explained in follow-up calls that agents at General Artists Corporation had decided that a much larger venue was needed and Dillard's business proposition was politely rebuffed.

The Washington Coliseum (1140 3rd Street NE, Washington, D.C.) was a logical choice to host the British invaders, as it was the largest available indoor facility in the city that hosted live music events. Prior to the arrival of the Beatles in America, there had been at least seven noteworthy popular music concert presentations in the coliseum: "The Biggest Show of Stars for 1961 Spring Edition" which featured Fats Domino and His Orchestra, the Shirelles, Chubby Checker, the Drifters, Bo Diddley, Ben E. King, Chuck Jackson, the Shells, Harold Cromer, Paul Williams and His Show of Stars Orchestra (Sunday, April 2, 1961); "The Biggest Show of Stars '61" which featured Brook Benton, the Platters, Del Shannon, Dee Clark, the Drifters, Gary U.S. Bonds, Gene McDaniels, the Jarmels, Curtis Lee, the Cleftones, Phil Upchurch, Harold Cromer and Paul Williams and His Show of Stars Orchestra (Sunday, October 15, 1961); "Dick Clark's Caravan of Stars" which featured Paul Anka, Chubby Checker, Duane Eddy, Linda Scott, Clarence "Frogman" Henry, the Shirelles, the Jive Five and Jules Lavan and the Caravan of Stars Orchestra (Sunday, November 12, 1961); "The Biggest Show of Stars for '62 Spring Edition" which featured Brook Benton, Fats Domino, Gene Chandler, Bruce Channel, Don and Juan, the Impressions, Marie Knight, Harold Cromer, Lou Parks, the Twisting Parkettes and Paul Williams and His Biggest Show of Stars Orchestra (Sunday, April 22, 1962); Harry Belafonte and Miriam Makeba (Saturday, April 28, 1962); Joan Baez and Pete Seeger (Saturday, April 27, 1963); and "The Original Hootenanny U.S.A." which featured the Journeymen, the Halifax III, the Geezinslaw Brothers, Jo Mapes and Glenn Yarbrough (Wednesday, November 27, 1963).

The Beatles landed in America on Friday, February 7, 1964 at New York's John F. Kennedy Airport and appeared live on "The Ed Sullivan Show" on the evening of Sunday, February 9, performing five songs over two separate sets on the hour-long program and drawing the largest audience in television history. Their performance, which had registered more than 50,000 ticket requests, took place in CBS's Studio 50 in front of 728 people and to this day remains one of the most important milestones in rock and roll history. More than 73 million people – approximately 40% of the American population at the time – viewed the historic broadcast. On Monday, February 10 a snowstorm dumped eight inches of snow on New York and Washington, D.C. and at 12noon the following day the Beatles boarded a train and headed towards a musical date in the nation's capital.

Two agents from General Artists Corp. in New York, Norman Weiss and Jerry Perenchio, had agreed to financial terms with Harry Lynn, owner of the Washington Coliseum in Washington, D.C., and the Beatles' first American concert was scheduled for the night of Tuesday, February 11, 1964. It remains one of the greatest and most important concerts in the history of rock and roll music.

The Beatles arrived at Union Station in Washington, D.C. at 3:09pm on the afternoon in question, where an estimated crowd of more than 3,000 fans (and innumerable police officers) anxiously awaited them. The band was then pulled aside by WWDC vice president of programming Irv Lichtenstein, who ushered them into his 1962 Rambler station wagon and safely transported them to the coliseum to conduct a general press conference with the local media on the square stage that had been constructed in the center of the cavernous building's ground floor.

The band subsequently gave a brief interview with disc jockey Carroll James at 5pm inside a makeshift WWDC satellite radio station that had been constructed to the left of the

Coliseum's front entrance (during the interview, James actually introduced the Beatles to Marsha Albert, the teen who had requested their music be played on WWDC). The band members then napped on the studio's floor until the afternoon concluded and a limousine arrived to take them to the Shoreham Hotel (2500 Calvert Street NW; today the hotel is known as the Omni Shoreham Hotel), where the entire seventh floor had been reserved for them and their entourage. After settling in, John Lennon scribbled down the evening's set list on a sheet of Shoreham stationery. Sometime between 8pm and 8:30pm, the band headed back to the coliseum for the show.

A lone ad in the Friday, January 31, 1964 edition of the Washington Post newspaper declared showtime as 8:30pm and listed ticket prices at $2, $3 and $4. While this ad proclaimed "A Complete Show With Other Big Acts," it did not actually name any of the show's opening bands (Washington Coliseum owner Harry Lynn ran the same ad three other times – in the Washington Daily News of January 31, 1964, the "Teen" section of the Evening Star on the same date, and again in the Evening Star on Tuesday, February 4, 1964).

It is known that six supporting acts did appear onstage that evening, though the exact order of appearance and exactly who provided their musical backing has never been conclusively verified. Beginning shortly after 8:30pm, two-song performances were given by Jay and the Americans, the Caravelles, singer Tommy Roe, the Righteous Brothers and the Chiffons. There was also a one-song performance by singer Donna Lynn, who sang her Capitol Records novelty single, "My Boyfriend Got a Beatle Haircut" (which was written by Jack Wolf and "Bugs" Brower).

When the Beatles took the stage at approximately 9:35pm the Washington Coliseum was filled with 8,092 screaming teens (slightly above the facility's 8,000 capacity). Band members Paul McCartney, John Lennon, George Harrison and Ringo Starr worked their way from the dressing rooms to the center of the floor and climbed onto what appeared to be a makeshift, boxing ring-like stage that hosted a round, rotating drum set platform that was flanked by three amplifiers. Four local radio station disc jockeys sporting Beatles wigs emceed the show – Carroll James (WWDC), Johnny Dark (WCAO of Baltimore), Jack Alix (WEEL) and Dean Griffith (WPGC). As Paul McCartney walked across the stage, one emcee, Jack Alix, reached out and shook his hand.

The Beatles appeared onstage in matching Edwardian gray suit coats over white shirts and black ties and performed an electrifying set of 12 songs: "Roll Over Beethoven," "From Me to You," "I Saw Her Standing There," "This Boy," "All My Loving," "I Wanna Be Your Man," "Please Please Me," "Till There Was You," "She Loves You," "I Want to Hold Your Hand," "Twist and Shout," and "Long Tall Sally." The band had actually begun playing one minute and 56 seconds after all four musicians had taken the stage. They completed their final song some 34 minutes and 45 seconds after having taken the stage. They then left the stage 14 seconds later. All told, the Beatles had spent a total of 34 minutes and 59 seconds on the stage, of which 32 minutes and 49 seconds had been spent playing their 12 songs. The mostly female crowd was reportedly screaming at the top of their lungs throughout the entire Beatles performance and hurled a steady stream of jelly beans at the Fab Four as they performed. The entire historic concert, for which the Beatles were paid $12,184.76, was recorded on black-and-white videotape by CBS Television for closed circuit presentation that later aired at theatres and arenas throughout the United States on Saturday, March 14 and Sunday, March 15, 1964. Millions attended those viewings.

After the Washington Coliseum concert the Beatles returned to the Shoreham Hotel, but left after midnight to attend a charity ball for the National Society for the Prevention of Cruelty to Children at the British Embassy (3100 Massachusetts Avenue NW) hosted by British Ambassador to the United States David Ormsby-Gore. The following morning limousines escorted the band back to Union Station, but stopped along the way so group photographs of the Beatles could be taken with the Capitol in the background. At 11:46am the Fab Four boarded their train and headed back to New York where they would perform two separate concerts at Carnegie Hall that evening.

The Beatles and the British Invasion had an amazing effect on every aspect of the Washington, D.C. area rock and roll scene. Local teens, like others all over the world, went absolutely nuts over the rock stars from England. Beatles-type bands proliferated in the metropolitan area as the Fab Four saturated the popular music charts with a seemingly endless stream of hit singles and albums. Accordingly, the weekly "Teen" section of the Evening Star newspaper overflowed with announcements and articles on local teen musicians and their bands, thus adding considerable fuel to a popular culture force that was already on fire.

In the aftermath of the Beatles' Washington, D.C. invasion, many of the adult bands that worked the local rock and roll night clubs began covering the songs of the British Invasion. In addition, the Beatles' appearance led local promoters to accelerate the practice of presenting visiting national rock and roll acts in larger venues, thus steering such groups away from the area's night clubs, armories, fire departments and theatres.

When the Beatles returned to Washington, D.C. on Monday, August 15, 1966 to headline District of Columbia Stadium (unofficially known at the time as D.C. Stadium, the facility was later renamed Robert F. Kennedy Memorial Stadium in January 1969), their concert marked another milestone in local rock and roll history – the placing of superstar acts into sports stadiums. The show that evening in the 50,000-seat facility, which included four opening acts – The Remains, singer Bobby Hebb, the Ronettes, and the Cyrkle (the Remains were the backing band for both Bobby Hebb and the Ronettes) – drew a total of 32,164 fans. The Beatles had successfully revolutionized popular music and the British Invasion's infiltration of American music and culture had been activated.

CHAPTER SEVENTY-FIVE
FROM THE STREETS OF ALEXANDRIA

There are many music historians who do not consider the Northern Virginia region to be a part of the Washington, D.C. area for two reasons: the fact that the town of Alexandria retroceded from the District of Columbia in March 1847; and that Virginia itself was a member of the Confederate States of America during the Civil War – two historical footnotes that resulted in Virginians establishing social and political identities apart from their neighbors to the north. With regards to geographic layout, the Potomac River has long served as a permanent boundary line that reinforces a sense of physical separation between the two regions.

When reviewing local music history, the case has been presented that the city of Alexandria is the one section of Northern Virginia that could be granted consideration for inclusion into the historical spectrum of Washington, D.C. area rock and roll. The reasons for Alexandria's prominence are that several performing artists of note – including John Phillips, Cass Elliot, Scott McKenzie and Jim Morrison – spent considerable portions of their formative years living in the city, and that a prominent rock and roll venue, the Alexandria Arena (commonly referred to as the Alexandria Roller Rink), offered significant rock and roll shows from 1964 to 1974, many of which included performances by bands from around the Washington, D.C. area.

John Edmund Andrew Phillips was born Friday, August 30, 1935 in Parris Island, South Carolina, grew up in Alexandria, Virginia (he resided with his family at 4 Oxford Avenue in the Del Ray neighborhood of the city from 1939 to 1956), and attended George Washington High School, though he was expelled in December 1953 in the middle of his senior year. He went on to graduate in June 1954 from Bullis School, which at the time was located in Silver Spring, Maryland.

Late in his high school years Phillips began receiving informal guitar lessons from his brother-in-law Bill Throckmorton. The two would get together in Throckmorton's house and play along to pop and jazz records, with Philips on guitar and Throckmorton on drums and piano. During this time Phillips also began singing doo-wop songs on street corners in Alexandria with numerous friends from the area including Bill Cleary and Phil Blondheim. Phillips went on to attend several colleges including the United States Naval Academy, American University, George Washington University, the University of Virginia and Hampden-Sydney College.

It will be noted here that Phillips remained in Alexandria for several years after graduating high school. For several months from late 1956 to early 1957 he resided in an apartment at 3902 Executive Avenue #A12. He married Susie Adams in May 1957 and the couple then moved into her brother Tom's house at 213 Ramsey Alley, remaining through November of that year. Finally, from December 1957 to the end of 1960, Phillips and his wife had their own apartment at 917 Potomac Avenue #B1. In 1961 he left Alexandria and moved to New York City.

In the spring of 1959 Phillips formed a folk music vocal quartet called the Abstracts with the aforementioned Cleary and Blondheim, and Mike Boran. A year later the Abstracts changed their name to the Smoothies (with Blondheim changing his name to "Scott McKenzie") and performed in night clubs throughout the Eastern United States. The Smoothies were signed to a major record company and released two singles: "Joanie" backed with "Softly" (The Smoothies; Decca Records, June 1960); and "Ride, Ride, Ride" backed with "Lonely Boy and Pretty Girl" (The Smoothies; Decca Records, October 1960).

In 1961 Phillips, as a singer-guitarist, formed a new folk trio in New York City called the Journeymen, retaining singer-guitarist McKenzie and acquiring singer-banjoist Dick Weissman. The Journeymen gained national attention and released a total of three albums: "The Journeymen" (The Journeymen; Capitol Records, 1961), "Coming Attraction – Live!" (The Journeymen; Capitol Records, 1962), and "New Directions in Folk Music" (The Journeymen; Capitol Records, 1963).

In early 1964 Phillips formed a new folk trio called the New Journeymen, rounding out the lineup with singer Michelle Phillips (his wife) and singer-banjoist Marshall Brickman. Later in the year he went looking for an accomplished vocalist to add to the group and recruited singer-guitarist Denny Doherty, a Canadian native who had previously been a member of the folk trio known as the Halifax Three, and, more recently, a Washington, D.C.-based folk rock band known as the Mugwumps.

In December 1964 Phillips booked the New Journeymen into a two-week Christmastime engagement opening for comedian Bill Cosby in the Blue Room of the Shoreham Hotel in Washington, D.C. The engagement lasted from Tuesday, December 22, 1964 through Saturday, January 2, 1965, with the New Year's Eve entertainment lineup consisting of Cosby, the New Journeymen, the Tee Carson Trio, Gretchen Wyler, Bob Cross and His Orchestra and Steve Kisley and His Orchestra. Several weeks later Brickman quit the group and was replaced by guitarist-banjoist Eric Hord for the few remaining dates on their schedule. Shortly thereafter the New Journeymen called it quits.

Sometime in the spring of 1965 Phillips gathered up his wife Michelle, Denny Doherty and several friends and associates and headed for St. Thomas in the Virgin Islands, where they set up camp for an extended stay and performed informally in a boardinghouse night club called Duffy's (the exact length of their 1965 Virgin Islands vacation has never been conclusively established – almost all of the published works on the Mamas and the Papas give conflicting dates of their arrival and departure).

The group was soon joined by Cass Elliot, who had previously been a member of the folk trio the Big Three and had spent most of 1964 in the Mugwumps with Doherty (Elliot had spent much of her teen years living in Alexandria, Virginia and had briefly attended the same high school as Phillips, though the two were five years apart and their paths had never crossed). Elliot, a talented singer and actress, accompanied the band onstage at Duffy's and worked well with the musicians around her.

After the Virgin Islands excursion ended sometime around August 1965, the entire crew moved back to the United States and the quartet of John and Michelle Phillips, Denny Doherty and Cass Elliot soon found themselves together in Los Angeles, California where they began working on songs together. In the fall of 1965 singer Barry McGuire heard them rehearsing and introduced them to Lou Adler who was then president, co-owner, and chief record producer of Dunhill Records. A deal with Dunhill was reached, Adler took the quartet into the studio, and the band chose the Mamas and the Papas as their title.

From 1966 to 1971 the Mamas and the Papas released a total of five studio albums on Dunhill Records: "If You Can Believe Your Eyes and Ears" (1966), "The Mamas and the Papas" (1966), "The Mamas and the Papas Deliver" (1967), "The Papas and the Mamas" (1968) and "People Like Us" (1971). They also released 17 singles, six of which reached the top ten on Billboard's "Hot 100" popular music chart, and one of which, "Monday, Monday," went to number one on Saturday, May 7, 1966.

The Mamas and the Papas were inducted into the Rock and Roll Hall of Fame in the "Performers" category on Monday, January 12, 1998. After the original version of the group broke up, John Phillips remained active in the popular music world as a songwriter and performer. He maintained a band called the New Mamas and the Papas and performed with them throughout the 1980s and 1990s. The band endured numerous lineup changes and later versions included his longtime friend Scott McKenzie. John Phillips died of heart failure on Sunday, March 18, 2001 at the age of 65.

Cass Elliot was born Ellen Naomi Cohen in Baltimore, Maryland on Friday, September 19, 1941 and was raised in Baltimore and Washington, D.C. Her family moved to Alexandria, Virginia and resided at 1445 Arlington Terrace from 1953 to 1955 (today this house is marked 2215 Arlington Terrace), during which time Cohen attended Mount Vernon Junior High School. From 1956 to 1958 the Cohen family resided in an apartment at 1502 Commonwealth Avenue #2 in Alexandria, and Cohen spent her freshman and sophomore years at George Washington High School (the 1956-1957 and 1957-1958 school years). In the summer of 1958 her family left Alexandria and moved to Baltimore, Maryland where Cohen attended Forest Park High School for her junior and senior years (the 1958-1959 and 1959-1960 school years), dropping out two weeks before she was scheduled to graduate. It was during her high school years that Cohen took on the name "Cass" and it was shortly thereafter that she adopted the surname "Elliot" in memory of a deceased friend.

Cass Elliot first began singing and acting in her high school years, during which time she appeared in various plays and musicals and was noted for her powerful, distinctive voice. In the early 1960s she continued these artistic pursuits and moved back and forth between New York and the Washington, D.C., attending American University for a brief period. From 1961 to 1965 her permanent address was 1710 Crestwood Drive in Alexandria, Virginia, a house owned and occupied by her mother.

In late 1962 Elliot met singer-banjoist Tim Rose at a private party in Georgetown. Rose suggested they relocate to Chicago, Illinois and Elliot complied. There, they met up with a friend of Rose's who played banjo named John Brown and together formed a folk trio called the Triumvirate. The band embarked on night club tours in the Midwest in 1963 and while performing in Omaha, Nebraska they replaced Brown with a singer-guitarist named Jim Hendricks.

With the personnel shift Triumvirate changed its name to the Big 3 and moved back to the East Coast, alternating engagements at the Bitter End in New York City's Greenwich Village and the Shadows in Washington, D.C.'s Georgetown neighborhood. The band signed a major record deal and released two albums: "The Big 3" (The Big 3; FM Records, 1963); and "The Big 3 Live at the Recording Studio" (The Big 3; FM Records, 1964).

In the summer of 1964 Tim Rose left the Big 3 and the group disbanded. Elliot and Hendricks then teamed with singer-guitarists Denny Doherty and Zal Yanovsky, two Canadians who had both been members of the Halifax Three, to form an electric folk rock group called the Mugwumps. The band made a permanent move down to Washington, D.C. and performed as the nightly house band at the Shadows in Georgetown from Monday, July 13 to Saturday, November 8, 1964. A part-time member of the band was a harmonica player from Greenwich Village in New York City named John Sebastian, who would later form the Lovin' Spoonful with Yanovsky.

The Mugwumps were signed by Warner Bros. Records and recorded an album in 1964 entitled "The Mugwumps," which was released posthumously in 1967. From that album came two singles, also posthumously released: "Here It Is Another Day" backed with "Searchin'" (The Mugwumps; Warner Bros. Records, 1967) and "I Don't Wanna Know" backed with "I'll Remember Tonight" (The Mugwumps; Warner Bros. Records, 1967). Neither single release made the Billboard charts.

After a short engagement at the Peppermint Lounge in Manhattan (a borough of New York City) the band received a call from John Phillips, who wanted to enlist the services of Denny Doherty for a two-week New Journeymen gig at the Shoreham Hotel in Washington, D.C. in late December 1964. With Doherty's departure, the Mugwumps broke up.

In the spring of 1965 Elliot performed irregularly as a solo act at the Shadows in Georgetown. Doherty, meanwhile, remained with the New Journeymen for their last round of performances early in the year. That summer he accompanied Phillips and an entourage of friends and musicians to St. Thomas in the Virginia Islands for an extended vacation. Elliot, who was without a steady singing job at the time, flew down and joined the camp and would sing informally at a night club called Duffy's with Phillips' pickup band, which included his wife Michelle and Doherty.

That August Elliot returned to the United States and moved to Los Angeles, where several weeks later she reunited with John and Michelle Phillips and Denny Doherty and engaged in a series of rehearsals. The quartet was signed by Lou Adler of Dunhill Records, became the Mamas and the Papas, and went on to become one of the most popular folk rock vocal groups in the world. Cass Elliott died of a heart attack in her sleep in London, England on Monday, July 29, 1974 at the age of 32.

Scott McKenzie was born Phil Blondheim on Tuesday, January 10, 1939 in Jacksonville, Florida and spent his youth living with relatives in North Carolina, Kentucky and Rhode Island. In 1946 he moved with his mother Dorothy W. Blondheim to Washington, D.C. where they took an apartment at 1413 Girard Street NW #38. They remained there through 1948 and then moved to Falls Church, Virginia, where they resided in a house which was then-marked 6724 Lake Street from 1949 to 1954. In 1955 Blondheim and his mother moved to 3573B South Stafford Street in Arlington, Virginia, a dwelling that would remain his home for the next 11 years.

During his teen years Blondheim sang and played guitar along to jazz albums and formed a band called the Singing Strings with a friend from Arlington named Tim Rose. Blondheim graduated high school from St. Stephen's School in Alexandria in 1957 and shortly thereafter attended a party in the apartment of John Phillips, with whom he began a musical association that would span several decades.

In the spring of 1959 Blondheim joined the Abstracts, a folk group whose lineup also included fellow Alexandrians John Phillips, Bill Cleary and Mike Boran. In 1960 the band changed its name to the Smoothies, and while performing an engagement at the Elmwood Casino in Windsor, Ontario, Canada, Blondheim changed his name to "Scott McKenzie." The change came about when Blondheim, after complaining at an after-show party that no one could properly pronounce his name, combined two off-handed suggestions he culled from the performers around him. First, comedian Jackie Curtis told him he resembled a Scottie dog, an image the Smoothies band members wouldn't let Blondheim live down; second, John Phillips suggested that the stage name be completed with the insertion of "Mackenzie" – his daughter Laura's middle name. Hence, after some spelling alterations, "Scott McKenzie" was born. The Smoothies toured the Eastern United States and released two singles for Decca Records before disbanding late in 1960.

From 1961 to 1963 McKenzie was a member of the Journeymen along with John Phillips and Dick Weissman. The popular folk group released three albums on Capitol Records and frequently performed at the Shadows in Washington, D.C.'s Georgetown neighborhood. The band shared the same manager as the Kingston Trio (the folk group they modeled themselves after) and enjoyed considerable success.

The Journeymen's first job was at a night club called Gerde's Folk City in New York's Greenwich Village where they shared a bill with Lightnin' Hopkins and Bob Dylan. They subsequently performed around the country and made stops at folk music venues in Los Angeles, Boston and Chicago. When performing at the Shadows in Washington, D.C. their frequent opening act was a young comedian named Bill Cosby. The band was also booked on a number of multi-band "Hoot" tours where one of their fellow acts was the Halifax

Three, a band whose singer, Denny Doherty, greatly impressed John Phillips and was later recruited into the Mamas and the Papas.

In 1964 McKenzie embarked on a solo career, mixing folk with acoustic-oriented pop music. He signed with Ode Records, a company in Los Angeles, California created by former Dunhill Records founder-president-chief producer Lou Adler, and released two albums: "The Voice of Scott McKenzie" (Scott McKenzie; Ode Records, 1967); and "Stained Glass Morning" (Scott McKenzie; Ode Records, 1970).

From McKenzie's first album came the now-classic single "San Francisco (Be Sure to Wear Flowers in Your Hair)," which reached number four on the "Billboard Hot 100" popular music chart on Saturday, July 1, 1967. After his second album was released on Ode Records, McKenzie faded from view and was inactive for most of the 1970s. He later returned to the popular music scene when he reunited with John Phillips and performed in various versions of the New Mamas and the Papas throughout the 1980s and 1990s. Scott McKenzie died from complications of Guillain-Barre syndrome on Saturday, August 18, 2012 at the age of 73.

Jim Morrison is Alexandria, Virginia's greatest rock and roll icon. He resided in the town from January 1959 until August 1961 – a period that covered most of his high school years – and while he never was part of a rock and roll band during his time there, he certainly gathered creative inspiration by exploring local night clubs and observing various bands and poets in action. It was these experiences that led him to become a performing artist as lyricist-vocalist with the Doors, one of the greatest American rock and roll bands in history.

James Douglas Morrison was born on Wednesday, December 8, 1943 at Brevard Hospital (a facility that has since been renamed the Holmes Regional Medical Center) in Melbourne, Florida. His father, George Stephen "Steve" Morrison, a career naval officer, and his mother, Clara, eventually added two more children, Anne and Andy, to the fold, and as a military family endured numerous moves about the country.

Prior to turning 14, Jim Morrison had resided in no fewer than 14 different homes, including stops in Florida, California, Pennsylvania, Maryland, New Mexico, Virginia and Texas. From August 1950 until January 1953, the Morrison family resided in the city of Falls Church, Virginia at 813 Jefferson Avenue (today the house is marked 6913 Jefferson Avenue). During that time Morrison attended Oak Street Elementary School for all of his second and third grade school years, and the first half of his fourth grade year (today this school is currently in operation as Thomas Jefferson Elementary School and is still situated at 601 S. Oak Street, Falls Church). After several additional moves around the country, the Morrison family eventually landed in Alameda, California in the late 1950s, where Jim spent his freshman year and the first half of his sophomore year at Alameda High School in Alameda, California.

In late 1958 Steve Morrison was promoted from commander to captain and was informed that he had been assigned to the Pentagon in Arlington County, Virginia. In January 1959 the family moved to a home at 310 Woodland Terrace in the Jefferson Park neighborhood of Alexandria, Virginia and Jim Morrison enrolled at George Washington High School just as the second semester of his sophomore year was starting.

Although the subsequent 32-month portion of Jim Morrison's life has largely been largely ignored by his various biographers, it was indeed a fascinating period where he spent much of his time in his basement bedroom reading, drawing and painting. When the urge to see the outside world overcame him, he would venture off on foot and explore the surrounding terrain, with the Alexandria Library and the docks along the Potomac River waterfront rating as favorite hangouts. He also journeyed on occasion into Washington, D.C. where he visited book shops and night clubs. At this point he had yet to express any interest in singing, though he was known to have been filling notebooks with poetry and at times had exhibited some strange behavior for the benefit of his friends and classmates.

It has been verified that Morrison frequented several different night clubs during his teen years in Alexandria that in all likelihood contributed to his later decision to become a performing artist. He was sighted by friends on many occasions at the Club Log Tavern on Richmond Highway, down in the Hybla Valley neighborhood of Alexandria. There, he had the opportunity to observe the performances of a teen rock band called Ronnie and the Off Beats (which included guitarist Danny Gatton) and talk on the breaks with lead singer Ron MacDonald about his song selections.

Morrison also ventured into Washington, D.C. to such bars as the Brickskeller in the Dupont Circle neighborhood where he would cavort with friends, and Bohemian Caverns in the You Street area, the jazz night spot that boasted the JFK Quintet as its house band at the time.

Perhaps the most significant of all of Morrison's nocturnal hangouts was Coffee 'n' Confusion, the beatnik coffee house at 10th and K Streets NW in Washington that offered live folk music and open poetry readings. According to several of his George Washington High School classmates, on one occasion Morrison actually got up onstage in the dingy basement club and gave a poetry recital that turned out to be his first known public performance. It was an event that must have been an exhilarating experience for the high school student who was just beginning to explore the boundaries of personal artistic creativity and expression.

Jim Morrison graduated from George Washington High School in June 1961. Despite his high intelligence, he initially sidestepped the major universities and attended St. Petersburg Junior College (today known simply as St. Petersburg College) in Florida and Florida State University in Tallahassee before moving to Los Angeles, California in January 1964 and enrolling in UCLA. There he studied in the Department of Theater Arts (erroneously referred to by most Morrison biographers as the UCLA Film School, this department has since switched its title from the Department of Theater Arts to the UCLA School of Theater, Film and Television) and in June 1965 he earned a Bachelor of Arts in theater arts, a program which at the time allowed him to take a series of courses in film production. It was at UCLA where Morrison reportedly escalated his drinking habits and experimented with drugs such as marijuana and LSD. He continued filling notebooks with thoughts, observations, poetry and lyrics.

Jim Morrison's career as a rock and roll singer began in the spring of 1965 when fellow UCLA theater arts student Ray Manzarek, who was then singing and playing keyboards in a rock and roll band called Rick and the Ravens that included his brothers Rick (on guitar) and Jim (on harmonica) and a drummer named Vince Thomas, invited him out to observe his group play in a bar called the Turkey Joint West in Santa Monica. Morrison went out and watched the band perform on several occasions. One time, when the group was hired to work a high school graduation dance at Ports O Call in the San Pedro Marina on Friday, June 11, 1965, Manzarek called upon Morrison to help the band fulfill a contractual obligation by standing onstage and pretending to play an unplugged guitar.

A little over a month later, Ray Manzarek was renting a house on Fraser Avenue in the Ocean Park neighborhood of Santa Monica, California and, unbeknownst to him, Jim Morrison, with his UCLA theater arts degree already forgotten, was unemployed and living nearby on the roof of a friend's apartment building in Venice. On a bright afternoon in July 1965 Manzarek was sunbathing on the Pacific Ocean beach directly down the street from his house when Morrison unexpectedly came strolling along. When Manzarek asked his friend what he had been up to, Morrison responded by telling about the lyrics he had been writing and recited the song "Moonlight Drive" while kneeling in the sand.

Manzarek, who was significantly impressed by the impromptu performance, suggested they begin working on songs together, and invited the rooftop dweller to join Rick and the Ravens. Morrison told Manzarek he had been entertaining the idea of forming a band and making a million dollars, voicing his desire to call the group "The Doors," a name he took from a book about hallucinogenic drugs entitled "The Doors of Perception" by Aldous Huxley. (Huxley, in turn, had taken that title from a line in the 1792 William Blake poem "The Marriage of Heaven and Hell" that went, "If the doors of perception were cleansed, everything would appear to man as it is: infinite.")

In August 1965 Ray Manzarek met a drummer from West Los Angeles named John Densmore who had previously played in a rock and roll band called the Psychedelic Rangers. The two became acquainted in a meditation class and Densmore was recruited to replace Vince Thomas in Rick and the Ravens. Densmore participated in a few rehearsals in the band, which had evidently run out of jobs and was running out of steam.

On Thursday, September 2, 1965 Rick and the Ravens changed its name to the Doors and recorded a six-song demo, which included a version of the future hit song "Hello, I Love You" at World Pacific Studios in Los Angeles. The lineup for this session included Jim Morrison, the three Manzarek brothers, John Densmore, and a bassist named Patty Sullivan. Shortly after this session Rick and Jim Manzarek and Patty Sullivan left the fold.

In the final week of September guitarist Robby Krieger, who had previously played with Densmore in the Psychedelic Rangers, was asked to join the band. The classic Doors lineup of Morrison, Manzarek, Densmore and Krieger was then complete. The band then conducted most of its earliest rehearsals at the home of a friend named Hank Olguin, whose residence has only been identified as being a pink house situated in an alley behind a greyhound bus station somwhere in Santa Monica.

Reportedly, on Saturday, September 4, 1965 Jim Morrison wrote his parents, who were then living in London, England, and informed them of his decision to sing in a rock and roll band. His father allegedly wrote back and told his son he did not think highly of his decision and Jim's response was to never write them again. Jim had last seen his folks sometime in late 1964 and this latest incident was his last attempt to contact them in any manner. (Clara Morrison passed away on Thursday, December 29, 2005 and George Stephen Morrison passed away on Monday, November 17, 2008.)

The Doors emerged from an electric Los Angeles, California rock and roll scene that had kicked into overdrive with the opening of the now-legendary Whisky A Go Go night club at 8901 Sunset Boulevard on Wednesday, January 15, 1964. Scores of exciting new rock bands like Buffalo Springfield, the Byrds, Iron Butterfly, the Leaves, Love, the Mothers of Invention, Rhinoceros, the Seeds, the Standells, Steppenwolf and the West Coast Pop Art Experimental Band were spawned in various clubs on and around the famed Sunset Strip during the 1960s. All of these groups and many others contributed to a new cultural movement that had originated in a string of music-oriented hot spots like Ciro's, the Galaxy, Gazzarri's, Pandora's Box, the Sea Witch, the Trip, and the top Los Angeles establishment of the era, the Whisky itself.

The Doors initially landed a steady gig in February 1966 at the London Fog, a smallish rock and roll bar located on the Strip at 8909 Sunset Boulevard. While the club's outside marquee read: "The Doors – Band from Venice," few who entered the night club could imagine what was really unfolding before their very own eyes. The inexperienced foursome on the towering stage, despite the seemingly bashful lead vocalist who sang with his back to the audience, was embarking on a mystical mission that would land them the number one song in America some 17 months later and firmly establish them as rock and roll superstars.

On Saturday, May 7, 1966 the Doors gave their final performance at the London Fog, though before being released by the night club's manager Jim Morrison had captured the interest of Ronnie Harran, a talent agent for the Whisky A Go Go a few doors away. The group auditioned for a job at that prestigious night club the following Monday and were hired by owner Elmer Valentine for house band duties beginning Monday, May 23, 1966. From this date until late August 1966 the Doors opened at the Whisky for acts like Buffalo Springfield, Captain Beefheart and His Magic Band, the Chambers Brothers, Gene Clark and the Group, Johnny Rivers, Love, Them (featuring singer Van Morrison) and the Turtles.

Consequently, at some point in August the Doors attracted the attention of Elektra Records president and founder Jac Holzman, who, on the advice of Love lead singer Arthur Lee, scouted the Doors at the Whisky and ultimately signed the group to a record deal (evidently just before they were fired from the night club for Morrison's onstage profanity during a now-legendary performance of "The End").

Combining poetic lyrics with piercing guitar leads, haunting keyboard melodies, and jazzy, blues-influenced percussion, the Doors would go on to release six studio albums for Elektra Records: "The Doors" (January 1967), "Strange Days" (October 1967), "Waiting for the Sun" (July 1968), "The Soft Parade" (July 1969), "Morrison Hotel" (February 1970) and "L.A. Woman" (April 1971). The band also hit the Top 40 a total of eight times, with two singles topping the charts: "Light My Fire," which reached number one on "Billboard's" "Billboard Hot 100" popular music chart on Saturday, July 29, 1967; and "Hello, I Love You," which reached number one on the same chart on Saturday, August 3, 1968. Their other Top 40 hits were "People are Strange," "Love Me Two Times," "The Unknown Soldier," "Touch Me," "Love Her Madly" and "Riders on the Storm."

Jim Morrison embarked on a strange homecoming when the Doors worked a rare double-header on Friday, August 18, 1967, appearing at the Annapolis Armory in Annapolis, Maryland at 7:30pm and then that same night performing at 10pm at the Alexandria Arena in Alexandria, Virginia. The band would later return to the nation's capital when they performed on Saturday, November 25, 1967 at the Hilton Hotel International Ballroom in Washington, D.C., a night that saw Morrison's mother and brother show up in an unsuccessful attempt to visit with their long-lost family member.

When the Doors had arrived in the Washington, D.C. area for their August 18 concert doubleheader, they were shaking off the rust of a week-long layoff. At this point in time nobody seems to know where or how the band members spent their free time during the days leading up to the Alexandria Arena gig or why there was such a time gap in their increasingly cramped schedule. There are no published statements by any of the surviving members of the Doors pertaining to any comments made by Jim Morrison regarding his return to Alexandria to perform at this concert. If Morrison said anything to anyone about this homecoming, his words evaporated without notice. It seems like the Doors simply breezed into the area to work two shows in one night and when the job was done they packed and departed as quickly as they had arrived.

The concerts in Annapolis and Alexandria had been booked by agent Todd Schiffman and had been promoted locally in the Washington, D.C. area by Bud Becker of Domestic Sound Productions, a music management and booking company based out of Falls Church, Virginia. Nothing at all is known about the Doors' 7:30pm performance at the Annapolis Armory in Annapolis, Maryland that night, aside from the fact that they did indeed show up and work the show (for which they were paid a flat fee of $3,000 – the same amount they received for playing the Alexandria concert).

Additional information has surfaced regarding the Alexandria Arena gig, which was advertised as "The Flower Power Show," an event emceed by the popular WPGC disc jockey Jack Alix that included a supporting performance by the Blades of Grass and a 12-

band competition from 7pm to 10pm in which the winner was supposedly granted an audition with Columbia Records in New York City. Competing teen bands that performed onstage that night were December's Children, the Warlox, the Hounds of Baskerville, Gary Scott and the Classics, the Fantastic Plastic, the McCormick Tool Company, the Corporation, the Shades, the Brotherhood, Essex, the Tornadoes and the New York Public Library. The winner of the contest was a band from Northern Virginia called Gary Scott and the Classics, though reportedly they never did receive that audition with Columbia Records.

The Friday night doubleheader kicked off in uneasy fashion for the Doors, as something strange apparently happened at the concert in Annapolis that resulted in Jim Morrison being separated from the other band members. While the Doors were onstage in Annapolis performing before a sold-out crowd of more than 3,000 fans, Kerby Scott, a disc jockey at local radio station WYRE who served as emcee for the early show, reportedly called Bud Becker, promoter of the Alexandria concert, and told him to have someone drive to Annapolis as fast as possible to retrieve Morrison, who had somehow alienated himself from the other three members of the group before they had even taken the stage. Becker complied and when Morrison arrived in Alexandria, he was clearly inebriated and exhibiting bizarre behavior.

The Doors concert at the Alexandria Arena lasted approximately 45 minutes, consisted of seven or eight songs, and, from most accounts, was an exceptional performance, an amazing fact given Jim Morrison's alleged state of mind that evening. Tickets for the event were only $3 and the facility filled up early in the evening, with a reported 4,000 attendees having stuffed their way into the huge building. The doors to the facility opened at 7:30pm and the opening 12-band competition lasted for two hours, after which the Blades of Grass performed an abbreviated set.

Shortly after 10pm the sweaty, agitated members of the Doors emerged from the dressing room (in reality a small space behind the stage used to store skates) and briefly greeted some fans as they made their way to the stage. Cheers erupted from the crowd as the band members solemnly mounted the steps in single file: Robbie Krieger, his hair thick and bunched above the collar, dressed in a long-sleeved, button-down, white shirt and tan slacks; John Densmore, his dark hair relatively short from a recent style job, wearing a white, pull-over tee-shirt, a black suit coat, and white slacks; Ray Manzarek, his straight brown hair parted on the side from left to right and dangling to his collar, sporting a button-down, striped white shirt and dark pants; and then Morrison himself, drenched in perspiration with matted, dark brown hair framing his features, decked out in a button-down, black shirt, black leather jacket, and black vinyl pants.

When the band members took their positions onstage, emcee Jack Alix quickly approached each musician with microphone in hand and asked them to introduce themselves individually to the audience. Krieger, Densmore and Manzarek respectfully complied. Morrison just stared straight ahead into the audience with both hands tightly gripping the microphone, silently ignoring the simple request.

Attempts to definitively state what songs were played that evening by the Doors have been futile, as there are no known existing bootleg recordings of the concert. It has been reported by many who allegedly attended the concert that the band came out and opened the show with "Break on Through" and finished with extended versions of "Light My Fire" and "The End." Many have stated that the band also played "Soul Kitchen" (most likely the second song of the evening) and "Back Door Man." Other songs that may have been performed that evening include "The Crystal Ship," "Alabama Song," and a version of Bo Diddley's "Who Do You Love?" At this point there is no way to verify any of this information and fans can only hope that in the future a soundboard tape or an audience recording emerges that will solve the mystery.

Confounding this unusual homecoming at Alexandria were subsequent reports of strange behavior allegedly displayed by Morrison throughout the show. It's a given that Morrison was inebriated when he arrived in Alexandria and remained that way for the duration of the night. It had been a hot one in Alexandria that Friday with the temperature reaching 91 degrees in the late afternoon and thunderstorms firing up as dusk approached. The atmosphere was steamy and there was no air conditioning inside the facility.

Several individuals have noted that Morrison looked sweaty and drained backstage before the Alexandria concert began. Reports later surfaced that towards the end of the concert as the band played "The End," he allegedly threw something into the audience, alternately described as either a cymbal or a drumstick, which possibly struck a teenager sitting in one of the front rows. There are reports that Morrison was seen briefly scuffling onstage with emcee Jack Alix at the conclusion of the show, and one account has the Doors lead singer berating the crowd and waving one-fingered peace signs at his fans before stumbling off the stage.

Only one picture of the Doors taken at the Alexandria Arena that night is known to exist, a group photo of the band backstage that appeared in Heather Owens' "Teen Tempo" column in the "Star Leader" (Clinton, Maryland) newspaper of Wednesday, August 23, 1967. The photograph shows the band members in various states of disinterest: Krieger, eyes closed, holds a crumpled copy of WPGC's "Go" magazine; Densmore looks silly with a large flower lodged in his hair above his left ear; Manzarek appears on the outer edge as a distant spectator, apparently sitting on a chair; and Morrison, clad in black, is cupping his mouth with his left hand, apparently yelling something at the concert emcee Jack Alix, who is bent over, a copy of "Go" clenched in his teeth. Three members of the Blades of Grass and two Jackettes Go-Go Girls complete the crowded scene.

Immediately after the Alexandria Arena concert, the Doors disappeared into the hot August night and presumably made a hasty exit from town, though their activities for the remainder of that weekend remain undocumented. It is known that on Monday, August 21, 1967 all four band members were back in Hollywood, California where they began recording sessions for their second album at Sunset Studios #1. The following Friday they performed a concert at the Las Vegas Convention Center in Nevada.

For all practical purposes, the Alexandria concert evidently was soon considered a thing of the past by the members of the Doors, as Morrison himself never publicly commented on the strange return he made to his old hometown. It will never be known what he was thinking when he mounted the stage at the Alexandria Arena or how he felt when he departed Alexandria for the last time. If he did, in fact, flip off the crowd as he left the stage that night, it would indicate he harbored some resentment for the city in which he spent his high school years. Unfortunately, the Lizard King chose not to share his inner feelings on this matter with anyone around him. Undeniably, the Dionysian forces were in full swing with Morrison that night and despite his concert preparation, which included a complete derangement of the senses, he gave an intense homecoming performance cloaked in controversy.

Many fans of the Doors believe that part of the reason for the band's rise to prominence in the rock and roll world during the 1960s was Jim Morrison's personal charisma and omnipotent stage presence. During much of the first half of the band's existence he embodied the Lizard King mystique, with long brown hair dangling towards his shoulders, the black leather jacket and black vinyl pants on display, and the elements of drama and theater etched in his stage presentation. He writhed, rolled, danced like an Indian shaman, jumped into the audiences, and, at times, attempted to incite riots. Poetry was evident in his vocal performances, as dark symbolism meshed with themes of love, longing, pain, and death to create a stunning panorama of musical imagery. With Morrison out front, the

Doors assumed a prominent role in bringing theater and rock music together in the sixties, a practice that would be liberally borrowed by throngs of bands in the coming decades.

The Doors performed before a sold-out crowd at New York's Madison Square Garden on Friday, January 24, 1969, augmented by former Bob Dylan bassist Harvey Brooks and a small orchestra. Back in Los Angeles, Morrison spent the last week of February attending performances of the Living Theater, an avant-garde repertory acting company, on the campus of the University of Southern California. This troupe saw themselves as seekers of total liberation and staged four guerrilla theater performances, the last of which, "Paradise Now," was offered on Friday, February 28 and concluded with the actors stripping down onstage past the legal limit and being busted by the police for their display. Unfortunately, Morrison, who had been observing from the front row, was duly inspired.

The very next night, Saturday, March 1, 1969, the Doors performed a legendary, abbreviated concert at the steamy and overstuffed Dinner Key Auditorium in Miami, Florida, an event now simply referred to as "Miami." The band appeared that night on a rickety stage for one hour and five minutes while Morrison – bearded, inebriated, and with the Living Theater antics fresh in his mind – stumbled, cursed and shouted his way through an embarrassing and incoherent public display that culminated in him allegedly exposing himself onstage.

Although band members and others from the Doors contingency maintained that Morrison never actually did whip it out, he was eventually arrested on Sunday, November 9, 1969 and charged with four counts: lewd and lascivious behavior, indecent exposure, open profanity, and drunkenness. On Sunday, September 20, 1970, Morrison was convicted in the Dade County Courthouse of indecent exposure and open profanity (both misdemeanors). On Friday, October 30, 1970 he was sentenced to six months in jail and given a $500 fine. Morrison's attorney Max Fink appealed the decision and Morrison was freed on $50,000 bail. In the immediate aftermath of Miami, scores of Doors concerts were cancelled, as few promoters were willing to take chances with Morrison's unpredictable stage habits.

The Doors did not appear again onstage until a Saturday, June 14, 1969 concert at the Chicago Auditorium Theatre in Illinois, a two-show performance that drew rave reviews and was watched closely by promoters from around the country who were wary of allowing the band to enter their territories. The band continued to perform during the latter half of 1969 and into 1970, though occasional cancellations continued to surface. Morrison spent much of the month of August on trial in Miami as the star in the case of "The State of Florida vs. James Douglas Morrison," a legal debacle that stemmed from his arrest for the Dinner Key Auditorium incident from the previous year.

On Friday, December 11, 1970 the Doors gave a concert at the State Fair Music Hall in Dallas, Texas. The next night they appeared at the Warehouse in New Orleans, a disastrous event that saw Morrison sputter through songs and reach a point where all he did was limply cling to the microphone stand as if the life had left his body. Sensing imminent disaster, the band reportedly broke into "Light My Fire," with a despondent Morrison taking a seat near the drum set during the instrumental break. After finally stepping forth and finishing the song he smashed the microphone stand into the stage repeatedly, tossing what was left of it into the audience before walking off for good. It was the last concert the Doors ever performed with Jim Morrison.

Jim Morrison, smarting from Miami and obviously physically and mentally exhausted from life in the rock and roll world, took an extended vacation from the band after the recording of the "L.A. Woman" album and left Los Angeles for Paris, France on Thursday, March 11, 1971. There, he rejoined his girlfriend Pamela Courson, who had left Los

Angeles in February and had been awaiting his arrival, and together they took a third-floor apartment at 17 rue Beautreillis, Paris, 4th Arrondissement.

The activities of Morrison in Paris are shrouded in mystery and have been subject to wide speculation. It appears that while abroad he did little more than go for long walks around the city and occasionally scribble in notebooks. Reportedly, his health was poor, as he had allegedly taken a fall from a balcony at the Chateau Marmont Hotel in Los Angeles just before leaving for France and suffered from undiagnosed internal injuries (believed to have been broken or cracked ribs and possibly a punctured lung). Various accounts have him suffering respiratory problems during his time in Paris including bouts of asthma and fits of coughing and hiccupping. Photographs from France show him clean-shaven with darkish, gray-streaked hair approaching his shoulders, and seemingly carrying more body weight than ever before.

Early on the morning of Saturday, July 3, 1971, Jim Morrison was found dead in the bathtub of his Paris apartment. To this day, not a living soul really knows what happened during those early morning hours or how he actually died. Since that date, various circumstances surrounding his death have been embellished and even fabricated by journalists and other individuals who claimed to have had reliable information regarding what had "really" happened.

Rumors aside, here is the information that appeared in official documents filed with the 4th Arrondissement Police of Paris regarding the death of Jim Morrison. Pamela Courson, in a statement given to Officer Jacques Manchez, related that Morrison had dinner by himself at a restaurant on the evening of Friday, July 2, 1971, after which the two of them attended a movie entitled "Death Valley" at a local cinema. She claimed they returned to their third-floor apartment at 17 rue Beautreillis at approximately 1am, at which time she began cleaning dishes and Morrison began watching an amateur film on a projector. They proceeded to lie on a bed and listen to Doors records until they went to sleep at approximately 2:30am. At 3:30am Courson claims she awoke to the sounds of her mate's "noisy" breathing and believed that he may have been choking. She woke Morrison, who then decided to take a bath. While bathing, he complained of feeling ill, called Courson over, and vomited three separate times into a bowl she held, with the last eruption yielding visible blood clots. He then told Courson he felt better and sent her back to bed. Courson claimed she awoke at an undisclosed time during the early morning hours, noticed Morrison was not in their bed, and ran to the bathroom where she found him dead in the tub, with a little blood running from one of his nostrils. She claimed she next called her Parisian friends Alain Ronay and Agnes Varda and believed they called either the fire brigade or the police.

In a report filed with the Paris Police Criminal Investigations Department, Lieutenant Alain Raisson of the Paris Fire Brigade claimed that he appeared on the scene with his unit at 9:20am that morning and found Jim Morrison completely naked in the bath with his head resting on the edge above the water and his right arm resting on the side of the bath. He described the water in the bath as slightly pink in color and still lukewarm. He and his men took Morrison's body from the bath and laid it on the bedroom floor, where he attempted heart massage to no avail. Lieutenant Raisson ended his report by stating that he had Morrison's body placed on the bed. (It is still not clear who actually summoned the Paris Fire Brigade, as Alain Ronay said in his statement to police that when he arrived at the apartment, the firemen were already on the scene.)

At 6pm on the evening of Saturday, July 3, 1971, a forensic doctor named Dr. Max Vassille examined Morrison's body and then prepared a medical report for Robert Berry, superintendent of the Arsenal District Police, which later became the basis for the death certificate. The body, according to Dr. Vassille, did not show "any signs of suspicious traumatism or lesions of any kind." He did observe a little blood around the nostrils and provided a brief recent history of Morrison's aliments, mentioning that friends reported he had been complaining for a few weeks of chest pains and dyspnea. He noted Morrison's coronary problems, suggesting they had possibly been aggravated by excessive drinking. Dr. Vassille concluded that "death was caused by heart failure (natural death)."

Reportedly, Morrison's body was placed on a bed in the bedroom in an ice-packed plastic bag by an unnamed mortician at approximately 8pm that Saturday evening. On Monday, July 5, unnamed undertakers finally arrived at the apartment, dressed Morrison's body in a suit, and placed him in a coffin. The burial took place at 11am on Wednesday, July 7, 1971 at Pere Lachaise Cemetery near Paris, with the ceremony being attended by: Pamela Courson; Doors manager Bill Siddons; friends Alain Ronay, Agnes Varda and Robin Wertle; an unnamed undertaker; and several pall bearers (reportedly, no priest was present at the burial, which lasted under 10 minutes).

Of course the mystery deepened and the controversy raged on, as volumes have since been written suggesting drugs played a role in Jim Morrison's death. Despite what has been published by the rock and roll press, there isn't one shred of evidence that suggests Morrison died of a heroin overdose. No drugs were found in the Paris apartment he shared with Pamela Courson (who later died in Los Angeles under mysterious circumstances of an apparent heroin overdose on Thursday, April 25, 1974), no needle tracks scarred his arms, and the various stories that blamed Morrison's demise on a late-night bout with smack are unverifiable.

It seems logical that Morrison's excessive consumption of alcohol and complications from internal injuries sustained in his recent balcony flop (not to mention his reported medicinal intake for asthma) could have been contributing factors to the deterioration of his coronary system. Therefore, while no one knows for sure what caused the death of Jim Morrison, it's a certainty that the rock and roll world was never the same after the fateful morning of Saturday, July 3, 1971.

After Morrison's passing, the three surviving Doors members opted to carry on as a trio and released two albums, "Other Voices" (The Doors; Elektra Records, 1971) and "Full Circle" (The Doors; Elektra Records, 1972).

In the 1980s there was renewed interest in Morrison's life, the Doors' catalog was released on CD to a new generation of fans, and books on the band and biographies on their lead singer began to appear on the market. An Oliver Stone movie, "The Doors" (Tri-Star Pictures, 1991) focused on Morrison's individual legend and sensationalized his exploits, immortalizing him for all the wrong reasons. The Doors were inducted into the Rock and Roll Hall of Fame in the "Performers" category on Tuesday, January 12, 1993. Today, Jim Morrison rates with the likes of Frank Sinatra and Elvis Presley as one of popular music's all-time great vocalists.

CHAPTER SEVENTY-SIX
WISCONSIN AND M

Prior to the British Invasion of the 1960s, the bars and night clubs in the historic Georgetown neighborhood of Northwest Washington, D.C. offered a variety of live entertainment that spanned the spectrum of popular music. During the 1950s as established restaurants changed management and new restaurants multiplied along M Street NW, the status of live music became a primary issue with Georgetown's entrepreneurs. A number of long-standing establishments opted to either add live music to their calendars or change their offerings to what management perceived to be more popular musical styles. Newer night clubs to the scene were faced with the option of offering live music, and, if the decision to add such entertainment was affirmative, choosing a particular style that would attract a desired customer base.

During the 1950s the Bayou, located near the intersection of Wisconsin and K Streets NW, emerged as Georgetown's most popular live music night spot and maintained its lofty status into the middle 1960s. During those years the prevailing style of music at this night club was Dixieland jazz, with regular appearances made by such bands as Wild Bill Whelan and His Dixie Six, Wild Bill Davison and His All Stars, Big Bill Decker and His Dixie Six, Joe Renaldi and the Foggy Bottom Six, Wally Garner and His New Orleans Jazz Band and Eddie Dimond and the Foggy Bottom Six.

A special attraction at the Bayou during this time was exotic dancer Julie Gibson, a longtime entertainer in various Washington, D.C. night clubs who had found a home in the former gambler's den by gyrating to the music of the jazz giants behind her and creating nightly spectacles for her enthusiastic following. In the late 1960s a band called the Telstars introduced rock and roll music to the Bayou and the night club went in a new musical direction.

On nearby M Street NW, the musical offerings were diverse. Several night clubs offered live C&W music in the early 1960s, which had long been a neighborhood tradition: the Shamrock Restaurant (3295 M Street NW) featured the popular bluegrass band the Country Gentlemen, as well as the Woodward Brothers, Mickey and Roger, who not only owned the establishment but served as the venue's main entertainers for years; the Corral (3267 M Street NW) offered Wade Holmes and His Town and Country Boys; and the Frog, a basement night club situated below the Corral, was booking Danny Denver and the Sound Tracks.

Other night clubs along this main avenue turned towards jazz in the early 1960s including: the B&J Restaurant (3236 M Street NW), which had hosted C&W singer-guitarist Roy Clark at various times during the 1950s and had switched to modern jazz at the turn of the decade when they brought in the Bohemian Quintet (pianist Norman Edwards, saxophonist Jay Kaiser, vibraphonist Van Byrd, bassist Sonny Powell and drummer Ted Porterchinko); and the French Quarter (3263 M Street NW), a basement night spot which had opened in November 1962 and featured performers such as Jose Donza, the Tommy Gwaltney Trio (clarinetist-vibraphonist Tommy Gwaltney, singer-guitarist Steve Jordan and singer-pianist John Eaton), the Eddie Phyfe Combo (featuring singer Ann Read) and the Joe Bovello Combo.

Contributing to Georgetown's colorful musical spectrum during these years were the Silver Dollar Restaurant (3124 M Street NW), which featured accordionist-pianist Nat Bader and pop singer-pianist Frances Kuhn; and the Goat and Compass (3003 M Street NW), which had a guitar duo known as the Matadors entertaining their patrons.

The status of Georgetown as a live music hot spot significantly increased with the opening of a folk music night club called the Shadows in early 1962. In April 1961 two Georgetown University students named Frank Weiss and Bob Cavallo leased a building that had been standing vacant on the northeast corner of 34th and M Streets NW for the previous six years. This former home of Quaker City Motor Parts occupied a prominent spot on M Street's far western edge and upon its reopening was granted a new front door on the building's west side and a new street address of 1201 34th Street NW.

Weiss and Cavallo had the floor of this building restructured with gray tiles, added sections of burlap and pine over the exposed brick walls throughout, and installed a burlap-covered jukebox. A total of 25 tables (which could accommodate 100 patrons), each adorned with a candle and a hand-written menu, were placed within the original room's 750 feet of floor space, and the small stage was originally constructed against the wall directly opposite the 34th Street side entrance. A single string of lights wrapped around the walls illuminated the premises.

The Shadows had its grand opening on the night of Friday, January 12, 1962 with a lineup of emcee-comedian Bob Caputi, dramatic reader Mike Byrne, and two folk music singer-guitarists, Pete Warner and John Keats. Live music was featured every night except Monday, and the opening night entertainers remained on the Shadows schedule for several months. A variety of folk musicians and groups were scheduled throughout the year, including a number of national acts. Among those to perform at the club were the Hard Travelers Trio, Ian and Sylvia, Dave Guard and the Whiskeyhill Singers, the Halifax Three, the Phoenix Singers, the Tarriers, the Ivy League Trio, and such singer-guitarists as Don Paulin, Judy Collins, Donald Leace and Josh White Jr.

As the Shadows closed in on its one-year anniversary, Weiss and Cavallo decided the night club had outgrown its space and relocated the business to a larger, two-story building farther east on M Street NW that had previously hosted a long line of restaurants, the most recent of which had been the Publick House. On the night of Friday, December 21, 1962 the Shadows had a new grand opening in its new quarters at 3125 M Street NW with the Journeymen serving as the headlining act. The night club's new structure consisted of a ground floor main room that could accommodate 135 patrons and featured a stage against its back wall, and a long, narrow upstairs "Dark Room" that could accommodate 108 occupants and featured a long bar along its right side and a small stage against its back wall.

Throughout 1963 the Shadows featured a steady stream of folk music acts including the likes of the Big Three, the Gaslight Singers, the Travelers Three, the Country Gentleman, the Modern Folk Quartet and singer-guitarist Tom Paxton. In addition, headlining comedians included Bill Cosby and Woody Allen. (Most bands and comedians worked the main room of the Shadows, while many solo performers and lesser-known comedians were booked into the Dark Room.)

In 1964 the main room of the Shadows was the home of the electric folk group known as the Mugwumps, which held house band duties from July to October of that year. The Mugwumps lineup consisted of singer Cass Elliot and singer-guitarists Denny Doherty, Zal Yanovsky and Jim Hendricks, along with several musicians who passed in-and-out including harmonicist John Sebastian and numerous bassists and drummers. A year later Elliot and Doherty would become founding members of the Mamas and the Papas, while Yanovsky and Sebastian resurfaced in the Lovin' Spoonful.

Rock and roll began making its presence felt on M Street NW in 1964 and to combat the new wave of music the Shadows brought in some intriguing pop and jazz acts in 1965 including the Miles Davis Quartet, the Modern Jazz Quartet and singer-guitarist Johnny Rivers. Ultimately the night club closed its doors that summer, as it could not compete with the sheer number of new establishments that were turning Georgetown into the city's new live music mecca.

As a side note, original Shadows co-owner Bob Cavallo went on to make his mark in the popular music industry, managing acts such as the Lovin' Spoonful, Little Feat and Prince, and today is the chairman of the Buena Vista Music Group, overseeing all of the Walt Disney Company's recorded music and music publishing operations.

While the Shadows was in full swing in the new location, its original building at 34th and M Streets NW was hosting another folk music night club called the Cellar Door that would go on to establish legendary status in the local music scene for not only serving as a spawning ground for local talent, but also for hosting a plethora of musical performers who went on to achieve national recognition for their work.

The Cellar Door was originally owned by a budding entrepreneur named Jack Boyle, who hailed from Youngstown, Ohio and had graduated from Georgetown University. Boyle had first gotten into the local night club business in 1961 when he purchased part of a struggling bar called Mac's Pipe and Drum Restaurant, which was situated at 3401 M Street NW and sat facing the western 34th Street NW face of the vacant building that would soon house the Shadows. When the Shadows later moved over to 3125 M Street NW, Boyle was quick to move a new musical venue into its former space.

The Cellar Door opened under Jack Boyle's ownership at 1201 34th Street NW on the night of Friday, February 15, 1963 with the Jimmy Crawford Trio placed as headliners. Crawford was a talented singer-pianist whose vocal stylings strongly resembled Nat King Cole and his outfit was employed by Boyle as the house band for several months. In July of that year WAVA disc jockey Dick Cerri began holding a Sunday evening "Hootenanny" (commonly referred to as "The Hoots") that began at 5pm and allowed local folk musicians to take the stage in open mic sessions and show their wares (Cerri continued to host the "Hootenanny" on a regular schedule until October 1966). The Cellar Door's original seating capacity was 140, though, after interior alterations, it eventually expanded to 199 (in 1978 the night club's floor space was measured by city officials to be 1,250 square feet and its capacity was subsequently reduced down to 124 occupants).

Among the folk music entertainers who were featured in the Cellar Door during its first year were a number of singer-guitarists including Bob Grossman, Donald Leace, Carolyn Hester, Mike Boran, Shawn Phillips, Don Paulin, Mike Settle and Judy Roderick. Appearances were also made by singers Lydia Wood and David Troy and folk groups such as the Eddie Phyfe Three, Addis and Crofut, and the Tri-Adds, as well as flamenco guitarist Juan Serrano.

In 1964 the Cellar Door brought back many of its first-year performers in addition to introducing new folk music acts. Some of the newcomers to the night club that year included: acts such as Brown and Dana (a folk duo consisting of banjoist-guitarist Garrett Brown and singer-guitarist Al Dana), Ian and Sylvia, the Gaslight Singers, the Phoenix Singers, the Roy Thompson Singers, the Mandrell Singers, the Simon Singers, Knob Lick Upper 10,000, the Goldbriars, the Gateway Trio and the Country Gentlemen; singers Leon Bibb, Carol Hedin and Gale Garnett; singer-guitarists Judy Collins and Allen Damron; and comedians Sandy Baron, Fred Smoot, Simmy Bow and the duo of Greco and Willard.

As the 1960s advanced, the Cellar Door went through a series of different owners including Tom Lyons and Charlie Finchman before being sold back to Jack Boyle in October 1970. In 1971 Boyle founded Cellar Door Productions, which went on to become one of the biggest concert promotion agencies in the United States. Some of Boyle's later partners in Cellar Door Productions included Sam L'Hommedieu and Dave Williams.

Changes in ownership aside, the night club continued to host different headlining acts nearly every week, with an incredible array of local and national talent passing through its space. From 1965 to 1969, in addition to repeat visits from several of the night club's previous performers, popular folk music groups to appear on the Cellar Door stage included the Highwaymen, the Modern Folk Quartet, the Lettermen, the Mitchell Trio (singers Joe Frazier, Mike Kobluk and John Denver), Ian and Sylvia, the Backporch Majority, the Bitter End Singers, the Rooftop Singers, the Womanfolk, the Pozo-Seco Singers, the Serendipity Singers, the Jim Kweskin Jug Band, the Everly Brothers and the Fifth Avenue Band.

Folk singer-guitarists to headline the Cellar Door during those years included Dave Van Ronk, the duo of Bud and Travis, Tom Rush, David Bushkin, Elyse Weinberg, Buffy Sainte-Marie, Gordon Lightfoot, Tom Paxton, Judy Collins, Joni Mitchell, Carol Hedin, John Phillips, Eric Andersen, Richie Havens, Tim Buckley, Jake Holmes, John Denver, Neil Young, James Taylor and John Sebastian. Solo folk singers to appear included Glenn Yarbrough, Geula Gill, Chad Mitchell and the duo of Miriam Makeba and Odetta. Singer-pianists to appear included Biff Rose and Tom Lehrer.

Other styles of music were also represented at the Cellar Door during the late 1960s. Among the R&B entertainers to be featured included: acts such as the Platters, the Coasters, Little Anthony and the Imperials, the Drifters, Peaches and Herb, Gladys Knight and the Pips and Martha and the Vandellas; singers Jerry Butler, O.C. Smith, Maxine Brown and Oscar Brown, Jr.; singer-guitarists Muddy Waters, B.B. King, Albert King; and singer-keyboardist Stevie Wonder.

Among the jazz acts to appear were: bands such as the Ramsey Lewis Trio, the Young Holt Trio and Art Blakey and the Jazz Messengers; guitarist Charlie Byrd; singer-pianist Mose Allison; pianists Thelonius Monk and Count Basie; organist Jimmy Smith; flutist-saxophonist Herbie Mann; saxophonists Stan Getz and Julian "Cannonball" Adderley; and trumpeters Hugh Masekela and Miles Davis.

Other Cellar Door attractions of the late 1960s included: the rock and roll band Bill Haley and His Comets; the jazz rock band Love Cry Want; C&W singer-guitarist Jerry Jeff Walker; rock and roll singer Chubby Checker; rock and roll singer-guitarist Ricky Nelson; and a litany of comedians including Zack Norman, Patchett and Tarses, Jackie Mason, Mort Sahl, Redd Foxx, Uncle Dirty, David Steinberg, Jack E. Leonard, Richard Pryor and Irwin S. Watson.

In the early 1970s the Cellar Door booked an impressive number of entertainers from every section of the popular music scene and gained recognition as one of the area's most prestigious night clubs. Many of these bands, musicians and comedians were in the process of building their careers and were about to break on a national level, while others were already well-established in the entertainment industry.

Among those to perform at the Cellar Door in the early 1970s were Brewer and Shipley Loudon Wainwright III, Dizzy Gillespie, Seals and Crofts, Linda Ronstadt, Fat City, Emmitt Rhodes, the Paul Butterfield Blues Band, the Flying Burrito Brothers, Jonathan Edwards, Kris Kristofferson, Spencer Davis, the James Cotton Blues Band, Long John Baldry, Carly Simon, Weather Report, Al Kooper, America, Gary Puckett and the Union Gap, Rita Coolidge, Lily Tomlin, Dan Hicks and His Hot Licks, Jim Stafford, Neal Sedaka, Cheech and Chong, Wet Willie, John Prine, Country Joe McDonald, Bill Withers, the Dillards, Herbie Hancock, Jackson Browne, Harry Chapin, Bonnie Raitt, Taj Mahal, the Nitty Gritty Dirt Band, Tim Hardin, Jim Croce, Dr. Hook and the Medicine Show, Phil Ochs, Chick Corea, the Pointer Sisters, Alex Harvey, Looking Glass, the Nighthawks, Leo Kottke, Orleans, Randy Newman, Delaney Bramlett, Jesse Colin Young, the Country Gentlemen, Bob Brown, Bill and Taffy, Ashford and Simpson, Steve Martin, Martin Mull, Herbie Hancock, Papa John Creach, B.J. Thomas, Barry Manilow, Johnny Nash, the Rosslyn Mountain Boys, Michael Murphy, Larry Burnett, Lenny Bruce, Janis Ian, Kinky Friedman, the Chambers Brothers, Tom Waits, Al Stewart, Jimmy Buffet, the Beau Brummels, Buddy

Rich, J.D. Souther, Jean-Luc Ponty, the Chris Hillman Band, the Roger McGuinn Band, Willie Dixon, Leon Redbone, Leonard Cohen, Don McLean, John Fahey and Asleep at the Wheel.

The Cellar Door night club was sold by then-owners Jack Boyle and Sam L'Hommedieu to the partnership of Paul Kurtz and Howard Bomstein on Friday, January 30, 1981, who, six months later, changed the name of the night club to the Door (Boyle remained a co-owner of Cellar Door Productions until 1998). The legendary night spot then remained one of the Washington D.C. area's top live music venues until its closing on the night of Thursday, January 7, 1982 after a sold-out, two-performance show by Aztec Two Step. The following morning the club's marquee simply read "Goodnight D.C."

After a period of vacancy, the Cellar Door building hosted a short-lived comedy club called the Comedy Shop from January to June 1987. After sitting unoccupied for more than a dozen years, a business called the Philadelphia Cheesesteak Factory opened on the premises in 2001 and lasted until March 2011 (at this time the listed address was switched to 3347 M Street NW). Next up, Capriotti's Sandwich Shop operated within the Cellar Door's former space from Monday, December 15, 2014 through Thursday, March 31, 2016. The building has been vacant since Friday, April 1, 2016. As a side note, the concert promotion agency known as Cellar Door Productions was sold to SFX Entertainment in 1998 for $106 million.

One Georgetown night club that has endured through the years is Blues Alley (1073 Wisconsin Avenue NW), which was opened by Tommy Gwaltney on Wednesday, January 13, 1965 and remains in operation today. While it was not a rock and roll establishment, Blues Alley made its mark as one of the nation's best blues and jazz clubs by bringing in some of the best musical acts in the country.

Blues Alley is situated just a few steps away from the southeast corner of Wisconsin and M Streets NW inside a renovated carriage house that had been constructed sometime around 1800. When Gwaltney opened the night club, its main ground floor contained seating for 124 patrons, with an adjoining cocktail lounge that sat 30. He installed Tim Colgan as his manager and for its first year the house band was his own bluesy invention – the Tommy Gwaltney Trio – which consisted of Gwaltney himself on clarinet and vibraphone, singer-guitarist Steve Jordan and pianist Newton Thomas. (The group subsequently converted into a quartet when they were joined by bassist Norman Williams.)

Other jazz musicians to play Blues Alley in 1965 included: singers Lurlean Hunter, Louise Tobin and Maxine Sullivan; clarinetist Peanuts Hucko; trumpeter Billy Butterfield; and guitarist-harmonicist Toots Thielemans. Among the jazz headliners in 1966 were singer Irene Kral, cornetist Wild Bill Davison and trumpeter Henry "Red" Allen. The club was successful in attracting its own audience in the heart of what was a developing rock and roll zone and in the grand scheme managed to outlive all of Georgetown's competing night clubs and restaurants.

Rock and Roll hit Georgetown hard in the wake of the British Invasion, with a number of night clubs throughout the neighborhood offering this style of musical entertainment throughout the middle and late 1960s and into the 1970s. M Street NW remained the area's main drag and live music bars lined both sides of the street, causing intense competition among the establishments and their owners. Crowds flocked to Georgetown on a nightly basis during these years, with long-haired teenagers and college-aged kids swarming the sidewalks and jamming their way into their favorite night spots where hard-rocking house bands worked their followings into frenzied conditions.

As one entered Georgetown from the eastern end of M Street NW and moved in a westerly direction, a number of dynamic rock and roll night clubs offered their wares. First up was the Roundtable (2813 M Street NW), a small, narrow, ground-floor room that had a capacity of 98 occupants. This night spot was owned by Riley Carter and George Berman and opened for business on Friday, November 27, 1964. During its three-year run the Roundtable was known for being the home of the British Walkers, whose original lineup consisted of lead singer Bobbie Howard, lead guitarist Roy Buchanan, bassist Junior Gill and drummer Mike Kennedy. Other acts to play there included Ronnie Jones and the Superiors, the Chartbusters, the Dominoes, the English Nobles and Gary U.S. Bonds.

On Wednesday, November 1, 1967 the Roundtable became the Hurricane, which, during its relatively short lifespan, offered performers such as the Count Five, Chuck Berry, the Young Rascals, the Animals, the Shangri-Las and local psychedelic band Wild Honey. The Hurricane quickly blew over and closed its doors on Monday, February 26, 1968.

After the passing of the Hurricane, its vacant space was targeted by a group of young entrepreneurs who opened up a non-alcoholic night club on the premises called Emergency, which offered a record store in its front portion and catered to local and national rock and roll bands that performed original material.

Emergency opened for business on Wednesday, August 6, 1969 and lasted into the morning hours of Saturday, January 1, 1972. During its time some of the bands and musicians to appear in the night club were Love Cry Want, Tractor, the Fallen Angels, Fat City, Sageworth and Drums, the Northside Blues Band, Crackers, Claude Jones, Grin, Crank, Itchy Brother, Grits, Emmylou Harris, Sky Cobb, Evernow, Desdemona, Stillroven, Rent's Due, J.B. Hutto, the Blues Project, Dave Griggs, Rory Gallagher, Boomerang, Exuma, Freddie King, David Griggs, Cold Blood, American Dream, Elizabeth, Catfish (Catfish Hodge), Asleep at the Wheel, Fairport Convention, Bob Seger, It's A Beautiful Day, Renaissance, the Greg Kihn Band, Buddy Guy, Junior Wells, the Amboy Dukes (featuring guitarist Ted Nugent) and the Kinks. Since August 1976 Emergency's old digs have been occupied by a French restaurant called La Chaumiere.

Across the street and a few blocks due west sat the Silver Dollar Restaurant (3124 M Street NW), a narrow, rectangular, ground-floor room that had a capacity of 75 occupants (but reportedly packed in dozens more on a regular basis). The Silver Dollar had replaced the Max Rosenthal Dry Goods Store in 1938 and during the late 1950s and early 1960s gained popularity as a piano bar, featuring accordionist-pianist Nat Bader, pop singer-pianist Frances Kuhn, and a house band known as Josey's Combo. By the middle 1960s the Silver Dollar Restaurant was featuring the jazz-oriented Tee Carson Trio, and a popular music outfit known as the Tommy Cole Trio, which backed singers such as Lonnie Sattin, Lucien Farrar, Andy Thomas and Richie Kay.

In 1967 the format of the Silver Dollar Restaurant was permanently switched to rock and roll for owners Mike Bakhtiar and Max Berg, and manager Leon T. Petrossian. In the late 1960s bands and musicians to headline the night club included Mickey's Monkeys, the Playmakers, the Partymakers, Tuesday Boots, Willie and the Hand Jives, the Fourmost, the Uncalled Four (featuring guitarist Roy Buchanan) the Cherry People (who held down house band duties for much of 1968), Big Al Downing and His Band, Hillow Hammet, Rooth, Gnus, and Renthra.

Bands to work the Silver Dollar Restaurant in 1970 and 1971 included Sudden Rush and Three Easy Pieces. In September 1971 the Silver Dollar underwent a change in ownership and became the M Club, which closed four years later. From September 1975 to May 2016 the former Silver Dollar Restaurant space housed a French restaurant called Bistro Francais; after a short period of vacancy its premises were taken in November 2016 by a men's footwear and apparel store called UBIQ Georgetown, which is still in business at that address today.

Just west of the intersection of Wisconsin and M Streets NW was a night club called JamF (3218 M Street NW), which replaced a discotheque called the Whiskey A Go-Go in

1970, and, before that in the late 1960s, had been a restaurant called the Scarlet Garter. During its relatively short early 1970s existence JamF, whose ground-floor space had a capacity of 120 occupants, booked such diverse acts as Woody Herman and His Orchestra, the John Wells Delegation, Second Eagle, Fat City (which featured future Starland Vocal Band members Bill Danoff and Taffy Nivert) and the rock band Sageworth and Drums. Today this building, which has been reconfigured in recent years and has absorbed neighboring structures, hosts a saloon called J. Paul's.

One of Georgetown's rock and roll mainstays was the Crazy Horse (3259 M Street NW), which was opened up by Joseph and Sanford Bomstein in December 1964 in a building formerly occupied for more than 50 years by the P.T. Moran Hardware and Feed Store. The Crazy Horse, with a capacity of 150 occupants, became known as the home base for the Chartbusters, the popular, Washington, D.C.-based rock and roll band that had been formed in response to the success of the Beatles and scored with the hit single "She's the One" which was released on the Mutual Record Company label in June 1964 and peaked at number 33 on Billboard magazine's "Billboard Hot 100" popular music chart on Saturday, August 15, 1964. The Chartbusters based out of the Crazy Horse from 1965 to 1969 and helped define Georgetown's burgeoning rock and roll scene.

When the Chartbusters were working other jobs, some of the bands to fill their spot at the Crazy Horse in the late 1960s were Don Downing and the Crazy Horsemen, Willie and the Hand Jives, Barry Seidel and the Sellouts, Sal Masi and the Untouchables, Tuesday Boots and special attractions such as the Coasters, singer Dee Dee Sharp and the Shangri-Las. In the 1970s the Crazy Horse remained one of the area's top rock and roll night clubs and hosted such bands as the Magic Touch, Fats Domino, Sun Country, the Reasons Why, Evensong, Natural Bridge, the Cherry People, the New Censation, the Danny Gatton Band, Charlie and the Pep Boys, the Grimes Brothers, Hot Rocks, Summersalt, Redemption, Little Brother, Sinbad, Touch and Central Heat.

The Crazy Horse carried on with live music in the 1980s, but by the 1990s was mainly offering disc jockeys and piped-in music and eventually closed its doors for good in 1998. Since 2004 the former Crazy Horse space has been occupied by a leather goods store called Coach.

In the middle 1960s the building next door to the Crazy Horse was marked 3263 M Street NW and hosted two live music night clubs, the Peppermint Lounge on the street level and the French Quarter in the basement. The Peppermint Lounge, with a capacity of 84 occupants, offered local rock and roll bands such as the Young Rabbits, the English Setters, Kangaroo and the Fallen Angels. The French Quarter, with a capacity of 94 occupants, spent much of the early part of the decade as a jazz club with house bands like the Tommy Gwaltney Trio and the Eddie Phyfe Trio.

After the Beatles and other English bands emerged, the French Quarter's management changed the entertainment schedule and brought in younger, up-and-coming rock and roll groups like the Dagenites, Tuesday Boots and the Nooks. By 1968 both night clubs were out of business and the entire building was occupied by the French Montmartre Gourmet Shop. Throughout the 1970s the space was occupied by one of Georgetown's most popular countercultural supply stores, the Bird Cage Head Shop.

Right next-door at 3267 M Street NW sat another dual night club set-up, with the Corral situated on the street level and the Frog in its basement. Both establishments had capacities of 100 occupants. The Corral, owned by Ernest Byrd, had been in operation since 1952 and had long been a C&W bar, with Wade Holmes and His Town and Country Boys performing nightly just as the Beatles hit in early 1964. Downstairs, the Frog was relatively new to the scene, opening in early 1964, and during its first several months offered C&W music as well, with Danny Denver and the Sound Tracks holding down house band duties.

In the summer of 1964, several months after the Beatles had invaded the nation's capital and performed their now-legendary concert at the Washington Coliseum, both the Corral and the Frog switched to rock and roll formats. The Corral rated as one of the first Georgetown night clubs to switch to rock and roll that summer when they brought in a young, Alexandria, Virginia-based trio called the Stingers, which played Merseybeat and R&B covers. The Stingers consisted of guitarist Mike Boyd, lead singer-bassist Billy Hancock and drummer Gary Bowles and immediately became a hot commodity on M Street NW.

Simultaneously, another hot rock and roll band, this one called the Tejuns, had settled down below in the Frog where they sported the look and the sound of the Beatles and covered all of the current British hits. The Tejuns consisted of singer-guitarist Stan Doucette, guitarist Fred Long, bassist Dale Chafin and drummer Rocky Isaac and maintained house band duties at the Frog from June to December 1964.

Other Georgetown night club owners took notice of the crowds of long-haired teen-agers from the Maryland and Virginia suburbs that were packing the Corral and the Frog and in time several made the decision to begin booking similar bands into their establishments in an effort to keep up with the changing musical trend. The music that permeated the streets of Georgetown was rapidly changing.

During the middle and late 1960s both the Corral and the Frog featured a variety of younger rock and roll bands and some overlap in bookings occasionally took place. The Corral brought in groups like the English Setters, the Creatures, the Reachers, the Mosaic Virus, Tuesday Boots, Kangaroo, the Roaches, the Fallen Angels, the Crystal Mesh, the Nooks, the Yarbs, Froggy Little, and the Eightfold Path. Down below, the Frog responded with groups like the Fallen Angels, the Members, the Creatures, the Scorpions, the Nooks and Sonny and the Night People. By late 1967 both clubs had gone out of business, with the building subsequently occupied by Georgetown Leather Design.

As M Street NW advanced towards its western end, one of its main night clubs of the day was Apple Pie (3350 M Street NW), which was situated within the Forrest-Marbury House, one of the city's oldest buildings. A three-story structure built in 1787 by Colonel Uriah Forrest, this building, which served as the private residence of William Marbury from 1800 to 1835, is now a Category 1 Landmark with the National Register of Historic Places. During more recent times it housed a ground-floor folk music night club called Smokey's from June to August 1965 and a small movie house called Groovy's from August 1965 to February 1969.

After a period of vacancy that lasted several months, a night club called Apple Pie opened on the premises in June 1969 with a capacity of 183 occupants. Apple Pie lasted into 1976 and during its time featured some of the area's best rock and roll bands including Stillroven, Bobby and Friends, the John Wells Delegation, the Nighthawks, the Dubonnettes, D.C. Dog, the Nils Lofgren Band, the Flying As, Sun Country, Fargo, Mystic Blue, Summersalt, the Boyz, Pacer, the Pits, the Brad Smiley Band, the Boyz and Sadbird.

After a short spell as the Casablanca Tavern, a new night club called Desperado's opened in the Forrest-Marbury House in January 1977 and became one of the more popular night clubs in the nation's capital, booking a wide range of blues, pop, R&B, and rock and roll acts. Some of the top local and national bands and musicians that worked Desperado's included the Rosslyn Mountain Boys, the Nighthawks, the Martin Welling Band, the Danny Gatton Band, Yellow Rose, singer-guitarist Bobby Radcliff, Smalltalk, Sadbird, Fireside, the John Wells Delegation, the Catfish Hodge Band, Fireside, the Rhythm Masters, Silverspring, Big Yankee Dollar, the North Star Band, the Slickee Boys,

Double Trouble (featuring singer-guitarist George Thorogood), Son Seals, the Blues Prophets, NRBQ, Tex Rubinowitz and the Bad Boys, the Good Humor Band, Mike Cotter Band, the Puppets, Tru Fax and the Insaniacs, Billy Price and the Keystone Rhythm Band and Jr. Cline and the Recliners. Desperado's closed in September 1982 and since 1995 the Forrest-Marbury House has been occupied by the Embassy of Ukraine.

Georgetown's rock and roll strip came to an end on its far western end with the two smallish night clubs known as Mac's Pipe and Drum Restaurant (3401 M Street NW) and Nu-Mac's (3403 M Street NW), both of which had capacities of 50 occupants. Of the two, Mac's Pipe and Drum Restaurant had a far more extensive history. It replaced Gem Lunch in 1958 for original owner Frank McCarthy and originally served as a Scottish-themed restaurant with walls covered with travel posters, newspaper clippings and paintings – all from Scotland – and featured the playing of bagpipes every hour on the hour from 9pm until closing.

In 1961 Mac's Pipe and Drum Restaurant was sold to Jack Boyle, who eventually ushered in rock and roll music in the late 1960s. Among the bands that appeared there late in the decade were the Four Coachmen, the Mad Hatters, Boa, the Wolfpack, the British Walkers and Rooth. Meanwhile, in February 1964, Boyle and Tim Colgan had opened up a night club next door called Nu-Mac's (3403 M Street NW), which during the late 1960s brought in such rock and roll acts as the Stingers, the Button, Jimmy Eller and His Little People, Ronnie Wilson and the New Telstars, the British Walkers, Ginger Vein and Troy. While Nu-Mac's was relatively short-lived, Mac's Pipe and Drum Restaurant lasted until 1981.

CHAPTER SEVENTY-SEVEN
THE COMMIES AND THE COUNTERCULTURE

During the latter part of the 1960s hippies began magically materializing in America, energizing a new and different cultural movement characterized by their long hair and unique dress, allegiance to rock and roll, unbridled drug use, and opposition to the Vietnam War, capitalism and conservative principles. Most every major city in the country had a specific neighborhood where members of the burgeoning hippie counterculture gathered, socialized and resided. Perhaps the most publicized of all hippie neighborhoods was San Francisco's Haight-Ashbury, which, because of its flower children, the prevailing peace-and-love ethic that permeated the land, and rock band denizens like the Grateful Dead, achieved work-wide attention during 1967's Summer of Love.

As the decade progressed an emerging counterculture based in the Dupont Circle neighborhood of Washington, D.C. intertwined itself with the local rock and roll scene, whose function was consequently transformed from being a source of human entertainment to being a tool of human manipulation. At the heart of this transformation was the Communist Party, which sought to dismantle capitalism in the United States of America and replace it with a political and economic system that championed the redistribution of wealth, goods and services.

To achieve their goal, the Communist Party's primary strategy was to strengthen the liberal base in America, while creating chaos and conflict among the country's conservatives. The party's efforts were largely directed at White young adults, who were lured into the "hippie" movement through exposure to folk and rock and roll music, offerings of drugs such as marijuana and LSD, and invitations to partake in demonstrations and protests of particular social issues such as civil rights and the Vietnam War. What happened with the Washington, D.C. area's counterculture in the 1960s was a microcosm of what was taking place throughout the country.

At the forefront of the Communist Party's agenda was the promotion of civil rights, a strategy whose ultimate goal was to strengthen the economic, political, and social status of Blacks and other non-Whites (then labeled as "minorities") while simultaneously dispossessing White Americans of any measure of power in such matters. Their first major Communist-backed course of civil rights action during this decade was the "March on Washington, D.C. for Jobs and Freedom" which took place on Wednesday, August 28, 1963 and featured Rev. Martin Luther King, Jr.'s widely publicized "I Have a Dream" speech.

The Communist agenda was further strengthened by the "Civil Rights Act of 1964" – An act to enforce the constitutional right to vote, to confer jurisdiction upon the district courts of the United States of America to provide injunctive relief against discrimination in public accommodations, to authorize the Attorney General to institute suits to protect constitutional rights in public facilities and public education, to extend the Commission on civil rights, to prevent discrimination in federally assisted programs, to establish a Commission on Equal Employment Opportunity, and for other purposes – which was enacted by the 88th Congress and signed into law by democrat President Lyndon B. Johnson on Thursday, July 2, 1964.This bill impacted later civil rights legislation and mainly served to trigger change in the demographics in the two major political parties, the polarizing ramifications of which are strongly felt to the present day.

While civil rights became a major rallying point for Communist sympathizers, its importance was matched by the party's collective opposition to the Vietnam War (1956-1975), a conflict in which the United States of America sought to prevent a Communist takeover of South Vietnam by North Vietnam. The American side saw the war as an important containment strategy in its plan of ending the spread of global communism. As American combat units were deployed to fight the North Vietnamese in 1965, the growing college-aged counterculture in the United States was worked into a frenzy of defiance by Communist agitators.

Almost every weekend from 1965 to 1969 there were meetings, marches, demonstrations and protests throughout the city of Washington, D.C. calling for an end to the Vietnam War. These events drew gatherings of all sizes, with two of the decade's largest and most intense protests being the March on the Pentagon in October 1967 and the Moratorium to End the War in Vietnam in November 1969.

"The March on the Pentagon" was a large-scale protest march against the Vietnam War that took place on the afternoon of Saturday, October 21, 1967. The days preceding the March featured a series of anti-war speeches, demonstrations and related events at various locations around the city.

The festivities began with a benefit by the Artists of Conscience at the Ambassador Theatre on the night of Thursday, October 19 that featured anti-war talks by a number of high-profile writers and social critics including Norman Mailer, Paul Goodman, Robert Lowell and Dwight McDonald. All proceeds from this event went to the National Mobilization to End the War in Vietnam, a coalition of approximately 150 leftist groups that was sponsoring the following Saturday's March on the Pentagon.

The rally itself, coordinated by David Dellinger and directed by Yippie Jerry Rubin, saw an estimated 70,000 protestors assemble at the Lincoln Memorial on the morning of Saturday, October 21, 1967. The participants spent hours giving speeches and singing songs, after which approximately half proceeded to march across the Potomac River and take up position outside the Pentagon. More than 10,000 armed and helmeted federal law enforcement officials were guarding the property when the protestors invaded.

The actual demonstration was largely nonviolent, though not without its share of theatrics – Beat poet Allen Ginsberg bellowed out Tibetan chants (the intended effect of which is still undetermined, but it sounded cool); Yippie Abbie Hoffman attempted to levitate the Pentagon itself, during which time he claimed the structure would hover 300 feet in the air, turn orange, have its evil spirits vanquished, and cause the war to end (in reality the building never budged, its hue never changed, the spirits were unmoved and the war trudged on for six more years); and, as the Fugs performed on a flat-bed truck in an adjacent parking lot, leader Ed Sanders led a group exorcism of the building (thousands shouted "Out, Demons, Out" in unison, but the only noticeable departures from the grounds were throngs of hippie protestors who headed for home after the rally permit expired at 7pm). An account of the March's festivities was provided by Norman Mailer in his book "The Armies of the Night" (1968).

Towards the end of the 1960s Washington, D.C. was the site of what at the time was the largest and youngest antiwar demonstration ever assembled in the United States of America. At 2pm on Saturday, November 15, 1969 more than 250,000 protestors gathered on the Washington Monument grounds and participated in the "Moratorium to End the War in Vietnam," a relatively peaceful rally that highlighted a four-day collection of speeches, talks and marches organized by the New Mobilization Committee to End the War in Vietnam – an updated version of the same basic collection of Communist, Socialist, radical and liberal political groups that had staged the March on the Pentagon two years earlier.

Aside from the large number of participants – of which the Washington Post said nearly all were "young, White and middle-class" – the most interesting observation to be taken from the demonstration was that a Saturday afternoon musical performance on the Monument grounds featured American folk music performers Arlo Guthrie and Pete

Seeger, who led the rallying cries against their own country's involvement in the fight against global communism. Despite the songs, slogans and posturing of the demonstrators, the Vietnam War raged on for years.

CHAPTER SEVENTY-EIGHT
THE LSD TRIP

In the middle 1960s psychedelia invaded the Washington, D.C. area's social and music scenes, with its powerful presence strongly impacting the rock and roll community. The primary ingredient of this new equation was lysergic acid diethylamide – better known as LSD – a hallucinogen drug that left the mind of its user pulsating with color, strange imagery and frenetic movement. LSD was first synthesized on Wednesday, November 16, 1938 by Swiss-born chemist Albert Hoffman (1906-2008), who, as an employee in the pharmaceutical research department of Kern and Sandoz (a chemical company located in Basel, Switzerland that changed its name to Sandoz Ltd. In 1939), came across the chemical while conducting purification and crystallization experiments on the fungus ergot, with the goal of developing a new circulatory heart-lung stimulant.

Hoffman's LSD work was set aside for nearly five years until he embarked on a re-examination of his research, a process during which he accidentally absorbed a small quantity of the drug through his fingertips and fortuitously experienced its mind-altering effects.

Hoffman introduced the world to his new discovery with the following laboratory notebook entry: "Last Friday, April 16, 1943 I was forced to stop my work in the laboratory in the middle of the afternoon and to go home, as I was seized by a peculiar restlessness associated with a sensation of mild dizziness. Having reached home, I lay down and sank in a kind of drunkenness which was not unpleasant and which was characterized by extreme activity of imagination. As I lay in a dazed condition with my eyes closed (I experienced daylight as disagreeably bright) there surged upon me an uninterrupted stream of fantastic images of extraordinary plasticity and vividness and accompanied by an intense, kaleidoscopic-like play of colors. This condition gradually passed off after about two hours."

During his time Hoffman authored more than 100 scientific articles and numerous books including "LSD: My Problem Child" (1980).

From 1953 to 1966 Sandoz Ltd. distributed large quantities of LSD to qualified scientists throughout the world for use in biochemical and animal behavior research. By the middle 1960s large quantities of illegally manufactured LSD of unknown purity had hit the streets in the United States and Sandoz Ltd. passed its responsibility for the legal distribution of the drug to the federal government. At that point in time the drug's standing with teenagers and young adults began experiencing a sharp increase in popularity, though irresponsible use resulted in innumerable mental catastrophes.

As negative reports of the drug's powerful effects proliferated in the mainstream media, various individual states began making possession and distribution of LSD illegal. Ultimately, a federal law that made possession of LSD illegal in the United States of America was introduced to the 90th Congress, 2nd Session 1968. Recorded as Public Law 90-639 and officially entitled "AN ACT To amend the Federal Food, Drug and Cosmetic Act to increase the penalties for unlawful acts involving lysergic acid diethylamide (LSD) and other depressant and stimulant drugs, and for other purposes," the law was enacted by the Senate and House of Representatives of the United States of America in Congress Assembled on Thursday, October 24, 1968 and served to legally supersede possession laws of the individual states.

During the 1960s the greatest LSD guru in the world was Dr. Timothy Leary (1920-1996), who, from March 1962 to April 1963, worked as a lecturer on clinical psychology at Harvard University's Center for Personality Research, during which time he, along with Dr.

Richard Alpert (who later became known as Baba Ram Dass), studied the effects of hallucinogens such as psilocybin and LSD on graduate student subjects. Leary, who held a Bachelor of Arts in psychology from the University of Alabama, a Master of Science in psychology from Washington State University, and a Doctorate in clinical psychology from the University of California, Berkley, went AWOL from Harvard in the spring of 1963 to establish his own drug research organizations.

From August 1963 to February 1968 Dr. Leary was encamped at the 64-room, 2,500-acre estate known as "Millbrook" (today known as "Daheim Castle") in Dutchess County, New York where he and an ever-changing collection of scientists, teachers, hippies, and LSD devotees called themselves the Castalia Foundation (the name of this organization was later changed in 1966 to the League for Spiritual Discovery) and partook in a series of drug-fused, psychedelic research adventures, which ultimately led to several highly publicized drug-related arrests (during the 1960s and 1970s his run-ins with the law resulted in stays in 29 different prisons).

As the world's leading advocate of psychedelic drugs, Leary thought LSD showed therapeutic potential in psychiatry and sought to expand the range of human consciousness through the use of various hallucinogens. He achieved worldwide notoriety for his classic slogan, "Turn on, tune in, drop out."

The introduction of LSD to the counterculture of Washington, D.C. can directly be traced to Dr. Leary's first drug-related promotional visit to the nation's capital. This three-day affair began when Dr. Leary and Dr. Ralph Metzner presented what was advertised in the local media as an "LSD Lecture" entitled "Sober Reflections on the Ecstatic Experience" at 8:30pm on the night of Friday, October 29, 1965 at All Souls Unitarian Church (1500 Harvard Street NW). The evening consisted of a talk and question-and-answer session by the two hosts, followed by what they called "practical demonstration sessions" where the LSD experience was simulated through a series of non-drug psychedelic effects projected through taped music, slides, light shows and movies.

The Leary-Metzner demonstration at All Souls set the tone for the weekend, as the next two days were set aside for a couple of fascinating nine-hour programmed psychedelic sessions that only the most adventurous devotees from Washington's fledging psychedelic community could endure.

An article in the Washington Post of Monday, November 1, 1965 entitled "Sex, Music, Poetry: LSD Simulation Session Lures 16 to 'Ecstatic Experience'" by Nancy Moran told how Dr. Leary and five assistants set up camp in a small, dark room in a private residence within the Airy View Apartments at 2415 20th Street NW for a nine-hour "Ecstatic Experience" session that took place on Saturday afternoon beginning at 2pm. According to the article, the room itself, designed to give the feeling of being in another space-time dimension, was littered with fur pillows, the walls covered with Oriental print cloth, and four candles burned in a corner next to a plant in an aluminum foil-covered cup.

A total of 16 people, all of whom had paid $40 to attend the session, were instructed by Leary to lie prone on the floor and were then told by the good Doctor, "Nothing exists but your consciousness – your consciousness is all that exists." Dr. Leary and his helpers then conducted a series of programmed exercises intended to make the minds of the participants aware of the bodies. Everyone meditated, watched a movie of a psychedelic experience and stood up to do exercises. The sensation of sexual energy was created through the use of tapes, recordings and rainbow-colored slides transposed over pictures of erotic statues.

Through similar methods, Dr. Leary then simulated heart, throat and brain energy before closing the experiment with rapid-fire images of galaxies and planets being flashed on the room's walls and ceilings. A similar nine-hour session was to be conducted the following afternoon at the same location.

In the aftermath of his Washington, D.C. experiment, things did not go well for Dr. Leary. He was busted by police in Laredo. Texas on Wednesday, December 22, 1965 and indicted on three counts for offenses pertaining to "marihuana:" Count 1, which charged the smuggling of marihuana into the United States (charges dismissed); Count 2, which charged transportation, and facilitation of transportation, and concealment of marihuana after importation (guilty); and Count 3, which charged transportation and concealment of marihuana by defendants as transferees, required to pay the transfer tax imposed by the Internal Revenue Code (guilty). On Friday, March 11, 1966 a federal judge in Laredo sentenced Dr. Leary to a maximum of 30 years in prison on the two marijuana charges.

While Dr. Leary was dealing with the legal system, the Student-Faculty Union, a University of Maryland discussion group, had invited him to appear as a featured participant in "The FSU Drug Symposium," a two-day event that would feature several presentations providing the latest information on LSD and other hallucinogens that was scheduled to be held on campus in Ritchie Coliseum on Tuesday, April 26 and Wednesday, April 27, 1966. Leary was tagged to appear as a speaker and demonstrator on the first night and a panel participant on the second. However, his appearance, as well as the entire symposium, was canceled when Robert A. Beach, Jr., Director of University Relations, publicly stated: "Members of the administration have in this case and will in future cases act to prevent having on campus a speaker who is under sentence for criminal action of such significance as to be detrimental to the University of Maryland."

An alternate venue was located nearby and Dr. Leary went on to present a demonstration-type program about LSD before a capacity crowd of 2,000 at American University's Leonard Gymnasium on Thursday, May 5, 1966. His presentation, advertised as "Leary Speaks," consisted of films, a stroboscope and attempts to stimulate psycho-halucinant effects by what he called "more conventional means."

Ultimately, Dr. Leary sought to have Congress pass legislation permitting responsible adults to use hallucinatory drugs to expand their consciousness and for the benefit of themselves and mankind. He later embarked on a successful invasion of the University of Maryland's College Park campus when he debated Los Angeles psychologist Sidney Cohen on the potential of LSD in the University's Fine Arts Theater on Thursday, August 17, 1967 as part of "The First National Conference on Student Drug Involvement" (sponsored by the United States National Student Association). More than 1,300 spectators attended the event.

Because of Dr. Leary's adventures and exploits, LSD use in the Washington, D.C. escalated during the late 1960s, but subsequently subsided in the early 1970s due to government restrictions and public fear of the publicized dangers of such drugs. A 1974 report conducted by a National Institute of Mental Health (NIMH) task force on hallucinogenic research entitled "Research in the Service of Mental Health, Research on Drug Abuse, National Institute of Mental Health, Pub No (ADM) 75-236" (edited by J. Segal, US Department of Health, Education and Welfare, Washington, DC, 1975, US Government Printing Office) concluded: "Virtually every psychological test had been used to study persons under the influence of LSD or other such hallucinogens, but the research has contributed little to our understanding of the bizarre and potent effects of this drug." With that finding, interest in LSD dwindled in both the nation's scientific community and youth-oriented counterculture.

CHAPTER SEVENTY-NINE
THE CULTURAL TRANSFORMATION OF DUPONT CIRCLE

The Dupont Circle neighborhood of Washington, D.C. had steadily been attracting artists, bohemians, musicians and homosexuals for several years, and ultimately became a mecca for the city's hippies and counterculture devotees by the middle of the 1960s. The cultural transformation from stately residential neighborhood to Psychedelic Garden of Eden was a fascinating process that was impacted by a number of factors that altered the landscape's social composition.

The history of Dupont Circle dates back to 1871 when the Corps of Engineers constructed what they initially called Pacific Circle at the point where Connecticut Avenue, Massachusetts Avenue, New Hampshire Avenue, P Street and 19th Street NW all converge. The Act of February 25, 1882 – 64th Congress, 2d Session, House of Representatives Report No, 1376, "Dupont Memorial" – authorized the construction of a memorial statue of Rear Admiral Samuel Francis DuPont (1803-1865) in Pacific Circle (DuPont was an officer of the United States Navy who fought gallantly for the Union in the Civil War). This act also included a provision that changed the name of the location in question to "Dupont Circle." (It should be noted here that the circle and its surrounding neighborhood was actually being informally referred to as "Dupont Circle" in articles in the Washington Post as far back as April 1880.) The bronze statue of DuPont, sculpted by Launt Thompson, was unveiled during an afternoon ceremony on Saturday, December 20, 1884 before a crowd of 2,500 on-lookers.

In 1920 members of the DuPont family, feeling the existing memorial figure was too insignificant to honor their ancestor, commissioned architect Henry Bacon and sculptor Daniel Chester French to design a fountain to replace the statue. The double-tiered, white marble fountain featured a carving of three classical figures on its central shaft that symbolized the sea, the stars and the wind. It was installed late in the year, though the fountain did not become fully functional until water started coursing through its pipes in early March 1921. The Samuel Francis DuPont Memorial Fountain was officially dedicated on Tuesday, May 17, 1921.

The neighborhood surrounding Dupont Circle was largely developed during the last quarter of the 19th century, with large, spacious mansions mixing with multi-floored row houses on the area's side streets. The boundaries of Dupont Circle have varied through time according to who is telling its tale, but have usually been defined as Florida Avenue NW to the north, 16th Street NW to the east, 22nd Street NW to the west, and M Street NW to the south.

By the late 19th century the Circle's mansions had filled with politicians, diplomats, dignitaries and high-society millionaires, but in the wake of World War II most of the houses in the area had changed owners and were broken up into apartments and boarding rooms, with the neighborhood becoming a fresh destination for transients and unsettled government employees searching for cheaper, temporary rentals.

During the 1950s the Dupont Circle neighborhood filled with students from area colleges and universities, artists attracted by the presence of galleries such as the Phillips Gallery (1600 21st Street NW), the Corcoran Gallery of Art (500 17th Street NW), the Whyte Gallery (1518 Connecticut Avenue NW) and the Jefferson Place Gallery (1216 Connecticut Avenue NW), and bohemians who gathered at welcoming watering holes such as the Ben Bow Restaurant (1636 Connecticut Avenue NW; 1941-1979), Crystal City (1647 Connecticut Avenue NW, 1941-1974), Rand's Restaurant (1712 Connecticut Avenue NW, 1947-1971), Charlie's Café Lounge (1359 Connecticut Avenue NW; 1958-1966), the Brickskeller (1523

22nd Street NW, 1957-2010) and the Trio Restaurant (1537 17th Street NW, 1945-Present). A later addition to this collection was Tasso's (1307 17th Street NW, 1963-1971), which served as a mixing place for leftover wandering beatniks and newer hippies from the hood. The 1950s also saw the P Street Beach along Rock Creek to the west of the Circle develop into a popular daily gathering spot for the neighborhood's entire spectrum of residents and visitors.

While Dupont Circle had long been a popular daytime gathering spot for the upper-class citizenry of Washington, its social composition took on a noticeable change in the early 1960s as more and more bohemians and persons that defied categorization began draping themselves over the fountain's surrounding landscape.

On Friday, February 16, 1962 the University of Maryland's "Diamondback" newspaper became the very first local publication that attempted to capture the neighborhood's uniqueness within its pages. In an article entitled "Never a Dull Moment on D.C.'s Melting Pot," reporter Bob Levin wrote: "The Dupont Circle area is one of the most interesting locations in Washington... It is the kind of place that native Washingtonians like to go just to watch cars with out of town license plates go around and around as their bewildered drivers wish they had stayed home in Kansas...One Sunday afternoon, two years ago, the American Nazi Party (Lincoln Rockwell's friends), had a rally on the circle. Simultaneously a large group pf bearded folk singers and their only slightly unsanitary chicks decided to get together for some kind of jamboree. Finally, the confused police dept. solved all problems by shoving everybody into paddy wagons...this is typical. The area includes the embassy row section of Mass. Ave., a very sophisticated shopping area on Connecticut Ave., a large Spanish speaking population, a large Negro population (both American and African), a section devoted to rooming houses filled with country folk who came to the big city to make their marks, a poor man's Georgetown, a fair number of Orientals, luxury hotels and apartment buildings, shop lifters, perverts, derelicts, drunks, religious fanatics, beatniks and state department types."

The reputation of Dupont Circle changed forever with the highly publicized arrest of a somewhat mysterious wandering troubadour who had taken a seat on the Circle's grassy lawn around the fountain and began harmlessly singing and playing guitar for a small group of admirers that had gathered around him. In what turned out to be an incident of epic proportions, the troubadour in question, 25-year-old Eddie Hicks, was arrested on the afternoon of Wednesday, June 12, 1963 by United States Park Police officer James E. Thomas and was subsequently found guilty in the Court of General Sessions of vagrancy.

Hicks, who hailed from Southwestern Virginia, was a University of California, Berkley dropout and had appeared in productions for the Abingdon Playhouse the previous winter. Prior to his arrest, he had been in Washington, D.C. for four weeks and had been staying with a friend nearby in an apartment at 1617 15th Street NW. On weekday afternoons he would take to the Circle and play, and in the process drew the ire of Officer Thomas, who testified he had first seen Hicks informally performing at the Circle on Sunday, May 19 and several times since.

Thomas claimed he had told Hicks he couldn't play his guitar and sing because he was disturbing others. Hicks kept showing at the Circle, causing Thomas to ultimately take action. Despite the fact Hicks testified he had shown Officer Thomas a $20 bill as proof he wasn't a bum, Judge Scalley, as quoted by the Washington Post, determined "There is no question his actions come under the vagrancy statute" and found him guilty of vagrancy. However, on Thursday, June 13, Hicks was given a suspended sentence.

The Hicks case was given plenty of link in the local dailies and on Friday, June 14 dozens of musicians, artists, students and friends collected at the fountain throughout the day to argue the conviction and formulate plans for a series of future protests and "Hootenanny" gatherings.

A local musician named John Barker organized a "Strum-In" featuring singing, guitar and banjo-playing for Sunday, June 16 in support of Hicks and the right to perform music on the Circle grounds. On the day in question, more than 700 protestors showed up at the Circle at 2:15pm as 15 guitarists and one banjoist kicked off the festivities by performing their specialty song "He's Got the Park Police in His Hands" (to the tune of the traditional American spiritual "He's Got the Whole World in His Hands").

The day marched on with throngs of supporters circling the main group of musical performers. Eddie Hicks himself, smoking a pipe and enjoying the aura, was observed engaging in a duet with an old Circle panhandler. While the Hicks debacle soon faded from consciousness, Dupont Circle subsequently became the location of impromptu Saturday and Sunday folk music performances that endured for years, further cementing its status as the city's most popular bohemian gathering spot.

CHAPTER EIGHTY
THE NOW FESTIVAL

One of the most significant presentations of art and music to occur in Washington, D.C. during the 1960s was "The NOW Festival," a collection of avant-garde events and happenings that was staged in the spring of 1966 by the Private Arts Foundation, an organization which had recently been founded and incorporated by Alice Denney, one of the local art community's most important figures.

Denney was a longtime figure in the Dupont Circle arts scene, having served as the original director of the Jefferson Place Gallery, which had opened on the second floor of 1216 Connecticut Avenue NW on Thursday, October 10, 1957 under the collective ownership of 10 local artists, all of whom either taught or had previously taught at American University. (The Jefferson Place Gallery later moved closer to Dupont Circle when it took over a space at 2144 P Street NW in 1965.)

Denney left the Jefferson Place Gallery in 1962 to open the Washington Gallery of Modern Art just off the Circle at 1503 21st Street NW, where she served as assistant director and Adelyn Breeskin served as director. During her two-year stay with the new gallery, Denney's goal was to show Washingtonians the best in contemporary art and to present the latest avant-garde productions.

Denney drew substantial attention with a "new art" exhibition she staged at the Washington Gallery of Modern Art entitled "The Popular Image" which ran from Friday, April 19 to Sunday, June 2, 1963. This presentation featured visual and graphic works by 12 artists including Claes Oldenburg, Andy Warhol, Roy Lichtenstein, Verne Blossum, Jim Dine and Jim Rosenquist and rated as one of the very first art exhibitions of its kind in the United States.

Presented in conjunction with "The Popular Image" was an event she advertised as a "Pop Festival" that mainly took place in the Gallery and featured programs in music, dance, cinema and drama. This festival featured: an electronic music performance by John Cage entitled "Where Are We Going and What Are We Doing?" on Friday, April 19, 1963 (the presentation consisted of three tape recordings of him speaking that he played simultaneously as he spoke); a "Happening" ("an ephemeral form of theater that involves people, objects, sounds, and construction, in which all these things are moved about in situations which reflect the artist's experience of the real world") entitled "Stars" on Wednesday, April 24 and Thursday, April 25 by Ray Gun Theater, under the direction of Claes and Patty Oldenburg, that consisted of 19 participants performing 48 actions in 48 minutes – blue ice cream was served on plates, a performer dressed as Abe Lincoln was assassinated several times, children of the artists roller skated about, a woman cleaned her face vigorously, another ironed a flaccid Washington Monument, and the entire episode ended with Olga Adorno descending a staircases in a red dress and stripping down to a bikini before making a mad dash out of the room; a four-hour performance on Thursday, May 9 by the Judson Dancers at the National Arena on Kalorama Road NW in Adams Morgan where a choreographer pointed out different sites at different times and the audience migrated from piece to piece as the evening progressed (included in this event was a presentation of Robert Rauschenberg's happening "The Pelican"); and a closing lecture on contemporary art in the Gallery on Thursday, May 16 by Robert Rosenblum, professor of art history at Princeton University.

Alice Denney left the Washington Gallery of Modern Art in 1964 to work for a year as vice commissioner of the Venice Biennale art exhibition in Italy under Commissioner Alan Solomon. Upon returning to Washington, D.C. she founded her own arts organization – the

Private Arts Foundation – and one of her first projects was the organization of "The NOW Festival" in the spring of 1966. The six-day festival was a bit different from the previous Pop Festival in that this time around Denney booked a couple of high-powered rock and roll acts for the festivities, including the Velvet Underground from New York and local favorites the Hangmen.

Quoted in the local dailies as saying that "Experimentation is the life blood of art," Denney's conviction for assembling the program was her belief that Washington needed to be exposed to the mainstream of artistic thought, instead of just reading about it in the out-of-town newspapers.

The NOW Festival:

Tuesday, April 26, 1966, 8:30pm
National Arena, 1661 Kalorama Road NW
"Theatre Event"
The following happenings were presented: "The Pelican" by Robert Rauschenberg – a rehearsed performance in which a girl in tights tiptoed onto the roller rink followed by two guys on bicycles in gray sweat suits who carried giant Japanese umbrella-like parachutes on their backs and finished up by roller skating around the rink with arms entwined as the girl danced; "Prune Flat" by Robert Whitman – a color film that used real live people as shadows in the foreground and included on-screen gallops through city streets and forests, a sequence where a nude girl daubed herself with pig fat, and an end scene where a live young nymph all in white threw bashes out a bare light bulb with a glass; "Linoleum" by Robert Rauschenberg – a brand new happening that featured a guy laying prone in a wire cage full of clicking chickens, a girl in a Victorian chair with a pot of noodles in her lap, a cut-up travelogue-type film shown on a sheet pinned up on a clothesline, a squirming man with his feet stuck inside a bedspring and his upper torso covered by a paper egg shell, and a woman named Deborah Hay who was clad in a transparent plastic clothes hamper and wore a plexiglass Buck Rogers mask; "Untitled New Piece" by Robert Whitman – a series of short surgical films that highlighted incisions and operative techniques; and "Velvet Underground" by Andy Warhol and Cast – a live concert presentation by the Velvet Underground, a rock and roll group from New York, which, at the time, consisted of singer Nico, singer-guitarist Lou Reed, guitarist Sterling Morrison, bassist John Cale and drummer Maureen Tucker. Attendance for the three-hour event was 800.

Wednesday, April 27, 1966, 8:30pm
Pan American Union Building Auditorium, 200 17th Street NW
"Concert by John Cage and David Tudor"
A live performance of Cage's "Variations VI" – A two-hour dissonant symphony of sound to introduce our ear to our daily lives created with a complex jumble of electronic gear including seven tape recorders, two record players, 12 photo-electric cells triggered by floor spotlights, three audio-generators, seven short-wave receivers, six amplifiers and six speakers.

Thursday, April 28, 1966, 10:15pm and 11:45pm
Janus I and Janus II Theatres, 1600 Connecticut Avenue NW
"Underground Films"
A series of short experimental films by Red Groom, Bruce Connor, John Jones and Tony Conrad.

Friday, April 29, 1966, 8:30pm
National Arena, 1661 Kalorama Road NW
"Dance Concert"
Dance presentations by Trisha Brown, Deborah Hay, Alex Hay, Yvonne Rainier and Steve Paxton.

Saturday, April 30, 1966, 10pm
L'Aiglon Building, 1808 Adams Mill Road NW
"The Mad Camp Ball"
A live musical rock and roll concert by the Hangmen, a pop fashion show, and continuous light shows and movies. The pop fashion show included a girl wearing only leg tights and thickly applied whipped cream, a girl with plastic bags of live goldfish pinned to her outfit and a hat filled with foaming dry ice, and another girl who went out on the runway covered with electric glowing artificial flowers. The location was the then-empty former home of L'Aiglon, a Prohibition-era dance hall that was in operation from 1923 to 1935 – in more recent years it had served as office space to numerous businesses, but was vacant for much of the 1960s. The evening was emceed by Allen Ginsberg.

Sunday, May 1, 1966, 3pm
Grace Church, 1041 Wisconsin Avenue NW
"The NOW Festival Symposium"
An open forum discussion of the Festival moderated by Alan Solomon (former director of the Jewish Museum of New York and a former commissioner of the Venice Biennale art exhibition in Italy) whose panel featured Rafael Squirru, John Jones, Billy Kluver, Robert Rauschenberg, Robert Whitman, Yvonne Rainier and other Festival participants. This symposium closed out "The NOW Festival."

CHAPTER EIGHTY-ONE
BOO HOOS, GURUS AND ACID ACOLYTES

There is no way of determining the exact date that LSD hit the streets in Washington, D.C., though it began making local headlines in 1966 as Metropolitan Police began administering drug raids in a number of hippie pads in the Dupont Circle area. The drug had already been making national headlines for several years thanks to the various adventures of Dr. Timothy Leary, which had included forays into the nation's capital where he spread the word of his favorite brain-changing hallucinogen through demonstrations and programmed sessions. As the decade progressed, other homegrown acid proselytizers followed his lead in similar fashion, including Judith Kuch, a well-publicized leader in the Neo-American Church, and Ian Fralich, Washington's first high-profile psychedelic guru and commune leader. The publicity given to these LSD promoters, users and abusers mainly served to bolster public awareness of the counterculture and its psychedelic state of affairs. Underground newspapers emerged to advance the cause of the counterculture and local night clubs and venues began offering bands that had adopted the psychedelic rock and roll style. The Psychedelic Revolution had been activated.

With the psychedelics on the rise, the Narcotics Squad of the Metropolitan Police of the District of Columbia set up shop in scattered hideouts around Dupont Circle in the summer of 1966 and looked on in dismay as hippies engulfed the area and reportedly engaged in round-the clock pot smoking and LSD gobbling. In what developed into an epic police scene right out of your most intriguing Hollywood production, a 39-year-old law enforcement official named Sgt. David Paul personally took on the responsibility of nailing every drug-using hippie in town and his crusade kicked into high gear as the summer of 1966 wore on.

Sgt. Paul, a decorated 17-year veteran of the force who had been with the Narcotics Squad since 1957, had long been monitoring the city's beatnik coffee house scene and had been involved in numerous marijuana busts through the years. He was energized by the throngs of long-haired, joint-sucking invaders that permeated the Dupont Circle neighborhood and seemingly forged personal vendettas against every budding user, dealer and psychedelic guru that passed through the immediate vicinity.

A major drug bust that Sgt. Paul had spearheaded occurred when a total of 14 suspected drug dealers were arrested on Thursday, September 1, 1966 in the Dupont Circle residential area. The bust included the arrest of six persons at a suspected dope pad at 800 L Street NW that was set up through six weeks of undercover work by a 19-year-old police officer named Edward Varon, who had been working the area as "Danny Boy" and had successfully infiltrated the Circle's hippie scene.

That particular series of arrests, which netted needles, syringes, marijuana, heroin and LSD, set the stage for a second highly publicized raid on Tuesday, October 25, 1966 that became known as the "Psychedelic Basement Bust." In this episode, six men were arrested in a house just off of Dupont Circle at 1301 21st Street NW that included a basement "psychedelic room" for taking trips, the walls and ceiling of which were decorated with colorful and exotic drapes and pictures illuminated by colored lights. This house, in which authorities reportedly found marijuana, a Turkish pipe and other chemicals, had been rented at the time by 32-year-old William S. Marshall. Those arrested were booked on charges ranging from marijuana possession to being present in an establishment where illegal narcotics are used.

Creating substantial public interest in the area's counterculture scene was local media coverage given to some of the movement's more colorful characters. In its July 1966 issue, the Washingtonian magazine featured an article entitled "LSD: A New Religion Comes to Washington" by John Davenport that had a tremendous impact on the local counterculture. The article profiled Mrs. Judith "J.D." Kuch, the recently appointed "Washington Boo Hoo" of the Neo-American Church, a year-old, 500-member cult-like congregation that embraced LSD, cannabis, peyote and mescaline as sacraments.

Kuch and her church-goers seemingly believed that these drugs served as the true Hosts of God and they sought to promote and defend a psychedelic religion that believed the transcendental experience produced by the sacred substances led to a better understanding life and an improved condition of man on earth.

The Neo-American Church, led by Chief Boo Hoo Art Kleps, had actually been incorporated in California in 1965 as a non-profit corporation and had established other headquarters in Miami, Florida and Cranberry Lake, New York. The church operated under a pecking order that included Patriarchs of the East and West, Primates (analogous to bishops) and Boo Hoos (common clergy), the latter of which were assigned one per city. The Washington, D.C. branch of the Church claimed a modest membership of 25 that met informally in various homes. LSD use among members was encouraged, but not required.

The article in the Washingtonian served to introduce Washington Boo Hoo J.D. Kuch to the local heads – as well as unamused officers of the Metropolitan Police of the District of Columbia – and to further publicize the growing presence of LSD and similar chemicals in the nation's capital. A somewhat mysterious figure that seemingly materialized on the scene in hallucinogenic fashion, Kuch, as various court records would later declare, had been born on Monday, November 11, 1940 and had attended the University of Massachusetts where she reportedly had studied psychology with research interests in abnormal sexual behavior. At the time of her arrival in the Washington, D.C. area in the middle 1960s she was married to a man named Terrence Kuch and together they initially resided in Arlington, Virginia. Kuch claims she first took LSD in December 1965 and her membership in the Neo-American Church followed shortly thereafter. She presented herself to all as an "ordained minister of the Neo-American Church."

Kuch claimed in her various writings and public statements that she was recognized within the Church as the "Primate of the Potomac," a position analogized to bishop. She reported that there were more than 300 Boo Hoos throughout the country and that she supervised an untold number of Boo Hoos in her geographic area. A Boo Hoo was ordained without any formal training. He or she guided members on psychedelic trips, acted as a counselor for individuals having a spiritual crisis, administered drugs and interpreted the church to those interested.

The Church seemingly mocked established institutions by officially stating in its "Catechism and Handbook" that "we have the right to practice our religion, even if we are a bunch of filthy, drunken bums." Members of the Church were instructed that anyone should be taken as a member "no matter what you suspect his motives to be." The Church symbol was a three-eyed toad. Its bulletin was entitled "The Divine Toad Sweat." The Church key was a bottle opener. The official songs were "Puff, the Magic Dragon" and "Row, Row, Row Your Boat." The Church motto was "Victory over Horseshit." A review of the handbook showed no regard for a Supreme Being, law, or civic responsibility.

In order to join the Neo-American Church, prospective members were asked to subscribe to three basic principles: everyone has the right to expand his consciousness and stimulate visionary experience by whatever means he considers desirable and proper without interference from anyone; psychedelic substances, such as LSD, are the true Host of the Church, not drugs; and the ingestion of psychedelics by those who are unprepared is not encouraged.

Kuch's publicity did not work in her favor. She was placed under constant surveillance by both local and federal law enforcement authorities and became the favorite target of the zealous detective Sgt. David Paul. Kuch was arrested several times in the late 1960s on drug possession charges by federal agents who were working in conjunction with Sgt. Paul and his team of officers and the busts were well-publicized in the local media.

On Wednesday, September 13, 1967, after selling LSD to an undercover federal agent, Kuch was arrested at her home by Detectives David Paul and Edmund MacKinnon along with other offices of the Narcotics Squad and agents of the Bureau of Drug Abuse. These law enforcement officials had executed a U.S. Commissioners search at Kuch's residence at 2323 Nebraska Avenue NW in Washington, D.C. where quantities of marijuana, hashish, LSD, other dangerous drugs and smoking pipes were seized on the premises. Kuch was indicted for violation of the Marijuana Tax Act and the Drug Abuse Control Act.

A second raid on the Kuch empire took place on Friday, December 22, 1967 when she was arrested with seven other persons by Detectives David Paul and Edmund MacKinnon at her new home at 5333 MacArthur Blvd NW in Washington, D.C. This time around the officers caught Kuch and her cohorts with quantities of marijuana, opium, hashish, LSD, and various types of paraphernalia. She was indicted on five counts charging violations of the Uniform Narcotics Act and the Marijuana Tax Act.

One last bust was conducted on Thursday, July 11, 1968 where Kuch was arrested on her back porch along with three other people, including two minors, and again charged with violations of the Uniform Narcotics Act and the Marijuana Tax Act after marijuana and other drugs were found in her home.

By the summer of 1968, Kuch had so many drug charges against her one needed a score card to keep track of her legal entanglements. When her day in court arrived, she sought to have all charges against her dismissed on the defense was that her convictions for the sale and possession of marijuana and LSD violated her free exercise of religion.

Unfortunately for Boo Hoos everywhere, Judge Gerhard A. Gesell of the United States District Court for the District of Columbia ruled on Wednesday, July 3, 1968 that "The practices of the Neo-American Church involving the use, possession, transfer and sale of marijuana and LSD are contrary to criminal law" and concluded that the Church was "mocking established institutions" and that its written material was "full of goofy nonsense, contradictions, and irreverent expressions."

In his Opinion, Judge Gesell wrote, "In short, she has totally failed in her burden to establish her alleged religious beliefs, an essential premise to any serious consideration of her motions to dismiss...in summary the Court concludes that the motions to dismiss in all respects are denied. The Neo-American Church is not an establishment of religion and defendant Kuch has not sustained her burden of demonstrating that her religious beliefs require her to ingest psychedelic drugs."

With her defense rejected, Kuch was shuffled through the courts and was eventually found guilty on a number of drug offenses. She reportedly did time in a federal penitentiary and never returned to the Washington, D.C. counterculture scene, though she has remained one of the city's legendary psychedelic figures. She would later reappear in the Midwest where she remarried two more times and spent her final years living a quiet life in River Rouge, Michigan. Judith H. Kuch-Payne died on Monday, June 3, 2002 at the age of 61.

Arriving on the local counterculture scene during J.D. Kuch's reign was a charismatic young man who would not only befriend the Washington Boo Hoo and her cohorts, but came to quickly surpass her and her herd in psychedelic significance and local drug scene status. Though still a teenager, John Henry "Ian" Fralich was a remarkable individual whose sincere belief in the expansion of consciousness and maximization of human potential through the use of LSD cultivated a legion of hippie followers and firmly placed him at the forefront of the pulsating psychedelic movement that was bursting in the nation's capital. Fralich walked his talk, opening one of the area's first head shops, creating his own psychedelic commune (the members of which he personally recruited and supported), and organizing the city's first Be-Ins which he staged at Dupont Circle and the nearby P Street Beach. However, like the other acid pied pipers that were roaming the country, he also sold drugs, an illegal activity that eventually led to his personal downfall.

Ian Fralich quietly arrived in Washington, D.C. in the fall of 1966 with visions of world peace and what he called the "Awareness Movement" dancing in his head. His background was unusual – born in Lancaster, Pennsylvania and raised in nearby Millersville, he left home at age 14 but stayed in the area and finished high school a year early and subsequently headed for the woods of Tennessee. He enrolled at Tusculum College in the fall of 1966 at age 17 as a philosophy major, but dropped out after a few weeks and retreated to a cabin in the mountains where for three months he meditated, read philosophy and painted. In November 1966 he hitchhiked to Washington, D.C. and headed straight to the front gates of the White House, where he set up camp and spent a week on the sidewalk holding a sign that read, "Fast for Peace." It was an eventful week, as word of the intrepid teenager quickly spread to a group of young burgeoning Dupont Circle hippies, one of whom ventured to the White House gates and slipped Fralich a tab of righteous acid. After embarking on that first trip, Fralich's mission came into focus.

After a second week in Washington where he became better acquainted with his new, like-minded friends, Fralich went back to the Tennessee hills for a short Christmas stay. Back in the nation's capital as the year 1967 arrived, he took a job refinishing paintings for an art dealer in the city and went to work spreading the word on the potential of LSD with help from the colorful array of spacey followers that were gathering around him.

First, Fralich opened up a store he called "The Source" at 2151 K Street NW in Washington, D.C., which served as a head shop and headquarters for an organization he founded called D.C. Psychedelic Information Center. The shop sold everything one needed to embark on the Hippie Trip – posters, buttons, pipes, rolling papers and drug-related odds and ends galore. The information center flooded local media outlets with written material on the potential of LSD and other chemical goodies believed to help one better understand the capabilities and possibilities of the human mind, increase their awareness of the world around them and lead to other avenues beneficial to the survival and evolution of all mankind. He also edited and published a newsletter, also called "The Source," which reflected his philosophy on drugs and consciousness.

One of Fralich's more remarkable cosmic accomplishments during his stay in the nation's capital was the administration of several "Be-Ins" that were modeled after similar gatherings in New York and California that had transpired in late 1966 and early 1967. Through press releases produced for the public by his Psychedelic Information Center, the young hippie leader claimed the first Washington, D.C. Be-In, which was held on the afternoon of Saturday, January 14, 1967 on the grounds surrounding Dupont Circle, was a "shrine of vigils, love in the streets, loft parties and mass turn-ons."

J.D. Kuch was tagged as High Priestess of the Be-In and in the celebration's aftermath was quoted in the local dailies as saying it was "the most beautiful thing Washington has ever seen." The turnout for the first gathering was reportedly very small, with only a couple dozen hippie participants "being in" by the time the clock had struck 2pm. All of the participants hailed from Fralich's developing drug circle and all sported orange "psychedelic movement" buttons and passed out leaflets that urged "psychedelic people" to "combat sensationalist journalism with facts and truth – straight from the heads' mouths." Featured musicians at the Be-In were Rusti Taylor and Connie Taylor, who performed Beethoven duets on violin and cello, respectively. It was a fun and peaceful afternoon that inspired Fralich to stage more elaborate Be-Ins at the nearby P Street Beach on Saturday afternoons throughout the months of April and May 1967.

Perhaps the most interesting of all of Fralich's exploits was the establishment in early 1967 of what became known as "The Psychedelic House," a commune of LSD devotees that resided in a three-story house leased by Fralich at 1132 25th Street NW, not far from Dupont Circle. Fralich decorated the hallways of the residence with multi-colored lights, psychedelic art and posters of countercultural luminaries such as Allen Ginsberg. Reportedly, the Psychedelic House was home to several employees of the Source and served as a crash pad, dope lair and hippie hangout. Those in the local bohemian community regarded the residence as one of the city's earliest functioning communes. Fralich did little to hide the psychedelic veneer of his not-so-humble abode and it quickly attracted the attention of Detective Sgt. David Paul and his band of narcs.

At 4am on the morning of Sunday, April 30, 1967, Sgt. Paul and members of the Narcotics Squad executed a D.C. Court of General Sessions search warrant at the Psychedelic House and arrested a total of 26 persons – a sweep that tallied 22 adults, one unidentified woman and three juveniles. Charges against those arrested included vagrancy, being present in an illegal establishment, maintaining a common nuisance, violation of the Marijuana Tax Act, violation of the Uniform Narcotics Act, violation of the Dangerous Drug Act and violation of the Federal Drug Abuse Control Act.

In an article in the Washington Post of Monday, May 1, 1967 entitled "25 Arrested in Raid at 'Psychedelic' House," Carl Bernstein reported that police, who had been posing undercover and had been purchasing drugs from frequenters of the house for several months, confiscated a quantity of marijuana, amphetamines, barbiturates and a substance they believed to be LSD. (Although the title of this article stated that 25 persons were arrested, the actual number was 26.) Fralich, according to the article, said the house was a demonstration workshop of the movement he was heading which he called humanism and he approved of house members taking marijuana, LSD and other consciousness-expanding drugs. At the time of the raid, about 15 individuals were staying at the house in preparation for the Be-In that was going to take place at the P Street Beach that weekend.

In that Washington Post article, 21 of the persons said to have been arrested in the raid were identified. Whether or not they should be condemned as drug fiends or praised as Washington's first contingency of psychedelic vanguards is open to debate, but they do hold a prominent place in local counterculture history for their documented involvement in the Psychedelic House bust.

According to the Washington Post account, those charged were: Lucy Carmichael (29), John P. Schneider (19), Brian B. Fleisher (18), William B. Gillespie (20), Michael J. Huntzberry, Stuart E. Francke (21), John C. Wallraff (21), James Black (24), Donald J. Leach (20), Michael J. Friedman (18), Alexander W. Bartlett (23), William H. Bordenave (27), Raymond Urgo (23), Richard G. Browning Jr. (18), Michael J. Britt (20), Pamela Collins (21), John T. Leonard (24), Ann B. Leonard (22), Robert W. Freeman (20),Diana Carolyn Moore (18), Richard R. Zwible (age not provided), and Michael J. Huntzberry (age not provided). Ian Fralich, who was leasing the house, was also arrested in the raid and charged with maintaining a common nuisance, though his name did not appear in the article as one of the culprits.

The short-lived existence of the Psychedelic House came to an abrupt end with the bust, causing Ian Fralich, still the hippie movement's primary leader, to search for territories that were beyond the reach of the local heat. He looked to form a new psychedelic community similar to what Dr. Timothy Leary had established in Millbrook, New York and realized his new Utopia had to be well outside of the Washington, D.C. area.

As the Summer of Love progressed, the LSD evangelist set his sights on the rural stretches of Virginia, northwest of the nation's capital and well outside of Sgt. Paul's reach. He didn't realize the feds were watching his every move. After the conclusion of a short "business trip" to California, Fralich began leasing a 35-acre farm on Thursday, August 3, 1967 for $135 per month in an unincorporated village called Bluemont, situated in Loudon County, Virginia at the base of Snickers Gap in the Blue Ridge Mountains. Fralich moved a dozen cronies into the compound's 12-room farmhouse and immediately embarked on a new round of psychedelic adventures.

Unfortunately for Fralich and his new Bluemont family members, law enforcement officials from the Federal Narcotics Bureau were well-informed of the guru's adventures. When he settled in at the Virginia farm he and his friends became little more than sitting ducks for the Feds, who were determined to extinguish the joints, eradicate the acid tabs, and send the hippies at the foothill off to jail once and for all.

At 4:30pm on the afternoon of Tuesday, August 22, 1967 a contingency of federal agents, United States Customs Police officers, the Loudon County Sheriff, Loudon County Police officers and Virginia State Police officers descended upon the property with a warrant for Fralich's arrest on a charge of conspiring to smuggle 225 pounds of marijuana across the Mexican border into California. The warrant was issued on a July 19 indictment by a federal grand jury in San Diego for smuggling and concealing marijuana, aiding and abetting, and conspiracy to smuggle marijuana.

Upon their arrival at the farm, the officers nabbed Fralich and then ripped up a one-acre patch of land that contained some 300 marijuana plants that they estimated could produce $100,000 worth of marijuana in a single harvest. They also confiscated a variety of materials that led them to conclude the farm was functioning as a marijuana processing and packaging plant for East Coast distribution. Arraigned with Fralich in Alexandria Federal District Court on various drug charges were individuals named Dwight Tolliver (23), Michael Friedman (19) and Gerry Peake (20).

To further complicate matters, Fralich was arraigned in the Court of General Sessions on Thursday, August 24, 1967 for having sold 21 tabs of LSD to an undercover District of Columbia Metropolitan Police officer back on Monday, June 5, 1967. At this point there seemed to be little wiggle room for Fralich on all of the charges pending against him and a federal pen vacation seemed inevitable. Incredibly, a mysterious benefactor, or group of benefactors, repeatedly posted bond for the acid guru and he remained on the loose in Washington, D.C. where he crashed with friends and was seen on a daily basis hanging out at Dupont Circle and frequenting the Ambassador Theatre, where psychedelic rock and roll concerts featuring local and national talent were being offered.

Despite the serious legal issues he faced, Fralich was immortalized in a feature story in Washingtonian magazine of October 1967 entitled "Ian Fralich: Chief Prophet of Washington Hippies" by Phil Stanford. The article proclaimed that "New York hippies have their Galahad, San Francisco has Ken Kesey. And Washington, the third largest hippie center in the nation, with a population of between 500 and 1,000, has Ian Fralich."

Sanford went on to document Fralich's arrival in the nation's capital and his mercurial rise as the leading figure in the city's counterculture community. Ample space was also given to Fralich's psychedelic colleagues at the Source and their drug-fueled philosophies and activities. The piece wrapped up with a detailed account of how Fralich and crew, in fine hopped-up fashion, invaded the grounds of the Washington Monument on the 5th of July for a rescheduled fireworks demonstration that was referred to by the author as the "Super Psychedelic Light and Power Show of the Century." Claiming "a person who is high on LSD acts very much the same as anyone else" and "The Hippies, the disciples and their prophet, were just watching the fireworks," the article reached its anticlimactic conclusion with the question, "Wow, wow, wow, wow, WOW! And what will they do when the lights go out?"

Just as the Washingtonian issue was making the social rounds in the nation's capital, Fralich again made headlines for the wrong reasons. On Monday, October 16, 1967 he was one of three persons arrested in a narcotics raid at a top-floor apartment at 1737 F Street NW in Washington, D.C. When Metropolitan Police invaded they found three king-size marijuana cigarettes that were wrapped in copies of indictments against Fralich. They also confiscated 20 pounds of marijuana found in two suitcases in the apartment, which was located less than one block from the White House. Fralich was charged with violation of the Marijuana Tax Act and being in an illegal establishment. Arrested on the same charges was Jean Ann Lesar (19), for whom police had a warrant, charging violation of the Drug Abuse Act, and Nancy L. Marnette (19), who was charged with being in an illegal establishment.

The apartment where the bust occurred was leased to John Steinbeck IV (21), son of the Nobel Prize-winning novelist, who also faced charges of marijuana possession and maintaining a common nuisance. When Steinbeck, who was a Vietnam veteran with an honorable United States Army discharge, went to trial in December, he testified that the marijuana did not belong to him, but that he smoked marijuana infrequently as part of his preparation for two separate articles he was writing for Washingtonian magazine on the sociological use of marijuana. He claimed it was these journalism projects that led him to invite Ian Fralich to live with him. The jury bit and Steinbeck was acquitted of all charges.

As the 1960s came to a close Ian Fralich's luck ran out. There were so many drug charges piled up against him even the prosecuting attorneys had trouble keeping them straight. After a series of trials in late 1967 and early 1968 Fralich was ultimately found guilty on multiple counts and ended up receiving a five-year sentence on the Bluemont bust, with other sentences to be served concurrently. He ended up doing 30 months in Virginia's Lorton Reformatory. Upon his parole he returned to Lancaster, Pennsylvania where he married, had children, and embarked on a rather normal, drug-free life. In 1978 he relocated to Fort Meyer, Florida and spent more than 35 years working in the wellness, conservation and construction industries. At last report he was residing in Hawaii.

As a curious end note to the psychedelic hijinks that had swirled around Dupont Circle in the late 1960s, the Washington Post ran the following article entitled "'Hippie Buster' to Retire" in their edition of Friday, September 20, 1968: "Det. Sgt. David Paul, an 18-year veteran of the Metropolitan Police Department, yesterday was recommended by the Police Retirement Board for retirement for a medical disability incurred in the line of service. Paul, 40, who lives in Rockville, is a native of Brooklyn who came to Washington in 1950. He worked in the Eighth and Second Precincts before being assigned to the Narcotics Squad in 1957. He has been prominent in recent years in 'busting' hippies. His retirement will become effective at the end of September."

CHAPTER EIGHTY-TWO
NOTES FROM THE UNDERGROUND

Washington, D.C.'s counterculture thrived during the late 1960s thanks to the Vietnam War, communist operatives, brainwashed activists, hippies, drugs, drug users, drug gurus, head shops, psychedelic music and underground publications. Perhaps the movement's most significant instrument of communication during this period was the Washington Free Press, a radical newspaper published on a somewhat irregular schedule that provided all the information the hippies of the nation's capital needed to sustain what they saw as a cultural, political and social revolution. The paper was a vital piece of the 1960s cultural puzzle, but ultimately could not overcome the philosophical clashes of its ever-changing staff members and did not survive the decade. The Washington Free Press, and others of its ilk that were published in and around the city during the late 1960s and early 1970s, remain fascinating artifacts of its time.

In early 1966 two Howard University students, Art Grosman, a physics major, and Frank Speltz, a history major, discovered they had similar social and philosophical interests and became determined to enlighten Black students at Howard about the Vietnam War and White students at George Washington University about the civil rights movement. They got together at Tasso's Restaurant near Dupont Circle and decided to put together an intercollegiate newspaper to inform students about the Revolution that was taking place around them. Seven universities were targeted – Trinity University, the Catholic University of America, American University, Georgetown University, George Washington University, Howard University and the University of Maryland – and students from each campus were approached about getting involved in their media project.

The first issue of the Washington Free Press was pasted together at a friend's apartment just off of Dupont Circle on Newport Street NW and was issued in March 1966. Thereafter, newspaper headquarters were established nearby in a commune at 1737 Q Street NW and a total of three additional conventional-looking issues were published before the school session ended that spring.

The Washington Free Press was not without competition. First on the block to challenge was the appropriately named "Underground" which was a very short-lived paper published by 24-year-old Tom DeBaggio (1942-2011) of Arlington, Virginia. Later in his life DeBaggio gained widespread recognition as an author of several books on herbs including "Growing Herbs from Seed, Cutting & Root" (1985) and for his research into Alzheimer's disease.

The first issue of Underground was published in May 1966 and featured United Press Syndicate dispatches, reports from the editor of a Detroit Marxist newsletter, stories on pot, perversity, plays, politics, progress reports from a correspondent in Honduras who was setting up a free love vacation resort, news on West Coast folk heroes by a San Francisco bartender, ads placed by a psychedelic mail-order house, and the musings of Washington Boo Hoo J.D. Kuch on morning glory seeds and aphrodisiacs. Only four issues were published before DeBaggio pulled the plug and directed his attention towards plants and herbs. A much more ambitious and intriguing hippie newspaper entitled "Quicksilver Times" would later emerge in Washington, D.C. in June 1969 and endure a tumultuous, three-year run.

In its second year of publication the dynamics of the Washington Free Press changed dramatically. Grosman and Speltz brought in Conrad Averett, who had worked on the Berkley Barb in California, who added a psychedelic flavor to the paper's artwork and philosophy. The Washington Free Press, now fully embraced by the city's hippies, was being strategically placed in the mailboxes of every reporter of each of the city's three main dailies and was frequently being quoted in mainstream press, thus adding to its notoriety and general exposure.

The staff of the newspaper gradually grew in size with the most notable addition being Peter Novick, a Bowie, Maryland native who would write the publication's drug column under the pen name "Fooman Zybar." Novick had the distinction of being one of three persons busted for possession of narcotics and dangerous drugs in a highly publicized Prince George's County's LSD-marijuana drug sweep at a commune at 4302 Queensbury Road in Hyattsville on Friday, December 9, 1966. As the Washington Free Press gained popularity and its circulation increased, government infiltrators came and went, but the hardcore staff could not have cared less.

The Washington Free Press, which was an early member of the United Press Syndicate, moved its headquarters several times during its existence. In December 1967, after having spent more than seven months at 1703 R Street NW, the paper's offices were relocated to a three-story building at 3 Thomas Circle NW, a structure that also housed the Liberation News Service, the Washington Draft Resistance Union, a local chapter of the anti-draft group Resistance, a print shop, and a plethora of other activist groups that seemingly came and went with frenetic abandon. The newspaper covered every topic germane to the counterculture community – the antiwar movement, civil rights issues, police busts and brutality, college campus activism, leftist politics, demonstrations, drugs, welfare, coffee house events, local music and every imaginable type of hippie propaganda it could fit within its pages.

The prevailing attitude of the local counterculture was succinctly captured in an innocuous post from the staff of the Washington Free Press in the "What the Hell is Going On" calendar section of their December 31, 1967 issue. Under the entry "Monday – January 1," the following statement was listed: "Today being New Year's Day, the Washington Free Press suggests that you make a resolution to move out of that house in Bethesda, take a pad around Dupont Circle, turn-on with some grass, tune-in to all the games you've been playing, and drop-out of that government job you hate and join the peace movement."

While it is not exactly clear as to how many of the newspaper's constituents acted on the advice bestowed upon them by the wise men and women of the Washington Free Press, the general message reached a sizeable chunk of the area's hippie population, as the circulation of the publication reportedly topped off in the 25,000 range during its height of popularity.

With its existence always threatened by a lack of funding, the local music community was frequently called upon to help the Washington Free Press pay its bills. Benefits occurred with regularity and many of these were concert presentations featuring the best local rock and roll bands available. Churches within the city, permissive in terms of entertainment offerings and receptive to the plight of the local hippies, were often called upon to host these spectacles.

A prime example of this type of event was the "Forget Pearl Harbor and General Hershey Birthday Party" benefit which was staged for the newspaper on Saturday, December 7, 1968 at the Concordia United Church of Christ (1920 G Street NW) in Washington, D.C. This event, emceed by popular local disc jockey Barry Richards, featured the Fallen Angels, Flavor and the Cherry People, three of the very best rock and roll bands the Washington, D.C. area has ever produced.

Unfortunately for counterculture devotees, the Washington Free Press was a rather short-lived venture. In its final two years the staff turned over with regularity and its only founding member, Art Grosman, left the area in 1968 for an 18-month journey through Central and South America. When he returned to Washington, D.C., he discovered that the newspaper had published an obscene cartoon that infuriated a local judge and caused staff members and associates to waste a lot of time in the court system. As the end neared, the publication was being run by people whose philosophy was "Rip Off the State." In accordance, their main course of action against the System was to stop paying their printing bill, thus bringing an anticlimactic end to Washington, D.C.'s first underground newspaper with issue number 67 in December 1969.

As the Washington Free Press grinded to a halt, a new underground publication, the Quicksilver Times, came along to take its place. To this day, the very nature of this publication is a popular topic among counterculture historians. A book entitled "Secrets: The CIA's War at Home" (1999) by Angus Mackenzie, a study of the CIA's resistance to the Freedom of Information Act, maintains what was long-suspected of the newspaper – that it was heavily infiltrated by CIA and FBI undercover agents who were attempting to create chaos within the Washington, D.C. counterculture.

The book maintains that one of the Quicksilver Times' main contributors, Sal Ferrera, a 24-year-old Chicago native with a master's degree from Loyola University Chicago who had relocated to Washington, D.C. to work on a Doctorate in political science at George Washington University, was, in reality, an undercover CIA agent sent to damage the movement. Ferrera reportedly specialized in analyzing the operations of different antiwar groups and his very first assignment with the agency in 1969 was to infiltrate the Quicksilver Times and report on the activities of its staff members and associates. Ferrera wrote one article for the newspaper in its first issue under his own name, and then assumed the pen name "Sal Torey" for future articles. The book maintains that as many as seven FBI informants had been deployed to work for the publication with the ultimate goal of creating dissension within antiwar protest groups in the nation's capital.

The Quicksilver Times was founded by one Terry Becker, Jr., a former college newspaper editor and reporter for the Newhouse News Service. Their initial headquarters was inside a converted row house in the Dupont Circle area at 1932 17th Street NW. It's first issue was published on Monday, June 16, 1969, and its staff listing read: editorial group – Terry Becker, Steven Guss, John Hagerhorst; art directors – Don Perry Jack Dempsey; photography – Val DuBasky, Richard Harrington; copy editor – Peggy O'Callaghan; contributors – Bill Blum, Sal Ferrera, Ekim Boerman, Kyla Bowles, Lenore Patterson; graphics: Jeanette Bender, Bobbi Wheeler, and a person named Arthur.

The Quicksilver Times was a member of the Liberation New Service and the Underground Press Syndicate and ran articles supporting the antiwar movement, drug use, and anything promoting leftist-hippie-countercultural causes. In May 1970 the newspaper relocated to a basement office in the same neighborhood at 1736 R Street NW. At its peak, circulation reportedly topped the 20,000 mark. In all, a total of 77 issues were published, with the paper folding after the August 2 to August 18, 1972 (Volume 4, Number 9) edition.

CHAPTER EIGHTY-THREE
THE AMBASSADOR THEATRE EXPERIENCE

In 1967 the Summer of Love commenced with psychedelic social explosions in cities across America. One of the cultural staples of the season was the psychedelic ballroom, a large, indoor space where contemporary hippie bands, accompanied by kaleidoscopic light shows, blasted acid rock to predominantly young and stoned audiences. San Francisco had the Avalon Ballroom and the Fillmore Auditorium, Portland had the Crystal Ballroom, Detroit had the Grande Ballroom, Boston had the Boston Tea Party, and New York City had the Electric Circus. Joining the festivities was Washington, D.C., which offered the Ambassador Theatre, a long-standing, traditional movie theatre at 2454 18th Street NW that had been converted into a swirling, colorful concert hall that attracted a plethora of nationally known rock and blues performers including such now-legendary acts as the Jimi Hendrix Experience, John Lee Hooker, Canned Heat and Moby Grape. The Ambassador Theatre was in operation as a concert venue for a scant six months, but despite its brief existence, left a deep imprint in the local music scene as one of the most intriguing concert venues the region has ever experienced.

The Ambassador Theatre was the brainchild of the three-man team of Tony Finestra, Court Rodgers and Joel Mednick. Finestra and Rodgers had known each other since their high school days in Harrisburg, Pennsylvania. After graduating from their respective schools in 1961 they were employed for a couple years as district managers for the Master Sales Company of America, a door-to-door sales organization based in LeMoyne, Pennsylvania.

On Tuesday, December 17, 1963 Finestra and Rodgers started their own business in Harrisburg called the Eastern States Chemical Company. This new outfit sold fire extinguishers to a varied clientele around the country that included students on college campuses, Future Farmers of America chapters and Boy Scouts of America councils. In 1965 they relocated their operation to Washington, D.C. and rented an office on the second floor of 2234 Wisconsin Avenue NW, just above the Luros Carry Out Shop. During the summer seasons of these years when sales were slow, Finestra and Rodgers operated coffee houses called the Gypsy Rover in Ocean City, New Jersey, Erie, Pennsylvania and Harrisburg, Pennsylvania. The coffee house experience provided a solid foundation for what was on the horizon.

The third piece of the Ambassador triumvirate was Joel Mednick, a native Washingtonian who had grown up in the Tenleytown neighborhood of the city and had attended Woodrow Wilson High School before graduating from Montgomery Blair High School in Silver Spring, Maryland in 1962. As a youth Mednick had been exposed to the rock and roll of Bill Haley and His Comets and Elvis Presley through his older brother. Later, while attending American University as an economics major, he became involved in the local anti-war movement.

In 1965 Mednick embarked on a four-month tour or Europe that saw him travel through England, France, Germany, Spain, Sweden, Switzerland and Denmark. When he returned to the nation's capital, a friend picked him up at the airport and told him about Bob Dylan's new song "Like a Rolling Stone." They went back to the friend's house to listen to the song and it marked a turning point in Mednick's life – he started smoking marijuana, stepped up his involvement in the local counterculture, and never returned to American University.

In 1966 a friend told Mednick, who at that time was living in an apartment in Washington, D.C. at 2319 40th Street NW, about a couple of acquaintances who were running a small business a few blocks away on Wisconsin Avenue NW called the Eastern

States Chemical Company. Mednick dropped in on the company office and found the two fellows running it, Finestra and Rodgers, to be pretty hip dudes. He signed up to be a sales representative and in one of his first feats with the company Mednick introduced his two new bosses to marijuana. The three soon discovered that they shared the same anti-war philosophy and a love of rock and roll music. With fire extinguishers in tow the trio traveled the Midwest, staying in hotels, getting stoned, and selling their goods by day.

In early 1967 Finestra, Rodgers and Mednick finished a sales job in Oklahoma and, upon reading an article in Ramparts magazine about the burgeoning hippie scene in the Bay Area of California, flew out to San Francisco to check out the situation first-hand. They stayed at the apartment of a friend named Silver Dawn, a woman who had worked as a waitress for Finestra and Rodgers in one of their coffee houses and was now employed as a stripper in a North Beach night club. Their stay in Frisco lasted two weeks, during which time they attended concerts at the Avalon Ballroom and the Fillmore Auditorium, with the music and general ambiance of the venues leaving a strong impression on the young entrepreneurs. With two members of the team having ample coffee house management experience behind them, they consulted with legendary promoter Bill Graham and subsequently decided to open their own psychedelic ballroom back in the nation's capital just as the approaching Summer of Love began to take shape.

It did not take long for Finestra, Rodgers and Mednick to come up with a suitable concert hall in Washington, D.C. The first facility the trio scouted was the then-vacant D.C. Transit System Streetcar Barn at 3222 M Street NW in the heart of Georgetown, a building whose office space had been rented out during the middle 1960s by various government agencies. However, they soon discovered that the Ambassador Theatre, a vacant, boarded-up and worn-out movie house on 18th Street NW in the heart of the city's Adams Morgan neighborhood, was available for rent, and its architectural design provided greater concert space potential.

The Ambassador Theatre boasted a fascinating history. It was located southwest of the 18th Street-Columbia Road NW intersection in the heart of Adams Morgan. It had originally opened as the Knickerbocker Theater, which had been constructed in 1915 for Harry Crandall, who owned several movie houses in the city including the Lincoln Theatre and the Metropolitan Theatre. The three-story structure was designed by Reginald Geare, featured Neo-Classical styles in both its façade and interior designs, and seated 1,700. The Knickerbocker's grand opening occurred on Friday, October 12, 1917 with the historical drama "Betsy Ross," and featured a personal appearance by the film's star, Alice Brady.

The Knickerbocker Theatre was immediately considered to be one of Washington, D.C.'s most aristocratic picture houses. Tragedy struck the theatre, when, at approximately 9pm on the night of Saturday, January 28, 1922 as a capacity crowd was being seated for the second showing of the celebrated comedy "Get-Rich-Quick Wallingford," the theatre's steel-and-concrete roof caved in under 24 inches of snow. According to an article in the Washington Post of Monday, January 30, 1922 entitled "Full Lists of Dead and Injured in Theater Tragedy: The Dead, Reported Missing, the Injured," a total of 106 persons were killed in the accident, two were reported missing, and 133 were injured. It was, up to that point, the worst disaster in Washington, D.C. history.

In 1923 Crandall hired Thomas W. Lamb, the foremost theatre architect in America, to design and construct a new picture house to be called the Ambassador Theatre on the Knickerbocker's former site. The new theatre featured an interior of Italian renaissance design in black and gold with seats of old gold velvet and draperies of gold and dahlia purple. A new stage featured elaborate frame and background drapes and the main ceiling lighting fixtures offered domes of leaded work, with crystal trimming and amber glass. The lobby was finished in marble with pendant lighting fixtures and decorative poster frames, with the promenade lounge and auditorium proper decorated in restful tones of satins and silks. The new theatre was equipped with 1,500 seats.

The Ambassador Theatre opened on the night of Thursday, September 20, 1923 with a featured showing of “Main Street,” and a comedy offering of “High Life.” Music during the screenings and between programs was provided by the 20-member Ambassador Grand Orchestra under the conductorship of Mr. Bailey Alart.

For decades the Ambassador Theatre rated as one of the city’s most prestigious movie houses, but by the early 1960s its attendance dipped as the popularity of television increased and home entertainment became a viable option for theatre-goers. The building itself was also wearing out in many different structural areas and was falling into a state of disrepair. After several months of dismal turnouts and exorbitant utility bills, a decision was rendered to discontinue the business.

On the night of Tuesday, April 26, 1966 the Ambassador Theatre offered the final night of a week-long bill that featured “Spy Who Came In from the Cold” starring Richard Burton at 6pm and 9:40pm, and “Never Too Late” starring Connie Stevens at 7:55pm. After the 9:40pm showing, the theatre shut down operations and closed its doors as a movie house for good. Some 11 months later the team of Finestra, Rodgers and Mednick approached owner Maurice Shapiro about leasing the vacant facility for their ambitious musical venture.

Beginning Saturday, April 1, 1967, Finestra, Rodgers and Mednick, originally calling themselves “The Psychedelic Power and Light Company,” began leasing the Ambassador Theatre for $2,300 per month. The name didn’t go over well with the local Adams Morgan Citizens Association and the Metropolitan Police, and the three soon changed the name of their outfit to “Finestra, Rodgers and Mednick, Inc.” (Later, in November 1967 they would change their name again to “Mother Frog Productions,” with the original moniker being handed over to two friends of theirs, Jerry Marmelstein and Michael Saaks, who operated the venue’s light show and assumed the name for their two-man company.)

The theatre, after a year of inactivity, had fallen into a state of neglect. When the new lessees entered the shuttered, musty building they discovered that all the seats had been removed and the theatre was filled with little more than ghosts and cobwebs. Undaunted, they cleaned the premises, had a new air conditioning system installed, and began assembling a staff to help make their rock and roll ballroom dream a reality.

Many individuals, some still familiar to the Washington, D.C. area rock and roll community, were brought in to make the Ambassador happen. Those who were a part of the experience included: Paul Hawken and Scott Bartlett, who were flown in from San Francisco to design and construct the initial light show; Jerry Marmelstein and Mike Saaks, who together comprised the Psychedelic Power and Light Company and maintained and operated the light show throughout the theatre’s concert hall run; Mike Schreibman, who served as the publicity director and concessions manager; Steve Barker, a mainstay concession stand worker; Walter Hart, who operated a head shop entitled “Bleecker Street Shop” (identical to his store of the same name in Georgetown) in the theatre’s lobby; Norman Welles, the theatre’s initial stage announcer; Mike Paper, who worked the sound board, created concert posters, and replaced Welles as the Ambassador’s stage announcer; and a collection of individuals that designed and produced the concert posters which included Mike Paper, Phil Kautsky and Steve Barker.

Word spread fast throughout the city about the Ambassador Theatre’s new inhabitants and the management team quickly went to work on booking bands into the storied venue. Finestra negotiated with the William Morris Agency in New York, which offered him a platter of both up-and-coming and already-established blues and rock and roll acts that were available for short engagements in the $1,500-$2,000 price range. The first choice for their grand opening was the Grateful Dead, who were booked for a five-night stand from

Tuesday, June 20 through Saturday, June 24, 1967. The opening band for this engagement was supposed to be the Children of Paradise. Unfortunately, in a situation that was hazy on detail at the time, entertainment permits and licenses were initially denied by mysterious bureaucratic figures for no apparent reason, and the concert was nullified, despite the fact the band had shipped their equipment to the Ambassador ahead of schedule, where it sat for days untouched on the open stage. The Grateful Dead couldn't wait for a makeup date and carried on with their tour, leaving the Washington, D.C. gig behind them.

The truth of the Ambassador's roadblock was soon revealed. When Capt. Charles M. Monroe of the Metropolitan Police discovered that a group calling itself the Psychedelic and Power and Light Company was coming in to take over the Ambassador Theatre, he embarked on a personal one-man campaign to keep the young entrepreneurs out of the facility. He wrote a letter urging area merchants and residents to protest the opening of the Ambassador and along with other policemen distributed it to residents and merchants in the immediate area of the theatre. The ploy temporarily worked, as the Government of the District of Columbia Department of Licenses and Inspections initially denied the dance hall permit, forcing the Grateful Dead concert to be cancelled.

A hearing regarding this situation was called before the Government of the District of Columbia Department of Licenses and Inspections on Thursday, June 29, 1967. A total of 12 neighbors of the Ambassador Theatre protested against its opening, complaining it would cause parking problems, increase the crime rate and cause elevated noise levels. Many at the hearing expressed concern over the negative connotation raised by the term "psychedelic." The oldest witness of the day, 86-year-old Gover M. Koockogey testified that the hall would attract the "disgraceful set of people" he'd seen at Dupont Circle and on the P Street Beach. A group of people that testified on behalf of the Ambassador Theatre – promoters of the hall, several young people, one clergyman and lawyer John Diguid – insisted that no harm would come from the venue, only good.

After considering the mountain of testimony and evidence, the Government of the District of Columbia Department of Licenses and Inspections announced on Thursday, July 13, 1967 that the promoters of the dance hall would be given a license to operate, concluding that there were "no legal grounds" for denying their application.

Finestra, Rodgers and Mednick then obtained the required permits and kicked things off with a two-night grand opening show on Friday, July 28, 1967 and Saturday, July 29, 1967 featuring the Peanut Butter Conspiracy and the Mandrake Memorial. More than a thousand fans showed for the gig and the Ambassador Theatre entrepreneurs were in business. It was the start of an amazing and tumultuous six-month run.

One of the highlights of the Ambassador Theatre experience was the psychedelic light show that dazzled the audience as the music blared. Designed by author-environmentalist Paul Hawken and abstract filmmaker Scott Bartlett, who were brought over from San Francisco to create the system, the light show itself consisted of 16 rotary slide projectors, eight 16-mm movie projectors and four overhead transparency projectors that provided for a continual flow and ebb of light and color. When the concerts were in session the light show was operated by Jerry Marmelstein and Mike Saaks, whose objective was to have form replace formlessness within a psychedelic backdrop.

One of the Ambassador Theatre's greatest presentations took place early in its existence. During negotiations with the William Morris Agency, the opportunity was presented to book a new band from England called the Jimi Hendrix Experience, which was coming off a sensational performance at the Monterey Pop Festival that had thrust them into the forefront of rock and roll in America. The band could be had for a five-night stand at the total cost of $1,500. The deal was sealed and Jimi Hendrix, Mitch Mitchell and Noel

Redding breezed into town, checked into the Shoreham Hotel on Calvert Street NW and settled in for what is now a legendary week-long stay in the nation's capital.

The Jimi Hendrix performed at the Ambassador Theatre from Wednesday, August 9 through Sunday, August 13, 1967, with most reports telling the evening concerts were sparsely attended at first, but grew as word spread. During their stay, the band reportedly made daily visits to the Showboat Lounge across the stage for their afternoon meals, showed up at parties at various communes in and around the Dupont Circle area, and spent some of their down time hanging out in Georgetown, including one instance where Tony Finestra took Hendrix to the Silver Dollar Restaurant on M Street NW to witness and jam with guitarist Roy Buchanan, who was working the club with a band called the Uncalled Four.

During their Ambassador run, the Jimi Hendrix Experience also performed at the "Youth Concert" that was staged in the theatre on Thursday, August 10, 1967. This event, which was planned and administered by a team of local night club owners, the Adams Morgan Community Council and the DC Federation, began at 3pm and also featured such musical acts as the Family Album, Les McCann Ltd., Donald Leace, the Paul Hawkins Latin Jazz Quintet and Natty Bumpo. This particular performance was especially noteworthy for the fact that when the Jimi Hendrix Experience performed their three-song set, Natty Bumpo drummer Bill Havu was called upon to sub for an ailing Mitch Mitchell and reportedly did an exceptional job filling the drum seat.

Another historic rock and roll moment occurred at the Ambassador Theatre when, at the conclusion of the band's second show on the night of Saturday, August 12, Hendrix burned his guitar onstage for the third time ever in his career. In addition, at the conclusion of the band's final show on Sunday, August 13, Hendrix reportedly smashed his black Stratocaster onstage, the signed body of which, after spending time on display in the Ambassador's lobby until its closing, ultimately ended up in the possession of Ambassador announcer-poster artist Mike Paper, who maintained possession of the unique souvenir for years before it was taken away in a home robbery in the early 1970s. (According to Mike Paper, Hendrix signed the white pick guard: "Good luck, be cool, Jimi Hendrix, 8/13/67.")

Some of the musical performers that graced the Ambassador stage during its run were truly amazing and many went on to help define the rock and roll culture of the 1960s. Among these acts were Vanilla Fudge, Canned Heat, the Youngbloods, the Paul Butterfield Blues Band, John Lee Hooker, Strawberry Alarm Clock, Moby Grape and the Hollies. Local bands that were frequently called upon to perform on these shows included Natty Bumpo, the Fallen Angels, the Mosaic Virus, the Reachers, Clockwork Orange and the Crystal Mesh (which included a young guitarist named Nils Lofgren).

There was also a number of unique counterculture presentations staged at the Ambassador Theatre, including a weekend of activities surrounding "The March on the Pentagon," a protest march against the Vietnam War that took place on Saturday, October 21, 1967, beginning at the Lincoln Memorial and finishing outside the Pentagon building. The Ambassador served as the weekend's starting point when it hosted a benefit by the Artists of Conscience on the night of Thursday, October 19 that featured anti-war presentations by several writers and social critics including Norman Mailer, Paul Goodman, Robert Lowell and Dwight McDonald. Proceeds from this event went to the National Mobilization to End the War in Vietnam, a coalition of leftist organizations that sponsored Saturday afternoon's march. Live entertainment was offered at the Ambassador Theatre throughout the weekend, with the Fugs and the Mosaic Virus headlining the venue Friday through Sunday nights.

As the months wore on, the task of operating the Ambassador Theatre became problematic, with growing overhead costs, escalating band fees, erratic attendance figures and ever-present police pressure all contributing to a precarious financial situation that became increasingly difficult to manage. An unusual "Happening" was staged in the Ambassador on Sunday, January 7, 1968 that paired journalist Art Buchwald with avant-garde silk screen artist Sister Mary Corita (then an art professor at Immaculate Heart of Mary College in Los Angeles, California), who displayed her latest works to the beat of piped-in Beatles music.

After the Sunday "Happening," the closing of the theatre became inevitable. Two nights of soul music by local bands were offered, but the venue's fate was sealed. On Wednesday, January 10, 1968 the equipment was moved out, the doors were locked and its various managers and employees bid farewell and prepared to move on to other ventures. The Ambassador Theatre was closed for good. The building then sat vacant until falling to the wrecking ball on or around Monday, September 29, 1969. The theatre's former site currently hosts a SunTrust bank marked 1800 Columbia Road NW.

In retrospect, the Ambassador Theatre, although short-lived, played an important role in the Washington, D.C. area rock and roll scene for several reasons. It placed Washington, D.C. on the country's psychedelic rock and roll ballroom circuit, making the city a destination for many of the national acts that specialized in this type of music; it provided special opportunities for select local rock and roll bands to open concerts for prestigious, touring headlining groups; and it existed as a place of live music within walking distance of Dupont Circle, the city's primary countercultural neighborhood. A legendary musical institution of the nation's capital, the Ambassador Theatre, though longtime gone, lingers in flashback fashion in the memories of many of the area's rock and roll veterans.

*The following is a list of the Ambassador Theatre's advertised performances from its opening on Friday, July 28, 1967 until its closing on Wednesday, January 10, 1968:

Friday, July 28, 1967 and Saturday, July 29, 1967
Peanut Butter Conspiracy, the Mandrake Memorial, Natty Bumpo

Wednesday, August 2 to Sunday, August 6, 1967
The Free Spirits, the Ragamuffins

Wednesday, August 9 to Sunday, August 13, 1967
The Jimi Hendrix Experience, Natty Bumpo

Wednesday, August 16 to Sunday, August 20, 1967
The Wildflower, Natty Bumpo, the U.S. Male

Wednesday, August 23 to Saturday, August 26, 1967
Vanilla Fudge, Lothar and the Hand People, the Fallen Angels

Wednesday, August 30 to Sunday, September 3, 1967
The Paupers, the U.S. Male

Tuesday, September 5, 1967
"The Psychedelic Ball" featuring December's Children

Friday, September 8 to Sunday, September 10, 1967
Keith and the Wild Kingdom

Friday, September 15 to Sunday, September 17, 1967
The Critters, the U.S. Male

Thursday, September 21, 1967
The Lady Bird Johnson Counter Inaugural Ball

Friday, September 22 to Sunday, September 24, 1967
Junior Wells and His Chicago Blues Band, the U.S. Male, Clockwork Orange

Friday, September 29 to Sunday, October 1, 1967
Canned Heat, Clockwork Orange

Friday, October 6 to Sunday, October 8, 1967
The Youngbloods, Clockwork Orange

Friday, October 13 to Sunday, October 15, 1967
The Paul Butterfield Blues Band, the Mosaic Virus, Trip Ship

Thursday, October 19, 1967
A benefit by the Artists of Conscience with proceeds going to the National Mobilization to End the War in Vietnam, a coalition that was sponsoring the March on the Pentagon – this event featured speeches by a number of writers and social critics including Norman Mailer, Paul Goodman, Robert Lovell, Dwight Macdonald

Friday, October 20 to Sunday, October 22, 1967
The Fugs, the Mosaic Virus

Friday, October 27 to Sunday, October 29, 1967
John Lee Hooker, the Mosaic Virus

Tuesday, October 31, 1967
The Jokers Club Presents Halloween Hallucinations

Friday, November 3 to Sunday, November 5, 1967
The Cousin Duffy Show

Friday, November 10 to Monday, November 13, 1967
Strawberry Alarm Clock, the Mosaic Virus

Tuesday, November 14, 1967
Thorinshield

Friday, November 17 to Sunday, November 19, 1967
The Fallen Angels

Thursday, November 23 to Sunday, November 26, 1967
"Psychedelic Spectacular" featuring the Sunshine Company, the Reachers (opening act on Thursday's night show)

Wednesday, November 29, 1967
Benefit Concert for the Concerned Citizens for Peace featuring Tom Lehrer, the New Lost City Ramblers, the Lion's Den, Donald Leace

Friday, December 1, 1967 and Saturday, December 2, 1967
Moby Grape, the Crystal Mesh, the Mosaic Virus

Friday, December 8, 1967 and Saturday, December 9, 1967
The Children of Paradise, three other bands

Sunday, December 10, 1967
The Hollies, the Crystal Mesh, the Mosaic Virus, the Plain Brown Wrapper, the Children of Paradise

Friday, December 15 to Sunday, December 17, 1967
Circus Maximum

Thursday, December 21, 1967
The Fallen Angels, the Telstars, the Reachers, the Chocolate Snowflake, the Mosaic Virus

Wednesday, December 27 to Friday, December 29, 1967
Circus Maximus

Sunday, December 31, 1967
The Children of Paradise

Thursday, December 21, 1967 to Monday, January 1, 1968
Open every night with local bands

Sunday, January 7, 1968
Sister Mary Corita, Art Buchwald

Monday, January 8 and Tuesday, January 9, 1968
Local soul music bands

Wednesday, January 10, 1968
The Ambassador Theatre closes

CHAPTER EIGHTY-FOUR
MONUMENTS OF THE LOCAL ROCK AND ROLL SCENE

Throughout the 1950s, 1960s and early 1970s a number of individuals contributed to the local rock and roll scene by promoting live music events and concerts, writing about local music in various publications, or working in some other aspect of the music industry such as night club administration, management, radio programming, or record production and sales. The teen dance scene remained strong during the 1960s with promoters staging these functions in one of two ways: through organized teen clubs that held events and activities in set locations such as schools, churches, public facilities or privately owned buildings; or as privately administered live music events that utilized a wide range of locations and venues. In the 1970s, with increases in the number of bands and musicians on the scene and advances in technology, the presentation of live music swayed towards night club engagements and larger concerts with a growing emphasis on the pursuit of record deals and album production. In the nation's capital several persons made unique contributions to the evolution of rock and roll music.

During the late 1950s as "The Milt Grant Show" was the most popular live music television show in the Washington, D.C. area, a 250-watt radio station in Wheaton, Maryland called WDON was broadcasting a popular rock and roll program called "The Record Club." Hosted by an energetic disc jockey named Don Dillard, this innovative production drew an enthusiastic listening audience and significantly increased the popularity of rock and roll music with local teens. The man behind the microphone, Don Dillard, was an industrious music industry entrepreneur and was one of the first local promoters to take national popular music acts, mix them together with the top teen bands of the regions and present them in live teen dance record hop formats at area armories and halls before large, enthusiastic crowds.

Donald Everett Dillard was born on Friday, February 8, 1935 in Kansas City, Missouri and moved with his family to Silver Spring, Maryland at age five. His father Everett was an audio engineer who traveled the country designing and constructing radio stations. In the nation's capital he created station WASH-FM in 1944 and was co-founder and president of the Continental FM Network, an organization of 52 stations. In 1947 he established WDON-AM, a 250-watt AM station at 2647 University Boulevard in Wheaton, Maryland that he named after his son.

Don Dillard graduated from Montgomery Blair High School in 1953 and briefly attended the University of Maryland. After serving in the United States Air Force he began working as a disc jockey at WDON-AM in 1955. At the time of his arrival, the station was broadcasting jazz and classical music, but in 1956 Dillard went against the established order created a new program that featured a raucous mix of rock and roll and R&B. He called his new show "The Record Club" and it initially aired at 1540 on the AM dial from Monday to Friday, 6am to 9am and 3:30pm to 6:45pm and on Saturdays from 2pm to 6:45pm.

Dillard was impressed with the teen dance scene that was developing in the area and he began negotiating with national record companies to bring in some of their acts for live local performances. At the same time, dance show host Milt Grant entered the fray and the two went head-to-head in friendly competition, taking turns booking the same local facilities for teen dances and concerts.

Dillard initially called his events "Record Hops" and throughout the late 1950s utilized the local group Terry and the Pirates as his teen dance house band. His first show was held in the spring of 1957 in Rosensteel Hall at the Knights of Columbus Father Rosensteel

Council 2169 in Silver Spring, Maryland. Reportedly, over one thousand teens showed up at that event to see the Starlighters (featuring singer Van McCoy) and Terry and the Pirates.

Dillard's larger live music shows in the late 1950s and early 1960s were held at a variety of locations including the Silver Spring Armory, Glen Echo Park's Spanish Ballroom, the Hyattsville Armory and the Bladensburg Volunteer Fire Department. From 1957 to 1959 he regularly offered shows topped by Ray Vernon and Terry and the Pirates at the Silver Spring Armory and Terry and the Pirates at the Hyattsville Armory. In the early 1960s Dillard presented and emceed shows at the Bladensburg Volunteer Fire Department that were headlined by such acts as Link Wray and His Ray Men, Bo Diddley, the Hot Tamales, Barry Darvell and the Blazers, Chubby Checker, the Miracles, the Shangri-Las, Danny and the Juniors and Joey Dee and the Starlighters.

When the Beatles and the bands of the British Invasion began changing the course of rock and roll in 1964 Dillard began to slowly retreat from the teen dance business, leaving those bookings to a younger WDON employee named Barry Richards, who would go on to become one of the most celebrated rock and roll disc jockeys and television music show hosts the nation's capital has ever known. In 1966 WDON switched to a C&W music format and Dillard left the station for good. He went on to spend more than two decades as a circulation distributor for the Baltimore Sun newspaper. He died on Thursday, May 28, 2009 at the age of 74.

The next prominent teen dance promoter on the scene was John Anthony "Jack" Alix, who was born in Chicago, Illinois on Sunday, October 4, 1942 and grew up with his single mother on Hawaii Avenue NE in Washington, D.C. During his teen years at Archbishop Carroll High School, he danced on "The Milt Grant Show" and attended Grant's live record hops, activities that inspired him to begin booking teen dances on his own.

Alix was shrewd and just as Milt Grant's show was taken off the air he began placing ads under "Notices" in the "Teen" section of the Evening Star (Washington, D.C.). Alix placed his teen dance notice in the Evening Star of Sunday, April 2, 1961 for a "Teen Music Marathon Record Hop" to take place on Friday, April 7 featuring the Hot Tamales at the Clinton Volunteer Fire Department in Prince George's County, Maryland. Reportedly, the dance was a rousing success and Jack Alix was in the music business.

Throughout the summer and fall months of 1961 Alix held regular "Teen Marathon Record Hops" at Washington, D.C. locations such as the Shrine of the Sacred Heart Teen Club, Mackin High School and St. Anthony's School. He booked shows in the suburbs as well, with a "Jack Alix Dance Spectacular" on Friday, July 21, 1961 at the Silver Spring Boys Club featuring Link Wray and His Ray Men, the Hot Tamales, the Chessmen, the Rhythm Masters and Bristow Hopper. Alix also booked several Clinton, Maryland facilities for his dances including Church of St. John the Evangelist, the Clinton Volunteer Fire Department, American Legion Clinton Post 259 and Surrattsville High School. By September 1961 he was advertising his popular dances as "Teen-Athons."

In January 1962 Alix was hired as a full-time pop music disc jockey at station WEEL in Fairfax, Virginia. It was his introduction to the world of radio broadcasting and he followed up his two-year stint at that station with stops as a rock and roll jock at such Washington, D.C. area stations as WEAM (1964-1966, and again in the early 1970s) and WPGC (1966-1969). In 1969 he returned to WEEL with a progressive rock and roll program entitled "Jack Alix Underground." A personal highlight for Alix during this period occurred when he was chosen to be one of four emcees to host the Beatles' first American concert that took place at the Washington Coliseum on Tuesday, February 11, 1964. When Paul McCartney first hit the stage that evening, it was Alix who greeted him with a handshake.

Alix's stature as a radio personality grew and during the late 1960s he was frequently called upon to emcee local rock and roll concerts for promoters such as Bud Becker and Durwood Settles. Some of the shows Alix was hosted included: a WPGC happening entitled "Psychedelia" at the Alexandria Arena on Saturday, May 6, 1967 headlined by December's Children and the Town Criers, the latter of which was christened as the "J.A. the D.J. Band of the Year;" a "Flower Power Show" at the Alexandria Arena on Friday, August 18, 1967 that was booked by Bud Becker and Domestic Sound Productions and featured the Doors, the Blades of Grass, and a 12-band competition for a Columbia Records recording contract – it was at this now-legendary event that Alix, who was acting as emcee for the night, got into an onstage altercation with Jim Morrison over control of the main microphone; and a multi-act show Alix himself promoted and emceed at W.T. Woodson High School in Fairfax, Virginia on Saturday, November 11, 1967 that featured the Chartbusters, the Sweet, the New Delphonics, the McCormick Tool Company and the Apollos.

A music television program entitled "Wing Ding" first aired on WDCA-TV Channel 20 on Thursday, April 21, 1966 with Kerby Scott as the initial host. Broadcasting live from the WDCA-TV studio at 5202 River Road in Bethesda, Maryland, the show initially aired from 4pm to 5pm on a Monday-to-Saturday schedule and was similar in format to "American Bandstand" in the way if featured live pop and rock and roll bands performing in front of a studio audience consisting of dancing teens.

Jack Alix was recruited to take over as host of "Wing Ding" beginning with their Thursday, May 23, 1968 broadcast, replacing Scott Wallace. During its run the program offered a mix of local and nationally known pop and rock and roll bands. On Monday, December 2, 1968 WDCA-TV officially changed the name of the program from "Wing Ding" to "The Jack Alix Show." The newly named program continued on with the same format as its predecessor for another seven months, with its final episode airing on Sunday, July 13, 1969.

Alix relocated to the Richmond, Virginia area in the early 1970s and worked in sales and promotions for a number of different radio stations. During the late 1970s and early 1980s he hosted a nationally syndicated radio show entitled "Rock 'n' Roll Roots" which broadcast over 140 stations nationwide. He later held management positions at radio stations in Florida, Michigan, Missouri, West Virginia and Virginia before returning to Washington, D.C. in the middle 1990s as operations manager and co-host of a morning drive show on WXTR-FM. During this time he also served as director of the Columbia School of Broadcasting in Washington, D.C. More recently he served as head of marketing and promotions for Clear Channel Communications in Richmond, Virginia. Jack Alix died at on Wednesday, November 15, 2006 at the age of 64.

One of the most popular disc jockey-promoters to ever emerge from the nation's capital is Barry Richards, who, for more than 20 years, had a hand in almost every aspect of the administration of rock and roll music in the Washington, D.C. area. In an amazing and colorful career, Richards went from local roles as radio station employee, on-air personality (where he was unabashedly hailed as "The Boss with the Hot Sauce"), teen dance organizer, concert emcee and music television program host, to radio executive positions around the country, and ultimately, to his current position as one of the leading record company consultants in Hollywood. His showcasing of local bands and musicians through live events and radio and television broadcasts combined with his work in bringing nationally known rock and roll acts to town stimulated the local music scene throughout the 1960s and 1970s and earned him recognition as an iconic figure in local rock and roll history.

Most of the early personal history of Barry Richards is locked in obscurity, largely because of conflicting information provided to various journalists by Richards himself. It is believed that he was born Barry Benjamin Richards on Monday, November 23, 1942 and grew up in Washington, D.C. Reportedly he attended Paul Junior High School in the Northwest neighborhood of the city and Chamberlain Vocational High School in the Southeast quadrant of the city, ultimately graduating from Emerson Preparatory School in 1962. As a teen he developed a love for all types of popular music and became an avid follower of "The Milt Grant Show."

At some point, probably around 1960, Richards was hired as a personal assistant to Don Dillard at radio station WDON in Wheaton, Maryland. As the popular story goes, Richards had been hitchhiking down Georgia Avenue with a friend when police took after them in hot pursuit, leading the teenager to run into the radio station where Dillard impulsively hid him under a stereo console. The two then talked for a while, got along well, and Richards was hired to sweep floors, get coffee and carry cargo to and from teen dances. He eventually began filling in for Dillard on the air when the disc jockey was running late or feeling ill. From there Richards was granted a program on WDON entitled "Spotlight on Teens" which featured a mixture of R&B and rock and roll songs and served as his very first on-air radio show.

In 1961 Richards began assisting Don Dillard on his various live music record hops around the Washington, D.C. area. He observed Dillard closely and began using these events as a springboard for his own promotions and live music events. In 1962 he left WDON and took a disc jockey position at WHMC, a brand new station owned by Nick Chaconas on a patch of rolling farmland in Gaithersburg, Maryland. His stint at the small Montgomery County station saw him host a daily rock and roll show from 12am to 6am, but after a seven-month run he opted to leave the station and book, promote and emcee local teen dance events.

In one of his more interesting ventures of this time, Richards hosted "Beatle Night" on Monday, February 10, 1964 at the Shelter Room, a somewhat rough, subterranean night club in the Congress Heights neighborhood of Southeast Washington, D.C. Staged the night before the Fab Four made their United States concert debut at the Washington Coliseum, this unique party offered Beatles wigs and souvenirs, a dance contest, 59-cent drinks, and music by the Shelter Room's house band, the Dominoes.

The following Monday Richards was back at the Shelter hosting "Party Night" with R&B singer Jimmy Velvet, along with the ever-present Dominoes. He then followed up those ambitious ventures with something advertised as the "Barry Richards Swing Soiree" at Strick's Restaurant in Prince George's County, Maryland on Sunday, March 8, 1964. The all-day event, which ran from 2pm to 12am, featured performances by the Kingsmen (a nine-piece local R&B band) and Tommy Cole and the Belvederes. Other offering included 50-cent drinks, free 45rpm single records to the first 100 ladies, a cash money dance contest and free movie tickets.

During the latter half of the 1960s, Richards worked in the area as a rock and roll disc jockey at several different radio stations, booked numerous live music shows, and was called upon by various promoters to emcee some of the region's top concerts. He spent the summer of 1964 working his own radio show at WMID in Atlantic City, New Jersey and then went through a succession of stations including WYRE (Annapolis, Maryland), WITH (Baltimore, Maryland) WUST (Washington, D.C.), WINX (Rockville, Maryland), and WANN (Annapolis, Maryland).

In September 1968 Richards returned to station WHMC where he hosted a free-form progressive music show entitled "The Barry Richards Underground Show," in the process becoming known over the airwaves as "The Heavy Head Leader." Richards's slot began as a two-hour Saturday program and achieved such immediate popularity it soon turned into a daily show, leading owner Chaconas to switch the entire station to a 24-hour underground music format. Other disc jockeys to work at WHMC during this time were Nick Chaconas Jr., Steve Walker, Ed Painter and Mike Scott. Richards remained at WHMC until April 1973. Afterwards he spent the remainder of the 1970s working for a succession of radio stations including WKTK (Baltimore, Maryland), WEEL (Fairfax, Virginia), WMOD (Washington, D.C.) and WEAM (Arlington, Virginia).

It was during the 1960s that Richards achieved his status as one of the most sought-after rock and roll personalities in the area through his involvement in the administration of live music events. Seemingly he was everywhere, hosting teen dances in local community centers and churches, promoting his own shows, and emceeing concerts by nationally known performing artists in some of the region's larger venues. Several nights per week he was on the move and became an instantly recognizable figure on the local music scene. He left his mark on the local airwaves, negotiated dates with the area's top bands, and made preparations for some of the major incoming rock and roll acts that were readying their visits to the nation's capital.

The list of concerts and dances Richards was involved with during these years is impressive. Even a limited sample of some of the events he was involved with will sufficiently illustrate his importance to a music scene that championed both R&B and rock and roll and attracted a following of teens and young adults who were changing with the times around them.

From March to October 1966 Richards hosted what he advertised as a "Swing Soiree" on Friday nights at the Bladensburg Volunteer Fire Department in Bladensburg, Maryland, bringing in headliners such as Link Wray and His Ray Men, Bo Diddley, the Coasters, the British Walkers, the Hot Tamales, T.N.T. Turner and His Band, Phil Flowers and the Flower Shop and Big Al Downing and His Band.

On Wednesday, July 20, 1966, in conjunction with radio station WUST, Richards hosted a performance by Little Richard and his 15-piece band at Glen Echo Park's Spanish Ballroom; on Saturday, April 8, 1967 he hosted a concert by Wilson Pickett and the Marvelettes at Walt Whitman High School in Bethesda; on Saturday, April 15, 1967 he kicked off a summer-long series of dances at the Gaithersburg Agricultural Center with a bill that featured the Kitchen Cinque, Bob Brady and the Concords and King's Row; on Saturday, January 20, 1968 he hosted a "Soul Battle of the Bands" at the Wheaton Youth Center featuring the Laymen and four other bands; and on Friday, September 6, 1968 he did a rare double-shift, presenting shows by the Drifters at two separate facilities in the same night – the Wheaton Youth Center and the Greenbelt Youth Center.

Perhaps the greatest concert Richards was ever responsible for was the now-legendary Led Zeppelin show that is believed to have taken place at the Wheaton Youth Center in Wheaton, Maryland on Monday, January 20, 1969. Booked on short notice and reportedly only advertised for approximately 72 hours on Richards' WHMC radio program, the Zep concert was crammed into the band's first Unites State tour in between shows at the Grande Ballroom in Detroit and an as-yet-unidentified concert somewhere in Pennsylvania.

As the story goes, Richards guaranteed Led Zeppelin a mere $225 for the concert. An estimated 60 concert-goers showed up and the band performed for a scant 40 minutes before manager Peter Grant pulled the plug and demanded additional money from Richards for gas. The problem with this event is that there is no verifiable evidence to conclusively prove the concert ever actually took place, aside from the eyewitness testimony of Richards and a couple-dozen individuals who claimed to have been in attendance that night. No ticket stubs, no posters, no photographs, no contracts, no audio tapes and no reviews of the show have ever surfaced. In 2013 a feature-length independent documentary film entitled "Led Zeppelin Played Here" (produced by Jeff Krulik, John Heyn and Brad Dismukes) made its debut, providing a detailed story about this particular concert and including on-screen commentary from Richards himself.

From 1969 to 1972 Richards booked and emceed (usually in partnership with Bud Becker of Domestic Sound Productions) a number of shows at the Wheaton Youth Center including concerts by the likes of the Stooges (featuring lead singer Iggy Pop), Faces (featuring lead singer Rod Stewart), Grin, Dr. John, Spirit, Rare Earth, Rory Gallagher, the Bob Seger System, and numerous others. He was also called upon to emcee most of the shows at the Alexandria Arena during these years – many of which were booked by promoter Durwood C. Settles in conjunction with Giant Music Centers – that featured such headliners as Blood, Sweat and Tears, Canned Heat, Jethro Tull, Black Sabbath, Alice Cooper, T. Rex and Emerson, Lake and Palmer.

With his reputation as one of the area's top rock and roll personalities intact, Richards was called upon to host a local music television program entitled "Sears Sound Revolution." Airing at 8:30pm on Tuesday, August 19, 1969 on WMAL-TV Channel 7, this one-hour special was co-hosted by Richards and a local model named Dorris Biscoe and featured a mix of progressive rock and roll and soul music, along with a fall fashion show segment. Performing artists on this special show included singer O.C. Smith, Iron Butterfly, Creedence Clearwater Revival, Janis Joplin, Ten Years After, the Impressions, comedian Richard Pryor, and three local bands: Flavor, El Corals, and the Magic Reign. Richards would use this program as a springboard for future television projects.

Nearly a year later, Richards again appeared on local television when WTOP-TV Channel 9 aired a special program of his own making entitled "Barry Richards Presents." This 30-minute musical show was broadcast at 11:15pm on the night of Saturday, June 13, 1970 and featured in-studio performances by Richie Havens, Little Richard, Jamal, Zephyr and the comedian Uncle Dirty. Hosting television programs of this nature seemed a logical extension of his concert work and he pressed on for a local network to hold a regular show of his own.

It didn't take Richards long to find a television station that would give him the opportunity to lead a weekly music program of his own aimed directly at the audiences who for years had been tuning into his radio broadcasts and attending his live music shows. The station in question was WDCA-TV Channel 20, which operated out of a station at 5202 River Road in Bethesda, Maryland. The shows Richards would direct and host for this station were "Turn On," "the Barry Richards Rock Show" and "Barry Richards Rock and Soul."

The first of his WDCA-TV ventures, "Turn On," was presented in a unique, open-ended format with no fixed sign-off time. Richards was allowed to broadcast for as long as he liked – or until the musicians ran out of material and got tired of playing – and he would often keep the show going until the station's morning programs signed on at 7am. The show debuted at 11pm on Saturday, September 12, 1970 with the inaugural program featuring performances by B.B. King, Biff Rose, taped interview segments with actor Buster Crabbe, a Flash Gordon serial, and a Charlie Chaplin movie. The show aired for 10 months and featured some of the top musical guests of the time such as Richie Havens, Little Richard, Ten Years After, Arlo Guthrie, Sea Train, Dr. John, Captain Beefheart, Alice Cooper, Humble Pie, Rory Gallagher, Ace Trucking Company, and dozens of others. The final episode of "Turn On" aired on Saturday, July 17, 1971.

Next up on WDCA-TV was "The Barry Richards Rock Show," a program which featured live in-studio musical performances similar to what was offered on "Turn On," but adhered to a one-hour time limit and aired at various times on Saturdays. The very first episode aired at 9:30am on the morning of Saturday, April 6, 1974 with the first guest being the band Alice Cooper, which was fresh off its "Billion Dollar Babies" tour. "The Barry Richards

Rock Show" last aired under this name on Saturday, May 17, 1975. A name change then occurred and one week later at 10:30pm on Saturday, May 24, 1975, the show was replaced by "Barry Richards Rock and Soul." This program carried on until its final episode aired at 8pm on Saturday, September 6, 1975.

Despite the cancellation of his WDCA-TV shows, Richards remained a force in the Washington, D.C. area's music scene. As the 1970s pressed on, he continued to work at various local radio stations and hosted dance events at local night clubs. He also hosted yet another local television program, this one a short-lived disco show on WMAL-TV entitled "Studio 78." By September 1979 he had slowed down his operations and that month he began presenting disc jockey shows at a night club called Club Images on K Street NW in Downtown Washington, D.C.

In 1980 Barry Richards left the Washington, D.C. area and moved to New Orleans, Louisiana where he spent several years working for a number of different radio and television stations. In 1985 he relocated to Los Angeles, California and became a key figure in the national entertainment industry as a writer, analyst, producer, promoter, administrator and occasional on-air radio personality. He remains based in Hollywood and is currently a highly sought-after entertainment corporation consultant.

Bud Becker, who hails from Oneonta, New York, was a 23-year-old audio specialist in the United States Army when he was assigned to Fort Myer in Arlington County, Virginia in 1965. His involvement in the local popular music scene took place when he formed a Washington, D.C.-based disc jockey service called Lape the Ape and Blimp the Chimp that serviced the area's military base officers' clubs. In due time he was organizing teen dances at local churches, community centers and schools and before the year was out he formed a Falls Church, Virginia-based booking agency called Domestic Sound Productions.

Becker specialized in teenaged rock and roll bands and among the more than 200 groups he booked were such popular acts as the Plum Beach Incident, December's Children, the New Del-Phonics, Gnu Generation, the Warlox, Michael and the Power, the Gents, Venus and the Fly Traps, the Village Squires, the Lemon-Blues, the Incredible Fog, Cape Breton Union, Fantastic Plastic, the Hounds of Baskerville, the Magic Reign and Penny Arcade. Domestic Sound Productions quickly developed into the largest rock and roll booking outfit in Northern Virginia.

Most of the younger bands that went through Domestic Sound Productions worked teen dances throughout Northern Virginia, Washington, D.C., and Montgomery and Prince George's Counties, Maryland. However, as Becker's roster grew in quantity and quality in the late 1960s, a number of local promoters began approaching him with offers to hire his clients as opening acts for nationally known rock and roll acts that would be performing concerts in and around the nation's capital. As a result, local entrepreneurs such as Jack Alix and Barry Richards began to partner with Becker on larger shows that were staged at facilities like the Alexandria Arena, the Wheaton Youth Center and the Falls Church Community Center.

Becker was brought on board as a booking agent, arranger and producer for a number of now-legendary local rock and roll concerts. One of the venues he was very involved with was the Alexandria Arena where, during the late 1960s alone, he helped stage shows by such major performers as the Yardbirds, the Buckinghams, Neil Diamond, the Count Five, the Turtles, the Doors, and numerous others. Becker maintained Domestic Sound Productions as a major source of talent for the local rock and roll dance scene through 1973.

Becker has remained tied to the local entertainment industry for years as a consultant and marketing specialist through his own company, Bud Becker Consultants. From 1986 to 1992 he served as an advertising and promotions consultant and national talent buyer for

Hammerjack's Night Club and Concert Hall in Baltimore, Maryland. In recent years he has owned Digital Sound DJ Service, in addition to working with other DJ services throughout Maryland, and was a co-founder of College Underground Radio. He currently maintains an Ebay memorabilia site called Saintlun Emporium and has produced a series of "Memories of the Road" CDs that chronicle his personal experiences in the popular music industry.

Another noteworthy proponent of the Washington, D.C. area music scene is Charlie Tompkey, who has served in several fascinating capacities since the 1960s. Tompkey was born in East Stroudsburg, Pennsylvania in 1942, raised in nearby Coolbaugh Township, and grew up listening to such musical performers as Gene Vincent, Little Richard and Chuck Berry.

Tompkey moved to Groveton, Virginia in 1965 and spent the next four years as a Fairfax County police officer. He became a part of the local music scene through his work as a uniformed police security guard at rock and roll teen dances and shows at a number of area facilities including St. Alban's Episcopal Church in Annandale, where regular performers included the English Setters and the Hangmen. In an unusual chain of events, he worked security for a concert by Vanilla Fudge at the B.P.O. Elks Lodge No. 2188 Arlington-Fairfax in Fairfax, Virginia in the late 1960s, met the band members backstage and got along with them very well, and began entertaining thoughts of getting into the local music business as a manager and booking agent.

On Friday, August 18, 1967 the Doors performed a concert at the Alexandria Arena in Alexandria, Virginia. Tompkey was in attendance and was intrigued by the opening rock and roll attraction – a 12-band competition for an audition with Columbia Records in New York City which was won by a Northern Virginia group called Gary Scott and the Classics. He subsequently formed his own Annandale-based booking agency, T.O.P. Productions, and began placing Gary Scott and the Classics into local teen dances, with nearby St. Alban's Episcopal Church becoming a regular gig. He began booking local bands into teen dances throughout Northern Virginia and in the late 1960s brought several national acts to the area including the 1910 Fruitgum Company and the Ohio Express, both of whom performed concerts at his favorite venue, St. Alban's Episcopal Church in Annandale.

Tompkey remained the head of T.O.P. Productions from 1968 to 1973. He then worked as a booking agent for Barry Rick Associates from 1973 to 1975 where he handled the agency's placing of bands that were based in Northern Virginia. In the early 1970s one of the most popular bands he worked with was Steve Bishop and the Chessmen. In addition, a top professional night club band he managed early in the decade was Starr, a rock and roll group that worked long engagements at the Bayou in Georgetown. Starr's lineup consisted of singer Lorraine Cohen, guitarist Joe Reino, bassist Tim Wynne, keyboardist George Rivers and drummer Vince Santoro.

In October 1976 Mike Munley, owner of the newly opened night club Louie's Rock City in Bailey's Crossroads, Virginia, hired Tompkey to manage his establishment. The emphasis during the club's first year was on local rock and roll bands and among the acts to perform there were Face Dancer, Sinbad, Grande Hotel, Artful Dodger, the Roadducks, the Nowhere Men, Wizzard, Tahoka and the Nighthawks, among others. In the ensuing years the night club brought in such national acts as Johnny Winter, Chuck Berry, Canned Heat, the Ramones and Judas Priest. Tompkey remained at Louie's Rock City for over a year, but in 1978 he worked for a time as an agent for P.H.L. Associates, a Silver Spring-based jazz music booking agency run by Peter Lambros, before accepting the management offer from a band in Los Angeles that was breaking on the national music scene.

In 1971 Tompkey witnessed a pop-rock band from Richmond, Kentucky called the Exiles perform at a night club in Washington, D.C. called My Mother's Place. He was impressed with what he saw and arranged future performances for the band at two different Alexandria, Virginia locations, Fort Hunt High School and T.C. Williams High School. These shows led to an association with the group (which changed its name to "Exile" in 1973) that lasted through 1978. Tompkey booked the band throughout the Washington, D.C. area for several years in the 1970s at venues like the Bayou and then served as their full-time manager in Los Angeles for several months in 1978. The group released the single "Kiss You All Over" (Exile; Curb Records, 1978), which peaked at number one on Billboard's "Billboard Hot 100" pop music chart on Saturday, September 30, 1978. Under Tompkey's guidance the band then toured the United States, performing in arenas and concert halls co-billed with such acts as Aerosmith and Seals and Crofts. Tompkey's association with Exile ended in January 1979.

Back in the Washington, D.C. area, Tompkey rejoined P.H.L. Associates as a booking agent in 1979 but resigned in 1980. After being employed for several years in private industry, he worked as a real estate agent in Northern Virginia from 1988 to 2014. In 2012 he re-entered the local music scene by re-establishing T.O.P. Productions in Oakton, Virginia and serving as owner and president. He currently continues to scout and consult with local musical artists.

One of the most influential figures on the local popular music scene is Mike Schreibman, who was born in 1944, is a native Washingtonian, and graduated from the city's Western High School in 1962. Through the years he has experienced nearly every aspect of the local music industry, working behind the scenes in night clubs, booking and promoting concerts and shows, and serving as a co-founder and current director of the Washington Area Musicians Association (WAMA).

Growing up in Washington, D.C., Schreibman avidly listened to music on the radio and on jukeboxes, with Elvis Presley becoming a personal favorite. Friends of his played in bands and in the early and middle 1960s he began hanging out at two folk music night clubs in Georgetown, the Shadows and the Cellar Door. In 1965 he got a job as the light and sound man at Smokey's, a folk music night club that had replaced Julie's Café at 3350 M Street NW and was owned at the time by Jack Boyle and Frank Reis. In the fall of that year the owners changed the establishment into a Cinemateque called Groovy's and Schreibman took over the projectionist position. From there he became a roving manager for Jack Boyle and worked in his various Georgetown night clubs, a lot that included Mac's Pipe and Drum Restaurant, Nu Mac's and the Crazy Horse.

After a six-month stay in Puerto Rico, Schreibman returned to Washington, D.C. in 1967 and worked as a bartender at several local restaurants including the Journey Inn and the Mike Palm Restaurant Rathskeller. He fell in with the team that was staging rock and roll concerts at the Ambassador Theatre and served the operation as a consultant, publicist and snack bar attendant, most often taking the visiting performers out to local radio stations for interviews. At the end of the 1960s he was managing the Showboat Lounge, the basement bar that had previously hosted jazz guitarist Charlie Byrd for years and was located directly across 18th Street NW from the Ambassador. During that time he was also a photographer for a media service called Washington News and became the light man at the Cellar Door.

Schreibman entered the concert arena when he promoted his first large-scale show, an event headlined by Country Joe and the Fish and Iron Butterfly at Merriweather Post Pavilion in Columbia, Maryland on Saturday, August 24, 1968. One of his next major ventures saw him book a concert with Lester Grossman at Merriweather Post Pavilion featuring The Who and Led Zeppelin on Sunday, May 25, 1969. These early examples set the stage for a long list of live concert events that Schreibman staged in and around the nation's capital over the next 35 years.

In August 1969 a new night club called Emergency opened up in Georgetown at 2813 M Street NW, a building that had previously been the site of such establishments as the Roundtable and the Hurricane. The club, which did not have a liquor license and was devoid of tables and chairs, was a long, sloping, narrow room that could hold 200 people. Its front space housed a record store and farther back was a stage and a small dance floor area. Schreibman was part of the club's evolving management team and during its two-year run he was responsible for bringing in a mix of rock and roll acts including local favorites such as Claude Jones, Love Cry Want, Tractor, Grin, and Crank, and national acts like the Rory Gallagher, the Blues Project, the Amboy Dukes (featuring lead guitarist Ted Nugent) and the Kinks. Emergency closed its doors in December 1971, and, after serving for a while as publisher of an arts publication called Woodwind, Schreibman began focusing most of his attention on concert promotion and booking acts into local night clubs such as the Bayou, the Psyche Delly, and, in the 1980s, the Wax Museum.

In 1984 Schreibman became part of a group with Michael Jaworek, then a booking agent at the Warner Theatre, that planned on forming an organization that would stage an annual awards show for local musicians. Thus, the Washington Area Music Association (WAMA) was formed with their first show – "The Washington Area Music Awards" (AKA "The Wammies") – being held at Lisner Auditorium in Washington, D.C. on Sunday, September 29, 1985. At that initial outing more than 40 different music awards were granted to musicians among more than 200 nominees from jazz to pop, go-go to gospel, rap to rock, and bluegrass to hardcore.

The organization's promotional literature states: "WAMA is a non-profit tax exempt organization of music industry professionals committed to raising the profile of the region's diverse music community. WAMA's main goal is to promote Washington area music in general and to achieve national recognition of the region as an important center for live and recorded music." Among WAMA's programs are the Wammies (career achievement awards for area musicians), charitable events including the annual WAMA Crosstown Jam, WAMA Pages (a 100-page directory of Washington area music), seminars, calendars, compact disc compilations of local artists, and the WAMA News newsletter. While Mike Schreibman gave up concert promotion in 2004, he remains involved in the local music scene and currently serves as president and executive director of WAMA.

Richard Harrington was born in Switzerland in 1947 and lived in Europe until age nine, at which time his father, who was employed in the United States Foreign Service, moved the family to Washington, D.C. He attended grade school in the city at Annunciation Catholic School before being enrolled at the Harvey School, a college prep school in Katonah, New York. It was there that he developed an interest in folk music and sang and played guitar in an unnamed folk trio group with fellow singer-guitarists Loudon Wainwright III and John Coster. After graduating from the eighth grade at the Harvey School in 1961 he attended the Hotchkiss School, an elite prep school in Lakeville, Connecticut, for ninth and tenth grades. He then returned to the nation's capital where he passed through Woodrow Wilson High School, the Hawthorne School and Western High School, the last of which he dropped out of just before graduation because he found life on the streets of Georgetown to be far more interesting.

In the middle and late 1960s Harrington became immersed in music and listened to blues, folk and rock and roll. He participated in poetry readings at Coffee 'n' Confusion, hung out at the Unicorn near Dupont Circle, and worked as a bouncer at the French Quarter, a basement rock and roll bar on M Street NW in Georgetown. He played 12-string guitar at the Cellar Door's "Hootenanny" shows, worked at the Washington Free Press answering phones, and, late in the decade, was employed at an independent record shop called Soul Shack.

Harrington had been keeping journals for years and in 1969 he began writing for Quicksilver Times, one of Washington, D.C.'s primary counterculture newspapers. In 1970, with an interest in non-political culture and music, he began publishing Woodwind, which advertised itself as "An Arts Paper." Mike Schreibman handled the publication's advertising and for more than two years the publication existed as a two-man venture. In 1972, Harrington, with an eye on new adventures, bowed out of the picture and Schreibman assumed total control over the magazine's operations. Woodwind kept going until February 1974.

In the wake of his Woodwind experience, Harrington took over the weekly "Music Makers" column in the Evening Star and Washington Daily News newspapers. The column had previously been penned by Michael Oberman, and, as one of the area's most popular recurring music articles, enjoyed a large readership. Harrington's first column appeared in the publication's Saturday, March 31, 1973 edition and featured singer Colin Blunstone (formerly of the Zombies). He continued to write the feature for more than a year, providing coverage on a mix of local and national performing artists. His final "Music Makers" column appeared in the Saturday, May 11, 1974 edition of the Washington Star-News (the newspaper's new name) and profiled the rock band Mott the Hoople.

Harrington then went on to spent time in Boston, Massachusetts before returning to Washington, D.C. where he worked for a while at Discount Records on Connecticut Avenue NW near Dupont Circle. In 1975 he began writing for a music-oriented newspaper called Unicorn Times at the request of editor-publisher Elliot Ryan.

In August 1977 Harrington began writing concert reviews for the Washington Post and was occasionally called upon to provide feature articles for the paper's Style and Show sections. He soon became Washington, D.C.'s premier music journalist and in 1984 the Washington Post finally granted him a full-time, salaried position as the paper's pop music critic. He remained in that capacity until his retirement on Friday, May 30, 2008.

One of the Washington, D.C. area music scene's most endearing and enduring personalities is Joe Lee, who is noted for having been the longtime proprietor of the popular record store, Joe's Record Paradise, and for his contributions to the local music scene as a manager, promoter and entrepreneur. Lee was born in 1947, raised in Montgomery County, Maryland in the city of Silver Spring and the community of Colesville, and graduated from Springbrook High School in 1965. He was raised in a political family as his father Blair Lee III was a democrat politician who served as the second-ever Lieutenant Governor of Maryland from 1971 to 1979 and as Acting Governor of Maryland from Tuesday, January 4, 1977 to Monday, January 15, 1979 (during Marvin Mandel's suspension of gubernatorial duties).

Joe Lee was introduced to music at a young age through the radio and became interested in rock and roll because he wasn't interested in politics. In 1954 at the age of seven he saw his first live band when Vernon Taylor was hired to perform at a private party at his parents' house. He collected records by Elvis Presley and as a teenager he obtained a fake ID and familiarized himself with the local bus system, enabling him to venture downtown and hangout in night clubs where he witnessed musical performers like Phil Flowers at the Hayloft and the British Walkers at the Roundtable. He developed a love for soul music and became a faithful listener of such local radio stations as WOOK, WOL and WUST.

From 1968 to 1970 Lee sang and played drums in a local rock and roll band called Beverly Pureheart, whose lineup included singer-guitarist-trombonist Dick Bangham, lead guitarist Dave Panzer and bassist Neil Thompson. During its time, the group performed locally at a coffee house called Sagitta in Takoma Park, Maryland, some outdoor concerts, and at Nu-Mac's in Georgetown. The group recorded and issued a five-song EP entitled

"Beverly Pureheart" (Beverly Pureheart; Adelphi Records, 1970) and disbanded shortly after its release. In the wake of Beverly Pureheart, Lee relocated to California in 1970 and took a job in a used record store called Platypus Records on Pico Boulevard in Los Angeles. He quickly was promoted to assistant manager of their store on Hollywood Boulevard and remained on the West Coast for four years.

Joe Lee returned to the Washington, D.C. area in 1974 and in September of that year he opened up the first version of Joe's Record Paradise at 7054 Carroll Avenue in Takoma Park, Maryland. The store became a favorite of record collectors from all over the Delmarva region and a focal point for musicians who would gather and hang out on the premises, talking music and soliciting free information from Lee regarding the local music scene and its opportunities. Joe's Record Paradise remained at that location until 1982, after which the store moved through several different locations in Silver Spring and Rockville, Maryland over a period of more than 30 years. The shop is still in business and is currently located in the basement of the Suntrust building at 8700 Georgia Avenue in Silver Spring, Maryland.

One of Joe Lee's most famous adventures was the time he spent managing the notorious singer Root Boy Slim, a bluesy rock and roll frontman whose penchant for partying was as legendary as the lofty reputations of the talented musicians he employed in his various bands. In 1976 Root Boy Slim, real name Foster MacKenzie, would regularly visit Joe's Record Paradise and on one occasion inquired about the whereabouts of Adelphi Records, a business which, at the time, was renting out office space in the back of the record store building. Lee pointed him in the right direction, but, after a brief meeting, a dejected Slim informed the record store proprietor that the record label administrators were not impressed with a demo tape of his band that was played for them. Lee asked to hear the tape, which had been made in Florida and consisted of members of the original Sex Change Band (who were mainly from Florida). He was impressed by the James Brown-like vibe, humorous lyrics and bluesy music and played it for his friend and associate Dick Bangham. Lee and Bangham eventually took Root Boy Slim and his band into Track Recorders in Silver Spring, Maryland to cut a new demo tape.

Lee delivered a copy of the new demo tape to disc jockey Weasel at progressive radio station WHFS, who frequently played the cut "Mood Ring" on the air. Lee then booked Root Boy Slim and his band into local night clubs such as the Psyche Delly, the Varsity Grill Back Room and the Cellar Door. WHFS disc jockey Josh Brooks acquired one of the demos and gave it to an old college friend named Donald Fagen, who was part of the group Steely Dan, which at that point in time had had their first six albums for ABC Records produced by Gary Katz. Fagen liked the tape and gave it to Katz, who had just been hired as an A&R man for Warner Bros. Records. Katz contacted Joe Lee and Dick Bangham and made arrangements to bring Slim and the band into Criteria Studios in Miami, Florida for a recording session. The result of this project was the band's first album, "Root Boy Slim & the Sex Change Band with the Rootettes" (Root Boy Slim & the Sex Change Band; Warner Bros. Records, 1978).

Unfortunately, due to circumstances beyond human control, Warner Bros. never followed through with a second Root Boy Slim album (the record label actually paid the band a healthy sum not to record for them anymore), though Slim continued performing with a variety of local musicians and went on to record and release several more albums on mostly independent labels in the ensuing years. By 1985 Joe Lee had backed out of the Root Boy Slim picture, though he stayed active in the local music scene by maintaining his popular record store, booking and promoting live shows, and generously providing advice, contacts and information for a plethora of players and personalities within the local music scene.

After a transitional period, Joe Lee retired to Hardy County, West Virginia in 2006 and transferred Joe's Record Paradise to his son Johnson Lee. Joe Lee still occasionally promotes live music shows in the Washington, D.C. area.

Michael Oberman was born in Baltimore in 1947 and was mainly raised in Silver Spring, Maryland. He was introduced to music through his father, who sang in the choir at the Chaizuk Amuno synagogue in Baltimore, and his brother Ron, who was four years older and developed an interest in rock and roll in the middle 1950s, with artists such as Elvis Presley, Carl Perkins and Hank Ballard becoming favorites. The Oberman family had a console in their living room and music was an integral part of their lives.

In addition to music, both Michael and Ron Oberman developed interests in journalism during their teen years. In the early 1960s Ron Oberman obtained a job with the Evening Star newspaper as copy boy and was soon promoted to dictationist, typing reporters' stories as they called them in. He impressed the powers at the paper with his writing ability and eventually took over the "Top Tunes" column from reporter James Lee, with his first installment appearing on Friday, February 7, 1964. His initial column of that date – credited to "Ronnie Oberman" – covered a surf band from Los Angeles called the Marketts, who were then making waves with a hit song entitled "Out of Limits." Appearing weekly, "Top Tunes" provided facts and information on a variety of local and national popular music artists.

Michael Oberman followed in his brother's footsteps and took a job as a copy boy at the Evening Star in 1963 at the age of 16. At the time he was still a student at Northwood High School in Silver Spring and was inspired to develop an identity as an artist through two of the institution's faculty members, an art teacher named Frances Avila and a beatnik-styled English instructor named William Tunis. During his teenage years he also began accompanying his brother Ron to local live music shows, including the Beatles' now-historic first United States concert which took place at the Washington Coliseum on Tuesday, February 11, 1964. After graduating high school in 1965, he enrolled at the University of Maryland to study journalism, all the while maintaining his employment with the Evening Star newspaper.

In early 1967 Ron Oberman accepted a job as director of publicity for Mercury Records in Chicago, Illinois and made plans to leave the Evening Star. His final "Top Tunes" column ran on Saturday, February 11 of that year. As Ron was in the process of leaving the newspaper, Michael Oberman approached the paper's editor about replacing his brother as the column's writer and was eventually granted the job. His first "Top Tunes" column – credited to "Mike Oberman" – appeared in the Saturday, February 18, 1967 edition of the Evening Star and profiled R&B singer Freddie Scott, who had recently been in town performing at the Howard Theatre. His column also included a "Notes and Halfnotes" section that provided bits of information on local and national performing artists.

Shortly after Michael Oberman took over "Top Tunes," the column was syndicated to the Elizabeth Daily Journal newspaper in Elizabeth, New Jersey. The name of the column was later changed to "Music Makers" in the Saturday, September 4, 1971 issue. Ultimately, Michael Oberman's last "Music Makers" column appeared in the Saturday, March 10, 1973 edition and profiled folk-pop singer-guitarist Jonathan Edwards, who had grown up in Northern Virginia and was appearing at the Cellar Door at the time. During his time as a columnist for the newspaper he interviewed more than 300 major artists including Janis Joplin, Jim Morrison, James Brown, Otis Redding, Led Zeppelin and David Bowie, who, on his very day in America on a publicity tour in January 1971, spent an evening with Oberman at his parents' home at 9714 Admiralty Drive in Silver Spring. (Later that evening Oberman took Bowie back to his then-Takoma Park residence where he visited with members of the band Sky Cobb, a band he was managing at the time.)

In 1968 with his reputation as one of the area's top music journalists already established, Michael Oberman began mentoring local musicians and participating in the local counterculture, taking special interest in the antiwar movement. One of the area's top booking agencies, Barry Rick Associates, recognized his ability to work with local original rock and roll bands and added him to their staff. One day he was approached by a local musician named Reggie Brisbane, who invited him to check out a rehearsal involving a band he was in called Claude Jones. Oberman visited the group in Washington, D.C. at their band house entitled "Little Gray," liked what he heard, and agreed to become their manager. At the time the lineup of Claude Jones consisted of lead singer Joe Triplett, guitarist Peter Blachly, bassist Frank Sprague, keyboardist Mike Henley and drummer Reggie Brisbane.

Claude Jones went on to become one of the Washington, D.C. area's most popular rock and roll bands of the late 1960s and early 1970s, appearing at night clubs such as Emergency, the Showboat Lounge and the Cellar Door, performing shows and concerts at the P Street Beach off of Dupont Circle and at local colleges, and playing benefits and special events at churches around the city and on the Mall. Oberman negotiated a record deal for the band with Mercury Records that included a $40,000 guarantee, which the group voted on and ultimately rejected. Claude Jones disbanded at the end of 1971.

During the early 1970s, in addition to maintaining his "Music Makers" column at the Evening Star, Michael Oberman spent a year managing Sky Cobb, another top Washington, D.C. area rock and roll band. After leaving the newspaper in early 1973 he worked for a time as a Maryland salesman for Warner Elektra Atlantic (WEA) and in 1974 he became an assistant to Jack Boyle, owner of the Cellar Door night club in Georgetown and president of the concert booking agency Cellar Door Productions (Oberman, whose job titles also included media manager and production coordinator, mainly handled radio and print advertising for the night club).

In late 1974 former Grin drummer Bob Berberich visited Oberman at his Cellar Door office and asked him to manage a new band he was in called the Rosslyn Mountain Boys, a country rock group that included former Claude Jones lead singer Joe Triplett. Oberman quit his job with Jack Boyle and booked the Rosslyn Mountain Boys into local night clubs such as the Birchmere, the Italian Gardens, the Shamrock Restaurant and Desperado's. The group released one album under Oberman's management, "The Rosslyn Mountain Boys" (The Rosslyn Mountain Boys; Adelphi Records, 1976), but interest in their mixed style of music among the major record labels was slow to develop and the band members began looking at other musical options. In August 1979 the group changed their name to Payday, but after a round of local gigs and a short time in New York, the band called it quits.

Oberman spent part of the early 1980s partnering in a store in the Adams Morgan neighborhood of Washington, D.C. called Blue Moon that specialized in clothing, folk art and esoterica. Later in the decade while living in the city on Rodman Street NW a house painter he had hired spied his music memorabilia and offered to play him a demo of his songs. The painter turned out to be Gene Ryder, a rock and roll singer-guitarist from Falls Church, Virginia who had a collection of songs at this disposal but no backing band to work with. Oberman sent him into the studio with a group that included guitarist Steuart Smith, shopped the resulting demo tape to music industry executives, and set up a three-gig showcase in Los Angeles for Ryder and a backup group. Polygram (the parent company of Mercury Records) signed Ryder and after sessions in Florida and Texas his debut solo album, "Last Cigarette and a Blindfold" (Gene Ryder; Mercury Records, 1989) hit the record bins.

In the 1990s Oberman went on to manage such acts as the Shy (a power pop band from Detroit, Michigan), Radioblue (a Washington, D.C.-based rock and roll group), and Les Lokey (a New Mexico-based blues-jazz singer-guitarist) and went on to spend several years working for private companies including a position as the national QSR account executive for DMX Music in Gaithersburg, Maryland. Today Michael Oberman is a nature photographer living in Columbia, Maryland and spends his time teaching photography and displaying his work in galleries and shows around the world.

Skip Groff is known among local music aficionados for being the proprietor of Yesterday and Today Records, a store he has operated in Montgomery County, Maryland since September 1977. However, his experiences with the local music scene extend far beyond that venture and encompass time spent as a music journalist, radio disc jockey and music director, independent record label owner, and music producer, arranger and engineer.

Skip Groff was born in Waltham, Massachusetts in 1948, and, since his father served in the United State Air Force, moved several times as a youth, living in Washington, D.C. and spending several years in Japan. As a teenager his family resided in District Heights, and, a little later, Temple Hills, Maryland, with Groff graduating from Suitland High School in 1966. During his sophomore year of high school he began listening to the Beatles and in late 1964 saw the popular rock and roll band the British Walkers (with lead guitarist Roy Buchanan) perform at a WPGC-sponsored concert at Marlboro Race Course in Upper Marlboro, Maryland.

During his high school years Groff also saw a local rock and roll band called the Adam's Apples perform at a Suitland High dance. He was impressed with the band – which soon changed its name to Nobody's Children – and played one of their demo records over the school's public address system during the morning announcements. He was initially the sports editor for the school's newspaper, the Suitland Echo, but as his interest in the local music scene grew he began writing music articles and record reviews for the paper as well.

After graduating from Suitland High School Groff enrolled at the University of Maryland as a radio and television major and remained a full-time student for three years. During his time there he worked at WMUC, the college's radio station, serving in various capacities including disc jockey, record librarian, assistant program director, program director and music director. He also wrote record reviews and music articles for the university's newspaper, the Diamondback. During the late 1960s Groff branched out and worked as a progressive rock and roll disc jockey at radio station WSID in Baltimore, as well as hosting weekend Top 40 shows on station WINX in Rockville, Maryland.

In early 1970 Groff held various part-time jobs including stints with the S. Klein department store in Greenbelt as an in-store announcer and with the Varsity Grill in College Park as a disc jockey. In August 1970 he was drafted into the United States Army and spent time at Fort Dix in New Jersey and then at Hunter Army Airfield, a military installation of Fort Stewart in Savannah, Georgia where he wrote concert and record reviews for the base's Flight Trainer newspaper. In August 1971 he was transferred to Walter Reed Army Medical Center in Washington, D.C. where he worked on public relations assignments, wrote music articles for their Stars and Stripes newspaper, and spent his weekends as a popular music disc jockey at WINX. He was discharged from the United States Army in February 1972.

With his years in the service behind him, Groff continued working at WINX from 1972 to 1974, where he served in a variety of positions including disc jockey, program director and music director. In 1973 he began hosting an on-air show entitled "Heavy Metal Thunder" that aired on weeknights from 9pm-12am. During this time he began venturing into the world of music production, first co-producing with Dave King and Bill Campbell the 45rpm single record "Bip Bop" backed with "Signal for a Stop" (Toothpick Tommy and the

Truckers; Era Records, 1973). He then became involved with the local heavy metal band Pentagram, producing a five-song demo by the group as well as two singles on his own independent labels: "Earth Flight" backed with "Hurricane" (Pentagram; Boffo Socko Records, 1973); and "Under My Thumb" backed with "When the Screams Come" (Pentagram; Gemini Records, 1974).

In March 1974, after his time with WINX had ended, Groff spent a year writing a weekly record review column for the Evening Star newspaper entitled "L Pinions." His other endeavors included publishing a music and record review fanzine called Graffiti, working for Empire Records as a store manager and for Variety Records in Wheaton Plaza as a manager and buyer for the chain. He cultivated an interest in how records were made and how they came to be played on the radio and contemplated a career in the recording industry as a record company promotions or A&R (artist and repertoire) man. Following that path, in 1975 he moved to St. Louis, Missouri and for the next year worked as the Midwest promotions manager for RCA Records. After returning to the Washington, D.C. area, Groff spent two months in the summer of 1977 working with local entrepreneur Al Ercolani in a store called Hit and Run Records in Kensington, Maryland.

On Friday, September 16, 1977 Groff founded his own business, Yesterday and Today Records, which operated out of a storefront marked 1327-J Rockville Pike in Rockville, Maryland. Yesterday and Today Records gained prominence for offering the latest releases in punk music and specialized in vinyl EPs and 45rpm single records. The store became a focal point for local punk musicians and fans and through the years employed such local hardcore music scene figures as singer Ian MacKaye and his Fugazi bandmates Guy Picciotto and Brendan Canty, Razz bassist Ted Niceley, guitarist Kim Kane of the Slickee Boys, and singer-guitarist Archie Moore and drummer Jim Spellman, both of Velocity Girl. A frequent volunteer at the store was future Black Flag singer Henry Rollins. Yesterday and Today eventually closed its doors at the Rockville location on Monday, September 16, 2002, but Groff has since continued the operation as an Internet-based mail-order business.

From 1978 to 1982 Groff operated an independent record label called Limp Records out of Rockville, Maryland that specialized in releasing music from the Washington, D.C. area punk music scene. The label emphasized EPs and 45rpm single records with its very first release being the four-song EP "Mersey, Mersey Me" (The Slickee Boys; Limp Records, 1978). Groff produced many of the early Dischord bands and among the more than two-dozen Limp releases were records by artists such as the Slickee Boys, Tina Peel, the Shirkers, D.Ceats, the Nurses, the Reind Dears, Nightman, (the) Razz, Killer Bees, the Dark, Black Market Baby, Minor Threat, the Stiff All-Stars, the Korps and the Pagans. The label also released several compilations, including "The Best of Limp (...Rest of Limp)" (Various Artists; Limp Records, 1980), a 13-selection album that included songs by the Slickee Boys, Nightman, D.Ceats, the Nurses, Tex Rubinowitz, (the) Razz, the Shirkers, the Penetrators and Bad Brains.

Other Endeavors of Groff's include having published two separate music fanzines, Hit and Run and Yesterday and Today, hosting the radio programs "Sunday Night Oldies" on WPGC in the early 1980s and "Rock of the 90s" on WAVA in the early 1990s, and issuing 45rpm single records in the 1990s by groups such as Manifesto, Strange Boutique, Black Market Baby and Bad Brains on Yesterday and Today Records, another of his independent record labels.

Today Skip Groff continues to operate Yesterday and Today Records as a mail order business based in Olney, Maryland. He is active on the Internet and Ebay and his inventory exceeds more than one million 45rpm single records and over 50,000 albums in such categories as country & western, girls, metal, punk, rare, and Top 40, with new items arriving on a daily basis.

CHAPTER EIGHTY-FIVE
JOURNEY TO THE CENTERS OF THE TEEN DANCE SCENE

Throughout the 1960s and into the early 1970s the Washington, D.C. area teen music scene was comprised of hundreds of bands and thousands of musicians. Teen dances and concerts were being staged several nights per week at almost every school, church, community center, fire department, armory and private hall that was receptive to the scheduling of such events. Rock and roll was by far the preferred style of music of the bands that performed at these functions, with R&B coming in a distant second, and C&W music, once so popular with young adult audiences in the 1950s, now being almost overlooked completely by young musicians.

As the popularity of rock and roll grew and teen participation in the music increased, a behind-the scenes management trend seemed to emerge. In the 1950s, many of the area's new teen bands booked themselves into the area's facilities, while others attempted to join forces with top promoters Don Dillard or Milt Grant who were staging larger live-music record hops. As the 1960s progressed and the sounds of R&B and the British Invasion gave way to harder rock and roll, just about all the bands had to align themselves with booking agencies like Domestic Sound Productions (operated by Bud Becker in Falls Church, Virginia), Barry Rick Associates (operated By Barry Rick in Kensington, Maryland) and Washington Talent Agency (operated by Jeff Rubin in Wheaton, Maryland) in order to work the local teen dances. While the total number of teen dance bands continued to increase into the early 1970s, the percentage of these bands that were actually doing their own booking greatly decreased.

In the summer of 1976 the teen dance scene, after more than 20 years of growth and relative prosperity, came to an abrupt halt. There were a few glaring reasons for its demise. With the spread of the counterculture, the hot rods, crew cuts, record hops, and saxophones of the 1950s had morphed into a swirl of long hair, drugs, concerts, and wailing electric guitars that permeated the late 1960s and early 1970s teen culture. Rock and roll music was heavier than ever and marijuana had become the drug of choice of suburban teens, with PCP looming on the scene.

Simultaneously, the demographics began changing in the Maryland suburbs, with Prince George's County in particular being divided along racial lines when a court-ordered system of public school busing was implemented in January 1973. Whites fled the county and were quickly replaced by Blacks, with the ensuing turbulence caused by this cultural shift resulting in racial skirmishes between teens in both the schools and community centers. Most of the teen dances, once fun and safe, had become tense and perilous. Consequently, community center directors and school officials stopped calling the booking agencies, took the dances off their schedules, and the teen music scene unceremoniously expired as the nation's bicentennial arrived.

During this era a number of venues achieved tremendous popularity for the memorable shows they presented and became favorites of musicians and fans alike. One of the area's most esteemed locations for teen dances was the Greenbelt Youth Center, which, after its opening in 1960, had carried on the long tradition of the town's Drop Inn as a hangout for the city's teens. The Greenbelt Youth Center was a facility often used by the Greenbelt Teen Club, which was operated by the Greenbelt Recreation Department and was completely autonomous from the Prince George's County Recreation Department. The Greenbelt Youth Center was unique in that its teen club dances were held in one of two locations within the one-story building: the gymnasium, which had a capacity of 520 occupants for such events; or the much smaller Multi-purpose Room adjacent to the building's lobby, which could hold approximately 50 teens.

The bookings for the teen dances in the Greenbelt Youth Center during the 16 years that such events were scheduled were done by the sitting teen club director, a position that was first held in the early 1960s by Joe O'Loughlin, and then changed through time. The bands that played the teen dances as the Greenbelt Youth Center were always among the best that were working the region's teen dance circuit. From 1960 to 1963 their dances featured such groups as the Capris, the BJs, the Savoys, the Galaxies, the Belvederes, the Montereys, the Rockin' Rejects, the Rip-Tydes and the High Tones.

A now-legendary event occurred at the Greenbelt Youth Center when a Valentine Dance was presented by Don Dillard for the Greenbelt Teen Club in the gymnasium on the night of Saturday, February 10, 1962. A very rare double-header was presented that evening featuring two of the top rock and roll singers in the world at the time, Freddy Cannon, who was in the area working the Rocket Room, and Gene Chandler, who was working a week-long engagement at the Howard Theatre.

Freddy Cannon, who grew up in Lynn, Massachusetts (north of Boston) and recorded for Swan Records, had already scored with two major popular music singles, "Tallahassee Lassie," which had reached number six on the Billboard magazine's "The Billboard Hot 100" chart on Monday, June 29, 1959, and "Way Down Yonder in New Orleans," which had reached number three on "The Billboard Hot 100" chart on Monday, January 11, 1960. Cannon's forthcoming hit song "Palisades Park" would go on to peak at number three on the "Billboard Music Week Hot 100" chart on Saturday, June 23, 1962.

Gene Chandler, a Chicago native who recorded for Vee Jay Records, had just released what was unexpectedly becoming a smash hit entitled "Duke of Earl," which had entered Billboard Music Week magazine's "Billboard Music Week Hot 100" chart on Saturday, January 13, 1962, climbed to number two on the day of his Greenbelt Youth Center appearance, and peaked a week later at number one on Saturday, February 17, 1962. The two stars reportedly gave separate live performances that evening, singing along to their records to a capacity crowd. Their show that evening still rates as the most prestigious live musical performance ever presented within the Greenbelt Youth Center.

From the beginning of 1964 through the end of 1966 the Greenbelt Teen Club brought to the Greenbelt Youth Center a band called Lawrence and the Arabians, who would arguably develop into the region's most popular teen dance group, booking them as often as twice a month. During this time, when Lawrence and the Arabians performed elsewhere, other attractions offered at the Greenbelt Teen Club dances included such groups as the High Tones, the Twilights, the Jaguars, the Majestic Neons, the Rockin' Rejects, the Corvettes, the Runabouts, L.B. and the Classics, Jay and the Continentals, the Aardvarks, the Secret G's, Donnie and the Deablos, the Hangmen, the Group, the Midnight Marauders, the Pagans, the Knightmen, the Fifth Edition and the Emotions.

The popularity of Lawrence and the Arabians at the Greenbelt Youth Center reached such proportions that the band eventually outgrew the facility. On Saturday, December 10, 1966 they co-headlined, along with the English Setters, a concert at the Greenbelt Armory that drew an estimated crowd of over 700 attendees. It was this event that led the band to rent out the more spacious armory for its own dances in the ensuing years.

In 1967 and 1968 bands that performed at the Greenbelt Teen Club dances at the Greenbelt Youth Center included Lawrence and the Arabians (on an infrequent basis), the Soul Searchers (a band that included singer-guitarist Chuck Brown), the Fifth Edition, the Lancers, the Pagans, the Soulmen, the McConkey Brothers, the Mystic Knights, the Knightmen, the Webb, the Reflections, the Soul Masters, the Counts, the Butlers, Lloyd the Lonely Souls, the Mystairs, the Manchurian Candidates, Us and Others, the Soul

Organizations, the Daytons, the Nitehawks, El Corals, the Soul Syndicate, the New Breed and the Impalas, the Great Expectations and the Syndicates. The highlight of this period was a Friday, September 6, 1968 doubleheader staged by Barry Richards that featured the Drifters and the Nowhere Men.

On Saturday, March 8, 1969 the Greenbelt Teen Club changed its name to "Kava" and continued to hold its dances at the Greenbelt Youth Center. At this time the roster of bands appearing at the Youth Center changed noticeably, with some newer psychedelic rock and roll groups mixing in with the more established headliners of the 1960s. Some of these newer rock and roll bands that landed at the Kava events at the Greenbelt Youth Center in 1969 and 1970 included the Spades and the Rainbows, Dawn's Dusk, Illusion of Sound, the New People, the Fog, the Edge, Bob Brady and the Concords, Blue Mist, Mystic Blue, JV Voight, Beginning End, Rose, the Asian Flu, the Arctic Fox, No Name Crisis, the Elevation, Syllabus, Day Break and the Sound of Time.

In 1971 the Kava dances at the Greenbelt Youth Center featured groups such as Scorpius, Mystic Blue, Mean Feet, Stonehenge, Fresh Air, Last Exit, Wild Rice, Spectrum and Medullah. The 1972-75 period saw the Kava dances headlined by the likes of Woodpecker, Sassafras Tea, Last Exit, Confection, Heaven Earth Power and Light, Mystic Blue, Early Morning, Friends of the Family, Green Eggs, the Summerfield Smith Band, GMC (God Mother Country), Musique, Before and After, the Murray Spoons Band, Looney Tunes, Prelude, Southbound and Stone Granite.

While Kava at the Greenbelt Youth Center was autonomous in nature, a similar situation had evolved at the Prince George's Plaza Community Center at 6600 Adelphi Road, Hyattsville, Maryland, which was operated by the Prince George's County Department of Recreation. Bands that performed at the teen dances there were scheduled by the community center director, but the live music events were subject to the rules and final approval of the county's recreation department.

Construction of the Prince George's Plaza Community Center was completed in 1968 and on Wednesday, June 19 of that year the Nowhere Men were the featured band at their very first teen dance. The musical entertainment at this center was recruited through either Barry Rick Associates or Washington Talent Agency and was similar to what was being offered at other teen dance venues throughout the Washington, D.C. area.

From its opening until the shut-off date of 1976 bands that headlined the Prince George's Plaza Community Center teen dances included the Starliters, Lawrence and the Arabians, Jay and the Inspirations, the Speculations, El Corals, the Continentals, the Hi-Notes, the Condors, the Invention, the Other Side, Bob Brady and the Concords, the Inspiration, the New People, the Clique, Liberation, Sudden Rush, Dawn's Dusk, Spectrum Ltd., Syllabus, Rushmore, the Upsetters, the New Breed, Day Break, Devil's Track, Friends of the Family, Confection, GMC (God Mother Country) and Sassafras Tea. The most surprising booking the Prince George's Plaza Community Center ever offered was an appearance by Mitch Ryder and the Detroit Wheels at their Halloween Dance on Friday, October 30, 1970, courtesy of Barry Rick Associates.

On the eastern edge of Prince George's County in Bowie, Maryland – an area that basically serves as the outermost boundary of the Washington, D.C. area – there were no fewer than five different school-affiliated teen clubs in operation during the prime rock and roll era of the late 1960s and early 1970s. A mix of bands played these events, with the numbers being evenly distributed between Bowie-based groups and more seasoned rock and roll bands that were booked through either Barry Rick Associates or the Washington Talent Agency.

The two most popular of these teen clubs were the Belair Junior High School Teen Club and the Bowie Senior Teen Club (which held their dances at Bowie High School and variously advertised these events as Senior Teen Club Dances or Teen Drop-Ins). Bands that performed at the Belair Junior High School Teen Club included the Reflections, Quality Unlimited, the Showmen, the Loving Kind, the Jeff Street Band, Midnight Mass at Charlie's, Daybreak, Genesis, Harwood Tapestry, Confection, Rushmore, Cerberus, Spring Well, Winterland Wilderness, Black-Eyed Susan, the Heat Band, Synge, Summer, Last Exit, Fragile, Blue Steel, Sweet Meat, Springfield, Hard Cider, Oasis, Legend and Sweet Water. Meanwhile, bands performing at the Bowie Senior Teen Club during this time included the Banned, the Mod Squad, Bob Brady and the Concords, D.C. and the Capitals, Terry and the Uptights, Lawrence and the Arabians, the Soul Block, the Scattered Moss, the Harrison Act, the Talativ, Quality Maintenance, the Knightmen and the Counts, Rob Strong and the Dynamics, Dawn's Dusk, Sudden Rush, the Reflections, Midnite Mass at Charlie's, the Reactions, the Rising Sun, the Jeff Street Band, Dawn's Dusk, the Continentals, the Scene, the Loving Kind, the Dynamics and the Palantirs.

In the southern section of Prince George's County, one of the most popular teen dance sites was the Tucker Road Community Center in Fort Washington, Maryland, which introduced their teen dances in the late 1960s and continued into the following decade. Some of the bands that performed at the dances here included the Dagenites, the Continentals, the Soul Sisters, The Solutions, the DC Playboys, the Uptowners, This End Up, Madwort, Syn, Ulysses, Scar, Troy, Truck, Circus, Fluorescent Rainbow, Bob Brady and the Concords, Trestle, Wild Rice, Rushmore, Morning Rain, Maypole, Lite, Syllabus, Interprise, the Bouys, Gas, Stark Naked, Brainsand, Spring Fever, Butler's Orchard and Devil's Track.

As the rock and roll got heavier and the American youth culture seemingly joined up with the Woodstock Nation, a new outdoor venue opened up in Prince George's County during the summer of 1969 called the Oxon Hill Free Stage. Formulated by a 17-year-old Oxon Hill High School junior named Steve Shultz, the concerts were held on a makeshift stage on the grounds of Thomas Addison Elementary School (7100 Oxon Hill Road, Oxon Hill, Maryland) and were modeled after the outdoor weekend concerts that were being held at the P Street Beach in the Dupont Circle neighborhood of Washington, D.C.

The free concert idea became a reality when Shultz, who wanted to see some of the area's up-and-coming hard rock and roll bands on his own turf, took it upon himself to walk in on a meeting of the River Ridge Recreation Council early that summer and suggest to the elders that the neighborhood would benefit from a community stage. His proposal was met with interest and he assembled a management team entitled Billy Crunche Productions that consisted of himself and two fellow 17-year-old Oxon Hill High School students, Al Swearingen and Mike Workinger, along with 16-year-old Fred Johnson, who attended the Canterbury School in nearby Accokeek. Together, they went door-to-door around Oxon Hill, collected $140, and hired a small team of carpenters, painters and electricians to build a wooden stage adjacent to the school. They next went about putting the word out that they were looking for some of the area's hardest-rocking combos for their presentations, with the understanding that the bands would not be paid and the concerts were open to the public free of charge. Numerous bands volunteered their services.

The Oxon Hill Free Stage got underway late in the summer of 1969, just as Woodstock fever was infecting teenagers and young adults across America. A total of six shows were presented there on Sunday afternoons over a course of five weeks: August 31 – Crystal Ship, Group Therapy, Madwart (8pm-11pm); September 7 – Natty Bumpo, Sunday (3pm-6pm); September 14 – The Northside Blues Band, Witches Sabbath (6pm-9pm); September 21 – Earth, Sunday, the March of Time (5:30pm-9pm); September 28 – Stillroven, Chi Square (3pm-6pm); October 5 – Tractor, Natty Bumpo, Sunday, Swirl, Bitter Sweet, Power House, Inside Strait, Valarthaphume (12pm-7pm).

The Oxon Hill Free Stage returned in the summer of 1970 with a round of three Sunday afternoon shows, all of which drew several hundred spectators. Despite the strong attendance figures, the concerts were subsequently discontinued, reportedly because various obscure county ordinances were being violated. The three shows of that second season were: June 7 – Madwart, Grace (3pm-5pm); July 5 – The Greg Murphy Group, Nitty Gritty (5pm-7pm); August 16 – Sea and the East Utopian Mission, the Greg Murphy Group, Renthra, the Yancie Street Gang, Nitty Gritty (4pm-9pm).

In Montgomery County, Maryland there were teen dances in schools, churches and community center buildings, with two of the more prestigious venues for such events being the Bethesda Youth Center and the Wheaton Youth Center. The first of these facilities, the Bethesda Youth Center, began offering teen dances in the early 1960s, but started calling these events "The Wedge" with a dance on Saturday, April 15, 1967 that featured two rock and roll bands, the Butlers and the Herd. From 1967 to 1969 bands that performed at the Wedge included the Resumes, the Showmen, the Nightcaps, the Midnight Stalkers, the Thyme Beings, the Epsilons, the Uncalled 4, the Nowhere Men, El Corals, Bob Brady and the Concords, the Essence, the New Breed, the Expressions, the Expectations, the Laymen, the Continental Rockers, the Deltas, Lawrence and the Arabians and the Cherry People.

One of the most unique teen dance venues in the Washington, D.C. area during the rock and roll era was the Wheaton Youth Center, a one-story facility at 11711 Georgia Avenue which had opened on Saturday, December 7, 1963. It featured a large gymnasium which had an event capacity of 700 occupants, but could hold well over 1,000 standing patrons for dances and concerts.

The facility's first director, Ron Crane, oversaw the scheduling of bands for the first two years, with Sharon Ward replacing him in 1966 and remaining in charge throughout the rock and roll concert years. It became a favorite location of several area music promoters including radio personality Barry Richards of WHMC, Bud Becker of Domestic Sound Productions and Barry Rick of Barry Rick Associates, all of whom booked both local and national acts into the spacious facility. The Wheaton Youth Center quickly became Montgomery County's most prestigious venue for bands on the teen dance circuit and drew large crowds to its live music shows from 1964 to 1972.

From its inception through the end of the 1960s some of the local bands and musicians that played dances at the Wheaton Youth Center were K.M. and the Marauders, the Medallions, the Del Fis, the Renegades, the Nomads, the Emeralds, the Thrillers, the Blazers, the Scarlets, JD and the Jesters, the Velours, Billee Jones, Little Valentine, the Tornadoes, the Nowhere Men, Inside Strait, the Showmen, Lee Edwards and the Continentals, Lawrence and the Arabians, the Soul Syndicate, the Laymen, Cream and Cocoa, the Highlighters, Louie and the Uptights, the Mirells, the Twilighters, TNT Tribble and the Midnight Souls, the Sand Pebbles, the Esquires, the combined outfit of the Expressions and the Velours, the Bitter Sweet, the Spades, the Expectations and El Corals.

During this time a few nationally known performing artists were booked into the Wheaton Youth Center that greatly raised the venue's status. The first of these events was a show that featured the Drifters, Bobbie Lucas, and the Starliners on the night of Thursday, December 23, 1965. Another concert of this sort was staged there on Friday, May 3, 1968 that was headlined by the Dells and supported by the Curfews and Louie and the Uptights. Perhaps the most remarkable show of this time was a performance at this facility on Thursday, July 25, 1968 headlined by singer Etta James, who was supported by a local band called the Spades. These shows and their big-name performers were just a prelude to what was on the horizon.

WHMC disc jockey Barry Richards had been booking teen dances and concerts featuring the best local rock and roll and R&B bands for years and understandably targeted the Wheaton Youth Center for many of his live music shows. When rock and roll took a heavier turn in the late 1960s, he decided to try bringing in some of the bigger name bands that employed this style and were touring the Eastern United States. One of the very first hard rock bands he reportedly brought in was a new group from England named Led Zeppelin, whose alleged Monday, January 20, 1969 performance in the Wheaton Youth Center now rates as the greatest unsolved mystery in the history of Washington, D.C. area rock and roll.

The Led Zeppelin story unfolds as follows: the band, consisting of singer Robert Plant, former Yardbirds guitarist Jimmy Page, bassist John Paul Jones and drummer John "Bonzo" Bonham, formed in England in October 1968 and in December of that year embarked on its very first United States tour in support of their soon-to-be-released first album for Atlantic Records (the tour, which ran for 51 days – from Thursday, December 26, 1968 to Saturday, February 15, 1969 – saw the band reportedly perform 33 concerts in 20 different cities, including two gigs in Canada). Three weeks into the tour the band performed for three consecutive nights – Friday, January 17 to Sunday, January 19, 1969 – at Detroit's Grande Ballroom and then had a gap in their schedule before resuming the tour at the Boston Tea Party in Boston, Massachusetts on Thursday, January 23.

According to legend, Barry Richards heard of the opening, got on the telephone, and reportedly negotiated an under-the-table $225 cash deal with manager Peter Grant for the band to perform a one-hour, 9pm show at the Wheaton Youth Center on the night of Monday, January 20 – a school night which was also the very same night of President Richard M. Nixon's inauguration. Richards only had approximately 72 hours to publicize the show on his radio show on WHMC, a 500-watt station that could only be heard throughout central portions of Montgomery County, Maryland. It remains unclear if he referred to the band as "Led Zeppelin" or "The New Yardbirds" or both during his broadcasts that weekend.

According to sources who claim to have witnessed the show, the Led Zeppelin entourage, consisting of some eight persons in two vehicles, pulled into the Wheaton parking lot about an hour early, visibly exhausted from their 10-hour journey from the Motor City. They proceeded to set up their equipment on the floor in front of the gymnasium's stage and sometime after 9pm hammered out 40 minutes of songs off of their first self-titled album, which had just been released in the United States some eight days earlier on Sunday, January 12.

People who claim to have been in attendance that night have estimated the size of the crowd at approximately 60 individuals. Peter Grant, it has been told, was miffed at the poor turnout and collared Richards in the gymnasium, threatening violence if the promoter didn't turn over additional gas money so the band could make it to their gig the following night (rumored to have been held at Hunt Armory in Pittsburgh, Pennsylvania). Reportedly, Richards ponied up an extra $50 for Grant, who cut the concert short and instructed the band to unplug their instruments and pack their gear. With little fanfare, the Zeppelin entourage quickly boarded their vehicles and departed in the night for Parts Unknown.

Although this Led Zeppelin concert allegedly took place in 1969, the question of its authenticity unexpectedly became a hot topic of conversation among Washington, D.C. area music fans approximately 30 years later, thanks in part to the advent of the Internet and corresponding advancements in communications technology. It developed into a heated argument that persists to this day. On the one hand there are scores of individuals who claimed to have been in attendance that evening and can provide details of the concert itself. On the other hand, there are skeptics who point out that there is not one shred of hard evidence, aside from eyewitness testimony, to support the notion the concert ever took place – no posters, no handbills, no print or audio advertisements, no newspaper or magazine advertisements, no ticket stubs, no contracts, no photographs, no bootleg recordings of the show itself, no post-concert reviews, no private journal or diary entries, and, in the years that have since passed, not any reference to the concert in any books about Led Zeppelin or rock and roll, or in any published or recorded interviews with any of the band's members, managers or associates.

Through the years there have been a couple of published tidbits that seem to refer to the mysterious Led Zeppelin-Wheaton Youth Center saga. The first of these was an article entitled "Hairy Barry" by Chris Hutton and Tom Carrico that appeared in the Friday, November 20, 1970 edition of the Spur, the newspaper of what was then called Montgomery College (Rockville, Maryland campus).

This piece, which profiled Barry Richards, included the following: "He continues to bring in some of the semi-big rock groups at the few small halls left in the area, despite the recent trashings that have accompanied local rock concerts. He sees the current situation as unnecessary, and blames the disturbances mostly on the 'boppers.' One of his fondest memories is that of a concert he presented at the Wheaton Youth Center in the fall of '68 which had a pitiful turnout of only 200 people. The featured group was Led Zeppelin, at the time virtually unknown." (This article was recently brought to attention by researcher Ron Fritts.)

Another account to take into consideration is an article in the Washington Post of Sunday, December 25, 1977 entitled "Front Page People: D.C.'s Boogie Man Tried Disco TV" by Cyndy Loomis that, when discussing Barry Richards various exploits, states: "In the sixties he began the first progressive rock show on AM radio in the area (on WHMC) and hosted concerts in local recreation centers where he was lucky if 200 people showed up to hear unknown acts such as Led Zeppelin, Rod Stewart and Jethro Tull."

Next, in the book "Stairway to Heaven: Led Zeppelin Uncensored" (by Richard Cole with Richard Turbo, 1992) road manager Richard Cole writes in Chapter 11 ("Back to Reality") that critics of the band seemed to ignore the fact that during their first American tour Led Zeppelin played for as little as $200 per gig – a figure not far from the $225 fee that Barry Richards claimed he paid the band.

Most recently, filmmaker Jeff Krulik of Silver Spring, Maryland completed an 81-minute independent documentary film entitled "Led Zeppelin Played Here" (Produced by Jeff Krulik, John Heyn and Brad Dismukes, 2013), which examines every aspect of the story of Led Zeppelin's alleged landing at the Wheaton Youth Center. The movie includes on-screen interview segments with a number of Washington, D.C. area rock and roll luminaries including Barry Richards, Bud Becker, Skip Groff, Mike Schreibman, Richard Harrington, Dave Nuttycombe and Michael Oberman, along with commentary from numerous individuals who claimed to have attended the concert in question. The film has been featured at theatres and independent film festivals across the country and has raised the concert to legendary proportions with Led Zeppelin fans throughout the world.

In the wake of Led Zeppelin's possible visitation, the Wheaton Youth Center slowly backed away from presenting local teen bands and increasingly hosted nationally known rock and roll acts, many of which were just in the process of beginning their ascent to legendary status. Some of the major bands that performed here in the 1970-1972 time period were Orpheus, Zephyr, Atomic Rooster, Chicken Shack, Faces (featuring lead singer Rod Stewart), Grin, Dr. John the Night Tripper, Brownsville Station, If, Rare Earth, the Stooges (featuring lead singer Iggy Pop), Crow, the Bob Seger System, Spirit, Long John Baldry, Rory Gallagher, Pacific Gas and Electric, and scores of others.

However, despite the cavalcade of some of the rock and roll world's most revered performers, the live music shows of the Wheaton Youth Center were destined to go the way of all the other church and community center events. In December 1973 the Capital Centre opened in Landover, Maryland with a seating capacity of 18,756 and throughout the 1970s the top touring acts strived to play the spaceship-shaped arena. Those that were overlooked opted to work other area venues such the William P. Cole, Jr. Student Activities Building (University of Maryland; commonly referred to as Cole Field House), D.A.R. Constitution Hall, Shady Grove Music Fair, and even the Kennedy Center.

In the middle 1970s changes rapidly took place in Prince George's County's teen culture that impacted the corresponding music scene. One of the most popular teen clubs in the area, Kava, abruptly discontinued its practice of staging dances at the Greenbelt Youth Center after a performance by the hard-rocking band Menagerie on Saturday, March 6, 1976. Word of Kava's decision quickly spread to the Prince George's County Recreation Department, which opted to follow suit and end the teen dances at all of their participating community centers by the conclusion of that summer. In similar fashion, community centers and churches in Montgomery County, Washington, D.C. and even Northern Virginia opted to pull the plug on their teen dances and live music events. What was once a vibrant teen dance scene had grinded to a complete stop by the end of the summer of 1976.

In retrospect, more than 2,000 rock and roll bands actively performed on the Washington, D.C. area teen dance scene in the 1960s and 1970s. Thousands of young players participated in these bands, with the teen dance events serving as a fertile spawning ground for youths who later pursued music on a professional or semi-professional basis. The demise of the teen dance scene in 1976 marked the end of a cultural movement that encouraged and showcased the work of young musicians and subsisted on the support of their peers.

To provide a clearer understanding of the essence and magnitude of the Washington, D.C. area's teen dance scene, a partial list of its participating rock and roll bands from the 1960s and 1970s reads as follows: the Aardvarks, Acephalous, the Aces of Spade, Act V, the Adam's Apples, Alfred and the New Men, All the King's Men, the All-Night Diner Band, the Amazing Raisin, the Ambers, the American Cheese Band, Animal Farm, Anne's Badstreet Band, the Answer, the Anthill Convention, the Apollos, the Arachnids, Archaic Love Machine, Arctic Fox, the Aristocrats, the Arrangement, Artificial Energy, the Ascots, the Asian Flu, the Assassins, the Atlantic Cable, the Atlantics, the Attractions, the Authentics, the Authors, the Avalons, the Avantes, the Avengers, the Axemen, Axis, the Babbling Brooks, Back Bay, Badge, the Banned, the Banshees, the Barons, the Barren Straits, Barry and the Fantastics, the Battery Operated Pineapple, the Beachcombers, B.E.A.T. Ltd., the Beau Havens, the Bedlams, Before and After, Beginning End, Belinda and the Playmates, Ben Franklin's Electric Company Band, the Bent Penny Blues Band, the Berkshires, Black-Eyed Susan, the Blazers, Blinks and the Midnight Soul, the Blue Chords, the Blue Cinder, Blue Diamond, the Blue Grass, Blue Max, Blue Mist, the Blue Penny, Blue Steel, the Blues Bag, the Blues Dimension, Bob Brady and the Concords, Bob Conley and the Classics, Bobby and the Day Breakers, Bobby and the Starliners, the Bobcats, Bolt, the Boss Five, the Boston Monkeys, Boston Tea, Brainsand, the Brass Tacks, Brat, the Brave Maggots, the Brighton Crew, the British Crowns, the British Stompers, the Broken Limbs, the Brookwoods, the Brotherhood, Buckwheat, Burgundy Sunset, Burn, the Burning Sensation, Bush, the Butlers, the Candy Stripers, the Canterbury Tales, the Cape Breton Union, the Capris, the Captivators, the Carefrees, the Carnaby Street Set, the Carpetbaggers, the Castells, the Casuals, the Cat Thieves, the Cavaliers, the Cavalleros, the Celestials, the Cellar Dwellers, the Cellar Wall, the Cellmates, the Centurions, Cerberus, the Chancellors, the Changing Tides, the Chantels, the Chaotics, the

Chaparrals, the Charlie Browns, the Chasers, the Cherry Pink Reason, the Chessmen, the Chessmates, the Children of Discord, the Chordones, the Chosen Few, the Citations, the Classics, the Clique, the Clockwork Orange, the Coachmen, C.O.D., Cold Sweat, the Collection, the Collegians, the Colonials, the Coming Generation, the Community Toothbrush, Concert, the Condors, Confection, the Confusions, the Congressionals, Contents Under Pressure, the Continentals, the Contrasts, the Cornerstone Rockers, the Cornerstones, the Coronas, the Corporation, the Corpse Combo, the Corsairs, the Corvettes, Cosmic Rainbow, the Counts, the Creations, the Crescendos, the Crescents, the Crestwoods, the Cromwell Translucent Expedition, Crusader Rabbit, the Crypt Kickers, Crystal Silica Ashbury, Crystal Tower, the Cutaways, the Czars, Daddy Lean and the Bacons, the Daltons, Dave and the Defiants, Dawn's Dusk, Day Break, the Daytons, D.C. and the Capitals, the DC Playboys, the DCvers, the Dead Ends, the Deadbeats, Deaf Mute, the Debonaires, December's Children, the Del-Fis, the Del Rays, the Delmors, the Deltones, the Devil's Advocates, the Devotions, the Diamonds, Dickey and the Dynamics, the Dimensions, the Discorporated Blues Band, the Distortions, the Disturbances, the Divine Comedies, DK and the Witnesses, the Domains, the Dominoes, 007 and the Galores, the Door Knockers, the Dorian Grays, the Downbeats, the Drop Outs, the Druids, Duke and the Rhythm Aces, the Dukes, the Duo-Sonics, the Duquesnes, the Dyals, the Dynamic Twilighters, the Dynamic Viscounts, the Dynamics, Early Morning, Earth, Earth Power and Light Company, the Earthdogs, the East Side Kids, Easy, the Ebb Tides, the Echoes, the Ecstatic Group, the Edge, the Egyptians, El Corals, the Electras, the Electratones, Electric Circus, the Electric Twinkie, the Elegants, the Elevations, the Elites, the Emanons, the Embers, the Emeralds, the Emotions, the Empty Set, the English Nights, the Epics, the Epsilons, the Eruptions, the Escorts, the Esquires, the Essence, the Essex Set, the Evening People, Everyday People, the Examples, the Executioners, the Exotics, the Expressions, the Exterminators, the Extremes, the Fables, the Fabulous Hi-Notes, the Fabulous Kingsmen, the Fantastic Plastic, the Fantasticks, the Fascinations, Fast Break, Feedback, the Fender Benders, the Fidelities, the Fifth Amendment, the Fifth Dimension, the Fifth Edition, the Figments of Imagination, the Fisks, the Five Js, the Five of Us, Flagg, the Flames, Flesh and Blood, Fluorescent Rainbow, the Flower of London, Fluffy Sidewalk, Fly By Night, the Flying Circus, the Flying Hospital, the Flys, the Fog, the Forbidden Minors, Formula One, the Four Joys, the Four Quarters, 14th Street Chaos, Fragile, the Franklin Park Zoo, Free Country, Free Joe and the Rest of the World, Free Spirit, the Freedom, Freeway Jam, Fresh Air, Friends of the Family, Fringe, Froggy Little, the Fugitive Sound, the Fugitives, the Future Tense, the Fuzz, Gallery 28-40, the Gargoyles, Gary Scott and the Classics, Gas, the Gaylords, the General Analytics, the Generation, Genesis, the Gents, Gideon, Giles Cook and the Soul Binders, the Glass Hour, Glass Menagerie, the G-Men, the Gnu Generation, the Golden Souls, the Gondoliers, the Good Samaritans, the Grand Prees, the Grass, Gratitude, the Graven Images, the Great Expectations, the Gremlins, the Grenadiers, the Grog, the Group, Hailstone, the Handful, Happy Feet, Hard Cider, the Harrison Act, Harwood Tapestry, the Hayze, the Hazy Daye, the Heard, the Hearsemen, the Heaters, the Heathens, Heaven Earth Power and Light, the Henchmen, Herbie and the Originals, the Herd, the Hi Fis, the Hi-Notes, the High Beams, the High Tides, the High Tones, High Voltage, the Highwalkers, the Hinges of Fate, the Hiram Walkers, Hot Lather, the Hot Tamales, the Hounds of Baskerville, the Huns, the Hunted For, the Huntingtons, the Hustlers, the Ice Cream Grenade, the Id, the Idols, Illusion of Sound, the Illusions, the Immortals, the Impacts, the Imperials, the Imposters, the Impressions, the In Crowd, the Incredible Fog, Incubus, the Inklings, the Inmates, the Inside Outs, Inside Straight, the Inspiration, the Interludes, Interprise, the Invaders, the Invention, the Ivymen, the Jaguars, Jay and the Continentals, Jay and the Inspirations, Jay and the Techniques, the

Jaywalkers, the Jazz Masters, JC and the Disciples, J.C. and the 3Ds, the Jeff Street Band, the Jesters, Jett, Jimmie and the Newspeeds, Jimmy and the Blendells, JJ and the Invaders, JK and the Hurricanes, the Joint Possession, the Jokers Wild, the Joyful Noise, Judgment, the Justins, the Juveniles, JV Voight, the Karavans, Keep off the Grass, the Keggs, the Kegsmen, the Keynotes, the Keysers, the King Cobras, King's Row, the Kitchen Cinque, KM and the Barons, KM and the Marauders, Knee Deep, the Knightmen and the Counts, the Knights, Kriss Kross, the Lamonts, the Lamplighters, the Lancers, Last Exit, the Last Remains, the Laymen, the Lazy Loafers, L.B. and the Classics, LD and the Classics, the Leaves of Grass, the Leftovers, Legend, the Lemon Blues, Les Couleurs, Liberation, Life, the Lighter Shades of Dark, the Limit, the Lion's Din, Lite, the Living End, Lloyd and the Lonely Souls, Lockhouse, Lodestone, the London Fogs, the London Heirs, the London Lymes, the London Stompers, the Londoners, the Looms, the Looney Tunes, the Lost Souls, Louie and the Uptights, the Love Children, the Love Company, the Lovin' Mood, the Loving Kind, LSD Sounds Ltd, the Luvable, the Madcaps, Madwort, the Magical Popcorn Machine, the Majestics, the Malibus, the Manchester Squires, the Manchurian Candidates, the March of Time, the Marquees, Maximus Septum, Maxwell, Maxwell Parachute, Maypole, the McConkey Brothers, the McCormick Tool Company, Mean Feet, the Medallions, Medullah, Medusa, the Melodaires, Menagerie, Mercury, the Merry Five of Windsor, the Midnight Blues, the Midnight Haze, Midnight Mass at Charlie's, the Midnight Stalkers, the Midnighters, the Mighty Tundra, the Minus Four, the Minx, the Mirells, the Misfits, the Missing Links, they Missing Lynx, the Modern Music Makers, the Mod Squad, Mods and Rockers, the Mods of Quinn, the Monarchs, the Monks, the Monsters, the Montells, the Montereys, the Moonlighters, Morning Rain, the Morticians, Mother, Motley Crew, the Muddy Waters, the Murray Spoons Band, the Music Men, Musique, the Mustangs, the Mystairs, Mystic Blue, the Mystic Knights, the Mystics, Nasty Habits, the Natives, the Nelltones, the Neon Flag, the Neptunes, the Never Never Boys, the New Colonial Blues Band, the New Deadheads, the New Delphonics, the New Found Sound, the New Generation, the New People, the New Vagabonds, the Newtrons, the Next Times, the Night Raiders, the Night Walkers, the Nightcaps, Nitty Gritty, the Nomads, No Name Crisis, the Nooks, the Novocaines, the Null Set, the Nutones, Oasis, the Occidentals, the Omegas, the Ones, Only After Dark, Opal City, the Open Road Band, the Open Roads, the Organic Cavemen, Organization Man, Orondous, the Other Five, the Other Side, the Out Crowd, the Outlaws, the Outcast Set, the Oxford Reformers, the Pagans, Pain, the Palantirs, Paragon, the Paramounts, the Pastels, the Patriots, the Paupers, the Pearls, Peat Moss, the Pendletons, the Penetrators, Penny Arcade, Perry Gray and the Other Side, the Personalities, the Persuaders, the Phantoms, Phoenix, Pink Marmalade, the Plague, the Playboys, the Playmates, the Plum Beach Incident, the Poet Souls, Polyhymnia, Poor Richard, the Potomac Rhythms, Powerhouse, Prelude, the Premiers, the Primitive Sect, Prince and the Paupers, the Profiles, Project Sound, Promise, the Prophets, the Purple Existence, the Quaker Blues, Quality Maintenance, Quality Unlimited, the Quarrymen, the Quotations, the Radical Five, Rage, Rainbow, Ramp, Random Choice, the Rare Breed, the Rat Finks, the Rat Pack, the Razor's Edge, Ray and the Authentics, the Reactions, the Red Coats, Red Dog, the Redwoods, the Reflections, the Renaissance, Renaissance Blues, the Renditions, the Renegades, the Revelations, the Rhythm Masters, the Rhythm and Blues Express, the Rhythmaires, Riddle, Rik and the Illusions, the Rip-Tydes, the Rippers, the Rising Sun, the Rising Tides, RJ's Hustlers, the Roaches, the Road Runners, Road Work, Rob Strong and the Dynamics, Rock Bottom, the Rockin' Rebels, the Rockin' Regals, the Rockin' Rejects, Rocking Horse, Rocky and His Friends, the Rogues, the Roguesmen, Ronnie and the Walkers, the Roots of Evil, the Roustabouts, the Roulettes, the Royaltons, Rokx, Rose, RSVP Blues Group, the Rubber Band, the Rubber

Souls, the Runabouts, the Runarounds, Rushmore, Sagebrush, Salt and Pepper, the Santells, Sassafras Tea, Satan's Playmates, Satan's Sweet Souls, the Satanic Mill Blues Band, Saturn, Savage Rose, the Savages, the Saxons, the Scarlet Monopoly, Scar, the Scarlet Onyx, the Scarlets, the Scattered Moss, the Scene, Scorpio, the Scorpions, Scorpius, the Scoundrels, Second Generation, the Secret Gs, the Sensations, the Sentimentals, the Sextans, the Shackles, the Shades, Shades of Darkness, the Shadows, Shadows of Soul, the Shags, the Shantels, the Shayes, the Shapes of Things, the Sheffields, the Shot, the Shy Ones, the Sights and Sounds Revolution, the Silencers, the Silvertones, Simon Soul and the Knight Raiders, Sir John and His Knights, Skyhawk, Skyware, the Sledde, the Sleepless Knights, Slo Frate, Slow Rush, Smokey and the Casanovas, Snake Eyes, Snow, Society's Prisoners, the Solar Eclipse, the Solutions, the Sonnets, Sonny and the Temps, the Sonny Boy Reed Organization, the Sonotones, the Sons of Adam, the Soothsayers, the Soul Block, the Soul Invention, the Soul Knights, the Soul Masters, the Soul Organizations, the Soul Providers, the Soul Revolution, the Soul Searchers, the Soul Seekers, the Soul Set, the Soul Sisters, the Soul Specters, the Soul Syndicate, the Soul System, the Soulastics, the Soulful Progressions, the Soulmen, Sound Investment, the Sound Story, the Sounds of Time, Southbound, the Sovereigns, Space Meat, the Spades and the Rainbows, the Spartans, Spectrum Ltd, the Spectrums, the Speculations, Spread Eagle, Spring Fever, Spring Well, Springfield, Springtime, the Squire Five, the Squires, Stark Naked, the Starlighters, the Starliners, the Starliters, the Startones, Starrs, the Statics, the Stingrays, Stone Granite, Stonehenge, Storm, the Straight Eight, the Strange Bedfellows, Strange Bru, Strawberry Rag, Stronghold, the Styles Anonymous, the Suburbans, Sudden Rush, the Suds, Summer, the Summerfield Smith Band, the Sunsets, the Superiors, Sweet Meat, Sweet Water, the Swinging Agents, the Syke Machine, Syllabus, Syn, the Syndicate, Synge, the Syze Five, the Talativ, Tangerine Flake, Ted Veneman and the Impalas, the Tee Jays, Tequila Sunset, Terry and the Uptights, the Testaments of Time, Them Things, the Thin Men, Third Stone, Third Stone from the Sun, Third Street West, This End Up, the Thrillers, the Thyme Beings, T.L. and the Barons, Together Now, Tom Terrific, the Tomcats, Tommy Bryant and the Giants of Sound, the Tormentors, the Tornadoes, the Torquays, Total Eclipse, the Town Criers, Transition, the Trees, the Tremolos, the Trend, the Trend-ells, Trestle, the Triads, the Triumphs, the Trixons, the Troubadours, Troy, Truck, Truth, the Turbines, the Turncoats, the Twang Gang, the Twilights, the Twilighters, the Tytans, the Ultimate Sound, the Uncalled 4, Uncle Sam's Traveling Band, Ulysses, Undecided, the Undertones, the United Orange, the Unknown Kind, the Uptowners, the US, Us and Others, Turning Point, the Uninhibited, the Unique Shadows, Uncle Truck, the Undertakers, the Unknown Kind, the Upper Four, the Upsetters, the Vagrants, the Vandels, the Vanguards, the Varsells, the Velours, the Velvet Haze, the Venjures, Venus and the Fly Traps, the Vertations, the Vibratones, the Vibratos, the Victors, the Village Rats, the Village Set, the Villagers, Vince and the Brothers of Soul, the Viper Blues Band, the Voices of Time, the Void, the Voodoos, the Waifs, the Wailers, Wake, the Wakes, Walrus, the Wanderers, the Wandering Souls, the Warlocks, the Warlox, the Warringtons, We the People, the Webb, the Weekenders, Wes and the Weasels, the West Street Extended, the Whigs, Whiskey and Automobiles, White Fool, Wide Load, the Wild Alfalfa, the Wild Ones, Wild Rice, Winterland Wilderness, Winthrop Savage, the Wolfpack, Woodpecker, the Wrong Way Inn, the XKEs, the Yankee Doodle Dandies, the Yarbs, Yellow Brick Road, the Yorkshires, the Young Ones, the Young Rabbits, the Zebes, Zillion, the Zipp Tones, the Zodiacs, and the Zoo.

CHAPTER EIGHTY-SIX
LINK WRAY

From the middle 1950s to the early 1970s, Link Wray rated as one of the most talented lead guitarists the local rock and roll scene ever celebrated. During the 1960s he inspired a legion of young guitarists by turning up the volume louder than anyone else in town and churning out gut-wrenching power cords and screaming leads years before the notion of heavy metal playing took hold.

Link Wray arrived in Washington, D.C. via Portsmouth, Virginia in the middle 1950s with his brothers Vernon and Doug in tow, and together they set the local music scene on fire. While Vernon – as "Ray Vernon" – initially established himself as a viable solo artist with musical backing from both of his brothers, Link developed his own raunchy style of play and eventually became the focus of the family unit, with the band becoming known as "Link Wray and His Ray Men." The band's legend spread throughout the 1960s as they cranked out their fired-up brand of rock and roll at a succession of rough-edged, Southern-tinged bars and night clubs throughout the Washington, D.C. area.

Long regarded as the Father of the Power Chord, Link Wray earned his legendary status by chiseling out gritty, savage guitar work that left his listeners reeling. Having blitzed the national charts with snarling instrumental hits like "Rumble" in 1958, "Rawhide" in 1959, and "Jack the Ripper" in 1963, Link Wray's enormous talent, everlasting energy, and innovative use of distortion and volume has inspired and influenced guitarists all over the world.

The Wray family saga begins in the small rural town of Dunn, North Carolina. Fred Lincoln "Link" Wray (son of Fred L. Wray Sr. and Lillian M. Wray) was born at Fort Bragg, North Carolina on Thursday, May 2, 1929, chronologically sandwiched between older brother Vernon Aubrey Wray, born Monday, January 7, 1924, and Douglas Leon Wray, born Tuesday, July 4, 1933. The Wray family spent their early years in Dunn and Link reportedly began playing guitar at the age of eight through the urging of his older brother Vernon.

In 1943 Fred and Lillian Wray moved the family to Portsmouth, Virginia and the Wray boys were soon playing together in various C&W combos throughout the region. The three brothers had worked hard to become accomplished musicians, with Vernon becoming proficient on rhythm guitar and vocals, Doug having taught himself drums, and Link having developed into a talented lead guitarist.

The brothers worked together in the Portsmouth area in a group called the Melody Four before Link joined the United States Army in 1950, where he was stationed in Germany and served as a medical assistant for most of his two-year hitch. When Link Wray returned to Virginia in 1952 he rejoined brothers Vernon, now called "Lucky," and Doug, and along with close family friend Brantley "Shorty" Horton Jr., they formed a group called Lucky Wray and the Lazy Pine Wranglers. After several months they changed the name of the band to Lucky Wray and the Palomino Ranch Gang. The group performed the country music tunes of Hank Williams, Hank Thompson and Bob Wills, and played all over the Norfolk-Portsmouth area at night clubs like the White Rabbit, the Rathskeller, the Lazy Pine Ranch and Fernwood Farms Picnic Ranch.

In the summer of 1954 the Wray brothers moved to Washington, D.C., with Link and his first wife Elizabeth taking an apartment in Brentwood Village at 1345 Saratoga Avenue NE #463D, Vernon and his wife Evelyn renting a unit in the same complex at 1339 Saratoga Avenue NE #493A, and Doug Wray reportedly alternating on couches in both apartments. Working under the name "Lucky Wray," the three brothers – Vernon Wray singing and playing rhythm guitar, Link Wray on lead guitar, Doug Wray on drums, along with the ever-present Shorty Horton on bass – first assumed house band duties at the Rendezvous, a roughshod Downtown night club at 409 10th Street NW that was owned at the time by Constantine and Pandora Gogos and offered a mix of live C&W and rock and roll music.

A year later, with the same lineup intact, the quartet began working the Ozarks Restaurant on 10th Street NW as "Lucky Wray and the Ozark Four," a job that caught the attention of Washington, D.C. record producer Ben Adelman. The Wray brothers recorded a number of songs under Adelman's direction with the end result being three separate 45rpm single records that were leased to Starday and released to the public over the course of the next year: "It's Music She Says" backed with "Sick and Tried" (Lucky Wray; Starday Records, 1956); "What-Cha Say Honey" backed with "Got Another Baby" (Lucky Wray; Starday Records, 1956); and "Teenage Cutie" backed with "You're My Song" (Lucky Wray with Link and Doug Wray; Starday Records, 1957).

In March 1957 the Wray brothers and their families moved across the city to what was then called the Bolling View Apartments in Southeast Washington, D.C. Vernon and Evelyn took a unit at 210 Orange Street SE #1 while Link and Elizabeth, along with brother Doug, moved into unit #4. The three Wray brothers and Shorty Horton continued to work the Rendezvous throughout the year, where they still appeared as "Lucky Wray" and also worked engagements at two other Washington, D.C. night clubs that were flirting with rock and roll, Bob White's Hideaway on Pennsylvania Avenue SE in Capitol Hill and the Charles Café on upper 14th Street NW in Columbia Heights. Link Wray had been sidelined for several months in the latter half of 1956 with tuberculosis and had one of his lungs removed, but Lucky Wray continued on, often times with guitarist Dick Williams taking Link's place.

In the spring of 1957 Link Wray was on the mend, and, although his recovery was reportedly far from complete, he valiantly returned to the local stages with his brothers. In April of that year, while working the Charles Café, Lucky Wray was observed by a booking agent with ties to Cameo Records in Philadelphia, Pennsylvania and was transformed into a teen idol under the new stage name "Ray Vernon." (From this point on he will be referred to by his new moniker.)

Link worked numerous recording sessions with Ray Vernon in Philadelphia that month and would also back him up on live performances throughout the remainder of the year. However, once he returned to Washington, D.C. that spring Link also began working jobs in a trio format with Shorty Horton on bass and Doug Wray on drums, simply billed as "Link Wray." Throughout much of 1957 and most of 1958 "Link Wray" gigged at local night clubs such as the Rendezvous, the Ozarks Restaurant, Guy's Place, the Round Up Club, the Red Robin Restaurant, Benny's Rebel Room, the Shelter Room, the Shanty, the Moulin Rouge, and over the Maryland line on Bladensburg Road at the Dixie Pig.

During this period Ray Vernon befriended local television host Milt Grant and secured Link a position as the house guitarist on his WTTG Channel-5 music-and-dance television program "The Milt Grant Show," a steady engagement that lasted until the show's demise in April 1961. Ray Vernon also began making live appearances, most always with Link and Doug and Shorty backing him up, on the various record hops that Grant staged at schools, armories and fire departments in and around the nation's capital. Link Wray, sometimes billed as a separate act, often appeared at these record hops which were regularly staged at such facilities as the Silver Spring Boys Club, the Silver Spring Armory, the Hyattsville Armory, Glen Echo Park's Spanish Ballroom and the Bladensburg Volunteer Fire Department. In addition, Ray Vernon and Link Wray also worked similar record hop jobs for radio disc jockey-promoter Don Dillard, who had a long-running friendly feud going with

Grant. Strangely enough, working for both promotions did not cause any known conflicts among the parties involved.

In the late 1950s Link Wray began making records as a featured rock and roll artist and it was by accident that his biggest hit – "Rumble" – was conceived. The scene was a Milt Grant Record Hop held at the Fredericksburg Arena in Virginia on the night of Friday, July 12, 1957. While several accounts have been circulated regarding what transpired that evening, one of the most popular tales is that at one point in Link Wray's stage performance Grant leaned over to the guitarist and requested that he play "The Stroll," a popular hit song by a band called the Diamonds. Link's alleged deadpan response, "I don't know any strolls," left Grant nonplused, who further requested that Link play something that "sounds like a stroll." Doug Wray thought he knew what Grant was talking about and cut in with a beat. Link jumped right in and improvised "Rumble" on the spot, causing the teens to rush the stage and demand a repeat performance. It was evident a major hit song had just been created.

Shortly after this record hop, Milt Grant took a demo of that very song, originally entitled "Oddball," to Archie Bleyer, who at the time was president of Cadence Records in Philadelphia, Pennsylvania. Bleyer was unimpressed, but the tune reportedly went over big with his daughter, who renamed it "Rumble" and talked her dad into signing the band to a one-shot record deal and releasing the song as a single on the Cadence label.

Ray Vernon booked time at the United States Recording Company at 1121 Vermont Avenue NW in Washington, D.C. in early 1958 and "Rumble" was rerecorded, with Link being backed up by his usual bandmates: bassist Shorty Horton, drummer Doug Wray and Ray Vernon himself playing acoustic rhythm guitar. When the tape of the session was sent to Bleyer, he placed the artist name "Link Wray & His Ray Men" on the single and a new band was born. For sake of uniformity, the band will from this point forward be referred to as "Link Wray and His Ray Men," though it should be noted that for the remainder of their time in the Washington, D.C. area, the band was variously referred to, both in night club ads and on recordings, as "Link Wray and His Ray Men," "Link Wray and His Raymen," "Link Wray and the Ray Men," "Link Wray and the Raymen," "Link Wray and His Wray Men," and "Link Wray and the Wraymen."

The single in question, which was the first recorded instance of what we call fuzz-tone, thanks to Link's 1953 Gibson Les Paul being blasted through a Premier amp filled with pencil holes, was a huge success. "Rumble" (Link Wray & His Ray Men; Cadence Records, 1958) was released in April 1958 and peaked at number 16 on the Billboard magazine's "Best Selling Pop Singles in Stores" music popularity chart on Monday, June 30, 1958. Curiously, the song's writing credits were listed as "M. Grant – L. Wray," though in reality the former had nothing to do with writing the instrumental.

Link Wray and His Ray Men spent the spring months of 1958 touring theatres and ballrooms in the Midwest and then spent much of that summer working concert shows in the Mid-Atlantic and New England states. With "Rumble" on the charts, the band settled back into the Washington, D.C. area and worked local night clubs and record hops on a nightly basis, with their main home base for the remainder of the 1950s being the Rendezvous.

In 1959 other musicians entered the fold, with Link, Doug and Shorty being joined on most nights by two young musicians from Arlington, Virginia – guitarist Johnny Sneed and singer-guitarist-keyboardist Bobbie Howard. Both men periodically worked with the band into the early 1960s. Sneed was a fine rock and roll guitarist in his own right and performed on some classic Link Wray material, including many of the Swan-era recordings. He also appeared with the band on releases by such artists as Bunker Hill and Marvin Rainwater, in addition to numerous other Ray Vernon-produced singles and albums. Bobbie Howard later fronted his own bands with names like the Dial Tones, the Ponies, and the Hi-Boys. In 1964 he became a founding member of the British Walkers, a group that would become one of the Washington, D.C. area's most popular rock and roll bands.

In the wake of "Rumble," Ray Vernon had secured a record deal for Link Wray and His Ray Men with Epic Records. From January 1959 until August 1961 they released at least six different singles for the label, along with their first long-playing album, "Link Wray & The Wraymen" (Link Wray & The Wraymen; Epic Records, 1960). The band's first single for their new record company, "Raw-Hide" (Link Wray and the Wraymen; Epic Records, 1959), was released in January 1959 and peaked at number 23 on the Billboard magazine's "The Billboard Hot 100" chart on Monday, March 23, 1959.

A high point for the band was an appearance in support of their new single release on "American Bandstand" hosted by Dick Clark on Tuesday, February 10, 1959. Epic ultimately tried to tone down Link's raunchy guitar style and get him to record more pop-oriented songs with full orchestras, a move that led to the rock and roller making a clean split with the company.

While Link Wray and His Ray Men were recording for Epic Records, Ray Vernon had gone into music production and in October 1960 opened his own recording studio in the Portland Building at 1129 Vermont Avenue NW, room 327. For two years he recorded many of the best rock and roll and C&W acts in the Washington, D.C. area. When his lease in the Portland Building expired in October 1962, he moved his Ray Vernon Recording Studio to new quarters at 527 9th Street NW, though within a mere two months the business had had closed its doors.

Throughout 1960 and into early 1961 Link Wray and His Ray Men continued to work the Rendezvous and the Ozarks Restaurant and also kept a schedule of live appearances for Milt Grant, both on his popular television program and at local record hops. When "The Milt Grant Show" went off the air in April 1961, Ray Vernon hooked up Link and the band with budding promoter and future WEAM disc jockey Jack Alix, who booked them at teen dances and record hops throughout the spring and early summer months all over the nation's capital. Consequently, Link Wray and His Ray Men gigged in Washington, D.C. at dances held at the Shrine of the Sacred Heart Teen Club, Mackin High School and St. Anthony's School. They also headlined in Maryland at the Silver Spring Boys Club in Montgomery County and a number of venues in the Prince George's County community of Clinton including the Clinton Volunteer Fire Department, American Legion Clinton Post 259, Church of St. John the Evangelist and Surrattsville High School.

During the late summer of 1961 Ray Vernon decided the financial opportunities were greater if Link and the band concentrated on working Washington, D.C.'s night club scene. An offer for their services came from Isidor Schonberger, who had purchased the Madrid Grill at 1001 H Street NW from Fred Fernandez in August 1960 and transformed it into a live C&W music night club called Vinnie's Grill. Within a year the visiting country bands began to fizzle, the business dropped, and the remaining clientele began to besiege the owner with requests for live rock and roll music. Going on the recommendations of several of his regular customers, Schonberger checked with the owners of the nearby Rendezvous, which had discontinued live music and was about to close its doors for good, about acquiring their former house band. In a smooth transition, Link Wray and His Ray Men then began appearing nightly at Vinnie's Grill.

A sweeping social transformation instantly took place at Vinnie's Grill when the new house band began their run. Despite abstaining from alcohol and drugs, Link Wray projected a menacing image with his black leather jacket, no-nonsense demeanor and hard-edged guitar slinging. In similar fashion, the Ray Men were not a group to be messed with and their presence commanded respect. Perhaps because of the booming power cords and heavy-handed rock and roll the band churned out, they developed a devoted following of motorcycle club members and their associates who craved the music they offered. Vinnie's Grill became flooded with bikers who loved Link Wray, but also loved to party and fight – seemingly with anyone who dared walk through the front door.

Schonberger's establishment soon earned the reputation of being one of Washington, D.C.'s toughest night clubs. Wild stories abounded regarding the happenings inside, including one bizarre account about a crazed drunk, who, whenever the band broke into "Run Chicken Run," would start screaming at the top of his lungs, lift the cash register off the counter, and heave it through the front window (it has never been explained why the patron in question was never arrested or barred from the premises for his behavior, but multiple eyewitnesses have verified the authenticity of the tale).

From 1961 to 1964 when Link Wray and His Ray Men had a break in their Vinnie's Grill schedule, they worked one-nighters or short engagements at many other Washington, D.C. night clubs including Benny's Rebel Room, the Rocket Room, Rand's Night Club, the Shelter Room, the Skylark and the Alpine Room. They also ventured into Maryland on occasion and headlined shows at two popular locations, the Bladensburg Volunteer Fire Department and Glen Echo Park's Spanish Ballroom.

During this time the band also welcomed in a number of different area musicians into their expanded family including singer-guitarists Chuck Bennett and Mike Hunnicutt, singer-keyboardist Max Navarro, keyboardist Bill Hodges, guitarist Jack Van Horn and singers Lee Best and Dave Martin. While the trio of Link, Shorty and Doug remained intact, any combination of these individuals could and would show up to work with the band whenever their services were needed and all were considered part of the extended Wray family.

During the band's run at Vinnie's Grill, a major event took place in the life of the Wray family. In December 1962 Ray Vernon and his wife left the apartment building at 210 Orange Street SE and purchased a home deep in the woods of Southern Prince George's County, Maryland at 16706 Livingston Road in Accokeek. Several other family members – including his parents Fred L. Wray Sr. and Lillian Wray – also went with him. The sprawling, wooded property was equipped with one main house, two smaller guest houses in the backyard, and a large, crumbling chicken coop. When Ray relocated to Accokeek, he also took his recording business with him, first setting up his Ampex three-track recorder in the basement of the main house before moving it into the converted backyard chicken coop, which he then officially dubbed "Wray's Shack 3 Tracks."

Innumerable musicians began visiting the property for informal jam sessions and studio work and Ray seemed determined to capture all of them on tape. In the 1960s alone he produced more than 100 singles and two-dozen albums on a plethora of obscure record labels for an array of different musical artists from the Washington, D.C. area.

From 1961 to 1967 Ray Vernon produced dozens of songs for Link Wray and His Ray Men, many of which were recorded at Wray's Shack 3 Tracks and issued as 45rpm single records under different artist names on various labels. More than a dozen 45rpm single record releases appeared on the Swan Records label alone. In addition, this period saw a total of three long-playing albums released under the Link Wray banner: "Great Guitar Hits by Link Wray" (Link Wray; Vermillion Records, 1962); "Jack the Ripper (Link Wray; Swan Records, 1963); and "Link Wray sings and Plays Guitar" (Link Wray; Vermillion Records, 1964).

It was during this time that one last popular instrumental became a national hit – "Jack the Ripper" (Link Wray and the Raymen; Rumble Records, 1963), which was released in June 1963 and peaked at number 64 on Billboard magazine's "Billboard Hot 100" pop music chart on Saturday, July 27, 1963. To promote the single, Link Wray and His Ray Men made their second and final appearance on "American Bandstand" on Wednesday, July 10,

1963. During his career more than 30 Link Wray albums were issued in either record or compact disc format on a number of different independent and major record labels.

In March 1964 Isidor Schonberger closed Vinnie's Grill and Ray Vernon, acting on information provided by one of Vinnie's bouncers who had worked at several bars throughout Washington, D.C., found a new house band gig for Link Wray and His Ray Men across the Anacostia River at a raunchy, live-music dive called the 1023 Restaurant. Offering loud and primitive rock and roll music and tolerating any type of behavior from its ferocious, Southern-flavored clientele, the 1023 Restaurant was owned at the time by a gentleman named Robert Taylor and located at 1023 Wahler Place SE in Washington, D.C.

While Vinnie's Grill had been considered to be one of Washington, D.C.'s roughest night clubs in memory, the 1023 Restaurant appeared fully equipped to give it a run for its money. To this day the folks that frequented the 1023 back in the middle 1960s find it difficult to describe what would take place on a nightly basis inside the gritty box-like building that was built into a sloping hillside surrounded by decaying public housing projects. It was a different place in a different time and it hosted an entirely different culture.

From 1964 to 1967 Southeast Washington, D.C. was rapidly losing its traditional White, working-class population and those that remained were throwbacks to years past when hard-living Southerners, duck-tailed greasers, and proud, take-no-nonsense folks of Caucasian persuasion ruled the neighborhood streets and bars with iron fists. Government-subsidized public housing quickly changed that, spurring an influx of Blacks, first to the fast-decaying apartment complexes that littered the area, and, secondly, to certain blocks of older housing units throughout the entire Southeast quadrant. The social atmosphere was rapidly changing.

As a neighborhood bar and hangout near the Prince George's County, Maryland line in far Southeast, the 1023 Restaurant was caught in the crossfire of drastic demographic and cultural change. Despite the increasingly darkened complexion of the neighborhood's residents, the 1023 became known as home base to both White neighborhood toughs who refused to leave their home turf behind, as well as select White motorcycle clubs such as the Pagans, the Phantoms, the Knight Riders, the Kamikazes, and their associates and followers. Brutal bar fights between the crazy White folks, trouble of every sort, and brain-shattering rock and roll were always on the menu at the 1023 Restaurant.

When they first landed at the 1023 Restaurant, the steady lineup for Link Wray and His Ray Men was the faithful core trio of Link, Shorty Horton on bass and Doug Wray on drums. They were soon joined by an impressive array of talented musicians, some of whom had worked with the band in the past at Vinnie's Grill and the Rendezvous. This collection consisted of several holdovers including Chuck Bennett, Bill Hodges, Jack Van Horn, Max Navarro and Lee Best, along with newer, highly regarded arrivals such as bassist Ed Cynar of McLean, Virginia, bassist Richie Mitchell of Arlington, Virginia, and bassist Ellwood Brown of Oxon Hill, Maryland.

The band's lineup changed frequently with the aforementioned musicians moving in and out on an almost nightly basis. At different times, Link Wray himself would only work the weekend shift, while weeknights were handled by "The Ray Men" alone. During the 1023 Restaurant run, the band worked six nights per week, playing five separate 45-minute sets from 9pm to 2am. With the volume turned up to ear-splitting levels, the band cranked out high-octane Link Wray originals, treatments of classic and obscure blues songs, and plenty of Elvis Presley covers.

Link Wray and His Ray Men worked the 1023 Restaurant for nearly two years before their run was unceremoniously ended as a result of extreme acts of stupidity by the neighborhood's criminal denizens. In a now-legendary, small-scale riot that served as a prelude to the forthcoming unrest that would rock the city, a mob of young Black thugs inexplicably attacked the 1023 Restaurant and its White patrons shortly before midnight on the evening of Saturday, August 13, 1966.

In a series of criminal and violent actions that began at 5pm that evening and lasted for more than eight hours, Blacks assaulted White citizens, smashed windows of local businesses, and threw rocks and stones at passing automobiles in the 4100 block of Wheeler Road SE. Just before midnight that evening the activity shifted towards the 1023 Restaurant, when a 23-year-old White American named Wallace Poole was attacked as he left the night club by a large group of Blacks who hit him with bricks and sliced off one of his ears with a knife. They then attacked the ambulance that arrived on the scene to transport Poole to the hospital.

According to numerous individuals who claimed to have been in the 1023 Restaurant that evening, the neighborhood thugs cut the club's electrical lines, vandalized automobiles and motorcycles in the outdoor parking lot, smashed the establishment's windows with bricks, rocks and bottles, and attacked customers as they frantically fled the premises. Reportedly, Link Wray and his bandmates somehow survived the melee and made it to their respective homes safely, but the 1023 Restaurant went out of business after this savage ambush.

After leaving the 1023 Restaurant, Link Wray and His Ray Men, now mainly consisting of Link, Doug on drums, Bill Hodges on keyboards, and assorted bass players and guest singers, spent a few months working a number of one-shot jobs and weekend gigs at night clubs like the Bee Hive in Southeast Washington, D.C., the Sunnybrook Tavern in Oxon Hill, Maryland, the Frontier Restaurant in Waldorf, Maryland, and the 1320 Club on Richmond Highway in Alexandria, Virginia.

In early 1967 Link Wray and His Ray Men moved over to the Famous Restaurant on New York Avenue NW in Washington, D.C., where they appeared as the house band for the remainder of the year and into early 1968. When taking a break from the Famous, the group performed at Strick's Restaurant in Silver Hill, Maryland, which became a fairly regular gig for them throughout the remainder of 1968 and all of 1969.

Link Wray, who had three different wives during his time in the nation's capital, had moved away from Orange Street SE in January 1967 to a new apartment just over the Washington, D.C. line in Prince George's County, Maryland at 403 Kennebec Street #1 in the Glassmanor neighborhood of Oxon Hill (today marked 1005 Kennebec Street #1A). In early 1969 he moved into a guest house at his brother Ray's Livingston Road property in Accokeek.

In 1970 and 1971 the guitar great was winding down his time in the area, performing simply as "Link Wray" with different musicians behind him farther south in Charles County, Maryland at night clubs such as Smitty's Steakhouse and Stables Restaurant and Lounge (both in Bryans Road), and a number of night spots in Waldorf including the 301 Ranch, the Wigwam Restaurant, the Loft Room in the Waldorf Restaurant, and the Stardust Inn.

In January 1971 Link Wray moved into his brother Doug's house at 311 Rivermont Drive in Waldorf, Maryland. That year he released the critically acclaimed solo album "Link Wray" (Link Wray; Polydor Records, 1971), a work which had been recorded at Wray's Shack 3 Tracks and was the first of three albums that he would eventually release on that particular major record label. In the fall of that year Ray Vernon cleared the people off his Accokeek property, sold the estate, and relocated to Tucson, Arizona, taking the recording equipment from Wray's Shack 3 Tracks with him. In February 1972 Link Wray left Maryland and joined his brother in Tucson.

From that point on Link Wray would only return to the Washington, D.C. area on rare occasions. He picked up wife number four and moved to Denmark in 1980, a location that would become his final resting place. He continued to record and tour through his remaining years and his music appeared in numerous television programs and movies. Accolades came from every part of the entertainment industry, with legendary rock and roll guitarists like Pete Townshend, Neil Young and Jimmy Page citing him as a major influence on their musical careers.

Link Wray was a musical innovator, incorporating feedback, fuzztone and power chords into a thunderous heavy metal style of savage playing that was years ahead of its time and remains unique and fresh to the present day. Among the better CD compilations that have reissued his work are: "Rumble: The Best of Link Wray" (Rhino Records, 1993); "Mr. Guitar: Original Swan Recordings" (Norton Records, 1995); and "Guitar Preacher: The Polydor Years" (Polydor/Polygram Records, 1995). Link Wray died of heart failure at his home in Copenhagen, Denmark on Saturday, November 5, 2005 at the age of 76.

CHAPTER EIGHTY-SEVEN
ROY BUCHANAN

Roy Buchanan is considered by many in the music industry to have been one of the greatest blues rock guitarists of all-time and was a favorite of such musical artists as John Lennon, Jimi Hendrix, Jeff Beck and Nils Lofgren. He possessed tremendous musical ability, appeared quiet and detached when observed in public or around other musicians, and seemingly shunned the rock and roll spotlight, preferring to simply be his own man in his own time, without regard to the demands of the music business. A Washington, D.C. area resident from 1961 until his untimely death at the age of 48 in 1988, Buchanan was an enigmatic performing artist whose unique style of play made him a legendary guitarist in the nation's capital and around the world.

Roy Buchanan was born in Ozark, Arkansas on Saturday, September 23, 1939 and moved with his parents to Pixley, California at the age of two. When he was five years old he strummed a guitar for the first time and later took lessons from a local music teacher named Clara Presher. At age 13 he purchased a brand new 1953 Fender Telecaster and in the ensuing years was influenced by such guitarists as Roy Nichols, Chet Atkins, Hank Garland, Grady Martin, Pee Wee Crayton, Scotty Moore, Jimmy Nolen and Barney Kessel, among others.

In various interviews throughout the years, Buchanan repeatedly told stories of how he left home in his teens and traveled with different country, jazz and rock bands to perform in such locations as Los Angeles, San Francisco and Las Vegas, though there is almost no existing documentation to verify exactly what bands he was in, what venues he performed at, and what years such adventures may have taken place.

Reportedly, sometime in 1956, Buchanan joined a Los Angeles-based rock and roll band called the Heartbeats, whose drummer Spencer Dryden later went on to play in Jefferson Airplane. A year later the Heartbeats were performing on a Tulsa-based musical variety television show entitled "Oklahoma Bandstand" when he met rockabilly singer-guitarist Dale Hawkins, who recruited the young guitarist into his band. Buchanan toured and recorded extensively with Hawkins from 1957 to early 1961, reportedly playing on no fewer than eight different 45rpm single record releases by the rockabilly great during those years. His most notable recorded work with Hawkins was the single "My Babe" backed with "A House, a Car and a Wedding Ring" (Dale Hawkins; Checker Records, 1958).

Roy Buchanan first paid a visit to Washington, D.C. in late 1957 when Dale Hawkins was booked to make a live appearance on "The Milt Grant Show." Buchanan had been doing studio work on the side and had worked several months as house guitarist on the popular television show "Louisiana Hayride" when Hawkins called him back into the fold for some dates up and down the East Coast.

During this time Dale Hawkins added to his group a saxophone player from Mantua, New Jersey named Ed Montini, who quickly became Buchanan's best friend and roommate on the road. At a gig in Somers Point, New Jersey during the summer of 1960 they met a talented drummer named Stan Weinberg, who hailed from the nation's capital. Weinberg was playing a number of Jersey clubs with the Peppermint Stix, a Washington, D.C. band that was backing the wild lead singer Tito Mambo at the time. Weinberg was greatly impressed by Dale Hawkins and his band and expressed his desire to work with both Buchanan and Montini should the opportunity ever present itself.

On Tuesday, October 18, 1960, Dale Hawkins and his band were booked into the Rocket Room in Washington, D.C. and began working a Tuesday-through-Sunday engagement that lasted until Sunday, October 30. During this booking Hawkins inquired about available musicians he could add to the band and brought in local saxophone great Joe Stanley from the Saxtons. Stanley struck up immediate friendships with both Buchanan and Montini and discussed plans of forming future bands with the pair. When the Rocket Room engagement ended Hawkins left town and continued touring with Buchanan in tow, but in January 1961 the guitarist decided to embark on a new musical project.

At the urging of Ed Montini and Stan Weinberg, Roy Buchanan returned to the Washington, D.C. area in February 1961 and took an apartment with Joe Stanley at the Gregory Arms Apartments on George Palmer Highway in Seat Pleasant, Maryland. (The apartment building that Stanley and Buchanan lived in still stands today at 6000 Martin Luther King Highway in the Pleasant Homes Apartments complex. Also renting apartments in that particular building back in 1961 were Jimmy Dean and Charlie Daniels.) Buchanan joined up with the Saxtons, whose revamped quintet was rounded out with Stanley on saxophone and handling lead vocals, Montini on saxophone, Weinberg on drums and Vince Brando on bass. From February to April of that year the band performed locally at Guy's Place, the Round Up Club, the Rocket Room and the 4400 Club.

In May 1961, Joe Stanley opted out and took the band's name with him. Buchanan, Montini, Weinberg and Brando then took an apartment together on Georgia Avenue NW in Washington, D.C. and formed a new rock and roll band they called the Bad Boys. From May to July 1961 the Bad Boys based out of the Alpine Room and worked one-nighters at the Rocket Room, Rand's Night Club, and Benny's Rebel Room. In July 1961 the Bad Boys traveled to Virginia Beach, Virginia and worked the Tropicana Ballroom and the Top Hat Club.

During their stay Roy Buchanan and Judy Owens, his girlfriend from Mt. Rainier, Maryland, were married on Thursday, July 20, 1961 by a justice of the peace in Elizabeth City, North Carolina. However, the trip down yonder came to an abrupt end when Buchanan and Ed Montini were in a bad automobile accident. The Bad Boys were forced to cancel their remaining engagements and return home to the Washington, D.C. area.

In August 1961 Roy and Judy Buchanan moved in with Judy's mother at 4215 31st Street in Mt. Rainier, Maryland. As soon as they settled, Buchanan was called to Canada where he worked with rock and roll singer-guitarist Ronnie Hawkins and allegedly gave guitar lessons to a young Robbie Robertson. It was a short stay north of the border. In the fall Buchanan relocated to Bellmawr, New Jersey and began a two-year period of playing and recording for such Philadelphia artists as Bobby and the Temps, Freddy Cannon, Cody Brennan and the Temptations, Danny and the Juniors and Bobby Gregg and His Friends.

In the summer of 1963 Buchanan returned to the Owens residence in Maryland and became reacquainted with the Washington, D.C. rock and roll scene by participating in late-night jam sessions at Bass' Restaurant and Bar, then located on Rhode Island Avenue in Mt. Rainier, just a few blocks from home. He spent much of the next 12 months again working with the Saxtons at such local night clubs such as Strick's Restaurant, Benny's Rebel Room, the Rocket Room, the Senate Inn and Rand's Night Club.

In September 1964 Buchanan joined forces with Bobbie "The Kid" Howard, a singer-guitarist-keyboardist who had worked in the past with Link Wray and His Ray Men. He became lead guitarist in Howard's latest venture, a rock band called Bobbie Howard and the Hi Boys, and worked with them on-and-off for more than two months at two of Washington, D.C.'s more popular night spots, Benny's Rebel Room and Rand's Night Club.

In November 1964 Howard reorganized the band and came up with a quartet that included Buchanan, bassist Junior Gill and drummer Mike Kennedy. Bobby Poe came on board to handle the management chores and the group changed its name to the British Walkers. With the new name came a change in style as well, with a combination of British

Invasion and R&B covers dominating their sets. They settled in at the Roundtable, a new rock and roll night club on M Street NW in the city's Georgetown neighborhood.

With Buchanan in the fold, the British Walkers enjoyed tremendous popularity and in December released the single, "I Found You" backed with "Diddley Daddy" (The British Walkers; Try Records, 1964) which received extensive radio airplay in the nation's capital and became a regional hit of great acclaim. Inexplicably, in January 1965 Buchanan suddenly left the British Walkers.

At this point tracking the Washington, D.C. area groups that Buchanan passed through during the remainder of the 1960s becomes an insurmountable task, as he worked pickup jobs and short engagements with a plethora of rock and roll bands, rarely staying in one place for any length of time. In 1965 he had his own short-lived band, the Royal Buchanans, passed through a rock and roll band called the Jumping Jax, and briefly backed up singers Big Al Downing at Rand's Night Club and Phil Flowers at the Hayloft. He spent the summer months working with Danny Denver and the Sound Tracks at the Crosstown Restaurant, McGuire's Pub, the Shelter Room, Benny's Rebel Room, the 4400 Club, Bass' Restaurant and Bar and Strick's Restaurant. He then spent September and October 1965 working a Washington, D.C. night club called the Starlite Restaurant with a rock and roll group called the Outcasts.

From November 1965 through August 1966 Buchanan played lead guitar for the Kalin Twins. Ironically, his bandmates included former British Walker mates Junior Gill and Mike Kennedy. This outfit worked the Rocket Room, Rand's Night Club, Benny's Rebel Room, the Crazy Horse, the Rabbit's Foot, the Skylark and the Turntable Lounge in the basement of Bass' Restaurant and Bar.

After another flurry of jobs with different area rock and roll groups, Buchanan put together a quartet called the Fourmost which took over as the house band at the Silver Dollar Restaurant on M Street NW in Georgetown in March 1967. This particular outfit consisted of Buchanan on lead guitar, singer-bassist Stan Doucette (formerly of the Tejuns, Ray Rock and the Revlons, Stan D and the Profiles and the Four Coachmen), keyboardist Dennis "Stoney" Lucci (formerly of the Creatures) and drummer Bobby Jones. In June the band changed its name to the Uncalled Four. They played everything from R&B to rockabilly and rock and roll classics. As the Summer of Love wore on, they also added tinges of psychedelia to their sets, thanks to Buchanan's versatility and penchant for experimentation.

In August 1967 an event allegedly occurred that has since grown to legendary proportions. As the story goes, Jimi Hendrix was in town playing a five-night stand at the Ambassador Theatre (August 9th through the 13th) up in Adams-Morgan and reportedly stopped by the Silver Dollar Restaurant with Tony Finestra (one of the Ambassador Theatre's managers) to personally observe Buchanan's guitar work. According to information supplied to various media outlets by several individuals including then-Silver Dollar Restaurant manager Leon Petrossian and Buchanan's own bandmates Doucette and Jones, Hendrix got up on the stage with the Uncalled Four that evening and he and Buchanan jammed for approximately 30 minutes. Possibly adding further corroboration to the story, Buchanan himself discusses this alleged Washington, D.C. jam session with Jimi Hendrix in a published article in the August-September 1982 edition of Harmonix magazine entitled "Exclusive Interview with Roy Buchanan" by Harry Folsom.

In September 1967 the Uncalled Four left the Silver Dollar Restaurant, changed its name to Roy Buchanan and the Poor Boys, and entered into a management contract with the Jolly Joyce Agency in Philadelphia. They proceeded to work for several months at such night clubs as the Aztec Club in Bethlehem, Pennsylvania, the Cameo Lounge in Allentown, Pennsylvania, Dick Lee's Musical Bar in Bellmawr, New Jersey, and Joe Pop's

Shore Bar in Long Beach, New Jersey. In early 1968 the band broke up and Buchanan spent several months doing session work in studios from New York City to Nashville, Tennessee.

Since 1965 Buchanan and his family had lived in various apartments in Mt. Rainier and Silver Spring and in the spring of 1968 he began renting a house at 4925 56th Place in Hyattsville, Maryland. At that time he joined forces once again with Danny Denver, who now named his backup band the Soundmasters. The band at that time consisted of Denver handling lead vocals, Buchanan on guitar, bassist Shorty Horton and drummer Richard Maughn. They mainly worked in Waldorf, Maryland at the Loft Room of the Waldorf Restaurant and the Stardust Inn, where they performed C&W classics, Elvis Presley covers and pop songs. They also began working off-nights at the Cross Roads in Bladensburg for owner George Saslaw, who was mainly booking C&W acts, but seemed intrigued with the wide range of musical material Danny Denver and the Soundmasters offered.

Buchanan started the year 1969 off by moving from 56th Place to a rented home at 5724 Eastpines Drive in Riverdale, Maryland. Danny Denver and the Soundmasters worked wherever they could at this time, including engagements at Frank Gosman's Dawnrose Big Dipper in Beltsville, the Tick Tock Restaurant in Hyattsville, and the Turf Club in Laurel. Late in the year Denver moved the band over to the Cross Roads in Bladensburg on a full-time basis, a move that resulted in what many believe to have been Roy Buchanan's finest hour.

When Danny Denver and the Soundmasters invaded the Cross Roads, the night club already had an incredible history of legendary entertainment under its belt, having been home to big band orchestras in the 1940s, pop singers like Tony Bennett and Patti Page and strippers like Blaze Starr in the 1950s, and C&W legends like Little Jimmy Dickens and Ernest Tubb in the 1960s. With Buchanan on the Cross Roads scene, the club was suddenly packed with imported long-haired hippies from Georgetown and Dupont Circle, out-of-place University of Maryland students, and fellow musicians from all over the area anxious to witness what ads in the Washington Post proclaimed as "The finest rock guitarist in the world." The new arrivals were forced to rub shoulders with the club's long-standing, blue-collar, country music-loving clientele and for the most part it was not a smooth mix. The contrast only added to the night club's unique flavor.

Danny Denver and the Soundmasters worked the Cross Roads throughout all of 1969 and 1970 and into early 1971. In 1970 Buchanan left the home on Eastpines Drive and moved his wife and kids to the Whitfield Towne Apartments in Lanham, Maryland where they took a unit at 5626 Whitfield Chapel Road. By that time the band's lineup consisted of Denver, Buchanan, keyboardist Joe Bayliss, bassist Don Monahan (replacing Shorty Horton) and drummer Ricky Rohme (replacing Richard Maughn).

Buchanan built a large following at the Cross Roads and began receiving coverage in the local dailies for his prowess on the guitar. Journalist Tom Zito was an enthusiastic supporter of the guitarist and wrote a feature article on him entitled "Only a Guitar Player: A Legend Among Musicians," which appeared in the Washington Post on December 9, 1970. A slightly different version of the same piece titled "Roy Buchanan, Heavy Axe" was published in Rolling Stone in their Thursday, February 18, 1971 issue.

Zito became linked with Buchanan and when touring big-name rock and rollers hit the nation's capital and were looking for something to do after their gigs, he would usher them to the Cross Roads to see the living legend in action. During the course Buchanan's Cross Roads run, some of the rock and rollers who made pilgrimages to the Bladensburg night club to catch the guitarist on his home turf included Kim Simmonds, Brian Auger, Peter Green, Leon Russell, Jerry Lee Lewis, Ry Cooder, Rory Gallagher, Paul Rodgers, Simon Kirk, Mike McGear (brother of Paul McCartney), Robbie Robertson, Jerry Garcia, Duane and Gregg Allman, Pete Townshend, Frank Zappa, Eric Clapton, Charlie Daniels, Sly Stone and a number of local guitar heroes including Nils Lofgren and Danny Gatton.

In the spring of 1971 Buchanan decided to leave Danny Denver's outfit and from his own band. Simply billed as "Roy Buchanan," his new group continued to work the Cross Roads on a regular basis. The lineup of his first group consisted of himself, singer Lee Best, bassist Billy Hancock, keyboardist Vince Barrett and drummer Mike Cannon. It was a short-lived affair and a few months later Buchanan put together another band that included lead singer Chuck Tilley, bassist Pete Van Allen, keyboardist Dick Heintze, percussionist Marc Fisher and drummer Michael "Pokey" Walls. Later in the year the band's lineup was again shuffled and they re-emerged as Roy Buchanan and the Snake Stretchers with a lineup of Buchanan, Tilley, Van Allen, Heintze, rhythm guitarist Ted Irwin and drummer Ned Davis.

Tom Zito's published articles on Buchanan in 1970 and 1971 had intrigued a group of filmmakers from National Education Television in New York who decided to produce a biographical documentary on Buchanan. The result was "Introducing Roy Buchanan," a 90-minute film of music, live performances and commentary interspersed with footage of Buchanan's return to Pixley, California. The movie aired on public television stations across the United States on Monday, November 8, 1971.

In the aftermath of this documentary, Polydor Records called and after several months a deal with Buchanan was hatched. In February 1972 Roy Buchanan and the Snake Stretchers left the Cross Roads behind and moved over to a night club a few blocks east of Georgetown called My Mother's Place at 18th and M Streets NW in Washington, D.C. They remained there into the month of July. When this booking ended in the middle of the summer season it marked the conclusion of Roy Buchanan's time as a Washington, D.C. area rock and roll commodity.

Roy Buchanan's popularity was now beyond cult status. Despite the fact he had no major label record album to promote and was not actively touring, he headlined as a solo artist at Carnegie Hall in New York on Wednesday, June 21, 1972. The concert completely sold out. In August of that year Polydor Records released the guitarist's debut album, simply titled "Roy Buchanan" and he began embarking on concert tours around the country to support his releases. Four more records on Polydor followed: "Second Album" (1973), "That's What I Am Here For" (1973), "In the Beginning" (1974) and "Live Stock" (1974). He then made a switch to Atlantic Records and over the next few years released the albums "A Street Called Straight" (1976), "Loading Zone" (1977) and "You're Not Alone" (1978). In the ensuing years a number of different Roy Buchanan albums and compilations were released on a variety of different record labels.

When Buchanan began receiving his payments from Polydor in 1973 he moved away from Prince George's County, Maryland and relocated to Lovettsville, Virginia. In 1985 he moved his family to 2325 Harleyford Court in Reston, Virginia and began working in a trio with Crack the Sky singer-bassist Carey Ziegler and singer-drummer Vince Santoro. Then, suddenly, Buchanan's odyssey came to an end on the night of Sunday, August 14, 1988. Arrested near his home that evening on a drunk-in-public charge, he was placed in a holding cell at the Fairfax County Adult Detention Center. On a routine check, officers found him hanging from his shirt at 11:16pm. Attempts to revive him were unsuccessful and he was pronounced dead one minute before midnight. His death was officially ruled a suicide.

CHAPTER EIGHTY-EIGHT
DANNY GATTON

Danny Gatton was a master popular music guitarist whose artistry encompassed every conceivable musical style from blues to jazz to rock and roll. Widely known as "The World's Greatest Unknown Guitarist" (a moniker placed on him by Guitar Player magazine), Gatton worked his way through the local teen dance scene in the 1950s, performed with scores of talented musicians in local night clubs in a plethora of bands, and signed a lucrative record deal with Elektra Entertainment, only to have his life come to an untimely end before his full potential was realized.

Daniel Wood Gatton Jr. was born in Washington, D.C. on Tuesday, September 4, 1945 and first learned guitar from his father. His early influences included Les Paul, Chet Atkins, Wes Montgomery, Charlie Christian, Hank Thompson, Cliff Gallup, Hank Garland, Carl Perkins, James Barton and Scotty Moore. Gatton grew up in Washington, D.C. at 88 Elmira Street SW and two of his biggest influences as he practiced on guitar as a teenager in the late 1950s were guitarists Jack Reid and Gene Newport, both of whom lived in close proximity and played in a popular local teen dance band called the Thunderbirds.

Gatton attended Hart Junior High School and then spent two years at Ballou High School in Southeast Washington, D.C. before a move to Oxon Hill, Maryland led him to graduate from Oxon Hill High School in 1963. During his junior high and high school years he played in such local teen bands as the Lancers, the Rockin' Minors, the Phaetons and the Off Beats (a different group from the area Dixieland jazz-pop teen band of the same name that was active in 1940s and 1950s). When Gatton was 15 years old, as the Off Beats were working the 1320 Club in Alexandria, Virginia, he began sitting in during his off-nights with Dub Howington and His Tennessee Haymakers at such Maryland night clubs as the Cross Roads, the Dixie Pig and the Las Vegas Club.

After the Off Beats disbanded in 1964 Gatton spent the remainder of the decade working with a series of bands including the Superiors, who had a house band position at the Red Fox Inn in Bethesda, Maryland, and the Take Five, a four-piece band whose lineup at the time included bassist John Koslin, keyboardist Dick Heintze and singer-drummer Ron MacDonald. The Take Five became one of the region's most popular jazz-pop-rock combos, working throughout 1965 at such night clubs as the Belby House in Rockville, Maryland and the Crazy Horse and the Paul Mall Restaurant in Georgetown. They then spent most of 1966 at Tom Sarris' Orleans House Restaurant on Wilson Boulevard in Arlington, Virginia.

In the late 1960s Gatton played briefly in a local band called the Soul Mates with former members of the Off Beats, a project which produced the single "Moonlight Cruise" backed with "How's Your Sister" (The Soul Mates; Wilson Line Records, 1966). He then went on the road, first spending time in Nashville where he played with a band called John Richard Jarvis and the Church Street Gathering, and then touring the Midwest with jazz organist Bobby Charles and appearing on the album "Bobby Charles!!!!! Invades the Wells Fargo Lounge" (Bobby Charles; Fenton Records, 1968).

Back in the Washington, D.C. area in the summer of 1968, Gatton returned to the band called Take Five, which was now a quintet with the addition of saxophonist Roger McDuffie, and spent the next two years with them performing at two night clubs in Silver Hill, Maryland, the Quonset Supper Club and Strick's Restaurant. In the early 1970s, the band worked a night club called Gus and John's Italian Villa in Camp Springs Maryland under the name the East Coast Express. The lineup of the group at that time consisted of Gatton, lead singer Ron MacDonald, bassist Jimmy Welsh, keyboardist Dick Heintze and drummer Michael "Pokey" Walls.

In 1971 Gatton got together with singer-bassist Billy Hancock and drummer Dave Elliott and formed the country rock band Fat Chance. They first worked at Hillbilly Heaven in Lorton, Virginia and a series of local Village Inn restaurants (Springfield, Bailey's Crossroads and Rockville). After a short stint as Heavy Duty, the band changed its name to Danny and the Fat Boys. During their reign from 1971 to 1976 (which included a period where the three were absorbed by a larger band called Liz Meyer and Friends), Danny and the Fat Boys worked a wide range of Washington, D.C. area night clubs including the Childe Harold, the Crazy Horse, the Cross Roads, Bass' Restaurant and Bar, Apple Pie, the Keg, Ernie's Place, the Stardust Inn, the Varsity Grill Back Room, the Psyche Delly and My Friend's House. During this period the band also recorded and released an album entitled "American Music" (Danny and the Fat Boys; Aladdin Records, 1975).

In late 1976 Gatton joined forces with bassist John Previti and over the next 18 years assembled a series of bands and musical projects with such names as the Danny Gatton Band, the Redneck Jazz Explosion, the Drapes, and Funhouse. He also worked with other performing artists such as C&W singer-guitarist Roger Miller, rockabilly singer-guitarist Robert Gordon and blues singer-guitarist Tom Principato.

As a solo performer and bandleader, Gatton headlined throughout the 1980s and early 1990s at some of the Washington, D.C. area's top venues including Wolf Trap National Park for the Performing Arts, the Birchmere, the Bayou, Club Soda, Nightclub 9:30 and Tornado Alley. He was written up in numerous national music publications, including Rolling Stone, which featured Gatton in an article by David Fricke in their edition of Thursday, May 18, 1989 entitled "Hot Guitarist: He is the Fastest Player Alive – So How Come Nobody Knows His Name?"

In 1990 Gatton was signed to Elektra Records and two albums resulted: "88 Elmira St." (Danny Gatton; Elektra Entertainment, 1991); and "Cruisin' Deuces" (Danny Gatton; Elektra Entertainment, 1993). Throughout his career, he recorded or appeared with other musical acts on more than 20 albums, most of which were issued on different independent record labels. One of the best of the many compilations of Gatton's career is a two-disc, 27-track collection entitled "Hot Rod Guitar: The Danny Gatton Anthology" (Danny Gatton; Rhino Entertainment Company, 1999). Danny Gatton died suddenly on Tuesday, October 4, 1994 at the age of 49.

CHAPTER EIGHTY-NINE
THE NEWPORTS

During the early 1960s, the Newports emerged as one of the most dynamic and highly sought-after rock and roll bands on the Washington, D.C. area teen dance scene. Forming in Montgomery County, Maryland under the leadership of Blaine Smith and Scott Mitchell, they achieved the goals of every young band in the region – headlining teen dances and shows at the area's most popular churches, community centers and armories, appearing with and backing up a number of nationally known performing artists, and recording and releasing several 45rpm single records that were well-received throughout the region. As the decade progressed, the Newports experienced numerous personnel changes, adapted to the changing musical times, and added engagements at local night clubs to their schedule. The Newports are still performing today and are one of the very few rock and roll bands in the nation's capital that have survived the times and have continued to add to their impressive musical legacy.

The roots of the Newports go back to a popular teen rock and roll band from Montgomery County, Maryland called the Galaxies, who formed in February 1958 and consisted of four students from Leland Junior High School in Bethesda, Maryland: singer-guitarist Blaine Smith, saxophonist Donald Shook, pianist Bob Oberlander and drummer Allen Gutheim (later additions included bassist Bill White and singer Jim Osmond). The band played songs by such artists as Chuck Berry, Duane Eddy and Link Wray, and stayed together through late 1960.

As the Galaxies wound down, leader Blaine Smith was approached by a drummer from Bethesda named Scott Mitchell, who asked if he would be interested in putting together a new group that culled members from the Galaxies and his own band, the Scott Mitchell Band. Smith agreed, and one of the area's first young super groups emerged.

The Newports, as the new outfit was called, first gathered and rehearsed on Sunday, January 1, 1961 at the Garrett Park Recreation Center. The band's initial lineup consisted of singer-guitarist Blaine Smith (Bethesda-Chevy Chase High School, Class of 1963), former Galaxies bassist Bill White (Bethesda-Chevy Chase High School, Class of 1963), drummer Scott Mitchell (Walter Johnson High School, Class of 1961), saxophonist Paul D'Amatto from Garrett Park, Maryland (Walter Johnson High School, Class of 1961) and pianist Dick Heintze from the Tenleytown neighborhood of Washington, D.C. (Woodrow Wilson High School, Class of 1957; he had previously played in the Triumphs with bassist Jack Casady and guitarist Jorma Kaukonen, and the Off Beats with guitarist Danny Gatton).

The Newports played originals and most everything that was on the Billboard popular music charts including songs by Chuck Berry, Fats Domino, Bill Haley and His Comets and Elvis Presley. They immediately rose to the top of the local teen dance circuit and during their first six months performed shows at the North Bethesda Teen Club (North Bethesda Junior High School), the Our Lady of Lourdes Catholic Church Teen Club (Bethesda), the Shrine of the Sacred Heart Teen Club (Washington, D.C.), the St. John Baptist de la Salle Catholic Church Teen Club (Chillum), the St. Mark the Evangelist Catholic Church Teen Club (Hyattsville), Northwestern High School (Hyattsville), Frederick Sasscer High School (Upper Marlboro), the Arlington County Fire Department (Arlington) and Club Waysons (Lothian, in Anne Arundel County, Maryland).

Other major Newports performances of the day included: co-headlining with the Naturals at the Silver Spring Armory on Saturday, April 15, 1961; co-headlining with Link Wray and His Ray Men at the "Jack Alix Dance Spectacular" at the Silver Spring Boys Club on Friday, July 21, 1961; and headlining at the Bladensburg Volunteer Fire Department on Wednesday, July 26, 1961.

The Newports were somewhat unique in that they managed to stay together as a unit despite some significant personnel changes. In many instances younger bands would lose their focus when key players moved on, but Blaine Smith kept tabs on local musical talent and skillfully replaced departing members with equally gifted musicians.

Both Scott Mitchell and Paul D'Amatto graduated from Walter Johnson High School in June 1961 and left the Newports soon after as they prepared for college. Smith revamped the band that July and introduced several newcomers to the fold, most of whom were from Montgomery County, Maryland. Joining holdovers Smith, White, and Clarke in the second edition of the Newports were lead singer Calvin Linthicum (who used the stage name "Cal Linley"), guitarist Larry Swacker, saxophonist Don Shook, drummer Pepper Archenbeau, and two female background singers, Diane Meenahan and Pat Brown (who were collectively known as "The Filterettes"). A pianist named Mike Smith also joined that summer, but left after a few months and was not replaced.

The second edition of the Newports remained intact from July 1961 through January 1963 and during this time the band regularly headlined large teen dances at the Silver Spring Armory, a facility that, for all practical purposes, became a home base for the band. They also spent much of 1962 performing on Saturday and Sundays at Glen Echo Park's Spanish Ballroom in Montgomery County, Maryland. In addition, during this time they appeared in Washington, D.C. at Mackin High School, St. Albans School and Trinity Episcopal Church; in Maryland at the St. Bartholomew School Teen Club (Bethesda), the Holy Redeemer Catholic Church Teen Club (Kensington), the Palmer Park Teen Club (Kent Junior High School), the Garrett Park Recreation Center (Garrett Park) and Walter Johnson High School (Bethesda); and in Virginia at Yorktown High School (Arlington) and the American Legion Fairfax Post 177 (Fairfax).

The evolution of the Newports continued as the decade moved forward. From 1963 to 1967, musicians periodically left the fold and new ones emerged to take their places. Three more versions of the band manifested through this time. From February 1963 to February 1964 the band consisted of seven musicians: lead singer Tom Willett, lead guitarist Blaine Smith, bassist Bill White, organist John Hurd, saxophonist Greg Novick, trumpeter Bill Behr and drummer Don Williamson. The fourth main version of the band, which lasted roughly from February 1964 to March 1966, consisted of lead singers Tom and Charlie Willet, lead guitarist Blaine Smith, bassist Bill White, organist John Hurd and drummer Don Williamson.

The final run of the Newports, from April 1966 to June 1967 saw several members weave in and out including guitarist Chris Tobey and organist Bob Koch, with the most stable roster consisting of lead singer Robert Gordon (who later went on to some measure of fame as a solo rockabilly artist), lead guitarist Larry Swacker, bassist Bill White, organist Bob King and drummer Bruce Davis. This part of the 1960s saw the band headline shows at such facilities as the Wedge (Bethesda Youth Center), the Wheaton Youth Center (Wheaton), the Kensington Armory (Kensington), Northwestern High School (Hyattsville) and the Arlington County Fire Department (Arlington).

As the 1960s advanced the Newports began adding more prestigious concert and night club dates to their work schedule – achievements that few of their contemporaries on the teen dance scene could equal. These performances established the band as one of the region's most talented young rock and roll outfits. While they continued to work dances at the local schools, churches and community centers during these years, they also began playing events at area colleges, opening concerts for various nationally known performing artists, and securing engagements at some of the very best rock and roll night spots in

Washington, D.C. area including the Roundtable, the Crazy Horse, the Bayou, the Rocket Room, the Keg, the Rabbit's Foot and the Red Fox Tavern in Bethesda, Maryland.

During their time the Newports recorded and released several 45rpm single records on both independent and national labels. Early in their career they backed rockabilly singer Doug Powell on his single "Ft Lauderdale," backed with "Big City Walk" (Doug Powell; Mercury Records, 1962). The band only performed on the A-side of this release, which was released and distributed nationally, but failed to make the Billboard popular music charts.

The Newports also released seven singles of their own: "(Don't You Ever) Mess Around" backed with "Can't Find A Girl" (Cal Linley and the Newports; DC Records, 1962); "Deep Blue" backed with "Questions" (Blaine Smith with the Newports; Limo Records, 1962); "Big Boy Pete" (Credited to "Blaine Smith and His Beat Guitar with the Newports") backed with "I Won't Cry" (Credited to "Cal Linley and the Newports") (Limo Records, 1963); "Magic Potion" backed with "Love Works From Town to Town" (Cal Linley with the Newports; Limo Records, 1963); "C'Mon Part Two" (Credited to "Blaine Smith and the Newports") backed with "I Won't Cry" (Credited to "Cal Linley and the Newports") (Mibus Records, 1963); "Little Heart" backed with "Maybe You've Changed" (The Newports; BSM Records, 1965); and "The Trouble Is You" backed with "I Want You" (The Newports; BSM Records, 1965; this single was reissued on the major label Laurie Records that same year).

After the Newports disbanded in 1967 founding member Blaine Smith put together a highly acclaimed Christian music band called Sons of Thunder that performed on college campuses throughout the Mid-Atlantic states throughout the late 1960s and early 1970s. Smith remained active in music through the years and in December 2001 he reformed the Newports. They are still performing today throughout the Washington, D.C. area with their current lineup consisting of singers Debbie Halverson, Arlene Jay and Becky Briggs ("The Filterettes"), guitarist Blaine Smith, bassist Mike DeGraba, keyboardist Mike Henley and drummer Rob Dyer.

CHAPTER NINETY
THE MAJESTIC NEONS

One of the area's most talented teen bands of the 1960s was the Majestic Neons, who got their start in Prince George's County, Maryland, went through a significant shift in personnel early in their existence, and, after becoming a top attraction on the area's teen dance circuit, became the only local band of its kind to perform live at the World's Fair in New York in 1964. The Majestic Neons specialized in the rock and roll songs that dominated popular music during the early 1960s, but their vast repertoire included standard pop songs, R&B and rockabilly. In an era where musical specialization was the trend, the Majestic Neons displayed versatility in their performances and a high level of musicianship that placed them among the very best young bands in the region.

The roots of the Majestic Neons go back to a teen band entitled the Rhythm Rockers who based their operations out of the Colmar Manor Teen Club adjacent to the Bladensburg Road Strip in Prince George's County, Maryland. The band came into existence in 1959 with a lineup of three Colmar Manor teens in rhythm guitarist Theodore "T.S." Wright, bassist Joel "Spike" Gundersheimer and drummer Bobby Klein, along with a talented singer-lead guitarist from Northeast Washington, D.C. named Milford Chick Hall (commonly referred to as "Chick Hall, Jr.").

Chick Hall, Jr. was born on Monday, December 24, 1945 in Norfolk, Virginia. His father, Milford Willard "Chick" Hall, a great country and jazz guitarist, relocated to Washington, D.C. in 1949 in search of better musical opportunities. Chick Jr. and his mother joined the senior Chick Hall a year later and after a couple moves around the city the family settled in 1953 at 4202 14th NE. Chick Hall Jr. entered St. Anthony's School in sixth grade and remained there throughout his high school years, graduating in 1963.

The senior Chick Hall worked his guitar magic at various venues throughout the Washington, D.C. area in the early and middle 1950s and in December 1955 he purchased the Surf Club on Bladensburg Road in Colmar Manor, Maryland. As a youth Chick Jr. tried his hand at piano and clarinet and sang with his father on occasion, but it wasn't until a visit to the Surf Club to watch his father play on Easter Sunday 1958 that he started playing the guitar in serious fashion. During this time he became friends with a slightly older bass-playing Colmar Manor teen named Spike Gundersheimer, whose father worked as a cook at the Surf Club. Within a year the two had recruited two other teen-aged musicians name T.S. Wright and Bobby Klein into a band they called the Rhythm Rockers.

In 1960 the Hall family relocated from Washington, D.C. to a house at 4506 24th Street in Mt. Rainier, Maryland. The Rhythm Rockers remained together into the latter half of 1960, holding down house band status at the Colmar Manor Teen Club (located within the Town of Colmar Manor Municipal Building, 3701 Lawrence Street, Colmar Manor, MD; today it is known as the Town of Colmar Manor Community Center and Town Hall). The performed at the teen club every other Friday night and played early-era rock and roll songs by artists such as Chuck Berry, the Ventures and Duane Eddy. They also occasionally performed at the Surf Club on nearby Bladensburg Road.

During the course of the year drummer Bobby Klein left the band and was replaced by a teenager named Tommy Haughawout, who had grown up in Colmar Manor, but was living in Berwyn Heights, Maryland and attending Greenbelt Junior High School when he joined the group.

Soon after connecting with the band Haughawout moved back to his grandmother's house in Colmar Manor and entered the 10th grade at Bladensburg High School, a school from which he would graduate in 1964. He brought impressive bloodlines to the band, as his father Frank was a greatly respected steel guitar player who had backed Patsy Cline and had worked with singer Jimmy Dean on the "Town and Country Jamboree" shows at the Joe Turner Arena. Late in 1960 the Rhythm Rockers splintered, but much of group's lineup decided to continue playing together in a new rock and roll band.

In early 1961 the first edition of the Majestic Neons emerged with a lineup of singer-guitarist Chick Hall, Jr., bassist Spike Gundersheimer, drummer Tommy Haughawout, and a saxophonist named George Wright, who hailed from Silver Spring, Maryland. Though the details on the circumstances behind the band's unique name are sketchy today, it is generally agreed upon that the name "Neons" was first introduced by Wright, with Haughawout suggesting "Majestic" as the lead-in.

The Majestic Neons kept busy by playing their popular brand of rock and roll music – everything from Link Wray and His Ray Men to Bo Diddley to Gene Vincent – at dances at the Colmar Manor Teen Club (Colmar Manor), the Seabrook Teen Club (Seabrook), the Nativity Catholic Church Teen Club (Washington, D.C.), the Cottage City and Colmar Manor Fire Department (Cottage City), the Bladensburg Volunteer Fire Department (Bladensburg), St. Anthony's School (Washington, D.C.) and scores of private parties. On occasion, the band was also booked by Hall's father into his Surf Club on Bladensburg Road, which proved quite an experience for a group of musicians just entering their high school years.

It is noteworthy that during this time Hall, Jr., Gundersheimer, and Wright sharpened their musical skills by working together in a band called the Misfits with drummer Ray Tanguay and singer-pianist Eddie Stitt. This outfit played a mix of C&W and rockabilly music on a steady basis at the Ranch House, a night club on Brightseat Road in Seat Pleasant, Maryland.

In late 1962 the Majestic Neons shifted their lineup and became a trio, with Gundersheimer and Wright departing, and Hall, Jr. and Haughawout being joined by bassist Brendan Pelan, who was also a member of St. Anthony's School Class of 1963. Pelan was born in Belfast, Ireland on Wednesday, October 31, 1945, moved to America with his family in 1949 and was raised in College Park, Maryland. As a child learned the violin from his father, who had been a champion fiddler back in Dublin.

As he entered his teens Pelan decided he wanted to play the guitar after hearing Elvis Presley's "Jailhouse Rock" over a friend's house. During his ninth grade year at St. Anthony's School he formed a rock and roll band called the Runarounds with three of his friends. The Runarounds worked private parties and shopping mall events for two years and Pelan developed a reputation for his singing and playing. During his junior year of high school at St. Anthony's School, Chick Hall, Jr. approached Pelan and asked him to join his band, offering to teach his new recruit the bass guitar. The pair worked out songs by the Everly Brothers, Dion and the Belmonts, the Five Satins, the Drifters and others, and Brendan Pelan became a full-time member of the Majestic Neons.

Before 1962 was finished Tommy Haughawout opted to leave the Majestic Neons and make a go of it as a full-time drummer in bands that worked the Washington, D.C. night club scene. Upon notifying Hall and Pelan of his impending departure, he recommended a friend and drummer from school named Rick Stubblefield as his replacement. Stubblefield was born on Friday, January 21, 1944 and had grown up in Bladensburg, Maryland, where he had attended Bladensburg Junior High School and then Bladensburg High School. As a senior at Bladensburg during the 1962-1963 school year he became a member of the Majestic Neons.

With a new three-man lineup of Chick Hall, Jr., Brendan Pelan and Rick Stubblefield, the Majestic Neons plugged in and took off. The band worked out more sophisticated tunes from the Billboard popular music charts and specialized in three-part harmonies, an offering few other area teen dance bands could match. Artists they covered included Elvis Presley, Link Wray and His Ray Men, the Everly Brothers, Roy Orbison, the Ventures, Del Shannon, Bobby Vee, Rick Nelson, Booker T. and the M.G.s, the Drifters and the Crickets (featuring singer-guitarist Buddy Holly).

From late 1962 to 1964 the Majestic Neons were in great demand on the local music scene and performed at dances at the Hyattsville Teen Club (Hyattsville), the Greenbelt Teen Club (Greenbelt Youth Center), the Laurel Teen Club (Laurel), Bladensburg High School (Bladensburg), Northwestern High School (Hyattsville), St. Anthony's School (Washington, D.C.), St. Vincent Pallotti High School (Laurel), DeMatha Catholic High School (Hyattsville), the Bladensburg Volunteer Fire Department (Bladensburg), the Cottage City and Colmar Manor Fire Department (Cottage City), the St. Mark's Catholic School Teen Club (Hyattsville), the St. John Baptist de la Salle Catholic Church Teen Club (Chillum), St. Mary's Church (Rockville), the St. Bernadette Catholic Church Teen Club (Silver Spring), the St. Bernard Catholic Church Teen Club (Riverdale) and the Holy Redeemer Parish Teen Club (College Park). They also occasionally performed at dances at the VFW Kent Memorial Post 5730 (then-located at 1000 Brightseat Road in Landover, Maryland).

The Majestic Neons had taken to working in blue monogrammed blazers – a dress-up trend that other teen bands emulated – and were became known for being the regular Friday night house band at the College Park Teen Club which was located in the basement of the City of College Park Municipal Building at 4500 Knox Road. When they had started performing at College Park in 1962 the teen club was struggling. However, the band quickly attracted a large following and began packing the room on a regular basis, leading the City of College Park to present them with a special award of appreciation in the summer of 1963 for their contributions to the city's youth.

Things got interesting for the Majestic Neons in 1964. During the spring months they attracted the attention of Elliot Ryan, a local entrepreneur who owned a beatnik-styled coffee house on 17th Street NW in Washington, D.C. called the Unicorn and had his hand in many local music projects (in 1973 Ryan founded a Washington, D.C. music newspaper called Unicorn Times). He took the band into the studio and produced two original songs, resulting in the single "Swingin' Thing is Summertime" backed with "My Baby Don't Love Me" (The Neons; Unicorn International Productions, 1964).

One of the greatest accomplishments of the Majestic Neons was a one-hour afternoon performance they gave in the United States Pavilion at the New York World's Fair, located in Flushing Meadows-Corona Park in the Borough of Queens, New York City, New York, on Saturday, August 14, 1965. It was a hectic live music weekend in the City, with the Beatles performing the very next day at Shea Stadium. The Majestic Neons then rounded out the year with a co-headlining performance with the Hangmen at the St. Jerome Catholic Church Teen Club in Hyattsville on Friday, November 5, 1965.

As the late 1960s rolled around the Majestic Neons began cutting back on their schedule. They still gave well-received performances, including an appearance at the Hyattsville Armory on Saturday, March 19, 1966 where they were on a multi-act bill with the Hangmen, the Plague and the Outcast Set. The group took a hit when Brendan Pelan left the fold and was replaced on bass by Jesse Ayers, but continued on as the Neons Band. After playing several dances at the American Legion College Park Post 217 from January to March 1967, the band folded for good.

CHAPTER NINETY-ONE
LAWRENCE AND THE ARABIANS

During the 1960s there were dozens of talented bands that enjoyed tremendous success on the local teen dance scene. One of the very best groups to emerge from Prince George's County, Maryland was Lawrence and the Arabians, who became known for their repertoire of R&B covers of such performers as James Brown, Otis Redding, Wilson Pickett, the Temptations and innumerable others. A top attraction throughout the region, this band held tight to their soulful style and provided an alternative to the British Invasion cover bands that proliferated during the decade. Lawrence and the Arabians, with their impressive musical talent and polished stage demeanor, were a strong influence on all of the other young musicians in the area and during their time rated as one of the most popular and influential teen dance bands to grace the nation's capital.

Lawrence and the Arabians formed in the autumn of 1963 with its initial lineup consisting of singer-keyboardist Larry Kidwell of Hyattsville (Northwestern High School, Class of 1965), bassist Bill Caron of Silver Spring (Montgomery Blair High School, Class of 1966), saxophonist Dennis Monke of Hyattsville (High Point High School Class of 1965) and drummer Mike Zack of Beltsville (a ninth-grader at Beltsville Junior High School at the time, he would go on to attend High Point High School).

The band first rehearsed together in the basement of Kidwell's house at 3904 Longfellow Street in Hyattsville, Maryland and gave its first performance at a March of Dimes benefit held that fall at the Berwyn Heights Teen Club in the Berwyn Heights Elementary School. Shortly after forming, Caron departed and was replaced by guitarist Johnny Ellison of Chillum (Northwestern High School, Class of 1963).

While the Beatles changed the course of popular music in 1964 by spearheading the British Invasion, Lawrence and the Arabians resisted the popular trend and opted to play R&B at local teen dances. Throughout that year they performed their music in the area for functions at the College Park Teen Club (College Park Municipal Building), the Berwyn Heights Teen Club (Berwyn Heights Elementary School), Beltsville Junior High School (Beltsville), the Hyattsville Teen Club (Prince George's Plaza), the St. Jerome Catholic Church Teen Club (Hyattsville), the St. Camillus Catholic Church Teen Club (Silver Spring), St. Vincent Pallotti High School (Laurel) and the Greenbelt Teen Club (Greenbelt Youth Center).

Beginning in late 1964 Lawrence and the Arabians experienced a string of personnel changes. Dennis Monke and Johnny Ellison departed. In due time Kidwell and Zack expanded the band's size and sound by welcoming in several new members from around the region. The new additions were: guitarist George Bold; saxophonists Mike Fried and Mike Kidwell; trumpeters Gerry Bowles and Bruce Morris; and trombonist Tom Blair. With the new additions, the popularity of Lawrence and the Arabians soared. They showed up onstage wearing matching blue tuxedos, traveled to jobs by van and worked up to four gigs per week playing almost every church, school and teen club event in the area.

From 1965 to 1969 Lawrence and the Arabians frequently performed at the Greenbelt Teen Club dances which were held in the gymnasium of the Greenbelt Youth Center. At the time, the facility had a capacity of 520 occupants and the band drew near that number of patrons on a regular basis, leading them to rent out the neighboring Greenbelt Armory every few months for their own concert shows. The first of these Armory events took place on the night of Saturday, December 10, 1966 when Lawrence and the Arabians co-headlined with the English Setters and brought in more than 700 fans for a display of R&B and British Invasion music at its finest.

Other major shows for Lawrence and the Arabians included: competing with the Hangmen in a "Battle of the Bands" competition at Northwestern High School (Hyattsville) on Saturday, November 13, 1965; appearing with the Delphonics, the Epsilons and the Villagers at "The Big Beat" music festival at the Sheraton Park Hotel (Washington, D.C.) from Thursday, August 17 to Saturday, August 19, 1967; and appearing with the Turtles and the Thyme Beings at the Reckord Armory (University of Maryland) on Friday, March 15, 1968.

During the late 1960s Lawrence and the Arabians continued to perform at teen dances all over the Washington, D.C. area at such locations as the Greenbelt Teen Club (Greenbelt Youth Center), the St. James Catholic Church Teen Club (Mt. Rainier), the St. Matthew's Parish Teen Club (Hyattsville), the St. Elizabeth Catholic Church Teen Club (Rockville), the St. Bernadette Catholic Church Teen Club (Silver Spring), the St. Hugh's Catholic Church Teen Club (Greenbelt), the St. Jerome Catholic Church Teen Club (Hyattsville), the St. Ambrose Parish Teen Club (Cheverly), the St. Mary's Catholic Church Teen Club (Landover Hills), the St. Bernard Catholic Church Teen Club (Riverdale), the Our Lady of Sorrows Parish Teen Club (Takoma Park), the Hollywood Teen Club (College Park), Robert Goddard Junior High School (Lanham), Northwestern High School (Hyattsville), Bowie High School (Bowie), Sherwood High School (Sandy Spring) and Wheaton High School (Wheaton).

The band also headlined some of the area's bigger and better facilities such as the Hyattsville Armory (Hyattsville), the Prince George's Plaza Community Center (Hyattsville), the Wheaton Youth Center (Wheaton), the Wedge (Bethesda Youth Center), Indian Springs Country Club (Silver Spring), the Colony Ballroom (University of Maryland), Ritchie Coliseum (University of Maryland) and Novak Field House (Prince George's Community College).

The popularity of Lawrence and the Arabians was such that arrangements were made for the band to lay down several tracks in Ed Green's Edgewood Recording Studio in Washington, D.C. for regional and, possibly, national release. From these sessions came two singles: "Coincidence" backed with "Ooh Baby" (Lawrence and the Arabians; Hem Records, 1967); and "Money" backed with "I'll Try Harder" (Lawrence and the Arabians; Hem Records, 1967). The first single attracted the attention of executives at Atlantic Records, who switched the sides and reissued the 45rpm single record on one of their subsidiaries as "Ooh Baby" backed with "Coincidence" (Lawrence and the Arabians; Shout Records, 1967). Though the reissue failed to make the Billboard popular music charts, the release of this single on a major record label served as one of the band's proudest moments.

As the 1960s came to a close Lawrence and the Arabians experienced numerous changes in personnel as they ventured into the Washington, D.C. area night club world. During this period they played engagements at such area night spots as the Quonset Supper Club, the Keg, the Rocket Room, the Crazy Horse, the Hedin House, the Bastille Supper Club and the Act IV Supper Club.

One of the last versions of Lawrence and the Arabians consisted of singer-keyboardist Larry Kidwell, guitarist George Bold, bassist Terry Gorka, keyboardist Jim McAndrew, saxophonist Mike Kidwell, trumpeters Gerry Bowles and Bruce Morris, trombonist Dick Hoeltze and drummer Bill Caron. Saxophonist Kirk McGetrick also played passed through the band during its night club phase. In 1970, with the popularity of hard rock and roll on the rise in area venues, interest in horn bands began to wane and the reign of Lawrence and the Arabians came to an end.

CHAPTER NINETY-TWO
THE CHARTBUSTERS

As the British Invasion swept America and bands across the land emulated its style of rock and roll, a group called the Chartbusters materialized in the Washington, D.C. area and made a national impact when their Beatles-like single release "She's the One" cracked the Billboard Top 40 popular music chart in 1964. The Chartbusters became wildly popular in the nation's capital with their English sound, enjoyed a four-year residency in Georgetown at a night club called the Crazy Horse, and included in their various lineups many of the region's most talented musicians. The Chartbusters were a musical force that helped define the 1960s Washington rock and roll scene.

The roots of the Chartbusters can be traced to a band that formed in 1956 in Coffeyville, Kansas called Bobby Poe and the Poe Kats. The band's lineup consisted of lead singer Bobby Poe, singer-guitarist Vernon Sandusky, singer-pianist Al Downing and drummer Joe Brawley. The band played a mix of R&B and rock and roll material, covering such artists as Fats Domino, Jerry Lee Lewis and Elvis Presley, and worked as rockabilly singer Wanda Jackson's backup band throughout 1957 and 1958. Downing, Sandusky and Brawley performed on Jackson's debut album, "Wanda Jackson" (Wanda Jackson; Capitol Records, 1958) and played on her hit single "Let's Have a Party," which peaked at number 37 on the Billboard's "The Billboard Hot 100" popular music chart on Monday, October 10, 1960.

In 1959 Bobby Poe and the Poe Kats headed east and performed in night clubs in Scranton, Pennsylvania and Boston, Massachusetts. In 1960 Bobby Poe switched from singer to manager and the band relocated to Washington, D.C. where a house band job at Rand's Night Club awaited them. When they hit the nation's capital, the band changed its name to Big Al Downing and the Rhythm Rockers, with the new quartet maintaining holdovers Downing and Sandusky and adding two Pennsylvania imports, bassist John Dubas from Scranton and drummer Mitch Corday from Philadelphia. Big Al Downing and the Rhythm Rockers remained at Rand's Night Club all the way into May 1964.

As the Beatles took the music world by storm, manager Bobby Poe sent most of the Rhythm Rockers into the recording studio in May 1964 to record a two-song demo consisting of "She's the One" backed with "Slippin Thru Your Fingers" that emulated the British Invasion rock and roll style. Performing on the recording under the new name "The Chartbusters" were Sandusky (who handled lead vocals on the songs), Dubas, rhythm guitarist-saxophonist Vince Gedeon (formerly of the Belvederes and Terry and the Pirates), and drummer Chib Holmes, who had replaced the regular Rhythm Rockers percussionist Mitch Corday.

Poe sent the completed demo around to a number of record companies, with the Mutual Record Company offering a contract to release the single. As a result of this transaction, "She's the One" (The Chartbusters; Mutual Record Company, 1964) was released in June 1964 and peaked at number 33 on Billboard magazine's "Billboard Hot 100" popular music chart on Saturday, August 15, 1964. After the single had become the property of Mutual, Poe enlisted the services of Mitch Corday to become his business partner and co-manager of the band and assigned guitarist Vernon Sandusky the additional duty of Chartbusters road manager.

The Chartbusters spent the summer months of 1964 performing British Invasion music at Rand's Night Club, often appearing on the same bill with Big Al Downing and a new backup group he had put together. In October they began a round of bookings at the Rocket Room which was situated two blocks away. When the Roundtable opened on M

Street NW in Georgetown that November, they alternated engagements in the club with the British Walkers for several weeks.

The Chartbusters spent the first half of 1965 at the Rocket Room, played short engagements in the area at the Shelter Room in Southeast Washington, D.C. and Glen Echo Park's Spanish Ballroom, and were then hired as the house band at the Crazy Horse in Georgetown that summer, a job that would endure for the next four years. The highlight of this period was an appearance on a concert bill at the District of Columbia National Guard Armory in Washington, D.C. on Saturday, June 5, 1965 where they appeared with Herman's Hermits and the British Walkers.

From 1964 to 1969 the Chartbusters were one of the city's top popular music attractions. For most of the decade they rated as one of the best rock and roll bands in the Washington, D.C. area, along with groups like the British Walkers, the Cherry People, the Fallen Angels, and the Reachers. For much of this time they interspersed their Crazy Horse engagements with occasional appearances at local dances, concerts, and regional tours around the country in support of their various single releases.

When the Beach Boys came to town and appeared at the Washington Coliseum on Saturday, April 15, 1967, the Chartbusters were one of the supporting acts on the bill, along with the Casinos, Jim and Jean, the Minus IV and Natty Bumpo. Other gigs that pulled them away from the Crazy Horse included: participating in a concert show that was headlined by Dee Dee Sharp and also included appearances by Gary Scott and the Classics, the Hounds of Baskerville, the McCormick Tool Company, the Project LTD and the Coming Thing at George C. Marshall High School (Falls Church) on Saturday, September 30, 1967; and co-headlining a concert show with Bobbie Howard and the Sweet that also included appearances by the New Delphonics, the McCormick Tool Company and the Apollos at T.C. Williams High School (Alexandria) on Thursday, November 23, 1967.

In the 1960s it was difficult for many local rock and roll bands to maintain stability in terms of personnel. Like so many other groups, the Chartbusters experienced numerous changes in their lineups through time. The original quartet of Sandusky, Dubas, Gedeon and Holmes remained intact for about a year before various players began moving in and out.

The first series of changes for the Chartbusters saw drummer Gary Kingery (formerly of the British Walkers), replace Holmes, rhythm guitarist-saxophonist Eddie Kopa replace Vince Gedeon, and Ronnie Welborne (also formerly of the British Walkers) replace John Dubas on bass, though Dubas would return after a brief respite. Next, Kopa was replaced by singer-guitarist Frank Dillon (formerly of the Fablons, Kenny Dino, and Ali Baba and the Four Thieves), and Kingery was replaced by drummer Stuart Ross, who was later replaced by Mike "Pokey" Walls (formerly of Willie and the Handjives). Other musicians to work in the quartet through time included guitarists Chuck Bennett and Tiny Jenkins and drummers Kip Ford, Danny Motta and Ronnie Stevens.

In terms of recorded output, after their hit "She's the One," the Chartbusters released six additional singles, though no original albums of their work were ever issued: "'Why' (Doncha Be My Girl)" backed with "Stop the Music" (The Chartbusters; Mutual Record Company, 1964); "You're Breakin' My Heart" backed with "Can't You Hear Me Callin'" (The Chartbusters; Mutual Record Company, 1965); "New Orleans" backed with "Lonely Surfer Boy" (The Chartbusters; Crusader Records, 1965); "One Bird in the Hand is Like Two in the Bush" backed with "Maybe" (The Chartbusters; Crusader Records, 1966); "One Bird in the Hand is Like Two Birds in the Bush" backed with "Leavin' You" (The Chartbusters; Bell Records, 1966); and "Dance Dance" backed with "Glass Houses" (The Chartbusters; Bell Records, 1967). More recently a 30-track compilation of the band's work has been issued on compact disc: "She's the One" (The Chartbusters; Eagle Records, 1996).

By April 1969 lead guitarist Vernon Sandusky was the last original standing Chartbuster and the group's final lineup was rounded out by lead singer Chuck Bennett, bassist Ronnie Welborne and drummer Kip Ford. The group was still working both the Crazy Horse and the Rocket Room at that time, but Sandusky had grown weary of the steady stream of roster changes and when an offer came from his longtime friend Big Al Downing to join his backup band for a tour of Europe, he consulted with Bobby Poe and told him the Chartbusters had run its course. Sandusky began working again with Downing and later went on to spend more than 20 years with Rodney Lay and the Wild West, the backup band for C&W singer-guitarist Roy Clark. While the Chartbusters were no more, their position as one of the greatest rock and roll outfits the Washington, D.C. area has ever known was firmly cemented.

CHAPTER NINETY-THREE
THE BRITISH WALKERS

The Washington, D.C. area was rich with hard-rocking bands in the 1960s and one of the very best was the British Walkers, who, like others in the music scene around them, formed as the British Invasion was taking America by storm. Unique in that they performed both covers of Beatles songs and other English-styled bands, along with R&B classics, the band developed a strong following in the night clubs of Georgetown and included in their various lineups some of the best musicians the area has ever offered. Early editions of the band centered around the talented and charismatic front man Bobbie Howard, while the later versions that carried on without him more than held their own in terms of talent and energy. The British Walkers were best seen and heard in a live setting and although they recorded and released several 45rpm single records on various labels, they never developed the internal stability that would have allowed for a proper album release that could have made them one of the biggest rock and roll bands in the world.

The Founding Father of the British Walkers was Bobbie Howard, who was born in Southern Virginia, spent most of his teen years in Miami, Florida, and after finishing high school in the Sunshine State moved with his family to Arlington, Virginia in 1958. He became a proficient vocalist, guitarist and keyboardist and met Link Wray at the Rendezvous in Washington, D.C., becoming an active member of Link Wray and His Ray Men. In the early 1960s he fronted his own bands, Bobbie Howard and the Ponies and Bobbie Howard and the Hi-Boys. By the fall of 1964 the Hi-Boys, whose lineup had settled to include Howard, guitarist Roy Buchanan (formerly of the Saxtons and Dale Hawkins), and two Northern Virginia musicians, bassist Junior Gill and drummer Mike Kennedy, were working regularly in Washington, D.C. at Rand's Night Club and the Alpine Room.

In November 1964 manager Mitch Corday changed the name of Bobbie Howard and the Hi-Boys to the British Walkers and moved the band over to a new night club called the Roundtable, which was located at 2813 M Street NW on the far eastern edge of Georgetown. Although the band was presented in the local media as an offshoot of the British Invasion bands that were strongly impacting the world of popular music, the British Walkers repertoire mainly consisted of R&B covers, with Beatles-type music thrown in for good measure. They were an immediate hit in the city and during their first few weeks, in addition to holding their regular slot at the Roundtable, they made appearances at Benny's Rebel Room on the infamous 800 block strip of 14th Street NW.

By January 1965 the British Walkers had developed a devoted following at the Roundtable and would remain the club's main attraction through October 1967. However, a scant 10 weeks after they had formed, the band began experiencing significant changes in personnel, a problem that would plague them throughout their existence. The first departures in early 1965 were Roy Buchanan and Junior Gill, who were replaced by guitarist Jimmy Carter and bassist Ronnie Welborne, respectively. Soon after, Mike Kennedy left the band and was replaced by drummer Gary Kingery.

The quartet of Bobbie Howard, Jimmy Carter, Ronnie Welborne and Gary Kingery remained together into the fall of 1965, at which time two major changes in the band took place. First, Kingery was replaced by a 19-year-old drummer from Alexandria, Virginia named Steve Lacey, who had previously played with a band called the Cavaliers. Next, Ronnie Welborne was replaced by 21-year-old bassist Jack Brooks, also from Alexandria, who had previously played with the Saxtons, the Wolfpack and Jimmy Eller and His Little People. Lacey and Brooks would become mainstays in the British Walkers and remained with the band until its final day.

Throughout 1965 the British Walkers took occasional dates when they had time off from the Roundtable. Some of these jobs included: opening for the Beach Boys at the Washington Coliseum on Saturday, April 24, 1965, sharing the bill with the Chartbusters and Little D and the Reflections; opening for Herman's Hermits at the District of Columbia National Guard Armory in Washington, D.C. on Saturday, June 5, 1965, again sharing the bill with the Chartbusters; and performing at several dances and social functions at Georgetown University. They also appeared as headliners at concerts at venues such as the Silver Spring Boys Club, the Hyattsville Armory and the Bladensburg Volunteer Fire Department.

The lineup of Bobbie Howard, Jimmy Carter, Jack Brooks and Steve Lacey remained intact throughout most of 1966. Still basing out of the Roundtable, the band was a part of some prestigious local concert bills during the year. These included: appearing on a concert bill headlined by the Byrds and supported by the Chiffons and Tommy Vann and the Echoes at the Baltimore Civic Center on Friday, June 17, 1966; appearing at a concert show entitled "Summertime Hullabaloo" that was headlined by Neil Diamond and supported by Bobby Parker, the English Setters, the Minutemen, the Marvels, the Rip-Tydes and the Sidekicks at the Manassas Armory in Virginia on Saturday, August 6, 1966; appearing on a concert bill headlined by the Yardbirds and supported by the English Setters, the New Delphonics, the Jay Walkers, the New Found Sound, December's Children, the Sheffields, the Gents, Fugitive Sound and the Villager Go-Go Girls at the Alexandria Arena on Friday, September 9, 1966; co-headlining a "Fall Festival" concert with the Shirelles at McDonough Gymnasium (Georgetown University) on Saturday, October 15, 1966; and appearing in-concert with the Coasters and the Chartbusters at the Marriott Twin Bridges Motor Hotel in Arlington, Virginia on Tuesday, November 22, 1966.

In late 1966 the quartet of Howard, Carter, Brooks and Lacey was joined by a guitarist from England named Paul Downing, though he only stayed a few weeks before moving on. Next to depart late in the year was Jimmy Carter, whose replacement was a 15-year-old rock guitar prodigy from Vienna, Virginia named Ted Spelios, who was still attending James Madison High School and had previously played in a teen dance band called the US.

In March 1967 Bobbie Howard left the British Walkers and after a short stay in the Mad Hatters he formed another group he called Bobbie Howard and the Sweet. His replacement in the band was lead singer-rhythm guitarist John Hall from Baltimore, who had been playing in Georgetown in a band called the Wad and years later would resurface in the band Orleans. The band spent the spring months playing dates at the Roundtable and the Rabbit's Foot, which was north of Georgetown on upper Wisconsin Avenue NW in Washington, D.C. In June 1967 Spelios and Hall departed and joined a rock and roll band called Kangaroo.

In the summer of 1967, at the urging of manager Mitch Corday, Jack Brooks and Steve Lacey went to England to recruit two new members for the British Walkers. There, they auditioned numerous musicians and eventually settled upon guitarists Geoff Richardson (formerly of the Attack) and Tony Fallows, and brought the pair back to Washington, D.C. in January 1968. For practical purposes, this would be the final edition of the British Walkers, who saw their existence end without any original members on board.

The British Walkers spent the early months of 1968 as the house band at Nu-Mac's on M Street NW and participated in some impressive concert shows. These included: opening for Mitch Ryder and the Detroit Wheels at McDonough Gymnasium (Georgetown University) on Friday, March 22, 1968; and appearing on a concert bill headlined by Vanilla Fudge and supported by Ultimate Spinach, the Curfews and Wild Honey at the Alexandria Arena on Sunday, April 21, 1968. After spending the month of May performing at the Keg, the British Walkers informed Corday they were disbanding.

During their time the British Walkers did not record or release any albums, though five different 45rpm single records did appear under the band's name. Cataloging these releases is problematic, as much of the published information regarding the recording of these songs is erroneous. The singles that were issued under the band's name are: "I Found You" backed with "Diddley Daddy" (The British Walkers; Try Records, 1964); "The Girl Can't Help It" backed with "Lonely Lover's Poem" (The British Walkers; Charger Records, 1965); "Watch Yourself" backed with "Bad Lightnin'" (The British Walkers; Manchester Records, 1965); "The Story of My Life" backed with "Bad Lightnin'" (The British Walkers; Manchester Records, 1966); and "Shake" backed with "That Was Yesterday" (The British Walkers; Cameo Records, 1967).

Of these five singles, only two were actually recorded by legitimate British Walker lineups. The first single release, "I Found You" and its B-side, were recorded by the original lineup of Howard, Buchanan, Gill and Kennedy. The second release, "The Girl Can't Help It" and its B-side, were recorded by the lineup of Howard, Carter, Welborne and Kingery. Bobbie Howard sang lead vocals on all four songs. The third single "Watch Yourself" and the fourth single "The Story of My Life," and their B-sides, were done in Nashville, Tennessee with Bobbie Howard handling lead vocals and rhythm guitar and Nashville studio musicians providing the rest. Reportedly, guitarist Robbie Robertson, bassist Rick Danko, harmonica player Charlie McCoy and drummer Ken Buttrey rounded out the musical backing on these tracks. The last single's A-side, "Shake," was a Chartbusters project that came out under the British Walkers name, with Chuck and Tom Willett of the Newports sharing lead vocals, Vernon Sandusky playing lead guitar, Jack Brooks playing fuzz guitar, Johnny Dubas on bass, and Mike "Pokey" Walls on drums. The B-side of that single, "That Was Yesterday," was recorded with Frank Dillon singing lead and playing rhythm guitar, Vernon Sandusky playing lead guitar, Johnny Dubas playing bass, Larry Kidwell on keyboards and Mike "Pokey" Walls on drums.

It should be noted that, contrary to other published reports, the British Walkers single release of "Shake" was never a top 100 hit, as it peaked at number 106 on Billboard's "Billboard Hot 100" chart on Saturday, May 20, 1967. In 2009 these and other rarities were reissued on the compact disc compilation "The British Walkers Are Coming" (The British Walkers; Turkey Mountain Records, 2009). In recent years Bobbie Howard has put together numerous British Walker reunion shows in the Washington, D.C. area with a mix of old and new bandmates participating.

CHAPTER NINETY-FOUR
THE HANGMEN

The Hangmen rate as one of the legendary rock and roll bands in Washington, D.C. area popular music history. Although the group's members were a bit older than most of their competitors, they became one of the most popular bands on the area's teen dance scene, where their dynamic appearances attracted throngs of screaming young fans and brought on comparisons to the Beatles in the way they presented high-energy musical performance that generated manic responses from their fans. Playing concerts, drawing hundreds to promotional appearances and releasing an album on a major record label, the Hangmen were a 1960s phenomenon that helped redefine rock and roll music in the nation's capital.

The Hangmen formed in March 1965 and based out of the town of Garrett Park in Montgomery County, Maryland. The band's original lineup consisted of: lead guitarist Tom Guernsey, born July 5, 1944 and raised in Garrett Park (Walter Johnson High School Class of 1962); rhythm guitarist George Daly, born June 10, 1945 and raised in Silver Spring (Northwood High School Class of 1963); drummer Bob Berberich, born December 23, 1947 and raised in Silver Spring (St. John's College High School Class of 1965); lead vocalist Dave Ottley, born in 1943 in Glasgow, Scotland and raised in London, England; and bassist Mike West (whose real name reportedly was Mike Walters), who was born in 1943, hailed from Prince George's County, Maryland, and was attending the University of Maryland when he joined the band.

The driving force behind the Hangmen was Tom Guernsey, who had previously led a band of Walter Johnson High School alumni called the Reekers which had scored a local hit with the single "Don't Call Me Flyface" backed with "Grindin'" (The Reekers; Ru-Jac Records, 1964). Guernsey pulled in drummer Bob Berberich, who had done session work on occasion with the Reekers, and met George Daly in classes at Montgomery Junior College, who, in turn, recruited the Scottish singer Dave Ottley (supposedly Daly called the British Embassy and asked the night attendant who answered the phone if he any suitable rock and roll singers for a new Beatles-styled band in America; the attendant recommended his own daughter, who, after failing her audition with the band, recommended her hairdresser who happened to be Dave Ottley). Mike West rounded out the group after answering a "Musician Wanted" ad in a local newspaper and passing an audition in the basement of Guernsey's Garret Park home where the band rehearsed.

The Hangmen, performing songs of the British Invasion and other popular rock and roll tunes, quickly ascended to the top of the local teen dance scene and created Beatles-like fervor wherever they appeared. They employed three different managers during their two-year reign – Larry Sealfon, Mike Klavans and Arnold Stahl.

Things took off for the Hangmen when, during the summer of 1965, Sealfon and Klavans played a demo recording made by the Reekers of a song entitled "What A Girl Can't Do" for administrative employees at local radio station WWDC. Present at the time was an individual named Joe Cash, who worked for Schwartz Brothers Record Distributors and also happened to be a national promotion manager for Monument Records, a major record company based in Nashville, Tennessee.

Cash played the demo for Monument president Fred Foster in Nashville, who was impressed by the song and contacted Tom Guernsey, who informed him that the Reekers were no longer in existence but that he had a new band called the Hangmen that were fast becoming one of Washington, D.C.'s top rock and roll acts. Foster and Guernsey struck a deal to release the demo as a 45rpm single record under "The Hangmen" moniker. The resulting single, "What A Girl Can't Do" backed with "The Girl Who Faded Away" (The Hangmen; Monument Records, 1965) was released in September and became a local smash in the Washington, D.C. area, but was never properly marketed by Monument Records on a national level.

Not long after this first single was released, a couple of incidents exemplified the intense popularity of the Hangmen in the nation's capital. The first event occurred on the afternoon of Friday, February 4, 1966 when the band gave a live, in-store promotional performance at Giant Music Center at 110 West Broad Street in Falls Church, Virginia, which reportedly had sold more than 2,500 copies of "What A Girl Can't Do" in previous weeks.

According to different articles that were published on Saturday, February 5, 1966 – one in the Washington Post entitled "Rock 'N' Roll Frolic Wrecks Record Shop: The Hangmen packs 'Em In" by James T. Yenckel, and another in the Washington Daily News entitled "Falls Church Shop Turns Into a Discowreck" (uncredited) – the band began playing at 4pm before an overflow crowd of more than 400 teens who had jammed their way inside Giant Music Center some two hours before the start time. As the indoor mob stood on chairs and stools and swayed to the music, another 1,500 teens flooded the sidewalk outside the store and blocked traffic on West Broad Street. After the band had performed for 15 minutes, the situation got out of hand. Four display cases were tipped over, several record bins were overturned resulting in hundreds of records being trampled and broken, several fans fainted, and two of the eight sales clerks on duty sought refuge by climbing up into the front display window, drawing jeers from the fans outside. Store owner Jack Shaver had little choice but to call the Falls Church Police, who dispatched five officers to the scene to disperse the crowd. It took the authorities one hour to clear the store and two teen-agers were arrested for disorderly conduct. Shaver estimated the total damage at more than $500.

While the abbreviated Giant Music promotional appearance increased the Hangmen's notoriety, a second significant factor contributing to their overall popularity occurred when their single "What A Girl Can't Do" reached the number one position on radio station WEAM's publicly issued Top 40 listing on Monday, February 7, 1966, unseating the Beatles' "We Can Work It Out" from the top slot. It was a high point in the band's career and afterwards they began changing with the times. They grew their hair long, sported paisley-designed shirts and pants, added more psychedelic-edged music to their repertoire, and traveled to assorted gigs in a black 1953 Hearse.

The Hangmen had established themselves as one of the most popular bands in the region and gave live performances at all types of events. In 1965 and 1966 they played teen dances at the area's most popular facilities including the St. Camillus Catholic Church Teen Club (Silver Spring), the St. Jerome Catholic Church Teen Club (Hyattsville), the Our Lady of Lourdes Catholic Church Teen Club (Bethesda), Northwestern High School (Hyattsville), the Shaare Tefila Congregation (Silver Spring), the Hyattsville Armory (Hyattsville), Sherwood High School (Sandy Spring), Montgomery Blair High School (Silver Spring), Bishop Ireton High School (Alexandria), Robert E. Lee High School (Springfield), and the Greenbelt Teen Club (Greenbelt Youth Center).

The Hangmen were also called upon to play some major social events including Alice Denney's NOW Festival's "Mad Camp Ball" inside the L'Aiglon Building in Adams Morgan on Saturday, April 30, 1966, a concert emceed by Beat poet Allen Ginsberg. They also performed at a charity picnic staged by Senator Robert F. and Ethel Kennedy at Hickory Hill, their stately mansion at 1147 Chain Bridge Road in McLean, Virginia.

In addition, the Hangmen participated in many local concert shows including: opening for the Yardbirds and the Shangri-Las at the Alexandria Arena on Saturday, January 1, 1966; opening for the Dave Clark Five at Shady Grove Music Fair (Gaithersburg) on

Monday, July 18, 1966; opening for the Lovin' Spoonful at Shady Grove Music Fair (Gaithersburg) on Monday, August 8, 1966; appearing at the "End of Summer Blast" along with the English Setters, the Flys, the Tytans and the Organic Cavemen at the Bayou (Washington, D.C.) on Sunday, September 4, 1966; appearing at a concert headlined by Neil Diamond and supported by the English Setters, the Brave Maggots and 20 other groups at the Alexandria Arena on Saturday, October 1, 1966; appearing on a concert bill co-headlined by the Count Five and Martha and the Vandellas and supported by the English Setters at the Alexandria Arena on Wednesday, November 23, 1966; and opening for the Young Rascals at the Alexandria Arena on Friday, December 23, 1966.

In 1966 the Hangmen experienced a rapid-fire series of changes. First, Paul Dowell, a graduate of Wheaton High School who had met George Daly in classes at Montgomery Junior College, replaced bassist Mike West in February of that year. Next, encouraged by the regional success of "What A Girl Can't Do," Fred Foster pulled the band back into the studio in the spring and produced their second single, "Faces," backed with "Bad Goodbye" (The Hangmen; Monument Records, 1966). In July, vocalist Tony Taylor of the Roaches, a Springfield, Virginia native who had graduated from Robert E. Lee High School in 1964, was called upon to replace Dave Ottley, who was returning to London, England.

In August 1966 the Hangmen returned to Nashville, Tennessee and embarked on recording sessions in an effort to gain national attention for their music. The result of this studio work was their third single "Dream Baby" backed with "Let It Be Me" (The Hangmen; Monument Records, 1966) and the album "Bitter Sweet" (The Hangmen; Monument Records, 1966). Neither the single nor the album were given any semblance of national promotion, aside from nationwide shipments to various radio and record store outlets that were void of any communication or action pertaining to on-air interviews, regional tours or band appearances.

While the Hangmen did occasionally venture outside the Washington, D.C. area for work, a promotional push by the record label into national markets never materialized. Monument Records simply shipped the records, ignored the band, and turned their attention towards other recording artists in their fold. In the aftermath of what should have been a celebrated album release, the Hangmen were inexplicably left to their own devices.

Late in 1966 as the "Bitter Sweet" album was being prepped for release, Tom Guernsey and Paul Dowell scouted a young, talented guitarist who was playing in psychedelic rock and roll band called the Seldom Scene at the Brickskeller off of Dupont Circle in Washington, D.C. The guitarist in question was 22-year-old Jorge Strunz, who had been born in Costa Rica and raised in England and Canada before moving as a teenager to Arlington Virginia where he graduated from Yorktown High School in 1962. Strunz had played in folk groups while in high school and in 1963 joined Joe Corey and the Bristol Singers, a folk group that held house band duties at the Brickskeller. After spending a year in Spain he found himself back at the Brickskeller with the Seldom Scene, a rock and roll band that let him stretch his playing into broader territories. Guernsey brought Strunz into the Hangmen to replace rhythm guitarist George Daly.

As 1967 rolled around the Hangmen lineup consisted of lead singer Tony Taylor, lead guitarist Tom Guernsey, rhythm guitarist Jorge Strunz, bassist Paul Dowell and drummer Bob Berberich, a roster many felt was the band's strongest. They kicked off the year as the "Band of the Week" on the local WDCA-TV Channel 20 music program "Wing Ding," performing live in the studio and having their recordings featured on episodes that aired from Monday, January 2 through Saturday, January 7, 1967. Throughout the early months of the year the band steadily worked the Rabbit's Foot on upper Wisconsin Avenue NW in Washington, D.C., a night club engagement that signaled a move away from the teen dance scene they had previously dominated.

In April 1967, with nothing in the way of support from Monument Records and the musical interests of the individual group members taking different directions, the Hangmen decided to disband. Though their reign lasted a scant two years, their status as one of the most popular rock and roll bands the nation's capital had ever known was firmly established.

In the aftermath of the Hangmen, several of the band members embarked on impressive musical journeys: Tom Guernsey reformed the Reekers and became a highly sought-after local studio musician; Paul Dowell formed a band called Paul Dowell and the Dolphin with singer-guitarist Nils Lofgren, bassist George Daly and drummer Bob Berberich, and then went on to a long career as a soundman with Jefferson Airplane; Bob Berberich went on to drum for the Button, Paul Dowell and the Dolphin, Grin and the Rosslyn Mountain Boys; George Daly played in Paul Dowell and the Dolphin and Grin, and then became a high-level music executive with such record companies as Columbia, Elektra/Asylum, Atlantic and Zoo Entertainment; Tony Taylor later sang with the Button, Graffiti, the Collection, Tony Taylor and the Looking Glass, and spent several years as a solo folk music performer in New York City; and Jorge Strunz passed through such bands as the Button, the Collection, Aims Oka, Snake, Spectrum and the jazz rock band Caldera (which released four records on Capitol Records from 1976-1979) – in recent years he has been a member of the nationally acclaimed acoustic world jazz duo Strunz Farah.

CHAPTER NINETY-FIVE
THE SHOWMEN

During the 1960s most of the bands on the teen dance circuit in the Washington, D.C. area were divided into two camps – those that specialized in basic rock and roll, and those that concentrated on R&B. This division was especially pronounced during the middle part of the decade, before the advent of psychedelic and harder-edged rock and roll that came on fast and strong as the 1970s approached. While Prince George's County primary contribution to the R&B contingency was the Hyattsville-based outfit Lawrence and the Arabians, their main soul music counterparts in Montgomery County were the Showmen, a horn-flavored band that hailed from Chevy Chase, Maryland and performed at some of the area's largest teen club gatherings. While the Showmen did not play together beyond this decade, they are remembered as one of the most talented soul music outfits the region has produced.

The Showmen formed in September 1965 with an initial lineup of 11 pieces: lead singer Tommy Peters, co-lead singer Judy Fisher, lead guitarist Les Hatley, rhythm guitarist Rick Dashner, bassist Tom Carrico, pianist Kevin Walsh, keyboardist Mike Urciolo, saxophonist Doug Fahey, saxophonist Adam Wenner, trumpeter Gary Gaulette and drummer Ricky Rodgers. Two of the band's primary members were Carrico, who had previously played in an R&B basement band called the Apollos and was a member of Bethesda-Chevy Chase High School's Class of 1968, and Hatley, who had been in a band with Carrico called the Delmors and was a member of Bethesda-Chevy Chase High School's Class of 1967. Throughout the pair's tenure with the band, the Showmen largely featured Montgomery County musicians and rehearsed and operated out of Carrico's house in Chevy Chase, Maryland.

From the very beginning, the Showmen were champions of R&B and among the artists they covered were James Brown, Wilson Pickett, Otis Redding, Little Richard, Ben E. King, Sam and Dave, Junior Walker and the All Stars, the Temptations, Martha and the Vandellas and innumerable others of that style. During its final days the band would reluctantly follow the changing times and added songs by the Jimi Hendrix Experience and Cream to their repertoire, but they largely remained devoted to R&B to the very end.

Midway through their career the Showmen were profiled in the "Teen" section of the Evening Star (Washington, D.C.) newspaper. The uncredited article, which appeared in the weekly "Teen Music Makers" column of Saturday, February 11, 1967, read in part: "The Showmen specialize in James Brown numbers. In their reddish tuxedo jackets, except for the singer who sports a gold one, the boys open up with a couple of instrumentals such as 'Bootleg' and 'Twine Time.' Then Tommy Peter, their soul singer, who used to be with the Crescendos, let's go with 'Mr. Pitiful," an Otis Redding number...The Showmen have played 14 times at St. John's College High School dances, once for a crowd of 4,200, says Les (Hatley). The Showmen have also played nine times at the Bethesda Youth Center, five times at the Wheaton Youth Center, plus lots of proms, teen clubs and private parties. The Showmen have also been seen at dances at Stone Ridge, Ursuline, Holy Cross, Gonzaga, LaReine and Walt Whitman. Tonight the Showmen will be at the Cheverly Teen Club at Tuxedo Elementary School from 7:30 to 10:30."

Other teen dances the Showmen performed at in the area during this time were: the St. Thomas Moore Parish Teen Club (Arlington), the Our Lady of Mercy Parish Teen Club (Potomac), the St. Camillus Catholic Church Teen Club (Silver Spring), the Our Lady of Lourdes Catholic Church Teen Club (Bethesda), the St. Bernadette Catholic Church Teen

Club (Silver Spring), the St. Elizabeth Catholic Church Teen Club (Rockville) and the Belair Junior High School Teen Club (Bowie).

Unfortunately, the Showmen never signed with any local, independent or national record labels, though their lack of recorded output did not hinder their popularity. While many local bands produced single record releases and promoted their wares at their live appearances, the Showmen passed on studio work and instead concentrated on their live performance schedule, which saw them work steadily on weekends throughout their four-year lifespan.

One of the Showmen's highlights occurred when they appeared with the Fantastic Johnny C at the Wedge (Bethesda Youth Center) in Montgomery County. This presentation took place on Friday, March 29, 1968 and consisted of the Showmen first performing a solo act and then returning to the stage and backing up the Fantastic Johnny C himself as he worked through a number of songs the Showmen had already performed earlier in the evening. The night's feature was the playing of Johnny C's hit single "Boogaloo Down Broadway" (The Fantastic Johnny C; Phil-L.A. of Soul Records, 1967), which had peaked at number seven on Billboard's "Hot 100" popular music chart on Saturday, December 23, 1967 and was later picked up by both London Records and Polydor Records for worldwide releases. As was the case with many solo performers of the era, Johnny C, 24 years old and based out of the Philadelphia area at the time, embarked on short regional tours and relied upon top local bands to back him up on these live performances. The Showmen, with their outstanding musicianship, were pegged as the perfect band to accompany the soul singer for his nation's capital debut.

Throughout the late 1960s the Showmen experienced numerous changes in personnel. While Tom Carrico, Les Hatley and Tommy Peter remained with the band from beginning to end, a steady stream of quality musicians passed through the band. Among the musicians who played in the group included singer Stanley Burley, keyboardist Paul Blustein, saxophonist Lewis Burley, trombonist Steve Stoll, trumpeters Steve Sharpe and Bob Butcher and drummers Gordon Moss, Mickey Gorman and Mark McInturff. In one of their final performances, the Showmen participated in a show at the Walt Whitman High School Field House (Bethesda) on Monday, December 2, 1968 that also featured jazz guitarist Charlie Byrd, R&B singer Roberta Flack and popular comedian Sam Levinson.

CHAPTER NINETY-SIX
THE FALLEN ANGELS

The Fallen Angels are one of the finest psychedelic rock and roll bands the Washington, D.C. area has ever produced. Original members Charlie "C.J." Jones, Wally Cook, Jack Bryant, and Ned Davis brought a mélange of musical styles to the group and collectively made a strong and lasting impact on the city's growing rock and roll following as the British Invasion advanced. They established a reputation for excellence on the competitive Georgetown night club circuit during the late 1960s, performed at countercultural benefits around the nation's capital, and were a popular concert attraction up and down the East Coast. The band saw many talented musicians pass through its ranks, released critically acclaimed 33rpm long-play records and 45rpm single records, and performed everywhere around the area from the Ambassador Theatre to the P Street Beach to the Wheaton Youth Center. Though the Fallen Angels lost momentum as the 1960s came to an end, their legacy as a monumental entry in the annals of local rock and roll history lives on.

In the fall of 1965 the quartet of lead guitarist Charlie "C.J." Jones, rhythm guitarist Wally Cook, lead singer-bassist Jack Bryant and drummer Ned Davis first came together. Wally Cook had grown up in Oxon Hill, Maryland and had lived in Hillcrest Heights during his years at Crossland High School, where he was a member of the Class of 1966. As a 16-year-old in 1964 he first played in a rock and roll band called Herbie and the Originals. Through connections he made with his cousin George Cook, he next joined a band called the Young Rabbits, which included a drummer from Alexandria, Virginia named Ned Davis. The Young Rabbits maintained house band status at the Peppermint Lounge at 3263 M Street NW in the Georgetown neighborhood of Washington, D.C. throughout the summer of 1965.

Across the way Jack Bryant had been raised in Bethesda, Maryland and graduated from Walter Johnson High School in 1965. He spent his teen years playing the local teen dance circuit with a band called the Dynamic Viscounts. Upon graduating he joined an R&B band called the Abstracts that worked a night club called the Americana in Odenton, Maryland. The guitarist in that band was Charlie "C.J. Jones, who wanted to form a Beatles-type rock band and have Bryant join him.

The man who would become the early focal point of the Fallen Angels, C.J., was born and raised in Washington, D.C., lived on Otis Street NE during his teen years, and graduated from St. Anthony's School in 1960. He played guitar in rock and roll bands on the local teen dance circuit called the Four of Us (with bassist Jack Casady) and the Eddie Stitt Combo. After he completed high school his family moved to New Carrollton, Maryland. In 1965, after passing through several bands, he joined a group called Stephen Charles and the Abstracts, whose roster included bassist Jack Bryant. On his off-nights he was playing jam sessions in Georgetown when he heard a band rehearsing in the French Quarter called the Young Rabbits and asked if he could sit in. Impressed with Wally Cook and Ned Davis, he asked the pair to join a new British Invasion-styled rock and roll band he was putting together.

In the fall of 1965 C.J., Bryant, Cook and Davis began playing together as the Disciples during the evening hours at the Peppermint Lounge. During the daytime hours they rehearsed in the basement night club below, the French Quarter. Within weeks they had changed their name to the Uncalled Four, but upon discovering the name was already in use by other groups, they switched their moniker to the Fallen Angels, a name taken from the John Milton novel "Paradise Lost."

In early 1966 the Fallen Angels left the Peppermint Lounge and after a short engagement in the basement at the French Quarter the group was hired as the house band at the Frog, a night club situated a couple doors away in the basement of the Corral at 3267 M Street NW. There, they mixed the latest songs of the British Invasion with R&B classics, performing sets of Beatles, Sam and Dave, and James Brown covers.

The Fallen Angles remained at the Frog for most of the spring of 1966. That summer drummer Ned Davis was replaced by Rocky Isaac, a 1963 graduate of Anacostia High School and former drummer for two popular Georgetown rock and roll bands, the Tejuns and the Creatures. With Isaac on board the group accepted a house band offer from the owners of the Keg, a popular rock and roll night club on Wisconsin Avenue NW in the city's Glover Park neighborhood. They remained there until March 1967, offering an increasingly complex and heavy rock and roll sound that mixed original compositions with their regular repertoire of rock and R&B covers. It was at the Keg that the Fallen Angels built a sizeable following and challenged other popular Washington, D.C. rock and roll bands like the British Walkers, the Chartbusters, the Cherry People, the Telstars, the Reachers and the Mad Hatters for local superiority.

In 1966 the Fallen Angels recorded four songs which were released as singles by Laurie Records, a New York City-based national record label. The first, "Every Time I Fall in Love" backed with "I Have Found" (The Fallen Angels; Laurie Records, 1966) was recorded by the band's original lineup at Rodell Audio Services in Georgetown and was released in May of that year with little promotional activity behind it. The second release, "A Little Love From You Will Do" backed with "Have You Ever Lost A Love" (The Fallen Angels; Laurie Records, 1966), was a mixed bag with the A-side having been recorded by the band's original lineup at Rodell Audio Services, and the B-side having been recorded in New York with Rocky Isaac taking the place of Ned Davis. Released in December 1966, it too suffered from a lack of company support and failed to make the Billboard charts.

In what rates as two of the early band's more interesting gigs, the Fallen Angels first took a night off from the Keg and opened for the Young Rascals at the Alexandria Arena on Friday, December 23, 1966, serving as a supporting act along with the English Setters, the Hangmen and the Surf Boys. Next up, they headlined a concert at the Annapolis Armory on Saturday, February 11, 1967, a spacious venue they would periodically return to in the months ahead. In the coming year the band would experience significant shifts in musical style and band composition. They added psychedelic elements to their rock and roll, became more theatrical in their stage presentations, and endured numerous personnel changes.

In March 1967 the Fallen Angels bid farewell to the Keg and as the spring progressed they began venturing into previously unexplored territories. In the weeks ahead they had engagements in Washington, D.C. at the American Palace, which was a night club inside of the Dodge House Hotel, and Mac's Pipe and Drum Restaurant in Georgetown. They also performed at the "Festival of Visual and Performing Arts" at the Washington Gallery of Modern Art (1503 21st Street NW) on Saturday, May 27, 1967 along with the Reachers, the Telstars and December's Children.

The Summer of Love saw the band work two new rock and roll night clubs in the rougher and more remote Northeast quadrant of town: the Rogue, which was located at 2315 Bladensburg Road NE and booked such local bands as the English Setters and the Fugitive Sounds, as well as out-of-place out-of-towners like singer-pianist Jerry Lee Lewis; and the Purple Finger, a stranger and more psychedelic dive which was just down the street at 2301 Bladensburg Road NE and featured local band Natty Bumpo.

In one of its more unlikely outings the Fallen Angels headlined a "Sears Fashion Bash" at the Sheraton Park Hotel in Washington, D.C. on Sunday, August 13, 1967 that included a set by the Outsiders and a runway show by the Yardley London Look Girls. The band also took its psychedelic stylings to the Ambassador Theatre in Adams Morgan multiple times including a four-night stand from Wednesday, August 23, 1967 to Saturday, August 26, 1967 where they opened for Vanilla Fudge and Lothar and the Hand People; a three-night engagement that saw them headline on their own from Friday, November 17, 1967, through Sunday, November 19, 1967; and a special one-nighter on Thursday, December 21, 1967 where they co-headlined a bill that included the Telstars, the Reachers and the Mosaic Virus.

Other notable performances that year included a headlining position at "The Montrose Park Be-In" in Georgetown on Sunday, October 8 and a slot on a special concert presented by the Springfield East Teen Club at Robert E. Lee High School in Springfield, Virginia on Saturday, December 30 that also included the Telstars, the Reachers, the Mosaic Virus and Lawrence and the Arabians.

The year 1967 also saw the Fallen Angels work through several changes in personnel. C.J. left in March and was replaced by guitarist Jack Lauritsen, who had been raised in Bethesda, Maryland, had graduated from Maret School in Washington, D.C., and had previously played with a local teen band called the Velours. Drummer Rocky Isaac then departed and was replaced for a short while by Mike Kennedy, previously of the British Walkers and the Jumping Jax, who, in turn, was replaced by Richard "Spider" Kumer, previously of the Mad Hatters. Next, a fifth member was added to the band in keyboardist Howard Danchik, who, like Lauritsen, was a graduate of Maret School. Late in the summer, drummer Spider Kumer was replaced with John "Thumper" Molloy, formerly of the Reachers.

Manager Barry Seidel had secured a record deal for the band with New York-based national record company Roulette Records and during the course of 1967 the Fallen Angels traveled to New York City on multiple occasions and ultimately recorded two albums for the label. The first of these, "The Fallen Angels" (The Fallen Angels; Roulette Records, 1967) featured the lineup of Bryant, Cook, Lauritsen, Danchik and Kumer and was released in September 1967. The second album release, "It's A Long Way Down" (The Fallen Angels; Roulette Records, 1968) featured the lineup of Bryant, Cook, Lauritsen, Danchik and new drummer Molloy and was released in July 1968.

Singles released from these albums were: "Room at the Top" backed with "Your Friends Here in Dunderville" (The Fallen Angels; Roulette Records, 1967); "Hello Girl" backed with "Most Children Do" (The Fallen Angels; Roulette Records, 1968); and a rarity that was leased by Roulette to a European company, "I Don't Want to Fall" backed with "Most Children Do" (The Fallen Angels; London Records, 1968). Although the psychedelic-tinged albums and singles received critical acclaim from various publications, Roulette Records seemed disinterested in giving them proper promotional consideration, and, consequently, the records failed to make the national charts.

The Fallen Angels remained active in 1968. They passed on regular house band jobs and appeared at all manner of rock and roll functions. These performances included: headlining a concert supported by the Plum Beach Incident and the Dead Ants at T.C. Williams High School (Alexandria) on Friday, March 8, 1968; headlining a concert, supported by Velvet Haze, at Thomas A. Edison High School (Alexandria) on Saturday, March 16, 1968; co-headlining, along with the Scattered Moss, a benefit for the Mustard Seed Coffee House at St. Stephen and the Incarnation Episcopal Church (Washington, D.C.) on Sunday, May 5, 1968; co-headlining, along with the Telstars, "The Washington Pop Music Festival," a 20-band event which was staged at the P Street Beach near Dupont Circle (Washington, D.C.) on Sunday, August 4, 1968; co-headlining, along with Flavor and Puzzle, a benefit for the Washington Free Press at St. Thomas Parish (Washington, D.C.)

on Friday, November 1, 1968; and headlining a concert Northern Virginia Community College Alexandria Campus on Friday, August 23, 1968.

During the year the band had one more personnel change when former drummer Ned Davis returned, but this time around came back to the fold as a keyboard player in replace of Howard Danchik.

The year 1969 saw the Fallen Angels maintain a busy live performance schedule, though the band was headed for a breakup by the year's end. They started things off by performing live on Sunday January 19, 1969 at "The Counter-Inaugural Ball," a protest event arranged by the National Mobilization Committee to End the War in Vietnam. The concert was held in "The Counter-Inauguration Tent" which was situated just south of the Sylvan Theater on the Mall in Washington, D.C. in a grassy location bounded by 15th Street NW, and Maine and Independence Avenues SW. The event began at 7pm, lasted for several hours, and, in addition to the Fallen Angels, featured live appearances by Phil Ochs, the Fugs, Urch Perch, Paul Krassner, the Hog Farm, members of SDS organizations, and people of the movement. The event reportedly drew a crowd of more than 8,000 and portions of the festivities, including footage of the Fallen Angels in action, later appeared in the underground movie "The Revolution is in Your Head" (Adelphi Films, 1970).

From March to August of 1969 the Fallen Angels held down house band duties at a Washington, D.C. night spot called Sam's Place (3333 Connecticut Avenue NW), a club which in previous decades had operated as the Brown Derby. Other times during the year they headlined a range of shows and concerts. These dates included: co-headlining a concert with Flavor and Puzzle at the Walt Whitman High School Field House (Bethesda) on Friday, January 31, 1969; headlining a concert, supported by the Foggy Bottom Blues Band, at New Lecture Hall (American University) on Friday, February 21, 1969; headlining a concert, supported by Urch Perch and the Atlanta Blues Band, at St. Stephen and the Incarnation Episcopal Church (Washington, D.C.) on Sunday, March 2, 1969; headlining a concert at the Falls Church Community Center (Virginia) on Saturday, March 8, 1969; participating on a concert bill headlined by Buffy Sainte-Marie and supported by Puzzle, Burt Mason, the Charles River Valley Boys and the New Lost City Ramblers at McDonough Gymnasium (Georgetown University) on Saturday, March 15, 1969; headlining a concert, supported by the Broom, at St. Stephen and the Incarnation Episcopal Church (Washington, D.C.) on Sunday, April 13, 1969; and headlining a concert, supported by Penny Arcade and Stone Bridge, at the Wheaton Youth Center (Wheaton) on Saturday, June 14, 1969.

Late in 1969 the Fallen Angels succumbed to various forms of long-simmering internal pressure and their time as one of the Washington, D.C. area's best rock and roll bands came to a halt. One of their last live gigs was also one of their strongest, as they opened for the Velvet Underground at the Multipurpose Building (gymnasium) at the University of Maryland Baltimore County (Catonsville) on Saturday, September 20, 1969. Reportedly, their performance far outshined the headliners. The band then expired after an engagement at Emergency in Georgetown from Monday, November 10 to Saturday, November 15, 1969. (Band members and followers still like to say the Fallen Angels unofficially died in the Emergency room.)

In 1970 singer-bassist Billy Hancock regrouped a version of the Fallen Angels with long-standing guitarist Wally Cook, former drummer Richard "Spider" Kumer and singer-keyboardist John Petrini. This reconstituted lineup performed dates at Nu-Mac's in Georgetown, Dick Poole's Supper Club in Annapolis, Club 175 in Jessup, and Cousin Nick's in Washington, D.C. In 1971 the band changed its name to Love and Trust and continued on for several months. Original member Jack Bryant was not a part of this venture.

Through the years the Fallen Angels have reunited on several occasions with both former members and new musicians joining in on the celebrations. Notably, in June 1997 the band recorded a collection of new material under the direction of jazz aficionado Pierre Sprey at Mapleshade, a private estate in Upper Marlboro, Maryland that houses a state-of-the-art recording studio. The result was the CD "Rain of Fire" (The Fallen Angels; Wildchild!, 1998) which featured a reconstituted lineup of longtime members Jack Bryant, Jack Lauritsen and Wally Cook, who were joined by bassist Kevin Armstrong, keyboardist Larry Willis and drummer Tom Mansell.

CHAPTER NINETY-SEVEN
THE NOWHERE MEN

When the song "Nowhere Man" by the Beatles raced up the Billboard popular music charts and peaked at number three on their "Hot 100" list on Saturday, March 26, 1966, it became an immediate favorite with the majority of the British Invasion-influenced teen dance bands throughout the Washington, D.C. area. One local group that materialized in the aftermath of that song's meteoric rise went so far as to use its title as the inspiration for their name, a unique course of action that drew substantial attention to their musical ventures. This particular band, the Nowhere Men, formed in Hyattsville Maryland and initially concentrated on the more pop-oriented Top 40 rock and roll material that went over so well on the teen dance circuit. It didn't take long, however, for the band to add horn players to their roster and introduce soul and R&B songs to its repertoire. Their expanded format went over so well that the Nowhere Men went on to rival Lawrence and the Arabians for popularity in Prince George's County and acquire bookings into many of the top night clubs throughout the region. For more than a decade the Nowhere Men were regarded as one of the Washington, D.C. area's highest quality R&B-rock bands.

The Nowhere Men formed in the summer of 1966 with a lineup of lead guitarist Steve Valenti (Archbishop Carroll High School, Class of 1970), lead singer-rhythm guitarist Bruce Gardner (Northwestern High School, Class of 1968), bassist Tommy Rodante (Northwestern High School, Class of 1968), keyboardist Richard Purvis (Northwestern High School, Class of 1967) and drummer Miles Sheetz (Northwestern High School, Class of 1968). All five of these initial members grew up in Hyattsville, Maryland and it was there in their hometown that the band played its first gig at a Magruder Park outdoor holiday celebration on Monday, July 4, 1966. Staying true to the music that gave them their name, the band originally specialized in songs by the Beatles, the Rolling Stones, the Kinks, the Buckinghams and other similar groups that were dominating the pop music charts.

Shortly after their fireworks-fused debut at Magruder Park, the Nowhere Men enthusiastically delved into the local teen dance world. They obtained a spot in the prestigious "Middle Atlantic Rock and Roll Tournament," a nine-band live music presentation that was sponsored by the National Tea Council and staged at Wheaton Plaza in Montgomery County, Maryland on Saturday, July 30, 1966 (other participating bands that afternoon were the Beau Havens, the Henchmen, the Trespassers, the Dead Beats, Act V, Blues British, 24-Karat Five and the Sheratons).

In the aftermath of that tournament performance, the Nowhere Men entertained steady offers to play dances at schools and teen clubs throughout the Washington, D.C. area. During the next year they headlined at William Wirt Junior High School (Riverdale), DeMatha Catholic High School (Hyattsville), Winston Churchill High School (Potomac), the College Park Teen Club (City of College Park Municipal Building), the St. James Catholic Church Teen Club (Mt. Rainier), the Wedge (Bethesda Youth Center), the St. John Baptist de la Salle Teen Club (Chillum), the St. Camillus Catholic Church Teen Club (Silver Spring), the St. Mark the Evangelist Catholic Church Teen Club (Hyattsville), the Our Lady of Sorrows Church Teen Club (Takoma Park), the St. Jerome Catholic Church Teen Club (Hyattsville), the St. Bernard Catholic Church Teen Club (Riverdale), the St. Bernadette Catholic Church Teen Club (Silver Spring), the St. Francis Xavier Parish Teen Club (Southeast Washington, D.C.), and the St. Ambrose Parish Teen Club (Cheverly).

In late 1967 the Nowhere Men began expanding in size and significant changes in their musical output ensued. The original quintet was first joined by saxophonist Bruce Horton, and then by trombonist Danny Nelson and trumpeter Joe McColly. In 1968 the band went through additional changes and its lineup consisted of Gardner, Valenti, Rodante, Purvis, Sheetz, McColly, saxophonist Jimmy Robinson, trumpeters Gary Gaulette and Chris Heer, and a second drummer named Tommy Wright. That year Gardner departed and three new lead singers were added in Don Halcombe, Billy Vabolis and Charlie Taylor. Shortly thereafter in 1969 original member Steve Valenti left the band and was replace by guitarist Mike Pirko.

Throughout the late 1960s and into the 1970s the Nowhere Men moved forward as a larger and more musically complex group. During that time they concentrated on performing the songs of bands such as the Righteous Brothers, the Temptations, the Association, the Four Tops, James Brown, Otis Redding, Wilson Pickett, Rare Earth, Chicago, Tower of Power and Blood, Sweat and Tears, in addition to such popular rock and roll groups as the Beatles, the Rolling Stones and Cream.

The Nowhere Men played a wide variety of jobs during this period, including a headlining performance on Wednesday, June 19, 1968 at the grand opening of the brand new Prince George's Plaza Community Center in Hyattsville Maryland. They also played teen dances at the Church of St. Matthias the Apostle Teen Club (Lanham), the Mt. Rainier Teen Club (Mt. Rainier Junior High School), the Little Flower Parish Teen Club (Bethesda), the Wedge (Bethesda Youth Center), the St. Elizabeth's Catholic Church Teen Club (Rockville), the Holy Redeemer Catholic Church Teen Club (Kensington), the St. Hugh's Catholic Church Teen Club (Greenbelt) and Our Lady of Good Counsel High School (Wheaton).

The Nowhere Men developed particularly strong followings in Greenbelt, Maryland and at the University of Maryland in College Park, where their shows at various venues drew capacity crowds. One well-publicized show in Greenbelt that was booked and emceed by disc jockey-promoter Barry Richards saw them co-headline with the Drifters at the Greenbelt Youth Center on Friday, September 6, 1968. They also appeared on numerous bills at the larger Greenbelt Armory including a double-header with Lawrence and the Arabians on Monday, November 4, 1968, a triple-header with the Coasters and the Syndicate on Wednesday, November 27, 1968, another concert with Lawrence and the Arabians on Thursday, October 16, 1969, and a three-band record hop staged by radio stations WWDC and WPGC on Sunday, December 14, 1969 with the Magic Touch and Jay and the Inspirations.

The University of Maryland campus was also a favorite haunt of the Nowhere Men and the band frequently made appearances on the school's larger stages. On Monday, February 17, 1969 they were part of a multi-band presentation in the Grand Ballroom in the Adele H. Stamp Student Union with the New Breed, the Continental Rockers, the Novells, the Speculations, Lloyd and the Lonely Souls, and Jay and the Inspirations. They also performed at Ritchie Coliseum on numerous occasions including: a concert they headlined on Friday, February 28, 1969; an extravaganza on Friday, September 19, 1969 where the appeared on a bill with the Speculations, the Soul Lighters, the Magic Touch, Syfiun, God Mother Country, the New Breed, the Magic Touch, and Movus Quofe; a headlining position at "The Moratorium Rock Festival" on Sunday, November 9, 1969, an event that also included Parsec, Bob Brown and Claude Jones; and another concert event they headlined on their own on Friday, December 5, 1969.

Early in the 1970s a major transition took place in the Nowhere Men when Tommy Rodante, Donnie Halcombe, Charlie Taylor and Tommy Wright broke away from the band, and, along with keyboardist Mike Sarigumba, formed an R&B-rock band called Second Coming that began working the local supper club circuit. With their departure the Nowhere Men regrouped with a lineup of returning singer Bruce Gardner, returning guitarist Steve Valenti, singer-bassist Bob McCoy, keyboardist Richard Purvis, trumpeters Gary Gaulette and George Kindrock, trombonist Clark Kendrick and drummer Mike Valenti. It was this lineup of the band that was called upon to participate in one of the area's biggest concerts of the time when they opened for Three Dog Night at the William P. Cole, Jr. Student Activities Building (University of Maryland; commonly referred to as Cole Field House) on Sunday, April 25, 1971, an event that sold out the facility.

During the remainder of the 1970s the Nowhere Men experienced innumerable changes in personnel. Tracking the band through the decade is problematic, as subsequent lineups contained no original members and were subject to constant change. Musicians to pass through the group included: singer Mike Buker; guitarists Vic Jenkins, Steve Bishop and Mike Ault; singer-keyboardist Steve Hatfield; keyboardist Rick Aurich; saxophonist Larry Mason; trumpeters Warren Grimes, Richard Seeley and Craig Balliette; and drummers Mike Zack, Matt Abts and Jimmy Baker.

The Nowhere Men mainly concentrated on playing night clubs during these years, both locally and across the eastern half of the United States from Michigan to Pennsylvania to Florida. When they worked the nation's capital, they embarked on night club dates at establishments such as the Act IV Supper Club, the Bastille Supper Club, My Mother's Place, the Quonset Supper Club, Cesare's II, Fran O'Brien's Anthony House Restaurant, Ventuno 21 Supper Club, the Black Greco, Black Ulysses, the Cave, the Crazy Horse and the Bayou.

Record deals never materialized for the Nowhere Men, as they always concentrated on performing covers of popular songs as opposed to playing original material. For this reason national recognition eluded this talented outfit. In addition, the high quality of the group's musicianship caused other local bands to constantly attempt to recruit players from the fold. In 1978, with the music scene changing and the practice of hiring house bands slowly evaporating, the initial 12-year run of the Nowhere Men came to a close.

In recent times the Nowhere Men have regrouped with a number of different musicians coming and going. The current lineup of the band consists of lead singer-percussionist Joe Roundtree, lead singer-guitarist Vince Campanella, bassist Tommy Rodante, keyboardist Wayne Brown, saxophonist Tommy Ruggieri, trumpeters Richard Kessler and Steve Kaufmann, trombonist Dave Cannon and drummer Joe Consorti.

CHAPTER NINETY-EIGHT
THE NEW BREED

The New Breed was a talented, horn-oriented R&B-rock band that was originally based in the Lewisdale community of Prince George's County, Maryland and was a hot commodity on the both the local teen dance scene and night club circuit. The band had an auspicious beginning in the late 1960s and evolved into one of the region's most talented and highly sought-after musical outfits, performing all manner of R&B and rock and roll, eventually specializing in the work of the popular band Chicago, whose brassy sound they embraced, perfected and displayed during their exciting six-year run. Many alumni of the New Breed went on to work with nationally recognized performing artists and several of these musicians are still active in the music world today.

In the spring of 1967 the New Breed formed when five young musicians from various local teen rock and roll bands intersected and decided to put together a new group. The very first lineup of this outfit consisted of singer-keyboardist Mike Eccard of Lewisdale (Northwestern High School, Class of 1969), lead guitarist Gerry Hemming of Hyattsville (St. John's College High School, Class of 1967), bassist Bobbie Colie of Takoma Park (Northwestern High School, Class of 1970), saxophonist Jamie MacKinnon of Lewisdale (Northwestern High School, Class of 1970) and drummer Jim Fauntleroy of White Oak, a community in neighboring Montgomery County, Maryland (Springbrook High School, Class of 1969).

The New Breed first set up shop and rehearsed in the basement of Jamie MacKinnon's home at 2405 Amherst Road in Lewisdale, a community situated between the Northeast Washington, D.C. line and Adelphi, Maryland. During its first year together, the band expanded, bringing in a horn section consisting of saxophonist Ronnie Rudkin, trombonist Kim Cissel, and trumpeter Clark Forcey, all of whom were students at nearby Northwestern High School in Hyattsville, Maryland. At times the band also performed onstage with an all-Black four- or five-person vocal team out of Northwestern High School called the Impalas.

At this point in time the repertoire of the New Breed consisted of covers of performing artists such as James Brown, the Delfonics, Sam and Dave, the Temptations, Otis Redding, Herbie Hancock, Junior Walker and the All Stars, Martha and the Vandellas, the Miracles, Archie Bell and the Drells, the Soul Survivors, Aretha Franklin, Eddie Floyd, Ben E. King, the Everly Brothers, the Drifters, Cliff Nobles and Company, the Intruders, Dionne Warwick, Tom Jones and the Beatles. The great majority of the area's teen dance bands of the 1960s tended to concentrate on either the sounds of the British Invasion or straightforward R&B, with little mixing of the two styles taking place. The New Breed tended to buck that trend, leaning towards R&B, but including healthy doses of the era's rock and roll hits in their sets as well. Their mix of music attracted a devoted following that strongly supported their local appearances.

Throughout 1967 and the first half of 1968 the New Breed performed at local teen dances at the Cottage City and Colmar Manor Fire Department (Cottage City), the Adelphi Mill (Adelphi), the Holy Redeemer Parish Teen Club (College Park), Northwestern High School (Hyattsville), Laurel High School (Laurel), the Mt. Rainier Teen Club (Mt. Rainier Junior High School), the Brentwood Teen Club (Bartlett Park, Wohlfarth Building, 4300 39th Place, Brentwood, Maryland), the St. Ambrose Parish Teen Club (Cheverly), the St. Bernard Catholic Church Teen Club (Riverdale), the St. Bernadette Catholic Church Teen Club (Silver Spring), the St. Jerome Catholic Church Teen Club (Hyattsville), the St. John Baptist de la Salle Catholic Church Teen Club (Chillum), the St. Mark the Evangelist Catholic Church Teen Club (Hyattsville), the Church of St. Matthias the Apostle Teen Club

(Lanham), the St. Michael the Archangel Parish Teen Club (Silver Spring), the St. Thomas Moore Parish Teen Club (Arlington), the Greenbelt Teen Club (Greenbelt Youth Center), the Prince George's Plaza Community Center (Hyattsville), the Wedge (Bethesda Youth Center), the Wheaton Youth Center (Wheaton), the Greenbelt Armory (Greenbelt), Henderson Hall Officer's Club (A military installation of the United States Marine Corps in Arlington County, Virginia) and the Wilson Line's M.V. George Washington cruise ship. During this time the band also stepped up and made its first night club appearances at two prominent Washington, D.C. establishments, the Gentlemen II and the Hayloft.

During the two-year period from 1968 to 1970 the New Breed experienced a number of personnel changes in fairly steady succession. Guitarist Bruce MacKinnon, brother of Jamie MacKinnon, came and went. Rudkin and Forcey departed, and a trumpet player named George Kindrock, another Northwestern High School graduate, joined the band. Kurt Gibbons, a College Park native who had graduated from High Point High School in 1969 and had previously played in a band called the Soul Revolution, replaced Mike Eccard and came on board as lead singer and keyboardist and assumed leadership duties. David Platshon, a West Hyattsville resident and 1969 graduate of Northwestern High School who had previously played with Nitty Gritty and the Epsilons, replaced Jim Fauntleroy on drums.

During this time the New Breed continued playing the local teen dance scene and made appearances at the Wedge (Bethesda Youth Center), the St. Elizabeth Catholic Church Teen Club (Rockville), the St. Mary's Catholic Church Teen Club (Landover Hills), the Mt. Rainier Teen Club (Mt. Rainier Junior High School), the Prince George's Plaza Community Center (Hyattsville), and Albert Einstein High School (Kensington). During the summer of 1969 the band was called upon to perform several times at the large weekend hippie gatherings at the P Street Beach near Dupont Circle in Washington, D.C.

Throughout 1969 and 1970 the New Breed also preformed regularly at the University of Maryland in College Park at both Ritchie Coliseum and the Grand Ballroom in the Adele H. Stamp Student Union, sometimes as part of multi-act presentations and sometimes as concert headliners. In one of the largest concert attractions of the era that featured local rock and roll bands, the New Breed headlined with the Cherry People and the Young Senators at Ritchie Coliseum on Thursday, April 30, 1970. This particular event not only sold out the 1,500-seat facility, but brought in offers from several night club owners who sought the band's services for the coming summer months.

After weighing its options, the New Breed opted to spend the summer of 1970 in Somers Point, New Jersey and perform at the Attic, one of the Jersey Shore's most popular night clubs. There, they worked the 10pm-6am graveyard shift. During this year they had made two more major replacements, with lead guitarist Mike Pirko – an Adelphi native and member of the High Point High School Class of 1968 – replacing Gerry Hemming and trumpeter Bruce Morris – a Beltsville native and member of the High Point High School Class of 1966 – replacing Kindrock. The band was now a seven-piece consisting of lead singer-keyboardist Kurt Gibbons, lead guitarist Mike Pirko, bassist Bobby Colie, drummer David Platshon, saxophonist Jamie MacKinnon, trombonist Kim Cissel and trumpeter Bruce Morris.

The New Breed was a tight operation that now specialized in the big horn sound of the band Chicago, and, to a lesser extent, groups like Ten Wheel Drive, Tower of Power, Ides of March, the Isley Brothers, Blood, Sweat and Tears and others of that style. At the conclusion of the summer the band returned to the Washington, D.C. area and secured an engagement at the local version of the Attic, a sister club to the New Jersey establishment they had just left behind.

In 1970 the New Breed made one last personnel change, when lead guitarist Bobby Manriquez was chosen to replace Mike Pirko. Manriquez, a Silver Spring, Maryland native who had graduated from Montgomery Blair High School in 1969 and had previously been in such bands as the Madcaps, Nitty Gritty and Desdemona, was a highly sought-after guitarist in the region and his signature blues-based style fit the band well.

The New Breed carried on into 1971, most notably co-billed with Crank and Tractor at Our Lady of Good Counsel High School in Wheaton, Maryland on Friday, February 26, and then with Sageworth and Drums and Claude Jones at Archbishop Carroll High School in Washington, D.C. on Sunday, April 25. They spent that entire summer again working the Attic in Somers Point, but upon returning home to the Washington, D.C. area most of the band members decided to tap into the area's more lucrative night club scene and began moving in different directions. Gibbons, Manriquez and Platshon, for example, got together with bassist Greg Hemming (brother of original New Breed guitarist Gerry Hemming) to form Bobby and Friends, a rock and roll band that became the house band at Apple Pie in Georgetown. After one last performance at a dance held at the Prince George's Plaza Community Center in Hyattsville on Friday, September 17, the New Breed disbanded.

CHAPTER NINETY-NINE
THE CHERRY PEOPLE

The Cherry People emerged from the 1960s as one of Washington, D.C.'s top rock and roll bands, a dynamic group noted for its tremendous talent, command of the local night club scene, and impressive recorded output. The band formed in Southeast Washington, D.C. during the British Invasion of 1964 as the Intruders, quickly switched its name to the English Setters, and ultimately became the Cherry People, in the process becoming one of the region's hardest working and most talented musical outfits. Early on the band was a force on the local teen dance scene with a repertoire that mixed Beatles covers and original material, and by the end of the 1960s had turned up the volume and taken the Georgetown night club scene by storm. A deal with Heritage Records in New York saw the band release an album and embark on regional promotional tours, spreading their rock and roll legend far beyond the nation's capital.

The roots of the Cherry People go back to Southeast Washington D.C. – perhaps the city's most fertile spot for developing rock and roll and C&W musicians during the 1950s and 1960s. It was there in the Barnaby Terrace neighborhood (a short distance from the homes of Danny Gatton, Roy Clark and Link Wray) where the quartet of Chris and Doug Grimes, Edwin "Punky" Meadows and Larry Gray were raised, became interested in music, and began following the Beatles and other British Invasion bands. In 1964 these four youngsters, who ranged in age from 13 to 16, formed their first band, the Intruders.

When the Intruders first got together, Doug Grimes was attending Draper Elementary School, while Chris Grimes, Punky Meadows and Larry Gray were all students at nearby Charles Hart Junior High School. All four band members were basically self-taught, with the Grimes brothers and Meadows playing guitars and Gray handling the drums. Doug Grimes took on the role of lead singer and the band rehearsed in Gray's house at 849 Xenia Street SE (the Grimes and Meadows families lived on Varney Street SE at the time, though both families moved around the neighborhood quite a bit).

In April 1964 the Intruders gave their very first public performance at a talent show entitled "The Spring Festival" at Charles Hart Junior High School, performing two Beatles songs, "Long Tall Sally" and "I Saw Her Standing There." They spent the remainder of the year performing at parties and area military base establishments such as the Bolling Air Force Base Officers' Club (Washington, D.C.), the Andrews Air Force Base Officers' Club (Prince George's County, Maryland) and the Fort George G. Meade Officers' Club (Anne Arundel County, Maryland).

In an effort to accentuate their British Invasion influence, the band changed its name to the English Setters in early 1965. That year saw band members Doug and Chris Grimes and Punky Meadows move with their families from Southeast Washington, D.C. to Arlington, Virginia. The relocation uprooted Chris Grimes from Ballou High School in Southeast and forced Doug Grimes to enroll in Stratford Junior High School in Arlington. Punky Meadows, who had also been a student at Ballou High School in Southeast, now had to attend T.C. Williams High School in Alexandria.

The English Setters became a quintet when they added drummer David Alves of Southeast Washington, D.C., another Ballou High School student, a move that pushed Larry Gray, who by this time was attending Chamberlain Vocational High School in Washington, D.C., over to bass guitar. The band spent the year working officers' clubs on local military bases as well as the area's teen dance circuit. They were a featured attraction at the St. Andrew's Episcopal Church Teen Club (Arlington), the St. Mary Catholic Church Teen Club (Alexandria) and the St. Agnes Catholic Church Teen Club (Arlington). They also performed at school dances held at the Cameron Club (Alexandria), the Roger B. Taney Teen Club (at Roger B. Taney Junior High School in Temple Hills, Maryland) and Oxon Hill Junior High School (Oxon Hill).

In late 1965 the English Setters signed a management contract with Lionel Hampton, who had the band record several original songs in a New York City studio and then perform live dates in Philadelphia, Atlantic City and New York City. Two singles were released from those sessions: "Tragedy" backed with "If She's All Right" (The English Setters; Glad-Hamp Records, 1966), and "Someday You'll See" backed with "It Shouldn't Happen to a Dog" (The English Setters; Glad-Hamp Records, 1966). Back in the Washington, D.C. area, the band then built a large following during the summer of 1966 as the house band at the Corral on M Street NW in Georgetown.

In 1966 the English Setters also performed some memorable live music shows. These performances included: appearing at a concert presentation entitled "Summertime Hullabaloo" headlined by Neil Diamond and supported by Nobody's Children, Bobby Parker, the British Walkers, the Minutemen, the Marvels, the Rip-Tydes and the Sidekicks at the Manassas Armory in Virginia on Saturday, August 6; appearing at the "End of Summer Blast" along with the Hangmen, the Flys, the Tytans, the Organic Cavemen, the Jon Norvell Combo, Diane Joyce, Johnny Wooten and Sharon 'N' Karen at the Bayou on Sunday, September 4; appearing at a concert headlined by the Yardbirds and supported by the British Walkers, the New Delphonics, the Jay Walkers, the New Found Sound, December's Children, the Sheffields, the Gents, Fugitive Sound and the Villager Go-Go Girls at the Alexandria Arena on Friday, September 9; opening for the Beau Brummels in a street dance at Robert E. Lee High School in Springfield, Virginia on Saturday, September 24; serving as the backup band for headliner Neil Diamond at a concert supported by the Hangmen, the Brave Maggots and a rally that included more than 20 teen bands (that evening the English Setters also performed their own set) at the Alexandria Arena on Saturday, October 1; appearing at a concert headlined by the Count Five and Martha and the Vandellas and supported by the Hangmen at the Alexandria Arena on Wednesday, November 23; co-headlining with Lawrence and the Arabians at the Greenbelt Armory on Saturday, December 10; and appearing at a concert headlined by the Young Rascals and supported by the Hangmen, the Fallen Angels and the Surf Boys at the Alexandria Arena on Friday, December 23.

The English Setters kicked off the year 1967 with another single release in January, "Wake Up" backed with "She's In Love" (The English Setters; Jubilee Records, 1967). The band continued to work around the Washington, D.C. area, performing engagements at such night clubs in the city as the Corral, the Frog, the Peppermint Lounge and the American Palace (inside the Dodge House Hotel).

That year the English Setters also played WPGC-sponsored teen dances at Washington-Lee High School (Arlington), the St. Mary's Catholic Church Teen Club (Landover Hills), Indian Head Elementary School (Accokeek) and Clinton Regional Park (located in Clinton, Maryland, this recreational area was renamed Louise F. Cosca Regional Park in 1970). In the summer months the band spent time in New York City, where they played several different Greenwich Village night clubs including the Café Wha?

Personnel changes ensued, with bassist Pick Kelly, an Arlington, Virginia native who had formerly played with the Briars, passing through, and bassist Jan Zukowski, a Forestville, Maryland resident who had formerly played with Nobody's Children and Tuesday Boots, taking his place. In addition, former Fallen Angels drummer Rocky Isaac, an Anacostia High School graduate, replaced David Alves. This version of the band, with the classic lineup of Doug and Chris Grimes, Punky Meadows, Jan Zukowski and Rocky

Isaac, spent the fall months working on the far side of the city at a psychedelic night club called the Rogue on Bladensburg Road NE.

While performing in New York City in the fall of 1967 the English Setters signed a deal with Heritage Records, a subsidiary of MGM Records. The producers brought in studio musicians to perform on the sessions, which did feature vocal work by the actual band members. The result was a new name for the band, "The Cherry People," and a strange-sounding album released the following May, "Cherry People" (The Cherry People; Heritage Records, 1968), which came across as a burst of bubblegum pop music that was not indicative at all of what the group was really about.

Several singles off the album were released, most notably "And Suddenly" (The Cherry People; Heritage Records, 1968), which peaked at number 45 on Billboard magazine's "Billboard Hot 100" popular music chart on Saturday, August 31, 1968. Although the band remained based in Washington, D.C., they embarked on several short regional tours around the country in support of the album and performed at such faraway places as the Whisky a Go Go on the Sunset Strip in Los Angeles and Caesar's Palace in Las Vegas, Nevada. Heritage Records, however, failed to provide the band with proper financial backing and a follow-up album was never recorded.

In July 1968, right in the midst of the push for their eponymous album on Heritage Records, the Cherry People turned up their hard rock volume and began working periodically at the Silver Dollar Restaurant on M Street NW in the Georgetown neighborhood of Washington, D.C. After several months of short engagements, the night club granted them house band status, a position that had the group working the establishment up to seven nights per week for months at a time throughout 1969 and 1970.

When breaks came up during the Silver Dollar Restaurant run, the band embarked on some interesting rock and roll adventures. These included: headlining a dance at the St. Ambrose Parish Teen Club (Cheverly) on Sunday, September 7, 1969; headlining a dance at the Wedge (Bethesda Youth Center) on Saturday, October 18, 1969; appearing along with Love Cry Want, Claude Jones, and Jabberwok at "The Intercollegiate Music Festival" which was held in the Sylvan Theatre on the Mall in Washington, D.C. on Sunday, October 19, 1969; co-headlining a triple bill with the Nowhere Men and Curfew at the Falls Church Community Center (Virginia) on Saturday, March 7, 1970; and headlining a concert supported by the New Breed, the Young Senators, Easy, and David at Ritchie Coliseum (University of Maryland) on Thursday, April 30, 1970.

The early 1970s saw the Cherry People perform at some of Georgetown's best night clubs including the M Club (formerly the Silver Dollar Restaurant), the Bayou and the Crazy Horse, as well as the Keg in Glover Park. They also ventured back into the recording studio and recorded and released one last single, "Sea and Me" backed with "Come on Over" (The Cherry People; Hot Cotton Records, 1971).

After the departure of strongholds Punky Meadows (who would go on to be a founding member of the hard-rocking band Angel), Rocky Isaac and Jan Zukowski, the band went through a whirlwind of personnel changes with musicians coming and going on a regular basis. Among those to pass through the group included: guitarists Chris Noe and Wayne Tomlinson and drummers Mike Zack and T.C. Tolliver. By late 1973 the band had settled on a lineup of Doug and Chris Grimes, lead guitarist Rick Benick, bassist Andre Sokol and drummer Barry Brandt.

After more than a year as the house band at the Keg, the band replaced Chris Grimes with guitarist David Namerdy and Barry Brandt, who left to join Angel, with drummer Steve Riley, a native of Boston, Massachusetts who had previously played in Max and years later would play in such bands as Steppenwolf, Keel, W.A.S.P. and the L.A. Guns.

In early 1975 the final version Cherry People took up residence at the Varsity Grill Back Room in College Park, Maryland. The night club was trying to recover from its early 1970s period of drugs and rampant violence and the owners felt that bringing in one of Washington, D.C.'s best working bands was the shot in the arm the business needed. While the band drew throngs of followers to the club, the stress of keeping the outfit together began wearing on Doug Grimes. After dominating the Washington, D.C. area rock and roll scene for over 11 years, the Cherry People played their final gig with a three-night stand at the Varsity Grill Back Room from Thursday, June 19 to Saturday, June 21, 1975.

Like other local stalwart bands from their era, different versions of the Cherry People still assemble on occasion under the direction of Doug and Chris Grimes for recording sessions and live performances. In recent years the band has issued two albums: a new studio recording, "Nobody's Perfect" (The Cherry People; Dischord Records, 2010); and a compilation of older material, "Whoopin' & a Whoppin'" (The Cherry People; Angel Air Records, 2011).

During its long and colorful lifespan, the Cherry People ran the entire rock and roll spectrum of the Washington, D.C. area rock and roll scene. They were early heroes of the teen dance circuit, became a national act that released an album and singles and toured the country, and ultimately established themselves as one of the very best original hard rock night club bands the region has ever experienced.

CHAPTER ONE HUNDRED
THE TRIP WINDS DOWN

As the 1960s progressed the sounds that constituted rock and roll music diversified in style and expanded in complexity. Certain trends in rock and roll emerged, developed and evolved during the decade as different bands immersed themselves in different types of music, with the shifts moving through pop, rockabilly and C&W in the early years; R&B and soul during the middle portion; the British Invasion in the last half; and psychedelia and hard rock in the latter part. The 1960s came to pass as a dynamic decade where the boundaries of rock and roll transformed through the discovery, experimentation and implementation of different musical elements.

In the nation's capital the social climate was changing with the music and as the 1960s came to a close the two became intensely intertwined. The Washington, D.C. area popular music scene was greatly impacted by the Riots of 1968. The violence and destruction began in the nation's capital when, shortly after 8pm (EST) on the night of Thursday, April 4, 1968, Dr. Martin Luther King, Jr., a Black co-pastor of Ebenezer Baptist Church in Atlanta, Georgia and president of a civil rights promotional organization known as the Southern Christian Leadership Conference, was shot and mortally wounded while standing on the balcony outside his second-floor room at the Lorraine Motel in Memphis, Tennessee. King, 39, had actually been shot at 6:01pm (CST) and was pronounced dead at 7:05pm at St. Joseph Hospital in Memphis. News of his assassination quickly spread, with rioting commencing in cities across the United States.

The rioting in Washington, D.C. began that Thursday evening when hundreds of Blacks began clustering in groups within a corridor that stretched from 2800 to 2000 14th Street NW, north of the intersection of U Street NW. The rioters began throwing rocks, smashing windows, igniting fires, looting stores and attacking innocent bystanders and uniformed police officers. They savagely ravaged three Black commercial corridors of the city: 14th Street NW (from the 2800 block south to Thomas Circle NW); 7th Street NW (mainly in the 1800 block and areas south); and H Street NE (from the 200 block eastwards to the 1400 block). In addition, smaller-scale rioting broke out in various neighborhoods and commercial areas throughout the District. While the most intense rioting took place on Thursday and Friday nights, disturbances continued on for much of the following week, with Metropolitan Police being augmented by thousands of United States Army troops and D.C. National Guard military police in combined efforts to quell the disorder.

Assessing the damage caused during the Riots of 1968 has been problematic. The reported numbers have changed through the years and to this day vary from source to source. In terms of number of deaths directly caused by the rioting, the most reliable source seems to be an article in the Washington Post of Wednesday, April 10, 1968 entitled "City's 10 Riot Fatalities: Witnesses Describe Deaths" that sets the number of fatalities at 10 (the article was assembled by Washington Post staff writers Ivan C. Brandon, Hollie I. West, Leonard Downie Jr. and Jim Hoagland).

Other riot statistics gleaned from various Washington Post articles published in the disturbance's aftermath reveal that from April 4 to April 10 the city experienced 1,166 injury incidents, 1,062 fire incidents, and more than 5,500 arrests. A total of 15,246 United States Army troops were dispatched to Washington, D.C. to help Metropolitan Police and local military police combat the disturbances. Damages attributed to the seven-day rioting period totaled $12,703,661.00.

The riots had an immediate impact on the Washington, D.C. area's music scene and solidified the notion among White Americans that Washington, D.C. had transitioned from a

White city to a Black one both symbolically and demographically. In reality the demographic change had been steadily in motion since the early 1950s. To this day, the exact date that Washington, D.C. transformed from a White-majority city to a Black one has never been conclusively verified, though foundationless estimates by various social service agencies in the nation's capital claim the change may have taken place as early as 1956 or 1957. The United States Bureau of the Census – the only government agency capable of conducting an accurate and final population count for the city – first officially reported a Black majority in 1960. They recorded the following statistics:

1950: Total (802,178); White (517,865; 64.5%); Black (280,803; 35.0%)
1960: Total (763,956); Black (411,737; 53.8%); White (345,263; 45.1%)
1970: Total (756,510); Black (537,212; 71.0%); White (209,272; 27.6%)

By the early 1970s the changes to the popular music scene in Washington, D.C. were extensive. The city's White Southerners were all but gone, the country music scene was near extinction, and the number of traditional rock and roll night clubs that had either changed musical styles to accommodate the new population or had simply closed their doors significantly outweighed the opening of new establishments.

While the Georgetown neighborhood of the city maintained its status as a rock and roll stronghold with night clubs like the Bayou, the Cellar Door and the Crazy Horse soldiering on, many of the city's other long-standing, live music clubs were in transition: Benny's Rebel Room in the vibrant 800 block of 14th Street NW last featured live rock and roll bands in December 1974 and then converted into an exotic dance club, officially changing its name to Benny's Home of the Porno Stars in January 1982; the Rocket Room next to the bus station on New York Avenue NW dropped rock and roll and began exclusively booking R&B bands in late 1969 – in April 1970 the night club had its name changed to the Room, began catering to predominantly Black audiences, and managed to stay in business until 1987; the Shelter Room in the Congress Heights neighborhood of Southeast Washington, D.C. lost its White patronage after the riots, began emphasizing soul and R&B bands in 1969, and closed its doors for good in 1973; and the Starlite Restaurant at 14th and Irving Streets NW, once the home of Jimmy Dean and the Texas Wildcats, Patsy Cline, Curly Slider and Butterball Paige, switched over to Black soul bands in 1968 and eventually went out of business in 1974. The area's live music scene had undergone a dramatic transformation.

Although the Washington, D.C. area's rock and roll scene was in a state of transition during the late 1960s and early 1970s, it was, in part, supported by a small number of "progressive" or "underground" local radio programs that were steadily emerging. These programs served a purpose in that they played various shades of album rock and roll music targeted at college-aged, leftist hippies. In addition to the progressive rock and roll they aired, the stations also relayed information regarding countercultural services and events, provided advertisements for rock and roll concerts and performances, and stayed faithful to the music of the day, rarely playing rock and roll from the 1950s or early 1960s.

Initially there were three underground radio programs in the Washington, D.C. area that began airing in February 1968 and targeted the college-age crowd: "Subterranean Sound Experiment" (hosted by Jack Jeffries on WOL; specializing in psychedelic blues and rock and roll); "Electric Brew" (hosted by Blair Newman, Frank Richards and Paul Dowell on WASH; specializing in acid rock and old blues); and "Music Americana" (hosted by Mary Cliff on WAVA; a successor to Dick Cerri's previous program of the same name; specializing in folk rock). As notice of these three relatively short-lived radio programs spread throughout the local counterculture community, two area stations, WGTB and WHFS, decided to devote all of their on-air broadcasting towards the growing movement.

WGTB, a 6,700-watt radio station, operated out of the basement of Copley Hall on the Georgetown University campus that first went on the air on the AM dial in 1946. In 1960 the station switched to 90.1 FM and offered a combination of pop music and spiritual programming throughout the decade. Major changes took place in 1970 when radicals took over the 10-member operations board and turned it into a leftist and subversive politics station that mainly played progressive rock and avant-garde jazz.

WGTB featured a free form radio philosophy with no playlists and no commercial support. Local rock and roll bands were sporadically featured on its various segments and the station became a support system for the area's musicians and fans. Among the more popular radio programs the station aired during its countercultural prime were "Mystic Eyes" hosted by Steve Lorber, "The Abstraction Show" hosted by John Paige, "Tea Time" hosted by Mark Garbin and "The Hard Implosion" hosted by Fred Cresce. WGTB experienced waves of highs and lows during its existence and eventually signed off from the local airwaves on Monday, January 29, 1979.

The other main underground radio station of the era, WHFS, first went on the air on Saturday, November 11, 1961 at 102.3 FM and initially offered a mix of pop, jazz and classical music. The 2,300-watt station initially broadcast from a makeshift studio in the basement of the Bethesda Medical Building. Later in the decade, after moving through two other Bethesda addresses, the station set up quarters in a studio on the second floor of Triangle Towers, a 15-story luxury condominium in Bethesda at 4853 Cordell Avenue, directly across the street from the Psyche Delly.

In 1967 station part-owner Jake Einstein became general manager and the following year implemented a free-form, progressive rock and roll format, which, like WGTB, emphasized album tracks and gave airtime to Washington, D.C. area bands. Many disc jockeys at WHFS achieved great heights of local popularity during the 1960s and 1970s including Frank Richards, Sara Vass, Mark Gorbulew, Don "Cerphe" Colwell, Mick Sussman, John "Littlejohn" Hendricks, Jonathan "Weasel" Gilbert, David Einstein, Damian Einstein, Bob "Here" Showacre, Diane Divola, Tom Grooms, Josh Brooks, Don Grossinger and Adele Abrams. In October 1983, WHFS left Bethesda and was moved to Annapolis, Maryland, where it was granted new call letters, and, with the counterculture a thing of the past, struggled for on-air survival.

Despite the perseverance of a small collection of hard-rocking night clubs in Georgetown and the presence of underground radio, the Washington, D.C. area's counterculture began unraveling in the early 1970s with three momentous events contributing to its eventual demise: the Richard Mattingly Murder; the folding of the Quicksilver Times underground newspaper; and the end of the Vietnam War.

In the first event, hippie innocence took a hit when 63-year-old Richard L. Mattingly Sr., executive secretary of the District of Columbia Board for the Condemnation of Insanitary Buildings, was brutally murdered in his home at 4413 N. 15th Street, Arlington, Virginia on Thursday, January 8, 1970. In what was called a Charles Manson copycat murder, Mattingly was confronted in his home at 5pm that evening by a gaggle of four deranged Dupont Circle hippies: 21-year-old Kenneth W. Hitner (an AWOL United States Marine), 19-year-old self-appointed biker Eugene L. "Spirit" Comeau, 15-year-old runaway Patricia "Pegasus" Truax, and his own adopted daughter, 14-year-old Debra "Muffin" Mattingly, all of whom reportedly were tripping on LSD at the time and had invaded the premises to assist Muffin in the retrieval of some of her personal clothing and photographs.

Upon entering the premises, an argument between Muffin and her father ensued and Richard Mattingly was subsequently attacked by Hitner, struck in the head with a claw hammer by Comeau, and strangled to death with a crowbar by both assailants. The four invaders all lived together at the time on the fourth floor of a commune at 1752 N Street NW in Washington, D.C. and were well-known in the Dupont Circle hippie community, having originally met some time earlier at the Switchboard, a social center of the counterculture which operated out of the basement of the Church of Pilgrims at 2201 P Street NW. Hitner in particular was a highly visible part of the scene, as he volunteered for several antiwar organizations in the Dupont Circle neighborhood.

The murder, for which Comeau and Hitner both were convicted on first-degree murder charges and given 30-year sentences (Muffin was slapped with a juvenile detention center stay at a "special school" in Florida and Truax avoided prosecution in exchange for damning testimony against her cohorts), served to skewer the prevailing hippie Utopian vision in the nation's capital by casting a veil of darkness and evil over the Dupont Circle scene that lingered for years.

In the second event, the underground press in the Washington, D.C. area, for all practical purposes, came to an end when the Quicksilver Times newspaper closed up shop in August 1972. The counterculture had lost its last remaining source of communication and without the paper a major point of identification and unifying instrument for the hippies and radicals was gone. By that point in time, however, the staff of the Quicksilver times was reportedly heavily infiltrated with CIA and FBI undercover agents who were basically using the publication to spy upon and subtly infuse confusion and chaos into what was left of the Movement.

With the counterculture on the skids, the publication no longer posed a threat to the prevailing capitalist system and the Quicksilver Times' resident government agents decided to pull the plug on its production after the publication of its August 2 to August 18, 1972 (Volume 4, Number 9) edition. When its successor, the Unicorn Times, hit the streets with it first issue in October 1973, it focused solely on the local popular music scene and was void of the radical commentary, pro-drug propaganda and anti-war rhetoric that the Washington Free Press and Quicksilver Times had thrived upon.

The third and final event that damaged the Washington, D.C. area's counterculture was the end of the Vietnam War, a near-20-year conflict that included the involvement of the United States, which had attempted to prevent a communist takeover of South Vietnam and stop the spread of global communism. When the war concluded on Wednesday, April 30, 1975, the purveyors of communist mind control were stymied as America continued on with its system of free market enterprise. The counterculture devotees in America were now left to their own devises and without anything to protest many of them unwittingly embraced the American Dream and began aspiring to make money, acquire material possessions, and raise kids. It was a sudden change, with most of the hippies either taking jobs or starting their own businesses and eventually cleaning up and becoming part of the very same capitalist system they had been railing against for years. While many continued to do drugs and embrace left-wing politics, the fire was gone from the Revolution. Being a long-haired freak that tripped on LSD and waved protest signs was no longer cool – at least not for the time being.

With the Utopian hippie vision temporarily damaged, the sources of leftist communication disintegrating, and no immediate social or philosophical cause to rally behind, the hippies started blending into the establishment and the music of the counterculture began losing its intensity and meaning. What then transpired during the middle 1970s in the Washington, D.C. area music scene was: a gaggle of local bands playing Top 40 covers in supper clubs; a somewhat depleted night club scene littered with short-lived rock and roll groups serving up everything from light rock to heavy metal; and the unsettling presence in venues throughout the region of entirely new sub-genres of music such as disco, new wave and punk. The opening of the Capital Centre in Landover, Maryland in December 1973 introduced the notion of arena rock to the industry and drastically changed the local concert scene, effectively eliminating the practice of local independent promoters booking bands into smaller local venues such as community centers. The teen dance scene – because of the presence of harder drugs such as PCP and problems associated with race mixing – was terminated throughout the region by the summer of 1976.

On a larger scale, rock and rock and roll music in general lost its fundamental back beat in the late 1970s and became an amorphous art form that could encompass almost any musical genre and still retain a fundamental identity. At that point in time computers had not yet dehumanized the production of music on a global level, but the dawning of a technological revolution fueled by the Internet and digital downloads was in the planning stages. Its arrival in the ensuing years would alter the way music was performed, recorded and disseminated and drastically change the very nature of the popular music industry in the Washington, D.C. area and around the world.

PART TWO
EARLY-ERA ROCK AND ROLL: A SELECTION OF NIGHT CLUBS, STAGES AND FESTIVALS

In this volume many of the historic live music venues of the nation's capital have been discussed and analyzed. Such establishments remained a vital component of the region's music scene as rock and roll emerged in the early 1950s and continuously evolved through the 1960s and into the early 1970s. The following entries rate as some of the more significant venues and events – night clubs, stages and festivals – that, in some manner, assisted in defining early-era rock and roll in the Washington, D.C. area.

NIGHT CLUBS

The Alpine Room, Benny's Rebel Room, Bob White's Hideaway, the Charles Café, the Childe Harold, the Crosstown Restaurant, the Famous Restaurant, the 4400 Club, Gus and John's Italian Villa, Guy's Place, the Hayloft, Jack Rowe's Restaurant, the Keg, Maynard's Restaurant, the Moulin Rouge, the Ozarks Restaurant, the Psyche Delly, Rand's Night Club, the Rendezvous, the Rocket Room, the Shelter Room, Some Place Else, the Starlite Restaurant, the Varsity Grill and the Varsity Grill Back Room

THE ALPINE ROOM

312 Kennedy Street NW, Washington, D.C.

Years of operation at this address: 1957-1967

In October 1957 the Alpine Room opened at this address in the city's Brightwood Park neighborhood in a one-story building that had previously housed a night club called Woody's, and, before that, the Concord Restaurant. The first band to perform in the Alpine Room was an R&B act called the Crawford Brothers, who regularly performed there for more than three years. Other R&B and rock and roll bands and musicians to appear at the night club in the late 1950s were singers Jimmy Kuhn and Angel Face, the Three of Us Trio, the Jones Boys and Bernie Kessler and His Rhythm Rockers.

In the 1960s the Alpine Room continued to offer R&B and rock and roll bands and among the acts to perform there were singer Elaine Gay, Ronnie and the Off Beats, Reggie and the Bermudas, Bobby Ellis and His Thunderbirds, Charlie Daniels and the Jaguars, the Rainbows, the Capris, Tommy Cole and the Belvederes, the Intruders, Chet Ivey and the Fabulous Avengers, the Perry Mates, the Medallions, the Eddie Stitt Combo, Chuck Booker and His Blues Messengers, the Four Horsemen, the Three of Us Trio, the Prodigals, the Newport Rhythmaires, the Stingers, the Memories, Bobbie Howard and the Ponies (featuring drummer Trudy Cooper), Chuck Bennett and His Fender Benders, the Riffs, Wild Bill and His Thunderbirds, the Hot Tamales, Lamont and His All Stars, Jimmy D and the Melodaires and Leroy Taylor and the Four Kays.

The Alpine Room closed in 1967 and in the ensuing years a succession of restaurants and night clubs occupied its former space. The building that once housed this night club (a mere 980 square feet in size) is still standing, though it has been absorbed by a connected, neighboring building and currently serves as the fitness room for the Hattie Holmes Senior Wellness Center, whose main front entrance is now marked 324 Kennedy Street NW.

BENNY'S REBEL ROOM
829 14th Street NW, Washington, D.C.
Years of operation at this address: 1947-1984

For decades Benny's Rebel Room was a fixture on "The Strip" – the famed stretch of glitzy night clubs on 14th Street NW from New York Avenue NW to Thomas Circle in Washington, D.C. It was opened by Benjamin L. Mendelson (a transplant from Atlanta, Georgia who had migrated to the nation's capital in 1932 and had been employed as a cab driver for years) as Benny's Tavern in February 1947, replacing the John Benson Grocery. Throughout the late 1940s and early 1950s the tavern, which was situated on the building's ground floor, offered jazz and pop entertainment by such acts as singer Bill "Boogie Woogie Man" Randle and the musical trio the Three Aces (pianist Woody Woods, reed player Billy White and bassist Pete Moss).

In March 1955 Benny's Tavern had its name changed to Benny's Rebel Room and the live music offerings became a curious mix of Dixieland jazz and rock and roll. Among the featured attractions throughout the remainder of the 1950s were the Capital City Dixielanders (featuring saxophonist Country Thomas), Big Steve and His House Rockers, the Saxtons and the popular Philadelphia rock and roll band Jimmy Cavallo and His House Rockers.

The 1960s saw both local and out-of-town rock and roll groups perform at Benny's Rebel Room. Among those bands to work the establishment that decade were the Paul King and the Blue Knights, Ronnie and the Off Beats, the Saxtons, Charlie Daniels and the Jaguars, Barry Darvell and the Blazers, the Carmen Canavo Quintet, the British Walkers, the Esquire Boys; the Untouchables, Georgie Young and His Big Revue, the Holidays, the Ink Spots, the Van Dykes, the Untouchables, the Kalin Twins, the Naturals, Gabriel and His Angels, the Furys, Judy and the Misfits, Ali Baba and His Four Thieves, Phil Flowers and His Flower Shop, the Red Caps, the Jaguars, the Rockin' Superiors, Kim and the Esquires, the Coasters, Billy Joe and the Confidentials, Tommy Cole and the Belvederes, Jimmy Eller and His Little People, the Memories, the Starlighters, Joe Banana and the Bunch, the Loved Ones, Tricycle and Archie and the Stereos.

In 1970 Benjamin Mendelson sold Benny's Rebel Room to the three-man team of Kenny Snyder, Max Berg and Leo Halpert. The new management continued to book live rock and roll bands throughout the early 1970s and among their top attractions during that period were Rooth, Animal Farm and Devil's Track. Reportedly, the last band to ever perform in the night club was the Cherry People, who headlined their New Year's Eve show on Tuesday, December 31, 1974. In the ensuing years the night club focused on adult entertainment.

In January 1982 Benny's Rebel Room officially became Benny's House of Porn. On Saturday, November 10, 1984 the business shut its doors for good and the building was unoccupied until its demolition in April 1986. The land then sat vacant until construction began in 1988 on a new structure. Since 1989 the former site of Benny's Rebel Room has been occupied by a 12-story office building called 1350 Eye Street (which covers the area that had previously hosted buildings marked 829-833 14th Street NW).

BOB WHITE'S HIDEAWAY
319 Pennsylvania Avenue SE, Washington, D.C.
Years of operation at this address: 1948-1960

In March 1948 the Bob White Seafood House opened up in this Capitol Hill building that dated back to the late nineteenth century. Its previous occupants had been businesses known as Visual Art and Advertising and Vincent Connolly Photographer. The basement of the Bob White Seafood House was outfitted as a live music night club and christened Bob White's Hideaway.

From its inception through 1955 entertainment in Bob White's Hideaway mainly consisted of C&W bands and a smattering of pop music performers. Some of the more notable performing artists to work the night club during those years included Frankie Robinson and the Virginia Playboys (featuring singer Miss Dale Turner), Dub Howington and the Tennessee Haymakers, singer-guitarist Roy Clark, Jimmy Dean and the Texas Wildcats, Fiddlin' Clyde and His String Dusters, the Four Pirateers, the Four Hillbilly Kids, Tom Williams' Runaway Four, Danny Powell's Combo, the duo of Tom and Kay, Smitty Ervin and the Tri-State Ramblers, the Hillbilly Harmoneers, Jack Huff and His Tri-State Ramblers, the Four Jacks, and a number of headlining singers such as Jerry Toronto, Jean Muncy, George Eades, Shirley Altine, Sterling Singleton and Billy Stanton.

In 1956 Bob White's Hideaway began offering live rock and roll music. Among the performers to appear in the basement night club were Bernie Kessler's Rhythm Rockers, Lucky Wray and His Rock and Roll Trio (Lucky being Ray Vernon – real name Vernon Wray – with bassist Shorty Horton and drummer Ray Scearce), and singer-guitarist Link Wray.

A mix of musical styles was presented in Bob White's Hideaway in the late 1950s. Everything from C&W to pop to R&B to rock and roll was presented to the public, making it one of the city's most eclectic live music venues of the era. Among the night club's headliners during those years were organist Dick Frank, pianist Ted Darios, the Bob Koethe Trio, the Bob Brooks Trio, Roger Allen and His Western Swing Boys, the Moonlighters Trio, the Starlanders Trio, Al Batista's Trio, the Cave Men, the Billy Williams Combo, the Luel Hayes Combo, Calvin Ruffin and His Band, the Krazy Kats, Billy Fair and His Fair Notes, Bill Ritchie and the Dixie Kats, the Chet Ivey Combo, Hayes and His Combo, the Billy Clark Combo, and Link Wray and His Ray Men.

Bob White's Hideaway closed in February 1960 and a month later was replaced by a night club called the Cloak Room. This basement space went on to host a number of different restaurants and night clubs through the years. Currently the entire building at 319 Pennsylvania Avenue SE (basement, ground floor and second floor) is occupied by a cocktail bar called Stanton and Greene.

THE CHARLES CAFÉ
3201 14th Street NW, Washington, D.C.
Years of operation at this address: 1925-1958

In September 1925 Paul Allen purchased the long-standing Hampton Swan Department Store on upper 14th Street NW and converted it into the Charles Cafeteria. In November 1936 a new owner named Joseph M. Gailliot came on board and changed the name of the establishment to the Charles Grill, later updating the name in 1950 to the Charles Café and Grill.

In November 1956 Gailliot shortened the name of his restaurant to the Charles Café and began offering live C&W and rock and roll music as entertainment. For the next two years some of the local performers to work this rough-edged night spot were singers Lee Richardson, Toni Vargas and Jackie Harris, singer-guitarist Kenny Fisher, singer-guitarist-mandolinist Pete Potter, Stoney Rigsby and His Dixie Dudes, Tommy Woods and His Rhythm Rockers, the Crazy Bops, the Southland Boys, Bee Dempsey and Her Little Bees, and singer-guitarist Link Wray, who, beginning in the spring of 1958, began calling his band Link Wray and His Ray Men.

Perhaps the most noteworthy aspect of the Charles Café is that from 1957 to 1959 a regular headliner was singer Lucky Wray, who performed there in a trio with guitarist Dick

Williams and bassist Shorty Horton, and also played rhythm guitar with Link Wray and His Ray Men. Lucky, of course, was the first stage name for Vernon Wray, brother of guitarist Link Wray. While performing at the Charles Café, Lucky was discovered and signed to Cameo Records, which released his single "Evil Angel" and prompted another change in his stage name, this time to Ray Vernon.

In October 1958 the Charles Café underwent a change in ownership, was converted into Joe's Burdland Bar and Café, and subsequently booked Black R&B entertainers until its closing in 1969. The building then housed different businesses before being razed in 1986. After 20 years as a vacant lot, the former site of the Charles Café welcomed the opening of an apartment building called Park Triangle in March 2006. This six-story structure, whose street address is now 1375 Kenyon Street NW, is located at the hub of the intersection of 14th Street NW, Kenyon Street NW, and Park Road NW.

THE CHILDE HAROLD
1610 20th Street NW, Washington, D.C.
Years of operation at this address: 1967-2007

The Childe Harold opened for business in an old Victorian building adjacent to Dupont Circle in July 1967 and owner Bill Heard, Jr. offered live music in the main, walk-up dining room for his customers from 1971 until 1981. The early and middle 1970s saw a variety of local musicians from the fields of blues, C&W, folk and rock and roll perform in the night club including singer-guitarists Emmylou Harris, Jack Bond and Bobby Radcliff, Evernow, Breakfast Again, Liz Meyer and Friends, Grits, Babe, Danny Gatton and the Fat Boys, the Catfish Hodge Band, the Star Spangled Washboard Band, Bill Holland and Rent's Due, Hickory Wind and the Rosslyn Mountain Boys.

In the late 1970s some of the local bands to play the Childe Harold included Terry Plumeri and Evolution, the Nighthawks, Smalltalk, Tim Eyermann and East Coast Offering, Tex Rubinowitz and the Bad Boys, Original Fetish, Billy Hancock and the Tennessee Rockets, Urban Verbs, Slickee Boys, the D.Ceats, Tears, the North Star Band, Root Boy Slim, Cryin' Out Loud and Rhythm Method. In 1980 and 1981 groups to appear included the Rhythm Masters, the Mike Cotter Band, the Nurses, 4 out of 5 Doctors, Tru Fax and the Insaniacs and the Insect Surfers.

During its lifetime numerous out-of-town bands and musicians performed at the Childe Harold, including several that had already established national reputations or were on their way to some measure of popular music stardom. Among these acts were Townes Van Zandt, Ramblin' Jack Elliott, David Allan Coe, Leon Redbone, Mose Allison, comedian Martin Mull, Elvin Jones, Willie Dixon, Luther Allison, Asleep at the Wheel, Powerhouse, the Little River Band, Firefall, Captain Beefheart and His Magic Band, the Ramones and George Thorogood and the Destroyers. Perhaps the most famous performer to work the night club was Bruce Springsteen, who made his Washington, D.C. debut at the Childe Harold with a three-night stand from Thursday, May 24 to Saturday, May 26, 1973 (he and his band were reportedly paid a total of $750 for the entire engagement).

Live music was discontinued at the Childe Harold in 1981. Bill Heard, Jr. sold the business in 1982 to Hossein Shirvani who maintained the restaurant until rent increases forced him to close its doors on Saturday, November 3, 2007. The building is currently occupied by a restaurant called Darlington House.

THE CROSSTOWN RESTAURANT
3102 Mount Pleasant Street NW, Washington, D.C.
Years of operation at this address: 1947-1972

In 1947 the Crosstown Restaurant replaced Baird's Electric Service Company on the ground floor of a former row house in the heart of Washington, D.C.'s Mount Pleasant neighborhood. During its first three years the regular headliner was its owner, C&W singer George Saslaw.

Throughout the 1950s the Crosstown Restaurant offered an eclectic schedule of C&W, jazz and pop music acts. Musical entertainers to grace its stage during that era included: singers George Lowe, Joyce Kerr, Joyce Norman and Terry Doyle; pianists Jo Freedman, Tommy Chase and Sammy Marks; C&W singer-guitarist Kenny White and guitarist Zeb Turner; jazz guitarists Charlie Byrd (who made his night club debut here in 1952) and Bill Harris; accordionist Lew Rossi; and a variety of bands such as the Sammy Krupit Unit with bassist Jack Wyatt (also billed as "The Guy and I"), Dave Amram's Symphonic Sextette, the Lloyd Lillie Trio, Norval Reid and His Three Cs, Sammy Ferro and His Trio, Johnny Sweet's Combo, Bill Beach's Combo, Music in the Modern Mood (a jazz group consisting of pianist Gene Bonnike, bassist Ron Greer, trombonist Earl Swope, trumpeter Ted Efantis and drummer Don Daumit) and Three Kings and a Queen.

In the 1960s the Crosstown Restaurant brought in a number of R& B entertainers such as the Van Perry Trio (featuring singer Laura Joy), the Jerome Hopkins Trio, and singer Angel Face, along with such pop music combos as the Tony Matos Quartet, Jimmy Adams and the Crescendos and singer Larry Mason. Several country rock bands frequently worked the establishment during those years including Danny Denver and the Sound Tracks (featuring guitarist Roy Buchanan), the Skeeter Cooper Band, Bobby Stephenson and the Crosstowners and Johnny Hopkins and the Crosstowners. A regular headliner from 1965 until the night club's closing in 1972 was the popular local rock and roll band Ray Rock and the Revlons. The building that once housed the Crosstown Restaurant has hosted many different eateries through the years and is currently occupied by Haydee's Restaurant.

THE FAMOUS RESTAURANT
1215 New York Avenue NW, Washington, D.C.
Years of operation at this address: 1945-1968

In March 1945 the Famous Restaurant replaced the Jerome Oxenburg Restaurant in a bustling row of bars and restaurants clustered around two main bus lines – the Greyhound Lines at 1110 New York Avenue NW and the Trailways Bus Terminal at 1201-1205 New York Avenue NW.

The Famous Restaurant was long regarded as one of the city's C&W music strongholds and throughout the 1950s was known as the unofficial home base of the dynamic singer-guitarist Roy Clark, who performed at the night club in combinations with many of the region's top players. In the early 1950s Clark liked to work the club with singer-guitarist Dick Williams and steel guitarist Tommy "Cuz" Johnson in a trio often billed as Roy Clark and His Gang. During those years other C&W headliners at the Famous Restaurant included yodeler Flossie Lee, singer-guitarist Marvin Rainwater, Mickey Woodward's Famous Four, Dub Howington and the Tennessee Haymakers, Jimmy Dean and His Texas Wildcats, Buddy Hawk and His Band and Jimmy Short and His Silver Saddle Ranchers.

The year 1955 was a banner period for the Famous, as its primary attractions were Bill Peer and His Melody Boys featuring singer Patsy Cline, Buzz Busby and His Bayou Boys and the Blue Grass Champs (featuring fiddlers Pop Stoneman and Scotty Stoneman). The Blue Grass Champs would retain house band honors throughout 1956 and 1957, though they often shared the bill with Roy Clark, who would alternately bill his backup band as the Country Kut-Ups, the Country Cousins or the Country Stylists (his usual bandmates in these aggregations were steel guitarist Tommy Johnson, singer-rhythm guitarist Freddie Stafford, bassist Roy Brown and drummer Duke Maddox). Other popular performers at the night club during the latter part of the decade included Jack Rodgers and His Country Cousins, the Stanley Brothers, Dub Howington and His Tennessee Haymakers, Zeb Turner and His Band and the Melody Sweethearts.

In December 1958 the Famous began adding rock and roll to its bills, as a new band from Wilmington, North Carolina called Charlie Daniels and His Rockets made their Washington, D.C. debut there, fresh off an engagement at Rose's Musical Bar in North Beach, Maryland.

In the 1960s the Famous Restaurant largely retained its C&W identity and throughout the decade featured such performers as Pee Wee "Slowpoke" King, Red Allen, Red Sovine, Benny Martin and His 8-String Fiddle, Lou Childe, Roy Self, Roy Drusky, Dick Williams, Bill Emerson, Mac Wiseman, Frank Wakefield, Miss Dale Turner, Jack Rodgers and the Suburbans, the Stanley Brothers, the Clinch Mountain Boys, the Twist Clicks, the Stoneman Family, the Blue Grass Champs, the Country Kats, Patsy Stoneman and the Troubadours, Barbara Lease and Her Buddies, the B.B. Combo, Johnny Hopkins and the Fire Fountains, Jimmy Case and the Cherokees, the Yates Brothers, Bill Harrell and the Virginians, Chubby Wise and His Tennesseans, the Outlaws, Johnny Downs and the Famous Trio, Little Jimmy and the Rangers, Red Allen and the Kentuckians, Jimmy King and the Tune Kings and the Cimarrons.

During the 1960s there was also a steady helping of rock and roll acts on the Famous Restaurant bills, with some of the more popular bands on its schedule being the Peppermint Stix, Stan D and the Profiles, Bobbie Howard and the Ponies, Lloyd Bell and the Four Bells, Jimmy D and the Impacts, the Dimensions, the Three Tones, the Scoundrels and the Boston Monkeys. The Famous Restaurant ultimately adopted rock and roll on a full-time basis late in the decade, with the house band for all of 1967 and most of 1968 being local favorites Link Wray and His Ray Men.

In October 1968 the Famous changed owners and gave way to a strip club called Dolly's, which eventually closed in 1975. In 1976 the building was torn down and in 1988 construction began on a new office complex that would dominate the avenue. Since 1989 the former site of the Famous (the first half of the north side of the 1200 block of New York Avenue NW) has been occupied by a 13-story office property called 1201 New York Ave NW.

THE 4400 CLUB

4400 Rhode Island Avenue, Brentwood, Maryland

Years of operation at this address: 1945-1964; 1967 to 1979; 1985 to 1995

The building at 4400 Rhode Island Avenue in Brentwood, Maryland was under construction in 1944 and 1945 and opened to the public as the 4400 Club on Friday, June 7, 1945. The establishment was basically a neighborhood bar for its first several years, but entered the local night club competition in January 1951 when it was purchased by a former Cross Roads bartender named James J. "Jimmy" Comber. The new owner hailed from Philadelphia and brought in different pop and jazz groups from his native city as entertainment, most notably the Four Tunes, who played the night club frequently in 1953 and 1954 (the proprietor later transferred ownership of the restaurant to his wife Irene Comber in September 1955).

On Thursday, May 10, 1956 ownership of the 4400 Club changed once again, this time from Irene Comber to Herbert Hertz and John Frostbutter. With Hertz in control of entertainment, the musical offerings included pop, jazz and rock and roll. The first group to play the 4400 Club under Hertz's watch was Murray Schaff's Aristocrats. Other groups that played the club that summer included the Jodimars Quintet (featuring three original members of Bill Haley and His Comets), the Leonard Sues Quintet, Herbie Fields, the Johnny Hamlin Quintet, Benny Ventura and Group, the Jimmy Cavallo Quintet, the Block Busters featuring drummer Al Pometto, the Del Lucas Quartet, Don Haven and the Hi Fis, the Four Tunes, the Pete Rubino Quintet, Illinois Jacquet and His Orchestra and Bull Moose Jackson and His Buffalo Bearcats.

Hertz maintained ownership of the 4400 Club throughout the decade and from 1957 to 1959 he booked an impressive procession of bands and musicians into his night club. These included singer Bobby Sherwood, singer-guitarist Roy Clark, the Four Tunes, the Ray Reynolds Quintet, Frankie Mayo and His New Yorkers, the Treniers, the Johnny Hamlin Quintet, Georgie Young and His Rockin' Bocs, Murray Schaff and His Aristocrats, the Frank Moore Four, Jimmy Cavallo and His House Rockers, Jimmy Dean and the Texas Wildcats, Illinois Jacquet and His Orchestra, the Twin Tunes, the King Pins, the Thompsonaires (featuring singer Ann Marie Moss), the Al Belletto Sextet, singer Jerri Winters, Joe Renaldi's Sextet, the Nite Caps, Five Sharps and a Flat, Mario and the Flips, the Tyrones, the Saxtons, the Three of Us Trio, the Tyrones, Dave Appell and the Applejacks, the Honey Cones, Red Prysock and His Band, singer-guitarist Conway Twitty, the Playboys, the Stardusters, the Nu-Tornados and the High Hopes.

In December 1959 Herbert Hertz and John Frostbutter sold the 4400 Club to the trio of George Heyman, Ellis Coles and Robert L. Mandris, who carried on its rock and roll tradition into the middle 1960s.

From January 1960 to November 1963 some of the pop and rock and roll acts that appeared at the 4400 Club were the High Hopes, Georgie Young and the Rockin' Bocs, the Bobby Chick Quintet, the Del Lucas Quintet, the Frankie Brent Sextet (featuring singers Jay Price and Babs Tino), Gene Labati and the Toppers (featuring singer Connie Lynn), the Del Tones, the Kings V, George Forte and the Originals, the Skylarks, the Chick Brothers, the Virginia Beach Boys (featuring guitarist Roy Buchanan), Bertie Castle and the Stardusters, Terri Cirrel and the Back Beats, Jimmy J and the Js, Ralph Emmel and the Counts, the Jay Price Quintet, Robbie and the Ramblers, the Algiers, the Headliners, the Fabulous Magnatones, the Fall Guys, the Play Timers, the Knightcaps, the Rockatones, Frank Verna and the Profiles (featuring the singing Brigette Sisters), the Headliners, the Shyndells, Three Sharps and a Flat, the Embers Five, Sonny Richards and the Panics, the Hot Tamales and the Roof Toppers.

The 400 Club closed for the first time in July 1964. Through the years a number of restaurants have occupied its former space including two other incarnations of the original occupants – a second version of the 4400 Club from September 1967 to September 1979, and a third version called Gee's 4400 Club from June 1985 to February 1995 (Gee's version regularly offered live R&B music). The storied building at 4400 Rhode Island Avenue currently sits vacant.

GUS AND JOHN'S ITALIAN VILLA
6503 Old Branch Avenue, Camp Springs, Maryland
Years of operation at this address: 1969-1979

Gus and John's Italian Villa opened in a newly constructed building in July 1969 for owners John Linthicum, Gerald LeCompte and Constantine "Gus" Petrides. During its 10-year existence this night club was home to some of the area's top pop and rock and roll acts including the Naturals, the Memories, the Joe Stanley Band, the East Coast Express, the Danny Gatton Band, Mother Nature, Second Coming, Ron MacDonald and Nightwatch, the Tommy Cole Trio, Classic, Flying Start, Bentwood Rocker and Phil Haynes and the Inner Circle. The building that once hosted this establishment currently houses J.K. Johnson Funeral Home, P.A.

GUY'S PLACE
529 8th Street SE, Washington, D.C.
Years of operation at this address: 1947-1968

In the middle 1950s the C&W bar known as Guy's Place changed with the times and transformed into a rough rock and roll dive where the music was ear-splitting and any type of behavior was acceptable. Some of the rockin' bands that owner Guy Interdonato brought into his establishment during the latter half of that decade were Dick Vigue and His Band, the Super Jets, Leo the Lion, the Scarfers, Del Lucas and His Band, the Mad Caps, the Rockin' Horses, the Jimmy Kent Quartet, the Fabulous Dynatones, the Jerry Garo Quartet, the Cyclones (featuring singer Lyn Lori), George Ross and the Red Tops, Birdie Castle and His Star Dusters, Joe Bruce and His Steppers, the Ramparts, the Don Palmer Quintet, the Five Screwballs, Bob and Ray's Dynamics, Sal Tucker and His Quintet, Joe Pasko and His Rockin' Maniacs, the Saxtons, the Imperials Quintet, the Krazy Kats, Link Wray and His Ray Men and Bobby Stephenson and His Rock and Roll Boys.

Throughout the 1960s Guy's Place primarily remained a rock and roll night club, though the occasional country rock group was brought in to appease the Southern holdovers. Bands to play there in the 1960s included Charlie Daniels and the Jaguars, the Perry Mates, the Peppermint Stix, Stan D and the Profiles, Ray Rock and the Revlons, the Four Guys, the Taken, Bobby Brosh and the Surfside Four, Skeeter Cooper and His Sound Tracks, the Four Speeds, Dave Martin and the Chargers, Billy and Donna Strickland, Danny Denver and the Versatiles, Ben Langley and the Hi-Lo Jacks and the In Crowd.

Guy's Place closed in 1968 and its building went on to host a number of different restaurants through the years. In recent times this structure was reconfigured and the space that once held Guy's Place is now occupied by a Greek restaurant named Cava Mezze (marked 527 8th Street SE) and a vacant restaurant area which had previously been the site of Today's Pizza (marked 531 8th Street SE).

THE HAYLOFT
1409 H Street NW, Washington, D.C.
Years of operation at this address: 1957-1971

The Hayloft Building, as it will be called here, was another one of those early 20th century structures in the 14th Street zone that housed a succession of businesses in its early stages before hosting the A.B. Dick Company (a mimeo machine business) from 1922 to August 1943. From Thursday, October 7, 1943 to Sunday, May 20, 1951 a night club called the Windsor Room occupied the premises, which was originally marked 1411 H Street NW. Pop music entertainers to appear there included: singers Nora Williams, Jean Lee, Ann Bruck, Anna Sablavoka, Dorothy Byrd, June Elliot, Kitty McCormick, Rebecca Whitehurst, Quita Brazil, June Beverly, and the VocaLovelies; guitarist Jack Norman; singer-pianist Harvey Chown; pianists Matt Windsor and Jack Neal; groups such as the Four Duchesses, the Four Dukes, Clarence Jackson and His Four Notes of Rhythm, Bill Johnson and His Musical Notes, Buddy Hawkins and His Keynotes and the Jones Brothers; and comedian Louise Potter.

On Monday, May 21, 1951 owner Maynard Wayne converted the Windsor Room into the Wayne Room, with an opening night floorshow featuring Jack "Jive" Schafer and His Orchestra and the Harding and Moss Revue starring singer Carol Blaine. Schafer's outfit would remain the house band and primary attraction all the way through June 1953.

Throughout 1951 and 1952 the Wayne Room maintained the floorshow format, with a number of different exotic dancers sharing billing with Schafer's band and a variety of comedians, singers and guest musical outfits. Some of the more accomplished entertainers to appear at the Wayne Room during these years were: singer-pianist Harvey Chown; singers Carmen Sutton, June Elliot, Stuart Harris, and Al Antonio; comedians Jack Norman, Dick Shawn, the duo of Davis and Reese, Ned Walsh, Harry Shafran, Jay Jason, and Ken Barry; exotic dancers Divena, Bubbles Darlene, Syra, June Allen, Betty Allyn, Cleo Shore, Solitaire, Carmen del Carmen, Bonnie Lorraine, the Manhattan Models, and Irma the Body; and special attractions such as the Stan Nelson Trio, the Ronalds Brothers (a musical comedy trio), the R&B act the Jones Brothers, and the Mary Kaye Trio.

For the first six months of 1953 Jack "Jive" Schafer and His Orchestra were joined on a nightly basis at the Wayne Room by owner Maynard Wayne himself, who served as emcee of the shows, and a band called the Condijacs. These mainstays performed as a succession of entertainers came and went including pianist Jack Holliday, singer Jack Maggio, comedians Allen Stone, Jimmy Casanova, and Jack DeLeon, and dancer Maureen Marsh.

A landmark event took place at the Wayne Room on Monday, July 20, 1953, when a new, week-long, five-hour exotic revue was introduced that featured singer Bobbie Todd, dancers Ellen Leigh, Debbie Lawrence, and Diane Karlisle, and comedian Frank Keenan. Also featured as part of this package was a 27-year-old comedian from Queens, New York named Don Rickles, who made both his professional night club act and his Washington, D.C. debuts on this evening and would prove to be so popular, he remained a featured attraction at the Wayne Room for 20 straight weeks. Rickles, who came to be nicknamed "Glasshead" during his Wayne Room stay, would eventually leave Washington, D.C. and go on to fame and fortune as one of the greatest American comedians of all-time.

During the remainder of 1953 some of the other entertainers to appear in conjunction with Don Rickles included pop singers Jack Maggio, Bobbie Todd, and Betty Allyn; exotic dancers Aida and Blaze Starr; and other comedians including Allen Stone, Jimmy Casanova, Dick Havilland, Patsy Abbott, Lou Daley, Vicki Villani, Frank Keenan and Ken Barry.

From January to September 1954 entertainers to make appearances at the Wayne Room included pop singers Kay Gayle, Betty Allen, Betty Durrell, and Bonnie Moore; exotic dancers Terry Jean, Louise Angel and Betty Ray; and comedians Danny Rogers and Tony Santoro. Exotic queen Blaze Starr had been featured for much of the month of February of that year, and Don Rickles returned that March and stayed on for several weeks in a floorshow that included Blaze Starr and pop singer Ricky Lynch.

On Monday, October 4, 1954 owner Maynard Wayne abruptly introduced a change in the night club's musical policy, with the featured music now being "Bop City Jazz." Starting that night were two jazz bands, Charlie "Hound Dog" Hall and His Jazz Band and Ed "Mad-Man" Madison and His Krazy Kats.

On Monday, October 25, 1954 Maynard Wayne changed the name of the Wayne Room to Jazzland (advertising it in local newspapers as "Washington's Newest Jazz Spot") and for the next eight months relied upon Frank "Dual Trumpets" Motley and his singer Angel Face as his main attraction. Other bands to perform there included drummer Paul Crawford and His "Shake a Hand" Trio (featuring singer-pianist Curly Bridges and saxophonist King Herbert), organist Big John Greer and His Band, Billy Fair and His All-Stars, and a C&W-jazz act called the Pioneers (singer Dick Thomas, guitarist Pete Pepper, steel guitarist Bill Bagent and drummer Jesse Parish).

The jazz format evidently failed to pay dividends and on Friday, July 1, 1955 Maynard Wayne changed the name of the night club back to the Wayne Room. That night he offered a new revue headlined by the popular comedian Don Rickles and complemented by dancer Jo-Ann Ryan and pop singers Judy Santino and Beverly Styles. The show packed the Wayne Room for several weeks, resulting in Rickles being installed as the headliner for another six months. During this period some of the other acts to work underneath Rickles were: pop singers Pat Storme, Kathy Dennis and Randy Robbins; dancers Honey B. Heller, Betty Biddle, Bonnie Bell and Margie Grey; and fellow comedians Buzz Barrie and Jeff Davis. Rickles departed as the new year rolled around and in 1956 the Wayne Room's main features were pop singer Joe Lagana, the Crackerjacks, and exotic dancers such as Terry Miller and Tinker Bell.

In February 1957 another change took place with the Wayne Room being converted into a new night club called the Hayloft. This new enterprise initially struggled to develop its own identity, with a variety of musical styles being offered during its first year to see what would register with the old Wayne Room crowds. The Hayloft started off with the C&W band Jimmy Dean and the Texas Wildcats as their featured act. For several months thereafter a number of C&W and popular music acts worked the night club including singer Bud Isaacs, the Cyclones, Bobby Stephenson and His Hayloft Boys, Billy Clark and His Band and the Screwballs. Late in the year the R&B outfit Frank Motley and His Band (featuring drummer T.N.T. Tribble and singer Angel Face) were called upon to resume house band duties, an assignment they kept for the remainder of the decade.

The Hayloft remained one of the city's top R&B-rock night clubs throughout the 1960s and was home to Phil Flowers and His Flower Shop for most of the decade. Other popular groups to make appearances during those years were the 7-Ups, Jay Granger and the Persuasions and the Jade Brothers. In November 1966 the address for the Hayloft building was inexplicably changed from 1411 to 1409 H Street NW.

Unfortunately, the Hayloft was destroyed in a fire on Sunday, January 10, 1971 and its remains cleared away. Since 1992 the former site of the Hayloft – half of the north side of the 1400 block of H Street NW – has been occupied by a 12-story office building called City Center (1401 H Street NW).

JACK ROWE'S RESTAURANT
913 11th Street SE, Washington, D.C.
Years of operation at this address: 1943-1964

Jack Rowe's Restaurant, which was once listed at 913 11th Street SE, has a somewhat mysterious history. This night club, which evidently disappeared from sight at some point in the early 1960s, had an almost identical sister building next-door at 911 11th Street SE, leading many local historians to speculate that said sister building had been the actual location of Jack Rowe's Restaurant, with the address numbers of the entire block having been confusingly changed at some point in time. Historian Mara Cherkasky, in an effort to clarify the Jack Rowe's Restaurant situation, went to great lengths to uncover the various property maps, applications, permit requests and other relevant documents stored away at the DC Archives pertaining to the establishment in question. Her meticulous research provided clarity to the restaurant's interesting and somewhat murky story.

Here is what is known about Jack Rowe's Restaurant. In 1928 a two-story, 25x50-foot building was constructed at 913 11th Street SE at the end of a stretch of row houses and commercial structures on the edge of a quiet residential area. The first occupant of this building was the short-lived Victory Grocery Store, which opened in 1929 and went out of business a year later. In 1931 the family operated Milton Rowe Sea Food Restaurant opened for business on the premises. In 1943 Milton F. "Jack" Rowe converted the operation into a live pop music night club and changed the name to Jack Rowe's Restaurant. He then hired Harry Snider to serve as manager and the business thrived despite its somewhat offbeat location three blocks east of the commercial strip along 8th Street SE which was then-called Sailor's Row (today known as Barracks Row).

Jack Rowe's Restaurant liked to serve up multi-act bills featuring a variety of local entertainers. Among those to perform in the night club during the 1940s were: pop music bands such as the Three Jays, the Manhattan Trio, the Clinton Hobbs Quartet (featuring Hobbs on saxophone, guitarist Kenny White, pianist Bill Trauble and bassist John Keys), the Nu-Tones and the Harold Lowd Trio (featuring singer George Stribling and pianist Sammy Marks); pop singers Nora Wells, Audrey Reed, Gertrude Bond and the duo of Fred and Fay Wakefield; guitarist Roy Laconia; pianists Jean Foster, Jo Freedman and Tony Ryan; accordionist Dick O'Lare; comedians Louise Potter, Denny McCurtin, Jack Ryan, Jack "Quickie" Griffen, Tony Zero, Lennie Blush and the team of LaMont and Hagan; and dancers Jean Duncan, Bette Allen and Lillian Stuart.

From 1950 to 1956 Jack Rowe's Restaurant continued to stage nightly floorshows that mixed a wide assortment of entertainers. During these years the musical acts offered by the establishment ran the gamut from pop to jazz to R&B, with a smattering of rock and roll added to the mix as the decade wore on. Bands and musicians to appear at Jack Rowe's Restaurant during this time included: groups such as the Al Shea Trio, the Beach Johnson Quartet, the Johnny Lawrence Trio, the Jack McCullum Trio, Frank Condon and His Band, the Johnny Sweets Combo, the Merry-Tones, the Jack Holliday Trio, the Angelo Tompros Trio, Charlie Parrish and His Combo, the Tony Rand Trio, Stan Smith's Combo and the Dick Griffin Trio; singers such as Fay Wakefield, Sonny Kast, Nora Wells, Gracie Smith, Lew Jenkins, Jerry Ward, Florence Frye, Diane Jayson, Lois Kerber, Jerry Toronto, Norman Summers, Bill Norman, Rena Lyndon, George Eades, Bob McQuain, Grady Wilson, Amanda Thigpen, Peggy Clarke, Texas Jim Robertson, Joe Lagana, Don Stephan, Tommy Zang, Buddy Ladd, Bill Jackson, Helen O'Brien, Carolyn Wood, Tony Messina, Kim Elliot, Pat Grady, Diane Jayson and Bonnie Windsor; keyboardists Lucille Mallory and Jean Foster; and saxophonist Paul East.

In addition, comedians to appear during this period included Louise Potter, Andy Phillips, the Park Avenue Jesters, Pat Taylor, Danny Bishop, Tubby Boots, Joe Blow, Sally Rowe, Jay Kirk, Jay Weston, Dick Havilland, Buzz Barrie and Paul Neff. Rounding out the bills were assorted dancers that offered everything from tap displays to burlesque routines. Their ranks included Bunny Holliday, Eddie Darnell, Walter Long, Terry Miller, Judy Gibbs, Louise Angel, Jean Russell, Lynn Storm, Bonita Secret, Lorraine DeBoe, Sue Travers, Terri Lane, Donna Lee, Laura Patterson, Bobbie Layne, Tina Christine, Donna Christie and Jesse Ricks.

According to advertisements published in the Washington Daily News, this establishment operated as Jack Rowe's Carousel from September 1956 to September 1957. During that year-long period the night club's headliners included: the C&W band the Country Lads; pop bands such as Charlie Parrish and His Band and the Dynatones; the rock and roll group Spud Spuduto and the Carousers; pop singers Patsy Grady, Toni Price and Toni Raye; R&B singer Don Covay; and rock and roll singer Joe Lagana. In addition, regular burlesque dancers on the bills included Judy Gibbs, Lana London, and Toni Gayle and the comedy team of Laine and Hines.

Changes occurred to the operation in late September 1957. First, the name of the business was changed back to Jack Rowe's Restaurant. Next, according to various applications for building permits on file with the DC Archives, the owners of Jack Rowe's Restaurant merged the restaurant with the vacant next-door building and adopted the official street address of 911-913 11th Street SE. It appears that from this point forward the sister building marked 911 served as a liquor store and front lobby area for the entire establishment, while the restaurant and night club operations remained rooted in the building marked 913.

For the remainder of 1957 and all of 1958 the entertainment bill of Jack Rowe's Restaurant steadily consisted of emcee-comedian Louise Potter, a house orchestra called Buddy Garrison's Band, a headlining pop music outfit called Ray Marshall and the Ko-Ko Nuts and various burlesque dancers. The venue then cut the dancers loose and changed its musical format. For all of 1959, 1960 and early 1961 the primary headliner was the C&W music act Jimmy Case and the Country Kats. Live music was discontinued in April 1961.

From that point forward it became difficult to track exactly what happened to Jack Rowe's Restaurant. The newspaper advertisements for the night club's live music stopped in 1961 and both 911 and 913 11th Street SE were inexplicably omitted from Washington, D.C.'s city directories of 1963, 1964, 1965 and 1966, leaving researchers to wonder what happened to the buildings in question.

According to documents unearthed at DC Archives by Mara Cherkasky, an Application for Permit to Raze Building at 913 11th Street SE was filed by owner Martin Kopit (who had just recently purchased the 911-913 structures and Jack Rowe's Restaurant business) with the Government of the District of Columbia Department of Licenses and Inspections on Monday, October 12, 1964. The application was approved on Wednesday, November 18, 1964, with an expiration date of Friday, December 11, 1964. Related documents showed that Jack Rowe's Restaurant was occupied and in operation through October 1964. Presumably, the building at 913 11th Street SE was razed sometime in late November or early December 1964.

Shortly after the demolition of the restaurant building was complete (probably in early 1965) a business called Kopit's Wine and Liquor opened within the confines of 911 11th Street SE. A visit to the property today reveals that this building is still standing and houses a business called Gingko Gardens, with the leveled space where 913 once stood currently serving as its outdoor storage yard.

THE KEG
2205 Wisconsin Avenue NW, Washington, D.C.
Years of operation at this address: 1963-1979

In December 1963 a night club called the Keg (which, at different points in its existence, was also advertised as the Keg Tavern) replaced the U.S. Merchandise Mart Furniture Store in a small Glover Park strip mall, just north of Georgetown. The Keg quickly became one of Washington, D.C.'s most popular hangouts and during its impressive run developed a reputation for offering a variety of rock and roll bands with an emphasis on those that played loud and hard.

Popular local acts to perform at the Keg in the 1960s included the Van Dykes, Big Al Downing and His Band, Shep and the Limelights, the Marylanders, the Prodigals, Tommy Cole and the Belvederes, the Newports, the Mad Hatters, Tuesday Boots, the Fallen Angels, Bobbie Howard and the Sweet, the Washington Monuments, Jimmy Eller and His Little People, Kangaroo, the Reachers, the British Walkers, Lawrence and the Arabians, Innocent Color, the Resumes, Second Eagle, Hillow Hammet, Puzzle, Stillroven, Renthra and Tractor.

Many of the area's top rock and roll groups made appearances at the Keg during the 1970s and late in the decade the night club was credited for helping to usher in the punk rock movement that was gaining momentum in Washington, D.C. at the time. Bands to work the Keg during those years included Rooth, the Magic Reign, Goosby-Pegalo, Danny and the Fat Boys, Black On White, Devil's Track, Second Eagle, Liz Meyer and Friends, Crank, the Cherry People, Sun Country, Gravity, Ichabod Crane, Summerfield Smyth, DC

Dog, Rocking Horse, Jive Bomber, Daylight, Daddy Warbux, the Dubonnettes, Cherry Smash, Witness, the Sound Investment, Griffin, Overkill, Razz, Two-Headed Dog, the Rage, Lash, Thundergun, the Slickee Boys, Magnum, Crash, Worlds, Legend, Fargo, the Boys and Dirty Work.

The Keg closed in 1979 and was subsequently torn down. Since 1981 its former space has been occupied by a five-story, mid-rise apartment building called the Meridian (2201 Wisconsin Avenue NW).

MAYNARD'S RESTAURANT
1508 14th Street NW, Washington, D.C.
Years of operation at this address: 1940-1957

In 1905 this building was constructed for John J. Kolb who operated a confectionary on the premises until 1923 (the business was listed in local city directories as "John J. Kolb Confectioner"). The Kolb Building, as it is still known today, later housed businesses entitled Charles E. Schaffner Confectioner and Caterer in 1924 and Hubert Corens Confectioner from 1925 to early 1934. With Prohibition repealed, restaurateurs James and Lillian Duffy took over the premises and in February 1934 opened Duffy's Sea Grill, a seafood restaurant that lasted until February 1940. The business was subsequently sold to Harry Maynard, who opened Maynard's Restaurant in the space in March 1940.

At first, the main entertainment at Maynard's Restaurant was pianist Howard Cooper, who performed pop music favorites for the dinner customers. In 1946 the Gay Nineties team of singer Rudy Ferris and pianist Jack Neal became the featured attraction and remained in place for several years. In 1949 the pop music ensemble Sammy Ferro and His Trio took over house band duties.

From 1950 to 1953 Maynard's Restaurant kept the Sammy Ferro Trio as its house band while a variety of different blues, pop and R&B entertainers worked week-long engagements. Among the night club's featured attractions during those years were: singers Mary Martell, Roy Roberts, Norval Reid, Betty Jane, George Eades and Fats Pinere; and a variety of bands including the Marshall Brothers, the Merry-Tones, the Four Js, the Rhythm Rascals, the Skylighters, the Van Perry Quartet (featuring singer Eva Foster), Al Dunn and His Rhythm Kings (featuring singer VeRonnee), the Frankie Condon Combo, the Johnny Lawrence Trio, Bob Lawrenson's Trio, the Lou Muschell Trio, the Al Shea Trio, the Jo Ann Jordan Trio and the Tri Lane Trio.

In December 1953 Maynard's Restaurant began booking the popular local rock and roll band the Three Jacks, further expanding its already eclectic entertainment menu. The Three Jacks remained the main headliner at the night club throughout 1954 and into 1955. Among the establishment's featured attractions in 1956 and 1957 were: pop singer Laura Jay; the Latino group Los Americanos Mambo Band with the Stan Kelly Dancers; and R&B acts such as Two Jacks and A Queen (featuring saxophonist VI Burnsides), Al Dunn and His Orchestra (featuring singer VeRonnee) and the Three Kings. Maynard's Restaurant closed its doors in 1957 and its former ground floor space in the Kolb Building is currently occupied by a chain restaurant called Chipotle Mexican Grill.

THE MOULIN ROUGE
407 11th Street NW, Washington, D.C.
Years in operation at this address: 1954-1961

In November 1954 the Moulin Rouge replaced the long-standing Merchant's Lunch Room at this address and began a six-year run as one of the city's more interesting R&B-rock hangouts. Some of the musical acts to work this night club during its time were: singer Anna Thompson; and a number of bands such as Sterling Singleton and His Band (featuring singers Rea Parker and George Eades), Three Kings and a Queen (a group consisting of singer-saxophonist VI Burnside, pianist Warren Jackson, bassist Henry Outlaw and drummer Calvin Jackson), Billy Fair and His All-Stars, the Three of Us Trio, Ivory Joiner and His Men of Rhythm, Paul Kline and His Mellow-Ds, Bobby Marshall's Quintet, the Prince Shannon Trio, the Three Aces, the Carrington Visor Quartet, Frank Motley and His Band (featuring singer Angel Face), the Jones Brothers and Link Wray and His Ray Men.

The Moulin Rouge closed in August 1961 and in September 1962 a night club featuring burlesque entertainment called Al's Show Spot opened on the premises, eventually giving way in March 1967 to a very similar establishment called the Paper Doll. In the ensuing years various restaurants passed through this building, which was ultimately torn down in 1982. Today, the lot that once hosted the Moulin Rouge is the site of a 14-story office property called 1001 Pennsylvania Avenue that was opened in 1987 and occupies the entire east side of the 400 block of 11th Street NW.

THE OZARKS RESTAURANT
931 10th Street NW, Washington, D.C.
Years of operation at this address: 1955-1968

On the night of Wednesday, August 10, 1955 the Ozarks Restaurant opened at this address in a space that had most recently hosted an R&B night club called the Birdcage. This new establishment catered to a Southern-flavored, working class clientele that loved C&W music. Accordingly, acts to work the Ozarks Restaurant for the remainder of the 1950s included Lucky Wray and the Ozark Four (featuring banjoist Smitty Irvin and guitarist Pete Pike), the Ozark Boys (featuring accordionist Stoney Edwards), Dub Howington and His Tennessee Haymakers, the Blue Grass Champs, Link Wray and His Ray Men (who introduced rock and roll to the night club) and comedian Tiny Jenkins.

From 1960 to 1962 Link Wray and His Ray Men continued to headline the Ozarks Restaurant, usually featuring Ray Vernon as their primary lead singer. Other rock and roll groups to make appearances during those years included the Jesters and Tommy Riddle's Versatones. During that period the C&W music was also included in the mix and among the bands to perform on the Ozarks stage were Johnny Hopkins and His Band, the Stoneman Family, Jimmy Case and the Cherokees, Jack Rodgers and the Suburbans and Lloyd Bell and the Ozark Boys.

From 1963 to 1968 the nightly C&W house band was Jimmy Case and the Country Cats, who hold the distinction of being the last group to ever perform in the night club prior to it being burned to the ground during the riots that scorched the city after the assassination of Dr. Martin Luther King. Jr. in April 1968.

After the riots, the charred remains of the Ozarks Restaurant were cleared away and for decades a vacant lot was all that remained. Since 2005 the night club's former site has been occupied by an 11-story triangular office building called 901 New York Avenue NW that takes up the entire east side of the 900 block of 10th Street NW.

THE PSYCHE DELLY
4846 Cordell Avenue, Bethesda, Maryland
Years of operation at this address: 1971-1985
(Late in the Psyche Delly's existence the address of the building was changed to 4844 Cordell Avenue)

The Psyche Delly opened up in 1971 in a building previously occupied by Calvert Builders, Inc. and ultimately closed in 1985. The establishment began booking live blues and rock and roll music in 1973 and after Lou Sordo took over ownership in 1974 the night club quickly became one of the Washington, D.C. area's most popular venues.

During the 1970s, the Psyche Delly featured such acts as singer-guitarist Bobby Radcliff, the Slippery Eels, the Shonettes, the Reekers, the Flying As, the Rosslyn Mountain Boys, Grits, Barrelhouse, Danny and the Fat Boys, the Nighthawks, Rose Valley Special, Smalltalk, the Charlottesville Blues All Stars, Face Dancer, Bill Holland and Rent's Due, Pegasus, Pegasus, Happy the Man, the Richard Sales Band, Ravenstone, Windwater, Original Fetish, Richard Hell and the Voidoids, Rhythm Method, the James Cotton Blues Band, Root Boy Slim, Big Yankee Dollar, the Sliders, Departure, Tex Rubinowitz and the Bad Boys, the North Star Band, the Blue Rockers, the Rhythm Masters, Artful Dodger, Rocks and Razz.

Headliners at the Psyche Delly from 1980 to 1985 included New Riders of the Purple Sage, Deuce's Wild, the Method, the Slickee Boys, Martha Hull and the Steady Jobs, the Kids, Switchblade, Evan Johns and the H-Bombs, Billy Hancock and the Tennessee Rockets, and a special appearance by Black Oak Arkansas. The building that once housed the Psyche Delly is currently occupied by a restaurant called Flanagan's Harp and Fiddle.

RAND'S NIGHT CLUB
1414 Eye Street NW, Washington, D.C.
Years of operation at this address: 1951-1980
(The address of this building was listed as 1416 from 1951-1959; 1414-1416 from 1960-1966; and 1414 from 1967-1980)

In October 1951 Rand's Night Club replaced Baum's Furniture House in this ancient Eye Street NW building and remained in operation until July 1980. Some of the night spot's earliest headliners in the 1950s included: pop music performers such as singers Frances Kuhn, Terry Doyle, Brad Haynes, the band the Soft Winds, and the trio known as the Tunetwisters; and jazz performers such as singer Lionel Richardson, pianist Willie Jackson and saxophonists Gene Ammons and Billy Clark.

Beginning in 1960 and continuing into early 1964 the house band at Rand's Night Club was a rock and roll band called Big Al Downing and the Rhythm Rockers. Downing was then forced to put together another backup band in June of that year when all of the Rhythm Rockers morphed into a Beatles-type group called the Chartbusters and moved over to the Crazy Horse in Georgetown. Rand's Night Club was then forced to bring in other R&B and rock and roll acts to fill its bills.

From the summer months of 1964 to the final weeks of 1967 acts that appeared at Rand's Night Club included, in addition to Big Al Downing and his various backup bands: the Invictas, the Satans, Jimmy Vee and the Scamps, the Untouchables, Sal Massi and the Untouchables, the Sterling Brothers, Vince Carmen and the Frantic Six, Carol and Her Four Knights, Willie and the Handjives, Hank Ballard and the Midnighters, the Chartbusters, Bobbie Howard and the Hi-Boys, the Del Vikings, the Buddy Borda Four, the Beetles, Johnny Maestro and the Crests, the Encores, Farrel and the Flames, Sonny Richards and the Panics, the Dimensions, the Marvels, the Five Knights, the Crew Cuts, Rickey and the Gents, Angelo and the Initials, the Chariots, the Wise Guys, the Flamingos, the Tejuns, the Prodigals, the Intruders, Sonny Gordon and the Outcasts, Rick O'Dell and the Soul Senders, the Meditations (featuring singer Carol Gordon), the New Breed, the Persuasions, the Wolf Pack, the Surf Boys, the Heatwaves, Frankie Gracie and the Soul Brothers, the Wheels of Progress, the Saxtons, Jay and the Techniques, the Sonny Gordon Five (featuring singer Chuck Bennett) and the Adapters. Some of the major stars to headline the club during those years were R&B singer-pianists Fats Domino and Clarence "Frogman" Henry, rock and roll singer Gary U.S. Bonds and rock and roll singer-guitarist Bo Diddley.

In late 1967 singer Phil Flowers began performing at Rand's Night Club, with his act being billed the Phil Flowers Revue. From that point on the venue booked only R&B talent and other bands to appear onstage in the late 1960s included the Soul Brothers Six, the Showstoppers, and the Mellow Fellows. The night spot soldiered on throughout the 1970s with local soul music bands providing the entertainment.

Rand's Night Club ultimately closed its doors in 1980 as commercial developers descended upon the city's Downtown area looking to replace the long-standing night clubs with office building complexes. Since 1982 the former site of Rand's Night Club (the first half of the south side of the 1400 block of I Street NW) has been occupied by a 12-story office property entitled "1400 Eye St NW."

THE RENDEZVOUS
409 10th Street NW, Washington, D.C.
Years of operation at this address: 1951-1962

In 1951 the Rendezvous replaced Jimmie's Restaurant in deep Downtown Washington, D.C. and owners Constantine and Pandora Gogos, capitalizing on the city's Southern culture, immediately brought in C&W entertainers to attract customers. One of the most popular country music bands to perform in the night club during the middle and late 1950s was Roy Clark and the Power Pacs (featuring steel guitarist Bill Bagent). Several acts that mixed C&W with rock and roll also played there during that period including singer-guitarist Lucky Ray, Bobby Stevenson and His Rock and Roll Band, Stoney Rigsby and the Rock and Roll Westerners and the Three of Us Trio.

From 1957 to 1959 the main attractions at the Rendezvous was guitarist Link Wray, who, beginning in the spring of 1958, began calling his band Link Wray and His Ray Men, with Ray Vernon (formerly Lucky Wray) often featured as the lead vocalist. Late in the decade the Rendezvous brought in a young teen-aged rock and roll band called the Triumphs, which consisted of guitarist Jorma Kaukonen and bassist Jack Casady, both future members of the bands Jefferson Airplane and Hot Tuna. From 1960 until its closing in 1962, a regular attractions was the C&W band Jimmy Case and the Country Cats.

The building that housed the Rendezvous was torn down in 1963 and since 1975 its former site – the entire east side of the 400 block of 10th Street NW – has been occupied by the J. Edgar Hoover F.B.I. Building (935 Pennsylvania Avenue NW).

THE ROCKET ROOM
1200 New York Avenue NW, Washington, D.C.
Years of operation at this address: 1960-1970

On Thursday, June 30, 1960 the Rocket Room was opened by Joseph and Sanford Bomstein at 1200 New York Avenue NW in the Downtown area of Washington, D.C. (during the 1960s the Bomstein Brothers also owned three other night clubs in the city – the Crazy Horse, the Famous Restaurant, and the Shelter Room). The very first headliner at the Rocket Room was the Naturals, one of the area's top rock and roll bands. The building that housed the Rocket Room had hosted many different restaurants and businesses through the years and had most recently been occupied by a C&W night club called Harry's Tavern.

Prior to the British Invasion, the Rocket Room was the place to go in the nation's capital for rock and roll. During the remaining months of 1960 acts to appear there included: singers Richie Adams and Dick Webb; and bands such as Big Man Daniels and His Six Jaguars (a group alternately known as Charlie Daniels and the Jaguars), singer-guitarist Dale Hawkins and His Band (whose first engagement began on Monday, October 17, lasted through Sunday, October 30, 1960, and featured guitarist Roy Buchanan and saxophone player Ed Montini), the Day Brothers, the Perry Mates and the Joy Riders.

From 1961 to 1964 the Rocket Room offered the best in local, regional and national pop and rock and roll entertainment. Among the bands and musicians to work engagements there during this period included: singers Al Antonio, Barry Darvell, Freddy Cannon, Ray Peterson, Brian Hyland, Del Shannon, Jo Ann Campbell, Lou Christie, Johnny Cymbal and Jimmy Velvet; and bands such as the Moditones, Audrey and the Riot Men, Charlie Daniels and His Jaguars, the High Hopes, the Counts, the Perry Mates, the Five Musketeers, the Hot Tamales, the Naturals, the Jumping Jax, Frankie Mayo and the New Yorkers, the Twin Toppers, the Magnatones, Tito Mambo and the Upsetters, Dale Hawkins and the Escapades, the Peppermint Stix, the Blue Flames, Dion and the Belmonts, Don Russele and His Twisting Quartet, the Starlighters, Joey and the Twisters, Bobby Comstock and the Counts, Jay and the Americans, Ed and the Twisters, Little Hugh and the Embers (featuring singer Linda Lou), Ali Baba and His Four Thieves, the Imperials, Tommy Cole and the Belvederes, Ronnie Dove and the Belltones, Chuck Dehn and the Diplomats, the Holidays, the Kalin Twins, the Rockin' Blazers, the Escapades, the Romans, Johnny Caswell and the Magnificent Six, the Chuck-A-Luks, the Seven Dardanelles, Sonny Richards and the Panics, Bobby August and the Beachcombers, the Jokers, the Beetlenicks, the Saxtons, the Green Men (featuring singer Misty), the Encores, the Elegants, the Kingsmen (featuring singer-saxophonist Barry Petri), the Bill Black Combo, the Dovells, Dee Robb and the Robb-ins, the Lee Allen Revue, the McGraw Brothers, the Personalities, Terry Stafford, the Prodigals, the Preachers, the Off Beats, the Dominoes, the Riffmen, the Chartbusters, Bobby Paris and the Show Offs, the Rag Dolls, the Roger Pace Revue and the Barbarians.

From 1965 to 1968 the Rocket Room continued to offer a steady menu of pop, R&B and rock and roll entertainment. Among the bands and musicians to make appearances during the last half of the decade were: singers such as Ronnie Dove, Steve Alaimo, Monti Rock III, Dee Dee Sharp, Freddy Cannon, Len Barry and Memphis Gold; singer-pianist Jerry Lee Lewis; and bands such as the Chartbusters, the Prodigals, the Newbeats, the Saxtons, Mike Scott and the Niteriders, the Dominoes, Big Al Downing and His Band, the Executives, the Rag Dolls, the Morticians, Frankie Rondell and the Saints, the Lucky Seven, the Newports, the Prophets, the Boomerangs, Harvey Kaye and the Larks, the Four Evers, the Vibrants, the Dovells, the Cross Fires, the New Beats, Steve Colt and the 45s, Freddie and the Freeloaders, Joey Powers and the Vanguards, the Halos, the Four Reasons, the Shangri Las, Erin Farley and the Ovations, Little Anthony and the Imperials, the Johnny Walker Revue, the Devil's Disciples, the Happenings, the Frankie Brent Revue, the Spiders, the In Crowd, the Marketts, the Kalin Twins, Jimmy Eller and His Little People, the Hard Guys, the Curfews, the Soultastics, the Jimmy Jones Show, the Energy Pack, the Holidays, the Jade Brothers, the D.C. Riders, the Bluebeards, the Shirelles, the Morgan Pirates, the Patriots, Sonny Gordon and the Mustangs, the Words of Love, Tuesday's Boots, Flavor, the Spectrums, the Great Dames, the Devil's Children, Take Five, the Washington Monuments, Angel and the Devils, the Capers, the D.C. Love Train, Carl Edwards and the Combo-Nation, the Young Breed, Ron E. Jones and the Nomads, the Reasons Why, Wild Honey, Steve Charles and the Soul Syndrome, Willie and the Handjives, the Platters, Wally and the Capers, the Electric Flowers, Lunatic Fringe, Peppermint Rainbow, Nobody's Children, the Wet Paint, Today's Special and Cook E. Jar and the Krums.

In 1969 the Rocket Room booked both R&B and rock and roll performers, though its clientele had changed in the wake of the Riots of 1968. Among the acts to appear in the club that year were the King's Men, Boston Cream, the Winstons, Ronnie Jones and the Incidents, the Broom, the Shades of Autumn, Puzzle, Confection, Steve Charles and the

Soul Syndrome, the Flames (featuring singer Little Milton), Sedatrius Brown and the El Dorados, the Coordinators, the Boston Monkeys, Peaches and Herb and Phil Flowers and His Flower Shop.

In January 1970 the Rocket Room abandoned rock and roll and adopted R&B as its music of choice. For the first three months of the year the night club's headliners included Phil Flowers and His Flower Shop, Peaches and Herb, Big Al Downing and the Bruthers, and the Heavyload. In April 1970 the Rocket Room was transformed into a new night club called the Room that maintained the practice of booking local R&B bands. The Room eventually closed in 1987 and its building was torn down in 1988.

Since 1989 the former site of the Rocket Room (the first half of the south side of the 1200 block of New York Avenue NW) has been occupied by a 12-story building that currently houses the American Association for the Advancement of Science (1200 New York Avenue NW).

THE SHELTER ROOM
1357 Savannah Street SE, Washington, D.C.
Years of operation at this address: 1962-1973

The Shelter Room was one of several night clubs that existed in Southeast Washington, D.C. during the 1960s that offered rock and roll music for a quadrant of the city that was going through a major demographic and cultural transformation. Unbeknownst to most of its current-day residents, the vast majority of Southeast Washington's population was White and Southern from the 1940s to the middle 1960s and during those years many of its live music establishments catered to the culture of its people. This meant that C&W and rock and roll were prevalent in many of the bars, night clubs and taverns of such Southeast neighborhoods as Anacostia and Congress Heights up to the time of the Riots of 1968, at which point White Flight from the area accelerated greatly. Among the now-legendary watering holes that characterized Southeast Washington during the 1960s were places like the Anchor Grill, the Bee Hive, the Shanty, the Skylark (which became the Naylor Restaurant), the Stage Coach Tavern, the 1023 Restaurant, Walker's Tavern and others.

Joining the night club scene of Southeast Washington, D.C. in 1962 was the Shelter Room, whose listed address was 1357 Savannah Street SE at the far eastern end of the Congress Heights neighborhood. This particular space was a basement room that sat below the Park Shopping Center, a small mall constructed in 1949, which, on the surface, initially housed Park Rexall Drug (1355 Savannah Street SE), Park Barbershop (1359 Savannah Street SE), and the Park Theatre (1361 Savannah Street SE). The basement space of the shopping center was there from the beginning, but served as storage area for the various businesses above from 1949 to 1954. In 1955 the basement was cleared out and the Congress Park Bowling Center opened in its space with an address of 1357 Savannah Street SE. In early 1962 the bowling alley closed and in April of that year Joseph and Sanford Bomstein, owners of several Washington, D.C. live music night clubs, opened the Shelter Room in its place.

From 1962 to 1966 the Shelter Room featured local and national entertainers of various musical styles, but was mainly known for its pop and rock and roll acts. Headlining singers that performed there included Jimmy Clanton, Jo Ann Campbell, Jimmy Velvet, Lou Christie, Johnny Cymbal, Terry Stafford, Steve Alaimo, Ronnie Dove and Freddy Cannon; singer-guitarist Turley Richards; and singer-pianist Jerry Lee Lewis. Among the bands that appeared there during those years were the Rhythm Makers, the Green Men (featuring singer Misty), the Dovells, the Preachers, the Riffmen, the Dominoes, the Reflections, the Encores, the Chartbusters, the Acoustics, Bill Black and the Elegants, Herbie and the Originals, the Roger Pace Revue, the Morticians, the Rag Dolls, J.D. and the Expressions, the Celestials, Sonny Gordon and the Panics, the Joey Welz Band, Little Anthony and the Imperials, Vic and the Versatiles, the Jades, Erin Farley and the Ovations and the Magnatones.

In 1967 the Shelter Room underwent a change in ownership and was changed into an R&B night club. Among the better-known performers to perform there in the late 1960s and early 1970s were the Manhattans, the Parliaments, King Henry and the Knights, the Soul Brothers, the Dynamic Superiors, the Aylords, the Brother Jack McDuff Quartet and singer Mary Wells. In one of its most famous bookings, the nationally known rock and roll band Rare Earth appeared at the Shelter Room from Friday, April 3 to Sunday, April 5, 1970.

The Shelter Room closed in 1973 and a year later the entire Park Shopping Center was razed. In 1975 a new building marked 1345 Savannah Street SE was constructed on the land where the Shelter Room once existed and through the years various businesses have passed through the premises. Currently this structure houses the Congress Park Plaza Apartments Rental Office.

SOME PLACE ELSE
19 Atlantic Street SW, Washington, D.C.
Years of operation at this address: 1964-1978

Some Place Else was a night club whose building address was officially registered with the Government of the District of Columbia Alcoholic Beverage Control Board as 19 Atlantic Street SW. This is a highly significant fact because word-of-mouth in the rock and roll community usually had it residing in Southeast Washington, D.C. and ads in various local publications (and phone directories) would alternately list its address as "17 Atlantic Street SE," "19 Atlantic Street SE," "17-19 Atlantic Street SE," "17 Atlantic Street SW," "17-19 Atlantic Street SW," "21 Atlantic Street SE," "21 Atlantic Street SW," and, in most instances, "19 Atlantic Street SW" (its correct listing). The building actually sat in Southwest in what is known as the Bellevue neighborhood of the city only a few feet away from the Southeast Washington, D.C. border. For the record, the Polk city directories for Washington, D.C. correctly identify Atlantic Street SW as being west of South Capitol Street and north of Chesapeake Street, while Atlantic Street SE lies east of South Capitol Street.

Some Place Else was a rock and roll night club that operated from 1964 to 1978 and never strayed from its hard-rocking entertainment policy. In the 1960s bands that performed there included the Stingers, the Spyders, the Dagenites, the In Crowd, the Group, the Carpetbaggers, Beauty and the Beasties, the Rubber Band and Slow Rush. Top local bands to work its stage its stage in the 1970s included Curfew, Trestle, Squeeze, Sassafras Tea, Diamond, Trix, Fast Eddy, Fargo, Griffin, Starz and Aspex.

The building that housed Some Place Else hosted many different businesses through the years and was ultimately torn down in 2013. Since May 2015 its former lot has been occupied by a four-story apartment complex called Trinity Plaza (21 Atlantic Street SW).

THE STARLITE RESTAURANT
1419 Irving Street NW, Washington, D.C.
Years of operation at his address: 1954-1974

This storied building which had been situated near the intersection of 14th and Irving Streets NW in the Columbia Heights neighborhood of Washington, D.C. was constructed in 1910 and during its first two years served as headquarters for the Washington Horse Show Association. From 1912-1919 it housed the Mount Pleasant Stables (a livery owned by John O. Gheen), and then for the next 20 years it housed a succession of motor companies: Nash-Rinker Motor Company (January 1929-October 1930); McDevitt Motor Company (November 1930-August 1933); Britt Motors (September 1933-July 1934); Logan

Motor Company (August 1934-December 1936); and Arcade Pontiac (January 1937-February 1940).

After a 20-month period during which time the vacant, two-story structure was given substantial alterations, Burton's Restaurant opened on the ground floor of the premises on the night of Friday, November 28, 1941. Billed as "Uptown's Finest Restaurant," evening entertainment during its lifespan was provided by such pop music bands as Burton's Quartette, Jimmy Ellison and His Orchestra, Jack Morton's Orchestra and Charlie Corcoran and His Orchestra. Burton's Restaurant closed in March 1944.

New owners emerged and in April 1944 the Ding How Restaurant was opened in the former quarters of Burton's Restaurant. A live pop music schedule was maintained and bands to perform there in the 1940s and early 1950s included Woody Pittman and His Orchestra, Paul Kline and His Orchestra, Bob Siedell and His Orchestra, Jimmy Bright and His Orchestra and Johnny Fichette and His Orchestra. The Ding How Restaurant closed in December 1953.

After a period of vacancy the empty building at 1419 Irving Street NW was purchased and refurbished by Herman Savage and Hilton Ethridge, who decided to call their new business venture the Starlite Restaurant. On Monday, July 19, 1954 the Starlite celebrated its grand opening with a night of live C&W music by Jimmy Dean and His Texas Wildcats (featuring lead guitarist Roy Clark), which remained the house band throughout the summer months. During the final six months of the year other C&W bands that worked the night club were Butterball Paige and His Band (featuring singer-guitarists Tom "Butterball" Paige and Carl "Curly" Sluder), and Bill Peer and His Melody Girls and Boys (featuring the now-legendary singer Patsy Cline).

For the remainder of the 1950s, other C&W performers to headline the Starlite Restaurant included: bands such as Butterball Paige and the Starliters (as his new outfit was called), Sonny James and the New Starliters, Curly Sluder and the Twilighters (featuring drummer Al Denunzio), and the Country Kats (featuring the Case Brothers); singers such as Dick Williams and Bobby Collins; singer-fiddler-guitarist Blackie Skiles; guitarist Pete Pepper; and singer-accordionist Stoney Rigsby.

When the 1950s concluded the Starlite Restaurant abandoned its C&W format and began booking local rock and roll acts. Bands to appear in the night club from 1960-1967 included Bob Hirschmann and His Six Originals, the Rhythm Makers, the Fabulous Rivieras, the Peppermint Twisters (featuring drummer Al Pometto), the Dominoes, the Satellites, the Texans, the Prodigals, Tommy Cole and the Belvederes, Ken Case and the Versatiles, the Bad Boys, the Billy Kidd Combo, the Rocking Mar-Vels, the Rocking Chuckles, the Poodles, the Personalities, the Mad Hatters, the Outcasts (featuring guitarist Roy Buchanan), the Jumping Jax, the Abstracts (featuring singer Steve Charles), Little Joe and the Impossibles, the In Crowd, the Blue Feelin' (featuring guitarist Tiny Jenkins), the Saxtons, Harry Johnson and the Sonics, the Foremost (featuring guitarist Roy Buchanan), the D.C. Riders and Sonny and His Playmates.

During the late 1960s the Columbia Heights neighborhood in which the Starlite Restaurant was located underwent a fast demographic transformation, changing from White, Southern and working class to Black in just a couple short years. To keep pace with the new faces, the night club's management saw fit to bring in more R&B acts, with Steve Charles and the Soul Syndrome being the first group to usher in the new style in 1967. By early 1968 they had assumed house band duties and were on hand the night Washington, D.C. experienced rioting in the wake of Dr. Martin Luther King, Jr.'s assassination in April of that year. Steve Charles and the Soul Syndrome survived the melee and continued to headline at the Starlite Restaurant throughout 1968 and 1969 and into the early 1970s.

Other featured acts during those years were Big Al Downing and His Band and Chuck Booker and the Messengers.

The Starlite Restaurant closed in 1974 and in its final days was reportedly little more than a run-down neighborhood bar with no live music. Shortly after its closing the building was demolished and for more than 30 years a vacant lot marked its former location. Developers eventually swooped in as Columbia Heights underwent another cultural change, with Latinos displacing most of the neighborhood's Black residents. Since 2008 the Starlite Restaurant's former site on the north side of what was once the 1400 block of Irving Street NW, has been occupied by DC USA, an 890,000 square foot, $145 million pedestrian-oriented retail complex (shopping mall) whose street address is listed as 3100 14th Street NW.

THE VARSITY GRILL AND THE VARSITY GRILL BACK ROOM
THE VARSITY GRILL
7410 Baltimore Avenue, College Park, Maryland
Years of operation at this address: 1932-1980
THE VARSITY GRILL BACK ROOM
4410 Knox Road, College Park, Maryland
Years of operation at this address: 1974-1983
From 1950 to June 1974 the entire establishment (front room and Quonset building together) was called "The Varsity Grill"
Beginning in June 1974 the Quonset building, with a separate entrance marked 4410 Knox Road, was officially named "The Varsity Grill Back Room"
The Varsity Grill (front room) closed in 1980
The Varsity Grill Back Room closed in March 1983

The building at 7410 Baltimore Avenue was a square, one-story structure with a 2,250 square foot interior that was constructed in 1925, and, after briefly serving as makeshift dormitory space for University of Maryland students, operated for several years as a tea room. In August 1932, after rezoning was completed, Emanuel Francis ("Zal") Zalesak, a 1925 graduate of the University of Maryland, opened the Varsity Grill at 7410 Baltimore Avenue as a soda shop aimed at University students.

After Prohibition was repealed the Varsity Grill was converted into an alcohol-serving restaurant and fraternity brothers and sorority sisters flocked to the evolving establishment. (Much of the Varsity Grill's early history is recounted in an uncredited article in the Diamondback newspaper of Wednesday, September 10, 1959 entitled "Grill Room To Be Rebuilt: Fire Forces Face Lifting.")

In 1950 a separate, two-story, 4,050 square foot Quonset building was constructed at 4410 Knox Road, just west of and behind the Varsity Grill's Baltimore Avenue structure. Zalesak took over the new property and installed a covered 10-foot walkway that led from the back of the main Varsity Grill building into the Knox Road Quonset structure. He then installed a bar and a stage in the newer building, which had a capacity of 450 occupants and was commonly referred to as the Quonset building of the Varsity Grill. During the 1950s pop music bands to appear on the Varsity Grill's Quonset building's stage included Tony Smith and the Boys and the Varsity Six.

From 1960 to 1966 a variety of R&B and rock and roll bands appeared at the Varsity Grill in its back Quonset building. These performers included Billy Duke and the Comets, the Rivieras, the Rocking Valiants (featuring singer Lady Chi Chi), the Van Dykes, the Shirelles, Lamont and the All Stars, the Infernos, Bobby Ellis and the Thunderbirds, Phil Flowers and His Flower Shop, the Versailles, the Playmates, Tommy Vann and the

Echoes, Sir Charles and the Twilighters, the Tytans, Gene Austin and the Downbeats, the Esquires, the Pipe Dreamers and the Prophet and His Disciples.

Changes occurred in ownership with Zal Zalesak selling the business to Francis Gaegler in 1964, who, in turn, sold the night club to Washington, D.C. restaurateur Leon Zeiger in April 1966. Zeiger placed a stronger emphasis on booking rock and roll bands. He also adorned his "discotheque room" (as he began calling the Quonset building) with flashing strobe lights and dancing go-go girls. The night club's largely college-aged clientele rapidly changed from crew cut, beer drinking frat boys and their neatly dressed sorority dates to long-haired pot smokers, protestors and hippies of all persuasions. Throughout the late 1960s and early 1970s, the venue's more popular bands included Upstairs and the Attics, the Banned, Brownie, and G.A.S.

In June 1974, just as the Varsity Grill was becoming known as a haven for hardcore drug users and local motorcycle clubs like the Pagans, the Quonset building officially took on the name "The Varsity Grill Back Room." For the remainder of the 1970s the emphasis was on hard rock and roll, though all types of bands were given chances. Among the local groups to perform in the Varsity Grill Back Room during those years were Half Moon, Flush, Shannon, Happy Jack, Face Dancer, the Blue Meanies, the Nighthawks, Orange Wedge, Wolfgang, Sinbad, the Rock 'n' Roll Express, Razz, Danny and the Fat Boys, Foxie, Daddy Warbux, the Cherry People, Sly Fox, Tramp, Windjammer, Truk, Secunda, the Now Band, Monster Rabbit, Earth Bound, Black on White, Bill Holland and Rent's Due, Artful Dodger, Slow Rush, Flight, Train Wreck, Hard Bark, Star Machine, Genghis Kahn, Silver Queen, Sadbird, Smalltalk, Shock, Starz (before they became DC Star), the Boyz, the Kid Band, Original Sin, Edge, Root Boy Slim and the Sex Change Band, Urban Verbs, the Rosslyn Mountain Boys, D.C. Star, the Rage, Lash, Grande Hotel, Cherry Smash, Plymouth Rock, the Grimes Brothers, High Roller, the Country Gentlemen and Tsakanikas.

In addition, the late 1970s saw a number of national acts appear in the Varsity Grill Back Room. Among those that worked engagements there were Chuck Berry, Steppenwolf, Jan and Dean, Long John Baldry, the Buddy Miles Band, Iron Butterfly, the Ramones, Rick Derringer and David Johansen.

Several other rock and roll bars emerged in College Park during the 1970s to cash in on the rock and roll crowd the Varsity Grill had fostered. Their ranks included the Bastille (9098 Baltimore Avenue), which opened just north of the University of Maryland campus in a long-standing building that had previously hosted such establishments as the Villa and the Knotty Pine. The Bastille brought in Ted Nugent and the Amboy Dukes as one of their earliest headliners. As legend has it, Nugent and company were a bit too wild for the crowd of 50 persons and were booted off the stage by management on the opening night (Wednesday, January 30, 1974) of their three-night booking. Nugent released a multi-million-selling album the very next year, "Ted Nugent" (Ted Nugent; Epic Records, 1975), and headlined at the Capital Centre in support of the album. In 1977 he had a huge single (and album) entitled "Cat Scratch Fever" and was the year's top-grossing live rock and roll act. Through the years the Bastille was home to such top local bands as Daddy Warbux, Face Dancer, Sinbad, the Nighthawks and DC Star. It closed on Tuesday, April 3, 1984.

The other main College Park rock and roll bar was the Paragon (7416 Baltimore Avenue), which opened on the top floor of the Italian Gardens right next door to the Varsity Grill in December 1975. The Paragon went through many formats (it operated as a heavy metal venue called the Attic from September 1982 to March 1987) and was a favorite of local bands like Face Dancer and DC Star. In 1987 and 1988 an attempt was made to draw in national acts and such bands as Kix, Crack the Sky, Nantucket, Foghat, Three Dog Night, Savoy Brown, Dr. Hook, Helix, Pat Travers, Blackfoot, Blue Oyster Cult, Frank Marino and Mahogany Rush, and Molly Hatchet all appeared at the night club. The

Paragon closed in August 1995 and many different restaurants and live music venues have since occupied its former site.

The Varsity Grill's front room closed in August 1980 and in the ensuing years a number of different businesses occupied its former quarters. In recent years the 7410 Baltimore Avenue building was reconfigured and today hosts three separate storefronts – 7408 (Revo Nail and Spa); 7410 (Jimmy John's Gourmet Sandwiches); and 7412 (Pizza Mart). Meanwhile, the Varsity Grill Back Room, which discontinued live music in 1979, remained in operation as a non-descript college beer bar until March 1983. It subsequently sat vacant for more than three years, hosted the Santa Fe Café from June 1986 to May 2010, and then was again empty for three more years. Since Thursday, October 3, 2013 the former Varsity Grill Back Room at 4410 Knox Road has been the home of a restaurant called Terrapin's Turf.

The Varsity Grill's indescribable atmosphere was so unique that famed author Toby Thompson donated an entire opening chapter to it in his non-fiction classic "Saloon: A Guide To America's Great Bars, Pubs, Saloons, Taverns, Drinking Places, and Watering Holes" (1976).

STAGES

Alexandria Arena, the Birchmere, the Capital Centre, DAR Constitution Hall, Falls Church Community Center, the John F. Kennedy Center for the Performing Arts, Ritchie Coliseum, Shady Grove Music Fair, Warner Theatre, William P. Cole, Jr. Student Activities Building

ALEXANDRIA ARENA

801 N. St. Asaph Street, Alexandria, Virginia
Years of operation at this address: 1948-1986
Commonly known as the Alexandria Rock Arena; the Alexandria Roller Rink
Capacity: 3,000

The Alexandria Arena was an enormous, Quonset-styled, yellow, brick-and-concrete structure located in the Old Town neighborhood of Alexandria, Virginia. Approaching the front of the building, one was greeted by a massive slab of architecture that featured porthole windows, an arched roof and a walk-up platform porch with stairways on both sides leading to four large entrance doors. On top of this front entrance was a sign in red letters that spelled out "Alexandria Arena." The building itself cost more than $1 million and was first opened to the public on the night of Tuesday, November 23, 1948. Primarily used as a roller skating rink, local music promoters began utilizing the building in the 1950s for sporadic big band or C&W music concert performances, citing its abundant floor space as its most attractive feature.

Things changed at the Alexandria Arena in the 1960s. The popularity of rock and roll music skyrocketed with the introduction of the British Invasion and the cavernous building was targeted by representatives from local radio stations such as WEAM, WEEL and WPGC as the perfect concert facility. The arena's manager, Thomas Brown, was happy to comply with the wishes of his new suitors and when promoters booked the concrete monstrosity for concert shows, the first thing they did was to change the name of the facility in their advertisements to either the Alexandria Roller Rink or the Alexandria Rock Arena, with the given address usually marked as either 805 or 807 N. St. Asaph Street.

The Alexandria Arena had a capacity of 3,000 occupants and patrons had little choice but to sit on the open maplewood floor, with folding chairs only being used in rare situations. The relatively low overhead of the facility earned it special designation among local music promoters as one of the Washington D.C. area's most desirable concert halls.

Kicking off the incursion of new bands into the facility was Peter and Gordon, who headlined there on Wednesday, June 24, 1964. The next concert staged at the Alexandria Arena was the Beach Boys, who performed there before a sold-out audience on Wednesday, September 23, 1964, with more than a thousand fans reportedly being turned away. The following year a unique, festival-styled concert using the theme "It's What's Happening, Baby!" was presented by radio station WEAM at the arena on Thursday, August 12, 1965 featuring the Strangeloves, the McCoys, the Haloes, Bobbi Martin and Lenny Welch. Major national acts that headlined the arena in 1966 included the Yardbirds, Neil Diamond, the Count Five and the Young Rascals (a number of top local Washington, D.C. area rock and roll bands like the English Setters, the Hangmen and the British Walkers were called upon to open for these headliners).

The Alexandria Arena continued to maintain its status as the Washington, D.C. area's top concert venue into the 1970s and hosted some amazing bills including Black Sabbath and Humble Pie; Alice Cooper and Edgar Winter's White Trash; Jethro Tull and Yes; T. Rex and Grin; Nazareth and Blue Oyster Cult; and Lou Reed and Hall and Oates. However, the opening of the Capital Centre in Landover, Maryland in December 1973 caused a downturn in business for smaller concert halls and the Alexandria Arena eventually went back to its designated function as a skating rink for the locals.

In the 1980s, developers descended on N. St. Asaph Street and the property was sold to Development Resources, Inc., who planned on erecting a $45 million dollar hotel-office complex on the prized piece of real estate. The Alexandria Arena closed for business on Sunday, November 30, 1986 and the building was razed in April 1987. Today its former site is occupied by a hotel called Sheraton Suites Old Town Alexandria (801 N. St. Asaph Street), though memories of all the great rock and roll bands that once performed on the block still linger in the air.

Rock and roll concerts held at the Alexandria Arena:
Peter and Gordon, the Roaches (Wednesday, June 24, 1964)
The Beach Boys, the Mugwumps, Steve Alaimo and the Dynamos (Wednesday, September 23, 1964)
"It's What's Happening, Baby!" featuring the Strangeloves, the McCoys, the Haloes, Bobbi Martin, Lenny Welch (Thursday, August 12, 1965)
"WEAM Holiday A Go Go" featuring the Yardbirds, the Shangri-Las, the Hangmen, Joey Welz, the Open Roads, the Plague, the Beau Street Runners (Thursday, December 23, 1965)
The Yardbirds, the English Setters, the British Walkers, New Delphonics, the Jay Walkers, the New Found Sound, December's Children, the Sheffields, the Gents, Fugitive Sound, the Villager Go-Go Girls (Friday, September 9, 1966)
Neil Diamond, the English Setters, the Hangmen, the Brave Maggots, 20 other bands (Saturday, October 1, 1966)
Richard and the Young Lions, the Chiffons (Friday, November 4, 1966)
The Count Five, Martha and the Vandellas, the English Setters, the Hangmen (Wednesday, November 23, 1966)
The Young Rascals, the English Setters, the Hangmen, the Fallen Angels, the Surf Boys (Friday, December 23, 1966)
"The Vox Band Battle for Stardom" featuring the Reachers, the Warlox, Rokx, the Hearsemen, the Tornados, Contents Under Pressure, the Hayze, the Brotherhood and the London Stompers (Sunday, April 2, 1967)
Vanilla Fudge, the British Walkers, the Curfews, Wild Honey, the Magic Reign (Sunday, April 23, 1967)

"Psychedelia" featuring the Town Criers, the Warlox, Rokz, the Reachers, the Hearsemen, the Tornados, the Hayze, the Brotherhood, the London Stompers, Contents Under Pressure, the Hounds of Baskerville, the British Crowns, PJ and the Nitecaps (Saturday, April 29, 1967)
"Sockeroonie" featuring Question Mark and the Mysterians, the American Breed, the Telstars (Friday, June 23, 1967)
The Doors, the Blades of Grass, December's Children, the Warlox, the Hounds of Baskerville, Gary Scott and the Classics, the Fantastic Plastic, the McCormick Tool Company, the Corporation, the Shades, the Brotherhood, Essex, the Tornados, the New York Public Library (Friday, August 18, 1967)
Keith and the Wild Kingdom, Peaches and Herb with the Six Pack, the Gents, December's Children (Saturday, September 23, 1967)
The Turtles, Bobbie Howard and the Sweet (Wednesday, November 22, 1967)
The Buckinghams, December's Children, the Plum Beach Incident, the McCormick Tool Company, the Wakes (Saturday, December 23, 1967)
Vanilla Fudge, Ultimate Spinach, the British Walkers, Wild Honey, the Curfews, the Magic Reign (Sunday, April 21, 1968)
Big Brother and the Holding Company (featuring singer Janis Joplin), the Jeff Beck Group (featuring singer Rod Stewart) (Sunday, October 20, 1968)
Vanilla Fudge, the Steve Miller Band, Rhinoceros (Sunday, November 24, 1968)
Blood, Sweat and Tears, Spirit, Dr. John (Sunday, January 26, 1969)
Canned Heat, B.B. King (Sunday, February 16, 1969)
The Jeff Beck Group, Jethro Tull (Saturday, March 1, 1969)
Black Sabbath, Humble Pie (Sunday, April 14, 1971)
Emerson, Lake and Palmer (Sunday, May 16, 1971)
Alice Cooper, Edgar Winter's White Trash, Grin (Sunday, June 13, 1971)
Jethro Tull, Yes (Sunday, July 11, 1971)
T-Rex, Grin (Sunday, February 20, 1972)
Alice Cooper, Mitch Ryder and the Detroit Wheels (Sunday, March 12, 1972)
Humble Pie, King Crimson, Alexis Korner (Sunday, March 26, 1972)
The J. Geils Band, Dr. John the Night Tripper (Sunday, April 9, 1972)
Nazareth, Blue Oyster Cult (Sunday, June 30, 1974)
Ted Nugent and the Amboy Dukes, Cactus (featuring singer-guitarist Mike Pinera) (Sunday, July 28, 1974)
Rory Gallagher, Status Quo, Hearts Field (Sunday, August 25, 1974)
Lou Reed, Hall and Oates (Sunday, October 13, 1974)

THE BIRCHMERE
3701 Mount Vernon Avenue, Alexandria, Virginia
Years of operation at this address: 1997-Present
Capacity: 500
Previous addresses:
2723 South Wakefield Street, Arlington, Virginia (1966-1981)
3901 Mount Vernon Avenue, Alexandria, Virginia (1981-1997)

Greg Oelze took over a 100-seat restaurant called the Birchmere at 2723 South Wakefield Street in Arlington, Virginia on Monday, April 4, 1966 and immediately turned it into a live music night club. He brought in a variety of bluegrass and country rock bands as entertainment and during his 15-year run at that address some of the acts to appear onstage included the Old Five and Dimers (his own band, for which he played guitar), Hickory, Fireside, the Rosslyn Mountain Boys, the Seldom Scene, the Bluegrass Cardinals and Grass Menagerie, among others. The Birchmere closed at this address on Wednesday, May 13, 1981 and the building was razed later that month.

Oelze had been searching for a new location for his restaurant business and discovered a building at 3901 Mount Vernon Avenue in Alexandria, Virginia which could accommodate 300 patrons. Finalizing a seamless transition, he opened up the second version of the Birchmere at that address on Thursday, May 14, 1981.

The Birchmere continued its tradition of hosting bluegrass and contemporary acoustic music and for most of the 1980s continued to feature the Seldom Scene as its regular headliner. Popular out-of-town performers such as Guy Clark, John Hartford and Jonathan Edwards also made appearances. In the 1990s big-name acts came through including the Nighthawks, Livingston Taylor, Jorma Kaukonen, Alison Krauss and Union Street, Kelly Willis, Tom Rush, Lowen and Navarro, and Taj Mahal. The Birchmere closed its 3901 Mount Vernon Avenue location with a performance by the jazz band Ritmo Junction on Friday, June 27, 1997, but reopened the very next day in a new space a mere two blocks away.

The Birchmere's third stop was in a large building at 3701 Mount Vernon Avenue in Alexandria. Opening night, Saturday, June 28, 1997, saw the Average White Band headline. This latest version of the night club seated 500 people, had the feel of a concert hall, and placed an emphasis on booking national talent, courtesy of promoter Michael Jaworek (who still serves the Birchmere in that capacity today). During its first weeks some of the acts to perform there included Rodney Crowell and the Cicadas, Roger McGuinn, Nils Lofgren, Bruce Cockburn, Richard Thompson and Delbert McClinton.

In time the Birchmere came to shed its long-standing bluegrass image and hosted most every genre of popular music. In recent years some of the better-known rock and roll acts to headline the night club have been Todd Rundgren, 38 Special, Three Dog Night, the Marshall Tucker Band, the Ventures, Robin Trower, and the Outlaws.

THE CAPITAL CENTRE
1 Harry S. Truman Drive, Landover, Maryland
Years of operation at this address: 1973-1999
Also operated as:
USAir Arena (1993-1996)
US Airways Arena (1996-1997)
Capacity: 18,756

The Capital Centre was a spacious arena that opened on Sunday, December 2, 1973 with an NBA basketball game between the Washington Bullets and the Seattle Supersonics and during its existence was regarded as one of the country's premiere concert venues. The very first concert in the building saw the Allman Brothers Band perform on Tuesday, December 4, 1973. Two nights later the Who performed to a packed house on their "Quadrophenia" tour.

Over the next two decades most every major act in popular music made stops in the arena. The biggest names in rock and roll performed on the Capital Centre stage in the 1970s including such acts as Alice Cooper, Ted Nugent, the Rolling Stones, Led Zeppelin, Fleetwood Mac, Elvis Presley, Paul McCartney and Wings, Kiss, Bad Company, Pink Floyd and innumerable others. On Saturday, May 31, 1986, independent filmmakers Jeff Krulik and John Heyn immortalized the Capital Centre when they shot their now-legendary short movie "Heavy Metal Parking Lot" on the premises, a documentary that captured the tailgate party activities of fans of the band Judas Priest, who were appearing inside the arena that evening.

The Capital Centre closed in 1999 and was demolished on Sunday, December 15, 2002. Its former site now hosts an open-air shopping center called the Boulevard at the Capital Centre (880-G Shoppers Way, Largo, Maryland).

DAR CONSTITUTION HALL
1776 D Street NW, Washington, D.C.
Years of operation at this address: 1929-Present
Capacity: 3,702

DAR Constitution Hall was opened in 1929 by the Daughters of the American Revolution to serve as the site of its growing annual convention. Decades later, during the rock and roll era, it became one of Washington, D.C.'s primary stops for visiting national acts on the rise. Some of the rock and roll bands to perform concerts there in the 1960s included the Who, the Dave Clark Five, the Lovin' Spoonful, Buffalo Springfield, Strawberry Alarm Clock, Eric Burdon and the Animals, the Box Tops and Procol Harum. Among the dozens of acts to appear in the hall in the 1970s were the J. Geils Band, Rare Earth, Argent, Fleetwood Mac, Billy Joel, Elton John, Kansas, and Frank Zappa and the Mothers of Invention.

FALLS CHURCH COMMUNITY CENTER
223 Little Falls Street, Falls Church, Virginia
Years of operation at this address: 1968-Present
Capacity: 700

The Falls Church Community Center opened in September 1968 and, because of its spacious basketball gymnasium, was quickly targeted by local music promoters as a viable concert hall. Local historian Jack Maier has done an impressive job of researching the facility's music history and has compiled an exhaustive list of local and national rock and roll bands that performed there from 1968 to 1974.

According to Maier, local groups that performed at this venue included the Magic Reign, Penny Arcade, the Yorkshires, the New Delphonics, the Gents, Scarlet Onyx, the King Cobras, the Fallen Angels, December's Children, the Incredible Fog, Slow Rush, Flavor, Grin, Ulysses, January Tyme, American Dream, Greasy Pig, the Cherry People, the Nowhere Men, Curfew, Second Eagle, Crank, Earth, Tahoka, Claude Jones, Sageworth and Drums, Badge, Star, Razz, and Sky Cobb. In addition, Maier also reports that national acts to headline the Falls Church Community Center included the McCoys, the Bob Seger System, the Stooges (featuring lead singer Iggy Pop), Sir Lord Baltimore, Dust, the Groundhogs, Brownsville Station, Mitch Ryder and the Detroit Wheels, Mother Earth, the Doobie Brothers, Matthews' Southern Comfort (featuring singer-guitarist Iain Matthews), Atomic Rooster, singer-keyboardist Bobby Whitlock (formerly of Delaney and Bonnie and Derek and the Dominoes), and the Stories.

THE JOHN F. KENNEDY CENTER FOR THE PERFORMING ARTS
2700 F Street NW, Washington, D.C.
Years of operation at this address: 1971-Present
Commonly known as the Kennedy Center
Capacity (Concert Hall at the Kennedy Center): 2,442

In the early 1970s the John F. Kennedy Center for the Performing Arts regularly booked rock and roll concerts in its Concert Hall, with the very first popular music act to perform there being the Fifth Dimension on Monday, September 13, 1971. Over the next three years some of the many rock and roll shows in the Concert Hall included Chicago, Murray the K's Rock Revival (featuring Little Richard, the Coasters, the Drifters, the Shirelles and

Clyde McPhatter), the Eagles and Spooky Tooth, Pink Floyd, Badfinger, the James Gang, Deep Purple, the Hollies, Neil Young, Mott the Hoople and Iggy and the Stooges, Roy Buchanan, Bruce Springsteen, Black Oak Arkansas, Lou Reed, Steely Dan, Poco, Electric Light Orchestra, Todd Rundgren, Procol Harum, Grin, King Crimson and many others.

RITCHIE COLISEUM
7675 Baltimore Avenue, University of Maryland, College Park, Maryland
Years of operation at this address: 1931-Present
Capacity: 1,500

Of all the colleges in the Washington, D.C. area, the University of Maryland stands out in that it boasted two major venues of the early rock and roll era, Ritchie Coliseum, and the William P. Cole, Jr. Student Activities Building (commonly known as Cole Field House). The smaller of the two, Ritchie Coliseum, was built in 1931 as a multi-purpose athletic facility and began hosting live music events in 1956 with appearances by such jazz performers as Eddie Condon and His All Stars and Duke Ellington and His Orchestra.

The first rock and roll concert to be held at Ritchie Coliseum was a multi-act show on Friday, May 16, 1958 featuring the Terp Tones, the Belvederes, the Playboys and the Cameos. Later that year the venue was the site of a "Rock 'N Roll Spectacular" on Saturday, December 27, 1958 that offered a bill headlined by Bill Haley and His Comets and supported by the Kingsmen, the Mellow Kings, Vernon Taylor, the Crystals, Jerry Dallman and the Knightcaps, the Cool Breezes, Terry and the Pirates and the Starlighters.

Throughout the 1960s a mix of local rock and roll bands and national pop and rock acts periodically headlined at Ritchie Coliseum. Local bands to perform there included the Van Dykes, Doug Clark and the Hot Nuts, Lawrence and the Arabians, the Nowhere Men and Claude Jones. Among the nationally known outfits to make appearances were the Four Seasons, the Buckinghams, Vanilla Fudge, Booker T. and the M.G.s, Neil Diamond, Jefferson Airplane and Tommy James and the Shondells.

The 1970s saw Ritchie Coliseum continue its practice of offering rock and roll shows that alternately featured both local and touring groups.

Among the local favorites that headlined during that decade were the Cherry People, the New Breed, the Nowhere Men, Crank, Sky Cobb and Grin. Among the majors that made stops here during that time were Chicago, Rhinoceros, Poco, Youngbloods, the Kinks, the James Brown Revue, Kenny Rogers and the First Edition, Steppenwolf, Sugarloaf, Chuck Berry, Blue Oyster Cult, Commander Cody and His Lost Planet Airmen, Looking Glass, Don McLean, Focus, the New York Dolls, Frank Zappa and the Mothers of Invention, and the Mahavishnu Orchestra.

In addition, some of the more interesting rock and roll concerts that Ritchie Coliseum has hosted through the years include: the Clash (Saturday, September 29, 1979); U2 (Monday, April 25, 1983); and a triple-billed show featuring Black Sabbath, Motorhead and Morbid Angel (Wednesday, February 16, 1994).

SHADY GROVE MUSIC FAIR
Shady Grove Road, Gaithersburg, Maryland
Years of operation at this address: 1962-1978
Capacity: 5,000

Shady Grove Music Fair opened in 1962 as a summer tent theatre with a capacity of 2,000. In 1967 it was converted into a 5,000-seat, permanent, year-round facility. The venue closed after the 1978 season and was torn down in 1979.

During the 1960s, in addition to plays and theatre productions, Shady Grove Music Fair offered live concerts by a variety of popular music entertainers. Among the rock and roll acts to perform there late in the decade were the Dave Clark Five, the Lovin' Spoonful and Jefferson Airplane. A number of top rock and roll bands appeared there in the 1970s including the James Gang, Sly and the Family Stone, Bread, Rare Earth, the Allman Brothers Band, Faces (featuring lead singer Rod Stewart), Savoy Brown, Lou Reed, the Steve Miller Band, Leon Russell, the Byrds, Humble Pie, Yes, Looking Glass, Canned Heat, Bruce Springsteen, and New Riders of the Purple Sage.

Today the former site of Shady Grove Music Fair is occupied by a sprawling business park called the Grove 270 with a new listed address of 9201 Corporate Boulevard, Rockville, Maryland.

WARNER THEATRE
513 13th Street NW, Washington, D.C.
Years of operation at this address: 1947-Present
Capacity: 1,847

This venue was opened to the public in 1924 as the Earle Theatre and in 1947 was renamed Warner Theatre in honor of Harry Warner, one of the founders of the American entertainment company Warner Bros. For decades, Warner Theatre has hosted rock and roll shows and during the 1970s headliners included the James Brown Revue, Hawkwind, Wishbone Ash, the Climax Blues Band and Rush. In one of the facility's most surprising bookings, the Rolling Stones performed a concert at Warner Theatre on Thursday, June 15, 1978.

WILLIAM P. COLE, JR. STUDENT ACTIVITIES BUILDING
4095 Union Lane, University of Maryland, College Park, Maryland
Years of operation at this address: 1955-Present
Commonly known as Cole Field House
Also operated as Student Activities Building (1955-1956)
Renamed William P. Cole, Jr. Student Activities Building in 1956
Capacity: 14,596

The Student Activities Building is an indoor sports arena that opened on the University of Maryland's College Park campus in 1955. It was renamed William P. Cole, Jr. Student Activities Building in 1956 and rates as the largest of all the local college auditoriums. From its inception it was commonly known as Cole Field House and served as a popular venue for all manner of live folk, jazz, pop and R&B music events.

In the 1970s rock and roll concerts became a major attraction in the William P. Cole, Jr. Student Activities Building and some of the performers in the arena that decade included Janis Joplin, Van Morrison, Grand Funk Railroad, Steppenwolf, Three Dog Night, the James Gang, the Guess Who, the Grateful Dead, the Beach Boys, Leon Russell, Jethro Tull, Chicago, Santana, the Doobie Brothers, Seals and Croft, Faces (featuring lead singer Rod Stewart), Peter Frampton, Frank Zappa, Queen, Thin Lizzy and Emerson, Lake and Palmer.

Three of the more interesting shows to ever take place in the facility were: Black Sabbath, Black Oak Arkansas and Blue Oyster Cult (Friday, July 28, 1972); Chuck Berry, Jerry Lee Lewis and Bruce Springsteen (Saturday, April 28, 1973; Springsteen and his band opened the concert with their own set and then were called upon to back up the headliner Chuck Berry with no rehearsal and no sound check); and Elvis Presley (two nights – Friday, September 27 and Saturday, September 28, 1974).

FESTIVALS
The Washington Pop Music Festival, the Laurel Pop Festival, Caravan of Love, Livestock, Berlin Airlift

THE WASHINGTON POP MUSIC FESTIVAL
Sunday, August 4, 1968; 1pm
P Street Beach, 22nd and P Streets NW, Washington DC
Attendance: 1,000

"The Washington Pop Music Festival" is considered to be the first large-scale outdoor concert festival to feature rock and roll bands that was ever held in the Washington, D.C. area. It was presented by the National Park Service through its "Summer in the Parks" program, produced by Unlimited Projects Company, and organized by George Hauer. George Daly, formerly of the Hangmen, served as the event's master of ceremonies. This 10-hour outdoor festival, which predated "Woodstock" by a full year, was held at the P Street Beach near Dupont Circle and featured more than 20 local musical acts of various styles. Bands and musicians that performed at this event included: blues singers Mother Scott and John Jackson; the blues-folk band the Third World; the C&W group the Rounders; the folk band the Joe Latham Trio; folk singers Dawn Thompson, Pat Bernstein and Dave Wall; the jazz groups Bobbi Woods and Her Men, the Steve Nathan Quintet and Jambo; pop music pianist Jay Levy; the R&B act Bunky McCreary and the Expressions; rock and roll pianist John Guernsey; and the rock and roll bands the Fallen Angels, the Telstars, the Shot, the Dolphin, the Harrison Act and Today's Special.

THE LAUREL POP FESTIVAL
Friday, July 11 and Saturday, 12, 1969, 8pm
Laurel Race Course, 198 Laurel Race Track Road, Laurel, Maryland
In 1994 the facility was renamed Laurel Park
Attendance: 15,000

"The Laurel Pop Festival" was a two-day event held during the season of "Woodstock" at what was then called Laurel Race Course in Anne Arundel County, Maryland. The show was organized by a trio consisting of two Baltimore concert promoters, Elzie Street and James Scott, and large-scale festival promoter George Wein. Friday evening's advertised performers were Jethro Tull, Led Zeppelin, Al Kooper, the Edwin Hawkins Singers, Johnny Winter and Buddy Guy. Saturday's bill consisted of Jeff Beck, Ten Years After, the Guess Who, the Mothers of Invention, Sly and the Family Stone and the Savoy Brown Blues Band.

CARAVAN OF LOVE
Tuesday, August 25, 1970, 12pm
L'Enfant Square, 9th Street NW and Constitution Avenue NW, Washington, D.C.
Attendance: 8,000

In August 1970 more than 150 hippie freaks from San Francisco banded together, and, taking inspiration from American novelist Ken Kesey and His Merry Pranksters who had already done this sort of thing years prior, piled into a procession of buses and other vehicles and embarked on a tour of America, staging a series of free rock and roll concerts along the way. Warner Bros. funded the journey – basically a roadshow version of "Woodstock" – and filmed much of the ensuing action with the end result being the commercial feature film "Medicine Ball Caravan" (Warner Bros., 1971). When the oversized tribe hit the nation's capital, the resulting festival concert, "Caravan of Love," was staged on the grounds of L'Enfant Square near the Mall (not to be confused with L'Enfant Plaza) on a sweltering late August weekday afternoon. The show, scheduled for 12noon to 8pm, actually began at 2pm and ended at 9:40pm. The performing acts were (in order of appearance): Sageworth and Drums, folk singer-guitarist Mimi Farina, Asleep at the Wheel, Hot Tuna (featuring Washington, D.C. natives Jorma Kaukonen and Jack Casady), Stoneground and Alice Cooper. Details on the entire "Caravan of Love" adventure, including a chapter on this particular concert, are available in the book authored by John Grissim, Jr., "We Have Come for your Daughters: What Went Down on the Medicine Ball Caravan" (1972).

LIVESTOCK
Saturday, August 29, 1970, 11am
Fort Reno Park, 4000 Chesapeake Street NW, Washington, D.C.
Attendance: 500

During the summer of 1968 a Jesuit priest named Father George Dennis and members of the Tenleytown Neighborhood Planning Council No. 3 began staging rock and roll concerts in Fort Reno Park, a Civil War fort and park maintained by the National Park Service. The free shows became very popular despite a lack of sponsorship or advertising and are still being presented today. Focusing on younger, local talent, the 1970s concerts mainly featured blues bands and heavy, psychedelic rock and roll groups, while the 1980s events were driven by area punk and new wave bands. Late in the summer of 1970 Fort Reno Park was the site of "Livestock," one of many themed festivals that took place on its grounds through the years. That particular event featured the following local rock and roll outfits: Crank, Grin, Claude Jones, Fat City, Sageworth and Drums, Wayne Feeds, Sea and the East Utopian Mission and Renthra.

BERLIN AIRLIFT
Sunday, September 20, 1970, 3pm
Robert F. Kennedy Memorial Stadium, 2400 E. Capitol Street NE, Washington, D.C.
Attendance: 21,000

"Berlin Airlift" was a massive, six-hour rock and roll festival that was headlined by Grand Funk Railroad and included sets by Pacific Gas and Electric, the Allman Brothers Band, Crow, and two top local bands, Crank and Sageworth and Drums. The gates opened at 1:30pm and tickets were a whopping $6.50 each.

PART THREE
A PROCESSION OF CAPITOL ROCKERS

During the early era of rock and roll music – a period generally defined as the years 1951 to 1975 – there was a large number of bands and musicians performing this style on the teen dance and night club circuits in the Washington, D.C. area. Many of these artists faded before they reached their full potential, while others prospered through time and contributed to the region's rich musical heritage. The rock and roll landscape was vastly different back in those days: night clubs brought in ensembles to work "house band" engagements; bands and musicians secured managers and strived to sign record deals for the recording and release of 33rpm long-play records and 45rpm single records; and the Internet and music downloads were not yet a part of the overall popular music process. From this formative period emerged many bands and musicians who, in retrospect, were either seminal in nature with regards to the way they had influenced the evolution of local music, or had gone on to impact the national rock and roll scene in some manner – usually through major label record releases or significant work with renowned performing artists. Presented here are groups and individuals that started their musical careers at some point during this general period and in some manner helped advance the progress of the Washington, D.C. area's rock and roll scene.

The Bands and Musicians:
Abaad Behram, Adam Wenner, Andre Sokol, Andy Hamburger, Andy Rutherford, Angel, Ashwood, Aspex, Babe, Barry Darvell, Barry Hart, Barry Holober, Barry Seidel, the Beatnik Flies, Becky Woo, the Bedforde Set, Ben Mason, Benny Mardones, Big Al Downing, Big Boy Little, Big Joe Maher, Bill Caron, Bill Craig, Bill Holland and Rent's Due, Bill Starks, Bill Verrill, Billy Coulter, Billy Hancock, Billy Poore, Billy Woo, Blaine Smith, Blitz, Bo Diddley, Boa, Bob Berberich, Bob Brown, Bob Coleman, Bob Embrey, Bob Farris, Bob Mallardi, Bob McCoy, Bob Reilly, Bob Shade, Bobbie Howard, Bobby Jones, Bobby LaKind, Bobby Manriquez, Bobby Radcliff, Boyd Farrell, Brendan Pelan, Brent Woodall, Brian Wagner, Bud Harner, Butler's Orchard, Carl Anderson, Catfish Hodge, Cathy Ponton King, Charlie Burgee, Charlie Daniels, Cherry Smash, Chip Clemmer, Chris Noe, Chris Shaw, Christopher Zell, Chuck Bennett (Blonde Chuck or Clean Chuck), Chuck Bennett (Dirty Chuck), Chuck Sullivan, Chuck Underwood, Circus, Clarence Perry, Claude Jones, Clint Holmes, Conte Bellucci, the Country Gentlemen, Craig Thomas, Crank, the Crawling King Snake Blues Band, the Creatures, Crusader Rabbit, the Crystal Mesh, Curfew, Daddy Warbux, the Dagenites, Dan Hovey, Danny Denver, Danny Frankel, Danny Stellabotte, Daryl Cline, Daryl Davis, Dave Chappell, Dave Elliott, Dave Johnson, Dave Koplow, Dave Long, Dave Panzer, Dave Reynolds, Dave Sherman, Dave West, David Arnson, David Gabaldon, David Kitchen, David Lourim, David Platshon, David Simmons, Dawn's Dusk, DC Dog, the D.C. Magnatones, DC Star, Del Puschert, Demetri Callas, Dennis Monke, Deuce, Devil's Track, Dexter Dunn, Dick Heintze, Dick Moody, Dick Webb, Don Duvall, Don Monahan, Donal Leace, Donnie and the Diablos, Doug Tull, Drake Allen, the Dubonnettes, Duke Ayres, Ed Crowley, Ed Cynar, Eddie Becker, Eddie Day, Eddy Ottenstein, Ellwood Brown, Emmylou Harris, Eric Wilfong, Erich Seehafer, Eva Cassidy, Evan Johns, the Eye, the Fablons, the Fabulous Hubcaps, Face Dancer, Fireside, Flavor, Frank Dillon, Frank Radice, Frank Shegogue, Fred Jaeschke, Fritz Carney, Gantt Kushner, Gary St. Clair, George Dively, Gil Goldstein, God Mother Country, Green Eggs, Greg Hardin, Greg Pugliese, Gregg Karukas, Gregg Wright, Grin, Grits, Gui Bokoles, Guy Taylor, Hal Lindes, the Hall Brothers, Hank Burnett, Happy the Man, Harvey Nussbaum, Hawaii,

Henry Rollins, Hillow Hammet, Ian MacKaye, Ichabod Crane, Innocent Color, Irvin Utz, Jack Brooks, Jack Casady, Jan Zukowski, Jay Nedry, J.D. and the Jesters, Jeff Archer, Jeff Lodsun, Jerome Monroe, Jerry Mercer, Jim Cerone, Jim Colby, Jim Robeson, Jim Snidero, Jim Stephanson, Jimbo Manion, Jimmy Earl, Jimmy Eller and His Little People, Jimmy Marcos, Jimmy Nalley, Jimmy Nalls, Jimmy Robinson, Jimmy Thackery, Joe Bayliss, Joe Goulait, Joe Hasselvander, Joe Lagana, Joe Martone, Joe Ray Realité, Joe Roundtree, Joe Stanley, Joe Tass, John Fahey, John Guernsey, John Herbert, John Jennings, John Koslin, John Molloy, John Molo, John Previti, John Van Horn, the John Wells Delegation, John Whipple, Johnny Castle, Johnny Hopkins, Johnny Seaton, Johnny Tsakanikas, Jon Carroll, Jonathan Edwards, Jorge Strunz, Jorma Kaukonen, the Kalin Twins, Kangaroo, Keith Grimes, Keith John, Ken Briley, Ken Fiester, Kim Kane, Kim Tsoy, Kurt Gibbons, Lance Quinn, Larry Burnett, Larry Rice, Lawrence Green, Lee Dorman, Les Hatley, Linwood Taylor, Liz Meyer, Louie Newmyer, Love Cry Want, the Mad Hatters, the Mad River Blues Band, the Magic Reign, Malcolm Lukens, the March of Time, Marianna Previti, Mark Francis Nickens, Mark Noone, Mark Stutso, Mark Wenner, Marshall Keith, Martha Hull, Marty Friedman, Mary Blankemeier, the Marylanders, Matt Abts, Max Navarro, the Medallions, the Memories, Michael Fath, Michael Smith, Michael Tash, Michael Walls, the Midnight Marauders, Mike Colburn, Mike Hurney, Mike Johnstone, Mike Mautino, Mike Melchione, Mike Persh, Mike Pirko, Mike Reidy, Mike Stern, Mike Toole, Mike Tramonte, Mike Valenti, Mike Weber, Mike Zack, the Mosaic Virus, the Muffins, Murray Schaff's Aristocrats, the Mydnight Sonn, Natty Bumpo, the Naturals, the Nighthawks, Nightman, Nils Lofgren, Nobody's Children, the North Star Band, the Off Beats, the Omegas, Original Fetish, Overkill, Patsy Stephens, Patty Reese, Paul Bell, Paul Goldstein, Paul Jones, Paul Mastradone, Paul Reed Smith, Paul Sears, Pedro Sera, Pegasus, Pentagram, the Peppermint Stix, the Perry Mates, the Personalities, Pete Kennedy, Pete Ragusa, Pete Van Allen, Peter Bonta, Phil Flowers, Phil Mathieu, Phil McCormack, Phil Wahle, Philip Shimmel, Pierre Beauregard, the Profiles, Punky Meadows, Puzzle, Randy Hart, Ratso, Ray Lombardo, Ray Rock, Ray Tilkens, Razz, the Reachers, the Reasons Why, the Reekers, the Renegades, the Resumes, Rich Eckhardt, Richard X. Heyman, Richard Tipton, Richie Mitchell, Rick Benick, Rick Berberich, Rick Davis, Rick Ransom, Rick Thompson, Ricky Rohme, Rico Petruccelli, Ritchie Burns, the Roadducks, Rob Duprey, Rob Petrie, Robbie Magruder, Robert Fiester, Robert Gordon, the Rockin' Rejects, Rocky Isaac, Roger Edsall, Rolf Hanson, Ron Bushy, Ron Culbertson, Ron Fetner, Ron Holloway, Ron MacDonald, Ron Newmyer, Ron Widman, Root Boy Slim, the Rosslyn Mountain Boys, Ruth Newton, Ruthie Logsdon, Sageworth and Drums, Sam Paladino, Sammy Blair, Sane Day, Scott McKnight, Scott Weinrich, Second Coming, the Seldom Scene, Seth Justman, Shep Tullier, Silverspring, Sinbad, Sky Cobb, the Slickee Boys, Sonny Gordon, the Soul Mates, Spats, Spring Fever, Stan Weinberg, Starland Vocal Band, Stephen Geyer, Steuart Smith, Steve Bishop, Steve Carey, Steve Hatfield, Steve Jacobs, Steve Lacey, Steve Long, Steve Spurling, Steve Wolf, Stevie Sparks, Stock Wilson, Susan Jones, the Sweet, Switchblade, T.C. Tolliver, Tears, the Tejuns, the Telstars, Terry Gleason, Terry Jones, Terry Plumeri, Tex Rubinowitz, Three Easy Pieces, the Three Jacks, the Three of Us Trio, the Tikis, Tim Eyermann, Tim Rose, Tim Wynne, Timm Biery, Tinsel'd Sin, Tiny McCloud, Tod Cornett, Tom Jones, Tom Maynard, Tom McCarthy, Tom Principato, Tommy Auldridge, Tommy Haughawout, Tommy Keene, Tommy Lepson, Tommy Panella, Tony Denikos, Tony Grasso, Tony Jordan, Tractor, the Triumphs, Tuesday Boots, Urban Verbs, the Velours, Vince Santoro, Vince Vigliotti, Wade Matthews, Wade Richards, Wally Cook, Wayne Tomlinson, Whitewater, Wild Honey, the Winstons, and Wolf Crescenze.

ABAAD BEHRAM

Guitarist Abaad Behram was born in India and raised in Arlington, Virginia. In the early 1970s while attending Washington-Lee High School he played in a rock and roll band called Sway that specialized in Rolling Stones covers. In 1972 Behram was called upon to play in the hard-rocking band Razz, whose lineup at the time was rounded out by singer Mike Reidy, guitarist Bill Craig, bassist Ted Nicely and drummer Pete Ragusa. He remained with Razz until May 1978, playing with them through their heyday as house band at the Keg and Varsity Grill Back Room.

Behram next took a position as lead guitarist in the band Artful Dodger, a group from Fairfax, Virginia that had previously recorded for Columbia Records. Behram went on to spend much of the 1980s playing for the Smash Band and during the late 1980s and into the 1990s played in Johnny Bombay and the Reactions, a band that included former Razz members Bill Craig and Doug Tull. He has since been active in several Razz reunions and more recently was a member of a band called the Howling Mad, which consisted of former Razz members Mike Reidy, Bill Craig, Doug Tull and a succession of bass players.

ADAM WENNER

Saxophonist Adam Wenner grew up in Chevy Chase, Maryland and as a teenager in the late 1960s played the local teen dance scene in such bands as the Showmen and the Midnighters. In the late 1970s and early 1980s he occasionally sat in with the Nighthawks, of which is brother Mark Wenner was founding father. Later, in the 1990s, Wenner spent time playing saxophone for Butch Grant and Crossfire at such Washington, D.C. night clubs as the Round Table on Wisconsin Avenue NW and the Saloon in Georgetown.

ANDRE SOKOL

Bassist Andre Sokol spent much of his youth living in Southeast Washington, D.C. before moving out to Oxon Hill, Maryland as a teenager in the late 1960s. He learned the bass guitar by watching his older brother practice in the family's basement and during his years at Oxon Hill High School in the early 1970s he played in such hard-rocking bands as Powerhouse, Earth and Hailstone. During this time, Sokol would often venture to Georgetown and watch the Cherry People perform at the Silver Dollar and actually sat in with the band on several occasions when Jan Zukowski would take a break.

After finishing high school in 1972 Sokol spent a year in Michigan, where he played in an R&B band called Billy Cox's Nitro Function featuring Char – the Electric Lady (Char Vinnedge). Upon returning to the Washington, D.C. area Sokol played bass in the Moon Band before joining the Cherry People in the fall of 1973, a group that was still considered to be one of the best rock and roll bands in the Washington, D.C. area, but was then undergoing a major transformation in personnel.

For much of Sokol's tenure with the Cherry People the band's lineup also included lead singer Doug Grimes, lead guitarist Rick Benick, rhythm guitarist Chris Grimes and drummer Barry Brandt. He remained with the group until its demise in June 1975. Sokol went on to play bass in such rock and roll bands as the Paul Spence Band, Merlin, Sex, the Michael Fath Group and Escape.

ANDY HAMBURGER

Drummer Andy Hamburger was born in Baltimore, Maryland and moved to Silver Spring as a teenager in the middle 1960s. He had taken up drumming in his pre-teen years and was inspired by the likes of the Beatles, the Rolling Stones, Led Zeppelin, Alice Cooper and jazz drummers such as Buddy Rich and Louie Bellson. As a teenager at John F. Kennedy High School in Silver Spring in the late 1970s he drummed for a theatrical touring company called the Young Columbians. He then studied jazz percussion at the University of Maryland and continued performing in live settings for plays, theatrical presentations and dinner theatre programs.

In the early 1980s Hamburger began playing with rock and roll bands throughout the Washington, D.C. area and since that time his music career has seen him perform with a vast assortment of performing artists of almost every imaginable style from blues to jazz to rock. For years he has been one of the region's most sought-after session drummers for recordings, studio productions, commercials, jingles, films and movie trailers.

Some of the rock and roll bands Hamburger drummed for in the 1980s included the Third Degree, the False Alarm, and Out of the Dark. During that decade he also worked with: blues singer-pianist Mary Blankemeier; the jazz band Al Williams and Friends; the R&B group Downtown (now known as Jeff Watson and Downtown Band); and R&B singer Julia Nixon.

Since the 1990s some of the musical artists Hamburger has drummed for include: blues performers such as singers Little Margie Clark and Nadine Rae, singer-guitarist Cathy Ponton King and singer-harmonicist Anthony "Swamp Dog" Clark; the blues-jazz band the Natty Beaux; C&W singer-guitarist Randy Thompson; folk singer-guitarists Russ Glenn and Robbie Schaefer; jazz singer Barbara Gracewood, saxophonist Jacques "Saxman" Johnson, and the bands Tim Eyermann and East Coast Offering and Jazz on L; the pop group Classified Frequency; pop-jazz singer-guitarist Mary Fagan; pop-rock singer-guitarist Patty Reese; R&B singers Mary Ann Redmond and Julia Nixon; the R&B band the Junkyard Saints; rock singer-guitarist John Palumbo; rock singer-bassist Holly Montgomery; rock and roll bands such as Vulture, the Michael Sheppard Group, Op-Critical, Side FX and Big Cam and the Lifters; and the world beat music outfit Wynne Paris and Groovananda.

Hamburger has also toured and performed with such national R&B acts as singer Chick Willis, the Platters, the Coasters, the Drifters, the Marvelettes, the Temptations, the Ink Spots, Harold Melvin's Blue Notes, and Peaches and Herb. He is currently drumming for one of the region's most highly regarded blues groups, the Big Boy Little Band.

ANDY RUTHERFORD

Guitarist Andy Rutherford was born in St. Louis, Missouri and moved to Lorton, Virginia in 1966 at the age of six. He started singing and playing guitar two years later, with his earliest influences being the Beatles, the Monkees and other pop and rock and roll bands. During his high school years at Hayfield High School in Alexandria in the 1970s he spent four years in the school's jazz band while jamming with friends at parties and sessions to the songs of Aerosmith, Bad Company, Led Zeppelin and Yes.

Rutherford attended the University of Virginia in the late 1970s and early 1980s and earned a Bachelor of Science in computer science. While there he played lead guitar in such rock and roll bands as the Chameleons, Yon Youn Son and the Mechanix, and Redline. He returned to the Washington, D.C. area in 1984 and for the remainder of the decade played in a succession of rock and roll bands including Hank Burnett and Exit, the Incident, Athena and the Virgins, and the Shivers.

In the 1990s Rutherford was in demand as a guitarist and some of the bands he performed with included a wedding band called Evergreen, Ingus (a rock and roll band that backed up Douglas "Greaseman" Tracht), and a country-rockabilly group called the Coolerators. More recently he has played guitar for such acts as: blues singer-guitarist Cathy Ponton King; the blues band Sookey Jump; the blues-jazz group the Natty Beaux; the Cajun band Zydeco Crayz; the C&W bands Mary Battitia and Little Pink and J.P. McDermott and Western Bop; and the rockabilly act the Thrillbillys. He has also performed onstage with such artists as rockabilly singer-guitarist Bill Kirchen and the rock and roll instrumental band Los Straightjackets.

In 2008 Rutherford began subbing on guitar with the C&W band Ruthie and the Wranglers and became a full-time member in 2011. He is still performing with that band today and also remains a mainstay in the Thrillbillys.

ANGEL

The roots of Washington, D.C.'s first glam rock band, Angel, go back to a hard-rocking quintet from Boston called Daddy Warbux. That particular group landed in the nation's capital in September 1974 at a night club called Bogie's which was located on the second floor of the building at 1214 Connecticut Avenue NW. When the band hit the nation's capital, its personnel included two former Cherry People members, guitarist Punky Meadows and bassist Mickie Jones. Daddy Warbux began to splinter and Meadows and Jones began rehearsing different musicians at Bogie's for future musical projects. In December 1974 the pair changed the name of their band-in-progress to Foxie, with rehearsals at Bogie's continuing into early 1975.

In April 1975 Foxie became Angel with a new lineup of Punky Meadows, Mickie Jones, lead singer Frank DiMino (from Revere, Massachusetts), keyboard player Gregg Giuffria (from Biloxi, Mississippi) and drummer Barry Brandt (another former member of the Cherry People). After showcasing at Bogie's for several more weeks, the band signed with Casablanca Records and went on to release six albums for the label from 1975 to 1980: "Angel" (1975), "Helluva Band" (1976), "On Earth as It Is in Heaven" (1977), "White Hot" (1978), "Sinful" (1979) and "Live Without a Net" (1980).

After its third album, Angel brought in bassist Felix Robinson to replace Mickie Jones. A St. Louis native, Robinson had previously played with several groups in the Midwest including a 1971 to 1973 stint with Bob Kuban and the In-Men. Angel disbanded in 1982, but in recent years Frank DiMino and Barry Brandt have reformed the band on several occasions with different musicians.

ASHWOOD

Ashwood was a hard-rocking band of the early 1970s that based out of Camp Springs, Maryland. They formed from the remnants of another rock and roll band from the area called Saturn, whose ever-changing lineup had included such musicians as singer Bill McGunigal, singer-guitarist Frankie Clark, guitarist Ron Thomasson (who had replaced Clark), saxophonist Jim Snidero, several bassists including Phil Chappell, Mark Liebe and Steve Shoap, and drummer Mark Newcastle.

In 1974 Saturn disbanded and Ashwood was formed with an initial lineup of singer-lead guitarist Frankie Clark, rhythm guitarist Ron Thomasson, bassist Steve Shoap and drummer Mark Newcastle. Three of the band members had attended Crossland High School in Camp Springs, while Shoap had gone to Surrattsville High School in Clinton. The band rehearsed at Newcastle's house in Camp Springs and mixed originals with covers of songs by Aerosmith, Blue Oyster Cult, Deep Purple, Eric Clapton, Kiss, Free, Led Zeppelin, Black Sabbath and Grand Funk Railroad, among others.

Ashwood worked a variety of events and venues during its time including: private parties; teen dances at Surrattsville High School (Clinton) and Church of St. John the Evangelist Parish (Clinton); night clubs such as Jimmy's Fireplace (Waldorf) and the Stardust Inn (Waldorf); and engagements at the Andrews Air Force Base Officers' Club (Prince George's County, Maryland), the National Naval Medical Center Officer's Club (at the time the facility was informally known as the Bethesda Naval Hospital; today it is officially called the Walter Reed National Military Medical Center), and Congressional

Country Club (Bethesda). The band dissolved in 1977, with singer-guitarist Frankie Clark going on to front his own popular rock and roll band, Frankie and the Actions.

ASPEX

Aspex was one of the more talented and versatile rock and roll bands to emerge from the Washington, D.C. area in the 1970s, offering a variety of rock and roll and R&B material as they advanced beyond the local music scene and toured night clubs from Virginia to Florida. The band formed in the summer of 1976 in Oxon Hill, Maryland with the original lineup consisting of lead singer-keyboardist Ricky Chrismer, guitarist Mike Miller, guitarist Charley Bass, bassist Ron Chrismer, drummer Rodney Chrismer and percussionist Mike Brown. The group experienced a round of personnel changes during its time, with drummer Vince Galeano replacing Rodney Chrismer, Mike Brown departing, and Ivan Silva joining as lead singer. Silva soon departed and in late 1977 when the band moved on as a quintet, Ricky Chrismer and Charley Bass began sharing the lead vocal duties.

In terms of musical material, Aspex started out playing contemporary rock and roll, covering such bands as the Beatles, Led Zeppelin, Bruce Springsteen and Frank Zappa. With the addition of Ivan Silva, the group expanded their sound and added in songs by Aerosmith, Bad Company, the Eagles, Steely Dan, Kansas, the Rolling Stones, and even covered Root Boy Slim's, "Mood Ring." They worked such area night clubs as the Varsity Grill Back Room (College Park), the Paragon (College Park), Frankie and Freddie's (Hyattsville), the Crazy Horse (Washington, D.C.), Louie's Rock City (Bailey's Crossroads) and worked a long house band engagement at Some Place Else in Southeast Washington, D.C. The band also performed several times on the University of Maryland's College Park campus including concerts at the Grand Ballroom and Ritchie Coliseum.

Aspex often performed outside the immediate area at Pier 7 (Annapolis), the Library (Annapolis), Garfield's (Arlington), the Fancy Dancer (Alexandria), the Waldorf Inn (Waldorf), Reb's Fireplace (Waldorf), the Country Castle (Waldorf), the Leonardtown Wharf (Leonardtown) and the Dungeon (Ocean City). They also embarked on regional tours up and down the Atlantic Coast, performing at the China Garden (Dover, Delaware), the Wing Ding (Norfolk, Virginia), Big Daddy's (Jacksonville, Florida) and the Looking Glass Lounge (Fort Myers, Florida), where they once opened two shows in the summer of 1977 for the band Cactus. Aspex remained atop the local rock and roll scene through 1979.

BABE

Babe emerged in August 1968 out of the remnants of an Annapolis, Maryland-based teen rock and roll band called the Dead Beats. The group's original lineup consisted of lead singer-bassist Bob Coleman, singer-keyboardist Mitch Collins, guitarist Ed Eastridge (all graduates of Annapolis High School) and drummer Wayne Jordan (who resided in the Ardmore community of Prince George's County and had graduated from DuVal High School). Shortly after its formation the band relocated to Washington, D.C. and its first performances in the nation's capital were at a night club called Victoria Station, which was then-located in the basement of the Stratford Hotel (25 E Street NW).

Babe spent the late 1960s mixing original material with Top 40 covers at such city night clubs as Sam's Place (formerly the Brown Derby on Connecticut Avenue NW), both Chadwick's restaurants (3205 K Street NW in Georgetown and 319 Pennsylvania Avenue SE in Capitol Hill), the Showboat Lounge in Adams Morgan, and the Garage (1122 18th Street NW). In 1969 Jeff Lodsun replaced drummer Wayne Jordan and the band entered a long run as the house band at Mr. Henry's Tenley Circle (4323 Wisconsin Avenue NW) that stretched throughout the early 1970s. At the time they covered such bands as the Beatles, the Rolling Stones, CSN&Y, the Steve Miller Band and Frank Zappa. Babe eventually began adding more R&B material to its sets, with Chuck Berry becoming a favored artist.

During the early 1970s Babe also performed at such Washington, D.C. night clubs as JamF, the Cellar Door, My Mother's Place, the Reading Gaol, Cousin Nick's, and, in 1974, the Childe Harold. In 1975 Babe underwent a major transformation, with holdovers Coleman, Eastridge and Collins being joined by two former members of Barrelhouse – guitarist Steuart Smith and drummer Steve Dennis. This version of the group primarily performed R&B covers and worked extensively at the Childe Harold for several years.

Babe experienced one last round of changes in personnel in 1977 with Collins, Smith and Dennis being joined by bassist Michael Maye and lead singer Kathe Russell, formerly of Gravity. They remained a top band on the local night club scene, performing at Mr. Henry's Tenley Circle (Washington, D.C.), Timothy's Pub (Rockville) and Fred and Sully's (Wheaton). Babe ultimately disbanded in 1978. During its time, the group recorded and released two singles: "Phoebe" backed with "Why is the Sky" (Babe; Unicorn Records, 1969); and "Smile Again" backed with "It's a Long Road" (Babe; Aladdin Records, 1974).

BARRY DARVELL

Born Barry Peregoy, this rock and roll singer spent his teen years in Alexandria, Virginia and graduated mid-year from George Washington High School in December 1960. During his time in high school he assumed the stage name "Barry Darvell" and fronted a group entitled Barry and the Blazers that performed on the Northern Virginia teen dance circuit and was a particular favorite at such Alexandria locations as the Franconia Volunteer Fire Department, the Fraternal Order of Eagles and the B.P.O. Elks Lodge No. 758 Alexandria.

While still in high school, Darvell signed with local independent record company Colt 45 Records and in 1959 and 1960 performed as a solo act at such Washington, D.C. night clubs as the Parkside Café and Benny's Rebel Room, as well as the Las Vegas Club on Marlboro Pike in Coral Hills, Maryland. He also enjoyed a long residency in the city at the Rocket Room on New York Avenue NW, performing there on a regular basis from 1961 to 1963. During his time at the Rocket Room he was a featured recording artist for Atlantic Records, one of the industry's major record labels.

Barry Darvell left the rock and roll world behind in 1967 and subsequently concentrated on a career in real estate. He released numerous 45rpm single records during his time including: "How Will It End?" backed with "Geronimo Stomp" (Barry Darvell; Colt 45 Records, 1959); "Teenage Love" backed with "Geronimo Stomp" (Barry Darvell and the Blazers; Colt 45 Records, 1959); "Butterfly Baby" backed with "Send Me Some Loving" (Barry Darvell; Colt 45 Records, 1960); "Little Angel Lost" backed with "Fountain of Love" (Barry Darvell; Cub Records, 1961); "Lost Love" backed with "Silver Dollar" (Barry Darvell; Atlantic Records, 1961); "A King for Tonight" backed with "Adam and Eve" (Barry Darvell; Atlantic Records, 1962); "Seek and You Will Find" backed with "You Can Have Her" (Barry Darvell; Colt 45 Records, 1962); "Run Little Billy" backed with "All I Need is You" (Barry Darvell; Atlantic Records, 1963); and "When You're Alone" backed with "It's Rainin', It's Pourin'" (Barry Darvell; Providence Records, 1964).

BARRY HART

Hailing from Oxon Hill, Maryland, Barry Hart entered the world of professional music during his teen years at Oxon Hill High School in the middle 1960s and is noted for his long tenure as drummer for the great multi-styled guitarist Danny Gatton. Hart is a master of many styles and has performed with an impressive array of bands and musicians including: the blues band Moonshine Society; the blues-jazz bands the J Street Jumpers, and David Wright and the Wright Touch; the blues rock group the Dave Chappell Band; the jazz acts the Tommy Dorsey Orchestra, Bob Hope's Orchestra, Cab Calloway's Orchestra and Steve Wolf and Swing Speak; jazz guitarist Rick Whitehead; R&B singer Lou Rawls; and R&B acts the Ink Spots, the Drifters and the Ron Holloway Band.

BARRY HOLOBER

Drummer Barry Holober grew up in Prince George's County, Maryland in the city of Hyattsville and the town of Riverdale and began playing drums at the age of five. His father played piano and kept a variety of instruments in the basement of their Hyattsville home, where Holober discovered a drum set and began playing along with Benny Goodman records. During his years at Parkdale High School in the late 1960s he played the local military officers' club circuit in a Top 40 rock and roll band called the Graduates with former Natty Bumpo guitarist Dee Clay and a revolving cast of musicians.

In 1970 Holober joined a 13-piece R&B band called the Ovations and remained their drummer for approximately one year. Over the next few years he played in several bands including the Bill Black Combo, a quartet which covered the Top 40 hits of the day and was rounded out by singer-guitarist Dee Clay, singer-bassist Aaron Ellison and saxophonist Joe Stanley; and a Southern Maryland-based Top 40 band called Critical Point, which consisted of singer-keyboardist Doug Gwin, guitarist Coe Anderson, bassist John Gwin, singer-saxophonist Joe DeFelice and Holober on drums. In 1972 Holober joined a Northern Virginia-based progressive rock band called Lyceum, a quartet whose lineup also included lead singer-guitarist Tim Tanner, bassist Fred Crittenden and saxophonist Bobby Reid.

In 1974 the popular rock and roll band Cherry Smash was undergoing a transformation and absorbed the entire Lyceum group. The new Cherry Smash lineup consisted of Brent Woodall, Doug Allen, Tim Tanner, Fred Crittenden, Bobby Reid and Holober. That rendition of the band performed in Washington, D.C. at the Crazy Horse, the Keg, and the Act IV Supper Club before becoming one of the house bands at the Bayou in Georgetown. Holober remained with Cherry Smash through 1979.

After leaving Cherry Smash, Holober drummed for an Annapolis-based group called the Band of a Thousand Names, which included lead singer-bassist Carey Ziegler, guitarist Paul Reed Smith and keyboardist Russell Stone. In 1981 he received a call from Coe Anderson to sit in for the ailing drummer of the Hubcaps. He fit the group so well he was soon offered a full-time position in the band and has remained their drummer ever since.

BARRY SEIDEL

Rock and roll singer Barry Seidel grew up in Northern Virginia and during the early 1960s he regularly performed (often times as Barry Seidel and the Sellouts) at such Washington, D.C. night clubs as Benny's Rebel Room, the Hayloft, the Rocket Room, the Crazy Horse, and Captain Guy's. During his career he recorded and released several 45rpm single records including: "Too Late" backed with "I Know Loneliness" (Barry Seidel; Florentine Records, 1961); "Did You Hear" backed with "Through the Looking Glass" (Barry Seidel; Dayhill Records, 1962); and "Wonders of Love" backed with "It Happens Every Time" (Barry Seidel; Belinda Records, 1962). During the late 1960s he managed several Georgetown-based rock and roll bands including the Reachers, the Telstars, the Fallen Angels and the Mad Hatters.

THE BEATNIK FLIES

The story of the Beatnik Flies begins with singer-guitarist Joe Dolan, who grew up in Bethesda, Maryland, and, while attending Pyle Junior High School in the middle 1960s, drummed in such rock and roll bands as the Rat Finks and Blue Diamond. Later in the decade during his time at Walt Whitman High School he switched to guitar and played in a rock and roll band called the Miss Fay's Neighbors. In the middle 1970s he put together a trio with neighborhood friends Ken Bugg on bass and Larry Fornia on drums and began informally playing folk music at parties and local coffee houses such as the Iguana Coffeehouse, which was located in the basement of Luther Place Memorial Church in Washington, D.C. During this period they also made their night club debut when they performed at a "Hootenanny" at the Cellar Door in Georgetown.

In 1977 the three musicians were given a copy of New York Rocker, a contemporary rock and roll magazine from Manhattan that ran a pictorial on the burgeoning punk rock scene that was taking shape in New York City. Although unaware of what the music actually sounded like, they decided to put aside the folk style and morph into a punk rock band, thus marking the beginning of the Beatnik Flies. Dolan, Bugg and Fornia took a while before they attempted to play their new style of music in public, first performing as a trio at the "New Wave Night" Monday evening sessions at One Flight Up (4934 Wisconsin Avenue NW, Washington, D.C.) in 1981. Personnel changes ensued, with drummer Drew Vogelman replacing Larry Fornia. In 1982 the band added a fourth piece in lead guitarist Joe Stone. Later on they replaced Vogelman with drummer Britt Conley, who remained with the band for 22 years.

The Beatnik Flies were one of the top attractions on the Washington, D.C. area rock and roll scene of the 1980s and 1990s, blurring distinction between the musical styles of punk, psychedelia, new wave and hard rock and roll. Among the band's favorite stops during these years were such area night clubs as D.C. Space, the Psyche Delly, Nightclub 9:30, Desperado's, Columbia Station, Friendship Station and the Gentry.

The band has four albums to its credit: "From Parts Unknown" (The Beatnik Flies; Dacoit Records, 1985); "Behind These Walls" (The Beatnik Flies; New Rose Records, 1988); "PsychoMetalPop: The Lost Cause of the Beatnik Flies" (The Beatnik Flies; Dacoit Records, 2001); and "Drunk on Incense" (The Beatnik Flies; Beatscene Records, 2007). The Beatnik Flies are still together today with a lineup of singer-guitarist Joe Dolan, lead guitarist Joe Stone, bassist Ken Bugg and drummer Bidjje Kavanaugh.

BECKY WOO

Born Becky Rice in Clinton, Massachusetts, this popular music singer moved to Takoma Park, Maryland as a teenager and joined up with the Sound of Peace, a musical youth witness group associated with Columbia Union College and the Seventh Day Adventist Church that performed at youth conferences up and down the East Coast in the early 1970s. From there she auditioned for – and was granted – the lead vocalist position in the local rock and roll band Sauce, performing with the group in the late 1970s. Rice went on to sing in several other Washington, D.C. area popular music groups including Sweetwater, MacArthur Park, Sky King and Fallen Angel.

In 1979 Becky Rice moved to Los Angeles, California and married singer-guitarist Billy Woo. She then began co-writing and recording music for feature-length motion pictures, including a number of films produced by Roger Corman, Fred Olen Raye and Dan Golden. Some of the movies that contain songs she composed and/or sang include "Uncaged" (Concorde-New Horizons, 1991); "Kiss Me a Killer (Concorde-New Horizons, 1991); "Dance With Death" (Concorde-New Horizons, 1992); "Bloodfist V: Human Target" (Concorde-New Horizons, 1994); and, more recently, "Bikini Jones and the Temple of Eros" (Retromedia Entertainment, 2010) and "Supershark" (BoomGates, 2011). Becky Woo is currently serving as a studio singer at Jade Dragon Studio in West Los Angeles, California and performs with her husband Billy Woo in the band Bronco Billy.

THE BEDFORDE SET

The Bedforde Set was a British Invasion-styled rock and roll outfit based in Silver Spring, Maryland that was a featured attraction on the area's teen dance scene from 1965 to 1969. Forming from the remnants of a band called the Jaguars, the group's initial lineup consisted of four musicians from the cities of Rockville and Silver Spring in Montgomery County, Maryland: lead guitarist Bill Singer (Walter Johnson High School, Class of 1962); lead singer-bassist Norm Bull (Robert E. Peary High School, Class of 1966); keyboardist Louie Miller (Northwood High School, Class of 1965); and drummer Steve Schein (Northwood High School, Class of 1965). The band also performed at times as "The New Bedforde Set."

The Bedforde Set performed most of the top pop and rock and roll hits of the 1960s, with an emphasis on the English sound. Among the many groups they covered were the Beatles, the Rolling Stones, the Kinks, the Hollies, the Yardbirds, Procol Harum, Cream, the Jimi Hendrix Experience, the Monkees, the Young Rascals, the Beach Boys, Buffalo Springfield, Jefferson Airplane, the Association, Paul Revere and the Raiders, the Temptations and Otis Redding.

The Bedforde Set performed at events all over the region including teen dances at the Silver Spring Boys Club (Silver Spring), the Forest Glen Teen Club (Silver Spring), the Sligo Park Teen Club (Silver Spring), St. Andrew's Episcopal Church Teen Club (Arlington), Northwood High School (Silver Spring), Montgomery Blair High School (Silver Spring), Walter Johnson High School (Bethesda), Albert Einstein High School (Kensington), George C. Marshall High School (Falls Church) and T.C. Williams High School (Alexandria), among others.

The band was also booked into the hotel ball circuit which included dates in Washington, D.C. at the Ambassador Hotel, the Shoreham Hotel, the Annapolis Hotel, the Willard Hotel and the Cosmos Club. In addition, the band worked private parties at facilities in Montgomery County such as the Brooke Manor Country Club (Olney), the Blair Mansion Inn (Silver Spring), the Shady Grove Country Club (Gaithersburg), the Woodmont Country Club (Rockville), the Congressional Country Club (Bethesda) and the Chevy Chase Country Club (Chevy Chase). The group regularly headlined dances at local colleges such as American University, George Washington University, Georgetown University, the University of Maryland, Gallaudet University and the United States Naval Academy.

One of the Bedforde Set's most exciting moments occurred when they opened up for the Beach Boys at the District of Columbia National Guard Armory in Washington, D.C. on Sunday, September 9, 1965 (also on the undercard were El Corals and Little Wimpy). The band released two 45rpm single records during its time, the first as a backup group and the second as featured artists: "Little Girl" backed with "Oh Don't You Know" (Ronnie Dean & His Bedford Set; Dean Records, 1965); and "The World Through a Tear" backed with "Girl, Go Run Away" (Bedforde Set; RCA Victor Records, 1967). They made an appearance in 1967 on the local music television show "Wing Ding" and spent time in the late 1960s touring night clubs from Massachusetts to Florida in support of their singles. The Bedforde Set disbanded in the summer of 1969.

BEN MASON

Multi-instrumentalist Ben Mason was raised in Annandale, Virginia, where, as a teenager during the middle 1960s, he first drummed for a rock and roll band called the Infernos that worked the local teen dance scene. At age 16 in 1967 while attending Annandale High School he joined the John Wells Delegation, a quartet that mixed the British Invasion sound with folk rock. During his 10-year tenure with the band, the John Wells Delegation became one of the region's most popular groups, working extended engagements at such establishments as the Lancer Restaurant (Bethesda) and numerous night clubs in Washington, D.C. including the Zodiac, Apple Pie, the Act IV Supper Club, Mr. Henry's Tenley Circle and Fat Howard's.

In the late 1970s and into the early 1980s Mason drummed for Primadonna, a rock and roll band that headlined at such local night spots as the Bayou, the Crazy Horse and the Varsity Grill Back Room. Primadonna also performed in night clubs up and down the Atlantic Coast from New York to Florida.

In 1981 Mason switched gears and embarked on a solo career as a singer-pianist. Through the years he has headlined at such local venues as the Cellar Door, the Birchmere, Jammin' Java, Gypsy Sally's, Villain and Saint, and the Kennedy Center. On Friday, June 20, 2014, Mason was the solo opening act at Jiffy Lube Live in Bristow, Virginia on a concert featuring Styx, Foreigner and Don Felder.

To date, Mason has four solo pop-rock albums to his credit: "River Deep in Me" (Ben Mason; Masonic Music, 1989); "48 States of Love" (Ben Mason; Masonic Music, 2004); "Loveland" (Ben Mason; Masonic Music, 2009); and "Flesh and Bone" (Ben Mason; Masonic Music, 2018).

BENNY MARDONES

Benny Mardones was born in Cleveland, Ohio, raised in the Howard County community of Savage, Maryland, and graduated from Howard High School in Ellicott City in 1964. After a stint in the United States Navy he gravitated toward the Washington, D.C. rock and roll scene.

In 1970 Mardones approached the band Boa while they were performing at Nu-Mac's in Georgetown and asked if he could become their lead vocalist. Shortly after joining the group, they changed their name to Troy, and Mardones, as one of two lead singers in the band, assumed the stage name Benny Troy. Basing out of Silver Spring, Maryland, Troy's lineup consisted of singers Benny Troy and Danny Goers, guitarist Dave Alexander, bassist Dale Marcks, keyboardist John Macuci and drummer Ronnie Fulkersin.

Troy based out of a night club called My Mother's Place at 18th and M Streets NW in Washington, D.C. for most of 1970 and into 1971. They also ventured into the area's teen dance territory, performing at such venues as the Tucker Road Community Center (Fort Washington), and gave performances at a variety of USO shows at area military bases and installations such as Walter Reed Army Medical Center. Troy's repertoire consisted of originals and covers of such artists as Ten Years After, Three Dog Night, Traffic, Joe Cocker and others of that vein. The band released one single: "Stand and Be Counted" backed with "Then Go" (Troy; White Whale Records, 1970).

After Troy disbanded in 1971, Mardones went to New York City, embarked on a solo career as a pop singer, and eventually signed with Polydor Records. He scored with one major hit single, "Into the Night" (Benny Mardones; Polydor Records, 1980), which peaked at number 11 on the "Billboard Hot 100" pop music chart on Saturday, September 6, 1980. It was rerecorded and rereleased and then charted again as "Into the Night" (Benny Mardones; Curb Records, 1989), reaching number 20 on the "Billboard Hot 100" chart on Saturday, July 1, 1989. That particular song rates as one of only 10 singles in Billboard history to make their pop music chart on two separate occasions.

BIG AL DOWNING

A singer-pianist from Lenapah, Oklahoma, Al Downing is unique in that he is one of the very few Black performing artists to gain fame in the field of C&W music. While a favorite of country music fans around the world, his career saw him perform almost every known popular musical style.

As a teenager in the late 1950s Downing moved to Coffeyville, Kansas and became an early member of Bobby Poe and the Poe Kats, a rock and roll band that included guitarist Vernon Sandusky. The group toured as the backup band to rockabilly singer Wanda Jackson and Downing played piano on her single "Let's Have a Party" (Wanda Jackson; Capitol Records, 1960), which peaked at number 37 on "The Billboard Hot 100" pop music chart on Monday, October 10, 1960.

In 1960 Downing relocated to Washington, D.C. with Poe and Sandusky and became the headlining solo performer at Rand's Night Club in the heart of Downtown Washington, D.C. For four years he played a mix of rockabilly and rock and roll until his backup band, which included guitarist Vernon Sandusky, left him behind in 1964 and evolved into the Chartbusters. Downing then put together a new backup band and went in a stronger R&B direction, remaining at Rand's Night Club throughout the remainder of the decade.

In the late 1970s Downing returned to his roots and concentrated on performing C&W material, signing with Warner Bros. Records in 1978 and scoring with three Top 20 country hit songs during an 11-year association. During his long and colorful career, Downing recorded albums and singles for more than two-dozen different record labels.

In 1974 Downing scored with the disco single "I'll Be Holding On" (Al Downing; Chess Records, 1974), which peaked at number one on Billboard's "Disco Action – By Audience Response" disco music chart on Saturday, December 28, 1974. During his time with Warner Bros. Records, his highest charting C&W music single was "Touch Me (I'll Be Your Fool Once More)" (Big Al Downing; Warner Bros. Records, 1979), which peaked at number 18 on the "Billboard Hot Country Singles" chart on Saturday, June 30, 1979. Downing passed away on Monday, July 4, 2005 at the age of 65.

BIG BOY LITTLE

Born Bret Littlehales in Washington, D.C. and now known professionally as Big Boy Little, this esteemed blues musician grew up in Chevy Chase, Maryland and was first exposed to folk music at a young age by his father, who listened to the Memphis Jug Band and blues-folk singer-guitarist-harmonicist Robert Johnson. Littlehales began listening to R&B artists such as Jimmy Reed and B.B. King on radio station WOL as a teenager in the middle 1960s and took up guitar and harmonica.

Littlehales attended St. Albans School in Washington, D.C., and, while in the ninth grade in 1965, joined his first musical group, the Bent Penny Blues Band. Next, he played in local groups called the Robert Dusty Blues Band and Duke and the Rhythm Aces.

During his junior year at St. Albans School in 1968 Littlehales became a founding member of the Northwest Blues Band, which quickly changed its name to the Northside Blues Band, a group that included guitarist Rob Ewan (later known as Bobby Radcliff). The band specialized in classic blues by artists such as singer-harmonicist Junior Wells and singer-guitarist Buddy Guy. They performed in Washington, D.C. at teen dances at St. Albans School and Sidwell Friends School, events at the P Street Beach near Dupont Circle, and night clubs such as Emergency, the Showboat Lounge and the Childe Harold. After Littlehales graduated from St. Albans School in 1969, the Northside Blues Band carried on without him.

Littlehales entered Cornell University in the fall of 1969 and remained for a short while. He spent a total of four years in Ithaca, New York and during his time there he played in such blues groups as Egret Brand, his own Bret Littlehales Band, and Brute. He also frequently sat in with Slippery Elm, a rock and roll band that featured Hugh Craig (the future Huey Lewis).

Littlehales eventually finished college in 1976 at the Rhode Island School of Design with a degree in photography. He returned to the Washington, D.C. area in 1978, but concentrated on his family and his photography career throughout the 1980s. In the early 1990s Littlehales returned to the local blues music scene and during the decade he played with two bands, Terence McArdle and Big Trouble (harmonica, rhythm guitar and vocals), and Steve Smith and His Meteors (harmonica and vocals).

In 1999 Littlehales joined a blues group called the Fabulous Merkins which consisted of himself handling vocals and harmonica, guitarist Rusty Bogart, bassist Steve Shaw, keyboardist Arthur Gerstein, saxophonist Charlie Hubel and drummer Jeff Lodsun. In 2000 Hubel left the Fabulous Merkins. Littlehales regrouped with the band's remaining players, assumed a new stage name, and the Big Boy Little Band came into existence. His new group played a mix of blues and jazz and worked the Zoo Bar Café (3000 Connecticut Avenue NW, Washington, D.C.) for years. Changes in personnel occurred through time and among the musicians to pass through the Big Boy Little Band were guitarists Irving Bannister and Matt Kelley, bassists Steve Potter and Kevin Forder, and drummer Robbie Leebrick.

Today the Big Boy Little Band consists of lead singer-harmonicist Big Boy Little, guitarist Steve Jacobs, bassist Steve "Wolf" Crescenze and drummer Andy Hamburger. They remain one of the premier blues band in the nation's capital and frequently appear at such establishments as the Old Bowie Town Grille (Bowie), JV's Restaurant (Falls Church), the New Deal Café (Greenbelt), Blair's Londontowne Pub and Grill (Edgewater), Two Nineteen Restaurant (Alexandria) and Acadiana (Washington, D.C.). The band has one official CD to its credit, "Live From the XM Satellite" (The Big Boy Little Band; Big Train Records, 2010).

BIG JOE MAHER

Blues drummer Big Joe Maher was raised in Bowie, Maryland and through the years has worked with some of the Washington, D.C. area's top musicians including rock and roll saxophonist Joe Stanley, blues singer-harmonicist Mark Wenner, blues singer-guitarist Tom Principato, jazz guitarist Rick Whitehead and jazz bassist Steve Wolf. In his career he has also drummed for such noted blues musicians as singers Nappy Brown and Jimmy Weatherspoon; singer-guitarists Bob Margolin, Duke Robillard, Otis Rush and Earl King; and singer-saxophonist Bull Moose Jackson.

During his years at Bowie High School in the late 1960s and early 1970s Maher drummed for an R&B band called Mother that performed on the Bowie teen dance circuit. At the time he also drummed for his high school jazz band, the Starliners. In 1970s he was a member of a blues-jazz outfit called the Mickey Basil Trio and then a Minneapolis, Minnesota-based R&B band called Roy Hunt and the Dimensions. In the 1980s Maher drummed for a number of different groups including the R&B band Floating Opera, a blues act called Sneaky Pete, a blues band called the Rhythm Masters (featuring singer Cathy Ponton King) and a popular R&B outfit known as the Uptown Rhythm Kings.

In 1987 Maher put together Big Joe and the Dynaflows, a band that quickly became recognized as one of the nation's very best jump-blues bands. Albums by Maher and his cohorts include: "Good Rockin Daddy" (Big Joe and the Dynaflows; Powerhouse Records, 1991); "Layin' in the Alley" (Big Joe and the Dynaflows; Black Top Records, 1994); "Mojo" (Big Joe Maher, Jeff Sarli, and Their New Band Big Blues; Wildchild!, 1994); "Cool Dynaflow" (Big Joe and the Dynaflows; Tramp Records, 1997); "I'm Still Swingin'" (Big Joe and the Dynaflows; Severn Records, 1998); "All Night Long" (Big Joe and the Dynaflows; Severn Records, 2000); "I Warned You Baby!" (Big Joe and the Dynaflows; Gutter Records, 2008); and "You Can't Keep a Big Man Down" (Big Joe and the Dynaflows; Severn Records, 2011).

BILL CARON

Bill Caron grew up in Silver Spring, Maryland and as a teenager in the early 1960s played in several bands that worked the local teen dance circuit – he drummed for a pop trio called the Classics; played bass for such rock and roll bands as the Gondoliers and the Revelaires; became a founding member of Lawrence and the Arabians as their bassist; then switched back to drums and played with two top R&B bands, the Illusions and the Nightcaps.

After graduating from Montgomery Blair High School in June 1966 Caron passed an audition in New York City for the drum seat in Jay and the Americans. He toured with the band for a little under a year, performing with the band at concerts and shows all over the United States and Canada. When he returned he rejoined Lawrence and the Arabians, this time as a drummer, and worked engagements with them during the late 1960s at such Washington, D.C. night clubs as the Bastille Supper Club, the Act IV Supper Club and the Cave.

From 1969 to 1972 Caron drummed for the Admirals, a longstanding popular music act that performed at night clubs, supper clubs and hotels from New York to Florida. When performing in the nation's capital, the Admirals made appearances at the Bastille Supper Club and the Act IV Supper Club.

In November 1972 Caron joined the very successful R&B-rock band Second Coming, taking over drums in a six-piece group which at the time included singers Charlie Taylor and Joe Saitta, guitarist David Fultz, bassist Tommy Rodante and keyboardist Mike "Pineapple" Serigumba. Caron remained with the band for nine years, during which time they worked long engagements at such area night clubs as Fran O'Brien's Anthony House Restaurant, Ventuno 21 Supper Club, the Cave, the Act IV Supper Club and the Classic III Supper Club. Caron stopped playing in bands in 1981 and in 1986 he co-founded a concert promotion agency called National Artists Corporation.

BILL CRAIG

Guitarist Bill Craig grew up in College Park, Maryland and during his years at High Point High School in the late 1960s he played the local teen dance circuit in such bands as the Null Set and the Mods of Quinn. Upon graduation he passed through several local rock and roll bands including Morning Star, Easy and Warm as Toast.

In 1970 Craig formed a rock band called the Hot Crabs, which included singer Mike Reidy, bassist Fred Gallagher and drummer Scott Galloway. The Hot Crabs frequently performed at shows and events on the University of Maryland's College Park campus. In early 1971 Craig and Reidy moved Gallagher over to rhythm guitar, recruited a rhythm section of bassist Ted Niceley and drummer Pete Ragusa, and gave their new band the name Razz. For the remainder of the 1970s Razz was considered one of the very best rock and roll bands in the Washington, D.C. area. The group endured several personnel changes, with one of their most popular lineups consisting of Reidy, Craig, Niceley, guitarist Abaad Behram (who was replaced late in the decade by Tommy Keene) and drummer Doug Tull.

After Razz broke up in 1979 Craig went on to perform with a number of different rock and roll acts including Nightman, Other World, Jr. Cline and the Recliners, Johnny Bombay and the Reactions, the Chasers, Johnny and the Ringers, Groovy, singer Cal Everett, the Howling Mad, and the Billy Coulter Band. He also spent more than a decade as a featured guitarist for BandHouse Gigs, a not-for-profit production company founded by Chuck Sullivan and Ron Newmyer that produces musical tribute shows.

Craig is currently playing guitar at night clubs in and around the nation's capital with the VI-Kings, a band that specializes in covering rock and roll bands of the 1960s.

BILL HOLLAND AND RENT'S DUE

Differing from many of his musical colleagues, Bill Holland never played in bands on the local teen dance circuit as a teenager. One of the most talented singer-pianists the nation's capital has produced, Holland grew up in Silver Spring, Maryland, graduated from Archbishop Carroll School in 1959, and, upon graduating from St. Vincent College in Latrobe, Pennsylvania, spent time working for the Peace Corps in Liberia. In the middle 1960s he returned to the nation's capital and began devoting time to songwriting and making music.

Holland has the distinction of having been the original keyboardist in 1972 for the now-legendary blues group the Nighthawks. He then put together a band he called Rent's Due that mixed different styles of jazz, R&B and rock and roll. He kept the group going for seven years, utilizing many of the area's finest musicians in the process, performing in the Washington, D.C. area's best night clubs and recording many critically acclaimed albums.

In 1974 the very first lineup of Bill Holland and Rent's Due rehearsed in the basement of Holland's home in the Adams Morgan neighborhood of Washington, D.C. and consisted of singer-pianist Holland, guitarist Gerry Mule, bassist Mac Cridlin, saxophonist Kurt McGettrick, and two alternate drummers who were called upon separately, Scott Taylor and Rick Anderson. Personnel changes were steady and through the band's tenure members to pass through included: guitarists John Bohanan, John Jennings, Pete Kennedy and Keith Grimes; bassists Steve Wolf, Eliot Jagoda, Gary Starr and Wade Matthews; drummer Carl Holzapfel; and saxophonist Mike Roll.

The band's final lineup in 1981 consisted of Holland, guitarist Paul Bell, bassist Ron Newmyer, saxophonist Larry Strother and drummer Chuck Sullivan. During its time, Bill Holland and Rent's Due appeared at a variety of Washington, D.C.'s top night clubs including Rocky Raccoon's Saloon, Ernie's Place, the Corsican, the Childe Harold, Desperado's, the Cellar Door and Columbia Station.

Albums featuring Bill Holland include: "If It Ain't One Thing..." (Bill Holland & Rent's Due; Adelphi Records, 1975); "It's About Time" (Bill Holland & the Rent's Due Band; Dutch Treat Records, 1980); "Let It Go Live" (Bill Holland and the Rent's Due Band; Dutch Treat Records, 1980); "True Blue Trio" (Bill Holland; Dutch Treat Records, 1993); "Players, Fools & Thieves" (Bill Holland; Dutch Treat Records, 1995); "Way Overdue" (Bill Holland and the Rent's Due Band; Dutch Treat Records, 1998); and "By Heart" (Bill Holland & the Rent's Due Band; Dutch Treat Records, 2003).

BILL STARKS

Singer-pianist Bill Starks was born in Washington, D.C. and raised in Montgomery County, Maryland in the town of Kensington and the city of Rockville. As a youth he played drums and trumpet and started on the piano at age 10. Largely self-taught, he would play along in his basement to the Beatles, Bob Dylan, and various Christmas songs. During his years at Robert E. Peary High School in Rockville in the early 1970s he hung out with musicians and frequented jam sessions in the homes of friends where he played everything from songs by Cream to classic R&B tunes. After graduating from Robert E. Peary High School in 1972 he attended Montgomery College (Rockville campus) and went on to earn a Bachelor of Arts in radio-television-film from the University of Maryland in 1978.

In December 1977 Starks became a founding member of a Rockville-based pop-R&B band called Shadowbox. He sang and played piano for the band, whose lineup also included guitarist Chuck Underwood, singer-bassist Greg Hardin and drummer Kendall Diehl. The group lasted through November 1978 and covered everything from Little Feat to Jackson Browne to Marvin Gaye. Shadowbox performed at a number of local night clubs including Mr. Henry's Tenley Circle (Washington, D.C.) and Fred and Sully's (Hyattsville).

In December 1978 Shadowbox disbanded, with Starks, Underwood and Hardin regrouping with singer-guitarist Steve Bernd, saxophonist Joe Reiff and drummer Joe Daugherty to become the pop-R&B group Rhythm Method.

In November 1979 Starks left Rhythm Method and joined a rock and roll cover band called Smalltalk. With his arrival the Northern Virginia-based band's new lineup consisted of singer-guitarist-steel guitarist Bob Garrison, lead guitarist Sam Catalona, bassist Gary Falwell, drummer Keith Edwards, and Starks on piano. They played material by the likes of Little Feat, Steely Dan and Pure Prairie League and were regulars in Washington, D.C. at Mr. Henry's Tenley Circle, Desperado's, and Columbia Station; in Virginia at the Shed (Alexandria); and in Maryland at the Varsity Grill Back Room (College Park), Italian Gardens (College Park), Bambino's (Riverdale), and the Outside Inn (Rockville). Starks remained with Smalltalk through late 1981.

In the early 1980s Starks spent a brief period playing piano with a jazz-pop outfit called Melissa Berman and the Thin Man Band and then from 1982 to 1986 was a member of the popular R&B-rock act Jr. Cline and the Recliners. In 1988 he began playing piano for blues singer Cathy Ponton King and continued to perform and record with her for more than 25 years. In the 1990s he played piano with several Washington, D.C. area rock and roll bands including the Chasers and the Dynettes.

In 2004 Starks began playing in the various BandHouse Gigs tribute shows. In 2006 he became the full-time singer-pianist with the C&W band Ruthie and the Wranglers, first performing with them at the Half Moon Bar-B-Que in Silver Spring, Maryland. He is still with the band today.

Through the years Starks has played keyboards on albums by such musicians as rock and roll singer-guitarist Mike Cotter, the folk music duo of singer-guitarist-banjoist Cathy Fink and guitarist-mandolinist Marcy Marxer, folk rock singer-guitarist David Massey, and the rock and roll band One Nite Stand. He has two solo albums to his credit: "Starksongs" (Bill Starks; Bill Starks, 1984); and "I See Trouble" (Bill Starks; Azalea City Recordings, 2015).

BILL VERRILL

Drummer Bill Verrill was born in Washington, D.C. and lived in the Southeast quadrant of the city until the age of nine. At that point his family moved to Oxon Hill, Maryland and in 1964 while in the eighth grade at John Hanson Junior High School he joined his first rock and roll band, the Assassins. While this band was playing in basements and at local parties, Verrill would venture out on weekends to the John Hanson Teen Club at his school and watch frequent headliners Lawrence and the Arabians perform, with drummer Mike Zack becoming a major inspiration for his musical career.

In 1965 Verrill began drumming for another rock and roll band, the Wrong Way Inn, which, in early 1966, changed their name to the Love Children. The band played British Invasion tunes, standard rock and roll hits and classic R&B. In 1966 Verrill played his first-ever night club date at the 1023 Restaurant in Southeast Washington, D.C. when Link Wray told the Love Children's lead singer, Lee Best, that he needed a one-night substitute for ailing drummer Doug Wray. Verrill took the job and performed all evening with Link Wray and His Ray Men in what was considered one of the city's roughest rock and roll night spots.

The Love Children stayed together throughout 1968, performing at such local night clubs as the Quonset Supper Club (Silver Hill), the Hayloft (Washington, D.C.) and the Beehive (Washington, D.C.). They also took out-of-town jobs at establishments such as Uncle Billy's (North Beach, Maryland) and the Wig Wam (Waldorf, Maryland). Late in the year the band changed its name to Heaven.

In June 1969, Heaven, with Verrill fresh out of Oxon Hill High School and still on drums, was recruited to back rock and roll singer Chubby Checker for his week-long engagement at the Wig Wam. This experience led Verrill to accept short-notice freelance jobs for whatever performing artists needed a drummer for gigs and abbreviated regional tours. In 1969 and 1970 he was called upon on several occasions to again drum for Chubby Checker, as well other national acts such as the Drifters, the Platters and Gene Vincent at shows and concerts throughout the Midwest and South.

When Verrill came off the road in 1972, he joined an Oxon Hill-based rock and roll band called Fargo, which performed at such Washington, D.C. night clubs such as the Crazy Horse, the Bayou, Fran O'Brien's Anthony House Restaurant and Some Place Else, in addition to embarking on occasional night club tours up and down the East Coast. He was with Fargo until 1975 and then spent time as a drummer-for-hire through the Barry Rick Associates booking agency.

From 1978 to 1986 Verrill drummed for a popular rock and roll band called Sugar Bear, which held down house band duties at the Marco Polo Restaurant in Vienna, Virginia. From 1987 to 2000 he drummed for a Top 40 rock and roll band called Ravin' that frequently performed at Sam's Crabhouse in Clinton, Maryland. From 2000 to 2013 Verrill drummed for the band Route 66, a Northern Virginia-based outfit that specialized in oldies and classic rock.

BILLY COULTER

Singer-guitarist Billy Coulter was born in Baltimore, Maryland and raised in Montgomery County in the city of Rockville. At age 10 he briefly took guitar lessons and learned basic chords, but opted to leave his guitar unattended for several years. While attending Thomas Sprigg Wooton High School in the middle and late 1970s a guitarist in his sister's rock and roll band showed him a few chords and from there he was self-taught. He purchased his first guitar during his junior year of high school, listened to Mott the Hoople and David Bowie, was influenced by the songwriting of John Lennon and Bob Dylan, and began playing music with friends at parties.

In 1979 Coulter played guitar in a rock and roll cover band called Vision that performed at the Red Fox Inn in Gaithersburg. He started writing songs in 1980 and from 1981 to 1982 he played in a rock and roll band called the Inserts. They played original rock and roll and performed in Washington, D.C. at the Chancery, Friendship Station, Desperado's and the Gentry; and in Maryland at the Psyche Delly (Bethesda). In the middle 1980s he played guitar in such local rock and roll bands as the Diversions and the Bomb Squad.

Coulter graduated from American University with a Bachelor of Arts in journalism in 1984 and then withdrew from the local music scene for several years. In the middle 1990s he picked up his acoustic guitar and returned to action in a rock and roll band called Butterface that performed for two years at the Grog and Tankard on Wisconsin Avenue NW in Washington, D.C. He moved to Takoma Park, Maryland and resumed songwriting activities.

While vacationing in Mexico in March 1999 Coulter struck up a friendship with a keyboardist named Steve Thoma, who had performed with Fleetwood Mac and singer-guitarist Glenn Frey. Thoma played in the resort's rock and roll house band, which also included musicians such as singer-bassist Tim Scott (formerly of Tower of Power) and drummer Denny Seiwell (formerly of Paul McCartney and Wings). At Thoma's urging, Coulter sat in with the band several times.

Coulter and Thoma kept in touch. A rough mix recording of songs Coulter had worked up in his home studio was sent to Thoma in California, who, in turn, offered to produce a demo. Coulter went West, recorded several tracks, and played some new compositions for the producer. A new band was then assembled consisting of Coulter, guitarist Brian Villalva (whom Coulter had previously worked with in the Diversions), bassist Tim Scott and drummer Danny Pucillo, Jr. This group recorded four additional tracks which would become the foundation for Coulter's first solo album. With the sessions completed in 2001, Coulter returned to Maryland and began assembling a new rock and roll band in Takoma Park to perform the material.

Back in Takoma Park, the Billy Coulter Band was pieced together in late 2001 with an initial lineup of Coulter on lead vocals and guitar, guitarist Tommy Derr, bassist Willard Morris and former Razz drummer Doug Tull. Musicians to pass through the group in the ensuing years included guitarist John Penovich and bassists Barry Warsaw, Chuck Dolan and Arch Alcantara.

The Billy Coulter Band has appeared as an opening act at the Iota (Arlington), the Birchmere (Alexandria) and Rams Head On Stage (Annapolis). They now regularly headline in the area at the Music Café (Damascus), the New Deal Café (Greenbelt), Blueside Tavern (Frederick), Bump 'n Grind (Silver Spring) and at various festival and concert events. The band mainly performs original material and currently consists of Coulter, Tull, singer-bassist Hollie Montgomery and lead guitarist Max Evans.

Coulter has also been a member of the blues-jazz group the Natty Beaux since 2006, has played numerous BandHouse Gigs tribute concerts, and in recent years has performed onstage with the likes of rockabilly singer-guitarist Bill Kirchen, rock and roll guitarist Eric Ambel, rock and roll singer-guitarist John Eddie, rock and roll singer Janine Wilson, and the C&W band Ruthie and the Wranglers. Coulter has four albums to his credit thus far: "Billy Coulter" (Billy Coulter; Confluence Records, 2003); "Dose" (Billy Coulter; Confluence Records, 2008); "Trace: Live Goose Creek" (Billy Coulter; Confluence Records, 2010); and "Back and Fourth" (Billy Coulter; Confluence Records, 2014).

BILLY HANCOCK

Hailing from Alexandria, Virginia, Billy Hancock was an extraordinary singer-bassist-guitarist with an impressive body of work that encompasses many musical styles including rock and roll, rockabilly, blues, C&W and jazz. He took up guitar at age 11 and during his teen years in the early 1960s he first played the local teen dance circuit in a rock and roll band called the Torquays.

Hancock entered the local night club scene after graduating from George Washington High School in Alexandria in 1964, working with guitarist Mike Boyd in a band called the Stingers at the Corral on M Street NW in Georgetown. The Stingers were playing different types of rock and roll and R&B and also worked at other Washington, D.C. night clubs such as the Frog, the Hayloft, the Alpine Room, the Shanty, the 1023 Restaurant and Some Place Else.

After a stay in New York City Hancock returned to the nation's capital in 1966 and put together a rock band called the In Crowd that worked in Washington, D.C. at the Rocket Room, Guy's Place, the Beehive, the Shanty and Some Place Else. He then spent the late 1960s playing rhythm guitar and bass with such local bands as Steve Charles and the Soul Syndrome, the Package, Danny Denver and the Sound Tracks, and a final version of the Fallen Angels, which morphed into the band Love and Trust as the 1970s arrived. In 1968 Hancock also worked a tour playing bass for legendary rock and roller Gene Vincent.

In 1971 Hancock worked with blues rock guitarist Roy Buchanan and different versions of his band at the Cross Roads in Bladensburg, Maryland. He then spent much of that decade working with multi-styled guitarist Danny Gatton, first in a band called Fat Chance, and then as a trio called Danny and the Fat Boys which included drummer Dave Elliott. Since that time Hancock has performed and recorded with innumerable rockabilly, rock and roll, and R&B artists including Joe Stanley, the Clovers, Fats Domino, Charlie Feathers and Amos Milburn.

In recent times Hancock has gained national recognition for his own rockabilly bands, Billy Hancock and the Tennessee Rockets and Billy Hancock and the Sidekicks. Through the years, Billy Hancock has recorded extensively for a number of American and European record labels. Among his many popular album releases are: "American Music" (Danny and the Fat Boys; Aladdin Records, 1975); "Shakin' That Rockabilly Fever" (Billy Hancock & the Tennessee Rockets; Solid Smoke Records, 1981); "Hey! Kittle Rock and Roller" (Billy Hancock; Big Beat Records, 1983); "Wanted: True Rock 'n' Roll" (Billy Hancock; Ripsaw Records, 1985); "Passions" (Billy Hancock; Turkey Mountain Records, 2005); and "Out of the Darkness" (Billy Hancock; Turkey Mountain Records, 2008). Billy Hancock passed away on Monday, January 22, 2018 at the age of 71.

BILLY POORE

Rockabilly singer Billy Poore was raised in Brentwood, Maryland and in the early 1960s during his time at Northwestern High School he sang lead with a popular, Louisville, Kentucky-based rock and roll group called the Trend-Els. In the early and middle 1960s he also performed and recorded with other rock and roll bands including the Sultans and the Recalls. Poore went on to become one of the best-known producers, concert promoters, record company owners, radio show hosts and authors in the field of rockabilly music. He also established a solo career as a rockabilly singer-songwriter, having appeared at festivals and concert halls all over the United States and Europe. He is the author of the best-selling book "RockABilly: A Forty-Year Journey" (1998).

Poore's early singing can be heard on the singles "I'm So Young" backed with "Don't You Hear Me Calling Babe" (The Trend-Els; Tilt Records, 1961), "It'll Be Easy" backed with "You Got Me Goin'" (The Sultans; Tilt Records, 1961), and "The Lonely Wait" backed with "No Reason" (The Recalls; Arrow Records, 1965). More recently, as a solo rockabilly artist, he has released the single "A Whole Lotta Racket" backed with "Fool Fool Fool" (Billy Poore; Rock-A-Billy Record Co., 1995), and the albums "Last of the Renegades" (Billy Poore; Renegade Records, 2011), and "50 Years of Flatout Rock'n'Roll: 1961-2011" (Billy Poore; Renegade Records, 2012). Billy Poore passed away on Saturday, July 23, 2016 at the age of 71.

BILLY WOO

Billy Woo is a singer-guitarist who played in several prominent rock and roll bands during his years in the nation's capital and is also noted for his more recent work within the Hollywood film industry, having written and performed music and songs for a variety of feature-length motion pictures. Woo grew up in Washington, D.C. and attended DeMatha High School and Woodrow Wilson High School in the middle and late 1960s. After a tour of duty in the United States Navy he sang and played guitar for such local rock and roll acts as the Montells, Sweetwater, Fantasy, Diamond, Blitz, Sauce, Fairchild, keyboardist Arlene Quatro, and Merlin.

In 1979 Woo relocated to Los Angeles, California and played with a band called Crank that included Kim Turner and performed at the Hong Kong Café in L.A.'s Chinatown district, opening for punk bands such as the Germs, Social Distortion and Fear. He has since played in the Los Angeles area in a variety of popular music bands including Bronco Billy and his own rock group, the British Woos.

In the 1980s Woo began writing and recording songs at Jade Dragon Studio in West Los Angeles for famed movie producer-director Roger Corman and the film production-distribution company Concorde-New Horizons, with more than 30 of his works having been placed in various major motion pictures. For one particular motion picture, "Naked Obsession" (Concorde-New Horizons, 1990), Woo either wrote or co-wrote the songs "Welcome to the Darkside" (which featured lead vocals by James Manzie of Midnight Oil), "Be My Slave," "One Night With You," "Was It All in Vain?" and "Tonight, Tonight" (Woo handled lead vocals on the latter two songs).

Other well-known movies that used music written and performed by Woo include "Kiss Me a Killer" (Concorde-New Horizons, 1991), "Body Waves" (Concorde-New Horizons, 1992), "The Liars' Club" (Concorde-New Horizons, 1993) and "Stripteaser" (Concorde-New Horizons, 1995). He has since written and recorded songs for movies produced by Retromedia Entertainment and a number of films produced and directed by Fred Olen Ray and Dan Golden.

BLAINE SMITH

Singer-guitarist Blaine Smith was raised in Montgomery County, Maryland where he spent his teen years living in Chevy Chase. He taught himself guitar and his early influences included Chet Atkins, Elvis Presley, Bo Diddley, Chuck Berry, Link Wray and Duane Eddy. While attending Leland Junior High School in the late 1950s he was a member of the Galaxies, a popular rock and roll band on the local teen dance circuit. While a student at Bethesda-Chevy Chase High School in the early 1960s he became a founding member of the Newports, one of the region's top rock and roll bands, and remained a pivotal member of the group for five years.

In 1964 Smith underwent a religious conversion and in 1966 he felt God was telling him to leave the Newports. He formed Sons of Thunder, the first active Christian rock and roll band in the Eastern United States, and served as a singer-guitarist with the band from June 1967 to December 1974.

Sons of Thunder performed concerts in front of large gatherings on college campuses and released four albums: "Till the Whole World Knows" (Sons of Thunder; Zondervan Records, 1968); "Day Follows Night" (Sons of Thunder; Bronte Records, 1972); "Live at Virginia Beach" (Sons of Thunder; Bronte Records, 1973); and "Rock Gospel: Sing & Sign" (Sons of Thunder; Bronte Records, 1973). They also released the single "'On the Right Path the Limping Foot Recovers Strength and Does Not Collapse" Otherwise Known as 'The Limping Foot'" (Sons of Thunder; Omega Records, 1970).

Devoting his life to Christian service, Smith holds degrees from Georgetown University, Wesley Theological Seminary and Fuller Theological Seminary, is an ordained Presbyterian minister, and has served as an assistant pastor at Memorial Presbyterian Church in St. Louis, Missouri. Returning to Maryland, he served as director of Nehemiah Ministries from 1978 to 2009. To date he has authored eight books on spiritual and Christian topics and still publishes an on-line newsletter entitled "Nehemiah Notes." In 1995 Sons of Thunder reformed and recorded and released the CD "Treasures" (Sons of Thunder; Bronte Records, 1998).

In December 2001 the Newports reformed with Smith at the helm. They are still performing today and frequently appear at such Maryland establishments as the Outta the Way Café (Derwood), Hershey's Restaurant (Gaithersburg) and La Mexicana (Gaithersburg).

BLITZ

Specializing in progressive rock and roll music and noted for its versatility and high-quality musicianship, Blitz was on the local scene from 1973 to 1975 and held the distinction of being a favorite on both the local 14th Street NW Strip in Washington, D.C. and various stages on the University of Maryland's College Park campus. Basing out of

Olney, Maryland, the band's best-known lineup consisted of singer-lead guitarist Billy Woo, guitarist Joe Sofet, bassist Larry Sullivan, keyboardist Danny Garrett and drummer Roger Fallin.

A group with wide appeal, Blitz was the house band at the Butterfly on 14th Street NW for most of 1973 and 1974. During that time they were also a regular attraction at the Pub, which was located inside the Adele H. Stamp Student Union Building on the University of Maryland campus (College Park).

Blitz specialized in covering more complex material, offering its own arrangements of both obscurities and radio hits of such bands as Yes, Queen, Mott the Hoople, Elton John, the Allman Brothers Band, Thin Lizzy, Aerosmith, Rod Stewart, Mountain and Emerson, Lake and Palmer. A high point for the band was its opening slot position for a concert headlined by the New York Dolls at Ritchie Coliseum (University of Maryland) on Sunday, January 13, 1974.

BO DIDDLEY

Born Otha Ellis Bates in McComb, Mississippi on Sunday, December 30, 1928, Diddley was adopted by his mother's cousin in Chicago in 1933 and had his name changed to Ellas McDaniel. As rock and roll singer-guitarist Bo Diddley he rose to national prominence in the 1950s for his various albums and singles on two different labels, Checker Records and Chess Records.

From 1958 to 1967 Diddley lived in Washington, D.C. at no fewer than three different addresses including 2614 Rhode Island Avenue NE (1958-1964), 1724 Newton Street NW in Mount Pleasant (his wife resided here in a first floor apartment during the summer of 1962 and Diddley was a regular guest) and 812 Rittenhouse Street NW (1964-1967).

From the late 1950s to the middle 1960s Diddley regularly performed in the Washington, D.C. area at such venues as the Hyattsville Armory, the Bladensburg Volunteer Fire Department, the Kentland Volunteer Fire Department and the Howard Theatre. Bo Diddley passed away on Monday, June 2, 2008 at the age of 79.

BOA

The rock and roll group Boa formed in 1968 in Silver Spring, Maryland and worked as the house band at Nu-Mac's on M Street NW in Georgetown for more than two years. After a series of personnel changes, the group settled on a lineup consisting of lead singer Danny Goers, guitarist Dave Alexander, bassist Dale Marcks, keyboardist John Macuci and drummer Ronnie Fulkersin. In 1970 Boa picked up a second lead singer named Benny Troy – he later changed his name to Benny Mardones – and the band promptly changed its name to Troy.

After working My Mother's Place at 18th and M Streets NW for most of 1970, Benny Troy departed and the band reclaimed the Boa moniker. In 1971 Boa regrouped with a lineup of Goers, Alexander, Marks, Fulkersin, and two new keyboardists, Marc Fellows on organ and synthesizer, and Jeff Fellows on piano and mellotron. For the next five years the group gave concerts and toured night clubs up and down the Atlantic Coast, playing original rock and roll compositions and covering progressive material by bands such as Led Zeppelin, Yes, Jethro Tull, David Bowie and Frank Zappa. When in the nation's capital during this time, Boa frequently performed at the Bayou and the Act IV Supper Club.

BOB BERBERICH

Bob Berberich grew up in Silver Spring, Maryland and began playing drums at age 14. In 1965 during his senior year at St. John's College High School in Washington, D.C. he was recruited by Tom Guernsey and George Daly into their newly formed rock and roll band, the Hangmen. For the next two years this group reigned as one of the Washington, D.C. area's most popular attractions, especially with the younger teen crowd.

In May 1967 the Hangmen disbanded, with holdovers Berberich, lead singer Tony Taylor and guitarist Jorge Strunz forming a new rock and roll band called the Button, which played several weeks at Nu-Mac's in Georgetown before relocating to New York City.

Berberich returned to the Washington, D.C. area at the end of 1967, moving to a popular group house entitled "Toad Hall" in Takoma Park, Maryland where he lived for most of 1968 and spent his time jamming with friends at parties. Later that year he joined forces with guitarist Nils Lofgren and former Hangmen George Daly and Paul Dowell in a short-lived band called Paul Dowell and the Dolphin.

In April 1969 Dowell departed for San Francisco where he became the soundman for Jefferson Airplane, while Lofgren, Daly and Berberich stayed together as a trio and a month later put together a new rock and roll band called Grin. Within a year Bob Gordon replaced George Daly on bass and in 1972 Tom Lofgren was added on keyboards and guitar. For more than five years Grin was at the top of the local music scene, headlining teen dances as well as large concert events throughout the region. The band released a total of six albums on four different major record labels and played its farewell show at the John F. Kennedy Center for the Performing Arts Concert Hall on Saturday, June 8, 1974.

Berberich went on to spend the rest of the 1970s drumming for the Rosslyn Mountain Boys, an extremely popular country rock band in the nation's capital. Through the years he has drummed for an array of different musical acts including Payday, Joe Triplett and the Hired Hands, Goin' Goin' Gone, the Sliders, Switchblade, the Dynettes, and Mike Cotter and the Usual Suspects. More recently, Berberich has drummed for blues singer-guitarist Cathy Ponton King, Ottley! (a hard rocking power trio rounded out by his wife and lead singer Martha Hull and former Slickee Boys guitarist Marshall Keith), and two blues acts, the Bruce Ewan Band, and singer-guitarist Bobby Radcliff. Berberich is currently drumming for the VI-Kings, a band devoted to recreating the hard-rocking music of the 1960s.

BOB BROWN

Bob Brown grew up in Clinton, Maryland and began singing and playing guitar after discovering Tom Paxton, Judy Collins and Peter, Paul and Mary while in the ninth grade at Surrattsville Junior High School. During his years at Surrattsville High School in the middle 1960s he was a member of the Folk Club and performed at school "Hootenanny" shows. He attended the Newport Folk Festival in both 1965 and 1966 and witnessed many of his musical heroes in action including Bob Dylan, Donavan, Joan Baez, Tim Harden, Eric Anderson and Richie Havens. In the middle and late 1960s he entered the Washington, D.C. folk music circuit and performed at coffee houses such as Through-the-Gates Coffee House (Capitol Hill Presbyterian Church in Southeast Washington, D.C.) and the Crow's Toe (formerly Coffee 'n' Confusion).

During the summers of 1967 and 1968, while a student at the University of Maryland, Brown hitchhiked to Boston, Massachusetts, where on one excursion he met and befriended Richie Havens at the Blues Bag in Provincetown on Cape Cod. He then spent the late 1960s performing in Washington, D.C. at places like the Iguana Coffeehouse (Luther Place Memorial Church) and the summertime gatherings at the P Street Beach just off of Dupont Circle. During that time he put together a folk group (simply billed as "Bob Brown") with guitarist Orin Smith, pianist-saxophonist Joe Clark and viola player Roland Hendricks, which often opened at Ritchie Coliseum (University of Maryland) for national acts such as Neil Diamond and Renaissance. On one occasion, Brown's band opened for the hard-rocking band Razz at the Adele H. Stamp Student Union on the Maryland campus.

As the decade ended, Richie Havens asked Brown to sign with his record label Stormy Forest, a subsidiary of MGM Records. Brown released two solo albums on the label, "The Wall I Built Myself" (Bob Brown; Stormy Forest Records, 1970), and "Willoughby's Lament" (Bob Brown; Stormy Forest Records, 1971). He then opened at the Cellar Door for such acts as Eric Anderson, Neil Young, Albert King and Earl Scruggs. He also worked with bassist Terry Plumeri and performed at Mr. Henry's Capitol Hill.

Brown toured in support of his solo albums as the opening act for Richie Havens and played all manner of venues from 1969 to 1972, including a sold-out concert at the Royal Albert Hall in London, England. He later went on to open up in night clubs and concert halls for such performing artists as Linda Ronstadt, Bonnie Raitt, James Taylor, Randy Newman, Harry Chapin, Kris Kristofferson and Emmylou Harris. Brown continued to travel, record and perform into the early 1980s. He is currently working as a restaurant consultant.

BOB COLEMAN

Multi-instrumentalist Bob Coleman was raised in Hyattsville, Maryland and moved to Annapolis at the age of 14 in 1963. He grew up listening to R&B, Elvis Presley, the Everly Brothers and the folk music of the Kingston Trio and Pete Seeger. During his years at Annapolis High School in the middle 1960s he played guitar in a rock and roll band called the Dead Beats, which played the local teen dance scene and recorded and released the single "She Don't Love Me" backed with "I'm Sure" (The Dead Beats; Gray Ant Records, 1966).

In August 1968 the Dead Beats morphed into a rock and roll band called Babe, with Coleman switching to bass. Babe became one of the Washington, D.C. area's most popular groups and Coleman remained a primary member until 1977.

Coleman spent most of 1977 and 1978 playing bass for the popular bluegrass band Liz Meyer and the Midnight Flyers, a group that had a strong following at the Childe Harold at Dupont Circle in Washington, D.C. He then spent most of 1979 playing bass in Cryin' Out Loud, the esteemed R&B group that included singer-keyboardist Tommy Lepson and guitarist Steuart Smith in its lineup and worked such Washington, D.C. night clubs as Mr. Henry's Tenley Circle and Columbia Station.

Coleman went on to embark on a career in engineering. He currently resides in Sebastian, Florida and since 2007 has served as lead singer in a blues rock band called the Coolers.

BOB EMBREY

Singer-bassist Bob Embrey grew up in Manassas, Virginia and during his years at Stonewall Jackson High School in the middle 1960s he played in such rock and roll bands as Sonny and the Nite People, the Monongahelians, the Heard, and the Goosebumps. Of these groups, it was Sonny and the Nite People who invaded the Washington, D.C. night club scene with engagements in 1966 at the Rocket Room and the Frog.

Embrey served in the United States Army from 1968 to 1971 and then spent the 1970s playing in such Manassas-based rock and roll bands as Little Home and Little Bit. He then spent the early 1980s playing the military base officers' club circuit with a C&W band called the Country Diamonds.

Embrey then took a break from performing but remained involved with local music by publishing D.C. Monuments, a fanzine that chronicled the Washington, D.C. area's 1960s rock and roll scene, from 1995 to 2000. He then returned to the music world in 2002 and spent the year playing in a Manassas-based rock and roll trio called the Gallowtones that covered such acts as Link Wray and His Ray Men, Paul Revere and the Raiders and Chuck Berry.

Since November 2011 Embrey has been a singer-bassist in the Classic Spotlight Band, a Manassas group that specializes in 1950s and 1960s rock and roll and covers such bands as the Beatles, Paul Revere and the Raiders, the Jimi Hendrix Experience and the Association.

BOB FARRIS

Singer-guitarist Bob Farris was raised in Adelphi, Maryland and as a youth was inspired by the likes of Chet Atkins and James Burton. During his years at High Point High School in the middle and late 1960s he was the bass player in a British Invasion-styled rock and roll band called the Outcast Set that performed on the local teen dance scene. Late in the decade he played guitar in two other rock and roll bands on the same circuit, the Soul Revolution and the Clique.

In the early 1970s Farris played guitar in a rock and roll band called Musique. This group played teen dances at the Prince George's Plaza Community Center (Hyattsville) and for the teen club Kava at the Greenbelt Youth Center (Greenbelt). They also worked local night clubs like Jimmy Comber's Restaurant (Hyattsville). Musique was noted for its horn section and covered bands such as Blood, Sweat and Tears, Chicago, Tower of Power, Little Feat and the Who.

Farris next played in such local groups as Springfield (another rock and roll band with horns) and Nightwatch (a popular music group fronted by Ron MacDonald). In 1976 he put together his own short-lived rock and roll band, Farris Wheel, whose lineup consisted of lead singer Tom McWhirter, Farris on guitar, bassist Ronnie Newmyer, keyboardist Elliot Wolff and drummer Paul White.

In December 1976 Farris joined a Silver Spring-based pop-rock band called Our Pleasure, which appeared at local night clubs and hotels and worked jobs up and down the East Coast. When Farris joined, the lineup consisted of lead singer Tom McWhirter, Farris on guitar, bassist Chuck Lawhorn, keyboardist Verlon Brickey and drummer Charlie Crowder. Our Pleasure remained a full-time venture through 1991 and then continued playing on a part-time basis until 2012. Personnel changes occurred through time, but Farris remained with the band throughout its entire run.

In recent years Farris has continued to periodically work with Nightwatch and has also played in such bands as the Southern rock group One Way Out and the blues-rockabilly act Retro Deluxe. Since February 2014 he has been the lead guitarist for Johnny Seaton and Bad Behavior, a band that features the work of Elvis Presley and other classic rock and rollers. In addition, Farris has been performing on occasion with the Takoma Park-based rock and roll group GrooveQuest.

BOB MALLARDI

Singer-bassist Bob Mallardi was born in Washington, D.C. and grew up in Greenbelt, Maryland. Raised in a musical family – his father sang and his mother sang and danced – he took up the guitar at age six and listened to R&B artists such as Chuck Berry, James Brown and Ray Charles as a youth. As a teenager he began attending local teen dances and was inspired by such area bands as the Nowhere Men and the Soul Syndicate. While attending Greenbelt Junior High School in the late 1960s he joined a rock and roll band called Aardvark and served as lead vocalist.

During his years at Parkdale High School in the early 1970s Mallardi sang and played bass in a jazz rock band called the M&Ms, an outfit that included guitarist-keyboardist Joe Martone and mainly performed at local parties. He spent the middle and late 1970s singing and playing bass for a local blues band called Blue Steel.

Later, in the 1980s, Mallardi played bass in yet another area blues group, the Bluescasters. In 1993 he first sat in with the blues band Bad Influence, a group put together by guitarist Michael Tash, and became their full-time singer-bassist shortly thereafter. He is still with the band today. In addition Mallardi currently serves as the lead singer-bassist for Pete Kanaras and the Hi-Fyers, a blues band that regularly performs at the Cat's Eye Pub in Baltimore, Maryland.

BOB MCCOY

Singer-bassist Bob McCoy was born in Bluefield, West Virginia and raised in Rockville, Maryland. He took up the bass guitar at the age of 10 in 1964 and was largely self-taught, listening to and playing along with such musicians as pop-rock bassist Carol Kaye, R&B bassist James Jamerson, R&B-rock bassist Donald "Duck" Dunn, jazz bassist Keter Betts and Beatles bassist Paul McCartney. While attending Randolph Junior High School in 1967 he joined his first rock and roll band, the Casuals, and served as their lead singer-bassist.

McCoy attended Wheaton High School in the early 1970s and while a student there he joined one of the top R&B-rock bands in the region, the Nowhere Men. He sang and played bass for the band from 1970 until their final days in 1978. After leaving the Nowhere Men he joined the R&B band Spats, which often performed at the Cellar Door in Georgetown, and remained with them into the early 1980s. Other popular music bands McCoy worked with in the 1980s include the Jan Davis Group, In A Pinch, and his own rock and roll group, McCoy.

From 1985 to 2004 McCoy played in the Gaithersburg, Maryland-based pop-rock band Classified. The original lineup was McCoy handling lead vocals and bass guitar, singer-guitarist Mike Nelson, singer-keyboardist John Cleveland and drummer Mike Gibney. Cleveland was eventually replaced by Don Duvall, who was later replaced by Essie Tovia. The group's final lineup consisted of McCoy, Nelson, Gibney and Tovia.

In 2004 McCoy joined the Main Event, a Gaithersburg, Maryland-based pop-rock band, and is still with them today. For seven years this group was the featured attraction at Timpano Italian Chophouse, a restaurant in Rockville, Maryland. Through the years McCoy has performed onstage with an array of local and national popular music bands and musicians including jazz bassist Jaco Pastorius, jazz rock saxophonist Tim Eyermann, blues singer-guitarist Memphis Gold, and the classic rock cover band the Fabulous Dialtones.

BOB REILLY

Bob Reilly hails from New Carrollton, Maryland and entered the local music scene when he served as the lead vocalist for the Sensations during his years at Parkdale High School in the late 1960s.

The Sensations were a large R&B group consisting of Reilly, lead guitarist Dave Long, rhythm guitarist Gary Leibrich, bassist John Russell, keyboardist Mark Kowaleski, saxophonist Eddie Kowaleski, saxophonist Michael "Whitey" White, trumpeter Doug Hollowboch, trumpeter Larry Mackey and drummer Bill Wilson. Based in New Carrollton, the band covered such musical artists as James Brown, Otis Redding, and Sam and Dave. They regularly performed at teen dances at the St. Ambrose Parish Teen Club (Cheverly), the St. Mary's Catholic Church Teen Club (Landover Hills), the St. Bernard Catholic Church Teen Club (Riverdale), the Greenbelt Teen Club (Greenbelt Youth Center), the Charles Carroll Teen Club (Charles Carroll Junior High School in New Carrollton), the New Carrolton Pool (New Carrollton) and social functions at Parkdale High School (Riverdale).

As the 1960s gave way to the 1970s, the Sensations dropped the horn section and transitioned to more psychedelic rock and roll band, covering such groups as Cream,

Vanilla Fudge, the Doors and Tommy James and the Shondells. In the 1970s Reilly concentrated on singing and playing guitar and performed in two bands, a light jazz duo with flutist-guitarist Ellen Rosch called Bob and Ellen that played local coffee houses and college events, and a more popular pop-rock band called Watercress, which performed in Washington, D.C. at the Iguana Coffeehouse (Luther Place Memorial Church), Gallagher's Pub and Desperado's.

Throughout the early and middle 1980s Reilly was singer-guitarist for the band Chula, whose lineup also included guitarist-keyboardist-clarinetist Mike Callahan, bassist Rob O'Steen and drummer Dave Sheib. Chula performed original rock and covered popular groups like the Beatles, Yes and the Eagles. They appeared in Washington, D.C. at such night clubs as Mr. Henry's Tenley Circle, Mr. Henry's Capitol Hill, Gallagher's Pub, the Brickskeller and Food For Thought; in Maryland at the Varsity Grill Back Room (College Park) and the Pour House Pub (Chester); and in Virginia at the Warehouse (Alexandria).

From 1989 to 1999 Reilly was a member of the spiritual group Open Circle, which recorded and released two albums and performed at coffee houses and churches around the Washington, D.C. area. The band's lineup consisted of Reilly handling guitar and vocals, guitarist-keyboardist Mike Callahan, keyboardist-flutist Cheryl Suhari, trumpeter Jimmy Martin and drummer Chris Moline.

From 2002 to 2005 Reilly performed and recorded with the Bridge, another spiritual band that was rounded out by bassist Rick Mastroianni, keyboardist-guitarist Bobby Walters, keyboardist Suraj Sukamuran and drummer Mike Walls.

More recently Reilly has been a part of an original rock and roll studio project with bassist Jerry Stroup and drummer George Sheppard entitled, appropriately enough, "Reilly, Stroup, Sheppard." This trio recorded and released two CD albums. Reilly has also been a part of a pop-R&B trio called RGR that performed at corporate events. This group included bassist Joe Goulait and singer-guitarist-keyboardist Steve Rosch.

Since 2010 Reilly has been a singer-guitarist in the Reilly Goulait Band, a trio that also includes bassist Joe Goulait and drummer Mike Ross. Just recently this outfit began occasionally adding a fourth piece in guitarist Ray Tilkens. They perform pop and rock and roll covers – everything from the Beatles to Van Morrison to Wilson Pickett – at area establishments such as the Judge's Bench (Ellicott City), the New Deal Café (Greenbelt), the River Hill Sports Grille (Clarksburg), Sullivan's Steak and Beverage Company (Laurel), Oliver's Old Towne Tavern (Laurel), Looney's Pub (Fulton), McGinty's Pub (Silver Spring) and the Twist and Turn Tavern (Highland).

Reilly's album discography is as follows: "Unity" (Open Circle; Open Circle Ministries, 1994); "Children of God" (Open Circle; Open Circle Ministries, 1997); "The Journey Home" (Reilly, Stroup & Sheppard; Bob Reilly & Jerry Stroup, 2002); "Perfect Love" (Reilly, Stroup, Sheppard; www.truthbridge.org, 2003); "Songs for a Season" (Reilly – Callahan; www.truthbridge.org, 2003); "Unexpected Ways" (The Bridge; Weinot Productions, 2005); and "Work in Progress" (The Reilly Goulait Band; Weinot Productions, 2018).

BOB SHADE

Drummer Bob Shade grew up in Hyattsville, Maryland and during the middle 1970s while attending Nicholas Orem Junior High School and Northwestern High School he played in a rock and roll group called the American Cheese Band that performed everything from the Beatles to Buck Owens on the local teen dance scene. Towards the end of his high school years in the late 1970s he joined a harder-rocking, Aerosmith-styled band from Silver Spring called Feedback, which was rounded out by lead singer Mike Buff, guitarist Rodney Harris and bassist Shane Bogan.

Shade next joined band called Purlz, which changed its name to Shatter and settled on a lineup of singer-guitarist Brian Sylvester, lead guitarist Benny Backover, bassist Mike O'Connor and Shade on drums. From 1979 to 1982 Shatter played at a number of local night clubs including the Bastille (College Park), the Varsity Grill Back Room (College Park), the Paragon (College Park), the Riverside Inn (Riverdale) and Louie's Rock City (Bailey's Crossroads).

In late 1982 Shade joined Darius, a Northern Virginia-based rock and roll band that was rounded out by lead singer Eddie Day, guitarist Dave Koval and bassist Tim Jones. Darius covered acts such as the Scorpions and Ozzie Osborne and performed at the Riverside Inn (Riverdale), the Outside Inn (Rockville) and the Stardust Inn (Waldorf).

In 1983 he again joined forces with guitarist Mike Buff, who had assumed the stage name "Mike Feeedbak" (that is the wat Buff spells his stage name), and while drumming for the band appeared on their 45rpm single record, "Red Rock" backed with "Jenny Whooo" (Mike Feeedbak and the Nuclear Warriors; N.U.K.-Fire Rock Records, 1983).

In the summer of 1985 Shade was recruited by Eddie Day into the revamped version of the hard-rocking band Hawaii which included mainstay guitarist Marty Freidman and Mike "Feeedbak" Buff, who was brought in to play bass. The band went through personnel changes, including the loss of Friedman and the acquisition of guitarist Robert Fiester, and worked local night clubs such as the Bayou, with a high point being an opening act performance for Emerson, Lake & Powell at the Capital Centre in Landover, Maryland on Friday, September 19, 1986.

Hawaii broke up in 1987 and Shade, after abbreviated stays in New York and California, embarked on a six-week tour of Europe in 1989 with the band Anthrax as their drum technician. At the conclusion of the tour he returned to Hyattsville, Maryland and in 1991 he again worked with Mike Feeedbak, this time drumming on the album "Cruel World" (Mike Feeedbak; N.U.K.-Fire Rock Records, 1991).

Shade moved to Greenbelt, Maryland and from 1992 to 2002 he owned and operated a store called Greenbelt Video; the space it occupied on Centerway is today the back bar and performance space of the New Deal Café. In 2001 he pursued his passion for making guitars and founded a separate business called Hallmark Guitars which is still in existence today.

BOBBIE HOWARD

Bobbie Howard was raised in Miami, Florida and began playing guitar during his teen years in the 1950s. After finishing high school in the Sunshine State he moved to Arlington, Virginia, where, in 1958, he put together a rock and roll band with guitarist Johnny Sneed called Bobbie Howard and the Ponies that worked local teen dances and night clubs. In 1959 he and Sneed met guitarist Link Wray at the Rendezvous in Washington, D.C. and the pair then spent most of the following three years working with Link Wray and His Ray Men at Vinnie's Grill on 10th Street NW.

Howard put together a new rock and roll band and from 1962 to 1964 Bobbie "The Kid" Howard and the Ponies, as he called his reconstituted outfit, worked at such Washington, D.C. night clubs as the Round Up Club, the Famous and the Alpine Room. The regular lineup for this group consisted of Howard handling lead vocals, guitar and keyboards, lead guitarist Johnny Sneed, either Jack Casady or Mike Hunnicutt on bass, and female drummer Trudy Cooper.

In September 1964 Howard put together a new band he called Bobbie Howard and the Hi-Boys that consisted of himself, lead guitarist Roy Buchanan, bassist Junior Gill and drummer Mike Kennedy. The band performed for several weeks in Washington, D.C. at Rand's Night Club and the Alpine Room and then in November of that year the band changed its name to the British Walkers and moved to the Roundtable on M Street NW in Georgetown.

Howard stayed with the British Walkers until March 1967, at which time he briefly took over as lead singer for the Mad Hatters, who were then playing at Nu-Mac's in Georgetown. In May of that year Howard put together a new band, the Sweet (often billed as "Bobbie Howard and the Sweet"), which consisted of himself handling vocals and keyboards, lead guitarist Tommy Curley, bassist Curt Jonnie and drummer Mike Kennedy. The band released singles on Smash Records and spent most of the year performing at the Keg on Wisconsin Avenue NW.

In 1970 Howard was singing and playing bass in a band called Goosby-Pegalo that also included lead guitarist Lance Quinn, rhythm guitarist Billy Patterson and drummer Mike Zack. The short-lived quartet performed in Washington, D.C. at the Keg and the Bayou.

Howard remained in the area into the middle 1970s, but gradually withdrew from the local music scene. He recorded an album under the name Mordicai Jones at Wray's Shack 3 Tracks in Accokeek, Maryland which was released on Polydor Records in 1971. In 1975 he relocated to Florida and left the music world behind, until being called back to the Washington, D.C. area for a series of British Walker reunion performances in 2009.

Singles that feature Bobbie Howard include: "The Pony" backed with "Stupid Pony" (The Kid; Okeh Records, 1960); "Sleep Tight" backed with "True Love (is hard to find)" (The Kid; Rumble Records, 1961); "Sh' Mon" backed with "Sh' Mon (Part Two)" (The A-side is credited to Mr. Dynamite, arranged and conducted by Charlie Hampton; the B-side is credited the Dynamite Orchestra, arranged and conducted by Charlie Hampton; Sue Records, 1966) – the lineup for these recordings was lead singer Bobbie Howard, lead guitarist Jimmy Carter, bassist Jack Brooks, drummer Steve Lacey, and the Howard Theatre Orchestra conducted by Charlie Hampton; "Broken Heart Attack" backed with "Don't Do It" (The Sweet; Smash Records, 1967); "Got To Have More Love" backed with "You Can't Win At Love" (The Sweet; Smash Records, 1967); and "Rockin Gambler" backed with "Alabama Guitar Man" (Goosby-Pegalo; Paramount Records, 1970).

Album releases that feature Bobbie Howard include: "Mordicai Jones" (Mordicai Jones; Polydor Records, 1971); "The British Walkers Are Coming" (The British Walkers; Turkey Mountain Records, 2009); and "The Kid" (Bobbie Howard; Turkey Mountain Records, 2009).

BOBBY JONES

Drummer Bobby Jones grew up in Charles County, Maryland in the town of Indian Head and during his time at Lackey High School in the late 1950s he first played in a rock and roll band called the Rhythm Makers that specialized in covering songs by Carl Perkins and Elvis Presley. In the early 1960s Jones entered the Washington, D.C. area night club scene and drummed for a rock and roll band called the Prodigals at such establishments as Rand's Night Club, the Starlite Restaurant and the Keg.

From 1964 to 1966 Jones drummed for the Dominoes, a rock and roll band that performed for stretches at two Washington, D.C. night clubs, the Shelter Room in the Southeast quadrant of the city and the Rocket Room in the Downtown area. While working the Shelter Room, the band backed up several national acts including pop singers Terry Stafford and Jo Ann Campbell.

In 1967 Jones joined a rock and roll band called the Uncalled Four which featured guitarist Roy Buchanan and performed in Washington, D.C. at the Silver Dollar Restaurant and the Hayloft; and in Maryland at the Half Shell Restaurant on Branch Avenue in Silver Hill.

In the late 1960s Jones worked short engagements for a number of different rock and roll acts in the Washington, D.C. area including Danny Denver and the Sound Tracks at the Starlite Restaurant and Strick's Restaurant, the Fourmost at the Silver Dollar Restaurant, Link Wray and His Ray Men at the 1023 Restaurant, the Van Dykes at Benny's Rebel Room, and the Joey Welz Band at the Gold Rush. Jones still drums for the Rhythm Makers, who periodically reunite for performances in Charles County, Maryland.

BOBBY LAKIND

Bobby LaKind was raised in Teaneck, New Jersey, graduated from Teaneck High School in 1963, and attended the University of Kentucky. In the late 1960s he enrolled in law school at the University of Maryland, lived near the campus in College Park, and began exploring the local music scene. During this time he sang and played percussion in a rock and roll band called the Manchester Squires that performed at local teen dances.

In 1969 LaKind became the lead singer and conga player in a local band called Rock Bottom, which performed a mix of R&B and rock and roll covers and mainly performed at My Mother's Place, a popular night club at 18th and M Streets NW in Washington, D.C. Though Rock Bottom was a short-lived venture, the band boasted an impressive roster of local talent that included several members that had previously been a part of a local soul band called Jerome and the Good Knights.

Rock Bottom's main lineup consisted of LaKind, guitarist Richard Solow, bassist Alan Bennett, keyboardist Gil Goldstein, trumpeter Gerry Bowles, trombonist Mark Swartz and drummer Gary Shofnos. In the band's last performance on Sunday, July 20, 1969, they appeared at My Mother's Place and were called upon to back up all three of the evening's feature acts: pop singer Andy Kim; Peaches and Herb; and singer-keyboardist Billy Preston.

In the early 1970s LaKind moved to Los Angeles, California and became an equipment manager and lighting technician for the Doobie Brothers, occasionally joining them onstage as an extra percussionist and background vocalist. By 1979 he had become a full-time member of the band as a conga player and singer, a position he retained through 1988.

During his career, LaKind performed with such popular music acts as: country rock singer-guitarist Chris Hillman; C&W singer Karen Brooks; pop singers Lauren Wood, Greg Guidry, Nicolette Larson and Linda Ronstadt; R&B-rock singer-keyboardist Michael McDonald; rock and roll singer Johnny Van Zant; rock and roll singer-guitarist Paul Berrere; and the bands Spirit, the Nitty Gritty Dirt Band and Little Feat. Bobby LaKind passed away on Thursday, December 24, 1992 at the age of 47.

BOBBY MANRIQUEZ

Guitarist Bobby Manriquez was raised in Washington, D.C. and Silver Spring, Maryland and graduated from Montgomery Blair High School in 1969. During his teen years he played lead guitar in several different rock and roll bands including the Madcaps, Axis, and Nitty Gritty. He then spent time in the early 1970s playing in such popular local groups as Desdemona and the New Breed.

After leaving the New Breed in 1971 Manriquez put together his own band called Bobby and Friends that included three transfers from his previous group – bassist Bobby Colie, keyboardist Kurt Gibbons and drummer David Platshon, with Greg Hemming eventually replacing Colie. The band worked a long engagement out of the Apple Pie on M Street NW in Georgetown. In the early 1970s he also passed in and out of the Dubonnettes and was called upon to work live dates with singer-guitarist Nils Lofgren, an association that would endure throughout the decade.

In 1973 Manriquez was recruited by record producer David Briggs to put together a touring band for San Francisco-based blues rock singer and Capitol Recording artist Kathi McDonald. The band Manriquez assembled included himself on lead guitar, bassist Wornell Jones, keyboardist Kurt Gibbons, saxophonist Boots Hughston and drummer Vince Santoro. Manriquez toured with McDonald for two years and then in 1975 was called upon to again perform dates with the Dubonnettes, this time in London, England and Marbella, Spain. During this time he also played guitar in Charlie and the Pep Boys (the Dubonnettes under a different name).

In 1976 Manriquez was called upon to again join forces with singer-guitarist Nils Lofgren, whose new band also included guitarist Tom Lofgren, bassist Scotty Ball and drummer Mike Zack. That outfit lasted for most of the late 1970s and embarked on concert tours throughout the United States and Europe.

In an article entitled "Central Park Rock & Roll Hoochie Koo" that appeared in Rolling Stone on Thursday, September 9, 1976, reporter Dave Marsh favorably writes of Nils Lofgren's performance, and Manriquez in particular, at the Schaefer Music Festival (Wollman Rink, Central Park, New York City, New York, Monday, July 26, 1976): "Lofgren's voice never sounded better and his band, which now features a good second guitarist, Bobby Manriquez (late of Charlie and the Pep Boys), Is his best yet. He came on less of a punk and more of a guitar hero than ever before, and that's a distinct advantage."

Manriquez toured as Wilson Pickett's lead guitarist in 1994 and 1995 and more recently has fronted his own blues bands. His albums include: "Daddy's Girl" (Charlie and the Pep Boys; A&M Records, 1976); "Live on the Test" (Nils Lofgren; Windsong International, 1993 – Manriquez appears on the portion recorded live in 1976 on "The Old Grey Whistle Test," a musical television show that broadcasted from the fourth floor of the BBC Television Centre at White City in West London, United Kingdom; the band for this performance included, besides Nils Lofgren and Manriquez, Tom Lofgren, Scotty Ball and Mike Zack); "Another Shade of Blue(s)" (Bobby Manriquez; Time Blues, 2000); and "Prayin' the Blues (blu funk)" (Bobby Manriquez; B-Side Blues Publishing, 2005).

BOBBY RADCLIFF

Internationally-known blues guitarist Bobby Radcliff grew up in Chevy Chase, Maryland and graduated from Bethesda-Chevy Chase High School in 1970. Born Robert Ewan, he started playing guitar at age 12 and was heavily influenced by the Ventures, Elvis Presley, the Beatles, Link Wray and Buck Owens. The first band he was in as a teenager was called the Yarbs, which played blues and progressive rock and roll on the area's local teen dance circuit during the middle 1960s. In 1967 the band began performing at the Corral in Georgetown and soon changed its name to Froggy Little.

During his years at Bethesda-Chevy Chase High School, Ewan was first a member of a band called Hunk of Funk which included future Nighthawks founder Mark Wenner. He then joined a band called the North Side Blues Band, a group that consisted of himself handling lead vocals and lead guitar, harmonica player Bret Littlehales, bassist Bill Bowman, keyboardist Guy Dorsey and drummer Richard Murray (later drummers in the band included Van Holmead and Walter Sheridan; and later bassists included Steve Shaw and Tom Slavin).

After graduating high school Ewan began performing simply as "Bobby Radcliff" with assorted musicians in his various backup bands. He often played in a trio format with either Tom Slavin or Steve Shaw or Dave Walker on bass, and drummer Victor Spano. Radcliff headlined throughout the early and middle 1970s in Washington, D.C. at such night clubs as Top O' Foolery, the Far Inn, Buddy's Place, Cousin Nick's and the Childe Harold; and in Maryland at the Psyche Delly (Bethesda).

Radcliff relocated to New York City in 1977 where he has maintained his career as one of the world's best blues musicians. Among the albums he has released are: "Early in the Morning" (Bobby Radcliff; A-Okay Records, 1985); "Dresses Too Short" (Bobby Radcliff; Black Top Records, 1989); "Universal Blues" (Bobby Radcliff; Black Top Records, 1991); "There's A Cold Grave in Your Way" (Bobby Radcliff; Black Top Records, 1994); "Live at the Rynborn" (Bobby Radcliff; Black Top Records, 1997); "Natural Ball" (Bobby Radcliff; Rollo Records, 2004); and "Freaking Me Out" (Bobby Radcliff; Krellno Records, 2011).

BOYD FARRELL

Singer Boyd Farrell was born in Swindon, Wiltshire, United Kingdom and as a youth and teenager moved about England, Texas and the Washington, D.C. area. While living in Bowie, Maryland in the middle 1970s he attended Largo High School and was influenced by such performers as Iggy Pop, David Bowie, Alice Cooper, the Rolling Stones, the Ramones, as well as punk rock bands like the Damned, the Clash, the Sex Pistols, the Stranglers and the Germs.

While in high school Farrell first sang in a local hard-rocking party band called Brat. He next sang for the band Crash, a heavy metal group that performed in the late 1970s at such area night clubs as the Varsity Grill Back Room in College Park and the Keg in Washington, D.C. In 1978 and 1979 he handled vocals for a punk rock cover band called Snitch, which gave performances at a Washington, D.C. night club called the Atlantis prior to its conversion into Nightclub 9:30.

In 1980 Farrell formed what would become one of the Washington, D.C. area's most heralded punk rock bands, Black Market Baby. The group's lineup consisted of Farrell handling lead vocals, guitarist Keith Campbell, bassist Paul Cleary and drummer Tommy Carr. The band lasted through 1988 and then had another run from 1993 to 1997. Farrell went on to sing for other local rock and roll bands including Shatterbox in 1988, the Vile Geezers from 1991 to 1995, and RUSTBUCKiT from 2005 to 2008.

BRENDAN PELAN

Multi-instrumentalist Brenda Pelan was born in Belfast, Ireland in 1945 and came to the United States in 1949. He was raised in College Park, Maryland by his mother, who sang and danced, and his father, a plasterer by profession who also played violin for the Irish American Society in Baltimore. Pelan learned the violin from his father and took piano lessons in grade school. After hearing the Elvis Presley song "Jailhouse Rock" while in the seventh grade at Holy Redeemer School in College Park he took up guitar and started hanging out with some fellow musicians.

Pelan and a friend from his neighborhood named Dennis Brown put together a rock and roll band called the Runarounds which lasted from 1958 to 1960, his eighth and ninth grades school years. He played rhythm guitar for the group, which performed covers of such artists as Little Richard, Jerry Lee Lewis and Gary U.S. Bonds at local parties and a few shopping center promotional events.

In the spring of 1962, near the conclusion of his junior year of high school at St. Anthony's School in Washington, D.C., Pelan was approached by a classmate named Chick Hall, Jr., who played guitar and asked him to play bass and sing in a band he was putting together. Although Pelan was not a bassist, Hall showed him the basics and the two began collaborating on vocal harmonies. Together they worked on songs by Dion and the Belmonts, the Five Satins and the Everly Brothers, among others. That summer they added drummer Rick Stubblefield and called their new band the Majestic Neons. The group quickly built a following at the College Park Teen Club in the city's municipal building and went on to become one of the best young bands on the local teen dance circuit. Pelan remained a member of the Majestic Neons into 1966.

In 1968 Pelan put together a band called the Four Reasons Why which was based in Clarksville, Maryland (Howard County) and performed pop and rock and roll songs at area church functions, high school reunions, weddings and military base officers' clubs. He served as the band's lead singer and bassist and guitarist Chick Hall, Jr. frequently sat in with the group.

In the early 1980s he changed the name of the group to the Reasons, led them into a jazz rock direction, and booked the group into area hotels and weddings. The band experienced changes in personnel and since 1990 have been performing as the Rockin' Reasons. The group's current lineup consists of Pelan on lead vocals and bass, guitarist Brian Lite and drummer Frank Cucuzzi.

In recent years Pelan has performed with Chick Hall, Jr. in a singer-guitarist duo called Class Reunion that performs all manner of C&W, jazz, pop and rock and roll at night spots like the Limerick Pub in Wheaton, Maryland. He is also performing today as an Irish folk music solo artist, singing and playing acoustic guitar at such night clubs as Molloy's Irish Pub and Grill (Gambrills), the James Joyce Pub (Baltimore), the Kilkarney House (Davidsonville) and the Limerick Pub (Wheaton). Pelan has also performed as a solo artist at various Irish music festivals throughout Maryland, and his native Ireland as well.

BRENT WOODALL

Singer Brent Woodall was born in Baltimore, Maryland and raised in nearby Howard County in the community of Dorsey. During his years at Waterloo Junior High School in the early 1960s he sang for a British Invasion-influenced band on the local teen dance circuit called Sir Brent and the Mystics. During his time at Howard High School in the middle and late 1960s he sang in a nine-piece horn band called the Coming Generation that played country club functions around the Washington, D.C. area.

In 1967 Woodall formed a rock and roll band called Cherry Smash that initially played Beatles songs and Top 40 material at the Gaslight Lounge inside the Howard Johnson's Motor Lodge in Catonsville, Maryland. He remained with the band until 1978. In its lifetime, Cherry Smash had more than 40 musicians pass through its roster and was regarded as one of the Washington, D.C. area's top bands, particularly during the early and middle 1970s when they regularly appeared at the Bayou in Georgetown.

Woodall spent the early 1980s in San Francisco, California drumming for rock and roll singer-guitarist Barry "The Fish" Melton and then gave up music for more than 10 years. In 1993 he returned to the music world as lead singer of River's Edge, a C&W band from Winchester, Virginia that went from playing in a garage to playing Farm Aid within four years of its inception. More recently he has performed and recorded with his own C&W group, Brent Woodall and the Natchez Trace Band, which includes several former members of Cherry Smash.

BRIAN WAGNER

Bassist Brian Wagner was born in Baltimore, Maryland, where, during his junior high school years in the middle 1960s, he listened to groups like the Beatles, the Rolling Stones and the Dave Clark Five and first played bass in a rock and roll band called the Gremlins. When he was 14 years old his family moved to Lanham, Maryland and while in the ninth grade at Robert Goddard Junior High School he played in a rock and roll band on the local teen dance circuit called the Zoo.

Wagner attended DuVal High School in the late 1960s and in September 1968 he formed the rock and roll band God Mother Country. The group was based in Lanham,

Maryland and had an original lineup of lead singer-guitarist Dave Williams, guitarist Jeff Greene, Wagner on bass, keyboardist Sherman Griffith and drummer Birdie Williams. They originally covered such artists as the Doors, Cream, Steppenwolf, the Troggs and the Young Rascals and initially performed at private parties and teen dances at the Seabrook Teen Club (Gaywood Elementary School) and the Carleton East Teen Club (Lanham). God Mother Country went on to become a top attraction at teen dances and night clubs throughout the Washington, D.C. area. They disbanded in 1974.

From January 1977 to April 1978 Wagner played bass in a local R&B-rock band called Sky King. In 1979 he joined the Washington, D.C.-based rock and roll band Tears, which, prior to his arrival, had released an eponymous album for Backstreet Records. From February 1980 until March 1981 Wagner was the bass player for Fast Eddie, a hard-rocking outfit on the Washington, D.C. area night club scene that also included singer-guitarist David Utter, guitarist Wayne Tomlinson and drummer Timm Biery.

BUD HARNER

Drummer Bud Harner was raised in McLean, Virginia and while attending Langley High School during the late 1960s and early 1970s he played with a number of rock and roll bands on the local teen dance circuit including the Yorkshires. He went on to drum for such national acts as C&W singer Jim Stafford and pop singer Paul Anka and was a member of pop singer Barry Manilow's backup band for most of the 1980s. Most recently he drummed for a jazz band called Uncle Festive.

BUTLER'S ORCHARD

Butler's Orchard was a notable rock and roll band that formed in the summer of 1971 in Clinton, Maryland. Most of the band's members were sons of military parents and were born in other regions of the United States or other countries altogether. Military transfers to nearby Andrews Air Force Base brought these families to Clinton, which was served by Surrattsville High School. All but one of the various musicians to pass through the group attended Surrattsville from 1971 to 1974, with most band members graduating in either June 1972 or June 1973.

The original lineup of Butler's Orchard, which was an outgrowth of an earlier rock group called Acephalous, consisted of singer-rhythm guitarist Roger Owens, singer-lead guitarist Ray Gibbs, bassist Mike Mihlbauer and drummer Micheal Mello. Soon after forming, Mihlbauer was replaced on bass by John Previti and a flutist-saxophonist named Don Stapleson was added. Several months later the band brought in rhythm guitarist Neal Dawson, who had previously played with a band called Winthrop Savage. Drummer Mike Mello was the only non-Surrattsville member of the band, having graduated from Bishop McNamara High School in 1971.

The initial six-piece edition of Butler's Orchard debuted with a standing-room-only performance at the Surrattsville Senior Teen Club (Surrattsville High School) in the fall of 1971, an event that saw them feature selections from Jethro Tull's popular "Aqualung" album.

The repertoire of Butler's Orchard included both original compositions and covers of such popular rock and roll bands as CSNY (Crosby, Stills, Nash and Young), Traffic, Spirit, Cream, the Beatles, the Rolling Stones, the Moody Blues, Three Dog Night and others.

From 1971 to 1977 the band performed at dances at Tucker Road Community Center (Fort Washington), the Surrattsville Senior Teen Club (Surrattsville High School in Clinton), the Surrattsville Junior Teen Club (Surrattsville Junior High School in Clinton), Friendly High School (Fort Washington), Bowie High School (Bowie), the Stephen Decatur Teen Club (Stephen Decatur Junior High School in Clinton), the Eugene Burroughs Teen Club

(Eugene Burroughs Junior High School in Accokeek), the John Hanson Teen Club (John Hanson Junior High School in Oxon Hill), the Lord Baltimore Teen Club (Lord Baltimore Junior High School in Fort Washington), the Benjamin D. Foulois Teen Club (Benjamin D. Foulois Junior High School in Suitland), the Volunteer Fire Department of Brandywine (Brandywine), Tantallon Country Club (Fort Washington), Thomas Stone High School (Waldorf) and Frostburg State College (Frostburg, Maryland).

Butler's Orchards experienced numerous personnel changes during its time. In 1972 Don Stapleson departed, John Previti was replaced on bass by Danny Cross, and Bill Smith was added on keyboards and rhythm guitar. In the fall of 1972 Ray Gibb departed, reducing the band to a quintet. In the spring of 1973 the band regrouped with Owens and Cross remaining, three members leaving, and three new members in guitarist Glenn Morris, drummer Dave Danielson and lead singer Kathy Shelow completing the arrangement. After a brief hiatus, the band reorganized again and from the summer of 1976 to the summer of 1977 the group's final lineup featured singer-lead guitarist Ray Gibb, singer-rhythm guitarist Roger Owens, bassist Danny Cross and drummer Mike Mello.

Butler's Orchard was well-respected in the Washington, D.C. area during its time for the solid instrumental and vocal abilities of its members. The band was a major influence on numerous rock and roll bands from around the region including DC Star, which also hailed from Clinton, Maryland and went on to achieve some measure of national recognition.

Several Butler's Orchard alumni went on to work with musicians of note, including bassist John Previti who worked for several years with guitar great Danny Gatton, and reed player Don Stapleson, who has performed with the likes of Ray Charles and Martha Reeves. In addition, Mike Mello and Roger Owens worked together in several top bands around the nation's capital including High Roller and the Fox Chase Band; guitarist Ray Gibb has spent several years with country rock singer-harmonicist Rich Layton and Canadian-based blues pianist David Vest; and guitarist Neal Dawson has toured with the Last Psalm, a nationally known contemporary Christian music band.

Butler's Orchard has reunited several times in recent years to headline the various "Surrattstock" events staged by the Surrattsville High School Alumni Foundation. In addition, Neal Dawson, Roger Owens and former Crusader Rabbit member Henry Smith currently perform together in the Back Pages Band.

CARL ANDERSON

Singer Carl Anderson was born and raised in Lynchburg, Virginia, and, after a two-year stint in the United States Air Force, relocated to the Washington, D.C. area at the age of 24 in 1969. Upon arrival in the nation's capital he began singing R&B covers with the house band at a night club called the Hollywood Restaurant on 9th Street NW, a block south of U Street NW and two blocks away from the Howard Theatre.

Not long after his arrival, Anderson, who was Black, fell in with some long-haired White musicians from Annapolis, Maryland who had previously played together in a rock and roll band called Innocent Color and were now playing as a trio called Second Eagle at the Keg in Glover Park. The threesome, consisting of lead guitarist Dick Rausch, bassist Lee Craig and drummer Vernon Smith, asked Anderson to take over the lead vocalist position.

Second Eagle continued to rehearse and perform at the Keg as a four-piece unit throughout the fall of 1969. In the months ahead the band added a keyboardist named Tim Burleson, lived for a spell on a farm called Buck Mountain Farm near Browntown outside of Front Royal, Virginia, and later replaced Burleson with Mark Redd of Silver Spring, Maryland.

In early 1970 the owners of the Bayou recruited Second Eagle away from the Keg and installed them as their house band, a position they maintained for most of the year. During this time the group was mixing unique original material with heavy, Vanilla Fudge-styled covers of songs by such artists as the Beatles, the Rolling Stones, Jethro Tull, Rhinoceros, Iron Butterfly and Richie Havens.

When not playing the Bayou, Second Eagle appeared at another Georgetown night club by the name of JamF and was also a popular attraction at functions on local college campuses such as American University and the University of Maryland, where they headlined a concert at Ritchie Coliseum on Friday, September 18, 1970.

Second Eagle presented songs outside the mainstream in their own heavy style, with a typical set consisting of tunes by musicians as diverse as John Lennon, George Gershwin and Burt Bacharach – all served up in a trippy, psychedelic style. While rehearsing at Mark Redd's house in Silver Spring, Maryland in late 1970, the band began working up selections from the album "Jesus Christ Superstar" ("Jesus Christ Superstar," A Rock Opera by Andrew Lloyd Webber & Tim Rice; Decca Records, 1970) for inclusion in their stage act.

On Palm Sunday, April 4, 1971, Second Eagle gave a performance at St. Stephen and the Incarnation Episcopal Church in Washington, D.C. that featured a 40-minute medley of songs from the "Jesus Christ Superstar" album. More than 1,000 people jammed into the church to see the rock and roll spectacle. Reportedly, among those observing the performance was a talent agent from the William Morris agency who set up an audition for Anderson with a team of producers who were organizing an on-the-road play production of "Jesus Christ Superstar."

Anderson made the cut and was signed up as Ben Vereen's understudy in the role of Judas, eventually taking over the lead as the play gained popularity on Broadway. Anderson was then given the role of "Judas" in the movie "Jesus Christ Superstar" (Universal Pictures, 1973) and was nominated that year for two Golden Globe awards as "Most Promising Newcomer" and "Best Musical Actor."

Anderson went on to enjoy a long career on stage and screen, appearing in numerous movies, television shows and theater productions. He also enjoyed a long recording career as a solo jazz and R&B singer, releasing albums for such major record labels as Epic, Polydor, and GRP. Carl Anderson passed away on Monday, February 23, 2004 at the age of 58.

CATFISH HODGE

Blues rock singer-guitarist Bob "Catfish" Hodge hails from Detroit, Michigan, where, in the late 1960s, he played in a popular local rock band called Wicked Religion. In 1969 he put together a band called Catfish which signed with Epic Records and embarked on regional tours, including stops in the Washington, D.C. area where they first played the night club Emergency in 1970. Though a short-lived venture, Catfish released three albums in its time: "Get Down" (Catfish; Epic Records, 1970); "Catfish" (Catfish; Epic Records, 1970); and "Live Catfish Featuring Bob Hodge" (Catfish; Epic Records, 1971).

In the fall of 1974 Hodge relocated to McLean, Virginia and put together a new band of local musicians that focused on playing in and around the nation's capital. During the 1970s the Catfish Hodge Band performed in Washington, D.C. at such night clubs as the Childe Harold, Mr. Henry's Tenley Circle, Rocky Raccoon's Saloon, Columbia Station, Desperado's and the Cellar Door; and in Maryland at the Psyche Delly (Bethesda).

In 1982 Hodge moved to California and remained there for 17 years, furthering his status as an American blues rock legend. Hodge has more than two-dozen albums on a variety of independent record labels to his credit and still performs throughout the United States today.

CATHY PONTON KING

Blues singer-guitarist Cathy Ponton King was born in Washington, D.C. and raised in what was then an Irish community in Hyattsville, Maryland. She lived with her parents and her grandmother, who hailed from Moycullen, Galway, Ireland, and the family home was a gathering place for locals of Irish descent. Ponton began singing at the age of five at parties hosted by her grandmother. Her father was musical as well, once winning the "Best Harmonica Player in Washington" contest at the age of 10, a competition hosted by the Washington Daily News newspaper.

Ponton attended high school at St. Anthony's School in Northeast Washington, D.C. in the early 1970s. In the ensuing years while attending the University of Maryland she became a featured performer at the Dubliner in Washington, D.C., first starting out singing Irish songs from her family's history and then gradually adding songs by Little Feat, Bonnie Raitt, Join Mitchell and others. A frequent visitor to the Dubliner was blues guitarist Jimmy Thackery, who would take the stage and play while Ponton sang.

During the early 1970s Ponton also performed as a solo artist at Gallagher's Pub on Connecticut Avenue NW in Washington, D.C. Ponton increasingly want to explore the worlds of blues and rock and roll and began writing original songs and material. In the late 1970s she worked at ABC News Radio and also took a position as news director at WLMD, a rock and roll radio station in Laurel, Maryland. There she hosted an on-air interview program entitled "90 Seconds." During this period she moved in with Jimmy Thackery and his wife in Bethesda, Maryland and delved further into the local blues scene.

In 1979 Ponton formed her own blues band, the Rhythm Masters. Musicians came and went and the group eventually settled on a lineup of singer-guitarist Ponton, lead guitarist Dave Sherman, bassist Russ Dunlap, harmonicist Pat Day and drummer Corey Hackett. Other musicians to pass through the band during its early stages included bassist Leo Aspiras and drummer Mike Parrell.

The Rhythm Masters covered such blues artists as Magic Sam, Muddy Waters, Little Walter and Big Joe Turner. Locally, they performed in Washington, D.C. at such night clubs as Desperado's, Columbia Station, Mr. Henry's Tenley Circle, the Gentry, the Childe Harold and the Wax Museum; in Maryland at the Psyche Delly (Bethesda), the Italian Gardens (College Park) and the Takoma Tap Room (Silver Spring); and in Virginia at Beacon's Backstage (Falls Church) and the Warehouse (Alexandria). The band also embarked on night club tours and made festival appearances up and down the East Coast. The Rhythm Masters endured several changes in personnel during their time and remained one of the region's top blues band until dissolving in 1986.

Ponton married producer-engineer Jeff King of Falls Church, Virginia in 1986 and became Cathy Ponton King. After a break in the action she returned to the local music scene in 1990, gathered musicians around her, and began performing under the banner of either "Cathy Ponton King" or "The Cathy Ponton King Band."

Through the years a large number of local musicians have performed and recorded with her including: guitarists Mike Dennis, Jimmy Thackery, Bill Thomas, James Mabry, Mike Lessin, Chick Hall, Jr., Dan Hovey and Andy Rutherford; bassists Jim Robeson, Wade Mathews, Carl Peachey, Dave Besley, Rolf Hanson, Eric Scott and Jan Zukowski; keyboardists Bruce Harrison, Bill Starks, Jon Carroll, Tommy Lepson, Mike Kelley and Tim Ford; saxophonists Tim Eyermann, Alex Holland, Joe Stanley, Chris Watling and Ron Holloway; trumpeter Curtis Pope; and drummers Andy Haley, Big Joe Maher, Robbie Magruder, Bob Berberich, Pete Ragusa, Paul Goldstein and Andy Hamburger.

The current Cathy Ponton King Band consists of King, lead guitarist Mike Melchione, bassist John Previti, keyboardist Sam Paladino and drummer Antoine Sanfuentes.

To date, Cathy Ponton King has released a total of four albums: "Lovin' You Right" (Cathy Ponton King; Long Gone Records, 1993); "Undertow" (Cathy Ponton King; Long Gone Records, 2007); "The Crux" (Cathy Ponton King; Long Gone Records, 2012); and "Quartet/Duet" (Cathy Ponton King; Long Gone Records, 2013). She currently performs at Madam's Organ in Washington, D.C., Flanagan's Irish Pub in Bethesda, Maryland (its space formerly housed the Psyche Delly), and at festivals and shows throughout the Washington, D.C. area.

CHARLIE BURGEE

Billed as "Rock and Roll Charlie," this saxophone player from the Hillside neighborhood of Capitol Heights, Maryland was instrumental in introducing rock and roll music to a number of Prince George's County, Maryland night clubs in the late 1950s that had previously been C&W strongholds. During its time, Charlie Burgee and His Sophisticators, as he called his rock and roll outfit, were a popular attraction in the southern part of the county at Strick's Restaurant in Silver Hill and a number of Marlboro Pike establishments including the Campus Club, the Senate Inn, Billy's Tavern and the Homestretch Tavern.

CHARLIE DANIELS

Charlie Daniels was born on Wednesday, October 28, 1936 in Wilmington, North Carolina and arrived in North Beach, Maryland on the Chesapeake Bay with his rock and roll band, then-called Charlie Daniels and the Rockets, in the summer of 1958. They spent the remainder of the year working there as the house band at a night club called Rose's Musical Bar.

Daniels moved his band to Washington, D.C. in December 1958 where they spent the month playing the Famous Restaurant. In April 1959 the group began a lengthy engagement at the Dixie Pig in Cottage City, Maryland where they assumed the name Charlie Daniels and the Jaguars. A record deal with Epic Records was completed and the group recorded and released two singles: "Jaguar" backed with "Roundabout" (The Jaguars; Epic Records, 1959); and "Drive-In" backed with "Exit 6" (The Jaguars; Epic Records, 1959).

From 1959 to 1961, Charlie Daniels and the Jaguars played in Washington, D.C. at such night clubs Benny's Rebel Room, the Alpine Room, Guy's Place and the Rocket Room; and in Maryland at the Dixie Pig (Cottage City), Strick's Restaurant (Silver Hill) and the Turf Club (Laurel). Daniels remained a constant presence on the Washington, D.C. area music scene throughout the 1960s and was a frequent visitor to the night clubs along the Bladensburg Road Strip, with the Dixie Pig, the Surf Club and the Cross Roads rating among his favorite hangouts. His band released one more single during this period, "The Middle of a Heartache" backed with "Skip It" (Charley Daniels & the Jaguars; Paula Records, 1966).

A Hero of the South, this singer-guitarist-fiddler later went on to fame and fortune with his unique brand of Southern rock. During his career Daniels has released more than 30 albums, the first of which was "Charlie Daniels" (Charlie Daniels; Capitol Records, 1971). He has also released more than two-dozen compilation and live albums on more than a dozen different record labels including Kama Sutra, Epic, Liberty, Sparrow, Blue Hat, Sony Music, Audium, Koch and Mega Force.

Daniels has released singles that have cracked the Top 40 six times (for the Kama Sutra and Epic labels) from 1973 to 1982. His biggest hit to date is the single "The Devil Went Down to Georgia" (The Charlie Daniels Band; Epic Records, 1979), which reached number three on the "Billboard Hot 100" pop singles chart on Saturday, September 15, 1979.

CHERRY SMASH

The first version of Cherry Smash appeared in 1967 and played Beatles covers and Top 40 rock and roll songs five nights per week at the Gaslight Lounge (Howard Johnson's Motor Lodge, 5701 Baltimore National Pike, Catonsville, Maryland). The band consisted of a few holdovers from a Howard County, Maryland teen dance band called Sir Brent and the Mystics. The group's initial lineup consisted of singer-drummer Brent Woodall, lead guitarist Mike O'Connell, bassist Ken Johnson and keyboardist Paul Lorenz.

The late 1960s saw Cherry Smash perform regularly at Sarano's Lounge in West Friendship, Maryland and the Pirate's Den in Baltimore. During that time the band added a lead singer named Bonnie Cole and a second guitarist named Dale German, who was then replaced by guitarist Bob Flurie. At this time the band also added a second drummer named Dave Reid. From that point on, Cherry Smash experienced numerous personnel changes, with players coming and going at a rapid pace.

In the early 1970s Cherry Smash moved its operations to Washington, D.C. and played such night clubs as the Butterfly, the Crazy Horse, the Far Inn, and the Pub inside the Adele H. Stamp Student Union Building on the University of Maryland campus. Eventually they settled in as the semi-regular house band at the Bayou, a position that lasted from 1973 until 1978.

In the middle of the Bayou run in 1975 one of the band's best-known lineups consisted of lead singer and only original holdover Brent Woodall, lead guitarist Tim Tanner, guitarist Doug Allen, bassist Fred Crittendon, keyboardist-woodwind player Lee Foy (who was replaced by Ron Fetner) and drummer Barry Holober. During the Bayou run the band also opened for dozens of national acts including Aerosmith, the Beach Boys, Foreigner and Dire Straits.

Cherry Smash continued performing into the early 1980s with more than 40 members ultimately passing through its ranks before folding. Some of the more notable musicians to play in the band included saxophonist-keyboardist Bobby Read, who has been a member of Bruce Hornsby and the Noisemakers for more than 20 years, and keyboardist Chuck Ansell, who became a founding member of the rock and roll band Appaloosa and is still performing with them today.

Cherry Smash released one single during its existence: "She Loves You" backed with "Bug Huntin' Monkey" (Cherry Smash; Fayette Records, 1969).

CHIP CLEMMER

Growing up in Farmington, Connecticut, drummer Chip Clemmer studied percussion at the Hartford Conservatory of Music during his teen years at Rogers Junior High School and Farmington High School. Although primarily influenced by big band drummers such as Gene Krupa, Buddy Rich and Louie Bellson, he also listened to rock and roll drummers like Carl Palmer and Barriemore Barlow of Jethro Tull. He spent two years in the early 1970s studying music education at Bowling Green State University in Ohio, during which time he played in the college's symphony orchestra, chamber orchestra and concert bands. In addition he performed in the college lounge with a jazz trio called Music This Week. He later studied music for a year at Western Connecticut State College.

In 1977 Clemmer joined the United States Air Force. He was accepted into the Air Force Music Program and assigned to McGuire Air Force Base in Burlington County, New Jersey. There, he was a member of the 590th Air Force Band for two years, serving as a percussionist in the concert band. During that time he also drummed with the Jazz Ambassadors, who once backed up Doc Severinsen at a National Quarter Horse Association convention in Newport, Rhode Island.

In December 1979 Clemmer accepted the position of drummer in the United States Air Force Band and was relocated to Bolling Air Force Base in Washington, D.C. He ultimately spent 26 years in the United States Air Force and during his enlistment drummed and percussed for several components including the Singing Sergeants, the Airmen of Note, the United States Air Force Symphony Orchestra and the United States Air Force Concert Band, where he occupied the principal drum chair on their pop music show tours. During his last seven years of service he drummed for the Air Force's C&W band, the Silver Wings.

While stationed at Bolling Air Force Base, Clemmer performed onstage at DAR Constitution Hall in Washington, D.C. with the United States Air Force Concert Band as they backed up a number of nationally known musical artists who made appearances in conjunction with the Guest Artist Series. His performances in these concert events included drumming for Henry Mancini, Richard Carpenter, Clinton Gregory, Marie Osmond, Janie Fricke, Margaret Whiting, Mitch Miller and Roy Clark.

The United States Air Force Concert Band, with Clemmer on drums, also backed up Patti Austin at the Lightings of the National Christmas Tree on the Ellipse near the White House on Monday, December 7, 1987. On another occasion they backed up Gary Morris at an Air Force Association Convention at the Washington Hilton. Clemmer retired from the United States Air Force on Saturday, November 1, 2003 as a senior master sergeant.

While stationed At Bolling Air Force Base, Clemmer drummed for various local jazz and big band ensembles. In the 1980s and 1990s he worked extensively around the nation's capital with the Bob Tennyson Orchestra, the Tom Cunningham Orchestra, D.C. Authority, Trux Baldwin and the Starlite Octette and Frankie Condon's Big Band.

After his retirement from the United States Air Force Clemmer began freelancing and drumming at blues jams with scores of different musicians and groups at such area night clubs as Taliano's Restaurant and Bar (Takoma Park), the Surf Club (Hyattsville), Lasick's College Inn (College Park), Bangkok Blues (Falls Church), the Old Bowie Town Grille (Bowie) and Sapphire's Restaurant and Lounge (Laurel). Some of the blues and rock and roll bands he has played with in recent times include the Paulverizers, the Sherwood Blues Band, the Big Boy Little Band, Blue Lou and Friends, the Roadhouse Crew, Treated and Released, the Musician's Protection Program and the Roustabouts.

On Thursday, December 1, 2011 Clemmer and bassist Steve Carey played with country rock singer-guitarist Shane Dwight on "B.B. King's Bluesville," a blues radio program hosted by Bill Wax on Sirius XM Radio in Washington, D.C. As a trio they performed several songs on the air in a live setting from the XM Radio studio on Eckington Place NE.

Clemmer is currently drumming on a regular basis for three of the area's top musical acts, the Hall Brothers, the Joy Bodycomb Band (alternately known as the Joy B Band) and singer Patsy Stephens. Clemmer has appeared on three commercially issued albums: "Sophisticated Lady" (The Frankie Condon Orchestra; North Star Music, 2004); "Nuke the Juke" (Chick Hall Jr. with the Mustangs; Patuxent Music, 2010); and "Just Livin'" (Joy B Band; Self-Released, 2013).

CHRIS NOE

Guitarist Chris Noe was raised in Camp Springs, Maryland and during his teen years in the late 1960s he played the local teen dance circuit in bands called the Living End and Spread Eagle. As a senior at Crossland High School during the 1969-1970 school year he joined the band Devil's Track, a rock and roll band that performed at local teen dances and went on to become one of the top night club bands in the area.

Noe left Devil's Track in the summer of 1972 and briefly played in a popular Georgetown-based rock and roll band called Black On White, which regularly performed at the Act IV Supper Club and the Keg. In the fall of that year he joined the Cherry People, one of the best rock bands to ever emerge from the nation's capital. Noe lasted several months with the band, performing with them on a tour of New England and working an engagement with them at the Keg.

In 1973 Noe relocated to California and has since played with some of the best bands and musicians in the Los Angeles area, as well as a number of national acts. In 1974 he joined a hard rock band called Angel (different from the Casablanca group that featured Punky Meadows) and from there spent the rest of the 1970s playing with such rock and roll acts as Odyssey, singer-keyboardist Michael McDonald, Iron Butterfly, White Horse, Holy Smoke, Vendetta, and Flight 19.

In the 1980s some of the bands Noe played guitar for included Vixen, Lori and the Look-a-Likes, Mars, and Pentagon. He then spent the 1990s playing in the L.A. All-Stars and also worked with hip hop rapper Puff Daddy (Sean Combs), appearing in the 1997 video for the single "It's All About the Benjamins." Since 2000 Noe has been a part of the popular music duo Chris and Lisa. He currently owns and operates Allstars Studio in Long Beach, California.

CHRIS SHAW

Chris "Sky" Shaw is a Washington, D.C. native who spent his youth living in the city's Spring Valley neighborhood before moving over the line to Bethesda, Maryland as a teen. His first instrument was piano, but during his high school years in the early 1970s he began playing guitar and became enamored with blues players like James Cotton and Junior Wells, as well as local guitar heroes Bobby Radcliff, John Fahey and Danny Gatton.

As a teenager Shaw first played in a rock band called Hot Lather, which included future Urban Verbs drummer Danny Frankel. After graduating from Whitman High School in 1972 he passed through several local rock and roll bands including the Dorian Grays and the Monsters. He then took to the road and journeyed to the Midwest where, in 1975, he played lead guitar with the now-legendary blues singer-harmonicist Junior Wells at Theresa's Lounge in Chicago, Illinois, establishing himself as a top blues player and fulfilling a lifelong dream in the process.

After pursuing an acting career in New York City, Shaw returned to Washington, D.C. in 1986 and began performing in pickup blues bands on a nightly basis in night clubs around the city with the New Vegas Lounge on P Street NW becoming a favorite haunt. He was a founding member of a blues-based band called the Unforgiven in 1991 and two years later he formed the band Blues Museum, a group that headlined at such establishments as Blues Alley in Washington, D.C. and the State Theatre in Falls Church, Virginia.

In 2005 Shaw formed another band called White Whale, employing a revolving group of blues musicians that he directed towards a New Orleans jazz-styled type of music. A year later Shaw changed the name of the band to Whale Etouffee and they performed regularly at St. Elmo's Coffee Pub in Alexandria, Virginia. Shaw has since changed the name of this evolving musical project to Etufe and is recognized as one of the region's top pure blues guitarists.

CHRISTOPHER ZELL

Born in Washington, D.C. and raised in the Southwest and Southeast quadrants of the city, Christopher Zell was introduced to music at age nine when his mother taught him some old blues songs on the guitar.

In the middle 1960s while attending Ballou High School in Southeast Washington, D.C. he began frequenting a coffee house called the Crow's Toe, which had previously operated as the Open Way, and, before that, Coffee 'n' Confusion. Musicians he saw perform there included Fletcher Dubois, Joe Latham, Dawn and Joe, and Mississippi John Hurt. Zell began performing there with a fellow Ballou classmate named Garry Walker in an acoustic folk duo called the Tea Leaves. The Crow's Toe gave way to the Womb's Tomb, and then the Lute and Lyre, and in 1966 owner Ted Porterchinko changed its name to the Blue Sparrow, maintaining the beatnik coffee house vibe and the folk music entertainment. In 1966 and into 1967 Zell and Walker performed at the Blue Sparrow as "Chris and Garry."

In 1966 Zell briefly attended Prince George's Community College in Largo, Maryland where he played in a rock and roll band called the Magic Shop. After a two-year stint in the United States Navy he returned to Washington, D.C. in 1969 and reunited with Garry Walker, naming their new folk music project St. John's Churchyard. They initially performed folk music at such Washington, D.C. night clubs as the Zodiac and the Red Coach Inn, and tapped into the city's coffee house circuit, appearing at the Iguana Coffeehouse (Luther Place Memorial Church), the Through-the-Gate Coffee House (Capitol Hill Presbyterian Church) and the Wits End Restaurant (3709 Macomb Street NW), among others.

Zell took a break in 1972 and spent some time in Cape Cod, Massachusetts, where he performed with a folk act called Bell, Book and Candle. Late in the year he moved back to the nation's capital. He returned to St. John's Churchyard, which continued on as a duo, and, at times, with other musicians in the fold. The band played throughout the 1970s, covering the Everly Brothers, the Beatles and a wide range of folk and soft rock artists. Among the Washington, D.C. night clubs they performed at during those years were Jason's, Tammany Hall, the Exchange, Mr. Henry's Tenley Circle, the Act IV Supper Club and Rocky Raccoon's Saloon. In addition, St. John's Churchyard often participated in the Cellar Door "Hootenanny" shows and gave outdoor concerts organized by the city's "Summer in the Parks" program.

CHUCK BENNETT ("Blonde Chuck" or "Clean Chuck")

Chuck Bennett is a West Virginia native who moved to the Hillside neighborhood of Capitol Heights, Maryland at the age of 21 in 1963. At that time he learned to play bass guitar from his neighbor Jimmy Case, who was an established C&W guitarist in the area. He became a member of the backup band for the Ralph Case Square Dancers, an outfit which included guitarist Jimmy Case and singer-fiddler-guitarist Blackie Skiles. Bennett also worked with Case in his full-time C&W-rockabilly band Jimmy Case and the Cherokees at the Ozarks Restaurant in Washington, D.C. for most of 1963 and 1964.

Bennett spent the remainder of the 1960s playing in such Washington, D.C. bands as Ray Rock and the Revlons, a trio which at the time consisted of singer-guitarist Wally Simms, Bennet on bass and drummer Ray Rock and performed rock and roll at the Crosstown Restaurant in the Mount Pleasant; and Big Al Downing and His Band, whose R&B outfit consisted of Downing handling vocals and piano, Bennett, guitarist Tiny McCloud, saxophonist Vince Gedeon and drummer Dave West, and performed regularly at Rand's Night Club.

From the late 1960s to the early 1970s Bennett worked with many of the Washington, D.C. area's finest musicians and bands including a long stint with King Henry and the Knights, who played in Washington, D.C. at the Starlite Restaurant; and in Maryland at the Senate Inn (Capitol Heights), Strick's Restaurant (Silver Hill), the Quonset Supper Club (Silver Hill) and Sonny's Turntable Lounge in the basement of Bass' Restaurant and Bar (Mt. Rainier). During those years he also worked with other groups including the Joe Stanley Band, Little Joe and the Impossibles and Danny Denver and the Soundmasters (featuring guitarist Roy Buchanan). Bennett spent most of the 1980s with the C&W band Cool Country.

From 1961 to 1990 Bennett lived at 6711 Cipriano Road in Lanham, Maryland, a house that became a legendary hangout for the area's country and rock and roll musicians, with weekend after-hours jam sessions regularly lasting until dawn. In 1990 Bennett relocated to Huntington, West Virginia where he still resides.

CHUCK BENNETT ("Dirty Chuck")

Born Charles Avery in Washington, D.C. in 1942, Chuck Bennett, as he came to be known, was a singer and multi-instrumentalist who spent his entire life in and around the nation's capital and worked with some of the very best bands and musicians the region had to offer. Often called "Dirty Chuck" by his fellow musicians because of his dark hair (which distinguished him from the blonde-haired bassist of the same name in the area who was tagged "Clean Chuck"), Bennett entered the local music scene as a teenager playing rhythm guitar and bass with Link Wray and His Ray Men in Washington, D.C. night clubs such as the Rendezvous and Vinnie's Grill, as well as "The Milt Grant Show."

Later in his career Bennett served as a lead singer, rhythm guitarist, or bassist for such acts as the Fender Benders, the Chartbusters, the Warlox, Hillow Hammet, Gravity, Roy Buchanan, and Willie and the Hand Jives. He worked for many years in the 1960s and 1970s with the Winstons and in the 1980s toured extensively as a bassist with the Clovers. As a solo singing star, he released one single, "Seven Days (Are Made For Love)" backed with "I Went to Your House" (Chuck Bennett; Bonnie Records, 1962). Bennett passed away on Thursday, January 29, 2009 at the age of 66.

CHUCK SULLIVAN

Chuck Sullivan was raised in Bethesda, Maryland and as a teen in the late 1960s he drummed in a number of R&B and rock and roll bands on the local teen dance circuit including the Remains, the Tremolos, Elijah Jackson and the Fantastics, the Hinges of Fate, and Lockhouse. During his years at Winston Churchill High School in the early 1970s he was a member of the trippy rock band Sagebrush, which also included singer-guitarist Tim Kugel, singer-bassist Mark Walston and keyboardist Peter Stone. Sagebrush performed in Washington, D.C. at Nu-Mac's and Fort Reno Park; and in Maryland at the Wheaton Youth Center in Montgomery County and the Greenbelt Armory in Prince George's County, where on one occasion they opened a concert for the Damnation of Adam's Blessing.

While attending the University of Maryland in the middle 1970s Sullivan worked with several wedding bands through the Washington Talent Agency including Tic Tac and Rhapsody. During that time he also played in a country-pop-rock band called Off Balance. In 1979 he formed the band Big Yankee Dollar, a pop-rock band in the vein of Steely Dan and Dire Straits that included singer-guitarist John Jennings, bassist Gary Starr and keyboardist Bill Greer. Big Yankee Dollar performed in Washington, D.C. at the Cellar Door; in Maryland at the Psyche Delly (Bethesda) and the Italian Gardens (College Park); and in Virginia at Beacon's Backstage (Falls Church) and the Shed (Alexandria).

In 1980 Sullivan drummed for the final edition of Bill Holland and Rent's Due, whose lineup at the time also consisted of singer-keyboardist Bill Holland, guitarist Paul Bell, bassist Ron Newmyer and saxophonist Larry Strother. In 1981 he joined the R&B-rock band Jr. Cline and the Recliners, whose lineup at the time consisted of singer Daryl "Jr." Cline, guitarist Paul Bell, bassist Ron Newmyer, keyboardist John Hurd, saxophonists Wayne Sulc and Jeremy Schuhmann, and Sullivan on drums, with singer Tommy Lepson being a later addition to the mix.

In 1982 Sullivan, Lepson, Bell, Newmyer and Strother formed a new R&B band called Soul Crackers, which was noted for its versions of soul classics and became one of the region's most popular night club bands.

In 1984 Soul Crackers mainstays Sullivan, Bell and Newmyer teamed up with singer-guitarist Tom Lofgren to form an all-original pop band called Newkeys, which remained intact for six years and backed singer-guitarist Nils Lofgren on several East Coast tours. (Later additions to Newkeys were keyboardist Spencer Hoopes and singer Diane Rosenthal.) Among the major rock and roll musicians to join Newkeys for onstage jam sessions during its time were Joe Walsh and Bruce Springsteen.

From 1990 to 1994 Sullivan drummed for Tommy Lepson and the Lazy Boys. In one of his career highlights, he drummed in the backup bands for both Chuck Berry (along with bassist Ron Newmyer) and the pop vocal group known as Starland Vocal Band (along with the band Soul Crackers) at President William Clinton's Georgetown University Class of 1968 25th Anniversary party on the White House South Lawn on Saturday, June 5, 1993.

More recently Sullivan has played in the band Groovy, a group that rearranged classic songs of the 1960s using Latin, African and reggae grooves and included Ron Newmyer and Tom Lofgren. Additions to Groovy included guitarist Bill Craig and singers Mike Downey and Deeme Katson. Another recent band that Sullivan performed and recorded with was Paper Umbrella, which also included Ronnie Newmyer and Tom Lofgren, as well as guitarist Dave Egelhofer.

In 2004 Sullivan and Ronnie Newmyer co-founded BandHouse Gigs, a not-for-profit production company that organizes tributes to iconic artists or musical movements and typically combines over 50 local musicians for each concert.

CHUCK UNDERWOOD

Singer-guitarist Chuck Underwood was born in Milwaukee, Wisconsin, and, as a child in a military family, moved around the country frequently as a youth. His family moved to Rockville, Maryland in 1968 and two years later at the age of 12 he started playing guitar. He began making music with friends while attending Wheaton Woods Elementary School and in the sixth grade he sang pop songs in a neighborhood band called the Village Rats. During his time at Parkland Junior High School in the early 1970s he jammed in garages to the music of Jimi Hendrix and Alice Cooper and during his 8th and 9th grade years he sang and played guitar in a rock and roll band called White Fool.

During his years at Robert Peary High School in the middle 1970s Underwood sang and played lead guitar in a power trio called Third Stone From the Sun, a group rounded out by bassist Rob Williams and drummer Joe Daugherty. This band mainly appeared at local parties where they performed covers of songs by Cream, Robin Trower, the James Gang, the Jimi Hendrix Experience and the Allman Brothers Band.

Underwood graduated high school in 1976 and a year later became a founding member of a band called Shadowbox, an Aspen Hill-based group which performed a mix of pop music and R&B. The band's lineup was Underwood on guitar, singer-bassist Greg Hardin, singer-pianist Bill Starks and drummer Kendall Diehl, with a later addition being guitarist Steve Bernd. Shadowbox worked a number of local night clubs including Mr. Henry's Tenley Circle (Washington, D.C.) and Fred and Sully's (Silver Spring).

In December 1978 Underwood, Hardin, Starks and Bernd started a new pop-R&B group based in Wheaton called Rhythm Method, with the lineup being completed by saxophonist Joe Reiff and drummer Joe Daugherty, who was later replaced by Mike Cullens. The group initially played in Washington, D.C. at the Childe Harold, Mr. Henry's Tenley Circle, the Far Inn and Beneath It All (in the basement of the Crazy Horse); in Maryland at the Psyche

Delly (Bethesda) and Fred and Sully's (Silver Spring); and in Virginia at Eskimo Nell's (Arlington).

In 1981 a new version of Rhythm Method emerged consisting of Underwood, Reiff, Cullens, bassist Dean Carrigan and lead singer-keyboardist Richard Whiting. This version of the band concentrated on jazz material and performed originals and covers of artists such as Weather Report, Jeff Lorber, Charlie Parker and others. After a year additional changes came about, with the next version of the band consisting of Underwood, Cullens, bassist Scott Ambush, singer-keyboardist John Young and saxophonist Russell Lyles. The band was now playing original fusion jazz and appeared locally in Georgetown at Desperado's and the Cellar Door in addition to playing night clubs and shows from New York to Virginia. Rhythm Method won the "DC 101 Battle of the Bands" competition at the Bayou in December 1982 and broke up shortly thereafter.

In the early and middle 1980s Underwood played guitar in a succession of wedding bands including Chesapeake and Playing Favorites. During this time he also worked a series of jazz gigs and from 1985 to 1988 he appeared regularly at Takoma Station (Washington, D.C.) as the lead guitarist for the club's main attraction, saxophonist Marshall Keys, whose instrumental jazz band was rounded out by bassist Scott Ambush, keyboardist Dan Reynolds and drummer Keith Killgo.

In June 1988 Underwood became the lead guitarist for R&B singer Patti LaBelle, first passing an audition in Philadelphia and then immediately embarking on a tour of Japan. He remained with her until September 1989, playing theatres, concert halls, festivals, arenas and stadiums. During his final months with her band, they performed on several major television shows including an appearance on "The Tonight Show Starring Johnny Carson" on Friday, August 18, 1989 (Show #4026).

In the early 1990s the Underwood-Cotter Band emerged, a rock and roll group which consisted of Underwood on guitar and vocals, lead singer-guitarist Mike Cotter, bassist John Dawson and drummer Mike Aubin. This outfit performed locally at Durty Nelly's (Bethesda) and the Grog and Tankard (Washington, D.C.). Next up was the Chuck Underwood Group, a trio consisting of Underwood on guitar and vocals, bassist Bill Monroe and drummer Mike Aubin. This band played old blues and songs by the likes of Jimi Hendrix, Robin Ford and Eric Clapton, and performed in Maryland at Fatty's (Rockville), Durty Nelly's (Bethesda), the Outta the Way Café (Derwood) and Parker's American Grill (Bethesda). They added singer-keyboardist Jeff Hall and played original, pop-styled music before disbanding in 1994.

In 1992 Underwood joined a 10-piece Top 40 band called Odyssey and remained its guitarist until 2004. Simultaneously, from 1995 to 2004 he had his own band, the Chuck Underwood Trio, with bassist Paul Phillips and drummer Byron McWilliams, playing jazz instrumentals at the Bentz Street Raw Bar in Frederick, Maryland. In addition, in 2004 he and Byron McWilliams formed an instrumental jazz duo called Monkey Paw, which still exists to this day.

In 2008 Underwood became lead guitarist for the Dixie Power Trio, a four-piece Cajun-Zydeco band rounded out by singer-trumpeter Zack Smith, tuba player Andy Kochenour and drummer Byron McWilliams. The group performs in Virginia at the Ice House Café (Herndon), the Colonial Tavern (Fredericksburg) and the Mad Fox Brewery (Falls Church).

Underwood is currently playing in an instrumental jazz rock quartet called Beast from the East with guitarist Dan Hovey, bassist Mike Tony Echols and drummer Deren Blessman. He also performs at the various tribute shows staged by BandHouse Gigs. For more than 20 years he has been a guitar instructor at the Landon School in Bethesda, Maryland, where he is currently an adjunct music faculty member. His wife is the internationally renowned glass artist Nancy Weisser.

CIRCUS

Circus was an Oxon Hill, Maryland-based heavy rock and roll band that consisted of five members of the Potomac High School Class of 1972: lead singer Tim Rose, lead guitarist Larry Green, rhythm guitarist George Dobbs, bassist Charlie Phelps and drummer Conrad Ornstein.

Circus worked the Southern Prince George's County teen dance circuit in the years 1969 and 1970, performing at venues such as the Marlow Heights Community Center (Marlow Heights), Tucker Road Community Center (Fort Washington), Potomac High School (Oxon Hill), the Church of Jesus Christ of Latter-Day Saints (Camp Springs) and Holy Family Catholic Church (Hillcrest Heights). They also performed at dances in Washington, D.C. at Anacostia Lodge No. 21 F.A.A.M. and in Virginia at Annandale Virginia Stake (Temple of the Church of Jesus Christ of Latter-Day Saints).

Circus covered the top rock and roll bands of the day including the Beatles, Grand Funk Railroad, Cream, the Jimi Hendrix Experience and Three Dog Night and attracted fans that followed the area's changing music culture of the early 1970s. Members of this group later resurfaced in other top bands of the area including Gideon and Devil's Track.

CLARENCE PERRY

Born in Camden, Arkansas and raised in Bladensburg, Maryland, Clarence Perry employed a flashy and flamboyant style of rock and roll guitar playing during his tenure with the Off Keys in the late 1950s, a teen dance band best known locally for its long run as headliners at the Bladensburg Volunteer Fire Department.

Perry went on to sing and play lead guitar with the Saxtons before fronting his own band, the Perry Mates, from 1960 to 1961. Perry then spent most of the 1960s in Bay Town, Texas working the Nesa Dale Club with different versions of the Perry Mates. At one point Perry brought the band up to Prince George's County for a one-week gig at the Dixie Pig in February 1965. They hold the distinction of being the last rock and roll band to ever play that legendary night club before it closed its doors for good.

In 1969 Perry took the Perry Mates to Nashville, Tennessee and while playing the Coral Club the group was recruited to become the backup band for singer-guitarist Roy Orbison. At that point Perry changed the name of his band to Clarence Perry and the Mercy Blues and spent the next three years backing the C&W music superstar.

Perry went on to own night clubs in Tennessee and Texas and in 1975 he hosted "The Clarence Perry Mercy Blue Show" on Saturday nights on WLAC-TV Channel 5 in Nashville. During this time he and his band were signed to a major record label and released the 45rpm single record "Woman Stealer" backed with "Shape Up or Ship Out" (Clarence Perry and the Mercy Blues; Epic Records, 1976). Perry has since continued to own night clubs in Tennessee and Texas and in recent times has played lead guitar for rock and roll singer-guitarist Dale Hawkins.

CLAUDE JONES

Claude Jones formed in the summer of 1968 as a psychedelic trio consisting of guitarist Peter Blachly, bassist Frank Sprague and drummer Reggie Brisbane. Residing together in a group house in Washington, D.C. they called "Little Gray" (3717 Military Road NW), the band, which was named after their then-equipment manager, initially worked out long, spacey instrumentals and songs in the vein of Cream, the Jimi Hendrix Experience and early Pink Floyd.

One day in the summer of 1968, shortly after forming, the band picked up a hitchhiker on Connecticut Avenue NW who turned out to be former Reekers keyboardist Mike Henley. They invited him to partake in an afternoon of jamming and soon enlisted him as a full-time band member. Henley brought in fellow Reekers alum Joe Triplett as lead vocalist and Claude Jones soon expanded to a seven-piece unit with the additions of a second vocalist named Francis Day and a second keyboardist named John Guernsey.

As Claude Jones grew in size, they changed their sound and in time became known as Washington's answer to the Grateful Dead, though their repertoire encompassed everything from country-tinged, Guernsey and Triplett originals to covers of such artists as the Temptations, Smokey Robinson and the Miracles, Bob Dylan, the Band, and Country Joe McDonald. The band spent much of 1970 living communally on a farm outside of Warrenton, Virginia, during which time Blachly was replaced by guitarist Happy Acosta.

Claude Jones became a favorite of the local hippies and a centerpiece of the Washington, D.C. area's counterculture, playing leftist benefits, protests and festivals throughout its existence. The band played regularly at Emergency in Georgetown from 1969 to 1971, but also played other venues and opened concerts for a number of major acts.

Claude Jones was the house band at the Showboat Lounge in the Adams Morgan neighborhood of Washington, D.C. for most of the summer of 1969. That year the band also participated in several other local concert shows including: opening for Tim Buckley at Leonard Gymnasium (American University) on Friday, October 17, 1969; appearing with the Cherry People, Love Cry Want and Jabberwok at "The Intercollegiate Music Festival" at the Sylvan Theatre on the Mall in Washington, D.C. on Sunday, October 19, 1969; headlining a triple bill with the Magic Touch and the Young Senators at "The Homecoming Thing" at the Reckord Armory (University of Maryland) on Friday, November 7, 1969; and performing on a bill with the Nowhere Men, Parsec, and Bob Brown at "The Moratorium Rock Festival" at Ritchie Coliseum (University of Maryland) on Sunday, November 9, 1969.

In 1970 Claude Jones headlined concerts at Leonard Gymnasium (American University) on Friday, February 6, 1970 and the Stone Ridge School on Friday, May 8, 1970. Other noteworthy performances included: serving as the opening act and then backup band for Chuck Berry at the Ark (Alexandria) on Friday, May 22, 1970; appearing along with Grin, Crank, Fat City, Renthra, Sageworth and Drums, and Sea and the East Utopian Mission at "Livestock," a festival held at Fort Reno Park (Washington, D.C.) on Saturday, August 29, 1970; headlining at the Brickskeller near Dupont Circle for most of September 1970; appearing with the Cherry People, Sageworth and Drums, Claude Jones, Meretrix, Babe, Sea and the East Utopian Mission, the El Corrals, Fat City, Scott Taylor, and the John Wells Delegation at the second version of "The Intercollegiate Music Festival" at the Sylvan Theatre on the Mall in Washington, D.C. on Sunday, October 18, 1970; opening for the Allman Brothers Band at Leonard Gymnasium (American University) on Sunday, December 13, 1970; and headlining the Falls Church Community Center (Virginia) on Saturday, December 5, 1970.

In 1971 Claude Jones continued to be a part of the local concert scene and participated in numerous shows including: being co-billed with Grin at Bishop McNamara High School (Forestville) on Sunday, January 17, 1971; headlining a concert at the Falls Church Community Center (Virginia) on Saturday, January 30, 1971; appearing on a triple bill with Sageworth and Drums and the New Breed at Archbishop Carroll High School (Washington, D.C.) on Sunday, April 25, 1971; headlining a show at Fort Reno Park (Washington, D.C.) on Friday, July 23, 1971; headlining at the Cellar Door (Washington, D.C.) on Saturday, October 16, 1971; performing with Delaney and Bonnie, Alex Taylor, Bill Withers, Country Joe, the Blues Project, Jerry Jeff Walker, Bob Seger, and Teagarden and Van Winkle at a concert at Rosecroft Raceway (Fort Washington) on Sunday, October 17, 1971; opening for Brownsville Station at the Falls Church Community Center (Virginia) on Sunday,

October 31, 1971; and playing a farewell show at Emergency (Washington, D.C.) on the evening of Friday, December 31, 1971.

Claude Jones released one record during its time, a five-song EP that came out three months before they disbanded: "Sykesville" (Claude Jones; Sweet Breeze Records, 1971).

CLINT HOLMES

Clint Holmes is a Black singer-songwriter who scored with the major hit song ""Playground in My Mind" in 1973 and is currently a headline performer at hotels and night clubs in Las Vegas, Nevada. Born in Bournemouth, England, he was raised in Farnham, New York and served three years in the United States Army where he sang with the United States Army Chorus. Upon his discharge he settled in Washington, D.C. at the age of 23 in 1969 and began singing in such city night clubs as the Judge's Inn and Mr. Henry's Capitol Hill.

In 1970 Holmes began an engagement as the featured attraction at the Port O' Georgetown in Washington, D.C., a run that lasted all the way until his popular hit single topped the pop charts in the summer of 1973. During that stretch he also headlined in the city at Mr. Day's in Georgetown and the Blue Room at the Shoreham Americana; and in Maryland at the Stardust Inn (Waldorf) and the Galaxy Room (Sheraton-Silver Spring).

Reportedly, while performing at a resort hotel in the Bahamas in 1972, Homes caught the attention of a producer at Epic Records and was offered a record contract. His very first single release, "Playground in My Mind" (Clint Holmes; Epic Records, 1972), ultimately reached number two on the "Billboard Hot 100" pop music chart on Saturday, June 16, 1973.

Holmes continued to periodically perform in the Washington D.C. area throughout the 1970s, appearing at such venues as the ever-present Port O' Georgetown, the Classic III Supper Club in Camp Springs, Maryland, and Images on K Street NW in Washington, D.C.

CONTE BELLUCCI

As the son of local legend jazz drummer Louie Bellucci, Conte grew up in Riverdale, Maryland with rhythm in his blood. During his early teen years he would often help his father set up his gear and then watch him perform in such Washington, D.C. night clubs as the Gaslight Room and the Blue Mirror. Conte initially played the trumpet, but switched gears at the age of 14 in 1967 when he was given a drum set by his father. He would visit his father at his home in Southeast Washington, D.C. and receive instruction in percussion and would then play at home to the records of the Beach Boys, Herman's Hermits, James Brown, Blood, Sweat and Tears and others.

During his years at William Wirt Junior High School in the late 1960s Bellucci played in a local teen dance rock and roll band called the Midnighters. He then began playing out at parties during his high school years in the early 1970s at Parkdale High School with a rock and roll band called Fly By Night.

Bellucci spent much of the 1970s hitchhiking and traveling around the country. He eventually returned to the Washington, D.C. area and in the early 1980s settled into the music scene, drumming for such rock and roll bands as Kid Blue, Georgie Jessup and the Jewels, and Bad Habit. He then spent the rest of the 1980s drumming for the Bel Airs, a Baltimore-based pop band which at the time was one of the top touring acts on the East Coast. During Bellucci's time with them, the Bel Airs performed locally at the Cross Roads in Bladensburg and Club Soda in Washington, D.C.

In 1997 Bellucci joined the Bad Weather Boyz, one of the area's top rock and roll bands, and remained their drummer through 2014. For most of those years the band's lineup consisted of lead singer Irvin Utz, singer-guitarist Robert Fiester, bassist Ken Fiester, keyboardist Jeff Archer and Bellucci on drums.

THE COUNTRY GENTLEMEN

The Country Gentlemen formed on Thursday, July 4, 1957 when several members of the bluegrass band Buzz Busby and His Bayou Boys landed at Rose's Musical Bar in North Beach, Maryland for a night of informal playing and partying. That evening, on the way back to Washington, D.C., the car carrying Busby, Bayou Boys bassist Vince Truell, fellow musician Eddie Adcock and a friend of Adcock's named Sonny Preston veered off the highway and struck a utility pole head-on at over 70 miles per hour. The crash sent Busby to the hospital for over three months and rendered his band temporarily inactive and unable to fulfill its band duties at the Admiral Grill on Columbia Pike in Bailey's Crossroads, Virginia. Bayou Boys singer-banjoist Bill Emerson, in an effort to keep the job alive, immediately put together a quartet with fellow Bayou Boys singer-guitarist Charlie Waller, and two other area musicians, singer-mandolinist John Duffey and bassist Larry Lahey. The new bluegrass group was dubbed the Country Gentlemen and they took over at the Admiral Grill without missing a beat.

From 1960 to 1964 the Country Gentlemen consisted of lead singer-guitarist Charlie Waller, singer-mandolinist John Duffey, banjoist Eddie Adcock and bassist Tom Gray. Personnel changes were constant in the years ahead. Despite being defined as a bluegrass band, the group also performed a mix of folk, C&W and rock and roll tunes and was noted for modernizing their basic style of music without forsaking its traditions.

From 1957 to 1972 the Country Gentlemen were regularly featured at the Shamrock Restaurant in Georgetown. In the 1960s and early 1970s they also performed at such Washington, D.C. night clubs as the Shadows, the Brickskeller, the Cellar Door and Hall's on the River.

More than 100 musicians passed through the Country Gentlemen from beginning to end. Charlie Waller remained the group's sole original member until his death in 2004, an event that signaled the end of the band. Through the years the Country Gentlemen released more than 40 albums on more than a dozen different record labels including Folkways, Starday, Vanguard, Rebel and Mercury. The band remained a popular attraction at bluegrass festivals around the country until Waller's passing.

CRAIG THOMAS

Craig Thomas is a talented singer and multi-instrumentalist who has worked with some of the biggest names in popular music. A native of Kensington, Maryland, he attended Albert Einstein High School in Kensington the late 1960s, during which time he played saxophone in an R&B band called the Eruptions, who performed in conjunction with a vocal group called the Majestics. After finishing high school he sang and played saxophone, clarinet, flute, guitar and percussion with a series of local R&B and rock bands such as the Great Expectations, Animal Farm and Everyday People.

In 1971 Thomas joined a Kensington-based, jazz rock band called Spectrum, whose lineup, after some shuffling, consisted of Thomas handling lead vocals and saxophone, guitarist Jorge Strunz, keyboardist Hillary Hamburg, bassist Arne Frager and drummer Dave Smith. In July 1973 Spectrum moved to Los Angeles, California and Thomas remained with the band for several years.

Since relocating to the West Coast, Thomas has played with an impressive array of bands and Musicians. From 1978 to 1981 he toured and recorded with soft rock singer-guitarist Jim Messina, providing vocals and playing saxophone and flute on his albums "Oasis" (Jimmy Messina; Columbia Records, 1979) and "Messina" (Jim Messina; Warner

Bros. Records, 1981). In the 1980s he also recorded, performed and toured with the pop music act Captain and Tennille, pop singer Johnny Mathis, R&B saxophonist Clarence Clemons, and a number of R&B singers including Aretha Franklin, Audrey Wheeler, Tyka Nelson, Jermain Jackson and Smokey Robinson. During this time Thomas also fronted his own band, C.T. and the Soul Rockers.

In the 1990s Thomas performed with such artists as jazz saxophonist Warren Hill, pop singers Christopher Cross and Tom Jones, R&B singer Kathy Sledge, and the jazz group Domino Affect. More recently, he has played with a number of nationally known R&B performing artists including the Stylistics, singer Freda Payne, singer-pianist Les McCann and pianist Billy Shields.

Thomas continues to perform with the R&B Bombers, a band he first started playing with back in the 1980s, and since 2010 he and his saxophone have been touring with Jim Messina. In 2014 was called upon to tour and play sax in Olivia Newton John's backup band.

CRANK

From 1969 to 1974 one of the very best hard-rocking bands in the Washington, D.C. area was Crank, a group that emerged in the post-riots period and became a featured attraction at night clubs, concert events, and festivals throughout the region. Crank's best-known lineup consisted of lead singer Guy Bokoles, singer-guitarist Geoff Richardson (formerly of the British Walkers), singer-bassist Johnny Castle (who had previously played in a band called the Blues Idiom with Richardson), flutist-saxophonist Bill Blessington and drummer Guy Gengrass.

Crank showed great versatility with its range of rock and roll material, playing originals and well as covers of songs by bands such as Blodwyn Pig, Jethro Tull, Spooky Tooth, Free and early Fleetwood Mac. They became an immediate favorite with the local rock and roll crowd for their heavy style and played most of the city's top night clubs of the time including Emergency, My Mother's Place, the Keg, the Crazy Horse, the Bayou and the Godfather Restaurant.

Crank also headlined their own shows at such local schools as Groveton High School (Alexandria), Our Lady of Good Counsel High School (Wheaton), Northwood High School (Silver Spring), Stone Ridge School of the Sacred Heart (Bethesda), St. John's College High School (Washington, D.C.), T.C. Williams High School (Alexandria) and Robert E. Lee High School (Springfield).

In addition, Crank headlined its own concerts and worked shows with a number of national acts. These local performances included: opening for Manfred Mann at the New Students Center (George Washington University) on Tuesday, May 5, 1970; appearing with Grin, Crank, Claude Jones, Fat City, Renthra, Sageworth and Drums, and Sea and the East Utopian Mission at the festival called "Livestock" at Fort Reno Park (Washington, D.C.) on Saturday, August 29, 1970; co-headlining with Grin at Gaston Hall (Georgetown University) on Saturday, January 30, 1971; headlining a concert at Ritchie Coliseum (the University of Maryland) on Sunday, March 7, 1971; headlining a show at the Bethesda Youth Center (Bethesda) on Saturday, May 8, 1971; opening for the Steve Miller Band at McDonough Gymnasium (Georgetown University) on Sunday, February 6, 1972; and co-headlining a concert with Spectrum at the Trinity Theatre (Georgetown) on Saturday, January 6, 1973.

One of Crank's biggest moments occurred when they performed at "Berlin Airlift," a massive rock and roll show held at Robert F. Kennedy Memorial Stadium in Washington, D.C. on Sunday, September 20, 1970 that drew over 21,000 fans. Grand Funk Railroad headlined the six-band event, which also included appearances by the Allman Brothers Band, Pacific Gas and Electric, Crow, and Sageworth and Drums.

Other musicians to pass through Crank included keyboardist Big McCoy and drummers William "Duke" Ayres, Mike James and Rick Anderson. Crank disbanded after finishing an engagement at the Crazy Horse in February 1974.

THE CRAWLING KING SNAKE BLUES BAND

The Crawling King Snake Blues Band was a Washington, D.C.-based group that formed in 1970, rehearsed in the basement of a house at 30th and T Streets NW in Georgetown, and consisted of singer-guitarist Jimmy Cole, guitarist Jimmy Thackery, bassist John Curlin, harmonicist Pierre Beauregard, keyboardist Jeff Cole and drummer Richard Murray.

The band played in Washington, D.C. at private parties, church benefits, college events, the St. Alban's Episcopal Church Friday Coffeehouse, and night clubs such as Emergency and My Mother's Place; and in Maryland at Club 175 (Jessup). After disbanding in 1971 several of the band members resurfaced two years later in Boston, Massachusetts in a band called Powerhouse that included guitarist Tom Principato and bassist Steve Jacobs.

THE CREATURES

The Creatures were a British Invasion-styled rock and roll quartet that achieved great popularity on the Washington, D.C. night club scene, particularly in Georgetown during the years 1965 and 1966. The band's best-known lineup consisted of lead singer-bassist Dale Chafin (formerly of the Tejuns), singer-guitarist Chris Creature, keyboardist Dennis "Stoney" Lucci and drummer Rocky Isaac (another former member of the Tejuns).

The Creatures performed at such Washington, D.C. night clubs as the 1023 Restaurant, the Roundtable, the Frog, the Corral and the Rocket Room. During its time the band recorded and released two singles: "Letters of Love" backed with "Stop Your Sobbin'" (The Creatures; Jet Set Records, 1965); and "All About Love" backed with "Letters of Love" (The Creatures; Oxon Hill Records, 1965).

CRUSADER RABBIT

Crusader Rabbit was a Clinton, Maryland-based, hard-rocking cover band that was considered to be one of the best musical outfits on the dynamic Southern Prince George's County music scene from 1970 to 1973. The group's original lineup consisted of lead vocalist Guy Singer (Bowie High School, Class of 1971), lead guitarist Ed Foy (Oxon Hill High School, Class of 1970), rhythm guitarist Chris Baker (Oxon Hill High School, Class of 1970), bassist John Koory (Oxon Hill High School, Class of 1970) and drummer Chris Dickson (Sherwood High School, Class of 1970).

In April 1972, rhythm guitarist Henry Smith (Surrattsville High School, Class of 1971) replaced Chris Baker. Among the many musical acts of the day they covered were the Rolling Stones, the Beatles, Johnny Winter, Cream, the Jimi Hendrix Experience, Led Zeppelin, Free, Savoy Brown, Jethro Tull and Humble Pie.

Crusader Rabbit was unique in that, despite the fact they formed and maintained a home base in Clinton, Maryland, all band members, upon graduating from their respective high schools, attended Frostburg State College (now Frostburg University) in Frostburg, Maryland. During the school terms the band performed at parties, beer bashes, and fraternity events on the Frostburg campus and gave concerts at the nearby Frostburg Armory.

While on break from college Crusader Rabbit reconvened back in Clinton and played dances at Sandy Spring Friends School (Sandy Spring), the Andrews Air Force Base Teen Club (Prince George's County, Maryland), and at both the Surrattsville Junior Teen Club

(Surrattsville Junior High School) and the Surrattsville Senior Teen Club (Surrattsville High School).

In one memorable performance at the latter facility, the band set up on the floor of the school's Multi-purpose Room (as opposed to the gymnasium stage), kept the lights on for the entire show, and, as the crowd of several hundred sat cross-legged on the floor, embarked on an intense, three-hour concert-like experience. Another time in the "front porch" area of the outdoor parking lot in front of Surrattsville High School, they set up their equipment on a summer Saturday night and drew hundreds of Clinton teens to an impromptu open-air concert.

Crusader Rabbit released a radio and television station promo 45rpm single record that contained the song "There is a Man" on the A-side which served as the official theme song for the 1972 presidential campaign of Democrat George McGovern, the United States Senator from South Dakota. The B-side contained the selection "McGovern Speaks" which consisted of excerpts of the senator speaking on various policy issues – the 45rpm single vinyl record itself contained no label information or credits.

THE CRYSTAL MESH

This bluesy psychedelic rock band of the Summer of Love era consisted of five musicians of the local teen dance circuit, all of whom hailed from Bethesda in Montgomery County, Maryland, had attended Walter Johnson High School, and had previously been a part of the band the Renegades: lead singer Tom Birks, guitarist Nils Lofgren, guitarist Rolf Hanson, bassist Scotty Ball and drummer Mark "Sid" Sithens.

The Crystal Mesh formed in the fall of 1967 and was best known for having performed on two now-legendary bills at the Ambassador Theatre: a two-show engagement by Moby Grape on Friday, December 1, 1967 and Saturday, December 2, 1967; and a concert headlined by the Hollies on Sunday, December 10, 1967.

All of the members of the Crystal Mesh were heavily recruited by various local budding super-groups and the band dissolved shortly after a teen dance extravaganza at George Mason High School (Falls Church) on Saturday, March 2, 1968 where they appeared with the New Delphonics, December's Children, the Gnu Generation, the Warlox, and the Plum Beach Incident.

CURFEW

Curfew was a psychedelic rock and roll band that formed in Rockville, Maryland in 1966 as "The Curfews," worked the local teen dance circuit for several years (changing its name to "Curfew" in 1969), recorded an album for United Artists in 1970, and remained one of the local music scene's favorite bands until 1974. Curfew experienced some personnel changes along the way, with its best-known lineup consisting of lead singer Gui Bokoles, lead guitarist Rick Rowe, bassist Stephen Geyer, keyboardist Stephen Spencer and drummer Dave Eaton (whose later replacement was Rick Anderson).

Curfew ran the entire gamut in terms of local performances. Early in their career they were favorites at teen dances held by St. Sophia Greek Orthodox Cathedral (Washington, D.C.), Our Lady Queen of Peace Catholic Church Teen Club (Arlington), St. Rita Catholic Church Teen Club (Alexandria) and the Our Lady of Lourdes Catholic Church Teen Club (Arlington). They also performed in Washington, D.C. at such night clubs as the Rocket Room, Sam's Place, Some Place Else and the Brickskeller.

Some of Curfew's bigger moments included: appearing with the Dells, Louie and the Uptights, and PJ and the Pitifuls at the Greenbelt Armory in Greenbelt, Maryland on Thursday, April 11, 1968; appearing at a concert headlined by Vanilla Fudge and supported by Ultimate Spinach, the British Walkers and Wild Honey at the Alexandria Arena on

Saturday, April 27, 1968; again appearing with the Dells and Louie and the Uptights, this time at the Wheaton Youth Center on Friday, Mary 3, 1968; and appearing with the Cherry People and the Nowhere Men at the Falls Church Community Center (Virginia) on Saturday, March 7, 1970.

Curfew recorded one psychedelic rock and roll album for a major label: "Let There Be Dark; And There Was Dark" (Curfew; United Artists Records, 1970).

DADDY WARBUX

Daddy Warbux was a hard-rocking band from Cape Cod, Massachusetts that was formed in the late 1960s by a guitarist named Jimmy Newlon. The band went through numerous personnel changes as they established themselves on the Boston night club scene and by 1973 Newlon had added several transplanted Washington, D.C. area musicians to the fold.

In June 1974 the lineup of Daddy Warbux consisted of Newlon, singer Ralph Morman, lead guitarist Punky Meadows (formerly of the Cherry People), bassist Mickie Jones (formerly of Max) and drummer Rocky Isaac (formerly of the Creatures, the Fallen Angels and the Cherry People). At that time the band moved to Washington, D.C. and spent the summer months working the Keg on Wisconsin Avenue NW in the Glover Park neighborhood of the city.

In the fall of 1974 Daddy Warbux moved over to Bogie's on Connecticut Avenue NW, just below Dupont Circle, where they worked into the month of December. At that point the band splintered, with Meadows and Jones putting together musicians that became the bands Foxie, and, in the spring of 1975, Angel. Daddy Warbux, with various musicians in and out of the band, continued to work in Washington, D.C. at the Bayou and in College Park, Maryland at the Bastille and the Varsity Grill.

Daddy Warbux disbanded in 1976. Ralph Morman went on to become lead vocalist for Savoy Brown and the Joe Perry Project. The band had one posthumous album release on a major label, "We Come to Play" (Bux; Capitol Records, 1976), which had actually been recorded in 1973 when Punky Meadows was still in the fold.

THE DAGENITES

The Dagenites were a hard-edged rock and roll band with an early punk attitude that formed in September 1964 and originally consisted of four Oxon Hill High School students: lead guitarist John Bardi, singer-rhythm guitarist Bruce Kennett, lead singer-bassist Geoff Robinson and drummer Roger Fallin. In June 1965 the lineup changed, with Kennett and Robinson departing, and John Bardi and Roger Fallin adding lead singer Jimmy Musgrove, rhythm guitarist Jon Rowzie and bassist Julian Bardi to the mix.

The Dagenites covered all the popular recording acts of the era including Duane Eddy, Link Wray and His Ray Men, Roy Orbison, the Everly Brothers, the Ventures, the Beatles, Gerry and the Pacemakers, the Kingsmen, Peter and Gordon, the Searchers, the Yardbirds, the Hollies, the Animals, the Kinks, the Dave Clark Five, Herman's Hermits and the Zombies.

During its two-year run the band worked parties in the Oxon Hill area and also performed at teen dances that were staged at Oxon Hill Junior High School, Oxon Hill High School, the Oxon Hill Volunteer Fire Department, the Surrattsville Junior Teen Club (Surrattsville Junior High School), the Surrattsville Senior Teen Club (Surrattsville High School), the Clinton Volunteer Fire Department, Tantallon Country Club (Fort Washington) and Tucker Road Community Center (Fort Washington).

The Dagenites were also somewhat unique in that they often ventured into the area's night club scene, despite the relatively young age of the various band members. They appeared in Washington, D.C. at such establishments as the Bolling Air Force Base Officers' Club, the Casino Royal Theatre Restaurant, the Crow's Toe, the French Quarter, the Hayloft, the Roundtable, Some Place Else and the 1023 Restaurant; and in Maryland at the Andrews Air Force Base Officers' Club (Prince George's County) and VFW Scott-Johnson-Pollins Post 9619 (Morningside).

Especially noteworthy is the fact that the band frequently opened for Link Wray and His Ray Men at the 1023 Restaurant in Southeast Washington, D.C. and also performed with the guitar great on several occasions as his onstage backup band at teen dances throughout the area.

During its time the Dagenites released three 45rpm single records: "I Don't Want To Try It Again" backed with "Now That Summer's Gone" (The Dagenites; Pixie Records, 1965); "I'm Gone Slide" also backed with "Now That Summer's Gone" (The Dagenites; Heigh-Ho Records, 1965); and "The Fugitive" backed with "Poison Ivy" (The Dagenites; Heigh-Ho Records, 1966).

DAN HOVEY

Dan Hovey is a guitarist from Hyattsville, Maryland who first played in a rock and roll band called the Contrasts during his junior high school years in the late 1960s. During his teen years in the early 1970s he played in such rock bands as Lodestone, Cosmic Rainbow, and Cold Sweat. During the middle 1970s while finishing up at Northwestern High School he sang and played guitar in a jazz-rock band called A Special Blend, which included bassist Jimmy Earl and performed regularly at Strick's Restaurant (Silver Hill).

After spending time playing with a rock and roll road band called Tony Tillman and the East Coast Brass, Hovey began working with rock and roll singer Root Boy Slim, playing in his various bands throughout the early 1980s and appearing on his album "Dog Secrets" (Root Boy Slim; Congressional Records, 1983). He next played briefly with a reggae band called Black Sheep and then from January 1987 to January 1988 played guitar in Washington, D.C. area night clubs with the popular R&B-rock band Jr. Cline and the Recliners.

Hovey next took his musical talents in a different direction, accepting a position in the guitar chair in the orchestra at the National Theatre on Pennsylvania Avenue NW in Washington, D.C. At the National he performed in stage productions for a number of touring companies in 1987 and 1988, including presentations of the musicals "Sweet Charity" and "Cats."

In 1989 Hovey moved to Manhattan, a borough of New York City, where he spent the next 15 years as a professional musician. During his time there some of his many musical accomplishments included: playing on two critically acclaimed albums, "PTTM" (Wiseblood; Big Cat Records, 1991) and "Prince of the Deep Water (The Blessing; MCA Records, 1991); and fronting his own blues band, the Dan Hovey Group. He also performed and/or recorded with such blues-based groups as the Long Shadows and the Haunted Lobsters, and the jazz band Ron Sunshine and Full Swing. Other musicians he performed with include: folk singer-guitarists Jim Allen and Janet Burgan; folk singer-guitarist-pianist Eric Anderson; jazz clarinetist-saxophonist Don Byron; and R&B singers Ben E. King and Rosco Gordon.

Hovey also worked on Broadway – a descriptive moniker for theatrical performances presented in 40 professional theatres located in the Theater District and Lincoln Center along Broadway in the New York City borough of Manhattan – where he played guitar in different orchestras for a number of live musicals including "The Full Monty," "Thoroughly Modern Millie," "Mamma Mia!" and a 14-month run in 1999 and 2000 with the stage production of "Swing!"

In 2004 Hovey returned to Washington, D.C. and has since played guitar for R&B singer Mary Ann Redmond, fronted his own blues group Dan Hovey and Bad Daddy (a trio rounded out by bassist Rico Petruccelli and drummer Dave Elliott), and sang and played in a band called GHz with singer-bassist Scott Giambusso and drummer John Zidar that specializes in classic rock works by bands such as Cream, the Jimi Hendrix Experience, Led Zeppelin, Jethro Tull and the Who. Since 2014 he has been a member of an R&B act called the Soul Serenaders, a band rounded out by singers Billy Price and Tommy Lepson, bassist Jan Zukowski, saxophonist Bruce Swaim and drummer Pete Ragusa.

Most recently Hovey has played guitar in such theatre productions as "Diner," which showed at the Signature Theatre in Arlington, Virginia from December 2014 through January 2015; "Freedom's Song: Abraham Lincoln and the Civil War," which showed at Ford's Theatre in Washington, D.C. in March 2015; and "The Book of Mormon," which had an engagement at the John F. Kennedy Center for the Performing Arts Opera House in Washington, D.C. in the summer of 2015.

Among Hovey's more popular album appearances are: "The Dan Hovey Group" (The Dan Hovey Group; Aquatone Music, 1994); "The Haunted Lobsters" (The Haunted Lobsters; 1997); "There's Trouble Coming" (GHz; New Door Productions, 2009); "Morbid Curiosity" (GHz; New Door Productions, 2010); and "The Cheap Stuff" (GHz; New Door Productions, 2013).

DANNY DENVER

He was born Cole Blease Ghoens, Jr. on Wednesday, June 23, 1937 in Hartsville, South Carolina, but this C&W and rock and roll singer-guitarist was known throughout the Washington, D.C. area as Sammy Gowans, and then later as Danny Denver, and achieved cult status for fronting bands that featured the now-legendary blues rock guitarist Roy Buchanan.

Ghoens, Jr. moved to Washington, D.C. at the age of 18 in 1955 and for several years worked as a rhythm guitarist and backup singer for a variety of C&W bands at such Washington, D.C. night clubs as the Kit Mar Restaurant, the Covered Wagon, and the Town and Country jamborees at the Joe Turner Arena. In the late 1950s he was courted by United Artists Records, who signed him to one-shot deal under the stage name Sammy Gowans and released the single "Kissin' at the Drive-In" backed with "Rockin' By Myself" (Sammy Gowans; United Artists Records, 1958).

In 1962 Ghoens, Jr. assumed a new stage name and put together a trio called Danny Denver and the Sound Tracks with bassist Buck Tickle and drummer Skeeter Cooper that played a mix of C&W and rock and roll. That year they performed at the Crosstown Restaurant (Washington, D.C.) and Strick's Restaurant (Silver Hill), and then spent the rest of the early 1960s working in Washington, D.C. at such night clubs as the Frog, the Corral, Guy's Place and the Round Up.

In 1965 Denver met blues rock guitarist Roy Buchanan and brought him into the Sound Tracks, a move that led him to give up the guitar for good and focus on singing and frontman duties. That summer alone the band made appearances in the city at the Crosstown Restaurant, McGuire's Pub, the Shelter Room and Benny's Rebel Room, and in Prince George's County, Maryland at the 4400 Club (Brentwood), Bass' Restaurant & Bar (Mt. Rainier) and Strick's Restaurant (Silver Hill).

Innumerable musicians passed through Denver's band in the 1960s. Late in that decade he changed the name of his group to Danny Denver and the Soundmasters and settled on a lineup that consisted of himself handling lead vocals, guitarist Roy Buchanan, drummer Richard Maughn, and either Shorty Horton or Steve Spurling on bass. During that period the band worked such Maryland night clubs as the Loft Room of the Waldorf Restaurant

(Waldorf), the Stardust Inn (Waldorf), the Senate Inn (Capitol Heights), the Big Dipper (Beltsville), the Tick Tock (Hyattsville), the Turf Club (Laurel) and the Cross Roads (Bladensburg).

In the early 1970s one of the most highly regarded editions of the Soundmasters had Denver and Buchanan being joined by bassist Don Monahan, keyboardist Joe Bayliss and drummer Ricky Rhome. This outfit worked as the house band at the Cross Roads, a lengthy engagement that helped Roy Buchanan establish himself as one of the world's best blues rock guitarists. Denver went on to surround himself with many of the area's top musicians and work a long engagement at the TD Diner in Laurel, Maryland before retiring from the music scene in the early 1980s.

In his career Denver recorded and released a number of singles including: "You're My Girl" backed with "Image of Love" (Danny Denver; Chancellor Records, 1962); "Baby One More Chance" backed with "Only You" (Danny Denver; Deville Records, 1966); "Long Hairy Arms" backed with "I Didn't Want to Do It" (Danny Denver; Deville Records, 1967); "The Shoes That Jesus Wore" backed with "Spring is a Woman" (Danny Denver; Wrayco Records, 1971); and "My Woman's Love" backed with "Mother Nature" (Danny Denver; Wrayco Records, 1971).

Denver also released two rare albums, now both collector's items: "Live On Stage at the Stardust Inn" (Danny Denver; Go-Go Records, 1970; it is known that the musicians on this recording were Denver, Roy Buchanan, Shorty Horton and Dicky Maughn); and "The Best of Denver with Roy Buchanan" (Danny Denver; Wrayco Records, 1970). Danny Denver died on Saturday, November 15, 2003 at the age of 66.

DANNY FRANKEL

Danny Frankel is considered to be one of the very best drummers to ever emerge from the Washington, D.C. area and has recorded and performed with some of the biggest pop, rock and roll and avant-garde artists in the music business. Raised in Silver Spring, Maryland, Frankel mainly jammed with friends at parties during his years at Bethesda-Chevy Chase High School in the late 1960s and early 1970s.

Frankel spent much of the 1970s drumming for various local performers including blues singer-guitarist Bobby Radcliff, and rock and roll acts such as the Calypso Gypsies, the Choadsmen, the Mystery Band, the John Guernsey Band, the Humans, the Look, the Nurses, the Reind Dears, the Sick Band, and Root Boy Slim. In 1977 he joined Urban Verbs, a local art rock band that became very popular locally and went on to release two albums on Warner Bros. Records.

In 1983 Frankel relocated to Los Angeles, California and has since become one of the music industry's most heralded drummers. Among the major national popular music acts he has recorded, toured and performed with through the years are: folk singer-guitarist Victoria Williams; folk singer-pianist Robin Holcomb; pop singer K.D. Laing; pop singer-guitarists Jewel and Beck; pop singer-violinist-keyboardist Laurie Anderson; pop singer-pianist Fiona Apple; the rock and roll band the Rentals; rock and roll singers Rikki Lee Jones and Marianne Faithful; rock and roll singer-guitarists Bo Diddley, Lou Reed, Moris Tepper and Michael Penn; rock and roll singer-bassist John Cale; the juggling-comedy troupe known as the Flying Karamazov Brothers; and rapper-singer-guitarist Everlast.

Frankel has released four avant-garde solo albums that run the gamut from rock to jazz: "Jupiter, Now!" (Danny Frankel with Kid Conga Powers and Patrick Warren!!!; WIN Records, 1995); "New Thing on Jupiter" (Danny Frankel; WIN Records, 1997); "The Vibration of Sound" (Danny Frankel; True Classical Records, 2007); and "The Interplanetary Note/Beat Conference" (Danny Frankel with Nels Cline & Larry Goldings; Self-Released, 2010).

DANNY STELLABOTTE

Danny Stellabotte grew up in Silver Spring, Maryland and started playing guitar at age 10, taking one lesson at Veneman Music in his hometown before teaching himself to play. At age 11 in 1965, while attending Sligo Junior High School, he joined his first band, a rock and roll group called the Cellar Wall that performed at local parties and covered bands such as the Rolling Stones, Them, and the Kingsmen. During his years at Northwood High School in the early 1970s he played guitar in a band called Mods and Rockers, which performed songs by groups such as the Who, Spirit, the James Gang and Johnny Winter at school dances, teen clubs and American Legions.

Stellabotte next spent much of 1975 in an R&B band called Flush, which performed frequently at Bogie's (Washington, D.C.). From 1976 to 1978 he was in a Top 40 rock group called the Night People, which was booked through the Washington Talent Agency, specialized in material by popular acts like Fleetwood Mac, Heart and Lynyrd Skynyrd, and performed at a variety of events from the St. Camillus Teen Club (Silver Spring) and the St. Bernadette's Teen Club (Silver Spring) to University of Maryland fraternity parties.

After a decade of jamming with local musicians and occasionally playing out, Stellabotte embarked on a 1988-1990 run with a blues-C&W trio called High Ballin' that worked in Montgomery County, Maryland at such night clubs as Hunter's (Wheaton), the Layhill Café and Lounge (Silver Spring) and Normandie Farm Restaurant (Potomac).

After another long spell of informal playing, Stellabotte became a founding member of Cold Hard Cash in 2005, a musical outfit devoted to performing the songs of Johnny Cash and other artists such as Buck Owens and Merle Haggard. This group, which first came together at Stellabotte's home in Silver Spring, initially consisted of singer-guitarist Rob Petrie (formerly of the Dixie Cannonballs), bassist Karen Taylor and Stellabotte on lead guitar.

Cold Hard Cash initially performed at the Savory Café (Takoma Park) and at local festivals. Changes ensued within the band and from 2006 to November 2009 the outfit operated as a quartet with Petrie and Stellabotte being joined by bassist Bill Maron and drummer Lester King. This version of the band played carnivals and special events around the state of Maryland and were a regular attraction at the New Deal Café (Greenbelt).

From 2005 to 20010 Stellabotte was also a part of the Takoma Zone, a revolving group of musicians that performed bluegrass, C&W and folk music on a weekly basis at the Savory Café. After taking time off from performing, Stellabotte rejoined Cold Hard Cash in June 2011, joining Petrie, drummer Mark Lucas, and assorted bassists. He left the band in May 2018.

Since 2011 Stellabotte has also been a member of Birds on a Wire, a blues-bluegrass-pop group of musicians, usually rounded out with singer-mandolinist Eric Vesper and singer-guitarist Gary Markwood, that performs from April-to-November on Sunday mornings at the College Park Farmer's Market. In recent years Stellabotte has backed Elvis Presley-Johnny Cash tribute performer Jed Duval, and also played onstage at the New Deal Café in December 2015 with City Bus, a blues rock band that features Cheryl Poirier, former lead vocalist of Kid Creole and the Coconuts.

DARYL CLINE

Singer-guitarist Daryl Cline was born in Gilbert, West Virginia and raised in Wheaton, Maryland. As a youth his family often played bluegrass music in the home, though as he entered his teens his interests switched to soul music with Otis Redding and Ray Charles becoming personal favorites. Along the way, in addition to developing his vocal skills, he taught himself guitar.

In the late 1960s Cline attended Wheaton High School and then Montgomery Blair High School, during which time he was the lead singer in an R&B band on the local teen dance scene called the Varsells. He went on to sing in other bands and in 1973 became the lead singer in the first version of Barrelhouse, a local blues group that included guitarist Steuart Smith and regularly performed in Washington, D.C. at such night clubs as Mr. Henry's Tenley Circle and the Far Inn.

In the late 1970s Cline put together his own musical outfit, Jr. Cline and the Recliners, a band that would become one of the Washington, D.C. area's most popular and long-standing R&B-rock acts. The original lineup of this band consisted of lead singer Cline, guitarist Rusty Bogart, bassist Barry Foley, keyboardist Tammy Sullivan, saxophonists Jeremy Stone and Wayne Sulc, and drummer Joey Romero.

Jr. Cline and the Recliners specialized in classic and contemporary R&B and rock and roll songs and their repertoire included original compositions and covers of such artists as Junior Walker, Wilson Pickett, Sam Cooke, Otis Redding, the Temptations and Van Morrison. Early on the band performed in Washington, D.C. at such night clubs as Desperado's, the Bayou, Columbia Station, Rumors, Mr. Henry's Tenley Circle and the Childe Harold; in Northern Virginia at Louie's Rock City (Bailey's Crossroads) and Eskimo Nell's (Arlington); and in Maryland at the Psyche Delly (Bethesda).

In the ensuing 40-plus years Jr. Cline and the Recliners endured numerous personnel changes, appeared at the top venues in the Washington, D.C. area, and played night clubs, shows, concerts, and festivals up and down the Atlantic Coast from New York to Florida. Top local musicians to pass through the band included guitarist Paul Bell, bassists Ron Newmyer and Greg Hardin, pianist Bill Starks, saxophonist Bruce Swaim, trumpeter Vince McCool and drummer John Lee.

Through the years Jr. Cline and the Recliners have recorded and released several albums and singles, beginning with their debut album, "Jr. Cline and the Recliners" (Jr. Cline and the Recliners; Apogee Records, 1985). Most recently, Cline has issued a solo album, "Anywhere the Wind Blows" (Daryl Junior Cline; Clone Records, 2017), which covers a variety of styles including C&W, R&B and rock and roll.

Cline currently sings and plays guitar with two R&B-rock bands – an updated, nine-piece version of Jr. Cline and the Recliners, and a smaller group without a horn section called the Daryl Jr. Cline Band ("soul with a rockin' edge"), whose lineup is completed by bassist Doug Meyer, percussionist Tim Cutrona and drummer Todd McDaniel.

DARYL DAVIS

Singer-keyboardist-guitarist Daryl Davis was born in Chicago, Illinois, and, with parents employed in the United States Foreign Service, lived all over the world as a youth including Africa and Europe. He was exposed to popular music at an early age through the radio, with some of his favorite performers being Chuck Berry, Elvis Presley, Little Richard, Jerry Lee Lewis and Fats Domino. Later in his youth, while visiting his grandparents in Roanoke, Virginia, he discovered C&W music through "The Porter Wagoner Show," which often featured singer Dolly Parton.

As a teenager Davis lived with his family in Potomac, Maryland and during his years at Thomas Sprigg Wooton High School in Rockville in the middle 1970s he decided to become a professional musician. He first sang in his high school's choir, and on breaks between classes he taught himself to play boogie woogie piano in the school's music room. He had friends show him guitar licks and he eventually taught himself to read music.

In 1975 Davis put together his first band, Daryl and the Dayrells, which covered 1950s rock and roll. Shortly after its formation, the band was hired to perform as the onstage backup band for the Coasters and the Drifters at a show at the Stardust Inn in Waldorf,

Maryland. In the ensuing years the band backed up such R&B acts as the Shirelles, the Platters, Rosemary Clooney and Bobby Lewis.

Davis earned a Bachelor of Arts in music from Howard University (majoring in jazz performance) and in the 1980s played piano with various blues bands including the Wild Cards and Johnny and the Headhunters. In 1981 he began playing piano for the legendary rock and roll singer-guitarist Chuck Berry, an association that lasted for more than 30 years and included numerous East Coast and Midwest tours.

From 1985 to 1988 Davis toured and performed with the Legendary Blues Band. He also kept Daryl and the Dayrells going strong throughout much of the decade, performing at such Washington, D.C. night clubs as Desperado's, the Cellar Door, the Bayou and the Wax Museum. In 1988 this band became the Daryl Davis Band.

The 1980s also saw Davis cross over and work with many of the Washington, D.C. area's top C&W groups. Among the bands of this genre he worked with include the Mary Dallas Band, Benny Dean and the Shades of Blue, Heavy Country, Stoneridge, the Baxter Brothers, the Stardells, Notorious, and Sho-Gun. Some of the top musicians of this style he performed with included guitarist Randy "Red Dog" Leith, singer-guitarist Chick Hall, Jr. and singer-pianist Big Al Downing.

Other bands and musicians Davis has recorded and/or performed with through the years include: the blues vocal duo Cephas and Wiggins (singer-guitarist John Cephas and singer-harmonicist Phil Wiggins); blues singer-harmonicist Billy Branch; blues singer-pianist Pinetop Perkins; blues pianist Johnnie Johnson; jazz drummer Joe Dyson; the pop vocal group the Jordanaires; R&B singers Percy Sledge and Sam Moore; rock and roll guitarist James Burton, rock and roll singer-guitarists Ted Nugent and Bo Diddley, rock and roll singer-bassist-guitarist Billy Hancock and rock and roll singer-pianist Jerry Lee Lewis; rockabilly singer-guitarist Tex Rubinowitz; and multi-styled guitarist Danny Gatton.

Davis continues to perform throughout the Washington, D.C. area with his own band and regularly tours the United States with a plethora of R&B acts.

DAVE CHAPPELL

Dave Chappell is a blues rock guitarist who currently leads his own band and has performed with an array of local and nationally known musicians. He was born in Washington, D.C., and, as the son of an Air Force serviceman, grew up on Andrews Air Force Base in Camp Springs, Maryland. His grandfather played guitar and fiddle and Chappell was exposed to music at an early age. He began taking guitar lessons at age nine and shortly thereafter began attending the Andrew Air Force Base Teen Club dances where he saw local musicians like guitarist Jeff Avery and bassist John Previti perform.

During his younger years Chappell played along to records of the Allman Brothers Band and the Rolling Stones and was influenced by other guitarists such as Eric Clapton, Buddy Guy and Muddy Waters. He also had the opportunity to see local guitar legends Roy Buchanan and Danny Gatton perform and became a devoted fan of their work.

Chappell played guitar informally during his years at Central High School and after his graduation in 1975 he joined a rock and roll band called Freeway Jam, which was based in Largo, Maryland, covered bands like the Rolling Stones, Steely Dan and Led Zeppelin, and performed locally into the late 1970s at several night clubs in College Park, Maryland including the Varsity Grill Back Room, the Bastille and Yesterday's Inn.

From 1979 to 1980 Chappell and a guitarist from Bethesda, Maryland named Tim Kugel lived in Hollywood, California where they played blues jam sessions and open mics at night clubs like the Central on Sunset Boulevard. After returning to the nation's capital, Chappell joined Elvis Presley impersonator Johnny Seaton's band in 1981 and remained his lead guitarist throughout 1982. Chappell then spent the early and middle 1980s working with a

C&W music band from Baltimore called Barbed Wire. Later in the decade he worked with guitarist Danny Gatton in the American Music Company, a band than included many of Gatton's old bandmates from the Off Beats.

In the 1990s Chappell's reputation soared and he became in demand as a lead guitarist. He spent much of that decade playing a mix of C&W, jazz and rockabilly music in the Hula Monsters and working in various bands fronted by rockabilly singer-bassist Billy Hancock.

Through the years he has performed and/or recorded with some of the region's top blues, jazz and rock and roll performers including the Joe Stanley Band, the Patty Reese Band, the Jim Stephanson Band, the Rhodes Tavern Troubadours, Swing Speak, the Darryl Davis Band, Billy Kemp and the Paradise Rockers, and Kevin Johnson and the Linemen. Other musicians he has played guitar with include: C&W singer-guitarists Marge Calhoun and Arty Hill; folk singer-guitarist Lisa Moscatiello; jazz saxophonist-clarinetist-flutist Seth Kibel; rockabilly singer-guitarist Bill Kirchen, and rockabilly guitarist Evan Johns.

In terms of working with nationally known performing artists, Chappell has performed onstage as a lead guitarist for such artists as: blues pianist Johnnie Johnson; blues rock singer-pianist Johnny Neal; R&B singers Sam Moore, Percy Sledge and Nappy Brown; and rock and roll singer-pianist Jerry Lee Lewis.

Chappell recently released his first solo album, "Dave Chappell & Friends" (Dave Chappell; Sunburst Records, 2014), and currently leads his own blues rock quartet, the Dave Chappell Band.

DAVE ELLIOTT

Drummer Dave Elliott, while living in Falls Church, Virginia and attending George Marshall High School in the middle 1960s, played the local party and teen dance scene in such rock and roll bands as the Apollos and the Attic. Later in the decade he was drumming for a local Top 40 rock and roll band called the Velvet Underground at a restaurant called Pizza King in Fort Belvoir, Virginia, which was owned by Earl Dixon, who was also proprietor of a night club a little further south on Richmond Highway in Lorton called Hillbilly Heaven.

In 1972 Elliott was drumming at Hillbilly Heaven for the C&W-oriented Larry Black Band, when he happened to meet guitarist Danny Gatton and singer-bassist Billy Hancock, who were at the club talking with Dixon about putting together a replacement house band. The three musicians decided to form a rockabilly trio and performed at Hillbilly Heaven for a week as Heavy Duty. They next performed for a short time as Fat Chance before changing their name in 1973 to Danny and the Fat Boys. They performed at several Village Inn pizza restaurants in the area and also appeared at some of the most popular night clubs in the area including a long engagement at the Chide Harold in Washington, D.C. and several Maryland establishments including Bass' Restaurant and Bar (Mt. Rainier) and the Psyche Delly (Bethesda).

For Elliott it was the start of a musical association with Gatton that would endure for more than 20 years. During that time he performed with Danny and the Fat Boys until October 1976. He then played in several of Gatton's groups including the Danny Gatton Band and the Redneck Jazz Explosion. In addition, he drummed on a number of Gatton's single recordings and albums.

In the late 1980s Elliott formed his own trio, the Dave Elliott Band, which was initially rounded out by singer-guitarist Bill Kirchen and bassist John Previti. The band played a mix of C&W, rock and roll and rockabilly and had a steady engagement at the Sunset Grille in Annandale, Virginia. When Kirchen moved on, his place was taken by guitarist Dave Chappell.

In the early 1990s Elliott reconnected with Kirchen in the rockabilly band Bill Kirchen and Too Much Fun, which was initially a trio consisting of Kirchen, Elliott and bassist Jeff Sarli. Since that time Elliott has performed with a number of top local blues, C&W and rock and roll bands and musicians including blues guitarist Dave Sherman, Honky Tonk Confidential, the Rockin' Bones, the Hall Brothers, the Dave Chappell Band, the Marianna Previti Band, Dagmar and the Seductones and the Swingin' Daves.

In addition to his long association with guitarist Danny Gatton, Elliott has also performed with a number of national acts through the years including the Clovers, the Spaniels, legendary guitarist Les Paul, Hot Tuna, blues singer-guitarist Robert Ward (he and bassist Jeff Sarli worked a tour of Europe with Ward in 1995), blues singer-harmonicist Flatfoot Sam, Elvis Presley impersonator Johnny Seaton and rockabilly singer Robert Gordon.

Elliott has also performed in recent years with the blues group Dan Hovey and Bad Daddy, and an updated Dave Elliott Band, which consisted of himself on drums, singer-guitarist Jim Stephanson, guitarist Dave Chappell and bassist Claude Arthur. Currently he drums for Andrew Acosta, a singer-guitarist-mandolinist who plays acoustic bluegrass and C&W music at shows around Northern Virginia.

DAVE JOHNSON

Singer-keyboardist Dave Johnson was born in Erwin, Tennessee but was mainly raised in Rockville, Maryland, where, during his years at Parkland Junior High School in the middle 1960s, he played drums in his first rock band, the New Generation. In the early 1970s while attending Robert E. Peary High School he played keyboards and guitar in a blues group called Daddy Lean and the Bacons and then concentrated on keyboards in his next group, Bacon's Blues Band, which performed at fraternity parties at the University of Maryland and the night club Mr. Henry's College Park.

From 1972 to 1975 Johnson sang and played keyboards in a succession of local blues and rock and roll bands including Sleaze, the Josh Howl Blues Band (which performed for several months in 1973 in Boston, Massachusetts), Earthbound, Uncle Cup, and Highway.

In 1975 Johnson brought his vocal and keyboard skills to the first edition of the Gaithersburg-based rock and roll band Pegasus, whose lineup was rounded out by singer-guitarist Stephan Spano, guitarist Chris Grigsby, singer-bassist Joey Tarbell and drummer Mike Custer. Pegasus went to the top of the local music scene, playing over 300 gigs per year, covering everyone from the Moody Blues to Little Feat, and working nearly all of the region's top night clubs from the Crazy Horse to the Bayou to the Wax Museum. In 1982 Pegasus changed its name to Force of Habit and Johnson remained with the band until its final gig at the Paragon in College Park, Maryland in April 1985.

Through the years Johnson has performed with a number of different local bands of varying styles including the Kid Band, Smalltalk, Tough Luck, the Fabulettes, Honky Tonk Confidential, and the Sookey Jump Blues Band. More recently he was a member of the rock and roll groups Redline (1995 to 1997), the Sandra Dean Band (1997 to 2010) and Johnny and the Stingrays (2011 to 2012).

DAVE KOPLOW

Singer Dave Koplow was born in Washington, D.C. and spent his teen years living in Potomac, Maryland. As a youth he sang along to movie theme songs, performed in the Washington National Cathedral Choir, and listened to the hits on such local radio stations as WINX, WEAM and WPGC. His early musical tastes ranged from Joe Tex to doo-wop to groups such as the Rolling Stones, the Kinks, Cream and the Allman Brothers Band. During his time at Herbert Hoover Junior High School in the early 1970s he was the lead singer in a rock and roll band called the Burning Sensation (which also went by the name Burn) that performed at parties and local teen dances.

In the late 1970s, while attending Winston Churchill High School, Koplow sang in a rock and roll band called Paragon, which covered such artists as Led Zeppelin, Peter Frampton, and Mountain. He then sang in a rockabilly group called the Trouble Boys before leaving the area to attend Boston University, where he sang in an acoustic folk rock duo that went by the name Jim Daly and Dave Koplow.

After finishing college, Koplow returned to the Washington, D.C. area but faded from the local music scene. After a long hiatus, he took the stage at Chief Ike's Mambo Room in the Adams Morgan neighborhood of Washington, D.C. in February 2012 and sang three songs with a Grateful Dead cover band called the Wharf Rats. A month later, he again sang with the band, this time at the New Deal Café in Greenbelt, Maryland.

Koplow then decided to resume his singing career and in February 2013 he joined a blues rock band from Colesville, Maryland called Intone Nation. He is still with the band today and among their regular stops are the New Deal Café (Greenbelt), Sullivan's Steak and Beverage Company (Laurel), Oliver's Old Towne Tavern (Laurel), T-Bonz Grille and Taphouse (Ellicott City) and the American Legion Laurel Post 60 (Laurel).

In addition to his position in Intone Nation, Koplow also currently handles lead vocals for two other Washington, D.C. area bands, a classic rock group called the Acme Band Company, and a rockabilly act called the Basset Hound Boys.

DAVE LONG

Guitarist Dave Long was born in Arlington, Virginia and raised in New Carrollton, Maryland, where, in the late 1960s while attending Charles Carroll Junior High School, he first joined an R&B band on the teen dance circuit called the Sensations. Long was influenced early on by a number of guitar-heavy rock and roll bands including Led Zeppelin, the Jimi Hendrix Experience, Cream, as well as a litany of blues and jazz guitarists.

While attending Parkdale High School in the early 1970s Long played guitar in a rock and roll band called Wake, which performed locally at parties and at dances held at Parkdale and Bladensburg High Schools. From 1972 to 1973 he played in a popular area rock and roll band called Woodpecker and from 1974 to 1978 he was the guitarist in a pop-disco band called Flight that worked weddings and school dances, and also performed at the Paragon in College Park, Maryland.

Long spent much of the 1980s playing music in Virginia on the Leesburg-to-Woodbridge American Legion-Moose Lodge-VFW circuit in a C&W band called Night Train. Later on he played guitar in another C&W group called No Alibi and for many years frequented blues jams including one staged by Mike Mautino at the Old Bowie Town Grille in Bowie, Maryland.

Since 2008 Long has been the lead guitarist for the Joy B Band (led by country rock singer-guitarist Joy Bodycomb) and appears on their album "Just Livin'" (Joy B Band; Self-Released, 2013). He has recently worked on occasion with the Hall Brothers at venues such as the American Legion College Park Post 217 in College Park, Maryland when lead guitarist Chick Hall, Jr. was busy with other engagements.

DAVE PANZER

A native of Silver Spring, Maryland and a 1970 graduate of Montgomery Blair High School, Panzer is a singer-guitarist who is best known for having performed and toured for five years during the 1990s with R&B singer Wilson Pickett. In the late 1960s he played in such local rock and roll bands as Axis and Beverly Pureheart. Through the years he has played guitar for such performers as: blues singer-guitarist Memphis Gold; blues saxophonist Jacques Johnson; the blues bands Moonshine Society and the Paulverizers; the blues-rockabilly band Retro Deluxe; R&B singers Skip Mahoney and Gene Chandler; and R&B bands such as the Orioles, Little Anthony and the Imperials, Bloodstone, the Platters and the Drifters.

Panzer has also played guitar for the Mustangs Band, a popular R&B outfit that performs at night clubs and private functions up and down the East Coast. More recently he has fronted his own blues bands in the Washington, D.C. area such as Dave Panzer and the Bluesicians and Dave Panzer and the Partnas in Kryme. He currently plays guitar in an R&B group called Soulville, Maryland.

DAVE REYNOLDS

Dave Reynolds was born in Dallas, Texas and moved with his family to Prince George's County, Maryland at the age of seven in 1946, first residing in Cottage City for a year before relocating to nearby Hyattsville. His first instrument was the harmonica, on which the first song he taught himself was "Silent Night."

In 1951, while in the seventh grade at Bladensburg Junior High School, he joined a pop-jazz trio called the Harmony Hounds with singer-accordionist Ken Selby and guitarist Jan Bisch. The trio played school variety shows, area USO shows, and the Landover Hills Teen Club. In 1954 as Reynolds began his sophomore year at Bladensburg High School, the band changed its name to the Harmony Boys, with singer-bassist Jack Otley replacing Bisch and Reynold switching from harmonica to drums. The trio expanded its repertoire to include jazz, Top 40 pop, and early-era rock and roll songs, and performed at school dances and local Moose Lodges.

Throughout his remaining years at Bladensburg High School Reynolds drummed on pickup jobs in jazz groups organized by fellow classmates-saxophonists Joe Stanley and Lewis Maddox. After graduating from Bladensburg High School in 1957, Reynolds continued to play pickup gigs as a drummer and frequently worked with the house band at a night club in Washington, D.C. called the Vineyard (732 14th Street NW).

In 1958 Reynolds received a call from Joe Stanley and joined the Saxtons, a band that was developing into one of the region's top rock and roll acts. He stayed with the band for nearly two years, touring the East and Midwest, and playing in Washington, D.C. at the Parkside Café and Benny's Rebel Room, and in Brentwood, Maryland and the 4400 Club and Jimmy Comber's Supper Club.

In 1960 Reynolds moved back to Dallas, Texas and drummed for a number of jazz greats in local night clubs including saxophonists John Hardee, James Clay and Gene Ammons. From 1961 to 1965 he resided in Tulsa, Oklahoma, where he drummed for the Sonny Gray Quartet, a group that served as the house band at a jazz night club called the Rubiot. During those years Gray's ensemble, with Reynolds on the skins, backed up such major jazz performers as: pianists Teddy Wilson, Mose Allison, Bubba Cobb and Warren Bernhardt; clarinetist Benny Goodman; saxophonist Zoot Simms; and vibraphonist Terry Gibbs. This period also saw Reynolds jam onstage with a number of other jazz stars including: pianist Bill Evans; saxophonist Charles Lloyd; and vibraphonists Cal Tjader and Gary McFarland. In 1965, while still in Tulsa, Reynolds also drummed for an R&B band called the Sunday Servants.

In the late 1960s Reynolds moved about North America and drummed for different psychedelic rock and roll bands including a group in Vancouver, British Columbia called Mother Tucker's Yellow Duck and a band in San Francisco called Peace and Love.

DAVE SHERMAN

Guitarist Dave Sherman was born in Washington, D.C., raised in Silver Spring, Maryland, and during his high school years in the middle 1960s (he attended Walter Johnson High School and Wheaton High School before moving to Kensington and finishing at Albert Einstein High School) he played the local teen dance circuit in such rock and roll bands as Dave and the Defiants, the Last Remains, and the Pastels.

In the late 1960s Sherman performed as a solo artist at Washington, D.C. coffee houses such as the Iguana Coffeehouse (Luther Place Memorial Church) and spent the early 1970s playing guitar in a local C&W band called Kinda Country. After living in Chester, Pennsylvania for several years he returned to the Washington, D.C. area and spent the late 1970s playing in a blues band called Sunset Strip and sitting in with other popular groups such as the Nighthawks.

In the 1980s some of the blues bands Sherman played guitar with included the Rhythm Masters (featuring singer-guitarist Cathy Ponton King), the Smokin' Presstones, the Uptown Rhythm Kings and Little Junior and the Hitmen. He then spent part of the 1990s fronting his own blues band, Dave Sherman and the Nightcrawlers.

Since 2001 Sherman has been the lead guitarist in the Smokin' Polecats, a blues band that alternates lead singers Marianna Previti and Mary Shaver. Some of the musical artists Sherman has played onstage with through the years include: R&B singer Nappy Brown; and a litany of blues performers including singer-guitarists Earl King, Hubert Sumlin and Otis Rush; singer-guitarist-harmonicist Jimmy Rogers; and singer-harmonicist James Cotton.

DAVE WEST

Drummer Dave West was raised in Chicago, Illinois and after a tour of duty in the United States Navy he moved to the Washington, D.C. area at the age of 21 in 1963. He began playing jam sessions and sitting in with various R&B and rock and roll bands in Downtown night clubs such as the Rocket Room, Benny's Rebel Room, Rand's Night Club and the Hayloft. From 1963 to 1971 West drummed for several top bands on the local scene including Phil Flowers and His Flower Shop, Big Al Downing and His Band, Sonny Gordon and the Outcasts and Joe Banana and the Bunch.

In 1971 West began a five-year stretch as the drummer for pop music singer Clint Holmes, during which time they regularly performed in Washington, D.C. at Judge's Inn on upper Wisconsin Avenue NW and the Port O' Georgetown. He played on all of Holmes' recordings of that period including the hit single "Playground in My Mind." In 1975 West returned to Illinois and left the world of professional music behind.

DAVID ARNSON

David Arnson was born in Manhattan, New York and grew up in Chevy Chase, Maryland, where, during the middle 1970s, he played bass in the rock and roll band Feedback Forever. After graduating from Bethesda Chevy-Chase High School in 1979, he formed Insect Surfers, whose initial lineup consisted of Arnson on bass and vocals, singer-guitarist Dave Peterson, keyboardist Michael Strider and drummer Dan Buccino.

Insect Surfers played a unique style of new wave surf music and performed in Washington, D.C. at Fort Reno Park, Madam's Organ, D.C. Space and Nightclub 9:30. The band also opened for several visiting national acts including: a show featuring Destroy All Monsters and the Model Citizens at the Wilson Theatre in Arlington, Virginia on Friday, August 24, 1979; a concert headlined by the B-52's at the Ontario Theatre in the Adams Morgan neighborhood of Washington, D.C. on Wednesday, October 17, 1979; and another show at the Ontario Theatre, this one a triple bill headlined by Iggy Pop and rounded out by Joan Jett on Thursday, December 4, 1980.

Insect Surfers experienced numerous changes in personnel through time and in the early 1980s its lineup consisted of singer-guitarist David Arnson, bassist Josh Arnson, keyboardist Tom Linson and drummer Drew Vogelman. From 1980 to 1984 the band headlined in Washington, D.C. at the Gentry, the Wax Museum and the Bayou. During this time they also toured the United States from Maine to Minnesota to Texas to Florida, and in 1984 they toured Canada and up and down the West Coast.

Arnson moved to Los Angeles, California in April 1985 and in June 1986 started a new, instrumental version of Insect Surfers which consisted of himself on guitar, guitarist-keyboardist-saxophonist Dan Sullivan) who would remain with the band for 22 years), bassist Richard D'Andrea and drummer Mike Parma. The group has endured numerous personnel changes through the years, but is still active today with a lineup of Arnson, guitarist Michael Abraham, bassist Jonpaul Balak and drummer Chris Roberts.

While based in the Washington, D.C. area, Insect Surfers released their first two albums "Wavelength" (Insect Surfers; WASP Records, 1981), and "Sonar Safari" (Insect Surfers; WASP Records, 1983. To date they have released more than a dozen albums on various independent record labels and their work has appeared on more than three-dozen different compilation albums, including "Cowabunga! The Surf Box" (Various Artists; Four-CD Compilation, Rhino Records, 1996).

DAVID GABALDON

Known to friends and fellow musicians as "Gabby," this rock and roll guitarist was born in Yardley, County of Birmingham, England and grew up in Falls Church, Virginia. While attending James Madison High School in Fairfax, Virginia in the middle 1960s he joined his first band, the Deltones, which would play Ventures covers in the school's dining hall before the start of classes. During this time he also played the teen dance scene in a local rock and roll band called the Escorts.

After a stint at Virginia Tech University, Gabaldon became a professional musician and during the late 1960s played both guitar and bass for Jimmy Eller and the Little People, which at the time held house band duties at the Rocket Room in Washington, D.C. He served in the Unites States Army, and in 1969 returned to the Washington, D.C. area and joined one of the regions' top jazz rock bands, the Eye.

When Gabaldon joined the Eye the band's lineup consisted of himself handling vocals and guitar, bassist-keyboardist Paul Brier, singer-keyboardist Guy Meredith and drummer Ronnie Stevens. The group headlined in Washington, D.C. at such night spots as the Montage, the Paul Mall Restaurant, the Cave and Black Ulysses. They were occasionally called upon to back up touring acts such as the Shirelles, the Coasters, rockabilly singer-guitarist Gene Vincent and rock and roll singer-guitarist Chuck Berry. The Eye endured numerous personnel changes, but Gabaldon remained a constant with the band through 1976.

In the late 1970s Gabaldon joined the R&B band Spats, a group that came off as a cross between Little Feat and Pablo Cruise. The band's initial lineup consisted of lead singer Michael Bradley, Gabaldon on lead guitar and vocals, bassist Johnny Castle, singer-keyboardist Ric Arenz and drummer Mike Zack. They had one album release, "Spats" (Spats; Good Sounds Records, 1978), and performed in Washington, D.C. at the Cellar Door, the Crazy Horse and on a concert bill headlined by Wild Cherry and Joe Cocker at the Warner Theatre on Sunday, October 1, 1978.

In the 1980s Gabaldon played guitar with a number of popular rock and roll bands including Network, the Kamikaze Pilots, McCoy, the Cutters, the Shades, DC Dog, and the

Original Sevilles. He also played guitar and bass on the new age album "Bodymusic" (Nicholas; Nuage Records, 1989).

More recently Gabaldon has played guitar in an updated version of the British Walkers (featuring singer-keyboardist Bobbie Howard) and has performed with Billy Hancock's Giants of Georgetown, a group of longtime rock and rollers who are veterans of Georgetown's rock and roll night club scene. He is currently performing in the Frederick, Maryland area with two classic rock bands, the Shades, and Gabby and the Leftovers.

DAVID KITCHEN

Singer-guitarist David Kitchen was born in Norfolk, Virginia, lived for a time in Hyattsville, Maryland, and during his junior high school years at Bladensburg High School he first played in a rock and roll band called the Cornerstone Rockers. He moved to Alexandria, Virginia as a teen and during his high school years at Hayfield Secondary School in the middle and late 1970s he played in the school jazz band and also in an art-rock band called Slander Rose. The latter group mixed originals with covers of songs by the Kinks and Mott the Hoople and performed in Virginia at the Fort Belvoir Teen Club (Fairfax County) and the Thomas Restaurant and Night Club (Fort Belvoir).

After a stay in Boulder, Colorado, Kitchen resided in Kingsport, Tennessee from 1979 to 1981 during which time he attended East Tennessee State University and played in a C&W band called Ivory Tower. He returned to Alexandria, Virginia in 1981, started a family and played music on an occasional basis. From 1985 to 1990 he sang and played guitar in a country rock band called Shoot the Messenger and spent much of the 1990s fronting his own country rock band, David Kitchen and the Demolition.

More recently, Kitchen has performed and recorded with the pop music band American Song and since 2005 he has been a singer-guitarist in the rockabilly band the Thrillbillys. He has also played with the rockabilly band Dagmar and the Seductones, the Cajun group Zydeco Craze, the multi-styled act Dave Elliott's Redneck Jazz, and the blues band the Cutaways. He currently performs throughout the Washington, D.C. area as a solo artist and also fronts the David Kitchen Band, which plays a mix of pop, country rock and rock and roll.

As a lead artist, Kitchen has an album with his band the Demolition and two other pop-rock solo albums to his credit: "Low Falutin'" (David Kitchen and the Demolition; RockMonger Records, 1998); "Underground" (David Kitchen; RockMonger Records, 2008); and "David Kitchen Live at Goose Creek" (David Kitchen; Goose Creek Entertainment; 2009).

DAVID LOURIM

Guitarist-keyboardist David Lourim, today known as David Christopher, was raised in Bowie, Maryland and grew up listening to Jimi Hendrix, Peter Frampton and Van Halen. During the late 1970s he frequently participated in the rock and roll jam sessions that were held at, of all places, the Bowie Branch Library in Prince George's County, Maryland.

During his years at Bowie High School in the early 1980s Lourim played in the progressive rock band Stonehenge, whose lineup consisted of lead singer Eva Cassidy, Lourim on guitar, bassist Larry Melton, keyboardist Ned Judy, fiddler Dan Cassidy and drummer Mark Merella. Stonehenge performed in Bowie at places like the Bowie High School Coffeehouse, Allen Pond Park, Boswell Hall inside the Knights of Columbus Sacred Heart Council 2577, and elsewhere at Prince George's Community College (Largo) and a night club called the Bratwursthaus (Falls Church). The group initially covered the music of Yes, Jean-Luc Ponty, Jeff Beck and King Crimson, eventually moving into lengthy, original compositions.

In 1986 Lourim began recording original pop-rock music at Black Pond Recording in Rockville, Maryland, a project which eventually produced the album "Method Actor" (Method Actor; BLP Records, 1988). The primary musicians on the album were singer Eva Cassidy, guitarist-keyboardist David Lourim, bassist Ken Fiester and drummer Jim Campbell.

As a band, Method Actor was based in Gaithersburg, Maryland and played out on several occasions including appearances at the Bayou in Georgetown. For those live appearances, the original quintet was often joined by keyboardist Tony Lord and fiddler Dan Cassidy (bassist Ken Fiester was later replaced by David Vespoint). During this time Lourim continued to conduct studio work and played guitar on a song called "God Bless the Child" which appears on the highly acclaimed blues-jazz indie album "The Other Side" (Chuck Brown and Eva Cassidy; Liaison Records, 1992).

When Method Actor disbanded in 1992, Lourim joined the rock and roll band She's Melting, a group that featured lead vocalist Yvonne Charbonneau and eventually included Method Actor holdovers Robert Fiester, Ken Fiester, Tony Lord and Jim Campbell. She's Melting covered the likes of Janis Joplin, Jimi Hendrix, Nirvana and the Black Crowes. Before disbanding in 1995 they appeared at many of the region's better night clubs including the Bayou in Georgetown and Jaxx Nightclub in Springfield, Virginia.

DAVID PLATSHON

Drummer David Platshon was raised in Hyattsville, Maryland and during his years at Northwestern High School in the late 1960s he played the local teen dance circuit with such rock and roll bands as the Nightwalkers and Nitty Gritty, as well as a 15-piece R&B band called the Epsilons. During his senior year in 1969 he joined the New Breed and remained with the popular R&B-rock band for three years.

Platshon spent the early 1970s playing night clubs in the Georgetown neighborhood of Washington, D.C. with the bands Three Easy Pieces and Bobby and Friends, and also tried his hand at C&W music by drumming for a spell with Tobacco Road at the Big Dipper in Beltsville, Maryland. In 1974 Platshon left for a 15-month stay in Hawaii where he drummed in an R&B band called Monkey Pai. In February 1976 he joined the backing band for Ike and Tina Turner, but was released in April while playing onstage at a Hilton Hotel in Las Vegas, Nevada. Later in 1976 he returned to the Washington, D.C. area and became the regular drummer for rock and roll singer-guitarist Nils Lofgren, touring and recording with his band from 1976 to 1979.

After concentrating on various business ventures, Platshon was hired to drum for the Motels in 1983 and stayed with the band for eight months, performing with them on their "Saturday Night Live" performance that aired on Saturday, January 21, 1984. He next worked with C&W singer Dolly Parton, drumming on her album "The Great Pretender" (Dolly Parton; RCA Records, 1984) and joining her band as a full-time member. He spent much of the late 1980s performing with the Sam Taylor Blues Band in Los Angeles, California. In the middle 1990s he co-founded Fat Box, an audio-visual production facility now located in Redwood City, California.

DAVID SIMMONS

Singer-guitarist David Simmons was raised in Clinton, Maryland and during his time at Surrattsville High School in the early 1970s played the Southern Prince George's County teen dance circuit in the rock and roll bands Spring Fever and Medusa. In June 1974 Medusa changed its name to Starz, and, in addition to working dances at facilities like the Tucker Road Community Center in Fort Washington, they began performing in Washington, D.C. at such night clubs as Some Place Else, the Crazy Horse and Bogie's. In November

1977 Starz changed its name to DC Star and became one of the top rock and roll bands on the East Coast. DC Star eventually disbanded in March 1987.

Simmons is still involved with the national music scene and since 1986 has officially served as the owner-president-head producer of David and Goliath Music, a Baltimore-based production company and record label he founded and currently operates with Ray McCrory.

DAWN'S DUSK

Based in Silver Spring, Maryland, this hard-rocking band of Albert Einstein High School and John F. Kennedy High School students came together in 1968 and originally consisted of singers Steve Anderson and Joanne Joynt, lead guitarist Vince Campanella, bassist Steve Gardosik, keyboardist Bill Carroll and drummer Bill Brasso.

Dawn's Dusk remained on the local scene for 10 years and hammered out the popular R&B and rock and roll tunes of the times. Among the performing artists they covered were the Beatles, the Rolling Stones, Janis Joplin, Big Brother and the Holding Company, Jefferson Airplane, the Who, the Four Tops, the Temptations and others.

The band was a major attraction at area teen dances and were especially popular at such events staged at the Montgomery Hills Teen Club (Montgomery Hills Junior High School in Silver Spring), the Argyle Teen Club (Argyle Junior High School in Silver Spring), the Rosemary Hills Teen Club (Rosemary Hills Elementary School in Silver Spring), the Homewood Teen Club (Homewood Capitol View Recreation Center in Kensington), John F. Kennedy High School (Silver Spring), Prince George's Plaza Community Center (Hyattsville), Kava (Greenbelt Youth Center), the Belair Teen Club (Belair Junior High School in Bowie), the Bowie Senior Teen Club (Bowie High School in Bowie) and the Bowie Community Center.

Dawn's Dusk also performed at area bar mitzvahs, University of Maryland fraternity parties, embassy engagements in Washington, D.C., summer appearances at the Carousel Club inside the Carousel Hotel in Ocean City, Maryland, and spent much of the 1970s working local gigs through the Washington Talent Agency.

DC DOG

During the middle 1970s one of the top rock and roll bands in the area was DC Dog, whose regular lineup consisted of singer-keyboardist Gary St. Clair, guitarist Jimmy Nalls, bassist Elliott Jagoda and drummer Mike Zack. The band based out of Apple Pie on M Street NW in Georgetown from 1974 to 1976 and covered such popular music artists as Van Morrison, Frank Zappa, Taj Mahal, Dr. John, the Isley Brothers and Little Feat. DC Dog also performed regularly in Washington, D.C. at such night clubs as the Crazy Horse, the M Club and the Keg.

DC Dog conducted innumerable recording sessions at Ted Bodnar's American Star Recording Studios in Merrifield, Virginia, with much of their work going uncredited. One record they did receive credit for was the classic R&B album "Music-Music" (Lloyd Price; LPG Records, 1976). For that recording, the band was joined by synthesizer-clavinet player Ric Arenz.

THE D.C. MAGNATONES

The D.C. Magnatones were a large and constantly evolving group of White Southeast Washington, D.C. teens – the vast majority of whom attended Anacostia High School during the middle and late 1960s – that specialized in doo-wop, soul and pop songs that emphasized perfect pitch vocals and tight harmonies. The band was active from 1962 to 1968 and originally came together through informal street corner singing sessions along both Nichols Avenue SE and Good Hope Road SE, particularly on and around the grounds of the Ruppert Home for Aged (then-located at 2300 Good Hope Road SE).

The band's early lineup was sizeable and consisted of lead guitarist Jay Soule, rhythm guitarist Tommy Simmons, bassist Spud Blake, saxophonist Tommy Distl, drummer Ron Covell, and singers Joe Saitta, Billy Vabolis, Hunter Phillips, Butch Boswell and Don Halcombe. A later addition to the band's team of singers was Charlie Taylor, who had originally lived in the Hillcrest neighborhood of Southeast Washington, D.C., but had moved across the line into Prince George's County, Maryland during his teen years and attended Oxon Hill High School. For much of its existence the band rehearsed at Ron Covell's house at 1514 U Street SE in Anacostia.

In addition to singing informally at places around the city like Union Station and the Rainbow Delicatessen (then-located on their home turf in Anacostia at 1533 Good Hope Road SE), the D.C. Magnatones played at local parties and at Anacostia High School-related social functions throughout Southeast Washington. In their immediate Southeast neighborhood they were regulars at dances at the Church of the Assumption Teen Club, the St. Teresa of Avila Catholic Church Teen Club and the St. Francis Xavier Parish Teen Club. They also ventured on occasion into neighboring Prince George's County, Maryland and performed at dances at Crossland High School (Camp Springs), Surrattsville High School (Clinton), and the Bladensburg Volunteer Fire Department (Bladensburg).

In their time the D.C. Magnatones performed a wide range of popular vocal-oriented songs, covering performers such as the Five Satins, the Contours, the Spaniels, the Moonglows, the Penguins, the Solitaires, Gene Chandler, James Brown, the Temptations, the Four Tops, the Isley Brothers, the Beatles and the Rolling Stones.

A high point for the band was the recording and release of a now-rare 45rpm single record they issued on their own independent label: "Not Room for Two" backed with "Does She Love Me" (The D.C. Magnatones; D.C. Magnatones Records, 1966). The band carried on until 1968, at which time singers Donnie Halcombe and Charlie Taylor were recruited into a newly formed R&B-rock band called Second Coming, effectively bringing the reign of the D.C. Magnatones to an end.

DC STAR

DC Star emerged from the remnants of several Southern Prince George's County, Maryland teen dance bands of the 1970s and became one of the Atlantic Coast's premier hard rock and roll groups. Exuding melodic rock and roll fueled by heavy metal power, the band was a hard-working outfit that went to the top of the local night club scene, signed up with a major record company, and opened arena concerts for some of the top rock and roll acts in the world. The band's best-known lineup – lead singer Ken Taylor, guitarists Dave Simmons and Jeff Avery, bassist Henry Farmer and drummer Glenn Jones – carried the torch into the late 1980s, an era that saw the band widely recognized as one of the Washington, D.C. area's top contributions to the world of rock and roll.

The roots of DC Star go back to the Southern Prince George's County community of Clinton, Maryland and Surrattsville High School, where a rock and roll scene was in full power during the early 1970s. In 1974 a Surrattsville High School-based band called Medusa emerged. After a little shuffling, the group's lineup consisted of: singer Ken Taylor, an Accokeek native who attended Friendly High School; guitarists Jeff Avery and Dave Simmons, both Surrattsville High students who had previously played together in the band Spring Fever; Henry Farmer, who lived in Camp Springs, attended Potomac High School and was called in to replace original bassist Bill Baker; and drummer Wade Richards, who also attended Surrattsville High School, had previously drummed in the bands Deaf Mute and Sassafras Tea, and was hired to replace drummer Warren Early.

In June 1974, Medusa changed its name to Starz and began performing in Washington, D.C. at the night clubs Some Place Else in Southeast and the Crazy Horse in Georgetown. The band then gained prestige by opening for Angel at Bogie's (south of Dupont Circle) for several weeks in the spring of 1975.

For the next two years Starz tirelessly worked night clubs including the Bayou in Georgetown and throughout Maryland at Tall Timbers (Calloway), the Varsity Grill Back Room (College Park), Mike's Place (Oxon Hill), Fred and Sully's (Wheaton), My Friend's House (Silver Spring) and the Stardust Inn (Waldorf). In September 1977 drummer Wade Richards left the band and was replaced by Pat McGowan, who hailed from Bethesda, Maryland and had most recently drummed for the band Gravity.

In November of 1977 the band released its first single under the altered name of D.C. Starz: "Blue Sparks" backed with "Keeper of the Keys" (D.C. Starz; Secant Records, 1977). Because of a legal conflict with a band from New York City calling itself Starz, the group then changed its name to DC Star.

With the new moniker in place, the band headlined locally in Washington, D.C. at the Bayou in Georgetown; in Maryland at the Varsity Grill Back Room (College Park), the Paragon (College Park), the Bastille (College Park), Michelle's (Camp Springs) and the Stardust Inn (Waldorf); and in Virginia at Louie's Rock City (Bailey's Crossroads). In 1979 drummer Pat McGowan was replaced by Glenn Jones, who had grown up in Riverdale, Maryland and had previously played in the band Cold Sweat.

In the early 1980s DC Star began focusing on the Baltimore night club circuit. One of their career highlights took place when they were called upon to open for Journey for two consecutive sold-out concerts before a combined total of over 40,000 people on the nights of Monday, May 2 and Tuesday, May 3, 1983 at the Capital Centre in Landover, Maryland. It marked the first time a Prince George's County, Maryland-based rock and roll group ever played the facility.

The band moved farther north in the middle 1980s, concentrating on the New York City night club scene and opening concerts up and down the East Coast for bands such as Blue Oyster Cult, Judas Priest, Iron Maiden and Twisted Sister. After a series of personnel changes, the group dissolved in March 1987.

DC Star recorded and released one EP and two albums during its time: "DC Star" (DC Star; Escape Records, 1982; a 5-song EP picture disc); "Livin' in a Rock & Roll Whirl" (DC Star; Escape Records, 1984); and "Rockin' in the Classroom" (DC Star; Mirage Records, 1985). In addition, four different compilations of the band's work have been released on CD: "DC Star Records" (DC Star; David and Goliath Music, 1999); "The Best of DC Star: Record Classics" (DC Star; Retrospect Records, 2009); "The Best of DC Star Records Vol #2" (DC Star; Retrospect Records, 2009); and "The Best of DC Star Records 1977-1983: The Last Master" (DC Star; D&G Music, 2015).

DEL PUSCHERT

Saxophonist Del "Big Daddy" Puschert grew up in Annapolis, Maryland and during the early 1950s played with several different rock and roll bands in and around his hometown. While in his early twenties during the middle 1950s he moved to Texarkana, Texas and became the main saxophone player for Elvis Presley, backing the King on gigs from Texas to Florida.

Puschert returned to Maryland in 1956 and began a 10-year tenure with the Van Dykes, a Baltimore-based R&B band that recorded for Atlantic Records and was frequently called upon to back up major performers of the day such as Otis Redding, Sam Cooke, James Brown, and Ike and Tina Turner, among numerous others. The Van Dykes frequently performed in the Washington, D.C. area during those years at such night clubs as Benny's

Rebel Room, the Keg and the Varsity Grill, in addition to headlining concerts at facilities like the Bladensburg Volunteer Fire Department and two halls on the University of Maryland campus, Ritchie Coliseum and Reckord Armory.

Puschert also played in a number of rock and roll bands in and around the nation's capital during the 1960s including the Perry Mates, the Fablons and the Sam Paladino Trio. From 1968 to 1972 he was a member of the Classics, a rock and roll quartet whose main lineup consisted of singer-guitarist Frank Shegogue, Puschert on saxophone, keyboardist Sam Paladino and drummer Jerry Zadera. The Classics were popular on the local military base officers' club circuit and enjoyed a long run at the Villa, a night club in College Park, Maryland that later became the Bastille.

Puschert played with several orchestras, pop groups and rock and roll bands from Annapolis to Baltimore to Washington, D.C. throughout the 1970s and into the 1980s. During his long and illustrious career he has played saxophone for such R&B artists as the Coasters, the Drifters, and singers Little Richard, LaVern Baker, Ruth Brown and Jackie Wilson. Others he has performed onstage with include Southern rock singer-fiddler-guitarist Charlie Daniels, and the C&W group Asleep at the Wheel. Puschert still occasionally sits in with various bands throughout the region.

DEMETRI CALLAS

Demetri Callas is a highly esteemed rock and roll singer-guitarist who grew up in Frederick, Maryland and spent his teen years in the late 1950s and early 1960s playing in such Frederick-based bands as the Playboys and the Shades. He then performed in C&W-pop singer Ronnie Dove's band and toured the East Coast with the Bill Black Combo.

In early 1964 Callas put together a rock and roll quartet called Demetri and the Bad Boys, which also included singer-keyboardist Al Ruzicka singer-saxophonist Larry Mann and singer-drummer Eddie Crocetti. The band worked a steady engagement at the Starlite Restaurant in Washington, D.C. through September 1964. Shortly thereafter, Callas and a singer-saxophonist named Billy Joe Ash joined forces with singer-keyboardist Gary St. Clair and drummer Danny Conway and formed a new band called Billy Joe and the Confidentials, which became the house band at Benny's Rebel Room on the 14th Street Strip. In June 1965, while performing at a night club in Orlando, Florida, Callas, St. Clair and Conway split from Ash and called their new trio the Bad Boys.

In the summer of 1965 the Bad Boys relocated to Washington, D.C. and worked the night club scene, with the Rabbit's Foot on Wisconsin Avenue NW becoming a favorite venue. In January 1968 the Bad Boys were signed to Columbia Records and changed their name to Flavor. They went on to become one of the biggest rock and roll bands in the nation's capital and released three 45rpm single records for Columbia before disbanding in 1969.

Callas went on to become lead guitarist for Frankie Valli and the Four Seasons, remaining with them from 1970 to 1974. In the 1980s and 1990s he played in a Frederick-based rock and roll band called Hollywood Cool Breeze and also fronted his own oldies rock band, Demetri and the Flashbacks. More recently, Callas has played lead guitar for Bill Haley's Original Comets at night clubs, casinos and resorts in Las Vegas, Nevada.

DENNIS MONKE

Saxophonist-keyboardist Dennis Monke was born in Baltimore, Maryland and raised within the state in the city of Hyattsville. While attending Hyattsville Junior High School in the early 1960s he first played saxophone in a rock and roll band called the Revelaires. In the middle 1960s, while attending Northwestern High School and then High Point High School, he played saxophone in a pop-rock band called Jimmy Dee and the Melodaires and then was a member of the first edition of the extremely popular local R&B band Lawrence and the Arabians, which became a dominant force on the local teen dance scene.

In the late 1960s Monke played saxophone with an area R&B-rock band called the Fifth Edition. He followed that stint by working with singer Steve Charles in two of his local R&B bands, the Infernos and the Soul Syndrome, often performing at Jimmy McPhail's Gold Room in Northeast Washington, D.C. In 1968 and 1969 he also played saxophone with an R&B-rock band called the Nightcaps at the Go Go 007 on New York Avenue NW in the Downtown area of the city.

Monke went on to work with a variety of Washington, D.C. area groups and musicians in the 1970s and 1980s including Walter Salb's Orchestra (as a clarinetist-saxophonist) and such rock and roll bands as the Classics, the Graduates, Eros, Octagon, Flight, Energy, and many others.

DEUCE

A heavy metal rock and roll band that formed in the latter-half of the 1970s in Laurel, Maryland, Deuce was one of the relatively few area groups that left the nation's capital to invade the Los Angles, California rock and roll scene and pursue the dream of musical stardom. The original lineup for Deuce consisted of singer-rhythm guitarist Tom Gattis, guitarist Marty Freidman, bassist Steve Leter and drummer Chris Tinto.

Deuce initially set up shop in a barn on the Gattis family property on Supplee Lane in Laurel and began playing local parties and night club gigs, but experienced regular changes in personnel. When guitarist Marty Friedman left the band in 1980 he was replaced by Timmy Meadows (Friedman went on to play in the bands Vixen, Hawaii and Megadeth before pursuing a solo career). Deuce usually consisted of four or five members and among the musicians that passed through in the late 1970s and early 1980s were lead singer Eddie Day, drummer Billy Giddings and a number of bassists including Mike Davis, Chris Hall, Mike Francis and Tim O'Connor.

In terms of night club work, Deuce performed in Maryland at the Big Dipper (Beltsville), the Riverside Inn (Riverdale), the Psyche Delly (Bethesda) and the Seagull Inn (Essex); and in Virginia at Louie's Rock City (Bailey's Crossroads).

In the middle 1980s Deuce relocated to Los Angles with a lineup of Gattis, Meadows, O'Connor and Giddings, and, at the insistence of its managers, changed its name to Tension. Under that moniker they recorded one album: "Breaking Point" (Tension; Torrid Records, 1987). Shortly thereafter, Tension disbanded. Guitarist Tom Gattis later played with the bands War Dog and Ballistic. The band's story has been commemorated in the feature-length DVD, "Tension – 25 Years Underground: A Documentary by Rudy Childs" (Rudy Childs, 2012).

DEVIL'S TRACK

One of the best hard-rocking bands to come out of Southern Prince George's County, Maryland in the late 1960s was Devil's Track, a group that formed in 1969 around the core of guitarist Chris Noe (a Camp Springs resident and member of Crossland High School's Class of 1970), singer-bassist Monte Norris (who hailed from Oregon, had graduated from Heidelberg American High School in Heidelberg, Germany in 1965, and, during the late 1960s, was a serviceman stationed at Andrews Air Force Base in Camp Springs and was living nearby in an apartment in Suitland), and drummer Craig Kellstrom (a Suitland resident who, like Noe, was a member of Crossland High School's Class of 1970).

Early in its history Devil's Track took on different musicians, but in 1970 settled on a lineup of Noe, Morris, Kellstrom, and two former members of the rock band United Orange, keyboardist Tom Dawson and lead singer Doug Allen, both of whom had graduated from Crossland High School in 1969. After a year Dawson and Allen left and the band was back down to its core trio, with Monte Norris then handling much of the lead vocal work.

Devil's Track got its start on the county's teen dance circuit and built a strong following with their electric performances at Crossland High School (Camp Springs), the Surrattsville Senior Teen Club (Surrattsville High School in Clinton), the Stephen Decatur Teen Club (Stephen Decatur Junior High School in Clinton), Bishop McNamara High School (Forestville), LaReine High School (Suitland), Kava (Greenbelt Youth Center), Marlow Heights Community Center (Marlow Heights), Tucker Road Community Center (Fort Washington), Prince George's Plaza Community Center (Hyattsville), the Wheaton Youth Center (Wheaton) and Tantallon Country Club (Fort Washington).

Throughout the early 1970s Devil's Track worked numerous night clubs in Washington, D.C. including Some Place Else, the Butterfly, the Silver Dollar, the Crazy Horse, the Paul Mall Restaurant, the Bayou, Benny's Rebel Room, My Mother's Place, the Keg, the Rabbit's Foot and the Bolling Air Force Base Officers' Club. They also appeared in Maryland at the Cross Roads (Bladensburg), the Stardust Inn (Waldorf) and the Ocean Underground (Ocean City). In addition, the band was a hot commodity on local college campuses and often played mixers, parties and fraternity social events at schools such as Prince George's Community College, Gallaudet University, Catholic University, American University, the University of Maryland, Georgetown University, St. Mary's College and Frostburg State College.

During its time Devil's Track concentrated on covering the top rock and roll bands of the day. Some of the artists whose work they presented included Free, Bad Company, Jethro Tull, Grand Funk Railroad, the Beatles, the Rolling Stones, Buffalo Springfield, Deep Purple, Neil Young, Jeff Beck, Mountain, the Yardbirds, the Edgar Winter Group, Chuck Berry, Spirit, Creedence Clearwater Revival, Elton John, Santana, Iron Butterfly and the Doors.

Devil's Track continued on until 1976 and during its final years experienced some changes in personnel. At some point in 1972 guitarist Chris Noe departed and joined the band Black on White before replacing Punky Meadows as lead guitarist in the Cherry People. With Noe gone, Devil's Track rebounded with a new lineup of lead guitarist Larry Green (formerly of the bands Circus and Gideon), singer-rhythm guitarist Monte Norris (moving over from bass), bassist Tom Herway (formerly of United Orange) and drummer Craig Kellstrom. For much of 1974 the band's lineup consisted of Green, Herway, Kellstrom and singer-keyboardist John Damba. In the group's final run Green, Kellstrom and Damba were joined by bassist Randy Kuklik.

DEXTER DUNN

Guitarist Dexter Dunn hails from Silver Spring, Maryland and in the early 1970s during his years at Montgomery Blair High School he first played in a series of R&B bands on the local teen dance scene, including one group that included saxophonist Ron Holloway. After high school he played guitar in Razz, one of the area's top rock and roll bands at the time.

Dunn went on to play guitar in a series of top local groups including: a rock and roll band called Majestic in the early 1980s; a multi-styled wedding group called Second Nature in the middle and late 1980s; a rock and roll band called Crazy Fingers from the middle 1980s to the early 1990s; a multi-styled wedding group called Brass Alley in the 1990s; and a pop-rock cover band called Peter North throughout the 1990s and into 2000.

More recently Dunn played guitar in the area's premiere Black Sabbath tribute band, Disciples of Sabbath. He is currently playing guitar in the Maryland-based, high-powered classic rock band Raized By Wolves.

DICK HEINTZE

Keyboardist Dick Heintze grew up in the Tenleytown neighborhood of Northwest Washington, D.C. and during his years at Woodrow Wilson High School in the late 1950s played the teen dance scene in a rock and roll band called the Triumphs, whose membership included guitarist Jorma Kaukonen and bassist Jack Casady. In the 1960s Heintze also performed in such local rock and roll bands as the Off Beats, the Newports, the Superiors, the Soul Mates and Take Five.

Heintze spent several years playing piano and other keyboard instruments for the National Symphony Orchestra in Washington, D.C. During the 1970s he played with some of the region's best musicians including blues singer-guitarist Bobby Radcliff, blues rock guitarist Roy Buchanan, rockabilly singer-bassist-guitarist Billy Hancock, and multi-styled guitarist Danny Gatton and his various bands, including the East Coast Express. Dick Heintze passed away on Tuesday, January 20, 1981 at the age of 42.

DICK MOODY

Saxophonist Dick Moody grew up in Landover Hills, Maryland and during his years at Bladensburg High School in the late 1950s he played in the Off Keys, a popular rock and roll band that performed on the local teen dance circuit and featured among its members keyboardist Sam Paladino. As a teenager, despite being underage, his father often took him to night clubs such as the Red Robin in Southeast Washington, D.C. and the 4400 Club in Brentwood, Maryland to see and hear live rock and roll music.

During his time with the Off Keys, Moody would venture on Friday nights to Capitol Arena (formerly Joe Turner Arena) and participate in the "Barn Dance" jam sessions that were being staged at the time by promoter Don Owens. There, he struck up a friendship with C&W singer-guitarist Roy Clark, who selected Moody and several of his Off Keys bandmates to play on his 45rpm single record "Please Mr. Mayor" (Roy Clark; Debbie Records, 1958). Moody often played saxophone for Clark in the ensuing years and appears on another one of his 45rpm single records, "Rock, Maggie, Rock" backed with "Man, Like Long Ago" (Roy Clark and the Versitals; Owens International Corp., 1960).

In the early 1960s Moody went on to play saxophone in such local rock and roll bands as the Off Beats (a four-man version that included guitarist Danny Gatton, bassist Jack Casady and singer-drummer Jack Kerge), the Savoys and the Belvederes. From 1963 to 1978 he was a member of the Personalities, a band that included singer-guitarist Mike Hurney among its featured players. When his time with the Personalities came to an end, Moody left the nation's capital. Through the years he continued playing music in the South. Today he resides in Key West, Florida and is a self-employed artist.

DICK WEBB

Raised in the Anacostia neighborhood of Southeast Washington, D.C. and a 1959 graduate of St. John's College High School, Dick Webb was a popular rock and roll singer who worked the local record hop scene in the late 1950s for promoters such as Don Dillard and Milt Grant. In the early 1960s he was a regular attraction at the Rocket Room in Washington, D.C. where he performed as a solo act as well as a guest vocalist with such bands as the Perry Mates and Charlie Daniels and the Jaguars. He also fronted his own bands in the city at Guy's Place and the Alpine Room before fading from the local scene in the middle 1960s. Webb had one single release for a major record company, "Land of Teenage Love" backed with "Just One More Kiss" (Dick Webb; Epic Records, 1960).

DON DUVALL

Keyboardist Don Duvall grew up in Laurel, Maryland and was introduced to music with piano lessons at the age of five. He started playing guitar at age 13 and in the late 1960s while attending Laurel Junior High School he played bass in his first band, a rock and roll group called the Colonials that mainly covered material by Paul Revere and the Raiders and performed at dances at the Fort George G. Meade Teen Club (Anne Arundel County, Maryland).

While attending Laurel High School in the early 1970s Duvall switched to keyboards and played in a succession of rock and roll bands including C.O.D., the Syke Machine, and Ramp. From 1973 to 1979 he played with such area rock and roll bands as Constellation, Patchwork, Flying Start and Fringe. He then spent most of the 1980s playing keyboards for such pop-rock bands as Friends form the Start, Joy Ride and Itchy Fingers. From 1986 to 1988 he performed as a solo singer-keyboardist act, simply billed as Don Duvall, headlining at night clubs all over Maryland including the Pirate's Cove (Galesville), the Holiday Inn Express Waldorf (Waldorf) and Johnny's and Sammy's Restaurant (Salisbury).

From 1989 to 2004 Duvall played keyboards in Classified, a Gaithersburg-based outfit that developed into one of the area's most sought-after pop-rock bands. For much of his time with the band the lineup was Duvall, singer-guitarist Michael Nelson, singer-bassist Bob McCoy and drummer Michael Gibney. Classified was a popular attraction at the Silo Inn (Olney), the Bethesda Marriott (Bethesda) and Harrington Raceway and Casino (Delaware). In 2004 Duvall joined the Main Event, another Gaithersburg-based popular music group, and remained with them into 2017. The Main Event served as the house band at Timpano Italian Chophouse in Rockville for more than seven years.

DON MONAHAN

Bassist Don Monahan was born a Navy brat and raised on St. George Island in St. Mary's County, Maryland. As a teen he was heavily influenced by the music of the Beatles and during his time at Great Mills High School in the late 1960s he played in pickup rock and roll bands with friends from similar Navy families. In the summer of 1967 Monahan was working as a busboy at a night club called Tall Timbers in Calloway, Maryland and was asked to replace the bassist in a rock and roll band called the Montels. He remained with the band for more than a year.

In early 1970, after taking some time off from music, Monahan began jamming with musicians from Takoma Park, Maryland, one of whom told him a band playing the Cross Roads in Bladensburg was looking for a bass player. He went to the night club and discovered the band in question was Danny Denver and the Soundmasters, a group that included lead guitarist Roy Buchanan. After a couple of nights of workouts, Monahan was offered a job with the group. He remained with the band at the Cross Roads into the summer months and on one occasion they worked a 90-minute set with visiting guest singer-pianist Jerry Lee Lewis.

In the early 1970s Monahan worked with several area blues and rock and roll bands and in 1972 became the first bassist in the Nighthawks, joining singer-harmonicist Mark Wenner, guitarist Jimmy Thackery, keyboardist Bill Holland and drummer Larry Bolet. During his tenure, the group performed in Washington, D.C. at the Far Inn and Mr. Henry's Tenley Circle, and in Prince George's County, Maryland at Mr. Henry's College Park. He later went on to play bass in Bill Holland and Rent's Due and then spent the late 1970s and early 1980s playing with a succession of C&W bands and musicians.

DONAL LEACE

Folk-pop singer-guitarist Donal Leace went to high school in Philadelphia, Pennsylvania, spent time in New York City in 1959, and came to Washington, D.C. in the early 1960s to attend Howard University. He was a popular figure on the local folk music circuit, appearing as a solo performer at such night clubs as Coffee 'n' Confusion, the Showboat Lounge, the Shadows and the Cellar Door. (For many years he performed under his given name, "Donald Leace," but for reasons that remain unclear he eventually dropped the letter "d" at the end of his first name and became "Donal Leace.")

Leace worked with many different area musicians throughout his career. One of his most popular backup bands in the middle 1970s consisted of guitarist Gerry Mule, bassist Pete Kessler and drummer Sid Sithens. This outfit regularly performed in Washington, D.C. at such night clubs as Mr. Henry's Tenley Circle, the Corsican and Fat Howard's. Leace also performed and toured with singer R&B singer Roberta Flack throughout the 1960s and 1970s and has recorded as a solo artist for Atlantic Records.

DONNIE AND THE DIABLOS

In the summer of 1965 the Greenbelt, Maryland soulful rock and roll band known as the Rockin' Rejects picked up a new lead vocalist from town named Donnie Dorsey, Sr. and instantly became Donnie and the Diablos, maintaining their position as one of the most popular bands to work the Greenbelt Teen Club dances at the Greenbelt Youth Center.

The original lineup of this outfit – lead singer Donnie Dorsey, lead guitarist Chris Peters, rhythm guitarist Leigh Dorsey, keyboardist Rick Ransom, bassist Dave Wigley and drummer Jerry McGuire – expanded its repertoire by adopting entries from the musical catalogs of such R&B performers as Wilson Pickett, Otis Redding, James Brown, Percy Sledge, the Miracles, along with popular rock and roll numbers by bands such as the Rolling Stones.

In addition to the Greenbelt Youth Center, Donnie and the Diablos spent their first couple of years giving performances at the American Legion Greenbelt Post 136, the Greenbelt Armory, St. Hugh's Catholic Church Teen Club, Greenbelt Center Elementary School, the Lakeland Tavern's outdoor beer garden (on Navahoe Street in College Park, Maryland), the Beverly Beach Pavilion (Anne Arundel County, Maryland), and private parties from Greenbelt to North Beach, Maryland.

By the summer of 1967 the band had ventured into the night club world and during that final year together worked at such hot spots as Nuzback's Bar (Laurel), the Turf Club (Laurel), the California Inn (Laurel), the Three Nines Tavern (Jessup), and a memorable two-week engagement at the Cross Roads (Bladensburg).

Like other bands around them, Donnie and the Diablos experienced a number of personnel changes and would alternately expand and then decrease in size, with such musicians as guitarist Joe Ecker, saxophonist Tom Baker and drummers Dennis Miller and Markus Cuff passing through in the group's final days.

DOUG TULL

Doug Tull lived in Camp Springs, Maryland, and Arlington, Virginia as a youth and during his years at Washington-Lee High School in the early 1970s he drummed in the rock and roll bands Horizon and Sway. He then spent the next couple of years in the soft rock band Cool Water, which held house band duties at a Washington, D.C. night club called Black Ulysses.

In 1974 Tull was recruited to drum for a short-lived rock and roll band in Seat Pleasant, Maryland called Bitch, which included two members of Razz (which was on a temporary hiatus), bassist Ted Nicely and guitarist Abaad Behram, and stayed around long enough to play one gig – a dance at Central High School. When Razz reconvened they asked Tull to take over the drums, joining lead singer Mike Reidy, guitarists Bill Craig and Abaad Behram and bassist Ted Niceley. This aggregation constituted one of Razz's strongest lineups and persevered until May 1978, at which time Behram left the band and was replaced by guitarist Tommy Keene.

After Razz disbanded in December 1979 Tull drummed for the band Nightman, a rock and roll group that consisted of four former members of Razz – Tull, lead singer-guitarist Mike Colburn, guitarist Bill Craig and bassist Ted Niceley – and released one album, "No Escape" (Nightman; Limp Record, 1981). Next, Tull, along with bassist Ted Nicely, joined forces with power pop singer-guitarist Tommy Keene and remained a part of his band from 1981 to 1986. At various points in time, Keene's group operated as a quartet, with either former Razz guitarist Mike Colburn or guitarist Billy Connelly in the mix.

Tull appears on the following Tommy Keene albums: "Strange Alliance" (Tommy Keene; Avenue Records, 1982), "Places That Are Gone" (Tommy Keene; Dolphin Records, 1984), "Back Again (Try...)" (Tommy Keene; Dolphin Records, 1984), "Songs from the Film" (Tommy Keene; Geffen Records, 1986) and "Run Now" (Tommy Keene; Geffen Records, 1986).

Tull went on to perform with such top local rock and roll bands as Johnny Bombay and the Reactions, the Billy Connelly Band and the Howling Mad. He is currently drumming for two rock and roll groups, the Billy Coulter Band and the Relics. Through the years he has also performed at numerous Razz reunion gigs in the nation's capital.

DRAKE ALLEN

Singer-guitarist Drake Allen was born in Ann Arbor, Michigan and raised in Greenbelt, Maryland, where he first took guitar lessons at a Veneman Music store in Beltway Plaza during his teen years. Allen was a devoted listener to local radio station WHFS and mainly taught himself guitar while listening to the music of Jimi Hendrix, Johnny Winter and Lightnin' Hopkins. During his years at Parkdale High School in the early 1970s he participated in private jam sessions with other local musicians such as guitarists Terry "T.I." Gleason and Armand Lenchek, bassists Ian Barber and Gary Colgan, and drummer Wayne Pugh.

In 1976 the Rockville-based singer-synthesizer player Rupert Chappelle enlisted the guitar services of Allen to complete the latest version of his avant-garde electronic music duo, Ozone Music. For more than a year they performed original compositions and Brian Eno covers in Washington, D.C. at events such as the 1976 Fourth of the July Smoke-In on the Mall and at night spots such as the Iguana Coffeehouse (Luther Place Memorial Church). Later in the 1970s Allen spent time playing guitar in a Bob Dylan-influenced duo with singer-guitarist Doug Stevens at Canal Square in Georgetown.

After taking time off from performing, Allen rejoined Ozone Music in the early 1990s and appeared with Rupert Chappelle at various open mic sessions at such Maryland night clubs as Manny's Restaurant and Lounge (Rockville), Taliano's Restaurant and Bar (Takoma Park) and the 8x10 (Baltimore). In 1996 Allen formed his own surf music act, Drake's Mojo, which performed at the Flower Theatre in Takoma Park and the New Deal Café, then-located in the Greenbelt Community Center. He performed as a solo guitarist at the 1996 Fourth of July Smoke-In on the Mall and began taking his surf guitar routine to various night club open mic sessions around the nation's capital.

More recently Allen has taken up playing hand drums and participates in drum circles and festivals throughout Washington, D.C. and Maryland. In addition, he occasionally picks up his guitar and haunts local open mic sessions at the New Deal Café and the Old Bowie Town Grille.

THE DUBONNETTES

A flashy, hard-rocking outfit that was based in Chevy Chase, Maryland and was popular in the night clubs of Georgetown from 1972 to 1976, the Dubonnettes consisted of lead singer Charles Pearson, lead guitarist Michael Stern, rhythm guitarist Alan Adkins, bassist Rolf Hanson and drummer Jim Sabot. For years they based out of Apple Pie in Georgetown and also worked engagements at nearby night clubs such as the Keg and My Mother's Place, playing everything from Sam Cooke to the Rolling Stones.

The Dubonnettes underwent changes in personnel during its run, with several musicians coming and going including guitarists Eric Rosenfield and Bobby Manriquez and drummer Mike Zack, and recorded and released an album under an assumed name, "Daddy's Girl" (Charlie and the Pep Boys; A&M Records, 1976). In the wake of the album's release, Pearson and Adkins led a revamped version of the Dubonnettes to Denver, Colorado that included guitarist Tony Grasso and keyboardist Gary St. Clair, but their time there was short-lived. Pearson and Adkins eventually returned to the nation's capital and were founding members of the band Tears.

DUKE AYRES

Drummer William "Duke" Ayres was born in Fort Benning, Georgia and, as an Army brat, grew up all over the United States and Europe. He began playing bongos at age 11, eventually took up the drums, and in the late 1950s and early 1960s listened to records by a mix of bands and musicians that included Chuck Berry, Fats Domino, John Coltrane, Miles Davis and Dizzy Gillespie.

After finishing high school in Newport, Rhode Island, Ayres moved with his family to Falls Church, Virginia at the age of 19 in 1967. There, he joined his first band, a psychedelic rock and roll group called the Mosaic Virus that performed original material as well as covers of such acts as the Beatles, the Animals, Pink Floyd and Jefferson Airplane.

During the Summer of Love the Mosaic Virus often performed at the Corral on M Street NW in Georgetown and also opened many concerts that fall at the Ambassador Theatre in the Adams Morgan neighborhood of Washington, D.C. In the late 1960s Ayres also drummed for the Northern Virginia-based rock and roll band the Magic Reign.

Ayres went on to drum for a number of rock and roll bands in the Washington, D.C. area. In the 1970s he played in such groups as Thurbr, Crank, Snake, Gravity, and the Fabulous Touchtones. Some of the bands he worked with in later years were Island, Pacer, SRO, the Dianna Crawford Band, the Erection Set and Uneven Numbers.

ED CROWLEY

Singer-harmonicist Ed Crowley was born in Washington, D.C. and raised in the Prince George's County, Maryland communities of Chillum and Adelphi. He became interested in music in grade school and initially took up the guitar. In the early 1970s, when he was in the eighth and ninth grades – at St. Joseph's Catholic School in Beltsville and Our Lady of Good Counsel High School in Wheaton, respectively – he played guitar in a teen rock and roll band called the High Boys that mainly performed at area American Legions and VFWs.

Crowley transferred to High Point High School in his sophomore year, took up the harmonica, and spent the middle 1970s checking out local blues bands, with the Nighthawks becoming a personal favorite. He attended Bethany College in West Virginia from 1976 to 1980 and participated in the blues music scene there. Crowley spent the early 1980s in Baltimore, Maryland and played in an acoustic blues band called the Self Destructive Fools for five years. He then took an extended break from music.

In the early 2000s Crowley picked up his harmonica and began participating in open mics at various night clubs around the nation's capital such as the J.V. Restaurant (Falls Church), Bangkok Blues (Falls Church), Sully's Restaurant and Lounge (Chantilly), Blair's Londontowne Pub and Grill (Edgewater), Old Bowie Town Grille (Bowie), the Zoo Bar Café (Washington, D.C.) and the Surf Club (Hyattsville). In 2009 he began singing and spent two years in an R&B group called the Blue Dog Band.

Crowley next put together a blues band to perform at "The DC Blues Society 7th Annual Fish Fry 'n' Blues Show" that was held at the American Legion Cissell-Saxon Post 41 in Silver Spring, Maryland on Saturday, July 16, 2011. He called his band Fast Eddie and the Slowpokes and the lineup that day consisted of Crowley singing and playing harmonica, lead guitarist Larry Younkins, bassist Charles Solomon, keyboardist Rick Jones and drummer Scott Chadwick.

Fast Eddie and the Slowpokes originally rehearsed at Younkins' home in Ellicott City, Maryland and in 2012 they endured personnel changes, with Solomon being replaced by bassist James "Cookie" Cook, and Jones being spelled by keyboardist Dave Gorozdos. On Saturday, October 13, 2012 the band won "The DC Blues Society's Battle of the Bands" at the American Legion Wheaton Post 268 in Wheaton, Maryland, with its prize being a bid to "The 2013 International Blues Challenge" in Memphis, Tennessee, a contest that lasted from Tuesday, January 29 to Saturday, February 2, 2013.

In 2016 Fast Eddie and the Slowpokes settled on a lineup of Crowley, lead guitarist Scott Mattern, Cook, Gorozdos and Chadwick. They rehearsed at Mattern's home in Wheaton and mixed original compositions with classic and obscure blues songs. The band has performed at local festivals such as "The Greenbelt Blues Festival" and "The Colonial Beach Blues Festival." They regularly work in Maryland at such night clubs as the New Deal Café (Greenbelt), Old Bowie Town Grille (Bowie), the Cat's Eye Pub (Baltimore) and Second Chance Saloon (Columbia); and in Virginia at JV's Restaurant (Falls Church), the Ice House Café (Herndon) and Nick's Nightclub (Alexandria).

On Saturday, October 1, 2016 Fast Eddie and the Slowpokes won "The DC Blues Society Memphis or Bust IBC Battle of the Bands," which was staged at the American Legion Cissell-Saxon Post 41 in Silver Spring, Maryland. First prize in this competition led to an entry in "The 2017 International Blues Challenge" in Memphis, Tennessee, a contest that lasted from Tuesday, January 31 to Saturday, February 4, 2017. In the wake of that experience, the band headlined at the John F. Kennedy Center for the Performing Arts Millennium Stage (Washington, D.C.) on Sunday, March 26, 2017.

In addition to fronting Fast Eddie and the Slowpokes, Crowley currently sings and plays harmonica for the Freestate Blues Revue, a band whose lineup is rounded out by guitarists Robert Frahm and Andy Poxon, bassist Steve Wolf and drummer Mark Stutso. Through the years Crowley has also performed onstage with such blues acts as the Nighthawks, Bad Influence, the Andy T. Nixon Band, singers Charlie Owens and Phil Pemberton, and singer-pianist Victor Wainwright.

ED CYNAR

Bassist Ed Cynar grew up in McLean, Virginia and started playing guitar at the age of 13. After a few lessons he took off on his own, learning a couple chords from friends and basically teaching himself how to play by listening to such musicians as Link Wray and His Ray Men, the Everly Brothers, Elvis Presley, the Crickets (featuring singer-guitarist Buddy Holly) and Dale Hawkins. While attending Bishop Denis J. O'Connell High School in Arlington in the early 1960s he played in a few different rock and roll bands including the Roadrunners, who were a popular commodity on the Northern Virginia teen dance scene.

In 1963 Cynar had a chance to see Link Wray and His Ray Men perform at Vinnie's Grill in Washington, D.C. He enrolled at the University of Virginia that year and actually got the band to come down and perform a concert on the campus, an event that saw Cynar actually take the stage and play bass with the band. In 1964 he joined a group called the Fender Benders which was rounded out by singer-guitarist John Van Horn, keyboardist Bill Hodges and drummer Bobby Jones (Cynar often alternated with bassist Richie Mitchell). This group performed regularly at the Oasis, a basement night club in the Mount Pleasant neighborhood of Washington, D.C. and it was there that Ray Vernon recruited various members from the band to work with Link Wray.

In early 1965 Cynar began playing with Link Wray and His Ray Men at the 1023 Restaurant in Southeast Washington, D.C. At that time the band consisted of singer-guitarist Link Wray, singer-rhythm guitarist Chuck Bennett, rhythm guitarist John Van Horn, drummer Doug Wray, and two bassists – Shorty Horton doing the back beats and Cynar handling the runs. After a week Horton left the band and Cynar became the full-time bass player. The group remained the house band at the 1023 Restaurant through August 1966, performing from 9pm to 2am, 40 minutes on and 20 minutes off. Cynar, however, was drafted into the United States Army in November 1965 with his place being taken by Richie Mitchell.

Back in the Washington, D.C. area, Cynar spent the late 1960s and early 1970s playing bass in the Fender Benders. He also worked with a rock and roll band called Face Value that performed in the city at such night clubs as the Golden Eagle and the Brickskeller. He attended Georgetown University, earning a Bachelor of Arts in English in 1971, and went on to work for the United States Department of the Navy and then the United States Department of the Interior.

In the ensuing years Cynar performed in bands with John Van Horn, most often in Fender Benders appearances, and Link Wray, when the guitarist would return to the Washington, D.C. area for gigs at places like the Psyche Delly, Nightclub 9:30 and the Wax Museum. Most recently, Cynar has been playing bass in a trio called Link Wray's Ray Men with singer-guitarist John Van Horn, Jr. and drummer Pat Greenwood.

EDDIE BECKER

Eddie Becker grew up in Montgomery County, Maryland in the community of Bethesda and the town of Kensington and began taking guitar lessons as a teenager in the early 1960s at Bethesda Music and Art. Among his early influences were Link Wray and His Ray Men, the Ventures, Duane Eddy, Lonnie Mack, Chet Atkins and local jazz favorite Charlie Byrd.

During his years at Walter Johnson High School in the middle 1960s he played in two popular teen dance bands, the Fidelities and the Velours, the latter of which played everything from British Invasion songs to R&B classics and expanded in size through time. The Velours were noted for performing at teen dances at facilities like the Bethesda Youth Center and the Wheaton Youth Center, and night clubs such as the Red Fox Inn in Bethesda, Maryland.

Becker played guitar for a short while in the Newports and then spent the late 1960s in a series of R&B bands in the Washington, D.C. area such as Jerome and the Good Knights, a 13-piece outfit called the Midnighters, and a dual-combo outfit known as the Spades and the Rainbows. In the summer of 1968 he played guitar for the R&B act Phil Flowers and the Flower Shop at the Hayloft in Washington, D.C.

In the early 1970s Becker was guitarist for a local rock and roll band known as Steve Smith and the Nakeds. In 1975 he relocated to Texas and spent several years performing slide and bottleneck guitar with the noted Houston-based Cajun singer-guitarist-harmonicist Gene Billeaudeaux.

Becker returned to the Washington, D.C. area in the middle 1980s and has since played with a variety of bands and musicians including: a bluegrass band called Phil Dirt and the Shovel Band; a blues rock band called Vital Signs; C&W guitarist Chick Hall, Jr.; rockabilly singer-guitarist Bill Kirchen; the Newports (again); a blues rock band called the Shakers; an R&B act called the Ten Most Wanted; and his own 9-piece R&B group, the Eddie Becker Band.

EDDIE DAY

Singer Eddie Day hails from New Carrollton, Maryland, attended Parkdale high School, and in the late 1970s joined the Laurel-based heavy metal band Deuce, whose roster at the time was filled out by lead guitarist Marty Friedman, rhythm guitarist Tom Gattis, bassist Steve Leter and drummer Billy Giddings.

In 1980 Day handled lead vocals for a heavy metal band from Northern Virginia called Overlord, and then in 1981 he joined Maxx, a hard-rocking outfit which included lead guitarist Terry "T.I." Gleason and covered such bands and musicians as Pat Travers, Judas Priest and Frank Marino and Mahogany Rush. Day next sang in another Northern Virginia heavy metal band called Darius, which headlined in Virginia at night clubs such as Louie's Rock City (Bailey's Crossroads), the Wild West (Springfield) and the Fancy Dancer (Alexandria); and in Maryland at the Outside Inn (Rockville).

After a short stay in Hollywood, California, Day returned to the Washington, D.C. area in late 1982 and sang for a rock and roll band called Action. A call from his former Deuce bandmate Marty Friedman led Day to venture to Hawaii in January 1984 and take over lead vocals for the heavy metal band Hawaii. He sang on the band's second and third albums, "Loud Wild and Heavy" (Hawaii; Cavern Productions, 1984) and "The Natives are Restless" (Hawaii; Shockwaves Records, 1985). In the summer of 1985 Friedman and Day returned to Prince George's County, Maryland and regrouped Hawaii. Day remained the band's lead vocalist until its breakup in 1987.

After a long hiatus, Day returned to the local music scene in 1992 as lead singer of the Beltsville, Maryland-based rock and roll band Idlewild, which regularly appeared at the Paragon in College Park. In 1993 he became a founding member of the Rockin' Bones, a popular rockabilly band whose current lineup consists of Day, rhythm guitarist Kent Lopez, bassist Paul Cleary, drummer Mark Lucas, and either Robert Frahm or Bruce Katsu on lead guitar.

EDDY OTTENSTEIN

A Washington, D.C. native, singer-guitarist Eddy Ottenstein played with Willie and the Handjives at the Rocket Room in the late 1960s before moving to the West Coast in 1971 and embarking on a career that saw him play with a number of national acts including the Youngbloods, Jesse Colin Young, Van Morrison, the Steve Miller Band, Il Big, and Gone Johnson.

ELLWOOD BROWN

Ellwood Brown first saw Link Wray and His Ray Men perform at his Oxon Hill High School prom at the American Legion Oxon Hill Post 248 in June 1964. Two years later he began playing bass for the group at the 1023 Restaurant in Southeast Washington, D.C., and remained a fixture with the band until 1970. During that period the group worked in Washington, D.C. at the Famous Restaurant; and in Maryland at Strick's Restaurant (Silver

Hill), Stables Restaurant and Lounge (Bryans Road), Smitty's Steakhouse (Bryans Road), the Stardust Inn (Waldorf), the Wig Wam (Waldorf) and the Frontier Restaurant (Waldorf).

Brown later jammed with such guitar greats as Roy Buchanan and Danny Gatton and went on to work with such local rock and roll acts as singer Ray Vernon, the Doug Wray Group, Danny Denver and the Soundmasters, Rambunctious, J.C. and the Goodtimers (featuring guitarist Johnny Hopkins) and Frenchy and the Heartthrobs.

EMMYLOU HARRIS

Today singer-guitarist Emmylou Harris is a superstar in the field of C&W music, but back in the early 1970s she was a fixture in the night clubs of the Washington, D.C. area, spending her nights singing country, bluegrass, gospel, folk, and even a few rock and roll numbers as her following grew.

Harris was born in Birmingham, Alabama, but was largely raised in Woodbridge, Virginia where she attended Garfield High School in the middle 1960s. Late in the decade she moved with her family to the community of Clarksburg in Montgomery County, Maryland and in 1969 she released her debut album, a folk music record under a mistaken name: "Gliding Bird" (Emmy Lou Harris, Jubilee Records, 1969).

From 1970 to 1975 Harris performed at such Washington, D.C. night clubs as the Assembly Restaurant, Emergency, the Reading Gaol, the Childe Harold, the Chancery, as well as the Red Fox Inn in Bethesda, Maryland.

Things changed in a big way for Harris when she met country rock singer-guitarist-keyboardist Gram Parsons, formerly of the Byrds and the Flying Burrito Brothers. Parsons had been invited by his previous band, the Flying Burrito Brothers, to join them onstage during their engagement at the Cellar Door in Georgetown which lasted from Monday, September 13 to Saturday, September 18, 1971. While on break one evening, Parsons ventured across M Street NW and saw Harris singing at Clyde's Restaurant in front of an audience of three people. Reportedly, he was greatly impressed by her performance and took her on the road with him.

The death of Gram Parsons on Wednesday, September 19, 1973 led Harris to return to Washington, D.C. where she formed the Angel Band, whose initial lineup consisted of lead guitarist Bruce Archer, bassist Tom Guidera, steel guitarist Danny Pendleton and drummer Mark Cuff.

Harris' reputation became well-established in the music industry and in 1975 she released her major label debut album, "Pieces of the Sky" (Emmylou Harris; Reprise Records, 1975), with the original Angel Band backing her. She then unceremoniously dropped the band despite the album's success.

Harris has since recorded and released more than two-dozen albums of C&W music on a variety of record labels including Reprise, Warner Bros. and Elektra, and no fewer than 10 compilations of her work have been issued through the years. She remains one of the biggest stars in C&W music today.

ERIC WILFONG

Bassist Eric Wilfong was born in Washington, D.C. and raised in Chevy Chase, Maryland. While attending Kensington Junior High School in the early 1960s he joined his first rock and roll band, the Shadows, which worked the local teen dance circuit and specialized in Everly Brothers covers.

From 1965 to 1966, while attending Harker Preparatory School in Potomac, Maryland, Wilfong sang and played bass in the Velours, a Kensington-based group that initially was rounded out with guitarist Eddie Becker and drummer Mark McInturff and covered the popular rock and roll songs of the day. While a member of the Velours, Wilfong began hanging out at different Washington, D.C. night clubs and at one point in 1965 he worked several weekends at Rand's Night Club as the bassist for Little Willie and the Handjives.

Wilfong entered Colgate University in New York in the fall of 1966 and took a break from the local music scene. He returned in 1969 and for two years played bass in a rock and roll band called Sideshow that performed regularly in Washington, D.C. at the Brickskeller and Fran O'Brien's Anthony House Restaurant. He then spent the early 1970s playing bass for two local acts: Parsec, a trippy rock and roll band that played local festivals and University of Maryland functions; and blues singer-guitarist Bobby Radcliff, who was primarily working at the Far Inn on upper Connecticut Avenue NW in Washington, D.C.

Wilfong stepped away from the local music scene in 1973 and after a long hiatus he spent the 1990s playing bass in a large R&B group called the Blue Dog Band that featured guitarist Les Hatley. He later joined Hatley and guitarist Eddie Becker in a blues rock band called the Shakers. Eric Wilfong passed away on Saturday, January 4, 2014 at the age of 65.

ERICH SEEHAFER

Guitarist Erich Seehafer was born in Washington, D.C. and spent his teen years living in Fort Washington, Maryland, where he took up guitar at the age of 14 in 1965. He played in his first rock and roll band, a Fort Washington-based group called the DCvers, from 1965 to 1968. The band, whose lineup consisted of Seehafer on lead guitar, singer-rhythm guitarist Ralph Thompson, rhythm guitarist Ray Hume and drummer Scott Taylor, performed at local parties and teen dances and covered popular acts such as the Beatles and Wilson Pickett.

In 1968, during his senior year at Crossland High School, Seehafer joined a hard-rocking band called Trestle Special which was based in Fort Washington and mainly consisted of Crossland students. The group, which shortened its name to Trestle shortly after forming, consisted of Seehafer on lead guitar, lead singer-rhythm guitarist Ralph Thompson, bassist Tom McCarthy, keyboardist Clark Merritt and drummer Scott Taylor, who was later replaced by Don Maines.

Trestle covered such rock and roll bands as the Beatles, the Rolling Stones, the Moody Blues and the Strawberry Alarm Clock. In their time they performed at Tucker Road Community Center (Fort Washington), the Surrattsville Junior Teen Club (Surrattsville Junior High School in Clinton), the Surrattsville Senior Teen Club (Surrattsville High School in Clinton), the Andrews Air Force Base Teen Club (Prince George's County, Maryland) and a night club in Washington, D.C. called Gentlemen II.

Trestle disbanded in 1971 and Seehafer next joined another Fort Washington-based rock and roll band, this one named Summerfield Smyth. He played lead guitar and was joined in the group by lead singer-rhythm guitarist Ralph Thompson, rhythm guitarist Gary Pritchett, bassist Alan Wood and drummer Kenny Hayes. Summerfield Smyth mixed originals with covers of songs by the Rolling Stones, Steppenwolf, the James Gang, Led Zeppelin, Budgie and Grand Funk Railroad. They played teen dances at Oxon Hill Junior High School (Oxon Hill) and Kava (Greenbelt Youth Center), as well as Washington, D.C. night clubs such as Some Place Else, the M Club, the Crazy Horse, the Paul Mall Restaurant and the Keg.

In March 1974 Summerfield Smyth shortened its name to Summerfield and relocated to Reading, Pennsylvania. At that point the band's lineup consisted of Thompson, Seehafer, singer-keyboardist Rick McGale, bassist Ron Kalina and drummer Kenny Hayes (who was later replaced by T.C. Tolliver). Summerfield worked concerts and night clubs throughout Pennsylvania, New Jersey and New York before disbanding in 1977.

In the late 1970s and throughout the 1980s Seehafer played guitar in a Washington, D.C. area rock and roll band called Scarlet, which featured singer-guitarist-keyboardist-flutist Janine Davy. He spent several years in the late 1980s and early 1990s in a C&W band called Yellow Rose and since 2000 he has played guitar with Janine Davy and Heartspeak, as well as holding membership in another band with her called Touchstone that performs soft rock covers. Seehafer's recording credits include the album "Looking For You" (Janine Davy; Funkstown Records, 2005).

EVA CASSIDY

This blues-jazz-pop singer was born in Washington, D.C., mainly grew up in the Prince George's County, Maryland city of Bowie, and graduated from Bowie High School in 1981. In 1974 at age 11 she sang and played guitar in her first band, Easy Street, and during her high school years she sang in a rock and roll band called Stonehenge.

During the 1980s Cassidy sang in the rock and roll bands Characters Without Names and Method Actor. In 1990 she began fronting her own group, the Eva Cassidy Band, the lineup of which consisted of Cassidy handling lead vocals and guitar, lead guitarist Keith Grimes, bassist Chris Biondo, keyboardist Lenny Williams and drummer Raice McLeod. In the early 1990s Cassidy recorded and released several solo albums on independent record labels.

Eva Cassidy passed away on Saturday, November 2, 1996 at the age of 33. Since that time Blix Street Records has released albums of her previously recorded material and her popularity has posthumously soared throughout the world.

EVAN JOHNS

Rockabilly singer-guitarist Evan Johns was born in Washington, D.C. and raised in McLean, Virginia. As a youth he listened to the radio and became influenced by such musicians as the Beatles, the Everly Brothers, James Brown, Sam Cooke and Roy Orbison. Upon entering his teens in the late 1960s he began attending the Smithsonian Folklife Festivals on the Mall in Washington, D.C. and would take in the various live musical performances. It was at these events he met such performers as Mississippi John Hurt, Lightnin' Hopkins, Bill Monroe, Doc Watson, the Stanley Brothers and others.

Johns attended Langley High School before graduating from Emerson Institute in Washington, D.C. in 1974. During those school years he played guitar and sang on an informal basis with friends and on occasion appeared in bars in the Tyson's Corner area where he gave impromptu performances on acoustic guitar. In 1972 he began hanging out at Dupont Circle and met guitarist Danny Gatton at the Childe Harold, who was performing at the time with Liz Meyer and Friends.

After finishing at Emersion Institute Johns joined a local country rock band called the Cold Steel Benders and in 1976 he began singing and playing guitar with the Danny Gatton Band. Johns appears on the 45rpm single record "Ugly Man" backed with "Love is What You Need" (Danny Gatton Band; NRG Records, 1977) and the album "Redneck Jazz" (Danny Gatton; NRG Records, 1978). In 1978 Johns joined the Good Humor Band and also continued playing music with guitarist Danny Gatton on an occasional basis.

In 1979 he put together the first edition of Evan Johns and the H-Bombs, a rockabilly group consisting of Johns on lead vocals and guitar, guitarist Don Oehser, bassist Michael Maye and drummer Keith John. The band's first album was a four-song EP entitled "Giddy Up Girl" (Evan Johns and the H-Bombs; DECO Records, 1980). This record consisted of the songs "Giddy Up Girl" and "Don't Be Late" on the A-side and "Mind of My Own" and "Pain of Love" on the B-side. They remained one of the top rockabilly acts in the Washington, D.C. area until 1984, at which time Johns relocated to Austin, Texas.

In Texas, Johns spent played guitar for the Leroi Brothers on extensive tours of the United States and Europe from 1984 to 1986. In the late 1980s he reformed the H-Bombs in Austin, Texas and in the ensuing years the group endured numerous changes in personnel. Through the years Evan Johns and the H-Bombs have released several different albums on more than a half-dozen different independent record labels, and Johns himself has recorded with a variety of rock and roll and rockabilly artists.

Evan Johns stopped fronting his own band in 1996 and subsequently lived in Vancouver from 1998 to 2009. He then returned to Austin, where he lived until his passing on Saturday, March 11, 2017 at the age of 60.

THE EYE

The Eye was a popular Washington, D.C.-based dance band that played a mix of pop, jazz, R&B and rock and roll in some of the area's top night clubs. The group formed in 1969 and during its first few years the lineup consisted of singer-guitarist David Gabaldon, singer-bassist-keyboardist-saxophonist Paul Brier, singer-keyboardist Guy Meredith and drummer Ronnie Stevens. Changes in personnel ensued and in 1973 and 1974 the band carried on with Gabaldon and Brier being joined by bassist John Herbert, keyboardist Mike Zivodinovich and drummer Rick Davis. In 1975 Gabaldon, Brier and Davis were joined by newcomers David Banya on bass and Larry Strother on saxophone and flute.

Among the many Washington, D.C. night clubs the Eye performed at were the Paul Mall Restaurant, the Crazy Horse, the Bayou, Act IV Supper Club, the Montage, Black Greco, Black Ulysses, and Ventuno 21 Supper Club. The band also worked engagements up and down the Atlantic Coast.

Among the national acts the Eye backed up onstage through the years were the Shirelles, the Coasters, Gene Vincent, Chuck Berry and Del Shannon. Other local musicians to pass through the Eye during its time included guitarist Pete "Peaches" Williams, drummer Mike Zack and singer-keyboardist Larry Kidwell. The Eye disbanded in 1976.

THE FABLONS

The Fablons were an organ-based rock and roll trio that specialized in instrumentals and were especially popular on the military base circuit in the Washington, D.C. area from 1963 to 1970. The band consisted of lead singer-drummer Don Sylvia, keyboardist Sam Paladino and saxophonist Tony Romagna, and often appeared at Benny's Rebel Room on the 14th Street NW Strip in Washington, D.C., and the Cross Roads in Bladensburg, Maryland.

The Fablons regularly performed at officers' clubs on most of the area's military bases including Andrews Air Force Base (Prince George's County, Maryland), Bolling Air Force Base (Washington, D.C.), Fort Belvoir (Fairfax County, Virginia), Fort George G. Meade (Anne Arundel County, Maryland), Fort Myer (Arlington County, Virginia), Henderson Hall (Arlington County, Virginia) and Marine Corps Base Quantico (Prince William County, Virginia). The band recorded and released one popular single, "Organ-Ism" backed with "Rigatoni" (The Fablons; Sylvia Records, 1964).

THE FABULOUS HUBCAPS

The story of the Fabulous Hubcaps goes back to an oldies rock band called Harvey Hubcap and the Do Ron Ron, which was formed in 1972 by Rocky Simon of Clinton, Maryland. The group was put together with remnants of another band called Wally and the Starfires and initially rehearsed at the home of a friend named Dave "The Grit" Gebhardt in Clinton.

The original lineup of Harvey Hubcap and the Do Ron Ron consisted of singer-drummer-saxophonist Dale "Rocky" Simon of Clinton, singer-guitarist Maury Wahler of

Oxon Hill, bassist Tom Osborn of Westminster, and saxophonist Dan Mitchell, who at the time was a student at the Catholic University of America in Washington, D.C.

Harvey Hubcap and the Do Ron Ron debuted at a Lackey High School reunion in Charles County, Maryland in 1972. During their first year they played parties and teen dances throughout Southern Prince George's County and Charles County and worked a house band job at a night club in Washington, D.C. called Graffiti. Early on the group covered such pop and rock and roll artists as Chuck Berry, Link Wray and His Ray Men, Santo and Johnny, Dick Dale and His Del-Tones, Carl Perkins, Elvis Presley, the Crickets (featuring singer-guitarist Buddy Holly), and Fats Domino. Also offered were hit songs by many other popular performers of the day including Jodi Reynolds, the Earls, the Marcels and Larry Williams.

In the early 1970s Harvey Hubcap and the Do Ron Ron performed at such Maryland night clubs as the Hangar Club (Camp Springs) and the Quonset Supper Club (Silver Hill). Band members came and went during this period, but several musicians stayed the course and provided roster stability. Among the constant members of the band were singer-drummer-saxophonist Rocky Simon, lead singer Tommy "Nicky" Nichols of Hyattsville, singer-bassist Denny Cook of Hyattsville, singer-guitarist Richard "Fast Ricky Strings" Marcus of Arlington, and singer-saxophonist Mike "Spider" Kirk of Camp Springs.

One of the more interesting moments in Harvey Hubcap and the Do Ron Ron history occurred when three band members, bassist Denny Cook, keyboardist Steve Huey and drummer Rocky Simon, were recruited to play in the onstage backup band at a multi-act concert featuring Jerry Lee Lewis, Little Richard, the Coasters, the Five Satins, and the Crystals at the Capital Centre in Landover, Maryland on Friday, April 4, 1975.

In August 1975 after a jam session at a night club called Some Place Else in Southeast Washington, D.C., a merger took place between Harvey Hubcap and the Do Ron Ron and another rock and roll group called the Half Moon Band. The end result was a new musical outfit entitled Harvey Hubcap and the Moon Band, the lineup of which consisted of three singers – Rocky Simon, Denny Cook and Tommy Nichols – along with guitarist Billy Weir, bassist Willie Farrell, keyboardist Jimi Simon, saxophonist Mike Kirk and drummer Charlie Crowder. The band soon changed its name to T.S.M.B. featuring the Harvey Hubcap Show (T.S.M.B. standing for "The Southern Maryland Band"). They continued playing rock and roll favorites of the 1950s and 1960s.

In 1980 T.S.M.B. featuring Harvey Hubcap officially changed its name to the Hubcaps. At this time the band's lineup consisted of lead singer Denny Cook, singer-saxophonist Rocky Simon, guitarist Billy Weir, guitarist Coe Anderson, bassist Willie Farrell, keyboardist Jimi Simon, saxophonist Tiny Barge, trumpeter-trombonist Jeff Eckman and drummer Ron Correa. In 1981 Correa was replaced by former Cherry Smash drummer Barry Holober, who is still with the band today.

Throughout the 1980s the Hubcaps were working more than 200 dates per year, performing shows and concerts and opening for national acts up and down the Atlantic Coast, and appearing in the Washington, D.C. area at such venues as the Volunteer Fire Department of Brandywine (Brandywine), the Bladensburg Volunteer Fire Department (Bladensburg), the Cross Roads (Bladensburg), the Stardust Inn (Waldorf), the Classic III Supper Club (Camp Springs), Second Coming (Lanham), the Big Apple (Hyattsville) and innumerable American Legions and Moose Lodges. They were also a popular attraction at the Hollywood Palace (Catonsville), the Golden 40 Inn (Joppa), the Cadeaux Nite Club (Dover), the Hurricane (Ocean City) and the Prince George's County Fair in Upper Marlboro, Maryland, where they enjoyed a 15-year run.

In 1983 the Hubcaps recorded and released their first album, "Rock to the Beat" (The Hubcaps; T.S.M.B. Records, 1983). That year the band also changed its name to the

Fabulous Hubcaps and switched their home base to Dover, Delaware. In the ensuing years the Fabulous Hubcaps recorded and released several singles and CD albums.

The Fabulous Hubcaps have experienced a number of personnel changes through the years. Musicians that have played in the band include: guitarist Rod Hudson; keyboardist John Penue; keyboardist-saxophonist Steve Huey; singer-saxophonist-keyboardists Barbara Riehl and Mary McKenna; saxophonist-guitarist Kathy Martin; saxophonists Doug Mark, Ken Matthews and Steve Griffin; singer-bassist Jan Zukowski; bassist Doug Lewis; and drummers Dave Fletcher, Coco Russell and Lee Jordan.

Today the Fabulous Hubcaps are based in Greenbelt, Maryland and perform approximately 85 live dates per year. Their current lineup consists of singers Denny Cook and Lorraine Allen, guitarist Michael Shipley, bassist Dean Andrews, keyboardist Tommy Dildy, saxophonist Jay Cleaver and drummer Barry Holober.

FACE DANCER

Face Dancer was originally a progressive rock and roll band that formed on the University of Rhode Island party circuit in 1972 when the members of two top local bands, Jack and Shadowfax, merged together. The band's original lineup consisted of lead singer-drummer Carey Kress, guitarist Rob Mattera, bassist Mike Bassette, keyboardist Mark Roumelis and keyboardist D.J. Long.

In September 1973 Face Dancer moved south to play the nation's capital's rock and roll scene and rented a house at 12411 Littleton Street in Wheaton, Maryland. They became a top attraction at the Bayou in Georgetown and a restaurant inside the Adele H. Stamp Student Union Building on the University of Maryland campus called the Pub. The band experienced numerous personnel changes as their sound evolved from progressive rock and roll in the manner of Genesis and King Crimson to more hard-rocking material. The 1970s saw Bassette, Mattera, Roumelis, and Long depart the band at different times, with bassist Dale Marcks passing in and out.

Face Dancer signed with Capitol Records in July 1978 and several months later they released their first album for the label, "This World" (Face Dancer; Capitol Records, 1979). The album featured a lineup of lead singer Carey Kress (who had moved away from the drum set), guitarists David Utter and Jeff Adams, bassist Scott McGinn and drummer Bill Trainor. Kress and Utter left Face Dancer after their debut effort was released and for the follow-up, "About Face" (Face Dancer; Capitol Records, 1980), the roster included Trainor, McGinn, Adams and lead singer Mike Milsap from Atlanta, Georgia.

Since 1981 Face Dancer has shuffled its lineup several times and still periodically gives live performances. Their two most recent album release are: "Midnite Raid" (Face Dancer; Red Shoes Records, 1990); and "Face Dancer Alive: (Face Dancer; Self-Released, 2003).

FIRESIDE

One of the more unique groups to emerge in the Washington, D.C. area during the middle 1970s, Fireside rates as the only known band from the area to offer music that they called "AcidFolk" and "BlueRockGrass." The band came together in 1974 from the remnants of a Prince George's Community College-based group called Friends of the Family, which worked the local coffee house circuit and often appeared at the Italian Gardens in College Park, Maryland.

At the time of its formation, Fireside was based in College Park, with most of its membership attending the University of Maryland. The group's initial lineup consisted of singer-guitarist-mandolinist Terry Reynolds, singer-guitarist Wade Moroughan, guitarist-banjoist-harmonicist Rob Gibbs, and singer-bassist Joe Goulait, with singer-drummer-pianist-flutist Phil Shimmel added in 1975.

In 1976 Reynolds was replaced by singer-fiddler-mandolinist-guitarist Nat Winer. Further personnel changes ensued in 1977 with Goulait being replaced by singer-bassist John Spiro and Shimmel being replaced by drummer Scott Taylor. The band's final version in 1978 consisted of Gibbs, Moroughan, Taylor, singer-fiddler Michael Stein and singer-steel guitarist Bruce Bouton. John Spiro, Nat Winer, and Phil Shimmel all reappeared shortly thereafter in the band Silverspring, with Bruce Bouton later moving to Nashville where he became a member of C&W singer-mandolinist Ricky Scaggs' backup band.

Fireside performed original compositions and also covered such acts as the Beatles, the Eagles, John Denver, Jonathan Edwards, the Dillards, John Prine, the Pure Prairie League, the Byrds, and traditional bluegrass songs in what they called "RockGrass" style. During its time, Fireside appeared in Washington, D.C. at Rocky Raccoon's Saloon and Desperado's; in Maryland at the Italian Gardens (College Park), O'Brien's Pit Barbecue (College Park), the Village Pub (Seabrook), Timothy's Pub (Rockville), DiGennaro's (Laurel) and the Red Fox Inn (Bethesda); and in Virginia at the Birchmere (Arlington).

FLAVOR

In June 1968 Columbia Records issued a press release on a new Washington, D.C.-based acquisition. Its opening stanza read: "Flavor is a subtle experience: its music is changeable, provocative, original. The group can do a driving rock number and, moments later, ease into a slow, sophisticated love-lost song. Comprised of three young musicians, all of whom hail from the Washington, D.C. area, Flavor has been performing for enthusiastic college audiences in Georgetown's numerous clubs."

Flavor was an R&B-influenced rock and roll trio consisting of singer-keyboardist Gary St. Clair, who had grown up in Adelphi, Maryland, singer-guitarist Demetri Callas from Frederick, Maryland, and drummer Danny Conway, a native of Silver Spring, Maryland. The roots of the band go back to a quartet called Billy Joe and the Confidentials, which formed in September 1964 and consisted of lead singer-saxophonist Billy Joe Ash, along with Callas, St. Clair and Conway. The band primarily worked Benny's Rebel Room in Washington, D.C., but in the spring of 1965 they briefly relocated to Orlando, Florida and worked several night clubs in the Sunshine State.

In June of 1965 Callas, St. Clair, and Conway split from Billy Joe Ash and began performing as the Bad Boys. They returned to the Washington, D.C. area and from 1965 to 1967 headlined at such night clubs as the Silver Dollar and the Rabbit's Foot. A highlight from this period was a Charlie Daniels-produced 45rpm single record the band released, "Black Olives" backed with "Love" (The Bad Boys; Paula Records, 1966).

While performing at the Rabbit's Foot in Washington, D.C. in January 1968, the Bad Boys were signed to Columbia Records and changed their name to Flavor. They released a total of three singles for the record label: "Sally Had a Party" backed with "Shop Around" (Flavor; Columbia Records, 1968); "Heart-Teaser" backed with "Yea, I'm Hip" (Flavor; Columbia Records, 1968); and "Dancing in the Street" backed with "Comin' On Home" (Flavor; Columbia Records, 1969).

Flavor based out of Adelphi, Maryland and throughout 1968 and 1969 participated in a number of shows and concerts in the Washington, D.C. area including: appearing with the Fallen Angels and Puzzle at the Walt Whitman High School Fieldhouse (Bethesda) on Friday, January 31, 1969; co-headlining a concert with Bob Brady and the Concords at Novak Field House (Prince George's Community College) on Friday, April 25, 1969; and performing in Maryland at the St. Ambrose Parish Teen Club (Cheverly) and the Wheaton Youth Center (Wheaton); and in Virginia at the St. Rita Catholic Church Teen Club (Alexandria) and the Falls Church Community Center.

Flavor lasted until 1970, briefly performing during its final days in such faraway lands as Santa Monica, California and Las Vegas, Nevada. A compilation album of the band's recordings was recently issued on compact disc: "Sally Had a Party: Singles Collection" (Flavor; Sony BMG Music Entertainment, 2006).

FRANK DILLON

Singer-guitarist Frank Dillon was born in Salt Lake City, Utah and raised in Silver Spring, Maryland. During his years at Northwood High School in the early 1960s he sang in an R&B band on the local teen dance scene called the Illusions, which performed in Maryland at venues like the Silver Spring Armory and Bladensburg Volunteer Fire Department. In the middle 1960s Dillon played guitar with New York City-based pop singer Kenny Dino, a Philadelphia-based pop group called Ali Baba's Go-Go Revue which toured from New England to Atlantic City, New Jersey to Chicago, Illinois, and a Washington, D.C. area rock and roll band called the Fablons.

In 1965 Vernon Sandusky recruited Dillon to play guitar for the Chartbusters, one of Washington, D.C.'s most popular rock and roll bands, who were still riding high with their 1964 hit song "She's the One." The Chartbusters based out of the Crazy Horse in Georgetown for several years and Dillon remained with the group into 1968. Later that year he joined Jimmy Eller and His Little People as a second lead singer and worked several months with the band at the Cave in Washington, D.C.

In 1969 and 1970 Dillon mainly worked at a night club called the Montage in Washington, D.C., fronting such rock and roll bands as the American Express, Sky, and Quorum. In 1971 he relocated to Atlanta, Georgia where he sang in a rock and roll group called the Big 8 Band. A year later he retired from the music business.

FRANK RADICE

Bassist Frank Radice grew up in Chevy Chase, Maryland and joined his first teen dance band, an R&B outfit called the Flames, while attending Western Junior High School in the middle 1960s. During his years at Bethesda-Chevy Chase High School in the late 1960s he worked with a succession of bands on the teen dance circuit including the Continentals, the Twilighters, and an outfit called the Zebes and the Sparks. During that time he also began venturing to the 14th Street Strip in Washington, D.C. where he played bass in an R&B group fronted by Hiawatha Hatter at the Hayloft. From there he became the bassist for Phil Flowers and His Flower Shop and worked such establishments as Benny's Rebel Room, the Rocket Room, Rand's Night Club and the Hayloft.

In the early 1970s Radice played in local rock and roll bands such as Parsec, Snow, and Sideshow. He left the music scene behind in 1972 and entered the television industry, eventually producing such shows as the "ABC News" and "Entertainment Tonight." He served as executive vice president of NBC from 2004 to 2008 and as president and chief marketing officer of the National Academy of Television Arts & Sciences from December 2008 to September 2009. He is currently a managing partner of VIDA F.R. Company, a promotion, marketing, media and consulting firm with offices in New York, Los Angles and London.

FRANK SHEGOGUE

Frank Shegogue rates as one of the earliest rock and roll guitarists in the Washington, D.C. area. Born and raised in the Huntington neighborhood of Bowie, Maryland, Shegogue grew up in a musical family, with his mother playing piano, his father proficient on guitar, banjo and fiddle, and his older brothers playing the guitar as well. He learned the guitar from his various family members, and at age 12 in 1947 he embarked on his first paid job when he performed C&W songs with his brother George at the Snug Harbor Inn in Lanham, Maryland. The Shegogue brothers, along with another guitarist named Jack Marnell played the bar on a regular basis for several years.

During his years at Laurel High School in the early 1950s, Shegogue played lead guitar for singer-guitarist Reds Newkirk, whose backup band was rounded out by saxophonist Bobby Sauer and drummer Jimmy Hines. The quartet performed pop standards and C&W tunes at local parties, weddings and dances at the American Legion Disney-Bell Post 66 in Bowie.

In the summer of 1953 Shegogue's quartet, billed as either the Reds Newkirk Band or the Frank Shegogue Combo, began working at Chubby's Restaurant and Bar, a night club on Central Avenue in Seat Pleasant, Maryland. At that time they began playing covers of rock and roll tunes by Billy Haley and His Comets and various R&B artists. After a year of working as the house band at Chubby's, the Frank Shegogue Combo, as they were now exclusively being called, took their unique blend of C&W and rock and roll music across the eastern border into Anne Arundel County, Maryland to a night club in Crofton called the Pigeon House Inn. While working there, the Frank Shegogue combo picked up two more local musicians in pianist Bobby Charlton and saxophonist Lewis Maddox.

Shegogue left the area and joined the United States Navy in the spring of 1955. He returned to the area later in the decade and played with two different rock and roll bands – the Saxtons in 1958 and Al Pometto and the Jazz Bombers in 1959.

Shegogue spent the early 1960s fronting his own band, the Classics, which was rounded out by bassist Gene Newport, keyboardist Sam Paladino, saxophonist Tommy Norwood and drummer Stan Weinberg. The group played rock and roll covers at a night club called the Villa in College Park for several years. At one point they underwent a transformation and a name change, becoming Sam Paladino and the Classics, with the new lineup consisting of Shegogue, Paladino, saxophonist Del Puschert and drummer Jerry Zadera.

In the middle 1960s the Classics folded and Shegogue and Paladino joined forces with saxophonist Ralph McDuffie and drummer Ron McGehee to comprise a new version of the Naturals, a popular Washington, D.C. area rock and roll combo. Shegogue spent several years with the Naturals, and, later in the 1980s, he played lead guitar for a C&W band called Dallas County. In the ensuing years he would periodically perform at jam sessions and special musical events around the nation's capital.

In recent years Shegogue emerged with a new musical project called the Frank Shegogue Band, a rock and roll trio rounded out by keyboardist Sam Paladino and drummer Chip Clemmer that performed at the Old Bowie Town Grille. Another band he had recently started, the Frank Shegogue Trio, was rounded out by bassist John Previti and drummer Barry Hart, and most often appeared at the Westlawn Inn in North Beach, Maryland. He is considered to be one of the most influential and revered rock and roll guitarists to ever grace the Washington, D.C. area music scene. Frank Shegogue died on Tuesday, May 29, 2018 at the age of 82.

FRED JAESCHKE

Bassist Fred Jaeschke grew up in Colmar Manor, Maryland and started out playing in local C&W bands while attending Bladensburg High School in the middle 1950s. In early 1959 he was recruited by Luman Perry to play bass in the Off Keys, the popular Bladensburg-based rock and roll band that had been a longtime favorite at the Bladensburg Volunteer Fire Department and was in the process of becoming a regular attraction at the Dixie Pig on the Bladensburg Road Strip in Cottage City, Maryland.

After the Off Keys disbanded, Jaeschke began frequenting Coffee 'n' Confusion in Washington, D.C. and regularly sat in with the various folk musicians who would perform there. In the early 1960s he played bass for Paul King and the Blue Knights, a rock and roll band that initially included his former bandmate from the Off Keys, Sam Paladino. Jaeschke retired from the local music scene in 1962.

FRITZ CARNEY

Bassist Fritz Carney hails from Southeast Washington, D.C., where, while attending Ballou High School in the middle 1960s, he first played in the backup band for R&B singer Gene Austin on the local military base officers' club circuit. He next worked with another R&B singer, Little Marie Franklin, at the Journey's Inn on Pennsylvania Avenue NW in Washington, D.C. He then spent the late 1960s playing bass for several R&B performers in Washington, D.C. including singer Leroy Taylor at the Journey's Inn and singer-guitarist Bobby Parker at the Spa Restaurant. During that time he also worked pickup jobs in the city at Bob's Inn, the Byrdland and the Diamond Jim Club.

Carney moved to Los Angeles, California in December 1967 and in 1969 he entered the R&B music scene there, playing in a succession of bands through the early 1970s including the Mean Machine, Sweet Meat, the Thunder Brothers and Shotgun. In August 1976 he became the bassist for the Sweet Inspirations, a female R&B vocal group that recorded and toured with Elvis Presley and served as his onstage warm-up act and concert background singers. He remained with the band through December 1976.

Through the years Carney has also played bass with gospel singer J.D. Sumner and more recently has performed with the R&B act A Touch of Silk. He currently resides in Visalia, California and fronts his own R&B band, Fritz and the Cats.

GANTT KUSHNER

Guitarist Gantt Kushner was born in Baltimore, Maryland and after a series of moves as a youth was raised in Silver Spring, Maryland. He took up guitar at age 12 in the middle 1960s and began making music with friends and playing songs by the Beatles and the Ventures. He then began emulating the guitar playing of Eric Clapton, Jeff Beck and Jimmy Page, among others. During his years at Albert Einstein High School in the late 1960s he played in such local rock and roll bands as Random Choice, the Merry Five of Windsor, and Red Dog.

From 1970 to 1972, while still residing in the Washington, D.C. area, Kushner played guitar in a series of bands including the rock and roll group We the People, a C&W act called the Joe Corey Band, and R&B outfits such as the Mighty Intrepids Band and Show, Steve Charles and the Soul Syndrome, and singer Phil Flowers.

In 1972 Kushner moved to Venice, California and played guitar in the backup band for pop-R&B singer Paul Indelicato. They went on the road and landed in Allen Park, Michigan where they worked for six months at the Park Lounge. He next formed a jazz trio in Michigan called Bazooka with two other Washington, D.C. area natives, singer-keyboardist Malcolm Lukens and singer-drummer Tommy Panella, and continued on throughout the remainder of the year at the Park Lounge.

Kushner returned to the Washington, D.C. area in 1973 and backed jazz singer Lee Nelson at a night club called the Devil's Fork. Then, as Lee Nelson and Bazooka, the group took an engagement at Club 175 in Jessup, Maryland. Late in the year the act became Ron MacDonald and Bazooka and spent six months as the house band at the Key Bridge Marriott in Arlington, Virginia playing jazz tunes. The next couple of years saw Kushner play guitar for a husband-and-wife pop music act called Bill and Mo Moore in Denver, Colorado and then C&W singer-guitarist Bob Sanders in Nashville, Tennessee.

Back in the nation's capital, Kushner spent the remainder of the 1970s working with a number of different musical outfits including: a pop-rock band called the Show Biz Kids; a C&W group called the Virginia Rangers; the country rock group the North Star Band; and the popular C&W house band at Hunter's Lodge known as the Stringdusters. Late in the decade he ventured to Las Vegas, Nevada and played guitar for C&W singer Dick Trees and Jerry Lee Lewis performer Joe Hardin Brown.

Kushner eventually returned to the area and spent the 1980s playing in a variety of local bands including: a country rock group called That Damned Band; country rock singer Danny Denver; the R&B-rock band Second Coming; and a jazz-pop outfit called the Gene Donati Orchestra. From 1989 to 1993 he worked extensively with R&B singer Mary Ann Redmond at such venues as the Key Bridge Marriott and E.M. Magoo's in Wheaton, Maryland.

Among the many bands and musicians Kushner has played guitar for through the years are: the C&W band the Baxter Brothers; folk singer-guitarist Dusty Rose; jazz groups the Dixie Power Trio and the John Guernsey Band; R&B performers Tommy Lepson and the Lazy Boys, and Jr. Cline and the Recliners; rock and roll singer-guitarist Mike Cotter; and numerous tribute shows for BandHouse Gigs and Newmyer Flyer. Most recently he has been playing throughout the Washington, D.C. area with several country rock bands including Tony Denikos and the Working Poor, the Bill Baker Band and Lunch With Bob.

In addition to his band work, Kushner has owned and operated Gizmo Recording Company, currently located in Silver Spring, Maryland, since 1988.

GARY ST. CLAIR

Hailing from Adelphi, Maryland, Gary St. Clair is a talented singer-keyboardist who attended Buck Lodge Junior High School and then High Point High School for a year before shipping off to Florida where he graduated from Miami Military Academy in 1964. He joined his first band, the Duo-Sonics, while in the ninth grade at Buck Lodge. He started out as a drummer and gave his first public performances with the band at teen dances at Beltsville Junior High School and the Beltsville Teen Club.

When St. Clair returned to the Washington, D.C. area in 1964, he got together with drummer Danny Conway and the pair joined an R&B band called Duke and the Glissandos that worked Washington, D.C. night clubs such as the Carnival Café (4123 Georgia Avenue NW), Angie's Cozy Corner Restaurant (810 Bladensburg Road NE) and the Diamond Jim Club (2300 14th Street NW). In 1965 St. Clair and Conway were recruited by singer-saxophonist Billy Joe Ash and guitarist Demetri Callas to round out a quartet called Billy Joe and the Confidentials that obtained a house band job at Benny's Rebel Room in the heart of the 14th Street NW Strip.

In June 1965 St. Clair, Conway and Callas split from Ash and became the Bad Boys. While performing at the Rabbit's Foot in January 1968, the band signed with Columbia Records, changed its name to Flavor, and went on to become one of the Washington, D.C area's top rock and roll bands. Upon Flavor's demise, St. Clair went on to release a solo album, "Gary St. Clair" (Gary St. Clair; Paramount Records, 1972).

St. Clair remained active in the recording industry for years and in 1991 he became a producer and then head of A&R for Blitzz Records, a subsidiary of Atlantic Records. During the 1990s St. Clair co-produced albums for two of the world's best-selling vocal pop groups, All-4-One, and Nuflavor.

GEORGE DIVELY

The son of an Air Force officer, George Dively moved around the world as a youth, eventually settling in Springfield, Virginia where he attended Robert E. Lee High School in the middle 1970s. He took up guitar during his sophomore year, began practicing to players like Jimi Hendrix, Jeff Beck, Jimmy Page and Eric Clapton, and began playing informally at parties with friends and at a Saturday night coffee house at Grace Presbyterian Church in Springfield.

In 1975 a drummer from Woodbridge, Virginia named Michael Franklin, who played with various bands on the 1950s revival circuit up and down the East Coast, took Dively to New York City for an audition with rock and roll singer Gary U.S. Bonds. Dively passed the audition and became part of Bonds' backing band, working shows and concerts throughout the Eastern United States from the fall of 1975 to the spring of 1976.

After a stint in North Carolina with a Top 40 band called Contraband, Dively returned to the Washington, D.C. area in 1977 and formed a rock and roll band called the Penetrators, whose Northern Virginia-based lineup consisted of Dively handling lead vocals and lead guitar, rhythm guitarist Scott Logan, bassist Mike Crosson and drummer Larry Norton (who was later replaced by Tommy Carr).

The Penetrators became one of the area's top punk rock bands and performed shows at such Washington, D.C. night clubs as the Atlantis, D.C. Space, One Flight Up, and Louie's Rock City in Bailey's Crossroads, Virginia. A highlight for the band was opening for the Cramps at the LBJ Restaurant on Capitol Hill in Washington, D.C. on Friday, April 20, 1979. Dively is still active on the local rock and roll scene and has performed in the bands the New Standard and FreakTrain.

GIL GOLDSTEIN

Keyboardist Gil Goldstein was born in Washington, D.C., raised in Baltimore, and spent his teen years living in Silver Spring, Maryland. He started on the accordion at age five and switched to piano at age 10. During his years at Takoma Junior High School in the middle 1960s he first played the local teen dance scene in such rock and roll bands as the Fugitives and the Candy Stripers. While attending Montgomery Blair High School in the late 1960s he played keyboards in a local rock and roll band called Rock Bottom, which included singer-conga player Bobby LaKind, who several years later went on to become a member of the Doobie Brothers.

Goldstein spent the early 1970s studying music at the University of Maryland while working jazz gigs around the nation's capital. He then earned a Master of Music from the University of Miami in Florida in 1974. In 1975 he began touring and recording with jazz guitarist Pat Martino and appeared on three consecutive albums with him: "Exit" (Pat Martino; Muse Records, 1976); "We'll Be Together Again" (Pat Martino; Muse Records, 1976); and "Starbright" (Pat Martino; Warner Bros. Records, 1976).

Through the years Goldstein has recorded and released several jazz solo albums and has also performed and/or recorded with some of the top jazz musicians in the world including: guitarists Pat Metheny, Jim Hall, Romero Lubambo and Toninho Horta; bassists Jaco Pastorius, Stanley Clarke, Carles Benavent, and Richard Bona; pianists Gil Evans, Michel Petrucciani and Eliane Elias; saxophonists Lee Konitz, Eric Kloss, Wayne Shorter, Bob Berg, Bob Mintzer, James Moody, Joe Lovano and Pietro Tonolo; saxophonist-flutists Dave Liebman and Jorge Pardo; trumpeters Miles Davis, Quincy Jones and Tiger Okoshi; accordionist Richard Galliano; percussionist Ray Barretto; drummers Billy Cobham, Lenny White and Omar Hakim; singers Rachelle Ferrell and Bobby McFerrin; and bands such as Elements, and the Michael Brecker Quindectet. Two other major names in popular music he has performed and recorded with are singers Sting and Boz Scaggs.

Goldstein has also produced more than a dozen albums for various performing artists and has composed, arranged and produced music for numerous major motion pictures. He has won three Grammy Awards, two of which came from his production and arrangement credits for the jazz album "Wild Angles" (Michael Brecker Quindectet; Verve Records, 2003). Since 2003 he has been an adjunct music professor at the Steinhart School at New York University.

GOD MOTHER COUNTRY

God Mother Country was a rock and roll band that was formed by Brian Wagner in Lanham, Maryland in September 1968. The group's first lineup consisted of lead singer-guitarist Dave Williams, guitarist Jeff Greene, bassist Brian Wagner, keyboardist Sherman Griffith and drummer Birdie Williams (all of the original band members attended DuVal High School). During its first six months the group performed at private parties and dances at the Seabrook Teen Club (Gaywood Elementary School), the Carleton East Teen Club (Lanham) and covered such bands as Cream, the Doors, Steppenwolf, the Troggs and the Youngbloods.

In 1969 God Mother Country went through several changes. Early in the year the band became a quartet, with Greene and Griffith departing and keyboardist Jurgen Underwood being added. After a short while Underwood left and the band carried on for several months as a trio. In September of that year Wagner and the Williams brothers added a new lead singer named Guy Convoy. During this period the band added songs by the Beatles, Blue Cheer, Bob Dylan, the Grass Roots, the Guess Who, the Jimi Hendrix Experience and Led Zeppelin to its repertoire and performed at a wide array of venues including Robert Goddard Junior High School (Lanham), the Cheverly Tuxedo Fire Department (Hyattsville), Nuzback's Bar (Laurel), Ritchie Coliseum (the University of Maryland) and University of Maryland fraternity parties.

In June 1970 God Mother Country became a quintet consisting of Wagner, the Williams brothers, lead singer Bob Petty and keyboardist Larry Bird. In March 1971 drummer Birdie Williams departed and was replaced by Hank Burnett. Bob Petty then left, reducing the band to a quartet and in September of that year more changes ensued with Bird leaving and Wagner, Dave Williams and Burnett being joined by keyboardist Dana Cole.

During this period and into the summer of 1972 God Mother Country performed some original compositions on their live dates, in addition to adding covers of songs by the Allman Brothers Band, Badfinger, Black Sabbath, the Byrds, Deep Purple, the Kinks and Neil Young to its sets. At this juncture, in addition to its regular performances on the University of Maryland campus at fraternity parties and shows at Ritchie Coliseum, the band often appeared at Kava (Greenbelt Youth Center), VFW Free State Post 8950 (Lanham), the Charles Carroll Teen Club (Charles Carroll Junior High School in New Carrollton), Largo High School (Largo), the Vienna Community Center (Virginia), and events on various college campuses throughout Maryland and Virginia. They also worked in Washington, D.C. at such night clubs as My Mother's Place, the Crazy Horse and the Far Inn.

In August 1972 God Mother Country once again reorganized with a lineup of lead singer-flutist Charlie Hastings, guitarist Dave Williams, guitarist Brian Sperty, bassist Brian Wagner and drummer Hank Burnett. In January 1973 original member Dave Williams departed and was replaced by guitarist Mitchell Sperty. In May of that year the Sperty brothers moved on and the band reacquired Dave Williams and added guitarist Ray Tilkens. New material to their sets included songs by Fleetwood Mac and the J. Geils Band. The band remained a popular attraction at Kava (Greenbelt Youth Center) and the Crazy Horse (Washington, D.C.) and among their new haunts included two night clubs in St. Mary's County, Maryland – Tall Timbers and Capt'n Tom's Oar House.

God Mother Country made a final stand from November of 1973 to the spring of 1974 with a membership consisting of lead singer-flutist Charlie Hastings, guitarists Dave

Williams and Doug Hallobaugh, bassist Brian Wagner and drummer Hank Burnett. The band expanded its range during these final days, playing in Maryland at such venues as the Rabbit's Foot (Frederick), the Pier Ballroom (Ocean City) and Sarano's Lounge (West Friendship); and down the road in Tennessee at the Flamingo (Bristol).

GREEN EGGS

The hard-rocking band known as Green Eggs came out of Bladensburg, Maryland in May 1970 and for four years blitzed the local teen dances and night clubs with heavy heapings of the hard rock and roll that was gaining momentum in the wake of Woodstock. Originally known as Green Eggs and Ham, a moniker copped from the popular Dr. Seuss book by original members Gary Fitzhugh and Glenn Michaud during an inspirational, laugh-filled smoke session, the band spent much of their existence in the power trio mode and rated as one of the heaviest rock and roll outfits Prince George's County, Maryland had ever produced. Despite its talent and popularity, Green Eggs opted for covers over original material in its live performances, were consequently overlooked by the major out-of-town record companies, and, in time, ran its course with the members seeking other musical adventures. However, the band's thunderous sound continues to echo in the memories of those who witnessed the group in its heyday.

Green Eggs and Ham originally consisted of lead singer-bassist Glen Michaud (a native of Landover Hills, Maryland and a 1970 graduate of Archbishop Carroll High School), drummer Gary Fitzhugh (a native of Bladensburg, Maryland and a 1969 graduate of Bladensburg High School), and lead guitarist Stuart Paine (a native of Springfield, Virginia and a 1971 graduate of Robert E. Lee High School). The band members came together through a series of jam sessions with mutual friends and rehearsed in the basement of Fitzhugh's home at 5314 Crittenden Street in Bladensburg.

In 1971 the band shortened its name to Green Eggs and in March 1972 added a fourth piece in guitarist Wayne Tomlinson (a native of Landover Hills, Maryland and a 1972 graduate of Bladensburg High School) who had previously played in the New Colonial Blues Band and Bosco Pie. Paine departed in June 1972 and the trio of Michaud, Tomlinson and Fitzhugh carried on for the duration.

The members of Green Eggs loved the bands Vanilla Fudge and Cactus and regularly performed the works of those two hard-rocking bands. In addition, they covered such groups as the Beatles, the Rolling Stones, Johnny Winter, Cream, they Yardbirds, the Jeff Beck Group, Steppenwolf, Jethro Tull, Grand Funk Railroad, Ten Years After, Led Zeppelin, the Jimi Hendrix Experience, Grand Funk Railroad, Mountain, Black Sabbath, Free, the James Gang, the Who, the Moody Blues and Deep Purple. They also worked out a version of the orchestral musical piece "In the Hall of the Mountain King" by Edvard Grieg, an instrumental selection from Henrik Ibsen's 1876 play "Peer Gynt" (Paine learned the song from a 78rpm recording of "Peer Gynt, Suite No. 1, Op.46"). No other hard rock bands in the region had ever presented such an adventurous example of music and when played live by the band all three members were allowed to showcase their individual musical prowess.

During its tenure, Green Eggs was a hot commodity on the local teen dance circuit and performed at a wide range of venues throughout the suburbs of Virginia and Maryland. The band's Virginia gigs included dances and shows at Arlington United Methodist Church (Arlington), John Calvin Presbyterian Church (Annandale), Wakefield High School (Arlington), Washington-Lee High School (Arlington), T.C. Williams High School (Alexandria), Thomas A. Edison High School (Alexandria), Mount Vernon High School (Alexandria), Robert E. Lee High School (Springfield), Wilbert Tucker Woodson High

School (Fairfax), Northern Virginia Community College Annandale Campus and the Falls Church Community Center.

In Maryland Green Eggs appeared at the Charles Carroll Teen Club (Charles Carroll Junior High School in New Carrollton), Kava (the Greenbelt Youth Center), the Glenridge Teen Club (Glenridge Junior High School in Landover Hills), the Parklawn Teen Club (Parklawn Elementary School in Hyattsville), the St. James Catholic Church Teen Club (Mt. Rainier), the Church of St. Matthias the Apostle Teen Club (Lanham), the St. Mary's Catholic Church Teen Club (Landover Hills), the Sacred Heart Church Teen Club (Bowie), DuVal High School (Lanham), the Landover Hills Volunteer Fire Department (Landover Hills), Tucker Road Community Center (Fort Washington) and the cafeteria at Prince George's Community College Cafeteria (Largo). In addition, the band worked a number of local pool parties in the summer months at places like the Springfield Swim Club, the New Carrollton Pool, the Landover Recreation Center Swimming Pool and the Cheverly Swim Club.

Green Eggs also performed in a number of local night clubs including Bambino's in Riverdale, Maryland and two venues in Washington, D.C., the Act IV Supper Club and the Bayou. The band carried on into 1973, but before the year was out its individual members parted company and pursued other musical opportunities.

GREG HARDIN

Singer-bassist Greg Hardin was born in Knoxville, Tennessee and it was there that he took up the guitar at age nine. His father served in the United States Navy and after several moves Hardin arrived in Rockville, Maryland at the age of 15 in 1973. At that point his musical interests included the Beatles, the Who, Bruce Springsteen and Tom Waites. He switched to bass and learned to play off of records and from friends.

During his time at Colonel Zadok A. Magruder High School in the early and middle 1970s Hardin first played in a rock and roll band called Sleepy Creek that performed at local dances, parties and American Legions and covered the likes of the Rolling Stones, Steely Dan and Eric Clapton. He then spent the late 1970s playing in the pop-R&B bands Shadowbox and Rhythm Method, groups that included guitarist Chuck Underwood and pianist Bill Starks. Area bands he played bass for in the early 1980s included the R&B group Tough Luck (featuring singer-harmonicist Lips Lackowitz), and the pop group Melissa Berman and the Thin Man Band.

In 1982 Hardin joined the popular local R&B-rock band Jr. Cline and the Recliners and remained their bassist for more than 20 years. When he first joined the group the lineup consisted of singer-guitarist Daryl "Jr." Cline, guitarist Mike Dennis, Hardin on bass, pianist Bill Starks, saxophonist Bruce Swaim, trumpeter Scott Cunningham (who was soon replaced by Vince McCool) and drummer John Lee. Just prior to leaving the band the membership consisted of Cline, Hardin, guitarist Andy Shiver, keyboardist Arif Durrani, saxophonist Wayne Sulc, trumpeter Chris Hutton and drummer Byron McWilliams.

In 2001 Hardin began playing bass with the country rock band Ruthie and the Wranglers and became an official member of the group a year later. He ultimately left the band in 2017.

Through the years other musical artists Hardin has played bass for include such R&B performers as guitarist Eddie Hinton and saxophonist Ron Holloway; rock and roll singer Root Boy Slim; and rock and roll singer-guitarists Bo Diddley and Nils Lofgren. Hardin has recorded with numerous bands and musicians and has one solo rock and roll album to his credit, "Meet Mr. Knuckles" (Greg Hardin; Baggy Pants Music, 2009). He is currently playing bass for a country rock group called the 19th Street Band.

GREG PUGLIESE

Singer-keyboardist Greg Pugliese was raised in Adelphi, Maryland and during his years at Nicholas Orem Junior High School in the middle 1960s he played the local teen dance scene in such rock and roll bands as the Sunsets and the Revolution.

During his time at Northwestern High School in the late 1960s Pugliese played in a group called the Blues Bag, a band that performed at the Adelphi Friends Meeting House (the Religious Society of Quakers) on Metzerott Road. A late addition to the group was keyboardist Seth Justman, who went on to become a member of the J. Geils Band. The Blues Bag eventually changed its name to the Open Road Band. During this time Pugliese was also a member of a folk music group called the Jefferson Street Jug Band.

From June 1970 to May 1973 Pugliese sang and played keyboards in Sky Cobb, one of the Washington, D.C. area's top rock and roll bands. The group's lineup consisted of Pugliese, guitarist Bruce MacKinnon, bassist Craig Warner, guitarist-keyboardist Richard Sales, saxophonist Jamie MacKinnon and drummer Mark Cuff. The band was based in Hyattsville, Maryland, concentrated on original material, and opened concerts throughout the region, in addition to performing at night clubs like Emergency in Georgetown and headlining their own shows at facilities like the Falls Church Community Center in Virginia.

In 1978 Pugliese played in a College Park-based rock and roll band called the Trashmen. In 1980 he joined the Cranes, an original music rock and roll trio that was rounded out by guitarist Richard Sales and drummer Art Bessette. He then played in a Silver Spring-based rock and roll band called Freeze from 1981 to 1983.

In 1983 Pugliese joined a Hyattsville-based new wave rock and roll band called Model Prisoners, which concentrated on playing original music. The group's lineup consisted of Pugliese singing lead and playing keyboards, singer-guitarist Bruce MacKinnon, bassist Jay Dixon, saxophonist Jamie MacKinnon and drummer Art Bessette (subsequent bassists were Andy Margileth and Tony Flagg).

A high point for Model Prisoners was opening for Duran Duran at the Capital Centre in Landover, Maryland on Monday, April 2, 1984. They also worked several local night clubs including the Wax Museum, Club Saba, and the Bayou (where they opened shows for INXS, the Alarm, NRBQ and the Hooters, among others). The band has a six-song EP to its credit: "Model Prisoners" (Model Prisoners; Aratron Records, 1983).

In 1987 Model Prisoners morphed into a band called MPs, which was mainly Pugliese and Bruce MacKinnon working together with help from various musician friends. Under this banner they released one album: "Beater Release" (MPs; Aratron Records, 1987).

Pugliese spent much of the 1990s in a College Park-based rock and roll band which started out under the name Dog Bowl and finished up as the Splinters. This outfit covered groups like Rockpile, Elvis Costello and Bob Dylan, and mainly played private parties. The lineup for this band was Pugliese handling vocals and keyboards, guitarist Bruce MacKinnon, guitarist Phil Lazarus, bassist Craig Warner and a number of different drummers through time.

Pugliese has remained musically active in recent years. One thinly-disguised solo project saw him record and release the pop-rock CD album "Rubberballs N Liquor" (Rubberballs N Liquor; Self-Released, 2005). Since 2005 he has been singing and playing in a folk music guitar trio, the Bills, with Craig Warner and Carl Reuben Sosebee. His latest work is a C&W album he recorded with the help of 10 of his musician friends: "Dead Mother's Club" (The Royal Dominos; StrangeKey Records, 2015).

GREGG KARUKAS

Composer-keyboardist Gregg Karukas is a world-renowned figure in the field of smooth jazz. He grew up in Bowie, Maryland and one of his first musical experiences was playing keyboards in the rock and roll band Harwood Tapestry on the Prince George's County teen dance circuit in the early 1970s. He graduated from Bowie High School in 1974 and during his time there he switched musical styles and was a keyboardist in the school's jazz band, the Starliners.

After high school Karukas was a member of the Washington, D.C.-based jazz rock group East Coast Offering (featuring saxophonist Tim Eyermann), and remained with the band for five years. In 1979 he founded a local jazz group called Natural Bridge, which regularly opened shows at the Cellar Door in Georgetown.

In 1982 Karukas moved to Los Angeles, California and has since become one of the world's best-known performing artists in the fields of smooth jazz and world music. He has released over a dozen solo jazz albums including several on Nightowl Records and has performed with such jazz bands and musicians as the Rippingtons; singers Patti Austin, Shelby Flint and Melissa Manchester; guitarists Grant Geissman, Larry Carlton and Peter White; harmonicist Toots Thielemans; pianists Omar Akram and Sergio Mendes; singer-keyboardist Brenda Russell; saxophonists Richard Elliot, Ronnie Laws and Boney James; and trumpeter Rick Braun.

GREGG WRIGHT

Gregg Wright has performed with some of the biggest blues and rock and roll artists in the music industry and currently fronts his own blues rock band in Los Angeles, California. He grew up in Suitland, Maryland, where, during his years at Suitland High School in the early 1970s, he sang and played lead guitar in Kriss Kross, a Jimi Hendrix-influenced psychedelic trio rounded out by bassist Jimmy Barnett and drummer Jerry Najera. During its time, Kriss Kross performed in front of enthusiastic crowds at Marlow Heights Community Center (Marlow Heights), Central High School (Seat Pleasant) and Prince George's Community College (Largo).

Later in the 1970s Wright played guitar for such rock and roll bands as Red Hot Chicken and Shadowfax. In 1982 he relocated to Los Angeles, California, met Michael Jackson, and began recording and touring with the Jacksons, appearing on their album "Victory" (The Jacksons; Epic Records, 1984). He subsequently joined the rock and roll band Berlin and appeared on the album "Count Three & Pray" (Berlin; Mercury Records, 1986). Wright has since performed with R&B artists such as the Gap Band and singer Tracie Spencer, and a number of rock and roll acts including Mick Fleetwood's Zoo and singer-guitarist Spencer Davis.

Wright has released several solo blues rock albums through the years including: "Khamsin" (Gregg Wright; The Record Company of the South, 1978); "World Rock" (Gregg Wright; Quality Records, 1992); "Round One" (Gregg Wright's Left Hook; Left Hook Records, 1995); "Lightning Strike!!!" (Gregg Wright; Left Hook Records, 2003); and "King of the Rockin' Blues!" (Gregg Wright; Left Hook Records, 2009).

GRIN

In 1968 a band called Paul Dowell and the Dolphin came into existence when three former Hangmen members – bassist Paul Dowell, rhythm guitarist George Daly and drummer Bob Berberich – joined forces with singer-guitarist Nils Lofgren, formerly of the Crystal Mesh. This hard-rocking quartet stayed together long enough to attract the attention of some New York City record executives and release two singles: "Let's Get Together" backed with "Grubb's Blues" (Dolphin; Phoenix Records, 1968); and "It's Better to Know You" backed with "The Last Time I Saw You" (Paul Dowell and the Dolphin; Sire Records, 1969).

In April 1969, after Paul Dowell had moved to the West Coast to become the soundman for Jefferson Airplane, Lofgren, Daly and Berberich reformed as a trio called Grin. Within a year, George Daly was replaced by bassist Bob Gordon, formerly of the Renegades, and the band went on to become one of the biggest rock and roll attractions the Washington, D.C. area had to offer.

Originally based in Silver Spring, Maryland, Grin was propelled by the acrobatic singer-guitarist Nils Lofgren, who met Neil Young at the Cellar Door in May 1969 and maintained a lasting friendship with him. The band signed a record deal with the Spindizzy label, a subsidiary of Epic Records, and for more than five years primarily worked both the teen dance and concert scenes in and around the nation's capital. In 1972 Tom Lofgren joined the band as a keyboardist and rhythm guitarist and remained on board until the end.

Grin performed in Washington, D.C. at Emergency, Fort Reno Park, Gaston Hall (Georgetown University) and the John F. Kennedy Center for the Performing Arts Concert Hall; in Maryland at Bishop McNamara High School (Forestville), Friendly High School (Fort Washington), the Bethesda Youth Center (Bethesda) and the Wheaton Youth Center (Wheaton); and in Virginia at the Vienna Community Center and the Falls Church Community Center.

In addition, Grin also opened many concerts for a variety of national acts including: Faces (featuring lead singer Rod Stewart) at Northern Virginia Community College Alexandria Campus on Monday, March 30, 1970 and the next night, Tuesday, March 31, 1970, at the Wheaton Youth Center; Alice Cooper and Edgar Winter's White Trash at the Alexandria Arena on Sunday, June 13, 1971; T. Rex at the Alexandria Arena on Sunday, February 20, 1972; and the Steve Miller Band at Shady Grove Music Fair in Gaithersburg on Saturday, November 24, 1973.

Grin disbanded after a farewell concert at the John F. Kennedy Center for the Performing Arts Concert Hall in Washington, D.C. on Saturday, June 8, 1974. The band has six albums to its credit: "Grin" (Grin; Spindizzy Records, 1971); "1+1" (Nils Lofgren Grin; Spindizzy Records, 1972); "All Out" (Grin; Spindizzy Records, 1973); "Gone Crazy" (Grin; A&M Records, 1973); "The Best of Grin Featuring Nils Lofgren" (Grin; Epic Records, 1976); and "The Very Best of Grin featuring Nils Lofgren" (Grin featuring Nils Lofgren; Sony Music Entertainment, 1999).

GRITS

Grits was a progressive band that existed from 1970 to 1978 and mixed together elements of psychedelic rock, Frank Zappa-styled jazz and classical music. Originally based in Arlington, Virginia, its lineup consisted of four classically-trained musicians: singer-bassist-violinist Amy Taylor, singer-guitarist-violinist Tom Wright, singer-keyboardist Rick Barse and singer-drummer Bob Sims. Locally, they were favorites in Washington, D.C. at such establishments as the Corsican, Fat Howard's, and the Childe Harold; and in Maryland at the Italian Gardens (College Park), Mr. Henry's College Park (College Park) and the Psyche Delly (Bethesda).

Although Grits did not release any albums during its existence, three posthumous CDs of the group's work have been issued: "As the World Grits (Grits; Cuneiform Records, 1993); "Rare Birds" (Grits; Cuneiform Records, 1997; recorded live on August 21, 1976 in the backyard of the Muffins in Gaithersburg, Maryland); and "Rock and Roll Madness" (Grits; Self-Released, 2008).

GUI BOKOLES

Rock and roll singer Gui Bokoles was born in Washington, D.C. and raised in the city's Chevy Chase neighborhood. He became interested in music as a youth after his mother took him to a Harry Belafonte concert at Carter Baron Amphitheatre in the early 1950s. While attending Alice Deal Junior High School in the city he gained vocal experience by singing in the school's barbershop quartet. During his years at Woodrow Wilson High School in the middle 1960s he sang informally with different musicians at rock and roll jam sessions.

In 1966 at the age of 20 Bokoles became a founding member of a Montgomery County, Maryland-based rock and roll band called the Curfews, whose initial lineup included, along with Bokoles on lead vocals, guitarist Rick Rowe, bassist Stephen Geyer, keyboardist Stephen Spencer and drummer Dave Eaton. The Curfews, which later shortened its name to Curfew, developed into one of the area's top young bands, working teen dances at local schools and community centers and opening local concerts, in addition to performing at night clubs such as the Rocket Room in Washington, D.C. With Bokoles as the frontman, Curfew released the psychedelic album "Let There Be Dark; And There Was Dark" (Curfew; United Artists Records, 1970).

During his time with Curfew, Bokoles became recognized for his vocal ability and was recruited by Ray Vernon to provide background vocals on a number of recordings made by Link Wray and His Ray Men at Wray's Shack 3 Tracks, the famed recording studio in Accokeek, Maryland.

After leaving Curfew, Bokoles sang for a succession of bands in Washington, D.C. during the late 1960s and early 1970s including Hillow Hammet, Puzzle and Crank, all of which frequently appeared at the Keg in the city's Glover Park neighborhood. He then spent several years in the early and middle 1970s in the Georgetown-based rock and roll band Gravity, which endured numerous personnel changes and performed for long stretches of time in the city at the Crazy Horse and the Keg. For much of Bokoles' time with Gravity, the lineup consisted of two lead singers, Bokoles and Kathe Russell, lead guitarist Tony Grasso, bassist Bob Gordon and drummer William "Duke" Ayres.

In the 1980s Bokoles held lead vocalist duties in a succession of area pop, R&B and rock bands including the Kamikaze Pilots, Network, Spats, the Joe Stanley Band and McCoy. In the 1990s Bokoles sang on a sporadic basis with a number of different bands throughout the region.

Bokoles moved to Texas in 1999 and then in 2004 he relocated to Nashville, Tennessee where he spent the next seven years playing congas and providing backup vocals for the country rock singer-guitarist Paul Scott.

GUY TAYLOR

Guitarist Guy Taylor grew up in a military family and spent most of his early years living in Japan. His mother ran a teen club on a base in Okinawa and as a pre-teen in the late 1950s Taylor started playing guitar after his watching his older brother play. He then honed his craft by listening to Eddie Cochran and Duane Eddy records. In 1961 Taylor's family moved back to the United States and settled in Suitland, Maryland.

While attending Suitland High School in the middle 1960s Taylor began playing guitar in a local teen dance rock and roll band called the Leftovers, and later performed with another local rock band called the Del-Fis. In 1964 he became a founding member and singer-guitarist of a five-piece Suitland-based rock and roll band called the Phantoms, whose lineup was rounded out with singer-guitarist Rick Neri, bassist Mike Lyons, saxophonist Denny Selensky and drummer John Kincaid. For four years the Phantoms played local dances, parties and shows at facilities in Maryland like Suitland High School (Suitland), the Marlow Heights Community Center (Marlow Heights) and the District Heights Municipal Building (District Heights). They also worked in Washington, D.C. at events staged at St.

Elizabeths Hospital and engagements at a night club in the Southeast quadrant of the city called the Beehive.

The Phantoms were recruited into the studio by local music promoter Lillian Claiborne. Under her direction the band recorded and released a 45rpm single record, the A-side of which was "You Made My Heart Cry" (credited to Rick Neri and the Phantoms; Loop Records, 1964) and the B-side of which was "Lesa" (credited to Guy Taylor and the Phantoms; Loop Records, 1964). In addition to performing with the Phantoms, Taylor often sat in with Link Wray and His Ray Men at the 1023 Restaurant in Southeast Washington, D.C. in 1966. The Phantoms ultimately called it quits in 1968.

In late 1968 one of the area's most popular rock and roll bands, the Telstars, disbanded and leader Ronnie Wilson decided to reorganize the group. For his new venture he enlisted the services of two former members of the Reachers – singer-guitarist Jim MacFarlane and bassist Dickie Thompson – and rounded out the quartet with Taylor on guitar. The new band was dubbed Ronnie Wilson and the New Telstars and assumed house band duties at Nu-Mac's in the Georgetown neighborhood of Washington, D.C. This group, which soon switched its name to the New Telstars, remained active through 1969.

In 1970 Taylor worked as a solo singer-guitarist playing the latest pop and rock and roll tunes under the stage name "Brennan" at the Lord Telford Pub (2605 Connecticut Avenue NW) in Washington, D.C. He also performed as a solo act under his real name at such Washington, D.C. hotels as the Sheraton Park Hotel and the Washington Hilton Hotel, and in Baltimore at the Playboy Club.

Taylor then spent the early 1970s in New York City performing with an all-original soft rock band called the Road Apples, playing guitar with blues singer-guitarist-harmonicist John Hammond, and playing bass for a R&B outfit called Shinbone Alley.

During this time he was also recruited into the studio by producer Teo Macero of Columbia Records to sing on a number of recordings. The results of these sessions included his vocals on two folk songs in the movie "Tom Sawyer" (United Artists, 1973), "If'n I Was God" and "A Man's Gotta Be (What He's Born to Be)." Both of these songs appear on the album "Theme From 'Tom Sawyer' and 24 Other Riverboat Favorites" (Mississippi Banjo Band; Paramount Records, 1973).

For much of the late 1970s Taylor played guitar for a 1950s show band out of Charles Town, West Virginia called the Cruisers. He then spent most of the 1980s touring the United States in a rock and roll group called Hard to Get. More recently Guy Taylor has played guitar for several C&W acts including Chris Montgomery and Neon Moon, singer C.B. Wilson, singer Joey Dee, and the band Country Rose. In addition he has worked with an R&B band called the Champagne Brothers.

HAL LINDES

In the early 1970s guitarist Hal Lindes, who at the time was residing in Kensington, Maryland, was a member of the hard rocking band Sudden Rush. This group performed on a regular basis at the M Club in the Georgetown neighborhood of Washington, D.C. and also headlined teen dances at the Belair Junior High School Teen Club (Bowie), the St. Luke's Lutheran Church Teen Club (Silver Spring), the St. Alban's Episcopal Church Friday Coffeehouse (Washington, D.C.), Potomac High School (Oxon Hill), the Rockville Civic Center (Rockville), the Wheaton Youth Center (Wheaton) and the Falls Church Community Center (Virginia).

Later in the decade Lindes moved to the United Kingdom and in 1979 he was a member of a rock and roll band called Darling. A year later he joined the band Dire Straits and remained its rhythm guitarist through 1985. During his tenure with that band he played on three of their albums: "Love Over Gold" (Dire Straits; Warner Bros. Records, 1982);

"Extendedanceplay" (Dire Straits; Warner Bros. Records, 1983 – a 4-song EP); and "Alchemy Live" (Dire Straits; Warner Bros. Records, 1984). Today Lindes lives in Los Angeles, California and composes film soundtracks.

THE HALL BROTHERS

The Hall Brothers are a versatile trio consisting of singer-guitarist Milford Chick Hall ("Chick Hall, Jr."), singer-bassist Chris Hall and drummer Chip Clemmer. They perform a mix of C&W, rock and roll, and classic pop songs and instrumentals around the Washington, D.C. area before a loyal following that has supported them through their days at the Surf Club to the present. Chick and Chris Hall are the sons of Milford Willard "Chick" Hall, who was considered to be one of the region's best jazz and C&W guitarists from the 1950s to the 1980s.

From 1955 to 1975, Chick Hall owned and operated the Surf Club on Bladensburg Road in Colmar Manor, Maryland, holding court in his own country-flavored bands and leading his two sons into the world of popular music. The Hall family moved from Washington, D.C. to Mt. Rainier, Maryland in 1960, with Milford Chick Hall (commonly known as "Chick Hall, Jr.") graduating high school from St. Anthony's School in the city in 1963 and Chris Hall graduating from the same school in 1970. Learning guitar from their father, Chick Hall, Jr. played in a highly regarded rock and roll band called the Majestic Neons during his teen and young adult years, while Chris Hall did the vast majority of his playing in the late 1960s and early 1970s in the Surf Club, usually filling in on bass for absent members of his father's longstanding band, the Chick Hall Trio.

In early March 1975 Chick Hall closed the Surf Club in Colmar Manor, but reopened a few nights later at a new location on Kenilworth Avenue in Hyattsville, Maryland. From 1975 to 1991 the Chick Hall Band was the nightly attraction at the new Surf Club, with Chick on lead guitar and his son Chris Hall playing bass on Friday and Saturday nights. Chick Jr., meanwhile, spent the 1970s working from Baltimore to Frederick to Washington, D.C. in such C&W bands as 301 Country, On the Rise, and the American Heart Band. In the 1980s he was in demand as a lead guitarist and performed and toured such performing artists as: C&W singers Johnny Lee and Lorrie Morgan; C&W-pop singer Ronnie Dove; country-rockabilly saxophonist Ace Cannon; pop singers Billy J. Kramer and Jim Gold; pop-country singer Johnny Tillotson; and the R&B act the Platters.

In 1991 Chick Hall retired and Chick Jr. and Chris Hall put together a new Surf Club house band called Heroes and Friends, with the initial lineup consisting of singer-guitarist Chick Hall Jr., singer-bassist Chris Hall, keyboardist Brin Reed and drummer Tim Jarvis. Through the years musicians passed in and out of the band including steel guitarist Bob Gellison, guitarist Randy Leaf and drummers Lenny Davis and Nick Davis. Eventually Heroes and Friends settled on a trio format, with Chick Jr. and Chris being joined by drummer Mike Toole.

In 2008 the Hall connections sold the Surf Club to Jim Byrum. At that time Chick Jr. and Chris Hall formed a new trio with drummer Chip Clemmer called the Hall Brothers. They began regularly playing out in Maryland at the American Legion College Park Post 217 (College Park), the Old Bowie Town Grille (Bowie), the Sapphire Restaurant and Lounge (Laurel), Remington's of Laurel (Laurel) and the New Deal Café (Greenbelt); and in Virginia at JV's Restaurant (Falls Church).

The band is still playing out today and offers a wide range of material including covers of songs by Roger Miller, Bill Doggett, Big Joe Turner, Red Foley, Ray Price, Jimmy Buffet, and the Ventures. In addition, Chick Hall, Jr. and Chris Hall has recently played with Benny Potter and Western Electric, singer Patsy Stephens, the country-rockabilly band George Garris and Friends, and an oldies rock act called the Al Parsons Band.

Chick Hall, Jr. has one solo CD album to his credit: "Nuke the Juke" (Chick Hall Jr. with the Mustangs; Patuxent Music, 2010). He also currently plays guitar for his daughter, rock and roll singer-guitarist Rachel Hall, at several Maryland venues including the Cat's Eye Pub in Baltimore and Clyde's Restaurant in Columbia.

HANK BURNETT

Singer-drummer Hank Burnett was born in Washington, D.C. and raised in the Beacon Heights neighborhood of Riverdale, Maryland. During his years at Glenridge Junior High School in the middle 1960s he drummed in a rock and roll band called the Out Crowd, which performed on the local teen dance circuit. During his years at DuVal High School in the late 1960s he drummed in another teen dance rock and roll band called Slo Frate and followed that up with a stint in an R&B band called Illusion of Sound. He then spent time in Florida drumming for different bands, but soon returned to the Washington, D.C. area.

In March 1971 Burnett became the drummer of the one of the Washington, D.C. area's top rock and roll bands, God Mother Country. The group was a hot commodity on the local teen dance scene, but also headlined at local night clubs and performed at music festivals around the region. He remained with the band through 1974, at which time several members, including Burnett, formed a new, short-lived rock and roll outfit called Fast Eddie. He then spent the late 1970s drumming in a rock and roll group called the Kid Band which regularly performed locally at the Varsity Grill Back Room (College Park) and Mr. Henry's Tenley Circle (Washington, D.C.) and released the single "Working On You" backed with "Pet of the Month" (The Kid Band; Rude Record, 1978).

Burnett started the 1980s singing and drumming for his own rock and roll outfit, Hank Burnett with Exit, which recorded one single, "The Bullshit "Song" backed with "Getting Over" (Hank Burnett w/ Exit; Eastern Records, 1981). He then spent the early 1980s drumming in a local C&W band called Hurricane Dixie and late in the decade joined the Arlington-based rock and roll band the Redeemers, which performed at such Washington, D.C. night clubs as the Roxy and D.C. Space and released the album "Redeemers" (The Redeemers; One Horse Records, 1989).

In the 1990s Burnett drummed for a number of local bands including the rock and roll group the Van Dangos, the R&B-oriented Jim Price Band, and a multi-styled pop band called the Wild Bunch. Late in the decade he was called back to the Redeemers and appears on their second CD album, "She Rocks "N" Rolls All Night & Day" (The Redeemers; One Horse Records, 2002). Two recent album releases by the band also feature Burnett on drums, "Live At The Black Cat. DC" (The Redeemers; One Horse Records, 2017); and "Live at the Bayou" (The Redeemers; One Horse Records, 2017).

In recent years Burnett has drummed for such blues acts as the Railriders and the Little Muddy Jones Band, and the rock and roll group Boomerang. Since 2009 he has been a member of the local rock and roll band the Colliders and appears on both of their CD albums, "A Difficult Girl" (The Colliders; CatBug Records, 2011) and "Simone" (The Colliders; CatBug Records, 2016). He is also currently drumming in a multi-styled pop trio called the Tapestry Band, which can be seen on weekends at the Fort Myer Officers' Club (Arlington County, Virginia).

HAPPY THE MAN

Happy the Man is a progressive rock and roll group that formed in Harrisonburg, Virginia in 1972. Three years later they relocated to Arlington, Virginia and settled on a lineup of singer-guitarist Stanley Whitaker, keyboardist Kit Watkins, keyboardist-reed player Frank Wyatt, bassist Rick Kennell and drummer Mike Beck.

Throughout the late 1970s Happy the Man performed in Virginia at the Fairfax Theatre (Fairfax) and Cable Hall (University of Virginia); and in Washington, D.C. at the Carter Barron Amphitheatre, the Bayou and the Cellar Door. In the fall of 1977 they toured as the opening act for Hot Tuna and played colleges, theatres, concert halls and arenas from Virginia to New York.

In recent times Happy the Man has regrouped and performed on numerous occasions with various musicians in the fold. To date they have released a total of eight albums: "Happy the Man" (Happy the Man; Arista Records, 1977); "Crafty Hands" (Happy the Man; Arista Records, 1978); "3rd Better Late..." (Happy the Man; Azimuth Records, 1983); "Retrospective" (Happy the Man; East Side Digital, 1989); "Beginnings" (Happy the Man; Cuneiform Records, 1990); "Live" (Happy the Man; Cuneiform Records, 1997); "Death's Crown" (Happy the Man; Cuneiform Records, 1999); and "The Muse Awakens" (Happy the Man; InsideOut Music, 2004).

HARVEY NUSSBAUM

Drummer Harvey Nussbaum was born in Washington, D.C. and raised in Silver Spring, where, during his years at Northwood High School in the early 1970s, he first played in a rock and roll band on the local teen dance circuit called Apocalypse. He spent the remainder of the early and middle 1970s drumming for such Washington, D.C. area rock and roll bands as the Magic Touch, Rushmore, Razz, and Fargo.

Nussbaum next relocated to the Central United States where he played in the rock and roll bands Fourplay and Tram 86 in Kansas City, Missouri from 1975 to 1976, and the rock group Oz in Lawrence, Kansas from 1977 to 1978. He then returned to the Washington, D.C. area in 1978 and spent a year drumming for a multi-styled show group called the First National Band Featuring White Heat. He followed that engagement with a return to the rock band Fargo, remaining with them into the early 1980s.

After a long hiatus Nussbaum returned to the local music scene and from 2000 to 2004 served as the drummer for the Rock and Roll Relics, an aptly-named oldies group based in Gaithersburg, Maryland. During those years he also worked for "DayJams" (a rock music day camp operated by the National Guitar Workshop for youths aged 8-15) at some of their Montgomery County, Maryland locations, first serving as a drum inspector and later serving as a camp director.

More recently Nussbaum has performed and recorded with the Charlottesville, Virginia-based blues-jazz singer-guitarist-harmonicist Michael Mulvaney. He currently resides in Locust Grove, Virginia and is working on musical projects with rock and roll guitarist Nick Burgess.

HAWAII

Hawaii was a heavy metal rock and roll band that formed in the state of Hawaii in 1983, but had strong ties to the Washington, D.C. area. The group's original lineup consisted of lead singer-bassist Gary St. Piere, drummer Jeff Graves, and guitarist Marty Friedman, who hailed from Laurel, Maryland and had previously played in the heavy metal band Deuce.

Marty Freidman left Laurel and moved to the state of Hawaii in 1982 where he first played in a rock and roll band called Vixen. In 1983 he founded the band Hawaii, which entered the studio and recorded and released its debut album, "One Nation Underground" (Hawaii; Shrapnel Records, 1983). In January 1984 St. Piere left Hawaii and Friedman and Graves added two new recruits to the fold. The first addition was lead singer Eddie Day, who was from New Carrollton, Maryland, had graduated from Parkdale High School in 1977, and had previously worked with Freidman in the band Deuce. The other was bassist

Joey Galisha. With this new lineup, the band released its second album, "Loud Wild and Heavy" (Hawaii; Cavern Productions, 1984).

Hawaii next became a quintet by adding rhythm guitarist Tom Azevedo. The group then recorded and released its third and final album, "The Natives are Restless" (Hawaii; Shockwaves Records, 1985). In one of the band's highlights, this five-man version of Hawaii opened for Deep Purple at the Neal S. Blaisdell Arena in Honolulu, Hawaii on Friday, May 3, 1985.

In the summer of 1985 Hawaii splintered and Marty Friedman and Eddie Day opted to return to the Washington, D.C. area and reform the group with new players. They acquired bassist Mike "Feeedbak" Buff (that's how he spells it), who had grown up in the Green Meadows community of Maryland and had previously played in the band Feedback, and drummer Bob Shade, who hailed from Hyattsville and had previously drummed for such bands as the American Cheese Band, Feedback, Purlz, and Shatter.

The new version of Hawaii conducted rehearsals at Buff's house in Lanham, Maryland and performed in Washington, D.C. at the Bayou; and in Maryland at the Stardust Inn (Waldorf), Network (Pasadena) and Hammerjacks (Baltimore). However, before the year was out Friedman had departed. He would later re-emerge in the band Megadeth.

In early 1986 Hawaii again reorganized and resurfaced without any original members in the fold. The new lineup consisted of Day, Shade, and Feeedbak, along with new lead guitarist Robert Fiester of Bowie, Maryland. The group continued to shuffle its lineup and in the fall settled on a lineup of Day, Shade, Fiester, bassist Doug David and rhythm guitarist Danny Wright. This latest version of Hawaii opened for Emerson, Lake & Powell at the Capital Centre in Landover, Maryland on Friday, September 19, 1986. In the aftermath of this performance, Tim Stillwell of Baltimore, formerly of the band Trigger Happy, replaced Doug David on bass. In 1987 Hawaii disbanded, with the group's individual members going in different musical directions.

HENRY ROLLINS

Singer Henry Rollins was born and raised in Washington, D.C., and, while a student at Bullis School in Potomac, Maryland the late 1970s, he became a fan of the Ramones and served as a roadie for several local punk bands including the Teen Idles, a group that included Ian MacKaye. Reportedly, when the band's singer Nathan Strejcek was absent from practice sessions, Rollins would step in and handle vocals.

Rollins went on to serve as lead singer for the Washington, D.C.-based punk rock band S.O.A. (State of Alert) from 1981 to 1986 and then handled lead vocals for the Los Angeles, California-based hardcore punk band Black Flag from 1981 to 1986. He subsequently led his own rock and roll group, Rollins Band, from 1987 to 2003. In recent years he has been active as a writer, actor, radio personality and spoken word performing artist.

HILLOW HAMMET

Hailed as a high-powered, soul-influenced rock and roll band, Hillow Hammet came together in 1969 and based out of the Keg on Wisconsin Avenue NW in the Glover Park neighborhood of Washington, D.C. for much of its mercurial existence. The band was formed by Chuck Bennett, formerly of Link Wray and His Ray Men, who began rehearsing with several musicians who had previously been in a rock and roll band from Southern Maryland called the Leaves of Grass. Eventually, a lineup coalesced that consisted of lead singer Chuck Bennett, lead guitarist Pete "Peaches" Williams, rhythm guitarist Ronnie Barkley, bassist Jack Registers, keyboardist Steve Spencer, drummer Gregory "GC"

Coleman, and percussionist Mike Previti, who early on had replaced percussionist-equipment manager-soundman Frazier Botsford.

In addition to the Keg, Hillow Hammet worked engagements at other Washington, D.C. night clubs such as the Silver Dollar Restaurant, the Rocket Room (where they once backed up R&B singer-pianist Big Al Downing for a week), the Blue Mirror Club and the Butterfly.

Before the band's breakup in 1970, Chuck Bennett was replaced by former Crank frontman Gui Bokoles, and Gary Coleman's place was filled by Georgetown's resident drummer, Mike Zack. Although the group only existed for a little more than a year before its parts disengaged, they recorded and released one now-highly-sought-after album: "Hammer" (Hillow Hammet; House of the Fox Records, 1969).

IAN MACKAYE

Singer-guitarist Ian MacKaye was born and raised in Washington, D.C., where, as a pre-teen in the early 1970s, he took piano lessons and also began playing guitar. Reportedly, an early influence was Jimi Hendrix, with later inspirations being Queen, Ted Nugent, and the punk rock band the Cramps, among innumerable others.

In the late 1970s while attending Woodrow Wilson High School MacKaye began his punk rock journey as a member of a group called the Slinkees. In the 1980s he served as the frontman for several successive Washington, D.C. punk rock bands including the Teen Idles, Skewbald/Grand Union, Minor Threat, Embrace, Egg Hunt, and Pailhead.

From 1987 to 2003 MacKaye sang and played guitar in the post-hardcore punk rock band Fugazi, whose lineup was completed by singer-guitarist Guy Picciotto, bassist Joe Lally and drummer Brendan Canty. In addition, from 2001 to 2012 he sang and played guitar in a rock and roll duo called the Evens with singer-drummer Amy Farina. Since 1980 MacKaye has owned Dischord Records, a Washington, D.C.-based independent record label.

ICHABOD CRANE

Ichabod Crane was a rock and roll band that formed in Landover Hills, Maryland in 1973 from the remnants of the hard-rocking group Joint Possession. They worked dances, weddings, military base officers' clubs and night clubs throughout the Washington, D.C. area. The band's original lineup consisted of lead singer Irvin Utz, lead guitarist Andy Gardner, rhythm guitarist John Haughey, bassist Lee Page and drummer Steve Bryant. Early on, the group underwent a significant personnel shift when it replaced its rhythm section with bassist Donnie Bobic and drummer Timm Biery.

Ichabod Crane's reputation soared in 1974 when it became the regular attraction at the Back Alley Lounge, which operated in the back of the building that housed the Cross Roads night club in Bladensburg, Maryland. They also performed at Fort George G. Meade Officers' Club (Anne Arundel County, Maryland), Fort Belvoir Officers' Club (Fairfax County, Virginia), Andrews Air Force Base Officers' Club (Prince George's County, Maryland), Henderson Hall (Arlington County, Virginia), the West Lanham Hills Volunteer Fire Department (Hyattsville), the Sheraton Inn (New Carrolton) and the Ramada Inn (Lanham).

In terms of night club work, the band headlined in Washington, D.C. at the Keg, the Crazy Horse and the Top O' Foolery; and in Maryland at Jimmy Comber's Restaurant (Hyattsville), Mr. Henry's College Park (College Park) and the Quonset Supper Club (Silver Hill).

Ichabod Crane was noted for its versatility, covering everything from Led Zeppelin to Merle Haggard, favoring songs by the likes of the Beatles, Grand Funk Railroad, the Guess Who, Deep Purple, the James Gang and the Jeff Beck Group. One of the band's more impressive dates saw them perform in a stage presentation of the Woody Allen-authored play "Play It Again, Sam" that was presented by the Washington Theatre Group at the Paint Branch High School auditorium (Silver Spring) in 1974. They performed two songs that evening, "Johnny B. Goode" by Chuck Berry and "Walk Away" by the James Gang.

Ichabod Crane experienced one last personnel change when Jackie Dunn replaced Andy Gardner on lead guitar. The group ultimately disbanded in 1975.

INNOCENT COLOR

Innocent Color was a versatile rock and roll band that formed in 1967 and hailed from Annapolis, Maryland. The group consisted of recent Annapolis High School students and graduates and played original compositions, Motown-flavored R&B material, and pop songs in the vein of the Young Rascals. The band's original lineup consisted of lead singer Dale Rorer, lead guitarist Dick Rausch, bassist Sterling Spell, keyboardist Ray Brokamp and drummer Vernon Smith.

When they hit the nation's capital in 1968, Innocent Color first played the Keg on Wisconsin Avenue NW. The following year they replaced the Telstars as the house band at the Bayou in Georgetown, a prestigious position they held for much of the year.

In the fall of 1969 Innocent Color disbanded, with members Rausch and Smith teaming with bassist Lee Craig to form a new band called Second Eagle, which initially performed at the Keg. Second Eagle soon added lead singer Carl Anderson and went on to become one of the area's top rock and roll attractions.

IRVIN UTZ

Singer Irvin Utz grew up in Landover Hills, Maryland and during his time at Bladensburg High School in the early 1970s he sang in a popular rock and roll band called Joint Possession. The group's five-man lineup when Utz came on board as lead singer was rounded out with lead guitarist Henry Verdel, rhythm guitarist John Haughey, bassist Terry Selby and drummer Steve Bryant.

Joint Possession developed into one of the area's most popular bands with the younger crowd and regularly played in Prince George's County, Maryland at the St. Mary's Catholic Church Teen Club (Landover Hills), the Cooper Lane Teen Club (Cooper Lane Elementary School in Landover Hills), the Beacon Heights Teen Club (Beacon Heights Elementary School in Riverdale) and the Tuxedo-Cheverly Fire Department (Hyattsville). The group disbanded in 1973.

Utz next sang in the rock and roll band Ichabod Crane, which formed later in 1973 and was rounded out by Haughey and Bryant (also previous members of Joint Possession), along with bassist Lee Page and guitarist Andy Gardner. Ichabod Crane was best known for its lengthy run as the house band at the Back Alley Lounge, a night club situated in the back portion of the Cross Roads in Bladensburg, Maryland. The group was a popular attraction on the local music scene for more than two years.

Utz next went on to sing for other popular Washington, D.C. area rock and roll bands including Vintage (in the 1980s) and Random Access (in the 1990s).

In 1997 Utz put together the Bad Weather Boyz, a hard-driving rock and roll band whose original lineup consisted of Utz handling lead vocals, guitarist Robert Fiester, bassist Paul Jones and drummer Conte Bellucci. The group was especially popular in the Maryland suburbs at night clubs like Lasick's College Inn (College Park), the Riverdale Pizza Pub (Riverdale), Oliver's Saloon (Laurel), the California Inn (Laurel), Willy K's (inside the Holiday Inn Washington D.C.-Greenbelt) and Mike's Crab House (Riva). In 2000 Jones was replaced by bassist Ken Fiester. At one point Robert Fiester was replaced by guitarist Mike

Dunn for approximately one year. Fiester then returned to the fold and remained with the band through much of its existence.

One of the Bad Weather Boyz's longest running lineups consisted of Utz, the two Fiester brothers, Bellucci and keyboardist Jeff Archer. In 2013 Utz reorganized the band, with the new lineup consisting of Utz, Bellucci, guitarist Steve Long, original bassist Paul Jones and saxophonist Paul Shumate. The Bad Weather Boyz played their last gig in March 2015.

In recent years Utz has performed as a singer-guitarist with many other bands and musicians including Johnny Seaton and Bad Behavior, blues singer-guitarist Andy Poxon, rock and roll singer-guitarist Martha Capone, and rock and roll singer-guitarist Dan Dorsey. He has also appeared onstage at the New Deal Café in Greenbelt, Maryland with such performers as: a jazz group called the Susan Jones Quartet; blues singer-harmonicist Waverly Milor; and the rock and roll band T.C. and Friends, a band that featured singer-keyboardist Tom Constanten, who was a member of the Grateful Dead from 1968 to 1970, and, as part of that group, was inducted into the Rock and Roll Hall of Fame in the "Performers" category on Wednesday, January 19, 1994.

JACK BROOKS

Bassist Jack Brooks grew up in the Belhaven neighborhood of Alexandria, Virginia and as a teenager in the late 1950s became a fan of Ricky Nelson and took up guitar. During his time at Groveton High School in the early 1960s he first played guitar in a rock and roll teen dance band called Bobby and the Starliners, and then spent time playing in another group called the Off Beats. In the middle 1960s he played guitar for the Saxtons at the Quonset Supper Club (Silver Hill), the Wolfpack at Mac's Pipe and Drum Restaurant (Washington, D.C.), and Jimmy Eller and His Little People at Benny's Rebel Room (Washington, D.C.).

In 1965 Brooks was invited to play bass in one of the Washington, D.C. area's top rock and roll bands, the British Walkers. When he first joined the quartet the lineup was completed by singer-keyboardist-guitarist Bobbi Howard, lead guitarist Jimmy Carter and drummer Steve Lacey. The band's home base was the Roundtable in Georgetown and a number of musicians came and went during its time. Brooks remained their bassist until the group's demise in late 1967.

In 1969 Brooks joined a newly-formed rock and roll band called Tractor, whose initial lineup consisted of singer-keyboardist Bill Manning, guitarist Ron Culbertson, Brooks on bass and drummer Michael "Pokey" Walls (who was soon replaced by Steve Lacey). Tractor played Washington, D.C. night clubs such as Emergency and My Mother's Place and made several trips to New York City where they performed at the Electric Circus. The group endured changes in personnel and in 1973 relocated to California. Before the year was out the band had changed its name to Pony Express. In the ensuing years Brooks played bass for such rock and roll bands as Eddie Haddad and the Canyon Band, Cheryl Paris and the New People and the Mojo Mountain Band.

JACK CASADY

Today Jack Casady is considered to be one of the greatest bassists in rock and roll history. He was raised in the Tenleytown neighborhood of Washington, D.C. and graduated from Woodrow Wilson High School in 1962. In the late 1950s he had been a member of a teen rock and roll band called the Triumphs along with guitarist and neighbor Jorma Kaukonen. He then spent the early 1960s working with a variety of bands in and around the nation's capital including the Off Beats, the Medallions, Herbie and the Originals and Bobbie Howard and the Ponies.

Along the way Casady served as a pickup bass player for house bands in numerous night clubs in Washington, D.C. including the Rendezvous, Coffee 'n' Confusion, the Pine Tavern, Vinnie's Grill, the Famous Restaurant, Rand's Night Club, the Hayloft, Benny's Rebel Room and others.

In October 1965 Casady received a call from Jorma Kaukonen in the Bay Area of California and accepted his invitation to join Jefferson Airplane. The rest is history. After his time in that great psychedelic San Francisco band was up, he joined Hot Tuna, an outfit he continues to work with to this day. Casady, as a member of Jefferson Airplane, was inducted into the Rock and Roll Hall of Fame in the "Performers" category on Wednesday, January 17, 1996.

JAN ZUKOWSKI

Jan Zukowski is one of the finest bass players to ever emerge from the Washington, D.C. area. He grew up in Forestville, Maryland and during his teen years at Francis Scott Key Junior High School and Suitland High School in the middle and late 1960s he played in such rock and roll bands as the Coachmen, the Adam's Apples, Nobody's Children, the Surf Boys, Tuesday Boots and Boone's Farm.

From 1967 to 1973 Zukowski was bassist for one of the region's best rock and roll bands, the Cherry People. In 1974 he switched to the blues and joined the Nighthawks, remaining with them for 30 years during which time he worked thousands of gigs, played on over 20 of their albums, and appeared with them on such television shows as "Homicide" and "The Wire." Some of the blues artists the Nighthawks backed up with Zukowski on bass were singer-pianist Pinetop Perkins, singer-guitarists Muddy Waters and Otis Rush, and singer-guitarist-harmonicist John Hammond. From 2004 to 2013 Zukowski played bass for the Fabulous Hubcaps.

Zukowski has also played bass for a variety of nationally known performers from the fields of blues, R&B, and rock and roll including: singers Ben E. King and Jerry Lawson; singer-guitarists Chuck Berry, Bo Diddley, John Lee Hooker, Elvin Bishop, Jimmy Dawkins, J.B. Hutto and Warren Hayes; singer-harmonicist Jimmy Hall; and singer-keyboardist Gregg Allman.

In recent years Zukowski has also worked with such bands and musicians as Tough Luck, the Cathy Ponton King Band, the Big Money Band, the Soul Serenaders, the Dave Chappell Band, the Meena Cryle and Chris Fillmore Band, the Skyla Burrell Band, the Southern Soul Tribute Band, the Beat Hotel, Johnny and the Headhunters, Scott Ramminger and the Crawstickers, Johnny Seaton and Bad Behavior, the Billy Price Band, Mike Lapadula and the Lost Souls, the Ron Holloway Band, Rick Hogue and the Revolving Doors, the Linwood Taylor Band, the Kings (featuring guitarist Michael Fath), singer-guitarist Andy Poxon, singer-keyboardist Johnny Neel, guitarist Anthony Pirog, guitarist Dean Rosenthal, and French blues guitarist Fred Chapellier.

In 2015 Zukowski was a member of the Chesapeake Bay Blues Band along with singer-harmonicist Mark Wenner, guitarists Robert Frahm and Dean Rosenthal, keyboardist Tommy Lepson and drummer Pete Ragusa.

A personal highlight of Zukowski's musical career occurred when he was called upon to play bass for George Thorogood and the Destroyers at "Live Aid," a concert organized by Bob Geldof and Midge Ure for relief of Ethiopian famine, at John F. Kennedy Stadium in Philadelphia, Pennsylvania on Saturday, July 13, 1985. This dual venue concert was watched by an estimated global audience of 1.9 billion people across 150 nations.

JAY NEDRY

Drummer Jay Nedry was born in Chicago Illinois, and, after a short stay in Alexandria, Virginia, resided in Mount Vernon, Virginia until he began his high school years in the middle 1960s, just as the British Invasion arrived on our country's shores. At a young age he began listening to jazz, and, upon entering the sixth grade (1961-1962), he added local rock and roll stations to his radio selections.

Initially Nedry wanted to play saxophone, but, as he began seventh grade in the fall of 1962, his father had him switch to drums (in hopes he would eventually give up on music). Nedry took lessons for two years, bought his first drum set, and drummed for N.A.R.D. (National Association or Rudimental Drummers). During these formative years he championed such jazz drummers as Gene Krupa, Buddy Rich and Joe Morello, with rock and roll drummer Cozy Powell becoming a major inspiration further on down the road. After finishing the eighth grade at Walt Whitman Junior High School in 1964 Nedry and his family moved to the nearby community of West Springfield, Virginia.

As the Beatles and the Rolling Stones began making their marks on rock and roll Nedry began stepping out and attending live music shows at the American Legion Springfield Post 176 near his Virginia home. He also showed more interest in frequenting his neighborhood's bowling alleys, pool halls and teen dance venues than he did in attending his freshman year classes at Robert E. Lee High School. His activities during that time included serving as a roadie for one of the top young rock and roll bands on the local circuit, the Roaches. Consequently, after an aborted school year, he became a student at Staunton Military Academy in Staunton, Virginia, graduating in 1969.

During his breaks from Staunton in the late 1960s Nedry sharpened his music skills: he attended Band Camps as a drummer at the College of William & Mary in Williamsburg, Virginia during the summers of 1964 and 1965; he drummed for a rock and roll band on the Northern Virginia teen dance scene called the Surf Riders in the summer of 1965; and he later handled percussion for a local rock band called the Charlatans in the summer of 1967.

In September of 1969 Nedry enrolled at the College of William & Mary as an economics and philosophy major. A series of serious back injuries forced him to eventually leave school (though he later attended James Madison University in Harrisonburg, Virginia for the 1974-1975 school semesters). From August to December 1975 he drummed in a local rock and roll band called Leesburg Pike and right around Christmas of that year he ran into an old friend from the neighborhood named Bill Schmidle, who played guitar and was ready to start a new musical venture. A month later Nedry, Schmidle and guitarist Bob Gaynor grouped together in West Springfield and assembled the first edition of a Southern rock band they called the Roadducks.

In the late 1970s the Roadducks worked such night clubs as the Elbow Room (Harrisonburg, Virginia), the Psyche Delly (Bethesda), Louie's Rock city (Bailey's Crossroads) and the Bayou (Washington, D.C.). They spent time in New Haven, Connecticut and worked the night club scenes in New York City and Boston, Massachusetts. They then spent years touring concert halls and arenas as the opening act for such acts as Blackfoot, Foghat, Molly Hatchet, Stevie Ray Vaughan, the Outlaws and numerous others. The Roadducks endured rounds of personnel changes through the years and are still in existence today under Nedry's direction.

In the 1980s Nedry purchased a professional sound and lights system and familiarized himself with its installation and operation. He then became the sound and lights man at a live music night club called Zaxx at 6355 Rolling Road in Springfield, Virginia (which had replaced a similar establishment called the Copa), a position he maintained from 1989 to 1991. He subsequently served as the club's booking agent from 1992 to 1993.

Nedry branched out and owned and operated a night club called Honey Bear's in Martinsburg, West Virginia for much of 1993 (late in the year he changed the name of the venue to Boomer's). Meanwhile, Zaxx had been replaced by a night club called Boots, which was experiencing severe financial difficulties. In August 1994 Nedry and Nick Dukovich took over the business and began bringing in a variety of local and national rock and roll acts. They changed the name of the 550-person capacity night club/concert hall to Jaxx Nightclub in September 1994.

Dukovich backed out of the picture in December 1996 and on Wednesday, January 1, 1997, after paying off more than $200,000 in back taxes, Jay Nedry became the sole proprietor of Jaxx Nightclub. For years it was the Washington, D.C. area's premier rock and roll venue, with its owner using his extensive connections in the music industry to bring in the best available acts including Dokken, UFO, Foghat, Motorhead, Robin Trower, Blue Oyster Cult, Kix, Frank Marino and Mahogany Rush, John Paul Jones, Wishbone Ash, Mountain and hundreds of others. Every local rock and roll fan owes Nedry a debt of gratitude for the incredible music he brought to the nation's capital and his hard work for the cause. He ultimately sold Jaxx Nightclub on Sunday, January 1, 2012.

In the summer of 2014 Nedry re-enrolled at William & Mary College and ultimately earned a Bachelor of Arts in history from the storied institution in 2018. He is currently enrolled in a master's/doctoral program in history at George Mason University and is preparing for a career in teaching. Through it all he has maintained his position as drummer for the Roadducks. The band is still alive today and going stronger than ever.

J.D. AND THE JESTERS

This Silver Spring-based R&B-rock band formed in September 1964 and endured many changes in musical styles and personnel during its seven-year run. The original lineup for the group was lead singer Marlene Parker, lead guitarist Larry Gaiser, rhythm guitarist Dave "J.D." Palmer, bassist Dean Brand and drummer Terry Vipond, with all members attending Northwood High School except for Brand, who attended Takoma Park Junior High School and then Montgomery Blair High School.

Early on, players joined and left J.D. and the Jesters, with Gaiser departing and lead singer Doug Blanche and keyboardist Richard Willett joining the fold (at that point Dean Brand moved to lead guitar and J.D. Palmer switched to bass). As the band expanded its repertoire of R&B material, they introduced a horn section consisting of saxophonist Tom Young, trumpeter Doug Enfield and trombonist Jeff Kardos.

During its earlier years J.D. and the Jesters were a popular commodity on the local teen dance scene, particularly at places like the Silver Spring YMCA and the Wheaton Youth Center, where in one highly publicized event they were part of a "Shindig" on Saturday, November 27, 1965 that included Little Valentine, Billee Jones, the McConkey Brothers, T.N.T. Tribble and His Band and the Velours. The band experienced numerous personnel changes in the early 1970s, a period that saw them perform in Washington, D.C. at such night clubs as the Montage and the Cave.

JEFF ARCHER

Singer-keyboardist Jeff Archer grew up in the Montgomery County town of Brookeville Maryland and as a youth learned to play keyboards by ear. In the late 1960s while attending Sherwood High School he played the local teen dance scene in a rock and roll band called the Keysers. During this time he also played his first night club gigs with a band called Bittersweet at Clyde's Restaurant in the Georgetown neighborhood of Washington, D.C.

In 1970 Archer joined Inside Strait, a band that covered more progressive rock and roll bands such as Yes and King Crimson. He then spent much of the late 1970s with a rock and roll band called Revolver, which headlined in Washington, D.C. at such Georgetown night clubs as the Bayou and the Crazy Horse; and in Maryland at the Bastille (College Park). In 1978 he spent time in New York performing and recording with the legendary blues rock guitarist Lonnie Mack. In the 1980s Archer played keyboards for an R&B band called Osirius and a rock and roll band called the Bel Airs. In 1983 he began a 12-year run with the pop-rock band Our Pleasure.

Through the years Archer has played keyboards for such acts as pop singer B.J. Thomas; R&B bands the Coasters, the Drifters and the Clovers; and rock and roll bands Freak'n'Fuzz, and the Bad Weather Boyz. He is currently recording and performing with his own rock and roll band, the Jeff Archer Group.

Archer's discography as a lead performer includes the single, "Solar Cell" backed with "The Last Day of the World" (Jeff Archer and the Secret Band; Aradia Records, 1983), and the albums, "Angels Without Wings" (Jeff Archer; Jeff Archer, 2004); "Starrlite & Starrbrite: Songs for the Holidays" (The Jeff Archer Group; NAL Records, 2005); "The JA Project" (The Jeff Archer Group; NAL Records, 2006); "My Baby's From Ocean City Maryland" (The Jeff Archer Group; NAL Records, 2007); and "The U.K. Sessions" (The Jeff Archer Group; NAL Records, 2007).

JEFF LODSUN

Drummer Jeff Lodsun was born in Fort Belvoir, Virginia and raised nearby in Falls Church where he was exposed to all types of music at an early age. His father was in the military and played tuba in the marching unit of the United States Army Band and bass fiddle in the jazz concert unit. Lodsun began taking drum lessons at age 12 from a member of the United States Army Band and would listen to everything from Elvis Presley to Chuck Berry to Carl Perkins.

From 1964 to 1968 Lodsun drummed for King's Row, a popular rock and roll band on the Northern Virginia teen dance scene. Late in the 1960s while a student at Bishop Denis J. O'Connell High School in Arlington, Virginia he drummed in a blues band called Whiskey and Automobiles, which included guitarist Tom Principato.

In 1970 Lodsun joined the popular local rock and roll band called Babe, whose four-man lineup was rounded out at the time by Ed Eastridge, Mitch Collins and Bob Coleman. Lodsun remained with the group until 1975, during which time they appeared at such Washington, D.C. night clubs as Chadwick's (on Capitol Hill), Mr. Henry's Tenley Circle, Sam's Place, Cousin Nick's, Desperado's and the Childe Harold. Lodsun was instrumental in steering the band from a pop-rock style to a more R&B-influenced sound.

While working with Babe at the Childe Harold, Lodsun befriended owner Bill Heard, Jr., who installed him as the night club's house drummer. As a result, during the first half of the 1970s Lodsun drummed at the Childe Harold for a number of visiting nationally known blues performers including: singers Koko Taylor and Lefty Diaz; harmonicists Hammie Nixon, Carey Bell and Phil Wiggins; singer-guitarists Archie Edwards, Houston Stackhouse, Sam Chatmon, John Cephus, Otis Rush and Muddy Waters; guitarists Sleepy John Nixon, John Jackson and Lonnie Pitchford; singer-pianists Pinetop Perkins and Sunnyland Slim; and others such as the R&B vocal group the Clovers and rock and roll singer-guitarist Bo Diddley. Lodsun was also called upon to drum at other night clubs around town for a number of visiting blues acts such as singer Nappy Brown and singer-guitarists Jimmy Rogers and Hubert Sumlin.

In 1975 Lodsun left the nation's capital and moved to Colorado, where he played in the Mile High Blues Band, toured with blues guitarist-harmonicist Johnny Long, and drummed for blues guitarist Homesick James.

In 1978 Lodsun returned to the Washington, D.C. area and for two years hosted all-star jams at the Childe Harold with a house band that included guitarist Bob "Newscaster" Swenson, pianist Steve Kramer, bass fiddler Bryan Smith and harmonicist Phil Wiggins. Among the major popular music artists who took the stage and performed with them at these jams were blues singer Bonnie Raitt, country-gospel vocal group the Gatlin Brothers, rock and roll singer-guitarist Steve Miller and blues singer-harmonicist Paul Butterfield.

In the 1980s Lodsun drummed for a variety of blues, R&B and rock and roll artists including guitarist Bob Margolin, Swing Shift, Billy Hancock and the Tennessee Rockets, the Rhythm Masters, Andrea Brown and the Kokomo Mojos and Tough Luck (featuring singer-harmonicist Lips Lackowitz). More recently he has drummed for such blues bands as the J Street Jumpers, Bruce Ewan and the Solid Senders and the Big Boy Little Band; and the R&B group the Red-Hot Swinging Johnsons.

JEROME MONROE

Jerome "Stump" Monroe was raised in Washington, D.C. and taught himself the drums at age 13 by playing along to James Brown records in his basement. He left the nation's capital as a teenager in the early 1960s and went on to drum for such R&B greats as: singers Jerry Butler, Wilson Pickett, Dee Clark, Cuba Gooding, Sr., Betty Wright and Chuck Jackson; singer-pianist Billy Stewart; a number of bands including the Coasters, the Del Vikings, Gladys Knight and the Pips and Martha Reeves and the Vandellas; and pop-rock singer Ricky Nelson.

In the late 1960s Monroe became the full-time drummer for the Sweet Inspirations, the R&B female vocal group, who, from 1969 to 1977, served as the opening act for the Elvis Presley Show, a concert presentation highlighted by Elvis himself and the TCB Band.

During his time with the Sweet Inspirations Monroe was called upon to fill in for Presley's drummer Ronnie Tutt on three occasions. Each time Monroe worked the entire Elvis Presley concert as the King worked the stage in front of him. The three shows in question were: the Spectrum in Philadelphia, Pennsylvania on Monday, November 8, 1971; the Hilton Hotel in Las Vegas, Nevada on Sunday, December 7, 1975; and the Dane County Coliseum in Madison, Wisconsin on Friday, June 24, 1977.

More recently Monroe has drummed for the doo-wop vocal group the Flamingos and is currently drumming for a Las Vegas-based R&B band called A Touch of Silk.

JERRY MERCER

Drummer Jerry Mercer was born in Newfoundland (a Maritime Province of Canada) and worked with a Montreal-based rock and roll band called Mashmakhan in the early 1970s. He then relocated to Colmar Manor, Maryland, where he drummed for blues rock guitarist Roy Buchanan at the Cross Roads in nearby Bladensburg. Mercer appears on the record "Second Album" (Roy Buchanan; Polydor Records, 1973) and embarked on regional tours with the guitar great.

Mercer subsequently drummed with a rock and roll group called Band of Thieves, which featured prominent local guitarist Crazy Joe Tass, and held down house band duties at a night club called the Benedict Pier Restaurant in Benedict, Maryland (Charles County).

Mercer left Colmar Manor and later in 1973 joined the Canadian-based rock and roll band April Wine. He played on all of the group's albums and tours until his retirement from music in December 2008.

JIM CERONE

Guitarist Jim Cerone grew up in Takoma Park, Maryland and during his years at Montgomery Blair High School in the late 1960s he played the local teen dance scene in two top R&B-rock and roll bands, the Pagans (which included keyboardist Tommy Lepson), and the Spades and the Rainbows, a two-group, instrumental-vocal act.

Cerone went on to play guitar in Eastern Blend, one of the region's most celebrated pop-rock bands, from 1974 to 1997. The band had formed in Capitol Heights, Maryland in 1972 and covered everyone from James Brown to Chicago to Kool and the Gang. They performed at weddings, corporate events, private parties and at local military base establishments such as the Andrews Air Force Base Officers' Club (Prince George's County, Maryland), the Fort Belvoir Officers' Club (Fairfax County, Virginia) and the Marine Corps Base Quantico Officers' Club (Prince William County, Virginia). For years Eastern Blend's lineup consisted of lead singer John Kincaid, Cerone on guitar, bassist Marty King, trumpeter Mike Reuwer, saxophonists Don Antal and Mike Keegan and drummer Rob Forsee.

Cerone next played lead guitar from 1997 to 2015 in Pocket Change, a pop-rock band that was based in Crofton, Maryland and offered a repertoire of songs ranging from Engelbert Humperdinck to Bill Haley and His Comets to Van Morrison. The band consisted of Cerone on guitar, lead singer-keyboardist Brian Stevenson, bassist George Vermillion, saxophonist Ken Smith and drummer Rob Forsee. Pocket Change performed at concert shows and festivals throughout the region, and at Maryland venues such as the American Legion Wheaton Post 268, the American Legion College Park Post 217 and Boswell Hall inside the Knights of Columbus Sacred Heart Council 2577 in Bowie. Jim Cerone passed away on Tuesday, February 3, 2015 at the age of 66.

JIM COLBY

Bassist Jim Colby was born in Natick, Massachusetts and raised in Greenbelt, Maryland, where, as a teenager, he learned to play the bass through his two brothers, both of whom played guitar. While attending Eleanor Roosevelt High School in the middle and late 1970s he played bass in a local rock and roll band called Ace that covered such acts as the Rolling Stones, Robert Palmer, Kiss and Lynyrd Skynyrd. He next played in a Berwyn Heights-based new wave rock band called the Organism that included guitarist James "Butch" Smith, mainly performed at Captain Tom's Oar House in Park Hall, Maryland (St. Mary's County), and lasted from 1979 into 1980.

In the early 1980s Colby played bass in such Washington, D.C. area heavy metal rock bands as Rapid Fire and Wrathchild. From 1983 to 1985 he played in Insect Surfers, a largely instrumental surf rock band that featured guitarist Dave Arnson and at the time embarked on tours of the West Coast and Canada.

In the late 1980s Colby played bass in several local groups including a new wave band called the Famous Babies, an R&B act called the John Comstock Group, and a band called the Rhomboids that specialized in 1960s garage rock and was a favorite at such Washington, D.C. night clubs as D.C. Space, BBQ Iguana, Kilimanjaro and Nightclub 9:30.

After spending several years in Santa Monica, California where he played in church bands, Colby moved to College Park, Maryland in 1994 and played bass in the blues rock band One Thin Dime from 1995 to 2003. In 2005 he played in the surf music band Mega Tsunami, from 2006 to 2011 he was part of the surf band Reverb Galaxy, and from 2011 to 2014 he played bass and bass clarinet in a Hyattsville-based Cajun/zydeco/R&B group called the Wild Anacostians.

In 2014 Colby moved to the Orlando, Florida area and has recently played bass in several groups including the surf music band the Nova Rays, an oldies rock and roll act called the Silvertones Rock & Roll Revue, and the surf music bands the Midnight Surf and Agent Octopus.

JIM ROBESON

Singer-bassist Jim Robeson was born in Butler, Pennsylvania and raised in nearby Saxonburg. He began taking accordion lessons at age 10, started playing guitar at age 13 and shortly thereafter switched to bass. During his teen years in the 1960s he counted among his musical influences a variety of Motown, R&B and rock and roll artists including the Four Tops, the Temptations, James Brown, the Beatles, the Rolling Stones, Jimi Hendrix and Janis Joplin. During those years he became active in the recording and production of music, practices he has remained involved with to the present day.

In Robeson's first band job in the middle 1960s, he played accordion with Bill Abernathy and the Pennsylvania Hillbillies Square Dance Band, a C&W outfit based in Mars, Pennsylvania. During his years at Knoch High School in Saxonburg in the late 1960s Robeson played guitar in several rock and roll bands including the Lost Ones, the Kruisers, and Lite Rain. After finishing high school he served in the United States Army from 1969 to 1972.

Upon his discharge Robeson moved to Triangle, Virginia and took a job with Xerox. He then entered the Washington, D.C. area music scene, playing with an Arlington, Virginia-based country rock band called Newington Station. He relocated to Sterling, Virginia and built a home studio with one of his clients being singer-guitarist-harmonicist Al Johnson, who led his own Bethesda, Maryland-based country rock group called the North Star Band. In 1976 Robeson played some of his original songs for Johnson, who, in turn, asked him to become the North Star Band's new bassist. Robeson remained with the band throughout the remainder of the 1970s.

Since that time Robeson has played bass for a number of different bands and musicians on the local music scene including: the country rock bands All Night Long (with guitarist Mike Melchione) and Front Porch Swing (with singer-guitarist Pete Kennedy and drummer Robbie Magruder); the rock and roll bands Pete Kennedy and Good Rockin' Tonight, the Dynettes, the Chasers, and Pressure Drop; country rock singer-guitarist Dave Massey; and blues singer-guitarist Cathy Ponton King. Most recently, he has been a full-time member of two groups, Lunch With Bob (a rock and roll band he joined in 2017), and Ruthie and the Wranglers (a country rock group he joined in January 2018).

On another level, Robeson has been involved in the recording of music for decades. He worked as an engineer and producer for the local recording facility Bias Studios from 1978 to 2014 during which time he arranged, engineered, produced and played on hundreds of sessions. In 2014 he established Jim Robeson Productions, a production company and studio in Gaithersburg, Maryland that provides a range of music and video services.

JIM SNIDERO

Saxophonist Jim Snidero was born in Redwood City, California and raised in Camp Springs, Maryland. During his years at Crossland High School in the middle 1970s he played in a rock and roll band called Saturn, which performed on the local Prince George's County teen dance circuit. He went on to become one of the world's most renowned jazz saxophonists.

Snidero moved to New York City in 1981 and spent two years playing saxophone for jazz keyboardist Jack McDuff. In 1983 he joined the Toshiko Akiyoshi Jazz Orchestra and remained with the pianist's group for more than 20 years. He has worked with some of the biggest names in jazz music, including the Frank Wess Sextet in the 1980s and saxophonist Walt Weiskopf from 1994 to 2003.

Through the years Snidero has led his own quintet and has also worked as a sideman for such jazz greats as pianists David Hazeltine, Maris Achneider and Mike LeDonne; saxophonist David Murray; trumpeters Joe Magnarelli, Jim Rotondi and Brian Lynch; trombonist Conrad Herwig; French horn player Tom Varner; and drummer Mel Lewis. He has also recorded and performed with jazz bassist Dave Holland and jazz drummer Jack DeJohnette.

Snidero began making jazz recordings in 1984, and, as a leader, has more than 20 albums on more than a half-dozen different record labels to his credit. As a sideman he has also appeared on more than two-dozen jazz albums. His most recent album release is "MD66" (Jim Snidero; Savant Records, 2016).

JIM STEPHANSON

Blues-jazz-rock singer-guitarist Jim Stephanson grew up in Fort Washington, Maryland and as a youth was introduced to music by his parents – his mother Mary was a talented singer, as was his father Charles Stephanson, who had sung and played piano on "The Cherry Blossom Hour" radio show on station WJSV back in the 1930s. As a youth, Stephanson was initially started on guitar by his brother. During his teen years at Friendly High School in the middle and late 1970s he would get together with his brother and cousin and play along to records by such performers as the Beatles, Bob Dylan, Mississippi John Hurt, and heavier bands like Cream and Led Zeppelin.

In the early 1980s Stephanson played out as a solo blues-folk performer at the Tuesday night "Hootenanny" shows at Billy Jacks, a night club on Livingston Road in Oxon Hill owned by Billy Windsor and Jack Jensen. It was there that he struck up a friendship with guitarist Danny Gatton, who performed at the club on Wednesday nights with his band the Drapes. Later in the 1980s Stephanson played guitar in a jazz-rockabilly band called the Chromatics.

In the early 1990s Stephanson formed his own blues band, Jimmy and the Blue Dogs, which is still together today. The group originally consisted of lead singer-guitarist Stephanson, singer-bassist Matt Busby, pianist Mindy Hopson and drummer Pat Perry. They appeared regularly at a number of Northern Virginia night clubs such as the JV's Restaurant (Falls Church), the Luna Park Grille (Arlington) and Whitey's Restaurant (Arlington).

In recent years Stephanson has performed with a variety of bands and performers including the Blue Rhythm Boys, Hillbilly Jazz (a C&W quartet rounded out by guitarist Chick Hall, Jr., bassist John Previti and drummer Brooks Tegler), the blues-jazz band the J Street Jumpers, the jazz band Swing Speak, and blues-jazz singer Marianna Previti. He also performs with his own blues outfit, the Jim Stephanson Trio and recently recorded and released his first solo album, "Say Go" (Jim Stephanson; Clang! Records, 2010).

JIMBO MANION

Singer-guitarist Jimbo Manion grew up in McLean, Virginia and in the late 1970s was a founding member of the McLean-based Southern rock band Jazzbo McMann (along with lead singer Phil McCormack). He went on to play in such great Southern rock bands as Molly Hatchet and the Roadducks. He has also fronted his own rock band, the Jimbo Manion Group.

JIMMY EARL

Bassist Jimmy Earl is considered to be one of the top players in the jazz world and is currently a member of Cleto and the Cletones, the house band for the ABC late-night television show "Jimmy Kimmel Live!" Earl was raised in Hyattsville, Maryland and during his years at Northwestern High School in the middle 1970s he played in the rock and roll band Lodestone and the jazz-rock band A Special Blend, both of which included guitarist Dan Hovey.

In the fall of 1975 Hovey moved to Boston, Massachusetts and studied bass guitar for a year at the Berklee School of Music. From 1976 to 1985 he played with several Boston-based jazz-R&B acts including the Force, Sapphire, Joyous, Uptown Strut, Tavares, and trumpeter Tiger Okoshi. In 1985 he took to the road and toured with a band called the Jazz Explosion, a group that went around the country and backed up such jazz artists as singer Phyllis Hyman, saxophonists Gato Barbieri and Stanley Turrentine, keyboardists George Duke and Lonnie Liston Smith, pianist Ramsey Lewis, and trumpeters Freddie Hubbard and Tom Browne.

Since that time Earl has performed and/or recorded with such jazz artists as the Mark Varney Project, Joe Sample and the Crusaders, singers Angela Bofill and Colin Hay, bassist Stanley Clarke, keyboardist Chick Corea, and many guitarists including Larry Carlton, Pat Metheny, Pino Daniele and Robben Ford. He has three solo albums to his credit: "Jimmy Earl" (Jimmy Earl; EFA Records, 1995); "Stratosphere" (Jimmy Earl; Pacific Time Entertainment Company, 1999); and "Renewing Disguises" (Jimmy Earl; Severn Records, 2014).

JIMMY ELLER AND HIS LITTLE PEOPLE

Singer-saxophonist Jimmy Eller was born in North Wilkesboro, North Carolina and moved to Alexandria, Virginia as a teenager in the 1950s, where he attended Mount Vernon High School. In 1961 he was called up on the stage at the Rendezvous in Washington, D.C. by singer Ronnie Brent and asked to sit in with the band. He subsequently put together his very first rock and roll band, which he called Jimmy Eller and His Little People. The initial lineup of this group consisted of lead singer-saxophonist Eller, guitarist Dave Cleveland, bassist Glen Ball, keyboardist Tom Winkler and drummer Eddie Sellers.

Basing out of Alexandria, Virginia and playing everything from Bill Haley and His Comets to Elvis Presley to Gene Vincent, Jimmy Eller and His Little People spent the 1960s working such Washington, D.C. night clubs as the Rocket Room, Benny's Rebel Room, the Keg, the Crazy Horse, the Rabbit's Foot and the Shelter Room. They also appeared in Maryland at the Turntable Lounge (Mt. Rainier) and in Virginia at the 1320 Club (Alexandria).

In the 1970s Eller put together a new band, Jimmy Eller and the Presidents Band, and worked such Washington, D.C. establishments as the Montage and the Cave. Eller had dozens of local musicians pass in and out of his bands throughout the years before moving to Florida in 1978. During its time his band released the single "The Way of the Brokenhearted" backed with "Bad Luck" (Jimmy Eller and His Little People; Vermillion Records, 1966).

JIMMY MARCOS

Drummer Jimmy Marcos grew up in Bowie, Maryland, where, as a teenager in the middle 1970s he played in such rock and roll bands as Nasty Habits and Crystal Tower. While attending Bowie High School in the late 1970s he drummed for the power trio Tight Fit and developed a reputation as one of the area's best drummers.

Tight Fit formed in Bowie in 1978 with its original lineup consisting of Marcos, lead singer-guitarist Bob Atkins and bassist John Clark, who left the band in 1980 and was replaced by Mark Smoot. The band mixed Southern rock with heavy rock and covered such bands as Lynyrd Skynyrd, the Outlaws, Deep Purple and the Who. They performed in

Maryland at the Turf Club (Laurel), the Big Dipper (Beltsville) and the Paragon (College Park); and in Virginia at Louie's Rock City (Bailey's Crossroads). Tight Fit disbanded in 1983, but would often reunite in the ensuing years.

Marcos next joined Frank Marino and Mahogany Rush in 1985 and remained with the band for a total of two years. In the late 1980s he drummed for the rock and roll bands Last Child in Florida and RH Factor in Los Angeles, California. Marcos returned to Bowie in 1988 and has since drummed for a world music band called Khanfusion, a blues group called Blues Attitudes, and has participated in many Tight Fit reunion performances.

Marcos is currently drumming for the Crayfish, a hard rocking Bowie-based quartet that also includes lead singer-guitarist Terry Glaze (formerly of Pantera), bassist Tommy Rodante (formerly of the Nowhere Men and Second Coming), and guitarist Bob Porambo. They can frequently be found performing at T.J. Elliott's Restaurant in Bowie, Maryland.

JIMMY NALLEY

Keyboardist Jimmy Nalley was born in Washington, D.C. and raised in Silver Spring, Maryland. He was introduced to music through his parents, Marv and Bee Nalley, who avidly listened to Big Band jazz, and his older brother Ron Hurley, who played saxophone in a local R&B band called the Prophets during the 1960s and early 1970s. Nalley took piano lessons and played clarinet in his elementary school band, bass clarinet in his junior high school band and orchestra, and piano in its dance band. Among his early musical influences were Elvis Presley, James Brown, Wilson Pickett, the Young Rascals, Jimmy Smith, Sam and Dave, and the Four Tops.

During his years at Montgomery Blair High School in the middle and late 1960s Nalley played organ on the local teen dance scene in several different groups including an R&B band called D and the Twilights, a rock and roll band called the Reflections, a pop-rock group called the Impalas, and a pop-R&B band called the Vanguards.

As the end of the decade was approaching, Nalley joined a local R&B band led by guitarist Bobby Manriquez called the Funk Fair, which was combined with another band called Nitty Gritty to become the Nitty Gritty Funk Fair. In 1968 and 1969 he also played organ in a psychedelic rock and roll band called Axis, which, at different points, included such guitarists as Bobby Manriquez and Dave Panzer. Next up, Nalley played electric piano in a Hyattsville-based rock and roll horn band called the Starlighters, which covered groups such as Chicago and Blood, Sweat and Tears.

In 1970 and 1971 Nalley played keyboards in the rock and roll group portion of the All-American Entertainment Troupe, an outfit that was formed by a faculty sponsor at American University in Washington, D.C. and performed at United States Naval bases in Rota, Spain and Kenitra, Morocco. In 1971 most of the players in this band performed as Hulsi Fledge at several local venues including the night club Emergency in Washington, D.C. and Ritchie Coliseum on the University of Maryland campus.

In August 1971 Nalley joined the rock and roll trio Three Easy Pieces, replacing John Clark and joining singer-guitarist Mike Pirko and drummer Stuart Ross. In this band he began singing lead and holding down bass lines as well. With his arrival the band hit the road and rounded out the year playing hotel lounges and night clubs in Johnstown, Pennsylvania and Tarrytown, New York. They then headed south and spent most of 1972 playing club dates in Georgia and throughout Florida. The threesome went on to maintain a long-standing house band gig at the Paul Mall Restaurant in the Georgetown neighborhood of Washington, D.C. and Nalley and Pirko and a variety of drummers kept the group going through 1977. At that point guitarist Glenn Alexander replaced Pirko (and was quickly supplanted by guitarist Tony Grasso), and the trio – still moving drummers in and out – shorted its name to the Pieces and continued on into 1982.

Nalley spent the early 1980s singing and playing keyboards in such local rock and roll bands as the JP New Band (which sometimes appeared in a duo format with Wayne Tomlinson on drums, and sometimes in a trio format with Tomlinson switching to guitar and Michael "Pokey" Walls on drums) and Demetri and the Bad Boys, a group led by former Flavor guitarist Demetri Callas. Other musical artists he has backed up onstage include R&B singer Mary Wells and C&W-pop singer Johnny Tillotson.

In 1983 Nalley left live music behind and went on to own and operate a Gaithersburg, Maryland-based recording studio called Studio New Entry and a real estate resort property management business called Vacation Villas International, which had offices in Gaithersburg, Maryland and Poinciana, Florida. In 1991 he completed his Bachelor of Arts in radio-television-film from the University of Maryland. Since 1993 he has owned and operated another business in Gaithersburg, DJ Karaoke Allstars, and currently serves as a disc jockey and karaoke host for weddings, parties and corporate events.

Nalley re-emerged on the local music scene when he was recruited to join the British Walkers when they opened for the Zombies at the Robert E. Parilla Performing Arts Center at Montgomery College Rockville Campus in Rockville, Maryland on Friday, September 10, 2010. On that evening he sang and played keyboards and key bass in a lineup that also included lead singer Bobbie Howard, guitarist David "Gabby" Gabeldon and drummer Steve Lacey.

He next sang and played keyboards in his own rock and roll group, the Jimmy Nalley Band, at "Fireworks at Fairgrounds Park," a holiday celebration with live entertainment staged by the city of Hagerstown, Maryland on Monday, July 4, 2016. For that performance, his band was completed by guitarist Bryant Linthicum, bassist Danny Goers and drummer Mike Valenti.

JIMMY NALLS

Blues rock guitarist Jimmy Nalls was raised in Arlington, Virginia and during his years at Washington-Lee High School in the late 1960s he played with such Northern Virginia rock and roll bands as the XKE's, the Morticians, the Malibus, Skin Flower, the Chessmen, Prince and the Paupers, Penny Arcade, and Ulysses.

Nalls moved to New York City in the early 1970s and performed and recorded with such artists as: blues rock singer Bonnie Bramlett; blues rock singer-keyboardist Greg Allman; blues-jazz singer-keyboardist Dr. John; folk singer Gary Shearston; folk singer-guitarist Paul Stookey; folk rock singer-guitarist Don McLean; and Southern rock and roll singer Alex Taylor.

In the middle 1970s Nalls was back in the nation's capital playing guitar for DC Dog, a blues rock band that regularly performed at Apple Pie in Georgetown and the Keg in Glover Park. From 1976 to 1980 he was a member of Sea Level, a Southern rock band from Macon, Georgia that released albums on several record labels including Capricorn, Arista and Polydor.

Nalls went on to work with a number of other bands and musicians including the Nighthawks, C&W singer Charly McClain, pop singer B.J. Thomas and C&W singer T. Graham Brown. As a solo artist, he has recorded and released one blues album, "Ain't No Stranger" (Jimmy Nalls; MRL Records, 1999).

JIMMY ROBINSON

Saxophonist Jimmy Robinson grew up in College Park, Maryland and during his years at High Point High School in the middle and late 1960s he played the local teen dance circuit in an R&B band called the Soul Revolution. In 1969 he joined the Nowhere Men and remained with that popular R&B-rock band into 1970. Later in the 1970s he performed with

Blood, Sweat & Tears and jazz trumpeter Miles Davis and spent years recording and performing with rock and roll singer-drummer Buddy Miles.

Robinson was a skilled sound engineer and worked on songs by scores of musicians including Jimi Hendrix and David Bowie. Jimmy Robinson passed away on Saturday, January 6, 2018 at the age of 67.

JIMMY THACKERY

Blues singer-guitarist Jimmy Thackery was born in Pittsburgh, Pennsylvania and raised in Washington, D.C. where he attended Edmund Burke School in the late 1960s and early 1970s. As a teenager in the late 1960s he played guitar in the Cold Duck Blues Band, which, in 1970, morphed into a group called the Crawling King Snake Blues Band.

In 1972 Thackery became an original member of the Nighthawks, joining lead singer-harmonicist Mark Wenner, bassist Don Monahan, keyboardist Bill Holland and drummer Larry Bolet. He remained a member of that popular blues band until 1987 and appears on more than 20 of their albums. From 1987 to 1991 Thackery played guitar in an R&B band called the Assassins, who were based in Washington, D.C., but often embarked on tours of the Eastern and Southern states.

In 1991 Jimmy Thackery and the Drivers were formed and they remain active to this day. To date this blues band has released more than 20 albums on several different labels including Blind Pig Records and Seymour Records.

JOE BAYLISS

Singer-keyboardist Joe Bayliss was raised in Woodbridge, Virginia and began a career as a professional musician during his teen years in the late 1950s. For several years he sang and played guitar for a rock and roll group called Don Sylvia and his Midnight Moving Groovers on the local military base officers' club circuit, as well as such local night clubs as the Cross Roads in Bladensburg, Maryland and the Rocket Room in Washington, D.C.

In 1964 Bayliss put together the first version of Little Joe and the Impossibles, a rock and roll band that would employ dozens of Washington, D.C. area musicians in the ensuing years. Although the band was originally based in Woodbridge, they tapped into the Washington, D.C. night club circuit and throughout the rest of the decade worked at such establishments as the Famous Restaurant, the Starlite Restaurant, the Ozarks Restaurant, Vinnie's Grill, the Hayloft, the Shelter Room and the 1023 Restaurant.

Bayliss would go on to work extensively in the late 1960s and early 1970s with country rock singer Danny Denver and blues rock guitarist Roy Buchanan. More recently Bayliss worked with such C&W bands as Larry Eubanks and the Country Sessions and Terence Sullivan and the Sundance Band. Joe Bayliss passed away on Friday, February 2, 2018 at the age of 74.

JOE GOULAIT

Singer-bassist Joe Goulait was born in Cambridgeshire, England, moved to Landover Hills, Maryland early in life, and took up guitar at age 12. While attending Landover Hills Elementary School in the late 1960s he played bass in rock and roll bands called the Lost Souls and the Heard on the local teen dance scene.

In the early 1970s while attending Parkdale High School, Goulait played in a rock and roll band called Wake. The group's original lineup consisted of Goulait singing and playing bass, along with singer-guitarist Steve Rosch, singer-guitarist Dave Long, keyboardist David Pucillo and drummer Charlie Johnson. Wake covered songs by such groups as the Beatles, the Buckinghams, Three Dog Night, Santana, Badfinger, Spirit, Cream, the Rolling Stones and Grand Funk Railroad. They primarily performed on the Prince George's

County, Maryland teen dance circuit, including events at Parkdale High School (Riverdale) and the Robert Goddard Teen Club (Robert Goddard Junior High School in Lanham).

While still attending Parkdale High School, Goulait had played standup bass in the school's folk group. There, he met singer-guitarist Wade Moroughan. Upon graduating from Parkdale the pair spent the early 1970s performing as a folk music duo called Martin's Wood at local coffee houses.

In 1974 Goulait and Moroughan met the members of a band called Friends of the Family at the Prince George's Community College Coffee House. Musicians shuffled in and out and the resulting group became Fireside, an outfit that billed its music as "AcidFolk" and "BlueRockGrass." Fireside's initial lineup consisted of singer-guitarist-mandolinist Terry Reynolds, singer-guitarist Wade Moroughan, guitarist-banjoist-harmonicist Rob Gibbs and singer-bassist Joe Goulait. Singer-drummer-pianist-flutist Phil Shimmel was added to the group in 1975.

During its three-year existence Fireside mainly based out of the Italian Gardens in College Park, Maryland. They also performed at many of the area's other top night clubs including Desperado's (Washington, D.C.), the Birchmere (Arlington) and the Red Fox Inn (Bethesda).

After a lengthy hiatus Goulait returned to the local music scene in 2006 as the bass player for a rock and roll band called the Janglebachs. This group covered bands such as the Beatles, the Byrds, the Hollies, Bob Dylan and others, and are still together today.

In addition, since 2010 Goulait has been playing bass in a country rock band called the McDuffees. For several years Goulait has been making music with singer-guitarist Bob Reilly in a number of different projects. He is currently working with him in a rock and roll quartet called the Reilly Goulait Band.

JOE HASSELVANDER

Heavy metal singer-drummer Joe Hasselvander was raised in Woodbridge, Virginia and in the late 1960s and early 1970s he played in such rock and roll bands as the Midnight Riders, Bulldog, Tyme, and Odessa. While attending Garfield High School in the middle 1970s he drummed for Ra Notra Sextet and then became one of the area's top rock and roll drummers when he joined a popular, Washington, D.C.-based rock and roll band called the Boyz. He also drummed for the R&B vocal group the Platters, and rock and roll bands such as Friday's Children and Truk.

Hasselvander worked a one-night gig at a night club called Route One South in Alexandria, Virginia with Leslie West in 1976. He went on to drum for such rock and roll bands as Pentagram, Overlord, Death Row, Savoy Brown, the Kim Simmonds Band, Devil Childe, Phantom Lord, Raven, Armageddon, Black Manta, Jack Starr's Guardian of the Flame, Cathedral, Blue Cheer, and his own heavy metal band, the Hounds of Hasselvander.

Hasselvander has appeared on more than 30 albums by a variety of bands and musical artists in his career, and has two solo albums to his credit: "Lady-Killer" (Joe Hasselvander; Pentagram Records, 1985) and "Road Kill" (Joe Hasselvander; Bad Posture Records, 2000). He has also recorded and released two albums with his own band, the Hounds of Hasselvander: "The Hounds of Hasselvander" (The Hounds of Hasselvander; Rock Saviour Records, 2007) and "The Ninth Hour" (The Hounds of Hasselvander; Black Widow Records, 2011).

JOE LAGANA

An unsung hero of the 1950s popular music scene in Washington, D.C., Joe Lagana is remembered by survivors of that era as one of the most talented singer-frontmen to ever grace the night clubs of the nation's capital. Lagana remains a mysterious figure in the annals of local music history, materializing from nowhere and then silently disappearing after a few exciting years on the local scene.

Lagana emerged in the early 1950s as a headlining pop music singer and by 1954 was being billed at some of the area's top establishments as a rock and roll singing sensation. Among the Washington, D.C. night clubs he headlined at from 1954 to 1957 were Club Kavakos, Jack Rowe's Restaurant, the Coral Room, Club Players, the Wayne Room and the Showboat Lounge. In Prince George's County, Maryland he appeared at the Cross Roads (Bladensburg), the Las Vegas Club (Coral Hills), the Rustic Cabin Restaurant (Colmar Manor) and Strick's Restaurant (Silver Hill).

It is known that Lagana recorded and released one local single, "Nadine" backed with "Teaspoon Full of Lovin'" (Joe Lagana; Colt 45 Records, 1960). Another single attributed to Lagana is "My Little Home Town Girl" backed with "The Beating of My Heart" (Joe Lagana; Chant Records, 1965), though details regarding the sessions behind this recording are still a mystery.

JOE MARTONE

Singer-keyboardist Joe Martone was born in Cheverly, Maryland and lived in various locations in Maryland and Virginia during his younger years. He came from a large family and his brothers introduced him to British Invasion bands such as the Beatles, the Kinks and the Yardbirds during the 1960s, while his father was an avid listener of C&W music. He started playing guitar at age seven and at age 12 he began playing piano, primarily teaching himself to play both instruments. While living in College Park, Maryland and attending Beltsville Junior High School in the late 1960s he played guitar in a teen rock and roll band called the Jaguars that covered groups like the Animals and Monkees.

In the middle 1970s, after moving to Greenbelt, Maryland, Martone attended Parkdale High School. During those years he mainly jammed with friends at parties and in basement sessions. In 1974 he joined a Greenbelt-based heavy rock and roll trio called Menagerie, which consisted of Martone handling vocals and guitar, singer-bassist Kevin Grady and drummer John Novik. The group covered such bands as the Who, the Yardbirds, and the Kinks, and also played a number of Grady-penned original compositions that bordered on what would become punk rock. Menagerie performed in Maryland at the Holy Redeemer Parish Teen Club (College Park), the St. Hugh's Teen Club (Greenbelt), the Ridge Road Center (Greenbelt) and Kava (the name given to the Greenbelt Teen Club dances that were held inside the Greenbelt Youth Center). The band broke up in 1976.

Martone then played keyboards in a number of area rock and roll bands including Charlie Haley and the Avenue Boys in the late 1970s, the M & Ms in the early 1980s, the Smith-Tucker Band from the early 1980s to the early 1990s, and the Hurricanes throughout the middle and late 1990s.

Throughout the 1990s Martone also toured and played live revue shows with a number of R&B acts up and down the Atlantic Coast including the Coasters, the Drifters, the Platters, the Marvelettes, the Shangri-Las, the Chantels, the Soul Survivors, Pookie Hudson and the Spaniels, Harold Melvin's Blue Notes and singer-guitarist Chuck Berry.

In 2001 the Joe Martone Trio emerged, with the singer-pianist being joined by bassist Rick Tremble and drummer Karl Franklin. This group primarily performed blues and jazz selections at night clubs and concert halls across Maryland's Eastern Shore. Since 2010 Joe Martone has been a one-man blues-jazz show, singing and playing piano in Maryland at the Maryland Live! Casino (Hanover) and the Charles Street Brassiere (Solomons).

JOE RAY REALITE

Singer-guitarist-keyboardist-performance artist Joe Ray Realité, according to his promo materials, plays "hints of rockabilly, electronically tinged rock; Link Wray to Hasil Adkins to David Bowie and David Byrne" and "considers his recording software to be his main interest and digits streaming through the ether his main performance outlet; hopes to infect lovers of rock with his guitar-driven, lyrically engaging musical virus; employs a variety of styles to tell his tales of connection, conflict and hope of resolution." In reality, Joe Ray Realité is the other-world musical persona of Gregory Snook, a musician and graphic artist currently based in Arlington, Virginia.

Snook was born and raised in Lewistown, Pennsylvania where he took piano lessons as a youth and started on guitar at age 14 just as Beatlemania became infected with psychedelia. During his years at Lewistown Granville High School in the late 1960s and early 1970s he played guitar in rock and roll band called Sound Projection that covered everything from the Rolling Stones to the Amboy Dukes to Wilson Pickett. He graduated from the University of Pittsburgh with a Bachelor of Science in psychology and during his college years returned to Lewistown during the summers where he played in a rock and roll band called Pursuit of Happiness.

Visitations to the nation's capital in the 1970s led to a relocation to Rockville, Maryland in 1980, and a later move to Alexandria, Virginia in 1987. Snook spent much of that decade hanging out at such Washington, D.C. night clubs as 15 Minutes, Poseurs, Nightclub 9:30, D.C. Space, the Cellar Door and the Bayou. In his private time he experimented with guitars and synthesizers, pieced together fragments of songs, and created and recorded experimental soundscapes.

In the 1990s Snook joined forces with Washington, D.C. female performance artist-poet Dee Snyder and backed her on guitar while she took the stage and churned it out at such city venues as 15 Minutes, Perry's Restaurant and District of Columbia Arts Center (DCAC). At these happenings he would play experimental guitar background music – metal, crunchy, sometimes-distorted, sometimes-melodic – while Snyder wailed away to bohemian crowds. Throughout the decade he also performed with his own hard-to-define rock band, Waking the Dead, a group that employed a succession of different musicans and gave performances at favored Washington, D.C. spots such as 15 Minutes and District of Columbia Arts Center.

In the 2000s Snook resumed recording, this time utilizing computer software and multi-track systems. His work manifested in the emergence of singer-guitarist-keyboardist Joe Ray Realité, a rather mysterious Arlington-based musical artist who seamlessly weaves through both cyberspace and the real world, offering intriguing guitar-laden songs culled from personal thoughts, experiences and sojourns. Thus far, Joe Ray Realité has two albums to his credit: "State of the World" (Joe Ray Realité; Mutant Ray Records, 2006); and "Carnival Romance" (Joe Ray Realité; Mutant Ray Records, 2014).

JOE ROUNDTREE

Singer Joe Roundtree was born in Washington, DC and raised in Brentwood, Maryland. At the age of 12 in 1967 he saw Lawrence and the Arabians perform in a "Battle of the Bands" event at Prince George's Plaza in Hyattsville, Maryland. From that event he was inspired to play the organ, with friends showing him basic chords. He became a fan of Motown and frequently listened to the music of such groups as the Temptations and the Four Tops.

While attending eighth grade at Mt. Rainier Junior High School (the 1968-1969 school year) Roundtree played keyboards in a blue-eyed soul band called Free Country that played local teen dances and parties and covered bands like the Grass Roots and the

Young Rascals. He then spent his ninth grade year in the band Burgundy Sunset, which concentrated more on current pop and rock and roll songs and played local teen dances at the Brentwood Teen Club and the Edmonston Teen Club.

In the early 1970s, while a student at Northwestern High School in Hyattsville, Roundtree saw the Nowhere Men perform at the Mt. Rainier Teen Club, and, inspired by their trio of lead vocalists (Charlie Taylor, Don Halcombe and Billy Vabolis), decided to become a lead singer. During his high school years he sang lead in an R&B band called the Soul Syndicate that mainly worked private parties and fraternity events at the University of Maryland. In the early 1970s he was also the lead singer for a rock and roll band called Early Morning, another outfit that worked the local teen dance scene.

From the late 1970s to the late 1980s Roundtree was the lead singer in a Silver Spring-based wedding band called Odyssey. He followed that up with a 20-year run with Free Spirit, a Bethesda-based wedding band that offered everything from Top 40 rock and roll to pop standards. From 2007 to 2012 he handled lead vocals in a Rockville-based R&B-rock band called Off the Record, a group that covered popular horn bands such as Chicago, Tower of Power, and Blood, Sweat and Tears.

Since 2012 Roundtree has been the lead singer of the Nowhere Men, who currently perform at the Rod N' Reel Restaurant in Chesapeake Beach, Maryland and local events like the annual Greenbelt Labor Day Festival.

JOE STANLEY

Renowned saxophone player Joe Stanley was born in Washington, D.C., raised in Bladensburg, Maryland, and, after graduating from Bladensburg High School in the middle 1950s, put together a series of rock and roll bands with trombonist Robie Robinson. These combos worked under such names as Joe Stanley and His Building Rockers, Joe Stanley and the Sophistikats, and the Joe Stanley Combo, and appeared in Maryland at American Legions, VFWs, and night clubs such as Chubby's Restaurant and Bar (Seat Pleasant), Club LaConga (College Park) and the Wheel Bar (Colmar Manor).

In December 1956 Stanley and Robinson joined forces with a quartet called the Rhythm Rockets and called their new rock and roll group the Saxtons. They first played out in Washington, D.C. at such night clubs as the Moulin Rouge and the Parkside Café and made several appearances on "The Milt Grant Show." Stanley kept the Saxtons going, with dozens of different musicians passing through its ranks, for more than 30 years.

In the late 1950s Stanley began freelancing around the nation's capital and in the ensuing decades worked with some of the finest local and national C&W, R&B and rock and roll musicians in the business. He performed with Link Wray and His Ray Men at Vinnie's Grill; Charlie Daniels and the Jaguars at the Dixie Pig, the Rocket Room and the Turf Club; and worked a night club tour in New Jersey with C&W singer-guitarist Roy Clark. He played saxophone in an R&B outfit called the Rainbows, whose lead singer was Marvin Gaye, and when he was called upon to play in Dale Hawkins' rockabilly band at the Rocket Room in 1960, he recruited lead guitarist Roy Buchanan away from the group and brought him into the Saxtons when the engagement ended.

Stanley went on to perform and/or record with such musical artists as: blues singer Big Joe Turner; blues bands Big Joe and the Dynaflows, and the Big Four Combo; C&W singer Jimmy Dean; C&W band Heroes and Friends (featuring guitarist Chick Hall, Jr.); jazz saxophonist Sam Butera; multi-styled guitarist Danny Gatton; pop singers Bobby Darin, Bobby Rydell and Richie Kay; pop groups Dion and the Belmonts and the Ames Brothers; rock and roll singer Freddy Cannon; rock and roll bands the Bill Black Combo and the Naturals; rockabilly singer-bassist Billy Hancock; R&B singers Sam Cooke, Jackie Wilson, Lloyd Price and Don Covay; R&B singer-pianists Billy Stewart and Fats Domino; R&B

bands the Clovers, the Drifters, Little Anthony and the Imperials and the Red-Hot Swinging Johnsons; and innumerable others.

Stanley has two jazz-R&B albums to his credit, "King of the Honky-Tonk Sax" (Joe Stanley; Wildchild! Records, 1996), and the posthumously-released "Legend" (Joe Stanley; Eller Soul Records, 2015). Joe Stanley passed away on Sunday, January 7, 2007 at the age of 71.

JOE TASS

Known far and wide as "Crazy Joe," this guitarist was born in Alexandria, Virginia, and was raised in Takoma Park, Maryland. He moved to Hazel Park, Michigan as a teenager, finished high school there in the early 1960s, and returned to Takoma Park where he played guitar in a rock and roll band called the Runaways. He then returned to Michigan and in 1962 and 1963 played in such Detroit-based bands as Billy Lee and the Rivieras and the Chessmen.

Tass returned to the Washington, D.C. area in 1964 and for the rest of the decade played at almost every rock and roll night club in the nation's capital in a succession of bands including the Mount Pleasant Street Blues Band, Natty Bumpo, Ann Bradstreet's Band, the Pack, and the Souljures. He frequently backed up visiting performers, including a 1967 engagement at the Rogue on Bladensburg Road NE in Washington, D.C. where he played guitar for Jerry Lee Lewis. In 1969 Tass landed in San Francisco with a band called the Grapes of Wrath, which featured a female lead singer named Judy Jones. In 1970 he and Jones toured the Midwest together in a rock and roll band called the Lovin' Kind.

Tass moved to Colmar Manor, Maryland in the early 1970s and he and Judy Jones put together a new rock and roll group called Band of Thieves, which performed locally at the Godfather Restaurant in Washington, D.C., the Basin Street Lounge in Colmar Manor and the Cross Roads in Bladensburg. After a short tour of the Midwest, the group assumed house band duties at the Benedict Pier, a restaurant in the town of Benedict in Charles County, Maryland. At that time they also brought into the group a drummer from Canada named Jerry Mercer, who would go on to work with blues rock guitarist Roy Buchanan and the rock and roll band April Wine.

In 1973 Crazy Joe Tass and Judy Jones and the Rainbow City Rock Band emerged. They adopted a frenzied, high-energy style of hard rock and roll and an Alice Cooper-like stage act. After a short stay in Altoona, Pennsylvania they returned to the nation's capital and performed at the Basin Street Lounge and then in February 1974 moved over to the Back Alley Lounge of the Cross Roads. While at the Back Alley, Tass, who liked to spit flames as part of his performance, made local headlines one night by spilling some lighter fluid and accidentally setting himself on fire. He survived the incident, but his reputation for wild stage antics suddenly equaled his status as a blistering rock and roll guitarist.

Tass then played sporadically for several years, but resurfaced in the early 1980s in a rock and roll band called Cacophony that performed at Bambino's in Riverdale, Maryland. After another break in the action, he moved to Los Angeles, California and spent part of the early 1990s in a rock and roll group called the Los Angles Street Band, which then became the L.A. Toolz. He was last seen performing throughout 1992 at Carey's Pub in Hyattsville, Maryland in two different rock and roll bands, Rex Wilson and His New Thing and the Sin City Rhythm Section.

JOHN FAHEY

The renowned progressive folk guitarist John Fahey was raised in Takoma Park, Maryland and attended Northwestern High School in the late 1950s. Unlike most other young musicians in Prince George's County, Fahey never got involved with teen dance bands. Instead, he learned the instrument by trying to play along with the radio tunes of C&W performers like Hank Snow, Eddy Arnold, Bill Monroe, Hank Williams, Roy Acuff and others. During the warner months he would partake in informal acoustic guitar jam sessions on the outdoor grounds of nearby Coolidge High School in Washington, D.C.

Fahey went on to record and release more than 40 albums on a variety of record labels in his lifetime, including several for Takoma Records, an independent company he founded in 1959. In addition, more than a dozen compilations of his work and several tribute albums have been issued. Fahey frequently paid homage to his homeland by making reference to places and things in Prince George's County, Maryland in many of his song titles. He passed away on Thursday, February 22, 2001 at the age of 61.

JOHN GUERNSEY

While his brother Tom was playing rock and roll music with a band called the Reekers, John Guernsey was listening to his father's jazz record collection and learning the piano. Guernsey grew up in the town of Garrett Park in Montgomery County, Maryland and attended Walter Johnson High School in the middle 1960s. While he would sit in on occasion with the Reekers and play songs like "Louie, Louie" and "You Really Got Me," his first band experience during these years was with a jazz group called the Lost Souls who worked an engagement opposite the Smothers Brothers at the Brickskeller in Washington, D.C.

In the late 1960s Guernsey became a songwriter-keyboardist in a rock and roll band called Claude Jones, which became a favorite of the city's counterculture devotees. In the early and middle 1970s he led his own musical outfit, the John Guernsey Group, a quartet which was rounded out with three former members of Claude Jones – singer-guitarist Frannie Day, bassist Frank Sprague and drummer Reggie Brisbane. This outfit regularly performed in Washington, D.C. at night clubs such as Food For Thought and One Step Down; and in Maryland at the Psyche Delly (Bethesda).

Since the late 1970s Guernsey has mainly worked throughout the Washington, D.C. area as a solo artist or in small ensembles under the heading of the John Guernsey Group. Most recently he has served as the house pianist at the New Deal Café in Greenbelt, Maryland where he performs during the dinner hour every Friday and Saturday evening.

Guernsey's discography includes the following albums: "Sykesville" (Claude Jones; Sweet Breeze Records, 1971; five-song EP); "Twelve Songs by John Guernsey..." (John Guernsey/Mystery Band; Adelphi Records, 1976); "Rocketville" (John Guernsey; Subconscious Records, 1981); "Look the Other Way" (John Guernsey; Creative Records, 1984); "Sykesville" (Claude Jones; Sweet Breeze Records, 1993; LP); "Greatest Hits" (John Guernsey; Sweet Breeze Records, 2002); "The One Step" (John Guernsey; Sweet Breeze Records, 2004); "John Guernsey Meets the Beatles" (John Guernsey; Sweet Breeze Records, 2004); "Live at the New Deal Café" (John Guernsey Trio + One; Sweet Breeze Records, 2004); "Solo Piano (Volume One)" (John Guernsey; Sweet Breeze Records, 2005); "Solo Piano (Volume Two)" (John Guernsey; Sweet Breeze Records, 2007); "John Guernsey Group Meets the Beatles at the New Deal Café" (John Guernsey Group; Sweet Breeze Records, 2007); "Love at Last Sight" (John Guernsey; Sweet Breeze Records, 2008); "Dreams Gone By" (John Guernsey; Sweet Breeze Records, 2013); and "The Unusual Suspects: Music for the Younger Generation" (John Guernsey; Sweet Breeze Records, 2015).

His latest jazz instrumental offerings are the albums "Autumn Leaves" (John Guernsey Quartet; Sweet Breeze Records, 2015), which features a band lineup of pianist John Guernsey, guitarist Gantt Kushner, bassist Danny Griffin and drummer Gary Hacker; and

"Over the Rainbow – Solo Piano by John Guernsey" (John Guernsey; Sweet Breeze Records, 2017).

JOHN HERBERT

John Herbert, one of the region's top bass players, was raised in Southeast Washington, D.C. and as a teenager in the early 1960s moved to Hillcrest Heights in Prince George's County, Maryland. During his years at Bishop McNamara High School in the middle 1960s he played the local teen dance circuit as a guitarist in a rock and roll band called the Elites.

In 1963 Herbert joined a Hillcrest Heights-based rock and roll band called Herbie and the Originals, whose initial lineup consisted of Herbert on guitar, saxophonist Roger McDuffie, guitarist Dave McGinnis, bassist Harvey Kirschner and singer-drummer Herbie Bell. The group quickly graduated from playing local teen dances to working military base officers' clubs and Washington, D.C. night clubs such as the Shelter Room, the Starlite Restaurant, the Rocket Room and the Crazy Horse. They were also a popular attraction at Strick's Restaurant in Silver Hill, Maryland.

Numerous musicians passed through Herbie and the Originals, including bassist Jack Casady and trumpeter Gary McLean. In the middle 1960s this band backed up several major performers onstage at the Shelter Room and Herbert found himself playing guitar for such acts as the R&B group Little Anthony and the Imperials, R&B singer-pianist Fats Domino, pop singer Jimmy Clanton, and rock and roll singer-pianist Jerry Lee Lewis.

In the late 1960s Herbert switched to bass and joined a rock and roll band called Joe Banana and the Bunch. He performed with the group in Washington, D.C. at such night clubs as the Hayloft, Benny's Rebel Room and the Crazy Horse; and in Maryland at Rector's Restaurant (Marlow Heights) and the Senate Inn (Capitol Heights). During those years Herbert also worked with local R&B bands such as King Henry and the Knights and Little Willie and the Handjives, and rock and roll bands such as the Medallions and the Loved Ones.

Herbert then spent the early 1970s playing bass for the hard-rocking band Sun Country in Washington, D.C. at such night clubs as the Crazy Horse, the Montage and the Paul Mall Restaurant. Other pop-rock bands he played bass for during the decade were the Eye, Cool Breeze, Light Year, Phil Haynes and the Inner Circle, and the Jan Davis Group. He has also performed and recorded with a number of R&B artist including singer Gloria Gaynor and a vocal group called the Stylistics.

JOHN JENNINGS

A multi-instrumentalist who has worked in a variety of musical styles, John Jennings was born in Luray, Virginia and spent his teen years living in Arlington, Virginia. During his time in junior high school and at J.E.B. Stuart High School in nearby Falls Church in the late 1960s and early 1970s he played bass or guitar in a succession of Northern Virginia-based rock and roll bands including the Void, the Forbidden Minors, the Door Knockers, Space Meat, and Pentagram.

Later in the 1970s Jennings played in such rock and roll bands as Jimmy Russell and the Midnight Riders and the Sound Investment. He was then a member of Bill Holland and Rent's Due for two years, performing jazz, R&B, and rock and roll with them in Washington, D.C. at such night clubs as the Childe Harold and Harold's Rogue and Jar, and in Bethesda, Maryland at the Psyche Delly.

In the 1980s Jennings began a long association with C&W singer Mary Chapin Carpenter, serving as her guitarist, arranger and producer. He has also played on albums by a number of major C&W artists including singer-guitarists Kathy Mattea, Iris Dement and George Jones, and the folk music duo known as the Indigo Girls.

Jennings has five blues-folk solo albums to his credit: "Buddy" (John Jennings; Vanguard Records, 1997); "I Belong to You" (John Jennings; Vanguard Records, 1998); "It's All Good" (John Jennings; Impromptu Records, 2002); "Four" (John Jennings; Impromptu Records, 2006); and "More Noise from Nowhere" (John Jennings; Impromptu Records, 2007). John Jennings passed away on Friday, October 16, 2015 at the age of 61.

JOHN KOSLIN

Singer-bassist John Koslin was born in Johnstown, Pennsylvania and it was there that he first played accordion in dance bands before taking up the bass at age 20 in 1962. He moved to Glen Echo, Maryland in 1965 and joined a rock and roll band called the Superiors, which performed in Washington, D.C. at such night clubs as the Devonshire Grill and the Crazy Horse; in Maryland at the Red Fox Inn (Bethesda); and in Virginia at the 1320 Club (Alexandria) and the Fort Belvoir Officers' Club (Fairfax County). Other members to pass through the band included guitarist Danny Gatton, keyboardist Dick Heintze and singer-drummer Ron MacDonald. The Superiors disbanded in 1966.

Koslin played bass in several Washington, D.C. area rock and roll bands in the late 1960s with Gatton, Heintze and MacDonald including the Soul Mates and Take Five. In the early 1970s he played in a band called the East Coast Express, which also featured Danny Gatton, and he also handled lead vocals for a pop band called the Windjammers that regularly performed in Virginia at the Key Bridge Marriott (Arlington).

Koslin went on to serve as bassist for an area rock and roll band called the Personalities from 1972 to 1985. Since 1980 he has owned and operated a disc jockey service called JK Music Productions Inc. which is based out of Fairfax Station, Virginia.

JOHN MOLLOY

Drummer John "Thumper" Molloy lived in various locations around Prince George's County, Maryland as a youth including Kent Village, Landover Hills and Cheverly. His family ultimately moved back to Kent Village and during his years at Bladensburg High School in the middle 1960s he got together with a bunch of musicians from Cheverly with the intention of forming a Beatles-type band. Molloy started out as a singer, but after rounds of auditions that failed to produce a suitable drummer, he decided to give the skins a try. Entirely self-taught, he thus became the drummer for the Reachers, who went on to become a very popular band on the local teen dance circuit, and held down the house band position at the Corral in Georgetown for much of 1966.

During the Summer of Love in 1967 Molloy joined the Fallen Angels, one of the Washington, D.C. area's top psychedelic bands, who were especially noted for their performances at the Ambassador Theatre and recordings for Roulette Records. He remained with them through the end of the decade. After a break in the action, Molloy returned in 1971 and spent a year drumming for a rock and roll band called Sideshow, which performed in Washington, D.C. at such night clubs as the Paul Mall Restaurant, the Montage, My Mother's Palace, Fran O'Brien's Anthony House Restaurant and the Brickskeller. He spent most of 1972 working with the Swinglighters, a C&W band based in Dale City, Virginia, and in 1973 he drummed for another country music band called Straight from the Heart.

In 1977 Molloy moved to Frederick, Maryland, and, after an extended break from music, he played in a number of C&W bands in the early 1980s including Cross Country, West Wind, Sneaky Feelings, the Dusty Rhodes Band, and an oldies rock and roll group called

Backward Glance. In recent years he has participated in a number of Fallen Angels reunion performances.

JOHN MOLO

Drummer John Molo was born in Bethesda, Maryland and lived in Washington, D.C. before moving to Langley, Virginia as a teenager. During his years at Langley High School in the late 1960s and early 1970s he drummed for several local rock and roll bands including the Yorkshires. Molo is best known for being the drummer in the rock and roll band Bruce Hornsby and the Range from 1986 to 1990. After the Range disbanded he remained Hornsby's drummer until 2000.

Through the years Molo has also drummed for blues rock singer-guitarist Delaney Bramlett; the C&W trio Meisner, Swan and Rich (singer-bassist Randy Meisner, singer-keyboardist-guitarist Billy Swan and singer-keyboardist Charlie Rich, Jr.); the jazz band Modereko; jazz-rock trumpeter Willie Waldman; rock and roll bands Jemimah Puddleduck, the Other Ones and Phil Lesh and Friends; rock and roll singer-guitarists Paul Kelly, John Fogerty (formerly of Creedence Clearwater Revival), Keller Williams, David Nelson (formerly of the New Riders of the Purple Sage) and Mark Karan; and rock and roll singer-bassist Mike Watt.

JOHN PREVITI

John Previti grew up in Clinton, Maryland and while attending Surrattsville High School in the early 1970s he first played bass in the rock and roll band Butler's Orchard. In the ensuing years his interest in jazz grew and he spent time playing in a jazz band called Blue Horizon. In December 1976 he began playing bass for the Danny Gatton Band at the Crazy Horse in Georgetown, beginning an association with the legendary, play-everything guitarist that lasted until Gatton's untimely death in 1994.

Previti is a master of many different styles including blues, folk, C&W, jazz, R&B, rockabilly and rock and roll, and has played with some of the best musicians in the world. Besides the great Danny Gatton, the impressive list of musical artists he has performed and/or recorded with includes: blues guitarists Johnny Winter, Junior Watson, Jim Stephanson and Delbert McClinton; blues singer-pianist Jimmy McCracklin; blues-country-rock guitarist Arlen Roth; C&W singer-guitarists Dale Watson, Emmylou Harris and Chick Hall, Jr.; C&W steel guitarist Buddy Emmons; folk singer-guitarist-dulcimer player John McCutheon; jazz singer Jimmy "T99" Nelson; jazz guitarists Charlie Byrd, Herb Ellis, Lenny Breau, Rick Whitehead, Paul Wingo and Steve Abshire; jazz keyboardist Joey DeFrancesco; jazz clarinetist Allan Vache; jazz trumpeters Don Cheatham and Ed Pocler; jazz trombonist Bill Watrous; jazz drummers Barrett Deems, Brooks Tegler and Big Joe Maher; jazz-pop guitarist Les Paul; pop singer Paul Simon; R&B singer-pianist Floyd Dixon; rock and roll singer-guitarists Joe Walsh and Bill Kirchen; rock and roll singer-bassist Billy Hancock; rock and roll drummers Timm Biery and Gregg Bissonette; the folk-rock group Annette Wasilik and the Wonder Band; and his own jazz bands, the John Previti Mingus Monk Tribute and the John Previti Quartet.

Previti also has a solo jazz album to his credit, "Swinging Lullabies for my Rosetta" (John Previti Quartet; Mapleshade Records, 2003). For this project Previti was joined by guitarist Rick Whitehead, John Cocuzzi on piano and vibes, drummer Big Joe Maher and guest vocalist Marianna Previti.

JOHN VAN HORN

Guitarist John Van Horn grew up in Arlington, Virginia and put together the first version of a rock and roll band he called the Fender Benders in the late 1950s while attending

Washington and Lee High School. In 1965 a version of this band recorded and released the 45rpm single record "XKE" backed with "Drag Strip" (The Fender Benders; Vermillion Records, 1965). The band became a lifelong project for Van Horn, with a number of different musicians coming and going through the years.

In the early 1960s Van Horn became associated with Ray Vernon and Link Wray, and played rhythm guitar with Link Wray and His Ray Men in Washington, D.C. at Vinnie's Grill, the 1023 Restaurant and the Famous Restaurant.

After Link Wray left the area, Van Horn concentrated on a solo career and as a singer-guitarist recorded and released the album "Out Back Music" (John Van Horn; Mercury Records, 1972). His backup band at the time included bassist Richie Mitchell and drummer Lee Jeffries.

In the 1980s Van Horn often played guitar on live appearances in bands led by rock and roll drummer Mick Fleetwood. More recently he worked with a new Fender Benders lineup consisting of himself handling vocals and lead guitar, keyboardist-guitarist John Van Horn Jr., either Ed Cynar or Richie Mitchell on bass and drummer Pat Greenwood. The band has one album to its credit, "I've Got the Cure" (John Van Horn and the Fender Benders; Fender Bender Records, 1998).

THE JOHN WELLS DELEGATION

The John Wells Delegation was a difficult-to-label rock and roll band based in Great Falls, Virginia that mixed folk with rock in progressive fashion and enjoyed a 10-year run in the popular music scene of the nation's capital. The group, which mixed originals with covers of everything from Buck Owens to Little Richard to CSNY in art-rock fashion, formed in 1967 and consisted of guitarist-reed player John Wells, lead guitarist Tommy "Holly" Garber, bassist John Murtha and drummer Ben Mason. All four members contributed lead vocals and this lineup remained constant for the group's entire 10-year existence.

In the late 1960s the John Wells Delegation maintained house band duties at the Lancer Restaurant on Wisconsin Avenue in Bethesda, Maryland and then moved over to the La Boheme Restaurant on Arlington Boulevard in Falls Church, Virginia. They gradually took on a psychedelic edge and spent the 1970s working many of the more popular rock and roll establishments in Washington, D.C. including JamF, the Zodiac, the Act IV Supper Club, Apple Pie, the Corsican, the Reading Gaol, the Cellar Door, Babe's, and the Luau Hut.

From 1972 to 1977 the John Wells Delegation established Mr. Henry's Tenley Circle as its main home base and also worked regularly at Fat Howard's on Wisconsin Avenue NW. A highlight from this period was when they opened a concert for Poco and Dave Mason at the Baltimore Civic Center in Baltimore, Maryland on Tuesday, July 29, 1975. One of the last Washington, D.C. night clubs they appeared at in their final days in 1977 was Desperado's in Georgetown. The band also ventured to New York City on numerous occasions where they appeared at the Bitter End and Gerdes Folk City, and spent time recording a never-released album in Nashville, Tennessee.

During its time, the John Wells Delegation embarked on three recording projects that reached fruition. First they recorded the music for the NBC documentary "The Inside World of Outer Space" (NBC's American Rainbow; April 25, 1970), a 60-minute nationally televised special program designed for children that looked at American achievements in the realm of outer space and featured appearances by astronauts Charles H. (Pete) Conrad and Thomas Stafford, and Frederick C. Durant, Assistant Director of Aeronautics at the National Air & Space Museum.

Second, they recorded the soundtrack for the NBC documentary "Venice Be Damned" (NBC News Special; May 21, 1971), a 60-minute documentary narrated by Jose Ferrer that examined the reasons for the rapid environmental destruction of the city of Venice and how science and a national organization are trying to save the cultural heritage of the country.

Third, they recorded and released a straight-ahead rock and roll album, "One of These Days" (The John Wells Delegation; Sanctuary Records, 1975), which consisted entirely of original material.

After appearances at Desperado's in Georgetown in 1977, the John Wells Delegation dissolved, with Garber going on to establish a career as a solo artist, Mason going on to drum for the hard rocking band Primadonna, and Wells and Murtha relocating to Key West, Florida where they continued to play together in different bands.

JOHN WHIPPLE

Guitarist-bassist John Whipple was born in Washington, D.C. and raised in the Southeast quadrant of the city. As a pre-teen, while attending St. Francis Xavier Catholic School in the middle 1960s, he first played guitar in a rock and roll band called the Aces of Spade.

After the Riots of 1968 Whipple's family moved to Marlow Heights, Maryland. While attending St. John's College High School in the late 1960s and early 1970s he played the Southern Prince George's County teen dance scene in a band called Ulysses. He subsequently played in the rock and roll bands Truck, Scorpius, and Happy Jack.

In 1974 Whipple switched to bass and joined a local rock and roll band called Medullah, staying with them for over 20 years. He currently plays bass in a Southern Maryland-based classic rock and roll band called Four of a Kind.

JOHNNY CASTLE

Singer-bassist Johnny Castle was born in Albuquerque, New Mexico, graduated from Midway High School in Waco Texas, and, after an abbreviated stay at the University of Oklahoma, moved to Washington, D.C. in the fall of 1968. He played in a blues rock band called the Blues Idiom with former British Walkers guitarist Geoff Richardson before becoming a founding member of the band Crank, which during its 1969-1974 reign was considered to be one of the top rock and roll attractions in the nation's capital.

As one of the region's best all-purpose bass players, Castle has played with a variety of bands and musicians. Some of the musical artists he has performed and/or recorded with include: the bluegrass band IInd Generation (pronounced "Second Generation," this group featured banjoist Eddie Adcock); bluegrass singer-guitarists Liz Meyer and Mac Wiseman; bluegrass banjoist Jimmy Arnold; blues singer-guitarist John Lee Hooker; blues rock singer-guitarists Catfish Hodge and Elvin Bishop; C&W guitarist Joe Maphis; country rock groups the North Star Band and the Rosslyn Mountain Boys; R&B bands Spats and Tough Luck (featuring singer-harmonicist Lips Lackowitz); rockabilly bands Tex Rubinowitz and the Bad Boys, Switchblade, Bill Kirchen and Too Much Fun, and the Twangbangers; rock and roll singer Root Boy Slim; rock and roll band the Dynettes; and his own rock and roll band, Johnny Castle and the Hard Knights.

Castle is currently playing bass for the Nighthawks – the area's top blues band – and a rockabilly band called the Thrillbillys. Castle has one solo album to his credit, "Lifestyles of the Blitzed & Heinous" (Johnny Castle; Bloody Fingers Music, 1994).

JOHNNY HOPKINS

Guitarist Johnny Hopkins was born and raised in Washington, D.C. and developed into a master of both the C&W and rock and roll styles. While attending Coolidge High School in the middle 1950s he worked as an on-call house guitarist in Washington, D.C. at the Famous Restaurant and the Starlite Restaurant, and in Prince George's County, Maryland at Strick's Restaurant (Silver Hill), and the Village Barn (Morningside). In the early 1960s he was headlining as a solo C&W performer at the Ozarks Restaurant (Washington, D.C.).

Through the years Hopkins has toured and performed with such C&W musicians as singers Patsy Cline and Ronnie Dove; singer-guitarists Roy Clark, Dick Williams, Billy Grammer, Warner Mack, Buck Owens, Marvin Rainwater, George Jones and Johnny Dollar; and the C&W group the Compton Brothers (Bill and Harry). He also played throughout Canada with Bill Haley and His Comets on one of their final tours.

In the 1990s Hopkins mainly performed in the Washington, D.C. area with his C&W band J.C. and the Goodtimers at local American Legions, VFWs, and at a night club called El Rancho in Forestville, Maryland.

JOHNNY SEATON

Famed Elvis Presley impersonator Johnny Seaton was raised in Beltsville, Maryland and first started singing during his time at High Point High School in the middle and late 1970s. During those years his first band was a Top 40 rock and roll group called Fast Break, a Burtonsville-based outfit whose lineup initially consisted of Seaton handling vocals, guitarist Jim Jacobsen from Burtonsville, and three Silver Spring musicians – guitarist Jim Burras, bassist Mike Dameron and drummer Bill Bogus.

Fast Break played everything from Foghat and the Steve Miller Band to rockabilly classics and Elvis Presley covers, and first performed at a High Point High School Blue and Gold Talent Show. They proceeded to perform at University of Maryland fraternity parties and events, Prince George's County night clubs such as the Tin Dipper (Beltsville), the Paragon (College Park), the Bastille (College Park) and the Cross Roads (Bladensburg), and in Washington, D.C. at Columbia Station, Chances Are, and the Fancy Dancer. The band later added two female vocalists, Sharon Acres and Sharon Robey, and embarked on a 10-week Department of Defense-sponsored tour of Europe.

In the early 1980s Seaton spent time in Los Angeles, California, but returned to the Washington, D.C. area in 1981 and put together the Johnny Seaton Band, mainly concentrating on rockabilly covers. In 1982 his band consisted of himself as lead singer, guitarists Jay Monterose and Pete Flaotta, and two Fast Break holdovers in bassist Mike Dameron and drummer Bill Bogus. During this time the group performed at such Washington, D.C. night clubs as the Gentry, the Chancery, the Bayou, and the Wax Museum, as well as Remington's Restaurant in Beltsville, Maryland. Seaton's band endured several personnel changes in the 1980s and guitarists to pass through included Danny Gatton and Dave Chappell.

In 1988 Seaton relocated to Las Vegas, Nevada where he landed a starring role in a musical production entitled "Elvis: An American Musical" which was initially introduced that year at the Las Vegas Hilton. The show soon changed its name to "Elvis: A Musical Celebration" and evolved into a two-hour, 49-song, Elvis Presley tribute show with three Elvis singers. This high-tech, multi-media production played for several years in theatres, casinos and hotel ballrooms all over the United States and Canada.

From 1992 to 1997 Seaton had a prominent role in "Joseph and the Amazing Technicolor Dreamcoat," a two-act touring musical with music by Andrew Lloyd Webber and lyrics by Tim Rose that starred Donny Osmond as Joseph and Michael Fletcher as Jacob/Potiphar/Guru. In this production, Seaton was third-billed in the role of Pharaoh, an Elvis-like character. In the late 1990s Seaton was back in Las Vegas performing an Elvis Presley tribute entitled "The Johnny Seaton Show" at the MGM Grand Las Vegas Hotel and Casino.

More recently, Seaton has resettled in the Washington, D.C. area and performs as Johnny Seaton and Bad Behavior at local American Legions, festivals and night clubs. In addition to covering the songs of Elvis Presley, they perform the works of such musical artists as Johnny Cash, Conway Twitty, Tom Jones and Frank Sinatra. An array of top local musicians have worked with him in recent years including guitarists Chick Hall, Jr., Irvin Utz and Robert Fiester, and bassist Jan Zukowski. His current backup band is comprised of guitarist Bob Farris, bassist John Previti, keyboardist Jimi Simon and drummer Bill Bogus.

Johnny Seaton has two albums to his credit, "Uptown" (Johnny Seaton; Renegade Records, 1982), and "Reaction" (Johnny Seaton; Rounder Records, 1986).

JOHNNY TSAKANIKAS

Guitarist Johnny Tsakanikas grew up in Wheaton, Maryland, and began playing guitar as a teenager with Jimi Hendrix and Johnny Winter as major inspirational figures. While attending Albert Einstein High School in the late 1970s one of the local musicians he regularly jammed with was bassist Mark Nickens.

In the early 1980s Tsakanikas put together a power trio called Tsak, whose most popular lineup consisted of Nickens on bass, Michael Peck on drums, and Tsakanikas handling lead guitar and vocals. The band built strong followings at such Maryland night clubs as the Big Dipper (Beltsville), the Riverside Inn (Riverdale) and the Outside Inn (Rockville). Other musicians to pass through the band included drummers Mark Thompson and Kevin Morales.

In the early 1990s Tsakanikas moved to Los Angeles, California, assumed the stage name "Johnny Blaze," and played in a speed metal band called the Power Trio From Hell, which was rounded out by two other Washington, D.C. area musicians, singer-bassist Brian Fox and drummer Kevin Morales. The band stayed together long enough to release one major label album, "American Man" (The Power Trio From Hell; Reprise Records, 1993).

Tsakanikas returned to the Washington, D.C. area and for the remainder of the 1990s he worked with a number of bands and musicians including R&B singer-keyboardist Daryl Davis and the hard-rocking band Violet Says with bassist Mark Nickens and singer-drummer Kevin Morales. Violet Says also performed locally under Tsakanikas' new stage name, "Johnny Rushmore."

A highlight from this period was Johnny Rushmore's appearance at "Woodstock '99," a four-day, 110-act, large-scale music festival held from Thursday, July 22 to Sunday, July 25, 1999 on the grounds of the former Griffith Air Force Base in Rome, New York that attempted to emulate the original "Woodstock" festival of 1969. Johnny Rushmore performed on the "Emerging Artist Stage" on the festival's first day in front of an estimated audience of over 80,000.

Johnny Tsakanikas, as Johnny Rushmore, has one solo album to his credit, "Boogie Man" (Johnny Rushmore; PowerDog Records, 1998). Today, Johnny Rushmore fronts his own band and continues to perform throughout the Maryland-Virginia region.

JON CARROLL

Singer-keyboardist-guitarist Jon Carroll was born in Washington, D.C. and spent his early years in Fredericksburg, Virginia. In 1968 and 1969, while in the seventh and eighth grades at T. Benton Gale Junior High School in Fredericksburg, he played R&B and surf music in two teen bands, the Sound System, and the Blues Machine. At age 12 in 1969 he moved with his family to Washington, D.C. and six months later relocated to Alexandria, Virginia.

In 1970 during his freshman year at Bishop Ireton High School he formed a duo with classmate Mike Cotter called Sunshine, which he viewed as a type of Everly Brothers act playing at 78rpm. In Sunshine, both Cotter and Carroll sang and played guitar, and together they presented original material mixed with Grand Funk Railroad covers. Their home base was the Village Inn, a pizza parlor in Springfield, Virginia.

In 1971 Sunshine was observed by a woman named Sandy Jones, who told them her husband Bucky worked at the Cellar Door in Georgetown, and that they should perform their music at the night club's popular Sunday "Hootenanny" shows. Sunshine appeared at one of those events and was quickly signed up by a manager named Alan Cowell, who had them perform regularly at both the Cellar Door and a night club on Wisconsin NW called Fat Howard's.

After attending a Fat City show at the Cellar Door, Carroll and Cotter met Bill and Taffy Danoff and the four immediately became friends. Sunshine would frequently open local shows for Fat City, and the two musical outfits both appeared on a triple bill at the John F. Kennedy Center for the Performing Arts Concert Hall on Friday, May 26, 1972 that was headlined by comedian George Carlin.

In time Fat City became Bill and Taffy, and Sunshine became Cotter and Carroll. Carroll graduated from Bishop Ireton High School in June 1974 and that fall he left to attend the University of Miami in Coral Gables, Florida. While visiting home on his mid-semester break he worked as a backup musician for Bill and Taffy when they appeared as the opening act for Jackson Browne at DAR Constitution Hall on Sunday, October 27, 1974. This led to an offer from Bill and Taffy Danoff to join a vocal group they were putting together with singer Margot Chapman, formerly of the band Breakfast Again. A couple weeks later in November, Carroll accepted the offer and Starland Vocal Band was born.

Starland Vocal Band initially played local night clubs such as the Reading Gaol near Dupont Circle and the Cellar Door. During its six years together they recorded and released five albums, embarked on three national tours with John Denver, and headlined concerts and shows all over the country. Their hit single "Afternoon Delight" (Starland Vocal Band; Windsong Records, 1976) peaked at number one on Billboard's "Billboard Hot 100" popular music chart on Saturday, July 10, 1976.

In the 1980s and 1990s Carroll did studio work and performed with other bands and musicians. He played piano for C&W singer-guitarist Mary Chapin Carpenter. He also put his own four-piece pop-rock band together called Jon Carroll and Metro, which included guitarist John Jennings, bassist J.T. Brown and drummer Robbie Magruder. He also worked with C&W performers such as singer-guitarist Rodney Crowell, and the band known as the Dixie Chicks.

Carroll has recorded with a number of performing artists through the years and has three albums to his credit: "Love Returns" (Jon Carroll; Azalea City Recordings, 2007); "Live Returns" (Jon Carroll & Live Returns; Azalea City Recordings, 2008); and "Home & Away" (Jon Carroll; Cherry Lane Music, 2015). In recent years he has performed as a duo with his son, blues-folk singer-guitarist Ben Carroll. He is currently operating a private recording studio in Leesburg, Virginia called Ordinary World.

JONATHAN EDWARDS

Singer-guitarist Jonathan Edwards was born in Aitkin, Minnesota and raised in Alexandria, Virginia. He spent his high school years in the middle 1960s at Fishburne Military School in Waynesboro, Virginia. During that time he took up guitar and upon returning to the area on his breaks he would sing and play folk songs at the Blue Sparrow, a Washington, D.C. coffee house that had previously been the site of Coffee 'n' Confusion.

Edwards attended Ohio University in the late 1960s and played in the folk music band Sugar Creek for five years. In 1971 he went solo as a folk-pop singer-guitarist and scored with the hit single "Sunshine" (Jonathan Edwards; Capricorn Records, 1971), which peaked at number four on Billboard magazine's "Billboard Hot 100" pop music chart on Saturday, January 15, 1972.

Through the years Edwards has recorded more than 20 albums for more than a dozen different record labels including Capricorn, Atco, Warner Bros., and MCA.

JORGE STRUNZ

Jorge Strunz is a world-renowned jazz, flamenco and classical guitarist who has strong ties to the nation's capital and in the past has played in many popular rock and roll bands that graced this region. The son of a Foreign Service official, Strunz was born in Costa Rica and lived in many different countries around the world before his family settled in Arlington, Virginia in 1960. As a youth Strunz listened to the classical and Spanish music his parents played in the home, was turned on to Elvis Presley and the Everly Brothers by his peers, and had a friend show him some guitar chords.

In Northern Virginia Strunz attended Bishop Denis J. O'Connell High School and then Yorktown High School in the early 1960s. During his high school years he joined a folk music band called the Tokays. During that time he also began playing flamenco guitar as a solo performer at El Bodegon, a Spanish restaurant at 1637 R Street NW in Washington, D.C. After high school Strunz joined a folk music group called Joe Corey and the Bristol Singers who were the house band at the Brickskeller near Dupont Circle in Washington, D.C.

In 1964 Strunz went to Spain and attended the University of Barcelona for a year. He came back to the Washington, D.C. area in 1965 and rejoined with Joe Corey in a rock and roll band called the Seldom Scene, which performed British Invasion covers and also played regularly at the Brickskeller.

While performing with the Seldom Scene at the Brickskeller in 1966, Strunz was recruited by Tom Guernsey to take the guitar spot in the Hangmen, one of the area's most popular rock and roll groups. Strunz remained with the band into the spring of 1967. At that point members began leaving the band and the holdovers decided to continue on under a new name. The group then became Button and settled on a lineup consisting of lead singer Tony Taylor, lead guitarist Jorge Strunz, rhythm guitarist Allan Fowler, bassist John Cyr and drummer Bob Berberich. Button's first employment was at a Washington, D.C. night club called Nu-Mac's in Georgetown.

In the summer of 1967 Button moved to New York City where they soon splintered. Strunz and Taylor subsequently formed a new group called Graffiti. The original lineup of this psychedelic rock and roll band consisted of lead singer Tony Taylor, guitarist George Strunz, rhythm guitarist Jon St. John, bassist Steve Benderoth and drummer Richie Blakin. Graffiti played such New York City night clubs as the Electric Circus and Steve Paul's Scene. During its short existence, the group recorded and released one album, "Graffiti" (Graffiti; ABC Records, 1970).

In 1970 Strunz left Graffiti and moved to Baltimore, Maryland, where he played in a blues band called Aims Oak. Shortly thereafter he returned to the Washington, D.C. area and played in a blues rock band called Snake.

In 1971 Strunz joined a newly-formed jazz rock band called Spectrum, which included saxophonist Craig Thomas. A year after its formation Spectrum relocated to Los Angeles, California, but disbanded soon after its arrival. Strunz remained in Los Angeles and in the middle 1970s he joined the jazz rock band Caldera, which released a total of four albums: "Caldera" (Caldera; Capitol Records, 1976); "Sky Islands" (Caldera; Capitol Records, 1977); "Time and Chance" (Caldera; Capitol Records, 1978); and "Dreamer" (Caldera; Capitol Records, 1979).

In 1979 Strunz met fellow guitarist Ardeshir Farah and they formed the world jazz acoustic guitar duo Strunz & Farah. They have since released some 20 albums on such record labels as Ganesh, Milestone and Selva and are considered to be one of the top world music acts in the music industry today. Strunz also recently recorded and released a solo album, "Neotropical Nocturnes" (Jorge Strunz; Selva Records, 2010).

JORMA KAUKONEN

Jorma Kaukonen is a folk-blues-rock guitarist who spent part of his childhood living in Arlington, Virginia and his teen years in Washington, D.C. While attending Woodrow Wilson High School in the late 1950s he played guitar in the Triumphs, a rock and roll band that included guitarist-bassist Jack Casady and lead singer-drummer Ron MacDonald and performed on the local teen dance scene.

Kaukonen left for California in 1962 and fell in with the Bay Area's folk music circuit. He became a founding member of the rock and roll band Jefferson Airplane and in October 1965 invited his friend Jack Casady to join the band on bass guitar. They both remained with the group throughout its 1965-1972 existence.

Since 1969 Kaukonen and Casady have worked together in Hot Tuna, a blues rock band that is still recording and touring today. Through the years Kaukonen has released a total of 15 solo albums and several compilations of his work have been issued on a variety of record labels.

Kaukonen, as a member of Jefferson Airplane, was inducted into the Rock and Roll Hall of Fame in the "Performers" category on Wednesday, January 17, 1996.

THE KALIN TWINS

Herbert "Herb" Kalin and Harold "Hal" Kalin were born in Port Jervis, New York in 1934, began singing at school shows as part of an impromptu vocal group during their teens, and graduated from Port Jervis High School in 1952. Upon graduation Hal joined the United States Air Force while Herb relocated to Washington, D.C. in the summer of 1953 and began performing at a night club called Club Players at 5th and K Streets NW. Mainly covering Johnnie Ray songs, Herb first performed using his own name, but soon changed his stage moniker to Buddy Ladd.

In 1957 Buddy Ladd was joined by Hal Kalin and they continued on at Club Players as the Ladd Twins. The pair was then signed to Decca Records, eventually releasing more than a dozen singles for the label as the Kalin Twins. Their two biggest hit songs were: "When" (Kalin Twins; Decca Records, 1958), which peaked at number five on the Billboard magazine's "The Billboard Hot 100" music popularity pop records chart on Monday, August 4, 1958; and "Forget Me Not" (Kalin Twins; Decca Records, 1958), which peaked at number 12 on "The Billboard Hot 100" music popularity pop records chart on Monday, October 27, 1958.

The Kalin Twins toured the country from 1958 to 1961 in support of their Decca recordings. They then settled into the Washington, D.C. area night club scene, where from 1962 to 1967 they performed in the city at establishments such as the Rocket Room, Rand's Night Club, the Crazy Horse, the Rabbit's Foot, Benny's Rebel Room, the Skylark, and in Mt. Rainer, Maryland at Bass' Restaurant and Bar. The Kalin Twins continued to perform on a sporadic basis into the 1990s.

Hal Kalin passed away on Thursday, August 24, 2005 at the age of 71 and Herb Kalin passed away on Friday, July 21, 2006 at the age of 72. A 30-track compilation of the best of the Kalin Twins is available on compact disc – "When" (The Kalin Twins; Bear Family Records, 1992).

KANGAROO

Kangaroo was a popular, short-lived rock and roll quartet that performed in Washington, D.C. at such night clubs as the Peppermint Lounge and the Keg in 1967 and 1968. The group consisted of lead singer Barbara Keith, singer-bassist-keyboardist John Hall, guitarist Ted Spelios and drummer Norman D. "N.D." Smart III. During its brief existence the band released one album: "Kangaroo" (Kangaroo; MGM Records, 1968).

The individual members of Kangaroo had interesting backgrounds. Barbara Keith had previously been a popular singer-guitarist on the Greenwich Village folk scene. John Hall hailed from Baltimore, Maryland and had previously played in such Georgetown bands as the Wad, the Briars, the Chocolate Snowflake and the British Walkers. Ted Spelios had grown up in Vienna, Virginia and was a guitar prodigy, having played with the British Walkers as a teenager. N.D. Smart hailed from Dayton, Ohio and moved to New York City in 1966 where he met bassist-producer Felix Pappalardi and drummed for such rock and roll bands as the Remains and Bo Grumpus.

After Kangaroo disbanded in 1968, John Hall went on to release several solo albums and became a member of Orleans, which scored big with two radio hits "Dance With Me," which peaked at number six on Billboard magazine's "Billboard Hot 100" pop song chart on Saturday, October 18, 1975, and "You're Still the One," which reached number five on the "Billboard Hot 100" pop song chart on Saturday, October 23, 1976. Ted Spelios next joined the band Holy Moses, which recorded one hard-rocking album, "Holy Moses!!" (Holy Moses; RCA Records, 1971). N.D. Smart went on to drum on Leslie West's first solo album, "Mountain" (Leslie West; Windfall Records, 1969), and then became the original drummer for the band Mountain, joining West, Pappalardi and Steve Knight. He has drummed for a number of major acts in his career including Todd Rundgren and Gram Parsons. Barbara Keith next embarked on a solo career and today is still making music today as a member of the Stone Coyotes.

KEITH GRIMES

Guitarist Keith Grimes was born in Pittsburgh, Pennsylvania and mainly raised in Chevy Chase, Maryland. He began playing guitar at age 10, with his earliest musical influences being the Kingston Trio and the Beatles. As a teenager in the middle 1960s he became enamored with blues and R&B performers and began listening to Otis Redding, Sam and Dave, Aretha Franklin, B.B. King and Albert King.

In the late 1960s while attending Bethesda-Chevy Chase High School Grimes played guitar in an R&B band called the Midnight Blues. This group performed on the local teen dance scene, working venues such as the Wedge (Bethesda Youth Center). He spent 1968 and 1969 playing in a hard rock band called the Essence, which covered groups like Cream and the Jimi Hendrix Experience and often performed at the P Street Beach near Dupont Circle in Washington, D.C.

In the 1970s Grimes spent time in Baltimore, Maryland playing in a rock and roll band called Aux, attended the Berklee College of Music for a year, and played in several Washington, D.C. area bands including the C&W group the Yankee Rebels, the R&B band Bill Holland and Rent's Due, and a Top 40 outfit called New Censation that worked the East Coast hotel circuit. Grimes then spent the 1980s playing guitar for the R&B act Billy Price and the Keystone Rhythm Band and the blues band the Uptown Rhythm Kings.

From 1990 to 1996 Grimes was the lead guitarist for the popular blues-jazz singer Eva Cassidy. He appears on most of her recorded work including the highly acclaimed album "Live at Blues Alley" (Eva Cassidy; Blix Street Records, 1996). That decade also saw him work with a number of wedding bands in the Washington, D.C. area including Straight Up and Time Machine.

Through the years Grimes has also played guitar for such artists as blues singer Mary Shaver, blues-jazz singer-guitarist Esther Haynes, go go singer-guitarist Chuck Brown, the R&B band Soul Crackers, rock and roll drummer Mick Fleetwood and soft rock singer-guitarist-keyboardist-flutist Janine Davy.

Grimes has been a member of the wedding band Odyssey since 2010 and in 2015 he became the lead guitarist for the blues-pop-rock band Built For Comfort. He also plays guitar for the R&B-oriented Daryl Davis Band (with whom he backed up such blues artists as singer Nappy Brown and pianist Johnnie Johnson at the Bethesda Blues and Jazz Supper Club) and the rock and roll outfit Rick and the Rockers.

KEITH JOHN

Drummer Keith John grew up in Vienna, Virginia and during his time at James Madison High School in the late 1960s he played the local teen dance circuit in a rock and roll band called the Coachmen. He went on to drum in the 1970s for a variety of local pop, R&B and rock and roll bands and musicians including All of the Above, Starland Vocal Band, Evan Johns and the H-Bombs, singer-bassist Billy Hancock, multi-styled guitarist Danny Gatton, the Reasons Why and the Kids.

In 1981 John drummed for rock and roll singer Billy Idol on his first United States tour. He went on to drum for many other rock and roll acts in the 1980s including the Back Doors, Billy Vera and the Beaters, the Ventures, Buffalo Springfield, and blues singer-guitarist John Mayall.

In the 1990s he was drumming for Quaver, a hard-rocking band rounded out with Cherry People founders Doug and Chris Grimes and bassist Carl Jones.

KEN BRILEY

Saxophonist Ken Briley was born in Memphis, Tennessee and raised in Charles County, Maryland in the community of Fenwick. During his time at Lackey High School in the late 1950s he played in such rock and roll bands as the Blue Mooners and the Rhythm Makers.

In 1958 the Rhythm Makers began a two-year engagement as the house band at Guy's Place in Washington, D.C. In the early 1960s they mainly performed at two night clubs in the city, the Starlite Restaurant and the Shelter Room. In 1963 the Rhythm Makers changed its name to the Prodigals and worked at such night clubs as the Alpine Room, the Starlite Restaurant and Rand's Night Club. The Prodigals disbanded in 1965.

Briley spent the late 1960s playing saxophone in an R&B band called the Soul Syndrome that featured lead singer Steve Charles. They performed in Washington, D.C. at such area night clubs as the Starlite Restaurant, the Shelter Room and the Rocket Room; and in Maryland at the Hideaway (Waldorf) and the Senate Inn (Capitol Heights). When the 1960s ended, so did Briley's time as a full-time musician.

KEN FIESTER

Bassist Ken Fiester grew up in Bowie, Maryland and during his years at Bowie High School in the middle and late 1970s he played in a rock and roll band called Skyhawk, which performed at dances and shows in Bowie at Bowie High School, Allen Pond Park, the Belair Teen Club (Belair Junior High School) and the Samuel Ogle Teen Club (Samuel Ogle Junior High School).

Fiester spent much of the 1980s playing in such local rock and roll bands as Sorceress and Uncle Nasty, and a Baltimore-based hair band called Heartbreaker. Late in the decade he was recruited into the pop-rock group Method Actor, the core of which included, besides himself, lead vocalist Eva Cassidy, lead guitarist Robert Fiester, guitarist-keyboardist David

Christopher and drummer Jimmy Campbell. He played bass on their lone album, "Method Actor" (Method Actor; BLP Records, 1988).

In the 1990s Fiester played bass for a succession of rock and roll bands including Dreamer, She's Melting, and the Pallbearers. In 2000 he joined the Bad Weather Boyz and remained its bassist until 2012.

Recently Fiester has played in a variety of classic, modern and hard rock bands including High Test, Too Many Daves, the Brass Solution, Voyager, Speakeasy, and Spitfire. More recently he has subbed on bass for such groups as the Ron Hicks Band, Burn the House, Greydog, Destiny, Secret Addiction, Meridian One, Retro Deluxe, and the Grillbillies.

KIM KANE

Hard-rocking, psychedelic guitarist Kim Kane was born in Germany, and, as a result of his father's position with the United States Department of State, largely grew up in Europe and Asia. Kane spent his first two years of high school in Korea before his family relocated to Bethesda, Maryland in 1968 where he finished up at Walter Johnson High School.

While in Bethesda, Kane took two guitar lessons and in the process drove the teacher crazy, who requested he not come back for any further instructions. He was completely self-taught from that point on. In the late 1960s and early 1970s he regularly saw rock and roll groups perform at teen clubs and dances throughout Montgomery County, Maryland, with the band Grin becoming a particular favorite.

In 1975 Kane became a founding member of the Slickee Boys, the garage-psychedelic-hard rock band that today has legendary status in the Washington, D.C. area's music scene. Kane left the band in 1988.

Shortly after his Slickee Boys tenure ended, Kane joined Date Bait, a high-powered, garage-psycho-punk outfit that developed a devoted cult following during its 10-year run. Date Bait's original lineup consisted of lead vocalist Dan Bader, guitarist Kim Kane, guitarist Karl Straub, bassist Jeff Zang and drummer Brian D. Horrorwitz. Other musicians to pass through the band included guitarists John Stone and Vince Vigliotti, bassists Thomas Kane, Alex Schneider and Jonas Tavela, and drummers Bidjje Kavanaugh, Tim Scott and Doug Hoekstra.

KIM TSOY

Kim Tsoy was born on Seoul, Korea, and was raised in Washington, D.C. where he taught himself to sing and play guitar while attending John Phillip Sousa Junior High School in the late 1950s. At that time he played in his first band, an R&B group out of Bladensburg, Maryland called Starrs that worked local teen dances. He also sang with the Record Hoppers in the studio during their television appearances on "The Milt Grant Show," as well as performing with them at live shows at Glen Echo Park's Spanish Ballroom.

In 1959 Tsoy's family moved to Montgomery County, Maryland, residing in Chevy Chase before relocating to Silver Spring in 1960. In the early 1960s he attended Montgomery Blair High School and prepared for a career in professional music. In 1959 he began playing in a band called the Collegians at local parties, teen dances, and at the Village Barn in Morningside, Maryland. He next formed his own band, the Blazers, which became a featured attraction at record hops around the area promoted by WDON disc jockey Don Dillard.

In 1961 Tsoy became the guitarist for Barry Darvell and the Blazers, working with them on regional tours up and down the East Coast. He also played with the band on their local engagements at the Rocket Room in Washington, D.C. where they headlined on their own and also backed up visiting acts such as rock and roll singer-guitarist Del Shannon and pop singer-guitarist Brian Hyland.

In the early 1960s Tsoy also played guitar for a number of bands through the Jolly Joyce Agency in Philadelphia including Jeannie Dell and the Topics, a group that worked night clubs in Boston and New York City. Returning to the Washington, D.C. area, Tsoy began frequenting the Downtown night clubs such as the Rocket Room, the Parkside Café and Benny's Rebel Room, where he sat in with a plethora of rock and roll bands and made musical contacts.

In 1964 Tsoy put together his own group, Kim and the Esquires, and they performed as the house band at Benny's Rebel Room for more than two years. That particular quartet was comprised of Tsoy handling lead vocals and guitar, bassist Ron Widman, saxophonist Mike Sheer and drummer Gene Snyder. They played Top 40 hit songs and covered such acts as Tony Bennett, James Brown, the Temptations, the Beatles, the Rolling Stones, and Curtis Mayfield and the Impressions.

In June 1967 a new rock and roll group was formed, Kim Tsoy and the Sauce, and they assumed house band duties at the newly-opened Luau Hut, a restaurant owned and operated by Tsoy's family at 14 F Street NW in Downtown Washington, D.C. The initial lineup for this band consisted of Tsoy handling lead vocals and guitar, bassist Sam Creighton, keyboardist Malcolm Lukens, saxophonist Ronnie Williams and drummer Stan Sheltra. After a three-year stay, Tsoy moved forward with a new 13-piece jazz rock band called DRAGON that spent the early 1970s working at another one of his family's Luau Hut restaurants, this one at 1225 19th Street NW in Washington, D.C. During one engagement, DRAGON backed up a visiting Stan Getz.

Tsoy went on to establish himself as a major C&W singer-guitarist and spent years in Nashville, Tennessee where he performed locally in-concert and appeared at the Grand Ole Opry. Tsoy also recorded for Orbit Records, releasing the album "Pure Country" (Kim Tsoy; Orbit Records, 1989). He also scored with the single "I Need the Real Thing" (Kim Tsoy; Orbit Records, 1989), which went into the Top 10 of several different independent C&W music charts.

Other major hit singles Tsoy had on various independent and international C&W music charts were "I'll Be All Over You Tonight" backed with "The Sound of the Sun Going Down" (Kim Tsoy; Orbit Records, 1990), and "Happy For Your Sake" backed with "Now the Lonely Begins" (Kim Tsoy; Orbit Records, 1990).

Through the years Tsoy has performed so many musical tributes and concerts for the men and women of the United States Armed Forces he once had the American Flag flown over the Capitol building in his honor. Today Tsoy is still actively performing in Central Florida with his own oldies-classics pop-rock band, Kim and the Kadillacs.

KURT GIBBONS

Keyboardist Kurt Gibbons was raised in College Park, Maryland and as a teenager first played the teen dance scene in the middle 1960s in an R&B cover band called the Soul Revolution. He attended High Point High School, graduating in 1969, and during the late 1960s and into the early 1970s he handled lead vocals and keyboards for one of the area's most popular R&B-rock bands, the New Breed.

In 1971 Gibbons joined three fellow New Breed members – guitarist Bobby Manriquez, bassist Bobby Colie and drummer David Platshon – in a rock and roll group called Bobby and Friends which held down house band duties at Apple Pie in Georgetown. In 1973 Gibbons began a two-year stint as keyboardist for San Francisco-based blues rock singer and Capitol Recording artist Kathi McDonald. He toured the country in her band, which was rounded out by Manriquez on guitar, bassist Wornell Jones, saxophonist Boots Hughston and drummer Vince Santoro.

Gibbons is capable of performing in most any musical setting and through the years has performed with innumerable bands and musicians including: the C&W bands 301 Country and the Virginia Rangers; the pop-R&B band GTU; the pop-rock band the Show Biz Kids; the R&B-rock band Second Coming; the rock and roll band Sinbad; and blues singer-guitarist Memphis Gold. He is currently performing in the Washington, D.C. area in the multi-styled pop music band NightLife and also fronts his own R&B group, KGB (Kurt Gibbons Band).

LANCE QUINN

Guitarist Lance Quinn was born and raised in Pennsylvania and came to Washington, D.C. at the age of 18 in 1965 to attend Georgetown University. During the remainder of the 1960s and into the early 1970s he played the Georgetown and 14th Street NW night club scenes with a number of R&B and rock and roll bands and musicians including the Supreme Cosmic Benevolence, Willie and the Hand Jives, the Mount Pleasant Street Blues Band, Link Wray and His Ray Men, Goosby-Pegalo, singer-pianist Big Al Downing, singer-guitarist Robert Gordon and guitarists Roy Buchanan and Danny Gatton.

Through the years Quinn has played guitar for a number of national performing artists including: C&W singer Carlene Carter; jazz singer Marlene Shaw; jazz guitarist Jimmy Ponder; jazz keyboardists Jimmy McGriff and Webster Lewis; jazz saxophonist Gato Barbieri; jazz trumpeter Maynard Ferguson; jazz percussionist Mongo Santamaria; jazz singer-drummer Grady Tate; pop singers Grace Jones, Neil Sedaka, Carol Bayer Sager, Carol Douglas, Celi Bee and Engelbert Humperdinck; pop singer-keyboardist Franne Golde; pop singer-guitarist Linda Lewis; rock and roll singer Frankie Valli; rock and roll singer-guitarist Jess Roden; R&B singers Gloria Gaynor, Cissy Houston, Joe Simon and Ben E. King; the R&B bands Enchantment, and the New York City Band (featuring singer Luther Vandross); and the contemporary classical group the Kronos Quartet.

Quinn also established himself as one of the top producers in popular music, having produced albums by the Talking Heads, Nils Lofgren, Lita Ford, April Wine and Bon Jovi, among others.

LARRY BURNETT

Singer-guitarist Larry Burnett was born in Washington, D.C. and is known for being a founding member of the popular rock band Firefall. As a youth he moved about frequently and spent time living in Rhode Island, California and Silver Spring, Maryland. During his teen years in the middle 1960s he resided in Alexandria, Virginia, attended T.C. Williams High School, and played the teen dance circuit in a rock and roll band called the Broken Limbs.

After living for a few years in Ventura County, California, Burnett moved to Arlington, Virginia in 1970. He then began playing the Iguana Coffeehouse, a venue located in the basement of Luther Place Memorial Church in Washington, D.C. where he put together a folk music trio called the Heavy Metal Kids with Mark Greenhouse and a friend he brought over from California named George Hawkin. In the early 1970s he sang and played guitar at the Sunday "Hootenanny" shows at the Cellar Door in Georgetown, which led to opening act solo performances at the club for such headlining bands as Captain Beefheart and His Magic Band, Claude Jones, and Goose Creek Symphony.

In 1974 Burnett was introduced at the Cellar Door to country rock singer-guitarist Rick Roberts, the former Flying Burrito Brother who had been appearing there on occasion as a solo act. In August of that year he ventured to Boulder, Colorado at Roberts' request and

Firefall was formed, with their very first gig taking place at the Childe Harold back in Washington, D.C. Burnett stayed with the band until 1981 and appears on their first five albums.

Since that time Burnett has worked in the local restaurant industry and as a radio disc jockey at different stations in the Washington, D.C. area. On occasion he still gives live performances at area venues. He has two folk rock solo albums to his credit, "Confidence Game" (Larry Burnett; LB Records, 2004) and "Guitars & Vocals" (Larry Burnett w/ Don Chapman; 2009).

LARRY RICE

Singer/multi-instrumentalist Larry Rice (fiddle, mandolin, banjo, guitar, bass and ukulele) grew up in Annandale, Virginia, where, during his early teen years in the middle 1960s, he sang and played bass at parties and teen dances in such rock and roll bands as the Testaments of Time and Salt and Pepper. He then moved from the area and during his years at Rye Neck High School in Rye, New York during the late 1960s and early 1970s he played bass in a power rock trio called Andromeda.

Rice spent the 1970s in the Cleveland, Ohio area where he first sang and played bass in a C&W band called Skeeter Gulch before serving in a similar capacity for the country rock band Flatbush from 1974 to 1981 (in 1976, while with Flatbush, he began playing fiddle as well).

Rice returned to the Washington, D.C. area in the early 1980s but was absent from the local music scene until 2007, at which time he recorded and released the solo album "Little House" (Larry Rice; Larry Rice Music, 2007), a collection of fiddle-saturated country-folk songs which he sings and plays fiddle, guitar, banjo and bass.

In 2007 Rice became a part of the Big Cheese Band, a Falls Church, Virginia-based family bluegrass-folk trio rounded out by singer/multi-instrumentalists Lea Mae Rice Camarda and Julie Anne Greene (and sometimes Shannon Rice). The Big Cheese Band currently performs in Virginia at such night clubs as JV's Restaurant (Falls Church), the Old Brogue Irish Pub (Great Falls), Epicure Café (Fairfax) and Clare & Don's Beach Shack (Falls Church).

The Big Cheese Band has three albums to its credit: "Rumble in the Dairy Aisle: It's All Gouda" (The Big Cheese; The Big Cheese Music, 2009); "Live Culture" (The Big Cheese; Big Cheese Music, 2014); and "The Christmas Crocodile" (The Big Cheese Band; The Big Cheese Music, 2015).

LAWRENCE GREEN

Guitarist Lawrence Green was a big part of the flourishing early-1970s heavy rock and roll scene in Southern Prince George's County, Maryland. He was born and raised in Washington, D.C., spent much of his teen years living in Hillcrest Heights, Maryland, and during his years at Potomac High School in the early 1970s he played lead guitar for the hard-rocking bands Circus and Gideon.

From 1972 to 1976 Green was guitarist for Devil's Track, a band that worked its way from the local teen dance scene at places like Tucker Road Community Center to officers' clubs on local military bases and Washington, D.C. night clubs such as the Keg, My Mother's Place and the Bayou.

When Devil's Track disbanded Green concentrated on earning degrees in music, studying at Prince George's Community College, earning a Bachelor of Music in music performance from Brigham Young University in 1979, and a Master of Music in music from Arizona State University in 1985. He began teaching music at Brigham Young in 1982 and today is a senior lecturer in the Brigham Young University School of Music and coordinator of the school's guitar program.

Green has specialized in classical guitar and C&W music since the 1970s and has performed for years in a musical duo with his wife Robyn – today their family variety band in Utah is called Jerseystreet. He has played with a variety of bands and musicians through the years including a lead guitar position in 1988 for C&W singer and Capitol Records recording artist Chris LeDoux.

In 1997 Green became a member of the SurfNiks, a surf music band that included drummer Bruce Gary, formerly of the Knack, and released the album "One More Summer" (The SurfNiks; PST Music, 1997). Green also has two solo classical guitar albums to his credit, "Kingsfold" (Lawrence Green; Sanctus Records, 1996), and "At the River: Remembering Nauvoo" (Lawrence Green; Sanctus Records, 2000).

LEE DORMAN

Douglas Lee Dorman was born in St. Louis, Missouri and moved to Kensington, Maryland as a youth, where, during his years at Walter Johnson High School in the late 1950s and early 1960s he drummed for a rock and roll band on the Montgomery County teen dance circuit called the Dukes.

Shortly after Dorman finished high school his family relocated to California. In the middle 1960s he switched to bass and played for a variety of Top 40 cover bands in the San Diego area. He joined Iron Butterfly in Los Angeles in 1968 and remained the band's bassist through its various personnel changes until his health declined in late 2012. Lee Dorman passed away on Friday, December 21, 2012 at the age of 70.

LES HATLEY

A talented guitarist with roots in R&B and rock and roll, Les Hatley has performed with a wide assortment of local and nationally recognized bands and musical artists through the years, in addition to headlining as a solo artist at some of the Washington, D.C. area's top venues. Hatley grew up in Bethesda, Maryland and attended Bethesda-Chevy Chase High School in the middle 1960s. As a teenager he was influenced by musicians such as R&B guitarist Steve Cropper and folk singer-guitarist Leo Kottke, as well as local bands such as the Velours, the Newports, and various groups fronted by singer-guitarist Nils Lofgren.

In 1964 Hatley joined his first local rock and roll band, an instrumental trio called the Delmors, which included bassist Tom Carrico and drummer Bob Pavin, and spent time during his teen years watching bands perform at teen dances at the Bethesda Youth Center.

From 1965 to 1969 Hatley was a member of the Showmen, one of the Washington, D.C. area's top R&B bands. At one performance the Showmen appeared with the Fantastic Johnny C at the Wedge (Bethesda Youth Center) on Friday, March 29, 1968, performing a solo act show first, and then returning to the stage and backing up the visiting headliner. An evening highlight was the playing of Johnny C's hit single "Boogaloo Down Broadway" (The Fantastic Johnny C; Phil-L.A. of Soul Records, 1967), which had peaked at number seven on Billboard magazine's "Hot 100" popular music chart on Saturday, December 23, 1967.

Hatley spent the 1970s writing music and practicing guitar, and during the 1980s performed with the popular music wedding band Nite Life. In 1990 he became a founding member of an R&B band called the Blue Dog Band, which played around the nation's capital throughout the decade.

Other bands and musicians Hatley has performed and/or recorded with in recent times include: the contemporary gospel music bands Joyful Noise and Seneca; a blues rock band called the Shakers; a country-folk-pop duo with singer-guitarist Rick Crump called

Crumpled Hat (they also performed as Crump & Hatley); folk singer-guitarist Michelle Murray; the country-folk-pop group Only Restin'; the country-folk-pop-rock group the Second Wind Bandits; country-folk-pop singer-guitarist Don Bridges; former Brooklyn Bridge singer-keyboardist Jay Angoff; and the Ferrante-Hatley Show (a country-folk-pop duo with singer-guitarist Caroline Ferrante).

In the early 2000s Hatley worked several shows at the Outta the Way Café in Derwood, Maryland with Boston-based rocker Billy Bowman, a singer-guitarist who was named Billboard's "Best New Artist" in 2001.

In 2012 Hatley played guitar in a folk music duo with nationally recognized dulcimer player Dulcie Taylor. Together they appeared at numerous festivals and concerts including a performance at the Songwriters' Association of Washington Showcase at the John F. Kennedy Center for the Performing Arts Millennium Stage on Sunday, August 19, 2012.

Hatley is currently performing as a solo artist at venues around the Washington, D.C. area. He has two solo albums to his credit: "Second Chair" (Les Hatley; Second Chair Enterprises, 2009); and "Surge" (Les Hatley; Second Chair Enterprises, 2012).

LINWOOD TAYLOR

Singer-guitarist Linwood Taylor was born in Fort Lee, Virginia and raised in Lanham, Maryland. He began playing guitar at age 12 in the late 1960s and listened to a wide range of bands and musicians including the Jimi Hendrix Experience, the Animals, Booker T. and the M.G.s, Muddy Waters and the Beatles (later influences included Cream and Led Zeppelin).

While attending Archbishop Carroll High School in Washington, D.C. in the early 1970s Taylor played guitar in an R&B horn band called the Undercues that covered such groups as Mandrill, Curtis Mayfield, and Chicago. In the late 1970s he played in a number of Washington, D.C. area bands including a country rock group called the Patriots and a blues rock group called the Stags.

In 1980 Taylor began fronting his own blues rock group, the Linwood Taylor Band, serving as lead singer and guitarist. Early on he headlined in Washington, D.C. at such night clubs as the Gentry and Club Saba, and in Bethesda, Maryland at the Psyche Delly. He remains a featured attraction at the area's top venues to the present day. Through the years he has also performed throughout the United States and Europe and has employed many of the region's best blues musicians in various versions of his bands.

Taylor has performed onstage with innumerable bands and musicians including: blues singer-guitarists Albert Collins, Johnny Copeland, Coco Montoya, Luther Allison, Bernard Allison and Joe Louis Walker; blues guitarist Ronnie Earl; blues singer-guitarist-harmonicist Eddie Kirkland; blues singer-harmonica player Anthony "Swamp Dog" Clark; blues rock singer-guitarist Johnny Winter; country rock singer-keyboardist George "Commander Cody" Frayne IV; and R&B singer Sam Moore.

Currently the Linwood Taylor Band performs in a trio format with Taylor being joined by bassist Steve Wolf and drummer Joe Wells. He also performs with the blues groups Still Standing and the James Mabry Blues Band.

The Linwood Taylor Band has three albums to its credit: "Live at Colonial Seafood 1991" (Linwood Taylor Band; Linwood Taylor Band, 1991); "Take This and Stay Out of Trouble" (The Linwood Taylor Band; Linwood Taylor Band, 1993); and "Make Room for the Paying Customer" (Linwood Taylor Band; Mystery Media, 2000).

LIZ MEYER

Bluegrass singer-guitarist Liz Meyer was born in Washington, D.C. and raised in Bowie, Maryland. She entered the local music scene at the age of 18 in 1970 when she met banjoist-mandolinist J.B. Morrison at a coffee house called Sagitta in Takoma Park, Maryland. As a bluegrass-folk duo, they performed at Sagitta for six months and then moved their act to the Childe Harold in Washington, D.C. They soon became a quartet with the addition of bassist Ed Eastridge and fiddler Jeff Wisor.

Liz Meyer had several different names for her backup bands from 1972 to 1977. During those years they played bluegrass music in Washington, D.C. at such night clubs as the Childe Harold, the Chancery and Fat Howard's, and in College Park, Maryland at the Italian Gardens.

One of Meyer's most popular groups consisted of Meyer handling vocals and guitar, Morrison on banjo and mandolin, banjoist-steel guitarist Bob Siggins, bassist Chris Striker and drummer Seth Coit. For much of 1977 the outfit was billed as Liz Meyer and Friends, with the band consisting of Meyer, Morrison, Wisor, guitarist Danny Gatton, bassist Billy Hancock and drummer Dave Elliott.

In the late 1970s and early 1980s Meyer called her band Liz Meyer and the Midnight Flyers, with various musicians passing through the group. One of the more popular versions of the band consisted of Meyer, guitarist Chris Sonnenberg, steel guitarist Pete Finney, bassist Bob Coleman and drummer Dave Elliott (guitarist Tommy Lee Brooks later replaced Sonnenberg). This outfit performed in Washington, D.C. at such night clubs as the Childe Harold, Desperado's, Mr. Henry's Tenley Circle and Columbia Station; in Prince George's County, Maryland at Petrucci's (Laurel), Frankie and Freddie's (Hyattsville) and the Italian Gardens (College Park); and in Virginia at the Shed (Alexandria).

Meyer recorded and released several albums through the years on different independent record labels. Her first solo album was "One A Day" (Liz Meyer; Adelphi Records, 1982). She moved to the Netherlands in 1985 and went on to produce more than 30 albums for a variety of bluegrass and folk music artists including singer-guitarists David Olney and Jonathan Edwards. Liz Meyer passed away on Friday, August 26, 2011 at the age of 59.

LOUIE NEWMYER

Bassist Louie Newmyer works in many different styles of popular music. Growing up in Bethesda, Maryland, he learned his first guitar chords from neighborhood friend Rolf Hanson and joined his first band, the Night Raiders, at the age of 15 in 1965. In the late 1960s during his time at Walter Johnson High School he played bass in a popular Montgomery County rock and roll teen dance band called the Renegades that regularly performed at the North Bethesda Teen Club (Ayrlawn Recreation Center) and the Wedge (Bethesda Youth Center). Before the decade was out he played bass in a rock and roll band called Fleeboon, which performed at Sam's Place on Connecticut Avenue NW in Washington, D.C.

From 1969 to 1970 Newmyer played bass for the rock and roll band Stillroven, a quartet whose lineup also included lead singer-guitarist Steve Hubert, rhythm guitarist Alan Adkins and drummer John Patterson. Stillroven was a popular attraction at the night club Emergency in Georgetown where they headlined on their own and also opened for such national acts as the Kinks, the Bob Seger System, Cold Blood and Redbone. The band also performed at other night clubs in Washington, D.C. such as My Mother's Place, the Keg, and Apple Pie, and played concerts and events at the P Street Beach near Dupont Circle, and shows at colleges such as the University of Maryland and Catholic University.

After passing through the local rock group Little Willie and the Sweet Tarts, Newmyer played in the rock and roll band Itchy Brother from 1970 to 1972. This group's initial lineup was rounded out by lead singer-guitarist Phil Blum, pianist Guy Dorsey and drummer John Patterson. The band soon added reed player Mike Nash and trumpeter Randy Ottinger and played out in Washington, D.C. at the St. Alban's Episcopal Church Friday Coffeehouse, Emergency, Apple Pie, Nu-Mac's, Fort Reno Park and gatherings at the P Street Beach.

In 1972 Newmyer began a 13-year hiatus from playing music and concentrated on his family's restaurant business. He returned in 1985 and played in a succession of bands including the rock and roll group the Wilsons, and two blues-rock outfits, Step By Step and Visibly Shaken.

In 1991 Newmyer joined forces with rock and roll singer-guitarist Nils Lofgren and played bass with him on a European tour. In December 1991 while touring with Lofgren, he and the band performed onstage with Ringo Starr at a night club called Town and Country in London, England.

Since that time Newmyer has performed and/or recorded with: the C&W group the Hard-Core Troubadours; rockabilly acts such as the Peashooters, J.P. McDermott and Western Bop, the Collins Kids, the Old Line Skiffle Combo, and singer-guitarists Deke Dickerson, Bill Kirchen, and Marti Brom; and a number of rock and roll performers including guitarists Eric Ambel, Jeff "Skunk" Baxter and Tommy Keene.

Newmyer currently spends his time with four different musical outfits: the rockabilly band Jumpin' Jupiter, the garage rock band Jake Starr and the Delicious Fullness, a blues-jazz band called the Natty Beaux, and a rockabilly band called the Rock-A-Sonics.

LOVE CRY WANT

Love Cry Want was an avant-garde classical-jazz-rock instrumental trio of the late 1960s that performed in local night clubs, opened concerts for some of the major rock and roll bands that came to town, and mixed a myriad of musical styles in progressive fashion.

Love Cry Want consisted of three highly regarded musicians: guitarist Stephen J. Nicholas II, bassist Terry Plumeri and drummer-percussionist Michael Smith. In existence from 1968 to 1970, the band appeared in Washington, D.C. at jazz workshops conducted by the New Thing Art and Architecture Center at St. Margaret's Episcopal Church (1830 Connecticut Avenue NW); played night clubs such as the Showboat Lounge, Emergency and the Cellar Door; performed shows at the P Street Beach, the Corcoran Gallery of Art, the Washington Theater Club, and the Blessed Sacrament Teen Center; and opened concerts for a number of national acts including the Who at McDonough Gymnasium (Georgetown University) on Sunday, November 2, 1969.

In June 1970 guitarist Stephen J. Nicholas II parted ways with Plumeri and Smith and put together a new, five-man version of Love Cry Want that included contra bassist Rick Rozie, electric viola player Rusti Clark, saxophonist-clarinetist Joe Clark and drummer Leonard Cohen. This final version of the band broke up before the year was out.

Plumeri and Smith went on to perform and tour with R&B singer Roberta Flack from 1970 to 1973. Both would go on to achieve national recognition for their talents – Smith as a drummer for such great jazz musicians as Herbie Hancock, Adam Makowicz and Dave Liebman; and Plumeri as a bassist for innumerable jazz greats including Julian "Cannonball" Adderley, Frank Sinatra, and Quincy Jones, as well as for scoring for dozens of films and serving as conductor of the Moscow Philharmonic.

THE MAD HATTERS

The Mad Hatters were a British Invasion-influenced rock and roll band that hailed from Annapolis, Maryland and consisted of lead singer Dave Vittek, lead guitarist Tom Curley, bassist Allan Fowler and drummer Richard "Spider" Kumer. The Mad Hatters formed in 1964 and moved to the Georgetown neighborhood of Washington, D.C. in the summer of 1965 where they worked such popular night clubs as the Frog, Mac's Pipe and Drum Restaurant, and the Keg just up Wisconsin Avenue NW in the Glover Park neighborhood.

The Mad Hatters were noted for having a distinct garage band musical personality and a Rolling Stones sound. During their final months in the spring of 1967 Bobbie Howard (formerly of the British Walkers) was brought in to replace Vittek as lead singer. By the Summer of Love the Mad Hatters were no more.

During their time the Mad Hatters released two popular singles, "I Need Love" backed with "Blowin' in the Wind" (The Mad Hatters; Ascot Records, 1965) and "I'll Come Running" backed with "Hello Girl" (The Mad Hatters; Fontana Records, 1966).

THE MAD RIVER BLUES BAND

In April 1966 a psychedelic rock and roll group called the Mad River Blues Band formed at Antioch College in Yellow Springs, Ohio. They applied for a work-study program and were assigned to Washington, D.C. There, from June to September 1966, they served as the house band at the Blue Sparrow, a beatnik coffee house at 10th and K Streets NW that had formerly housed a legendary establishment called Coffee 'n' Confusion. During their time at the Blue Sparrow, the group performed a mix of blues, folk and psychedelic rock and roll.

The Mad River Blues Band's lineup at that time consisted of lead singer-bassist Lawrence Hammond, lead guitarist Dave Robinson, guitarist Greg Druian and drummer Greg Dewey (guitarist Tom Manning did not accompany the group to Washington, D.C.).

The band moved to Berkley, California in March 1967 and shortened its name to Mad River. They became a popular attraction in the Bay Area and signed with Capitol Records, releasing two albums on the label before disbanding in June 1969.

The full Mad River album discography reads as follows: "Mad River" (Mad River; Capitol Records, 1968); "Paradise Bar and Grill" (Mad River; Capitol Records, 1969); and "Jersey Sloo" (Mad River; Shagrat Records, 2011; previously unreleased material that was recorded in 1967 and 1968).

THE MAGIC REIGN

The Magic Reign formed in 1968 in Falls Church, Virginia with its original lineup consisting of lead singer-bassist Mike "The Fish" Buker and drummer William "Duke" Ayres (both former members of the Mosaic Virus), along with lead guitarist Mike Volk and keyboardist Bobby Winkler (both former members of the Chocolate Snowflake). Ayres was an early departure from the band, and the Magic Reign then became a sextet by adding three more musicians, bassist Picky Kelly, 12-string guitarist Robert "Chris" Christy and drummer Johnny Peters.

In 1969 Picky Kelly departed, and Christy was replaced by a guitarist named Steve Summers, who only stayed with the band for a short while. The remaining band members, Buker, Volk and Winkler, next replaced drummer Johnny Peters with Tommy Panella, who hailed from Anacostia in Southeast, Washington, D.C. and had previously played in the bands the Tomcats and the Quarrymen.

At one point a short-term member of the Magic Reign was guitarist Steve Croson, who hailed from Fairfax County, Virginia and had graduated from Herndon High School in 1968. Croson later moved to Nashville, Tennessee and performed and toured with some of the biggest names in C&W music including singers Louise Mandrell, Billy Joe Royal, Tanya Tucker, Dottie West and Jimmy C. Newman.

In the late 1960s the Magic Reign moved into a house on Jefferson Street in Arlington, Virginia, which later became the inspiration for a 45rpm single record they recorded and released to great acclaim. The band specialized in four-part harmonies and played both original compositions and covers of groups such as the Beatles, the Moody Blues, Paul

Revere and the Raiders, the Bee Gees, Moby Grape, Neil Young, Creedence Clearwater Revival and the Rolling Stones.

From 1968 to 1970 the Magic Reign played locally at a mix of teen dances and concerts, headlining on a regular basis in Virginia at the St. Rita Catholic Church Teen Club (Alexandria), the St. Mary Catholic Church Teen Club (Alexandria), John Calvin Presbyterian Church (Annandale), Bishop Ireton High School (Alexandria), Mount Vernon High School (Alexandria), Wakefield High School (Arlington), Northern Virginia Community College Alexandria Campus, the Vienna Community Center and the Falls Church Community Center; in Maryland at the Wheaton Youth Center; and in Southeast Washington, D.C. at the night club Some Place Else.

The Magic Reign participated in numerous local shows of interest including: participating in a concert show that was headlined by Vanilla Fudge and also included appearances by Ultimate Spinach, the British Walkers, Wild Honey, and the Curfews at the Alexandria Arena on Sunday, April 21, 1968; opening for the Fifth Dimension at DAR Constitution Hall in Washington, D.C. on Sunday, November 3, 1968; and appearing in a one-hour television special entitled "Sears Sound Revolution" that aired on WMAL TV-Channel 7 on Tuesday, August 19, 1969 that was hosted by Barry Richards and included performances by O.C. Smith, Iron Butterfly, CCR, Janis Joplin, Ten Years After, El Corals, Flavor, and the Impressions.

In 1970 the Magic Reign disbanded, only to be quickly reformed by promoter Bud Becker, who instructed drummer Tommy Panella to recruit a fresh set of musicians for a new band under the same name. This new version of the Magic Reign served as the house band at Some Place Else for several years, in addition to working other Washington, D.C. night clubs such as the Silver Dollar, the Keg and the Cellar Door. The band endured many personnel changes before dissolving in 1976.

During its time, the Magic Reign released two singles: "Pop Goes the Weasel" backed with "Mirrors" (The Magic Reign; Jamie Records, 1968); and "Jefferson Street" backed with "Charcoal Sketch" (The Magic Reign; Jamie Records, 1969).

MALCOLM LUKENS

Keyboardist Malcolm Lukens was born in Washington, D.C. and moved to Bethesda, Maryland as a teenager in the early 1960s. During his time at Walt Whitman High School in the middle 1960s he played in several teen dance rock and roll bands including the Wanderers. He also performed on occasion with the Reekers, a band led by Tom Guernsey that eventually morphed into the Hangmen.

In the late 1960s and early 1970s Lukens played keyboards for a number of rock and roll bands and musicians in the Washington, D.C. area including singer Bobbie Howard, singer Phil Flowers, guitarist Lance Quinn, Link Wray and His Ray Men, Kim Tsoy and the Sauce and the Joe Stanley Band.

From 1974 to 1977 Lukens performed and recorded with blues rock guitarist Roy Buchanan and played on three of his albums: "Live Stock" (Roy Buchanan; Polydor Records, 1975), "A Street Called Straight" (Roy Buchanan; Atlantic Records, 1976) and "Loading Zone" (Roy Buchanan; Atlantic Records, 1977).

In the 1980s Lukens worked in the Frederick, Maryland area with country-pop singer Michele Mauro and the rock and roll band Demetri Callas and the Flashbacks. He left Maryland for California in 1990 and today resides in Tarzana in Los Angeles County.

Through the years Lukens has played keyboards for some of the best popular music performing artists in the world, covering most every conceivable musical style. From the field of blues, he has worked with: singers Preston Smith, Janiva Magness and Maggie Parker Mayall; singer-harmonicists Kim Wilson and Mitch Kashmar; singer-harmonicist-guitarist Lazy Lester; guitarists Albert Lee, Cadillac Zack, Chris Cane, Kirk Fletcher, Robert "Bilbo" Walker Jr., Dave Melton, Jack Wargo, Alex Shultz and Debbie Davies; singer-guitarists Preston Shannon, Shawn Pittman, Phil Gates, Franck Goldwasser, Carlos Guitarios, Coco Montoya, Guitar Shorty, Junior Watson, Kal David, Arthur Adams, Chick Willis, Kenny Neal, Eugene "Hideaway" Bridges, Eddie C. Campbell and Steve Freund; singer-steel guitarist Sonny Rhodes; bassist Will Lee; singer-saxophonist Terry Hanck; the blues band the Moeller Brothers; blues rock singer-guitarists Wayne Baker Brooks and Kid Ramos; and the blues rock band Canned Heat.

Among the jazz musicians Lukens has played keyboards for are: guitarist Jeff Golub; bassists Stanley Clarke and Carlitos de Puerto; keyboardist Jan Hammer; drummer Billy Cobham; the duo known as the Brecker Brothers; the jazz band Bazooka; and jazz rock singer-guitarist Jimmy Vivino.

Lukens has also made music with a number of R&B greats including: singers Paul Indelicato and Billy Price; singer-guitarist Willie Chambers; guitarists Ray Gomez, Phil Upchurch and Steve Cropper; bassist Donald "Duck" Dunn; saxophonist Big Jay McNeely; and drummers Narada Michael Walden and Dave Garibaldi. Among the rock and roll performers he has worked with are singer Johnny Rivers, bassist Prescott Niles and the multi-styled guitarist Danny Gatton.

THE MARCH OF TIME

The March of Time was a versatile rock and roll band that was based in Oxon Hill, Maryland and existed from 1968 to 1971. The group originally consisted of four Oxon Hill High School students: lead singer-guitarist Dennis Parton, bassist John Parton (who was replaced early on by Rick Seal), electric pianist Alan Creveling (who was replaced in 1970 by Tony Chop) and drummer Davey Parton. Among the acts the March of Time covered were the Jimi Hendrix Experience, Buffalo Springfield, the Rolling Stones, the Doors, and Cream.

The March of Time was a popular attraction on the local teen dance scene and among the places in Maryland they performed at were the Tucker Road Community Center (Fort Washington), the Oxon Hill Free Stage (Oxon Hill), the Eugene Burroughs Teen Club (Eugene Burroughs Junior High School in Accokeek), the Surrattsville Senior Teen Club (Surrattsville High School in Clinton), the Oxon Hill Fire Department (Oxon Hill), the Allentown Road Volunteer Fire Department (Fort Washington), the Andrews Air Force Base Officers' Club (Prince George's County) and the Fort George G. Meade Officers' Club (Anne Arundel County). They also performed in Washington, D.C. at the Bolling Air Force Base Teen Club.

MARIANNA PREVITI

Singer Marianna Previti grew up in Silver Spring, Maryland. As a youth she sang and played the trumpet and learned pop standards of the 1930s and 1940s from her mother. As a teenager she held the first chair position as a trumpeter in the Montgomery County Concert Band and then the Montgomery County Youth Orchestra. She attended Springbrook High School in the early 1980s during which time she sang in the school's madrigals group, girl's chorus, and glee club, and often participated in jam session with a variety of local musicians.

After graduation Previti played trumpet in a band called Crazy Fingers, which performed at local college events and specialized in Little Feat and Grateful Dead covers. She then spent several years in the 1980s at St. Mary's College of Maryland (St. Mary's City) where she played in various instrumental and vocal groups.

In the early and middle 1990s Previti emerged as one of the area's top jazz singers, performing as a solo artist in Washington, D.C. at the Busara Restaurant; and in Virginia at the 219 Restaurant (Alexandria), Jacques (Arlington) and Fleetwood's (Alexandria).

During this period Previti also joined with singer-guitarists Ruthie Logsdon and Patty Reese in a C&W group called Plum Crazy, which performed in Washington, D.C. at D.C. Space (Washington, D.C.), McPherson Square (an open-air park area) and the Smithsonian Institution National Museum of Natural History; and in Maryland at Captain White's Seafood Restaurant (Silver Spring) and Tornado Alley (Wheaton).

Previti spent the late 1990s and early 2000s singing in the J Street Jumpers, a blues-jazz band whose lineup was rounded out by guitarist Rusty Bogart, bassist Adam Friedman, pianist Arthur Gerstein, saxophonists Charlie Hubel and Don Lerman, trumpeter Vince McCool, trombonist Steve Shaw and drummer Jeff Lodsun. The J Street Jumpers regularly appeared at Twist and Shout, a night club that operated inside the American Legion Fitzgerald-Cantrel Post 105 in Bethesda, Maryland.

Since 2004 Previti has been a lead singer for the Smokin' Polecats, a Silver Spring-based blues band that has played in Virginia at such night clubs as the Birchmere (Alexandria) and JV's Restaurant (Falls Church) and in Washington, D.C. at the Zoo Bar Café. They currently can be seen in Maryland at the New Deal Café (Greenbelt), Flanagan's Harp and Fiddle (Bethesda) and Hershey's Restaurant (Gaithersburg); and in Virginia at the Ice House Café (Herndon). The band's current lineup consists of either Previti or Mary Shaver on lead vocals, singer-guitarist Dave Sherman, singer-harmonicist Roger Edsall, bassist Leigh Olden and drummer Kevin Whisman.

In addition to all of her other musical accomplishments, Previti has been a general music teacher in Montgomery County, Maryland for more than 25 years.

MARK FRANCIS NICKENS

Guitarist-bassist Mark Francis Nickens was born in Los Angeles, California and moved to Washington, D.C. with his family as a youth. His father was a Duke Ellington fan and Nickens was influenced by Jimi Hendrix's performance in the movie "Monterey Pop" (Leacock-Pennebaker, 1968). At age 14 in 1974 he started taking lessons on acoustic guitar and began jamming with friends in basements and garages. That year he joined a local R&B band called Inner City Funk as a guitarist.

Nickens moved to Montgomery County, Maryland and spent the late 1970s living in Wheaton and Kensington and attending Albert Einstein High School. During those years one of the musicians he jammed with was blues rock guitarist Johnny Tsakanikas. In 1980 he became the bassist for a band based in Potomac, Maryland called the Blues Rockers, who played local parties and Maryland night clubs such as the Psyche Delly (Bethesda), the Varsity Grill Back Room (College Park) and the Paragon (College Park).

In 1980 Nickens joined the power trio known as Tsak, which was filled out by singer-guitarist Johnny Tsakanikas and drummer Michael Peck, who was later replaced by Mark Thompson. The band played heavy rock and roll and covered such artists as the Jimi Hendrix Experience, Frank Marino and Mahogany Rush, the Scorpions, Led Zeppelin, Van Halen and Y&T. Nickens remained with Tsak for more than two years during which time they performed in Maryland at such night clubs as the Big Dipper (Beltsville), the California Inn (Laurel), the Outside Inn (Rockville) and the Riverside Inn (Riverdale).

Nickens next joined an eight-piece R&B band called G-Force, which left the nation's capital and spent much of 1984 touring the West Coast and Big Sky country. In 1985 Nickens returned to the Washington, D.C. area and spent six months playing bass for R&B singer Phil Flowers.

In 1986 Nickens put together the first version of Skychurch, a Kensington, Maryland-based ambient music group that would endure numerous personnel changes and ultimately last for eight years. Skychurch first emerged as a trio, with Nickens handling guitar and vocals, Willard Morris playing bass and violin, and Mark Thompson playing drums. The band went through musical changes, playing jazz rock and straight rock and roll. They performed at local shows and concerts and worked such Washington, D.C. night clubs as the Hung Jury Pub, the Bayou, 15 Minutes and D.C. Space. In addition to working with Skychurch, Nickens became a street musician in 1987 and began busking on streets and Metro stations in Downtown Washington, D.C., an activity he engaged in for more than 20 years.

In the late 1990s Nickens joined the band Violet Says, whose original lineup consisted of lead singer Kevin Morales, guitarist Wayne Tomlinson, Nickens on bass, and drummer Michael Peck. Changes ensued and the band morphed into a trio consisting of guitarist Johnny Tsakanikas – who at this point was performing under the stage name Johnny Rushmore, Nickens and singer-drummer Kevin Morales. The group performed original heavy rock and roll and Jimi Hendrix covers, alternating between the band names Violet Says and Johnny Rushmore.

A high point for the band was its appearance – as Johnny Rushmore – at "Woodstock '99," a four-day, 110-act, large-scale music festival held from Thursday, July 22 to Sunday, July 25, 1999 on the grounds of the former Griffith Air Force Base in Rome, New York that attempted to emulate the original "Woodstock" festival of 1969. Johnny Rushmore performed on the "Emerging Artist Stage" on the festival's first day in front of an estimated audience of over 80,000.

Through the years Nickens has also performed onstage with such artists as blues singer-pianist Pinetop Perkins and keyboardist-Rock and Roll Hall of Fame inductee Tom Constanten, who had been a member of the Grateful Dead from 1968 to 1970. He has one solo space rock album to his credit, "MSAWBE" (Mark Francis Nickens; Highland Records, 2001).

MARK NOONE

Singer-bassist Mark Noone was born and raised in Washington, D.C. and was exposed to music at an early age through his family. His early influences ranged from singers such as Mario Lanza to bands like the Beatles and the Beach Boys. His parents bought him a Sears Silvertone acoustic guitar and at age 10 he joined a neighborhood rock and roll band called the Stingrays that performed at parties and informal gatherings. From there Noone took guitar lessons for a summer at the Chevy Chase Community Center, took up trumpet, and for several years played guitar in church services.

As a teenager in the late 1960s Noone played guitar in local coffee houses such as the St. Alban's Episcopal Church Friday Coffeehouse in Washington, D.C. In the early 1970s while attending Gonzaga College High School he played informally in various rock and roll pickup bands with a revolving cast of musicians that included guitarist Pedro Serra, rhythm guitarist Nick Buzzanca, bassist Kevin Connelly, and a number of different drummers including Ted Skowron, Doug Brennan and Mike Rinaldi.

In the middle 1970s Noone joined a reconstituted lineup of a pop-rock band called the Sound Investment, which at that time consisted of Noone on guitar and vocals, rhythm guitarist Allen Kelinsky, bassist Henry Arrington and drummer Dee Dee Hawkins. He next spent the 1975-76 school year at the Berklee College of Music in Boston, Massachusetts studying performance guitar, composition and arranging. After spending time in New Orleans, Louisiana, he returned to the nation's capital in early 1977 and joined a Top 40 pop-rock band, this one called the Crossroads, and began checking out local bands like Razz, the Slickee Boys, the Look and the Rage.

After responding to a band request in Unicorn Times, Noone auditioned with the Slickee Boys, a group that mixed punk, psychedelia and hard rock and roll. After several rehearsals he was selected as its new lead singer in the fall of 1978. When he came on board, the band consisted of Noone on lead vocals, guitarists Marshall Keith and Kim Kane, bassist Emery Olexa and drummer Dan Palenski.

The Slickee Boys quickly became one of the Washington's D.C.'s best and most beloved bands. They recorded albums, had videos aired on MTV and appeared at the area's most popular venues including the Psyche Delly in Bethesda, Maryland and several night clubs in Washington, D.C. including Desperado's, Friendship Station, the Bayou, and Nightclub 9:30, which they reportedly worked a total of 84 times in their existence, a venue record. Noone remained lead singer of the band through 1991, at which time the Slickee Boys began limiting their appearances to periodic shows that involved many of the musicians that had passed through the band.

In recent years Noone has sung and played bass for a variety of musical acts including the rock and roll bands the Wanktones and Frankie and the Actions, and the C&W groups Out Behind the Barn and Ruthie and the Wranglers. He currently has membership in a diverse lineup of rock and roll-based bands including the Rhodes Tavern Troubadours, the Hula Monsters, the Yachtsmen, and King Soul.

MARK STUTSO

Singer-drummer Mark Stutso was born in Welch, West Virginia and raised in nearby War, deep in the state's coal-mining country. His older brother received a snare drum as a gift and at a young age Stutso took an immediate interest. He started drumming in the second grade at War Elementary School and participated in their Toy Soldier Marching Band. His mother played boogie-woogie piano and Stutso would join her on the drums, with a favorite song becoming "St. Louis Blues" by W.C. Handy.

Stutso had a cousin who played guitar and at age 10 he joined him on drums and the pair performed instrumentals like "Wipe Out" (by the Surfaris) at the Town Tavern in War. At that time Stutso obtained his first full drum set from Sears and began making music in his basement with friends.

In 1968 while in the ninth grade at War Junior High School Stutso joined his first real band, a C&W group called Ron Dash and the Uniques, handling drums and lead vocals. He remained with that band into the early 1970s during his years at Big Creek High School. Stutso then drummed and sang with the rock and roll trio Tea & T Company in 1972 and 1973. He next performed with the rock and roll band Leather in 1974 and 1975, performing shows throughout West Virginia, Virginia and Kentucky.

In 1977 Stutso joined Tricks, a rock and roll band that was initially based in Blacksburg, Virginia and played at night clubs and concert halls up and down the East Coast and throughout the Midwest and South. It was with this band that Stutso first passed through Maryland, performing with the band at the Rabbit's Foot in Frederick. He remained with Tricks for seven years and appears on their one album "Turn a Trick" (Tricks; Loose Bid Music, 1981).

In 1984 Stutso joined the band Ruffryder, a Southern rock outfit led by former Black Oak Arkansas keyboardist Randy Ruff. He then rejoined Tricks and remained with them from 1986 to 1987. After leaving Tricks, Stutso and his wife moved to the Washington, D.C. area and he next joined a rock and roll band called the Smut Brothers, remaining with them from 1988 to 1989. The Smut Brothers performed in Washington, D.C. at the Grog and Tankard and the Roxy; in Maryland at the 8x10 (Baltimore); and in Virginia at Whitey's Restaurant (Arlington) and the Sunset Grille (Annandale).

In 1990 Stutso received a call from former Nighthawks singer-guitarist Jimmy Thackery, who wanted him to audition for the drummer position in his latest musical project. Stutso passed the test and became a member of Jimmy Thackery and the Drivers, which initially emerged as a trio consisting of Thackery, Stutso and bassist Wayne Burdette. He remained with Thackery and the band for 18 years, appearing on more than a dozen of their albums and extensively touring the United States and Canada.

In 2008 Stutso moved to Pittsburgh, Pennsylvania and drummed for such musicians as R&B singer Billy Price and rock and roll singer-guitarist Norman Nardini. During his stay there, he also recorded and released a solo blues album, "Rock My Soul" (Mark Stutso; Moondog Records, 2008).

In March 2010 Stutso got the call to replace longtime drummer Pete Ragusa in the popular Washington, D.C. area-based blues band the Nighthawks, joining frontman Mark Wenner, guitarist Paul Bell and bassist Johnny Castle. He is still with the band today.

MARK WENNER

Singer-harmonicist Mark Wenner was born in Washington, D.C. and raised in Chevy Chase, Maryland. Before he reached his teen years he became enamored with the blues and rock and roll and began collecting records and listening to such legendary performers as Jerry Lee Lewis, Carl Perkins, Chuck Berry and Little Richard. As a teen he ventured into Washington, D.C. and visited the Howard Theatre, where he witnessed the stars of the R&B Chitlin Circuit give live performances. He became a follower of legends such as James Brown, Ray Charles, Muddy Waters, Lightnin' Hopkins, Paul Butterfield and Charlie Musselwhite, among many others.

During his years at Bethesda-Chevy Chase High School in the middle 1960s Wenner began "noodling" on the blues harmonica. He attended Columbia University in New York City in the late 1960s and early 1970s, and during the summers he would return home to Chevy Chase and jam with friends like blues guitarist Bobby Radcliff in local night clubs. In one notable outing during the Summer of Love, he sang and blew the harp in a band with Radcliff called Hunk of Funk at an outdoor "Love-In" show at the P Street Beach off of Dupont Circle.

While a student at Columbia University, Wenner formed his first band, B-Town Slim and His Rhythm Review. He handled lead vocals for the group and led them through sets of classic blues and R&B songs at campus mixers and fraternity parties. Wenner graduated from Columbia University with a Bachelor of Arts in English in 1972. Upon the completion of his studies, he returned to the nation's capital.

In the spring of 1972, while on break from Columbia University, Wenner spent time participating in jam sessions with different musicians from the Washington, D.C. area and put together the first edition of the Nighthawks. The very first version of this now-legendary blues band consisted of Wenner on lead vocals and harmonica, guitarist Jimmy Thackery, bassist Don Monahan, keyboardist Bill Holland and drummer Larry Bolet. The group has experienced numerous changes in personnel through the years and to date has released more than 30 albums. The Nighthawks are still performing today with a lineup of Wenner, guitarist Paul Bell, bassist Johnny Castle and drummer Mark Stutso.

In addition to his enduring tenure with the Nighthawks, Wenner has performed and/or recorded with innumerable blues artists through the years including singers Juanita Williams, Cathy Jean, Kelly Bell and Janine Wilson; singer-guitarists Archie Edwards, Terry Garland, John Mooney, Carolyn Wonderland, Guitar Junior, Bob Margolin, Bobby Manriquez, Tom Principato, Charles "Big Daddy" Stallings, Ben Andrews, B.B. King, Muddy

Waters, Jimmy Rogers, Fenton Robinson, J.B. Hutto, Elvin Bishop, Bonnie Raitt, Otis Rush and John Lee Hooker; singer-guitarist-harmonicist John Hammond; singer-bassist Calvin Jones; singer-pianist Pinetop Perkins; singer-keyboardist Skeeter Brandon; singer-harmonicists James Cotton, John "Southside Johnny" Lyon and Jerry Portnoy; harmonicists Phil Wiggins and Big Walter Horton; and the bands the Thunderbirds, the Bel Airs, and the Blue Rider Trio.

Other musicians Wenner has worked with include folk singer-guitarist John McCutcheon; R&B saxophonist Ron Holloway; rock and roll singer-guitarists Nils Lofgren and Greg Kihn; Southern rock singer-keyboardist Greg Allman; and the rockabilly band Switchblade.

Wenner has also embarked on a number of side musical projects including his own band, Mark Wenner's Blues Warriors, whose current lineup is rounded out by singer-guitarist Clarence "The Bluesman" Turner, guitarist Robert Frahm, bassist Steve Wolf and drummer Mark Stutso.

Besides his voluminous recordings with the Nighthawks, Wenner's personal discography includes the albums "Fugitive" (Mark Wenner & Switchblade; Whitewall Records, 1984); "Nothin' But..." (Mark Wenner; Powerhouse Records, 1989); "Runs Good; Needs Paint" (Mark Wenner; Right on Rhythm, 2000); and "Mama Tried" (Mark Wenner and the Bel Airs; Right on Rhythm, 2002).

MARSHALL KEITH

Guitarist Marshall Keith spent part of his youth living in Rockville, Maryland before relocating to Washington, D.C. as a teenager in the middle 1960s. He passed through Paul Junior High School, Coolidge High School, Wilson High School, and studied for a year with the New Education Project. During these years he practiced guitar by tape recording music and playing along with it.

In the middle 1970s Keith was jamming with friends when he was introduced to fellow guitarist Kim Kane of Bethesda, Maryland. In late 1975 the two of them began putting together what would become the first version of the Slickee Boys, whose original five-person lineup was rounded out by lead singer Martha Hull, bassist Andy Von Brand and drummer Chris Rounds. The band was a high-powered outfit that combined garage rock and psychedelia with a punk attitude and striking stage attire. They experienced numerous personnel changes through the years and ultimately became one of the region's most popular and highly acclaimed rock and roll bands.

After the Slickee Boys folded in the late 1980s, Marshall worked with other groups into the early 1990s including the glam, wig-wearing rock and roll band the Upsetters and the rock and roll band Johnny Castle and the Hard Knights. After that time he mainly concentrated on his own private musical endeavors and individual recording projects. In the late 1990s he experimented with a customized baritone guitar and staged solo, one-man-band performances.

In 2006 Keith joined singer Martha Hull and drummer Bob Berberich in the hard-rocking trio Ottley! He remained with the band for more than three years, during which time they performed in Washington, D.C. at the Velvet Lounge and the 9:30 Club; and in Maryland at the Rodeo Restaurant (Silver Spring), Sangha (Takoma Park) and the Old Towne Tavern (Frederick).

More recently, Keith has concentrated on writing and recording his own music and has two solo albums to his credit: "Roadside Shrine" (Marshall Keith; Gakki Internazionale, 2010); and "On" (Marshall Keith; Gakki Internazionale, 2013).

MARTHA HULL

Singer Martha Hull grew up in Bethesda, Maryland and first performed as a fifth grader in 1964 in a folk group called Debbie and the Dawns. She went on to sing for a succession of local rock and roll bands in the 1970s including Lone Oak, the Slickee Boys, Afrika Korps, the Korps, and the D. Ceats.

In the 1980s Hull first recorded and released a rockabilly 45rpm single record, "Feelin' Right Tonight" backed with "Fujiyama Mama" (Martha Hull, backing by Tex Rubinowitz & the Bad Boys; Ripsaw Records, 1981). She then fronted her own band Martha Hull and the Steady Jobs and later went on to sing in the rock and roll band the Dynettes. From 2006 to 2009 she was the lead singer in the hard-rocking band Ottley!, a trio rounded out by guitarist Marshall Keith and drummer Bob Berberich.

MARTY FRIEDMAN

This renowned heavy metal guitarist hails from Laurel, Maryland, where he spent the late 1970s at Laurel High School as a member of the rock and roll band Deuce. He then spent the 1980s playing in such rock and roll bands as Vixen, Hawaii, and Cacophony. From February 1990 to December 1999 Friedman served as lead guitarist for Megadeth, touring the world and playing on six of their Capitol Records studio albums (which have sold more than 10 million units worldwide).

Through the years Friedman has recorded and released more than a dozen solo albums on such record labels as Shrapnel, MF Music, Avex Trax and Prosthetic that cover such guitar styles as instrumental rock, neo-classical, thrash and speed metal.

MARY BLANKEMEIER

Singer-pianist Mary Blankemeier was born in Chicago, Illinois and raised in Los Angeles, California. In the middle 1970s she relocated to Washington, D.C. to study nursing at Georgetown University. While in college she performed blues and folk music at the coffee house on campus. In addition, she also spent this time performing four nights per week at a nearby restaurant called Port O' Georgetown.

In the late 1970s and early 1980s Blankemeier had many local musicians pass through her bands. Longtime members of her group were guitarist Tom Principato and flutist Al Williams. Among her bassists were Steve Wolf, Ron Bolz and Steve Jacobs, and drummers she utilized included Shannon Ford, Warren Shadd and Tom Teasley.

The Mary Blankemeier Band performed blues and jazz at a number of area night clubs in the region. They performed in in Washington, D.C. at Desperado's, Beneath It All, Artie's, the Cellar Door, the Childe Harold, and Rumors; in Prince George's County, Maryland at Bambino's (Riverdale); and in Northern Virginia at the Wharf (Alexandria), the 219 Restaurant (Alexandria), the Shed (Alexandria), Eskimo Nell's (Arlington), Whitey's (Arlington), Beacon's Backstage (Falls Church) and Louie's Rock City (Bailey's Crossroads).

THE MARYLANDERS

The Marylanders formed in Silver Spring, Maryland in the summer of 1962 with an initial lineup of singers Carla Bean and Lorraine Bienvenue, lead guitarist Jim Ostmann, rhythm guitarist Kenny Laughlin, keyboardist Geoff Humphrey and drummer Russ Fleury. This dynamic pre-British Invasion outfit specialized in rock and roll instrumentals, with works by Link Wray and His Ray Men, Duane Eddy, and the Ventures prominently featured in their set lists. They also performed a variety of pop music standards such as "Harlem Nocturne" (a hit song in 1939 for the Ray Noble Orchestra), "Sentimental Journey" (a hit song in 1945 for Les brown and His Orchestra, vocal chorus by Doris Day), "Blue Moon" (popular versions hit the Billboard charts in 1949 for both Billy Eckstine and Mel Torme), and "Sleepwalk" (the 1959 instrumental by Santo & Johnny). They began working in the occasional Beatles song as the British Invasion moved forward.

The Marylanders lasted for more than two years, during which time they performed at private parties, fraternity functions at the University of Maryland, the St. Bernadette Catholic Church Teen Club (Silver Spring), the Bethesda Youth Center (Bethesda), the Bladensburg Volunteer Fire Department (Bladensburg), the Wheaton Youth Center (Wheaton), and, later in their career, the night club known as the Keg on Wisconsin Avenue NW in Washington, D.C.

Several musicians passed through the Marylanders during its time including singer Bill Swain, pianist Dick Brewer, and several saxophonists including Allen Kipnis, Stan Lipschitz, Tommy Tough and John Panzone.

MATT ABTS

Rock and roll drummer Matt Abts spent many years living in Fairfax, Virginia and attended Wilbert Tucker Woodson High School in the early 1970s. During that decade he drummed for many local rock and roll bands including Jeep, Rodeo, Steve Bishop and the Chessmen, the Nowhere Men, Liberation, Black on White, Merlin, and Orphan. In 1979 he moved to Florida where he drummed for a Southern rock group called the Dickey Betts Band.

In 1994 Abts joined up with singer-guitarist Warren Haynes and bassist Allen Woody (both former members of the Allman Brothers Band) to form the Southern rock power trio Gov't Mule. Today Abts continues to work with a version of Gov't Mule, in addition to a group that performs blues versions of Pink Floyd songs called Blue Floyd and his own blues rock band, Planet of the Abts.

MAX NAVARRO

Singer Max Navarro was born and raised in Washington, D.C. and grew up listening to James Brown, Little Richard and Elvis Presley. He attended Archbishop Carroll High School in the late 1950s and upon graduation began going to Vinnie's Grill in the city with friends Dave Martin and Lee Best, where they would see Link Wray and His Ray Men perform. The three of them began periodically doing backup singing for the band, with Navarro increasingly being called upon to augment the band onstage with his vocals.

Navarro taught himself piano and became a regular member of Link Wray and His Ray Men as a singer and keyboard player, working with the band throughout the 1960s during their engagements at such Washington, D.C. night clubs as the 1023 Restaurant, Vinnie's Grill and the Famous Restaurant. He also did backup vocal work with R&B singer Bunker Hill, appearing on his 45rpm single record "Red Ridin' Hood and the Wolf" backed with "Nobody Knows" (Bunker Hill; Mala Records, 1962). By the end of 1969 Navarro's active involvement in the local music scene had ended.

THE MEDALLIONS

The Medallions were a popular R&B-rock band on the local music scene in from 1960 to 1964, working both local teen dances as well as night clubs. The group formed in the Anacostia neighborhood of Southeast Washington, D.C. in 1960 with a lineup of lead singer Marty Kessler, guitarist Gary Cristy, bassist Jack Casady, saxophonist Bill "Mo" Blair, saxophonist Dave Wilson and drummer Bill Covey. Regular gigs for the band included dances held by the Mount Calvary Catholic Church Teen Club in Forestville, Maryland, the St. Francis Xavier Parish Teen Club in Washington, D.C., and a lengthy house band position at the Shanty, a night club in Anacostia.

In 1961 changes transpired within the Medallions, with Paul Kirkpatrick replacing Casady on bass and Rick Davis replacing Covey on drums. In 1962, while appearing at the Rocket Room in Washington, D.C., the Medallions backed up two national acts that appeared at the night club – pop singer Ray Stevens, who was touring at the time in support of his novelty single "Ahab the Arab," and local favorite Barry Darvell.

By 1963 the Medallions were performing with a lineup of Kessler, Kirkpatrick, Blair, Davis, singer-guitarist Dave McGinnis and saxophonist Tony Romagna. The band's final lineup in 1964 saw them perform as a quartet consisting of McGinnis, Blair, Davis and bassist Harvey Schwartz.

The Medallions primarily focused on R&B covers and played songs by such artists as Little Richard, Fats Domino, Ike and Tina Turner, the Dubs, the Five Satins, the Spaniels, the Isley Brothers, Chuck Berry, Hank Ballard and Ray Charles. During its time the band played fraternity events at the University of Maryland and University of Virginia, and also worked such Washington, D.C. night clubs as the Rocket Room, Benny's Rebel Room and the Alpine Room.

THE MEMORIES

In 1961 the Bobolinks, the popular vocal doo-wop band that had formed in the late 1950s in the Anacostia neighborhood of Southeast Washington, D.C., changed its name to the Memories. When the name changed occurred, the group's original five-man lineup remained Jim Durst, Ron Lutz, Robert "Boots" Dove, Lou Martin and Gene Fitzgerald.

In 1962 the Memories recorded and released the 45rpm single record "Love Bells" backed with "I Promise" (The Memories; Way-Lin Records, 1962). Throughout the 1960s and 1970s they appeared in Washington, D.C. at such night clubs as the Rocket Room, Benny's Rebel Room, the Alpine Room, the Shelter Room, Rand's Night Club, the Hayloft and the Crazy Horse; and in Prince George's County, Maryland at such night spots as the Cross Roads (Bladensburg), Strick's Restaurant (Silver Hill), and the Las Vegas Club (Coral Hills). They also held house band status at Gus and John's Italian Villa (Camp Springs) from 1971 to 1978; when the club changed over to Michelle's, they remained the main attraction through 1986.

The Memories went on to become a national attraction, performing shows and concerts and appearing on radio and television programs throughout the United States. While the band has always specialized in popular doo-wop and oldies hit songs, they also cover a wide variety of pop, rock, and R&B tunes. Through time the Memories evolved from a vocal quintet to a full-fledged band with various musicians passing through. Among those who have worked with the group are: guitarists Dennis Smith, Rudy Bautista and Vince D'Orazio; bassist Jim Morrow; keyboardist Bill Taylor; saxophonist Ralph McDuffie; drummers Jerry Wallmark and Tommy DiPietro; and singers Dennis Martin and Neil Arena (formerly of the Mello-Kings).

The Memories were enshrined in the Vocal Group Hall of Fame and Museum in Sharon, Pennsylvania in 1998 (today known as the Vocal Group Hall of Fame Foundation). Through the years they have released a number of albums on independent labels, with their most recent recording being "55th Anniversary Album" (The Memories; MAE Productions, 2013).

The band is still active today and performs concerts throughout the United States. Their current lineup consists of singers Lou Martin, Ron Lutz and June Flynn, singer-bassist Glen Bortz, guitarist Rick Williamson, keyboardist Charlie Helmick, saxophonist Mike Sheer and drummer Rob Dove, Jr.

MICHAEL FATH

Rock and roll guitarist Michael Fath was born in Washington, D.C. and raised in Sterling, Virginia where he started playing guitar at age 12. During his time at Broad Run High School in the late 1960s and early 1970s he played the Washington, D.C. area teen dance scene in the rock and roll bands the Love Company and Renaissance Blues.

Fath graduated from Emory and Henry College in Emory, Virginia with a Bachelor of Arts in kinesiology in 1974 and subsequently taught health and fitness at Sterling Middle School for a year. He then embarked on a career as a professional musician and in the late 1970s played lead guitar for such area rock and roll bands as Barefoot Trader, Teaser, and Heather. In 1977 he joined the national R&B act Peaches and Herb, performing with the band in Washington, D.C. at the Cellar Door and the Howard Theatre, and touring with them in Bermuda, Canada and the Eastern United States.

Fath spent all of 1978 and 1979 singing and playing lead guitar in the hard-rocking group Wizzard, which mixed originals with covers of bands such as Led Zeppelin, Deep Purple, Styx, and Queen, among others. Wizzard's lineup was rounded out by singer-guitarist Mark Mancini, singer-bassist Rich Chapin (who was later replaced by Steve Hatfield), singer-keyboardist Kris Fath and drummer Jimmy Orr (who was later replaced by Ned Liebman). Wizzard regularly performed in the Georgetown neighborhood of Washington, D.C. at the Bayou and the Crazy Horse and toured up and down the Atlantic Coast, from Massachusetts to South Carolina.

From 1980 to 1984 Fath played lead guitar in Orphan, one of the East Coast's most popular hard rock bands. The group's initial lineup consisted of Fath on lead guitar, lead singer Kris Fath, bassist Steve Hatfield and drummer Bobby Johnson. Lineup changes included Hatfield being replaced by bassist David Utter in 1982, who was then replaced by Berkley Royster in 1984, and Johnson being replaced by drummer Matt Abts in 1984. When working the nation's capital, Orphan headlined at such night clubs as the Bayou, the Wax Museum and the Crazy Horse, and also opened concerts for scores of national acts including Kix, whom they performed with on more than two-dozen occasions.

In July 1983 Fath was featured in the "Spotlight" section of Guitar Player magazine and soon afterwards recorded and released his first solo album, "Profile" (Michael Andre Fath; Platinum Records, 1985). These events launched him into a celebrated solo career that led to international acclaim.

In 1985 Fath became a founding member of the hard-rocking trio King Dazzle, which was rounded out by singer-bassist Berkley Royster and drummer Corey Holland. In 1986 he put together the Michael Fath Group, which featured himself on lead guitar and vocals, lead singer John Watson, bassist Andre Sokol, keyboardist Michael Salas and drummer Corey Holland. A later version of this group consisted of Fath, lead singer Rob Carroll, bassist Dave Crigger, keyboardist Lenny Gratz and drummer Jimmy Carroll.

From 1987 to 1994 Fath caught fire as a solo artist, concentrating on instrumental rock and roll guitar work. During that time he toured from Boston to Los Angeles with the ever-present rhythm section of bassist Dave Crigger and drummer Corey Holland. This period also saw him record and release several critically acclaimed albums including "Flick of the Wrist" (Michael Fath; Platinum Records, 1988); "Shake" (Michael Fath; R.E.D. Inc. Records, 1989); "Sonic Tapestries" (Michael Fath; R.E.D. Inc. Records, 1990); and "Suspended Animation" (Michael Fath; Music Maker Records, 1992).

Fath has since continued to record and perform as a solo artist and has headlined at such venues as Blues Alley (Washington, D.C.), the John F. Kennedy Center for the Performing Arts (Washington, D.C.), Wolf Trap National Park for the Performing Arts (Vienna, Virginia), the Sarah Gould Theatre (New York City), the Roxy (Los Angeles,

California), the Anaheim Civic Center (Anaheim, California), Exhibition Hall (Glasgow, Scotland), the Marquee (London, England) and Music Messe (Frankfurt, Germany).

Fath has continued to release solo albums and record with other artists, some 45 albums in all, in styles ranging from jazz to rock and roll. Most recently he has performed with his own country-jazz instrumental group, Michael Fath and the Virginia Rangers, and rock and roll bands such as the Cherry People, KINGs, and a progressive rock trio called Here, Now and Forever.

MICHAEL SMITH

Drummer Michael Smith is a native of Meadville, Pennsylvania and relocated to Washington, D.C. at the age of 21 in 1967 to attend Howard University. He became an integral part of the local music scene by spending most of that year drumming for jazz pianist Bobby Timmons at Bohemian Caverns.

From 1968 to 1970 Smith was recognized as one of the local music scene's top musicians for his role as drummer in the avant-garde classical-jazz-rock instrumental trio Love Cry Want. From 1970 to 1973, he, along with bassist Terry Plumeri, toured and performed with R&B singer Roberta Flack.

Smith went on to perform and/or record with such jazz notables as: the Entourage Music and Theater Ensemble; singers Billy Eckstine, Amanda Ambrose and Mose Allison; guitarists John Abercrombie, Herb Ellis and Nathan Page; keyboardist Herbie Hancock; pianists Tommy Flanagan, Milt Jackson, Steve Kuhn, Adam Makowicz, Gottfried Bottger and David Kane; pianist-bassist Don Thompson; saxophonist Dave Liebman; and trumpeters Randy Brecker and Freddie Hubbard, among many others. Michael Smith passed away on Monday, January 2, 2006 at the age of 59.

MICHAEL TASH

Guitarist Michael "Jr." Tash was raised in Silver Spring, Maryland and became hooked on rock and roll after seeing Kiss perform in-concert when he was 10 years old in 1975. Soon after that experience he took up guitar and began making music with friends. During his time at John F. Kennedy High School in the early 1980s he played in a Southern rock band called Back Alley and listened to bands such as Lynyrd Skynyrd, Black Sabbath, Van Halen, the Scorpions, Judas Priest, Iron Maiden and Def Leppard. Throughout the middle and late 1980s he played guitar at open mic sessions at Montgomery County, Maryland night clubs such as Hunter's (Wheaton) and Fatty's Restaurant (Rockville).

In 1988 Tash formed Bad Influence, a band that plays classic and original blues songs. During the group's first five years there were numerous changes in personnel. In 1993 the band settled on a basic, four-man lineup that remains intact to the present day: singer-bassist Bob Mallardi, guitarist Michael Tash, singer-harmonicist-guitarist Roger Edsall and drummer David Thaler.

Bad Influence has been a top attraction at in Washington, D.C. at Club Soda and the Hamilton; in Maryland at Bethesda Blues and Jazz Supper Club (Bethesda), the New Deal Café (Greenbelt), the Rams Head Savage Mill Tavern (Savage) and Rams Head On Stage (Annapolis); and in Virginia at the Ice House Café (Herndon). They have performed in-concert at the John F. Kennedy Center for the Performing Arts Millennium Stage (Washington, D.C.) and have appeared at shows and festivals all over the Eastern United States and as far away as Tennessee, Nevada and California.

Bad Influence has four albums to its credit: "Live at Bad Habits Café" (Bad Influence Featuring Whop Frazier and Guitar Star Junior Tash; Wildchild!, 1995); "Where We Been" (Bad Influence; Badblues Records, 1996); "Tastes Like Chicken" (Bad Influence; Badblues Records, 2001); and "Under the Influence" (Bad Influence; Badblues Records, 2011).

Through the years Tash has played onstage with a number of top blues performers including: singer-guitarist Albert Castiglia and Joy Bodycomb; guitarists Zac Harmon, Eddie "Devil Boy" Turner and John "Del Toro" Richardson; and harmonicist Lee Oskar.

MICHAEL WALLS

Drummer Michael "Pokey" Walls was born in Hamilton, Ohio, and, as part of a military family, moved about the United States frequently as a youth and teenager. He listened to blues and jazz and at age 16 in 1963 began drumming in a blues band called the Blades at Magoo's Lounge in Kansas City, Missouri.

In 1964 Walls moved with his family to Fairfax, Virginia and during his time at Fairfax High School in the middle 1960s he drummed for a rock and roll band called the Shadows on the local teen dance scene. In 1965 he was recruited by manager Mitch Corday to take over the drums in an R&B band called Willie and the Handjives, who were then working as the house band at the 1320 Club on Richmond Highway in Alexandria, Virginia. Later in the year Corday placed Walls with the popular Washington, D.C.-based rock and roll band the Chartbusters. Walls remained with the band for a couple of years during their heyday at the Crazy Horse in Georgetown.

In the late 1960s and early 1970s Walls passed through a number of top Washington, D.C. area rock and roll bands including Wild Honey, Puzzle, Tractor, the Reasons Why, Rooth, Happy Feet, and the Cherry People. He also drummed for blues rock guitarist Roy Buchanan at the Cross Roads in Bladensburg, Maryland and for the East Coast Express, a rock and roll band that featured guitarist Danny Gatton, at Gus and John's Italian Villa in Camp Springs, Maryland.

After spending part of the 1970s in Florida, Walls returned to the Washington, D.C. area and in the 1980s drummed for the rock and roll bands Three Easy Pieces and the JP New Band. He also worked with guitarist Demetri Callas in a number of his rock and roll bands including the Bad Boys and Demetri and the Flashbacks. In 1988 he moved to St. Petersburg, Florida, and has been a part of their music scene ever since.

THE MIDNIGHT MARAUDERS

The Midnight Marauders were a dynamic band from Greenbelt, Maryland that formed in 1965 with a lineup of budding young musicians from Greenbelt Junior High School who shared a love for R&B and rock and roll music. The band originally consisted of lead singer Duke Perry, guitarists Ken Nickolson and Tommy Hyland, bassist John O'Brien and drummer Norman Moran. Through time, the band members attended different high schools – Bladensburg, Parkdale and High Point – and during its three-year run the group served as the semi-regular house band of the Greenbelt Teen Club, which staged their weekly dances at the Greenbelt Youth Center. The band went through one significant personnel change with another Greenbelter named Dennis Miller replacing Norman Moran on drums.

Among the popular musical performers the Midnight Marauders covered were Wilson Pickett, James Brown, Little Richard, Otis Redding, the Temptations, Martha and the Vandellas, the Four Tops, the Ventures, Duane Eddy, the Rolling Stones and the Beatles.

In addition to appearing regularly at the Greenbelt Youth Center, the band appeared at local parties, worked wedding receptions at places like Lasick's College Inn (College Park) and the American Legion College Park Post 217 (College Park), played splash parties at the Greenbelt Swimming Pool and the annual Greenbelt Labor Day Festival, and performed at dances at Hyattsville Junior High School (Hyattsville), the Berwyn Heights Teen Club (Berwyn Heights Elementary School), the College Park Teen Club (City of College Park Municipal Building) and the Hollywood Teen Club (Hollywood Elementary School in College Park, Maryland).

MIKE COLBURN

Singer-guitarist Mike Colburn hails from Wheaton, Maryland and during his junior high school years first played in the Carpetbaggers, an R&B band that performed on the local teen dance scene in middle 1960s. He attended Wheaton High School in the late 1960s, during which time he played guitar in Nobody's Children, one of the area's more popular rock and roll bands.

Colburn went on to play in a succession of area rock and roll bands throughout the 1970s including the Magic Touch, Naked Dog, Razz, Skids, Diamond, and the Long Branch Band. In 1978 he formed the rock and roll band Nightman, a project that continued on for several years with various musicians in and out of the lineup. In the 1980s Colburn sang and played guitar with pop-rock singer-guitarist Tommy Keene, and worked for several years with his own rock and roll band, Other World.

In the 1990s Colburn handled lead vocals and guitar in the rock and roll power trio Dog Head. More recently, he spent several years playing guitar in the R&B-rock band Jr. Cline and the Recliners, and also sang and played guitar in the Silver Spring-based blues rock band Roaddog.

MIKE HURNEY

Singer-guitarist Mike Hurney was born in Washington, D.C. and spent his first 13 years in the city, learning violin and harmonica as a youth. His family then moved to Wheaton, Maryland and while attending high school in Montgomery County in the middle 1950s – Montgomery Blair High School and then Wheaton High School – he played violin in variety shows and local C&W concerts. During those years he also played fiddle in a bluegrass band led by the Marshall Twins and worked pickup jobs with bluegrass singer-mandolinists such as John Duffey and Buzz Busby.

While attending the University of Maryland in the late 1950s Hurney played fiddle in a local bluegrass trio with guitarists Mike and Dave Auldridge. In the 1960s he switched to guitar and worked with such top Washington, D.C. area rock and roll bands as Joe Stanley and the Saxtons, the Off Beats (a different band from the one that featured singer Ron MacDonald and guitarist Danny Gatton), the Perry Mates, and the Peppermint Twisters. Hurney then became a founding member of the Personalities in 1962 and remained with that rock and roll band until 1994.

MIKE JOHNSTONE

Guitarist Mike Johnstone was an Army brat who was born in Seattle, Washington and lived all over the United States and Europe as a youth, listening to such musicians as Scotty Moore, Chet Atkins, and the Ventures. He attended Hampton High School in Norfolk, Virginia for a year before enrolling at Castle Heights Military School in Lebanon, Tennessee. One of his dormmates at Castle Heights was a guitarist named Duane Allman, who recruited Johnstone to play bass in his rock and roll band, the Allman Joys. He remained at the military school for two years before moving to Newport News, Virginia where he graduated from Homer L. Ferguson High School in 1966.

Upon his high school graduation, Johnston began playing guitar with a Beatles-styled rock and roll band called the Wild Kingdom, which was recruited to be the touring backup band for the pop singer Keith. One of their stops in 1967 was a concert at the Ambassador Theatre in Washington, D.C.

In 1968 Johnstone returned to the Tidewater area of Virginia where he briefly worked with a new version of Wild Kingdom. He then put together a psychedelic blues band in Norfolk called Headstone Circus. In 1969 the band was working an engagement at the Peppermint Beach Club in Ocean City, Maryland when they hired a new drummer from the

Washington, D.C. area named Michael "Pokey" Walls. Headstone Circus finished the summer playing a night club called the Hideaway in Ocean City and then returned to Norfolk.

In 1970 another Norfolk-based rock and roll band called Rooth had relocated to an apartment complex in Silver Spring, Maryland and offered Johnstone its lead guitarist position. With their new guitarist on board, the band worked such Washington, D.C. night clubs as the Keg, the Silver Dollar, Mac's Pipe and Drum Restaurant, the Bayou, the Crazy Horse and the Hayloft. At Johnstone's urging, the band picked up drummer Michael "Pokey" Walls and then worked steadily at two night clubs in the city on 14th Street NW, the Butterfly and Benny's Rebel Room. Many musicians passed through Rooth during its time in the nation's capital, including a lead singer named Kris Peterson, who later went on to sing on Frank Zappa's "Waka Jawaka" album in 1972.

Johnstone and remnants of Rooth left the Washington, D.C. area in 1972 and returned to Norfolk where they regrouped and remained active under the name Rooth through the end of 1974. In 1975 Johnstone moved to Los Angeles and switched gears, taking up steel guitar and playing with a succession of C&W musicians. He toured with singer Charley Pride in the middle 1970s and performed with singer-guitarist J.J. Cale and singer Tex Williams. In 1977 struck up a friendship with Leon Russell and played guitar for him on live dates and recording sessions for the next four years.

Since that time Johnstone has played guitar for a number of C&W bands and musicians including Black Tie (a group that included ex-Poco and Eagles singer-bassist Randy Meisner and ex-Bread singer-guitarist Jimmy Griffin), singer-guitarist Jim Lauderdale, singer-guitarist Dale Watson, Buck Page's Riders of the Purple Sage, and singer Billy Swan.

MIKE MAUTINO

Drummer Mike Mautino was born in Darlington, South Carolina and raised in New Carrollton, Maryland. His father Robert "Buddy" Mautino played flute and saxophone in local big bands and Mike started on the drums at age six. While attending Charles Carroll Junior High School in the late 1960s he played the local teen dance circuit in a rock and roll band called Pain.

Mautino listened to such drummers as Louie Bellson, Richie Hayward, John Bonham and Carmine Appice, and during his years at Parkdale High School in the early 1970s he drummed in an R&B band called the Sensations. He went on to drum for a local rock and roll group called the Open Road Band from 1981 to 1993 and then played with the blues band Big Bill and That's Cool from 1995 to 2000.

More recently, Mautino has drummed for a number of Washington, D.C. area bands including the country rock group No Alibi, and the blues-rockabilly group Retro Deluxe. He currently drums for a blues-rockabilly band called the Low Rent Quartet that mainly performs at the Old Bowie Town Grille in Bowie, Maryland.

MIKE MELCHIONE

Multi-styled singer-guitarist Mike Melchione was born in Chicago, Illinois and raised in California, where, during the middle 1960s, he attended Antelope Valley High School in Lancaster, the alma mater of such rock and roll icons as Frank Zappa and Captain Beefheart. He was involved in its local music scene during his time there and then in the late 1960s he spent three years in the United States Navy.

Melchione moved to the Washington, D.C. area in the early 1970s, living for a time in Hyattsville, Maryland. While there, he befriended and played guitar with two of the area's music legends, Roy Buchanan and Danny Gatton. He went on to play guitar with a number of bands and musicians in the nation's capital, and spent the 1970s and early 1980s working with one of the region's top C&W bands, Heavy Country. This band regularly performed at the Cross Roads in Bladensburg, Maryland, a night club that had once been a showcase venue for Roy Buchanan, one of Melchione's favorite fellow guitarists.

In 1989 Melchione began playing guitar for Buckwheat Zydeco, a nationally known zydeco-jazz band that was named for its singer-accordionist-leader, Stanley "Buckwheat" Dural, Jr. The group changed its name to the Legendary ILS Sont Partis Band after Dural, Jr. passed away on Saturday, September 24, 2016. Melchione continues to perform with the band when called upon.

Through the years Melchione has played guitar with a number of great bands and musicians in the Washington, D.C. area including: blues singer-guitarist Cathy Ponton King; the blues trio Lords of the Strings (with guitarists Tom Principato and Dave Chappell); the blues band the Smut Brothers; the blues rock band LHB (Lost Highway Band); the country rock band All Night Long; R&B singer-pianist Big Al Downing; and rockabilly singer-bassist Billy Hancock. He was recently seen playing guitar with the newly formed rock and roll band Lunch With Bob.

MIKE PERSH

Drummer Mike Persh was born in Newport News, Virginia and moved to Glenside, Pennsylvania, where, in the early 1960s, he was exposed to music through his trumpet-playing father and took up drums at age 11. Among his influences were such drummers as Hal Blaine, Earl Palmer, Ringo Starr, Charlie Watts and Mitch Mitchell. As a Pennsylvania teenager in the middle 1960s he drummed for a rock and roll group called the Lost Souls.

In 1967 Persh's family moved to Annandale, Virginia and while attending Annandale High School in the late 1960s and into 1970 he drummed for two bands on the local teen dance scene, a rock and roll group called Incubus, and a jazz rock act called the New Jazz Epic. While attending Washington University in St. Louis, Missouri in the early 1970s he drummed for various rock and roll bands, and, upon graduation, spent the middle 1970s drumming for a rock and roll band called Rocking Horse in Greensboro, North Carolina. (Persh went on to earn additional academic degrees and eventually spent 27 years as an accountant.)

Persh returned to the Washington, D.C. area for good in 1975 and through the years has lived in Northern Virginia (Annandale, Falls Church and Arlington), and, more recently, in Colesville, Maryland. After a long hiatus from regular performing, he resumed a steady music schedule in the 2000s and has since drummed for such local bands and musicians as: the country rock group Bourbon Dynasty; the C&W band Busted Taillight; the rock and roll group Kid Goat; and rock and roll singer-guitarist Jason Meza. He is currently drumming for three Washington, D.C. area groups: the rock and roll outfit V6; the blues rock band Intone Nation; and the blues group DC Mudd.

MIKE PIRKO

Singer-guitarist Mike Pirko grew up in Adelphi, Maryland and during his years at High Point High School in the late 1960s he played the local teen dance scene in a series of rock and roll bands including the Pendletons, the Outcast Set, and the Electric Twinkie.

In 1969 Pirko joined the Nowhere Men, who at the time were transitioning into one of the Washington, D.C. area's top R&B-rock bands. When he joined the group on lead guitar, his bandmates were singers Donnie Halcombe, Charlie Taylor and Billy Vabolis, bassist Tommy Rodante, keyboardist Richard Purvis, saxophonist Jimmy Robinson, trumpeters Gary Gaulette and George Kindrock, trombonist Chris Heer and drummers Miles Sheetz and Tommy Wright.

At that point the Nowhere Men were performing in Washington, D.C. at such night clubs as the Bastille Supper Club and Fran O'Brien's Anthony House Restaurant, and in Prince George's County, Maryland at the Hangar Club in Camp Springs and on the University of Maryland campus at fraternity parties and shows at Ritchie Coliseum.

Pirko spent part of 1970 and 1971 playing guitar in the local R&B-rock bands Second Coming and the New Breed. Later in 1971 he joined Three Easy Pieces, a rock and roll trio which at the time was playing the Silver Dollar Restaurant in Georgetown and was rounded out by singer-bassist-keyboardist Jimmy Nalley and drummer Stuart Ross. The band went through numerous personnel changes throughout the decade, though Pirko remained in the lineup for several years.

In 1974 Pirko played guitar in a pop music band called Vic Dana and Sumpthin' Else that played Sheraton hotels in Pennsylvania and New York. When he left the band he returned to Washington, D.C. and joined a revamped version of Three Easy Pieces in 1975 that had shortened its name to the Pieces. The group now consisted of Pirko, Nalley and drummer Michael "Pokey" Walls and worked as the house band at the Paul Mall Restaurant in Georgetown.

From 1977 to 1979 Pirko sang and played guitar in a Rockville-based rock and roll group called the Bullet Band (later shortened to Bullet) which specialized in Eagles covers and whose lineup also included lead singer-bassist Danny Goers, singer-keyboardist Mike Joy and singer-drummer Roger Fallin. The group performed all over the region at such establishments as Fran O'Brien's Anthony House Restaurant (Washington, D.C.), the Colonial Manor Hotel (Bethesda), the Library (Annapolis), the Rabbit's Foot (Frederick), and once worked for a week backing singer-keyboardist Bruce Hornsby at a Ramada Inn in Williamsburg, Virginia.

In the 1980s Pirko played guitar in a series of pop bands in Florida including Primo, Hot Ice, Body and Soul, and the Tom Brickett Band. While in the Sunshine State he also played bass in the pop music band the Generation Gap and guitar for James Peterson and the Tou-Can Blues Band.

In the 1990s Pirko was in New York playing guitar for Gil Cruz and the Well Dressed Blues Band and later sang and played guitar in the blues rock band Michael Alan and the Sure Thing. More recently, he has been in New Mexico where he has worked with several rock and roll bands: he sang and played bass in the Grinders; and he sang and played guitar in 8-Track, and a group called Off the Record. He is currently playing guitar in a blues rock band called Unsigned.

MIKE REIDY

Singer Mike Reidy was born in Washington, D.C., and, as an Air Force brat, frequently moved about the country as a youth. At the age of 14 in 1964 he joined his first band, the Rhythm and Blues Express, while living in Omaha, Nebraska.

Reidy's family later moved to Camp Springs, Maryland and during the late 1960s while attending Crossland High School he sang in a group called the Red, White, and Blues Band that performed at the Roger B. Taney Teen Club (Roger B. Taney Junior High School in Temple Hills), the Surrattsville Senior Teen Club (Surrattsville High School in Clinton), the Hillcrest Heights Teen Club (Hillcrest Heights) and the Marlow Heights Community Center (Marlow Heights).

In 1970 Reidy sang in a rock and roll band called the Hot Crabs that included guitarist Bill Craig and played functions on the University of Maryland's College Park campus. In the fall of that year he sang in a short-lived rock and roll band called the Sonny Boy Reed Organization, a group that included Bill Craig on guitar and the talented Montgomery County triumvirate of guitarist Richard Marcello, bassist Donald "Mickie" Jones and drummer Barry Brandt (Brandt and Jones would later comprise the rhythm section for Angel). This band stayed together for two gigs, including one standing-room-only performance at the Marlow Heights Community Center in November 1970.

In early 1971 Reidy became a founding member of the seminal rock and roll band Razz, which initially rehearsed in his Camp Springs home at 5103 Wilkins Drive. The band's original lineup consisted of Reidy handling lead vocals, guitarists Bill Craig and Fred Gallagher, bassist Ted Nicely and drummer Pete Ragusa. Razz went on to become one of the most highly regarded rock bands to ever emerge from the Washington, D.C. area and Reidy remained the group's frontman until its demise in 1979.

In the spring of 1982 Reidy formed a new band that defied musical categorization, MWWW (Mick Way and the Wrong Ways). The group's lineup consisted of Reidy as lead singer, bassist Jim Crenca, keyboardist-saxophonist Max Surla and drummer Josh Rowley. They performed in Washington, D.C. at such night clubs as Desperado's, D.C. Space, the Bayou, the Wax Museum and Nightclub 9:30. MWWW disbanded in December 1982.

More recently, Reidy has participated in several Razz reunion concerts and briefly sang in the Howling Mad, a Razz offshoot that included guitarists Bill Craig and Abaad Behram, drummer Doug Tull, and a succession of bass players.

MIKE STERN

Jazz guitarist Mike Stern was born in Boston, Massachusetts and raised in Washington, D.C. After finishing high school at St. Albans School, he played lead guitar in the Dubonnettes, a popular rock and roll band that based out of the Georgetown night club known as Apple Pie in the early 1970s.

Stern went on to attend the Berklee College of Music in Boston, Massachusetts and later in the 1970s played guitar for Blood, Sweat and Tears and jazz drummer Billy Cobham. He then spent the 1980s and beyond performing and recording with such jazz artists as trumpeter Miles Davis, saxophonists David Sanborn and Joe Henderson, Jaco Pastorius' Word of Mouth, Steps Ahead, and the Brecker Brothers Band (a group led by saxophonist Michael Brecker and trumpeter Randy Brecker).

Stern was named "Best Jazz Guitarist of 1993" by Guitar Player magazine. As a solo artist, he has recorded and released some 16 albums on such record labels as Kenwood, Atlantic, ESC, and Heads Up International. His latest solo album is "All Over the Place" (Mike Stern; Heads Up International, 2012). He is still recording and touring today and is considered to be one of the finest jazz guitarists in the world.

MIKE TOOLE

Drummer Mike Toole was raised in Southern Prince George's County, Maryland, first residing in Oxon Hill, where, during the middle 1960s, he spent his time at John Hanson Junior High School playing in a rock and roll band called the Red Coats, who covered songs by the Animals, Herman's Hermits and the Rolling Stones on the local teen dance scene. His family then moved to District Heights, Maryland and late in the decade while attending Suitland High School he drummed in the school's concert and marching bands.

In the early 1970s Toole became involved in the area's music scene and spent the decade drumming for a succession of C&W acts including Danny Denver and the Soundmasters at the Cross Roads (Bladensburg), Smokey Mac at the Village Barn (Morningside) and the Jimmy Case Group at the Bolling Air Force Base Officers' Club (Washington, D.C.). During that time he also drummed for the C&W act Vallie Rae and the Raemen, and a rock and roll group called the Full Moon Jam Band, which covered Cream, Led Zeppelin and ZZ Top.

In the 1980s and 1990s Toole worked with a number of local bands including: Frenchy and the Heartthrobs, which specialized in the songs of Elvis Presley, Patsy Cline and Link Wray and performed at such area night clubs as El Rancho (Forestville), the Senate Inn (Capitol Heights) and the Trucker's Inn (Jessup); the Dixie Express, a C&W band that performed at the T.D. Lounge (Laurel); and the popular C&W band Oklahoma, which mainly worked area American Legions, Moose Lodges and VFWs.

In 2000 Toole joined Heroes and Friends, the C&W house band at the Surf Club in Hyattsville, Maryland, whose lineup also consisted of singer-guitarist Chick Hall, Jr., singer-bassist Chris Hall and guitarist Randy Leith. When Chris Hall sold the Surf Club to James Byrum in January 2008, Toole began filling in with bands that visited the venue on an on-call basis.

Today Toole regularly works with Chick Hall, Jr. and Chris Hall in the Hall Brothers, as well as C&W acts such as the band New South, singer Patsy Stephens, and country-rockabilly singer-guitarist George Garris.

MIKE TRAMONTE

Keyboardist Mike Tramonte was born in Washington, D.C. and raised in Arlington, Virginia. As a youth he was inspired by the Beatles and during his years at Williamsburg Junior High School in the middle 1960s he played the local teen dance circuit in a rock and roll band called the Cornerstones. While attending Yorktown High School in the late 1960s he played keyboards in a rock and roll band called Back Bay, which occasionally performed at the Bayou in Georgetown, the famed night club which at the time was owned by his father Vince Tramonte and his uncle Tony Tramonte.

In the early 1970s Tramonte moved his way up at the Bayou, working as a busboy and doorman, eventually becoming the night club's manager in 1974. In the late 1970s he also played keyboards for the Grimes Brothers, a rock and roll band featuring former Cherry People singer Doug Grimes and bassist Chris Grimes. During this time he worked with promoters like Mike Schreibman to bring national acts to the Bayou up until the time the Tramonte family sold the business to Cellar Door Productions in January 1980. Tramonte then spent more than two decades focusing on the Italian Store, a delicatessen in Arlington, Virginia owned by his family.

In recent years Tramonte has returned to Virginia's music scene: from 2005 to 2009 he played keyboards in the Natchez Trace Band, a country rock group that included several former members of Cherry Smash; from 2007 to 2008 he played in a classic rock band called King Willy and the Shadows; in 2012 he was a member of a classic rock band called the Phoenix Project; and since 2014 he has been playing in a blues band called the BlueHouse Project.

In addition, Tramonte was a part of the Last Call Band, a group of rock and roll musicians that performed at "The Bayou Presents Last Call," a live music tribute to the Bayou night club that took place at the Hamilton in Washington, D.C. on Sunday, February 17, 2013.

MIKE VALENTI

Drummer Mike Valenti grew up in Hyattsville, Maryland and was a fan of the Beatles and the popular local teen dance band Lawrence and the Arabians. He took drum lessons from the legendary jazz percussionist Bill Reichenbach and during his time at St. Jerome Catholic School in the late 1960s he drummed for a series of rock and roll bands on the local teen dance circuit including Second Generation, the Golden Souls, and the Superiors.

While attending Archbishop Carroll High School in the early 1970s Valenti began drumming for the Nowhere Men, the popular R&B-rock band his brother Steve Valenti had founded back in 1966. He worked with the Nowhere Men at different times all the way through the late 1970s. Other Washington, D.C. area rock and roll bands Valenti drummed for during that decade included the Starlighters, Liberation, the Reasons Why, and a disco group called Pinch. From 1978 to 1989 he drummed for the popular area rock and roll band Sinbad.

Valenti spent the 1990s drumming for the multi-styled pop music wedding band NightLife, reconfigured versions of Sinbad, and a pop-rock duo with singer-guitarist Bobby Stevens called Two Live Dudes that covered acts from the Doors to Otis Redding.

More recently Valenti drummed for more than 10 years with a Rockville-based R&B-rock band called Off the Record, a group that covered popular horn bands like Chicago, Tower of Power, and Blood, Sweat and Tears. He has also participated in many Nowhere Men reunion shows.

MIKE WEBER

Rock and roll singer Mike Weber was a featured performer at the popular Don Dillard record hops around the region throughout the early 1960s. He was born in Takoma Park, Maryland and raised in the Brightwood neighborhood of Washington, D.C. where he attended Coolidge High School before graduating from Chamberlain Vocational High School in 1961. During his school years Weber was introduced to the local rock and roll scene through his childhood friend Barry Richards at radio station WDON where they did odd jobs around the studio in exchange for 45rpm records, and, in the process, soaked up the popular music of the day.

After high school Weber began attending various night clubs in Washington, D.C., sitting in as a guest singer with Link Wray and His Ray Men at Vinnie's Grill and the Grand Café, and with Ray Rock and the Revlons at Guy's Place and the Round Up Club. He also performed with R&B singer-pianist Billy Stewart at Hillow's on 13th Street NW in 1963.

From 1961 to 1964 Weber was a regular performer at record hops around the region that were staged by various promoters including Don Dillard, Milt Grant and Barry Richards. The bulk of his live performances were for Dillard in Washington, D.C. at the Shrine of the Sacred Heart Teen Club and Mackin High School; and in Maryland at the Greenbelt Armory, the Hyattsville Armory, the Bladensburg Volunteer Fire Department, the Silver Spring Armory and the Silver Spring Boys Club. At these teen dances and record hops Weber was backed by local bands such as Barry Darvell and the Blazers and the Capris, and covered songs by the Drifters, the Platters, Larry Williams, Dion, Bobby Rydell, Ral Donner and Elvis Presley.

Weber's singing career came to a close when he was drafted into the United States Army in January 1965. He did, however, return to the stage in October 1966 at an officers' club on the Neureut Kaserne United States Army installation in Karlsruhe, Germany as a guest vocalist with Bill Pinkney and the Drifters.

MIKE ZACK

Drummer Mike Zack was born in Uniontown, Pennsylvania and raised in Beltsville, Maryland. In the fall of 1963, as a 14-year-old ninth-grader at Beltsville Junior High School, he became a founding member of Lawrence and the Arabians. The soul-styled band became the most popular entry on a large and competitive teen dance circuit and Zack's reputation as a talented drummer soared. Zack remained with Lawrence and the Arabians through November 1967, at which time he was out of High Point High School and exploring the Georgetown rock and roll night club scene.

In the late 1960s Zack drummed for a number of Washington, D.C.-based rock and roll bands including Wild Honey, the Reasons Why, Puzzle, and Hillow Hammet. During that time he also served as the house drummer at night clubs such as the Silver Dollar, the Crazy Horse and the Keg, and worked short engagements and on-call assignments with dozens of groups and solo acts at area night clubs. Among those he drummed for on a short-term basis were blues rock guitarist Roy Buchanan at the Silver Dollar Restaurant and the Hayloft; blues guitarist Bobby Parker at the Flamingo Lounge; the Winstons at Rand's Night Club; and Flavor at the Starlite Restaurant.

In the 1970s some of the rock and roll bands in the Washington, D.C. area Zack drummed for were Goosby-Pegalo, the Nowhere Men, the Cherry People, Sun Country, Gravity, the Young Senators, Gary St. Clair and Friends, Easy Street, Second Coming, D.C. Dog, Charlie and the Pep Boys, Bobby and Friends, various bands led by singer-guitarist Demetri Callas, and the R&B band Spats. He also toured and recorded with rock and roll singer-guitarist Nils Lofgren for a year beginning in late 1975 and again in 1979, the highlight of which was a live performance at London's Wembley Stadium on Saturday, August 18, 1979 where Lofgren and the band played on a triple bill with AC/DC and the Who before a crowd of over 80,000 fans.

In the early 1980s Zack toured with C&W singer Stella Parton and again worked with Nils Lofgren, though their association came to an end when the guitarist was called into Bruce Springsteen and the E Street Band in 1984. In recent years has cut back his playing, preferring to sit in with musician-friends in the Frederick, Maryland area on special occasions. Mike Zack passed away on Tuesday, August 21, 2018 at the age of 69.

THE MOSAIC VIRUS

The Mosaic Virus was a psychedelic-tinged rock and roll band that formed in early 1967, based out of Tyson's Corner, Virginia, and covered songs by such bands as Jefferson Airplane, the Beatles, the Animals, the Byrds, and the Youngbloods. The group's best-known lineup consisted of singer Fran Odenhall, guitarists Carl Grossman and Dave Buck, singer-bassist Mike Buker and drummer-percussionists Danny Coleman and William "Duke" Ayres.

The Mosaic Virus held down house band duties at the Corral in Georgetown throughout the spring and summer months of 1967 and late in the year were regularly called upon to open up at the Ambassador Theatre in the Adams Morgan neighborhood of Washington, D.C. for such visiting national acts as the Paul Butterfield Blues Band, the Fugs, Strawberry Alarm Clock, the Hollies, Moby Grape and others. They also worked an engagement at the Electric Circus in New York City before disbanding in March 1968.

Singer Fran Odenhall, under the name Fran Tate, later sang on albums by Little Feat and Robert Palmer. Mike Buker and Duke Ayres went on to form the rock and roll band the Magic Reign.

THE MUFFINS

The Muffins were a progressive jazz rock band in the vein of the Soft Machine, Caravan, and Henry Cow that came into existence in Gaithersburg, Maryland in the early 1970s, disbanded in the early 1980s, and then had another run from 1998 to 2016 that saw them perform at festivals and embark on recording projects.

The Muffins formed in 1973 and originally consisted of keyboardist-saxophonist Dave Newhouse, guitarist Michael Zetner and bassist Billy Swann. After a year of experimentation, they added saxophonist Thomas Scott to the group and began rehearsing with a succession of percussionists, eventually bringing in Stuart Abramowitz as a regular drummer. Abramowitz and Zetner both left the band in the summer of 1976 and the Muffins carried on as a trio. In late 1976 they added drummer Paul Sears and moved forward playing original instrumental music in an avant-garde, Canterbury-styled vein.

The Muffins' gigs were somewhat sporadic. In the 1970s they often played homegrown backyard concerts in Gaithersburg. When playing out they appeared in Washington, D.C. at the Washington Ethical Society, the Childe Harold, Columbia Station, the WAFU Coffeehouse, the Music Carryout and D.C. Space, and in Bethesda, Maryland at the Psyche Delly.

In 1977 the Muffins moved into a group house in Rockville, Maryland and founded an independent record company, Random Radar Records. They released two albums on the label before disbanding in 1981: "Manna/Mirage" (The Muffins; Random Radar Records, 1978); and "<185>" (The Muffins; Random Radar Records, 1981). The band also collaborated with avant-garde guitarist Fred Frith, backing him on his solo album "Gravity" (Fred Frith; Ralph Records, 1980).

In 1998, Newhouse, Swann, Scott and Sears reformed the Muffins and resumed work on recording projects and concert appearances. They performed at such festivals as the "Villa Celimontana Jazz Festival" in Rome Italy on Friday, July 28, 2000; the "North East Art Rock Festival" (NEARfest) at Baker Hall in the Zoellner Arts Center (Lehigh University, Bethlehem, Pennsylvania) on Sunday, July 10, 2005; and the "Rock in Opposition" festival at Maison de la Musique de Cap Decouverte in Carmaux, France on Sunday, September 20, 2009. The Muffins have released more than a dozen different albums on various record labels, including several new CDs through Cuneiform Records.

MURRAY SCHAFF'S ARISTOCRATS

The jazz band Murray Schaff's Aristocrats came into existence in Philadelphia, Pennsylvania in 1950. The group's initial lineup consisted of singer-saxophonist Murray Schaff, electric guitarist Al Carmen (his later replacement was Don Farrell), electric bassist Frankie Mayo, pianist Bobby Boyd and former Gene Krupa protégé Dave Black on drums. Shortly after forming they adopted R&B and in the fall of 1951 the band worked its way to Baltimore, Maryland where they regularly appeared at two separate night clubs, the Surf Club and the Spa Restaurant. Working down the road in the nation's capital was a logical extension for the band.

Murray Schaff's Aristocrats debuted in Washington, D.C. at the Blue Mirror Club where they were second-billed to the Billy Williams Quarter in an engagement that ran from Monday, November 19 through Sunday, November 25, 1951. The band's non-stop upbeat music – a mixture of traditional jazz covers and raucous R&B originals with a prominent backbeat – defied categorization and their dynamic stage show literally had night club audiences rocking and rolling in the seats. They were called back for an extended four-week stay that began on Monday, December 24, 1951 and lasted until Sunday, January 20, 1952, including a second-billing to jazz singer Ella Fitzgerald from Monday, January 14 to Saturday, January 19, 1952.

When the Blue Mirror Club bookings wound down, Murray Schaff's Aristocrats sought to capitalize on their popularity in the nation's capital and soon found an eager suitor in the Hilltop Restaurant just outside of the city's eastern limits on the developing Marlboro Pike in Prince George's County, Maryland. The night club, whose address at the time was 5211 Marlboro Pike (Coral Hills), was just steps away from the Washington, D.C. line and across the street from a couple of night clubs called the Campus and Mike Young's Café. The Hilltop had just changed hands again and was back under the ownership of Lucy M. Gentile and Bayless Smith, who were looking for new, dynamic ensembles who could offer their patrons many different styles of high-energy music and headline their bills that included assorted orchestras, jazz bands, pop singers, comedians and exotic dancers.

Murray Schaff's Aristocrats opening night of Tuesday, March 25, 1952 saw them headline a Hilltop Restaurant bill that also included trapeze artist Alma Bray and the duo of

Kast and Abernathy (Frank "Sonny" Kast and Bill Abernathy, "Washington's Favorite Jivesters"). A box advertisement in the Washington Daily News on their opening day announced, "HERE THEY COME. 1952'S Skyrocketing Quintet. Rock and Roll to Their Exciting Jazz." It was the first time the full term "rock and roll" was used to advertise the appearance of a live band in Prince George's County, Maryland.

Several days later, Hal Rosen, in his "Tips on Tables" column in the Saturday, March 29, 1952 edition of the Washington Daily News, wrote: "Here's a group who wants to make you rock and roll in your seats. It's Murray Schaff and his Aristocrats, currently featured at the Hilltop…the music these boys provide is more than slightly frantic." Reportedly, Schaff insisted to local reporters at this time that the music his band played was to be referred to as "rock and roll," but the term itself was still foreign to the Washington, D.C. media and journalists were slow to correctly apply it to the new phenomena unfolding before their eyes and ears.

Crowds packed the Hilltop Restaurant every single night to see Murray Schaff's Aristocrats, with people coming from miles around to view this new musical sensation. They played a variety of tunes – jazz and pop classics, covers of Treniers, Dominoes and Bill Haley songs, and their own originals such as "Believe Me" and "I Am Waiting for Ships That Never Come" – all of which were given their own rock and roll interpretation. The band remained at the Hilltop Restaurant through September 1953, during which time ads for the group in the night club section of the Washington Daily News screamed out "Go! Go! Go!," and "Still Rocking the Town."

Murray Schaff's Aristocrats, the region's original rock and roll invaders, remained in the nation's capital throughout the 1950s and displayed their musical talents in Washington, D.C. at such night clubs as the Blue Mirror Club, the Casino Royal Theatre Restaurant, and the Showcase, and in Prince George's County, Maryland at the Rustic Cabin Restaurant (Colmar Manor), the 4400 Club (Brentwood) and the Senate Inn (Capitol Heights). During these years the band recorded several singles for such labels as Essex, Jubilee, Sound, and Josie, though their efforts rated only as regional hits in the Northeast.

Despite their local success, the band members went their separate ways in 1960, with Murray Schaff moving to New York City where he formed a new jazz band, the Scott Murray Trio, which remained active through the 1970s. In the early 1980s Schaff returned to Philadelphia, where he owned and operated Murray's Variety Store in the city until his passing on Saturday, October 26, 1996 at the age of 69. Although Murray Schaff's Aristocrats never gained the national recognition they so richly deserved, their influence on Washington, D.C. rock and roll was greatly significant. Schaff broke new ground and his band's popularity caused other area night club owners to give careful consideration to this exciting new style of music.

THE MYDNIGHT SONN

The Mydnight Sonn was a rock and roll band from Oxon Hill, Maryland that formed in 1966 and for two years was a top attraction on the Washington, D.C. area's teen dance scene. The group's lineup consisted of five musicians, all of whom attended either Oxon Hill Junior High School or Oxon Hill High School during their time in the band: lead singer-lead guitarist Mark Ellis, rhythm guitarist Jerry Smith, bassist Rick Seal, electric organist Alan Creveling and drummer Steve Ellis.

The Mydnight Sonn offered the popular R&B and rock and roll hits of the day and covered such artists as the Beatles, the Rolling Stones, the Animals, Gerry and the Pacemakers, the Buckinghams, the Temptations and the Four Tops.

During its time the Mydnight Sonn performed in Maryland at weddings, pool parties and teen dances at such locations as Oxon Hill Junior High School (Oxon Hill), Oxon Hill High

School (Oxon Hill), the Eugene Burroughs Teen Club (Eugene Burroughs Junior High School in Accokeek), the John Hanson Teen Club (John Hanson Junior High School in Oxon Hill), the Roger B. Taney Teen Club (Roger B. Taney Junior High School in Temple Hills), the Wedge (Bethesda Youth Center), the Andrews Air Force Base Officers' Club (Prince George's County, Maryland), and the Saint Mark Presbyterian Church Coffee House (North Bethesda); and in Washington, D.C. at the Bolling Air Force Base Teen Club and the Congress Heights United Methodist Church in the Southeast quadrant of the city.

The Mydnight Sonn disbanded in 1968, with members Alan Creveling and Rick Seal soon resurfacing in another Oxon Hill-based rock and roll band, the March of Time.

NATTY BUMPO

Natty Bumpo emerged in the 1960s as one of the Washington, D.C. area's top psychedelic rock and roll bands and was best known for its position as house band at the Ambassador Theatre in 1967 where they opened for some for the best visiting national acts of the era.

The band formed in Wheaton, Maryland in 1963 as an acoustic folk music trio consisting of Wheaton natives Marty Baum and Chuck Smith on guitars and singer Judy Dalrymple. Baum, then attending the University of Maryland, and Smith, then a student at American University, had both been schooled in jazz and were multi-instrumentalists and accomplished songwriters. During its early years the group played coffee houses and special events on various college campuses around the nation's capital.

In the middle 1960s Natty Bumpo experienced changes in personnel and settled on a lineup of lead singer Cam Bruce, guitarist (and sometime drummer) Marty Baum, guitarist Arvil "Dee" Clay, bassist Stephen Baum, saxophonist-keyboardist-guitarist Chuck Smith and drummer Bill Havu. Later in the decade several musicians passed through the band including guitarists Jackson "J.R." Simms and Joe Tass, and keyboardists Tommy Lepson and Steve Spencer.

As the Summer of Love approached, Natty Bumpo evolved into a heavy psychedelic rock band that specialized in original material and intricate interplay. During this time the band worked local night clubs in Washington, D.C. such as the Purple Finger and the Rogue, both on Bladensburg Road NE, and performed concerts and shows at such locations as the P Street Beach near Dupont Circle and Christ Church Washington Parish (620 G Street SE, Washington, D.C.).

In one of the band's highlights, they appeared on the supporting bill for a concert by the Beach Boys at the Washington Coliseum on Saturday, April 15, 1967, a show that also included performances by the Casinos, Jim and Jean, the Chartbusters, and the Minus IV. When the Ambassador Theatre was utilized for rock and roll concerts during the second half of 1967, Natty Bumpo was called upon to work two engagements in the month of August: opening for the Jimi Hendrix Experience for five nights – Wednesday, August 9 through Sunday, August 13, 1967; and appearing on a triple bill headlined by the Wildflower and supported by U.S. Male for five nights – Wednesday, August 16, 1967 through Sunday, August 20, 1967.

During the week the Jimi Hendrix Experience was in town, Natty Bumpo drummer Bill Havu received a call to fill in for ailing drummer Mitch Mitchell for the band's appearance at a special event at the Ambassador Theatre entitled "Youth Concert." This program of jazz and psychedelic music was sponsored by the Adams Morgan Summer Program and took place on Thursday, August 10, 1967, 3 to 5pm. The show included performances by the Family Album, Les McCann Ltd., Donald Leace, the Paul Hawkins Latin Jazz Quintet, Natty Bumpo, and the Jimi Hendrix Experience. Havu played with the Jimi Hendrix Experience that day, completing an abbreviated, three-song set which included a rendition of "Purple Haze."

In 1969 Natty Bumpo worked a long engagement at the Showboat Lounge, which, ironically, was situated directly across the street from the Ambassador Theatre. They also made a couple of concert appearances at the Oxon Hill Free Stage in Oxon Hill, Maryland before disbanding late in the year.

In the 1970s founding member Marty Baum relocated to the West Coast and for several years put together different versions of Natty Bumpo in California and Oregon. During its time in the nation's capital, Natty Bumpo signed with Philips Records and recorded and released three 45rpm single records: "Theme from 'Valley of the Dolls'" backed with "Legends" (Natty Bumpo; Philips Records, 1967); "Carnival" backed with 'Nothin' Stones You Like Music" (Natty Bumpo; Philips Records, 1968); and "Our Love" backed with "I'll Follow You" (Natty Bumpo; Philips Records, 1968).

THE NATURALS

In 1957 a young rock and roll band called the Dyals performed at a talent contest hosted by Jerry Toronto at Strick's Restaurant in Silver Hill, Maryland. The group consisted of lead singer-guitarist Raymond McDuffie, guitarist Ronnie McDuffie, bassist Jack Aldrich and drummer Ralph McDuffie, with all four of the band members hailing from the Anacostia neighborhood of Southeast Washington, D.C.

Shortly after participating in the Strick's Restaurant talent contest, Ronnie McDuffie received an offer to play guitar in a country rock band led by Lonnie Spence at the North Inn in Waldorf, Maryland. The night club's owner took a liking to his style of play and asked him to put together a different group that would also work the North Inn. Ronnie McDuffie then recruited the drummer from Lonnie Spence's band, Ronnie McGehee, and formed a new R&B-rock band called the Naturals. The original lineup of this outfit consisted of lead singer Bob Raybold, keyboardist-guitarist Ronnie McDuffie, guitarist Ray McDuffie, bassist Jack Aldrich, saxophonist Ralph McDuffie (switching over from drums) and drummer Ronnie McGehee.

From 1957 to 1959 the Naturals performed in Maryland at such night clubs as the North Inn (Waldorf), the Midway (Waldorf), the Village Barn (Morningside), Strick's Restaurant (Silver Hill) and the Las Vegas Club (Coral Hills). They also made regular appearances on "The Milt Grant Show" where they competed in "Battle of the Bands" competitions and backed up various headline performers. Grant regularly booked the group into the live record hop shows he staged at venues throughout the Washington, D.C. area.

In terms of material, the Naturals covered a mix of bands and artists with one of their favorite artists being jazz singer-trumpeter Louis Prima. They also preferred to perform the music of several Philadelphia-based R&B-rock bands of the era such as Georgie Young and the Rockin' Bocs, the Tyrones, the Treniers, and the Playboys.

In the early 1960s the Naturals remained a popular commodity on the local music scene, performing at two Washington, D.C. night clubs, the Rocket Room and Benny's Rebel Room. In 1962 the band was hired to back the Kalin Twins on a United States and Canadian tour that lasted eight months. During that time several drummers passed through the band including Bobby Black, Joe Goss and Jack Kerge. When the Naturals came off the road with the Kalin Twins, they were hired as the house band at the Skylark on Naylor Road SE in Washington, D.C. When the Skylark closed in 1963 the Naturals temporarily disbanded.

In time the Naturals reformed with a new lineup and from 1966 to 1968 held house band duties at the Quonset Supper Club in Silver Hill, Maryland. During their time at the Quonset the group often played behind lead singers Richie Kay and Johnny Staggs. Personnel changes were constant and in 1969 the band moved to a night club called Gus and John's Italian Villa in Camp Springs, Maryland where they remained on the schedule into the early 1970s.

The Naturals remained active in the Washington, D.C. area with various lineups into the early 1980s (for part of the late 1970s Ronnie McDuffie also had a version of the band playing night clubs in Cocoa Beach, Florida). Through the years a variety of highly regarded musicians passed through the band including guitarists Frank Shegogue and Danny Gatton, bassists Jimmy LaComb and Mike Goins, keyboardist Sam Paladino, saxophonists Adrian "Switchy" Swicegood, Steve Reynolds and Mike Sheer, and drummer Ron MacDonald.

THE NIGHTHAWKS

The Nighthawks were formed in the spring of 1972 by singer-harmonicist player Mark Wenner, a Bethesda, Maryland native who had graduated from Bethesda-Chevy Chase High School and Columbia University. The group's original lineup consisted of: Wenner; guitarist Jimmy Thackery of Washington, D.C.; bassist Don Monahan, who was originally from St. George Island in St. Mary's County, Maryland; keyboardist Bill Holland from Silver Spring, Maryland; and drummer Larry Bolet of Laurel, Maryland.

The Nighthawks initially rehearsed in the basement of Don Monahan's Hyattsville home and got started by working most of 1972 at a night club in Washington, D.C. called the Far Inn. In 1973 the band performed regularly at two other Washington, D.C. night clubs, Graffiti on K Street NW, and the Reading Gaol off of Dupont Circle. They also opened at the Cellar Door in Georgetown for such acts as Linda Ronstadt and John Hammond. During this time the band's repertoire consisted of old blues tunes, material by 1950s rock and rollers such as Elvis Presley, Jerry Lee Lewis and Little Richard, and covers of songs by the J. Geils Band, the Allman Brothers Band and Little Feat.

Early on, the Nighthawks experienced personnel changes. Monahan, Holland and Bolet were eventually replaced by guitarist-keyboardist Peter Bonta, bassist Anton "Ace the Bass" Hansmann and drummer Lee Smith. In June 1974 Wenner revamped the band, maintaining Thackery and bringing in bassist Jan Zukowski (formerly of the Cherry People), and drummer Pete Ragusa (formerly of Razz). It was this quartet that came to be considered the band's classic lineup, remaining intact for over 12 years.

In the middle 1970s the Nighthawks performed in Washington, D.C. at such night clubs as Apple Pie, Mr. Henry's Tenley Circle, Cousin Nick's, the Act IV Supper Club, Fat Howard's, the Bayou and the Childe Harold; and in Maryland at the Psyche Delly (Bethesda) and Mr. Henry's College Park (College Park). They began touring the country and performed up to 300 shows per year, establishing themselves as one of the nation's most beloved blues bands, a position they have maintained to the current day. In 1974 the band recorded and released the first of their 30-plus albums, "Rock & Roll" (The Nighthawks; Aladdin Records, 1974).

One of the most talked-about events in Nighthawks history, "The M Street Shuffle," occurred on the night of Thursday, July 27, 1978 when George Thorogood and the Destroyers were appearing at the Cellar Door in Georgetown and the Nighthawks were right across the street at Desperado's. During Thorogood's second set that evening, the band launched into the song "Madison Blues," and the club's light man sent a signal across the street for the Nighthawks to strike up the same tune. Thorogood and Nighthawks guitarist Jimmy Thackery then simultaneously exited their respective clubs and met in the middle of a bustling M Street where they stopped traffic and jammed away on the tune for several minutes, with Thackery then moving over to the Cellar Door to join the Destroyers and Thorogood transferring to Desperado's to finish up with the Nighthawks.

In 1980 the Nighthawks signed with a major label and released the album "The Nighthawks" (The Nighthawks; Mercury Records, 1980). Subsequent album releases appeared on a variety of independent record labels.

In 1987 guitarist Jimmy Thackery left the Nighthawks and subsequently played in his own blues bands, Jimmy Thackery and the Assassins and Jimmy Thackery and the Drivers. In the post-Thackery years the Nighthawks went through a period where they were booked through the Rosebud Agency and served as the backup touring band for a number of national blues acts including singer-guitarists Elvin Bishop and John Lee Hooker, singer-guitarist-harmonicist John Hammond and singer-pianist Pinetop Perkins.

The Nighthawks had numerous musicians pass through its ranks in the 1980s and 1990s including keyboardists Greg Allman and Greg Wetzel, saxophonist-harmonicist Jimmy Hall, keyboardist Mike Cowan, and a number of guitarists including Jimmy Nalls, Steuart Smith, Jim Solberg, Pete Kennedy, Warren Haynes, Danny Morris and Pete Kanaras.

In 2004 Wenner and Ragusa introduced a new version of the Nighthawks completed by singer-guitarist Paul Bell and singer-bassist Johnny Castle. In February 2010 Ragusa left the group and was replaced by singer-drummer Mark Stutso, who had previously performed with Jimmy Thackery and the Drivers for more than 20 years. The band recently released its 31st album, "All You Gotta Do" (The Nighthawks; EllerSoul Records, 2017). The Nighthawks remain active today with a lineup of Wenner, Bell, Castle and Stutso.

NIGHTMAN

Nightman was a hard-rocking, Silver Spring-based band that formed in 1978 with a lineup of singer-guitarist Mike Colburn, bassist Jim Crenca and drummer Harvey Nussbaum. In March 1980 Colburn reorganized the band as a quartet, bringing in guitarist Bill Craig, bassist Ted Nicely and drummer Doug Tull (all former members of Razz).

Nightman opened shows in Washington, D.C. for a variety of visiting national acts including: Sylvain Sylvain at the Cellar Door on Monday, March 10, 1980; the Pretenders at the Bayou on Thursday, March 27, 1980; the Cure at the Bayou on Monday, April 14, 1980; and the Joe Perry Project at the Bayou on Sunday, May 24, 1981. In addition, they regularly appeared at such Washington, D.C. night clubs as the Cellar Door, the Childe Harold, Columbia Station, the Bayou and Desperado's; in Maryland at the Psyche Delly (Bethesda); and in Virginia at Louie's Rock City (Bailey's Crossroads).

In November 1981 Niceley and Tull left Nightman to become the full-time rhythm section for rock and roll singer-guitarist Tommy Keene. The band carried on as a trio with Colburn and Craig bringing in drummer Joey Romero. They subsequently worked Washington, D.C. night clubs such as Nightclub 9:30 and the Chancery, and in one outing opened for Eddie Money at the Wax Museum on Monday, October 18, 1982.

In March 1983, during an engagement at Friendship Station in Washington, D.C., Colburn changed the name of the band to Other World. Nightman has one album to its credit, "No Escape" (Nightman; Limp Records, 1981).

NILS LOFGREN

Singer-guitarist Nils Lofgren has long enjoyed a successful solo career, in addition to having been a member of Bruce Springsteen and the E Street band for more than 30 years. Born in Chicago, Illinois, he grew up in Bethesda, Maryland and during his years at Walter Johnson High School in the late 1960s he played in such rock and roll bands as the Waifs and the Grass.

In 1967 during his junior year of high school he was recruited into a Bethesda-based psychedelic rock band called the Crystal Mesh, whose lineup consisted of Lofgren on lead guitar, singer Tom Birks, guitarist Rolf Hanson, bassist Scotty Ball and drummer Sid Sithens. The Crystal Mesh was popular on the local teen dance circuit and garnered attention for opening concerts at the Ambassador Theatre for Moby Grape and the Hollies.

In the late 1960s Lofgren played in such rock and roll bands as Paul Dowell and the Dolphin and the Shot. In 1969 he formed the band Grin, which became one of the very best rock and roll bands in the nation's capital and gained national recognition for their record deals with the Spindizzy and A&M labels. Grin remained active through 1974.

Lofgren established a major contact in the music industry when, at the age of seventeen in May 1969, he snuck backstage at the Cellar Door in Georgetown, introduced himself to guitarist-singer Neil Young, and performed for him most of the songs that would later appear on Grin's first album. Young was duly impressed and had Lofgren play piano and acoustic guitar on his 1970 solo album "After the Goldrush" (Neil Young; Reprise Records, 1970).

In 1975 Lofgren began a solo career with his first band rounded out with rhythm guitarist Tom Lofgren, bassist Scotty Ball and drummer Mike Zack. He signed with a major record label and recorded and released his first solo album, "Nils Lofgren" (Nils Lofgren; A&M Records, 1975). His career took off and to date he has more than two-dozen solo albums to his credit.

In May of 1984 Lofgren was invited to join Bruce Springsteen and the E Street Band as a singer-guitarist. He has been a full-time member of the group ever since and appears on more than 10 of their albums. He has also recorded and toured with Neil Young and Ringo Starr's All Star Band.

Lofgren, as a member of the E Street Band (Bruce Springsteen's backup group), was inducted into the Rock and Roll Hall of Fame in the "Award for Musical Excellence" category on Thursday, April 10, 2014. He presently continues to record and tour as a solo artist and remains a permanent member of Bruce Springsteen and the E Street Band.

NOBODY'S CHILDREN

Nobody's Children formed in District Heights, Maryland in 1965 and became one of the top teen dance rock and roll bands of the Washington, D.C. area. Originally called the Coachmen, the initial lineup of the group consisted of: lead singer-guitarist Dennis Boone of Silver Spring; singer-guitarist Jan Zukowski of Forestville; bassist Willie Lucas of Silver Spring; and drummer Mark Mouhtouris of District Heights. The Coachmen covered the songs of the British Invasion and were regular attractions at the Francis Scott Key Teen Club (Francis Scott Key Junior High School in District Heights).

In the fall of 1965 the Coachmen were reorganized as the Adam's Apples. The lineup of this new rock and roll band consisted of lead singer-guitarist Dennis Boone, singer-lead guitarist Lee Travers, singer-bassist Jan Zukowski (switching over from guitar) and drummer Mark Mouhtouris. In May 1966 the band performed at a "Battle of the Bands" at Marlboro Speedway in Upper Marlboro, Maryland. It was there that they caught the attention of WPGC disc jockey Harv Moore, who took an interest in the group and began promoting them and booking them to perform at local record hops. Shortly after their performance at Marlboro Speedway, at Moore's urgings, the group changed its name to Nobody's Children.

On Friday, August 6, 1966, Nobody's Children opened for Neil Diamond at the Manassas Armory in Virginia, sharing the undercard with the British Walkers, the English Setters and the Rip-Tydes. In addition to its own performance, the group was also called upon to serve as Diamond's onstage backup band that evening. In November of that year they released their first single, "Jungo Partner (A Worthless Cajun)" backed with "Let Her Go" (Nobody's Children; United Artists Records, 1966).

In early 1967 Dennis Boone and Jan Zukowski left Nobody's Children and were replaced by two former members of an R&B band called the Carpetbaggers, singer-guitarist Mike Colburn and bassist Frank Crain. Throughout the year the revamped version of Nobody's Children (Travers, Colburn, Crain and Mouhtouris) worked dances in Maryland at the Clinton Fire Department (Clinton), Suitland High School (Suitland), Crossland High School (Camp Springs), Surrattsville High School (Clinton) and Bells United Methodist Church (Camp Springs). In January 1968 the band released the 45rpm single record "I Can't Let Go" backed with "Don'tcha Feel Like Cryin'" (Nobody's Children; Bullet Records, 1968), which was quickly picked up and rereleased on a national level by Buddha Records.

Nobody's Children toured the Eastern and Midwestern United States in support of its record in early 1968 and in April of that year gave a live performance on "Upbeat," a music variety program in Cleveland, Ohio. That summer they were back in the Washington, D.C. area and worked a two-week job with the psychedelic rock and roll group Wild Honey at the Rocket Room. In September 1968 Mark Mouhtouris left the band and was replaced by drummer Rick Miller. Nobody's Children still enjoyed great local popularity, but disbanded shortly after headlining a concert at Prince George's Community College's Novak Field House in Largo, Maryland on Saturday, February 15, 1969.

THE NORTH STAR BAND

The North Star Band was a popular, Bethesda-based country rock group that performed at night clubs throughout the Washington, D.C. area from the middle 1970s to the middle 1980s. The band experienced numerous personnel changes during its reign with one of its more popular lineups consisting of lead singer-guitarist-harmonicist Al Johnson, steel guitarist Jay Jessup, bassist Jim Robeson, keyboardist Louis Hager and drummer Paul Goldstein.

Among the other great area musicians that passed through the band included: singer-guitarist Liz Meyer; guitarists Mike Melchione, Gantt Kushner, Chris Sonneberg and Steuart Smith; bassists Bob Prader, Rico Petruccelli, David Besley and Johnny Castle; fiddler Bobby Spates; and drummers Dave Elliott and Robbie Magruder.

The North Star Band played a wide range of music including original country rock compositions, Hank Williams covers, and everything from swing jazz to R&B classics. They appeared in Washington, D.C. at such night clubs as the Childe Harold, Desperado's, the Far Inn, Rocky Raccoon's Saloon, Mr. Henry's Tenley Circle; in Maryland at the Italian Gardens (College Park), the Red Fox Inn (Bethesda), the Cross Roads (Bladensburg), Fred and Sully's (Wheaton), Timothy's Pub (Rockville), and Papa Joe's (Rockville); and in Virginia at the Annandale Grill (Annandale), the Shed (Alexandria), Quincy's (Arlington), Eskimo Nell's (Arlington) and the Birchmere (then-located in Arlington).

The band has two albums to its credit: "Tonight the North Star Band" (The North Star Band; Adelphi Records, 1979); and "'Burnin' 'Em Up' Live at Eskimo Nell's" (The North Star Band; Es-Ki-Mo Records, 1981).

THE OFF BEATS

The Off Beats were an early-era rock and roll band that was originally based in the Anacostia neighborhood of Southeast Washington, D.C. The group formed in 1958 with a roster consisting of lead guitarist Bob Hancock, rhythm guitarist Ernie Gorospe, lead singer-bassist Henry Pujol, saxophonists John Broaddus and Chuck Blonde, and drummer Jerry Wallmark (in addition, Henry's sister, Danielle Pujol, often performed with the band as a guest singer).

In the beginning, the band members, almost all of whom attended different high schools around the Washington, D.C. area, rehearsed at Gorospe's house at 2305 Chester Street

SE in the Anacostia neighborhood of the city. The group became a popular attraction at teen dances in Washington, D.C. at the St. Francis Xavier Parish Teen Club, the St. Teresa of Avila Catholic Church Teen Club, and the Order of Jobs Daughters Bethel No, 2 (a Masonic Temple at 5832 Georgia Avenue NW, Washington, D.C.). They also appeared in Prince George's County, Maryland at the Beltsville Volunteer Fire Department (Beltsville), the Branchville Volunteer Fire Company (College Park) and the Hyattsville Armory (Hyattsville).

The Off Beats specialized in the popular rock and roll songs of the day. Among the artists they covered included Gene Vincent, Elvis Presley, Duane Eddy, Little Richard, Fats Domino, Bo Diddley, Chuck Berry, the Crickets (featuring singer-guitarist Buddy Holly), Bobby Darin, Bobby Rydell, Dion and the Belmonts and Carl Perkins.

In 1959 the Off Beats underwent personnel changes. Original members Gorospe (now playing bass), Broaddus and Wallmark remained, while three newcomers were introduced. The additions were 14-year-old guitarist Danny Gatton, and two former members of the Triumphs, keyboardist Dick Heintze and singer Ron MacDonald.

With the new pieces the band changed its name to Ronnie and the Off Beats and for the next two years worked as a house band at the Club Log Tavern in Alexandria, Virginia. They also performed in Washington, D.C. at the Rocket Room and the Starlite Restaurant; and in Prince George's County, Maryland at Strick's Restaurant (Silver Hill). During this period the band embarked on studio work with one of the results being the 45rpm single record "Beggarman" backed with "Trouble in Mind" (Ronnie and the Off Beats; Norwood Records, 1959).

In the early 1960s the band had several musicians pass through and would alternately work under several different headings including "Ronnie and the Off Beats," "Ronnie and the Offbeats," "The Off Beats," and "The Offbeats." Among some of the better-known players to work with the band included rhythm guitarist-bassist Jack Casady (who had previously been a member of the Triumphs and went on to play with Jefferson Airplane and Hot Tuna), and saxophone players Dick Moody and Ronnie McDuffie.

In one unusual pickup job "The Offbeats" played a dance for the Greenbelt Junior Teen Club at North End School in Greenbelt, Maryland on Saturday, October 15, 1960. For this performance, the band's lineup consisted of lead guitarist Danny Gatton, rhythm guitarist Jack Casady, singer-saxophonist Dick Moody, and singer-drummer Jack Kerge.

Ronnie and the Off Beats spent much of 1962 and part of 1963 as the house band at the Champagne Room (1304 F Street NW, Washington, D.C.), where, for a spell, their performances were broadcast live on Friday evenings over radio station WEAM. During this time the band featured the now-legendary tandem of Danny Gatton on lead guitar and Jack Casady on bass, two of the greatest musicians the Washington, D.C. area has ever produced.

In 1964 the band worked such Washington, D.C. night clubs as the Devonshire Grill and the Bastille Supper Club. They disbanded before the year was out, with several members later reappearing in the bands the Soul Mates, the East Coast Express, and Take Five.

THE OMEGAS

The Omegas were a rock and roll band that formed during the summer of 1965 in Silver Spring, Maryland and performed at local parties, college fraternity events, and on the local teen dance circuit. The band's original lineup consisted of lead singer-bassist Art Brueggeman, lead guitarist Thurman Ryder, rhythm guitarist Steve Callahan, keyboardist Mike Sarigumba and drummer Mike McKeller. The group spent much of the summer of 1966 performing at the Paddock Supper Club in Ocean City, Maryland.

The Omegas experienced changes in personnel towards the end of its run and eventually disbanded in 1968. They have two 45rpm single records to their credit: "Mean Old Man Day" backed with "Mud" (The Omegas; Edgewood Records, 1966); and "I Can't Believe" backed with "Mr. Yates" (The Omegas; United Artists, 1968 – this recording features former Hangmen members Joe Triplett singing lead and Tom Guernsey on guitar).

ORIGINAL FETISH

Original Fetish was a unique rock and roll band that concentrated on humorous original material and followed the motto – "Music for people who burp and fart."

The group formed in the middle 1970s in Lewisdale, an unincorporated community in Prince George's County, Maryland, when singer-harmonicist David Doyle, who had previously performed with guitarist Jay Becker at open mics at the Varsity Grill Back Room in College Park, Maryland, joined forces with former members of a jazz outfit called So What? The original lineup of Original Fetish consisted of singers David Doyle (Oxie Scrubb) and Willie Doyle (Deadly Earnest), guitarist Phil Lazarus, bassist Gary Lasher, keyboardist Gary Harmon and drummer Art Bessette.

Original Fetish made its auspicious debut in August 1978 at El Brookman's, a comedy club in Southeast Washington, D.C., and subsequently became their long-running house band. During their two-year existence they also made appearances in Washington, D.C. at such night clubs as Mr. Henry's Tenley Circle, Columbia Station and the Childe Harold; in Maryland at the Italian Gardens (College Park), the Psyche Delly (Bethesda), the Marble Bar (Baltimore) and No Fish Today (Baltimore); and in Virginia at Beacon's Backstage (Falls Church).

The band's more infamous local performances were at the Outrageous Music Festival at the Warner Theatre in Washington, D.C. on Wednesday, May 9, 1979, where they appeared with Root Boy Slim, the Cramps, Gary Sinclair, Dimitri & Friends; and a headlining slot at the First Annual Primal Scream Dance Contest which was held at the Grand Ballroom (University of Maryland) on Friday, November 30, 1979.

Original Fetish thrived on off-the-wall originals, including such gems as "Give Me Money, Sex and Drugs" and "Ultraviolence is Fun." Other musicians to work with the group included singers Linda Paine and Jeanette Chamberlain; guitarists Bruce MacKinnon and Linwood Taylor; and saxophonists John Esquire, Jamie MacKinnon and Ron Holloway.

Original Fetish gave its final performance at the Psyche Delly in Bethesda, Maryland on Sunday, August 17, 1980. During its time the band released one single, "Standing in Line at Studio 54" backed with "I'm Glad Elvis is Dead" (Original Fetish; Warped Records, 1980); and one posthumous album, "Pink on the Inside: Rare Cuts 1978-80" (Original Fetish; Warped Records, 2005).

OVERKILL

Overkill came together in 1975 and during the summer of 1976 began playing on a regular basis at the Keg, a raucous night club in the Glover Park neighborhood of Washington, D.C. that had most recently housed such hard-rocking groups as the Cherry People, Razz, and the Slickee Boys.

Overkill's lineup at the time consisted of singer Barney Jones, guitarists Randy Austin and John Owens, bassist Harrison Sohmer and drummer Vance McCormick. They blitzed the Keg's patrons with a mix of unique hard rock originals, covers of 1960s bands such as the Seeds, the Velvet Underground and Roxy Music, and, in retrospect, bridged Washington, D.C.'s heavy rock scene of the early 1970s with the burgeoning punk rock movement that was in its formative stages at the time. Overkill endured several personnel changes during its run and reportedly lasted into early 1978.

PATSY STEPHENS

Singer-guitarist Patsy Stephens was born in Washington, D.C. and raised in the Prince George's county communities of Adelphi and Beltsville. As a teenager her mother was a fan of C&W music and Stephens listened to a variety of musicians including the Temptations, the Beach Boys, Ronnie Dove and Lesley Gore. While attending High Point High School in the late 1960s she participated as a singer-dancer in a presentation of the musical "Anything Goes" (music and lyrics by Cole Porter) Later, while attending Prince George's Community College in Largo, she took a similar role in a presentation of the musical "Mame" (music and lyrics by Jerry Herman).

In the late 1970s Stephens and her husband reconnected with the local music scene when they began attending DiGennaro's Restaurant in Laurel, Maryland where they enjoyed bluegrass bands such as Foggy Bottom. The pair would go and see performances by other bluegrass groups like the Country Gentlemen and the Seldom Scene and spent much of the 1980s attending picking parties where Patsy would sing and play guitar and her husband Sully played upright bass.

In 2000, after years of tending to her family, Stephens became a singer-guitarist in a bluegrass band from Columbia, Maryland called River's Edge. In 2002 she began frequenting jam sessions at a night club called the Friendly Inn in West Friendship, Maryland and it was there that she sang and played guitar in their bluegrass house band, Die Hausmusik. In 2004 the group changed its name to Keep Off the Grass and remained active through 2010. Separately, in 2002, Stephens had joined another bluegrass band called Mountain View and continues to play out with them today.

In 2010 Stephens sang with Celtic music specialist Brendan Pelan at a Friendly Inn session and then met C&W singer-guitarist Chick Hall, Jr. She subsequently sang with the Hall Brothers (featuring Chick Jr. and Chris Hall) at Remington's of Laurel and the American Legion College Park Post 217. It was those experiences that led her to form her own revue that would feature classic C&W artists and highlight the work of singer Patsy Cline.

In 2011 Stephens introduced "Patsy's Honky Tonk Torch & Twang," a show offering C&W, rockabilly and Patsy Cline covers with Stephens singing and playing guitar and musical backing provided by the Hall Brothers (guitarist Chick Hall, Jr., bassist Chris Hall and drummer Mike Toole). Besides Patsy Cline, Stephens cover songs by such C&W artists as Hank Williams, Patsy Montana, Kitty Wells, Loretta Lynn, Connie Smith and Hank Snow.

Stephens and the band perform at a wide range of area venues including the JV Restaurant (Falls Church), the New Deal Café (Greenbelt), the Old Bowie Town Grille (Bowie), and American Legions and festivals throughout the region. Currently, her outfit consists of Stephens, Chick and Chris Hall, steel guitarist Tommy Auldridge and either Chip Clemmer or Mike Toole on drums.

PATTY REESE

Singer-guitarist Patty Reese was raised in Silver Spring, Maryland and as a youth sang at Adelphi Presbyterian Church. While attending Francis Scott Key Junior High School in the middle and late 1970s she played in a folk guitar trio at the Iguana Coffeehouse (Luther Place Memorial Church) in Washington, D.C. During her time at Springbrook High School in the early 1980s she sang in musicals, talent shows and the choir, and was a regular participant in music department jam sessions.

Reese spent the middle 1980s as the lead singer in a pop-rock band called Island and from 1986 to 1989 she sang in the R&B-rock band Jr. Cline and the Recliners. From 1989 to 1992 she sang and played guitar in a C&W quartet called Plum Crazy, which was rounded out by singers Marianna Previti and Ruthie Logsdon, and bassist John Sprung. This outfit performed in Washington, D.C. at D.C. Space; in Maryland at Captain White's Seafood Restaurant (Silver Spring) and Big Lou's Crabhouse (Wheaton); and at festivals and shows throughout the region. In the early 1990s Reese also sang and played guitar in a Montgomery County-based rock and roll band called One Nite Stand.

In 1992 this singer-guitarist formed her own pop-rock group which she called the Patty Reese Band. The initial lineup of this outfit was Reese, guitarist David Bell, bassist Mark Easley and drummer John Tracey. Among the artists they covered were the Pretenders, Robert Palmer, Bonnie Raitt, Led Zeppelin, Janis Joplin and Patsy Cline. The band primarily performed in Maryland at two different night clubs, the 15 Mile House (Pikesville) and the Ritz (Rosedale). Late in the 1990s Reese went solo as a singer-acoustic guitarist. Among the area night clubs she performed at were the Round Table (Washington, D.C.), Kramerbooks and Afterwards (Washington, D.C.) and J.J. Muldoon's Restaurant and Saloon (Gaithersburg).

After a stay in California, Reese returned to the Washington, D.C. area in 2001 and put together a new version of the Patty Reese Band. This outfit served up a mix of blues and rock and roll and was completed by guitarist Dave Chappell, bassist Sonny Petrosky and drummer John Tracey.

Through the years Reese has employed some of the region's best musicians. Among those who have worked with her are guitarists Robert Fiester, Dan Hovey and Jeff Avery; bassists Steve Wolf, Mark Foster and Dennis Michaels; keyboardists Brian Simms and Wes Lanich; saxophonist Ron Holloway; and drummers John Thomakos, Brian Edwards and Robbie Magruder.

Reese has headlined the top venues in Washington, D.C. including Blues Alley, the Hamilton and Nightclub 9:30; in Virginia at the Birchmere (Alexandria), the Barns at Wolf Trap (Vienna) and Iota Club and Café (Arlington); and in Maryland at Strathmore (North Bethesda). She also regularly appears at jazz and blues festivals throughout the region such as the annual Chesapeake Bay Blues Festival.

The current Patty Reese Band consists of singer-guitarist Patty Reese, guitarist Jonathan Sloane, bassist Sonny Petrosky, keyboardist Tommy Lepson and drummer Andy Hamburger. She has four albums to her credit: "The Broad Highway" (Patty Reese Band; Patty Reese, 1995); "Here & Now" (Patty Reese; Patty Reese, 2004); "Strong Medicine" (Patty Reese; Azalea City Recordings, 2009); and "Let in the Sun" (Patty Reese; Azalea City Recordings, 2017).

PAUL BELL

Guitarist Paul Bell was born in Costa Rica and raised in several locations including Guatemala, Colombia and Chile. He briefly resided in Springfield, Virginia in the middle 1960s and returned to the area in 1971, living in Alexandria, Virginia. In the early 1970s while attending Thomas A. Edison High School he played guitar informally in jam sessions with friends.

After finishing school Bell began visiting local night clubs where he witnessed live performances by such musicians as blues rock guitarist Roy Buchanan and multi-styled guitarist Danny Gatton, who was then a part of the rockabilly trio Danny and the Fat Boys. He also had the opportunity to sit in with the Nighthawks in one of its early editions.

Bell spent the 1970s playing in such musical outfits as the pop-rock band Midnight Sun and the rockabilly group Swing Shift. He also performed and recorded with the highly regarded R&B band Bill Holland and Rent's Due. In the 1980s Bell performed with a number of the region's best R&B bands including Jr. Cline and the Recliners, Soul Crackers, the DV8s, and Newkeys, who backed singer-guitarist Nils Lofgren on several tours from 1987 to 1989 and performed onstage with Bruce Springsteen at the Stone Pony in Asbury Park, New Jersey in 1989.

The 1990s saw Bell begin a lengthy freelance period where he engaged in extensive studio work and performed with a plethora of area musical artists. Most notably he played lead and rhythm guitar for Nils Lofgren as a member of his backup band on several United States and European tours. In addition, he and Lofgren also performed many shows as an acoustic duo.

Other performing artists Bell played guitar with included: blues rock groups such as the Catfish Hodge Band and the Bill Baker Band; C&W singer Darren DeFoore; the jazz band Doc Scantlin's Imperial Palms Orchestra; the country rock band the Rosslyn Mountain Boys; the R&B-oriented Joe Stanley Band; and a rock and roll act called the Hanson Brothers.

Bell worked in an acoustic duo format with guitarists such as Mike Cotter and Tom Lofgren and spent several years playing guitar in the R&B outfits Tommy Lepson and the Lazy Boys and the Tommy Lepson Band. During this time he also appeared as a solo guitarist, performing a "Sunday Jazz Brunch" show at two different area restaurants, the Bistro Bistro in Arlington, Virginia and the Starland Café in Washington, D.C.

Since 2004 Bell has been playing lead guitar for the Nighthawks, the legendary Washington, D.C. area blues band whose current lineup also includes lead singer-harmonicist Mark Wenner, singer-bassist Johnny Castle and singer-drummer Mark Stutso. Recently, he has also been performing and recording with the pop-rock band Eureka Moment.

PAUL GOLDSTEIN

Drummer Paul Goldstein was born in Washington, D.C. and raised in Silver Spring, Maryland. He began playing drums at age 11 and initially took lessons at Smith's Drum Shop in Wheaton. During his teen years he listened and played along to records that featured such drummers as Ginger Baker, Elvin Jones, Al Jackson, Jr., and the James Brown tandem of John "Jabo" Starks and Clyde Stubblefield, learning the songs lick-for-lick. During his time at John F. Kennedy High School in the early 1970s he jammed with other musicians in the school's music room and drummed in a rock and roll band called Concert on the local teen dance scene.

Goldstein drummed for a multi-styled Top 40 band called the Four Seasons on the local hotel lounge circuit from 1972 to 1974 and then played in a local rock and roll band called Seneca from 1975 to 1976.

Goldstein next enjoyed a long run with the North Star Band, one of the region's top country rock bands, from 1976 to 1984. When he first joined up with that group the lineup was rounded out by singer-guitarist-harmonicist Al Johnson, guitarist Mike Melchione and bassist Bob Prader. Some of the area's top musicians passed through the North Star Band before its demise including guitarists Steuart Smith and Gantt Kushner, and bassists Jim Robeson and Johnny Castle.

After his time with the North Star Band ended, Goldstein spent several years drumming for a number of different bands including the local R&B band Tough Luck (featuring singer-harmonicist Lips Lackowitz) and two C&W groups, Whiskey River and the Gold Dust Band. In the early 1990s he began drumming for the rockabilly-styled Bobby Smith Band, a group he continues to work with to the present day.

Goldstein has also performed and/or recorded with such local bands and musicians as: multi-styled guitarist Danny Gatton; blues singer-guitarist Cathy Ponton King; blues rock singer-guitarist Tom Principato; the blues rock groups the Jimmy Cole Band and LHB (Lost Highway Band); country rock singer-guitarist Dave Allen (who made his mark as a songwriter both locally and in Nashville); the multi-styled R&B-rock band Bob Jenetes UpFront; and the multi-styled corporate band Fancy Pants.

Some of the nationally known artists Goldstein has drummed for include: blues rock singer-guitarist Duffy Kane; C&W singer Gene Watson; R&B singer Charlie Thomas; and the R&B vocal groups the Drifters and the Coasters.

Goldstein remains active on the Washington, D.C. area music scene and is currently drumming for two bands, the rock and roll group Lunch With Bob, and a Bob Dylan tribute act called the Bob Band.

PAUL JONES

Paul Jones was raised in Suitland, Maryland and as a youth learned to play the drums, piano and acoustic guitar, ultimately switching to bass guitar at age 10.

During his years at Suitland High School in the middle and late 1970s Jones played in the band High Voltage, a high-powered rock and roll quartet rounded out by lead singer Bobby Williams, guitarist David Brown, keyboardist Michael Salas and drummer Robert Dove. The band played in Prince George's County at private parties and competed in talent shows at venues like the John Eager Howard Community Center in Coral Hills and VFW Scott-Johnson-Pollins Post 9619 in Morningside.

From 1978 to 1979 Jones played bass in a short-lived rock and roll band out of Wheaton, Maryland called Dark Night. He then spent the early 1980s in a heavy rock and roll trio called Structure with singer-guitarist Steve Long and former High Voltage drummer Robert Dove. Structure covered bands such as Iron Maiden, Frank Marino and Mahogany Rush, Judas Priest and Rush, and played parties in Suitland and Temple Hills. He later took time off from the local music scene and concentrated on playing bass in the congregational band at Countryside Fellowship Church in Savage, Maryland.

In 1995 Jones joined Random Access, a Bowie, Maryland-based rock and roll band which also included lead singer Irvin Utz, lead guitarist Mike Dunn, rhythm guitarist John Haughey and drummer Freddie Ray. Covering groups like the Doobie Brothers, the Who, Stevie Ray Vaughan, Wilson Pickett and the Temptations, the group became a featured attraction at such Maryland establishments as Lasick's College Inn (College Park), the Riverdale Pizza Pub (Riverdale), Delaney's Irish Pizza Pub (Laurel) and Michael's Café (Columbia).

In 1997 Random Access disbanded and Utz and Jones put together a rock and roll band called the Bad Weather Boyz with guitarist Robert Fiester and drummer Conte Bellucci. The group quickly became one of the top night club attractions in the Washington, D.C. area, a status they maintained for years. Jones remained their bass player until 2001.

In recent years Jones has remained musically active in the region. He was part of an acoustic duo with singer-guitarist Steve Long called Two of a Kind, and played bass in the rock and roll bands Mirror Mirror and Group Therapy. In 2013 he was called back into the Bad Weather Boyz for a year's worth of gigs. That year he also filled in on bass at a concert performed by the legendary doo-wop band known as the Memories in Haymarket, Virginia. In 2015 Jones was playing in a Westminster, Maryland-based heavy metal band called Crash Course.

PAUL MASTRADONE

Blues rock singer-guitarist Paul Mastradone hails from Silver Spring, Maryland, where, during his years at Eastern Junior High School in the late 1960s he initially played bass in an R&B band called the Sounds of Time on the local teen dance scene. During his time at Montgomery Blair High School in the early 1970s he was bassist for Maxwell Parachute, a group that played a mix of R&B and rock and roll.

Mastradone left the local music scene behind and concentrated on education, eventually earning a PhD in chemistry from the University of Maryland. He returned to music in 1994 when he formed the Paulverizers, a Beltsville, Maryland-based blues band whose initial lineup consisted of singer-guitarist Charlie Havekost, Mastradone on bass and vocals, and drummer Rick Adenolfi. The group became a quartet when Adenolfi departed and singer-keyboardist Pete Locke and drummer Howard Moore were added. It was this lineup that recorded the album "Lunch Tent Revue" (The Paulverizers; PVZ Records, 1999). Thereafter, Havekost was replaced by singer-guitarist Walt Johns and guitarist Dave Panzer.

In time the Paulverizers experienced changes in personnel with one of its later lineups consisting of Mastradone handling vocals and guitar, guitarist Mike Kavanaugh, bassist Steve Carey, keyboardist Sam Paladino, saxophonist Scott Ramminger and drummer Chip Clemmer. Musicians to work with the band include guitarist Robert Frahm and harmonicist Bret "Big Boy Little" Littlehales. Today the Paulverizers are still performing, with Mastradone, Carey and Paladino being joined by drummer Steve Watson.

During its long reign, the Paulverizers performed in Washington, D.C. at the Zoo Bar Café; in Maryland at Lasick's College Inn (College Park), the Surf Club (Hyattsville), the Old Bowie Town Grille (Bowie) and the American Legion Greenbelt Post 136 (Greenbelt); and in Virginia at Bangkok Blues (Falls Church). They are also regularly featured at the annual Greenbelt Blues Festival.

Mastradone has performed onstage with many nationally known blues musicians including Lee McBee and the Confessors, guitarist Karl Angerer, and singer-guitarist Jim Weider (longtime guitarist for the Band; Mastradone has performed with Jim Weider's Project Percolators on several occasions, including a recent show at Rams Head On Stage in Annapolis, Maryland).

Mastradone is currently playing lead guitar with two blues bands around the Washington, D.C. area, the Capital Blues Ensemble and Steve Smith and His Meteors. He also plays upright bass with the Not So Modern Jazz Quartet.

PAUL REED SMITH

Paul Reed Smith, founder and proprietor of PRS Guitars, is recognized as being one of the finest guitar-makers in the world. Raised in Bowie, Maryland, this versatile guitarist spent the early 1970s at Bowie High School playing the local teen dance scene in a rock and roll group called the Murray Spoons Band. He went on to perform in such rock and roll groups as the Jude Band, Band of 1000 Names, Root Boy Slim and Capitol Offense, and the Dragons.

In recent years he has been leading his own Annapolis-based rock and roll outfit, the Paul Reed Smith Band. For its first album, "The Paul Reed Smith Band" (The Paul Reed Smith Band; Paul Reed Smith Music, 2007), the group's lineup consisted of lead singer Derek St. Holmes (of Ted Nugent fame), Smith on guitar, guitarist Michael Ault, bassist Gary Grainger and drummer Greg Granger. Smith has also recorded and released a pop-rock solo album "Look at the Moon" (Paul Reed Smith Nashville Sessions; Paul Reed Smith Music, 2011).

The current version of the Paul Reed Smith Band has Smith, Alt and the Grainger Brothers being joined by guitarist Bill Nelson and lead singer Mia Semone.

PAUL SEARS

Drummer Paul Sears was born and raised in Washington, D.C., where, as a youth, he learned to play such instruments as piano, autoharp, trumpet, guitar and bass. At age 13 he took up drums and began listening to such groups as the Beatles, the Rolling Stones, the Yardbirds and the Moody Blues. While attending Woodrow Wilson High School in the late 1960s he drummed for the rock and roll band Zapata, which covered bands such as Santana and Black Sabbath.

Sears next drummed for the local rock and roll band Sane Day from September 1970 to October 1972, and for Tinsel'd Sin from February 1973 to January 1974. After a short period in New Jersey where he played in a progressive rock and roll band called Whisk that covered King Crimson and Frank Zappa, he returned to Washington, D.C. and from 1975 to 1976 drummed for a jazz rock band called Magic Theatre that covered the likes of Miles Davis and Weather Report.

In September 1976 Sears joined the Muffins, a progressive jazz rock band which was originally based in Gaithersburg, Maryland. He performed and recorded with the group until their disbandment in 2016.

Through the years Sears has performed and/or recorded with some of the best avant-garde, progressive jazz and progressive rock and roll musicians in the world. Among the progressive rock (prog rock) bands and musicians he has drummed for include: the groups Spirits Burning, Karda Estra, Jack Dupon, Thee Maximalists, the Daevid Allen Weird Quartet, Nick Prol and the Proletarians, the Red Masque, Cloud Over Jupiter, and Clearlight; singer-guitarists Peter Blegvad, Steve Hillage, Jay Tausig, Kavus Torabi and Micahel Moorcock; singer-bassist John Greaves; bassists Alan Davey and Mike Howlett; bassist-keyboardists Harvey Bainbridge and William Kopecky; singer-keyboardist Tim Blake; keyboardist Doug Walker; flutist-saxophonist Didier Malherbe; violinist Cyndee Lee Rule; and percussionist Karen Stackpole.

Other musical artists Sears has drummed for include: avant-garde guitarist Fred Frith; experimental guitarist Henry Kaiser; folk singer Judy Dyble; the jazz group Michael Bass and His Moderately Sized Orchestra; jazz bassists Pepe Gonzalez and Linda Cushma; jazz woodwind player Yochk'o Seffer; jazz saxophonist-flutist Elliott Levin; jazz saxophonist T.S. Henry Webb; the jazz duo of keyboardist Don Preston and woodwind player Bunk Gardner; the jazz-rock band Chainsaw Jazz; the punk rock bands Braille Party and 9353; and the surf rock band Insect Surfers.

Sears has also drummed for a number of more straightforward rock and roll artists including: the band the Copper Angels; singer-guitarist Robert Berry; singer-guitarist-keyboardist Mike Keneally; guitarists John Ellis, David Byers, Yanni Papadopoulos and Glenn Phillips; singer-bassist Mahlon Hawk; bassists Bill Laswell, Bernie Wandel, Bryan Beller, Andy West and Jimmy Cavanuagh; keyboardist Jonathan Sindelman; and singer-drummer Al Bouchard. Sears has resided in Arizona since 2010 and is still actively performing and recording with a number of different musical artists.

PEDRO SERA

A native Washingtonian, Pedro Sera is a largely self-taught guitarist who, during his high school years at Georgetown Day School in the early 1970s, played in a rock and roll band called the Sound Investment. This group worked a wide range of gigs including private parties, teen dances at the Cooper Lane Teen Club in Landover Hills, Maryland, fraternity events on local college campuses, and engagements at the Keg in Washington, D.C.

Sera spent the late 1970s playing in several different bands including: the Viper Blues Band, which performed at high school dances, and in Washington, D.C. at Fort Reno Park and the Saloon in Georgetown; a heavy metal band called Stonehenge, which developed a following at Louie's Rock City in Bailey's Crossroads, Virginia; and the Erection Set, which worked such Washington, D.C. night clubs as the Chancery, Columbia Station, Nightclub 9:30 and D.C. Space.

From 1980 to 1982 Sera played guitar for the popular rockabilly band Evan Johns and the H-Bombs. During that time the band's lineup consisted of Sera, Johns on lead vocals and guitar, bassist Ivan Brown and drummer Giles Cook.

Sera then spent much of the early 1980s playing guitar in Elvis impersonator Johnny Seaton's band. He rounded out that decade playing with such rock and roll bands as the Essentials and the Vibrato Brothers, and the rockabilly bands Going Going Gone and Pink and Black.

From 1990 to 1994 Sera played guitar for a rockabilly band called the Choirboys and also performed live dates with R&B singer-pianist Daryl Davis. From 1994 to 1996 he switched gears and played with a power-pop band called Dream Kitchen.

Sera has also made appearances with such performing artists as the C&W bands Ruthie and the Wranglers and Virginia and the Blue Dots, rockabilly band Switchblade, rockabilly singer-guitarists Bill Kirchen and Sleepy LaBeef, blues-pop singer Janine Wilson, and blues singer-guitarist Linwood Taylor. More recently Sera has been playing guitar for such rockabilly acts as the Peashooters, Jumpin' Jupiter, and singer-guitarist Marti Brom.

PEGASUS

In 1974 singer-guitarist Stephen Spano of Gaithersburg, Maryland recorded and released the diverse rock and roll solo album "Eye to Eye" (Stephen Spano; Adelphi Records, 1974) and subsequently put together a band as a vehicle to promote his record. In 1975 this band became Pegasus, with an original lineup of singer-guitarist Stephen Spano, guitarist Chris Grigsby, singer-bassist Joey Tarbell, singer-keyboardist-guitarist Dave Johnson and drummer Mike Custer.

Pegasus became one of the most popular rock and roll bands in the Washington, D.C. area, performing original compositions and covers of such artists as the Moody Blues, Paul McCartney, Little Feat, Jackson Browne and most of the other top rock and roll groups of the day. During most of the band's existence, several members lived in a residence called "The Farmhouse" on Dufief Mill Road in Gaithersburg, a location they also used as their rehearsal space.

During its seven-year run, Pegasus performed up to 300 gigs per year. They appeared in Washington, D.C. at such night clubs as Mr. Henry's Tenley Circle, the Crazy Horse, the Bayou, Beneath It All, Desperado's, and the Wax Museum; in Maryland at the Italian Gardens (College Park), the Paragon (College Park), the Varsity Grill Back Room (College Park), Frankie and Freddie's (Hyattsville), the Back of the Rack (Ocean City), and the Hollywood Palace (Catonsville); and in Virginia at Louie's Rock City (Bailey's Crossroads) and the Wild West (Springfield).

Pegasus endured several personnel changes through the years. In 1977 Grigsby departed and singer-percussionist-harmonicist Josh Powell was added. A year later bassist Craig Carr replaced Tarbell and drummer Rob Hudgins replaced Custer. In 1979 the band underwent a transformation: Johnson and Powell stayed on and were joined by several new members in lead singer Bob Garrison, guitarist Brad Marshall, bassist Gary Falwell and drummer Phil Giordano (who was subsequently replaced by former drummer Mike Custer). In 1981 two more changes came about, with guitarist Mike Cavalier replacing Marshall and bassist Buck Rogers replacing Falwell.

Pegasus recorded and released one 45rpm single record during its time, "Winters Run" backed with The Hook" (Pegasus; Flying Horse Music, 1978). In 1982, after finding out there was a hard rock band in New Jersey also using the name Pegasus, the group elected to change its moniker to Force of Habit. They continued on for three more years before disbanding in 1985.

PENTAGRAM

Pentagram is a famed heavy metal band that formed more than 40 years ago under the direction of singer Bobby Liebling, an Arlington, Virginia native who, during his years at Wakefield High School in the late 1960s and early 1970s first sang in a rock and roll band called Shades of Darkness.

In 1971 Liebling put together the band Pentagram, the original lineup of which consisted of himself handling lead vocals, guitarist Geof O'Keefe, bassist Vincent McAllister, and drummer Steve Martin. Styled after Black Sabbath and Sir Lord Baltimore, but concentrating on original doom-laden material, the band initially rehearsed inside a building called the American Mailing Warehouse in Alexandria, Virginia.

Among the band's earliest recorded efforts were two 45rpm single records produced by Skip Groff: "Earth Flight" backed with "Hurricane" (Pentagram; Boffo Socko Records, 1973); and "Under My Thumb" backed with "When the Screams Come" (Pentagram; Gemini Records, 1974).

Personnel changes were fast and furious and through the years more than 30 musicians have passed through Pentagram, with guitarist John Jennings and drummer Joe Hasselvander being among the more noteworthy members. Through it all, Bobby Liebling has remained the only constant band member.

In 1985 the band recorded and released its first album, "Pentagram" (Pentagram; Pentagram Records, 1985). To date, the band has released 10 albums on a variety of independent labels and several compilations of their work have been issued. Pentagram is presently still recording and touring, and its current lineup consists of Liebling, guitarist Victor Griffith, bassist Greg Turley and drummer "Minnesota" Pete Campbell.

THE PEPPERMINT STIX

The Peppermint Stix rated as one of the Washington, D.C. area's top rock and roll bands from November 1961 to October 1962. The group's lineup consisted of four of the region's most popular musicians – singer-guitarist Duke Duquette, keyboardist Sam Paladino, singer-saxophonist Ed Montini and drummer Stan Weinberg.

The band covered such artists as Chubby Checker, Fats Domino and Louis Prima and most of the popular rock and roll bands of the era. They spent November and December of 1961 performing at the Rocket Room on New York Avenue NW in Washington, D.C.

In 1962, in addition to steady work at the Rocket Room (where they backed up such performers as pop singers Raty Peterson and Brian Hyland and rock and roll singer Barry Darvell), the Peppermint Stix performed at such Washington, D.C. night clubs as Guy's Place and the Famous Restaurant. They also spent much of that summer backing the wild singer-trumpeter Tito Mambo at venues in Somers Point New Jersey After an engagement at the Dixie Pig on Bladensburg Road in Cottage City, Maryland in October 1962, the Peppermint Stix disbanded.

THE PERRY MATES

In 1960 singer-guitarist Clarence Perry gathered up two of his former Off Keys bandmates – his bass-playing brother Luman Perry and keyboardist Sam Paladino – and added drummer Al Pometto, formerly of Al Pometto and the Jazz Bombers, to form the Perry Mates, a high-energy Bladensburg-based group that mixed the best R&B and rock and roll material of the day.

Though the Perry Mates were relatively short-lived, staying together a scant two years in the Washington, D.C. area, they enjoyed considerable local popularity with regular Saturday night shows at the West Lanham Fire Department and Sunday appearances at the Seat Pleasant Fire Department. The band also worked in Washington, D.C. at such night clubs as the Rocket Room, the Famous Restaurant, Guy's Place and the Alpine Room; and in Maryland at Chubby's Restaurant and Bar (Seat Pleasant) and the Las Vegas Club (Coral Hills).

Other members to pass though the Perry Mates during the group's local run included: guitarist Mike Hurney; saxophonists Del Puschert, Paul King and Ed Montini; and drummers Stan Weinberg and Johnny Robb. In December 1961 Clarence Perry relocated to Bay Town, Texas, where he kept different versions of the Perry Mates going throughout the decade.

In terms of recordings, the Perry Mates released the singles: "The Great Red Rat" backed with "It Was You" (The Pery Mates; Ca-Jo Records, 1961) – note the misspelling of the band's name; "Hang Your Head" backed with "Little Darlin' (Please Forgive Me)" (The Perry Mates; Lanar Records, 1962); "Kick Step" backed with "Gotta Go" (Perry Mates; San Records, 1963); and "Wake Up Sleeping Beauty" backed with "Crying My Heart Out" (Perry Mates; San Records, 1963).

THE PERSONALITIES

The Personalities were a versatile rock and roll band that was based in the Washington, D.C. area from the 1960s to the 1990s. The band formed in 1962 with its original lineup consisting of singer-bassist Dave Case, singer-guitarist Mike Hurney, saxophonist Paul King and drummer Al Pometto. Within a year former Off Keys singer-saxophonist Dick Moody replaced Paul King. Many musicians passed through the band in its lifetime including singer Jerome Powell, bassist John Koslin, pianist Brian Scott and singer-drummer Ron MacDonald.

The Personalities covered most of the top pop and rock and roll acts of their time, playing songs by everyone from Bo Diddley to Elvis Presley and occasionally working in musical comedy routines.

In the 1960s the Personalities performed in Washington, D.C. at such night clubs as the Starlite Restaurant and Rand's Night Club; in Maryland at the Village Barn (Morningside); and in Virginia at the 1320 Club (Alexandria). In its later years the band worked weddings, local military base officers' clubs, Moose Lodges and Elks Lodges. The group disbanded in 1994.

PETE KENNEDY

Singer-guitarist Pete Kennedy was raised in Arlington, Virginia and during his years at Bishop Denis J. O'Connell High School in the late 1960s he played guitar in a couple of Northern Virginia-based British Invasion teen dance bands, the Flying Hospital and the Figments of Imagination. In the 1970s he spent time in the rock band Grendel, mainly performing at a night club called the Godfather Restaurant on Wisconsin Avenue NW in Washington, D.C. His music career then took off and he took an interest in producing and engineering musical recordings.

For many years Kennedy was a house guitarist at the Birchmere in Alexandria, Virginia and was called upon to perform onstage with such performers as: acoustic blues duo Cephas and Wiggins (singer-guitarist John Cephas and harmonicist Phil Wiggins); bluegrass singer-guitarists John Starling and Peter Rowan; C&W singer-guitarist Keith Whitley; and folk singer-guitarists Tom Paxton, Bob Gibson, Steve Goodman, Jonathan Edwards, John Stewart, Peter Yarrow and Paul Stookey. He has also spent time as a house orchestra guitarist for stage productions at local theatres such as the Kennedy Center, the National Theatre and Ford's Theatre.

Through the years Kennedy has also performed with such bands and musicians as: blues singer-guitarist Tom Principato; blues rock singer-guitarist Catfish Hodge; the blues band the Nighthawks; bluegrass guitarist Tony Rice; bluegrass dobro player Mike Auldridge; the bluegrass duo of mandolinist Mike Marshall and fiddler Darol Anger; C&W singer-guitarists Emmylou Harris, Mary Chapin Carpenter and Patsy Montoya; C&W mandolinist Jethro Burns; the country rock band the Rosslyn Mountain Boys; folk singer-guitarists Kate Wolf, Nanci Griffith and Lucy Kaplansky; the folk music duo of singer-guitarist-banjoist Cathy Fink and guitarist-mandolinist Marcy Marxer; jazz singer Eartha Kitt; jazz guitarist Charlie Byrd; multi-styled guitarist Danny Gatton; pop singers Bob Hope and Joel Gray; pop singer-guitarist Bill Danoff; R&B bands Bill Holland and Rent's Due, Martha and the Vandellas, and the Fifth Dimension; and innumerable others.

Since 1993 Pete Kennedy has been, along with his wife Maura, one-half of the New York-based folk duo called, appropriately enough, the Kennedys. Locally, they have backed up numerous popular music acts at the current version of the Birchmere in Alexandria, Virginia (3701 Mount Vernon Avenue) including Nanci Griffith, Tom Paxton, the folk duo Lowen and Navarro, and rock and roll singer-keyboardist Bruce Hornsby.

To date the Kennedys have released a total of 10 albums, and Pete Kennedy himself has 10 folk music solo albums on a variety of independent labels to his credit. Currently, the Kennedys are a part of a folk-rock band called the Strangelings.

PETE RAGUSA

Drummer Pete Ragusa was raised in Cheverly, Maryland, and, during his years at Bladensburg High School in the late 1960s, he followed his favorite local band, Lawrence and the Arabians, and drummed in a rock and roll band on the teen dance circuit called the Manchurian Candidates.

From 1968 to 1970 Ragusa drummed for such local rock and roll bands as Easy, Warm as Toast, and Easy Street. In 1970 he became an original member of Razz, a seminal group that went on to become one of the area's hardest-rocking bands. He remained with Razz through 1973.

In 1974 Ragusa joined the Nighthawks and was part of the band's most celebrated lineup along with singer-harmonica player Mark Wenner, guitarist Jimmy Thackery and bassist Jan Zukowski. He appeared on more than two-dozen of the band's albums and remained with the Nighthawks for more than 35 years.

In his career Ragusa has performed with a number of local and nationally-known bands and musicians including: blues singer-guitarists Memphis Gold, Catfish Hodge, Cathy Ponton King and Tom Principato; blues singer-guitarist-harmonicist John Hammond; the R&B bands the Soul Serenaders and Urban Funk; and the rock and roll band Built for Comfort.

PETE VAN ALLEN

Bassist Pete Van Allen was born in Washington, D.C. and after several moves his family settled in Seabrook, Maryland in the late 1950s. He initially played the cello, but became an Elvis Presley fan and switched to guitar upon arriving in Maryland. During his time at Charles Carroll Junior High School in the early 1960s he played folk music at parties and basement jam sessions.

In 1961 Van Allen began a two-year tenure with a local rock and roll band called the Galaxies, which was based in Greenbelt, consisted of five guitarists and a drummer, and performed at teen dances staged by the Greenbelt Teen Club (Greenbelt Youth Center) and the Charles Carroll Teen Club (Charles Carroll Junior High School in New Carrollton).

While attending DuVal High School in the middle 1960s Van Allen played guitar in a succession of bands including: the Crypt Kickers, a rockabilly trio that worked the local teen dance circuit; the Manchester Squires, a teen dance band rock and roll band that featured lead singer Bobby LaKind (later of the Doobie Brothers); and the Members, a British Invasion cover band that performed at teen dances at the Congress Heights Boys Club (Southeast Washington, D.C.) and the St. Mary of the Assumption Catholic Church Teen Club (Upper Marlboro), as well as such Washington, D.C. night clubs as the Frog and the Tap Inn Restaurant. In 1966 he switched to bass and spent more than a year in an R&B group called Venus and the Fly Traps, an outfit that performed on both the teen dance and military base officers' club circuits.

Van Allen took to the road in 1967 and spent that Summer of Love in Laguna Canyon, California where he played with a rock and roll band called Limey and the Yanks. He returned to the nation's capital, enrolled at the University of Maryland where he studied art, and re-entered the local music scene.

As the 1960s wound down Van Allen played bass in two rock and roll groups that featured guitarist Dee Clay – first, the aptly-named Dee Clay Band, and then the Graduates, which worked local military base officers' clubs. In 1969 he played in such local R&B bands as the Talents and the Mount Pleasant Street Blues Band.

In 1970 Van Allen spent nine months in England where he lived in the same apartment building as the band Free and gave bass lessons to Paul Rodgers. Late in the year he returned to the Washington, D.C. area and rejoined the Mount Pleasant Street Blues Band at Cousin Nick's for a brief period. He next played bass with the Joe Stanley Band at Benny's Rebel Room on the 14th Street NW Block and remained with Stanley for his next band project, an R&B group called the Marquees that featured lead singer Johnny Staggs and performed at Club 175 in Jessup, Maryland. He also worked with both Dee Clay and Joe Stanley in the Bill Black Combo, a rock and roll outfit that worked local night clubs and at one point backed up the Platters at a night spot called the Peppermint Lounge in Virginia Beach, Virginia.

In the fall of 1971 Van Allen was chosen to replace Billy Hancock as bassist for blues rock guitarist Roy Buchanan, who had been working for years at the Cross Roads in Bladensburg, Maryland with various musicians and was in the process of putting together yet another new and different band. The initial version of his latest group, which was simply advertised in the local press as "Roy Buchanan," consisted of lead singer Chuck Tilley, guitarist Roy Buchanan, Van Allen on bass, keyboardist Dick Heintze, percussionist Marc Fisher and drummer Michael "Pokey" Walls. Later in the year the band's lineup was again shuffled and they re-emerged as Roy Buchanan and the Snake Stretchers with a lineup of Buchanan, Tilley, Van Allen, Heintze, rhythm guitarist Ted Irwin and drummer Ned Davis.

Van Allen remained with Buchanan throughout all of 1972 and into 1973, touring the country and appearing on the record "Second Album" (Roy Buchanan; Polydor Records, 1973. His bass playing also appeared on several future Roy Buchanan compilations).

Van Allen spent the remainder of the 1970s performing with a succession of bands and musicians including: C&W singer-guitarist Jack Bond at the Childe Harold (Washington, D.C.); a rock and roll band called Phase IV; the C&W band Danny Denver and the Soundmasters at various night clubs on the Eastern Shore of Delaware and Maryland; the rock and roll group Crazy Joe and Judy Jones and the Rainbow City Rock Band at the Back Alley Lounge of the Cross Roads (Bladensburg); Kim Tsoy and the Sauce at the Luau Hut (Silver Spring); a heavy rock and roll band called Cannon at the Quonset Supper Club (Silver Hill); and the R&B-oriented Joe Stanley Band at Rector's Restaurant (Marlow Heights).

After a hiatus where he concentrated on his career as a graphic designer, Van Allen spent the 1990s playing bass in a Baltimore-based rock and roll group called the Friday Night Basement Band. He currently plays in a classic rock band called Kelly's Secret, which regularly appears at the Judge's Bench in Ellicott City, Maryland.

PETER BONTA

Keyboardist-guitarist Peter Bonta was born in Fort Campbell, Kentucky, and, as an Army brat, lived all over the world before his family moved to Alexandria, Virginia in 1960. During his years at T.C. Williams High School in the late 1960s he played the local teen dance circuit in a psychedelic rock and roll band called the Ice Cream Grenade.

In the early 1970s Bonta played in a local rock and roll band called Harvest and was also an on-call organist in the house band at the Silver Slipper on 13th Street NW in Washington, D.C. From 1972 to 1974 he played keyboards in the Nighthawks and from late 1974 to 1979 he played bass in the country rock band the Rosslyn Mountain Boys, remaining with the group after their name was changed to Payday. In August 1979 he joined the rock and roll band Artful Dodger and toured and recorded with them into the early 1980s.

Through the years Bonta has performed with a plethora of bands and musicians including: the bluegrass band the Seldom Scene; the blues band Jimmy Thackery and the Drivers; blues singer-guitarist Tom Principato; blues singer-bassist Nick McAlister; C&W band Honky Tonk Confidential; C&W singer-guitarists Mary Chapin Carpenter and Emmylou Harris; folk singer-guitarists Kevin Marvelle, Bob Gramann and Dave Goodrich; the folk music duo of singer-guitarist-banjoist Cathy Fink and guitarist-mandolinist Marcy Marxer; rock and roll singer-guitarist Gene Ryder; and rockabilly singer-guitarists Marti Brom, Billy Hancock, Vernon Taylor and Bill Kirchen.

PHIL FLOWERS

Singer Phil Flowers born and raised in North Carolina. He joined the United States Air Force in 1951 and was stationed at Fort Myer in Arlington County, Virginia for much of his enlistment. In 1954 at the age of 20 he began singing at a Black night club called the Ebony Inn in Fairmount Heights, Maryland and then spent the late 1950s performing R&B material at such Washington, D.C. night clubs as Benny's Rebel Room and the Parkside Café.

In 1960 Flowers began working in a night club at 14th and H Streets NW called the Hayloft and remained a headliner there for most of the decade. He also performed at such nearby establishments as Rand's Night Club and the Rocket Room. Late in the 1960s he began calling his R&B act Phil Flowers and the Flower Shop.

Numerous musicians worked with Flowers through the years, but his longest-running Flower Shop aggregation consisted of guitarists Johnny Sneed and Tony Thomas, bassist Burch White, keyboardist Steve Sidor, saxophonist Rod Philips and drummer Rick Sheltra.

Flowers recorded prolifically through the years with albums and singles appearing on more than two-dozen different record labels including such majors as Dot, A&M, Columbia and Epic. In later years he performed on the Washington, D.C. area hotel circuit, played casinos and supper clubs around the country, and successfully mixed such musical styles as C&W and rock and roll into his stage act. He died on Monday, January 22, 2001 at the age of 66.

PHIL MATHIEU

Phil Mathieu was a guitarist well-versed in such musical styles as classical, C&W and Jazz. He was raised in Rockville, Maryland and before and during his years at Robert E. Peary High School in the late 1970s he played in area jazz groups and absorbed the work of such local guitarists as Charlie Byrd, Roy Buchanan and Danny Gatton.

His music career took off in the 1990 when he formed his own jazz outfit, the Phil Mathieu Trio. From 1992 to 2001 he was a member of the Washington Guitar Quintet (a jazz group which included the legendary Charlie Byrd); was lead guitarist for the C&W band

Ruthie and the Wranglers from 1996 to 2009; and also played in a classical music group known as the Potomac Guitar Quartet in 2006.

As a classical guitarist, Mathieu was a member of the house orchestra for a number of local theatre companies and performed in dozens of productions at such venues as the John F. Kennedy Center for the Performing Arts, Wolf Trap National Park for the Performing Arts, Ford's Theatre, and Arena Stage.

Through the years Mathieu performed and/or recorded with the internationally renowned classical-jazz Brazilian-born guitarist Carlos Barbosa-Lima, and a number of prominent Washington, D.C. area musical artists including folk singers Lisa Moscatiello and Carey Creed, classical guitarist Giorgia Cavallaro, and the blues-jazz band the Natty Beaux.

Mathieu released two solo albums, "Simple Gifts" (Philip Mathieu; Positive Music Records, 1993), and "Holiday Impressions" (Phil Mathieu; Self-Released, 2007). He passed away on Friday, February 10, 2012 at the age of 50.

PHIL MCCORMACK

Singer Phil McCormack was born in Milwaukee, Wisconsin in 1960, and, after living for several years in Dayton, Ohio, moved to McLean, Virginia in 1974. He spent the middle and late 1970s singing in the McLean-based Southern rock band Jazzbo McMann, a group that featured lead guitarist Jimbo Manion. McCormack was the lead singer for the Roadducks from 1981 to 1996. From 1996 to the present he has served as the lead vocalist and frontman for the great Southern rock band Molly Hatchet.

PHIL WAHLE

Bassist Phil Wahle was born in Riverdale, Maryland and was mainly raised in Wheaton, Maryland. As a youth he learned to play the organ and the violin and as a teenager in the middle 1960s he listened to a mix of folk and pop music, with the Beatles and Peter, Paul and Mary becoming favorites. He learned the guitar at age 13, and, during his years at Wheaton High School in the late 1960s, he played bass in a heavy rock and roll band called Sudden Rush (which shortened its name to Rush in 1970).

Wahle spent several years with Rush, remaining with the band into 1974. A number of musicians passed through the group including guitarist Hal Lindes, who hailed from Kensington, Maryland and later moved to England where he became a member of Dire Straits. Rush played originals and also covered such artists as the Rolling Stones, the Beatles, Iron Butterfly, Mott the Hoople and Deep Purple. They were regulars on the local teen dance scene for years and also headlined at University of Maryland fraternity parties, the Wheaton Youth Center, the Prince George's Plaza Community Center in Hyattsville, Maryland, and such Washington, D.C. night clubs as the Silver Dollar (they headlined this venue as Sudden Rush and then as Rush after it had transformed into the M Club) and This Is It.

In one of Rush's most unusual bookings, they opened for Ted Nugent and the Amboy Dukes at the Bastille in College Park, Maryland on the night of Wednesday, January 30, 1974. Scheduled to work a three-night stand, Nugent and his group followed Rush on the night in question and after an ear-splitting 20 minutes of screams, guitar feedback, and Nugent-atop-the-amps theatrics, management pulled the plug on the three Amboy Dukes, paid them their guarantee, and bid them farewell. Rush then headlined the Bastille for the remaining two nights.

Wahle went on to play bass for the Takoma Park, Maryland-based rock and roll band Revolver from 1976 to 1982. Covering everyone from the Beatles to David Bowie to Elvis Presley, Revolver headlined in Washington, D.C. at the Bayou and the Crazy Horse; in

College Park, Maryland at the Paragon; and at night clubs from Pennsylvania to South Carolina.

In 1983 Wahle joined a popular music act called Our Pleasure that became one of the Washington, D.C. area's most popular show bands. The group's longstanding lineup consisted of lead singer Tom McWhirter, guitarist Bob Farris, Wahle on bass and drummer Charlie Crowder. They remained a full-time operation until 1995, performing at night clubs in the nation's capital and up and down the East Coast. The group then continued to play out on a part-time basis through 2013.

Since 2015 Wahle has been the singer-bassist in a classic rock band called the Buddy Love Trio. They perform regularly at such Maryland venues as Hershey's Restaurant (Gaithersburg), the Highland Tavern (Highland), Rams Head Roadhouse (Annapolis) and the American Legion Laurel Post 60 (Laurel).

PHILIP SHIMMEL

Drummer Philip Shimmel was raised in Hillcrest Heights, Maryland and during his years at G. Gardner Shugart Junior High School in the late 1960s he played in a rock and roll band on the local teen dance circuit called the Czars. During his time at Potomac High School in the early 1970s he drummed for such rock and roll bands as Scorpius, the Neon Flag, and Happy Jack.

In the middle 1970s Shimmel did a six-month stint in New York with different pop music bands including the Maryland Trio and the Bonnie Boyer Show. After returning to the Washington, D.C. area he drummed for several different bands including the bluegrass group Fireside and a country rock group called the Joanne Dodds Band.

Late in the 1970s and into the early 1980s Shimmel sang and drummed for a bluegrass band called Silverspring, whose initial five-man lineup was rounded out with singer-guitarist John Fritz-Spiro, guitarist-violinist Frank Michels, bassist Sal DeRaffele and violinist Nat Winer. Silverspring worked up and down the Atlantic Coast, playing night clubs and college events. Locally, the band played in Washington, D.C. at such night clubs as Mr. Henry's Tenley Circle and Desperado's; and in Maryland at the Psyche Delly (Bethesda), DiGennaro's (Laurel) and the Italian Gardens (College Park).

In 1981 Shimmel, DeRaffele and Spiro were called out of Silverspring to back up blues singer-pianist Dr. John for an engagement at Desperado's in Georgetown. The performances went so well, the three remained his backup band for the following two years, during which time they played night clubs and shows up and down the East Coast. In the early 1980s Shimmel also played in the Washington, D.C. area with other groups including: a rock and roll band called the Peptones; an R&B act called Touch of Class; and a jazz ensemble called the Don Stapleton Quartet.

In 1985 Shimmel relocated to New York City and has since drummed for a number of popular music acts including: the blues band Michael "Murch" Powers and Frequency; the folk rock band Jeff Wilkinson and the Navigators; the jazz group Ron Sunshine and Full Swing; the multi-styled wedding bands the Klezmer Connection and the Avi Maza Orchestra; and the rock and roll bands Nick Palumbo and the Flipped Fedoras, and George Worthmore and the Dive Bombers.

Shimmel has also drummed for: blues singers Rosco Gordon, Moe Holmes, Roxy Perry and Joan Osborne; blues singer-guitarists Bobby Radcliff, Irving Louis Lattin, Junior Mack and Danny Draher; blues singer-pianist Pinetop Perkins; blues keyboardist Bobby Forrester; blues rock guitarist Dan Hovey; C&W singers Loey Nelson and Tanya Tucker; C&W guitarist John Leventhal; folk singer-guitarist Julie Grower; jazz guitarists Michael Powers and Grant Green; jazz singer-keyboardist Steve Lucky; jazz singer-saxophonist

Curtis Stigers; jazz saxophonist Pharaoh Sanders; rock and roll singers Gary U.S. Bonds and Dana Fuchs; and rock and roll singer-violinist Soozie Tyrell.

PIERRE BEAUREGARD

Singer-harmonicist Pierre Beauregard was raised in Bethesda, Maryland where he passed through the Landon School, Western Junior High School and the Eberhard School in Washington, D.C. While in the sixth grade at Landon in the middle 1960s he sang and played tambourine in a rock and roll band called Savage Rose. As a youth he had studied guitar, trumpet and drums and learned the harmonica at age 13.

Beauregard participated in jam sessions with friends during his junior high school years and in the late 1960s while in high school at the Eberhard School he joined a group called the Cold Duck Blues Band, which included guitarist Jimmy Thackery and performed in Washington, D.C. at the St. Alban's Episcopal Church Friday Coffeehouse.

In 1970 the Cold Duck Blues Band turned into the Crawling King Snake Blues Band. The group's lineup at this time was Beauregard, lead singer-guitarist Jimmy Cole, guitarist Jimmy Thackery, pianist Jeff Cole, bassist John Curlin and drummer Richard Murray. They rehearsed in the basement of a home at 30th and T Streets NW in Georgetown and played out at private parties, the St. Alban's Episcopal Church Friday Coffeehouse, Club 175 in Jessup, Maryland, and events at local churches and colleges.

In the summer of 1971 Beauregard moved to Boston, Massachusetts with remnants of the Crawling King Snake Blues Band. He then spent much of the decade singing and playing harmonica in a blues band called Powerhouse that included guitarist Tom Principato. The band often ventured south to Washington, D.C. where they performed in such night clubs as My Mother's Place, the Childe Harold, Desperado's, Apple Pie and the Cellar Door.

Since that time Beauregard has performed with the Memphis Rockabilly Band and the Cambridge Harmonica Orchestra. He has also played with such blues artists as guitarist J. Geils, singer-guitarists Geoff Muldaur, Muddy Waters, Arthur Crudup, Fred McDowell, John Jackson and Johnny Shines, singer-slide guitarist J.B. Hutto, singer-guitarist-harmonica player Jimmy Rogers, harmonicist Richard "Magic Dick" Salwitz and singer-pianist Sunnyland Slim. Beauregard stopped his regular playing schedule in 1980 and today he invents and designs harmonicas.

THE PROFILES

The Profiles were a group of Sherwood High School musicians that were based in Silver Spring, Maryland and formed in 1962. Their original lineup consisted of lead guitarist Al Butler, rhythm guitarist Bob Chambers, bassist Stu Sillery and lead singer-drummer Phil Martin.

The Profiles originally specialized in rock and roll instrumental music, with their sets dominated by the tunes of Link Wray, Duane Eddy and Al Butler. The band eventually added to its repertoire songs by the Crickets (featuring singer-guitarist Buddy Holly), the Kingsmen, the Safaris, the Shantays, the Rockin' Rebels, Bo Diddley, Ray Charles, Chuck Berry, and, ultimately, the Beatles. During its three-year run personnel changes occurred with pianist Geoff Humphrey, guitarist Jim Ostmann, saxophonist Barry Adamson, and others passing through the band.

The Profiles performed at teen dances in Maryland at places like: Sherwood High School (Sandy Spring), the Colesville Teen Club (Colesville), the St. Margaret of Scotland Catholic Church Teen Club (Seat Pleasant), the St. Bernadette Catholic Church Teen Club (Silver Spring), the Long Branch Teen Club (Long Branch Community Recreation Center in Silver Spring), Temple Emanuel (Kensington), the Takoma Park Teen Club (Takoma Park

Junior High School), Springbrook High School (Silver Spring), Gaithersburg High School (Gaithersburg), Robert E. Peary High School (Rockville) and Wheaton High School (Wheaton). They also headlined at several larger and more prestigious venues such as the Bethesda Youth Center (Bethesda), the Wheaton Youth Center (Wheaton) and the Bladensburg Volunteer Fire Department (Bladensburg), where their appearances for promoter Barry Richards in 1964 and 1965 necessitated the band members donning Beatles boots and wigs.

Late in the band's career the Profiles were booked into Dino's Ranch, an old-fashioned roadhouse on Georgia Avenue in Olney, Maryland, where, for several months in 1964, they alternated weekends with a popular band called the Monarchs. During this time Dino's Ranch was drawing capacity crowds and on one now-legendary evening the Profiles came full circle when they were called upon to serve as the backup band for headliner Link Wray, the legendary singer-guitarist who had been one of their strongest musical inspirations from their very first day.

PUNKY MEADOWS

Rock and roll guitarist Edwin "Punky" Meadows was born in Washington, D.C., raised in the Southeast quadrant of the city, and joined his first rock and roll band, the Intruders, in 1964 as the Beatles and the British Invasion began sweeping America.

The Intruders turned into the English Setters in early 1965 and became one of the Washington, D.C. area's top young bands, working local teen dances, night clubs such as the Corral in Georgetown, and appearing on local concert bills. The group was signed to Heritage Records in the fall of 1967 and officially changed its name to the Cherry People when their first and only eponymous album was released in May 1968. Meadows was still in high school at the time, attending Ballou High School in Southeast Washington, D.C. and later enrolling at T.C. Williams High School in Alexandria, Virginia.

Over the next few years the Cherry People became one of the area's very best rock and roll bands, working long engagements at such Washington, D.C. night clubs as the Silver Dollar, the Bayou and the Keg. They developed a national reputation and toured the country in support of their album.

Meadows left the Cherry People in 1972 and spent time playing music with keyboardist Gregg Giuffria in Biloxi, Mississippi and then with the band Daddy Warbux in Boston, Massachusetts. In the summer of 1974 Daddy Warbux moved to Washington, D.C. and in the fall months had settled in at Bogie's a night club on the second floor of 1214 Connecticut Avenue NW.

Daddy Warbux had several musicians come and go and remnants of the band ended up in another similar hard-rocking group called Foxie, which also based out of Bogie's. In early 1975 Meadows, bassist Mickie Jones and keyboardist Gregg Giuffria began auditioning different musicians at Bogie's. They eventually settled on lead singer Frank DiMino and drummer Barry Brandt and put together the glam-rock band Angel in April of that year. Angel quickly signed with Casablanca Records, moved to Los Angeles, toured the United States and countries such as Japan, and ultimately released six albums before disbanding in 1980.

Although Meadows had established himself as one of the best rock and roll guitarists in the world, he left the music world behind and in 1988 was back in the Washington, D.C. area, working as the disc jockey at the Crazy Horse in Georgetown. He remained there until the night club's closing in 1995, at which time he focused on operating the Tanfastic Tanning Club in Oakton, Virginia. Recently he returned to the world of rock and roll by recording and releasing the solo album "Fallen Angel" (Punky Meadows; Escape Music Ltd., 2016).

PUZZLE

Puzzle was a prominent, though short-lived, Georgetown-based psychedelic rock and roll trio that appeared on the local scene in November 1968 and disbanded in late 1969. The band's original lineup was: singer-guitarist Tony Grasso, who hailed from Oxon Hill, Maryland and had previously played in a rock group called the Rubber Band; singer-bassist Curt Jonnie from Wildwood, New Jersey; and singer-drummer Mike Zack of Beltsville, Maryland, previously of Lawrence and the Arabians, Wild Honey, and the Reasons Why.

A later replacement in Puzzle for Zack was former Chartbusters drummer Michael "Pokey" Walls. Changes were constant and the last version of the band consisted of lead vocalist Gui Bokoles, guitarist Tony Grasso, bassist Sam Powers and drummer Steve Lacey.

In 1969 Puzzle performed at such Washington, D.C. night clubs as the Keg, the Crazy Horse and the Silver Dollar. They also appeared on several concert shows, including a triple bill which included Flavor and the Fallen Angels at the Walt Whitman High School Field House in Bethesda, Maryland on Friday, January 31, 1969. Another event they participated in was "The Movement Caravan" at McDonough Gymnasium (Georgetown University) on Saturday, March 15, 1969 which was headlined by Buffy Sainte-Marie and included performances by, besides Puzzle, the New Lost City Ramblers, the Charles River Valley Boys, Rev. Gary Davis, the Fallen Angels and Bert Mason.

The band's original trio recorded and released one album, "Puzzle" (Puzzle; ABC Records, 1969), an effort that was produced by Eddie Kramer and Jay Senter.

RANDY HART

Keyboardist Randy Hart was born in Washington, D.C. and grew up in Falls Church, Virginia. He became involved in the local rock and roll scene as a teenager in the early 1970s when he contacted music promoter-manager Lester Grossman at his office on M Street NW in Georgetown to sell tickets at a Baltimore Civic Center event. Grossman was managing the rock and roll band Tractor at the time, and Hart, who had taken to informally working in Grossman's office, began booking he band to perform at local shows.

In 1971 Tractor was looking for a keyboard player and heard Hart playing piano backstage at one of their gigs. Although he was in his senior year at the Hawthorne School in Washington, D.C. at the time, he was added to the group as a full-time member. Hart began working with the group at My Mother's Place, a night club in Washington, D.C. at 18th and M Streets NW. He remained with Tractor all the way through October 1973. He then moved to California with bandmates Jack Brooks, Ron Culbertson and Steve Lacey and played in different groups with them on the West Coast for several years.

Hart went on to become the keyboard player for C&W singer Roger Miller and remained in his band from 1978 to 1985. He was instrumental in bringing guitarist Danny Gatton into Miller's band, a position Gatton maintained for several years.

In 1985 Hart relocated from Los Angles to Nashville, Tennessee and performed with such C&W artists as singer Gary Morris and singer-guitarist Steve Wariner. He went on to become the house pianist at the Grand Ole Opry, where he backed up almost every major performer in C&W music that appeared at the legendary venue.

RATSO

Singer-guitarist Ratso (real name Jimmie Silman III) hails from Texas, but was raised in Montgomery County, Maryland in the city of Silver Spring and the community of Bethesda. During his years at Thomas W. Pyle Junior High School in the middle 1960s he first took up the drums and sang and played in a series of rock and roll bands including the Rockin' Regals, the Squires, and the Gargoyles. In the late 1960s he attended high school at

Harker Preparatory School, listened to a range of music from R&B to bluegrass, and learned to play guitar.

In the early 1970s Ratso attended St. Andrews Presbyterian College in Laurinburg, North Carolina (today this institution is known as St. Andrews University) where he studied theater and English and spent time drumming in such acts as the A-Wop-Bop-A-Loo-Bop Blues Band and a rock and roll group called Underwear. After a brief return to Bethesda, he lived in Lynchburg, Virginia from 1973 to 1975 where he played guitar in a bluegrass outfit called Butch Bobbitt and the Tuckahoe Creek Band.

From 1975 to 1976 Ratso was back in the Washington, D.C. area where he sang and played guitar in a bluegrass group called the Lee Brothers Band and Show. He briefly lived in Richmond, Virginia and then moved across the state to Blacksburg where he sang and played guitar for a country rock band called Hardwood. In 1977 he moved to Colesville, Maryland where he spent the next couple of years sitting in with a variety of musical groups in local night clubs including the country rock act the North Star Band.

In 1979 Ratso brought his guitar skills to the rockabilly band Tex Rubinowitz and the Bad Boys, joining singer-guitarist Tex Rubinowitz, guitarist Steve Carr, bassist Mike Carr and drummer George Norris. The lineup soon changed to consist of Rubinowitz, Ratso, guitarist Eddie Angel, bassist Johnny Castle and drummer Scotty Flowers.

In 1980 Ratso, Angel and Castle joined forces with drummer Jim Dougherty and formed the psychobilly-rock band Switchblade, which enjoyed tremendous local success for many years. Later members of Switchblade included guitarist Steuart Smith and drummer Giles Cook. Throughout the decade he also appeared at local night clubs in Ratso and Friends, a band that covered such musical styles as bluegrass, C&W and rock and roll.

Ratso is best known for having been a guitarist and background vocalist for country rock singer-guitarist Kinky Friedman for the past 40 years. The association started when he got the call to join Friedman, who calls his band the Texas Jewboys, onstage for a two-night engagement at the Cellar Door in Georgetown on Tuesday, December 12 and Wednesday, December 13, 1978. He again played in Friedman's band when they were co-billed with the Doug Sahm Band at the Cellar Door on Saturday, March 10, 1979. Ratso subsequently became a fixture in the band and has recorded and toured extensively with Friedman ever since.

In recent years, when he is not working with Kinky Friedman, Ratso occasionally participates in Switchblade reunion performances in the Washington, D.C. area. In January 2017 he formed a rock and roll band in the nation's capital called Lunch With Bob, the lineup of which consists of Ratso handling vocals and guitar, singer-guitarist Gantt Kushner, singer-bassist Jim Robeson and singer-drummer Paul Goldstein.

RAY LOMBARDO

Drummer Ray Lombardo was raised in Southeast, Washington, D.C. and District Heights, Maryland. During his years at Bishop McNamara High School in the late 1960s he first played pop and rock and roll music in a teen dance band called Ray and the Authentics before being picked up by an older band called the Playboys, which played pop classics at social functions throughout Southern Maryland.

Lombardo then spent several months in 1968 drumming for Kim Tsoy and the Sauce at the Luau Hut in Washington, D.C. and followed that up studying music for the 1968-1969 school year at the Berklee School of Music (now Berklee College of Music) in Boston, Massachusetts. He enlisted in the United States Army and was stationed at Fort Myer in Arlington County, Virginia. There, from 1970 to 1973, he was the drummer for the U.S. Army Blues, the premier 18-piece jazz ensemble of the United States Army and part of the United States Army Band "Pershing's Own."

Lombardo was discharged from the United States Army in 1973 and in the 1970s and 1980s he drummed for a number of rock and roll bands around the Washington, D.C. area including Sunrise West, Bentwood Rocker, Linx, Demetri Callas and the Flashbacks, and Fresh Air. From 1992 to 1998 he drummed for the Admirals, a Baltimore-based multi-styled pop band that performed shows at some of the best night clubs and hotels in the Atlantic states.

In recent years Lombardo has drummed with a variety of musical acts including: the blues band B.G. and the Mojo Hands; the country-pop group known as the Joy Bodycomb Band; such jazz groups as the Martinsburg Jazz Orchestra, the Olney Big Band, and the Rick Whitehead Trio; such R&B groups as the Joe Stanley Trio and Rendezvous; and the multi-styled pop band 'Round Midnight. He is currently once again drumming for the Admirals.

RAY ROCK

Born Bebley Raymond Colie and known by the stage name Ray Rock, this multi-faceted singer-drummer grew up on Delafield Place NW in Washington, D.C. and began sitting in with various C&W and rock and roll bands in the bars of the nation's capital as a teenager in the middle 1950s.

In 1958 Rock sang and drummed in the first version of Stan D. and the Profiles, which was rounded out by singer Stan Doucette, guitarist Jay Thomas and bassist Tommy Dillinger. The band played a mixture C&W and rock and roll and held down house band duties at the Round Up Club in Southeast Washington, D.C. for several years.

In 1962 Stan D. and the Profiles morphed into a new band called Ray Rock and the Revlons. The group then carried on throughout the decade as a three-piece combo, most often performing in Washington, D.C. at such night clubs as the Crosstown Restaurant and Guy's Place. During those years many musicians passed in and out of the band. The initial version of Ray Rock and the Revlons consisted of lead singer-bassist Stan Doucette, guitarist Jay Thomas and Rock on drums. Another version of the group consisted of Rock singing lead and drumming, guitarist Wally Simms and bassist "Clean" Chuck Bennett. Later on, Rock was joined by guitarist Steve Reynolds and bassist Steve Spurling.

In the ensuing years Rock drummed for many major musical artists that performed in the area including: C&W singers Danny Denver and Stella Parton; C&W singer-guitarists Roy Clark, Marvin Rainwater, George Jones, Faron Young and Little Jimmy Dickens; pop singer Connie Smith; Southern rock singer-fiddler Charlie Daniels; and rock and roll guitarist Link Wray, among others.

In the 1990s Rock drummed with C&W guitarist Johnny Hopkins in the band J.C. and the Goodtimers at such Maryland night clubs as El Rancho Restaurant (Forestville) and the T.D. Lounge (Laurel). Bebley Raymond Colie passed away on Tuesday, April 16, 1996 at the age of 54.

RAY TILKENS

Guitarist Ray Tilkens was born and raised in Takoma Park, Maryland. He started at an early age on piano but switched to guitar after hearing the Beatles' "Day Tripper." His early influences included Jimi Hendrix, the Doors, Cream, Neil Young and various Motown artists. During his years at Montgomery Blair High School in the early 1970s he played in a number of rock and roll bands including Rocking Horse.

In 1972 Tilkens became the guitarist in a popular Lanham, Maryland-based rock and roll band called God Mother Country and remained with the group for two years. The band worked the local teen dance scene, played pool parties, and also appeared at such night clubs as Tall Timbers in Calloway, Maryland and the Crazy Horse in Washington, D.C. The band's lineup consisted of Tilkens on guitar, lead singer Charlie Hastings, bassist Brian Wagner and drummer Hank Burnett. Their repertoire consisted of covers of songs by such artists as Johnny Winter, Wishbone Ash, Jeff Beck, Jethro Tull, the Allman Brothers Band and numerous others.

Tilkens then spent the remainder of the 1970s playing in such local rock and roll bands as Flight, Mystic Blue, Smalltalk, and As Is. He rounded out the decade playing throughout 1978 and 1979 for R&B singer Big Al Downing. In the 1980s he played guitar for a variety of musical outfits including: the rock and roll bands Race the Rat, Root Boy Slim (and his various acts), and the Essentials; rock and roll guitarist Ed King (formerly of Strawberry Alarm Clock and Lynyrd Skynyrd); the pop group Hot Shot; and the R&B band Tough Luck.

A career highlight for Tilkens took place when he played guitar onstage with the Southern rock and roll band Lynyrd Skynyrd as they performed "Call Me the Breeze" during their concert at Merriweather Post Pavilion in Columbia, Maryland on Tuesday, July 23, 1991.

More recently Tilkens has performed with C&W singer-guitarist Mary Chapin Carpenter, blues singer-guitarist Cathy Ponton King, the blues band known as the Honeydrippers, the R&B group known as Hardaway Connection, and the country rock outfit Tony Denikos and the Working Poor.

Since 1980 Tilkens has been an engineer and producer at Ambient Recording, where he has worked on more than 300 music projects. He repairs guitars and is currently playing guitar in the Reilly Goulait Band, one of the Washington, D.C. area's most popular rock and roll groups.

RAZZ

Razz was one of the most highly regarded rock and roll bands to ever emerge from the Washington, D.C. area. The group, sometimes confusingly referred to as "The Razz" or "(The) Razz," formed in the Prince George's County, Maryland community of Camp Springs in 1970 with an original lineup of lead singer Michael Reidy of Camp Springs, guitarist Bill Craig of College Park, guitarist Fred Gallagher of Silver Spring, bassist Ted Niceley of Capitol Heights and drummer Pete Ragusa of Cheverly. The group endured a round of personnel shifts during its time, with Reidy, Craig, and Niceley forming a nucleus that endured until the band's dissolution in December 1979.

Razz came about when guitarist Bill Craig, who, during the late 1960s while attending High Point High School played the local teen dance circuit in such rock and roll bands as the Null Set and the Mods of Quinn, enrolled at the University of Maryland and passed through such rock bands at Morning Star, Easy and Warm as Toast. In 1970 during his sophomore year he transferred to Prince George's Community College in Largo, Maryland and put together a new rock and roll band called the Hot Crabs to perform at various GROK concerts on the University of Maryland's College Park campus. For this project he recruited lead singer Michael Reidy, guitarist-bassist Fred Gallagher and drummer Scott Galloway.

The Hot Crabs were short-lived and in late 1970 Craig decided to retain the services of Reidy and Gallagher for a new rock and roll band which he called Razz. He picked up drummer Pete Ragusa, who had previously played in the Manchurian Candidates while attending Bladensburg High School in the late 1960s and had then worked with Craig in the bands Easy and Warm as Toast. The group was then rounded out with bassist Ted Niceley, who was still attending Central High School in Seat Pleasant, Maryland at the time, and had previously played in several Capitol Heights-based rock and roll bands including Peat Moss, Rainbow, and Phoenix.

Over the next few years Razz underwent personnel changes, with Reidy and Niceley staying in place, Bill Craig taking a brief hiatus, and several musicians passing through including guitarists Mike Coburn, Dexter Dunn, and Abaad Behram, and drummer Harvey Nussbaum. In 1974 the band consisted of Reidy, Behram, Dunn, Niceley and a new drummer named Doug Tull, who lived in Arlington, Virginia and had previously played in the bands Horizon, Sway, Cool Water, and Bitch. In 1977 Razz settled on the classic lineup of Reidy, Craig, Behram, Niceley and Tull.

In the spring of 1978, while playing the Varsity Grill Back Room in College Park, Behram departed the group to join the rock and roll band Artful Dodger and was replaced by guitarist Tommy Keene, formerly of the Rage. Razz's final gig took place on Thursday, December 27, 1979 at Beacon's Backstage in Falls Church, Virginia, after which by mutual agreement the members parted ways.

During its early years Razz performed a mix of blues and rock, covering everything from the Rolling Stones to Rory Gallagher, though they concentrated on original material for most of the middle and late 1970s. They opened concerts for a number of visiting national acts including Roxy Music at the Grand Ballroom (University of Maryland) on Sunday, March 2, 1975; the J. Geils Band at McDonough Gymnasium (Georgetown University) on Saturday, February 4, 1978; and the Babys at the Ontario Theatre in Washington, D.C. on Tuesday, March 20, 1979.

Razz was a major attraction in Washington, D.C. at such night clubs as the Act IV Supper Club, the Keg, Bogie's, the Bayou, Columbia Station, the Cellar Door, Mr. Henry's Tenley Circle, Desperado's, the Childe Harold, the Far Inn and the Atlantis; in Maryland at the Psyche Delly (Bethesda), the Stardust Inn (Waldorf), the Varsity Grill Back Room (College Park) and the Marble Bar (Baltimore); and in Virginia at J.J.'s (Arlington). The band also traveled out of town on occasion and appeared at two famous clubs in New York City, CBGB's and Max's Kansas City.

In terms of recordings, Razz released two singles: "C. Redux" backed with "70's Anomie (Are You Single)" (Razz; O'Rourke Records, 1977); and "You Can Run" backed with "Who's Mr. Comedy" (The Razz; O'Rourke Records, 1979). They also issued an EP consisting of four selections taken from a live performance when they opened for Dave Edmund's Rockpile featuring Nick Lowe at the Grand Ballroom (University of Maryland) on Friday, November 3, 1978: "Air Time" (Side One – "Marianne," and "Cherry Vanilla;" Side Two – "Love is Love" and "Hippy Hippy Shake" ((The) Razz; O'Rourke Records, 1979).

THE REACHERS

The Reachers were a rock and roll band that got together in Cheverly, Maryland in the summer of 1964 and began playing out in the spring of 1965. The group originally consisted of four Bladensburg High School students: singer-guitarist Jim MacFarlane, singer-guitarist Mike Dixon, bassist Billy Dodd and drummer John Molloy.

The Reachers were born during the onset of the British Invasion and rehearsed in what they called "The Orange Room" – an orange-painted garage at the home of Jim MacFarlane at 2803 Crest Avenue in Cheverly, Maryland. Early on, the group specialized in covering bands such as the Beatles, the Rolling Stones, the Yardbirds and the Kinks. They were noted as being one of the few young rock and roll outfits that quickly graduated from the local teen dance scene to headline some of the best night clubs Georgetown had to offer.

The very first public performance the Reachers ever gave in 1965 was for the patients at the Spring Grove State Hospital, which was located outside of Baltimore in Catonsville, Maryland. They spent much of the next two years working teen dances in Maryland at the Cheverly Teen Club (Cheverly Tuxedo Elementary School in Cheverly), the Palmer Park Teen Club (Kent Junior High School in Palmer Park), the Kentland Teen Club (Kentland Elementary School in Kentland), the Cooper Lane Teen Club (Cooper Hill Elementary

School in Landover Hills), the Colmar Manor Teen Club (Colmar Manor), the Greenbelt Teen Club (Greenbelt Youth Center), the St. Ambrose Parish Teen Club (Cheverly), the Bladensburg Teen Club (Bladensburg Junior High School in Bladensburg) and St. Vincent Pallotti High School (Laurel).

In one of the Reachers' earliest night club jobs in 1965, they took a booking at the 1023 Restaurant in Southeast Washington, D.C. where they served as the misplaced opening act for Link Wray and His Ray Men. Later, in one of their brightest moments, the band was called upon to appear on the supporting bill for the Animals at the District of Columbia National Guard Armory in Washington, D.C. on Wednesday, April 13, 1966. This particular performance took place on the final evening of the "National Teen Show," a five-night concert series that featured some of the top popular music bands in the world. Joining the Animals and the Reachers on the bill that night were the British Walkers and the Jumping Jax. It was a monumental moment in the young band's history.

The Reachers experienced changes in personnel as time went by. In the spring of 1966 the band brought in John Gaines, another Bladensburg High School student, to play keyboards. A bit later Dixon and Dodd were replaced by two additional Bladensburg High School musicians, rhythm guitarist Randy Nelson and bassist Dickie Thompson (at this point Jim MacFarlane took over all lead guitar parts). During this time the band did an engagement at the Rocket Room in Washington, D.C. and performed at several area military bases including Fort George G. Meade Officers' Club (Anne Arundel County, Maryland), the Fort Belvoir Officers' Club (Fairfax County, Virginia) and the Marine Corps Base Quantico Officers' Club (Prince William County, Virginia).

At this point the groups' repertoire had expanded greatly and they were performing songs by more than three-dozen different pop and rock bands. Among the bands they had added to their mix were the Byrds, the Doors, the Hollies, the Jimi Hendrix Experience, Love, Procol Harum, the Rascals, Them, the Turtles, the Who and Wilson Pickett.

Things changed for the Reachers as the Summer of Love approached. First, they were offered a place in what was advertised as "The Vox Band Battle for Stardom," a multi-act competition held at the Alexandria Arena on Sunday, April 2, 1967 that was presented by the Sound Center of Falls Church, Virginia, produced by Bud Becker and Dick Kehoe, and hosted by WPGC disc jockey Cousin Duffy.

The competition, whose grand prize was an invitation to participate in a larger national competition for a movie contract with Hollywood-based American International Pictures, included, besides the Reachers, the Warlox, Rokx, the Hearsemen, the Tornados, Contents Under Pressure, the Hayze, the Brotherhood, and the London Stompers. Unlike the other bands on the bill, the Reachers positioned their speakers on poles some ten feet off the floor with their harmony-laden rendition of the Turtles' "Happy Together" resonating crystal clear throughout the arena.

While the winner of the "Band Battle" was a band called the Warlox, the Reachers impressed the judges enough to walk away with the second place prize. Perhaps more importantly, their performance that evening caught the attention of various local music promoters and contributed to the band's matriculation into the world of Georgetown night clubs.

The year 1967 proved to be a busy year for the Reachers. They were playing full-time at a mix of teen dances and night clubs and from January to the end of April that year they appeared in Maryland at the Cheverly Teen Club (Cheverly Tuxedo Elementary School in Cheverly), the Carrolton Teen Club (Charles Carroll Junior High School in New Carrollton), the West Lanham Hills Fire Department (Hyattsville), the Annapolis Armory (Annapolis) and the Fort George G. Meade Teen Club (Anne Arundel County); in Washington, D.C. at the

American Palace (the Dodge Hotel) and William Mitchell Hall (George Washington University); and in Virginia at the Fort Belvoir Officers' Club (Fairfax County).

From May to December of 1967 the Reachers served as the house band at a night club in Georgetown called the Corral, a job they obtained after being observed that spring by the club's managers as they were performing directly below in a basement night club called the Frog. When they weren't performing at the Corral, they filled in their schedule with one-nighters in Washington, D.C. at such night clubs as the Bayou, the Rogue, the Roundtable, the Hurricane and the Keg; in Maryland at the Crofton Teen Club (the Crofton Country Club) and the Fort George G. Meade Officers' Club (Anne Arundel County); and in Virginia at Fairfax High School (Fairfax), Leesburg High School (Leesburg), the East Springfield Teen Club (Springfield) and the Marine Corps Base Quantico Officers' Club (Prince William County).

The Reachers also performed at many special events that year. On Saturday, April 29, 1967 they participated in a multi-band show entitled "Psychedelia" at the Alexandria Arena that was booked and emceed by Jack Alix and also featured December's Children and the Town Criers, among others.

On Saturday, May 27, 1967 the Reachers were given the headlining 7:30pm slot in the "Festival of Visual and Performing Arts," a fund-raising event at the Washington Gallery of Modern Art (1503 21st Street NW, Washington, D.C.) staged for the gallery by the Junior Friends of the Gallery, a group of former students of Western High School art teacher Leon Berkowitz. This benefit, which ran from 1-9pm, advertised a symposium on contemporary art moderated by gallery director Charles Millard, poetry readings, daffodils, buttons reading "Art," dancing, experimental films, psychedelics, jazz, a continuous light and color show by artist Eric Rudd, perpetual happenings and a light show by artist Ian Fralich, and music by the Eddie Henderson Quartet, December's Children, Rusti Clark, the Jazz Advocates, the Fallen Angels, the Telstars, and the Reachers.

In addition, the Reachers shared a bill with the British Walkers and Skin Flower on a special concert presented by the St. Andrew's Episcopal Church Teen Club in Arlington, Virginia on Friday, June 30, 1967.

The popularity of the Reachers continued throughout the latter part of 1967. They were tagged as the featured attraction at the weekly, WPGC-sponsored teen dances staged by Cousin Duffy at St. Mary Catholic Church in Alexandria, Virginia that began on Friday, September 8 and ran through Saturday, December 23 of that year. Duffy also got the band to perform in an opening slot on the first night of a "Psychedelic Spectacular" featuring the Sunshine Company at the Ambassador Theatre on Thursday, November 23, 1967. The Reachers later returned to the Ambassador on Thursday, December 21, 1967 where they were part of a concert lineup that was co-headlined by the Fallen Angels and the Telstars and included opening acts the Chocolate Snowflake and the Mosaic Virus.

The Reachers experienced adversity late in the year after Randy Nelson called in sick for a series of performances at Mac's Pipe and Drum Restaurant in Georgetown. As a co-lead singer, his absence reduced the band to a quartet and forced Jim MacFarlane to carry the vocal load. Changes ensued, as Nelson was ultimately replaced by guitarist George Scutt. Drummer John Molloy then joined the Fallen Angels and was replaced by Jack O'Conner.

Confounding matters was the band's arrival at the Corral one day in January 1968, only to find the night club had shut down and shuttered its doors without warning. Shortly thereafter, drummer Ronnie Wilson of the Telstars notified manager Barry Seidel that he was looking to reorganize his band, and Jim MacFarlane and Dickie Thompson were recruited into his new project. The reign of the Reachers had come to a close.

THE REASONS WHY

Operating under such names as the Four Reasons, the Age of Reason, Reason, the Reasons, and the Reasons Why, this rock and roll band formed in 1966 and for more than a decade was a top attraction in such Washington, D.C. area night clubs as the Rocket Room, the Crazy Horse and Ventuno 21 Supper Club.

One of the group's most popular lineups consisted of singer-guitarist Billy Windsor, bassist Terry Gorka, singer-keyboardist Tommy Dildy and drummer Bill Manning. Other musicians to pass through the band included bassist Jack Jensen and drummer Mike Zack.

The group had one single release, "(Your Love is Like a) 'Magnet'" backed with "I'm a Fine Man" (The Age of Reason; Ascot Records, 1967), and also recorded and released one album, "The Age of Reason" (Reason; Georgetowne Records, 1969).

THE REEKERS

The Reekers were a rock and roll band that formed in late 1963 in Garrett Park, Maryland. They later evolved into the Hangmen, one of the most popular teen dance bands to ever grace the Washington, D.C. area. The group's initial lineup consisted of lead singer Joe Triplett, guitarist Tom Guernsey, bassist Richard Solo, keyboardist Mike Henley and drummer Jim Daniels.

The Reekers performed at private parties in Montgomery County, Maryland, at a night club called Ben's Hideaway in Northwest Washington, D.C., and a bar called the Zen Den in Rehoboth Beach, Delaware. They recorded and released on single, "Don't Call Me Flyface" backed with "Grindin'" (The Reekers; Ru-Jac Records, 1964).

In March 1965 Guernsey dissolved the band and put together a new group called the Hangmen, though he took a two-song demo previously recorded by the Reekers and had it released in September of that year as a single under the Hangmen name: "What A Girl Can't Do" backed with "The Girl Who Faded Away" (The Hangmen; Monument Records, 1965). In the ensuing years Tom Guernsey occasionally resurrected different lineups of the Reekers for local night club performances.

THE RENEGADES

The Renegades were a highly regarded rock and roll group on the local teen dance scene from 1965 to 1967. The band was based in Bethesda, Maryland with all of the band members at some point attending Walter Johnson High School. They cranked out the songs by the Rolling Stones, the Beatles, the Kinks, the Kingsmen, the Paul Butterfield Blues Band, the Blues Project and others while performing in cranberry and white shirts and white trousers.

The Renegades boasted a number of top musicians in its lineup who would remain on the local music scene for years to come. The original roster consisted of lead singer Tom Birks, lead guitarist Bob Gordon, rhythm guitarist Rolf Hanson, bassist Tom Babb and drummer Brooke Hall. Eventually, Mark "Sid" Sithens replaced Hall on drums, and Louie Newmyer replaced Babb on bass. Late in the band's reign bassist Scotty Ball joined up and Newmyer moved over to keyboards. For much of its time, the band's ambitious young roadie was a teenager named Nils Lofgren, who had yet to start playing guitar in his own bands.

The Renegades maintained a heavy work schedule and were popular attractions at dances in Maryland at the Ayrlawn Teen Club (Ayrlawn Recreation Center in Bethesda), the North Bethesda Teen Club (North Bethesda Junior High School in Bethesda), Northwestern High School (Hyattsville), the Wedge (Bethesda Youth Center), the Wheaton Youth Center (Wheaton) and University of Maryland fraternity parties. In the summer of

1967 Birks, Hanson, Sithens, Ball and roadie Nils Lofgren all resurfaced in the Crystal Mesh.

THE RESUMES

There were several bands in the Washington, D.C. area that went by the name "The Resumes," but the most popular of the bunch was a version out of Chevy Chase, Maryland that was in operation from 1965 to 1968. The original lineup of this particular group consisted of three Bethesda-Chevy Chase High School students – lead singer-rhythm guitarist Tom Tedrow, lead guitarist Alan Adkins and bassist Arthur Killick – along with drummer John Ridenour from Woodrow Wilson High School in Washington, D.C.

The Resumes headlined teen dances in Maryland at: the Leland Teen Club (Leland Junior High School in Bethesda), the Little Flower Parish Teen Club (Bethesda), the North Bethesda Teen Club (North Bethesda Junior High School in Bethesda), the Thomas W. Pyle Teen Club (Thomas W. Pyle Junior High School in Bethesda), the Western Teen Club (Western Junior High School in Bethesda), the Damascus Teen Club (Damascus Elementary School in Damascus), the Belt Teen Club (Belt Junior High School in Silver Spring), the White Oak Teen Club (White Oak Junior High School in Silver Spring), the Wedge (Bethesda Youth Center), River Road Unitarian Universalist Congregation (Bethesda), Springbrook High School (Silver Spring), Winston Churchill High School (Potomac) and Bethesda-Chevy Chase High School (Bethesda); and in Washington, D.C. at the Parish of Saints Paul and Augustine Teen Club, Chevy Chase Presbyterian Church, Maret School and Sidwell Friends School.

The Resumes played a mix of R&B and rock and roll including songs by James Brown, Sam and Dave, the Temptations, the Four Tops, the Beatles, the Rolling Stones, the Young Rascals, Them, Vanilla Fudge, and the Byrds. A high point was the release of the original 45rpm single record "Ain't Gonna Eat Out My Heart (Anymore)" backed with "One Day" (The Resumes; Sho-Time Records, 1966).

The final version of the Resumes in 1968 consisted of lead singer-rhythm guitarist Tom Tedrow, guitarists Alan Adkins and Steve Hubert, bassist Michael Blakeman and drummer John Patterson.

RICH ECKHARDT

Guitarist Rich Eckhardt grew up in Riverdale, Maryland and took up the guitar at age eight, listening and playing along to bands like the Ventures, the Beatles, the Monkees, the Beach Boys and the Grass Roots, and, after playing in local neighborhood bands, Cream, the Doobie Brothers, Foghat and Bachman-Turner Overdrive. At age 10 in the early 1970s he played in his own instrumental band called Scorpio that specialized in original compositions and Ventures covers.

During his time at Bladensburg High School in the middle and late 1970s Eckhardt played both bass and guitar in the Bladensburg Madrigals. During this time he also played guitar in the pit band for a theatrical show entitled "Music, Music, Music" at the Wild World theme park in nearby Largo, Maryland. In addition, during these years he first played the local teen dance scene in a rock and roll band called Storm, and followed that up with a run in a Top 40 pop music horn band called Gratitude. Later on, one of the most notable performing artists Eckhardt worked with in the Washington, D.C. area during the 1980s was blues-jazz singer Eva Cassidy.

In 1989 Eckhardt moved to Nashville, Tennessee, and, because of his talent and musical versatility, he quickly became the most sought-after guitarist in town, often backing up C&W headliners at the Grand Ole Opry. During his first 10 years in Nashville he performed, toured and/or recorded with such C&W acts as the James Brothers, singers

Eddy Raven and Shania Twain, and singer-guitarists Mel McDaniel, Becky Hobbs, John Berry and Clint Black. He also performed onstage and in-concert with the Charlie Daniels Band, a favorite of Southern rock fans.

In July 1998 Eckhardt joined forces with C&W singer-guitarist Toby Keith, taking on the lead guitar position in his Easy Money Band, and has remained Keith's main guitarist ever since.

Through the years a few of the innumerable major popular music artists Eckhardt has performed with are: blues singer-guitarist Delbert McClinton; C&W singers Scotty Emerick, Chalee Tennison, the Hager Twins and Lindsey Haun C&W singer-guitarists Willie Nelson, Merle Haggard, Glen Campbell, Rodney Atkins, Steve Azar, Terri Clark, Mark Nesler, John Anderson, Wade Hayes, Ty England, Blake Shelton, Connie Smith and Russell Smith; C&W singer-pianist Mickey Gilley; jazz bassist Sean O'Bryan Smith; R&B guitarist Steve Cropper; rock and roll singer Steven Tyler; rock and roll guitarists Nokie Edwards and Joe Perry; rock and roll singer-guitarists Ted Nugent, Derek St. Holmes and Sammy Hagar; and rock and roll singer-pianist Jerry Lee Lewis.

Eckhardt's extensive touring has taken him around the world and he has performed throughout the United States, Canada, Europe, and Asia. He has appeared in dozens of music videos, major motion pictures, television commercials, and television programs, including the ABC hit series "Nashville," where he has appeared in the role of "Bandleader" for character Luke Wheeler (portrayed by actor Will Chase).

In addition to his on-going work with Toby Keith, Eckhardt played lead guitar for Resurrection – A Journey Tribute, one of the top touring tribute bands in the United States, from 2014 to 2016. He is also currently playing guitar for C&W singer-guitarist Shane Owens. To date he has two solo albums to his credit: the jazz-influenced "Soundcheck" (Rich Eckhardt; Rich Eckhardt, 2005); and the rock and roll-oriented "Cottage City Firehouse" (Rich Eckhardt; Rich Eckhardt, 2009; the title of this album pays homage to guitarist Danny Gatton, who gave his first public performance at said facility).

RICHARD X. HEYMAN

Richard X. Heyman is a singer and multi-instrumentalist who was raised in Plainfield, New Jersey and was an original member of the Doughboys, a noted 1960s rock and roll garage band in his home state.

At the age of 26 in 1977 Heyman moved to Bethesda, Maryland, where he began playing guitar in a rock and roll band called the Rage, which also included guitarist Tommy Keene. For two years the Rage performed at local night clubs such as the Keg (Washington, D.C.) and the Varsity Grill Back Room (College Park), where they frequently opened shows for Razz, which at the time was one of the top rock and roll bands in the nation's capital.

Heyman went on to drum for such musical artists as the country rock group known as the Cooper Dodge Band, and such rock and roll performers as singer-guitarists Link Wray and Jonathan Richman, singer-keyboardist Brian Wilson, and keyboardist Michael Brown (formerly of the Left Banke). He also played keyboards for R&B singer Ben E. King and pop singer Mary Weiss (former lead singer of the Shangri-Las). Since 1988 he has recorded and released 10 albums as a solo rock and roll artist, including the major label release "Hey Man!" (Richard X. Heyman; Sire Records, 1991).

RICHARD TIPTON

Singer-guitarist Richard "Dickie Dog" Tipton was born in Washington, D.C. and spent his early years living in Hyattsville, Maryland, where he began teaching himself guitar at age eight. The first song he ever learned was "Secret Agent Man" (performed by Johnny Rivers) and as a youth he played along to the theme songs of various 1960s television programs including "Batman."

At the age of 10 in 1965 Tipton's family moved to Greenbelt, Maryland and the young guitarist began attending the rehearsals of a popular rock and roll band from town called the Midnight Marauders, who regularly performed at Greenbelt Teen Club dances at the Greenbelt Youth Center. In the ensuing years Tipton began playing along to recordings of such bands and musicians as the Beatles, Johnny Winter, Led Zeppelin and the Allman Brothers Band. During his time at Parkdale High School in the early 1970s he mainly sat in with other local rock and roll bands and jammed with fellow musicians at parties and shows.

Tipton joined the United States Army in 1973 and was stationed for three years in Hawaii. During his enlistment he played lead guitar in a 13-piece multi-styled Army band called Contents Under Pressure that played throughout the Islands and covered songs by such artists as Chicago, the Commodores and Earth, Wind and Fire. During his time with the group he performed onstage with such jazz musicians as trumpeters Maynard Ferguson and Chuck Mangione, and pop singer Don Ho. Tipton returned to Greenbelt in 1976 and spent several years sitting in with rock and roll bands at local night clubs such as the Paragon in College Park.

In the early 1980s Tipton switched his primary interests to C&W music and he spent several years singing and playing lead guitar in a band called Ralph and the Country Sound that performed at two night clubs in Laurel, Maryland, the Princess Bar and the Turf Club. He later did a long stint in another local C&W band called Oklahoma, whose home base was at the T.D. Lounge, also in Laurel. In the early 1990s he joined the Baltimore-based C&W band Four by Four and remained their lead guitarist for more than 10 years.

In 2002 Tipton relocated to Westminster, Maryland and in the ensuing years sang and played guitar in a duo format with such musicians as R&B-rock guitarist Greg Gottlieb and classical-jazz-rock singer-guitarist Ben Sherman. From 2010 to 2016 He was the lead guitarist for Mike Harrison and the Rivers Bend Band, a Mount Airy-based C&W group that performed at festivals, American Legions, Elks Lodges, Moose Lodges and VFWs throughout Central Maryland.

RICHIE MITCHELL

Bassist Richie Mitchell was born in Washington, D.C., raised in Arlington, Virginia, and was introduced to music at an early age by his guitar-playing father and rock and roll-loving older brothers. At age 12 his parents bought him a guitar and while attending Stratford Junior High School in the late 1950s he had a chance to see Link Wray and His Ray Men perform live in the school's cafeteria. After the show he passed the band in the parking lot as they were loading into a car, never suspecting he would become a member of their group a few years down the road.

Mitchell attended Washington-Lee High School and as a teenager in the early 1960s he spent time jamming with several friends including Jimmy Carter, who played in a local band called the Fender Benders and would later go on to play in the British Walkers. His father got him a Fender Jazzmaster guitar, and Mitchell, after practicing to Ventures instrumentals, formed a rock and roll band called the Del-Fis that worked the local teen dance circuit and select local night clubs like the Admiral Grill in Bailey's Crossroads. The Del-Fis were occasionally called upon by disc jockey-promoter Jack Alix to back visiting national acts such as pop singers Freddy Cannon and Bryan Hyland at some of his local record hops.

In 1962 Mitchell was recruited by singer-guitarist John Van Horn to play bass in his rock and roll band the Fender Benders. At that point in time group's lineup consisted of Van

Horn, Mitchell, keyboardist Bill Hodges and drummer Bobby Jones. The band played in Washington, D.C. at such night clubs as the Devonshire Grill and the Rabbit's Foot; in Maryland at the Sunnybrook Tavern (Oxon Hill); and in Virginia at the Fort Myer Officers' Club (Arlington County) and the Marine Corps Base Quantico Officers' Club (Prince William County).

That year Van Horn took Mitchell to Vinnie's Grill in Washington, D.C. and introduced him to guitarist Link Wray. Mitchell began filling in for Shorty Horton on bass and would play with Link Wray and His Ray Men for weeks at a time. During this time he also worked Sundays at Vinnie's Grill as the bassist for blues singer-guitarist Bobby Parker. In 1963 he played bass for the rock and roll band Bobbie Howard and the Ponies in Washington, D.C. at the Famous Restaurant and the Alpine Room.

In 1964, the Fender Benders, still consisting of Van Horn, Mitchell, Hodges and Jones, obtained a booking at a basement night club called the Oasis in the Mount Pleasant neighborhood of Washington, D.C. By that time the group was playing a mix of R&B and rock and roll and began adding songs of the British Invasion to its repertoire.

Late in the year the Fender Benders dissolved (Van Horn would keep different versions of the band alive in the ensuing years). Shortly thereafter, Mitchell, Hodges and Jones recruited singer-guitarist Jimmy Youngman and singer-keyboardist Bob Stoneman and formed a new rock and roll band called Lord Byron that spent much of 1965 playing in Georgetown at such night clubs as Nu-Mac's, the Roundtable, the French Quarter, the Corral, and the Frog (in this particular group all five members shared vocal duties).

During that year Mitchell also played bass for a rock and roll band called Barry Seidel and the Sellouts. This outfit worked in Washington, D.C. at such night clubs as Benny's Rebel Room, the Hayloft, the Rocket Room and the Crazy Horse. On one booking they were called upon to travel to Long Island, New York where they worked an engagement at the Shell House as Ronny and the Daytonas (backing up surf rock singer-guitarist John "Ronny" Wilkin). During this time Lord Byron was reorganized as a trio consisting of Mitchell, Jones and Youngman, and performed at another Washington, D.C. night club called Captain Guy's Club, which was located at 1212 New York Avenue NW.

In 1965 and 1966 Mitchell played bass for Link Wray and His Ray Men at the 1023 Restaurant in Southeast Washington, D.C. At this point the band had several musicians passing through and often times they worked weeknights at the 1023 without Link Wray himself, though the guitarist would always rejoin the outfit for their weekend appearances at the night club. While Vernon Wray managed the band and Doug Wray was a constant on the drum stool, musicians to fill out the lineups included guitarist John Van Horn, bassists Mitchell, Ed Cymer and Ellwood Brown, singer-bassist Chuck Bennett and keyboardist Bill Hodges. Mitchell also accompanied Link Wray and His Ray Men on numerous road trips throughout Pennsylvania, New York and the New England states where they would perform at college fraternity parties and night clubs.

In the early 1970s Mitchell again worked with John Van Horn and plays bass on his album "Out Back Music" (John Van Horn; Mercury Records, 1972). He has remained active on the Washington, D.C. area music scene and through the years he has played guitar (as opposed to bass) with a number of groups including the C&W bands Three + One and Good Time Country, and the rock and roll acts the Bank Street Band and Mid Life Crisis. In addition, he still picks up the bass when called upon and plays out with versions of the Fender Benders.

RICK BENICK

Guitarist Rick Benick grew up in Forest Heights, Maryland and attended Oxon Hill High School as the 1960s came to a close. As a teen he played in a Yardbirds-influenced rock and roll group called Ben Franklin's Electric Company Band and in the early 1970s was a member of the hard-rocking band Hailstone.

From November 1973 to June 1975 Benick was lead guitarist in the Cherry People, one of the Washington, D.C. area's most popular bands. He went on to play with such rock and roll acts as Roadmaster, singer-guitarist-keyboardist Henry Lee Summer, and Mitch Ryder and the Detroit Wheels.

Some of the albums Benick appears on include: "Sweet Music" (Roadmaster; Mercury Records, 1978); "Hey World" (Roadmaster; Mercury Records, 1979); "Fortress" (Roadmaster; Mercury Records, 1980); "Henry Lee Summer" (Henry Lee Summer; CBS Associated Records, 1988); and "I Got Everything" (Henry Lee Summer; CBS Associated Records, 1989).

RICK BERBERICH

Singer-bassist Rick Berberich was born in Washington, D.C. and grew up in Kensington, Maryland. He began playing bass at the age of 16 and during his years at Bethesda-Chevy Chase High School in the middle 1960s he played in such local R&B and rock bands as the Melodies, Joey and the Continentals, the Royals, and Herbie and the Soul Set. From the 1970s until just recently he would sing pop classics on an informal basis at local open mic sessions and in bars like Mr. Smith's in Georgetown and the Flaming Pit in Rockville.

In 2017 Berberich put together the rock and roll band Rick and the Rockers which can be seen in night clubs around the nation's capital. The current lineup of this group consists of singer Rick Berberich, guitarist Keith Grimes, bassist Rico Petruccelli and drummer Robbie Magruder.

RICK DAVIS

Drummer Rick Davis was born in Washington, D.C., raised in District Heights, Maryland, and joined his first band, a pop music group called Sam Weatherly and the Silvertones, at the age of 14 in 1960 while attending Francis Scott Key Junior High School.

During the early 1960s while attending Suitland High School he drummed for the Medallions, an R&B-rock band based in the Anacostia neighborhood of Washington, D.C. The band's main lineup during the years Davis was a member consisted of lead singer Marty Kessler, guitarist Gary Cristy, bassist Paul Kirkpatrick, saxophonists Bill "Mo" Blair and Dave Wilson, and Davis on drums. Musicians to pass through the Medallions included guitarist Dave McGinnis, saxophonist Tony Romagna and bassist Jack Casady.

The Medallions became a top attraction on the local teen dance circuit. The group also played fraternity parties at the University of Maryland and the University of Virginia and night club dates in Washington, D.C. at Benny's Rebel Room, the Rocket Room and the Alpine Room. In 1962 they backed up pop music singer Ray Stevens, who was touring at the time in support of his novelty single "Ahab the Arab," at the Rocket Room.

From 1964 to 1965 Davis drummed for Gil Clark and the Holidays, a rock and roll band that played the local military officers' club circuit and recorded and released one 45rpm single record, "The Middle of a Dream" (A-side credited to Gil Clark and the Holidays; Edgewood Records, 1965), backed with "How Does It Feel" (B-side credited to Gil Clark and Nancy Clifford with the Holidays; Edgewood Records, 1965).

Throughout the remainder of the 1960s Davis drummed with scores of rock and roll bands and musicians including the Classics (which included keyboardist Sam Paladino and saxophonist Del Puschert), the East Coast Express (which included guitarist Danny Gatton and keyboardist Dick Heintze), and the Naturals – a group he often sat in with at such Maryland night clubs as Strick's Restaurant (Silver Hill) and the Turntable Lounge (Mt. Rainier).

From 1967 to 1968 Davis was a member of Joe Banana and the Bunch, a pop-rock band that headlined in Washington, D.C. at such night clubs as Benny's Rebel Room and the Hayloft. At that time the band's lineup consisted of singer-keyboardist Kevin "Joe Banana" Fay, singer-bassist John Herbert, saxophonist Roger McDuffie, saxophonist Warren Smith and Davis on drums (the band had no guitarist). He also was occasionally called upon to back up R&B singer Leroy Taylor and jazz guitarist Fred Karnes at local night clubs.

In 1969 Davis became a founding member of the Georgetown-based rock and roll band Sun Country, whose initial lineup was rounded out by lead singer-guitarist Bobby Stevens, singer-bassist John Morrison and singer-keyboardist Jerry Stupp. During his two years with the band, musicians to pass through included singers Trudy Morgan and Mike Buker, guitarist Pete "Peaches" Williams and keyboardist Mike Zinodinovich. When Davis left the band he was replaced by drummer Mike Zack.

Sun Country played such Washington, D.C. night clubs as the Keg, the Crazy Horse, the Bayou, Gentlemen II, the Montage and Benny's Rebel Room. They released one single with Davis in tow, "Get Together" backed with "Things You Need" (Sun Country; Affiliated Records, 1969). During his time with the band, they also performed onstage with such nationally known R&B acts as the Drifters, and singers Gary U.S. Bonds and Jimmy Jones.

In the 1970s Davis drummed for a succession of bands and musicians including: a Baltimore-based jazz rock outfit called the Michael Goldberg Band; C&W singer-guitarist Emmylou Harris; the jazz rock band the Eye; and the multi-styled pop music groups Ron MacDonald and Nightwatch and McArthur Park. More recently Davis has drummed for the R&B-rock band Demetri and the Bad Boys, jazz rock guitarist Michael Fath, and a succession of jazz bands at Columbia Station in the Adams Morgan neighborhood of Washington, D.C.

RICK RANSOM

Singer-keyboardist Rick Ransom was raised in Greenbelt, Maryland and began taking piano lessons as a youth. During those early years he listened to such performers as Link Wray and His Ray Men, the Everly Brothers, Elvis Presley, and the sounds of R&B and soul. During his years at High Point High School in the early and middle 1960s he sang and played keyboards in a Greenbelt-based rock and roll band called the Rockin' Rejects, who played dances for the Greenbelt Teen Club at the Greenbelt Youth Center.

In 1965 the Rockin' Rejects morphed into an R&B-rock band called Donnie and the Diablos that also regularly performed at the Greenbelt Youth Center. Ransom remained a singer-keyboardist with the band for more than two years, during which time the group's popularity in its hometown rivaled that of Lawrence and the Arabians, leading the band to occasionally rent out the spacious Greenbelt Armory for its own concert performances.

In the late 1960s Ransom played in several different Washington, D.C. area rock and roll bands including the Fifth Edition, the Talents, Venus and the Flytraps, Chi Square, and Electric Fantasy. In the 1970s he worked with such rock and roll bands as Quinn and Candu, and the early 1980s saw him playing with the C&W group Jimmy Moore and the Rangers. In the 1990s Ransom performed as a solo act, singing and playing keyboards in a pop music format.

Since 1999 Ransom has been the lead singer-keyboardist in a Greenbelt-based rock and roll band called the Good Guys. For years the group performed as a trio, with Ransom being joined by guitarists Donald Nickolson and John "Rock" McBride, and percussion provided by a drum machine. They were joined in 2008 by Pat Fern, who played guitar at first but quickly switched to drums. Bassist Chuck Dumais joined the band in 2013.The group was a favorite at the American Legion Greenbelt Post 136, but has played out sparingly since McBride's untimely passing on Wednesday, November 26, 2014. Ransom is also currently playing keyboards in a Greenbelt-based classic rock and roll band called the Relics.

RICK THOMPSON

Saxophonist Rick "Hollywood" Thompson was raised in Hillcrest Heights, Maryland where he started on the clarinet at the age of eight. A year later in 1965 he became a clarinetist in the Metropolitan Police Department Boys' Club Band (Metropolitan Police Department, Precinct Station No. 1, 300 Indiana Avenue NW, Wash DC), a position he maintained for five years. In the late 1960s while attending Benjamin Stoddert Junior High School in Temple Hills, Maryland he played clarinet and saxophone in the school's concert and jazz bands.

Thompson attended Potomac High School in Oxon Hill, Maryland for two years in the early 1970s and played clarinet and saxophone in the school's concert, jazz and marching bands. His family then moved to Woodbridge, Virginia and Thompson graduated from Woodbridge High School. During his senior year there he played the reeds in the school's concert and marching bands.

In the early and middle 1970s Thompson played saxophone in a Washington, D.C. area rock and roll band called On Time. He then attended Marshall University in Huntington, West Virginia from 1974 to 1976. Shortly after arriving on campus he played in the onstage backup band for "Wolfman Jack's Rock and Roll 20-Year Anniversary Concert." While enrolled at Marshall, upon returning home on breaks, he played saxophone in an R&B band called Friday's Children. He remained with that group, which eventually changed its name to the Robert Byrd Blues Band, into 1977. In 1976 and 1977 he also played saxophone on the hotel circuit in several Washington, D.C. area big band jazz outfits including Trux Baldwin and the Starlite Orchestra.

Thompson entered the United States Navy in 1977 and spent the next 12 years playing saxophone and clarinet for the United States Navy Fleet Band, performing in such locations as the United States, the Caribbean, the Arctic Circle, the Pacific Islands and East Asia. He retired from the United States Navy in 1997 and relocated to the Washington, D.C. area in 2001.

Through the years Thompson has played saxophone onstage with such performers as: jazz saxophonist Richie Cole; pop singer Frankie Ford; and R&B singers Percy Sledge, Ernie K. Doe and Irma Thomas. Some of the more recent bands and musicians he has performed with include: the blues band B.G. and the Mojo Hands; blues singer-guitarist Terrence McArdle; the R&B vocal group the Drifters; R&B singer Julia Nixon; R&B singer-keyboardist-guitarist Daryl Davis; the R&B-rock band Jr. Cline and the Recliners; the multi-styled pop music band Ron MacDonald and Nightwatch; a classic rock cover band called the Fabulous Dialtones; and an outfit that plays traditional Bavarian music called the Edelweiss German Band.

Currently Thompson plays in his own longstanding group, the Rick Thompson Jazz Combo, which often performs in Virginia at such venues as the Ice House Café (Herndon), the Fort Myer Officers' Club (Arlington County) and the Fort Belvoir Officers' Club (Fairfax County). He estimates that since 1973 he has played with more than 60 different bands throughout the Washington, D.C. area.

RICKY ROHME

Drummer Ricky Rohme was born and raised in Washington, D.C., and, after returning from a stint in Vietnam in 1965 at the age of 20, first performed in a country rock band from Waldorf, Maryland called the Four Speeds, basically teaching himself how to play drums on-the-job. The group worked dances and bars in Charles County, Maryland and eventually played engagements at two night clubs in Southeast Washington, D.C., Guy's Place and the Round Up Club. He remained the drummer of the Four Speeds for approximately three years.

In the late 1960s Rohme spent time drumming for an R&B band called Steve Charles and the Soul Syndrome. Late in the decade he sat in with Danny Denver and the Soundmasters (featuring guitarist Roy Buchanan) at the Stardust Inn in Waldorf and was subsequently hired to be their full-time drummer. This group soon worked its way to the Cross Roads in Bladensburg, Maryland where Buchanan went on to establish himself as a blues rock guitar legend. Rohme drummed for Denver's band for more than two years after which he continued to drum for Buchanan in his various backup bands, primarily at the Cross Roads.

After Roy Buchanan embarked on a solo career, Rohme spent most of the 1970s drumming for country rock singer Danny Denver and his various bands throughout the Baltimore and Washington, D.C. areas. He then spent the early 1980s drumming for several different local C&W and rock and roll bands including a country rock group called the Wildcard Band that also included former British Walkers bassist Junior Gill. Rohme retired from the Washington, D.C. area music scene in 1984.

RICO PETRUCCELLI

Michael "Rico" Petruccelli grew up in Montgomery County, Maryland in the community of Aspen Hill, began on the bass guitar at age 14, and, during his years at Our Lady of Good Counsel High School in the late 1960s, played the local teen dance circuit in a variety of R&B and rock and roll bands including the Premiers, the Pastels, the Soul Syndicate and the Missing Lynx. In the late 1960s and early 1970s Petruccelli played bass in such Washington, D.C.-based rock and roll bands as Quorum, and Jimmy Eller and the Little People.

Since that time Petruccelli has played bass – and sometimes saxophone, flute and bass clarinet – with a variety of bands and musicians including: R&B singer Van McCoy (with whom he toured Japan and the Philippines); the country rock band the Rosslyn Mountain Boys; and from 1986 to 1992 he toured and recorded with C&W singer-guitarist Mary Chapin Carpenter.

Through the years Petruccelli has also performed with: the blues band Dan Hovey and Bad Daddy; the blues rock bands the Dan Hovey Group and the Dave Chappell Group; blues-pop singer Janine Wilson; bluegrass singer-guitarist Liz Meyer; bluegrass singer-dobro player Mike Auldridge; Celtic folk music band OCEAN (sometimes billed as Jennifer Cutting's Ocean Orchestra); C&W singer-guitarist Terri Allard; the country rock group the North Star band; the folk rock band the New St. George; folk singer Lisa Moscatiello; folk singer-guitarist John McCutcheon; folk duos the Kennedys and singer-guitarist-banjoist Cathy Fink and guitarist-mandolinist Marcy Marxer; folk-pop singer-guitarist Jonathan Edwards; jazz guitarists Charlie Byrd and Barney Kessel; the R&B vocal duo of Marilyn McCoo and Billy Davis Jr.; R&B singer Diahann Carroll; R&B bands Martha and the Vandellas, Little Anthony and the Imperials, the Drifters, the Coasters, the Crystals, and the Marvelettes; rock and roll singer-guitarist Chuck Berry; rock and roll bands the Hanson Brothers and Rick and the Rockers; and the rockabilly band Terri and the Back Alley Rhythm Cats.

RITCHIE BURNS

Singer-bassist-guitarist Ritchie Burns was born in Buffalo, New York and raised in Bethesda, Maryland, where he attended Bethesda-Chevy Chase High School in the middle

1950s. Upon graduating high school, he attended the University of Maryland for two years, during which time he was a member of the Sigma Alpha Epsilon fraternity and performed on ukulele at campus sorority and fraternity parties. In 1957 he moved to Los Angeles, California and for the next several years played in a variety of rock and roll bands including the Super Stocks, the Sunsets, the Weird-Ohs and the Four Speeds.

In 1964 Burns joined the Hondells, a group that originated as a special studio project put together by producer Gary Usher to make a series of surf music records. When the band's first album began to sell, Usher put together an actual band to go out and perform live in night clubs and on regional tours. The earliest lineup of the Hondells consisted of lead singer-bassist Ritchie Burns, lead guitarist Mike Hufford, keyboardist Randy Thomas and drummer Wayne Edwards. Several other musicians passed through the group as the 1960s progressed including guitarist Al Ferguson and keyboardist Dennis McCarthy.

The Hondells released three popular albums in the 1960s: "Go Little Honda" (The Hondells; Mercury Records, 1964); "The Hondells" (The Hondells; Mercury Records, 1964); and "Greatest Hits" (The Hondells; Curb Records, 1966). They also released several 45rpm single records, one of which, "Little Honda" (The Hondells; Mercury Records, 1964), peaked at number nine on Billboard magazine's "Hot 100" popular music chart on Saturday, October 31, 1964.

Burns remained with the Hondells through 1969 and then went on to spend many years in the music industry working for such record companies as Amos, RCA and Motown. He passed away on Sunday, August 29, 2010 at the age of 73.

THE ROADDUCKS

The Roadducks are a Southern rock band that formed in West Springfield, Virginia in the middle 1970s. They have performed some 5,427 live shows (and counting) from Maine to Texas (31 states in all), and are still going strong today. The band's original lineup consisted of lead singer Jay Kiernan, singer-rhythm guitarist Bob "The Bopper" Gaynor, lead guitarist Bill "The Senator" Schmidle, bassist Jody Chambers, keyboardist Dan Schrieber and drummer Jay Nedry.

Locally, the Roadducks were a popular night club and concert attraction and headlined in Washington, D.C. at the Bayou; in Maryland at the Psyche Delly (Bethesda) and the Outside Inn (Rockville); and in Virginia at Louie's Rock City (Bailey's Crossroads), the Fancy Dancer (Alexandria) and the Wild West (Springfield).

Throughout the 1980s the Roadducks regularly toured the United States with some of the top rock and roll bands in the world and appeared in-concert and at festivals with such acts as the Outlaws, the Marshall Tucker Band, Blackfoot, Molly Hatchet, the Allman Brothers Band, the Charlie Daniels Band, the Greg Allman Band, Lynyrd Skynyrd, Black Oak Arkansas, Foghat and Stevie Ray Vaughan.

Numerous musicians have passed through the Roadducks through the years including: guitarists Bill Culder, Jimbo Manion and Karl Zerambo; bassists Billy Cracknell, David Thorne, Rob Melchiorre and Mark Chandler; keyboardists Mark Sales, Ed Callan, Jeff Bean and Emit Carrol; drummers Jim Racey, Gino Chioffi, Dave Chase and Wayne Harrelson; and singers Phil McCormack (who was with the band for 15 years before departing in 1996 to become lead singer for Molly Hatchet) and Cindy Fullam. Roadducks founder Jay Nedry went on to operate Jaxx Night Club in Springfield, Virginia from 1994 to 2012.

The Roadducks have always mixed original compositions with covers of different bands from the Beatles and the Rolling Stones to ZZ Top and Lynyrd Skynyrd. The band has two albums to its credit: "Get Ducked" (Roadducks; Duxsongs Records, 1987); and "Get Ducked Again" (Roadducks; Duxsongs Records, 1990). The group's current lineup consists of lead singer-guitarist Gary Thomas, guitarist Kevin O'Brien, bassist Tom Sillis and drummer Jay Nedry.

The Roadducks currently perform at such Virginia establishments as the Electric Palm (Woodbridge) and Club Eclipse (Gainesville).

ROB DUPREY

Guitarist Rob Duprey grew up in Bethesda, Maryland and attended school locally at Landon School, Western Junior High School and Whitman High School, before graduating high school from Stockbridge School in West Stockbridge, Massachusetts in 1970. In the late 1960s, while living in Bethesda, he played the local teen dance scene in two rock and roll bands, the Warlocks and Gallery 2840.

In the 1970s Duprey moved to New York City where he played with the punk-glam rock band the Mumps. From February 1980 to December 1982 Duprey played lead guitar for Iggy Pop. He appears on two of Pop's albums: "Party" (Iggy Pop; Arista Records, 1981); and "Zombie Birdhouse (Iggy Pop; Animal Records, 1982).

Duprey recently returned to the Washington, D.C. area and currently plays in several rock and roll bands with guitarist Stock Wilson including the Stoats, the Loggers, and an acoustic trio project called Larry and the Lawn Chairs.

ROB PETRIE

Singer-guitarist-mandolinist Rob Petrie was born in Washington, D.C., raised in Oxon Hill, Maryland, and, during his years at John Hanson Junior High School in the late 1970s and Potomac High School in the early 1980s, sang in the school chorus and music theatre. During his high school years he also was a member of the Maryland All State Senior Chorus and the Prince George's County Public Schools Honor Chorus. During his teen years he was an avid listener of rock and roll bands such as Led Zeppelin, AC/DC and Kiss, and began playing guitar to the songs of Billy Joel and Elton John, among others.

In the 1980s and 1990s Petrie explored bluegrass and folk music and played guitar and mandolin at picking parties and informal gatherings of friends. In 1999 he joined a bluegrass band called the Dixie Cannonballs, serving as lead singer and mandolinist, and performed with the group at the Tiffany Tavern in Alexandria, Virginia through 2007.

In 2005 Petrie formed Cold Hard Cash, a band that specializes in covering the songs of the legendary C&W singer-guitarist Johnny Cash. The group's initial lineup consisted of Petrie handling lead vocals and guitar, lead guitarist Danny Stellabotte and bassist Karen Taylor. Changes ensued through the years with Taylor departing and singer-bassist Bill Maron and drummer Lester King joining the mix.

In 2009 Cold Hard Cash reorganized as a trio with Petrie being joined by bassist Beth LeaMond and various guitarists. The band soon morphed into a lineup consisting of Petrie, Stellabotte, drummer Mark Lucas, and different bassists. Cold Hard Cash is a popular attraction at carnivals, festivals and area night clubs such as Gypsy Sally's (Washington, D.C.), Hank Deitle's Tavern (Rockville) and the New Deal Café (Greenbelt).

In 2013 Petrie formed a separate bluegrass band called the Petrified Pickers. He sang and played mandolin and guitar with the group, and was initially joined by bassist John Nowakowski, banjoist-dobro player Dan Mazer (who was soon replaced by Matt Levins) and fiddler Tom Lyons. The band's current roster consists of Petrie, Nowakowski, Lyons and banjoist-steel guitarist Gary Lee Gimble. They frequently perform at the New Deal Café in Greenbelt, Maryland.

ROBBIE MAGRUDER

Drummer Robbie Magruder grew up in the Takoma neighborhood of Washington, D.C. and during his time at Calvin Coolidge High School in the middle 1960s he listened to jazz and R&B, drummed in his high school's marching band, and championed Art Blakeney and the Jazz Messengers and James Brown as favorite musical artists.

After graduating from Coolidge High School, the British Invasion hit America and Magruder played in a band called the Misfits that specialized in Beatles covers. He spent much of the late 1960s playing the local military base officers' clubs in a rock and roll band called the Ronnie Jones Incident. In the early 1970s he drummed for the R&B-styled Joe Stanley Trio at such local Maryland night clubs as Gus and John's Italian Villa (Camp Springs) and the Quonset Supper Club (Silver Hill).

In 1972 and 1973 Magruder performed and recorded with blues rock guitarist Roy Buchanan. He then spent the remainder of the 1970s and 1980s drumming for a variety of bands and musicians including: the multi-styled pop band Ron MacDonald and Nightwatch and multi-styled guitarist Danny Gatton Band; blues singer-guitarists Bobby Radcliff and Tom Principato; blues rock singer-guitarist Catfish Hodge; the country rock group the North Star Band; jazz singer Karen Henderson; the pop-rock band Jon Carroll and Metro; R&B-rock singer-keyboardist Bill Holland; and a rock and roll band called the Hanson Brothers. From 1989 to 1999 Magruder was the full-time drummer for C&W singer-guitarist Mary Chapin Carpenter, touring the world with her and appearing on eight of her albums.

In recent years Magruder has drummed for a variety of Washington, D.C. area bands and musicians including: the blues acts Johnny and the Headhunters, the Janine Wilson Band and the Mary Shaver Band; the Celtic folk music band OCEAN (sometimes billed as Jennifer Cutting's Ocean Orchestra); the C&W group Ruthie and the Wranglers; folk singer Lisa Moscatiello; the folk duo Lowen and Navarro; rock and roll bands the Usual Suspects and Rick and the Rockers; the rockabilly band the Thrillbillys; and the Odyssey Band of D.C., a mult-styled pop group that specializes in playing weddings and private events.

ROBERT FIESTER

As a youth, guitarist Robert Fiester listened to the Beatles and at age 11 took his first guitar lesson in a class at a community center in his hometown of Bowie, Maryland. He was soon listening to local radio station WGTB where he picked up on rock and roll bands like Deep Purple, Alice Cooper, Black Sabbath and Led Zeppelin and basically became a self-taught musician.

During his years at Bowie High School in the late 1970s Fiester began playing the local teen dance circuit in a rock and roll band called Skyhawk. In 1980 Skyhawk entered the local night club scene by playing Jimmy Comber's Restaurant in Hyattsville, Maryland. Next, while attending the University of Maryland in the early 1980s Fiester played in the rock and roll band Sorceress, which performed in Washington, D.C. at the Bayou; in Maryland at the Big Dipper (Beltsville) and the Paragon (College Park); and in Virginia at the Wild West (Springfield).

In 1984 Fiester took the lead guitar position in the band Dreamer, a Suitland-based quintet whose initial lineup also included lead singer Joe Long, bassist Greg Boulavsky, keyboardist Mike Solis and drummer Pat Montoya. Dreamer was geared towards more commercial, art rock material in the vein of Boston, Journey, Kansas, Styx and Yes. They headlined some of the top night clubs in and around the nation's capital including: in Washington, D.C. at the Bayou and the Wax Museum; and in Maryland at the Riverside Inn (Riverdale), the Big Dipper (Beltsville), the Stardust Inn (Waldorf) and the Paragon (College Park). They also performed at several establishments outside of Baltimore including the Sandbar (Pasadena), the Sea Gull Inn (Essex) and Coast to Coast (Catonsville).

While Dreamer was still active, Fiester got the call to join the band hard-rocking band Hawaii, whose previous guitarist had been Marty Freidman. He played lead guitar with the band from 1986 into 1987 during which time they performed at such night clubs as the Bayou in Washington, D.C. and Hammerjacks in Baltimore, and opened for Emerson, Lake and Powell at the Capital Centre in Landover, Maryland on Friday, September 19, 1986.

After his time with the bands Hawaii and Dreamer came to a close, Fiester spent the late 1980s playing guitar for the pop-rock band Method Actor, whose lead singer was fellow Bowie High School alumnus Eva Cassidy and included his brother Ken on bass. Method Actor made live appearances at the Bayou in Washington, D.C. and Fiester played lead guitar on their lone album, "Method Actor" (Method Actor; BLP Records, 1988).

During the 1990s Fiester played guitar for a number of bands and musicians including: a blues group called the Scrappy Harris Blues Band; pop singer-guitarist Angie Miller; rock and roll singer Brian Jack; and the rock and roll bands Horizon and Sinbad. From 1997 to 2012 he was the lead guitarist in the Bad Weather Boyz, one of the top rock and roll bands in the Washington, D.C. area.

In recent years Fiester has played guitar in such blues rock bands as the Greg Phillips Trio and the Patty Reese Band and has concentrated on his own blues outfit which he labels Tyrone Shuz and His Funky Blues. In addition he has played with C&W singer-guitarist T. Edwin Doss and such rock and roll acts as This World, Face Dancer Automatic, and Whiskerfish.

Fiester also played guitar in the Newmyer Flyer tribute presentation "Dream Discs: The Who's 'Who's Next' and Rod Stewart's 'Every Picture Tells A Story" that was staged at the Hamilton in Washington, D.C. on Saturday, September 20, 2014. He is currently playing guitar for blues singer-harmonicist Anthony "Swamp Dog" Clark, and a rock and roll duo with singer-guitarist Jimmy Brown called Radio Religion.

ROBERT GORDON

Rockabilly singer-guitarist Robert Gordon grew up in Bethesda, Maryland and during his time at Bethesda Chevy-Chase High School in the early and middle 1960s he was a member of the Confidentials, a popular rock and roll band on the local teen dance and college fraternity circuit.

When Gordon joined the Confidentials as lead vocalist, the band's lineup was rounded out by guitarist Paul Pisciotta, bassist John Driver, pianist Bob King and drummer Bruce Davis. The group was an especially popular attraction at the Bethesda Youth Center. During his time with the group, they released two singles: "Let's Picket" backed with "Leave Me Be" (The Confidentials; Loop Records, 1965); and "It's Summertime" backed with "She's Gone" (The Confidentials featuring Bob Gordon; Edgewood Records, 1965).

In 1965 Gordon and other members of the Confidentials joined another popular Montgomery County, Maryland rock and roll band called the Newports. At this time the Newports were transitioning into the Washington, D.C. night club world and during the late 1960s performed at such establishments as the Roundtable, the Rabbit's Foot, the Crazy Horse, the Keg and the Bayou.

Gordon moved to New York City in 1970 and spent the middle part of that decade singing in a punk rock band called the Tuff Darts. In the late 1970s he began his solo rockabilly career with the album "Robert Gordon with Link Wray" (Robert Gordon with Link Wray; Private Stock Records, 1977). In the 1980s he recorded and performed on occasion with guitar great Danny Gatton. To date Gordon has recorded and released more than a dozen solo albums, including several on RCA Records.

THE ROCKIN' REJECTS

The Rockin' Rejects was a group of teens from Greenbelt, Maryland that was active from 1962 to 1965, and, like a few other bands from their hometown, based out of the Greenbelt Youth Center where they played dances for the Greenbelt Teen Club. Like other teens from the city in the early 1960s, most of the band members had met each other at Greenbelt Junior High School and carried on their association into their secondary school years at either Bladensburg High School or High Point High School.

This particular outfit first got together in the pre-British Invasion years and its initial lineup consisted of lead singer Ronnie Hall, guitarists Lee Dorsey and Kenny Nickolson, bassist Dave Wigley, keyboardist Rick Ransom and drummer Wally Shultz (who hailed from Riverdale, Maryland, making him the only non-Greenbelter in the lineup). A few changes took place as the band matured, with Ronnie Hall departing and Rick Ransom assuming lead vocal duty, Jerry McGuire replacing Schultz on drums, and Chris Peters replacing Nickolson and taking over lead guitar duties. In addition, roadie Mike Magrum occasionally joined the band onstage as a part-time singer.

The Rockin' Rejects specialized in playing R&B and rock and roll songs by the likes of Chuck Berry, Fats Domino, Link Wray and His Ray Men, the Ventures, Duane Eddy, Bo Diddley, and others. In addition to their regular appearances at the Greenbelt Youth Center, they performed at dances staged by the Beltsville Teen Club (Beltsville Junior High School in Beltsville), the St. Joseph's Catholic Church Teen Club (Beltsville), the College Park Teen Club (City of College Park Municipal Building), the Cooper Lane Teen Club (Cooper Lane Elementary School in Landover Hills), the Berwyn Heights Teen Club (Berwyn Heights Elementary School in Berwyn Heights), and Hyattsville Junior High School (Hyattsville). In 1965 the Rockin' Rejects morphed into a new Greenbelt-based band called Donnie and the Diablos.

ROCKY ISAAC

Drummer Rocky Isaac was born in New Town, West Virginia, and, as a teenager, moved to Washington, D.C. where he attended Anacostia High School in the middle 1960s. After finishing school he began playing in rock and roll bands in the nation's capital, drumming for the Tejuns in 1964, the Creatures in 1965, and the Fallen Angels in 1966 and part of 1967.

In the summer of 1967 Isaac joined the English Setters, one of the area's most popular rock and roll bands. Shortly after his arrival, the English Setters changed its name to the Cherry People and Isaac remained with the band until 1972. He then spent the remainder of the 1970s drumming for a variety of bands including a touring C&W group called Head East, and rock and roll bands such as Estes and Daddy Warbux.

Issac's career highlights include two recording sessions he did with singer-guitarist Jimi Hendrix and bassist Billy Cox at the Record Plant in New York City on Tuesday, April 21, 1969 and Thursday, April 24, 1969. The trio recorded several songs on those dates, the total number of which has never been ascertained. Some of the songs they laid down on tape include "Bleeding Heart," "Crash Landing," "Hey Gypsy Boy," "Drone Blues," "Stone Free Again," and "Room Full of Mirrors." Selections from those two sessions have appeared on at least four different Hendrix posthumously-released albums: "Hear My Music" (Jimi Hendrix; Geffen Music, 2004); "The Jimi Hendrix Experience" (The Jimi Hendrix Experience; Sony Music Entertainment, 2009); "Valleys of Neptune" (Jimi Hendrix; Sony Music Entertainment, 2010); and "People, Hell and Angels" (Jimi Hendrix; Sony Music Entertainment, 2013).

ROGER EDSALL

Singer-harmonicist-saxophonist Roger Edsall was born in Alton, Illinois and spent his teen years living in College Park, Maryland. In grade school he played trombone and while attending High Point High School in the middle 1970s he would gather with friends in the building's stairwell and play harmonica. In 1976 he became a singer-harmonicist in the Kevin Hunter Band, a rock and roll group that covered such artists as the Rolling Stones and Rod Stewart. He then stopped playing in bands and concentrated on coaching high school football.

Edsall returned to the local music scene in 1989 when he began joining blues singer-guitarist Cathy Ponton King onstage at some of her live performances. That year he became a full-time member of Bad Influence, a blues band formed by singer-guitarist Michael Tash, and is still with the group today. In addition, since 2001 he has also been singing and playing harmonica with another Washington, D.C. area blues band called the Smokin' Polecats.

Through the years Edsall has performed with a number of blues acts including singer-guitarists Jimmy Thackery and Kenny Neal, guitarist David Earl, and such bands as Roger Edsall's Rollercoaster, Pork Chop and the Top Dogs, Delectrified, the Nightcrawlers, Big Joe and the Dynaflows and the James Mabry Blues Band.

ROLF HANSON

Rolf Hanson was raised in North Bethesda, Maryland and during his years at Walter Johnson High School in the middle and late 1960s he played guitar in such rock and roll bands as the Arachnids and the Renegades. In 1967 Hanson played guitar in the Crystal Mesh, a band that included singer-guitarist Nils Lofgren. As the 1960s came to a close, Hanson played bass with a hard-rocking local band called Desdemona.

In the early 1970s Hanson played bass in the Dubonnettes, a rock and roll band that based out of the Georgetown night club called Apple Pie. For a brief period in 1974 the group changed its name to Charlie and The Pep Boys.

Through the years Hanson has performed with a number of bands and musicians including: blues singer-guitarists Cathy Ponton King and Bobby Parker; the blues group Big Joe and the Dynaflows; a country rock band called the Cold Steel Benders; the R&B band the Red-Hot Swinging Johnsons; the R&B-rock group the Johnny Artis Band; and the rockabilly band Four Star Combo.

RON BUSHY

Drummer Ron Bushy was born in Washington, D.C. and spent several years of his childhood in the 1940s living in Greenbelt, Maryland. His father was in the United States Navy, and, accordingly, the Bushy family frequently moved about the country.

Bushy started playing drums while living in Clinton, Connecticut as a pre-teen. When he was 12 years old in 1953 his family moved to Alexandria, Virginia and he drummed in the Alexandria Police Boys Club Band. He attended George Washington High School (alma mater of Jim Morrison) for his sophomore year (1956-1957) and then spent part of his junior year at Francis C. Hammond High School in Alexandria. He did not play in any rock and roll bands during his high school years, preferring to listen to classical music.

Late in 1957 his family moved to San Diego, California and Bushy graduated from Mission Bay High School in 1959. In 1965 Bushy began drumming for a rock and roll band called the Voxmen, which eventually worked its way to Los Angeles where they performed in the night clubs of the Sunset Strip. In the summer of 1966 he was recruited into the rock and roll band Iron Butterfly and is still a member of the group today. Bushy's legendary drum solo on their 1968 17-minute-plus single "In-A-Gadda-Da-Vida" is today considered to be a seminal performance in modern rock and roll.

RON CULBERTSON

Guitarist Ron Culbertson grew up in Alexandria, Virginia and during his years at Francis C. Hammond High School in the early and middle 1960s he was involved with several musical acts including a folk duo called Ron and Buzz with bassist Buzzy Denholme that won a contest at the Shadows in Georgetown judged by Scott McKenzie, and a rock and roll band on the local teen dance circuit called the Ivymen.

In the late 1960s Culbertson played guitar for Today's Special, a rock and roll band that performed in such Washington, D.C. night clubs as the Rocket Room, Rand's Night Club and the Hayloft.

From 1969 to 1973 Culbertson played guitar in the local rock and roll band Tractor. When the band relocated to Los Angeles, California, he followed suit and remained with the group after its name was changed to Pony Express and subsequently served as a backup band for various popular music artists around the city.

Culbertson then spent the late 1970s performing and recording with country rock singer-pianist Bill LaBounty. In recent years he has been living in Arrowhead, California and has been playing guitar for pop singer Gloria Loring.

RON FETNER

Singer-guitarist Ron Fetner grew up in Vienna, Virginia, was schooled in several different musical instruments including piano, clarinet and saxophone, and was influenced at a young age by such performers as Elvis Presley, Jerry Lee Lewis and the Everly Brothers. During his years at James Madison High School in the middle 1960s he sang and played guitar on the local teen dance circuit in such rock and roll bands as Ronnie and the Walkers, the Scarlets, the Hiram Walkers, and the Chessmates.

After high school, Fetner attended the Berklee School of Music in Boston, Massachusetts for a year and a half. Upon his return to the Washington, D.C. area he sang and played bass (and, later on, guitar) in a rock and roll band called Sonny and the Shadows, which held house band duties at the Paul Mall Restaurant in Georgetown from 1968 to 1971. He then sang and played guitar and keyboards in a local pop-rock band called BIF from 1972 to 1974. During this time he also began working as soundman at the Bayou in Georgetown.

In 1975 Fetner joined the rock and roll band Cherry Smash as a keyboardist and saxophonist (and, later on, guitarist) and remained with the group through 1979. During that period the band based out of the Bayou and became one of the Washington, D.C. area's most popular musical attractions. In the wake of Cherry Smash, Fetner cooled his musical activities and moved on from the local scene. He attended college in Florida, earned a degree in aviation, and relocated to the Williamsburg, Virginia.

After a lengthy hiatus, Fetner slowly returned to the music world as a singer-songwriter-guitarist. In recent years his activities have included: singing and playing guitar and mandolin in the Natchez Trace Band, a Winchester, Virginia-based country rock group that included several former members of Cherry Smash; singing and playing guitar in a classic rock trio called King Willy and the Shadows, a Virginia band rounded out by keyboardist Mike Tramonte and singer-drummer Brent Woodall; playing with the Last Call Band, a group of rock and roll musicians that performed at "The Bayou Presents Last Call," a live music tribute to the Bayou night club that took place at the Hamilton in Washington, D.C. on Sunday, February 17, 2013; and performing and recording with the blues band Eddie Shaw and the 757 Allstars.

Recently, Fetner has led his own blues band – an outfit called BlueHouse – which transformed into his current group, Bluehouse Project. He also performs as a solo folk singer-guitarist at venues throughout Virginia.

Fetner has recorded various styles of music with a number of different bands and musicians through the years. He has also released several solo blues-folk albums and other recorded works of interest. Albums on his discography include: “This Box I'm Looking Through” (Ron Fetner; Cimirron/Rainbird Records, 1996); “Turning For Home” (Ron Fetner; Cimirron/Rainbird Records, 2001); Defying Gravity” (Ron Fetner; FetSong Music, 2004); “Sunday Morning Blue” (Ron Fetner; FetSong Music, 2008); “Watch Your Step” (Fetner & Dikon; FetSong Music, 2011 – six-song EP with harmonica player Tom Dikon); “Still Riding High” (Eddie Shaw & The 757 Allstars; Stringtown Records, 2012); and “BlueHouse Project” (BlueHouse Project; FetSong Music, 2016).

RON HOLLOWAY

Saxophonist Ron Holloway was born in Washington, D.C., spent his teen years in Takoma Park, Maryland, and has played with an array of local and national R&B, jazz and rock and roll bands and musicians. During his years at Montgomery Blair High School in the early 1970s he played with two popular R&B bands, the Sounds of Shea, and Mad Dog and the Lowlifers.

In the middle 1970s Holloway performed with jazz trumpeter Freddie Hubbard and on one occasion played alongside jazz saxophonist Sonny Rollins at a music clinic at Howard University. His music career took off in the late 1970s when he played in two top local groups, the rock and roll act Root Boy Slim and the Sex Change Band, and the R&B band Osiris. Since that time Holloway has been a highly coveted saxophonist by a vast range of musical artists.

Through the years Holloway has performed with: blues singer Shemekia Copeland; blues singer-guitarists Taj Mahal and Delbert McClinton; a blues rock group called the Susan Tedeschi Band; jazz singer Gil Scott-Heron; jazz trumpeter Dizzy Gillespie; jazz drummer Norman Connors; R&B singer Julia Nixon; Southern rock groups the Derek Trucks Band, the Allman Brothers Band, Gov't Mule, and the Warren Haynes Band; and the rock and roll band Little Feat.

Holloway has appeared on numerous blues and jazz recordings and has released several solo albums on the Milestone Records label. He currently works with his own R&B group, the Ron Holloway Band.

RON MACDONALD

Singer-drummer Ron MacDonald grew up in the Tenleytown neighborhood of Washington, D.C. and while attending Woodward School for Boys in the late 1950s he played in a teen dance rock and roll band called the Triumphs, whose lineup consisted of guitarists Jorma Kaukonen and Jack Casady (both would later play together in the bands Jefferson Airplane and Hot Tuna), bassist Mike Hunnicutt, and MacDonald handling vocals and playing drums. Like Jack Casady, MacDonald graduated from Woodrow Wilson High School in Washington, D.C. in 1962.

The Triumphs, in addition to working local teen dances, performed on “The Milt Grant Show” and regularly appeared at the now-legendary Washington, D.C. night club known as the Rendezvous, working opposite Link Wray and His Ray Men throughout 1958 and into 1959. During that period the band also performed on occasion nearby at the Famous Restaurant on New York Avenue NW.

From 1959 to 1964 MacDonald was the lead singer in a rock and roll band called the Off Beats (which was often billed as “Ronnie and the Off Beats”), which was noted for its lead guitarist Dany Gatton, and also for holding down house band duties for extended periods at the Club Log Tavern in Alexandria, Virginia and the Champagne Room in Washington, D.C., among other area night clubs.

After Ronnie and the Off Beats disbanded, MacDonald passed through a succession of rock and roll bands in the late 1960s with guitarist Danny Gatton and keyboardist Dick Heintze. One of these groups was called the Superiors. Another was Take Five, which initially consisted of MacDonald, Gatton, Heintze, bassist John Koslin and drummer Tommy Haughawout. This group performed in Washington, D.C. at the Paul Mall Restaurant, the Crazy Horse and the Rocket Room; and in Maryland at the Red Fox Inn (Bethesda), the Belby House (Rockville), the Quonset Supper Club (Silver Hill) and Strick's Restaurant (Silver Hill).

In the early 1970s MacDonald, Gatton, Heintze and saxophonist Roger McDuffie also worked together in a rock and roll band called the East Coast Express at two area night clubs, Tom Sarris' Orleans House in Arlington, Virginia and Gus and John's Italian Villa in Camp Springs, Maryland. Later, in the 1980s, MacDonald again worked with Gatton in a rock and roll band called the Drapes which performed at two area night clubs, Quincy's in Arlington, Virginia and Billy Jacks in Oxon Hill, Maryland.

In 1973 MacDonald formed a multi-styled pop music band which he called Ron MacDonald and Nightwatch. The group spent the remainder of the decade primarily performing at the Port O' Georgetown, a restaurant located in the Georgetown neighborhood of Washington, D.C. MacDonald kept the outfit going for more than 40 years, during which time the band headlined at night clubs and hotel lounges up and down the East Coast and endured innumerable changes in personnel.

RON NEWMYER

Bassist Ron Newmyer was born in Washington, D.C., raised in Bethesda, Maryland, and during his years at Herbert Hoover Junior High in the late 1960s played in a teen rock and roll band called Third Street West. He played sporadically during his time at Walter Johnson High School in the early 1970s, most notably with a short-lived rock and roll band called Bolt, which often performed at the popular Georgetown night club called Emergency.

In the 1970s Newmyer played bass in several local groups including the R&B band Black Heat, and rock and roll bands such as Farris Wheel, the Tom Lofgren Band, and the Mike Cotter Band. In the early 1980s Newmyer performed with such R&B bands as Bill Holland and Rent's Due, Jr. Cline and the Recliners, and Soul Crackers.

In 1984 Newmyer formed a rock and roll band called Newkeys, which remained active for more than six years and recorded two albums, "Acts of Love" (Newkeys; Ruby Records, 1986) and "Everything Goes" (Newkeys; Ruby Records, 1989). Newkeys also backed rock and roll singer-guitarist Nils Lofgren on several of his tours from 1987 to 1989, including an onstage performance with Bruce Springsteen at the Stone Pony in Asbury Park, New Jersey in 1989. Newmyer, along with drummer Chuck Sullivan, backed rock and roll singer-guitarist Chuck Berry at his performance for President Bill Clinton's Georgetown University Class of 1968 25th Anniversary on the White House South Lawn on Saturday, June 5, 1993.

Newmyer has since been involved in a number of musical ventures: he played bass for Nils Lofgren on tours throughout the United States and Europe from 1990 to 1996, and again from 2004 to 2006; he was a member of the R&B group Tommy Lepson and the Lazy Boys from 1992 to 1996; he played with the rock and roll bands Groovy from 1998 to 2002 and Paper Umbrella from 2006 to 2012; and, in conjunction with BandHouse Gigs and Happy Medium Productions, he produced "A Tribute to Nils Lofgren," a Washington Area Music Timeline Concert Series presentation staged in the Gudelsky Concert Pavilion at the

Mansion at Strathmore in North Bethesda, Maryland on Wednesday, August 25, 2004 – an event that featured numerous local musicians playing the music of Lofgren and a special Grin reunion featuring Lofgren himself.

During the time he spent with Nils Lofgren, Newmyer performed onstage with a number rock and roll's biggest names including guitarist Joe Walsh, saxophonist Clarence Clemons, and drummers Ringo Starr, Max Weinberg, Johnny "Bee" Badanjek and Andy Newmark.

Since 2004 Newmyer has produced more than two-dozen live music benefits, tributes and memorials for BandHouse Gigs, a not-for-profit musical organization dedicated to concert performance, production and promotion. In 2013 he formed Newmyer Flyer Productions, which has produced numerous live music presentations.

Newmyer still plays out and has recently performed with blues singer-guitarist Tom Principato and the country rock band Eric Brace and Last Train Home.

RON WIDMAN

Multi-instrumentalist Ronnie "Ronnie" Widman grew up in Silver Spring, Maryland and during his time at Montgomery Blair High School in the early 1960s played in two rock and roll bands on the local teen dance circuit, the Nightcaps and the Blazers, the latter of which included singer-guitarist Kim Tsoy and keyboardist Kevin Fay. Back then while Widman was playing tenor saxophone in these groups, he also played baritone saxophone in the Montgomery Blair High School Band.

Widman played with several Washington, D.C.-based rock and roll bands in the 1960s including the Highlights, which performed at the Devonshire Grill, and Kim and the Esquires, which held house band duties at Benny's Rebel Room. During his tenure with Kim and the Esquires, the band was called upon to back up the vocal group Danny and the Juniors on a two-week engagement at Corkey's Steak House in Cohoes, New York in 1966.

In the late 1960s, after a stream of musicians passed through Kim and the Esquires during its run at Benny's Reel Room, the band morphed into a new rock and roll outfit called the Loved Ones, with Widman switching to keyboards. In the wake of the Riots of 1968 Benny's Rebel Room soldiered on as the city's music scene began to change, with the Loved Ones eventually disbanding in 1970. Widman subsequently remained on at Benny's Rebel Room for several years as its daytime manager.

Later in the 1970s Widman played bass in a rock and roll band called Joe Banana and the Bunch, and from 1976 to 1988 he played bass for a C&W band in Mount Airy, Maryland called Allen Brown and the Wishing Well.

ROOT BOY SLIM

The now-legendary rock and roll singer Root Boy Slim was born Foster MacKenzie III in Asheville North Carolina and raised in Washington, D.C. He attended Sidwell Friends School as a teen before finishing his high school years at St. James School in Hagerstown, Maryland. He then attended Yale University, graduating in 1967 with a Bachelor of Arts in American studies.

While at Yale MacKenzie joined the Delta Kappa Epsilon fraternity and met Bob Greenlee, then-captain of the football team and a future music collaborator. Together they formed the band "The Duke of Dilemma Bobby Uptight and the Midnight Creepers featuring the Young Prince La La." This group mainly performed R&B songs at college fraternity and sorority parties and reportedly never played the same venue twice.

In the years following his Yale experience, MacKenzie divided his time between post graduate studies at various schools, driving a taxi cab in Washington, D.C., and periodically visiting Greenlee in Central Florida where he would sit in with his various bands. After successfully jumping the White House fence he was admitted to St. Elizabeths Hospital in Southeast Washington, D.C. where he was diagnosed as a paranoid schizophrenic. Assorted psychotic episodes in the late 1960s and early 1970s inspired many of MacKenzie's later songs.

In December 1976 MacKenzie made his first known local stage performances in a blues rock outfit called the Bethesda Sick Band at the Psyche Delly. The lineup of this short-lived venture consisted of lead singer Kenneth MacKenzie (as he was then called), guitarists Griff Hutton, Marc Halpern and John Hall, bassist John Bernstein and drummer Danny Frankel.

After conferring with Bob Greenlee, MacKenzie assumed the stage name Root Boy Slim and formed a new rock and roll act. This group, entitled Root Boy Slim and the Sex Change Band, consisted of Slim handling frontman duties and several Florida musicians providing the rest. They debuted on Friday, April 1, 1977 at the Psyche Delly with a lineup of lead singer Root Boy Slim, guitarist Ernie Lancaster, bassist Bob Greenlee, steel guitarist Walter Andrews, keyboardist Winston Kelly and drummer Tommy Ruger. Regular performers with the band included saxophonist Ron Holloway and a group of backup singers known as the Rootettes, which consisted of Cherie Grasso, Micki Lee Jonnie, Kathe "Special K" Russell, and Dick Bangham. The band specialized in satirical original material and offered up such favorite songs as "Boogie 'Till You Puke," "I Used to be a Radical," "Christmas at Kmart," "Laundromat Blues," "Dare to be Fat" and "Mood Ring."

Root Boy Slim and the Sex Change Band was managed by Joe Lee and six months after their debut were signed to Warner Bros. Records by Steely Dan producer Gary Katz, resulting in their first album, "Root Boy Slim & the Sex Change Band with the Rootettes" (Root Boy Slim & the Sex Change Band; Warner Bros. Records, 1978).

Through the years Slim employed more than two-dozen different musicians in his various backup bands, which performed under such names as Cryin' Out Loud, Capitol Offense, New Hope for the Criminally Insane, the Bar-B-Q Juiceheads, and the Humans. His groups performed in Washington, D.C. at such night clubs as the Childe Harold and the Roxy; in Maryland at the Psyche Delly (Bethesda), Bambino's (Riverdale) and the Varsity Grill Back Room (College Park); and at venues up and down the Atlantic Coast.

Some of the top area musicians to work in Slim's bands through the years included: guitarists Ray Tilkens, Dan Hovey, Wayne Tomlinson, Steuart Smith and Paul Reed Smith; bassists Dominic Vigliotti, Elliot Jagoda, Scott Ambush and Brett Mingoe; keyboardist Tommy Lepson and Jim Morr; saxophonists Deanna Bogart and Phil Berlin; and drummers Timm Biery, Steve Dennis and John Zidar.

Root Boy Slim recorded and released a total of six albums in his time. In addition to the debut album with Warner Bros., his albums were: "Zoom" (Root Boy Slim & the Sex Change Band; Illegal Records, 1979); Dog Secrets" (Root Boy Slim; Congressional Records, 1984); "Don't Let This Happen to You" (Root Boy Slim; Kingsnake Records, 1986); "Left for Dead" (Root Boy Slim & the Sex Change Band; Kingsnake Records, 1987); and "Root 6" (Root Boy Slim & the Sex Change Band; Ichiban Records, 1991). Foster MacKenzie III died in his sleep at his Florida home on Tuesday, June 8, 1993 at the age of 48.

THE ROSSLYN MOUNTAIN BOYS

The Rosslyn Mountain Boys were a country rock band that attained great heights of popularity in the Washington, D.C. area in the 1970s. They formed in 1973 with an original lineup of lead singer Joe Triplett, guitarist Happy Acosta, bassist Jay Sprague, keyboardist Peter Bonta, steel guitarist Tommy Hannum and drummer Bob Larrabee. Basing out of the

Psyche Delly in Bethesda, Maryland, the group mixed originals with covers of everything from Jimmie Rodgers to Hank Williams to Chuck Berry.

In 1970s the Rosslyn Mountain Boys also performed in Washington, D.C. at such night clubs as the 21st Amendment, the Shamrock Restaurant, Desperado's, Mr. Henry's Tenley Circle, the Chide Harold, the Chancery, the Far Inn and the Georgetown University Pub; in Maryland at My Friend's House (Silver Spring), the Red Fox Inn (Bethesda), the Tin Dipper (Beltsville), the Senate Inn (Capitol Heights), and the Stardust Inn (Waldorf); and in Virginia at the Birchmere (Arlington) and the 1320 Club (Alexandria).

Other musicians to work with the Rosslyn Mountain Boys through the years include bassists Barry Foley and Rico Petruccelli, and drummer Bob Berberich. The band has three albums to its credit: "The Rosslyn Mountain Boys" (The Rosslyn Mountain Boys; Adelphi Records, 1976); "Lone Outsider" (The Rosslyn Mountain Boys; Schizophrenic Records, 1982); and "Different Skyline" (The Rosslyn Mountain Boys; Sosumi Records, 2005).

RUTH NEWTON

Singer Ruth Newton was born in Polo, Missouri and mainly raised in Lake Lotawana, where, as a pre-teen in the late 1950s, she would sing with her sisters in church and at live performances given by her father's C&W music band. In the early 1960s her family made a series of quick moves from Independence, Missouri to Fountain Inn, South Carolina to Churchland, Virginia. There, in the Tidewater region, Newton and her sisters sang on local television shows, commercials, and stage presentations. At one live performance the young ladies were observed by musician-manager Vernon Wray (brother of guitarist Link Wray), who talked with their father and recommended the family relocate to the Washington, D.C. area.

Newton, still a teenager, and several family members, moved into the Wray family home in Accokeek, Maryland in 1963. There, she began providing background vocals on numerous rock and roll recordings made on the premises, both for Link Wray and other musicians. After a few months Newton moved with her family to the Mount Pleasant neighborhood of Washington, D.C. She then began singing with a rock and roll band called the Fender Benders at a night club called the Oasis on Mount Pleasant Street NW, a venue that also hosted Link Wray and His Ray Men on occasion.

Throughout the 1960s Newton moved about the Washington, D.C. area, staying for a while at the Wray's Accokeek house, and also living periodically in the Norfolk, Virginia area. One of her recording sessions in the basement of the Wray home resulted in a 45rpm single record release credited to herself and Sherry Wray (daughter of Vernon Wray), "Nothin' Much Tomcat" backed with "You're Gonna Be My Guy" (Ruth and Sherry; Swan Records, 1965). During this period she often sang with Link Wray and His Ray Men when they performed at the notorious 1023 Restaurant in Southeast Washington, D.C.

In the late 1970s, Newton, then-married to musician Ed Cynar, became the lead singer in a rock and roll band called the Pack. The group was based out of Falls Church, Virginia, and, in addition to Newton, originally consisted of singer-guitarist John "Jack" Van Horn, bassist Ed Cynar and drummer John Ossea. The band's first 45rpm single record release was "Get Off My Hog" backed with "Rawhide" (The Pack; Slash Records, 1977). For its second single, "Cadillac Joe" backed with "Run Chicken Run" (The Pack; Slash Records, 1978), the band essentially remained the same, with lone exception being the replacement of drummer Ossea with Pat Greenwood.

RUTHIE LOGSDON

Singer-guitarist Ruthie Logsdon was born in New London, Connecticut and raised in Rockville, Maryland. At the age of 10 she learned to play guitar from her father, later taking lessons and studying the stringed instrument in school. During her years at Richard Montgomery High School in the middle and late 1970s she would play guitar in her room, write lyrics, and listen to music by such artists as the Beatles, Stephen Stills, Loretta Lynn and Emmylou Harris. In addition, she would often watch music-oriented television shows with her father like "Hee Haw" and "The Johnny Cash Show." She and family members also attended live music performances by local bluegrass bands such as the Country Gentlemen, Hickory Wind and the Bluegrass Cardinals.

In the early 1980s Logsdon attended Montgomery College Rockville Campus and earned a degree from the Maryland Institute of Art. During that period she sang harmony and played rhythm guitar in the Painkiller, a Wheaton-based rock and roll band that specialized in covering songs of the 1960s.

Logsdon would often sing at parties with friends and in 1989 she put together a country rock band that consisted of herself handling lead vocals, guitarists Aiko Butler and Karl Straub, bassist Jeff Zang and drummer Matt Cook. The group went through several name changes including the Tune Wranglers and Little Ruthie and the Wranglers, before settling on the moniker that stands to this day, Ruthie and the Wranglers.

Simultaneously, as Ruthie and the Wranglers were still in the formative stages, Logsdon sang and played guitar in a C&W group called Plum Crazy, which was rounded out by singer-guitarist Patty Reese, singer-trumpeter Marianna Wasilik (later Previti) and bassist John Sprung. Plum Crazy would often cover the works of singer Patsy Cline.

In the 1990s Ruthie and the Wranglers performed in Washington, D.C. at such night clubs as the Grog and Tankard, and D.C. Space; and in Maryland at Hunter's (Wheaton) and Captain White's Seafood Restaurant (Silver Spring). The band also experienced gradual changes in personnel, eventually morphing into a unit consisting of lead singer-acoustic guitarist Logsdon, guitarist Billy Shelton, bassist Mark Noone (formerly of the Slickee Boys) and drummer John Shepherd.

By the late 1990s the group had reorganized again, with Logsdon and Noone being joined by guitarist Phil Mathieu and drummer Joel App. Other musicians to play in the band were bassist Rico Petruccelli and drummer Robbie Magruder. Most recently, singer-bassist Greg Hardin was a full-time member of the group from 2002 to 2017.

Ruthie and the Wranglers are a national attraction and have embarked on numerous regional tours and performed at venues and festivals from New York to Nashville to Florida, and as far west as Texas and Oklahoma. Locally they have performed in Washington, D.C. at Nightclub 9:30, the Hamilton, Gypsy Sally's and the John F. Kennedy Center for the Performing Arts Millennium Stage; in Virginia at the Birchmere (Alexandria), the State Theatre (Falls Church), Iota Club and Café (Arlington), Jammin' Java (Vienna) and the Barns at Wolf Trap (Vienna); and in Maryland at Strathmore (North Bethesda), the Surf Club (Hyattsville) and the Bethesda Blues and Jazz Supper club (Bethesda).

In addition, in the early 2000s, Logsdon began hosting "The New Old Jamboree" at the Half Moon Bar-B-Que in Silver Spring, a live music showcase that featured herself and the Wranglers, along with special guest performers. In 2011 she moved the presentation over to the New Deal Café in Greenbelt, Maryland where she continues to host the show on the first Tuesday of every month. The current lineup of Ruthie and the Wranglers consists of Logsdon, guitarist Andy Rutherford, singer-pianist Bill Starks, singer-bassist Jim Robeson and drummer Tom Fridrich.

Ruthie and the Wranglers have seven albums to their credit: "Wrangler City" (Ruthie and the Wranglers; Lasso Records, 1996); "Life's Savings" (Ruthie and the Wranglers; Lasso Records, 1998); "Live at Chick Hall's Surf Club" (Ruthie and the Wranglers; Lasso Records, 2000); "Someday" (Ruthie and the Wranglers; Lasso Records, 2003); "Americana Express" (Ruthie and the Wranglers; Azalea City Recordings, 2009); "Live at Goose Creek" (Ruthie and the Wranglers; Goose Creek Music, 2011); and the compilation "All Wrangled Up" (Ruthie and the Wranglers; Azalea City Recordings, 2018).

SAGEWORTH AND DRUMS

Sageworth and Drums was a Georgetown-based rock and roll band that was active in the late 1960s and early 1970s. The group was best known for having in its lineup singer-guitarist Walter Egan, who came down from New York to attend Georgetown University. The band formed in 1967 with its original lineup consisting of singer-lead guitarist Walter Egan, guitarist John Zambetti, bassist Ralph Dammann, keyboardist Frank Peters and drummer Tom Scarp. An early addition to the group was lead vocalist Anne Marie McLoone.

In early 1969 Sageworth and Drums changed over and Egan was then joined by lead singer-guitarist P.B. Chowka, bassist Tom Guidera and drummer Mat Sheppard. More changes ensued and late in 1969 the group consisted of Egan, Sheppard, singers Anne Marie McLoone and Jack Burkhardt, guitarist John Borger and original bassist Ralph Dammann. A later addition to the band was keyboardist Bing McCoy.

Sageworth and Drums played original, softer, blues rock and performed in Washington, D.C. at Emergency, JamF, My Mother's Place, and Fort Reno Park; in Maryland at Ritchie Coliseum (University of Maryland); and in Virginia at the Falls Church Community Center.

The band also participated in many local concert shows including: appearing with Grand Funk Railroad, the Allman Brothers Band, Pacific Gas and Electric, Crow, and Crank at "Berlin Airlift" at Robert F. Kennedy Stadium in Washington, D.C. on Sunday, September 20, 1970; appearing with Poco and Tractor at McDonough Gymnasium (Georgetown University) on Sunday, October 4, 1970; appearing with the Cherry People, Claude Jones, Meretrix, Babe, Sea and the East Utopian Mission, El Corrals, Fat City, Scott Taylor, and the John Wells Delegation at "The Intercollegiate Music Festival" at the Sylvan Theatre on the Mall in Washington, D.C. on Sunday, October 18, 1970; and opening for Wet Willie at Gaston Hall (Georgetown University) on Saturday, September 25, 1971.

Sageworth and Drums disbanded in March 1973 after an engagement at the Reading Goal, a night club located near Dupont Circle in Washington, D.C. Walter Egan later moved to Los Angeles, California and in February 1976 was heard auditioning at the Troubadour by producer Greg Lewerke, manager of Electric Light Orchestra. He was signed to Columbia Records and went on to enjoy a successful pop music solo career, the highlight of which was his single "Magnet and Steel" (Walter Egan; Columbia Records, 1978) which peaked at number eight on Billboard magazine's "Billboard Hot 100" popular music chart on Saturday, August 26, 1978.

SAM PALADINO

Keyboardist Sam Paladino was raised in Bladensburg, Maryland and as a youth became enamored with the music of such pianists as Fats Domino, Little Richard and Huey Smith. During his years at Bladensburg High School in the late 1950s he played piano in the Off Keys, one of the area's most popular rock and roll bands that started on the local teen dance circuit and worked its way up to the area's night club scene.

From the fall of 1959 to August 1960 Paladino was the piano player for Roy Clark and the Stardusters, a C&W band that worked some of the best night clubs in Prince George's County, Maryland including the Cross Roads (Bladensburg), Strick's Restaurant (Silver Hill) and the Village Barn (Morningside). They also performed at the weekend C&W "Town and Country" jam sessions that were held at the Capitol Arena (formerly Joe Turner Arena) in Washington, D.C. and featured stars such as Jimmy Dean and the Texas Wildcats, Dub Howington and the Tennessee Haymakers and singer-guitarist Billy Grammer. After Clark left this band he ventured to Las Vegas where he became the lead guitarist for rockabilly singer-guitarist Wanda Jackson and went on to fame and fortune as a C&W singer-guitarist and noted personality on the television show "Hee Haw."

In the 1960s and 1970s Paladino played keyboards with a number of Washington, D.C. area rock and roll bands and musicians including Paul King and the Blue Knights, the Perry Mates, the Peppermint Stix, Little Hugh and the Embers (featuring singer Linda Lou), the Fablons, guitarist Roy Buchanan, the Classics, the Naturals and the Joe Stanley Band. From 1975 to 1992 he was a member of Reliance, a band that specialized in performing classic rock and roll songs of previous years.

More recently Paladino has performed with such acts as: the C&W bands Detour and the Southern Drifters; the oldies pop-rock groups Avenue Grand and the Esquires; the R&B bands the Orioles and the Young Bucks (who backed up a number of artists including the Drifters and singer Gene Chandler); and such rock and roll outfits as singer-guitarist Frank Shegogue, the American Music Company (featuring guitarist Danny Gatton), the Shades, Great Train Robbery, Random Impact, the Dangertones and the Paulverizers. He is currently working with blues singer-guitarist Cathy Ponton King and the classic rock and roll band Rebound.

SAMMY BLAIR

Bassist Sammy Blair was born in Washington, D.C. and raised in District Heights, Maryland. As a youth he was introduced to music by his mother, who played piano, and his brother Bill, who played saxophone in a popular local R&B-rock band called the Medallions. He first learned to play saxophone, but switched to bass after watching a rock and roll band called Crank and its bassist Johnny Castle play a Christmas dance at Bishop McNamara High School in December 1969.

While attending Suitland High School in the early 1970s Blair played bass in Jett, a hard-rocking trio rounded out by singer-guitarist Ronnie Jett and drummer Jerry Roberts. The group often performed at the Tucker Road Community Center in Fort Washington, Maryland.

In 1975 Blair joined the heavy rock and roll band Griffin, a District Heights-based group that was proficient at covering Led Zeppelin, among other hard-rocking acts. Griffin's initial lineup included Blair on bass, guitarist Marvin Rainey, lead singer-guitarist Ronnie Coleman and drummer Vince Williams, and initially performed at such Washington, D.C. night clubs as the Fairfax Village Restaurant, Some Place Else and the Keg. Musicians to later pass through Griffin included guitarist David McGowan, keyboardist Larry Patterson and drummer Joey Forrester. Griffin changed its moniker and played out under the name Zelosa before disbanding in 1979.

In the 1980s Blair played bass in a succession of Washington, D.C. area rock and roll bands including Top Cat, Blitz (a couple of bands in the area have used this name and this particular version was based in Hyattsville, Maryland), Viper, the Pets, Attack, Arctic Fox and Kik the Dog.

The 1990s saw Blair play in such blues rock groups as Stevie B. and the Hungwells and Big Money Grip, and in 1996 he began a 16-year run with the Jack Diamond-Jim Steed Band, which opened arena concerts for such acts as Elton John, the Moody Blues, the Little River Band, Nils Lofgren, Kansas, 10,000 Maniacs, Pat Benatar, and the Gin Blossoms.

In recent years Blair has remained active on the local music scene and has played bass with a variety of rock and roll bands and musicians including singer-guitarist Jim Steed, the Idle Americans, the Jimbo Manion Group, the Smallwood Brothers, Bobby Howard's British

Walkers, Gabby and the Leftovers, the Shades, the 25th Hour Band, C. Bass and the Rockfish, and the Last Remains.

SANE DAY

Sane Day was a Washington, D.C.-based hard rock band that formed in June 1970 with a lineup of lead singer Matt McBride, guitarist Bob Siegel, bassist Peter Olson and drummer Jim Durham. That summer McBride left the band and Siegel took on lead vocal chores. In September 1970 drummer Paul Spears replaced Durham. An unusual side note is that the band rehearsed in the home of Siegel at 4921 30th Place NW, Washington, D.C., a house his father had purchased from Lyndon B. Johnson in 1961. J. Edgar Hoover lived directly across the street during the band's time together.

Sane Day specialized in original material, but occasionally covered such musical artists as Elvis Presley, the Allman Brothers Band, Alice Cooper and Donovan. They gave performances in Washington, D.C. at the St. Alban's Episcopal Church Friday Coffeehouse and Fort Reno Park; and in Maryland at Bethesda-Chevy Chase High School (Bethesda), Sandy Spring Friends School (Sandy Spring), the Andrews Air Force Base Officers' Club (Prince George's County, Maryland) and the Cedar Lane Unitarian Universalist Church Coffeehouse (Bethesda).

In the summer of 1972 Sane Day made several appearances at Fort Reno Park, with one of its concerts being recorded and released decades later as a CD album entitled "Live at Fort Reno" (Sane Day; Stampede Records, 2003). Sane Day disbanded in October 1972.

SCOTT MCKNIGHT

Singer-guitarist-bassist Scott McKnight was born in Washington, D.C. and raised in Arlington, Virginia (eventually moving to nearby Alexandria at age 16). He took up trombone at age 12 and at age 14 learned baritone horn, guitar and bass. While attending Gunston Junior High School in Arlington in the early 1970s he first played bass in a basement rock and roll band called Tequila Sunrise. In 1973 he also played baritone horn in the Wakefield Warriors Marching Band.

During his years at Fort Hunt High School in the middle 1970s McKnight played guitar, bass and harmonica (and sometimes keyboards) in such local rock and roll bands as Opal City, the All-Night Diner Band, and the Heaters, and also sang and played guitar in an acoustic duo with singer-drummer Steve Woehrle. He attended Northern Virginia Community College Alexandria Campus from 1978 to 1980 and graduated from George Mason University with a Bachelor of Arts in music in 1986.

In the 1980s McKnight played guitar with such local bands as the new wave-punk rock group Peter and the Noisemakers, and an instrumental rock and roll outfit called Bag 5. During that decade he also played bass in such prominent Washington, D.C. area pop-rock bands as Punch Me Judy and the Neighbors, both of which performed on occasion at D.C. Space and Nightclub 9:30.

In the 1990s McKnight sang and played lead guitar in a number of different bands including a pop-rock group called Naughty Pine (his stand with the band lasted from 1992-2006), a rock and roll act called the Mel Bays, and from 1994 to 2001 he was lead guitarist for the C&W group Kevin Johnson and the Lineman. During those years he also played bass with a number of different groups including a country rock band called the Grandsons, and an early version of the C&W group Last Train Home. In addition, from 1993 to 1998 he operated an eight-track recording studio in the basement of his Arlington, Virginia home called Extremely LTD.

More recently McKnight has sung and played either guitar or bass with a plethora of musical outfits including another stint with Last Train Home (from 2000 to the present), a country rock group called the Graverobbers, the blues rock band Exit 10, the Linemen (a reconfiguration of Kevin Johnson and the Linemen), and a country rock band called Dede and the Do-Rights. McKnight has recorded with many other bands and musicians through the years and has one solo rock and roll album to his credit: "It Works For Me" (Scott McKnight; SAM Records, 2000).

Since 2007 McKnight has been lead singer-guitarist in the Jelly Roll Mortals, a Silver Spring-based rock and roll band whose lineup is rounded out by singer-mandolinist Bill Williams, lead guitarist Arch Alcantara, bassist Jim Faris and drummer Steve Woehrle. They have appeared in Maryland at such establishments as the New Deal Café (Greenbelt), the Quarry House Tavern (Silver Spring) and El Golfo Restaurant (Silver Spring); and in Virginia at the Evening Star Café (Alexandria), Iota Club and Café (Arlington) and Clare and Don's Beach Shack (Falls Church).

SCOTT WEINRICH

Doom metal singer-guitarist Scott "Wino" Weinrich was raised in Rockville, Maryland, and, while attending Thomas Sprigg Wooton High School in the late 1970s, started his first rock and roll band, War Horse. In 1978 he put together the first version of the hard-rocking band the Obsessed, whose initial lineup consisted of, in addition to Wino, singer-guitarist Johnny Reese, bassist Mark Laue and drummer Dave Flood.

In the middle 1980s Wino relocated to California and became lead singer for the rock and roll band Saint Vitus, which recorded and released several albums for the SST and Hellbound record labels.

After working with such rock bands as the Mentors and the Lost Breed, Wino reorganized the Obsessed in 1990, whose recordings included the album, "The Church Within" (The Obsessed; Columbia Records, 1994). He next joined the Bullring Brummies, a heavy metal all-star band whose lineup also included lead singer Rob Halford (Judas Priest), guitarist Brian Tilse (Fight), bassist Geezer Butler (Black Sabbath) and drummer Bill Ward (Black Sabbath).

Wino returned to Montgomery County, Maryland in the late 1990s and played in rock bands such as Shine, Spirit Caravan, Place of Skulls, the Hidden Hand, Probot (a doom metal recording project of Dave Grohl's that also included singer-bassist Lemmy Kilmister of Motorhead), Punctuated Equilibrium, and Premonition 13. He is currently a member of the bands Shrinebuilder, and Royale Daemons, and performs and records as a solo artist under the name "Wino."

SECOND COMING

Second Coming was an R&B-rock band that formed in 1970 with several musicians who had broken away from another popular band on the local music scene, the Nowhere Men. The group's initial lineup consisted of lead singers Donnie Halcombe, Charlie Taylor and Joe Saitta, guitarist David Fultz, bassist Tommy Rodante, keyboardist Mike Serigumba and drummer Tommy Wright.

Musicians to pass through Second Coming during its lifetime included guitarists Mike Pirko, George Bold and Gantt Kushner; keyboardists Julio Fonseca, Tommy Dildy, Kurt Gibbons and Larry Kidwell; and drummers Bill Caron and Rick Davis.

Second Coming enjoyed great popularity throughout the 1970s and 1980s and performed up to 300 nights per year. They headlined at venues from New York to Florida to Nevada and throughout Canada.

Locally, Second Coming performed in Washington, D.C. at such night clubs as the Montage, the Act IV Supper Club, Ventuno 21 Supper Club, Fran O'Brien's Anthony House Restaurant, and the Cave; and in Maryland at the Classic III Supper Club (Camp Springs), the Quonset Supper Club (Silver Hill), Second Coming (a restaurant in Lanham owned for several years by band members Charlie Taylor and Joe Saitta) and the Hurricane (Ocean City).

THE SELDOM SCENE

The Seldom Scene is a bluegrass band that formed in Bethesda, Maryland in 1971. The group's original lineup consisted of: lead singer-guitarist John Starling, singer-dobro player Mike Auldridge, singer-mandolinist John Duffey, banjoist Ben Eldridge and bassist Tom Gray.

The Seldom Scene played bluegrass versions of C&W, pop, and rock and roll songs, and during its first six years held down house band duties at the Red Fox Inn in Bethesda. They later enjoyed a long residency at the Birchmere, which, at the time, was located in Arlington, Virginia.

The original group members reportedly had little interest in touring and only wanted to play locally once a week, hence the name the Seldom Scene. Beginning in 1977, numerous changes in personnel transpired, with a total of 13 different musicians passing through the band in the ensuing years. To date the group has more than 20 albums to its credit on such record labels as Rebel, Sugar Hill, and Smithsonian Folkways.

The Seldom Scene is still active today with its current lineup consisting of singer-guitarist Dudley Connell, singer-dobro player Fred Travers, singer-mandolinist-guitarist Lou Reid, banjoist-fiddler-guitarist Rickie Simpkins and bassist Ronnie Simpkins.

SETH JUSTMAN

Seth Justman was born in Atlantic City, New Jersey and raised locally in Maryland in the city of Greenbelt and the community of Lanham. He attended DuVal High School before graduating from the Hawthorne School in Washington, D.C. in 1969. During his teen years in the late 1960s he played keyboards in two rock and roll bands on the local teen dance scene, the Blues Bag and the Open Road Band.

In the fall of 1969 Justman moved to Boston, Massachusetts and joined the J. Geils Band, a rock and roll group that has more than 20 albums to its credit. Through the years the band has released 10 singles that have placed on the Billboard charts including "Centerfold" (The J. Geils Band; EMI America Records, 1981), which peaked at number one on Billboard magazine's "Billboard Hot 100" popular music chart on Saturday, February 6, 1982. Justman is still serving as singer-keyboardist for the J. Geils Band today.

SHEP TULLIER

Singer-bassist Shep Tullier was born in New Orleans, Louisiana and spent his teen years living in Annapolis, Maryland. He initially learned piano and guitar and grew up listening to artists such as the Crickets (featuring singer-guitarist Buddy Holly), Little Richard, Roy Orbison and the Ventures. During his years at St. Mary's Elementary School in the early 1960s he sang and played bass in a rock and roll band called the Torquays that performed on the Anne Arundel County teen dance circuit.

While attending St. Mary's High School in Annapolis in the middle 1960s Tullier sang and played bass in a rock and roll band called the Tower of London which released the 45rpm single record "Substitute" backed with "Perpetual Dreamer" (The Tower of London; Montgomery Records, 1967). The band played throughout Annapolis, Baltimore, and the

Washington, D.C. area, where they headlined on the Wilson Line's M.V. George Washington ship that sailed the Potomac River.

In the early 1970s Tullier was a member of the Washington, D.C. area-based rock and roll band David, which regularly performed at local teen dances and at University of Maryland parties and events, including multi-act concert shows at Ritchie Coliseum.

SILVERSPRING

Silverspring was a multi-styled, bluegrass-based band that advertised its music as "rock with violins." The group formed in Takoma Park, Maryland in the late 1970s and mixed original compositions with covers of songs by such artists as Bob Wills, Charlie Daniels, Dan Hicks and Jackson Browne.

Silverspring's initial lineup offered a mix of local and out-of-town musicians: lead singer-guitarist John Fritz-Spiro, guitarist-violinist Frank Michels, violinist-mandolinist Nat Winer, bassist Sal DeRaffele and drummer Phil Shimmel. Other musicians that later passed through the band were singer-guitarist Lois Fritz, guitarist Josh Rossy, keyboardists Tara Michaud and John Rosch, and saxophonist Ron Holloway.

For more than four years Silverspring headlined venues up and down the East Coast. In Washington, D.C. they performed at such night clubs as Mr. Henry's Tenley Circle and Desperado's; and in Maryland at the Psyche Delly (Bethesda), DiGennaro's Restaurant (Laurel), the Varsity Grill Back Room (College Park) and the Italian Gardens (College Park). The band has one album to its credit: "You Get What You Take" (Silverspring; Hitt Avenue Records, 1980).

SINBAD

Sinbad was an R&B-rock band that formed in the early 1970s and was noted for playing lengthy engagements at the Bayou in Georgetown, often alternating assignments with such bands as Cherry Smash, Face Dancer and the Nighthawks. The original version of Sinbad consisted of singer-guitarist Bobby Stevens, bassist Bobby Colie, keyboardist Mike Zinodinovich and singer-drummer Vince Santoro. One of the group's best-known lineups saw Stevens and Santoro joined by keyboardist Guy Meredith and singer-bassist Tim Wynne. Meredith was eventually replaced on by keyboards Donald Smallwood, previously of the bands Lightyear and Octagon.

In the late 1970s Sinbad experienced personnel changes, with Stevens, Wynne and Smallwood being joined by singer Danny Goers and drummer Mike Valenti. Another popular version of the band consisted of Stevens, Smallwood, Valenti and lead singer Lorraine Cohen.

Sinbad would survive all the way to the year 2000 with Stevens coming and going, and Valenti and keyboardist Kurt Gibbons keeping the operation going, usually as a trio or quartet, with a variety of musicians.

SKY COBB

Sky Cobb was a blues-based rock and roll band from Hyattsville, Maryland that emerged in 1970 and consisted of five former Northwestern High School students: singer-guitarist Bruce MacKinnon, singer-guitarist-keyboardist Richard Sales, singer-keyboardist Greg Pugliese, bassist Craig Warner and drummer Mark Cuff.

All five Sky Cobb members had previously played in various blues and rock and roll bands during their teen years in the late 1960s – MacKinnon had been with the Blues Bag and the Jefferson Street Jug Band; Sales had previously been a member of the Rivieras, Dick Gray and the Shadows, the Revelaires, and the Jefferson Street Jug Band; Warner had been with Ann Bradstreet's Band and the Jefferson Street Jug Band; Pugliese had worked with the Sunsets, the Revolution, the Blues Bag, the Open Road Band, and the Jefferson Street Jug Band; and Cuff had drummed for Donnie and the Diablos and Ann Bradstreet's Band.

In June 1970 these musicians came together, chose to call themselves Sky Cobb, and began rehearsing original compositions in the basement of MacKinnon's house at 2405 Amherst Road in Lewisdale, Maryland (an unincorporated community in Prince George's County). They emerged to play their first gig at Emergency in Georgetown on Saturday, January 23, 1971. Eventually they added former New Breed saxophonist Jamie MacKinnon to the group and then three female singers known as the Cosmic Colonels rounded out the lineup.

Sky Cobb mainly played local concert shows from 1971 to 1973, opening for the likes of Long John Baldry at the Wheaton Youth Center and Canned Heat at the William P. Cole, Jr. Student Activities Building (University of Maryland; commonly referred to as Cole Field House). They also appeared as headliners in Washington, D.C. at Fort Reno Park; in Maryland at Glen Echo Park's Spanish Ballroom (Glen Echo), Novak Field House (Prince George's Community College) and Ritchie Coliseum (University of Maryland); and in Virginia at the Falls Church Community Center.

THE SLICKEE BOYS

The Slickee Boys were a group from Bethesda, Maryland that formed in late 1975, combined elements of garage, punk and psychedelia in its high-powered music, and helped steer rock and roll in the nation's capital into an entirely different direction. The band's original lineup consisted of lead singer Martha Hull, guitarists Kim Kane and Marshall Keith, bassist Andy Von Brand and drummer Chris Rounds.

Sporting garish costumes and delivering intense stage performances, the Slickee Boys got their start at the Keg in Washington, D.C., a night club that was in the process of becoming a breeding ground for groups on the cutting edge of what would become the punk rock movement.

The Slickee Boys endured some changes in personnel over the next few years. Bassist Howard Wuelfing passed through and by 1978 the band consisted of Kane, Keith, lead singer Mark Noone, bassist Emery Olexa and drummer Dan Palenski. This version of the group stayed intact into 1982, at which time bassist John Chumbris replaced Olexa. From 1988 until its demise in 1991 the band consisted of Noone, Keith, Palenski, guitarist John Hanson and bassist Mike Maxwell.

The Slickee Boys established itself as a local rock and roll institution, headlining such establishments as the Psyche Delly in Bethesda and Nightclub 9:30 in Washington, D.C., where they appeared some 84 times during their existence. They often appeared at the Bayou in Georgetown, and opened for the band U2 at that venue on two separate occasions. The first time was on U2's Washington, D.C. debut on Sunday, December 7, 1980; and the second time was on U2's return trip on Tuesday, March 3, 1981 – an evening that included two separate shows at 8pm and 11pm.

The Slickee Boys recorded extensively, with the video for their single "When I Go to the Beach" placing second in MTV's "Basement Tapes" competition in 1983. The video then received heavy weekly rotation on the channel's "120 Minutes" program. They hold the distinction of being the first Washington, D.C. band to ever get a clip aired on the popular video channel. While the band emphasized original material, its traditional set-closing number was a heavily psychedelicized version of Status Quo's "Picture of Matchstick Men." Throughout the 1990s the Slickee Boys staged occasional performances that included many of its previous band members.

Albums by the band include: "Separated Vegetables" (The Slickee Boys; Dacoit Records, 1977); "Here to Stay" (The Slickee Boys; Line Records, 1982); "Cybernetic Dreams of Pi" (The Slickee Boys; Twin/Tone Records, 1983); "Uh Oh...No Breaks!" (The Slickee Boys; Twin/Tone Records, 1984); "Fashionably Late" (The Slickee Boys; New Rose Records, 1988); "Live at Last" (The Slickee Boys; Giant Records, 1988); "Somewhat of an Anthology" (The Slickee Boys; Dacoit Records, 2002); and "A Postcard From the Day" (The Slickee Boys; Dacoit Records, 2006).

SONNY GORDON

Born Sadi Maurice Pekerol in Augusta, Georgia, this rock and roller moved in with his grandmother in Washington, D.C. before his first birthday and began playing lead guitar and bass in local pickup bar bands at the tender age of 12 in the middle 1950s. In the early 1960s he assumed the stage name "Sonny Gordon" and performed as a singer-bassist in his own rock and roll bands such as Sonny Gordon and the Panics, the Sonny Gordon Five, and Sonny Gordon and the Mustangs.

One of his more popular groups, Sonny Gordon and the Outcasts, performed from 1965 to 1967 at three of Washington, D.C.'s most popular night clubs, the Starlite Restaurant, Rand's Night Club, and the Rocket Room, and, for a time, included blues rock guitarist Roy Buchanan in its lineup. In the late 1960s Gordon played bass for the Winstons, a Washington, D.C.-based R&B band that had a major hit single "Color Him Father" (The Winstons; Metromedia Records, 1969), which peaked at number seven on Billboard magazine's "Billboard Hot 100" popular music chart on Saturday, July 19, 1969.

Throughout the 1970s Gordon lived in Florida and played bass for several national acts including R&B singer Patti LaBelle and the major pop act the Jackson Five. Other rock and roll bands he performed with through the years in Florida included Street Life, the Rooster Band, Dr. Hoff's Prescription for Rock and Roll, and Taxi. Sonny Gordon passed away on Tuesday, November 28, 2006 at the age of 74.

THE SOUL MATES

The Soul Mates were a short-lived rock and roll band put together by several former members of Ronnie and the Off Beats that performed at dances that were offered on the Wilson Line's M.V. George Washington ship that sailed the Potomac River in 1966. The group's lineup consisted of guitarist Danny Gatton, bassist John Koslin, keyboardist Dick Heintze, saxophonist Roger McDuffie and singer-drummer Ron MacDonald. The band recorded and released one 45rpm single record, which they offered on their Wilson Line cruise appearances: "Moonlight Cruise" backed with "How's Your Sister" (The Soul Mates; Wilson Line Records, 1966).

SPATS

Spats was an R&B band that formed in February 1977 and consisted of singer Holly Sherwood, guitarist David "Gabby" Gabaldon, bassist Elliott Jagoda, keyboardist Ric Arenz and drummer Mike Zack. They performed in Washington, D.C. at such night clubs as the Crazy Horse and Mr. Henry's Tenley Circle; and in Maryland at the Italian Gardens (College Park). The group had one album to its credit, "Spats" (Spats; Good Sounds Records, 1978). Other musicians to pass through the band included singer Gui Bokolese, singer-guitarist Mike Bradley and bassist Johnny Castle.

SPRING FEVER

Spring Fever was a rock and roll band that emerged from Clinton, Maryland in the early 1970s and consisted of five musicians from Surrattsville High School: lead singer-keyboardist Bill Smith, lead guitarist Jeff Avery, rhythm guitarist Dave Simmons, bassist Bill Baker and drummer John Thomas. A later member was lead singer Bart Windsor. The group was active from 1972 to 1973 and covered such artists as the Rolling Stones, the Beatles, the Jimi Hendrix Experience, the Beach Boys, Little Richard, the J. Geils Band, Moby Grape, Three Dog Night and the Moody Blues.

Spring Fever was a popular commodity on the local teen dance circuit and gave performances in Maryland at the Tucker Road Community Center (Fort Washington), the Temple Hills Community Center (Temple Hills), the Stephen Decatur Teen Club (Stephen Decatur Junior High School in Clinton), the Eugene Burroughs Teen Club (Eugene Burroughs Junior High School in Accokeek), the Surrattsville Junior Teen Club (Surrattsville Junior High School in Clinton), the Surrattsville Senior Teen Club (Surrattsville High School in Clinton) and the Andrews Air Force Base Teen Club (Prince George's County). Members of Spring Fever went on to perform in the bands Medusa and DC Star.

STAN WEINBERG

Drummer Stan Weinberg was born in New York and moved to Washington, D.C. as a teenager in the 1940s. During his years at Thomas Jefferson Junior High School in Southwest Washington, he first drummed in a six-piece pop-jazz band called the Pastels. In the early 1950s while attending Eastern High School he became a member of the Dale Turner Orchestra, a 10-piece professional jazz band that regularly worked the Club Log Tavern in Alexandria, Virginia and Tall Timbers in Calloway, Maryland.

Upon graduating high school Weinberg joined the United States Navy and after his discharge in 1957 he freelanced as a drummer for various jazz bands around the nation's capital. Among the bandleaders he worked with during these years were saxophonist Lou Doren, saxophonist Ray Curry, and trumpeter-pianist Buddy Prima.

In June 1959 Weinberg put together an instrumental jazz band called the Stan Kaye Quartet. This group was recruited and funded by businessman and then-New York governor Nelson Rockefeller (who later served as the 41st vice president of the United States of America under president Gerald Ford from 1974 to 1977) to perform at politically-themed concerts and events in Paris, France and Vienna, Austria. The quartet, which toured Europe for three months, consisted of saxophonist Norman Katz, keyboardist Mike Brown, bassist Joe Broderick and Weinberg on drums.

In 1960 Weinberg switched his interest to rock and roll music and joined the Saxtons (featuring singer-saxophonist Joe Stanley). He worked with that band in Washington, D.C. at the Parkside Café and the Spotlite Room; and in Maryland at the 4400 Club (Brentwood), the Village Barn (Morningside), the Rustic Cabin Restaurant (Colmar Manor), the Dixie Pig (Cottage City) and the Cross Roads (Bladensburg). He then spent time drumming for another rock and roll band called the Perry Mates (featuring guitarist Clarence Perry and bassist Luman Perry) at the Senate Inn in Capitol Heights.

In 1961 Weinberg became the drummer for a rock and roll quartet called the Bad Boys, whose lineup was completed by singer-saxophonist Ed Montini, guitarist Roy Buchanan and bassist Vince Brando. That summer the band performed at night clubs on the New Jersey Shore and upon returning to Washington, D.C. worked such night clubs as Woody's, the Rocket Room and Rand's Night Club.

From October 1961 to October 1962 Weinberg drummed for a four-piece rock and roll band called the Peppermint Stix which included singer-guitarist Duke Duquette, keyboardist Sam Paladino and singer-saxophonist Ed Montini. The group held down house band duties at the Rocket Room for several months and often backed top visiting pop and rock and roll singers such as Ray Peterson, Freddy Cannon and Bryan Hyland. They also performed at night clubs on the Jersey Shore in the summer of 1962 where they backed vocalist Tito

Mambo. Late that summer and fall the Peppermint Stix worked engagements at Guy's Place in Washington, D.C. and the Dixie Pig in Cottage City, Maryland before disbanding.

During the early 1960s Weinberg also drummed for the pop vocal group the Kalin Twins for a six-month stretch, touring with them from Boston to Florida, and working local dates with them at Guy's Place in Washington, D.C. He also worked freelance drumming jobs for rock and roll bands that featured such musicians as guitarist Danny Gatton, bassist Jack Casady and keyboardist Dick Heintze, among others.

Other performing artists Weinberg drummed for before retiring from music in the late 1970s included a rock and roll band called the Classics (with keyboardist Sam Paladino and saxophonist Del "Big Daddy" Puschert), a jazz ensemble called the Gene Donati Orchestra, jazz pianist Ramon Ballve, and a pop music band called the Spirit of '76.

STARLAND VOCAL BAND

Starland Vocal Band was a popular, Georgetown-based, soft-rock vocal group that consisted of Bill Danoff, Taffy Nivert, Jon Carroll and Margot Chapman. Their roots go back to a folk music quintet called Fat City, which was formed in the fall of 1967 by singer-guitarist Bill Danoff, a native of Springfield, Massachusetts who was attending Georgetown University at the time, and Taffy Nivert, who had been raised in Falls Church, Virginia and had moved to Georgetown earlier in 1967 after spending a couple of years at the College of Steubenville in Ohio.

Nivert like to sing along to the jukebox at Clyde's Restaurant, a popular spot on M Street NW in Georgetown, and was introduced by bartender Bruce Adams to Danoff, who was working at the Cellar Door two blocks away as the club's door man and lights-and-sound man, in addition to performing at their Sunday "Hootenanny" shows. The pair added guitarist Steve Gray, bassist Jim Parker and drummer Larry Frederick, named themselves Fat City, and in the late 1960s and early 1970s performed at local benefit shows in churches and parks, as well as such Washington, D.C. night clubs such as Emergency, JamF, and Tammany Hall. The band recorded and released one album, "Reincarnation" (Fat City; ABC-Probe Records, 1969), with a follow-up album recorded and released as "Welcome to Fat City" (Bill Danoff and Taffy Nivert; Paramount Records, 1972).

Danoff knew rising folk singer-guitarist John Denver from his Cellar Door performances with the Chad Mitchell Trio. Along with Nivert, he penned two songs in their basement apartment at 3072 Q Street NW that Denver recorded: "I Guess He'd Rather Be in Colorado" (credited writers are Bill Danoff and Taffy Nivert Danoff) and the hit single "Take Me Home, Country Roads" (credited writers are Danoff-Nivert-Denver), which peaked at number two on Billboard magazine's "Billboard Hot 100" popular music chart on Saturday, August 28, 1971.

Fat City, which by that time had been reduced to just Danoff and Nivert, toured the country as Denver's opening act, and, later in 1971, toured with the Moody Blues for three weeks. Danoff and Nivert later released two additional albums, "Pass It On" (Bill & Taffy; RCA Victor Records, 1973) and "Aces" (Bill & Taffy; RCA Victor Records, 1974).

In November 1974 Danoff brought in two friends he knew from the Cellar Door who had been performing together in the band Sunshine, singer-keyboardist Jon Carroll of Alexandria, Virginia, and singer Margot Chapman, who had been born in Hawaii and raised in San Francisco, California. As a quartet they took the name Starland Vocal Band, and signed a contract with John Denver's Windsong Records label. They went on to release four albums for the company: "Starland Vocal Band" (Starland Vocal Band; Windsong Records, 1976); "Rear View Mirror" (Starland Vocal Band; Windsong Records, 1977); "Late Nite Radio" (Starland Vocal Band; Windsong Records, 1978); and "4 x 4" (Starland Vocal

Band; Windsong Records, 1980). They also recorded and released an obscure fifth album, "Christmas At Home" (Starland Vocal Band; Breaker Records, 1980).

Starland Vocal Band was known for its chart-topping, million-selling single "Afternoon Delight" (Starland Vocal Band; Windsong Records, 1976) which peaked at number one on Billboard magazine's "Billboard Hot 100" popular music chart on Saturday, July 10, 1976.

STEPHEN GEYER

Singer-guitarist Stephen Geyer was born in Lima, Peru and raised in a military family. In his younger years he traveled the world and lived in such places as Cyprus, the Philippines, Japan and England. As a teenager in the middle 1960s he began to teach himself rock and roll songs on a ukulele and developed chords by reading a Kingston Trio songbook and practicing on his older brother's guitar.

At one point Geyer's family lived in Rockville, Maryland, and, as the British Invasion hit, he played guitar in a rock and roll band on the local teen dance circuit called the Essex Set. A short time later while living in Oxford, England he began playing in a folk music duo with his brother Bruce Geyer in nearby pubs and churches. He also was a part of a four-piece rock and roll band called the Blues Dimension that performed at dances on the local military base.

In the late 1960s Geyer's family moved back to Rockville, Maryland and Geyer attended Wheaton High School, during which time he put together another edition of the Blues Dimension which performed on the local teen dance circuit. He next became the bassist in a rock and roll band called the Curfews, whose lineup also included lead singer Gui Bokoles, guitarist Rick Rowe, keyboardist Stephen Spencer and drummer Rick Anderson. Curfew, as they came to be called, was a classic psychedelic outfit whose style was a mix of Motown with Vanilla Fudge. For several years they were a popular attraction at local teen dances, night clubs and concert shows. Curfew released one album on United Artists Records.

In the early 1970s Geyer attended Towson State University in Maryland and performed as a solo folk singer-guitarist on the local coffee house circuit. During that time he also performed in tandem with folk singer-guitarist Ron Zuskin, as well as in an acoustic folk music duo called Together & Alone with singer-guitarist Tom Bolen.

In 1974 Geyer moved to California and while living in the Monterey area he performed and recorded with folk singer-guitarist Tom Jans. Geyer also backed up folk-pop singer-guitarist Jonathan Edwards on his United States and Canadian tours in 1977, and pop singer Carole Bayer Sager on her United States and European tours in 1978.

In the late 1970s Geyer moved down the coast and was introduced to the Los Angeles music industry by producer Mike Post, who hired him as a staff writer for his publishing company, Mike Post Productions. Geyer has since been a part of the Los Angeles entertainment industry for more than 40 years, writing, composing, arranging and producing songs and music for various television programs and major motion pictures.

A significant part of his time – the years 1980 through 1988 – were spent as a staff songwriter for the CBS publishing company April Blackwood Music (which became CBS Songs in 1982) where he produced material for some of the biggest names in the entertainment industry. Some of the musical artists Geyer has written songs for include Glen Campbell, Kenny Rogers, John Denver, Roberta Flack, and Latoya Jackson. His best-known writing credit is for the single "Believe It or Not (Theme from 'Greatest American Hero')" (Joey Scarbury, Music by Mike Post/Lyrics by Stephen Geyer; Elektra Records, 1981), which peaked at number two on Billboard magazine's "Billboard Hot 100" popular music chart on Saturday, August 15, 1981.

Through the years Geyer has served as a session guitarist for record albums, television shows and movie soundtracks alongside such musical artists as blues singer-harmonicist Paul Butterfield; blues-jazz guitarist Robben Ford; blues-jazz singer-keyboardist Dr. John; C&W singers Dolly Parton and Mac Davis; C&W singer-guitarist Herb Pedersen; jazz guitarists Larry Carlton and Lee Ritenour; jazz pianist David Benoit; jazz saxophonist Tom Scott; pop singer Kim Carnes; pop singer-keyboardist Bruce Hornsby; pop bassist Abe Laboriel; R&B singer Shirley Bassey; rock and roll guitarist David Lindley; rock and roll bassist Leland Sklar; and rock and roll drummers Hal Blaine, Russ Kunkel, Carmine Appice and Jeff Porcaro, among innumerable others.

Geyer has one pop music solo album to his credit, "Harlequin Wind" (Stephen George Geyer; Stephen George Geyer, 2007). Today he performs as a singer-guitarist solo act in night clubs throughout Southern California.

STEUART SMITH

Guitarist Steuart Smith was raised in Baltimore, Maryland, and, during his years at Baltimore City College High School in the early 1970s, listened to the Beatles and played in such rock and roll bands as the Norsemen, 2120 South Michigan Avenue, Moten Gator, and Aux.

In 1973 at the age of 20, Smith relocated to Takoma Park, Maryland, and, after a short stay, moved to nearby Kensington. He spent the remainder of the decade playing keyboards and guitar for some of the area's more popular groups including the R&B-rock bands Hickory and Barrelhouse, and the rock and roll band Babe.

From 1979 to 1985 Smith played with a number of different bands and musicians including: blues rock singer-guitarist Catfish Hodge; R&B bands Cryin' Out Loud, and Downtown (now known as Jeff Watson and Downtown Band); rock and roll singer Root Boy Slim; the rockabilly group Switchblade; and rock and roll singer-guitarist Gene Ryder.

In 1985 Smith moved to Arlington, Virginia, and, at the request of producer Rick Chertoff (then working with Sony Music) who had seen him performing with Switchblade, began flying down to Nashville, Tennessee to do recording sessions with various C&W musicians. Opportunities began opening up and in 1986 he began performing, recording and touring with country singer-guitarists Rodney Crowell and Roseanne Cash.

In the ensuing years Smith became a highly sought-after guitarist and performed and/or recorded with a plethora of bands and musicians including: the blues band the Nighthawks; C&W singers Patty Loveless, Kelly Willis, Trisha Yearwood, Wynonna Judd, Dolly Parton, Chely Wright, Lari White and J.C. Jones; C&W singer-guitarists Lionel Cartwright, James House, Mary Chapin Carpenter, Suzy Bogguss, Hal Ketchum, Kasey Chambers, Charlie Louvin, Emmylou Harris and Vince Gill; C&W singer-keyboardist Brady Seals; the C&W duo Thrasher Shiver (singer-guitarists Neil Thrasher and Kelly Shriver); the country rock band the Cicadas; folk singer John Stewart; folk singer-guitarists Shawn Colvin, Loudon Wainwright III, Susan Werner and Dar Williams; folk singer-guitarist-dulcimer player John McCutcheon; folk singer-guitarist-keyboardist Willie Nile; folk rock band Crash Test Dummies; folk vocal group the Roches; pop singers Julia Fordham and Crystal Bernard; pop singer-guitarists Joni Mitchell and Michelle Branch; rockabilly singer-guitarist Sonny Burgess; rock and roll guitarist Jules Shear; and rock and roll singer-guitarist Melissa Etheridge.

Smith landed his biggest gig when he was hired by the Eagles in 2001 after guitarist Don Felder was released by the band. He co-wrote several songs on their studio album "Long Road Out of Eden" (Eagles; Eagles Recording Co. II, 2007) and today is still a co-lead guitarist with the band, duties he shares with Joe Walsh. Smith is also a member of

Don Henley's solo touring band and in the past has performed in-concert with the late singer-guitarist Glenn Frey.

STEVE BISHOP

Guitarist Steve Bishop was born in Arlington, Virginia and raised in nearby Fairfax. During his time at Wilbert Tucker Woodson High School in the late 1960s and early 1970s he played in several rock and roll bands including Transition, Promise and his own group, Steve Bishop and the Chessmen. For much of the late 1970s and into the early 1980s he played guitar in the popular Washington, D.C. area R&B-rock band, the Nowhere Men.

Bishop moved to the West Coast in 1983 and went on to perform and/or record with a number of nationally known rock and roll musicians including singer Eddie Money, singer-guitarists Chris Isaak and Greg Kihn, guitarist Ronnie Montrose; and blues rock singer-pianist Johnny Neal. Steve Bishop passed away on Wednesday, December 22, 2010 at the age of 56.

STEVE CAREY

Bassist Steve Carey was born in Riverdale, Maryland and was mainly raised in Lanham, Maryland. He bought his first guitar at age 12 and a friend from the neighborhood named Larry Wilson taught him how to play. During his years at Robert Goddard Junior High School and DuVal High School in the late 1960s he played bass in a rock and roll band called the Unknown Kind, which performed on the local teen dance circuit. Carey then spent much of the early 1970s jamming with neighborhood musicians.

In 1975 Carey rented a house in Bowie, Maryland and put together a rock and roll band called T-Bone which consisted of Carey on bass, singer-guitarist Mitchell Sperty, guitarist Mark Land, harmonicist Bill Jasper, drummer Tom Brocato, and occasional guitarist Brian Sperty. The group covered such artists as the Eagles, Pure Prairie League, Bad Company, the Marshall Tucker Band and the Allman Brothers Band. T-Bone performed at private parties and dances in Maryland at the Beltsville Volunteer Fire Department (Beltsville) and the Branchville Volunteer Fire Company (College Park).

Late in 1975 T-Bone disbanded. Carey, Land and Mitchell Sperty then welcomed in singer-saxophonist-harmonicist Charlie Hastings and drummer Bobby Hawkins. The new quintet then began playing out as the Open Road Band, originally offering a Southern rock style before gradually adopting a more broad-based rock and roll format. In 1976 drummer Elliott Kessler replaced Bobby Hawkins. The group spent most of the 1970s performing at the Village Pub in Seabrook, Maryland.

In 1977 the Open Road Band underwent changes in personnel when Sperty and Kessler departed and were replaced by singer-guitarist Dave Williams and drummer Birdie Williams, both former members of the rock and roll band God Mother Country. For the next seven years the group performed in Washington, D.C. at the Crazy Horse, the Bayou and the Wax Museum; and in Virginia at Louie's Rock City (Bailey's Crossroads) and the Wild West (Springfield). In the late 1980s and early 1990s the band regularly appeared at such Maryland night clubs as Lasick's College Inn (College Park), the Princess Garden Inn (Lanham), Remington's Restaurant (Beltsville) and the Riverdale Pizza Pub (Riverdale).

The Open Road Band experienced personnel changes along the way. In 1983 Dave Williams was replaced by singer-guitarist Leon Jewett. After a break in 1984, the band was reorganized with a new lineup of bassist Steve Carey, guitarist Mark Land, lead singer-guitarist Mitchell Sperty, singer-keyboardist Dave Paolucci and drummer Mike Mautino. This version of the group lasted through 1994.

From 1995 to 2005 Carey played bass in the blues band Big Bill and That's Cool. The group's original lineup consisted of singer-harmonicist Bill Jasper, singer-guitarist David

Long, Carey on bass, and drummer Mike Mautino. He then spent the next few years frequenting blues jam sessions at such Maryland night clubs as the Surf Club (Hyattsville), Lasick's College Inn (College Park) and the Old Bowie Town Grille (Bowie). During these informal, onstage sessions he played bass alongside such musicians as: guitarists Chick Hall, Jr., Dave Chappell, Pete Kanaras, Robert Frahm, Paul Mastradone, Warner Williams, Mike Dutton, and Automatic Slim; singer-harmonicist Brett "Big Boy Little" Littlehales; keyboardist Sam Paladino; and drummers Chip Clemmer and Pete Ragusa.

Since 2005 Carey has been playing bass for the Paulverizers, a local blues band fronted by singer-guitarist Paul Mastradone. The group's main lineup consists of Mastradone, Carey, singer-guitarist Mike Kavanaugh, singer-saxophonist Scott Ramminger, keyboardist Sam Paladino and drummer Chip Clemmer (other regulars to work with the band include singer-guitarist Robert Frahm and drummer Steve Watson).

Carey has been playing bass with the Joy B Band since 2008, a Washington, D.C. area country rock quartet whose lineup is rounded out by singer-guitarist Joy Bodycomb, guitarist Dave Long and drummer Chip Clemmer. He plays on the band's recent album "Just Livin'" (Joy B Band; Self-Released, 2013). Carey wrote two songs included on that CD, "Open Road" and "Goin' Away Baby." In recent years he has also played bass for the original rock and roll group StradBoLand and such blues groups as Steve Smith and His Meteors, Scott Ramminger and the Crawstickers, the Swamp Keepers, Bad Influence, and the Andy Poxon Band.

On Thursday, December 1, 2011 Carey and drummer Chip Clemmer backed up nationally-recognized country rock singer-guitarist Shane Dwight during a live on-air performance on the satellite radio program "B.B. King's Bluesville." Hosted by Bill Wax, the performance took place in the studio at XM Satellite Radio (1500 Eckington Place NE, Washington, D.C.).

STEVE HATFIELD

Singer-guitarist-keyboardist Steve Hatfield was born in Schenectady, New York and raised in Fairfax, Virginia. During his years at Wilbert Tucker Woodson High School in the early 1970s his rock and roll resume included: singing lead and playing guitar in the band Jeep in 1971; singing lead in the band Stony Road from 1972 to 1972; singing lead and playing guitar with Steve Bishop and the Chessmen in 1973; and singing lead and playing keyboards in the horn band Redemption from 1973 to 1974.

From the middle 1970s on Hatfield played in some of the Washington, D.C. area's top bands. He was with the Nowhere Men from 1974 to 1977 serving as their lead singer as well as playing keyboards, guitar and bass. He rounded out that decade performing with three different rock and roll bands: from 1977 to 1978 he handled lead vocals and played bass for Merlin; in 1978 he sang lead and played keyboards in Anaconda; and from 1979 to 1980 he sang lead and played keyboards and bass in Wizzard.

In the early 1980s Hatfield sang lead and played bass in two area rock and roll bands, Orphan and High Roller. He then served as vocalist and keyboardist for the R&B band Downtown from 1982 to 1989 (now known as Jeff Watson and Downtown Band) and played on their albums "Band On a Budget" (Downtown; White House Tapes, 1984) and "Straight Ahead" (Downtown; Vanity Records, 1988). His professional music career came to a close after serving as a rock and roll keyboardist for the Gene Ryder Band from 1989 to 1992.

STEVE JACOBS

Guitarist Steve "Baby Jake" Jacobs was born in Newton, Massachusetts and raised in neighboring Newton Highlands. He grew up in a musical family, as his grandmother, Lena

Rockwell Jacobs, was a member of an all-female, Boston-based band called the Fadettes and was the country's first female saxophone soloist. In addition, his father Howard Jacobs played saxophone around Boston in the Savoy Hotel Orpheans.

Jacobs first picked up the bass guitar at age 17 while attending Newton South High School in Newton Center, Massachusetts and was largely self-taught. After finishing high school he spent the early 1970s in Massachusetts playing bass in the blues bands Hambone and Band of Swine.

At the age of 20 in May 1973 the bass-playing Jacobs joined a Boston-based blues band called Powerhouse, whose lineup was completed by four transplanted musicians from the Washington, D.C. area: singer-guitarist Jimmy Cole, guitarist Tom Principato, harmonicist Pierre Beauregarde and drummer Richard Murray. In 1974 Powerhouse began regularly playing the Washington, D.C. area with their first night club dates taking place at Apple Pie in Georgetown and the Psyche Delly in Bethesda, Maryland. Powerhouse remained active through 1978, often playing engagements in the nation's capital at the Childe Harold near Dupont Circle.

Jacobs next became the lead guitarist for a Boston-based blues band called George Leh and the Thrillers. The group appeared in 1978 in Washington, D.C. at the Cellar Door, in Alexandria, Virginia at the Shed, and in Bethesda, Maryland at the Psyche Delly. In 1979 he relocated to Fairfax, Virginia and played bass for blues-jazz singer-pianist Mary Blankemeier. He next played guitar for the blues rock singer-guitarist Catfish Hodge from 1980 to 1981 and appears on his album "Bout With the Blues" (Catfish Hodge; Adelphi Records, 1981). Jacobs then joined forces with the R&B band Tough Luck (featuring singer-harmonicist Lips Lackowitz), serving as their guitarist from 1982 to 1993.

While still performing with Tough Luck in 1988, Jacobs and Lips Lackowitz were called upon to put together a backup group for blues singer-harmonicist Carey Bell for some Washington, D.C. dates. Jacobs remained Bell's guitarist all the way through 2003, touring throughout the United States, Asia, Europe and Australia, and appearing on two of his studio albums: "Mello Down Easy" (Carey Bell & Tough Luck; Blind Pig Records, 1991) and "Good Luck Man" (Carey Bell; Alligator Records, 1997).

In recent years Jacobs has led his own blues band, Baby Jake and the Rattlers, and has played lead guitar for many blues artists including Bruce Ewan and the Solid Senders, singer-guitarist Cathy Ponton King, and singer-harmonicist Flatfoot Sam. Since 2009 he has been playing guitar in one of the Washington, D.C. area's top blues acts, the Big Boy Little Band.

Through the years Jacobs has performed on either bass or guitar with innumerable bands and musicians including such blues artists as: the band Bad Influence; singers Screamin' Jay Hawkins and Jesse Yawn; singer-guitarists David "Honeyboy" Edwards, Bonnie Raitt, Hubert Sumlin, Smokey Wilson and Rick Holmstrom; guitarist Ronnie Earl; harmonicist Big Walter Horton; singer-harmonicists James Cotton and Junior Wells; singer-harmonicist-guitarists Big Daddy Kinsey and Billy Boy Arnold; singer-pianists Pinetop Perkins and Sunnyland Slim; pianist Johnnie Johnson; keyboardist Mark Naftalin; singer-saxophonist Bull Moose Jackson; and drummer Bernard Purdie.

Other musical artists he has played with include: multi-styled guitarist Danny Gatton; blues rock singer-guitarist J. Geils; R&B singer Billy Price; R&B singer-guitarist Bo Diddley; rock and roll singer-drummer Levon Helm; rock and roll singer-guitarist Steve Miller (at a late-night jam session at the Childe Harold in Washington, D.C.); and the rock and roll legends guitarist Frank Zappa, drummer Terry Bozzio and singer Captain Beefheart at an onstage jam session in the middle 1970s at the Speakeasy in Cambridge, Massachusetts.

STEVE LACEY

Drummer Steve Lacey was born in Washington, D.C. and raised in Alexandria, Virginia. He was introduced to music at a young age – his parents listened to C&W music, his older brother played drums, and Lacey himself started taking drum lessons while in elementary school in the middle 1950s. He grew up listening to such popular performers as Elvis Presley, Conway Twitty, Danny and the Juniors, and Dion and the Belmonts.

In the early 1960s while attending Walt Whitman Junior High School Lacey drummed for a rock and roll band called Sonny and the Temps that performed on the local teen dance scene. Later, in the middle 1960s while attending Mount Vernon High School, he played drums in another teen dance rock and roll band called the Cavaliers. From 1965 to 1968 Lacey drummed for the British Walkers, the Georgetown-based rock and roll band that featured singer-guitarist-keyboardist Bobbie Howard and became one of the most popular musical attractions in the Washington, D.C. area.

In 1969 Lacey briefly drummed for Puzzle, another Georgetown-based band that specialized in psychedelic rock and roll. Later in the year after Puzzle disbanded, he joined Tractor, a rock and roll band that included one of his former British Walkers bandmates, bassist Jack Brooks.

In 1973 Lacey relocated to Los Angeles, California with Tractor, and remained with the band for three more years as they went through several name changes including the Pony Express and Eddie Haddad and the Canyon Band. Lacey retired from music in 1976, though in recent years he has resurfaced for several British Walkers reunions in the Washington, D.C. area.

STEVE LONG

Singer-guitarist Steve Long born in Washington, D.C. and raised in Temple Hills, Maryland, where, at age 15, he took up guitar and listened to such rock and roll players as Frank Marino, David Gilmour, Robin Trower and Michael Schenker. Largely self-taught, he often jammed during his teen years at John Hanson Junior High School in the late 1970s and Potomac High School in the early 1980s with local musicians such as bassist Paul Jones. During these years he played in a power trio called Structure with Jones and his brother Matt Long on drums that specialized in rock and roll instrumentals.

Along the way Long became a fan of such bands as Metallica, Iron Maiden and Judas Priest. In the late 1980s he became the guitarist in a Silver Spring-based, horror-themed heavy metal band called the Krypt which performed shows at the Paragon in College Park. Although relatively short-lived, the group took the stage in monster makeup, performed original material and was long-remembered for its dynamic stage shows.

Long spent the early and middle 1990s playing guitar in such local rock and roll bands as Escape, Kaos Choir, and Sister. He then spent the late 1990s singing and playing in a classic rock cover group called the Back Alley Band, which performed at a variety of Virginia night clubs including Sully's (Chantilly), the Sunset Grille (Annandale) and Fast Eddie's (Alexandria).

More recently, Long has performed with a number of area bands including: the acoustic rock and roll duo Two of a Kind (with bassist Paul Jones); a Baltimore-based jazz act called Boots Hatcher and the Stompers; a power rock and roll trio called Dirt; and the classic rock duos Fondu Blonde and Rock Me Sexy Jesus. He also handled lead guitar duties in the final version of the local rock and roll band the Bad Weather Boyz from 2014 to 2015.

STEVE SPURLING

Bassist Steve Spurling grew up in Bethesda, Maryland, and, in the middle 1960s after graduating from Walter Johnson High School, played in a succession of local rock and roll bands including the Duquesnes, the Nooks, the Lords of London, the English Muffins, the Mods, and Seventh Seal.

Later in the 1960s Spurling played in such Washington, D.C. rock and roll bands as the Mount Pleasant Street Blues Band at Cousin Nick's and Ray Rock and the Revlons at the Crosstown Restaurant. He also performed locally with R&B singer Big Al Downing, and with rock and roll acts such as Little Joe and the Impossibles and Frank Bilotti and the Heartbreakers. In addition, he spent time as the house band bassist at such Maryland night clubs as the Americana in Odenton and the Dairy-Land Restaurant in Jessup, where he backed up a number of headliners.

In the early 1970s Spurling played bass for the C&W outfit Danny Denver and the Soundmasters, whose band at the time included blues rock guitarist Roy Buchanan. He performed with Denver's band at such Maryland night clubs as the Frontier (Waldorf), the Cross Roads (Bladensburg) and the TD Lounge (Laurel). During this time he also worked engagements in Maryland with rock and roll bands such as the Superiors (featuring singer-keyboardist Joe Bayliss) at Uncle Billy's (North Beach), and Link Wray and His Ray Men at the Gentleman II (Baltimore). Another engagement saw him work with a multi-styled pop group called the First National Band (featuring singer Johnny Staggs) at Club 175 (Jessup).

Spurling rounded out the 1970s playing bass in such area C&W bands as Construction, Trilogy, Grapevine, and Vic Decker and Virginia Country. After another stint with Danny Denver at the TD Lounge in Laurel, Maryland 1982, he retired from the local music scene.

STEVE WOLF

Bassist Steve Wolf grew up in Oxon Hill, Maryland and as a teenager in the middle 1960s he first played the local teen dance circuit in such rock and roll bands as the Changing Tides and the Cutaways. During his time at Oxon Hill High School in the late 1960s he played in a psychedelic blues rock band called Sage, which frequently performed at a night club in Washington, D.C. called Cousin Nick's.

Wolf next began playing the Georgetown night club scene with a rock and roll band called Renthra, which from 1969 to 1970 worked engagements at Mac's Pipe and Drum Restaurant, the Silver Dollar Restaurant, and the Crazy Horse, along with a night spot in Glover Park called the Keg.

In the early 1970s Wolf played bass in a succession of area groups including the rock and roll band Gravity, a multi-styled pop music wedding group called the Shubert Quartet, and a pop-rock band called Magenta. He spent much of 1974 performing with classical-jazz pianist Ramon Ballve at the Twin Bridges Marriott hotel in Arlington, Virginia. Wolf then spent the remainder of the 1970s performing with a number of bands and musicians including the R&B group Bill Holland and Rent's Due and blues rock singer-guitarist Catfish Hodge.

In 1975 Wolf moved to Boston, Massachusetts, where, during the next three years, he played with ensemble classes and senior recitals at the Berklee College of Music, backed jazz pianist Jaki Byard on live performances, and played in a reggae band called Jamaica Way and a jazz rock group called the Isaacs Brothers.

In January 1978 Wolf received a call from guitarist Danny Gatton to return to the Washington, D.C. area and play bass in his band, Danny Gatton and the Redneck Jazz Explosion. Besides Gatton and Wolf, early versions of the band included keyboardist Dick Heintze, steel guitarist Buddy Emmons and drummer Dave Elliott.

In the 1980s and 1990s Wolf played bass for such musical artists as: comedian-pianist Mark Russell; blues singer Mary Blankemeier; blues singer-guitarists Tom Principato and Catfish Hodge; the blues band the band the Nighthawks (when called upon to sub for an ailing Jan Zukowski); his own jazz band Rockhouse; jazz guitarist Rick Whitehead; jazz saxophonist Deanna Bogart; and R&B singer-keyboardist Tommy Lepson.

In 1990 Wolf formed a jazz band called Swing Speak, whose original lineup consisted of himself on bass, singer-keyboardist Tim Ford, and drummer Barry Hart, with saxophonist Bruce Swaim soon making them a quartet. The group spent more than a decade as the featured attraction at the Two Nineteen Restaurant in Alexandria, Virginia. Through the years a number of top musicians have passed through the band including guitarists Rick Whitehead, Jim Stephanson, and Dave Chappell, and saxophonist Pete Barenbregge.

Swing Speak's current lineup consists of Wolf, Hart, lead singer Danielle Westphal, singer-keyboardist Barry Gurley, saxophonist Chris Watling, trumpeter Vince McCool and fiddler Robert Spates. The band has two albums to its credit: "Well Spoken" (Steve Wolf & Swing Speak; Powerhouse Records, 1997); and "Live in the Alley" (Swing Speak; Powerhouse Records, 2002).

In his career Wolf has also performed with other highly regarded musicians including: blues singer Jessie Yawn; blues singer-guitarists Cathy Ponton-King, Linwood Taylor, Guitar Junior and Memphis Gold; blues singer-harmonicist Charlie Musselwhite; blues singer-pianists Pinetop Perkins and Sunnyland Slim; blues-jazz singer-keyboardist Doctor John; jazz singer-drummer Big Joe Maher; rock and roll singer-guitarists Bo Diddley and Chuck Berry; rock and roll keyboardist Brian Auger; R&B groups the Coasters and the Marvelettes; and R&B saxophonist Clarence Clemons.

Wolf's most recent album appearance is on a collaborative blues effort with singer-guitarist Tom Principato, "The Long Way Home" (Tom Principato & Steve Wolf; Powerhouse Records, 2017).

STEVIE SPARKS

Stephen Fitch Hubert was born in Washington, D.C. and grew up in Chevy Chase, Maryland where he began playing guitar at age 13 in 1963. While attending Leland Junior High School in the middle 1960s he played in such rock and roll bands as the Chantones and the Elektras, both of which performed on the local teen dance circuit. During his time at Bethesda-Chevy Chase High School in the late 1960s he continued in similar fashion and played guitar in such rock and roll bands as the Vagrants and the Resumes.

In the summer of 1968, after Hubert graduated high school, his latest band the Resumes, while performing at a night club called the Pale Iguana in Ocean City, Maryland, went the psychedelic route and changed its name to Crystal Clear. Upon returning to the nation's capital that fall the band performed at such Washington, D.C. night clubs as the Rabbit's Foot, the Silver Dollar, the Keg and the Crazy Horse. During this time the group covered such artists as the Doors, Jimi Hendrix, Iron Butterfly, the Who and others. Hubert finished the decade playing with a rock and roll band called Fleeboon at Sam's Place in Washington, D.C.

In the summer of 1969 Hubert relocated to California and played with a rock and roll band called Albatross. He next began playing lead guitar for rock and roll singer Johnny Apollo and played on his major label single release, "I Don't Need No Doctor" backed with "Good, Good Woman" (Johnny Apollo; GNP Crescendo Records, 1969).

Hubert returned to the Washington, D.C. area in 1970, where he played guitar in the rock and roll band Stillroven, which regularly performed at the night club Emergency in Georgetown.

Hubert went on to become an integral part of the popular music scenes in various parts of the United States and Canada including Los Angles (California), Maui (Hawaii), Vancouver (British Columbia, Canada), Breckenridge (Rocky Mountains, Colorado), Austin (Texas), and Sandpoint (Northern Idaho). He sang and played guitar with esteemed bands and musicians in every region he concentrated on, assuming the stage names "Stevie Guitar" (1971-1987) and "Stevie Sparks" (1988-2005).

Among the work Hubert did with popular music national acts during his time were: playing lead guitar for pop singer Johnny Apollo in Los Angeles at different times in the 1970s; playing guitar and drums for the rock and roll act the Buddy Miles Band during their engagement at the Maui Belle in Maui in the summer of 1971; playing bass for the Mark Anthony Orchestra, a pop-jazz ensemble led by singer-pianist Mark Traversino, at various engagements around the Los Angeles area in the early 1970s; playing guitar for legendary folk singer-guitarist Ramblin' Jack Elliott at his appearances at the Lahaina Yacht Club and Silversword Inn in Hawaii in 1973; playing rhythm guitar for rock and roll singer-guitarist Boz Scaggs at one of his performances at the Wakefield Inn in Vancouver in July 1981; and playing guitar for famed folk singer-guitarist Ian Tyson, formerly of Ian and Sylvia, during his East Coast tour in 1987.

In 1994 Hubert put together a new blues rock band, Stevie Sparks and the Leisure Scientists, which performed club and concert dates in British Columbia and Hawaii and throughout the United States. In 2000 he returned to the Washington, D.C. area and legally changed his name to Stephen Mark Gray. He then spent time playing in a blues band called the Bay Boys, which also included guitarist Professor Mac Walter. Stevie Sparks passed away on Thursday, January 20, 2005 at the age of 54.

STOCK WILSON

Singer-guitarist Stock Wilson grew up in Bethesda, Maryland and took up music shortly after seeing the Beatles perform their first United States concert at the Washington Coliseum in 1964. During his time at Western Junior High School in the middle 1960s he played in a British Invasion cover band called Organization Man that played the local teen dance scene.

In 1966 Wilson became a founding member of another rock and roll band out of Western Junior High School called Liberation Front, whose initial lineup consisted of Wilson on vocals and lead guitar, singer Kevin Taylor, guitarist Fred Bruch and drummer Pat McGowan. Later additions to the lineup included bassist Tim Fenhagen and harmonicist Lee Daniels. The band covered such artists as Cream and the Yardbirds and performed at teen dances at the Western Teen Club (Western Junior High School in Bethesda), the Wedge (Bethesda Youth Center) and the St. Alban's Episcopal Church Friday Coffeehouse (Washington, D.C.). Liberation Front stayed together for four years and disbanded in late 1969 as Wilson was working his way through his senior year at Walt Whitman High School.

In 1970 Wilson went acoustic and formed a band called Betty Boop with Bosco's Baby in the Back, a folk music outfit that performed alternately as Paddlefoot Rat and specialized in original compositions. The group's lineup consisted of Wilson handling vocals and guitar, flutist Scott Dorman and saxophonist Bob Rath. They often appeared at such Washington, D.C. night clubs as Mr. Henry's Tenley Circle, Club Soda, and the Cellar Door, where they participated in numerous Sunday "Hootenanny" shows.

In 1971 Wilson played with the remnants of Liberation Front in a rock and roll band called Silver Arrow. Later in the year he became part of a new rock and roll band called OC Hopper, whose lineup consisted of Wilson as singer-guitarist, guitarist Scott Holland, bassist-flutist Scott Dorman, saxophonists Jimmy Heffron and Bob Rath and drummer Marshall Utterback (a later addition was bassist John Gillman). This group offered original material and performed in Washington, D.C. at Emergency, Jackie Lee's Lounge and concerts at the P Street Beach near Dupont Circle. The band subsequently moved over to Mr. Henry's Washington Circle and changed its name to Bifrost. In 1972 Wilson briefly played in a blues band called Ruby before taking a break from the local music scene.

Wilson re-emerged in the 1980s and played in an acoustic folk trio called Larry and the Lounge Chairs, and such rock and roll bands as the Megatones and the Loggers. In the 1990s some of the bands he worked with included a country rock group called the Slim Jims and the R&B bands Mud Turtle and Roundhouse. More recently he has sung and played guitar in a rock and roll band called the Sloats.

Since 2009 Wilson has played guitar in a classic rock and roll band called the VI-Kings, whose current lineup also includes guitarists Joe Dolan and Bill Craig, bassist Matt Maury and drummer Bob Berberich (all five band members handle lead and harmony vocal duties).

SUSAN JONES

Violinist Susan Jones was born in the Bronx (a borough of New York City), raised in Baltimore, Maryland, and moved to the Washington, D.C. area in the early 1970s to attend the University of Maryland. During that time she played electric viola with a group of rock and roll musicians at campus events under a constantly changing series of band names such as Witherstone, Green Plant Leadership, Laughing Cow Cheese, the Sensuous Woman, Speed Queen, and Band X.

Jones spent the middle 1970s playing viola and fiddle in a blues-folk band called Those Awkward Years that performed at the Berwyn Café in College Park, Maryland and other local coffee houses.

Jones spent the late 1970s playing fiddle for a country rock group that was first called Ladyfinger, and then, as it expanded in size, came to be called the Ladyfinger Band. Besides Jones, the outfit's membership also included singer-guitarist Lois Fritz, bassist John Previti, singer-keyboardist Sharon Gnatt and singer-drummer Larry Taylor. The Ladyfinger Band was one of the top local groups of its kind and performed in Washington, D.C. at Mr. Henry's Tenley Circle, the Biltmore Ballroom, Columbia Station, Desperado's, Food For Thought and Gallagher's Pub; in Maryland at the Bitter Lemon Pub (Rockville), the Italian Gardens (College Park), DiGennaro's (Laurel), the Psyche Delly (Bethesda) and the Takoma Tap Room (Silver Spring); and in Virginia at the Annandale Grill (Annandale).

Jones spent the 1980s and 1990s playing fiddle for several area C&W bands including 301 Country, Cowboy Jazz, the Freestate Cowboy Choir, Goldrush, Night Flight, the Dusty Rhodes Band, and Silverwings. She also performed with such rock and roll acts as the Visitors (a group that presented a rock opera about space aliens), Kit Kamien and the Backroom Players, and Jane Doe.

In addition, Jones has played violin in many different orchestras such as the University of Maryland Orchestra, the Kennedy Center Orchestra, the National Philharmonic and numerous others. She has also been the house violinist at several area theatres including the Harlequin Dinner Theatre, Ford's Theatre and the Warner Theatre.

Jones has two especially interesting musical ventures to her credit. First, she played violin in the house band for a show entitled "National 77th Birthday Tribute to Rosa Louise Parks" that was held at the John F. Kennedy Center for the Performing Arts Concert Hall on Sunday, February 4, 1990. During this evening she backed up such R&B performers as: singers Lou Rawls, Dionne Warwick, Melba Moore and Marilyn McCoo; singer-percussionist Cyril Neville; the vocal group Sister Sledge; and pop singer Melissa Manchester. Second, she played violin onstage for Jimmy Page and Robert Plant (former members of the rock and roll band Led Zeppelin) at their two-night concert at USAir Arena in Landover, Maryland on Wednesday, March 22 and Thursday, March 23, 1995.

Other artists Jones has performed with include: blues keyboardist-guitarist-vocalist Ann Rabson; classical cellist Yo-Yo Ma; the classical acts Mannheim Steamroller and the String of Pearls Quartet; C&W singer-guitarist Ray Price; jazz saxophonist Andrew White; the jazz bands Doc Scantlin and His Imperial Palms Orchestra, the Dixie Crawfish, the Bay Jazz Project, and String Shift; pop singers Tony Bennet, Bob Hope and Clay Aiken; R&B singers Ben Vereen, Dionne Warwick and Aretha Franklin; and R&B singer-keyboardists Stevie Wonder, Ray Charles, and Barry White (twice at D.A.R. Constitution Hall in the 1970s and then she became a part of White's orchestra for "The Icon Tour" in 1999). She has also recently been playing violin in the Washington, D.C. area for rock and roll singer-guitarist Kenny Holliday, Jr.

Jones currently leads her own band, the Susan Jones Jazz Quartet, the lineup of which consists of herself on violin, guitarist Pete Fields, bassist Bob Abbott and her husband-drummer Tom Jones. Other musicians to work with the group are guitarists Jerry Lynn, Brian Litz and Jim Cunningham, and bassists Scott Giambusso and James King. In existence since 1990, this outfit has recently performed in Washington, D.C. at Blues Alley and in Maryland at the New Deal Café (Greenbelt) and 49 West (Annapolis).

Susan Jones has recorded with a number of musical artists and as a lead performer has four albums to her credit: "Violin Dreams" (Susan Jones; Self-Released, 1999); "Nuts and Bolts" (Susan Jones and Seth Kibel; NB Records, 2004); "Violin Caliente" (Susan Jones; Self-Released, 2006); and "Exit 19 Future" (Susan Jones Jazz Quartet; Self-Released, 2011).

THE SWEET

The Sweet was a Georgetown-based R&B band consisting of singer-keyboardist Bobbie Howard (formerly of the British Walkers), guitarist Tom Curley (formerly of the Mad Hatters), bassist Curt Jonnie (a native of Canada who had previously lived in Wildwood, New Jersey and played in a rock and roll band called the Proverbial Knee-Highs) and drummer Mike Kennedy (formerly of the British Walkers). The group formed in March 1967 and spent most of the year performing at the Keg, where they were often billed as Bobbie Howard and the Sweet.

The Sweet was often called upon to appear on local concert bills and headline area teen dances. One of their more interesting gigs saw them open for the Turtles at the Alexandria Arena on Wednesday, November 22, 1967.

The Sweet has two 45rpm single records to its credit: "Got To Have More Love" backed with "You Can't Win At Love" (The Sweet; Smash Records, 1967); and "Broken Heart Attack" backed with "Don't Do It" (The Sweet; Smash Records, 1968). The Sweet disbanded in 1968.

SWITCHBLADE

The rockabilly band Switchblade formed in 1980 out of the remnants of Tex Rubinowitz and the Bad Boys, who had played their final show on New Year's Eve 1979. The band's roster included some longtime Washington, D.C. area music scene favorites and offered an original lineup of singer-guitarist Jimmie "Ratso" Silman III, guitarist Eddie Angel, singer-bassist Johnny Castle and drummer Jim Dougherty. Other musicians to pass through the band included guitarist Steuart Smith and drummer Giles Cook.

During its four years as a unit Switchblade played both originals and obscure rockabilly material and headlined in Washington, D.C. at D.C. Space, Nightclub 9:30, the Cellar Door, the Bayou, Desperado's, the Wax Museum, and the Gentry; and in Maryland at the Psyche Delly (Bethesda).

The original members of Switchblade all went on to work with performing artist of great stature: Ratso has long been performing and touring with Kinky Friedman, Eddie Angel went on to become a founding member of Los Straightjackets, Castle has been a long-standing member of the Nighthawks, and Dougherty moved to the West Coast where he drummed for Art Deco and the New Era.

Switchblade disbanded in 1984 and has since occasionally staged reunion performances. The band has two albums to its credit: "Fugitive" (Mark Wenner & Switchblade; Whitewater Records, 1984; the lineup for this recording was lead singer-harmonicist Mark Wenner, guitarist Jimmie "Ratso" Silman III, guitarist Steuart Smith, bassist Johnny Castle and drummer Giles Cook); and "Playing With Rats" (Ratso and Switchblade; Sphincter Records, 2001; this album was recorded live at the Bayou in 1986 and the lineup consisted of lead singer-harmonicist Mark Wenner, singer-guitarist Jimmie "Ratso" Silman III, singer-bassist Johnny Castle and singer-drummer Bob Berberich).

T.C. TOLLIVER

Drummer T.C. Tolliver was born and raised in Washington, D.C., where, in the early 1970s while attending Ballou High School, he played in his first band, an R&B outfit called J.J. and the Invaders. Other bands he drummed for throughout the decade include the rock and roll bands the Cherry People and Summerfield, and the R&B acts Peaches & Herb, and Symba.

In 1982 Tolliver relocated to New York City and spent two years drumming for the Plasmatics, the hard-driving rock and roll band fronted by singer Wendy O. Williams, who had a penchant for chainsawing guitars, blowing up speaker cabinets, sledgehammering television sets, and blowing up automobiles during the band's live stage performances. Tolliver appeared on their album "Coup d'Etat" (Plasmatics; Capitol Records, 1982). Although he left the Plasmatics in 1983, he did drum on Wendy O. Williams' debut studio album, WOW (Wendy O. Williams; Passport Records, 1984), and her second album, "Kommander of Kaos" (Wendy O. Williams; Gigasaurus Records, 1986). Tolliver spent much of the 1980s drumming for Williams on her tours of the United States and Europe.

Tolliver has since performed and/or recorded with such musical artists as: blues rock guitarist Eric Agales; classical-rock and roll guitarist Neil Zaza; jazz singers Angela Bofill and Jean Carn; jazz bassist Juma Sultan; jazz keyboardists Lonnie Liston Smith and Bobby Lyles; jazz saxophonists Marion Meadows, Ronnie Laws and Kim Waters; jazz flutists Bobbi Humphrey and Sherry Winston; jazz drummer Norman Connors; R&B singers Ali Woodson, Alyson Williams and Dawn Robinson; R&B guitarist Stevie Salas; R&B singer-bassist Michael Henderson; R&B keyboardist Bernie Worrell; the R&B trio Checkmate; rock and roll guitarist Vince Martell; rock and roll singer-bassist T.M. Stevens; and the heavy metal band the Hounds of Hasselvander.

TEARS

Tears was a Washington, D.C.-based rock and roll band whose best-known lineup consisted of lead singer Charlie Pearson, guitarist Erik Cartwright, guitarist Alan Adkins, bassist Brian Wagner and drummer Timm Biery. The group was active from 1979 to 1981 and performed in Washington, D.C. at such night clubs as the Childe Harold, Desperado's and Beneath it All; and in Maryland at the Psyche Delly (Bethesda). The band has one album to its credit, "Tears" (Tears; Backstreet Records, 1979).

THE TEJUNS

The Tejuns hold the distinction of being one of the very first bands to play British Invasion rock and roll in the night clubs of Georgetown and are credited with helping to pave the way for that popular style of music in the nation's capital.

The Tejuns formed in June 1964 and consisted of: lead singer-guitarist Stan Doucette (previously of Ray Rock and the Revlons and his own band, Stan Dee and the Profiles);

guitarist Fred Long (from Myrtle Beach, South Carolina); bassist Dale Chafin (from West Virginia); and drummer Rocky Isaac (who had moved from West Virginia to Southeast Washington, D.C. as a teen and was just finishing up at Anacostia High School).

The Tejuns sported the look and sound of the Beatles and shortly after their formation secured a spot as house band at a Georgetown bar called the Frog, which was located in the basement of a night club called the Corral and had previously been a C&W establishment. The group remained at the Frog for more than a year and then spent the summer of 1965 performing at night clubs in Myrtle Beach, South Carolina before disbanding.

The Tejuns were extremely popular during their time on the local scene and served to influence other area night club owners to book bands that offered the British sound. They have one 45rpm single record to their credit: "Girl" backed with "Nobody Knows" (The Tejuns; 100-Proof Records, 1964). Chafin and Isaac went on to play together in the Creatures and Doucette played on the local music scene for many years, including a noteworthy tenure with blues rock guitarist Roy Buchanan in the Uncalled Four.

THE TELSTARS

The Telstars formed in Norfolk, Virginia in 1963 and consisted of lead singer-drummer Ronnie Wilson, guitarist Gary Johnson, bassist Terry Gorka and rhythm guitarist-saxophonist Jimmy Maddox. The Telstars eventually moved north and spent the summer of 1965 playing at the Beachcomber, a night club in Ocean City, Maryland. In September of that year the band relocated to the Washington, D.C. area and began playing the Bayou, an engagement that ultimately turned into a house band position that lasted into 1968.

At one point in 1966 guitarist Gary Johnson was replaced by Jimmy Carter, formerly of the British Walkers. In September of 1968 Wilson disbanded the Telstars and put together an entirely new four-piece rock and roll band with singer-guitarist Jim MacFarlane, singer-guitarist Guy Taylor and bassist Dickie Thompson. He called this group Ronnie Wilson and the New Telstars and assumed the house band position at Nu-Mac's in Georgetown, remaining there into 1969. The Telstars have one 45rpm single record to their credit, "Keep On Running" backed with "Hold Tight" (The Telstars; Columbia Records, 1967).

TERRY GLEASON

Blues rock guitarist Terry "T.I." Gleason grew up in Greenbelt, Maryland and during the early 1970s while attending Parkdale High School he first played in a hard-rocking power trio called Orondous with bassist Kris Grempler and drummer Timm Biery. Orondous played private parties and teen dances in Greenbelt at the Greenbelt Volunteer Fire Department and the St. Hugh's Teen Club (St. Hugh's Catholic School).

Other rock and roll bands Gleason played guitar for during the 1970s included Felch, Stone Granite, Slow Rush, Zillion, Moonwind, Mercury, Mirage, and Rocks. In the spring of 1980 he joined a hard-rocking band called Maxx, which at the time consisted of Gleason on lead guitar, lead singer Eddie Day, rhythm guitarist Tim Jones, bassist Kris Grempler and drummer Paul Baker. Maxx became an integral part of what was then a dynamic rock and roll scene that had emerged at Bambino's, a night club in Riverdale, Maryland.

In May 1981 Gleason relocated to the Bay Area of California and over the next two years played in the rock and roll bands Kid Palomino, Autograph, and Vision. In 1983 he struck up a relationship with blues singer-guitarist John Lee Hooker and served as one of his main rhythm guitarists on live performances for most of the next 18 years.

Other bands and musicians Gleason played guitar for in the 1980s and 1990s included: blues singer Vala Cupp; blues singer-harmonicist Charlie Musselwhite; rock and roll singer

Eddie Money; rock and roll guitarist Carlos Santana; rock and roll bands Expressway, and Frank Marino and Mahogany Rush; and Southern rock singer-keyboardist Gregg Allman.

Gleason was featured in March 1994 issue of Guitar Player magazine, which chose his song "Stevie's Blues" as its "Demo of the Month" and featured him in their "Spotlight" section – he subsequently appeared in the magazine's "Auditions on Call" segment on several occasions.

In 1998 Gleason left California, and, after a brief stay in his hometown of Greenbelt, moved to Queenstown on the Eastern Shore of Maryland. There, he played in a local blues band called Blues Church and gave private guitar lessons. Terry Gleason passed away in December 2004 at the age of 49.

TERRY JONES

Singer-guitarist Terry Jones was born in San Diego, California and spent much of his teen years living in Marshall, Virginia. During his years at Woodward School for Boys in Washington, D.C. during the middle 1960s he learned to play guitar from John Hall (later of the bands the Wad, Kangaroo, the British Walkers, and Orleans) at Dupont Circle and sang and played guitar in a local rock and roll band called the Pride of Lions.

Jones spent most of 1969 as lead singer of the rock and roll band Holy Moses, whose lineup at the time was completed by lead guitarist Ted Spelios, rhythm guitarist Dave Vittek, bassist Marty David and drummer Jack O'Connor. Holy Moses was formed in Washington, D.C. and often performed at night clubs in New York City. After Jones left the band, Holy Moses continued onwards with different musicians and released the album "Holy Moses!!" (Holy Moses; RCA Victor, 1971).

In the early 1970s Jones sang and played guitar in a folk band based in Stratford, Ontario (Canada) called the Perth County Conspiracy, which recorded and released albums on several labels including Columbia Records. He went on to perform with a variety of musical artists including blues singer-guitarist Josh White and a Philadelphia-based rock and roll group called the Feds, which included keyboardist Don Preston and drummer Billy Mundi, both former members of the Mothers of Invention.

TERRY PLUMERI

Bassist Terry Plumeri was born in Greensboro, North Carolina and raised in Tampa, Florida where he attended George D. Chamberlain High School during the early 1960s. He then went on to attend the Manhattan School of Music in New York, during which time he performed with the likes of jazz singer-clarinetist-saxophonist Woody Herman and jazz flutist-saxophonist Yusef Lateef.

In the late 1960s Plumeri moved to the Washington, D.C. area and joined the avant-garde jazz rock instrumental trio Love Cry Want, which was rounded out by guitarist Stephen J. Nicholas II and drummer-percussionist Michael Smith. From 1968 to 1970 Love Cry Want was one of the region's most popular ensembles, playing a variety of shows, benefits and concerts around town, and appearing at such Washington, D.C. night clubs as Emergency, the Showboat Lounge and the Cellar Door.

From 1970 to 1973 Plumeri played bass for R&B singer Roberta Flack at Mr. Henry's Capitol Hill in Washington, D.C. During those years he also appeared on several of her albums and toured the country as a part of her backup band. In the middle and late 1970s he played locally in a jazz trio called Evolution and also served as an acoustic bassist for the Washington National Symphony.

Through the years other jazz artists Plumeri played bass for include: singers Arthur Prysock, Joe Williams and Frank Sinatra; guitarist John Abercrombie; singer-pianist Les McCann; keyboardist Herbie Hancock; saxophonists Julian "Cannonball" Adderley and

Wayne Shorter; and trumpeter Quincy Jones. In addition, he has recorded extensively as a solo performer, as well as with other musicians, and has scored music for a total of 57 feature-length motion pictures. Most recently, Plumeri held the role of composer-conductor of the Moscow Philharmonic Orchestra. Terry Plumeri died on Thursday, March 31, 2016 at the age of 71.

TEX RUBINOWITZ

Rockabilly singer-guitarist Tex Rubinowitz was born in Abilene, Texas and raised in Springfield, Virginia. He made an impact on the local music scene in the middle 1970s playing honky-tonk rockabilly with his band the Casaloma Cowboys, who later in the decade recorded and released the 45rpm single record, "That Old Patchwork Quilt" backed with "South of the Border (Down Mexico Way)" (Tex Rubinowitz and His Casaloma Cowboys; Aladdin Records, 1978). A year later he released the 45rpm single records, "Hot Rod Man" backed with "Ain't It Wrong" (Tex Rubinowitz; Ripsaw Records, 1979) and "Bad Boy" backed with "Feelin' Right Tonight" (Tex Rubinowitz; Ripsaw Records, 1979).

In the late 1970s he began calling his group Tex Rubinowitz and the Bad Boys and they remained one of the area's top bands throughout the 1980s, playing original material as well as covers of such rockabilly stars such as Carl Perkins, Charlie Feathers and Gene Vincent. During their time they performed in Washington, D.C. at such night clubs as the Childe Harold, Desperado's, Columbia Station, the Wax Museum, Rocky Raccoon's Saloon, the Cellar Door, Nightclub 9:30, Friendship Station, and the Gentry; in Maryland at the Italian Gardens (College Park), the Psyche Delly (Bethesda) and the Takoma Tap Room (Silver Spring); and in Virginia at the Annandale Grill (Annandale), Beacon's Backstage (Falls Church) and the Shed (Alexandria).

Rubinowitz's bands experienced constant personnel changes through the years. One of the most popular lineups of Tex Rubinowitz and the Bad Boys consisted of singer-guitarist Tex Rubinowitz, guitarist Jim "Ratso" Silman III, guitarist Steve Carr, bassist Mike Carr and drummer George Norris. The lineup soon changed to consist of Rubinowitz, Ratso, guitarist Eddie Angel, bassist Johnny Castle and drummer Scotty Flowers.

Other top local musicians to work with Rubinowitz through the years included guitarist Bob "Newscaster" Swenson and bassist Billy Hancock. Rubinowitz has three albums to his credit: "Hot Rod Man" (Tex Rubinowitz; Big Beat Records, 1980); "Tex Rubinowitz" (Tex Rubinowitz; No Club Productions, 1985); and "The Old Man Mississippi" (Tex Rubinowitz Bob Newscaster; Patuxent/No Club, 2017).

THREE EASY PIECES

Three Easy Pieces was a Washington, D.C.-based rock and roll band that formed in 1970 and initially appeared at the Silver Dollar Restaurant in Georgetown. One of its earliest lineups consisted of singer-guitarist Mike Pirko, keyboardist John Clark and drummer Stuart Ross. Clark was then replaced by singer-keyboardist-bassist Jimmy Nalley. During the early 1970s the band performed at night clubs in the South and for much of the decade maintained house band duties at the Paul Mall Restaurant in Georgetown. Musicians to pass through the band during those years included drummers Danny Conway, Mark Fincham, David Platshon and Joe Reckert.

Three Easy Pieces covered such popular artists as Bad Company, the Beatles, Grand Funk Railroad, the Steve Miller Band, Santana, Steppenwolf, Steely Dan, the James Gang, and the Who. In addition to the Paul Mall Restaurant, they performed in Washington, D.C. at the Crazy Horse, the Bayou and Mr. Henry's Tenley Circle, and in Maryland at the Back Alley Lounge in Bladensburg.

In 1976 the band shortened its name to the Pieces with Pirko and Nalley being joined by singer-drummer Michael "Pokey" Walls (formerly of the Chartbusters). They began performing more popular dance music and appeared at night clubs up and down the Atlantic Coast. Later in the 1970s the band consisted of Nalley, guitarist Tony Grasso (who had replaced interim guitarist Glenn Alexander) and a series of drummers that included Mike Zack, Michael "Pokey" Walls, Joe Reckert and Wayne Tomlinson (who was better known for his guitar playing abilities).

THE THREE JACKS

The Three Jacks were a rock and roll band that emerged on the local music scene in early 1953 with performances in Washington, D.C. at Maynard's Restaurant and in Maryland at the Quonset Supper Club in Silver Hill. They spent the first half of 1954 performing at the Romano Inn in Colmar Manor on the Bladensburg Road Strip before moving next door to the Wheel Bar in September of that year. It was there at the Wheel Bar that the group was prominently advertised in the pages of the Washington Daily News newspaper as a rock and roll band, with their Sunday afternoon appearances from 1954 to 1959 advertised as "Rock and Roll Sessions."

The problem with profiling the Three Jacks is that there is very little documentation available on the band, making them one of the more mysterious musical outfits in Washington, D.C. area rock and roll history. It is known is that when the group first arrived on the scene at the Quonset Supper Club in May 1953, an advertisement in the Washington Daily News listed the band as "Three Jacks and a Jill" with the Jacks being Bill Abernathy, Paul Rose and Paul "Sunny" Kline, and the Jill being pop singer Mary Martell.

Bill Abernathy had been a well-known local piano player and had previously headlined as a solo performer at the Chesapeake Musical Bar in Cottage City, Maryland in 1950, and, more recently, in a jazz duo with Sonny Kast ("Kast and Abernathy") at the Hilltop Restaurant in Coral Hills, Maryland in March and April of 1952. The pair subsequently added a third party in Paul "Sunny" Kline to the group, and, during the summer months of 1952, the trio of Kast, Abernathy and Kline headlined the Hilltop Restaurant.

Frank "Sonny" Kast was a musician from Southeast Washington, D.C., who had previously fronted his own bands under different names including: Sonny Kast and His Icelanders at the Penguin Restaurant in Southeast Washington, D.C. in 1948; Sonny Kast and His Jump Trio at the Hilltop Restaurant in 1949; and Sonny Kast and His Band at both the Hilltop Restaurant and Jack Rowe's Restaurant in Southeast Washington, D.C. in 1950.

When the Three Jacks started at the Wheel Bar in September 1954, their lineup was listed as Bill Abernathy, Paul "Sunny" Kline, and Joe Burch. In their Friday, October 12, 1956 edition, the Washington Daily News mentions the band has been at the Wheel Bar for 20 months and gives their lineup as Bill Abernathy, Joe Burch, and Jim Calomeris. All that is known about Calomeris is that he had previously headlined at the Hilltop Restaurant in 1948 and 1949 with a band called Jim Calomeris and His Musical Moods.

The Three Jacks later worked the Senate Inn on Marlboro Pike in Capitol Heights, Maryland for several months in 1960, and, late in that year, played a two-month engagement at the Romano Inn in Colmar Manor. After that, they faded from public view. Unfortunately, there is no evidence that the Three Jacks ever made any recordings of their music.

Apart from a few brief mentions in the Washington Daily News music columns of the 1950s, there are no known published articles or biographies on the band or any of its members. While it is known Abernathy was a keyboardist, the instruments played by the other band members cannot be determined. The few eyewitnesses who recall seeing the band can say they were a swinging trio that covered the top rock and roll songs of the era, but cannot provide details beyond that.

The Three Jacks had their roots in the various jazz-oriented bands that appeared at the Hilltop Restaurant of the late 1940s and early 1950s. They were an important early-era rock and roll group in the nation's capital during their eight-year existence event though most of their history has been lost through time.

THE THREE OF US TRIO

The Three of Us Trio was a rocking, three-man group that was regarded as one of the top musical acts of the 1950s and early 1960s in the Washington, D.C. area. The trio was unique in that although all three of its members were Black, they played an assortment of night clubs, some of which catered to Blacks and others that drew predominantly White audiences.

The Three of Us Trio consisted of lead singer-saxophonist Charles Kelley, guitarist Clarence Dillard and drummer Laurence Farrell. Forming in 1952, they were initially billed in local night clubs as an R&B act. During its first two years, the band played some extreme Washington, D.C. establishments – in November 1952 they were working an engagement at the Covered Wagon on upper 14th Street NW, a restaurant that was then considered a hillbilly hangout, and in February 1953 they had switched over to an all-Black bar called Club Afrique on Bladensburg Road NE, which offered blues music. Later in 1953 they had a long stay at Woody's on Kennedy Street NW, a club that mixed R&B with early rock and roll.

Throughout the remainder of the 1950s the Three of Us Trio were exclusively advertised in local newspapers as a rock and roll band. They appeared in Washington, D.C. at such night clubs as the Harmony, the Rendezvous, the Alpine Room, the Lyon's Den and the Moulin Rouge; and in Maryland at the Surf Club (Colmar Manor), the Rustic Cabin (Colmar Manor), the Wheel Bar (Colmar Manor), the 4400 Club (Brentwood), Strick's Restaurant (Silver Hill) and the Village Barn (Morningside). From 1960 to 1962 they concentrated on performing at the Spotlite Room (Washington, D.C.), the Las Vegas Club (Coral Hills) and the Dixie Pig (Cottage City).

From 1953 to 1957 the Three Of Us Trio was the house band on the weekly WTTG Channel 5 television show "Capital Caravan," which was advertised as featuring "all-Negro music and talent." The band has one 45rpm single record to its credit, "Telegram" backed with "Sugar Jump" (The Three-of-Us Trio and the Dillard-Kelley Orchestra, Vocal by Charles Kelley; York Records, 1959).

THE TIKIS

In the 1960s the Tikis were the pride of the burgeoning teen rock and roll scene in Bowie, Maryland. The band formed in the summer of 1965 with a lineup of three Bowie teenagers: singer-lead guitarist Jeff Webster; rhythm guitarist Steve DeCoste; and drummer Marc Connelly.

Initially rehearsing in the home of Connelly, the Tikis prepared to play out and worked on songs by the Kingsmen, Elvis Presley, Bill Haley and His Comets, and the Ventures. That fall DeCoste left the group and the Tikis subsequently became a quartet with the addition of two new Bowie High School musicians, rhythm guitarist Rick Myers and bassist John "Chip" McAuliffe. In the summer of 1966 they added an organ player named Rick Perry, also from Bowie, and became a quintet.

The Tikis performed the popular rock and roll songs of the era and first offered tunes by bands such as the Beatles, the Rolling Stones, the Yardbirds, the Kinks, the Who, the Knickerbockers, Paul Revere and the Raiders, James Brown, Johnny Rivers, and Chuck

Berry. Later, as they grew in size, they added to their repertoire songs by bands such as Sam and Dave, Muddy Waters, the Doors, the Young Rascals, the Turtles, Iron Butterfly, the Guess Who, and Mitch Ryder and the Detroit Wheels. On occasion they added several original ballads to the mix.

In terms of live performances, the Tikis worked parties around Bowie as well as teen dances at the Belair Junior High School Teen Club (Bowie), the Bowie Swim Club (Bowie), Hebrew Academy (Washington, D.C.), Beth Torah Congregation (Mt. Rainier), the Laurel Teen Club (Laurel High School), the Sacred Heart Church Teen Club (Bowie), the Fort George G. Meade Teen Club (Anne Arundel County, Maryland), the Fort Myer Officers' Club (Arlington County, Virginia), the Crofton Teen Club (dances in the Ballroom of the Crofton Country Club, as well as summer splash parties at the facility's outdoor pool), the Maryland City Teen Club (Maryland City Elementary School in Laurel), the Bowie Senior Teen Club (Bowie High School in Bowie) and the Annapolis Armory (Annapolis). They also performed at events on the Wilson Line's M.V. George Washington cruise ship that made regular journeys back-and-forth on the Potomac River from Washington, D.C. to Marshall Hall Park in Charles County, Maryland.

The Tikis also accepted numerous special offers far from its home base during its time, including a headlining concert position at the Fairgrounds in Ocean City, Maryland during the summer of 1967, and a lengthy engagement as the house band at Stanford's Cafeteria on Wilson Boulevard in Arlington, Virginia throughout much of the summer of 1968.

The Tikis were twice tagged to perform in supporting act positions for pop singer Neil Diamond, events that served as high points in the band's career. The first occurred at a concert event entitled "Summertime Hullabaloo" that was headlined by Diamond and also included appearances by, in addition to the Tikis, guitarist Bobby Parker, the English Setters, the British Walkers, the Minutemen, the Marvels, the Rip-Tydes, and the Sidekicks, and was held at the Manassas Armory in Manassas, Virginia on Saturday, August 6, 1966. Diamond was reportedly impressed with the band from Bowie and personally asked them to appear on another upcoming show in the area. The Tikis agreed and were on the bill when Neil Diamond headlined a concert that also included appearances by the English Setters, the Hangmen, and the Brave Maggots at the Alexandria Arena on Saturday, October 1, 1966.

The Tikis underwent one last major personnel shift in the late stages of its campaign, with all the band members dropping out with the exception of drummer Marc Connelly, who pulled in three new musicians to keep the charge going. In the fall of 1968 Connelly revamped the lineup by welcoming in lead singer Buddy Fowler, lead guitarist Danny Luckman and rhythm guitarist Andy Novik, all of whom were natives of Bowie and students at Bowie High School. This final version of the Tikis played fraternity parties at the University of Maryland and worked teen dances at the Springhill Lake Recreation Center in Greenbelt, Maryland before disbanding in June 1969.

TIM EYERMANN

Multi-instrumentalist Tim Eyermann, who was best known for playing the saxophone, was born in Philadelphia, Pennsylvania and raised in Pittsburgh, where he studied at Duquesne University in the late 1960s. He served in the United States Air Force for several years during which time he performed in their two premier jazz groups, the North American Air Defense Jazz Band and the Airmen of Note. Some of the nationally known musical artists he backed up while a member of those outfits included: jazz singer Sarah Vaughan; jazz pianist Count Basie; jazz trumpeters Maynard Ferguson and Clark Terry; pop singers Tony Bennett and Julie Andrews; R&B singer Anita Baker; and the R&B vocal group the Spinners.

In 1974 Eyermann relocated to the Washington, D.C. area and put together the jazz rock band East Coast Offering. The group, which mixed originals with covers of such artists as Frank Zappa, Chick Corea and Weather Report, kept going into the 1990s with an ever-changing lineup of local musicians.

As either a solo artist or with East Coast Offering, Eyermann released more than a half-dozen albums on no fewer than five different record labels. At his peak, two of these recordings were issued on a major label: "East Coast Offering" (East Coast Offering; MCA Records, 1984); and "Walkin' With You" (East Coast Offering; MCA Records, 1985).

In the 1970s and 1980s East Coast Offering (often billed as "Tim Eyermann and East Coast Offering") performed in Washington, D.C. at such night clubs as Harold's Rogue and Jar, Mr. Henry's Tenley Circle, the Biltmore Ballroom, Columbia Station, the Childe Harold, the Cellar Door, Blues Alley and One Step Down; in Maryland at the Psyche Delly (Bethesda) and the Takoma Tap Room (Silver Spring); and in Virginia at Beacon's Backstage (Falls Church).

In his career Eyermann performed with: jazz singers Nancy Wilson and Della Reese; jazz guitarists Earl Klugh and Larry Coryell; jazz saxophonist Anthony Braxton; jazz saxophonist-flutist James Moody; jazz trumpeters Maynard Ferguson and Dizzy Gillespie; and R&B singers Bubby Thurston, Gayle Adams and Evelyn "Champagne" King. Tim Eyermann passed away on Tuesday, May 1, 2007 at the age of 60.

TIM ROSE

Folk singer-guitarist Tim Rose was born in Washington, D.C. and raised in Arlington, Virginia. After finishing at Gonzaga College High School in the late 1950s he joined an Arlington-based folk group called the Swinging Strings, which included guitarist Phil Blondheim (who would soon change his name to Scott McKenzie). In 1962 he formed a short-lived folk duo with Mike Boran called Michael and Timothy (Boran had previously been a member of the Smoothies with John Phillips).

From 1962 to 1964 Rose was a member of the Big Three along with Cass Elliot and John Brown. He recorded two albums with the band: "The Big 3" (The Big 3; FM Records, 1963); and "The Big 3 Live at the Recording Studio" (The Big 3; FM Records, 1964).

In 1966 Rose embarked on a solo career playing folk, blues, and soft rock music. He was signed by CBS records to a multi-album record deal and released two solo albums on the label: "Tim Rose" (Tim Rose; CBS Records, 1967) and "Through Rose Colored Glasses" (Tim Rose; CBS Records, 1969). Rose went on to record and release more than a dozen solo albums on more than a half-dozen different record labels.

Among the musical artists Rose performed with during his career are: C&W banjoist Eric Weissbeg; C&W steel guitarist B.J. Cole; pop singer Tina Charles; rock and roll guitarist Andy Summers; rock and roll bassists John McVie and Pete Sears; rock and roll drummers John Bonham, Aynsley Dunbar and Russ Kunkel; and the folk rock band Priority of Brion (featuring singer Robert Plant). Tim Rose passed away on Tuesday, September 24, 2002 at the age of 62.

TIM WYNNE

Bassist Tim Wynne was raised in McLean, Virginia and became hooked on music as a teenager after hearing the Beatles and seeing a performance by a local teen band called the Organic Cavemen. While attending junior high school at St. John Academy in McLean during the middle 1960s he first played guitar in the Swinging Agents, a rock and roll group that performed on the local teen dance circuit and covered artists like the Ventures and the McCoys.

During his time at Bishop Denis J. O'Connell High School in Arlington in the late 1960s and early 1970s Wynne played bass in a rock and roll band called the Yorkshires. This group also worked the local teen dance circuit and covered bands such as the Beatles, the Rolling Stones, the Buckinghams and Steppenwolf. From 1971 to 1972 he played bass in a McLean-based rock and roll band called Star (they later changed their name to "Starr"), an outfit that included drummer Vince Santoro and performed at such Washington, D.C. night clubs as the Crazy Horse and the Bayou. He then spent two years in the United States Air Force during which time he played bass in the United States Air Force Band.

In 1974 Wynne joined the popular rock and roll band Sinbad, which was performing on a regular basis at the Bayou in Georgetown, alternating engagements with bands such as the Nighthawks, Cherry Smash, Face Dancer and the Cherry People. With the arrival of Wynne on bass, Sinbad's lineup was then completed by singer-guitarist Bobby Stevens, keyboardist Guy Meredith and drummer Vince Santoro. During his six years with the group, Sinbad also performed at the Crazy Horse in Washington, D.C., the Bastille in College Park, Maryland, and at colleges and night clubs throughout the Midwest and South.

In the early 1980s Wynne sang and played bass in a local, multi-styled pop-rock wedding band called Chesapeake. In 1984 he formed a 10-piece, multi-styled pop-rock band called the Odyssey Band of D.C., which became one of the top wedding acts in the region. He is still singing and playing bass for the group today.

TIMM BIERY

Drummer Timm Biery was born in Washington, D.C. and raised in the East Pines community of Riverdale, Maryland. His father introduced him to a small drum set at age five, he began taking lessons at age seven, and was subsequently turned on to the music of Steppenwolf, Jimi Hendrix and the Guess Who. At age 11 he gave his first public performance when a woman in East Pines recruited him to drum in a community band she had formed for a special town function – each member was given the opportunity to solo during the performance and Biery appropriately chose Iron Butterfly's "In-A-Gadda-Da-Vida" as his selection, a number that must have gone over big with the Prince George's County parents. He bravely took the stage, hammered out his solo, and firmly launched his career as rock and roll drummer extraordinaire.

During his years at Glenridge Junior High in the early 1970s Biery drummed for a number of local rock and roll bands, with the first being a Riverdale-based group called Fluorescent Rainbow. At that time the band's lineup consisted of singer-lead guitarist Craig Porter, singer-keyboardist Jeff Cole, rhythm guitarist Dave Cruit, singer-bassist Lee Dudley (who was later replaced by Kris Grempler), and Biery on drums. They covered a wide range of material from Crow to Black Sabbath to Iron Butterfly.

Fluorescent Rainbow was a popular attraction on the local teen dance circuit and performed in Maryland at the Colmar Manor Teen Club (Colmar Manor), the Beacon Heights Teen Club (Beacon Heights Junior High School in Riverdale), Cooper Lane Teen Club (Cooper Lane Elementary School in Landover Hills), the Brentwood Teen Club (Bartlett Park, Wohlfarth Building in Brentwood), and the Tucker Road Community Center (Fort Washington).

During his years at Bladensburg High School in the early 1970s Biery drummed for such rock and roll bands as Boston Tea, Orondous, and Felch. In the fall of 1973 he joined the rock and roll band Ichabod Crane, which had graduated from the area's teen dance circuit and performed in Washington, D.C. at such night clubs as Tom Foolery's and the Keg, and in Maryland at Jimmy Comber's Restaurant (Hyattsville) and the Back Alley Lounge (Bladensburg). He remained with Ichabod Crane into early 1975 and then spent the rest of the decade playing for such rock and roll bands as Sassafras Tea, Fast Eddie (the first edition; the band carried on into the 1980s with different lineups), Autumn Breeze, Sky King, Sauce, and Tears.

In February 1980 Biery and bassist Brian Wagner got together with former Face Dancer singer-guitarist David Utter to form a new three-man edition of Fast Eddie. This rock and roll trio recorded and released one single, "Cover Girl" backed with "I'm Not Your Kind of Fool" (Fast Eddie; Edsell Records, 1980). Later in the year they added guitarist Wayne Tomlinson. Fast Eddie played original material and also covered bands like Deep Purple, Humble Pie and Led Zeppelin. They performed in Washington, D.C. at such night clubs as the Bayou and the Cellar Door; in Maryland at Varsity Grill Back Room (College Park), the Stardust Inn (Waldorf) and Bambino's (Riverdale); and at other venues from New Jersey to West Virginia. They disbanded in early 1981.

While playing for Fast Eddie at Bambino's in late 1980 and early 1981, Biery often subbed on drums for one of the club's other attractions, a rock and roll band called Maxx. Guitarist Terry "T.I." Gleason, who has previously worked with Biery in the bands Orondous and Felch, was playing for Maxx and took the opportunity to introduce the drummer to rock and roll guitarist Frank Marino, who was then based in Montreal, Canada and was looking for a new percussionist to replace Jimmy Ayoub.

Biery passed his audition and from 1981 to 1991 he performed and recorded with Marino, who would appear live as either Frank Marino and Mahogany Rush, or just Frank Marino. Biery played on four of Marino's albums: "Juggernaut" (Frank Marino; Columbia Records, 1982), "Full Circle" (Frank Marino; Grudge Records, 1986), "Double Live" (Frank Marino & Mahogany Rush; Maze Music, 1988), and "From the Hip" (Frank Marino; SPV Records, 1990).

From August 1993 until October 1994 Biery drummed for the multi-styled guitarist Danny Gatton, whose trio at the time was rounded out by bassist John Previti. He appears on six of Gatton's albums in all, including "Cruisin' Deuces" (Danny Gatton; Elektra Entertainment, 1993).

From 1996 to 2006 Biery drummed for rock and roll singer-guitarist Nils Lofgren's band, which at the time also included guitarist-keyboardist Tom Lofgren and bassist Wade Matthews. He appears with this group on the multi-artist Bruce Springsteen tribute album "One Step Up/Two Steps Back: The Songs of Bruce Springsteen" (Various Artists; The Right Stuff, 1997), and five other Lofgren solo albums including "Sacred Weapon" (Nils Lofgren; Vision Music, 2006).

Through the years Biery has also performed and/or recorded with a variety of bands and musicians including: the multi-styled pop-rock Nightlife; multi-styled bassist Jay A. Turner; the blues groups the James Mabry Blues Band, Son O' Bop, and the Acme All Star Blues Band; blues singer-saxophonist-pianist Deanna Bogart; the blues rock band Dangerous Rhythm; blues rock guitarist Jeff Muller; blues singer-acoustic guitarist Mark Philips; country-folk singer-guitarist Tony Denikos; country rock singer-guitarists Greg Martin (of the Kentucky Headhunters) and Ron Diehms; C&W singer-guitarist Johnny Raimondo; the jazz bands Triplicity and the Rick Whitehead Trio; jazz saxophonists Jacques "Saxman" Johnson and Tim Eyermann; the jazz rock band the Aesthetics; pop singer Clint Holmes; pop-folk singer-guitarist Angie Miller; pop-rock guitarist Arlen Roth; R&B bands Martha and the Vandellas, Little Anthony and the Imperials, and Lee Atwater's Red, Hot & Blue Band; rock and roll bands August West, the Paul Reed Smith Band, the Dragons, and Jason and the Scorchers; rock and roll singer Root Boy Slim (and his various bands); rock and roll singer-guitarists Tommy Shaw (of Styx), Ric Ocasek (of the Cars), Murray Fentress, and drummer Mike Zack; Southern rock singer-guitarist Warren Haynes; and Senegalese koura player Djimo Kouyate.

In his career Biery has appeared on more than 50 albums, played on more than 300 recordings, engineered and/or produced more than 600 hundred recordings, and drummed on innumerable television programs, films, videos, DVDs and miscellaneous audio-visual presentations.

Biery has owned and operated his own recording studios in Beltsville, Maryland (Wizard Works, 1986-1989; Audio Artistry, 1989-1998; and Go! Digital, 1998-2001) and in Nashville, Tennessee (The Barn, 2004-2012; and the Dark Room, 2012-2017). Although he retired from public performance in 2012, he is still active in the music industry as a producer, teacher and clinician and has been based in Overland Park, Kansas since the fall of 2017.

As a lead artist, Timm Biery has 10 albums of various musical styles to his credit with the latest being the rock and roll collection "Too" (Timm Biery; Analemma Records, 2016).

TINSEL'D SIN

When the rock and roll band Sane Day disbanded in October 1972, three of its members, singer-guitarist Bob Siegel, bassist Peter Olson and drummer Paul Spears, joined forces with lead singer Lenny Puglisi, guitarist Carl Peachey and keyboardist Jim Panek to form a new six-piece rock band called Tinsel'd Sin. Singer Bill Curtis later replaced Puglisi as the frontman.

Tinsel'd Sin was in existence from February 1973 to January 1974, and, like its predecessor, became a favorite at Fort Reno Park in Washington, D.C. A surviving recording of a performance they gave there on Saturday, September 15, 1973 was later issued as a CD album entitled "Live at Fort Reno" (Tinsel'd Sin; Stampede Records, 2003).

While Tinsel'd Sin mainly played original material, they also covered songs by an array of artists such as Elvis Presley, Donovan, Alice Cooper, the Allman Brothers Band, Silverhead, and Russian composer Pyotr Tchaikovsky (a version of his composition "The Nutcracker Suite").

TINY MCCLOUD

Guitarist William "Tiny" McCloud was born and raised in Portsmouth, Virginia and moved to the Washington, D.C. area at the age of 18 in 1961. For more than 20 years he played guitar and bass with a succession of area bands and musicians including: blues rock guitarist Roy Buchanan; the C&W band Danny Denver and the Soundtracks; multi-styled guitarist Danny Gatton; R&B singer-keyboardist Big Al Downing; the R&B group Little Willie and the Handjives; and the rock and roll groups the Chartbusters, the Fourmost, and Little Joe and the Impossibles. Later in his career he performed and recorded with C&W singer Jeannie C. Riley. He is considered by his peers to be one of the great unheralded country rock guitarists in Washington, D.C. area music history. Tiny McCloud passed away on Monday, January 8, 1996 at the age of 53.

TOD CORNETT

Guitarist Tod Cornett was born in Washington, D.C. and raised in Greenbelt, Maryland. His first instrument was the trumpet, which he played in school concert and symphony orchestra bands from grades four through twelve. As a youth he listened to musicians such as Al Hirt, Herb Alpert and the Tijuana Brass, and the Beach Boys before graduating to the Beatles, Chicago, Boston, Rush, Ted Nugent, Foghat, Led Zeppelin, Aerosmith, Molly Hatchet, Yes and Jeff Beck.

Cornett took up guitar at age 13 and during his years at Eleanor Roosevelt High School in the middle and late 1970s he took elementary guitar and music theory classes and participated in jam sessions with classmates-musicians such as guitarist Tom Maynard, bassist Jim Colby and keyboardist J.B. Churchill. From 1978 to 1980 he played guitar in a local instrumental jazz rock band called Black Napkins, which covered songs by Frank Zappa, Billy Cobham, and Return to Forever.

In the 1980s Cornett played with a variety of Washington, D.C. area bands including: the heavy metal group Smokehatch; a jazz-pop outfit called the John Almond Band; a rock and roll band called Night Flight; a jazz group called the Arnold Wilson Band; and an R&B group called the Ray Sly Band. During those years he often jammed in a rock and roll trio format with bassist Bill Foster and drummer Andy Hamburger. On one occasion in Reisterstown, Maryland Cornett worked a session with Foster and famed rock and roll drummer Dennis Chambers.

Among the musicians Cornett performed and/or recorded with in the 1990s were: a Fairfax, Virginia-based rock and roll group called Sisters; folk singer-guitarist Paige Powell; rock and roll singer-guitarist Bill Cornett; and the jazz band Extraordinary Weapons. In recent years he has been focusing on a solo career as an instrumental jazz rock guitarist and collaborating on performances and recordings with drummer Joe Rooney.

TOM JONES

Drummer Tom Jones grew up in College Park, Maryland and played in his first band, Ted Veneman and the Impalas, while in the eighth grade at Greenbelt Junior High School from 1963 to 1964. Specializing in surf music, the band covered the Astronauts and the Beach Boys and performed at dances held by the Berwyn Heights Teen Club which then held its functions in private homes, and the Branchville Teen Club, which then held its events at the Berwyn Swim Club on Branchville Road in College Park. From 1963 to 1966 Jones also played drums and percussion in the Greenbelt Community Band, a 40-piece concert orchestra that performed different types of music with older musicians.

In the late 1960s, after graduating from High Point High School, Jones attended the University of Maryland and drummed for a pop-jazz band called the Jury Four, which performed at a night club in Washington, D.C. called the Judge's Inn. He then spent the summer of 1969 drumming for a Black female R&B vocal trio from Philadelphia called the Three Degrees, which performed shows at resorts and night clubs in the Poconos, the Catskills, and Atlantic City, New Jersey. During that summer the Three Degrees opened a concert at the Spectrum in Philadelphia, Pennsylvania for pop singer Tom Jones, then at the peak of his popularity, and Jones was called upon to remain in the orchestra pit and drum for the headliner as he performed the show.

Throughout the 1970s Jones drummed for a number of bands including: a jazz group called the New Jazz Coalition; and the pop-rock bands Ranny Pierce and the Prophets, All of the Above, Double Exposure, Top of the Town, and the Tiber Creek Pub.

From 1971 to 1975 Jones was the regular percussionist at Shady Grove Music Fair in Gaithersburg, Maryland. There, he played timpani, bells, xylophone, vibes and drums for visiting performing artists and stage productions. Among the acts he performed onstage with during those years were: the pop-jazz group the Buddy Rich Band; pop singers Tony Bennett, Jim Nabors, and the duo of Steve Lawrence and Edie Gorme; R&B singers Ben Vereen, Ike and Tina Turner, and the group Earth, Wind & Fire; and the musicals "Fiddler on the Roof" (featuring actor-singer Theodore Bikel) and "Hello, Dolly!" (featuring actress-dancer-singer Carol Channing).

Over the last four decades Jones has also drummed and percussed for stage productions at such local venues as Ford's Theatre, the National Theatre, Arena Stage, Warner Theatre, Olney Theatre Center, the John F. Kennedy Center for the Performing Arts, and several others. He has also performed with more than two dozen different symphony orchestras including the National Symphony Orchestra (at various locations in Washington, D.C.; conductors he drummed for included Leonard Bernstein, Antal Dorati and Marvin Hamlisch), the National Philharmonic (at the Strathmore in North Bethesda, Maryland), the Baltimore Symphony (Baltimore, Maryland), the Theater Chamber Players (Washington, D.C.), the Israeli Philharmonic (percussion; at both the John F. Kennedy Center for the Performing Arts Concert Hall and Carnegie Hall for conductor Zubin Mehta); and the Mormon Tabernacle Choir (at the John F. Kennedy Center for the Performing Arts in Washington, D.C.).

Of special interest is that Jones has drummed for both rock and roll singer-guitarist Elvis Costello and the rock and roll group Frankie Valli and the Four Seasons in concerts they performed through the Baltimore Symphony Pops at Joseph Myerhoff Hall in Baltimore. Over the years, other major popular music entertainers he has drummed for include: pop singers Cher, Helen Reddy, Jennifer Lawrence and Barbara Streisand; the pop group Tony Orlando and Dawn; R&B singers Mary Wells, Smokey Robinson, Patti LaBelle, Aretha Franklin, Dionne Warwick and Johnny Mathis; and R&B singer-pianist Ray Charles.

In terms of studio work, Jones has participated in innumerable recording sessions through the years in local studios. He has toured with and appeared on albums by the Appalachian folk band Trapezoid and folk singer-guitarist-dulcimer player John McCutheon, and has provided percussion for programs, documentaries and films produced by National Geographic, the Audubon Society and the Discovery Channel.

Jones performed on four different "Presidential Inaugural Gala" shows that celebrated the coming four-year term of the president of the United States of America. The four galas he participated in, along with the acts he drummed for, reads as follows: President Ronald Reagan (The Capital Centre, Landover, Maryland; Monday, January 19, 1981): Debbie Boone, Ethel Merman, Donny Osmond, Marie Osmond, Charley Pride, Dean Martin, Mel Tillis, Charlton Heston, Frank Sinatra, Mel Tillis, Ben Vereen, Rich Little and Johnny Carson; President Ronald Regan (The Washington Convention Center, Washington, D.C.; Saturday, January 19, 1985): Mac Davis, Ray Charles, Frank Sinatra, Pearl Bailey and the Beach Boys; President William Clinton (The Capital Centre, Landover, Maryland; Tuesday, January 19, 1993): Michael Jackson, Barbara Streisand, Elton John, and Fleetwood Mac; and President William Clinton (USAir Arena, Landover, Maryland; Sunday, January 19, 1997): Stevie Wonder, Aretha Franklin, James Taylor, Kenny G., Kenny Rogers, Trisha Yearwood and the Dave Matthews Band.

For 33 years Jones performed on every "Christmas in Washington" show that was staged each December at the National Building Museum in Washington, D.C. From 1982 to 1997 these programs aired on NBC television and from 1998 to 2014 they were broadcast over TNT. Each year the one-hour concert show featured several national performing artists of various musical styles with each act backed by a full orchestra and chorus. None of these performers brought their own back-up bands with them and local musicians were called upon to provide musical backing. The following is a list of performers on each "Christmas in Washington" program that Jones drummed for:

1982: Barbara Mandrell, Diahann Carroll, John Schneider, Dinah Shore, Ben Vereen
1983: Andy Williams, Julio Iglesias, Leslie Uggams
1984: The Osmonds, Frederica Von Stade, Nell Carter
1985: Pat Boone, Natalie Cole, Amy Grant
1986: Mac Davis, Sandi Patty
1987: Barbara Mandrell, Marilyn McCoo, Jack Jones
1988: Vikki Carr, Shirley Jones, Kathleen Battle, Gary Morris
1989: Olivia Newton-John, Diahann Carroll, Vic Damone
1990: John Denver, Reba McEntire, Aretha Franklin
1991: Anita Baker, Vince Gill, Johnny Mathis, Anne Murray
1992: Peabo Bryson, Neil Diamond, Midori

1993: Mary Chapin Carpenter, Patti LaBelle, Wynton Marsalis, Aaron Neville, Ricky Von Shelton
1994: Anita Baker, Jon Secada, Kathy Mattea, Tim McGraw, Kenny G.
1995: Clint Black, Gloria Estefan, Al Green
1996: Luther Vandross, Faith Hill, CeCe Winans, Ruth Ann Swenson
1997: Hanson, Deana Carter
TNT took over production in 1998
Brian Brake played drums from 1998-2007 and Ralph Humphrey played drums from 2008-2014; during that time Tom Jones performed on the shows as a percussionist, playing timpani, vibes, bells, chimes and congas.
1998: Kenny Loggins, Aretha Franklin
1999: Christina Aguilera, B.B. King, Jewel, 98 Degrees
2000: Marc Anthony, Chuck Berry, Jessica Simpson, the Corrs, Billy Gilman
2001: Tony Bennett, Charlotte Church, Mandy Moore, Usher
2002: Brooks and Dunn, Alison Krauss, the Brian Setzer Orchestra, Yolanda Adams
2003: Ashanti, Kenny Chesney, Joss Stone, Renee Fleming
2004: Leann Rimes, Jojo, Vanessa Williams, Ruben Studdard
2005: Rascal Flats, Carrie Underwood, Ciara, Jane Monheit, the Click Five, Cece Winans
2006: Taylor Hicks, Il Divo, Gretchen Wilson, Chris Brow, Corinne Bailey Rae, Bianca Ryan
2007: Ne-Yo, Vanessa Hudgens, Alan Jackson, Colbie Caillat, Heather Headley, Katharine McPhee, Andrea Bocelli
2008: Casting Crowns, Kristin Chenoweth, Julianne Hough, Darius Rucker, Straight No Chaser
2009: Mary J. Bilge, Neil Diamond, Sugarland, Rob Thomas, Usher, Justin Bieber
2010: Mariah Carey, Miranda Cosgrove, Andrea Bocelli, Annie Lennox, Maxwell, Matthew Morrison
2011: Justin Bieber, CeeLo Green, the Band Perry, Jennifer Hudson, Victoria Justice
2012: Diana Ross, Demi Lovato, Megan Hilty, Scotty McCreery, Chris Mann, Psy
2013: The Backstreet Boys, Sheryl Crow, Anna Kendrick, Janelle Monae, Pat Monahan
2014: Darius Rucker, Aloe Blacc, Christina Perri, Hunter Hayes, Rita Ora

Tom Jones currently drums and/or percusses for the Hall Brothers (a country-pop-rock group featuring guitarist Chick Hall, Jr.); a Latin folk music act called the World Jam Club; and rock and roll singer-guitarist Kenny Holliday, Jr. He also performs and records with his wife-violinist in the Susan Jones Jazz Quartet.

TOM MAYNARD

Guitarist Tom Maynard was raised in Riverdale, Maryland and while attending Glenridge Junior High School in the early 1970s he played in a rock and roll band called Cosmic Vision. This group, which covered such bands as Alice Cooper, Black Sabbath, Led Zeppelin and Grand Funk Railroad, was a featured attraction on the local teen dance circuit at the Cooper Lane Teen Club (Cooper Lane Elementary School in Landover Hills), the William Wirt Teen Club (William Wirt Junior High School in Riverdale) and the Glenridge Teen Club (Glenridge Junior High School in Landover Hills).

In the late 1970s Maynard transferred from Parkdale High School to Eleanor Roosevelt High School in Greenbelt, Maryland and joined a rock and roll band called M Street that played private parties, dances at Eleanor Roosevelt High School, and engagements at a night club called the Paragon in College Park, Maryland. He attended Frostburg State College in the late 1970s, during which time he played guitar in the Cumberland-based rock and roll bands Crescent and Full Steam Eddie.

In the early 1980s Maynard played lead guitar in BBC, a hard-rocking band out of Harrisburg, Pennsylvania that often performed in Washington, D.C. at such night clubs as the Bayou, the Crazy Horse, and the Paragon II; in Maryland at the Paragon (College Park) and Bambino's (Riverdale); and in Virginia at the Wild West (Springfield) and Louie's Rock City (Bailey's Crossroads).

In the summer of 1982 Maynard was back in Prince George's County, Maryland and joined a group called Forcer, which was one of the top heavy metal bands in the Washington D.C. area, and remained their lead guitarist for more than a year. Forcer performed at such Maryland night clubs as the Outside Inn (Rockville), the Big Dipper (Beltsville), the Paragon (College Park), and the Riverside Inn (Riverdale). He then spent the middle 1980s playing in the Cumberland, Maryland-based rock and roll bands Full Steam Eddie (again) and the Attack.

TOM MCCARTHY

Bassist Tom McCarthy grew up in Oxon Hill, Maryland and during his years at Crossland High School in the late 1960s he played in such rock and roll bands as the Collection and Trestle Special (which eventually shortened its name to Trestle).

From 1970 to 1972 McCarthy played bass for a Baltimore-based rock and roll band called North Wind and then returned to Trestle where he remained a member through 1975. Other area rock and roll bands he played with during the 1970s included Squeeze, Band Grenade, and the Grimes Brothers.

In the early 1980s McCarthy played bass in the local rock and roll band Nightman and became increasingly involved in the local music industry as a producer and engineer. He resurfaced as a bassist in the 1990s with the local rock and roll band the Reactions.

In 2003 McCarthy joined a revamped, hard-rocking version of the Cherry People, whose roster was rounded out by singer Doug Grimes, lead guitarist Michael Fath, rhythm guitarist Chris Grimes and drummer Corey Holland. He remained with the band for more than a decade. He is currently playing in a Virginia-based blues band called BlueHouse Project.

TOM PRINCIPATO

Blues rock singer-guitarist Tom Principato was born in Washington, D.C. and raised in Falls Church, Virginia. He started on the guitar at age 11 and grew up listening to the Ventures and guitarists such as Les Paul, Chet Atkins and Charlie Christian.

Mainly self-taught, Principato started playing in bands during his high school years. During his time at Falls Church High School in the late 1960s he played in several groups including: a rock and roll outfit called Electric Circus; a blues band called Whiskey Automobile which performed at such Washington, D.C. night clubs as the Roundtable and the Bayou; and another rock and roll group called Greasy Pig, which appeared at Brickskeller near Dupont Circle.

Principato then spent the early 1970s in Boston, Massachusetts, where he played guitar for blues singer-harmonicist James Montgomery (The James Montgomery Band).

In 1973 Principato joined a blues band in Boston called Powerhouse, which included several former members of a Washington, D.C.-based group called the Crawling King Snake Blues Band. With the edition of Principato on guitar, Powerhouse's lineup was completed by singer-guitarist Jimmy Cole, harmonicist Pierre Beauregard, bassist John Curlin and drummer Richard Murray. Musicians to later pass through the band included singer George Leh, bassist Stephen Jacobs, pianist Ben Kay, saxophonist Dave Birkin and drummer Steve Brown.

When visiting Washington, D.C. Powerhouse performed at such night clubs as the Childe Harold, My Mother's Place, Apple Pie, Desperado's and the Cellar Door, as well as the Psyche Delly in Bethesda, Maryland. The band remained active until the fall 1977 and has two albums to its credit: "Night Life" (Powerhouse; Aladdin Records, 1975); and "Lovin' Machine" (Powerhouse; Powerhouse Records, 1988).

In the late 1970s and early 1980s Principato performed with such artists as blues-folk singer-guitarist Pete Kennedy (in the Washington, D.C. area), blues-folk singer-guitarist Geoff Mildaur (in Boston), the R&B act Billy Price and His Keystone Rhythm Band (in Pittsburgh), and blues singer-pianist Mary Blankemeier (in the Washington, D.C. area).

In 1984 Principato began fronting his own Northern Virginia-based blues band and through the years has used some of the region's top musicians in his group including bassist Steve Wolf and drummer Big Joe Maher. In 1985 he released his first solo album, "Smokin'" (Tom Principato; Powerhouse Records, 1985) and has since recorded and released more than 20 albums as a featured artist. One of his most recent backup bands included bassist Matthew Everhart, singer-keyboardist Tommy Lepson, percussionist Josh Howell and drummer Joe Wells. His most recent album is a collaborative blues effort with singer-guitarist Tom Principato, "The Long Way Home" (Tom Principato & Steve Wolf; Powerhouse Records, 2017).

Through the years Principato has also performed and/or recorded with a number of bands and musicians including: blues guitarist Fred Chapellier; blues singer-pianist Sunnyland Slim; blues singer-harmonicist-guitarist Leadfoot Rivet; R&B singer Big Mama Thornton; and multi-styled guitarist Danny Gatton.

TOMMY AULDRIDGE

Steel guitarist Tommy Auldridge was born in Washington, D.C. and raised in Kensington, Maryland. As a child in the late 1940s he was first exposed to C&W and bluegrass music through his siblings and such local radio stations as WGAY and WDON. As a youngster he liked bands that employed steel guitarists and listened to the songs of Carl Smith, Ray Price, George Morgan, Eddy Arnold and Hank Williams.

During his years at Wheaton High School in the early 1960s Auldridge would often observe the rehearsals of a bluegrass band operated by his brothers Mike and Dave (who also had a bluegrass radio show on local station WDON). In 1967, at the age 24, Auldridge took up the steel guitar and in 1970 he joined the backup band for C&W singer Rita Kinnard who regularly performed at the Loyal Order of Moose Bethesda Lodge No. 1150 in Bethesda, Maryland. His brother Mike, meanwhile, became a founding member of the bluegrass band the Seldom Scene in 1971.

From 1975 to 2007 Auldridge played steel guitar in a C&W band called Pikesville Rye which performed at American Legions, Moose Lodges and VFWs throughout Maryland. In recent years he has also performed with such Maryland C&W artists as singer-guitarist Charlie Montalbano, Hat Creek Country (featuring singer-guitarist Marty Naugle), Mike Harrison and the Rivers Bend Band, Paul Wagner and the Country Swingers, and George Garris and Friends.

Since 2012 Auldridge has been playing steel guitar for the country-pop-rock band the Hall Brothers (Chick Hall Jr. and Chris Hall), a group that also provides the musical backing for "Patsy's Honky Tonk Torch & Twang," a country music extravaganza presented by singer-guitarist Patsy Stephens, who specializes in the songs of Patsy Cline.

TOMMY HAUGHAWOUT

Drummer Tommy Haughawout was raised in the Maryland towns of Colmar Manor and Berwyn Heights and was exposed to music as a youth through his father Frank, who played steel guitar for a number of local C&W bands in the 1950s including Jimmy Dean and the Texas Wildcats. Haughawout would often accompany his father to his band jobs at

Washington, D.C. night clubs like the Starlite Restaurant, as well as the "Town and Country Jamboree" shows at the Joe Turner Arena.

While attending Greenbelt Junior High School in 1960 he drummed for his first band, a rock and roll outfit on the local teen dance circuit called the Rhythm Rockers that included guitarist Chick Hall, Jr.

During his years at Bladensburg High School in the early 1960s Haughawout played with such rock and roll bands as the Majestic Neons (also with Chick Hall, Jr.), and the Jimmy Dee Trio (which also performed as Jimmy "D" and the "D-Lights), a group that performed in Washington, D.C. at such night clubs as Cap'n Guy's, Vinnie's Grill, Rand's Night Club and Benny's Rebel Room; and in Maryland at the Americana (Odenton) and Rose's Musical Bar (North Beach). Haughawout drummed on Dee's 45rpm single record "Dream World" backed with "Jeanie" (Jimmy "D" and the "D"-Lites; Start Records, 1963).

Haughawout spent the late 1960s drumming for numerous other rock and roll bands including: Little Joe and the Impossibles, a group that was fronted by singer-keyboardist Joe Bayliss and performed in Washington, D.C. at the Starlite Restaurant and embarked on night club tours up and down the East Coast; and Take Five, a quintet that included singer Ron MacDonald and guitarist Danny Gatton, and frequently worked at two night clubs in Silver Hill, Maryland, Strick's Restaurant and the Quonset Supper Club.

TOMMY KEENE

Singer-guitarist Tommy Keene was born in Evanston, Illinois and raised in Bethesda, Maryland, where, during his years at Walter Johnson High School in the middle 1970s, he played in such rock and roll bands as Blue Steel and Only After Dark.

In 1977 Keene joined a rock and roll band called the Rage, whose lineup consisted of Keene on lead guitar, lead singer-rhythm guitarist Richard X. Heyman, bassist Ricky Street and drummer Jim Dougherty. The group appeared regularly at the Varsity Grill Back Room in College Park, Maryland, where they were often billed with Razz, one of the Washington, D.C. area's best hard-rocking bands.

In 1978 the members of Razz persuaded Keene to leave the Rage and become a part of their lineup, where he served as a replacement for guitarist Abaad Behram. Following the breakup of Razz in December 1979, Keen relocated to New York City where he worked with new wave rock singer Suzanne Fellini. He appears on her only album, "Suzanne Fellini" (Suzanne Fellini; Casablanca Records, 1980). While in New York, he next played with a rock and roll band called the Pieces.

In 1981 Keene returned to the nation's capital and put together his own rock and roll band, the Tommy Keene Group, with three former Razz members, guitarist Mike Colburn, bassist Ted Niceley and drummer Doug Tull. This band released an EP, "Strange Alliance" (Tommy Keen; Avenue Records, 1982). At that point Colburn was replaced by guitarist Billy Connelly and the new lineup released two albums, "Places That Are Gone" (Tommy Keene; Dolphin Records, 1984), and "Back Again (try...)" (Tommy Keene; Dolphin Records, 1984).

During this period the Tommy Keene Group performed in Washington, D.C. at such night clubs as the Cellar Door, Desperado's, the Bayou, Nightclub 9:30, the Wax Museum, Friendship Station and the Roxy; and in Maryland at the Psyche Delly (Bethesda).

In 1986 Keene signed with Geffen Records and released an album titled "Songs from the Film" (Tommy Keene; Geffen Records, 1986) and a six-song EP titled "Run Now" (Tommy Keene; Geffen Records, 1986). For his 1989 Geffen release, "Based on Happy Times" (Tommy Keene; Geffen Records, 1989), Keene worked with a new backup band, but was subsequently dropped by the label.

In all Keene has more than 20 albums and compilations on various record labels to his credit. Tommy Keene passed away on Wednesday, November 22, 2017 at the age of 59.

TOMMY LEPSON

Singer-keyboardist-guitarist Tommy Lepson grew up in College Park, Maryland, where, during his teen years in the early 1960s at Hyattsville Junior High School, he first sang and played guitar (and then bass) in a rock and roll band on the local teen dance circuit called T.L. and the Barons.

Next, during his time at Northwestern High School in the middle 1960s, Lepson played bass in an R&B-rock band called the Pagans, whose lineup was rounded out by singer James Burris, lead guitarist Jim Cerone, rhythm guitarist Ken Crieser keyboardist Jeff Davidson, saxophonists Alan Jones and Dave Moltrup and drummer Al Davis. The Pagans covered acts such as Wilson Pickett and Paul Revere and the Raiders, and appeared in Maryland at teen dances staged by the Greenbelt Teen Club (Greenbelt Youth Center), the Edmonston Teen Club (Edmonston), the Brentwood Teen Club (Bartlett Park, Wohlfarth Building), the St. Mark the Evangelist Catholic Church Teen Club (Hyattsville) and the St. Jerome Catholic Church Teen Club (Hyattsville).

In the 1970s Lepson played with a succession of Washington, D.C. area rock and roll bands including Natty Bumpo, Renthra, Skids, Tricks, and Midnight Oil. In 1979 he joined a local R&B band called Cryin' Out Loud, whose initial lineup consisted of Lepson handling vocals and keyboards, guitarist Steuart Smith, bassist Bob Coleman, and drummer Steve Dennis. Cryin' Out Loud, which frequently backed singer Root Boy Slim, covered such artists as Marvin Gaye, Al Green and Ray Charles, and played in Washington, D.C. at such night clubs as Mr. Henry's Tenley Circle and Columbia Station.

Throughout the 1980s Lepson sang and played keyboards with several of the region's top acts including the R&B-rock band Jr. Cline and the Recliners, rock and roll singer Root Boy Slim and his various backup bands, and the R&B group the Assassins (featuring guitarist Jimmy Thackery).

In 1982 Lepson became a founding member of an R&B group called Soul Crackers, which has remained active to this day. The band's original lineup consisted of Lepson as singer and frontman, guitarist Paul Bell, bassist Ron Newmyer, keyboardist John Hurd, saxophonist Larry Strother and drummer Chuck Sullivan. The group went through early personnel changes with Hurd being replaced by keyboardist Spencer Hoopes and Sullivan being replaced by drummer Carl Holzapel. Larry Strother passed away in 1996 and the band subsequently added saxophonists Wayne Sulc and Jeremy Schuhmann, and percussionist Cesar Vanegas.

In the early 1980s Soul Crackers often performed at such Washington, D.C. night clubs as Desperado's, the Paul Mall Restaurant, Artie's After Dark, and the Wax Museum. The current edition of the band consists of singer-guitarist Tommy Lepson, guitarist Keith Grimes, bassist Ron Newmyer, keyboardist Spencer Hooes, saxophonist Wayne Sulc, trumpeter Chris Hutton, drummer Chuck Sullivan and percussionist Cesar Vanegas.

A highlight of the Soul Crackers experience was their appearance at President William Clinton's Georgetown University Class of 1968 25th Anniversary party on the White House South Lawn on Saturday, June 5, 1993, where they backed up the Starland Vocal Band. The band has three albums to its credit: "All You Squares Go Home" (Soul Crackers; Crossdog Music, 2003); "30 Years of Soul (Soul Crackers; Crossdog Music, 2011); and "30 Years of Soul Volume 2" (Soul Crackers; Crossdog Music, 2015).

In 1991 Lepson put together his own R&B band, Tommy Lepson and the Lazy Boys, and they remained one of the Washington, D.C. area's most popular groups through 1997. For this musical project he again took on the role of lead singer-keyboardist and called upon three familiar colleagues, guitarist Paul Bell, bassist Ron Newmyer and drummer Chuck Sullivan, to round out the lineup (they were joined by conga player Cesar Vanegas in 1993). The band covered such artists as James Brown, Aretha Franklin, Wilson Pickett, Stevie Ray Vaughan and John Hiatt.

Tommy Lepson and the Lazy Boys were popular in Maryland at such night clubs as the Outta the Way Café (Derwood), Durty Nelly's (Bethesda), Shootz Bar and Billiards (Bethesda) and Tornado Alley (Wheaton); and in Virginia at Whitey's (Arlington), Bad Habits (Arlington), and Nick's (Alexandria). The band has two albums to its credit: "Live & Durty" (Tommy Lepson & the Lazy Boys; Big Mo Records, 1995); and "Ready For This??!!!???" (Tommy Lepson and the Lazy Boys; Big Mo Records, 1996).

In 1997 Lepson reorganized the musicians he worked with and called his new R&B congregation the Tommy Lepson Band (in recent years he has also performed under the name the Tommy Lepson Group). The original lineup of this act consisted of Lepson handling lead vocals, guitar and keyboards, guitarist Paul Bell, bassist Wade Matthews, drummer Gary Crockett and percussionist Cesar Vanegas. Musicians to later pass through the operation included bassists Jay Turner and Spencer Leckliter, and drummers Steve Lozier and El Toro Gamble.

The Tommy Lepson Band's most recent lineup consisted of Lepson, guitarist John Bell, bassist Mike Davis and drummer Gary Crockett. The group has three albums to its credit: "AM 53" (Tommy Lepson Band; Powerhouse Records, 2002); "Live at Sweet Carolines" (Tommy Lepson Band; Powerhouse Records, 2006); and "Putty and Paint" (Tommy Lepson Band; Powerhouse Records, 2009).

Through the years Lepson has also performed with an array of local and national musical performers including: multi-styled guitarist Danny Gatton; the blues bands the Nighthawks and Blueheart Revival; blues singer-guitarist Duke Robillard; blues singer-harmonicists Jerry Portnoy and Kim Wilson (of the Thunderbirds); blues singer-guitarist Tom Principato; blues singer-keyboardist Johnny Neel; blues rock singer Bonnie Bramlett (formerly of Delaney and Bonnie); the folk music duo of singer-guitarist-banjoist Cathy Fink and guitarist-mandolinist Marcy Marxer; the R&B band the Soul Serenaders; rock and roll singer-guitarist Nils Lofgren; and rock and roll guitarist Skunk Baxter.

Tommy Lepson continues to perform as a singer-keyboardist throughout the Washington, D.C. area. Among his current projects are working onstage for tributes and memorials administered by BandHouse Gigs (a not-for-profit entity whose mission is to promote local music through unique, one-of-a-kind concerts), and playing in such local R&B outfits as the Dave Chappell Band, East Coast Sound, and Urban Funk. He also continues to make occasional appearances with his long-running band, Soul Crackers.

TOMMY PANELLA

Drummer Tommy Panella grew up in the Anacostia neighborhood of Southeast Washington, D.C. At the age of 12 in 1964 he saw the Beatles perform their first United States concert at the Washington Coliseum and subsequently joined his first rock and roll band, the Tomcats. The group performed British Invasion songs at local teen dances and were a featured attraction at the St. Teresa of Avila Catholic Church Teen Club in his Southeast neighborhood. Later on, after a change in name, the Tomcats became the Quarrymen.

In the late 1960s, while attending St. John's College High School, Panella joined one of the area's more popular rock and roll bands, the Magic Reign. The group played the local teen dance scene, worked night club engagements, and opened concerts for visiting national acts at venues such as the Wheaton Youth Center, the Alexandria Arena and Shady Grove Music Fair. In the early 1970s Panella put together a new version of the Magic Reign, which, for several years, held down house band duties at Some Place Else, a night club in the Southeast quadrant of Washington, D.C.

Panella moved to California in the 1980s and has since drummed for such national R&B performers as singer Percy Sledge, the L.A. Band, the Temptations, the Drifters and Bobby Day and the Hollywood Flames.

TONY DENIKOS

Singer-guitarist Tony Denikos was born in Washington, D.C. and raised in Laurel, Maryland where he began singing folk songs in grade school at local fairs and school functions. He took up guitar at the age of 14, was largely self-taught, and championed the music of Ray Charles, Louie Jordan, Roger Miller, the Beatles, the Animals, the Grass Roots and John Prine, among others. He initially played bass with several local rock and roll bands in the middle 1970s.

Late in the decade while attending Laurel High School Denikos was a member of the hard-rocking band Hat Trick, which covered such artists as the Jimi Hendrix Experience and Robin Trower and performed at area dances, parties, and Laurel night clubs such as the Turf Club and Nuzback's Bar.

After spending a summer performing as a solo folk rock singer-guitarist at a night club called Close Quarters in Virginia Beach, Denikos returned to the Washington, D.C. area and spent the 1980s and 1990s headlining night clubs throughout the region as a solo artist (often performing as "Tony De"). Mixing original material with covers of such artists as Neil Young, Creedence Clearwater Revival, Bruce Springsteen and John Prine, he appeared at venues from Washington, D.C. to Baltimore to Annapolis, and all points in between.

In recent years Tony Denikos and the Working Poor, as the group is now billed, has regularly headlined at such Maryland night clubs as the Music Café (Damascus), the Arts Barn (Gaithersburg), the Blue Side Tavern (Frederick) and the Cat's Eye Pub (Baltimore). Some of the area's top musicians have worked in Denikos' combos, with his regular lineup being rounded out by guitarist Gantt Kushner, bassist Mark Riddle and drummer Rick Weisenmiller.

Denikos has four country rock albums to his credit: "Naked & Smiling" (Tony De; Tony Denikos Music, 1999); "Time Tells Tales" (Tony Denikos; Tony Denikos, 2003); "Already Gone" (Tony Denikos; Tony Denikos, 2009); and "Under the Church" (Tony Denikos; Tony Denikos, 2012).

TONY GRASSO

Singer-guitarist Tony Grasso grew up in Oxon Hill, Maryland, and, during his years at Crossland High School in the middle 1960s, he first played the local teen dance circuit in a rock and roll band called the Castells. Next up he sang and played guitar in a harder-edged rock and roll group called the Rubber Band, which performed at such Washington, D.C. night clubs as Some Place Else and Benny's Rebel Room.

In the late 1960s Grasso was a founding member of Puzzle, the psychedelic rock and roll trio whose initial lineup was completed by bassist Curt Jonnie and drummer Mike Zack. Puzzle was based in Georgetown, performed at night clubs such as the Keg, the Silver Dollar and the Crazy Horse, and released an album on ABC Records. The band endured several changes in personnel, but Grasso remained a member until its demise in late 1969.

Grasso went on to spend much of the 1970s playing lead guitar for Gravity, a Washington, D.C. rock and roll band that, like Puzzle, appeared regularly at the Keg and the Crazy Horse.

Late in the 1970s Grasso ventured to Denver, Colorado where he played in a reorganized version of the Dubonnettes with Charlie Pearson and Gary St. Clair. He then returned to the Washington, D.C. area where he sang and played guitar in the Pieces, a rock and roll trio whose lineup at that time was rounded out by singer-keyboardist Jimmy

Nalley and drummer Joe Reckert. Tony Grasso passed away on September 6, 1984 at the age of 36.

TONY JORDAN

Saxophonist Tont Jordan was born in New York City and raised in the Hollin Hills neighborhood of Alexandria, Virginia. During his high school years at the Hawthorne School in Washington, D.C. in the middle 1960s he first performed in a McLean, Virginia-based rock and roll band called the Jazz Masters, which mainly concentrated on surf music and covered such artists as the Beach Boys and Duane Eddy.

In the late 1960s Jordan attended Colby College in Maine and then earned a Bachelor of Arts in music from Goddard College in Vermont. He spent the summer of 1970 studying at the Berklee College of Music in Boston. Upon returning to the Washington, D.C. area he took classes at Federal City College, where he also played in the Federal City College Jazz Ensemble.

Jordan spent the early 1970s playing saxophone in such area rock and roll bands as Sacred Heart, Matthews Drive, and John St. John and the Bandits. Among the local bands he performed with in the late 1970s and early 1980s were an R&B group called Mixed Breed and a pop band called Classic.

From the early 1970s to the late 1980s Jordan played saxophone in a local big band jazz outfit called the Tom Cunningham Orchestra. In the 1990s he played in a Latin music outfit called Glenn Crockwell and the World Community Orchestra that was based out of the Anacostia neighborhood of Southeast Washington, D.C. He was also a member of the Mount Vernon Swing Orchestra from 1998 to 2009.

In recent years Jordan has played saxophone with several different Washington, D.C. area bands. From 2006 to 2014 he was part of the Annandale Saxophone Ensemble, a jazzy, multi-styled pop music act which at times included up to five saxophones and a rhythm section.

Since 2009 Jordan has played with the Bob Gibson Big Band; since 2012 he has been a member of the Big Band Tradition; since 2013 he has played saxophone in an R&B group called the Java Kings with the Caffeines; and since 2014 he has been a part of a jazz band known as the Dukes of Rhythm.

TRACTOR

Tractor was a rock and roll band that emerged in the nation's capital in 1969 with its first lineup consisting of singer-keyboardist Billy Manning, singer-guitarist Ron Culbertson, bassist Jack Brooks and drummer Michael "Pokey" Walls. The group originally lived together on a farm in Catlett, Virginia and attempted to move beyond the Washington, D.C. area music scene, performing at such New York City venues as the Electric Circus and the Fillmore East. The band emphasized original material and conducted recording sessions in Philadelphia, Pennsylvania for Janus Records, though the finished album was never released.

Tractor experienced several personnel changes along the way, with singer Gene Johnson joining the band, Walls being replaced by drummer Steve Lacey, and Manning eventually being replaced by keyboardist Randy Hart. When appearing in Washington, D.C., the band performed at such night clubs as Emergency, the Keg, the Crazy Horse and My Mother's Place.

Tractor participated in several local concert shows including: opening for Canned Heat and the Youngbloods at Merriweather Post Pavilion (Columbia, Maryland) on Saturday, September 27, 1969; opening for Arlo Guthrie and Mountain at McDonough Gymnasium (Georgetown University) on Friday, October 10, 1969; opening for the Byrds at T.C.

Williams High School (Alexandria, Virginia) on Saturday, March 7, 1970; opening for Bo Diddley at the Ark (Alexandria, Virginia) from Friday, June 5 to Sunday, June 7, 1970; headlining at Bishop McNamara High School (Forestville, Maryland) on Friday, February 5, 1971; sharing a triple bill with Crank and the New Breed at Our Lady of Good Counsel High School (Wheaton, Maryland) on Friday, February 26, 1971; and sharing a double bill with Crank at Robert E. Lee High School (Springfield, Virginia) on Saturday, December 9, 1972.

Tractor's reign in the Washington, D.C. area came to an end when Culbertson, Brooks, Hart and Lacey relocated to Los Angeles, California in October 1973. There, they continued playing for several years under the name Pony Express.

THE TRIUMPHS

The Triumphs were a teen rock and roll band that formed in the Tenleytown neighborhood of Washington, D.C. in 1958 and consisted of guitarists Jack Casady and Jorma Kaukonen, bassist Mike Hunnicutt and singer-drummer Ron MacDonald. The group performed on the local teen dance circuit and shortly after forming worked its first night club dates at a rough-and-tumble establishment called the Rendezvous in the Downtown area of the city.

Casady, only 14 years old at the time, would later switch to bass guitar and went on to work in night clubs all over Washington, D.C. with such rock and roll bands as the Off Beats and the Medallions, and groups fronted by such musicians as C&W singer-guitarist Dick Williams and rock and roll singer-keyboardist-guitarist Bobbie "The Kid" Howard.

Jorma Kaukonen, who moved to the West Coast in the early 1960s, invited Casady to San Francisco and recruited him into Jefferson Airplane in 1965. The band was inducted into the Rock and Roll Hall of Fame in the "Performers" category on Wednesday, January 17, 1996. Casady and Kaukonen continue to work together today in the blues rock band Hot Tuna.

TUESDAY BOOTS

Tuesday Boots was a rock and roll band based in Clinton, Maryland that formed in October 1965 and was a popular attraction on the local teen dance circuit and in area night clubs. The group's best-known early lineup consisted of five Surrattsville High School students: singer-lead guitarist Ron Barkley, rhythm guitarist Ron Lilly, bassist Russ Barkley, keyboardist Bruce MacPherson and drummer Jerry Barkley. Having evolved from an earlier band called the Cavaliers, Tuesday Boots was noted for its polished musical performances and impressive, authoritative stage presence. Early on they appeared in matching white suits, paisley ascots, Beatles boots, and often previewed hit songs like "Revolution" before they had debuted on local radio.

The original version of Tuesday Boots covered songs by such bands as the Beach Boys, Paul Revere and the Raiders, the Beatles, the Rolling Stones, the Byrds, the Animals, the Beau Brummels, the Dave Clark Five, the Kinks, and other popular bands from the late 1960s. Later versions of the band changed with the musical trends and performed the material of groups such as the Jimi Hendrix Experience, Cream, Led Zeppelin and Buffalo Springfield, along with the R&B hits of James Brown, Wilson Pickett, and Sam and Dave.

From 1965 to 1967 Tuesday Boots performed in Maryland at teen dances staged by the Surrattsville Junior Teen Club (Surrattsville Junior High School in Clinton), the Surrattsville Senior Teen Club (Surrattsville High School in Clinton), Crossland High School (Camp Springs), the Roger B. Taney Teen Club (Roger B. Taney Junior High School in Temple Hills), the Church of Jesus Christ of Latter-day Saints (Camp Springs), Tantallon Country Club (Fort Washington), the Clinton Volunteer Fire Department (Clinton), the Silver Hill

Volunteer Fire Department (Suitland), and various military base teen clubs including the Andrews Air Force Base Teen Club (Prince George's County, Maryland).

Tuesday Boots also appeared on the local television show "Wing Ding" in 1966 where they performed a version of the song "Dirty Water" by the Standells. The band matured and entered into the Washington, D.C. night club world where they worked such establishments as the French Quarter, the Corral, the Crazy Horse, the Silver Dollar, the Keg and the Cellar Door.

In the late 1960s Tuesday Boots experienced changes in personnel. One edition saw Ron Lilly and Jerry Barkley reform the operation as a quartet with two former members of the popular teen band Nobody's Children, lead singer-guitarist Dennis Boone and bassist Jan Zukowski. Another version of the band consisted of lead singer John Jarvis, guitarist Scott Thompson, Ron Lilly (now on bass), keyboardist Doug Gwen and drummer Jerry Barkley (who was later replaced by Bob Venables). In its final days, Tuesday Boots relocated to Boston, Massachusetts, but disbanded in 1970.

URBAN VERBS

Urban Verbs formed in the late 1970s and became an integral part of what was then a developing scene that brought art and rock and roll together in Washington, D.C. The band consisted of lead singer Roddy Frantz, guitarist Robert Goldstein, bassist Linda France, keyboardist Robin Rose and drummer Danny Frankel. Offering music that sounded like a mix of the Doors and the Talking Heads, the group held its first performance at an art party in a loft above the Ben Bow Restaurant near Dupont Circle.

Urban Verbs performed in Washington, D.C. at such night clubs as the Atlantis, D.C. Space, Nightclub 9:30, the Childe Harold, the Bayou, and the Cellar Door. They also headlined concerts in the city at the Ontario Theatre, the Washington Project for the Arts, the Pension Building, and the Corcoran School of Art.

Urban Verbs recorded for a major record label and released two albums: "Urban Verbs" (Urban Verbs; Warner Bros. Records, 1980); and "Early Damage" (Urban Verbs; Warner Bros. Records, 1981). After the second album was released, Rose and France left the band, and bassist Billy Swann, formerly of the Muffins, was added. The group continued on as a quartet until its farewell show on Friday, October 29, 1982 at Nightclub 9:30.

THE VELOURS

The rock and roll band known as the Velours hailed from Kensington, Maryland and was a hot commodity on the local teen dance circuit from 1965 to 1966. The group began as a trio with a lineup of lead singer-bassist Eric Wilfong (Harker Preparatory School, Class of 1966), lead guitarist Eddie Becker (Walter Johnson High School, Class of 1966) and drummer Mark McInturff (Bethesda-Chevy Chase High School, Class of 1965). During its first year the band featured songs by Roy Orbison, the Kingsmen, the Kinks, the Beatles, the Rolling Stones, the Zombies, Chuck Berry and Bo Diddley.

In 1966 the Velours added a three-man horn section of trumpeter Bob Metz, trombonist Roger Newman and saxophonist Rick Wald (a later addition was saxophonist Jerry Freed). With the added instrumentation came a shift towards the R&B style of Otis Redding, Wilson Pickett, Bobby Byrd, the Drifters, the Coasters, Marvin Gaye, and Alvin Cash and the Crawlers. In addition, a full rendition of James Brown's classic album, "The Apollo Theatre Presents – In Person! The James Brown Show" (James Brown; King Records, 1963), becoming one of the group's featured live performance offerings.

The Velours performed in Maryland at teen dances staged by the Holy Redeemer Catholic Church Teen Club (Kensington), Stone Ridge School of the Sacred Heart

(Bethesda), and the Bethesda Youth Center (Bethesda). They also appeared at the Red Fox Inn, a long-standing night club in Bethesda, Maryland.

This original version of the Velours disbanded after Becker and Wilfong graduated from high school in 1966. The group's reputation was so strong another band of entirely different musicians appropriated their name a year later and remained active on the same circuit into the early 1970s.

VINCE SANTORO

Drummer Vince Santoro was raised in Alexandria, Virginia and took up the drums as a teen in the middle 1960s. During his time at T.C. Williams in the late 1960s he drummed on the local teen dance scene for such rock and roll bands as the Centers of Sound and Phoenix. In the early 1970s he worked with a succession of top local rock and roll bands including Navel, Starr, Glad Bag (with singer-keyboardist Larry Kidwell), Liberation, and Sinbad (known for their extended engagements at the Bayou in Georgetown).

Santoro went on to perform and/or record with an impressive array of popular music talent. Among the C&W artists he has worked with include singers Roseanne Cash, Shania Twain, Claudia Church, Jameson Clark, Jon Christopher Davis and Charlie Louvin; singer-guitarists Declan McGarry, Mary Chapin Carpenter, Rodney Crowell, Lari White, Josie Kuhn, Carlene Carter, G.B. Leighton, Jim Lauderdale and Hal Ketchum; and singer-pianist Annie Simms.

Musicians of other styles Santoro has drummed for include: blues rock singer Kathi McDonald; blues rock guitarist Roy Buchanan; blues rock singer-keyboardist Johnny Neel; the C&W super-group the Highwaymen (consisting of Kris Kristofferson, Johnny Cash, Waylon Jennings and Willie Nelson); the country rock groups the Nitty Gritty Dirt Band and the Cicadas (a band featuring Rodney Crowell); folk singer-guitarists Melissa Crabtree, Cheryl Wheeler, John Gorka, John Prine and Michael Reno Harrell; the folk-rock duo the Kennedys (Pete and Maura); pop singer Joe Croker; pop singer-guitarists Ashley Cleveland, Kristy Jackson and Vaughan Penn; pop singer-guitarist-harmonicist Julian Dawson; the pop-rock band Air Parma; rock and roll singer-guitarists John Palumbo and Todd Sharp; and rock and roll singer-keyboardist-saxophonist Edgar Winter. He is currently drumming for the rock and roll band Felix Cavaliere's Rascals.

VINCE VIGLIOTTI

Singer-guitarist Vince Vigliotti was born in Fort Meade, Maryland and mainly raised in Laurel, Maryland. He taught himself guitar as a teen and listened to such artists as Rory Gallagher, Johnny Winter, Wishbone Ash and Thin Lizzy. During his years at Laurel High School in the middle 1970s he played in a rock and roll band called Nimbus.

Through the years Vigliotti has played guitar in a number of top local rock and roll bands. In the 1970s he was in the band Shotel; in the 1980s he played in a band called Rave; and in the late 1980s and in early 1990s he worked in a multi-styled wedding band called Nightwatch. He went on to work with such acts as the punk rock band Date Bait and an R&B group called the Daryl Davis Band.

In 2007 Vigliotti formed a classic R&B-rock band called the 8 Balls. The group's original lineup consisted of lead singer Kathy Marr, singer-guitarist Vince Vigliotti, bassist Rick Norris, singer-keyboardist Mark Weaver and drummer Douglas Workman. The band is still together today with a lineup of Vigliotti, Weaver, Workman, bassist Erik Marks and singer Elle Christine Rubidoux. They currently perform in Maryland at such establishments as the New Deal Café (Greenbelt), Sullivan's Steak and Beverage Company (Laurel), and the American Legion Laurel Post 60 (Laurel).

WADE MATTHEWS

Bassist Wade Matthews was raised in Bethesda, Maryland and during his years at Rockville High School in the early 1970s he played in the rock and roll bands Stark Naked and the Cat Thieves, both of which covered such contemporary acts as Alice Cooper, Grand Funk Railroad, the Doors and the Rolling Stones.

Matthews worked with a number of bands and musicians throughout the 1970s including: folk-pop singer-guitarist Jonathan Edwards; jazz saxophonist Chris Vadala; the jazz rock group Tim Eyermann and East Coast Offering; the rock and roll band Fancy Colors; and the R&B band Bill Holland and Rent's Due.

Matthews went on to work with a variety of local and nationally known performing artists including: blues bands the Assassins, and the Mary Shaver Band; blues singer-saxophonist-pianist Deanna Bogart; blues rock singer-guitarist Tom Principato; C&W singer-guitarist Mary Chapin Carpenter; the folk duos Cathy Fink and Marcy Marxer, and the Kennedys; the jazz act the Gene Donati Orchestra; R&B singer-guitarist Lee Atwater; R&B band Tommy Lepson and the Lazy Boys; and rock and roll singer-guitarist Nils Lofgren. Wade Matthews passed away on Thursday, August 18, 2005 at the age of 50.

WADE RICHARDS

Wade Richards grew up in Clinton, Maryland where he started on the drums at age 12, inspired by such rock and roll groups as Steppenwolf, and, in the ensuing years, Grand Funk Railroad, Deep Purple and Led Zeppelin. In the early 1970s while attending Surrattsville Junior High School he began attending their weekend teen club dances and was particularly impressed with a rock and roll band he saw perform there called Trestle. In 1971, while in the ninth grade, he became the drummer for a hard-rocking trio called Deaf Mute, which performed Grand Funk Railroad and Creedence Clearwater Revival covers on the local teen dance circuit.

In the early 1970s while attending Surrattsville High School, Richards first drummed for a local rock and roll band called Scar before joining Sassafras Tea, another local rock and roll group that performed on the Washington, D.C. area teen dance circuit.

In the spring of 1974 Richards was recruited into the Clinton-based rock and roll band Starz, which at the time also included singer Ken Taylor, guitarists David Simmons and Jeff Avery, and bassist Henry Farmer. He remained with the band until September 1977, during which time they appeared at local teen clubs, as well as being a regularly featured at the night club Some Place Else in Southeast Washington, D.C. When Richards departed, Starz regrouped, changed its name to D.C. Star, and went on to enjoy tremendous success in the nation's capital, Baltimore, and up and down the East Coast.

Richards remained active on the local music scene throughout the late 1970s and early 1980s. He drummed for several bands during those years including two top rock and roll acts – Magnum, which often performed at the Keg in Washington, D.C. in 1979, and the Boyz, which during his 1980-1983 stint appeared in Maryland at such night clubs as the Outside Inn (Rockville), the Paragon (College Park), Jimmy Comber's Restaurant (Hyattsville) and the Riverside Inn (Riverdale); and in Virginia at the Fancy Dancer (Alexandria) and the Wild West (Springfield).

WALLY COOK

Guitarist Wally Cook grew up in the Prince George's County, Maryland communities of Oxon Hill and Hillcrest Heights where he began teaching himself guitar at the age of eight and was exposed to C&W music through his parents, who would take him to the Sunnybrook Tavern to see such artists as Jimmy Dean, Roy Clark and Patsy Cline perform live.

During his years at Benjamin Stoddert Junior High School in the early 1960s Cook played guitar in the rock and roll band Herbie and the Originals. Later, in the middle 1960s while attending Crossland High School, he played in another rock and roll band, this one called the Young Rabbits, who performed on the Georgetown night club scene.

In the fall of 1965 Cook became a founding member of a Georgetown-based folk rock band called the Disciples, which, within the span of a couple weeks, changed its name to the Uncalled Four. Shortly thereafter another name change ensued and the group became the Fallen Angels. This outfit eventually became one of the Washington, D.C. area's most popular rock and roll attractions. Cook remained with the Fallen Angels through 1969 and was also a part of a reconstituted version of the group put together by Billy Hancock in 1970.

Cook played with a number of Washington, D.C. area rock and roll bands in the 1970s including Love and Trust, Truckin', the Daylight Band and the Longbranch Band. He also played guitar in a C&W act called the Campbell Brothers, which held down house band duties at the Village Barn in Morningside, Maryland.

In the 1980s Cook stayed with country music and worked with such acts as the Carolina Band, the Gambler Band, and singers Danny Denver and Benny Dean. More recently, he has played guitar for the C&W band Seminole and a rock and roll group called the BackBeat Band.

WAYNE TOMLINSON

Multi-instrumentalist (guitar, bass, drums) Wayne Tomlinson grew up in Landover Hills, Maryland, and, learning from his percussionist father, began drumming before he could walk. When the Beatles hit America he picked up a friend's guitar and basically taught himself to play. As a teenager he became a fan of Jimi Hendrix and spent all his free time making music.

During his time at Glenridge Junior High School in the late 1960s Tomlinson first played guitar in the New Colonial Blues Band, a blues rock band that performed on the local teen dance scene. While attending Bladensburg High School in the early 1970s he played guitar in the rock groups Bosco Pie and Green Eggs, the latter of which was one of the area's more popular hard-rocking bands. He followed that experience with a stint in the Cherry People in 1973, a top local rock and roll band that was a featured attraction at the Keg in Washington, D.C. at the time.

Tomlinson went on to perform (mainly on guitar) with an impressive assortment of rock and roll bands in the ensuing years including Chesapeake, Sky High, Sauce, Pieces, Fast Eddie, the JP New Band, the Paul Reed Smith Band, Root Boy Slim (and his various backup groups from 1985-1993), Jr. Cline and the Recliners, Violet Says, and innumerable others.

In 1993 Tomlinson began working as an assembly line worker for PRS Guitars, a position he held for more than 20 years. Wayne Tomlinson passed away on Sunday, July 17, 2016 at the age of 61.

WHITEWATER

In the early 1970s a country rock band called the Don Revetta Trio held down house band duties at a restaurant called the Cock & Bull Inn on King Street in Alexandria, Virginia. The band's lineup originally consisted of singer-guitarist Don Revetta, bassist Chip Galeano and drummer John Bohonis. Throughout the middle 1970s musicians came and went and the group performed at parties and local bars under various names, most often appearing as the Don Revetta Group.

In 1977 the Don Revetta Group changed its name to Whitewater, with the initial lineup consisting of singer-guitarist Don Revetta, guitarist Mike Armstrong, guitarist Ted Seely, bassist Chip Galeano and drummer Keith Kendricks. At this time the band moved its base of operations to Suitland, Maryland, where Chip Galeano had been raised. They rehearsed in a studio they called Pexwater Sound in a small building adjacent to a house owned by Galeano's grandmother at 5501 Shadyside Avenue in Suitland (the rock band Aspex, which included Chip's brother Vince on drums, also rehearsed in the studio). The band then experienced a series of personnel changes, with Kendricks being replaced by drummer Ed Orendorff, who, in turn, was replaced by Gary Smith. A lead singer named Laurie Hyde was also added to the group.

In 1979 Whitewater regrouped and kicked into overdrive with a lineup of rhythm singer-guitarist Don Revetta, guitarist Mike Armstrong, guitarist Ted Seely, bassist Chip Galeano, pianist Ric Provanzano and drummer Vince Galeano. By this time the band was mixing original compositions with covers of songs by such artists as Merle Haggard, Waylon Jennings, Willie Nelson, the Allman Brothers Band, the Doobie Brothers and others.

Whitewater, which at times was also advertised in the local media as "Whitewater Band" and "The D.J. Whitewater Band," initially worked as the house band at a bar called El Brookman's on Pennsylvania Avenue SE in Washington, D.C. In their time they also appeared in the city at such night clubs as Mr. Henry's Tenley Circle, the Far Inn, Desperado's and Annie Oakley's Saloon; in Maryland at the Big Dipper (Beltsville), the Big Apple (Hyattsville), Billy Jacks (Oxon Hill) and the Cross Roads (Bladensburg); and in Virginia at Quincy's (Arlington), Eskimo Nell's (Arlington), Beacon's Backstage (Falls Church), the Annandale Grill (Annandale) and Louie's Rock City (Bailey's Crossroads). They also performed shows and concerts from New York to Ohio to Florida.

In the early 1980s Whitewater performed at the Lone Star Café in New York City three nights a week for the better part of two years, headlining on their own, as well as opening for such major acts as Johnny Paycheck, and Kinky Friedman and the Texas Jewboys. One time while performing at the Lone Star Café singer-guitarist Willie Nelson came in and worked a 90-minute set with the band, then, after a break, spent another 45 minutes onstage playing music with them. Another country music legend, fiddler Vassar Clemmons, also performed onstage with the band at the Lone Star Café.

A highlight in Whitewater's career was when they opened for Peter Frampton at Merriweather Post Pavilion in Columbia, Maryland on Friday, September 4, 1981 (advertised in local ads as "The D.J. Whitewater Band"). Whitewater remained a popular attraction on the Washington, D.C. area music scene until its disbandment in 1983.

WILD HONEY

In the late 1960s the night clubs of Georgetown hosted a plethora of hard-rocking, psychedelic-tinged bands that would suddenly emerge on the scene and then abruptly disappear. One such band that built a fast following but failed to stick around long enough to attract attention from the national record labels was Wild Honey, which holds the distinction of being the first Georgetown-based rock and roll band to be banned from performing in the neighborhood on the night of its very first gig due a legal conflict with a rival group.

Wild Honey formed in November 1967 with an original lineup of singer-keyboardist Billy Manning, guitarist Jimmy Carter, bassist Curt Jonnie and drummer Mike Zack. In what would have been its first Georgetown night club engagement, the band was initially booked into the Hurricane, which had formerly been in operation as the Roundtable at 2813 M Street NW. However, on opening night at the night club, local law enforcement officials descended upon the premises and prevented the band from taking the stage. The reason for the shutdown was that guitarist Jimmy Carter had an injunction filed against him by the Telstars (his previous band) that prevented him from performing in any other band in the Georgetown area for one full year.

Unable to perform at the Roundtable, Wild Honey switched operations to a night club across the city called the Go-Go 007, a psychedelic venue located at 1330 New York Avenue NW, just down the street from the Rocket Room and across from the Famous Restaurant. They based out of the Go-Go 007 for several months into 1968.

Wild Honey also participated in several local concert shows including opening for Vanilla Fudge at the Alexandria Arena (Alexandria, Virginia) on Sunday, April 21, 1968, an event that also included performances by Ultimate Spinach, the British Walkers, the Curfews and the Magic Reign. The band then spent the spring and summer months performing in Washington, D.C. at such night clubs as Benny's Rebel Room, the Rocket Room and the Scene.

During its run Wild Honey experienced changes in personnel, with its final lineup consisting of holdovers Manning and Carter, bassist Doug Farwig and drummer Mike "Pokey" Walls. The group disbanded in August 1968.

THE WINSTONS

The Winstons were a racially-mixed R&B band that formed in Washington, D.C. in early 1968 and lasted until November 1969. The band's most popular lineup consisted of lead singer-saxophonist Richard Spencer, guitarist Quincy Mattison, bassist Sonny Pekerol, singer-keyboardist Phil Tolotta, saxophonist Ray Maritano and drummer Greg Coleman. An early member of the band was singer-bassist Chuck Bennett.

The Winstons released several 45rpm single records on different labels during their short-lived career, including the popular hit "Color Him Father" (The Winstons; Metromedia Records, 1969), which peaked at number seven on Billboard magazine's "Billboard Hot 100" popular music chart on Saturday, July 19, 1969.

For several months the Winstons served as the onstage backup band for Curtis Mayfield and the Impressions. As headliners, they embarked on regional concert tours from Illinois to Florida and performed at such esteemed venues as the Apollo Theatre in New York City. Locally, the Winstons worked in Washington, D.C. at such night clubs as the Rocket Room, Rand's Night Club and the Hayloft.

WOLF CRESCENZE

Bassist Steve "Wolf" Crescenze was born in Washington, D.C. and grew up in a home that once stood on Walker Mill Road in what was then Seat Pleasant, Maryland (in recent years the mailing address of this property has been changed to Capitol Heights). He began playing bass in 1963 and during his years at Francis Scott Key Junior High School and Roger B. Taney Junior High School in the middle 1960s he first played in a local British Invasion rock and roll band called the Inside Outs.

During his senior year at Crossland High School Crescenze joined a Fort Washington-based rock and roll band called Sassafras Tea and served as its bass player from 1967 to 1970. At that point in time the band's lineup was rounded out by singer-lead guitarist Dave Olson, singer-rhythm guitarist Pat Packett and singer-drummer Stevie Packett, and they covered such artists as the Animals, the Beatles, Cream, the Doors and the Rolling Stones.

Sassafras Tea performed in Maryland at teen dances staged by the John Hanson Teen Club (John Hanson Junior High School in Oxon Hill), the Roger B. Taney Teen Club (Roger B. Taney Junior High School in Temple Hills), the Surrattsville Junior Teen Club (Surrattsville Junior High School in Clinton), and VFW Scott-Johnson-Pollins Post 9619 (Morningside); and in Washington, D.C. at such night clubs as the Rabbit's Foot and Some

Place Else. The band also spent the summer of 1968 performing in Virginia at night clubs called the Lighthouse in both Norfolk and Portsmouth.

Crescenze went on to earn bachelor's and master's degrees in industrial arts education from the University of Maryland and taught in his field at John Hanson Middle School in Charles County, Maryland for 32 years, retiring in 2004. After leaving Sassafras Tea in 1970 he left the local music scene and mainly concentrated on his teaching career.

In 2002 Crescenze returned to music and began participating in blues jams at night clubs throughout the Washington, D.C. area. From 2002 to 2004 he played bass in several bands including a blues rock group called Doctor Move and the Rocket Locomotive and a blues band called One Bad Jack. In 2004 he started a weekly blues jam at a night club called the Beach Cove in North Beach, Maryland that endured for nine years. Other area establishments where he has hosted blues jam in recent times include Bangkok Blues (Falls Church), Fat Boys Country Store (Leonardtown), JV's Restaurant (Falls Church), Old Bowie Towne Grill (Bowie) and Blair's Londontowne Pub and Grill (Edgewater).

During the last decade Crescenze has played bass for a number of blues acts in the Washington, D.C. area including the Acme Blues Company, the Idle Americans, Hot Rods and Old Gas, and Over the Limit. He is currently performing with such local blues groups as Still Standing (singer-guitarist Linwood Taylor, bassist Wolfe Crescenze and drummer Mike O'Donnell or Scott Rabino) and Along for the Ride (singer-guitarist Mike Pappas, bassist Wolf Crescenze and drummer Andy Hamburger; plus special guests). Since 2009 he has been a permanent member of the blues group the Big Boy Little Band (singer-harmonicist Bret "Big Boy Little" Littlehales, guitarist Steve Jacobs, bassist Wolf Crescenze and drummer Andy Hamburger).

Through the years, Wolf Crescenze has performed with such blues musicians as: the Skyla Burrell Band; singers Ruby Hayes and Nadine Rae; singer-harmonicists Steve Guyger and Mark Wenner; singer-guitarists Tab Benoit, Linwood Taylor and Andy Poxon; guitarists Guitar Shorty, Zac Harmon, Memphis Gold, Matt Kelley, Zach Sweeney and Clarence Turner; and singer-pianist Pinetop Perkins. Musicians of other styles he has worked with include: pop singer Paul Pfau; R&B singer-keyboardist-guitarist Daryl Davis; R&B harmonicist Frederic Yonnet; rock and roll singer-guitarist Lisa Lim; and rock and roll guitarist Tom Maxwell.

PART FOUR
ACKNOWLEDGMENTS AND SOURCES

ACKNOWLEDGMENTS

I would like to thank music historians Art Wray, Bob Embrey and Jeff Krulik for the extensive amount of information they contributed to this project. I would also like to extend my appreciation to the hundreds of musicians, music fans and music researchers who provided material used in this manuscript.

SOURCES

Books (Selected Bibliography):

Alan Virta. Prince George's County: A Pictorial History (Virginia Beach: The Donning Company/Publishers, 1984).

Ben W. Gilbert and the Staff of the Washington Post. Ten Blocks from the White House: Anatomy of the Washington Riots of 1968 (New York: Frederick A. Praeger, Publishers, 1968).

Benson J. Lossing (editor). The Diary of George Washington, from 1789 to 1791 (Richmond: Press of the Historical Society, 1861).

Billy Poore: RockABilly: A Forty-Year Journey (Milwaukee: Hal Leonard Corporation, 1998).

Bob Seymore. The End: The Death of Jim Morrison (London: Omnibus Press, 1990).

Carl Belz. The Story of Rock (New York: Oxford University Press, 1969).

Charlie Gillett. The Sound of the City (New York: Outerbridge & Dienstfrey, 1970).

Constance McLaughlin Green. Washington: A History of the Capital, 1800-1950 (Princeton: Princeton University Press, 1962).

Cynthia Connolly, Leslie Clague, and Sharon Cheslow (compilers). Banned in DC (Washington, D.C.: Sun Dog Propaganda, 1989).

Dorothy and Thomas Hoobler. Captain John Smith: Jamestown and the Birth of the American Dream. (Hoboken: John Wiley & Sons, Inc., 2006).

Doug Sundling. The Doors: A Guide (London: Sanctuary Publishing Limited, 2000).

Ellis Nassour. Honky Tonk Angel: The Intimate Story of Patsy Cline (Chicago: Chicago Review Press, Incorporated, 2008).

F.L. Brockett and Geo. W. Rock. A Concise History of the City of Alexandria, Va., from 1669 to 1883 with a Directory of Reliable Business Houses in the City (Alexandria: Gazette Book and Job Office, 1883).

German Arciniegas. Amerigo and the New World: The Life and Times of Amerigo Vespucci (New York: Alfred A. Knopf, 1955).

Grace Dunlop Ecker. A Portrait of Old Georgetown (Richmond: Garrett & Massie, Incorporated, 1933).

Hugh T. Taggart. Old Georgetown: District of Columbia (Lancaster: The New Era Printing Company, 1908).

Ivan M. Tribe. The Stonemans: An Appalachian Family and the Music that Shaped Their Lives (Chicago: University of Illinois Press, 1993).

J. Thomas Scharf. History of Maryland from the Earliest Period to the Present Day: Vol. I (Baltimore: John B. Piet, 1879).

Jack Lait and Lee Mortimer. Washington Confidential: The Low-Down on the Big Town (New York: Crown Publishers, Inc., 1951).

James Miller. Flowers in the Dustbin: The Rise of Rock and Roll 1947-1977 (New York: Simon & Schuster, 1999).

James Riordan and Jerry Prochnicky. Break On Through: The Life and Death of Jim Morrison (New York: William Morrow and Company, Inc., 1991).

Jay Stevens. Storming Heaven: LSD and the American Dream (New York: Grove Press, 1987).

Jim Dawson. Rock Around the Clock: The Record that Started the Rock Revolution! (San Francisco: Backbeat Books, 2005).

Jim Dawson and Steve Propes. What Was the First Rock 'N' Roll Record? (Winchester: Faber and Faber, 1992).

Mrs. Jimmie Rodgers. My Husband Jimmie Rodgers (San Antonio: San Antonio Southern Literary Institute, 1935).

Jimmy Dean and Donna Meade Dean. Thirty Years of Sausage, Fifty Years of Ham: Jimmy Dean's Own Story (New York: The Berkley Publishing Group, 2004).

John Clagett Proctor, LLM (editor-in-chief). Washington Past and Present: A History – Volume I (New York: Lewis Historical Publishing Company, Inc., 1930)

John Fahey. How Bluegrass Music Destroyed My Life (Chicago: Drag City Incorporated, 2000).

John Grissim, Jr. We Have Come For Your Daughters: What Went Down on the Medicine Ball Caravan (New York: William Morrow & Company, Inc., 1972).

John W. Haley and John von Hoelle. Sound and Glory: The Incredible Story of Bill Haley, the Father of Rock 'n' Roll and the Music that Shook the World (Wilmington: Dyne-American Publications, Inc., 1990).

John Tasker Howard and George Kent Bellows. A Short History of Music in America (New York: Thomas Y. Crowell Company, 1957).

John A. Jackson. Big Beat Heat: Alan Freed and the Early Years of Rock & Roll (New York: Schirmer Books, 1991).

John Phillips with Jim Jerome. Papa John: A Music Legend's Shattering Journey Through Sex, Drugs, and Rock 'N' Roll (Garden City: Dolphin Books, 1986).

Joseph E. Vaccarino. Baltimore Sounds: An Illustrated Encyclopedia of Baltimore Area Pop Musicians, Bands, and Recordings 1950-2000 (Catonsville: MJAM Press, 2nd edition, 2012).

Kate Van Winkle Keller. Dance and its Music in America 1528-1789 (Hillsdale: Pendragon Press, 2007).

Katherine K. Preston. Music For Hire: A Study of Professional Musicians in Washington (1877-1900) – Sociology of Music No. 6 (Stuyvesant: Pendragon Press, 1992).

Kenneth R. Bowling. The Creation of Washington, D.C.: The Idea and Location of the American Capital (Fairfax: George Mason University Press, 1991).

Lou Martin. The Memories: A Doo-Wop Journey (Bloomington: Cross Books, 2012).

Margaret Jones. Patsy: The Life and Times of Patsy Cline (New York: HarperCollins Publishers, 1994).

Mark Andersen and Mark Jenkins. Dance of Days: Two Decades of Punk in the Nation's Capital (New York: Soft Skull Press, 2001).

Martin A. Lee and Bruce Shlain. Acid Dreams: The Complete Social History of LSD – The CIA, the Sixties, and Beyond (New York: Grove Weidenfeld, 1992).

Mary Lou Williamson (general editor). Greenbelt: History of a New Town 1937-1987 (Norfolk: The Donning Company/Publishers, 1987).

Nicholas Cresswell. The Journal of Nicholas Cresswell 1174-1777 (New York: Dial Press, Incorporated, 1924).

Nolan Porterfield. Jimmie Rodgers: The Life and Times of America's Blue Yodeler (Jackson: University Press of Mississippi, 2007).

Odai Johnson and William J. Burling. The Colonial American Stage, 1665-1774: A Documentary Calendar (Madison: Fairleigh Dickinson University Press, 2001).

Paul E. Bierley. John Philip Sousa, American Phenomenon (Westerville: Integrity Press, 1973).

The Rev. Andrew Burnaby, A.M. Travels through the Middle Settlements in North America in the Years 1759 and 1760 with Observations upon the State of the Colonies (London: Printed for T. Payne at the Mews-Gate, 1775).

Robert Greenfield. Timothy Leary: A Biography (Orlando: Harcourt, Inc., 2006).

Robert K. Headley. Motion Picture Exhibition in Washington, D.C.: An Illustrated History of Parlors, Palaces, and Multiplexes in the Metropolitan Area, 1894-1997 (Jefferson: McFarland & Company, Inc., 1999).

Robert Kirk Headley Jr. Exit: A History of Movies in Baltimore (University Park: Robert Kirk Headley, Jr., 1974).

Roy Clark with Marc Eliot. Roy Clark: My Life in Spite of Myself (New York: Simon & Schuster, 1994).
Toby Thompson. Saloon: A Guide to America's Great Bars, Pubs, Saloons, Taverns, Drinking Places and Watering Holes (New York: Grossman Publishers, 1976).

Wayne E. Busbice Patricia Busbice. Uncovering the Secrets of a Southern Family: A Memoir (Bloomington: AuthorHouse, 2007).

Wilhelmus Bogart Bryan. A History of the National Capital From Its Foundation Through The Period of the Adoption of the Organic Act Vol. I 1790-1814 (New York: The MacMillan Company, 1914).

William V. Cox (compiler). Celebration of the One Hundredth Anniversary of the Establishment of the Seat of Government in the District of Columbia (Washington, D.C.: Government Printing Office, 1901).

William Tindall. Origin and Government of the District of Columbia (Washington, D.C.: Government Printing Office, 1909).

William Tindall. Standard History of the City of Washington from a Study of the Original Sources (Knoxville: H.W. Crew & Co., 1914).

William B. Wood. Personal Recollections of the Stage Embracing Notices of Actors, Authors, and Auditors, During a Period of Forty Years (Philadelphia: Henry Carey Baird, 1855).

Newspapers and Publications:
Alexandria Gazette (Alexandria, VA)
Billboard (New York, NY)
The Bowie Blade (Bowie, MD)
The Centinel of Liberty, and George-Town Advertiser (Georgetown; at the time an independent town on federal property)
The Columbian Chronicle (Georgetown; at the time an independent town on federal property)
The Columbian Mirror and Alexandria Gazette (Alexandria, VA)
Daily National Intelligencer (Wash DC)
DC Monuments (Manassas, VA)
The Diamondback (College Park, MD)
The Eagle (Wash DC)
The Evening Star (Wash DC)
The Fauquier Democrat (Warrenton, VA)
Greenbelt News Review (Greenbelt, MD)
The Hoya (Wash DC)

The Hyattsville Independent (Hyattsville, MD)
Maryland Gazette (Annapolis, MD)
Polk's Washington City Directory (Wash DC; various years)
The Prince Georgean (Mt. Rainier, MD)
The Prince George's Enquirer (Upper Marlboro, MD)
The Prince George's Journal (College Park, MD)
The Prince George's Post (Hyattsville, MD)
The Prince George's Sentinel (Hyattsville, MD)
Quicksilver Times (Wash DC)
Records of the Columbia Historical Society of Washington, D.C. (Wash DC)
Star Leader (Clinton, MD)
The Times and Potowmack Packet (Georgetown; at the time an independent town in MD)
Unicorn Times (Wash DC)
The Washington Afro-American (Wash DC)
The Washington Bee (Wash DC)
Washington City Paper (Wash DC)
The Washington Daily News (Wash DC)
Washington Free Press (Wash DC)
The Washington Post (Wash DC)
The Washington Tribune (Wash DC)
Woodwind (Wash DC)

Papers:
James Cobham Mackay III. The Development of Taverns in Alexandria, Virginia, 1750-1810 (A thesis submitted in partial fulfillment of the requirements for the degree of Master of Arts at George Mason University by James Cobham Mackay III; spring 1995, George Mason University, Fairfax, Virginia).

Repositories:
Frederick S. DeMarr Library of County History (Prince George's County Historical Society, Greenbelt, MD)
Greenbelt Branch Public Library – Tugwell Room (Greenbelt, MD)
Hornbake Library North – Special Collections and University Archives (University of Maryland, College Park, MD)
Martin Luther King, Jr. Memorial Library – Washingtoniana Division (Washington, D.C.)
McKeldin Library (University of Maryland, College Park, MD)

CPSIA information can be obtained
at www.ICGtesting.com
Printed in the USA
BVHW012143230119
538555BV00011B/110/P

9 781644 382837